SHOOT-EM-UPS

The Complete Reference Guide
to Westerns of the Sound Era

SHOOT-
EM-UPS

Les Adams & Buck Rainey

ARLINGTON HOUSE·PUBLISHERS
NEW ROCHELLE, NEW YORK

Manufactured in the United States of America

P 10 9 8 7 6 5 4 3 2 1

Library of Congress Cataloging in Publication Data

Adams, Les, 1934-
    Shoot-em ups.

    Includes index.
    1. Western films—History and criticism. 2. Moving-pictures—United States.
I. Rainey, Buck, joint author. II. Title.
PN1995.W4A3   791.43′0909′32   78-656
ISBN 0-87000-393-3

Dedicated to the Memory of

**HARRY CAREY
AND BUCK JONES**

. . . who loved children and took seriously the responsibility placed upon them by the adoration of millions of youngsters, demonstrating moral leadership and personal integrity which helped to sustain a depression-era generation

AND

HAL TALIAFERRO/WALLY WALES

. . . who, though he toiled in the shadows of fame, was cut from the same bolt of cloth

"They done themselves proud," and cowboyin', both real and reel, was a job they took pride in. To ride the trail with them over the years was an experience to be cherished for as long as the sun sets beyond the Rockies and the dreams of childhood are dreamed again

Acknowledgments

With love and appreciation we acknowledge the patience and understanding of our respective families during the two years that this book was in preparation. A tip of the hat to Mickye, Shannon, Brad, and Jill Adams and Rosalva, Rex, Tim, and Ken Rainey.

Our especial thanks to Ron AuBuchon, a researcher with few peers, whose work is reflected throughout the 1950-1977 coverage and who didn't need us as much as we needed him.

Thanks also to the following friends who were called upon for assistance and who generously shared their files and/or films:

Lewis Bagwell
Janus Barfoed
Eugene Blottner
Eddie Brandt
Ab Breeden
Wayne Campbell
Jack Clinger
Dennis Hahen
Mack Houston
Ed Hurley
Ken Jones
Ronnie Jones
Bill Lazear
Daria Littlejohn
Bertil Lundgren
Boyd Magers

Jack Mathis
Bill McDowell
Don Miller
Jim Murray
Cyril Nicholls
Vern O'Dell
Robert Pepe
Bob Slate
Garth Snowden-Davies
Ed Tabor
David Taylor
George Turner
Hames Ware
Nick Williams
Lee Roy Willis

Finally, a special thanks to Bob Smith and Victor Cornelius, two gentlemen who handled most of the source paper over the last four decades—and had the foresight not to destroy it.

KEY TO FILMOGRAPHY ABBREVIATIONS

AP	Associate Producer
Cont	Continuity
D	Director
Dial	Dialogue
Ed	Editor
P	Producer
S	Story
Scen	Scenario
SP	Screenplay

Contents

Preface

*S*hoot-Em-Ups: The Complete Reference Guide to Westerns of the Sound Era has been written for those who have long desired a reference book to which they could turn for information about Western films—*any* American-made Western of the last fifty years. No such book until now has attempted to chronicle *all* American Westerns of the sound era. One or two books have provided information of a limited nature on *selected* Westerns but have fallen short of even listing titles of a majority of such films. We have attempted to provide information on *every sound Western made since 1928*, whether it was a major studio production, a minor studio production, an "A," a "B," a full-length feature, a two-reel featurette, or a one-reel short. They are all here.

The authors hasten to add that there are a great many titles among the approximately 3400 listed in this book that in no way fit either's personal definition of a Western. Why include them? Well, primarily, because we have yet to find any two film fans, collectors, historians, or critics who can agree on what exact measurements frame this genre, and to limit the titles in this work to only those films that we call Westerns would be both a critical error and a disservice. Certainly, the shorts such as *Meet Roy Rogers*, or the ones we've included from the *Screen Snapshots* series featuring Western film clips and appearances by various Western stars, couldn't be classified as Westerns in any sense. But, as with the musical shorts featuring cowboy–hillbilly–country-western bands and performers, the inclusion is because their subjects or subject matter was closely (or wholly) identified with the Western film scene.

We have interpreted the term "Western" broadly and have chosen to include the "Northwest," "colonial frontier," and "country" stories, as well as all others that could even remotely be associated with Westerns. Our attitude has been that it is better to include fringe films than to be considered remiss in our obligations or research by those fans or historians who would be disappointed in not finding in this book a film that they consider to be a Western. The purists and nit-pickers (of which we are charter members) can in all justification object to finding *Coogan's Bluff* in a reference guide to Western films, as its story is one of a modern-day Arizona lawman showing the slicks in New York City how it is done. But if it is discarded on the basis of locale and time period, a fair and critical examination of other films would soon find *Headin' East* with Buck Jones, *Texas to Bataan* with the Range Busters, *Hollywood Cowboy* with George O'Brien, *Valley of Vanishing Men* with the Three Mesquiteers, all of the Roy Rogers films from mid-1941 on, and most of the Gene Autry films from Republic also having to be deleted. The authors were undivided in the opinion that they could live with such entries as *Coogan's Bluff* a lot longer than they could live without *Wall Street Cowboy* and *Hollywood Round-Up*. Reasons for most of the question mark entries should be obvious. Reasons for omissions we'll admit belong to "Those dummies left out . . ." School of Search, and we herein apologize. We make no apologies for the omissions of the X-rated Westerns, other than to profess the opinion that their subject matter is more suitable for participating than it is for spectating.

As far as possible, films have been listed chronologically by release dates, conveniently organized by chapters comprising approximately five years of Western movie history. The chronological presentation of the films will permit the reader to trace the rise and fall of any Western performer by reading through the book from front to back. It will be a fascinating journey when taken page by page, as long-forgotten or never-known movies, personalities, and studios make their appearance on the Western horizon, shine for a while, then become merely a part of yesteryear's memories. For those who want quick information about a particular movie, however, we have provided an alphabetical listing of the movies at the back of the book which will refer the reader directly to the data he is interested in. Thus, if one wants information on the movie *South of the Border*, he will find it appropriately listed in the "S" section of the alphabetical listing with the parenthetic notation "(1939, 1058)" beside it. This notation indicates that it was a 1939 movie and is entry number 1058 in the numbered entries starting with "1" and running consecutively through the film lists at the ends of the chapters.

For each film we have endeavored to list the production company, the releasing company (if different), the running time, the release date, the cast, the director, the story author, the screenplay author, and the producer. Such complete information was not available for some films, however, and for a few films we have listed additional information we thought would be of interest to Western film historians.

Casts are the most complete of any general Western movie reference book, and we are particularly proud with regard to what we have been able to do in assembling information on the "B" Westerns. Many months of research have been carried on to bring to life once again obscure, long-forgotten films of the early talkies, films produced by companies that burst into life overnight and died almost as quickly. We admit to a strong preference for the "B" Western and thus have gone to great lengths to chronicle these as completely as possible, gleefully shouting when—perhaps from a fellow historian in far-off England or Denmark—we have learned that Hank Bell or Silver Tip Baker or some other Western character actor was definitely spotted in the saloon free-for-all and could be added to the cast of a particular flick. It is the painstaking care with which we have attempted to add to the official pressbook casts for each movie listed herein that makes this book of particular value to movie historians.

Beginning with Chapter 2, each chapter encompasses a four- or five-year period of Western film history and the films, personalities, and state of the genre are briefly commented upon prior to presenting the films, listed year by year. The reader may disagree with some of our opinions and observations. Great! Take our thoughts with the proverbial grain of salt and figuratively drag us at the end of a rope across desert cacti and cow-dung pastures if such treatment be deserved. But we are optimistic in our belief that Western connoisseurs will find much more to agree with than to disagree with in our criticisms and evaluations of the cinema West.

We are not trying to excuse ourselves for blunders we might have made but do wish to point out that it has been a difficult task to determine the release dates and running times of many films. Thus, the film lists are chronological to the extent that we knew the exact release dates. When the release month of several films was known and not the exact day of release within that month, the films have been listed alphabetically behind the last exact release date for the month. When the year of release was known but not the month, the film has been listed following the entries for December, again alphabetically unless the sequence of release was known. For the most part, however, we have been able to determine release dates and have arranged the films accordingly. Running times are expressed mostly in minutes. With some of the early sound Westerns we have listed footage or reels since exact number of minutes was unknown. And for some few films, we have just not been able to determine the length either in minutes, footage, or reels. Many of the old Westerns are no longer physically in existence, nor are the records that would have provided information on the exact length.

We have tried our best. If a Western has somehow been left out or if we have made mistakes in our listings, we apologize and sincerely solicit the reader's information regarding the film so that in any revised edition the error can be corrected.

For the most part the photographic illustrations are "fresh" in the sense that they have not been published before. Thus, they should add immeasurably to the enjoyment of the book and bring back many pleasant memories of by-gone days at the movies.

One may wonder why Chapter 1 is included in a reference guide to sound Westerns, since it is a review of the Western genre of the silent era. To us it seemed illogical to begin talking about sound Westerns without some discussion—stage setting, if you will—of what had gone before. We think the reader will want to read this chapter carefully, much as one might read the Old Testament in order to better understand the New Testament. Many of the personalities involved in this book started their careers in the silent era; thus, it is helpful, we think, that some information on their early careers be included. Chapter 1 serves not only to introduce the book but to present important subject matter as well.

Likewise, we have added Chapter 12 in order that readers interested in them can have knowledge of the major foreign-made Westerns of the last several years. Nearly everyone has seen the Clint Eastwood "spaghetti" Westerns, for example, because, like many foreign films, they have been distributed in the U.S.A. Readers might therefore question the omission of these films from our work. And a number of Westerns filmed abroad were made by Hollywood producers using Hollywood personnel and for the U.S. market. Technically, these are not American-made Westerns since they were filmed outside the North American continent. But at least some of these films are important ones that need to be "in the record" when one is researching the films of various studios and personalities. Thus, a brief discussion and a selected foreign film list seemed to us to be desirable, and we thought it best to isolate the foreign films in a separate chapter.

We hope that our efforts will culminate in many hours of pleasure for the Western film buff who merely wishes to recall old Westerns that he has seen. For the film researcher, the guide should serve for years as an invaluable aid in the preparation of individual star filmographies, film histories, and so forth. For us, it has been a labor of love which has added a wealth of data and knowledge on a subject which we thought we were authorities on already. Once again we were boys living a thousand vicarious experiences from a time when heroes rode the Hollywood hills. Western filmdom had left us a dream that we found easy to reactivate. We dreamed our dreams of yesteryear and once again raced across the prairie with Reb Russell and "Rebel," dived into swirling rivers with Ken Maynard and "Tarzan," clowned around with Buck Jones and "Silver," paraded with Roy Rogers and "Trigger," and leaped chasms with Jack Perrin and "Starlight." Goosepimples long dormant erupted as we recalled a thousand and one scenes indelibly stamped on our minds for decades, visualized the lasses we loved and lost to our favorite heroes and the villains we loved to hate, heard again in our mind's ear the peculiar sounds of the early sound flicks and the chase and fight music which caused us to shrill with excitement in those carefree days of youth and innocence. Oh, the thrill of it all! Because of a boyhood never outgrown we have a release valve for life's mounting pressures—a valve that is easy to turn and does not need replacing. Closed eyes and a few quiet moments in recollections of yesterday's Saturdays bring tranquility of mind and soul that sustains us for yet more reality.

CHAPTER 1

The Silent Years
1903-1927

(RESCUED FROM THE ABYSS OF TIME)

As one of America's truly unique contributions to the theatre arts, the Western seems destined to live on forever in that favored corner of one's heart reserved for vicarious thoughts about experiences which—because of a combination of circumstance, era, and cowardice—one shall never have. The Western has served as our closest equivalent to a national myth, and the studios turned them out by the hundreds while the public mistakenly labeled them "cowboy pictures."

The beginning of what we shall call the Western genre pre-dated *The Great Train Robbery* (1903) by about five years, albeit a most inauspicious and shaky one—being a three- or four-minute tableau called *Cripple Creek Bar-Room*. Although they had no moving story and utilized only one set, the "actors" were coached in what they were to do and the film made a laudable attempt to realistically show life in a western saloon at the turn of the century. The seed was planted. And with *The Great Train Robbery* a second seed was sown that reaped a bountiful harvest.

Long for its time at 740 feet (about 9 minutes), *The Great Train Robbery* told a story, that of a western train robbery—although the "West" was actually a stretch of track of the Delaware and Lackawanna Railroad in New Jersey. Unlike most of the short films being produced for kinetoscope parlors by enterprising photographers out to shoot anything and everything that moved, this film told a complete story. It had a Western plot, sure to capture the public's fancy in the heyday of the pulp Westerns and Wild West shows. And it introduced many principles that became standard fare in motion picture production—the close-up, the chase, different locales, cutting from one scene to another, a climax, specially designed props, the escape, cliffhanger action, stop motion, and a musical interlude. All in all, it was quite a bundle of innovative film techniques wrapped up in such a short film produced by an erstwhile unknown by the name of Edwin S. Porter. And, as luck would have it, further icing was added to the cake in that the film served to introduce G. M. Anderson, who, three years later, started his fabulous career as the screen's first cowboy star under the name of Bronco Billy Anderson, grinding out nearly 400 one- and two-reel Westerns before his career collapsed in 1920.

Ironically, G. M. was no cowboy; rather, he was a photographer's model and salesman and of Jewish descent, having changed his name from Max Aronson. Nor could he ride a horse. Scheduled for an additional part in the film, he immediately fell off his horse and thus was not seen as a member of the posse. But he was beefy and courageous and he learned fast, eventually becoming a fair rider and stuntman. And to him must be given credit for realizing that America needed a popular hero. Luckily, he chose the cowboy to immortalize.

A thriving film industry sprang up in the first decade of the century, creating jobs for actors, distributors, writers, directors, theatre owners, producers, technicians, stable owners, costume renters, and . . . con men. Nickelodeons had caught on and had become cinema parlors, with the masses of lower and middle classes developing an edacious weekly habit of attendance. The motion picture industry was on its way, gradually casting off the nugatory and discrediting cloak of debasement with which its malevolent critics had wrapped it. The enthralling qualities of this flickering celluloid magic emanated from the screen, bathing viewers in exhilaration that seemingly was never satisfied, consequently bringing them back time and time again for further doses of fantasy—for the movies, with their magical powers of illusion and make-believe, would permanently preserve the fantasy and blow it up larger than life. American audiences rapidly developed a desire for action, thrills, catharsis, and escape while making it clear that they would accept education only in small, infrequent dosages.

Surprisingly non-insistent on realism, Western fans trekked to theatres on a weekly basis for half a century seemingly unbothered by the fact that their cowboy heroes seldom tended cattle; drank only milk or sarsaparilla; always had unerring accuracy in spite of the crudeness of 19th century firearms; easily fired a dozen shots from a six-shooter before finding it necessary to reload; were never encumbered with a wife or the responsibilities that beset the ordinary man; always had well-lodged hats in spite of knockdown-dragout fights; never endured winter; always bested the baddies; had bullet-proof horses; wore gaudy teflon-coated clothing immune to dirt; looked to be physical Adonises; invariably courted motherless heroines; indubitably were clean shaven, articulate, and comparable to Christ in their morals; and always remained cool and collected even though narrowly escaping death five times in as many minutes and killing off six or seven culprits during the same time interval. But so it was.

The early Western opuses churned out by D. W. Griffith and Thomas Ince appealed to the multitudes, seemingly possessed of an insatiable appetite for vicarious Western adventure and romance. Griffith had considerable finesse both as a director and film editor and developed to a fine art the use of panoramic shots and running inserts, both techniques adding a sense of reality to his own films as well as to the output of those who would follow in his footsteps. His intuition of the space and time fluidity of film technique and his development of the intensity of expressiveness of the close-up gave his films an exuberant uniqueness.

Ince, on the other hand, had a preference for strong plots and action sequences, as well as for telling the story of the Indian. Not surprisingly when one really stops to ponder upon it, the roots of both the "A" and "B" Westerns of later years—so far apart in the minds of the aficionados of each—lie in the films of these trailblazers who simply made semi-realistic little one- and two-reel Western gems unhampered by any semantic stigma. A Western was simply a Western and, independently, Ince and Griffith had concluded that frontier fantasy was ideally suited for the flickers they wished to peddle. Both men deserve much of the credit for setting the guidelines followed by later practitioners of the art of Western filmmaking.

And G. M. Anderson, too, has to be listed among the important Western directors, for he was almost literally the first one. It was he who developed by trial and error a number of techniques peculiar to Westerns, techniques that have been handed down to the present generation of movie and television directors. The same can be said of William S. Hart who, as actor-director, chartered directorial courses that men since have found convenient to follow. Hart scrupulously strived to depict the West truthfully, and, in this respect, he had much in common with Griffith, Ince, and John Ford. Ford? Yes, the name is a familiar one. Perhaps the greatest known of all Western filmmakers by the world at large, he became involved in the genre in the waning years of the pre-1920 era.

Salomy Jane (Liebler, 1914)—L to R: Mabel Hilliard, Fred W. Snook, House Peters, Bill Nigh (dir.), Beatrice Micheleana, Ernest Joy, Jack Holt (in the center background)

Ford learned quickly and seemed to sense, just as in later decades, what the public wanted in a Western. And he gave it to them—lots of action, panorama, a story worth telling, reasonable adherence to historical accuracy, romance, and liberal doses of sentimentality and humor.

And then there were Cliff Smith, Lambert Hillyer, Calvin Campbell, J. P. McGowan, B. Reeves Eason, Robert N. Bradbury, Cecil B. DeMille, W. S. Van Dyke, Tom Mix, William Duncan, and George Marshall, each earning a niche in film history as creative directors in the formative years of the Western genre.

The pre-1920's saw the star system developed, with seven Western stalwarts vying for top honors in what would lovingly become known as "hoss operas," "sagebrushers," "shoot-em-ups," "oaters," "programmers," and "series Westerns." G. M. "Bronco Billy" Anderson has already been mentioned as the screen's first cowboy star. Pete Morrison, Tom Mix, and William Duncan each became associated with Westerns around 1910, going on to achieve Western immortality in the Twenties. Harry Carey, William S. Hart, and Roy Stewart came along in 1914-1915 to quickly establish themselves as cowboy stalwarts. These seven were the frontrunners in a growing number of cowboy stars heading up Western dramas for Essanay, Selig, Triangle, Universal, Biograph, American, and at least seventy-five other smaller companies during the years 1905-1920.

It was William S. Hart who dominated Western films in the years 1915-1925, creating the good badman role that proved so appealing for cinema goers of that and later generations and introducing motifs which became classical ingredients. Hart's films inevitably contained a sentimental and highly emotional love story and his hero, with a past for which his present nobility is a kind of atonement, generally rode off into the sunset rather than commit another person to the burden of a lasting attachment. Invariably, his Westerns

Pete Morrison and friend from an un-identified Oater of the Twenties. Pete was one of the first pioneers of the Western and an ever-popular cowboy favorite, especially in 2-reelers

involved a transformation theme—either he was reformed by a good woman or a bad woman was reformed by him.

Early classics such as Griffith's *The Last Drop of Water* (1911) and *The Battle of Elderbush Gulch* (1913), Ince's *War on the Plains* (1912) and *The Indian Massacre* (1912), and DeMille's *The Spoilers* (1914) quickly cast the mold for the super, non-assembly-line Westerns as contrasted to the formula shoot-em-ups, epitomized best in the formative years by Anderson's "Bronco Billy" Westerns.

To perhaps a majority of Western aficionados, the occasional Westerns (by whatever name—"A," "Big," "Major," "Classic," or "Super") made by "dudes" (non-series stars) are somewhat repulsive and hardly deserving of serious consideration when speaking of Western films. Likewise, another significant portion of the movie-going public would tout the major Western and look down upon the lowly "B" with contempt. The die was cast in the early years, almost from the beginning. And as a result, otherwise sane, rational people will argue fervently the comparative merits of *Shane* (Alan Ladd), *The Virginian* (Gary Cooper), or *Duel in the Sun* (Gregory Peck) and such films as *The Fighting Sheriff* (Buck Jones), *The Durango Kid Returns* (Charles Starrett), or *The Man from Hell* (Reb Russell).

For the uninitiated, the allegiance that vast numbers of people have for the "B" Western is incomprehensible. They find it strange that one would cherish and remember forever Ken Maynard leaping along rooftops, Hoot Gibson's clowning, or Tom Mix's foolhardy stunts while at the same time rejecting as unimportant the super Westerns of the big studios, films starring dramatic actors of the calibre of Fonda, McCrea, Cooper, and Stewart. Yet, among the "outsiders" only John Wayne, who came up through the ranks of "B" Westerns and serials, and Randolph Scott, who voluntarily shifted almost entirely to Westerns, have been accepted by "B" devotees as worthy of much respect. Joel McCrea

Ace of the Saddle (Universal, 1919)— Harry Carey and Peggy Pearce

Tumbleweeds (United Artists, 1925) — William S. Hart and Lucien Littlefield

God's Gold (Pinnacle, 1920) — Neal Hart

ranks as a borderline case. All others who were not exclusively Western stars have been contemptuously labeled "frauds" and rejected. Such narrow-mindedness on the part of the "B" buffs can be forgiven, perhaps, if one will but imagine the reaction of a typical cosmopolitan audience at Grauman's Chinese Theatre or Radio City Music Hall to Lash LaRue or Sunset Carson in any shape, form, or fashion. One genre—two audiences—and seldom the twain did meet.

The Western, as a distinct form of motion picture entertainment, was born before hardly anyone knew the industry was pregnant with child. And like other infants the Western genre struggled to survive its own blunders and oppression from outside forces. But the "hoss opera" mastered life, grew rapidly, and prospered. By 1920 it was an industry within an industry, with its own horde of stars and technicians especially trained for bringing the wild West, as people wanted to imagine it, to life on the screen each week. The Western generally did not show the old West the way it really was but rather as a mythic past viewed nostalgically. The directors, for the most part, grasped the idea inherent in the silent Western; they served their art; they were inconsistent; they were guilty of mistakes and bad productions. But they worked and created. They were honorable and committed. While there were conventions to be built upon, individual directors made use of them for a wide variety of purposes. Taken together, their talents were as varied as they were personal and implied the maximum achievement of the film of their time.

As the nation entered upon the peaceful decade of the Twenties, Westerns—good, bad, mediocre—were rushing in to fill the need for films by the rapidly growing number of small town theatres, much as a thundering herd of buffalo in the real wild West of yesteryear might converge upon a valley of lush green grass and plentiful water. The star system was firmly entrenched. The early Twenties, however, saw a noticeable decline in enthusiasm for the Western and no really major ones had been produced in several years, although Hart and Mix and Carey were still doing well at the box office in minor ones. But the situation was changed with the release of *The Covered Wagon* (1923), a film that served as the diuretic needed to restore the well-being of the Western genre. As the first truly epic Western, it caught on to such an extent with a public that was tiring of such stories that a whole series of super Westerns followed. Costing nearly $800,000, the film ultimately grossed nearly $4 million for Famous Players Lasky Corporation.

And adding more impetus to the revival of the Western was John Ford's *The Iron Horse* (Fox, 1924, George O'Brien) and *Three Badmen* (Fox, 1926, George O'Brien), as well as Irving Willat's *North of '36* (Paramount, 1924, Jack Holt). These and other big-budget Western dramas changed somewhat the attitude toward Western films. Of no little consequence in this regard were the Paramount Zane Grey Westerns starring Jack Holt. So good were they, in fact, that the negatives were cannibalized and used in the sound remakes of the Thirties.

The really important Westerns of the Twenties, aside from the four just referred to, were *To the Last Man* (Paramount, 1923, Richard Dix), *Riders of the Purple Sage* (Fox, 1925, Tom Mix), *The Vanishing American* (Paramount, 1925, Richard Dix), *The Pony Express* (Paramount, 1925, Ricardo Cortez), *Tumbleweeds* (United Artists, 1925, William S. Hart), *The Thundering Herd* (Paramount, 1925, Jack Holt), *Wild Horse Mesa* (Paramount, 1925, Jack Holt), *The Winning of Barbara Worth* (Goldwyn-United Artists, 1926, Gary Cooper), *Forlorn River* (Paramount, 1926, Jack Holt), *Flaming Frontier* (Universal, 1926, Hoot Gibson), *Jesse James* (Paramount, 1927, Fred Thomson), *Red Raiders* (First National, 1927, Ken Maynard), and *The Mysterious Rider* (Paramount, 1927, Jack Holt). One would be treading on dangerous ice to attempt to make the ultimate decision as to just which Westerns of the Twenties would

The Enchanted Hill
(Famous Players-
Lasky, 1926)—Jack
Holt and Mary
Brian

North of '36 (Famous
Players - Lasky,
1924)—Jack Holt
and Noah Beery

28

be worthy of the title "important" and which would not be, but Western film historians generally concede the aforementioned ones to be among the important.

Movies in the Twenties seemed to capture a national tone, an innocent optimistic faith in progress and human potential, in the efficacy of change; a moralistic seriousness, a no-nonsense soberness; a mixture of sentimental idealism and gruff athletic confidence. Westerns were no exception.

Realizing there was still a profit to be made in Westerns, producers streamlined their "B" product and plowed more money into the budgets for programmers, as they began to be called by those in the trade. For, in a sense, the second-rate movie houses were in competition with the first-rate houses and their superior product. Since double features hardly existed, Westerns had to pull audiences on the strength of the feature (and perhaps the accompanying serial). Thus, Westerns in the Twenties were surprisingly good products considering their limited budgets. Unlike most Westerns of the Forties and Fifties, many had interesting plots and real production value. Only in the latter years of the decade did quality decline, mostly in the independent productions distributed on the states-right market. But the output of the major producers (Rayart, Fox, Pathe, Universal, FBO, Paramount, and First National), as well as independent producers like Sunset, IPC, and Associated Exhibitors, remained well above the quality level of the majority of "B" Westerns of the next two decades. This was especially true in story quality.

During the Twenties the "B" cowboys literally took over the Western cinema, stampeding across the "reel" range as if to escape forever the Pandora's Box that had held them in bondage. And the classic Western hero became a man possessed of fighting skill, courage, endurance, intelligence, sexual purity, and indifference to personal gain. He became an indestructible cowboy.

At Fox, Tom Mix and Buck Jones kept the studio financially afloat, with a little assistance from Will Rogers, while Hoot Gibson did the same for Universal, aided and abetted by Harry Carey, Jack Hoxie, Art Acord, Jack Perrin, Roy Stewart, Edmund Cobb, Pete Morrison, and a horde of other thrill-makers who blazed a wide swath across the celluloid heavens as if they were a mighty Pterodactyl gliding aloft in the Mesozoic Era, master of its domain.

Without question, Tom Mix was the embodiment of the world's yearning for a bigger-than-life hero, establishing a formula for the sexless Western that lasted into the Fifties. Tom created the character of the fun-loving loner who was always a clean-minded and right-livin' cowpuncher, always trying to do the right thing because it was the right thing to do. His films were breezy, cheerful, streamlined, aimed at a wide audience, and free of serious romantic entanglements. Above all, Tom and his horse Tony represented the finest in vicarious thrills and escapist entertainment.

Buck Jones, with a laconic personality and a true love of the West and its lore, seemed to be the epitome of masculinity, magnanimity, courageousness, and virtuousness, and he rode into the hearts of millions on his equally popular white horse Silver. Ultimately, in the sound era, he would overtake Mix in popularity.

Hoot Gibson dared to be human—and discovered a great secret. Audiences liked human beings. With Hoot you never could tell. He might well be the one on the floor after a fistic encounter, and audiences worried about him. His horse could throw him twenty feet. His gun would jam. His pack mule paid him "no never mind," and even the heroine blackened his eye. The action in his films was usually at a frenzied pace, the comedy refreshing. Strangely, Hoot's films appealed as much to mommy and daddy as to junior. Probably more so. By 1925 he was earning $14,000 a week, just $3,000 less than the salary commanded by

Harvest of Hate (Universal, 1929) — Tom London, Jack Perrin, and Helen Foster

The Cyclone Cowboy (Action, 1927) — Wally Wales and cigarette-smoking friends

Silver Comes Through (RC-FBO, 1927)— William Courthwright and Fred Thomson

Mix, and he remained a top star throughout the Twenties and into the Thirties, playing usually a clowning, bumbling, all thumbs hero.

Fred Thomson and his horse Silver King came along to earn several million dollars in a matter of six or seven years, and on their heels came Ken Maynard and Tarzan, appearing in as slick a series of Westerns at First National as was ever produced in the silent era. Ken had screen charm and a personality, quite different from his real one, that endeared him to millions of people of all ages and classes, and with Tarzan, a sensitive, highly intelligent animal, he rode through streamlined and showy Westerns specializing in action for its own sake and presenting a customary superficial and glamorized picture of the West.

Harry Carey was just about everyone's favorite, a cowboy, older in years, that one felt comfortable with. He was to the Western what Will Rogers was to the world, a kindly philosopher with winning ways and with a keen sense of humor. Beyond that he was one of the best actors the genre ever had.

Wally Wales, Jack Perrin, Buddy Roosevelt, Jack Hoxie, Bill Cody, Leo Maloney, and a host of others blazed a glory trail as celluloid heroes in the silent flickers, creating the memories that would sustain many of the children of the time along the treacherous trails of adulthood.

Even Metro-Goldwyn-Mayer jumped into the field with a series of frontier dramas starring Colonel Tim McCoy, one of the most authentic cowboys ever to appear on screen. McCoy presented a strong, handsome figure, with virile qualities that made him an appealing star. His first series, in 1927-1928, was a very realistic, high-budgeted group of historical Westerns featuring authentic Indians and locales. There was really no other cowboy star like McCoy in personality and manner. Throughout his long, illustrious career he maintained a military aloofness that set him apart from his contemporaries.

Serials in the Twenties were taken more seriously—by both the producers and the public—than they were in later decades, enjoying a measure of respectability granted only feature films in the sound era. And it was primarily Pathe and Universal that packed them in on a weekly basis with action oaters, although a number of companies made them. Ranking among the top serial performers of the time were William Desmond, Jack Daugherty, Art Acord, William Duncan, and a couple of ladies—Ruth Roland and beauteous Allene Ray, surely the reason for many a young boy's first terrible pangs of unrequited love.

The coins clinked in the coffers of serial producers as an enthralled, naive public streamed back week after week to see their heroes thwart death minute by minute. Toward the end of the decade Nat Levine's Mascot Pictures was created specifically to specialize in serial production, and the studio managed to market three Western serials of ten episodes each before switching to sound films and achieving a domination of the serial market in the early Thirties.

During the Twenties FBO vied with Universal for top-quality assembly-line shoot-em-ups, utilizing the services, at one time or another, of Fred Thomson, Tom Mix, Bob Steele, Bob Custer, Tom Tyler, Buzz Barton, and Yakima Canutt. Pathe, too, was in there giving all of them a run for their money with fine series starring Harry Carey, Bill Cody, Wally Wales, Buddy Roosevelt, Leo Maloney, Don Coleman, Buffalo Bill, Jr., and others.

Smaller outfits such as Arrow, William Steiner Productions, Action Pictures, William Pizor Productions, J. Charles Davis Productions, Weiss Brothers, Capital, Bud Barsky's Wild West Pictures, Aywon, IPC, Sunset, and PDC churned out low-budget Westerns like clockwork to supply the states-right market distribution system whereby regional distributors contracted for the right to market films in a given territory, thus relieving the

The Ramblin' Galoot (Action, 1926) — Buddy Roosevelt and Violet La Plante

Law of the Range (MGM, 1928) — Rex Lease and Tim McCoy

William Desmond and Yakima Canutt on the Universal backlot, circa 1925

Spurs and Saddles (Universal, 1927)—Art Acord and Fay Wray

A Man of Nerve (FBO, 1925)—Bob Custer and Jean Arthur

Scar Hanan (FBO, 1925) — Yakima Canutt seated; Palmer Morrison with arm around Dorothy Wood

Border Blackbirds (Pathe, 1927)—Leo Maloney hoping the horse stays put

Ace of Clubs (Anchor, 1926)—Jules Cowles and Al Hoxie

Rainbow Range (Anchor, 1929)—Cheyenne Bill, long a forgotten cowboy ace, beats the stuffin' out of Al Ferguson in one of the last of the silent Westerns

producer of any distribution headaches. And finding ephemeral stardom under this profitable distribution umbrella were such cowboys as Al Hoxie, Franklyn Farnum, Big Boy Williams, William Fairbanks, Bob Reeves, Neal Hart, Bill Patton, Yakima Canutt, and Art Mix, to name but a few.

And then, . . . sound! To draw a sort of parallel, if we may, Plato tells us of Atlantis and the great empire that existed on it. As the story goes, the island kingdom was rent by great earthquakes and torrential floods and, in the course of a day and a night, sank into the sea. Yet, until its sudden demise, it was reputed to be a powerful, conquering kingdom. And so it was with the Western, the Atlantis of the Twenties. Suddenly, instead of a conquering army at the apex of its glory, the Western genre became a crumbling, exploding continent with its inhabitants screaming in agony at the sudden realization that they might be doomed. Producers were not optimistic about the feasibility of outdoor films, and it was almost impossible to manipulate the awkward early sound equipment in the outdoors. No, instead of seeing cedars of Lebanon—straight, tall, and reaching eagerly for the heavens—producers' subconscious reflections on the future of the genre turned temerariously to castles built shoddily on the shifting sands of a tempestuous sea—decaying and crumbling with each licentious lapping of tenacious waves at their foundations. Pessimism was rampant. Even before sound there had been rumblings indicating the public might, after twenty years, be getting tired of seeing the cowboy hero come silently charging to the rescue of the fair maiden, saving her from the machinations of Black Bart and a "fate worse than death." Night was creeping over the cinema range, bringing eeriness and fear.

CHAPTER 2

The Transition Years
1928-1932

(THE PERILOUS PLUNGE INTO THE CHASM OF FEAR)

Sound, or the fear of it, almost laid to rest the Western before it became the rejuvenating force that would make horse operas more popular than ever. The period 1928-1930 was traumatic for the film industry as a whole and for Western filmmakers especially. Technical problems plagued outdoor productions. Early sound recording equipment was nothing to brag about under soundstage conditions; but when taken out-of-doors (and just getting it into the out-of-doors was somewhat of a challenge) it proved even more disappointing and unreliable. One could sympathize with studio moguls and cowboys who were apprehensive about the rigorous demands of the microphone. And such equipment was expensive. In a time of tumultuous change the Western was afloat, but pitching and drifting aimlessly in a tempestuous sea of uncertainty. But sound pictures were more than an evanescent novelty; they rejuvenated the entire motion picture industry and brought people back to the movie houses who had long since tired of silent dramas.

There was an obsession for dialogue and the action Western seemed doomed. Tim McCoy was given the heave-ho at MGM, as was Ken Maynard at First National and Tom Mix at Fox. Buck Jones had voluntarily left Fox in 1928, only to go bankrupt both as an independent producer and as a Wild West show impresario. And when he next appeared on the lot he had helped to build, William Fox turned a deaf ear. Harry Carey, Wally Wales, Buddy Roosevelt, and confreres were out at Pathe and Fred Thomson had bombed at Paramount prior to his sudden death.

Surprisingly, most of the Westerns turned out during this industrial changeover from silent to sound pictures were produced by poverty row studios willing to take the perilous plunge into crude sound and to gamble on the hopes of a big win. Syndicate, Big Four, Tiffany, and Superior were such companies. Of the majors, only Universal proceeded with little interruption of its Western shooting schedules. Early sound efforts left much to be desired, but those early "squeakies" were replaced by pictures whose sound qualities improved rapidly. By 1930 talkie movies were beyond the squeaks and squawks stage and were delivering to theatre patrons reliable reproductions of sound. By 1932 most of the technical problems associated with sound recording had been licked and most films released were talkies.

The phenomenon of sound caused a resurgence of interest in movies, a proven opiate for depressed societies. Consequently, the movie industry in general and Western filmmaking in particular prospered during the depression years as never before or since. The growing number of small theatres serving up a menu of double features caused independents to jump into the market in increasing numbers. Any movie was profitable, it seemed; the result, the production of innumerable Westerns by a score or more producers. Thus, by

The Big Hop (Buck Jones Productions, 1928) — Buck Jones talks to Jobyna Ralston as Edward Hearn looks on in Buck's one and only film fiasco (Photo courtesy Museum of Modern Art, Film Stills Archives)

their mere omnipresence, Westerns became the hub of social life for millions who made the trek to their hometown "picture shows" a weekly ritual.

Sound effects were hastily added to Buck Jones' *The Big Hop* (1928) to make it the first Western of record to employ sound in any form. It was a modest beginning, having no dialogue or music score, and the effort did not stave off financial disaster for Jones. Reputedly, he lost upward of $50,000 on the film, which was as much an air melodrama as it was a Western. Warner Brothers' Northwest melodrama, *Land of the Silver Fox*, released on October 13, 1928, was a legitimate sound film, and audiences listened—actually listened!—to the menacing growls of Rin-Tin-Tin as he thwarted villainous John Miljan and Tom Santschi in their attempts at despicable deeds. Old Rinty had been Warner's bread-and-butter for several years, earning the profits that enabled the company to indulge itself in more artistic films.

In January, 1929, Fox released its bombshell, Raoul Walsh's *In Old Arizona*, a smash hit at the box office. It earned star Warner Baxter an Academy Award for his portrayal of the Cisco Kid, a role minor Western star Buddy Roosevelt, a friend of Walsh, lost when he broke his leg and could not be tested for the part. The film was significant for several reasons, but none more important than the fact that outdoor dramas had been proven to be feasible.

In a gradual switchover many Westerns in 1929-1930 had only sound effects and/or music scores rather than dialogue, and even more were made as straight silent films. And it was not unusual to issue a film in both silent and sound versions to cater to both types of movie houses, for there were still many which were not equipped for sound. Universal's last silent serial, for example, was also its first sound one, *The Indians Are Coming*, made in 1930 and starring Tim McCoy and Allene Ray. Grossing over $1 million on an investment of under $175,000, it gave serial stature a needed shot of adrenalin and did possibly as much to stimulate enthusiasm for the Western as did the epics of the period. Certainly it built a fire of Western enthusiasm under Carl Laemmle, the feisty little giant who built Universal. He jumped at the chance to finance both a Hoot Gibson and a Ken Maynard series of sound Westerns budgeted at around $75,000 each, a tidy sum for a "B" Western.

FBO first employed sound effects and music scores on its series with Tom Tyler and Buzz Barton. Universal started out with music and limited talking sequences in its Ken Maynard and Hoot Gibson releases of 1929. Syndicate employed music scores only in its Bob Custer releases of that year. But Leo Maloney's independently produced *Overland Bound*, starring himself, Jack Perrin, Wally Wales, and Allene Ray, and the J. Charles Davis production *West of the Rockies*, starring Art Mix, were full-fledged talkies regardless of their many technical and artistic shortcomings.

The Virginian (Paramount, 1929) was Paramount's first sound Western and was produced on a large scale with Gary Cooper in the lead role. An archetypal Western, Cooper oversees the hanging of his best friend for cattle stealing. It was followed shortly by *The Spoilers* (1930), also starring Cooper. Both films were box-office bonanzas, much as *In Old Arizona* had been. And Raoul Walsh, fresh from his triumph in the latter film, directed for Fox one of the outstanding early sound epics, *The Big Trail*, released in 1930 and starring an unknown named John Wayne. The film was released first in 70mm, later in a standard 35mm version. Its artistic success exceeded its financial one, but it was an important film in the re-establishment of the Western genre as a major force in the film industry. King Vidor's *Billy the Kid* (1930) was MGM's entry to the major Westerns of the transition period. With William S. Hart serving as technical advisor, it is not surprising that it recaptured some of the grimness of *Hell's Hinges*, *White Oak*, and *Tumbleweeds*. But its

The Virginian (Paramount, 1929) — Mary Brian, Gary Cooper, and Richard Arlen

panorama and characterization found a receptive audience, and it served as a beginning for Johnny Mack Brown's long Western career. On a lesser scale, *Hell's Heroes* (1930), based on the Peter Kyne book *Three Godfathers*, was a surprisingly good Western produced on a modest budget by Universal. Likewise, Paramount's filming of Zane Grey's *The Border Legion* proved that there was still magic in the names of both Grey and star Jack Holt. And Cecil B. DeMille's *The Squaw Man* (1931), unusual both for its liberalism and its bigotry, pointed up rather vividly the inhuman role in which Westerners cast the American Indian. There was no question after this film that heavy drama could have a backdrop of the old West.

In 1931 RKO-Radio made *Cimarron*, Edna Ferber's spectacular account of the early history of Oklahoma. The film played to packed houses, copped the Academy Award as Best Film of the Year, and earned its star, Richard Dix, an Academy Award nomination. Undoubtedly, it was the most successful of the early sound Westerns, with good spectacle, superb acting, a keen sense of timing, and an especially enthralling landrush sequence in the film's first reel. Although far from being prairie cinema verite, it is clear that the intention was to create an illusion of reality in order to give the mammoth drama proper authority. The following year Universal released *Law and Order* with its John Huston screenplay, another film with roots in the William S. Hart brand of realism. It was possibly the best account yet of the Earp brothers and Doc Holliday at the O.K. Corral, with outstanding characterizations by Walter Huston, Harry Carey, and Raymond Hatton. Actually, the characters were not identified by name as being the Earps. Huston, for example, played "Frame Johnson." But it was obvious whom the characters were modeled after. The film recaptured much of the rugged austerity of the early Ince and Griffith films and those starring Hart, Carey, and Roy Stewart.

And so it was. A handful of epic films were produced and found favor with ever-expanding audiences. Some writers have credited the "B" boom of the Thirties to the renewed interest generated by these few outstanding Westerns, but that is a precarious point of view when the facts are examined closely. In 1930, before any of the big Westerns had yet had an opportunity to draw big at the box office, with the exception of *In Old Arizona*, the "B" boom had commenced. At Fox, George O'Brien was making a first-rate series of Westerns. Not to be confused with the low-budget, quickie programmers of the Forties and Fifties, the O'Briens were budgeted at up to $300,000 and utilized such locations as Monument Valley, various land cites in California, and distant locales in Arizona, Colorado, Montana, and Nevada. George brought to the genre a quality of acting and heroics seldom seen. An extrovert without equal, his personality, which was quite palatable, athletic prowess, dramatic ability, and comedy talents combined to make his films unique.

Hoot Gibson, Ken Maynard, and Ted Wells were in series at Universal. However, the Wells' series was a pedestrian affair with little enthusiasm for it shown by anyone, and it soon petered out. But Maynard and Gibson were riding tall in the saddle on Uncle Carl Laemmle's range. Maynard was fresh from his flamboyantly successful series at First National and was probably the most popular cowboy ace active at the time. On screen Ken projected as a shy, reticent cowpoke with the heroines, although he certainly had an eye for feminine pulchritude. Few could match him as an actioneer and his beautifully mounted films were expertly staged. With his own production unit and a six-figure budget, plus other niceties, Ken and Tarzan rode the crest of fame in the early depression years.

Gibson, too, was extremely popular at the turn of the Thirties and had a million-dollar contract with Laemmle. Known as the "Crown Prince of the Range," Gibson's bantering

The Lone Star Ranger (Fox, 1930) — Sue Carol and George O'Brien

Wild Horse (Allied, 1931) — Hoot Gibson and "Skeeter" Bill Robbins

comedy style had been well received during the Twenties, although many a child grew exasperated at the lack of action in some films, expectantly awaiting the final reel when Hoot invariably came to life in a whirlwind finale. Hoot's early sound films for Universal were generally light on action and heavy on bantering comedy but were good vehicles for him and were well received. However, Laemmle was running scared about the profitability of sound Westerns and decided not to renew Hoot's contract in 1931. So, Gibson signed with an independent, Allied Pictures, owned by Max H. Hoffman and serving the states rights market. Gibson's oaters for Allied were sadly lacking in production values as compared with the Universal product, but they were enjoyable. His characterization remained the same—that of the non-pistol-packing, rope-twirling, devilishly humorous, and bumbling cowboy who just happens into trouble. However, it was now downhill for the Hooter and he would never again be in the top echelon of cowboy favorites.

Bob Steele made his sound debut for Tiffany in *Near the Rainbow's End* (1930) and completed a total of eight films for the organization before moving to World Wide in 1932 for a series of six. Steele was one of the most handsome cowboy stars ever to appear on screen and also one of the smallest physically. But he was a whirlwind fighter, an excellent rider, an above-average actor, and possessed of a pleasant personality and voice. And not the least of his qualifications at this point was that he was young. Consequently, he seemed to be one of the brighter stars on the Western horizon and his legion of admirers was growing fast.

Buck Jones was hired by Sol Lesser in 1930 as a star for his Beverly Productions releasing through Columbia. After the first series of eight films Columbia took over production of the Jones pictures directly and he became a Columbia star *per se*. His first talkie was *The Lone Rider* (1930). Exhibitors and fans quickly re-established Buck at the box

Sunrise Trail (Tiffany, 1931) — Bob Steele and Jack Clifford

46

Men Without Law
(Columbia, 1930)—
Buck Jones and
"Silver"

Hello Trouble (Co-
lumbia, 1932) —
Buck Jones and
"Silver"

office and he and Silver were off and running to overtake Ken Maynard and Tarzan as the nation's favorite cowboy-horse twosome.

"Why not a second series of horse operas?" mused studio execs when it became apparent that they were making a bundle from the Jones films. Thus, Tim McCoy soon joined the Columbia stable. His first sound Western feature was *The One Way Trail* (1931), filmed for less than $20,000, directed by Ray Taylor, and featuring two comely prima donnas, Doris Hill and Polly Ann Young. McCoy took his acting seriously, as he had at MGM, and he quickly established his reputation as a stalwart, straight-forward Westerner in the twelve Columbias released during the Transition Years.

Tom Keene was in the saddle at RKO-Radio in one of the better and more popular series of the early Thirties. Lane Chandler was in a series at Big Four and Tom Tyler and Bob Custer were at work at Syndicate. Wally Wales, Buffalo Bill, Jr., and Jack Perrin were at work here and there among the smaller outfits. In 1932, the final year of the transition period, twenty-two "B" cowboys had identifiable series; others were appearing in non-series films.

Thus, the contention of numerous writers that the "A" Western carried the "B" product is highly questionable. The opposite side of that coin looks just as promising. The truth is that the "B" has always taken care of itself and, until the late Forties, did a better job of perpetuating itself and maintaining a consistent popularity than the "A" did. Both genres have borrowed extensively from the other. Many standard ingredients first appearing in "B" Westerns were carried over into the "A." Popular themes first used in "A's" have sifted down into the "B's." Neither type of Western has ever been dependent on the other for its survival, nor has either ever been responsible for any noticeable change in the popularity of the other.

Mention has already been made of *The Indians Are Coming* and its success, which resulted in part in giving the serial a new lease on life. Hoping to duplicate Universal's success, Mascot produced five cliffhangers during the Transition Years—two starring canine Rin-Tin-Tin, two with veteran Harry Carey, fresh from his MGM triumph *Trader Horn*, and one with Tom Tyler. Universal itself attempted to follow up on its success by offering another cowboy and Indian thriller, *Battling with Buffalo Bill*. Tom Tyler and Rex Bell headed up a rather impressive cast. Neither this serial, nor another, *Heroes of the West*, with young Noah Beery, Jr., matched the popularity of the earlier McCoy effort but they made money. Even the small indies Syndicate and Metropolitan came out with Western serials, the latter producing a fairly enjoyable one called *The Sign of the Wolf* and featuring a cast of old reliables headed by Rex Lease.

The transition had been made. It makes little difference whether the "B" drew its sustenance from the "A" or if the "A" was made possible because of a bedrock of "B's." Side by side they had weathered the perilous plunge into the chasm of fear, and the abyss of oblivion had failed to hold them.

FILMS OF 1928

1. THE BIG HOP
(Buck Jones Productions, August 31, 1928)   7 Reels
(Sound Effects and Synchronized Music)
Buck Jones, Jobyna Ralston, Ernest Hilliard, Charles
   K. French, Charles Clary, Duke Lee, Edward
   Hearne, Jack Dill
D: James W. Horne
S: J. B. Mack
P: Buck Jones

2. LAND OF THE SILVER FOX
(Warner Bros., October 13, 1928)   7 Reels
Rin-Tin-Tin, Leila Hyams, John Miljan, Carroll Nye,
   Tom Santschi, Princess Neola
D: Ray Enright
S: Charles Condon
Scen/Dial: Howard Smith

FILMS OF 1929

3. THE TRAIL OF '98
(MGM, January 5, 1929)   8799 Ft.
(Music and Sound Effects)
Dolores Del Rio, Harry Carey, Tully Marshall,
   Ralph Forbes, Tenen Holtz, Karl Dane, Russell
   Simpson, John Down, George Cooper
D: Clarence Brown
S: "The Trail of '98: A Northland Romance"—
   Robert William Service
SP: Benjamin Glazer

4. IN OLD ARIZONA
(Fox, January 20, 1929)   8724 Ft.
Warner Baxter, Edmund Lowe, Dorothy Burgess, J.
   Farrell MacDonald, Fred Warren, Henry Armetta,
   Frank Campeau, Tom Santschi, Pat Hartigan, Roy
   Stewart, James Bradbury, Jr., John Dillon, Frank
   Nelson, Duke Martin, James Marcus, Joe Brown,
   Alphonse Ethier, Soledad Jiminez, Helen Lynch
D: Raoul Walsh, Irving Cummings
SP: Tom Barry

5. THE RAINBOW
(Tiffany-Stahl, February 1, 1929)   6114 Ft.
(Sound Effects)
Dorothy Sebastian, Laurence Gray, Sam Hardy,
   Harvey Clarke, Paul Hurst, Gino Corrado, King
   Zany
D: Reginald Barker
S: L. G. Rigby

6. THE ROYAL RIDER
(First National, February 17, 1929)   67 Mins.
(One version released with synchronized effects, no
   dialogue)
Ken Maynard, Olive Hasbrouck, Phillipe De Lacy,
   Theodore Lorch, Joseph Burke, Harry Semels,
   William Franey, Frank Rice, Bobby Dunn, Johnny
   Sinclair, Benny Corbett, "Tarzan"
D: Harry Joe Brown

S: Nate Gatzert
P: Charles R. Rogers

7. TIDE OF EMPIRE
(Cosmopolitan/MGM, March 23, 1929)   6552 Ft.
(Music Score and Sound Effects)
Renee Adoree, George Duryea, George Faucett,
   William Collier, Jr., Fred Kohler, James Bradbury,
   Sr., Harry Gribbon, Paul Hurst
D: Allan Dwan
S: Peter B. Kyne

8. WOLF SONG
(Paramount Famous Lasky, March 30, 1929)
   6769 Ft.
Gary Cooper, Lupe Velez, Louis Wolheim, Constan-
   tine Romanoff, Michael Vavitch, Ann Brady, Russ
   Columbo, Augustina Lopez, George Regas
D: Victor Fleming
S: "Wolf Song" in *Red Book*—Harvey Ferguson
SP: John Farrow

9. IDAHO RED
(FBO, April 28, 1929)   4768 Ft.
(Music and Sound Effects)
Tom Tyler, Frankie Darro, Patricia Caron, Barney
   Furey, Lew Meehan
D: Robert De Lacey
S: Frank Clark

10. PALS OF THE PRAIRIE
(FBO, July, 1929)   4776 Ft.
(Music Score and Sound Effects)
Buzz Barton, Frank Rice, Tom Lingham, Duncan
   Renaldo, Milburn Morante, Natalie Joyce, Bill
   Patton
D: Louis King
S: Oliver Drake
SP: Frank Clark

11. THE WAGON MASTER
(Universal, September 8, 1929) 70 Mins.
(Talking Sequences and Music Score)
Ken Maynard, Edith Roberts, Tom Santschi, Jackie Hanlon, Al Ferguson, Bobby Dunn, Frank Rice, Fred Dana
D: Harry Joe Brown
S: Marion Jackson
P: Ken Maynard
Dial: Lesley Mason

12. RIDERS OF THE RIO GRANDE
(Syndicate, September 29, 1929) 4900-5277 Ft.
(Music Score)
Bob Custer, Edna Aslin, Horace B. Carpenter, Kit Cooper, Bob Erickson, Martin Cichy, Merrill McCormack
D: J. P. McGowan
S/SP: Sally Winters

13. IN OLD CALIFORNIA
(Audible, October 15, 1929) 5400 Ft.
Henry B. Wathall, Helen Ferguson, George Duryea (Tom Keene), Orral Humphrey, Larry Steers, Richard Carlyle, Henry Allen, Lew Stern, Paul Ellis, Charlotte Monti (Carlotti Monti), Gertrude Chorre, Ray Hazlor
D: Burton King
S: Fred Hart
SP: Arthur Hoerl

14. THE LONG, LONG TRAIL
(Universal, October 27, 1929) 5331 Ft.
(Part Talking)
Hoot Gibson, Sally Eilers, Walter Brennan, James Mason, Kathryn McGuire, Archie Ricks, Harold Truesdale
D: Arthur Rosson
S: "Ramblin' Kid"—Earl Bowman
SP: Howard Green
P: Hoot Gibson

15. ROMANCE OF THE RIO GRANDE
(Fox, November 8, 1929) 8652 Ft.
Warner Baxter, Mona Maris, Mary Duncan, Antonio Moreno, Merrill McCormack, Robert Edeson, Soledad Jiminez, Mabel Coleman, Charles Byer, Albert Roccardi, Agostino Borgato
D: Alfred Santell
S: "Conquistador"—Katherine Fullerton Gerould
SP: Marion Orth

16. THE VIRGINIAN
(Paramount, November 9, 1929) 8717 Ft.
Gary Cooper, Walter Huston, Richard Arlen, Mary Brian, Chester Conklin, Eugene Pallette, E. H. Calvert, Helen Ware, Vic Potel, Tex Young, Charles Stevens, Jack Pennick, George Chandler, Willie Fung, George Morrell, Ernie Adams, Ethan Laidlaw, Ed Brady, Bob Kortman, James Mason, Fred Burns, Nena Quartero, Randolph Scott (unbilled)
D: Victor Fleming
S: Owen Wister
SP: Howard Estabrook
Titles: Joseph L. Mankiewicz
Ass't D: Henry Hathaway
P: Louis D. Lighton

17. SENOR AMERICANO
(Universal, November 10, 1929) 71 Mins.
(Part Talking)
Ken Maynard, Kathryn Crawford, Frank Yaconelli, J. P. McGowan, Frank Beal, Gino Corrado, "Tarzan"
D: Harry Joe Brown
SP: Lesley Mason
P: Ken Maynard

18. THE GREAT DIVIDE
(First National, November 16, 1929) 6722 Ft.
Dorothy Mackaill, Ian Keith, Lucien Littlefield, Ben Hendricks, Myrna Loy, Frank Tang, Creighton Hale, George Fawcett, Jean Laverty, Claude Gillingwater, Marjorie Kane, Roy Stewart
D: Reginald Barker
S: William Vaughn Moody
SP: Fred Myton, Paul Perez

19. OVERLAND BOUND
(Rayton Talking Pictures/Presido, November 23, 1929) 5200 Ft.
Jack Perrin, Wally Wales, Leo Maloney, Allene Ray, Lydia Knott, Charles K. French, R. J. Smith, Joe Maloney, William Dyer, "Bullet," "Starlight"
D: Leo Maloney
SP: Ford Beebe, Joseph Kane
P: Leo Maloney

20. WEST OF THE ROCKIES
(Davis Productions, December 15, 1929) 6 Reels
Art Mix, Horace B. Carpenter, Henry Rocquemore, George Brown, Cliff Lyons, Bud Osborne, Fontaine LaRue, Inez Gomez, Ione Reed, Al Hewston, Pete Crawford, Antonio Sanchez
D: Horace B. Carpenter
S: Philip Schuyler

21. COURTIN' WILDCATS
(Universal, December 22, 1929) 5118 Ft.
(Part Talking)
Hoot Gibson, Eugenia Gilbert, Pete Morrison, Monte Montague, Joe Bonomo, Harry Todd, John Oscar, Joe Farley, Joseph Girard, Jim Corey
D: Jerome Storm
SP: Dudley McKenna
S: "Courtin' Calamity"—William Dudley Pelley

FILMS OF 1930

22. HELL'S HEROES
(Universal, January 5, 1930)   6148 Ft.
Charles Bickford, Raymond Hatton, Fred Kohler,
   Fritzi Ridgeway, Maria Alba, Jose De LaCruz,
   Buck Connors, Walter James
D: William Wyler
S: "Three Godfathers"—Peter B. Kyne
SP: Tom Reed

23. THE LONE STAR RANGER
(Fox, January 5, 1930)   5736 Ft.
George O'Brien, Sue Carol, Russell Simpson, Eliza-
   beth Patterson, Dick Alexander, William Steele,
   Bob Fleming, Caroline Rankin, Lee Shumway,
   Joel Franz, Joe Chase, Oliver Eckhardt, Billy
   Butts, Ralph LeFevre
D: A. F. Erickson
S: Zane Grey
SP: Seton Miller

24. PARADE OF THE WEST
(Universal, January 19, 1930)   75 Mins.
(Part Talking)
Ken Maynard, Gladys McConnell, Frank Yaconelli,
   Otis Harlan, Jackie Hanlon, Frank Rice, Fred
   Burns, Bobbie Dunn, Blue Washington, Stanley
   Blystone, "Tarzan," "Rex"
D: Harry Joe Brown
S: Bennett Cohen

25. FIREBRAND JORDAN
(National Players/Big 4, January 28, 1930)
   5400 Ft.
Lane Chandler, Yakima Canutt, Aline Goodwin,
   Tom London, Frank Yaconelli, Cliff Lyons, Fred
   Harvey, Al Hewston, Lew Meehan, Marguerite
   Ainslee, Sheldon Lewis
D: Alvin J. Neitz (Alan James)
S/SP: Carl Krusada
P: F. E. Douglas

26. COVERED WAGON TRAILS
(Syndicate, February 1, 1930)   4617 Ft.
(Music Score)
Bob Custer, Phyliss Bainbridge, J. P. McGowan,
   Charles Brinley, Martin Cichy, Perry Murdock
D: J. P. McGowan
S/SP: Sally Winters

27. THE MOUNTED STRANGER
(Universal, February 8, 1930)   5984 Ft.
Hoot Gibson, Louise Lorraine, Francis Ford, Fred
   Burns, Jim Corey, Walter Patterson, Milt Brown,
   Buddy Hunter, Francelia Billington, Malcolm
   White

D: Arthur Rosson
S: "Ridin' Kid from Powder River"—H. H. Knibbs
SP: Arthur Rosson

28. THE FIGHTING PARSON
(Hal Roach/MGM, February 22, 1930)   2 Reels
Harry Langdon, Thelma Todd, Nancy Dover, Eddie
   Dunn, Leo Willis, Charlie Hall
D: Charles Rogers, Fred Guiol
Story Ed: H. M. Walker

29. THE COWBOY AND THE OUTLAW
(Big Productions Film Corp./Syndicate,
   February 23, 1930)
(Music Score and Sound Effects)
Bob Steele, Edna Aslin, Bud Osborne, J. P.
   McGowan, Al Hewston, Tom Lingham, Cliff
   Lyons
D: J. P. McGowan
S/SP: Sally Winters

30. CALL OF THE DESERT
(Syndicate, March 1, 1930)   4800 Ft.
(Music Score)
Tom Tyler, Sheila LeGay, Bud Osborne, Cliff
   Lyons, Bobby Dunn
D: J. P. McGowan
SP: Sally Winters

31. PARTING OF THE TRAILS
(Syndicate, March 1, 1930)   5 Reels
(Music Score)
Bob Custer, Vivian Ray, Bobbie Dunn, George Mil-
   ler, Tom Bay, Henry Rocquemore
D/P: J. P. McGowan
SP: Sally Winters

32. BEAU BANDIT
(RKO-Radio, March 2, 1930)   6169 Ft.
Rod LaRocque, Doris Kenyon, George Duryea
   (Tom Keene), Barney Furey, Charles Middleton,
   Bill Patton, Mitchell Lewis, Walter Long, James
   Donlan, Charles Brinley, Ben Corbett, Gordon
   Jones, Ken Cooper, Buff Jones, Hank Potts, Walt
   Robbins
D: Lambert Hillyer
SP: Wallace Smith
P: William LeBaron

33. LUCKY LARKIN
(Universal, March 2, 1930)   66 Mins.
(Synchronized and Musical Effects)
Ken Maynard, Nora Lane, Paul Hurst, Blue Wash-
   ington, James Farley, Charles Clary, Harry Todd,
   Jack Rockwell, "Tarzan"

D: Harry Joe Brown
S/SP: Marion Jackson
P: Ken Maynard, Harry Joe Brown

34. THE LIGHT OF THE WESTERN STARS
(Paramount, March 3, 1930) 6219 Ft.
Richard Arlen, Mary Brian, Regis Toomey, Fred Kohler, Syd Saylor, Harry Green, George Chandler, Guy Oliver, Gus Saville, William LeMaine
D: Otto Brower
S: Zane Grey
SP: Grover Jones, William McNutt

35. SONG OF THE WEST
(Warner Bros., March 15, 1930) 7185 Ft.
(Technicolor)
John Boles, Vivienne Segal, Joe E. Brown, Edward Martindel, Harry Gribbon, Marie Wells, Sam Hardy, Marion Byron, Rudolph Cameron
D: Ray Enright
S: "Rainbow"—an operetta by Laurence Stallings and Oscar Hammerstein II
SP: Harvey Thew

36. MONTANA MOON
(MGM, March 20, 1930) 7917 Ft.
John Mack Brown, Joan Crawford, Cliff Edwards, Dorothy Sebastian, Ricardo Cortez, Benny Rubin, Karl Dane, Lloyd Ingraham
D: Malcolm St. Clair
S/SP: Sylvia Thalberg
P: Malcolm S. Clair

37. TRAILIN' TROUBLE
(Universal, March 23, 1930) 5198 Ft.
Hoot Gibson, Margaret Quimby, Pete Morrison, Olive Young, William McCall, Bob Perry
D: Arthur Rosson
S: "Hand 'Em Over"—Arthur Rosson
P: Hoot Gibson

38. UNDER A TEXAS MOON
(Warner Bros., April 1, 1930) 7498 Ft.
(Technicolor)
Frank Fay, Raquel Torres, Myrna Loy, Armida, Noah Beery, Sr., George E. Stone, George Cooper, Fred Kohler, Betty Boyd, Charles Selton, Jack Curtis, Sam Appel, Tully Marshall, Mona Maris, Francisco Maran, Tom Dix, Jerry Barrett, Inez Gomez, Bruce Covington
D: Michael Curtiz
S: "Two-Gun Man"—Stewart Edward White
SP: Gordon Rigby

39. THE FIGHTING LEGION
(Universal, April 6, 1930) 75 Mins.
(Part Talking)

Ken Maynard, Dorothy Dawn, Frank Rice, Charles Whittaker, Ernie Adams, Harry Todd, Robert Walker, Stanley Blystone, Les Bates, Bill Nestell, Jack Fowler, "Tarzan"
D: Harry Joe Brown
S: Bennett Cohen
SP: Bennett Cohen, Lesley Mason
P: Ken Maynard

40. BEYOND THE RIO GRANDE
(Biltmore Prod./Big 4, April 12, 1930) 5400 Ft.
Jack Perrin, Buffalo Bill, Jr., Charlene Burt, Pete Morrison, Franklyn Farum, Edmund Cobb, Henry Rocquemore, Emma Tansey, Henry Taylor, "Starlight" (the Wonder Horse)
D: Harry Webb
SP: Carl Krusada
P: F. E. Douglas

41. ROARING RANCH
(Universal, April 27, 1930) 6094 Ft.
Hoot Gibson, Sally Eilers, Wheeler Oakman, Bobby Nelson, Leo White, Frank Clark
D: B. Reeves Eason
S: B. Reeves Eason
SP: B. Reeves Eason
P: Hoot Gibson

42. THE ARIZONA KID
(Fox, April 27, 1930) 7902 Ft.
Warner Baxter, Carole Lombard, Theodore von Eltz, Hank Mann, Mona Maris, Soledad Jiminez, Wilfred Lucas, Jim Gibson, Larry McGrath, Jack Herrick, Walter Lewis, Arthur Stone, De Sacia Mooers
D: Alfred Santell
S: O. Henry
SP: Ralph Brock, Joseph Wright

43. THE TEXAN
(Paramount, April 27, 1930) 7142 Ft.
Gary Cooper, Fay Wray, Donald Reed, Emma Dunn, Soledad Jiminez, Cesar Vanoni, Enrique Acosta, Ed Brady, Vera Buckland, Romualdo Tirado, James Marcus, Russ Columbo
D: John Cromwell
S: "The Double-Dyed Deceiver"—O. Henry
SP: Daniel N. Rubin
Adaptation: Victor Milner
Ass't D: Henry Hathaway
(Remade in 1939 as The Llano Kid)

44. MOUNTAIN JUSTICE
(Universal, May 4, 1930) 6797 Ft.
(Title changed from Kettle Creek)
Ken Maynard, Kathryn Crawford, Fred Burns, Otis Harlan, Pee Wee Holmes, Paul Hurst, Richard

Carlyle, Les Bates, Blue Washington, "Tarzan"
D: Harry Joe Brown
S/SP: Bennett Cohen
P: Ken Maynard, Harry Joe Brown

45. CALL OF THE WEST
(Columbia, May 10, 1930) 6500 Ft.
Dorothy Revier, Matt Moore, Tom O'Brien, Victor
  Potel, Buff Jones, Nick DeCruz, Blanche Rose,
  Claire Ward, Gertrude Bennett, Allan Roscoe, Joe
  De LaCruz, Connie LaMont, Bud Osborne
D: Albert Ray
S/SP: Florence Ryerson, Colin Clements

46. SAGEBRUSH POLITICS
(Hollywood Pictures, May 15, 1930)
(Talking Sequences)
Art Mix, Lillian Bond, Jim Campbell, Tom Forman,
  William Ryno, Pee Wee Holmes, Jack Gordon,
  Wally Merrill
D: Victor Adamson
P: Victor Adamson

47. RIDIN' LAW
(Big 4, May 24, 1930) 5600 Ft.
Jack Perrin, Yakima Canutt, Rene Borden, Jack
  Mowers, Ben Corbett, Pete Morrison, Fern Em-
  mett, Olive Young, Robert Walker, "Starlight"
D: Harry S. Webb
SP: Carl Krusada
P: Harry S. Webb, F. E. Douglas

48. BORDER ROMANCE
(Tiffany, May 25, 1930) 5974 Ft.
Armida, Don Terry, Marjorie Kane, Victor Potel,
  Wesley Barry, Nina Martan, J. Frank Glendon,
  Harry von Meter, William Costello
D: Richard Thorpe
S/SP: Jack Natteford
P: Lester F. Scott

49. THE CANYON OF MISSING MEN
(Syndicate, June 1, 1930) 4742 Ft.
(Music Score)
Tom Tyler, Sheila LeGay, Tom Forman, Bud Os-
  borne, Cliff Lyons, Bobby Dunn, Arden Ellis, J. P.
  McGowan
D: J. P. McGowan
S: George Williams
SP: Sally Winters

50. TRIGGER TRICKS
(Universal, June 8, 1930) 5461 Ft.
Hoot Gibson, Sally Eilers, Neal Hart, Pete Morrison,
  Monte Montague, Max Asher, Walter Perry, Jack
  Richardson, Robert Homans

D: B. Reeves Eason
S/SP: B. Reeves Eason
P: Hoot Gibson

51. NEAR THE RAINBOW'S END
(Tiffany, June 10, 1930) 5169 Ft.
Bob Steele, Louise Lorraine, Al Ferguson, Lafe
  McKee, Al Hewston, Hank Bell, Merrill McCor-
  mack
D: J. P. McGowan
SP: Sally Winters
P: Trem Carr

52. ROUGH ROMANCE
(Fox, June 22, 1930) 4800 Ft.
George O'Brien, Helen Chandler, Antonio Moreno,
  Roy Stewart, Eddie Borden, John Wayne, Frank
  Lanning
D: A. F. Erickson
S: Kenneth Clark

53. THE BORDER LEGION
(Paramount, June 28, 1930) 6088 Ft.
Jack Holt, Richard Arlen, Fay Wray, Syd Saylor,
  Eugene Pallette, Stanley Fields, Ethan Allen, E. H.
  Calvert
D: Edwin H. Knopf, Otto Brower
S: Zane Grey
SP: Percy Heath

54. 'NEATH WESTERN SKIES
(Syndicate, June 29, 1930) 4924 Ft.
Tom Tyler, Lotus Thompson, Hank Bell, J. P.
  McGowan, Barney Furey, Bobby Dunn, Al Hews-
  ton, Harry Woods
D: J. P. McGowan
SP: Sally Winters

55. SONG OF THE CABALLERO
(Universal, June 29, 1930) 72 Mins.
Ken Maynard, Doris Hill, Francis Ford, Frank Rice,
  William Irving, Joyzelle Joyner, Evelyn Sherman,
  Josef Swickward, Gino Corrado
D: Harry Joe Brown
S: Kenneth Bonton
SP: Bennett Cohen
P: Ken Maynard

56. BAR L RANCH
(Big 4, July 1, 1930) 60 Mins.
Buffalo Bill, Jr., Wally Wales, Yakima Canutt, Betty
  Baker, Ben Corbett, Fern Emmett, Robert Walker
D: Harry S. Webb
S: Bennett Cohen
SP: Bennett Cohen, Carl Krusada
P: F. E. Douglas

57. THE DUDE WRANGLER
(Sono Art-World Wide, July 1, 1930) 6200 Ft.
Tom Keene, Lina Basquette, Francis X. Bushman, Clyde Cook, Ethel Wales, Margaret Sheldon, K. Sojin, Wilfred North, Jack Richardson, Virginia Sayles, Julia Gordon, Fred Parker, Aileen Carlyle
D: Richard Thorpe
S: Caroline Lockhart
SP: Robert Lee (Robert Lee Johnson)

58. THE LONE RIDER
(Beverly Productions/Columbia, July 13, 1930) 5118 Ft.
Buck Jones, Vera Reynolds, Harry Woods, George Pearce, "Silver"
D: Louis King
S: Frank Clark
SP: Forrest Sheldon
P: Sol Lesser
(Remade as *The Man Trailer* in 1934)

59. WAY OUT WEST
(MGM, August 2, 1930) 6407 Ft.
William Haines, Leila Hyams, Polly Moran, Cliff Edwards, Francis X. Bushman, Jr., Vera Marsh, Charles Middleton, Jack Pennick, Buddy Roosevelt, Jay Wilsey (Buffalo Bill, Jr.)
D: Fred Nilbo
S: Bryan Morgan, Alfred Brock

60. SONS OF THE SADDLE
(Universal, August 3, 1930) 76 Mins.
Ken Maynard, Doris Hill, Francis Ford, Joe Girard, Harry Todd, Caroll Nye, Frank Rice
D: Harry Joe Brown
S/SP: Bennett Cohen
P: Ken Maynard

61. THE LONESOME TRAIL
(Syndicate, August 7, 1930) 5786 Ft.
Charles Delaney, Virginia Brown Faire, Yakima Canutt, Ben Corbett, Lafe McKee, Monte Montague, James Aubrey, George Regas, George Berlinger, George Hackathorne, Bob Reeves, Art Mix, Bill McCall, William Von Bricken
D: Bruce Mitchell
S/SP: G. A. Durlam

62. OKLAHOMA CYCLONE
(Tiffany, August 8, 1930) 5916 Ft.
Bob Steele, Al St. John, Nita Ray, Charles King, Slim Whitaker, Shorty Hendricks, Emilio Fernandez, Hector Sarno, Fred Burns, Cliff Lyons, John Ince
D: John P. McCarthy
S: John P. McCarthy
SP: Ford Beebe
P: Trem Carr

63. THE STORM
(Universal, August 18, 1930) 7203 Ft.
Lupe Velez, Paul Cavanagh, William Boyd, Alphonse Ethier, Ernest Adams, Tom London, Nick Thompson, Erin LaBissoniere
D: William Wyler
SP: Wells Root
P: Carl Laemmle

64. SPURS
(Universal, August 24, 1930) 5303 Ft.
Hoot Gibson, Helen Wright, Robert Homans, Frank Clark, Buddy Hunter, Gilbert "Pee Wee" Holmes, William Bertram, Philo McCullough, Cap Anderson, Pete Morrison, Art Ardigan (Artie Ortego)
D: B. Reeves Eason
S/SP: B. Reeves Eason
P: Hoot Gibson

65. CANYON HAWKS
(National Players/Big 4, August 26, 1930) 5400 Ft.
Wally Wales, Buzz Barton, Rene Borden, Yakima Canutt, Cliff Lyons, Bobby Dunn, Bob Reeves, Robert Walker
D: J. P. McGowan, Alvin J. Neitz (Alan James)
S/SP: Henry Taylor, Alvin J. Neitz
P: F. E. Douglas

66. LAST OF THE DUANES
(Fox, August 31, 1930) 5580 Ft.
George O'Brien, Lucile Browne, Myrna Loy, Nat Pendleton, Walter McGrail, James Mason, Lloyd Ingraham, James Bradbury, Jr., Willard Robertson, Blanche Frederici, Frank Campeau
D: Alfred L. Werker
S: Zane Grey
SP: Ernest Pascal

67. UNDER MONTANA SKIES
(Tiffany, September 10, 1930) 5273 Ft.
Kenneth Harlan, Dorothy Gulliver, Lafe McKee, Ethel Wales, Harry Todd, Nita Martan, Christian Frank, Slim Summerville
D: Richard Thorpe
S/SP: James Aubrey, Bennett Cohen

68. THE BAD MAN
(First National, September 14, 1930) 7124 Ft.
Walter Huston, Dorothy Revier, Sidney Blackmer, Guinn Williams, James Rennie, O. P. Heggie, Marion Byron, Arthur Stone, Edward Lynch, Harry Semels, Erville Alderson, Myrna Loy
D: Clarence Badger
S: Porter Emerson Browne, C. H. Towne
SP: Howard Estabrook
Play: Porter Emerson Browne

The Bad Man (First National, 1930) — Walter Huston and Myrna Loy

69. THE SPOILERS
(Paramount, September 20, 1930) 8128 Ft.
Gary Cooper, Kay Johnson, Betty Compson, William "Stage" Boyd, Harry Green, Slim Summerville, James Kirkwood, Lloyd Ingraham, Oscar Apfel, George Irving, Knute Ericson, Merrill McCormack, Charles K. French, Jack Holmes, John Beck, Edward Coxen
D: Edward Carewe
S: Rex Beach
SP: Bartlett Cormack
Scen: Agnes Brand Leahy
P: Edward Carewe

70. MEN OF THE NORTH
(MGM, September 27, 1930) 5700 Ft.
Gilbert Roland, Barbara Leonard, Robert Greaves, Jr., Nina Quartero, Arnold Korff, Robert Elliott, George Davis
D: Hal Roach
S: Willard Mack
P: Hal Roach

71. SANTA FE TRAIL
(Paramount, September 27, 1930) 5839 Ft.
Richard Arlen, Rosita Moreno, Eugene Pallette, Mitzi Greene, Junior Durkin, Hooper Atchley, Luis Alberni, Lee Shumway, Chief Yowlachie, Blue Cloud, Chief Standing Bear, Jack Byron
D: Edwin Knopf, Otto Brower
SP: Sam Mintz

72. SHADOW RANCH
(Beverly Productions/Columbia,
    September 28, 1930) 5766 Ft.
Buck Jones, Marguerite De La Motte, Kate Price, Frank Rice, Ben Wilson, Al Smith, Ernie Adams, Slim Whitaker, Robert McKenzie, Lafe McKee, Fred Burns, Ben Corbett, Frank Ellis, Hank Bell
D: Louis King
S: George M. Johnson, Clark Silvernail
SP: Frank Clark
P: Sol Lesser

73. TRAILS OF PERIL
(National Players/Big 4, September 30, 1930)
    5400 Ft.
(Title changed from *Trails of Danger*)
Wally Wales, Virginia Brown Faire, Frank Ellis, Lew Meehan, Jack Perrin, Joe Rickson, Buck Connors, Bobby Dunn, Pete Morrison, Hank Bell
D: Alvin J. Neitz
S: Henry Taylor
P: F. E. Douglas

74. BEYOND THE LAW
(Syndicate, October 1, 1930)   4500 Ft.
Robert Frazer, Lane Chandler, Louise Lorraine, Charles King, William Walling, Robert Graves, Ed Lynch, Jimmy Kane, George Hackathorne, Franklyn Farnum
D: J. P. McGowan
S: G. A. Durlam

75. CODE OF HONOR
(Syndicate, October 1, 1930)   5400 Ft.
Mahlon Hamilton, Doris Hill, Lafe McKee, Robert Greaves, Jr., Stanley Taylor, Jimmy Aubrey, Harry Holden, William Dyer
D: J. P. McGowan
S: G. A. Durlam

76. PARDON MY GUN
(RKO-Pathe, October 5, 1930)   5650 Ft.
Tom Keene (George Duryea), Sally Starr, Harry Woods, Ethan Laidlaw, Robert Edeson, Lee Moran, Mona Ray, Hank McFarland, Lew Meehan, Tom McFarlane, Ida Chadwick, Al Narman, Abe Lyman's Band
D: Robert DeLacey
S: Betty Scott
SP: Hugh Cummings

77. THE GIRL OF THE GOLDEN WEST
(First National, October 12, 1930)   7276 Ft.
Ann Harding, James Rennie, Harry Bannister, Ben Hendricks, Jr., J. Farrell MacDonald, George Cooper, Johnny Walker, Richard Carlyle, Arthur Stone, Arthur Housman, Norman McNeil, Fred Warren, Joe Girard, Newton House, Princess Noola, Chief Yowlachie
D: John Francis Dillon
Play: David Belasco
SP: Waldemar Young

78. THE LAND OF MISSING MEN
(Tiffany, October 15, 1930)   5179 Ft.
Bob Steele, Caryl Lincoln, Al St. John, Fern Emmett, S. S. Simons, Emilio Fernandez, Noah Hendricks, Al Jennings, Eddie Dunn, C. R. DaFau, Fred Burns
D: John P. McCarthy
S/SP: John P. McCarthy, Robert Quigley
P: Trem Carr

79. MEN WITHOUT LAW
(Beverly Productions/Columbia, October 15, 1930)   65 Mins.
Buck Jones, Carmelita Geraghty, Tom Carr, Lydia Knott, Harry Woods, Fred Burns, Syd Saylor, Fred Kelsey, Victor Sarno, Ben Corbett, Lafe McKee, Art Mix (George Kesterson), "Silver"
D: Louis King

S: Lou Seiler
SP: Dorothy Howell
P: Sol Lesser

80. BILLY THE KID
(MGM, October 18, 1930)   8808 Ft.
John Mack Brown, Wallace Beery, Kay Johnson, Karl Dane, Wyndham Standing, Russell Simpson, Blanche Frederici, Roscoe Ates, Warner Richmond, James Marcus, Nelson McDowell, Jack Carlyle, John Beck, Marguerita Padula, Aggie Herring, Soledad Jiminez, Don Coleman, Christopher Martin, Lucille Powers, Hank Bell
D: King Vidor
S: Walter Noble Burns
Cont: Wanda Tuchock
Dial: Lawrence Stallings
Addit. Dial: Charles MacArthur

81. THE INDIANS ARE COMING
(Universal, October 20, 1930)   12 Chaps.
Tim McCoy, Allene Ray, Edmund Cobb, Francis Ford, Wilbur McGough, Bud Osborne, Charles Royal, "Dynamite" (a dog)
D: Henry MacRae
S: "The Great West That Was"—William F. Cody
SP: Ford Beebe, George Plympton
P: Henry MacRae
Chapter Titles: (1) Pals in Buckskin, (2) A Call to Arms, (3) A Furnace of Fear, (4) The Red Terror, (5) The Circle of Death, (6) Hate's Harvest, (7) Hostages of Fear, (8) The Dagger Duel, (9) The Blast of Death, (10) Redskin's Vengeance, (11) Frontiers Aflame, (12) The Trail's End

82. THE BIG TRAIL
(Fox, October 24, 1930)
   158 Mins. (70mm); 125 Mins. (35mm)
John Wayne, Marguerite Churchill, Ian Keith, Tyrone Power, Sr., Ward Bond, El Brendel, Tully Marshall, Charles Stevens, Andy Shuford, David Rollins, Frederick Burton, Jack Peabody, Russ Powell, Helen Parrish, Louise Carver, William V. Mong, Marcia Harris, Marjorie Leet, Frank Rainboth, Chief Big Tree, Emslie Emerson, Gertrude Van Lent, Alphonz Ethier, Lucille Van Lent, DeWill Jennings
D: Raoul Walsh
S: Hal G. Evarts
SP: Maria Boyle, Jack Peabody, Florence Postal

83. THE SILVER HORDE
(RKO-Radio, October 25, 1930)   6735 Ft.
Evelyn Brent, Louis Wolheim, Joel McCrea, Raymond Hatton, Jean Arthur, Gavin Gordon, Blanche Sweet, Purnell Pratt, William Davidson, Ivan Linow

D: George Archainbaud
P: William Baron
SP: Wallace Smith
S: "The Silver Horde"—Rex Beach

84. THE CONCENTRATIN' KID

(Universal, October 26, 1930) 5148 Ft.
Hoot Gibson, Kathryn Crawford, Duke Lee, Robert Homans, James Mason
D: Arthur Rosson
S: Harold Tarshis, Charles Saxton
SP: Harold Tarshis
P: Hoot Gibson

85. HEADIN' NORTH

(Tiffany, November 1, 1930) 5346 Ft.
Bob Steele, Barbara Luddy, Perry Murdock, Walter Shumway, Eddie Dunn, Fred Burns, Gordon DeMain, Harry Allen, Gunner Davis, S. S. Simon, James Welsh, Jack Henderson
D: J. P. McCarthy
S/SP: J. P. McCarthy
P: Trem Carr

86. PHANTOM OF THE DESERT

(Syndicate, November 1, 1930) 5220 Ft.
Jack Perrin, Eve Novak, Josef Swickard, Lila Eccles, Ben Corbett, Edward Earle, Robert Walker, Pete Morrison, "Starlight"
D: Harry S. Webb
SP: Carl Krusada
P: Harry Webb, F. E. Douglas

87. BREED OF THE WEST

(Big 4, November 12, 1930) 5400 Ft.
Wally Wales, Buzz Barton, Virginia Brown Faire, Robert Walker, Lafe McKee, Bobby Dunn, George Gerwin, Hank Cole
D: Alvin J. Neitz (Alan James)
SP: Henry Taylor, Alvin J. Neitz
P: F. E. Douglas

88. UNDER TEXAS SKIES

(Syndicate, November 15, 1930) 5119 Ft.
Bob Custer, Natalie Kingston, Bill Cody, Lane Chandler, Tom London, Bob Roper, William McCall, Joe Marba
D: J. P. McGowan
S/SP: G. A. Durlam
P: W. Ray Johnston

89. THE APACHE KID'S ESCAPE

(Robert J. Horner Productions,
    November 22, 1930) 4600 Ft.
Jack Perrin, Josephine Hill, Fred Church, Virginia Ashcroft, Henry Rocquemore, Bud Osborne, "Starlight"

D: Robert J. Horner

90. THE DAWN TRAIL

(Beverly Productions/Columbia,
    November 23, 1930) 66 Mins.
Buck Jones, Miriam Seegar, Charles Morton, Erville Alderson, Edward J. LeSaint, Charles King, Hank Mann, Vester Pegg, Charles Brinley, Charles Whittaker, Inez Gomez, Robert Burns, Robert Fleming, Violet Axzelle, Buck Connors, Jack Curtis
D: Christy Cabanne
S: Forrest Sheldon
SP: John Thomas Neville
P: Sol Lesser

91. THE UTAH KID

(Tiffany, November 27, 1930) 4408 Ft.
Rex Lease, Dorothy Sebastian, Tom Santschi, Walter Miller, Boris Karloff, Lafe McKee, Mary Carr, Bud Osborne, Jack Rockwell, Blackie Whiteford, Fred Burns, Bob Card, Al Taylor
D: Richard Thorpe
S: Frank Clark

92. THE RIVER'S END

(Warner Bros., November 1930) 75 Mins.
Charles Bickford, Evelyn Knapp, J. Farrell Mac-Donald, Zasu Pitts, Walter McGrail, David Torrance, Frank Coghlan, Jr., Tom Santschi
D: Michael Curtiz
S: James Oliver Curwood
SP: Charles Kenyon

93. ROUGE OF THE RIO GRANDE

(World Wide, December 7, 1930) 5146 Ft.
Jose Bohr, Myrna Loy, Raymond Hatton, William Burt, Florence Dudley, Carmelita Geraghty, Walter Miller, Gene Morgan
D: Spencer Gordon Bennet
S: Oliver Drake
P: George W. Weeks

94. FIGHTIN' THRU

(Tiffany, December 25, 1930) 61 Mins.
(Also known as *California in 1878*)
Ken Maynard, Carmelita Geraghty, Charles King, Wallace MacDonald, W. L. Thorne, Jeanette Loff, Fred Burns, Bill Nestell, Tommy Bay, John (Jack) Fowler, Charles Baldra, Art Mix, "Tarzan," Jack Kirk, Bud McClure, Jim Corey
D: William Nigh
S/SP: Jack Natteford
P: Phil Goldstone

95. THE LASH

(First National, December 28, 1930) 7169 Ft.

Richard Barthelmess, Mary Astor, Fred Kohler, Marian Nixon, James Rennie, Robert Edeson, Barbara Bedford, Arthur Stone, Erville Alderson, Mathilde Comont

D: Frank Lloyd
S: "Adios"—Lanier Bartlett, Virginia Stivers Bartlett
SP: Bradley King

96. THE CHEYENNE KID

(West Coast Pictures, 1930)

Buffalo Bill, Jr., Joan Jaccard, Yakima Canutt, Jack Mower, Frank Ellis, Fred Burns, Violet McKay, Tom Forman

D: Jacques Jaccard
S: Jacques Jaccard, Yakima Canutt

97. THE LONE DEFENDER

(Mascot, 1930)   12 Chaps.

Rin-Tin-Tin, Walter Miller, June Marlowe, Buzz Barton, Josef Swickard, Lee Shumway, Frank Lanning, Robert Kortman, Arthur Morrison, Lafe McKee, Bob Irvin, Julian Barlano, Victor Metzetti, Bill McGowan, Arthur Metzeth

D: Richard Thorpe
P: Nat Levine

FILMS OF 1931

98. THE PHANTOM OF THE WEST

(Mascot, January 1, 1931)   10 Chaps.

Tom Tyler, William Desmond, Tom Santschi, Dorothy Gulliver, Joe Bonomo, Tom Dugan, Philo McCullough, Kermit Maynard, Frank Lanning, Frank Hagney, Dick Dickinson, Halee Sullivan, Al Taylor, Ernie Adams

D: Ross Lederman
P: Nat Levine
Chapter Titles: (1) The Ghost Riders, (2) The Stairway of Doom, (3) The Horror in the Dark, (4) The Battle of the Strong, (5) The League of the Lawless, (6) The Canyon of Calamity, (7) The Price of Silence, (8) The House of Hate, (9) The Fatal Secret, (10) Rogues' Roundup

99. RED FORK RANGE

(Big 4, January 12, 1931)   59 Mins.

Wally Wales, Ruth Mix, Al Ferguson, Cliff Lyons, Bud Osborne, Lafe McKee, Will Armstrong, George Gerwin, Jim Corey, Chief Big Tree

D: Alvin J. Neitz (Alan James)
S: Henry Taylor
SP: Alvin J. Neitz

100. THE PAINTED DESERT

(RKO-Pathe, January 18, 1931)   80 Mins.

William Boyd, Helen Twelvetrees, William Farnum, J. Farrell MacDonald, Clark Gable, William Walling, Wade Boteler, William LeMaire, Dick Cramer, James Mason, Hugh Adams, Jerry Drew, Brady Kline, Charles Sellon, Edward Hearn, Cy Clegg, James Donlan

D: Howard Higgin
S/SP: Howard Higgin, Tom Buckingham
P: E. B. Derr

101. THE GREAT MEADOW

(MGM, January 24, 1931)   75 Mins.

John Mack Brown, Eleanor Boardman, Guinn Williams, Russell Simpson, Anita Louise, Lucille LaVerne, Gavin Gordon, Sarah Padden, Helen Jerome Eddy

D: Charles Brabin
S: Elizabeth Roberts

102. DESERT VENGEANCE

(Beverly Productions/Columbia, January 25, 1931)   59 Mins.

Buck Jones, Barbara Bedford, Buck Connors, Pee Wee Holmes, Slim Whitaker, Douglas Gilmore, Al Smith, Ed Brady, Robert Ellis, Bob Fleming, Joe Girard, Barney Bearsley, "Silver"

D: Louis King
S/SP: Stuart Anthony
P: Sol Lesser

103. WESTWARD BOUND

(Syndicate, January 25, 1931)   60 Mins.

Buffalo Bill, Jr., Buddy Roosevelt, Allene Ray, Yakima Canutt, Ben Corbett, Fern Emmett, Tom London, Robert Walker, Pete Morrison

D: Harry Webb
S: Carl Krusada
P: Harry Webb, F. E. Douglas

104. FAIR WARNING

(Fox, February 1, 1931)   74 Mins.

George O'Brien, Louise Huntington, Mitchell Harris, George Brent, Nat Pendleton, John Sheehan, Willard Robertson, Ernie Adams, Erwin Connelly, Alphonz Ethier

D: Alfred Werker
S: "The Untamed"—Max Brand
SP: Ernest Pascal

Hell's Valley (National Players/Big 4, 1931) — Wally Wales and Virginia Brown Faire

Red Fork Range (Big 4, 1931) — Ruth Mix and Wally Wales

105. SUNRISE TRAIL
(Tiffany, February 7, 1931)　65 Mins.
Bob Steele, Blanche Mehaffey, Jack Clifford, Eddie Dunn, Germaine De Neel, Fred Burns, Dick Alexander
D: J. P. McCarthy
S/SP: Wellyn Totman
P: Trem Carr

106. CIMARRON
(RKO-Radio, February 9, 1931)　124 Mins.
Richard Dix, Irene Dunne, Estelle Taylor, William Collier, Jr., Nance O'Neil, Edna May Oliver, Rosco Ates, George E. Stone, Stanley Fields, Robert McWade, Frank Darien, Eugene Jackson, Delores Brown, Otto Hoffman, Helen Parrish, Donald Dillaway, Bob McKenzie, Junior Johnson, Douglas Scott, Henry Rocquemore, Ann Lee
D: Wesley Ruggles
S: Edna Ferber
SP: Howard Estrabrook
P: Wesley Ruggles

107. FIGHTING CARAVANS
(Paramount, February 14, 1931)　91 Mins.
Gary Cooper, Lita Damita, Ernest Torrence, Fred Kohler, Tully Marshall, Eugene Pallette, Syd Saylor, Roy Stewart, May Boley, James Farley, James Marcus, Eve Southern, Donald MacKenzie, Charles Winninger, Frank Hagney, Frank Campeau, E. Allyn Warren, Merrill McCormack, Tiny Sanford, Jane Darwell, Irving Bacon, Harry Semels, Iron Eyes Cody, Chief Big Tree
D: Otto Brower, David Burton
S: Zane Grey
SP: Edward E. Paramore, Keene Thompson, Agnes Brand Leahy

108. TRAILS OF THE GOLDEN WEST
(Cosmos, February 15, 1931)　58 Mins.
Buffalo Bill, Jr., Wanda Hawley, Tom London, George Reed, Horace B. Carpenter, Merril McCormack, Chief White Eagle, William Bertram
D: Leander De Cordova
S: L. V. Jefferson

109. THE CONQUERING HORDE
(Paramount, March, 1, 1931)　75 Mins.
Richard Arlen, Fay Wray, George Mendoza, Ian MacLaren, Charles Stevens, Claire Ward, Claude Gillingwater, Arthur Stone, Frank Rice, James Durkin, Ed Brady, Bob Kortman, Harry Cording, John Elliott, Chief Standing Bear
D: Edward Sloman
S: Emerson Hough
SP: Grover Jones, William McNutt

110. WEST OF CHEYENNE
(Syndicate, March 1, 1931)　56 Mins.
Tom Tyler, Josephine Hill, Harry Woods, Robert Walker, Ben Corbett, Fern Emmett
D/P: Harry S. Webb
S/SP: Bennett Cohen, Oliver Drake

111. THE AVENGER
(Beverly Productions/Columbia, March 6, 1931)　65 Mins.
Buck Jones, Dorothy Revier, Edward Piel, Sr., Otto Hoffman, Sidney Bracey, Edward Hearn, Walter Percival, Paul Fix, Frank Ellis, Al Taylor, Slim Whitaker, "Silver"
D: Roy William Neill
S: Jack Townley
SP: George Morgan
P: Sol Lesser

112. HELL'S VALLEY
(National Players/Big 4, March 7, 1931)　60 Mins.
Wally Wales, Virginia Brown Faire, Walter Miller, Franklyn Farnum, Vivian Rich, Lafe McKee, Jack Phipps, Frank Lackteen, Bobby Dunn
D/S/SP: Alvin J. Neitz
P: F. E. Douglas

113. NOT EXACTLY GENTLEMEN
(Fox, March 8, 1931)　70 Mins.
Victor McLaglen, Fay Wray, Lew Cody, Eddie Gribbon, Robert Warwick, David Worth, Joyce Compton, Franklyn Farnum, James Farley, Carol Wines, Louise Huntington
D: Ben Stoloff
S: "Over the Border"—Herman Whitaker
SP: Dudley Nichols, William Counselman

114. WILD WEST WHOOPEE
(Cosmos/Associated Film Exchange, March 8, 1931)　57 Mins.
Jack Perrin, Josephine Hill, Buzz Barton, Fred Church, Horace B. Carpenter, John Ince, George Chesebro, Henry Rocquemore, Ben Corbett, Charles Austin, Walt Patterson
P/D/SP: Robert J. Horner

115. CLEARING THE RANGE
(Allied, April 1, 1931)　61 Mins.
Hoot Gibson, Sally Eilers, Hooper Atchley, George Mendoza, Robert Homans, Mme. Eva Grippon, Maston Williams, Edward Piel, Jack Byron, Edward Hearn
D: Otto Brower
S: Jack Cunningham
SP: Jack Natteford
P: M. H. Hoffman, Jr.

116. RIDERS OF THE NORTH

(Syndicate, April 5, 1931)   59 Mins.

Bob Custer, Blanche Mehaffey, Frank Rice, Eddie Dunn, George Regas, Buddy Shaw, William Walling

D: J. P. McGowan

S/SP: G. A. Durlam

117. GUN SMOKE

(Paramount, April 11, 1931)   71 Mins.

Richard Arlen, Mary Brian, Eugene Pallette, Louise Fazenda, Charles Winninger, Guy Oliver, James Durkin, Brooks Benedict, William (Stage) Boyd, J. Carroll Naish, William Arnold, Stanley Mack, William V. Mong, Jack Richard, Willie Fung, Dawn O'Day

D: Edward Sloman

S/SP: Grover Jones, William McNutt

118. PUEBLO TERROR

(Cosmos, April 15, 1931)   59 Mins.

Buffalo Bill, Jr., Wanda Hawley, Yakima Canutt, Art Mix, Hank Bell, Al Ferguson, Jack Harvey, Horace B. Carpenter, Robert Walker

D: Alvin J. Neitz (Alan James)

S: L. V. Jefferson

P: Robert J. Horner

119. GOD'S COUNTRY AND THE MAN

(Syndicate, May 1, 1931)   59 Mins.

(Changed from "Rose of the Rio Grande")

Tom Tyler, Betty Mack, George Hayes, Ted Adams, Julian Rivero, Al Bridge, John Elliott, Gordon DeMain, Artie Ortego

D: J. P. McCarthy

S/SP: Wellyn Totman

120. RIDER OF THE PLAINS

(Syndicate, May 3, 1931)   57 Mins.

Tom Tyler, Andy Shuford, Lillian Bond, Alan Bridge, Gordon DeMain, Jack Perrin, Ted Adams, Fern Emmett, Slim Whitaker

D: J. P. McCarthy

S/SP: Wellyn Totman

121. THE KID FROM ARIZONA

(Cosmos, May 10, 1931)   55 Mins.

Jack Perrin, Josephine Hill, Robert Walker, Henry Rocquemore, George Chesebro, Ben Corbett

D/S: Robert J. Horner

SP: Robert Walker

P: Robert J. Horner

122. THE TEXAS RANGER

(Beverly Productions/Columbia, May 10, 1931)   61 Mins.

Buck Jones, Carmelita Geraghty, Harry Woods, Ed Brady, Nelson McDowell, Billy Bletcher, Harry Todd, Budd Fine, Bert Woodruff, Edward Piel, Sr., Blackie Whiteford, Lew Meehan, "Silver"

D: D. Ross Lederman

S/SP: Forrest Sheldon

P: Sol Lesser

122a. THE COW-CATCHER'S DAUGHTER

(Mack Sennett/Educational, May 10, 1931)   22 Mins.

Andy Clyde, Harry Gribbon, Marjorie Beebe, Frank Eastman

D: Babe Stafford

S: John A. Waldron, Earle Rodney, Ewart Adamson, Harry McCoy

123. THE FIGHTING SHERIFF

(Beverly Productions/Columbia, May 15, 1931)   67 Mins.

Buck Jones, Loretta Sayers, Robert Ellis, Harlan Knight, Paul Fix, Lillian Worth, Nena Quartero, Clarence Muse, Lilliane Leighton, Tom Bay, "Silver"

D: Louis King

S/SP: Stuart Anthony

P: Sol Lesser

124. THE TWO GUN MAN

(Tiffany, May 15, 1931)   60 Mins.

Ken Maynard, Lucille Powers, Lafe McKee, Nita Martin, Charles King, Tom London, Murdock McQuarrie, Walter Perry, Will Stanton, William Jackie, Ethan Allen, "Tarzan," Buck Bucko, Roy Bucko, Jim Corey, Jack Ward

D: Phil Rosen

S/SP: Jack Natteford

P: Phil Goldstone

125. DUDE RANCH

(Paramount, May 16, 1931)   67 Mins.

Jack Oakie, Stuart Erwin, Eugene Pallette, Mitzi Green, June Collyer, Charles Sellon, Cecil Weston, George Webb, Guy Oliver, James Crane

D: Frank Tuttle

S: Milton Krims

SP: Percy Heath, Grover Jones, Lloyd Corrigan

126. IN OLD CHEYENNE

(Sono Art-World Wide, May 25, 1931)   60 Mins.

Rex Lease, Dorothy Gulliver, Harry Woods, Jay Hunt, Harry Todd

D: Stuart Paton

S: Bennett Cohen

SP: Betty Burbridge

127. THE RIDIN' FOOL

(Tiffany, May 31, 1931)   58 Mins.

Bob Steele, Frances Morris, Josephine Velez, Florence Turner, Eddie Fetherston, Ted Adams, Al Bridge, Fern Emmett, Gordon DeMain, Jack Hen-

In Old Cheyenne
(Sono Art-World
Wide, 1931) — Rex
Lease, Dorothy
Gulliver, and un-
impressed friend

derson, Artie Ortego
D: J. P. McCarthy
S/SP: Wellyn Totman
P: Trem Carr

128. THE VANISHING LEGION
(Mascot, June 1, 1931) 12 Chaps.
Harry Carey, Edwina Booth, Rex (King of the Wild
Horses), Frankie Darro, Philo McCullough, Wil-
liam Desmond, Joe Bonomo, Yakima Canutt,
Edward Hearn, Al Taylor, Lafe McKee, Dick
Hatton, Pete Morrison, Dick Dickinson, Bob
Kortman, Paul Weigel, Frank Brownlee, Tom
Dugan, Robert Walker, Olive Fuller Golden
D: B. Reeves Eason, Ford Beebe
SP: Wyndham Gittens, Ford Beebe, Helmer Berg-
man
P: Nat Levine
Chapter Titles: (1) The Voice from the Void, (2)
The Queen of the Night Riders, (3) The Invisible
Enemy, (4) The Fatal Message, (5) The Trackless
Trail, (6) The Radio Riddle, (7) The Crimson Clue,
(8) The Doorway of Disaster, (9) When Time
Stood Still, (10) Riding the Whirlwind, (11) The
Capsule of Oblivion, (12) The Hoofs of Horror

129. THE SHERIFF'S SECRET
(Cosmos, June 14, 1931) 58 Mins.
Jack Perrin, Dorothy Bauer, George Chesebro,

Jimmy Aubrey, Fred Hargreaves, Joe Marba, Billy
Franey, Monte Jones, "Starlight"
D: James Hogan
S/SP: James Hogan

130. DUGAN OF THE BADLANDS
(Monogram, June 24, 1931) 66 Mins.
Bill Cody, Andy Shuford, Blanche Mehaffey, Ethan
Laidlaw, Julian Rivero, Earl Dwire, John Elliott
D: R. N. Bradbury
S/SP: R. N. Bradbury
P: Trem Carr

131. SON OF THE PLAINS
(Syndicate, July 5, 1931) 59 Mins.
Bob Custer, Doris Phillips, Al St. John, J. P.
McGowan, Edward Hearn, Gordon DeMain
D: R. N. Bradbury
S/SP: R. N. Bradbury

132. RIDERS OF THE CACTUS
(Big 4, July 7, 1931) 60 Mins.
Wally Wales, Buzz Barton, Lorraine LaVal, Fred
Church, Ed Cartwright, Don Wilson, Joe Lawliss,
Tete Brady, Etta Delmas, Gus Anderson
D: David Kirkland
S: Charles Connell
SP: David Kirkland
P: David Kirkland, Charles Connell

133. CALL OF THE ROCKIES

(Syndicate, July 12, 1931)   60 Mins.

Ben Lyon, Marie Prevost, Russell Simpson, Anders
   Randolph

D: Ray Johnston

134. ALIAS THE BAD MAN

(Tiffany, July 15, 1931)   66 Mins.

Ken Maynard, Virginia Brown Faire, Charles King,
   Lafe McKee, Frank Mayo, Robert Homans, Irving
   Bacon, Ethan Allen, "Tarzan," Earl Dwire, Jack
   Rockwell, Jim Corey

D: Phil Rosen

S: Ford Beebe

SP: Earle Snell

P: Phil Goldstone

135. A HOLY TERROR

(Fox, July 19, 1931)   63 Mins.

George O'Brien, Sally Eilers, Rita LaFoy, Humphrey
   Bogart, James Kirkwood, Stanley Fields, Robert
   Warwick, Richard Tucker, Earl Pinegree

D: Irving Cummings

S: "Trailin"—Max Brand

SP: Ralph Brock

136. PARTNERS OF THE TRAIL

(Monogram, July 22, 1931)   63 Mins.

Tom Tyler, Betty Mack, Lafe McKee, Reginald
   Sheffield, Horace B. Carpenter, Pat Rooney

D: Wallace Fox

S/SP: G. A. Durlam

137. WILD HORSE

(Allied, August 2, 1931)   77 Mins.

Hoot Gibson, Alberta Vaughn, Stepin Fetchit, Neal
   Hart, Edmund Cobb, Skeeter Bill Robbins,
   George Bunny, Edward Piel, Sr., Joe Rickson,
   Glenn Strange

D: Richard Thorpe, Sidney Algier

S: Peter B. Kyne

SP: Jack Natteford

P: M. H. Hoffman, Jr.

(Reissued as *Silver Devil* by Astor Pictures)

138. CAUGHT

(Paramount, August 8, 1931)   68 Mins.

Richard Arlen, Frances Dee, Louise Dresser, Syd
   Saylor, Edward J. LeSaint, Tom Kennedy, Martin
   Burton, Marcia Manners, Guy Oliver, Charles K.
   French, Lon Poff, James Mason, Jack Clifford

D: Edward Sloman

S/SP: Agnes Brand Leahy, Keene Thompson

139. LAW OF THE RIO GRANDE

(Syndicate, August 9, 1931)   57 Mins.

Bob Custer, Betty Mack, Edmund Cobb, Nelson
   McDowell, Harry Todd

D: Bennett Cohen, Forrest Sheldon

S/SP: Betty Burbridge, Bennett Cohen

P: F. E. Douglas

140. THE MONTANA KID

(Monogram, August 11, 1931)   60 Mins.

Bill Cody, Doris Hill, Andy Shuford, W. L. Thorne,
   G. D. Wood (Gordon DeMain), John Elliott, Paul
   Panzer

D: Harry Fraser

S: Harry Fraser

SP: G. A. Durlam

P: Trem Carr

141. FLYING LARIATS

(Big 4, August 25, 1931)   60 Mins.

Wally Wales, Buzz Barton, Bonnie Gray, Sam Garrett, Etta Dalmas, Joe Lawliss, Fred Church, Tete
   Brady

D: Alvin J. Neitz (Alan James)

S: Henry Taylor

SP: Alvin J. Neitz

142. LIGHTNIN' SMITH RETURNS

(Syndicate, August 31, 1931)   59 Mins.

Buddy Roosevelt, Barbara Worth, Tom London, Pee
   Wee Holmes, Jack Richardson, Fred Parker, Wil-
   liam Bertram, Nick Dunray, Slim Whitaker, Sam
   Tittley

D: Jack Irwin

S: Jack Irwin

P: Jack Irwin

(Also known as *Valley of the Bad Men*)

143. THE ARIZONA TERROR

(Tiffany, September 1, 1931)   64 Mins.

Ken Maynard, Lina Basquette, Edmund Cobb,
   Hooper Atchley, Tom London, Charles King,
   Nena Quartero, Michael Visaroff, Murdock
   McQuarrie, Fred Burns, Jack Rockwell, "Tarzan,"
   Jim Corey, Roy Bucko, Buck Bucko

D: Phil Rosen

S/SP: Jack Natteford

P: Phil Goldstone

144. BRANDED

(Columbia, September 1, 1931)   61 Mins.

Buck Jones, Ethel Kenton, Wallace MacDonald, Fred
   Burns, Al Smith, Philo McCullough, John Oscar,
   Bob Kortman, Clark Burroughs, Sam MacDon-
   ald, "Silver"

D: D. Ross Lederman

S/SP: Randall Faye

145. THE SQUAW MAN

(MGM, September 7, 1931)   12 Reels

(English title: *The White Man*)

Warner Baxter, Lupe Velez, Eleanor Boardman,

Branded (Columbia, 1931) — Bob Kortman and Buck Jones

Paul Cavanagh, Lawrence Grant, Roland Young, Charles Bickford, Desmond Roberts, Mitchell Lewis, Luke Cosgrove, J. Farrell MacDonald, DeWitt Jennings, Frank Rice, Raymond Hatton, Frank Hagney, Victor Potel, Dickie Moore, Harry Northrup, Julia Faye, Eva Dennison, Ed Brady, Lillian Bond
D: Cecil B. DeMille
P: Cecil B. DeMille
SP: Lucien Hubbard, Lenore Coffee. Adapted from the play by Edwin Milton Royle

146. THE MAN FROM DEATH VALLEY
(Monogram, September 9, 1931) 64 Mins.
Tom Tyler, Betty Mack, John Oscar, Si Jenks, Gino Corrado, Stanley Blystone, Hank Bell
D: Lloyd Nosler
S/SP: George Arthur Durlam

147. BORDER LAW
(Columbia, eptember 15, 1931) 63 Mins.
Buck Jones, Lupita Tovar, James Mason, Frank Rice, Don Chapman, Louis Hickus, F. R. Smith, John Wallace, Robert Burns, Glenn Strange, Fred Burns, Art Mix, "Silver"
D: Louis King
S/SP: Stuart Anthony

148. HARD HOMBRE
(Allied, September 20, 1931) 65 Mins.

Hoot Gibson, Lina Basquette, Skeeter Bill Robbins, Mathilde Comont, Jesse Arnold, Raymond Nye, Christian Frank, Jack Byron, Frank Winkleman, Fernando Galvez, Rosa Gore, Robert Burns, Glenn Strange, Tiny Sanford
D: Otto Brower
S/SP: Jack Natteford
P: M. H. Hoffman, Jr.

149. HEADIN' FOR TROUBLE
(Big 4, September 22, 1931) 60 Mins.
Bob Custer, Betty Mack, Andy Shuford, Robert Walker, Jack Hardey, John Ince, Duke Lee
D: J. P. McGowan
S/SP: George Morgan

150. THE NEVADA BUCKAROO
(Tiffany, September 27, 1931) 59 Mins.
Bob Steele, Dorothy Dix, George Hayes, Ed Brady, Glen Cavander, Billy Engle, Artie Ortego, Merrill McCormack
D: John P. McCarthy
S: Wellyn Totman
P: Trem Carr

151. NEAR THE TRAIL'S END
(Tiffany, September 30, 1931) 55 Mins.
Bob Steele, Marion Shockley, Jay Morley, Si Jenks, Hooper Atchley, Murdock McQuarrie, Henry Rocquemore, Fred Burns, Artie Ortego

D: Wallace Fox
S: Robert Quigley
SP: G. A. Durlam
P: Trem Carr

152. WHITE RENEGADE

(Artclass, October 1, 1931)
Tom Santschi, Blanche Mehaffey, Philo McCullough, Reed Howes, Ted Wells, Donald Keith, Marjorie Keyes, Gene Layman, Billy Franey, Tom Murray, Mrs. Ted Wells
D: Jack Irwin
S: Jack Irwin
P: Jack Irwin
(Filming title was *The Empire Builders)*

153. OKLAHOMA JIM

(Monogram, October 3, 1931)   61 Mins.
Bill Cody, Marion Burns, Andy Shuford, William Desmond, Si Jenks, Franklyn Farnum, John Elliott, Ed Brady, G. D. Woods (Gordon DeMain), Iron Eyes Cody, J. W. Cody, Ann Ross, Art Ortego, White Eagle
D: Harry Fraser
S: Harry Fraser
SP: G. A. Durlam
P: Trem Carr

154. HURRICANE HORSEMAN

(Kent, October 11, 1931)   50 Mins.
Lane Chandler, Marie Quillan, Walter Miller, Lafe McKee, Yakima Canutt, Dick Alexander, Charles "Rube" Schaefer, Robert Smith, "Raven"
D: Armand Schaefer
S: Douglas Dawson
SP: Oliver Drake
P: Willis Kent

155. RANGE LAW

(Tiffany, October 11, 1931)   63 Mins.
Ken Maynard, Frances Dade, Charles King, Frank Mayo, Lafe McKee, Jack Rockwell, Tom London, Aileen Manning, William Duncan, "Tarzan," Blackjack Ward
D: Phil Rosen
S/SP: Earle Snell
P: Phil Goldstone

156. THE DEADLINE

(Columbia, October 14, 1931)   59 Mins.
Buck Jones, Loretta Sayers, Robert Ellis, Ed Brady, Raymond Nye, Knute Erickson, George Ernest, Harry Todd, Jack Curtis, James Farley, "Silver"
D: Lambert Hillyer
S/SP: Lambert Hillyer

157. THE ONE WAY TRAIL

(Columbia, October 15, 1931)   60 Mins.

Tim McCoy, Polly Ann Young, Doris Hill, Al Ferguson, Carrol Nye, Bud Osborne, Slim Whitaker, Jack Ward, Herman Hack
D: Ray Taylor
S: Claude Rister
SP: George Plympton

158. SUNDOWN TRAIL

(RKO-Pathe, October 18, 1931)   56 Mins.
Tom Keene, Marion Shilling, Nick Stuart, Hooper Atchley, Louise Beavers, Stanley Blystone, Alma Chester, William Welsh, Murdock McQuarrie
D: Robert Hill
S: Robert Hill

159. TWO-FISTED JUSTICE

(Monogram, October 20, 1931)   63 Mins.
Tom Tyler, Barbara Weeks, Bobby Nelson, Yakima Canutt, John Elliott, G. D. Wood (Gordon DeMain), Kit Guard, William Walling, Pedro Regas, Carl DeLoue, Joe Mills, Si Jenks
D: G. Arthur Durlam
S/SP: G. Arthur Durlam
P: Trem Carr

160. LARIATS AND SIXSHOOTERS

(Cosmos, October 25, 1931)   65 Mins.
Jack Perrin, Ann Lee, George Chesebro, Art Mix, Virginia Bell, Lafe McKee, Dick Cramer, Olin Francis, Jimmy Aubrey, Gloria Joy, "Starlight"
D: Alvin J. Neitz
S/SP: Carl Krusada

161. THE CYCLONE KID

(Big 4, October 28, 1931)   60 Mins.
Buzz Barton, Francis X. Bushman, Jr., Caryl Lincoln, Lafe McKee, Ted Adams, Blackie Whiteford, Nadja, Silver Harr
D: J. P. McGowan
S/SP: George Morgan
P: Burton King

162. RIDERS OF THE PURPLE SAGE

(Fox, October 28, 1931)   59 Mins.
George O'Brien, Marguerite Churchill, Noah Beery, Frank McGlynn, Yvonne Pelletier, James Todd, Stanley Fields, Lester Dorr, Shirley Nail
D: Hamilton McFadden
S: Zane Grey

163. FREIGHTERS OF DESTINY

(RKO-Radio, October 30, 1931)   60 Mins.
Tom Keene, Barbara Kent, Frank Rice, Mitchell Harris, Fred Burns, Tom Bay, Slim Whitaker, Billy Franey, William Welsh, Frederick Burton
D: Fred Allen
S/SP: Adele Buffington

164. SHOTGUN PASS

(Columbia, November 1, 1931)   58 Mins.

Tim McCoy, Virginia Lee Corbin, Frank Rice, Dick
 Stewart, Joe Marba, Monty Vandergrift, Ben
 Corbett, Albert J. Smith, Archie Ricks
D: J. P. McGowan
S/SP: Robert Quigley

165. LASCA OF THE RIO GRANDE
(Universal, November 2, 1931)   60 Mins.
Leo Carrillo, John Mack Brown, Dorothy Burgess,
 Slim Summerville, Frank Campeau
D: Edward Laemmle
S: Tom Reed
SP: Randall Faye

166. BRANDED MEN
(Tiffany, November 8, 1931)   70 Mins.
Ken Maynard, June Clyde, Charles King, Irving
 Bacon, Billy Bletcher, Donald Keith, Jack Rock-
 well, Hooper Atchley, "Tarzan," Edmund Cobb,
 Slim Whitaker, Roy Bucko, Buck Bucko, Al
 Taylor, Bud McClure
D: Phil Rosen
SP: Earle Snell
P: Phil Goldstone

167. THE CISCO KID
(Fox, November 14, 1931)   61 Mins.
Warner Baxter, Nora Lane, Edmund Lowe, Chris-
 Pin Martin, Willard Robertson, Douglas Haig,
 Charles Stevens, Conchita Montengro, George
 Irving, Marylin Knowden, Frederick Burton, Jack
 Dillon
D: Irving Cummings
SP: O. Henry
S: Alfred A. Cohn

168. CAVALIER OF THE WEST
(Artclass, November 15, 1931)   75 Mins.
Harry Carey, Carmen LaRoux, Kane Richmond,
 Paul Panzer, Theodore (Ted) Adams, George
 Hayes, Maston Williams, Ben Corbett, Christine
 (Carlotta) Monti
D/S/SP: J. P. McCarthy
P: Louis Weiss

169. THE RANGE FEUD
(Columbia, November 22, 1931)   64 Mins.
Buck Jones, John Wayne, Susan Fleming, Edward J.
 LeSaint, William Walling, Wallace MacDonald,
 Harry Woods, Frank Austin, Glenn Strange, Lew
 Meehan, Jim Corey, "Silver," Frank Ellis, Bob
 Reeves
D: D. Ross Lederman
S: Milton Krims
SP: George Plympton

170. BATTLING WITH BUFFALO BILL
(Universal, November 23, 1931)   12 Chaps.

Tom Tyler, Rex Bell, Lucile Browne, William Des-
 mond, Chief Thunderbird, Francis Ford, Yakima
 Canutt, Bud Osborne, John Beck, George Regas,
 Joe Bonomo, Jim Thorpe, Bobby Nelson, Edmund
 Cobb, Fred Humes, Art Mix, Franklyn Farnum
D: Ray Taylor
S: William Cody
SP: George Plympton, Ella O'Neill
P: Henry MacRae
Chapter Titles: (1) Captured by Redskins, (2) Cir-
 cling Death, (3) Between Hostile Tribes, (4) The
 Savage Horde, (5) The Fatal Plunge, (6) Trapped,
 (7) The Unseen Killer, (8) Sentenced to Death, (9)
 The Death Trap, (10) A Shot from Ambush, (11)
 The Flaming Death, (12) Cheyenne Vengeance

171. QUICK TRIGGER LEE
(Big 4, November 24, 1931)   59 Mins.
Bob Custer, Caryl Lincoln, Monte Montague, Lee
 Cordova, Richard Carlyle, Frank Ellis, Al Taylor
D: J. P. Morgan
S/SP: George Morgan
P: Burton King

172. THE FIGHTING MARSHAL
(Columbia, November 25, 1931)   58 Mins.
Tim McCoy, Dorothy Gulliver, Mathew Betz,
 Mary Carr, Pat O'Malley, Edward J. LeSaint, Lafe
 McKee, W. A. Howell, Dick Dickinson, Bob Perry,
 Harry Todd, Ethan Laidlaw, Lee Shumway, Black-
 Jack Ward, Blackie Whiteford
D: D. Ross Lederman
S/SP: Frank Clark

173. LIGHTNING WARRIOR
(Mascot, December 1, 1931)   12 Chaps.
Rin-Tin-Tin, Frankie Darro, George Brent, Georgia
 Hale, Yakima Canutt, Kermit Maynard, Bob
 Kortman, Lafe McKee, Hayden Stevenson, Pat
 O'Malley, Dick Dickinson, Ted Lorch, Frank
 Brownlee, Helen Gibson, William Desmond,
 Steve Clemente, Frank Lanning, Bertee
 Beaumont
D: Armand Schaefer, Benjamin Kline
SP: Wyndham Gittens, Ford Beebe, Colbert Clark
P: Nat Levine
Chapter Titles: (1) Drums of Doom, (2) The Wolf
 Man, (3) Empty Saddles, (4) Flaming Arrows, (5)
 The Invisible Enemy, (6) The Fatal Name, (7) The
 Ordeal of Fire, (8) The Man Who Knew, (9) Trai-
 tor's Hour, (10) The Secret of the Cave, (11) Red
 Shadows, (12) Painted Faces

174. MOUNTED FURY
(Sono Art-World Wide, December 1, 1931)
 63 Mins.
John Bowers, Blanche Mehaffey, Frank Rice, Lina
 Basquette, Robert Ellis, George Regas, John Ince

D: Stuart Paton
S/SP: Betty Burbridge

175. THE POCATELLO KID
(Tiffany, December 6, 1931)   61 Mins.
Ken Maynard, Marceline Day, Dick Cramer, Charles King, Lafe McKee, Lew Meehan, "Tarzan," Jack Rockwell, Bert Lindley, Bob Reeves, Jack Ward
D: Phil Rosen
S/SP: W. Scott Darling
P: Phil Goldstone

176. TWO GUN CABALLERO
(Imperial, December 15, 1931)   58 Mins.
Robert Frazer, Bobby Nelson, Consuelo Dawn, Carmen LaRoux, Pat Harmon, Al Ferguson, Diane Esmonds
D: Jack Nelson
S: B. Wayne LaMont
SP: Jack Nelson
P: William Pizor

177. RIDERS OF RIO
(Round-Up Pictures, December 31, 1931)
Lane Chandler, Karla Cowan, Sheldon Lewis, Bob Card, Sherry Tansey, Fred Parks
D/SP: Robert Tansey
P: Robert and John Tansey

178. THE MYSTERY TROOPER
(Wonder Pictures/Syndicate, 1931)   10 Chaps.
Robert Frazer, Buzz Barton, Blanche Mehaffey, Al Ferguson, Charles King, William Bertram, William Von Bracken, "White Cloud" (the Wonder Horse)
D: Stuart Paton
S: Flora E. Douglas
SP: Carl Krusada
P: Harry S. Webb, Flora E. Douglas

Chapter Titles: (1) The Trap of Terror, (2) Paths of Peril, (3) Fighting Fate, (4) The Cave of Horror, (5) The House of Hate, (6) The Day of Doom, (7) The Death Trail, (8) The Killer Dogs, (9) The Ghost City, (10) The Lost Treasure
(Reissued under the title of *Trail of the Royal Mounted*). Reissue chapter titles: (1) Clutches of Death, (2) The Perilous Trail, (3) Shadows of Evil, (4) The Pit of Doom, (5) Escape from Danger, (6) The Devil's Warning, (7) Path of Fate, (8) Fangs of the Killer, (9) The Phantom Warning, (10) Fight to the Finish)

179. THE SIGN OF THE WOLF
(Metropolitan, 1931)   10 Chaps.
(Reissued in 1932 as a feature called *The Lone Trail*)
Rex Lease, Virginia Brown Faire, Joe Bonomo, Jack Mower, Al Ferguson, Josephine Hill, Robert Walker, Edmund Cobb, Harry Todd, Billy O'Brien, "King" (a dog), Jack Perrin
D: Forrest Sheldon, Harry S. Webb
S/SP: Betty Burbridge, Bennett Cohen (credited for the feature version whereas Karl Krusada is credited for the serial version)
P: Harry S. Webb
Chapter Titles: (1) Drums of Doom, (2) The Dog of Destiny, (3) The Wolf's Fangs, (4) The Fatal Shot, (5) The Well of Terror, (6) The Wolf Dogs, (7) Trapped, (8) The Secret Mark, (9) Tongues of Flame, (10) The Lost Secret

180. YANKEE DON
(Talmadge/Capitol, 1931)   61 Mins.
Richard Talmadge, Lupita Tovar, Julian Rivero, Sam Appel, Gayne Whitman, Alma Reat, Victor Stanford
D: Noel Mason
S: Madeline Allen
SP: Frances Jackson
P: Richard Talmadge

FILMS OF 1932

181. RIDERS OF THE GOLDEN GULCH
(West Coast Studios, January 1, 1932)   52 Mins.
Buffalo Bill, Jr., Mary Dunn, Yakima Canutt, Pete Morrison, Edmund Cobb
D: Clifford Smith
S: Yakima Canutt

182. GHOST CITY
(Monogram, January 2, 1932)   60 Mins.
Bill Cody, Andy Shuford, Helen Forrest, Walter Miller, Charles King, Walter Shumway, Al Taylor, Jack Carlisle, Thomas Curran, Kate Campbell

D: Harry Fraser
S: Harry Fraser
SP: Wellyn Totman
P: Trem Carr

183. WITHOUT HONORS
(Artclass, January 2, 1932)   66 Mins.
Harry Carey, Mae Busch, Gibson Gowland, George Hayes, Lafe McKee, Mary Jane Irving, Tom London, Ed Brady, Jack Richardson, Partner Jones
D: William Nigh
S: Lee Sage
SP: Harry P. Crist (Harry Fraser)
P: Louis Weiss

184. RAINBOW TRAIL

(Fox, January 3, 1932) 60 Mins.

George O'Brien, Cecilia Parker, Roscoe Ates, James Kirkwood, Minna Gombell, Landers Stevens, Ruth Donnelly, Robert Frazer, Niles Welch, William L. Thorne

D: David Howard

S: Zane Grey

SP: Barry Connors, Philip Klein

185. RIDIN' FOR JUSTICE

(Columbia, January 4, 1932) 64 Mins.

Buck Jones, Mary Doran, Russell Simpson, Walter Miller, Bob McKenzie, William Walling, Billy Engle, Hank Mann, Lafe McKee, "Silver"

D: D. Ross Lederman

S/SP: Harold Shumate

186. THE SUNSET TRAIL

(Tiffany, January 7, 1932) 62 Mins.

Ken Maynard, Ruth Hiatt, Philo McCullough, Frank Rice, Buddy Hunter, Dick Alexander, Frank Ellis, Slim Whitaker, Jack Rockwell, "Tarzan," Lew Meehan, Bud Osborne, Bud McClure

D: B. Reeves Eason

S/SP: Bennett Cohen

P: Phil Goldstone

187. PARTNERS

(RKO-Radio, January 8, 1932) 58 Mins.

Tom Keene, Nancy Drexel, Ben Corbett, Fred Burns, Bobby Nelson, Billy Franey, Vic Potel, Lee Shumway

D: Fred Allen

S/SP: Donald W. Lee

188. SOUTH OF SANTA FE

(Sono Art-World Wide, January 8, 1932) 60 Mins.

Bob Steele, Janis Elliott, Chris-Pin Martin, Jack Clifford, Eddie Dunn, Robert Burns, Hank Bell, Allan Garcia

D: Bert Glennon

S/SP: G. A. Durlam

P: Trem Carr

189. THE CHEYENNE CYCLONE

(Kent/First Division, January 10, 1932) 57 Mins.

Lane Chandler, Connie LaMont, Frankie Darro, Yakima Canutt, Edward Hearn, Jay Hunt, Marie Quillan, J. Frank Glendon, Henry Rocquemore, Charles Whitaker, Jack Kirk

D: Armand Schaefer

SP: Adapted from "The Sagebrush Romeo"—Oliver Drake

P: Willis Kent

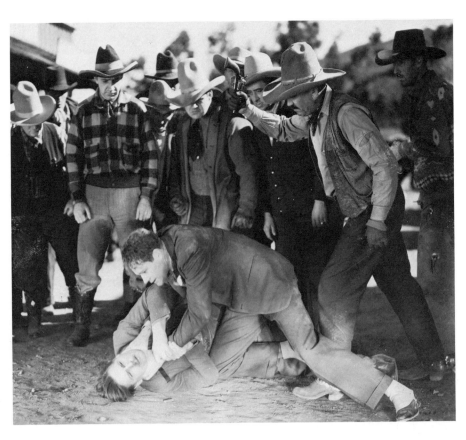

The Cheyenne Cyclone (Willis Kent, 1932) — Lane Chandler about to get bopped on the head by Charles "Slim" Whitaker

68

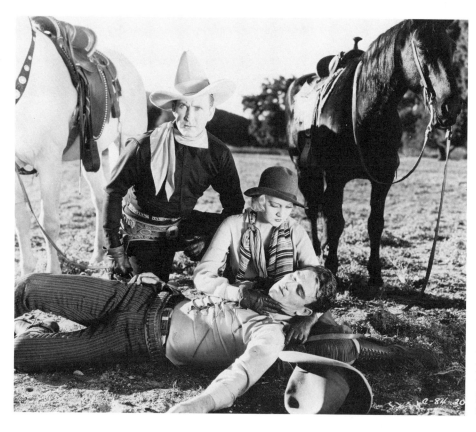

Texas Cyclone (Columbia, 1932) — Tim McCoy, Shirley Grey, and John Wayne

190. HUMAN TARGETS

(Big 4, January 10, 1932)

Rin-Tin-Tin, Buzz Barton, Francis X. Bushman, Jr.,
Tom London, Edmund Cobb, Ted Adams, Leon
Kent, Nanci Price, John Ince, Edgar Lewis, Pauline
Parker, Helen Gibson, Franklyn Farnum

D: J. P. McGowan

SP: George Morgan

P: Burton King

191. ONE MAN LAW

(Columbia, January 11, 1932)   63 Mins.

Buck Jones, Shirley Grey, Robert Ellis, Murdock
McQuarrie, Harry Todd, Henry Sedley, Ernie
Adams, Dick Alexander, Wesley Giraud, Edward
J. LeSaint, "Silver"

D: Lambert Hillyer

S/SP: Lambert Hillyer

192. THE LOCAL BAD MAN

(Allied, January 15, 1932)   59 Mins.

Hoot Gibson, Sally Blaine, Edward Piel, Sr., Hooper
Atchley, Milt Brown, Edward Hearn, Skeeter Bill
Robbins, Jack Clifford

D: Otto Brower

S: Peter B. Kyne

SP: Philip White

P: M. H. Hoffman

193. THE GAY BUCKAROO

(Allied, January 17, 1932)   61 Mins.

Hoot Gibson, Merna Kennedy, Roy D'Arcy, Edward
Piel, Sr., Charles King, Lafe McKee, Sidney
DeGrey, The Hoot Gibson Cowboys

D: Phil Rosen

S: Lee R. Brown

SP: Philip Graham White

P: M. H. Hoffman, Jr.

194. THE FIGHTING FOOL

(Columbia, January 20, 1932)   58 Mins.

Tim McCoy, Marceline Day, Robert Ellis, Ethel
Wales, Dorothy Granger, Bob Kortman, Arthur
Rankin, Harry Todd, William V. Mong, Mary
Carr

D: Lambert Hillyer

S/SP: Frank Clark

194a. THE TABASCO KID

(Hal Roach/MGM, January 30, 1932)   2 Reels

Charley Chase, Frances Lee, Billy Gilbert, Wilfred
Lucas, Julian Rivero, Leo Willis, Marvin Hatley,
Frank Gage, Jimmy Adams and the Ranch Boys

D: James W. Horne

195. TEXAS CYCLONE

(Columbia, February 4, 1932)   58 Mins.

Tim McCoy, Shirley Grey, Wheeler Oakman, John Wayne, Wallace MacDonald, Harry Cording, Vernon Dent, Walter Brennan, Mary Gordon, James Farley
D: D. Ross Lederman
S: William Colt MacDonald
P: Randall Faye

196. MARK OF THE SPUR
(Big 4, February 10, 1932) 58 Mins.
Bob Custer, Lillian Rich, Franklyn Farnum, Bud Osborne, Blackie Whiteford, Frank Ball, George Chesebro, Ada Bell Driver, Charles Edler, Lafe McKee
D: J. P. McGowan
S: Fredrick Chapin
P: Burton King

197. SINGLE-HANDED SANDERS
(Monogram, February 10, 1932) 61 Mins.
Tom Tyler, Margaret Morris, Robert Manning, G. D. Woods, John Elliott, Hank Bell, Lois Bridge, Fred Toones
D: Lloyd Nosler
SP: Charles A. Post
P: Trem Carr

198. THE GAY CABALLERO
(Fox, February 14, 1932) 60 Mins.
George O'Brien, Victor McLaglen, Cecilia Parker, Weldon Heyburn, Linda Watkins, Conchita Montengro, C. Henry Gordon, Willard Robertson, Wesley Giraud
D: Alfred Werker
S: Tom Gill
SP: Barry Connors, Philip Klein

199. TEXAS GUN-FIGHTER
(Tiffany, February 14, 1932) 63 Mins.
Ken Maynard, Sheila Mannors, Harry Woods, James Mason, Bob Fleming, Edgar Lewis, Lloyd Ingraham, Jack Rockwell, Frank Ellis, "Tarzan," Jack Ward, Roy Bucko, Buck Bucko, Bud McClure, Bob Burns
D: Phil Rosen
S/SP: Bennett Cohen
P: Phil Goldstone

199a. WIDE OPEN SPACES
(Masqueraders Club/RKO-Radio, February, 1932) 2 Reels
Ned Sparks, Antonio Moreno, Dorothy Sebastian, William Farnum, George Cooper, Claude Gillingwater, Frank McHugh, Tom Dugan, George Chandler
D: Arthur Rosson
S: Walter Weems, Edward Earle

200. SPIRIT OF THE WEST
(Allied, March 1, 1932) 60 Mins.
Hoot Gibson, Doris Hill, Lafe McKee, Hooper Atchley, George Mendoza, Walter Perry, Tiny Sanford, Charles Brinley, Al Bridge
D: Otto Brower
S: Jack Natteford
SP: Philip White
P: M. H. Hoffman, Jr.

201. HELL FIRE AUSTIN
(Tiffany, March 3, 1932) 70 Mins.
Ken Maynard, Ivy Merton, Jack Perrin, Charles LeMayne, Lafe McKee, Nat Pendleton, Allan Roscoe, William Robyns, Fargo Bussey, "Tarzan," Jack Rockwell, Jack Ward, Bud McClure, Lew Meehan, Ben Corbett
D: Forrest Sheldon
S: Forrest Sheldon
SP: Betty Burbridge
P: Phil Goldstone

202. SOUTH OF THE RIO GRANDE
(Columbia, March 5, 1932) 60 Mins.
Buck Jones, Mona Maris, Philo McCullough, Doris Hill, George J. Lewis, Paul Fix, Charles Reque, James Durkin, Harry Semels, Charles Stevens, "Silver"
D: Lambert Hillyer
S: Harold Shumate
SP: Milton Krims

203. LAW AND ORDER
(Universal, March 6, 1932) 7 Reels
(Reissued as Guns A' Blazing)
Walter Huston, Harry Carey, Raymond Hatton, Russell Hopton, Ralph Ince, Russell Simpson, Harry Woods, Dick Alexander, Andy Devine, Alphonz Ethier, Dewey Robinson, Walter Brennan, Nelson McDowell, D'Arcy Corrigan, George Dixon, Arthur Wanzer, Neal Hart
D: Edward Cahn
S: "Saint Johnson"—W. R. Burnett
SP: John Huston, Tom Reed

204. SADDLE BUSTER
(RKO-Radio, March 10, 1932) 60 Mins.
Tom Keene, Helen Forest, Charles Quigley, Ben Corbett, Fred Burns, Marie Quillan, Richard Carlyle, Robert Frazer, Harry Bowen, Al Taylor, Slim Whitaker
D: Fred Allen
S: Cherry Wilson
SP: Oliver Drake

205. LAW OF THE WEST
(Sono Art-World Wide, March 20, 1932) 58 Mins.

Bob Steele, Nancy Drexel, Ed Brady, Hank Bell, Charles West, Earl Dwire, Dick Dickinson, Rose Plummer, Frank Ellis
D: Robert N. Bradbury
S/SP: Robert N. Bradbury
P: Trem Carr

206. WHISTLIN' DAN
(Tiffany, March 20, 1932) 65 Mins.
Ken Maynard, Joyzelle Joyner, Georges Renevant, Don Terry, Harlan E. Knight, Jack Rockwell, Jessie Arnold, Bud McClure, Lew Meehan, Merrill McCormick, Roy Bucko, Buck Bucko, Frank Ellis, Hank Bell, Iron Eyes Cody, Wesley Giraud, "Tarzan"
D: Phil Rosen
SP: Stuart Anthony
S: Stuart Anthony
P: Phil Goldstone

207. THE MAN FROM NEW MEXICO
(Monogram, April 1, 1932) 60 Mins.
Tom Tyler, Caryl Lincoln, Robert Walker, Jack Richardson, Lafe McKee, Frank Ball, Lewis Sargent, Blackie Whiteford, Slim Whitaker, Frederick Ryter, Jack Long, William Nolte, C. H. (Fargo) Bussey, Lee Timm
D: J. P. McCarthy
S: "Frag Branded"—Frederick Ryter
SP: Harry O. Hoyt
P: Trem Carr

208. BORDER DEVILS
(Artclass, April 4, 1932) 65 Mins.
Harry Carey, Kathleen Collins, George Hayes, Murdock McQuarrie, Niles Welch, Ray Gallager, Olive Gordon, Al Smith, Maston Williams
D: William Nigh
S: Murray Lenister
SP: Harry C. Crist (Harry Fraser)
P: Louis Weiss

209. SCARLET BRAND
(Big 4, April 10, 1932) 58 Mins.
Bob Custer, Betty Mack, Duke Lee, Nelson McDowell, Blackie Whiteford, William Nolte, Robert Walker, Frederick Ryter, Jack Long, Frank Ball
D: Fred Allen
S: Frederick Ryter
SP: Oliver Drake
P: Burton King

Vanishing Men (Monogram, 1932) — John Elliott, Tom Tyler, and Robert Manning

210. VANISHING MEN
(Monogram, April 15, 1932) 62 Mins.
Tom Tyler, Adele Lacy, Raymond Keane, William L.
    Thorne, John Elliott, Robert Manning, Charles
    King, James Marcus, Dick Dickinson
D: Harry Fraser
S/SP: Wellyn Totman
P: Trem Carr

211. ARM OF THE LAW
(Monogram, April 20, 1932) 60 Mins.
Rex Bell, Lina Basquette, Dorothy Revier, Robert
    Frazer, Marceline Day, Gordon DeMain
D: Louis King
S: Arthur Hoerl
SP: Leon Lee
P: Trem Carr

212. RIDERS OF THE DESERT
(Sono Art-World Wide, April 24, 1932) 59 Mins.
Bob Steele, Gertrude Messinger, George Hayes, Al
    St. John, Greg Whitespear, Horace B. Carpenter,
    Louise Carber, Joe Dominguez, John Elliott
D: Robert N. Bradbury
S/SP: Wellyn Totman
P: Trem Carr

213. THE RIDING TORNADO
(Columbia, May 4, 1932) 64 Mins.
Tim McCoy, Shirley Grey, Wallace MacDonald,
    Russell Simpson, Art Mix, Montague Love,
    Wheeler Oakman, Vernon Dent, Lafe McKee,
    Bud Osborne, Hank Bell, Art Mix (George
    Kesterson), Silver Tip Baker, Tex Palmer, Artie
    Ortego
D: D. Ross Lederman
S: William Colt MacDonald
SP: Burt Kempler

214. MASON OF THE MOUNTED
(Monogram, May 15, 1932) 58 Mins.
Bill Cody, Andy Shuford, Nancy Drexel, Art Smith
    (Art Mix), Jack Carlisle, Blackie Whiteford, Nel-
    son McDowell, James Marcus, Joe Dominguez,
    LeRoy Mason, Dick Dickinson, Frank Hall Crane,
    Jack Long, Earl Dwire, Gordon McGee
D: Harry Fraser
SP: Harry Fraser
P: Trem Carr

215. THE LAST OF THE MOHICANS
(Mascot, May 17, 1932) 12 Chaps.
Harry Carey, Hobart Bosworth, Junior Coghlan
    (Frank Coghlan), Edwina Booth, Lucile Browne,
    Walter Miller, Bob Kortman, Walter McGrail,
    Nelson McDowell, Edward Hearn, Mischa Auer,
    Yakima Canutt, Chief Big Tree, Joan Gale, Tully

Marshall, Al Craven, Jewel Richford
D: B. Reeves Eason, Ford Beebe
S: James Fenimore Cooper
SP: Colbert Clark, Jack Natteford, Ford Beebe,
    Wyndham Gittens
P: Nat Levine
Chapter Titles: (1) Unknown, (2) Flaming Arrows,
    (3) Rifles or Tomahawks, (4) Riding with Death,
    (5) Red Shadows, (6) The Lure of Gold, (7) The
    Crimson Trail, (8) The Tide of Battle, (9) A Red-
    skin's Honor, (10) The Enemy's Stronghold, (11)
    Paleface Magic, (12) The End of the Trail

216. THE NIGHT RIDER
(Artclass, May 22, 1932) 72 Mins.
Harry Carey, Eleanor Fair, George Hayes, Julian
    Rivero, Jack Weatherby, Walter Shumway, Bob
    Kortman
D: William Nigh
SP: Harry P. Crist (Harry Fraser)
P: Louis Weiss

217. THE RIDER OF DEATH VALLEY
(Universal, May 26, 1932) 78 Mins.
Tom Mix, Lois Wilson, Fred Kohler, Forrest Stanley,
    Willard Robertson, Edith Fellows, Mae Busch,
    Edmund Cobb, Max Asher, Pete Morrison, Otis
    Harlan, "Tony," Iron Eyes Cody
S: Although most sources give story credit to Max
    Brand, the studio pressbook gives credit to
    Stanley Bergerman and Jack Cunningham
SP: Jack Cunningham
D: Albert Rogell

218. LAW OF THE NORTH
(Monogram, May 30, 1932) 55 Mins.
Bill Cody, Andy Shuford, Nadine Dore, Al St. John,
    William L. Thorne, Heinie Conklin, Gill Pratt, Jack
    Carlyle
D/SP: Harry Fraser
P: Trem Carr

219. TWO-FISTED LAW
(Columbia, June 8, 1932) 64 Mins.
Tim McCoy, Alice Day, Wheeler Oakman, Tully
    Marshall, Wallace MacDonald, John Wayne, Wal-
    ter Brennan, Dick Alexander, Wheeler Oakman
D: D. Ross Lederman
SP: Kurt Kempler
S: William Colt MacDonald

220. A MAN'S LAND
(Allied, June 11, 1932) 65 Mins.
Hoot Gibson, Marion Shilling, Skeeter Bill Robbins,
    Al Bridge, Charles King, Ethel Wales, Hal Burney,
    Robert Ellis, William Nye, Merrill McCormack,
    Slim Whitaker

D: Phil Rosen
SP: Adele Buffington
P: M. H. Hoffman, Jr.

221. MAN FROM HELL'S EDGES

(Sono Art-World Wide, June 15, 1932)   61 Mins.

Bob Steele, Nancy Drexel, George Hayes, Earl Dwire, Robert Homans, Gilbert Holmes, Dick Dickinson, Perry Murdock, Julian Rivero, Blackie Whiteford

D: Robert N. Bradbury
S/SP: Robert N. Bradbury
P: Trem Carr

222. TEXAS PIONEERS

(Monogram, June 18, 1932)   58 Mins.

Bill Cody, Andy Shuford, Sheila Mannors, Harry Allen, Frank Lackteen, Ann Ross, John Elliott, LeRoy Mason, Iron Eyes Cody, Chief Standing Bear, Hank Bell

D: Harry Fraser
S: Wellyn Totman
SP: Wellyn Totman, Harry Fraser
P: Trem Carr

223. HEROES OF THE WEST

(Universal, June 20, 1932)   12 Chaps.

Onslow Stevens, Diane Duval (Jacqueline Wells/ Julie Bishop), Noah Beery, Jr., William Desmond, Martha Mattox, Francis Ford, Philo McCullough, Harry Tenbrook, Frank Lackteen, Edmund Cobb, Jules Cowles, Grace Cunard, Chief Thunderbird

D: Ray Taylor
S: Peter B. Kyne
P: Henry MacRae

Chapter Titles: (1) Blazing the Trail, (2) The Red Peril, (3) The Avalanche, (4) A Shot from the Dark, (5) The Hold-Up, (6) Captured by the Indians, (7) Flaming Arrows, (8) Frontier Justice, (9) The Iron Master, (10) Thundering Death, (11) Thundering Hoofs, (12) End of the Trail

224. HONOR OF THE MOUNTED

(Monogram, June 20, 1932)   62 Mins.

Tom Tyler, Cecilia Ryland, Francis McDonald, Charles King, Tom London, Stanley Lystone, William Dyer, Arthur Millet, Gordon Wood (Gordon DeMain), Ted Lorch

D: Harry Fraser
S/SP: Harry Fraser
P: Trem Carr

225. TEXAS BAD MAN

(Universal, June 30, 1932)   60 Mins.

Tom Mix, Lucille Powers, Fred Kohler, Edward J. LeSaint, Willard Robertson, Dick Alexander, C. E. Anderson, Lynton Brent, Franklyn Farnum, Joseph Girard, Bob Milash, Buck Moulton, James Burtis, Slim Cole, Booth Howard, Frances Sayles, Richard Sumner, "Tony, Jr.," Theodore Lorch, George Magrill, Bud Osborne, Buck Bucko

D: Edward Laemmle
S/SP: Jack Cunningham
P: Carl Laemmle, Jr.

226. MYSTERY RANCH

(Fox, July 1, 1932)   65 Mins.

George O'Brien, Cecilia Parker, Charles Middleton, Roy Stewart, Charles Stevens, Forrest Harvey, Virginia Herdman, Noble Johnson, Russell Powell

D: David Howard
S: "The Killer"—Stewart Edward White
SP: Al Cohn

227. HELLO TROUBLE

(Columbia, July 15, 1932)   67 Mins.

Buck Jones, Lina Basquette, Russell Simpson, Otto Hoffman, Wallace MacDonald, Allan Roscoe, Morgan Galloway, Ruth Warren, Frank Rice, Lafe McKee, Ward Bond, Al Smith, Spec O'Donnell, King Baggott, "Silver"

D: Lambert Hillyer
S/SP: Lambert Hillyer

228. SON OF OKLAHOMA

(Sono Art-World Wide, July 17, 1932)   55 Mins.

Bob Steele, Carmen LaRoux, Earl Dwire, Julian Rivero, Josie Sedgwick, Robert Homans, Henry Rocquemore

D: Robert N. Bradbury
S: Wellyn Totman
SP: Burl Tuttle, George Hull
P: Trem Carr

229. DARING DANGER

(Columbia, July 27, 1932)   57 Mins.

Tim McCoy, Alberta Vaughn, Wallace MacDonald, Robert Ellis, Edward J. LeSaint, Bobby Nelson, Max Davidson, Dick Alexander, Vernon Dent, Murdock McQuarrie, Edmund Cobb

D: D. Ross Lederman
S/SP: William Colt MacDonald, Michael Trevelyan

230. DESTRY RIDES AGAIN

(Universal, July 27, 1932)   61 Mins.

Tom Mix, Claudia Dell, Zasu Pitts, Stanley Fields, Earle Fox, Edward Piel, Sr., Francis Ford, Frederick Howard, George Ernest, John Ince, Edward J. LeSaint, Charles K. French, "Tony, Jr."

D: Ben Stoloff
S: Max Brand
SP: Richard Schayer, Isadore Bernstein

231. THE VANISHING FRONTIER

(Paramount, July 29, 1932)   70 Mins.

My Pal, The King (Universal, 1932) — Tom Mix and Mickey Rooney

John Mack Brown, Evalyn Knapp, Zasu Pitts, Ben
Alexander, J. Farrel MacDonald, George Irving,
Raymond Hatton, Wallace MacDonald
D: Phil Rosen
S/SP: Stuart Anthony

232. DYNAMITE RANCH
(KBS/World Wide, July 31, 1932) 59 Mins.
Ken Maynard, Ruth Hall, Jack Perrin, Arthur Hoyt,
Allan Roscoe, Al Smith, John Beck, George Pierce,
Lafe McKee, "Tarzan," Martha Mattox, Edmund
Cobb, Charles LeMoyne, Cliff Lyons, Kermit
Maynard (stuntman and double)
D: Forrest Sheldon
S/SP: Barry Barrington, Forrest Sheldon
P: Burt Kelly, Sam Bischoff, William Saal

233. MY PAL, THE KING
(Universal, August 4, 1932) 74 Mins.
Tom Mix, Mickey Rooney, Stuart Holmes, Noel
Francis, Paul Hurst, James Kirkwood, Jim Thorpe,
Finis Barton, Christian Frank, "Tony, Jr.," Ferdi-
nand Schumann-Heink
D: Kurt Neumann
S/SP: Richard Schayer
P: Carl Laemmle, Jr.

234. CORNERED
(Columbia, August 5, 1932) 58 Mins.
Tim McCoy, Shirley Grey, Niles Welch, Raymond
Hatton, Lloyd Ingraham, Claire McDowell,
Charles King, John Eberts, John Elliott, Walter
Long, Bob Kortman, Art Mix, Merrill McCor-
mack, Noah Berry, Sr., Artie Ortego, Jim Corey,
Edward Piel, Ray Jones, Jack Evans, Blackie
Whiteford
D: B. Reeves Eason
S: Ruth Todd
SP: Wallace MacDonald

235. GHOST VALLEY
(RKO-Radio, August 12, 1932) 54 Mins.
Tom Keene, Merna Kennedy, Buck Moulton, Kate
Campbell, Harry Bowen, Mitchell Harris, Harry
Semels, Ted Adams, Al Taylor, Slim Whitaker
D: Fred Allen
S/SP: Adele Buffington
AP: Harry Joe Brown

236. McKENNA OF THE MOUNTED
(Columbia, August 26, 1932) 66 Mins.
Buck Jones, Greta Granstedt, James Glavin, Walter
McGrail, Niles Welch, Mitchell Lewis, Claude
King, Glenn Strange, Bud Osborne, Edmund
Cobb, "Silver"
D: D. Ross Lederman
SP: Stuart Anthony
S: Randall Faye

237. RIDE HIM, COWBOY
(Warner Bros./Vitagraph, August 27, 1932)
56 Mins.
John Wayne, Ruth Hall, Henry B. Wathall, Harry
Gribbon, Frank Hagney, Charles Sellon, Otis
Harlan, "Duke"
D: Fred Allen
S: Kenneth Perkins
SP: Scott Mason
P: Leon Schlesinger
(Remake of The Unknown Cavalier, a 1926 Ken May-
nard starrer)

238. KLONDIKE
(Monogram, August 30, 1932) 68 Mins.
Lyle Talbot, Thelma Todd, Tully Marshall, Henry B.
Wathall, Ethel Wales, George Hayes, Myrtle
Steadman, Pat O'Malley, Jason Robards, Lafe
McKee, Frank Hawks, Priscilla Dean
D: Phil Rosen
SP: Tristan Tupper
P: William T. Lackey
Supervisor: Trem Carr

239. FROM BROADWAY TO CHEYENNE
(Monogram, September 10, 1932) 60 Mins.
Rex Bell, Marceline Day, Robert Ellis, Roy D'Arcy,
Gwen Lee, George Hayes, Huntley Gordon,
Mathew Betz, John Elliott
D: Harry Fraser
S/SP: Wellyn Totman
P: Trem Carr

240. COME ON, TARZAN
(KBS/World Wide, September 11, 1932) 61 Mins.
Ken Maynard, Kate Campbell, Roy Stewart, Niles
Welch, Ben Corbett, Bob Kortman, Jack Rockwell,
Nelson McDowell, Jack Mower, Merna Kennedy,
"Tarzan," Edmund Cobb, Robert Walker, Hank
Bell, Jim Corey, Slim Whitaker, Al Taylor, Jack
Ward, Bud McClure
D: Alan James
SP: Alan James
P: Burt Kelly, Sam Bischoff, William Saal

241. BEYOND THE ROCKIES
(RKO, September 13, 1932) 60 Mins.
Tom Keene, Rochelle Hudson, Julian Rivero, Hank
Bell, Ernie Adams, Marie Wells, William Welsh,
Ted Adams, Tom London
D: Fred Allen
SP: Oliver Drake
S: J. P. McCarthy

242. THE WESTERN CODE
(Columbia, September 16, 1932) 61 Mins.
Tim McCoy, Nora Lane, Mischa Auer, Wheeler
Oakman, Gordon DeMain, Mathew Betz, Dwight

Frye, Bud Osborne, Emilio Fernandez, Chuck Baldra, Cactus Mack
D: J. P. McCarthy
SP: Milton Krims
S: William Colt MacDonald

243. COME ON, DANGER

(RKO-Radio, September 23, 1932) 60 Mins.
Tom Keene, Julie Hayson, Rosco Ates, Robert Ellis, Wade Boteler, William Scott, Harry Tenbrook, Bud Osborne, Roy Stewart, Frank Lackteen, Nell Craig, Monte Montague, "Flash" (a horse)
D: Robert Hill
S/SP: Bennett Cohen

244. THE LAST FRONTIER

(RKO-Radio, September, 1932) 12 Chaps.
Creighton Chaney (Lon Chaney, Jr.), Dorothy Gulliver, Mary Jo Desmond, Francis X. Bushman, Jr., Joe Bonomo, Yakima Canutt, Slim Cole, Judith Barrie, Richard Neil, LeRoy Mason, Pete Morrison, Claude Peyton, Benny Corbett, Fritzi Fern, Bill Nestell, Leo Cooper, William Desmond, Walt Robbins, Ray Steel, Fred Burns, Frank Lackteen
D: Spencer Gordon Bennet, Thomas L. Story
S: Courtney Riley Cooper
SP: George Plympton, Robert F. Hill
P: Fred McConnell
Chapter Titles: (1) The Black Ghost Rides, (2) The Thundering Herd, (3) The Black Ghost Strikes, (4) A Single Shot, (5) Clutching Hands, (6) The Terror Trail, (7) Doomed!, (8) Facing Death, (9) Thundering Doom, (10) The Life Line, (11) Driving Danger, (12) The Black Ghost's Last Ride

245. THE FOURTH HORSEMAN

(Universal, September 25, 1932) 63 Mins.
Tom Mix, Margaret Lindsay, Fred Kohler, Raymond Hatton, Rosita Marstini, Buddy Roosevelt, Edmund Cobb, Richard Cramer, Herman Nolan, Paul Shawhan, Donald Kirke, Harry Allen, Duke Lee, C. E. Anderson, Helene Millard, Martha Mattox, Frederick Howard, Grace Cunard, Walter Brennan, Pat Harmon, Hank Mann, Jim Corey, Delmar Watson, Fred Burns, Bud Osborne, Harry Tenbrook, Charles Sullivan, Sandy Sallee, Nip Reynolds, Henry Morris, Clyde Kinney, Jim Kinney, Ed Hendershot, Joe Balch, Augie Gomez, Frank Guskie, "Tony, Jr."
D: Hamilton McFadden
S: Nina Wilcox Putnam
SP: Jack Cunningham
AP: Stanley Bergman

246. HERITAGE OF THE DESERT

(Paramount, September 30, 1932) 63 Mins.
Randolph Scott, Sally Blaine, Vince Barnett, Guinn Williams, J. Farrell MacDonald, David Landau,

The Big Stampede (Warner Bros.-First National, 1932) — Luis Alberni, Noah Beery, and John Wayne

Gordon Westcott, Susan Fleming, Charles
  Stevens, Fred Burns
D: Henry Hathaway
S: Zane Grey
SP: Harold Shumate, Frank Partos

247. OUTLAW JUSTICE
(Majestic, October 1, 1932)   61 Mins.
Jack Hoxie, Dorothy Gulliver, Chris-Pin Martin,
  Donald Keith, Kermit Maynard, Charles King,
  Jack Trent, Walter Shumway, Jack Rockwell, Tom
  London
D: Armand Schaefer
S: W. Scott Darling
SP: Oliver Drake
P: Larry Darmour

248. GOLD
(Majestic, October 5, 1932)   58 Mins.
Jack Hoxie, Alice Day, Hooper Atchley, Jack Clif-
  ford, Bob Kortman, Tom London, Lafe McKee,
  Mathew Betz, Harry Todd, Archie Ricks, Jack
  Kirk, Jack Byron
D: Otto Brower
S: Jack Natteford
SP: W. Scott Darling
P: Larry Darmour

249. WHITE EAGLE
(Columbia, October 7, 1932)   67 Mins.
Buck Jones, Barbara Weeks, Ward Bond, Robert
  Ellis, Jason Robards, Jim Thorpe, Frank Campeau,
  Bob Kortman, Robert Elliott, Clarence Geldert,
  Jimmy House, Frank Hagney, Russell Simpson,
  "Silver"
D: Lambert Hillyer
S/SP: Fred Myton

250. THE BIG STAMPEDE
(Warner Bros.-First National, October 8, 1932)
  54 Mins.
John Wayne, Noah Beery, Mae Madison, Luis
  Alberni, Berton Churchill, Sherwood Bailey,
  Hank Bell, Paul Hurst, Lafe McKee, Frank Ellis,
  "Duke"
D: Tenny Wright
S: Marion Jackson
SP: Kurt Kempler
P: Leon Schlesinger
(Remake of Land Beyond the Law, a 1927 Ken Maynard
  starrer)

251. HIDDEN VALLEY
(Monogram, October 10, 1932)   60 Mins.
Bob Steele, Gerturde Messinger, Francis McDonald,
  Ray Haller, John Elliott, Arthur Millet, V. L.
  Barnes, Joe De LaCruz, Dick Dickinson, George
  Hayes, Capt. Verner L. Smith, Tom London

D: Robert N. Bradbury
S/SP: Wellyn Totman
P: Trem Carr

252. THE COWBOY COUNSELLOR
(Allied, October 15, 1932)   62 Mins.
Hoot Gibson, Sheila Mannors, Skeeter Bill Robbins,
  Bobby Nelson, Fred Gilman, Jack Rutherford,
  William Humphreys, Gordon DeMain, William
  M. (Merrill) McCormack, Sam Allen, Al Bridge,
  Frank Ellis
D: George Melford
S/SP: Jack Natteford
P: M. H. Hoffman, Jr.

253. BETWEEN FIGHTING MEN
(KBS/World Wide, October 16, 1932)   62 Mins.
Ken Maynard, Ruth Hall, Josephine Dunn, Wallace
  MacDonald, Albert J. Smith, Walter Law, James
  Bradbury, Jr., John Pratt, Charles King, "Tarzan,"
  Edmund Cobb, Jack Rockwell, Jack Kirk, Bud
  McClure, Roy Bucko, Jack Ward
D: Forrest Sheldon
S/SP: Betty Burbridge, Forrest Sheldon
P: Burt Kelly, Sam Bischoff, William Saal

254. TEXAS BUDDIES
(Tiffany/World Wide, October 19, 1932)   59 Mins.
Bob Steele, Nancy Drexel, George Hayes, Francis
  McDonald, Harry Semels, Dick Dickinson, Slade
  Harulbert, William Dyer
D: Robert N. Bradbury
S/SP: Robert N. Bradbury
P: Trem Carr

255. THE MAN FROM ARIZONA
(Monogram, October 21, 1932)   58 Mins.
Rex Bell, Charles King, Theodore Lorch, George
  Nash, John Elliott, Naomi Judge, Nat Carr, Les
  Lindsay, James Marcus, Henry Sedley, John Beck,
  Hank Bell, George Cooper, Bob McKenzie
D: Harry Fraser
S/SP: Wellyn Totman
P: Trem Carr

256. RENEGADES OF THE WEST
(RKO, October 25, 1932)   55 Mins.
Tom Keene, Betty Furness, Rosco (Roscoe) Ates,
  Rockcliffe Fellows, Jack Pennick, Max Wagner,
  James Mason, Joe Girard, Joseph Ramos, Billy
  Franey, Roland Southern
D: Casey Robinson
S: Frank Richardson Pierce
SP: Albert LeVine

257. THE FORTY-NINERS
(Freuler/Monarch, October 28, 1932)   59 Mins.
Tom Tyler, Betty Mack, Al Bridge, Fern Emmett,

Hidden Gold (Universal, 1932) — Raymond Hatton and Tom Mix

Gordon Wood (Gordon DeMain), Mildred Rogers, Fred Ritter, Frank Ball, Florence Wells
D: John P. McCarthy
S/SP: F. McGrew Willis
P: Burton King

258. FIGHTING FOR JUSTICE
(Columbia, October 29, 1932) 61 Mins.
Tim McCoy, Joyce Compton, Hooper Atchley, William Norton Bailey, Walter Brennan, Lafe McKee, Harry Todd, Harry Cording, Robert Frazer, Murdock McQuarrie, William V. Mong, Charles King
D: Otto Brower
S: Gladwell Richardson
SP: Robert Quigley

259. THE DEVIL HORSE
(Mascot, November 1, 1932) 12 Chaps.
Harry Carey, Noah Beery, Frankie Darro, Greta Granstedt, Barrie O'Daniels, Edward Piel, Jack Mower, Al Bridge, Jack Byron, J. Paul Jones, Carli Russell, Lew Kelly, Dick Dickinson, Lane Chandler, Fred Burns, Yakima Canutt, Jack Goodrich, Rube Schaefer, Ken Cooper, Wes Warner, Al Taylor, "Apache" (King of the Wild Horses)
D: Otto Brower, Richard Talmadge
SP: George Morgan, Barney Sarecky, Wyndham Gittens

P: Nat Levine
Chapter Titles: (1) Untamed, (2) The Chasm of Death, (3) The Doom Riders, (4) Vigilante Law, (5) The Silent Call, (6) The Heart of the Mystery, (7) The Battle of the Strong, (8) The Missing Witness, (9) The Showdown, (10) The Death Trap, (11) Wild Loyality, (12) The Double Decoy

260. HIDDEN GOLD
(Universal, November 3, 1932) 60 Mins.
Tom Mix, Judith Barrie, Raymond Hatton, Eddie Gribbon, Donald Kirke, Willis Clark, Roy Moore, "Tony, Jr."
D: Arthur Rosson
S: Jack Natteford
SP: Jack Natteford, James Milhauser

261. YOUNG BLOOD
(Monogram, November 5, 1932) 59 Mins.
Bob Steele, Helen Foster, Naomi Judge, Charles King, Henry Rocquemore, Art Mix, Hank Bell, Harry Semels, Lafe McKee, Perry Murdock, Roy Buck
D: Phil Rosen
S/SP: Wellyn Totman
P: Trem Carr

262. THE BOILING POINT
(Allied, November 12, 1932) 70 Mins.

Hoot Gibson, Helen Foster, George Hayes, Skeeter Bill Robbins, Lafe McKee, Tom London, Wheeler Oakman, William Nye, Charles Bailey, Billy Bletcher, Frank Ellis, Lew Meehan, Hattie McDaniels, Robert Burns, Art Mix, Merrill McCormack, Artie Ortego
D: George Melford
P: M. H. Hoffman, Jr.

263. FORBIDDEN TRAIL

(Columbia, November 18, 1932)   71 Mins.
Buck Jones, Barbara Weeks, Mary Carr, George Cooper, Ed Brady, Frank Rice, Al Smith, Frank LaRue, Wong Chung, Wallis Clark, Tom Forman, Gertrude Howard, Dick Rush, Charles Berner, "Silver"
D: Lambert Hillyer
S/SP: Milton Krims

264. WILD HORSE MESA

(Paramount, November 25, 1932)   65 Mins.
Randolph Scott, Sally Blaine, Fred Kohler, James Bush, George Hayes, Charley Grapewin, Buddy Roosevelt, Lucille LaVerne, Jim Thorpe, E. H. Calvert
D: Henry Hathaway
S: Zane Grey
SP: Frank Clark, Harold Shumate

265. LAW AND LAWLESS

(Majestic, November 30, 1932)   59 Mins.
Jack Hoxie, Hilda Moore, Wally Wales, Yakima Canutt, Julian Rivero, Jack Mower, J. Frank Glendon, Edith Fellows, Helen Gibson, Robert Burns, Alma Rayford, Joe De LaCruz, Fred Burns, Elvero Sonchez, William Quinn, Al Taylor, Dixie Starr
D: Armand Schaefer
S/SP: Oliver Drake
P: Larry Darmour

266. LUCKY LARRIGAN

(Monogram, December 1, 1932)   58 Mins.
Rex Bell, Helen Foster, George Chesebro, John Elliott, Stanley Blystone, Julian Rivero, G. D. Wood (Gordon DeMain), Wilfred Lucas
D: J. P. McCarthy
S/SP: Wellyn Totman
P: Trem Carr

267. TEX TAKES A HOLIDAY

(Argosy/First Division, December 2, 1932)   60 Mins.
(Natural Color)
Wallace MacDonald, Virginia Brown Faire, Ben Corbett, Olin Francis, George Chesebro, James Dillon, Claude Peyton, George Gerwing, Jack Perrin
D: Alvin J. Neitz
S: Robert Walker

268. THE GOLDEN WEST

(Fox, December 3, 1932)   74 Mins.
George O'Brien, Janet Chandler, Marion Burns, Onslow Stevens, Julia Swayne Gordon, Everett Corrigan, Edmund Breese, Sam West, Arthur Pierson, Bert Hanlon, Hattie McDaniel, Charles Stevens, Stanley Blystone, George Regas, Dorothy Ward, Sam Adams, Ed Dillon, Chief Big Tree, John War Eagle
D: David Howard
S: Zane Grey
SP: Gordon Rigby

269. GALLOPING THRU

(Monogram, December 5, 1932)   58 Mins.
Tom Tyler, Betty Mack, Al Bridge, Si Jenks, Stanley Blystone, G. D. Woods (Gordon DeMain), John Elliott, Artie Ortego
D: Lloyd Nosler
S/SP: Wellyn Totman
P: Trem Carr

270. END OF THE TRAIL

(Columbia, December 9, 1932)   59 Mins.
Tim McCoy, Luana Walter, Wheeler Oakman, Wally Albright, Lafe McKee, Wade Boteler, Chief White Eagle
D: D. Ross Lederman
S/SP: Stuart Anthony

271. THE FIGHTING CHAMP

(Monogram, December 15, 1932)   59 Mins.
Bob Steele, Arletta Duncan, George Hayes, Charles King, Lafe McKee, Kit Guard, George Chesebro, Frank Ball, Henry Rocquemore, Hank Bell
D: J. P. McCarthy
S/SP: Wellyn Totman
P: Trem Carr

272. HAUNTED GOLD

(Warner Bros.-First National, December 17, 1932)   58 Mins.
John Wayne, Sheila Terry, Erville Alderson, Harry Woods, Otto Hoffman, Slim Whitaker, Martha Mattox, Blue Washington, Jim Corey, "Duke"
D: Mack Wright
S/SP: Adele Buffington
P: Leon Schlesinger
(Remake of *The Phantom City*, a 1928 Ken Maynard starrer)

273. FLAMING GUNS

(Universal, December 22, 1932) 57 Mins.

Tom Mix, Ruth Hall, William Farnum, George Hackathorne, Clarence Wilson, Bud Osborne, Duke Lee, Pee Wee Holmes, Jimmy Shannon, William Steele, Walter Patterson, Fred Burns, "Tony, Jr.," Slim Whitaker, Clyde Kinney

D: Arthur Rosson

S: Peter B. Kyne

SP: Jack Cunningham

274. TOMBSTONE CANYON

(KBS/World Wide, December 25, 1932) 62 Mins.

Ken Maynard, Cecilia Parker, Lafe McKee, Sheldon Lewis, Frank Brownlee, Jack Clifford, George Gerwing, Edward Piel, Sr., George Chesebro, "Tarzan," Jack Kirk, Merrill McCormack, Bud McClure, George Chesebro

D: Alan James

S/SP: Claude Rister

P: Burt Kelly, Sam Bischoff, William Saal

275. THE DIAMOND TRAIL

(Monogram, December 30, 1932) 60 Mins.

Rex Bell, Frances Rich, Bud Osborne, Lloyd Whitlock, Norman Feusier, Jerry Storm, John Webb Dillon, Billy West, Harry LaMont

D: Harry Fraser

SP: Harry Fraser, Sherman Lowe

P: Trem Carr

276. BATTLING BUCKAROO

(Kent, 1932)

Lane Chandler, Doris Hill, Yakima Canutt, Lafe McKee, Ted Adams, Bill Patton, Olin Francis, "Raven," Herman Hack, Bart Carre

D: Armand Schaefer

S: Oliver Drake

P: Willis Kent

277. FORTY-FIVE CALIBRE ECHO

(Horner Productions, 1932) 60 Mins.

Jack Perrin, Ben Corbett, Eleanor Fair, Olin Francis, Dick Carmer, George Chesebro, Jimmy Aubrey, C. H. Bussey, Ruth Rennick

D: Bruce Mitchell

S: Carl Krusada

P: Robert J. Horner

278. THE GALLOPING KID

(Imperial, 1932)

Al Lane, Karla Cowan, Little Buck Dale, Fred Parker, Horace B. Carpenter, George Bates, Larry Warner, C. E. Anderson

D: Robert Emmett

SP: Robert Emmett

P: William Pizor

Tombstone Canyon (KBS/World Wide, 1932) — George Chesebro with rifle pointed at Ken Maynard and "Tarzan"

The Land of Wanted Men (Monogram, 1932) — Young Andy Shuford in the tub and Bill Cody on the pump

279. GUNS FOR HIRE
(Kent, 1932) 58 Mins.
Lane Chandler, Sally Darling, Neal Hart, Yakima Canutt, John Ince, Slim Whitaker, Jack Rockwell, Benny Corbett, Steve Clemente, Bill Patton, Hank Bell, John McGuire, Frances Morris, Nelson McDowell, John Bacon, Ed Porter, "Raven," Roy Bucko, Bud McClure, Buck Bucko, Bart Carre, Gene Alsace (Rocky Camron)
D: Lew Collins
SP: Oliver Drake
S: E. B. Mann
P: Willis Kent

280. LAND OF WANTED MEN
(Monogram, 1932) 60 Mins.
Bill Cody, Andy Shuford, Sheila Mannors, Gibson Gowland, Jack Richardson, Frank Lackteen, James Marcus
D: Harry Fraser
SP: Harry Fraser
P: Trem Carr

281. LAWLESS VALLEY
(Kent, 1932)
Lane Chandler, Gertrude Messinger, Richard Cramer, J. P. McGowan, Si Jenks, Anne Howard, Art Mix, Hank Bell, "Raven," Jack Kirk, Chuck Baldra
D: J. P. McGowan
SP: Oliver Drake
P: Willis Kent

282. THE LONE TRAIL
(Syndicate, 1932)
(Feature version of 1931 serial *The Sign of the Wolf*)
Rex Lease, Virginia Brown Faire, Joe Bonomo, Jack Mower, Josephine Hill, "King" (a dog), Al Ferguson, Robert Walker, Edmund Cobb, Harry Todd, Billy O'Brien, Jack Perrin
D: Forrest Sheldon, Harry S. Webb
SP: Betty Burbridge, Bennett Cohen
P: Harry S. Webb

283. THE RECKLESS RIDER
(Kent, 1932)
Lane Chandler, Phyllis Barrington, J. Frank Glendon, Neal Hart, Pat Rooney, G. Raymond Nye, Bart Carre, Ben Corbett, "Raven," Franklyn Farnum
D: Armand Schaefer
SP: Oliver Drake
P: Willis Kent

284. THE TEXAN
(Principal Attraction, 1932)
Buffalo Bill, Jr., Lucile Browne, Jack Mower, Bobby Nelson, Lafe McKee, Yakima Canutt, Art Mix

The Lone Trail (Metropolitan, 1932) — Harry Todd, Virginia Brown Faire, Rex Lease, and Joe Bonomo

D: Cliff Smith
P: William Pizor
(Filmed in 1930)

285. TEXAS TORNADO
(Kent, 1932)
Lane Chandler, Buddy Roosevelt, Doris Hill, Robert Gale, Yakima Canutt, Ben Corbett, Edward Hearn, Bart Carre, Mike Brand, Fred Burns, J. Frank Glendon, Pat Herly, Wes Warner, "Raven"
D: Oliver Drake
SP: Oliver Drake
P: Oliver Drake

286. WYOMING WHIRLWIND
(Kent, 1932)
Lane Chandler, Adele Tracy, Harry Todd, Loie Bridge, Yakima Canutt, Al Bridge, Bob Roper, Harry Semels, "Raven," Hank Bell, Ted Adams
D: Armand Schaefer
S: "Shootin' Straight" by Alan Ludwig in *Western Story* magazine
SP: Wallace MacDonald
P: Willis Kent

CHAPTER 3

The Boom Years
1933-1937

(COME ON, REBEL, WE'LL HEAD 'EM OFF AT THE PASS)

The years 1933 through 1937 were truly boom years for the "B" Western, which completely dominated the genre and made the bleak depression years a little more bearable for the whole family. The period was a veritable heaven for those millions who loved the escapist adventures of innumerable sagebrush cavaliers who galloped inexorably through film after film filled with exploding six-shooters, bone-crunching fist fights, and unbelievable stuntwork, but which were extraordinarily realistic. These galloping open-air yarns crackled with fiery, smashing action; volleys of whirring thrills; wild gun battles; mild romance; an occasional rousing musical score, beginning in 1935; breakneck streaks across the plains; cornball humor; and the greatest aggregation of performers ever assembled to provide mile-a-minute action entertainment with a thrill for every mile. The technical problems connected with sound had been licked and the movies were entering the era of glossy glamour.

Saturday afternoons or evenings at the movies became a tradition not only for kids but for moms and dads and grandparents who put away the frustrations of a meager existence to relax for an hour or two in a dream world housed in brick and mortar. It was a quarter well spent, and it was about the only amusement, except for radio, readily available to the masses. Thus, movies were never more popular than in the Thirties, and Westerns seemed to be in the vanguard of this popularity as audiences turned to them for an interlude of vicarious thrills. The Western was an escape from reality, and the escape was sorely needed for short intervals of time. Consequently, the Western profited and proliferated while large-scale Westerns were neglected by the major studios. The "A" films were risky and expensive. Sometimes they bombed. But the "B" could be counted on for consistent, predictable profits.

Of approximately 530 feature Westerns released during the five-year period, nearly 500 of them would have to be classified as "B's"—but what "B's" they were! And to these can be added 17 Western serials totaling 220 chapters, approximately 75 hours of pulsating cliffhanger action! The public was innundated with Westerns, which found a receptive, loyal, and large clientele in practically every hamlet in America.

If one were required to designate a single performer as *the* cowboy star of the period, it would undoubtedly have to be Buck Jones. With ten Columbia releases and twenty-two Universal feature releases plus four Universal serials, Buck dominated the Western screen in spite of the stiffest competition ever active in the Western cinema. And the competition was formidable! Inexorably so!

For years kids throughout America clip-clopped along neighborhood streets slapping their thighs while playing at being Buck astride Silver. In the sweltering heat of summer and the icy gusts of winter, loyal young fans (and older ones too) would brave the elements trudging to theatres showing the "new Buck Jones movie," never for one moment considering letting an ice storm or a heat wave deter them, even when—as was usually the case in the Thirties—there was no automobile transportation. And the fondest memories of childhood for tens of thousands of depression-era kids include backyard shootouts in which Buck and confreres such as Ken Maynard, Bob Steele, and Tim McCoy bested the dastardly villains who dared to usurp the forces of righteousness. Simply to say that the cowboy heroes of the day were a strong moral force is an understatement of their charisma and influence. Jones' films were a happy blend of action, humor, good stories, romance, and restrained realism. Furthermore, they did not have the assembly-line look to them. During the era of the Boom Years, Buck Jones was the best loved and most popular Western star in the world, for his films were shown on every continent. His reckless daring and courage were as well known to the Chinese and African children as they were to the two million American youths who enlisted in the proud ranks of the Buck Jones Rangers. And it was Buck Jones who, of all Hollywood cowboys, set the best example in morality, sportsmanship, and professionalism, always remaining loyal to his love for youth, his respect for all people, and his love of Western lore and the Western movie as a proud, distinct, unique facet of entertainment.

On the serial scene, Tom Mix starred in Mascot's *The Miracle Rider* in 1935, his last film and only serial. It was a profitable one even though Tom himself, at fifty-five, was just a shell of his former self. But he was still able to command $10,000 a week in salary and the fifteen-chapter opus was Mascot's most profitable serial. Profitable, too, was Ken Maynard's *Mystery Mountain*, and he, also, was able to garner $10,000 a week for his four weeks' saddle heroics on Tarzan thwarting the hellish "Rattler" and his gang while appropriately impressing the lovely Verna Hillie. John Mack Brown's *Fighting with Kit Carson*, Gene Autry's *Phantom Empire*, and the Bob Custer starrer *The Law of the Wild*, all for the same studio, were likewise money-makers. No serial producers in the sound era, even Republic into which Mascot evolved, could match the frenzy and exhilaration of Mascot's cliff-hangers, which had a special allure for audiences of the day. Universal and Republic, however, did their share to maintain the popularity of the Western serial. Because of his personal popularity, Buck Jones' four Universal films, *Gordon of Ghost City*, *The Red Rider*, *The Roaring West*, and *The Phantom Rider*, were instant winners in the serial sweepstakes as he rode into and homesteaded the hearts of a world audience. But Universal also scored with Tom Tyler's *Clancy of the Mounted* and Johnny Mack Brown's *Wild West Days*, while the new Republic growing out of a consolidation of Mascot, Monogram, Liberty, Select, Chesterfield, Invincible, and Consolidated Film Laboratories let it be known with *The Painted Stallion*, *Zorro Rides Again*, and *The Vigilantes Are Coming* that they would henceforth be formidable competition in the "Continued Next Week" market. Even RKO-Radio got the serial fever, releasing its only one, *The Last Frontier*, although it was an independent production. And Stage and Screen, a small independent outfit, undertook the ambitious task of telling the story of *Custer's Last Stand* in fifteen chapters, a rather dull production noteworthy only for the fine cast headed by Rex Lease. Probably few realized that the serial genre itself was making its last great stand; henceforth, with a few exceptions, the serial would decline in quality as well as in prestige and drawing power.

Since wild savages make for more interesting plots and an easier judgment of right and wrong than do tame Indians, Westerns of the post-Hart era exploited that idea to the fullest in getting more action. Especially was this true in the serials of the Thirties.

The best "B" Western series of the period, besides the two Jones series already referred to, were those starring George O'Brien at Fox, Tim McCoy at Columbia, Randolph Scott

The Miracle Rider (Mascot, 1935) — Wally Wales, Joan Gale, Tom Mix, and Jack Rockwell

Custer's Last Stand (Stage & Screen, 1936) — Rex Lease, Lona Andre, and Reed Howes

Gordon of Ghost City (Universal, 1933) — Buck Jones and Madge Bellamy

at Paramount, William Boyd at Paramount, Gene Autry at Republic, Charles Starrett at Columbia, and Ken Maynard at Columbia, Universal, and World Wide. Probably the high-class Westerns of O'Brien and Scott were the best. O'Brien's Westerns at Fox certainly were not "programmers" or common "B" Westerns as such, although not "A" Westerns either. They were expertly made and had about them a freshness and appeal not found in most of the competitive films. In fact, O'Brien's 1935 gem *When a Man's a Man* has been rated by some historians as one of the finest "little" Westerns ever made.

The Randolph Scott vehicles, likewise, were super "B's" and ranked with the O'Briens in quality although they were produced on smaller budgets, a feat accomplished through judicious surgery on old Jack Holt silent Westerns and the incorporation of panoramic and action sequences from those films into the Scott remakes of the same Grey stories. Those sequences had originally cost a tidy sum to film.

Tim McCoy, whether you realized it or not as a popcorn-munching kid, was different. You really didn't expect, if you will but think back, to see him crawl up on a bucking bronc *a la* Gibson or Mix, to engage in fantastic riding stunts such as were performed by Maynard or Canutt, or to give and take in a face-to-face slugfest with a half-dozen villains in every picture. Somehow it wasn't expected of this straight-backed, coldly reserved, glove-wearing protagonist with the distinguishing black outfit and wide-brimmed white stetson. It was expected, rather, that he would draw his pearl-handled pistol with the speed of greased lightning (Tim was acknowledged the fastest draw of the movie cowboys), foil the attempts of all who would despoil and bring dishonor to the range, win the hand of the comely damsel if he so pleased, and bring a quality of acting and charm to the screen not usually seen in Westerns of the "B" category. And this he did with gusto, becoming one of Western filmdom's all-time greats and sharing world acclaim for outstanding contributions to the genre with such other cowboy favorites as Buck Jones, Ken Maynard, Tom Mix, William S. Hart, Hoot Gibson, Harry Carey, and John Wayne.

Charles Starrett was a new personality—personable, good looking, athletic, and quite definitely of the new breed of cowboy heroes who emphasized flamboyancy over authenticity. His films of this period were meticulously made, shot around scripts that were serviceable if hardly exploratory, and overall were quite good. The action content was top grade, and the films benefited from both solid production values and good direction.

Gene Autry constituted the greatest phenomenon of the Boom Years, and his musical Westerns at Republic injected new life into the Western genre at a time when it was growing stale from a deluge of formularized sagebrushers that differed little in concept. Autry was a little-known Western singer from the National Barn Dance when he was signed, along with pal Smiley Burnette, to a contract by Nat Levine of Mascot, who detected an elusive quality about Autry that he thought might be worth an investment. Ken Maynard was acting up, Westerns were in a slump, and Nat was looking for something fresh. With a year of grooming and two small parts in Ken Maynard vehicles, Autry was put into his first starrer, *The Phantom Empire*, a twelve-chapter concoction combining both Western and science-fiction elements. It clicked. Levine's gamble that the shy Oklahoman's strange charisma and nasal tenor voice would find acceptance by audiences grown tired of standard Westerns paid off. With the merger of several small companies already mentioned to form Republic, Autry's first feature, *Tumbling Tumbleweeds*, came out under the Republic logo. Filmed for $18,000, *Tumbling Tumbleweeds* eventually grossed nearly $1 million. The singing troubadour was in vogue and with each new release Autry's popularity grew. Joseph Kane, as director, added his expertise to the Autry films, produced in the beginning under the supervision of Nat Levine himself. Good scripts, adroit directional finesse, flawless stuntwork, splendid photography, top-notch casts, superior editing, and the big ballyhoo push for him all helped to establish the star firmly in the Western skies. Republic's fortunes were built on the success of the Autry opuses, which more and more emphasized the musical element while playing down action and romance. By 1937 the sandy-haired, blue-eyed, gum-chewing vocalist had shot by the competition to become America's favorite cowboy. Personal appearances in rodeos and a string of hit records broadened his national following.

Autry's success quickly brought forth other singing cowboys in the persons of Dick Foran, Tex Ritter, Fred Scott, Smith Ballew, and Jack Randall. Ritter was the most successful and was an authentic Texan, although without any cowboy background. Ballew had the best voice of them all and was also a Texan. His background was in music, and during the late Twenties and early Thirties he was a popular band leader and vocalist. Foran was probably the most competent actor-singer and went on to become a successful dramatic actor after his stint as a singing cowboy. Dick had the advantage of working for Warner Brothers, which could give his Westerns more gloss than could the indies, and by 1937 he ranked fourth in popularity among cowboy stars behind Autry, Boyd, and Jones. Ballew's Westerns were produced by Sol Lesser but released through 20th Century-Fox, thus assuring them good bookings. Ritter, however, had to fight all the way to attain his popularity and sixth place in the cowboy rankings of 1937, as his Grand National releases were produced by Ed Finney, a shoe-string producer. Fred Scott did not even have the advantage of Grand National, which was "up town" as compared with Spectrum Pictures. Although Scott and sidekick Al "Fuzzy" St. John made some enjoyable oaters, there was really nothing to set them apart from other Western offerings and the Scott physique and voice were more suited for stage opera than hoss opry. Monogram's efforts to cash in on the singing Western with a Jack Randall series fizzled and the musical interludes were soon dispersed with in favor of straight action when distributors complained. The studio had envisioned him as another Gene Autry. Instead he became just another figure in the passing parade of cowboy actors.

Not only did Autry give the Western a needed boost but on his heels came another phenomenon, "Hopalong Cassidy." Harry "Pop" Sherman had intended to make one picture around Mulford's crusty character and had finally settled for a former DeMille star, William Boyd, for the lead. Boyd was a strange choice considering that he couldn't ride a horse. But with the help of stuntman Cliff Lyons who took his place in the chase and riding sequences, usually filmed in long shots to hide the deception, and the fact that Jimmy Ellison was given most of the action to perform, Boyd was successful in portraying not just a legendary screen hero but an ideal. He was everything his audiences supposedly aspired to be—kind, fair, temperate, witty, perceptive, above all human—and although he encountered opposition throughout the conflict at hand, he always emerged victorious. It was easy to see why this characterization was so popular with audiences. It could be said that Boyd was the "Ben Cartwright" of the pre-television era, and his distinct screen personality was one of the most pleasing ever presented to viewers. He exuded warmth and geniality. A good deal of money was spent on the Cassidy films and so longer running times, location shooting, and above-average scripts, photography, and casts were the usual rather than the exception. Release was through Paramount; thus a showing in houses not usually catering to "B" Westerns was assured.

Holdover stars from the Silent and Transition Years included ever-popular Bob Steele, featured in series for Monogram, Steiner, Supreme, and Republic; Tom Tyler, heading up series for Steiner, Reliable, Victory, and Monarch; Hoot Gibson, downgraded from his Universal pinnacle to stardom for Allied, First Division, and Diversion; Bill Cody, whooping it up in a cheaply made but entertaining series for Spectrum; Harry Carey, the old reliable, who, in his mid-fifties, was still sitting the saddle as a cowboy ace in a series for William Berke; and Tom Keene, holding down the lead in a series of historical Westerns for a small company called Crescent. And it might be mentioned that although the Keene series leaned toward realism and was made on a larger scale than most Western programmers, the films failed to win over the juvenile audience, who preferred the hell-for-leather, thrill-a-minute action provided by Maynard, Jones, Steele, and countless others who made escapist Westerns. One of his most delightful films was *Scarlet River*, in which he plays a cowboy movie star in a "movie-within-a-movie" story. Variations of this plot were later used by Columbia in *The Cowboy Star* with Charles Starrett and *Hollywood Roundup* starring Buck Jones and at RKO by George O'Brien in *Hollywood Cowboy* plus similar workings by Gene Autry in Republic's *The Big Show* and Fox's *Shooting High*, the only time he worked on loan-out. And there were a few other Westerns with the same basic theme, but Keene's was about the first.

John Mack Brown, the Three Mesquiteers (Ray Corrigan, Robert Livingston, Max Terhune), John Wayne, and Rex Bell all had popular series during the period and became mainstays in the Western field. Ironically, Bell was the least successful cowboy of this group even though he seemingly had the greatest potential. He was the most handsome; he was athletic and well built; he could act and was convincing in the romantic interludes; and he had a flair for light comedy. Yet things just didn't click any too well for him, his career being primarily stymied because of having to work for the small indies such as Colony and Resolute. Had he been able to remain at Fox after the transition to talkies or get with Columbia or Universal, his career quite possibly would have zoomed. As it was, he achieved only "minor star" status in the galaxy of cowboy stars. And Buster Crabbe, too, should be mentioned, as he was featured in six of Paramount's non-series Zane Grey Westerns, giving a good account of himself in superiorly scripted, adequately budgeted little Western gems. In 1936 he ranked tenth in cowboy popularity, but he left Westerns temporarily, returning to the genre in 1941. Paramount did not know exactly what to do with Crabbe and consequently wasted him in various features while he achieved screen immortality as "Flash Gordon" on loan-out to Universal.

For many a Western aficionado, the mid-Thirties are remembered for the numerous series produced at minimum cost for the states-right market and playing the smaller, less prestigious theatres across the nation. Wally Wales, Rex Lease, and Jack Perrin, three grossly underrated Western aces, were featured in fine little sagebrushers for Imperial, Superior, and Astor/Steiner/Atlantic respectively. Each man's talent should have carried him into the first echelon of stars, but it did not, circumstances working against them much as they had against Rex Bell. Only a small handful of people today remember these erstwhile heroes, such lack of recognition a sign that except for the favored few, fame is an ephemeral wisp of acknowledgment in the fleeting passage of time. But these stalwarts of sagebrush and serial were real troupers and their wide-awake wits and ready fists nonplused the villains throughout many a feature containing only a thread of a story but strengthened with the usual swift riding and heroics of these hold-overs from the silent era.

Kermit Maynard, another star who missed, had one of the better series of independent Westerns, his seventeen films for Ambassador being in many respects as good as anything his brother Ken was doing. There was as much difference between Westerns of the indies in the Thirties as there is in the taste of a fish fresh from the water and one a week old. Both are fish, but the similarity ends right there. The Ambassador policy on Maynard's Western features was to give spectators pictures stuffed with action, suspense, and romance, in entertainment value good enough for any show, but to keep down old man Overhead so that exhibitors could get them at prices at which they could make good money and yet have crowds asking for more. Ambassador utilized musical scores, running inserts, elaborate opticals, and other niceties that were not usually found in indies. Maynard carried the series in grand style. Fancy stunting and trick riding predominated, a logical outgrowth of Kermit's winning the World's Champion Trick Riding and Fancy Riding contests in the 1931 and 1933 competition. His first series had him starred as a Mountie in James Oliver Curwood tales; the second series was a straight Western one.

Superior provided the sad farewell series of starring Westerns for Buddy Roosevelt, a cowboy who should have hit the big time but who, instead, got stuck halfway up the ladder of success and eventually fell backward. But on neither the uphill climb nor the downhill slide did he ever forget that he was first a gentleman and only secondly a famous personage. Among the "inside" cowboys, he was a favorite. His worst stroke of luck occurred in the early Thirties as he was about to sign a contract to star in a series of talkies. As Buddy held the pen to sign, his wife blew up at the producer for some now-forgotten reason, calling him vile names and having a tantrum in general. The result was that Buddy got a divorce and the producer got a new star, a fellow by the name of John Wayne. While the plots of Buddy's Superior Westerns, which were similar to those mapped out for most indie oaters, did not arouse suspense, his riding and the several fights in which he usually took

Roaring Six Guns (Ambassador, 1937) — Mary Hayes and Kermit Maynard

92

Range Riders (Superior, 1934)—Buddy Roosevelt seems more impressed with the assistance offered by Barbara Starr than with that proffered by Merrill McCormack

The Man From Hell (Willis Kent, 1934) — Reb Russell seems to have Fred Kohler well in hand as Ann D'Arcy looks on

part in each film more than repaid the spectator for the sameness in story.

In 1934 a handsome young athlete fresh out of Northwestern University could be seen charging onto the screen as a rip-snortin', devil-take-the-hindmost cowboy in the tradition laid down by his mentor, Tom Mix. The picture was *The Man from Hell* and the star was Reb Russell, an All-American from Northwestern whom Knute Rockne called "the greatest fullback I ever saw." This Westerner lives up well to the stormy action suggestion contained in its title, for the notably energetic Russell cavorts around on horseback with the skill of a circus acrobat and the recklessness of a chap who doesn't appear to care whether he falls on his head or his heels. The pleasing personality of Reb Russell plus his unchallenged horsemanship and the fast tempo maintained throughout the reels sufficed to put over his Westerns in the type of theatre for which they were obviously produced. Russell proved that not every Hollywood cowboy is just a "pretty boy in chaps" who has his double do all his stunts for him. He was a great athlete and looked like a million dollars on his white gelding "Rebel." But in dialogue or romantic interludes he sounded and looked like considerably less. He had as much talent, though, as most of the cowboys and probably would have achieved greater fame had the market not been saturated with Westerns and had he been under contract to a major studio instead of Willis Kent Productions. After two series with Kent, Reb left pictures to tour with circuses, where his act put to shame anything that Mix had ever done under the Big Top.

Buffalo Bill, Jr., Big Boy Williams, Lane Chandler, Bob Allen, and Conway Tearle all had interesting, if not memorable, series before fading into oblivion. And in 1937, as the Boom Years were drawing to a close, Bob Baker, James Newill, and Ray Whitley appeared on the Western horizon as singing cowboys, hoping to capture some of the fame achieved by Autry, Foran, and Ritter. Only Baker, among all the saddle crooners who rode the cinema range, could lay claim to having been a real cowboy, working as such in Arizona prior to entering pictures. Interestingly, he was chosen by Universal over a fellow by the name of Leonard Slye, who was also trying to break into movies. The man was later hired at Republic and given the name Roy Rogers.

It would be a discourtesy, in writing about the Western, not to mention the contributions of the ladies who made "B" Westerns. Many of them, it is true, were just lovely props, without much functional value in the flicks in which they appeared. But others were given good, meaty roles and honestly contributed to the story development and enjoyment of the films. And although every little boy at the time would have denied it, many of them were secretly in love with beautiful and talented heroines such as Lucile Browne, Joan Barclay, Dorothy Revier, Allene Ray, Polly Ann Young, Marion Shilling, Claire Rochelle, Lois January, Louise Stanley, Eleanor Stewart, and Beth Marion. They were comely lasses, and both big and little boys could always imagine it was they being nudged into the arms of these pretty damsels by the hero's nag, which seemed to have more sense at the time than did the strong, bashful cowpoke who was shying away.

Most of the gals who made programmer Westerns on a consistent basis were courageous to say the least, for they were subjected to many indignities that modern-day actresses would not tolerate. Not only were they subjected to many unpleasant experiences, but they were often placed in dangerous situations. They were real troupers, these gals who sometimes played second fiddle to a horse. Long hours, grueling work, exposure to the elements, rough treatment in the action sequences, low pay—they took it in stride with nary a complaint and with a smile for all.

Coming closest to an epic Western during the Boom Years were Paramount's *The Plainsman* (1936, Gary Cooper, Jean Arthur) and *Wells Fargo* (1937, Joel McCrea, Frances

The Rangers Step In
(Columbia, 1937)
— Bob Allen and
Eleanor Stewart

The Fighting Ranger
(Columbia, 1934)
— Buck Jones,
Frank Rice, Ward
Bond, and Dorothy
Revier

Dee), Universal's *Sutter's Gold* (1936, Edward Arnold, Lee Tracy), and MGM's *Three God-fathers* (1936, Chester Morris, Walter Brennan, Lewis Stone). All were quite good, but hardly what one would call an epic of *The Covered Wagon* or *The Iron Horse* or *Cimarron* variety. The renaissance of the large-scale Western was short-lived.

Most of the interesting and novel Westerns of the period were products of 1936, with the exception of *Powdersmoke Range* (RKO, 1935, all-star cast), *Forlorn River* (Paramount, 1937, Buster Crabbe), and *Wells Fargo,* just mentioned. Somewhere between a "B" and an authentic "A" film were to be found *The Bold Caballero* (Republic), *Daniel Boone* (RKO), *Desert Gold* (Paramount), *End of the Trail* (Columbia), *The Last of the Mohicans* (United Artists), *The Last Outlaw* (RKO), *Rebellion* (Crescent), and *Arizona Mahoney* (Paramount).

Because they have attained the status of classics among "B" Westerns, special mention is made here of RKO's *Powdersmoke Range* (1935) and *The Last Outlaw* (1936). *Powdersmoke Range* was billed as the "Barnum and Bailey of Westerns" and just about lived up to it with its all-star cast headed by Harry Carey as "Tucson Smith," Hoot Gibson as "Stony Brooke," and Big Boy Williams as "Lullaby Joslin" in the first of the *Three Mesquiteers* films (although Williams and Al St. John had portrayed Tucson Smith and Stony Brooke in *Law of the 45's,* a non-trio film). Heading up the supporting cast as guest stars were Bob Steele as "The Guadalupe Kid" and Tom Tyler as "Sundown Saunders," a gunman. Former stars Buddy Roosevelt, Franklyn Farnum, Buzz Barton, Wally Wales, Art Mix, Buffalo Bill, Jr., William Desmond, and William Farnum were also in evidence.

The Last Outlaw has Carey cast as an aged ex-convict and Gibson as a cowboy in love with Carey's daughter. John Ford wrote the screenplay back in 1919 and filmed it as a two-reeler for Universal. Fred Scott, Tom Tyler, and Henry B. Walthall add much to the film, one of the best Westerns made by RKO and also one of the best talkies made by either Carey or Gibson.

End of the Trail (Columbia, 1936) is also singled out for special mention, since it was the last solo starring Western of Jack Holt. The screenplay is adapted from Zane Grey's novel, *Outlaws of Palouse,* although actually about all that remains of the Grey story in the film are the names of three of the characters. The plot is a direct remake of *The Last Parade* (1931) in a different time frame. Jack plays the role of a tough but lovable crook from the start to the touching scene where he walks bravely to the gallows, leaving behind the girl he loves and his best friend who was forced to bring him to justice. The film was a well-scripted, well-acted motion picture achieving high production values and tugging relentlessly at the heart strings of the viewer. And so it was in a figurative sense the end of the trail for Jack as a Western hero, although he would yet play in several action-packed shoot-em-ups and co-star in two well-made Westerns.

As the Boom Years melted into the Halcyon Years of 1938-1941, the Western genre's state of health was seemingly good, the popularity of the "B's" holding fast and giving possible support for the occasional production of more auspicious cinematic tales of the old West.

Strangely, numerous historians have put the cart before the horse in a sense by attributing the success of series Westerns to the stimulus generated by a few large-scale Westerns. As already brought out in this book, it just wasn't so. And it is even doubtful that the programmer Westerns provided much incentive for the extravaganza Westerns. In truth the Western is a loose, shifting, and variegated genre with many roots and branches. The "A" and "B" films, as roots of the genre, reached out into different soils to feed on unique nutrients. The markets and clientele were mostly different for the two

Powdersmoke Range (RKO-Radio, 1935) — Guinn "Big Boy" Williams, Hoot Gibson, and Harry Carey in the first of the *Three Mesquiteers* Westerns

End of the Trail (Columbia, 1936) — Jack Holt, Douglass Dumbrille, J. T. "Blackie" Whiteford, Art Mix (George Kesterson), and Jerome "Blackjack" Ward

types of film, and where they shared a common audience, the right hand was seldom influenced by what the left hand was doing.

Seeing an occasional Gary Cooper or Joel McCrea yarn certainly did not cause one to rush out and see even more Buck Jones or Jack Perrin sagebrushers. For, interestingly, major Western films, although touted by historians and Hollywood publicity departments, have, relatively speaking, had an insignificant influence in shaping the image of the West and the cowboy. Perhaps it is because there have been so few of them in comparison to the output of "B" Westerns, which number in the thousands. Seeing an occasional film such as *The Plainsman* or *Wells Fargo* could hardly have the lasting effect that the film output of Buck Jones, Rex Bell, Gene Autry, and confreres had from week to week, month to month, and year to year. Millions of boys and girls grew to adulthood thoroughly enmeshed in the continuing heroics of these bigger-than-life performers who were always cowboys, not something different each time they were seen. Thus we are tempted to hypothesize that the vast majority of Western fans have always cared more for the blood-and-guts action flicks of the "B" heroes who romped through wild Western adventures on a weekly basis than for the poetry and majesty of Ford or DeMille or Peckinpah or Boetticher. But perhaps we are wrong.

At any rate, the future seemed secure for the "B," and even those few cowboys whose range of thespian talents was limited to Expression Number 1 (constipation) and Expression Number 2 (relief) had little to fret about as long as they stayed in the saddle or in a brawl for the better part of an hour. Luckily, however, most of the cowboy aces were competent actors as well as showmen and capable of handling more creative rhetoric than "Come on, Rebel, we'll head 'em off at the Pass." But who would have had it otherwise? The simple, down-to-earth dialogue was part of the magic.

FILMS OF 1933

287. ROBBERS' ROOST
(Fox, January 1, 1933) 64 Mins.
George O'Brien, Maureen O'Sullivan, Maude Eburne, William Pawley, Ted Oliver, Walter McGrail, Doris Lloyd, Reginald Owens, Frank Rice, Bill Nestell, Clifford Santley, Gilbert Holmes, Vinegar Roan
D: David Howard
S: Zane Grey
SP: Dudley Nichols

288. WHEN A MAN RIDES ALONE
(Freuler/Monarch, January 15, 1933) 60 Mins.
Tom Tyler, Adele Lacy, Alan Bridge, Robert Burns, Frank Ball, Alma Chester, Duke Lee, Barney Furey, Lee Cordova, Lillian Chay, Jack Rockwell, Bud Osborne, Ed Burns, Jack Kirk, Herman Hack
D: J. P. McGowan
S: F. McGrew Willis
SP: Oliver Drake
P: Burton King

289. MAN OF ACTION
(Columbia, January 20, 1933) 57 Mins.
Tim McCoy, Caryl Lincoln, Wheeler Oakman, Walter Brennan, Stanley Blystone, Charles K. French, Julian Rivero
D: George Melford
S: William Colt MacDonald
SP: Robert Quigley

290. THE MYSTERIOUS RIDER
(Paramount, January 20, 1933) 61 Mins.
Kent Taylor, Lona Andre, Gail Patrick, Warren Hymer, Berton Churchill, Irvin Pichel, Cora Sue Collins, E. H. Calvert, Sherwood Bailey, Niles Welch, Clarence Wilson
D: Fred Allen
S: Zane Grey
SP: Harvey Gates, Robert Niles

291. CLANCY OF THE MOUNTED

(Universal, 1933)   12 Chaps.

Tom Tyler, Jacqueline Wells (Julie Bishop), William Desmond, Rosalie Roy, Francis Ford, Earl McCarthy, Tom London, Edmund Cobb, William Thorne, Leon Duval, Al Ferguson, Frank Lanning, Fred Humes, Monte Montague, Frank Lackteen, Steve Clemente

D: Ray Taylor

S: Based on the poem by Robert W. Service

SP: Basil Dickey, Harry O. Hoyt, Ella O'Neill

P: Henry MacRae

Chapter Titles: (1) Toll of the Rapids, (2) Brother Against Brother, (3) Ambuscade, (4) The Storm, (5) A Desperate Chance, (6) The Wolf's Fangs, (7) The Night Attack, (8) Crashing Timber, (9) Fingerprints, (10) The Breed Strikes, (11) The Crimson Jacket, (12) Journey's End

292. DRUM TAPS

(KBS/World Wide, January 24, 1933)   61 Mins.

Ken Maynard, Dorothy Dix, Hooper Atchley, Junior Coghlan, Charles Stevens, Kermit Maynard, Al Bridge, Harry Semels, Slim Whitaker, James Mason, "Tarzan," Leo Willis, Hooper Atchley, Los Angeles Boy Scout Troup No. 107

D: J. P. McGowan

SP: Alan James

P: Burt Kelly, Sam Bischoff, William Saal

293. TERROR TRAIL

(Universal, February 2, 1933)   57 Mins.

Tom Mix, Naomi Judge, Raymond Hatton, Francis McDonald, Arthur Rankin, Bob Kortman, Lafe McKee, John St. Polis, Frank Brownlee, Hank Bell, Jay Wilsey (Buffalo Bill, Jr.), Harry Tenbrook, W. J. Holmes, Leonard Trainer, Jim Corey, "Tony, Jr."

D: Armand Schaefer

S: Grant Taylor

SP: Jack Cunningham

294. VIA PONY EXPRESS

(Majestic, February 6, 1933)   60 Mins.

Jack Hoxie, Marceline Day, Lane Chandler, Julian Rivero, Doris Hill, Mathew Betz, Joe Girard, Charles K. French, Bill Quinlan

D: Lew Collins

SP: Lew Collins, Oliver Drake

P: Larry Darmour

295. TREASON

(Columbia, February 10, 1933)   63 Mins.

Buck Jones, Shirley Grey, Robert Ellis, Edward J. LeSaint, Frank Lackteen, T. C. Jacks, Charles Brinley, Charles Hill Mailes, Edwin Stanley, Art Mix, Frank Ellis, Ivar McFadden, Nick Cogley, "Silver"

D: George B. Seitz

S: Gordon Battle

296. SMOKE LIGHTNING

(Fox, February 17, 1933)   63 Mins.

George O'Brien, Virginia Sale, Douglass Dumbrille, Betsy King Ross, Nell O'Day, Frank Atkinson, Morgan Wallace, Clarence Wilson, George Burton, Fred Wilson

D: David Howard

S: "Canyon Walls"—Zane Grey

SP: Gordon Rigby, Sidney Mitchell

297. THE THUNDERING HERD

(Paramount, March 1, 1933)   59 Mins.

(Reissued as *Buffalo Stampede*)

Randolph Scott, Judith Allen, Barton MacLane, Harry Carey, Larry "Buster" Crabbe, Dick Rush, Frank Rice, Buck Conners, Charles Murphy, Noah Beery, Sr., Raymond Hatton, Blanche Frederici, Monte Blue, Al Bridge

D: Henry Hathaway

S: Zane Grey

SP: Jack Cunningham, Mary Flannery

298. SILENT MEN

(Columbia, March 3, 1933)   68 Mins.

Tim McCoy, Florence Britton, Wheeler Oakman, J. Carrol Naish, Walter Brennan, Joe Girard, Mathew Betz, Lloyd Ingraham, Steve Clark, William V. Mong, Syd Saylor

D: D. Ross Lederman

S: Walt Coburn

SP: Jack Cunningham, Stuart Anthony, Gerald Geraghty

299. THE PHANTOM THUNDERBOLT

(KBS/World Wide—Distributed by Fox, March 5, 1933)   63 Mins.

Ken Maynard, Frances Dade, Frank Rice, William Gould, Bob Kortman, Harry Holman, Frank Beal, Wilfred Lucas, William Robyns, "Tarzan," Nelson McDowell

D: Alan James

S: Forrest Sheldon, Betty Burbridge

SP: Alan James

P: Burt Kelly, Sam Bischoff, William Saal

300. SCARLET RIVER

(RKO-Radio, March 10, 1933)   57 Mins.

Tom Keene, Dorothy Wilson, Roscoe Ates, Edgar Kennedy, Creighton Chaney (Lon Chaney, Jr.), Billy Butts, Hooper Atchley, Betty Furness

D: Otto Brower

S/SP: Harold Shumate

301. RUSTLER'S ROUNDUP
(Universal, March 16, 1933)   56 Mins.
Tom Mix, Diane Sinclair, Noah Beery, Jr., Douglass Dumbrille, Roy Stewart, William Desmond, Gilbert Holmes, Bud Osborne, Frank Lackteen, William Wanger, Nelson McDowell, "Tony, Jr.," Walter Brennan
D: Henry MacRae
S: Ella O'Neill
SP: Frank Clark, Jack Cunningham

302. THE CALIFORNIA TRAIL
(Columbia, March 24, 1933)   67 Mins.
Buck Jones, Helen Mack, George Humbart, Luis Alberni, Charles Stevens, Emile Chautard, Evelyn Sherman, Chris-Pin Martin, Carmen LaRoux, Carlo Villar, Augie Gomez, John Paul Jones, Allan Garcia, Juan DuVal, William Steele, "Silver"
D: Lambert Hillyer
S/SP: Jack Natteford

303. THE TELEGRAPH TRAIL
(Warner Bros.-First National, March 28, 1933)   55 Mins.
John Wayne, Marceline Day, Frank McHugh, Yakima Canutt, Otis Harlan, Albert J. Smith, Clarence Gelbert, Jack Kirk, Lafe McKee, Slim Whitaker, Frank Ellis, "Duke"
D: Tenny Wright
SP: Kurt Kempler
P: Leon Schlesinger

304. GUN LAW
(Majestic, April 1, 1933)   59 Mins.
Jack Hoxie, Betty Boyd, J. Frank Glendon, Paul Fix, Mary Carr, Harry Todd, Ben Corbett, Dick Botiller, Edmund Cobb, Robert Burns, Jack Kirk, Horace B. Carpenter
D: Lew Collins
SP: Lew Collins, Oliver Drake
P: Larry Darmour

305. SOMEWHERE IN SONORA
(Warner Bros.-First National, April, 1, 1933)   57 Mins.
John Wayne, Shirley Palmer, Henry B. Wathall, J. P. McGowan, Ann Fay, Paul Fix, Frank Rice, Billy Franey, Ralph Lewis, Slim Whitaker, Blackie Whiteford, Jim Corey, "Duke"
D: Mack V. Wright
S: Will Comfort
SP: Joe Roach
P: Leon Schlesinger
(Remake of *Somewhere in Sonora*, a 1927 Ken Maynard starrer)

306. UNDER THE TONTO RIM
(Paramount, April 7, 1933)   63 Mins.
Stuart Erwin, Verna Hillie, Raymond Hatton, Fuzzy Knight, Kent Taylor, Fred Kohler, John Lodge, Pat Farley, Alan Garcia, George Narvie, Marion Bardell, Ed Brady
D: Henry Hathaway
S: "The Bee Hunter"—Zane Grey
SP: Jack Cunningham, Gerald Geraghty

307. THE WHIRLWIND
(Columbia, April 14, 1933)   62 Mins.
Tim McCoy, Alice Dahl, Pat O'Malley, J. Carrol Naish, Mathew Betz, Joe Girard, Lloyd Whitcomb, William McCall, Stella Adams, Theodore Lorch, Hank Bell, Mary Gordon, Joe Dominguez
D: D. Ross Lederman
SP: Stuart Anthony

308. THE THRILL HUNTER
(Columbia, April 30, 1933)   60 Mins.
Buck Jones, Dorothy Revier, Arthur Rankin, Robert Ellis, Edward J. LeSaint, Frank LaRue, Al Smith, Harry Semels, Eddie Kane, John Ince, Alf James, Harry Todd, Willie Fung
D: George Seitz
S/SP: Harry O. Hoyt

309. THE DUDE BANDIT
(Allied, May 1, 1933)   62 Mins.
Hoot Gibson, Gloria Shea, Skeeter Bill Robbins, Hooper Atchley, Neal Hart, Lafe McKee, Gordon DeMain, Fred Burns, Fred Gilman, Art Mix, George Morrell, Merrill McCormack
D: George Melford
S/SP: Jack Natteford
P: M. H. Hoffman, Jr.

310. DEADWOOD PASS
(Freuler/Monarch, May 5, 1933)   62 Mins.
Tom Tyler, Alice Dahl, Wally Wales, Buffalo Bill, Jr., Lafe McKee, Bud Osborne, Edmund Cobb, Slim Whitaker, Merrill McCormack, Charlotte (Carlotta) Monti, Duke Lee, Blackie Whiteford, Bill Nestell
D: J. P. McGowan
S: John Wesley Patterson
SP: Oliver Drake
P: Burton King

The Whirlwind (Columbia, 1933) — J. Carrol Naish, Tim McCoy, Pat O'Malley, and Theodore Lorch

311. SON OF THE BORDER

(RKO-Radio, May 5, 1933)   60 Mins.
Tom Keene, Edgar Kennedy, Julie Haydon, David
   Durand, Creighton Chaney (Lon Chaney, Jr.),
   Charles King, Al Bridge, Claudia Coleman
D: Lloyd Nosler
S: Wellyn Totman
SP: Wellyn Totman, Harold Shumate

312. UNKNOWN VALLEY

(Columbia, May 5, 1933)   69 Mins.
Buck Jones, Cecilia Parker, Bret Black, Carlota
   Warwick, Arthur Wanzer, Wade Boteler, Frank
   McGlynn, Charles Thurston, Ward Bond, Gay-
   lord Pendleton, Alf James, "Silver"
D: Lambert Hillyer
S: Donald W. Lee
SP: Lambert Hillyer

313. BREED OF THE BORDER

(Monogram, May 10, 1933)   60 Mins.
Bob Steele, Marion Byron, George Hayes, Ernie
   Adams, Wilfred Lucas, Henry Rocquemore, Fred

Cavens, Robert Cord, Perry Murdock
D: Robert N. Bradbury
S/SP: Harry O. Jones
P: Trem Carr

314. THE LONE AVENGER

(KBS/World Wide—Distributed by Fox,
   May 14, 1933)   61 Mins.
Ken Maynard, Muriel Gordon, Jack Rockwell,
   Charles King, Al Bridge, James Mason, Niles
   Welch, William N. Bailey, Ed Brady, Clarence
   Gelder, "Tarzan," Jack Rockwell, Lew Meehan,
   Horace B. Carpenter, Jack Ward, Roy Bucko, Buck
   Bucko, Bud McClure
D: Alan James
S: Forrest Sheldon, Betty Burbridge
SP: Alan James
P: Burt Kelly, Sam Bischoff, William Saal

315. TROUBLE BUSTERS

(Majestic, May 15, 1933)   55 Mins.
Jack Hoxie, Lane Chandler, Kaye Edwards, Ben Corbett, Harry Todd, Slim Whitaker, William Burt,

Roger Williams
D: Lew Collins
S: Oliver Drake
SP: Oliver Drake, Lew Collins
P: Larry Darmour

316. THE GALLANT FOOL
(Monogram, May 24, 1933)   60 Mins.
Bob Steele, Arletta Duncan, George Hayes, John
  Elliott, Theodore Lorch, Perry Murdock, George
  Nash, Pascale Perry
D: Robert N. Bradbury
SP: Robert N. Bradbury, Harry O. Jones (Harry
  Fraser)
P: Trem Carr

317. RUSTY RIDES ALONE
(Columbia, May 26, 1933)   58 Mins.
Tim McCoy, Barbara Weeks, Dorothy Burgess,
  Wheeler Oakman, Ed Burns, Rockcliffe Fellows,
  Edmund Cobb, Clarence Geldert, "Silver King"
D: D. Ross Lederman
S: Walt Coburn
SP: Robert Quigley

318. SUNSET PASS
(Paramount, May 26, 1933)   61 Mins.
Randolph Scott, Tom Keene, Kathleen Burke,
  Harry Carey, Fuzzy Knight, Noah Beery, Vince
  Barnett, Kent Taylor, Tom London, Pat Farley,
  Charles Middleton, Bob Kortman, James Mason,
  Frank Beal, Al Bridge, Leila Bennett, Nelson
  McDowell, George Barbier, Patricia Farley,
  Christian J. Frank
D: Henry Hathaway
S: Zane Grey
SP: Jack Cunningham, Gerald Geraghty

319. CRASHING BROADWAY
(Monogram, June 1, 1933)   55 Mins.
Rex Bell, Doris Hill, Harry Bowen, George Hayes,
  Charles King, Louis Sargent, G. D. Wood (Gor-
  don DeMain), Ann Howard, Blackie Whiteford,
  Perry Murdock, Henry Rocquemore, Max Asher,
  Allan Lee, George Morrell, Archie Ricks, Tex
  Palmer
D: John P. McCarthy
SP: Wellyn Totman
P: Paul Malvern
Supervision: Trem Carr

320. KING OF THE ARENA
(Universal, June 1, 1933)   59 Mins.
Ken Maynard, Lucile Browne, John St. Polis, Mi-
  chael Visaroff, Bob Kortman, James Marcus,
  Frank Rice, Fred McKay, Blue Washington, Wil-
  liam Steele, Jack Rockwell, Ed Coxen, Robert
  Walker, Jack Mower, Bobby Nelson, Steve Cle-
  mente, Robert Burns, Merrill McCormack, Artie
  Ortego, Chief Big Tree, Buck Bucko, Jack Kirk,
  Horace B. Carpenter, Pascale Perry, Bud McClure,
  Helen Gibson, Lafe McKee, Iron Eyes Cody,
  "Tarzan"
D: Alan James
S: Hal Berger, Ray Bouk
SP: Alan James
P: Ken Maynard

321. LIFE IN THE RAW
(Fox, July 7, 1933)   62 Mins.
George O'Brien, Claire Trevor, Warner Richmond,
  Francis Ford, Greta Nilsen, Gaylord Pendleton,
  Alan Edwards, Nigel De Brulier
D: Louis King
S: Zane Grey
SP: Stuart Anthony

322. THE CHEYENNE KID
(RKO, July 13, 1933)   61 Mins.
Tom Keene, Mary Mason, Roscoe Ates, Al Bridge,
  Otto Hoffman, Allan Roscoe, Anderson Lawler
D: Robert Hill
S: "Sir Peegan Passes"—W. C. Tuttle
SP: Keene Thompson

323. THE MAN FROM MONTEREY
(Warner Bros.-First National, July 15, 1933)
  57 Mins.
John Wayne, Ruth Hall, Luis Alberni, Francis Ford,
  Nena Quartero, Lafe McKee, Donald Reed, Slim
  Whitaker, Lillian Leighton, Jim Corey, "Duke"
D: Mack Wright
SP: Lesley Mason
P: Leon Schlesinger

324. THE FIDDLIN' BUCKAROO
(Universal, July 20, 1933)   65 Mins.
Ken Maynard, Gloria Shea, Fred Kohler, Frank Rice,
  Jack Rockwell, Joe Girard, Jack Mower, Slim Whit-
  aker, Al Bridge, Bob Kortman, "Tarzan," Bob
  McKenzie, Hank Bell, Frank Ellis, Roy Bucko,

Buck Bucko, Bud McClure, Pascale Perry
D: Ken Maynard
S/SP: Nate Gatzert
P: Ken Maynard

325. RAINBOW RANCH

(Monogram, July 25, 1933)   55 Mins.
Rex Bell, Cecilia Parker, Bob Kortman, Henry Hall,
George Nash, Gordon DeMain, Phil Dunham,
Jerry Storm, Tiny Sanford, Van Galbert, Jackie
Hoefley
D: Harry Fraser
S: Harry O. Jones (Harry Fraser)
SP: Phil Dunham
P: Trem Carr

326. THE FIGHTING TEXANS

(Monogram, July 26, 1933)   60 Mins.
Rex Bell, Luana Walters, Betty Mack, George
Hayes, Wally Wales, Yakima Canutt, Lafe McKee,
Anne Howard, Al Bridge, Frank LaRue, George
Nash, Gordon DeMain
D: Armand Schaefer

SP: Wellyn Totman, Charles Roberts
P: Trem Carr

327. FIGHTING WITH KIT CARSON

(Mascot, July, 1933)   12 Chaps.
John Mack Brown, Noah Beery, Betsy King Ross,
Noah Beery, Jr., Tully Marshall, Edmund Breese,
Robert Warwick, Edward Hearn, Lafe McKee,
Ernie Adams, Al Bridge, Lane Chandler, Reed
Howes, Jack Mower, DeWitt Jennings, Maston
Williams, William Farnum, Iron Eyes Cody, Frank
Ellis, Slim Whitaker

D: Armand Schaefer, Colbert Clark
SP: Jack Natteford, Barney Sarecky, Colbert Clark,
Wyndham Gittens
P: Nat Levine

Chapter Titles: (1) The Mystery Riders, (2) The
White Chief, (3) Hidden Gold, (4) The Silent
Doom, (5) Murder Will Out, (6) Secret of Iron
Mountain, (7) Law of the Lawless, (8) Red Phan-
toms, (9) The Invisible Enemy, (10) Midnight
Magic, (11) Unmasked, (12) The Trail to Glory

The Cheyenne Kid
(Radio, 1933) —
Tom Keene, Alan
Roscoe, and Mary
Mason

328. THE FIGHTING PARSON
(Allied, August 2, 1933)   61 Mins.
Hoot Gibson, Marceline Day, Robert Frazer, Stanley Blystone, Skeeter Bill Robbins, Charles King, Jules Cowan, Phil Dunham, Ethel Wales, Frank Nelson
D: Harry Fraser
S/SP: Harry Fraser
P: M. H. Hoffman, Jr.

329. GALLOPING ROMEO
(Monogram, August 5, 1933)   60 Mins.
Bob Steele, Doris Hill, George Hayes, Frank Ball, Ernie Adams, Lafe McKee, Ed Brady, George Nash, Earl Dwire
D: Robert N. Bradbury
S: Robert N. Bradbury
SP: Harry O. Jones (Harry Fraser)
P: Trem Carr

330. GORDON OF GHOST CITY
(Universal, August 14, 1933)   12 Chaps.
Buck Jones, Madge Bellamy, Walter Miller, William Desmond, Tom Ricketts, Francis Ford, Edmund Cobb, Hugh Enfield (Craig Reynolds), Bud Osborne, Ethan Laidlaw, Dick Rush, Jim Corey, William Steele, Bob Kerrick, Cecil Kellogg, Artie Ortego, "Silver"
D: Ray Taylor
S: "Oh, Promise Me!"—Peter B. Kyne
SP: Ella O'Neill, Basil Dickey, George Plympton, Harry O. Hoyt, Het Mannheim
P: Henry MacRae
Chapter Titles: (1) A Lone Hand, (2) The Stampede, (3) Trapped, (4) The Man of Mystery, (5) Riding for Life, (6) Blazing Prairies, (7) Entombed in the Tunnel, (8) Stampede, (9) Flames of Fury, (10) Swimming in the Torrent, (11) A Wild Ride, (12) Mystery of Ghost City

331. CROSSFIRE
(RKO-Radio, August 15, 1933)   60 Mins.
Tom Keene, Betty Furness, Edgar Kennedy, Edward Phillips, Lafe McKee, Charles K. French, Nick Cogley, Jules Cowan, Tom Brown, Murdock McQuarrie, Stanley Blystone
D: Otto Brower
S: Harold Shumate
SP: Tom McNamara

332. THE RANGER'S CODE
(Monogram, August 15, 1933)   59 Mins.
Bob Steele, Doris Hill, George Hayes, George Nash, Ernie Adams, Ed Brady, Hal Price, Dick Dickinson, Frank Ball
D: Robert N. Bradbury
S: John T. Neville
SP: Harry O. Jones (Harry Fraser)
P: Trem Carr

333. THE LAST TRAIL
(Fox, August 25, 1933)   59 Mins.
George O'Brien, Claire Trevor, El Brendel, Lucille LaVerne, Matt McHugh, Edward J. LeSaint, J. Carrol Naish, Ruth Warren, George Reed, Luis Albertson
D: James Tinling
S: Zane Grey
SP: Stuart Anthony

334. MAN OF THE FOREST
(Paramount, August 25, 1933)   62 Mins.
Randolph Scott, Harry Carey, Verna Hillie, Noah Beery, Larry "Buster" Crabbe, Barton MacLane, Guinn Williams, Vince Barnett, Blanche Frederici, Tempe Piggot, Tom Kennedy, Frank McGlynn, Jr., Duke Lee, Lew Kelly, Merrill McCormack
D: Henry Hathaway
S: Zane Grey
SP: Jack Cunningham, Harold Shumate

334a. THE FUGITIVE
(Monogram, August, 1933)   56 Mins.
Rex Bell, Cecilia Parker, George Hayes, Robert Kortman, Tom London, Gordon DeMain, Phil Dunham, Theodore Lorch, Dick Dickinson, Earl Dwire, George Nash
D: Harry Fraser
S/Adapt: Harry O. Jones (Harry Fraser)

335. THE TRAIL DRIVE
(Universal, September 4, 1933)   60 Mins.
Ken Maynard, Cecilia Parker, William Gould, Wally Wales, Ben Corbett, Lafe McKee, Alan Bridge, Bob Kortman, Frank Rice, Fern Emmett, Jack Rockwell, Slim Whitaker, Frank Ellis, Hank Bell, "Tarzan," Edward Coxen, Bob Reeves, Art Mix, Jack Kirk, Buck Bucko, Roy Bucko, Bud McClure
D: Alan James
S: Ken Maynard, Nate Gatzert

SP: Nate Gatzert
P: Ken Maynard

336. TO THE LAST MAN
(Paramount, September 15, 1933)   70 Mins.
Randolph Scott, Esther Ralston, Noah Beery, Jack LaRue, Larry "Buster" Crabbe, Fuzzy Knight, Barton MacLane, Gail Patrick, Muriel Kirkland, Egon Brecher, James Eagles, Eugenie Besserer, Harlan Knight, Shirley Temple
D: Henry Hathaway
S: Zane Grey
SP: Jack Cunningham

337. WAR ON THE RANGE
(Freuler/Monarch, September 22, 1933)   59 Mins.
Tom Tyler, Caryl Lincoln, Lane Chandler, Lafe McKee, Slim Whitaker, Ted Adams, Charles K. French, William Nanlan, Fred Burns, Billy Franey, Wesley Giraud
D: J. P. McGowan
SP: Oliver Drake
P: Burton King

338. RIDERS OF DESTINY
(Lone Star/Monogram, October 10, 1933)   58 Mins.
John Wayne, Cecilia Parker, George Hayes, Forrest Taylor, Al St. John, Earl Dwire, Heinie Conklin, Lafe McKee, Horace B. Carpenter, Yakima Canutt, Hal Price, Si Jenks, "Duke"
D: Robert N. Bradbury
S/SP: Robert N. Bradbury
P: Paul Malvern

339. STRAWBERRY ROAN
(Universal, October 26, 1933)   59 Mins.
Ken Maynard, Ruth Hall, Harold Goodwin, Frank Yaconelli, Charles King, William Desmond, James Marcus, Jack Rockwell, Robert Walker, Ben Corbett, Bill Patton, "Tarzan," Art Mix, Roy Bucko, Buck Bucko, Bud McClure
D: Alan James
S/SP: Nate Gatzert
P: Ken Maynard

340. KING OF THE WILD HORSES
(Columbia, November 10, 1933)   62 Mins.

William Janney, Dorothy Appleby, Wallace MacDonald, Harry Semels, Art Mix, Ford West, "Rex," "King," "Lady"
D: Earl Haley
S/SP: Fred Myton

341. FARGO EXPRESS
(KBS/World Wide—Distributed by Fox, November 20, 1933)   61 Mins.
Ken Maynard, Helen Mack, Roy Stewart, William Desmond, Paul Fix, Jack Rockwell, Claude Payton, Joe Rickson, "Tarzan," Bud McClure, Hank Bell
D: Alan James
SP: Alan James, Earle Snell
P: Burt Kelly, Sam Bischoff, William Saal

342. JAWS OF JUSTICE
(Principal, December 4, 1933)   58 Mins.
Richard Terry (Jack Perrin), Ruth Sullivan, Gene Tolar, Lafe McKee, Robert Walker, "Kazan"
D: Spencer G. Bennet
S: Joseph Anthony Roach
P: Sol Lesser

343. SMOKY
(Fox, December 8, 1933)   69 Mins.
Victor Jory, Irene Manning, Hank Mann, LeRoy Mason, Frank Campeau, Will James, Leonard Snegoff
D: Eugene Forde
S: Will James
SP: Stuart Anthony, Paul Perez

344. GIRL TROUBLE
(B 'n' B Pictures/Reliable, December 15, 1933)
Jack Perrin, Ben Corbett, Lola Tate, Mary Draper, Wally Turner
D: Bernard B. Ray
SP: Bennett Cohen
P: Bernard B. Ray
(Note: The "Bud 'n' Ben" series was produced by Bernard B. Ray doing business as Reliable Pictures Corporation which, in turn for this series of featurettes, did business as "B 'n' B Productions." All entries were distributed by William Steiner, either directly or through the Astor exchanges which, at that time, were an arm of the Steiner set-up. Astor was not, then or later, a production company. William Steiner supplied the financing, but B. B. Ray produced the films)

345. SAGEBRUSH TRAIL
(Lone Star/Monogram, December 15, 1933)   58 Mins.

John Wayne, Lane Chandler, Nancy Shubert, Wally
  Wales, Yakima Canutt, Henry Hall, William Dyer,
  Earl Dwire, Art Mix, Hank Bell, Slim Whitaker,
  Robert Burns, Hal Price
D: Armand Schaefer
SP: Lindsley Parsons
P: Paul Malvern

346. GUN JUSTICE
(Universal, December 16, 1933)   59 Mins.
Ken Maynard, Cecilia Parker, Hooper Atchley,
  Walter Miller, Jack Rockwell, Francis Ford, Fred
  McKaye, William Dyer, Jack Richardson, Ed
  Coxen, William Gould, Sheldon Lewis, Lafe
  McKee, Ben Corbett, Slim Whitaker, Hank Bell,
  Blackie Whiteford, Horace B. Carpenter, "Tar-
  zan," Bob McKenzie, Frank Ellis, Bud McClure,
  Roy Bucko, Buck Bucko, Pascale Perry, Jack Ward,
  Cliff Lyons
D: Alan James
S/SP: Robert Quigley
P: Ken Maynard

347. THE FIGHTING CODE
(Columbia, December 30, 1933)   65 Mins.
Buck Jones, Diane Sinclair, Ward Bond, Niles Welch,
  Dick Alexander, Louis Natheaux, Alf James, Er-
  ville Alderson, Gertrude Howard, Bob Kortman,
  Charles Brinley, Buck Moulton, "Silver"
D: Lambert Hillyer
S/SP: Lambert Hillyer

348. THE SUNDOWN RIDER
(Columbia, December 30, 1933)   65 Mins.
Buck Jones, Barbara Weeks, Pat O'Malley, Wheeler
  Oakman, Niles Welch, Bradley Page, Frank La-
  Rue, Ward Bond, Ed Brady, Harry Todd, "Silver"
D: Lambert Hillyer

S: John T. Neville
SP: Lambert Hillyer

349. SECRETS
(Mary Pickford Productions,
  United Artists, 1933)   90 Mins.
Mary Pickford, Leslie Howard, C. Aubrey Smith,
  Blanche Frederici, Doris Lloyd, Herbert Evans,
  Ned Sparks, Allan Sears, Mona Maris, Huntley
  Gordon, Ethel Clayton, Bessie Barriscale, Theo-
  dore von Eltz, Lyman Williams, Virginia Grey,
  Ellen Johnson, Randolph Connelly
D: Frank Borzage
S: Rudolf Besier, May Edgington
SP: Frances Marion

350. THE FIGHTING COWBOY
(California Motion Picture Enterprises/Superior
  Talking Pictures, 1933)   58 Mins.
Buffalo Bill, Jr., Genee Boutell, Allen Holbrook, Wil-
  liam Ryno, Marin Sais, Tom Palky, Bart Carre,
  Jack Evans, Boris Bullock, Ken Broeker, Betty
  Butler, Hamilton Steele, Clyde McClary, Ernest
  Scott, Bud Baxter, Jack Bronston
D: Denver Dixon (Victor Adamson)
S/SP: L. V. Jefferson
P: Victor Adamson

351. TRAILING NORTH
(Monogram, 1933)   60 Mins.
Bob Steele, Doris Hill, George Hayes, Arthur Ran-
  kin, Fred Burns, Dick Dickinson, Norma Fensler
D: J. P. McCarthy
S: Harry O. Jones (Harry Fraser)
SP: John Morgan
Supervisor: Trem Carr
P: Paul Malvern

FILMS OF 1934

352. POTLUCK PARDS
(B 'n' B Pictures/Reliable,
  January 15, 1934)
Walt Williams (Wally Wales), Ben Corbett, Jose-
  phine Hill, Harry Myers, James Aubrey, Robert
  Walker, George Chesebro, Murdock McQuarrie
D/P: Bernard B. Ray
SP: Bennett Cohen

353. FRONTIER MARSHAL
(Fox, January 19, 1934)   66 Mins.
George O'Brien, Irene Bentley, George E. Stone,
  Alan Edwards, Ruth Gillette, Berton Churchill,
  Frank Conroy, Ward Bond, Edward J. LeSaint,

Russell Simpson, Jerry Foster
D: Lewis Seiler
S: Stuart M. Lake
SP: Stuart Anthony, William Counselman

354. THE LUCKY TEXAN
(Lone Star/Monogram, January 22, 1934)
  56 Mins.
John Wayne, Barbara Sheldon, Lloyd Whitlock,
  George Hayes, Yakima Canutt, Jack Rockwell,
  Gordon D. Woods (Gordon DeMain), Earl Dwire,
  Edward Parker, Artie Ortego, Tex Palmer, Tex
  Phelps, George Morrell
D: Robert N. Bradbury

Frontier Marshal (Fox, 1934) — George O'Brien, Irene Bentley, and Ruth Gillette

S/SP: Robert N. Bradbury
P: Paul Malvern

355. THE LONE COWBOY

(Paramount, January 26, 1934)   64 Mins.

Jackie Cooper, Lila Lee, Barton MacLane, Addison Richards, Charles Middleton, Gavin Gordon, Herbert Corthell, John Wray, J. M. Kerrigan, Del Henderson, William LeMaine, George Pierce, Irving Bacon, Lillian Harmon, William Robyns, Leonard Kilbrick, Rose Levi
D: Paul Sloane
S: Will James
SP: Agnes Brand Leahy, Bobby Vernon

356. WEST OF THE DIVIDE

(Lone Star/Monogram, February 2, 1934)
   54 Mins.

John Wayne, Virginia Brown Faire, George Hayes, Yakima Canutt, Lloyd Whitlock, Billy O'Brien, Lafe McKee, Blackie Whiteford, Earl Dwire, Dick Dickinson, Tex Palmer, Artie Ortego, Horace B. Carpenter, Hal Price, Archie Ricks
D: Robert N. Bradbury
S/SP: Robert N. Bradbury
P: Paul Malvern

357. WHEELS OF DESTINY

(Universal, February 19, 1934)   63 Mins.

Ken Maynard, Dorothy Dix, Philo McCullough, Fred McKay, Jay Wilsey (Buffalo Bill, Jr.), Fred Sale, Jr., Jack Rockwell, Frank Rice, Nelson McDowell, William Gould, Ed Coxen, Merrill McCormack, Slim Whitaker, Hank Bell, Robert Burns, Artie Ortego, "Tarzan," Wally Wales, Jack Evans, Helen Gibson, Bud McClure, Fred Burns, Chief Big Tree, Roy Bucko, Marin Sais, Chuck Baldra, Arkansas Johnny, Blackjack Ward, Bobby Dunn
D: Alan James
S/SP: Nate Gatzert
P: Ken Maynard

358. NEVADA CYCLONE

(B 'n' B Pictures/Reliable,
   March 15, 1934)   33 Mins.

Fred Humes, Ben Corbett, Frances Morris, Lafe McKee, Walt Williams (Wally Wales), George Chesebro, Lew Meehan
D: Bernard B. Ray
SP: Bennett Cohen
P: Bernard B. Ray

358a. THE GOLD GHOST
(Educational, March 16, 1934) 2 Reels
Buster Keaton, Dorothy Dix, William Worthington,
  Lloyd Ingraham, Warren Hymer, Leo Willis, Joe
  Young
D: Charles Lamont
S: Ewart Adamson, Nick Barrows
P: E. H. Allen

359. THE FIGHTING RANGER
(Columbia, March 17, 1934) 60 Mins.
Buck Jones, Dorothy Revier, Frank Rice, Bradley
  Page, Ward Bond, Paddy O'Flynn, Art Smith,
  Denver Dixon, Frank LaRue, Jack Wallace, Mo-
  zelle Britton, Bud Osborne, Lew Meehan, Jim
  Corey, Steve Clemente, Frank Ellis, "Silver"
D: George B. Seitz
S: Stuart Anthony
SP: Harry O. Hoyt
(Remake of *Border Law*)

360. THE MAN TRAILER
(Columbia, March 24, 1934) 59 Mins.
Buck Jones, Cecilia Parker, Arthur Vinton, Clarence
  Geldert, Lew Meehan, Steve Clark, Charles West,
  Dick Botiller, Artie Ortego
D/SP: Lambert Hillyer

361. MYSTERY RANCH
(Reliable/William Steiner, April 12, 1934) 56 Mins.
Tom Tyler, Roberta Gale, Jack Gable (Jack Perrin),
  Frank Hall Crane, Louise Gabo, Charles King,
  Tom London, George Chesebro, Lafe McKee
D: Ray Bernard (Bernard B. Ray)
S: J. K. Henry
SP: Rose Gordon, Carl Krusada
P: Bernard B. Ray

362. ARIZONA NIGHTS
(B 'n' B Pictures/Reliable, April 15, 1934)
Jack Perrin, Ben Corbett, Al Ferguson, Charles K.
  French
D: Bernard B. Ray
SP: Bennett Cohen
P: Bernard B. Ray

363. HONOR OF THE RANGE
(Universal, April 16, 1934) 61 Mins.
Ken Maynard, Cecilia Parker, Fred Kohler, Jack
  Rockwell, Frank Hagney, James Marcus, Franklyn
  Farnum, Al Bridge, Jack Kirk, Art Mix, Eddie
  Barnes, Albert J. Smith, Charles Whitaker, Fred
  McKaye, Wally Wales, Hank Bell, Lafe McKee,
  William Patton, Bud McClure, Nelson McDowell,
  Ben Corbett, Pascale Perry, Jack Ward, Roy

Bucko, Buck Bucko, Fred Burns, "Tarzan"
D: Alan James
S/SP: Nate Gatzert
P: Ken Maynard

364. THE LAST ROUNDUP
(Paramount, May 1, 1934) 65 Mins.
Randolph Scott, Barbara Fritchie, Barton MacLane,
  Fuzzy Knight, Monte Blue, Charles Middleton,
  Richard Carle, Dick Rush, Ben Corbett, Fred Koh-
  ler, James Mason, Bud Osborne, Bob Miles, Buck
  Connors, Frank Rice, Jim Corey, Sam Allen, Jack
  M. Holmes
D: Henry Hathaway
S: "The Border Legion"—Zane Grey
SP: Jack Cunningham

365. FIGHTING TO LIVE
(Principal, May 6, 1934) 60 Mins.
Marion Shilling, Gaylord Pendleton, Reb Russell,
  Eddie Phillips, Ted Stroback, Bruce Mitchell,
  Lloyd Ingraham, Henry Hall, "Captain"
D: Edward F. Cline
S: Robert Ives
P: Sol Lesser

366. BLUE STEEL
(Lone Star/Monogram, May 10, 1934) 54 Mins.
John Wayne, Eleanor Hunt, George Hayes, Ed-
  ward Piel, Sr., Yakima Canutt, George Cleveland,
  George Nash, Artie Ortego, Hank Bell, Horace B.
  Carpenter, Ted Lorch, Earl Dwire, Lafe McKee,
  Silver Tip Baker
D: Robert N. Bradbury
S/SP: Robert N. Bradbury
P: Paul Malvern

367. THE MAN FROM UTAH
(Long Star/Monogram, May 15, 1934) 55 Mins.
John Wayne, Polly Ann Young, George Hayes, Ya-
  kima Canutt, Edward Piel, Sr., Anita Compillo,
  Lafe McKee, Earl Dwire, George Cleveland, Artie
  Ortego
D: Robert N. Bradbury
S/SP: Lindsley Parsons
P: Paul Malvern

368. RAWHIDE MAIL

(Reliable/William Steiner, June 8, 1934) 59 Mins.

Jack Perrin, Lillian Gilmore, Lafe McKee, Dick Cramer, Chris-Pin Martin, Nelson McDowell, George Chesebro, Jimmy Aubrey, Robert Walker, Lew Meehan, "Starlight"

D: Bernard B. Ray

S: Bennett Cohen

SP: Rose Gordon, Betty Burbridge

P: Bernard B. Ray

369. SMOKING GUNS

(Universal, June 11, 1934) 62 Mins.

Ken Maynard, Gloria Shea, Walter Miller, Harold Goodwin, William Gould, Bob Kortman, Jack Rockwell, Etta McDaniels, Martin Turner, Ed Coxen, Slim Whitaker, Hank Bell, Horace B. Carpenter, "Tarzan," Blue Washington, Wally Wales, Edmund Cobb, Bob Reeves, Fred McKaye, Jim Corey, Roy Bucko, Buck Bucko, Ben Corbett, Jack Ward, Bud McClure

D: Alan James

S/SP: Nate Gatzert

P: Ken Maynard

370. RAINBOW RIDERS

(B 'n' B Pictures/Reliable/Astor, June 15, 1934) 31 Mins.

Jack Perrin, Ben Corbett, Virginia Brown Faire, Ethan Laidlaw, Jim Corey, Jack Ward, Mack Wright, Grace Woods, "Starlight"

D: Bennett Cohen

SP: Bennett Cohen

P: Bernard B. Ray

371. RANDY RIDES ALONE

(Lone Star/Monogram, June 15, 1934) 54 Mins.

John Wayne, Alberta Vaughn, George Hayes, Yakima Canutt, Earl Dwire, Tex Phelps, Artie Ortego, Herman Hack, Mack V. Wright

D: Harry Fraser

SP: Lindsley Parsons

P: Paul Malvern

372. RACKETEER ROUND-UP

(Aywon, June 16, 1934) 50 Mins.

(Reissued by Beaumont in 1935, with some new footage, as *Gunners and Guns*)

Edmund Cobb, Edna Aslin, Edward Allen Bilby, Eddie Davis, Ned Norton, Lois Glaze, Felix Vallee, Jack Cheatham, Ruth Runnell

D: Robert Hoyt (possibly Robert J. Horner)

S: Eddie Davis

SP: Ruth Runnell

P: Nathan Hirsch

373. FIGHTING HERO

(Reliable/William Steiner, July 17, 1934) 59 Mins.

Tom Tyler, Renee Borden, Edward Hearn, Dick Botiller, Ralph Lewis, Murdock McQuarrie, Nelson McDowell, Tom London, George Chesebro. Rosa Rosanova, J. P. McGowan, Lew Meehan, Jimmy Aubrey

D: Harry S. Webb

S: C. E. Roberts (Charles)

SP: Rose Gordon, Carl Krusada

P: Bernard B. Ray

374. THE STAR PACKER

(Lone Star/Monogram, July 30, 1934) 60 Mins.

John Wayne, Verna Hillie, Yakima Canutt, George Hayes, Earl Dwire, Eddie Parker, George Cleveland, Tom Lingham, Davie Aldrich, Glenn Strange, Billy Franey, Tex Palmer

D: Robert N. Bradbury

S/SP: Robert N. Bradbury

P: Paul Malvern

375. BEYOND THE LAW

(Columbia, July 31, 1934) 60 Mins.

Tim McCoy, Shirley Grey, Lane Chandler, Addison Richards, Dick Rush, Harry Bradley, Morton Laverre (John Merton)

D: D. Ross Lederman

S/SP: Harold Shumate

376. THE RED RIDER

(Universal, July, 1934) 15 Chaps.

Buck Jones, Marion Shilling, Grant Withers, Walter Miller, J. P. McGowan, Dick Cramer, Margaret LaMarr, Charles K. French, Edmund Cobb, William Desmond, Mert Lavarre (John Merton), Frank Rice, Jim Thorpe, Monte Montague, Dennis Moore, Jim Corey, Bud Osborne, Al Ferguson, Artie Ortego, Tom Ricketts, J. Frank Glendon, Charles Brinley, William Steele, Fred Burns, Hank Bell, Chester Gan, Jim Toney, Art Mix, Jack Rockwell, Jack O'Shea, Frank Ellis, "Silver"

D: Louis Friedlander (Lew Landers)

S: "The Redhead from Sun Dog"—W. C. Tuttle

SP: George Plympton, Vin Moore, Ella O'Neill,

George Morgan

P: Henry MacRae

Chapter Titles: (1) Sentenced to Die, (2) A Leap for Life, (3) The Night Attack, (4) Treacherous Attack, (5) Trapped, (6) The Brink of Death, (7) The Fatal Plunge, (8) The Stampede, (9) The Posse Rider, (10) The Avenging Trail, (11) The Lost Diamonds, (12) Double Trouble, (13) The Night Raiders, (14) In the Enemy's Hideout, (15) Brought to Justice

377. A DEMON FOR TROUBLE

(Supreme/William Steiner, August 10, 1934)
58 Mins.

Bob Steele, Gloria Shea, Lafe McKee, Walter McGrail, Don Alvarado, Nick Stuart, Carmen LaRoux, Perry Murdock, Blackie Whiteford, Jimmy Aubrey, Buck Morgan

D: Robert Hill

S/SP: Jack Natteford

P: A. W. Hackel

378. RIDIN' GENTS

(B 'n' B Pictures/Reliable/Astor,
August 15, 1934) 32 Mins.

Jack Perrin, Ben Corbett, Doris Hill, George Chesebro, Alex Franks, Harry Myers, Lafe McKee, Charles K. French, Slim Whitaker, "Starlight"

D: Bennett Cohen

SP: Bennett Cohen

P: Bernard B. Ray

379. THE MAN FROM HELL

(Kent—Distributed by Cristo,
August 29, 1934) 58 Mins.

Reb Russell, Fred Kohler, Ann D'Arcy, George Hayes, Jack Rockwell, Yakima Canutt, Slim Whitaker, Roy D'Arcy, "Rebel," Tracy Lane, Mary Gordon, Tommy Bupp, Charles French, Murdock McQuarrie

D: Lew Collins

S: Ed Earl Repp

SP: Melville Shyer

P: Willis Kent

380. FIGHTING THROUGH

(Kent, August 29, 1934) 55 Mins.

Reb Russell, Lucille Lund, Yakima Canutt, Edward Hearn, Chester Gans, Steve Clemente, Bill Patton, Frank McCarroll, Ben Corbett, Hank Bell, Slim Whitaker, Nelson McDowell, Lew Meehan, Jack Jones, Jack Kirk, Chuck Baldra, Wally Wales, "Rebel"

D: Harry Fraser

S/SP: Harry Fraser

P: Willis Kent

381. THE LAW OF THE WILD

(Mascot, August, 1934) 12 Chaps.

"Rex" (King of Wild Horses), "Rin-Tin-Tin, Jr.," Bob Custer, Ben Turpin, Lucile Browne, Richard Cramer, Ernie Adams, Edmund Cobb, Slim Whitaker, Dick Alexander, Jack Rockwell, Wally Wales, Charles King, Lafe McKee, Hank Bell, Art Mix, Bud Osborne, Glenn Strange, Silver Harr, Al Taylor, Jack Evans, Bud McClure, Herman Hack

D: B. Reeves Eason, Armand Schaefer

S: Ford Beebe, John Rathmell, Al Martin

SP: Sherman Lowe, B. Reeves Eason

P: Nat Levine

Chapter Titles: (1) The Man Killer, (2) The Battle of the Strong, (3) The Cross-Eyed Goony, (4) Avenging Fangs, (5) A Dead Man's Hand, (6) Horse Thief Justice, (7) The Death Stampede, (8) The Canyon of Calamity, (9) Robber's Roost, (10) King of the Range, (11) Winner Takes All, (12) The Grand Sweepstakes

382. WAGON WHEELS

(Paramount, September 15, 1934) 56 Mins.

Randolph Scott, Gail Patrick, Billie Lee, Leila Bennett, Jan Duggan, Monte Blue, Raymond Hatton, Olin Howland, J. P. McGowan, James Marcus, Helen Hunt, James Kenton, Alfred Delcambre, John Marston, Sam McDaniels, Howard Wilson, Michael Visaroff, Julian Madison, Eldred Tidbury, E. Alyn Warren, Pauline Moore

D: Charles Barton

S: "Fighting Caravans"—Zane Grey

SP: Jack Cunningham, Charles Logan, Carl A. Buss

383. THE DUDE RANGER

(Principal/Fox, September 29, 1934) 65 Mins.

George O'Brien, Irene Hervey, Syd Saylor, LeRoy Mason, Henry Hall, James Mason, Sid Jordan, Alma Chester, Lloyd Ingraham, Earl Dwire, Si Jenks, Lafe McKee, Jack Kirk, Hank Bell

S: Zane Grey

SP: Barry Barringer

P: Sol Lesser, John Zanft

D: Edward F. Cline

384. ROCKY RHODES

(Universal, September, 1934) 7 Reels

Buck Jones, Sheila Terry, Stanley Fields, Walter Miller, Alf James, Paul Fix, Lydia Knott, Lee Shumway, Jack Rockwell, Carl Stockdale, Monte Montague, Bud Osborne, Harry Semels, "Silver"

D: Al Raboch
S: W. C. Tuttle
SP: Edward Churchill
P: Buck Jones

385. WEST ON PARADE

(B 'n' B Pictures/Reliable/Astor, October 15, 1934)

Denny Meadows (Dennis Moore), Ben Corbett, Jayne Regan, Franklyn Farnum, Fern Emmett, Philo McCullough, James Aubrey, Merrill McCormack

D: Bernard B. Ray
SP: Bennett Cohen
P: Bernard B. Ray

386. THUNDER OVER TEXAS

(Beacon, October 18, 1934) 61 Mins.

Big Boy Williams, Marion Shilling, Helen Westcott, Dick Botiller, Philo McCullough, Ben Corbett, Bob McKenzie, Claude Peyton, Victor Potel, Tiny Skelton, Jack Kirk, Hank Bell

D: John Warner (Edgar G. Ulmer)
S: Sherle Castle (Mrs. Edgar G. Ulmer)
SP: Eddie Granemann
P: Max and Arthur Alexander

387. THE TRAIL BEYOND

(Lone Star/Monogram, October 22, 1934) 55 Mins.

John Wayne, Noah Beery, Jr., Verna Hillie, Iris Lancaster, Robert Frazer, Earl Dwire, Eddie Parker, Artie Ortego, James Marcus, Reed Howes

D: Robert N. Bradbury
S: "The Wolf Hunters"—James Oliver Curwood
SP: Lindsley Parsons
P: Paul Malvern

Rainbow Riders (Reliable, 1934) — Veteran Western performers Jack Perrin and Benny Corbett starred as "Bud 'n' Ben" in the popular series of 3-reelers

388. THE FIGHTING TROOPER

(Ambassador, November 1, 1934) 61 Mins.

Kermit Maynard, Barbara Worth, Walter Miller, Robert Frazer, LeRoy Mason, George Regas, Charles Delaney, Joe Girard, George Chesebro, Charles King, Artie Ortego, Lafe McKee, Milburn Morante, Gordon DeMain, Nelson McDowell, George Morrell, Merrill McCormack

D: Ray Taylor

S: "Footprints"—James Oliver Curwood

SP: Forrest Sheldon

P: Maurice Conn

389. FRONTIER DAYS

(Spectrum, November 1, 1934) 61 Mins.

Bill Cody, Ada Ince, Wheeler Oakman, Franklyn Farnum, William Desmond, Bill Cody, Jr., Lafe McKee, Vic Potel, "Chico"

D: Bob Hill

S: Norman Springer

SP: James Shawkey

P: Al Alt (probably Ray Kirkwood)

390. OUTLAWS' HIGHWAY

(Trop Productions, November 1, 1934) 61 Mins.

(Reissued by Samuel S. Krellberg as *Fighting Fury*)

John King, Bonita Baker, Tom London, Lafe McKee, Philo McCullough, Bartlett Carre, Del Morgan, Jack Donovan, "Kazan"

D: Bob Hill

S/SP: Myron Dattlebaum

P: J. D. Trop

391. BRAND OF HATE

(Supreme/William Steiner, November 2, 1934) 63 Mins.

Bob Steele, Lucile Browne, William Farnum, Charles K. French, George Hayes, Jack Rockwell, Mickey Rentschiler, Archie Ricks, James Flavin

D: Lew Collins

S/SP: Jack Natteford

P: A. W. Hackel

392. THE PRESCOTT KID

(Columbia, November 8, 1934) 60 Mins.

Tim McCoy, Sheila Mannors, Alden Chase, Hooper Atchley, Joseph Sauers (Joe Sawyer), Albert J. Smith, Carlos De Veldez, Ernie Adams, Steve Clark, Slim Whitaker, Charles King, Bud Osborne, Art Mix, Tom London, Edmund Cobb, Walter Brennan, Lew Meehan, Jack Rockwell

D: David Selman

S: Claude Rister

SP: Ford Beebe

393. IN OLD SANTA FE

(Mascot, November 15, 1934) 64 Mins.

Ken Maynard, Evalyn Knapp, George Hayes, H. B. Warner, Kenneth Thompson, Gene Autry, Lester "Smiley" Burnette, Wheeler Oakman, George Chesebro, George Burton, Jack Rockwell, "Tarzan," Jim Corey, Jack Kirk, Edward Hearn, Frank Ellis, Horace B. Carpenter

D: David Howard

S: Wallace MacDonald, John Rathmell

SP: Colbert Clark

P: Nat Levine

394. LAWLESS FRONTIER

(Lone Star/Monogram, November 22, 1934) 59 Mins.

John Wayne, Sheila Terry, George Hayes, Lloyd Whitlock, Yakima Canutt, Gordon DeMain, Eddie Parker, Earl Dwire, Artie Ortego, Buffalo Bill, Jr., Herman Hack, Jack Rockwell

D: Robert N. Bradbury

S/SP: Robert N. Bradbury

P: Paul Malvern

395. WHEN A MAN SEES RED

(Universal, November 24, 1934) 60 Mins.

Buck Jones, Dorothy Revier, Syd Saylor, Peggy Campbell, LeRoy Mason, Frank LaRue, Libby Taylor, Jack Rockwell, Charles K. French, Bob Kortman, William Steele

D: Alan James

S: Basil Dickey

SP: Alan James

P: Buck Jones

396. MYSTERY MOUNTAIN

(Mascot, December 1, 1934) 12 Chaps.

Ken Maynard, Verna Hillie, Edward Earle, Edmund Cobb, Lynton Brent, Syd Saylor, Carmencita Johnson, Lafe McKee, Al Bridge, Edward Hearn, Bob Kortman, Gene Autry, Lester "Smiley" Burnette, Wally Wales, Tom London, George Chesebro, Philo McCullough, Frank Ellis, Steve Clark, James Mason, Lew Meehan, Jack Rockwell, Art Mix, William Gould, "Tarzan"

D: B. Reeves Eason, Otto Brower

S: Sherman Lowe, Barney Sarecky, B. Reeves Eason
SP: Bennett Cohen, Armand Schaefer
P: Nat Levine
Chapter Titles: (1) The Rattler, (2) The Man Nobody Knows, (3) The Eye That Never Sleeps, (4) The Human Target, (5) Phantom Outlaws, (6) The Perfect Crime, (7) Tarzan the Cunning, (8) The Enemy's Stronghold, (9) The Fatal Warning, (10) The Secret of the Mountain, (11) Behind the Mask, (12) The Judgement of Tarzan

397. WEST OF THE PECOS
(RKO-Radio, December 1, 1934) 68 Mins.
Richard Dix, Martha Sleeper, Samuel S. Hinds, Fred Kohler, Sleep 'n Eat (Willie Best), Louise Beavers, Maria Alba, Pedro Regas, G. Pat Collins, Russell Simpson, Maurice Black, George Cooper, Irving Bacon
D: Phil Rosen
S: Zane Grey
SP: Milton Krims, John Twist

398. THE WESTERNER
(Columbia, December 1, 1934) 58 Mins.
Tim McCoy, Marion Shilling, Joseph Sauers (Joe Sawyer), Hooper Atchley, Edward J. LeSaint, Edmund Cobb, John Dilson, Bud Osborne, Albert Smith, Harry Todd, Slim Whitaker, Lafe McKee, Merrill McCormack
D: David Sellman
S: Walt Coburn
SP: Harold Shumate

399. COWBOY HOLIDAY
(Beacon, December 15, 1934) 56 Mins.
Big Boy Williams, Janet Chandler, Julian Rivero, Dick Alexander, John Elliott, Alma Chester, Julia Bejarano, Frank Ellis
D: Bob Hill
S/SP: Rock Hawley (Bob Hill)
P: Max Alexander, Arthur Alexander

400. 'NEATH THE ARIZONA SKIES
(Lone Star/Monogram, December 28, 1934) 52 Mins.
John Wayne, Sheila Terry, Jay Wilsey (Buffalo Bill, Jr.), Shirley Ricketts (Shirley Jane Rickey), Earl Dwire, Weston Edwards, George Hayes, Yakima Canutt, Jack Rockwell, Phil Keefer, Frank Hall Crane, Artie Ortego, Tex Phelps, Eddie Parker
D: Harry Fraser
S/SP: Burl Tuttle
P: Paul Malvern

401. ARIZONA CYCLONE
(Imperial, 1934) 3 Reels
Wally Wales, Franklyn Farnum, Karla Cowan, "Silver King," Fred Parker, Barney Beasley
D: Robert Emmett (Tansey)
SP: Robert Emmett (Tansey)
P: William Pizor

402. BORDER GUNS
(Aywon, 1934)
Bill Cody, Blanche Mehaffey, Bill Cody, Jr., George Chesebro, Franklyn Farnum, William Desmond, Jim Pierce
D: Jack Nelson
P: Nathan Hirsh

403. THE BORDER MENACE
(Aywon, 1934)
Bill Cody, Miriam Rice, Ben Corbett, George Chesebro, James Aubrey, Frank Clark, Jim Donnelly, Lafe McKee
D: Jack Nelson
P: Nathan Hirsh
SP: Robert J. Horner

404. BOSS COWBOY
(Superior Talking Pictures, 1934) 5 Reels
Buddy Roosevelt, Frances Morris, Sam Pierce, Fay McKenzie, Bud Osborne, George Chesebro, Lafe McKee, Merrill McCormack, Clyde McClary, Allen Holbrook
D/P: Victor Adamson (Denver Dixon)
S/SP: Betty Burbridge

405. THE CACTUS KID
(Reliable, William Steiner, 1934)
Jack Perrin, Jayne Regan, Tom London, Slim Whitaker, Fred Humes, Philo McCullough, Joe De LaCruz, Kit Guard, Tina Menard, Lew Meehan
D: Harry S. Webb
S: Carl Krusada
SP: Carl Krusada
P: Bernard B. Ray

Fighting Through (Willis Kent, 1934) — Chuck Baldra, Jack Jones, Reb Russell, Jack Kirk, and Yakima Canutt

406. CARRYING THE MAIL
(Imperial, 1934)   3 Reels (27 Mins.)
Wally Wales, Peggy Djarling, Yakima Canutt, Al
  Hoxie, Sherry Tansey, Franklyn Farnum, "Silver
  King"
D: Robert Emmett
SP: Al Lane
P: William Pizor

407. CIRCLE CANYON
(Superior Talking Pictures, 1934)
Buddy Roosevelt, June Mathews, Clarise Woods,
  Bob Williamson, Allen Holbrook, Harry Leland,
  George Hazle, Clyde McClary, Mark Harrison,
  Ernest Scott, Johnny Tyke
D: Victor Adamson (Denver Dixon)
S: "Gun Glory"—Burl Tuttle
SP: B. R. (Burl) Tuttle
P: Victor Adamson

408. DESERT MAN
(Imperial, 1934)   3 Reels
Wally Wales, Peggy Djarling, Yakima Canutt,
Franklyn Farnum, Sherry Tansey, "Silver King,"
  Al Hoxie
D: Robert Emmett
SP: Robert Emmett
P: William Pizor

409. THE FEROCIOUS PAL
(Principal, Sol Lesser Productions, 1934)
Ruth Sullivan, Gene Tolar, Robert Manning, Tom
  London, "Kazan," Grace Wood, Ed Cecil
D: Spencer G. Bennet
S: Joe Roach
P: Sol Lesser

410. LIGHTNING BILL
(Superior Talking Pictures, 1934)
Buffalo Bill, Jr., Alma Rayford, Allen Holbrook,
  George Hazel, Nelson McDowell, Bud Osborne,
  William McCall, Lafe McKee, Eva McKenzie,
  Black Jack Ward
D: Victor Adamson (Denver Dixon)
P: Victor Adamson (Denver Dixon)
S: L. V. Jefferson

410a. LIGHTNING RANGE

(Superior Talking Pictures, 1934)   53 Mins.

Buddy Roosevelt, Patsy Bellamy, Betty Butler, Denver Dixon, Jack Evans, Si Jenks, Boris Bullock, Ken Broeker, Clyde McClary, Bart Carre, Olin Francis, Jack Bronston, Jack Evans, Lafe McKee, Genee Boutell, Anne Howard, Merrill McCormack

D/P: Victor Adamson (Denver Dixon)

S: L. V. Jefferson

411. THE LONE BANDIT

(Empire, 1934)

(*The Phantom Rider* Series)

Lane Chandler, Doris Brook, Wally Wales, Slim Whitaker, Ray Gallagher, Ben Corbett, Jack Prince, Philo McCullough

D: J. P. McGowan

S: Buck Parsons

SP: Ralph Consumana

P: Nathan Hirsh

412. THE LONE RIDER

(Imperial, 1934)

Wally Wales, Marla Bratton, Franklyn Farnum, James Sheridan (Sherry Tansey), Fred Parker, "Silver King"

D: Robert Emmett

SP: Al Lane

P: William Pizor

413. LOSER'S END

(Reliable/William Steiner, 1934)

Jack Perrin, Tina Menard, Frank Rice, William Gould, Fern Emmett, Elias Lazaroff, Robert Walker, Jimmy Aubrey, Rosemary Joye, Slim Whitaker

D: Bernard B. Ray

S: Harry Samuels (Harry S. Webb)

SP: Rose Gordon, Carl Krusada

P: Bernard B. Ray

414. THE OUTLAW TAMER

(Empire, 1934)

(*The Phantom Rider* Series)

Lane Chandler, Janet Morgan (Blanche Mehaffey), George Hayes, J. P. McGowan, Ben Corbett, Slim Whitaker, Tex Palmer, Herman Hack

D: J. P. McGowan

S: J. Wesley Patterson

P: Nathan and Fred Hirsh

415. PALS OF THE PRAIRIE

(Imperial, 1934)   28 Mins.

Buffalo Bill, Jr., Victoria Vinton, Charles K. French, Ben Corbett, Buck Owens, Sherry Tansey

D: Charles Hutchison

SP: Robert Emmett

P: William Pizor

416. PALS OF THE WEST

(Imperial, 1934)   29 Mins.

Wally Wales, Dorothy Gritten, Yakima Canutt, Franklyn Farnum, Al Hoxie, James Sheridan (Sherry Tansey), Fred Parker, "Silver King"

D: Robert Emmett

SP: Robert Emmett

P: William Pizor

417. THE PECOS DANDY

(Security, 1934)

George J. Lewis, Dorothy Gulliver, Betty Lee, Horace B. Carpenter, Robert Walker, Clyde McClary

D: Horace B. Carpenter or Victor Adamson (sources disagree)

SP: L. V. Jefferson

P: Victor Adamson (Denver Dixon)

418. RANGE RIDERS

(Superior Talking Pictures, 1934)

Buddy Roosevelt, Barbara Starr, Merrill McCormack, Denver Dixon, Fred Parker, Clyde McClary, Horace B. Carpenter, Herman Hack, Lew Meehan

D: Victor Adamson (Denver Dixon)

P: Victor Adamson (Denver Dixon)

SP: L. V. Jefferson

419. RAWHIDE ROMANCE

(Superior Talking Pictures, 1934)

Buffalo Bill, Jr., Genee Boutell, Lafe McKee, Si Jenks, Bart Carre, Boris Bullock, Jack Evans, Marin Sais, Clyde McClary, Ken Broeker

D: Victor Adamson (Denver Dixon)

SP: L. V. Jefferson

P: Victor Adamson (Denver Dixon)

420. THE RAWHIDE TERROR

(Security, 1934)   52 Mins.

Art Mix, William Desmond, Edmund Cobb, William Barrymore, Frances Morris, Bill Patton, Tommy

Bupp, George Holtz, Herman Hack, Ed Carey, George Gyton, Ernest Scott, Fred Parker
D: Bruce Mitchell
S: Victor Adamson (Denver Dixon)
SP: Jack Nelson
P: Victor Adamson (Denver Dixon)

421. RIDING SPEED
(Superior Talking Pictures, 1934)
Buffalo Bill, Jr., Joile Benet, Bud Osborne, Lafe McKee, Clyde McClary, Allen Holbrook, Ernest Scott
D: Jay Wilsey (Buffalo Bill, Jr.)
S: Ella May Cook
SP: Delores Booth
P: Victor Adamson (Denver Dixon)

422. THE SUNDOWN TRAIL
(Imperial, 1934)
Wally Wales, Fay McKenzie, James Sheridan (Sherry Tansey), Barney Beasley, Jack Kirk, "Silver King"
D: Robert Emmett
SP: Al Lane
P: William Pizor

423. TERROR OF THE PLAINS
(Reliable/William Steiner, 1934) 57 Mins.
Tom Tyler, Roberta Gale, William Gould, Charles

(Slim) Whitaker, Fern Emmett, Nelson McDowell, Frank Rice, Ralph Lewis, Robert Walker, Murdock McQuarrie
D: Harry S. Webb
S: Rose Gordon
SP: Jayne Regan, Carl Krusada
P: Bernard B. Ray

424. THE WAY OF THE WEST
(Empire/Superior, 1934)
Wally Wales, Marla Bratton, Bobby Nelson, William Desmond, Fred Parker, Sherry Tansey, Art Mix, Bill Patton, Tex Jones, Harry Beery, Helen Gibson, Tiny Skelton, Gene Raymond, Jimmy Aubrey
D/P: Robert Emmett (Tansey)
S: Barry Barringer
SP: Al Lane

424a. WEST OF THE LAW
(Imperial, 1934) 28 Mins.
Wally Wales, Marla Bratton, Franklyn Farnum, James Sheridan (Sherry Tansey), Fred Parker, "Silver King"
D: Robert Emmett (Tansey)
SP: Al Lane
P: William Pizor

FILMS OF 1935

425. UNCONQUERED BANDIT
(Reliable/William Steiner, January 8, 1935) 59 Mins.
Tom Tyler, Lillian Gilmore, Slim Whitaker, William Gould, John Elliott, Earl Dwire, Joe De LaCruz, George Chesebro, Lew Meehan, Dick Alexander, George Hazle, Ben Corbett
D: Harry S. Webb
S: Carl Krusada
SP: Rose Gordon, Lon Borden
P: Bernard B. Ray

426. SQUARE SHOOTER
(Columbia, January 21, 1935) 57 Mins.
Tim McCoy, Jacqueline Wells (Julie Bishop), Erville Alderson, Charles Middleton, John Darrow,

J. Farrell MacDonald, Wheeler Oakman, Steve Clark, William V. Mong
D: David Selman
S/SP: Harold Shumate

427. RUSTLERS OF RED DOG
(Universal, January, 1935) 12 Chaps.
Johnny Mack Brown, Raymond Hatton, Joyce Compton, Walter Miller, Harry Woods, Charles K. French, Fred McKaye, William Desmond, Wally Wales, Chief Thunder Cloud, Slim Whitaker, Art Mix, Jim Corey, Bill Patton, Cliff Lyons, Tex Cooper, Ben Corbett, Hank Bell, Bud Osborne, Edmund Cobb, J. P. McGowan, Monte Montague, Lafe McKee, Artie Ortego, Jim Thorpe, Chief Thunderbird, Ann D'Arcy, Fritzi

Burnette, Grace Cunard, Virginia Ainsworth

D: Louis Friedlander (Lew Landers)

S: Nathaniel Eddy

SP: George Plympton, Basil Dickey, Ella O'Neill, Nate Gatzert, Vin Moore

Chapter Titles: (1) Hostile Redskins, (2) Flaming Arrows, (3) Thundering Hoofs, (4) Attack at Dawn, (5) Buried Alive, (6) Flames of Vengeance, (7) Into the Depths, (8) Paths of Peril, (9) The Snake Strikes, (10) Riding Wild, (11) The Rustlers Clash, (12) Law and Order

428. HOME ON THE RANGE

(Paramount, February 1, 1935)   65 Mins.

Randolph Scott, Ann Sheridan, Dean Jagger, Jackie Coogan, Fuzzy Knight, Ralph Remley, Philip Morris, Frances Sayles, Addison Richards, Clarence Sherwood, Evelyn Brent, Allen Wood, Howard Wilson, Albert Hart, Richard Carle

D: Arthur Jacobson

S: "Code of the West"—Zane Grey

SP: Harold Shumate

P: Harold Hurley

429. NORTHERN FRONTIER

(Ambassador, February 1, 1935)   60 Mins.

Kermit Maynard, Eleanor Hunt, J. Farrell MacDonald, LeRoy Mason, Charles King, Ben Hendricks, Jr., Russell Hopton, Nelson McDowell, Walter Brennan, Gertrude Astor, Dick Curtis, Kernan Cripps, Jack Chisholm, Lloyd Ingraham, Lafe McKee, Tyrone Power, Jr., Artie Ortego, "Rocky"

D: Sam Newfield

S: "Four Minutes Late"—James Oliver Curwood

SP: Barry Barringer

P: Maurice Conn

430. SIX GUN JUSTICE

(Spectrum, February 1, 1935)   57 Mins.

Bill Cody, Wally Wales, Ethel Jackson, Budd Buster, Donald Reed, Ace Cain, Frank Moran, Bert Young, Buck Morgan, Roger Williams, Jimmy Aubrey, Blackie Whiteford

D: Robert Hill

SP: Oliver Drake

P: Ray Kirkwood

431. TEXAS TERROR

(Lone Star/Monogram, February 1, 1935)   51 Mins.

John Wayne, Lucile Browne, LeRoy Mason, George Hayes, Buffalo Bill, Jr., Bert Dillard, Yakima Canutt, Bobby Nelson, Fern Emmett, John Ince, Henry Rocquemore, Jack Duffy, Lloyd Ingraham

D/S/SP: Robert N. Bradbury

P: Paul Malvern

432. LAW BEYOND THE RANGE

(Columbia, February 15, 1935)   60 Mins.

Tim McCoy, Billie Seward, Robert Allen, Guy Usher, Harry Todd, Walter Brennan, Si Jenks, J. B. Kenton, Ben Hendricks, Jr., Jules Cowles, Tom London, Jack Rockwell, Alan Sears

D: Ford Beebe

S: Lambert Hillyer

SP: Ford Beebe

433. WHEN A MAN'S A MAN

(Atherton/Fox, February 15, 1935)   7 Reels

George O'Brien, Dorothy Wilson, Paul Kelly, Harry Woods, Jimmy Butler, Richard Carlisle, Edgar Norton, Clarence Wilson

D: Edward Cline

S: Harold Bell Wright

SP: Dan Jarrett

P: Sol Lesser, John Zanft

434. RUGGLES OF RED GAP

(Paramount, February 19, 1935)   76 Mins.

Charles Laughton, Mary Boland, Charlie Ruggles, Zasu Pitts, Roland Young, Leila Hyams, Maude Eburne, Lucien Littlefield, Leota Lorraine, James Burke

D: Leo McCarey

P: Arthur Hornblow, Jr.

S: "Ruggles of Red Gap"—Harry Leon Wilson

SP: Walter DeLeon, Harlan Thompson

Adaptation: Humphrey Pearson

435. THE PHANTOM EMPIRE

(Mascot, February 23, 1935)   12 Chaps.

Gene Autry, Frankie Darro, Betsy King Ross, Dorothy Christie, Wheeler Oakman, Charles K. French, Warner Richmond, J. Frank Glendon, Smiley Burnette, William Moore, Edward Piel, Jack Carlyle, Wally Wales, Jay Wilsey (Buffalo Bill, Jr.), Stanley Blystone, Richard Talmadge, Frank Ellis, Peter Potter, Bob Burns, Bob Card, Bruce Mitchell, "Champion"

D: Otto Brower, B. Reeves Eason

S: Wallace MacDonald, Gerald Geraghty, Hy Freedman, Maurice Geraghty

SP: John Rathmell, Armand Schaefer

P: Nat Levine

Chapter Titles: (1) The Singing Cowboy, (2) The Thunder Riders, (3) The Lightning Chamber, (4) Phantom Broadcast, (5) Beneath the Earth, (6) Disaster from the Skies, (7) From Death to Life, (8) Jaws of Jeopardy, (9) Prisoners of the Ray, (10) The Rebellion, (11) A Queen in Chains, (12) The End of Murania

(Two feature versions edited from this serial: *Men with Steel Faces* and *Radio Ranch*)

436. TRACY RIDES

(Reliable/William Steiner, February 26, 1935)
60 Mins.

Tom Tyler, Virginia Brown Faire, Edmund Cobb,
Charles K. French, Carol Shandrew, Lafe McKee,
George Chesebro, Robert Walker, Jimmy Aubrey

D: Harry S. Webb
S: Norman Hughes
SP: Rose Gordon, Betty Burbridge
P: Bernard B. Ray

437. OUTLAW RULE

(Kent, February, 1935)

Reb Russell, Betty Mack, Yakima Canutt, Jack Rockwell, John McGuire, Al Bridge, Joseph Girard, Jack
Kirk, Henry Hall, "Rebel"

D: S. Roy Luby
P: Willis Kent

438. ROCKY MOUNTAIN MYSTERY

(Paramount, March 1, 1935)   63 Mins.

Randolph Scott, Charles (Chic) Sale, Mrs. Leslie
Carter, Kathleen Burke, George Marion, Sr., Ann
Sheridan, James C. Eagles, Howard Wilson, Willie
Fung, Florence Roberts

D: Charles Barton
S: "Golden Dreams"—Zane Grey
SP: Edward E. Paramore, Jr., Ethel Doherty
P: Harold Hurley

439. THE CRIMSON TRAIL

(Universal, March 8, 1935)   60 Mins.

Buck Jones, Polly Ann Young, Carl Stockdale,
Charles K. French, Ward Bond, John Bleifer, Bob
Kortman, Bud Osborne, Charles Brinley, Hank
Pott, George Sowards, Paul Fix, Robert Walker,
"Silver"

D: Al Rabock
S: Wilton West
SP: Jack Natteford
P: Buck Jones

440. WILDERNESS MAIL

(Ambassador, March 9, 1935)   65 Mins.

Kermit Maynard, Fred Kohler, Doris Brook, Dick
Curtis, Syd Saylor, Paul Hurst, Nelson McDowell, Kernan Cripps, "Rocky"

D: Forrest Sheldon

S: James Oliver Curwood
SP: Bennett Cohen, Robert Dillon
P: Maurice Conn

441. RAINBOW VALLEY

(Lone Star/Monogram, March 12, 1935)   52 Mins.

John Wayne, Lucile Browne, LeRoy Mason, George
Hayes, Buffalo Bill, Jr., Bert Dillard, Lloyd Ingraham, Lafe McKee, Fern Emmett, Henry Rocquemore, Eddie Parker, Herman Hack, Frank Ellis,
Art Dillard, Frank Ball

D: Robert N. Bradbury
S/SP: Lindsley Parsons
P: Paul Malvern

442. THE CYCLONE RANGER

(Spectrum, March 15, 1935)   60 Mins.

Bill Cody, Nena Quartero, Eddie Gribbon, Soledad
Jiminez, Earle Hodgins, Zara Tazil, Donald Reed,
Colin Chase, Budd Buster, Jerry Ellis, Anthony
Natalie, "Chico"

D: Bob Hill
S/SP: Oliver Drake
P: Ray Kirkwood

443. THE REVENGE RIDER

(Columbia, March 18, 1935)   60 Mins.

Tim McCoy, Robert Allen, Billie Seward, Edward
Earle, Frank Sheridan, Jack Clifford, Jack Mower,
George Pierce, Alan Sears, Harry Semels, Joseph
Sauers (Joe Sawyer), Lafe McKee

D: David Selman
S/SP: Ford Beebe

444. RANGE WARFARE

(Kent, March, 1935)

Reb Russell, Lucille Lund, Wally Wales, Lafe McKee,
Roger Williams, Slim Whitaker, Ed Boland, Dick
Botiller, Chief Blackhawk, Ed Porter, Gene Alsace
(Rocky Camron)

D: S. Roy Luby
P: Willis Kent

445. STONE OF SILVER CREEK

(Universal, April 2, 1935)   61 Mins.

Buck Jones, Noel Francis, Niles Welch, Murdock

McQuarrie, Marion Shilling, Peggy Campbell, Rodney Hildebrand, Harry Semels, Grady Sutton, Kernan Cripps, Frank Rice, Bob McKenzie, Lew Meehan, "Silver"
D: Nick Grinde
S: R. R. Harris
SP: Earle Snell
P: Buck Jones

446. THE COWBOY AND THE BANDIT
(International/Superior, April 3, 1935) 57 Mins.
Rex Lease, Bobby Nelson, Janet Morgan (Blanche Mehaffey), Dick Alexander, Ada Belle Driver, Bill Patton, Wally Wales, William Desmond, Franklyn Farnum, Art Mix, Lafe McKee, Ben Corbett, Vic Potel, George Chesebro, Alphonse Martel, Jack Kirk, Fred Parker
D: Al Herman
SP: Jack Jevne
P: Louis Weiss

447. CYCLONE OF THE SADDLE
(Argosy/Superior, April 3, 1935)
Rex Lease, Janet Chandler, Bobby Nelson, William Desmond, Yakima Canutt, Art Mix, Chief Thunder Cloud, Helen Gibson, Milburn Morante, Chick Davis, George Chesebro, Chief Standing Bear, The Range Ranglers
D: Elmer Clifton
S/SP: Elmer Clifton, George Merrick
P: Louis Weiss

448. PALS OF THE RANGE
(Merrick/Superior, April 3, 1935) 57 Mins.
Rex Lease, Francis Wright (Morris), Yakima Canutt, George Chesebro, Robert (Blackie) Whiteford, Milburn Morante, Joey Ray, Tom Forman, Artie Ortego, Bill Patton, Art Mix, Bud Osborne, Ben Corbett, George Morrell
D: Elmer Clifton
SP: Elmer Clifton, George M. Merrick
P: Louis Weiss, George M. Merrick

449. SUNSET RANGE
(First Division, April 3, 1935) 60 Mins.
Hoot Gibson, Mary Doran, James C. Eagles, Walter McGrail, John Elliott, Eddie Lee, Ralph Lewis, Kitty McHugh, Martha Sleeper, Fred Gilman

D: Ray McCarey
S/SP: Paul Schofield

450. WAGON TRAIL
(Ajax, April 9, 1935) 55 Mins.
Harry Carey, Gertrude Messinger, Edward Norris, Earl Dwire, Chuck Morrison, Chief Thunder Cloud, John Elliott, Roger Williams, Dick Botiller, Lew Meehan, Francis Walker, Silver Tip Baker, Allen Greer
D: Harry Fraser
S/SP: Monroe Talbot
P: William Berke

451. FIGHTING SHADOWS
(Columbia, April 18, 1935) 58 Mins.
Tim McCoy, Robert (Bob) Allen, Geneva Mitchell, Ward Bond, Si Jenks, Otto Hoffman, Edward J. LeSaint, Bud Osborne, Alan Sears, Ethan Laidlaw
D: David Selman
S/SP: Ford Beebe

452. THE DESERT TRAIL
(Lone Star/Monogram, April 22, 1935) 54 Mins.
John Wayne, Mary Kornman, Paul Fix, Eddie Chandler, Carmen LaRoux, Lafe McKee, Al Ferguson, Henry Hall, Frank Ball, Artie Ortego, Lew Meehan, Wally West, Frank Brownlee, Frank Ellis, Dick Dickinson
D: Cullen Lewis (Lew Collins)
S/SP: Lindsley Parsons
P: Paul Malvern

453. THE COWBOY MILLIONAIRE
(Atherton/Fox, April 25, 1935) 74 Mins.
George O'Brien, Evelyn Bostock, Edgar Kennedy, Alden Chase, Maude Allen, Dan Jarrett, Lloyd Ingraham, Thomas Curran
D: Edward F. Cline
SP: George Waggner, Dan Jarrett
P: Sol Lesser

453a. UNCIVIL WARRIORS
(Columbia, April 26, 1935) 2 Reels
(*Three Stooges* Series)
Moe Howard, Larry Fine, Curly Howard, Dorothy Kent, Fred Kohler, Fred Kelsey

Sunset Range (First Division, 1935) — John Elliott and Hoot Gibson

D: Clyde Bruckman
S/SP: Felix Adler

454. CALL OF THE WILD

(United Artists, April 30, 1935) 91 Mins.
Clark Gable, Jack Oakie, Loretta Young, Reginald Owen, Frank Conroy, Sidney Toler, Charles Stevens, Lalo Encinas, Katherine DeMille, James Burke, John T. Murray, Bob Perry, Marie Wells, Sid Grauman, Herman Bing, Wade Boteler, John Ince, Syd Saylor, Joan Woodbury, Arthur Aylesworth, "Buck" (a dog)
D: William A. Wellman
S: Jack London
SP: Gene Fowler, Leonard Praskins
P: Darryl F. Zanuck

455. RUSTLERS' PARADISE

(Ajax, May 1, 1935) 61 Mins.
Harry Carey, Gertrude Messinger, Edmund Cobb, Carmen Bailey, Theodore Lorch, Roger Williams, Chuck Morrison, Allen Greer, Slim Whitaker, Chief Thunder Cloud
D: Harry Fraser
S: Monroe Talbot
SP: Weston Edwards
P: William Berke

456. THE TEXAS RAMBLER

(Spectrum, May 1, 1935) 59 Mins.

Bill Cody, Catherine Cotter, Earle Hodgins, Stuart James, Mildred Rogers, Budd Buster, Ace Cain, Roger Williams, Buck Morgan, Allen Greer, Colin Chase
D: Bob Hill
S/SP: Oliver Drake
P: Ray Kirkwood

457. THE SILVER BULLET

(Reliable/William Steiner, May 11, 1935) 58 Mins.
Tom Tyler, Jayne Regan, Lafe McKee, Charles King, Slim Whitaker, Franklyn Farnum, George Chesebro, Lew Meehan, Walt Williams (Wally Wales), Nelson McDowell, Robert Brower, Blackie Whiteford, Hank Bell, Allen Greer
D: Bernard B. Ray
S: William L. Nolte
SP: Rose Gordon, Carl Krusada
P: B. B. Ray

458. FIGHTING PIONEERS

(Resolute, May 21, 1935) 60 Mins.
Rex Bell, Ruth Mix, Buzz Barton, Stanley Blystone, Earl Dwire, John Elliott, Roger Williams, Guate Mozin, Chief Standing Bear, Chuck Morrison, Chief Thunder Cloud
D: Harry Fraser
S/SP: Harry Fraser, Chuck Roberts
P: Alfred T. Mannon

The Texas Rambler (Spectrum, 1935) — Earle Hodgins, Bill Cody, and Buck Morgan

459. JUSTICE OF THE RANGE

(Columbia, May 25, 1935)   58 Mins.

Tim McCoy, Billie Seward, Ward Bond, Guy Usher, Edward J. LeSaint, Alan Sears, Jack Rockwell, Jack Rutherford, George Hayes, Bill Patton, Stanley Blystone, Earl Dwire, Dick Rush, J. Frank Glendon, Frank Ellis, Tom London, Bud Osborne, Dick Botiller

D: David Selman

S/SP: Ford Beebe

460. GUNSMOKE ON THE GUADALUPE

(Kent, May, 1935)

Buck Coburn (Rocky Camron/Gene Alsace), Marion Shilling, Henry Hall, Roger Williams, Dick Botiller, Philo McCullough, Nelson McDowell, Lafe McKee, Bud Osborne, Benny Corbett, Lloyd Ingraham, Tracy Layne, Lew Meehan, Roy Bucko, Ralph Bucko

D: Bartlett Carre

S/SP: Paul Evan Leahman

P: Monte Montana (paid for use of name—Willis Kent actual producer)

461. TRAIL OF THE HAWK

(Affiliated Pictures, May, 1935)   60 Mins.

Yancie Lane, Dickie Jones, Betty Jordan, Lafe McKee, Don Orlando, Ramblin' Tommy Scott and Luke McLuke, Frankie Scott, Sandra Scott, Eddie Williams, Gaines Blevins, "Zandra" (King of Dogs)

D: Edward Dmytryk

S: "Pride of the Triple S" (author unknown)

P: H. A. Wohl

462. CIRCLE OF DEATH

(Kent, June 1, 1935)   60 Mins.

Monte Montana, Tove Linden, Yakima Canutt, Henry Hall, Ben Corbett, Jack Carson, John Ince, J. Frank Glendon, Princess Ah-Tee-Ha, Dick Botiller, Chief Standing Bear, Slim Whitaker, Marin Sais, Robert Burns, Olin Francis, George Morrell, Hank Bell, Budd Buster, Bart Carre

D: J. Frank Glendon

P: Willis Kent

463. CODE OF THE MOUNTED

(Ambassador, June 1, 1935)   60 Mins.

Kermit Maynard, Robert Warwick, Lillian Miles, Jim Thorpe, Syd Saylor, Wheeler Oakman, Dick Curtis, Stanley Blystone, Roger Williams, "Rocky"

D: Sam Newfield

S: "Wheels of Fate"—James Oliver Curwood

SP: George Sayre

P: Maurice Conn, Sigmund Neufeld

464. THE RED BLOOD OF COURAGE

(Ambassador, June 1, 1935)   55 Mins.

Kermit Maynard, Ann Sheridan, Reginald Barlow, Ben Hendricks, Jr., George Regas, Nat Carr, Charles King, "Rocky"

D: Jack English

S: James Oliver Curwood

SP: Barry Barringer

P: Maurice Conn, Sigmund Neufeld

465. BORDER BRIGANDS

(Universal, June 4, 1935)   56 Mins.

Buck Jones, Lona Andre, Fred Kohler, Frank Rice, Edward Keane, J. P. McGowan, Hank Bell, Al Bridge, Lew Meehan, "Silver"

D: Nick Grinde

S/SP: Stuart Anthony

P: Buck Jones, Irving Starr

466. THE DAWN RIDER

(Lone Star/Monogram, June 20, 1935)   57 Mins.

John Wayne, Marion Burns, Yakima Canutt, Reed Howes, Denny Meadows (Dennis Moore), Bert Dillard, Jack Jones, Nelson McDowell, Archie Ricks, Tex Phelps, James Sheridan

D: Robert N. Bradbury

S: Lloyd Nosler

SP: Robert N. Bradbury

P: Paul Malvern

467. THE OUTLAW DEPUTY

(Puritan, June 20, 1935)   59 Mins.

Tim McCoy, Nora Lane, Bud Osborne, George Offerman, Jr., Si Jenks, Jack Montgomery, George Holtz, Hank Bell, Tex Cooper, Jim Corey

D: Otto Brower

S: "King of Cactusville"—Johnston McCulley

SP: Ford Beebe, Dell Andrews

P: Nat Ross

468. RIDING WILD

(Columbia, June 28, 1935)   57 Mins.

Tim McCoy, Billie Seward, Niles Welch, Edward J. LeSaint, Dick Alexander, Dick Botiller, Edmund Cobb, Jack Rockwell, Bud Osborne, Wally West, Al Haskell, Si Jenks

D: David Selman

S/SP: Ford Beebe

469. THE VANISHING RIDERS

(Spectrum, July 3, 1935)

Bill Cody, Ethel Jackson, Wally Wales, Bill Cody, Jr., Budd Buster, Milburn Morante, Donald Reed, Francis Walker, Roger Williams, Bert Young, Buck Morgan, Ace Cain, Colin Chase, Bud Osborne

D: Bob Hill

S/SP: Oliver Drake

P: Ray Kirkwood

The Dawn Rider (Lone Star/Monogram, 1935) — John Wayne, Yakima Canutt, and Reed Howes

470. PARADISE CANYON

(Lone Star/Monogram, July 20, 1935) 52 Mins.

John Wayne, Marion Burns, Earle Hodgins, Yakima Canutt, Reed Howes, Perry Murdock, John Goodrich, Gino Corrado, Gordon Clifford, Tex Palmer, Herman Hack, Earl Dwire

D: Carl Pierson

S: Lindsley Parsons

SP: Robert Tansey, Lindsley Parsons

P: Paul Malvern

471. THE ARIZONIAN

(RKO, July 27, 1935) 8 Reels

Richard Dix, Preston Foster, Margot Grahame, Louis Calhern, James Bush, Ray Meyer, Francis Ford, J. Farrell MacDonald, Joe Sawyer, Edward Van Sloan, Bob Kortman, Ted Oliver, George Lollier, Willie Best, Etta McDaniels, Jim Thorpe, Podner Jones, Hank Bell

D: Charles Vidor

S/SP: "The Peacemaker"—Dudley Nichols

P: Cliff Reid

472. OUTLAWED GUNS

(Universal, July 29, 1935) 7 Reels

Buck Jones, Ruth Channing, Frank McGlenn, Sr., Charles King, Joan Gale, Monte Montague, Bob Walker, Carl Stockdale, Cliff Lyons, Babe De-Treest, Jack Montgomery, Pat O'Brien, Roy D'Arcy, Joseph Girard, Lee Shumway, Jack Rockwell

D: Ray Taylor

S: Cliff Farrell

SP: Jack Neville

P: Buck Jones

473. HOP-A-LONG CASSIDY

(Paramount, July 30, 1935) 63 Mins.

(First in the *Hopalong Cassidy* series—reissued by Screen Guild as *Hopalong Cassidy Enters*)

William Boyd, Jimmy Ellison, Paula Stone, Robert Warwick, Charles Middleton, Frank McGlynn, Jr., Kenneth Thompson, George Hayes, James Mason, Frank Campeau, Ted Adams, Willie Fung, Franklyn Farnum, John Merton, Wally West

D: Howard Bretherton

S: Clarence E. Mulford

SP: Doris Schroeder

P: Harry Sherman

474. BRANDED A COWARD

(Supreme/William Steiner, July, 1935) 57 Mins.

Johnny Mack Brown, Billie Seward, Syd Saylor, Yakima Canutt, Lee Shumway, Lloyd Ingraham, Roger Williams, Frank McCarroll, Mickey Rentschiler, Rex Downing, Bob Kortman, Ed Piel, Sr., Joe Girard

D: Sam Newfield

S: Richard Martinsen

SP: Earle Snell

P: A. W. Hackel

475. THE ROARING WEST

(Universal, July, 1935) 15 Chaps.

Buck Jones, Muriel Evans, Walter Miller, Frank McGlynn, Harlan Knight, William Desmond, William Thorne, Eola Galli, Pat O'Brien, Charles King, Slim Whitaker, Tom London, Edmund Cobb, Dick Rush, Cecil Kellogg, Paul Palmer, Harry Tenbrook, Jay Wilsey (Buffalo Bill, Jr.), Tiny Skelton, George Ovey, Fred Humes, Cliff Lyons, John Bose, Lafe McKee, "Silver"

D: Ray Taylor

S: Ed Earl Repp

SP: George Plympton, Nate Gatzert, Basil Dickey, Robert C. Rothafel, Ella O'Neill

P: Henry MacRae

Chapter Titles: (1) The Land Rush, (2) Torrent of Terror, (3) Flaming Peril, (4) Stampede of Death, (5) Danger in the Dark, (6) Death Rides the Plain, (7) Hurled to the Depths, (8) Ravaging Flames, (9) Death Holds the Reins, (10) The Fatal Blast, (11) The Baited Trap, (12) The Mystery Shot, (13) Flaming Torrents, (14) Thundering Fury, (15) The Conquering Cowpunchers

476. TRAILS OF THE WILD

(Ambassador, August 1, 1935) 60 Mins.

Kermit Maynard, Billie Seward, Fuzzy Knight, Monte Blue, Mathew Betz, Theodore von Eltz, Frank Rice, Robert Frazer, Wheeler Oakman, Roger Williams, Charles Delaney, John Elliott, Dick Curtis, "Rocky"

D: Sam Newfield

S: "Caryl of the Mountains"—James Oliver Curwood

SP: Joseph O'Donnell

P: Sigmund Neufeld, Maurice Conn

477. WESTERN FRONTIER

(Columbia, August 7, 1935) 59 Mins.

Ken Maynard, Lucile Browne, Nora Lane, Robert Henry, Frank Yaconelli, Otis Harlan, Harold Goodwin, Frank Hagney, Gordon S. Griffith, Jim Marcus, Tom Harris, Nelson McDowell, Frank Ellis, Art Mix, Slim Whitaker, William Gould, Dick Curtis, Budd Buster, Herman Hack, Horace B. Carpenter, Oscar Gahan, Joe Weaver, "Tarzan"

D: Al Herman

S: Ken Maynard

SP: Nate Gatzert

P: Larry Darmour

478. THE MAN FROM GUNTOWN

(Puritan, August 15, 1935) 61 Mins.

Tim McCoy, Billie Seward, Rex Lease, Jack Clifford,
Wheeler Oakman, Bob McKenzie, Jack Rockwell,
George Chesebro, George Pierce, Ella McKenzie,
Horace B. Carpenter, Hank Bell
D/S: Ford Beebe
SP: Ford Beebe, Thomas H. Ince, Jr.
P: Nat Ross

479. WESTWARD HO

(Republic, August 19, 1935) 60 Mins.
John Wayne, Sheila Mannors, Frank McGlynn, Jr.,
Jack Curtis, Yakima Canutt, Bradley Metcalf,
Hank Bell, Mary MacLaren, James Farley, Dickie
Jones, Glenn Strange, Lloyd Ingraham, Frank El-
lis, Earl Dwire, Fred Burns, Jack Kirk, Tex Palmer
D: Robert N. Bradbury
S: Lindsley Parsons
SP: Lindsley Parsons, Robert Emmett (Tansey),
Harry Friedman
P: Paul Malvern

480. TUMBLING TUMBLEWEEDS

(Republic, September 5, 1935) 57 Mins.
Gene Autry, Smiley Burnette, Lucile Browne,
Norma Taylor, George Hayes, Edward Hearn,
Jack Rockwell, Frankie Marvin, George Chesebro,
Eugene Jackson, Charles King, Charles Whitaker,
George Burton, Tom London, Cornelius Keefe,
Tommy Coats, Cliff Lyons, Bud Pope, Tracy
Layne, "Champion," Bud McClure, George Mor-
rell, Oscar Gahan
D: Joseph Kane
S: Alan Ludwig
SP: Ford Beebe
P: Nat Levine

481. WANDERER OF THE WASTELAND

(Paramount, September 9, 1935) 7 Reels
Dean Jagger, Larry "Buster" Crabbe, Gail Patrick,
Raymond Hatton, Fuzzy Knight, Edward Ellis,
Benny Baker, Al St. John, Trixie Frigans, Monte
Blue, Charles Walton, Anna Q. Nillson, Tam-
many Young, Stanley Andrews, Alfred Delcam-
bre, Pat O'Malley, Glenn (Leif) Erickson, Marina
Shubert, Kenneth Harlan, Jim Thorpe, Bud Os-
borne, Robert Burns
D: Otto Lovering
S: Zane Grey
SP: Stuart Anthony
P: Harold Hurley

482. THE THROWBACK

(Universal, September 17, 1935) 60 Mins.
Buck Jones, Muriel Evans, Eddie Phillips, George
Hayes, Paul Fix, Frank LaRue, Earl Pinegree, Bob
Walker, Charles K. French, Bryant Washburn,
Allan Ramsay, Margaret Davis, Bobby Nelson,

Mickey Martin, "Silver"
D: Ray Taylor
S: Cherry Wilson
SP: Frances Guihan
P: Buck Jones

483. MELODY TRAIL

(Republic, September 24, 1935) 60 Mins.
Gene Autry, Smiley Burnette, Ann Rutherford,
Wade Boteler, Willy Costello, Al Bridge, Marie
Quillan, Gertrude Messinger, Tracy Layne, Abe
Lefton, George DeNormand, Jane Barnes, Ione
Reed, Marion Downing, "Champion," "Buck" (the
Wonder Dog)
D: Joseph Kane
S: Sherman Lowe, Betty Burbridge
SP: Sherman Lowe
P: Nat Levine

484. POWDERSMOKE RANGE

(RKO, September 27, 1935) 6 Reels
(First of the *Three Mesquiteers* films)
Harry Carey, Hoot Gibson, Bob Steele, Tom Tyler,
Guinn "Big Boy" Williams, Boots Mallory, Wally
Wales, Sam Hardy, Adrian Morris, Buzz Barton,
Art Mix, Frank Rice, Buddy Roosevelt, Buffalo
Bill, Jr., Franklyn Farnum, William Desmond, Wil-
liam Farnum, Ethan Laidlaw, Eddie Dunn, Ray
Meyer, Barney Furey, Bob McKenzie, James Ma-
son, Irving Bacon, Henry Rocquemore, Phil Dun-
ham, Silver Tip Baker, Nelson McDowell, Frank
Ellis
D: Wallace Fox
S: William Colt MacDonald
SP: Adele Buffington
P: Cliff Reid

485. THUNDER MOUNTAIN

(Atherton/Fox, September 27, 1935) 7 Reels
George O'Brien, Barbara Fritchie, Frances Grant,
Morgan Wallace, George Hayes, Edward J. Le-
Saint, Dean Benton, William N. Bailey
D: David Howard
S: Zane Grey
SP: Dan Jarrett, Don Swift
P: Sol Lesser

486. THE NEW FRONTIER

(Republic, October 5, 1935) 60 Mins.
John Wayne, Muriel Evans, Warner Richmond, Al
Bridge, Mary MacLaren, Glenn Strange, Mur-
dock McQuarrie, Allan Cavan, Sam Flint, Earl
Dwire, Frank Ball, Hooper Atchley, Jack Kirk,
Sherry Tansey
D: Carl Pierson
S/SP: Robert Emmett (Tansey)
P: Trem Carr

487. THE EAGLE'S BROOD

(Paramount, October 10, 1935)   59 Mins.

(*Hopalong Cassidy* Series)

William Boyd, Jimmy Ellison, William Farnum, George Hayes, Addison Richards, Joan Woodbury, Frank Shannon, Dorothy Revier, Paul Fix, Al Lydell, John Merton, Juan Torene, Henry Sylvester

D: Howard Bretherton

S: Clarence E. Mulford

SP: Doris Schroeder, Harrison Jacobs

P: Harry Sherman

488. HIS FIGHTING BLOOD

(Ambassador, October 15, 1935)   60 Mins.

Kermit Maynard, Polly Ann Young, Ted Adams, Paul Fix, Joseph Girard, Ben Hendricks, Jr., Frank O'Connor, Charles King, Frank LaRue, Ed Cecil, Theodore Lorch, Jack Cheatham, The Singing Constables (Jack Kirk, Chuck Baldra, and Glenn Strange), "Rocky"

D: John English

S: James Oliver Curwood

SP: Joseph O'Donnell

P: Maurice Conn, Sigmund Neufeld

489. STORMY

(Universal, October 22, 1935)   7 Reels

Noah Beery, Jr., Jean Rogers, J. Farrell MacDonald, Raymond Hatton, Fred Kohler, Walter Miller, James Burtis, Cecil Kellogg, Ken Cooper, Jim Phillips, Bud Osborne, Jack Sanders, Jack Shannon, Glenn Strange, Jack Kirk, Chuck Baldra, "Rex," The Arizona Wranglers

D: Louis Friedlander (Lew Landers)

S: Cherry Wilson

SP: George H. Plympton, Bennett Cohen

P: Henry MacRae

490. ANNIE OAKLEY

(RKO, October 29, 1935)   90 Mins.

Barbara Stanwyck, Preston Foster, Melvyn Douglas, Moroni Olson, Pert Kelton, Andy Clyde, Chief Thunderbird, Margaret Armstrong, Delmar Watson

D: George Stevens

S: Joseph A. Fields, Ewart Adamson

SP: Joel Sayre, John Twist

AP: Cliff Reid

491. BETWEEN MEN

(Supreme/William Steiner, October 29, 1935)   59 Mins.

Johnny Mack Brown, Beth Marion, William Farnum, Earl Dwire, Lloyd Ingraham, Frank Ball, Harry Downing, Horace B. Carpenter, Forrest Taylor, Bud Osborne, Sherry Tansey, Milburn

Morante, Artie Ortego

D/S: Robert N. Bradbury

SP: Charles Francis Royal

P: A.W. Hackel

492. WESTERN COURAGE

(Columbia, October 29, 1935)   61 Mins.

Ken Maynard, Geneva Mitchell, Charles K. French, Betty Blythe, Cornelius Keefe, Ward Bond, E. H. Calvert, Renee Whitney, Dick Curtis, Bob Reeves, Wally West, "Tarzan," Roy Bucko, Buck Bucko, Bud McClure, Bart Carre, Arkansas Johnny

D: Spencer G. Bennet

S: Charles Francis Royal

SP: Nate Gatzert

P: Larry Darmour

493. MOONLIGHT ON THE PRAIRIE

(Warner Bros., November 1, 1935)   7 Reels

Dick Foran, Sheila Mannors, George E. Stone, Gordon (Bill) Elliott, Joe Sawyer, Robert Barrat, Herbert Heywood, Dickie Jones, Joe King, Milton Kibbee, Raymond Brown, Richard Carle, Bud Osborne, Ben Corbett, Gene Alsace (Rocky Camron), Glenn Strange, Vic Potel, Cactus Mack, Jack Kirk

D: D. Ross Lederman

S: "Boss of the Bar B Ranch"—William Jacobs

P: Bryan Foy

494. TIMBER WAR

(Ambassador, November 1, 1935)   60 Mins.

Kermit Maynard, Lucille Lund, Lawrence Gray, Robert Warwick, Lloyd Ingraham, Wheeler Oakman, Roger Williams, George Morrell, "Rocky," James Pierce, Patricia Royal

D: Sam Newfield

S: James Oliver Curwood

SP: Joseph O'Donnell

P: Maurice Conn, Sigmund Neufeld

495. LAWLESS RANGE

(Republic, November 4, 1935)   59 Mins.

John Wayne, Sheila Mannors, Earl Dwire, Frank McGlynn, Jr., Yakima Canutt, Jack Curtis, Wally Howe, Glenn Strange, Jack Kirk, Charles Baldra, Charley Sargent, Fred Burns, Slim Whitaker, Julia Griffin

D: Robert N. Bradbury

S/SP: Lindsley Parsons

P: Trem Carr

496. THE LAST OF THE CLINTONS

(Ajax, November 12, 1935)   59 Mins.

Harry Carey, Betty Mack, Del Gordon, Victor Potel, Earl Dwire, Ruth Findlay, Tom London, Slim

Whitaker, Ernie Adams, William McCall, Lafe McKee
D: Harry Fraser
S: Monroe Talbot
SP: Weston Edwards
P: William Berke

497. THE SAGEBRUSH TROUBADOR
(Republic, November 19, 1935) 54 Mins.
Gene Autry, Smiley Burnette, Barbara Pepper, J. Frank Glendon, Dennis Moore, Hooper Atchley, Fred Kelsey, Julian Rivero, Tom London, Wes Warner, Frankie Marvin, Bud Pope, Tommy Gene Fairey, "Champion," Art Davis
D: Joseph Kane
S: Oliver Drake
SP: Oliver Drake, Joseph Poland
P: Nat Levine

498. RIDIN' THRU
(Reliable/William Steiner, November 20, 1935)
Tom Tyler, Ruth Hiatt, Lafe McKee, Philo McCullough, Ben Corbett, Lew Meehan, Bud Osborne, Carol Shandrew
D: Harry S. Webb
S: Carl Krusada
SP: Rose Gordon
P: Bernard B. Ray

499. NEVADA
(Paramount, November 29, 1935) 7 Reels
Larry "Buster" Crabbe, Kathleen Burke, Monte Blue, Raymond Hatton, Glenn Erikson, Syd Saylor, William Duncan, Richard Carle, Stanley Andrews, Frank Sheridan, Jack Kennedy, Henry Rocquemore, William L. Thorne, Harry Dunkinson, Barney Furey, William Desmond, Frank Rice, Dutch Hendrian
D: Charles Barton
S: "Nevada"—Zane Grey
SP: Barnett Weston, Stuart Anthony

500. BAR 20 RIDES AGAIN
(Paramount, November 30, 1935) 65 Mins.
(*Hopalong Cassidy* Series)
William Boyd, Jimmy Ellison, Jean Rouveral, George Hayes, Frank McGlynn, Jr., Howard Lang, Harry Worth, Ethel Wales, Paul Fix, J. P. McGowan, Joe Rickson, Al St. John, John Merton, Frank Layton, Chill Wills and his Avalon Boys
D: Howard Bretherton
S: Clarence E. Mulford
SP: Gerald Geraghty, Doris Schroeder
P: Harry Sherman

501. GALLANT DEFENDER
(Columbia, November 30, 1935) 60 Mins.
Charles Starrett, Joan Perry, Harry Woods, Edward J. LeSaint, Jack Clifford, Al Bridge, George Billings, George Chesebro, Edmund Cobb, Frank Ellis, Jack Rockwell, Tom London, Stanley Blystone, Lew Meehan, Merrill McCormack, Glenn Strange, Al Ferguson, Slim Whitaker, Bud Osborne, Sons of the Pioneers (Roy Rogers, Bob Nolan, Tim Spencer, Hugh and Carl Farr)
D: David Selman
S: Peter B. Kyne
SP: Ford Beebe

502. THE IVORY-HANDLED GUN
(Universal, November, 1935) 60 Mins.
Buck Jones, Charlotte Wynters, Walter Miller, Carl Stockdale, Frank Rice, Joseph Girard, Robert Kortman, Stanley Blystone, Lafe McKee, Lee Shumway, Charles King, Ben Corbett, Eddie Phillips, Niles Welch, "Silver"
D: Ray Taylor
S: Charles E. Barnes
SP: John Neville
P: Buck Jones

503. LAW OF THE 45's
(Normandy/First Division, December 1, 1935) 57 Mins.
Big Boy Williams, Molly O'Day, Al St. John, Ted Adams, Lafe McKee, Fred Burns, Curly Baldwin, Martin Garralaga, Broderick O'Farrell, Sherry Tansey, Glenn Strange, Bill Patton, Jack Kirk, Francis Walker, Jack Evans, Tex Palmer, Merrill McCormack, George Morrell, William McCall
D: John P. McCarthy
S: William Colt MacDonald
SP: Robert Tansey
P: Arthur Alexander

504. LAWLESS RIDERS
(Columbia, December 6, 1935) 57 Mins.
Ken Maynard, Geneva Mitchell, Harry Woods, Frank Yaconelli, Hal Taliaferro (Wally Wales), Slim Whitaker, Frank Ellis, Jack Rockwell, "Tarzan," Bob McKenzie, Hank Bell, Bud Jamison, Horace B. Carpenter, Jack King, Bud McClure, Pascale Perry, Oscar Gahan
D: Spencer G. Bennet
S/SP: Nate Gatzert
P: Larry Darmour

505. LAWLESS BORDERS
(Spectrum, December 11, 1935) 58 Mins.
Bill Cody, Molly O'Day, Martin Garralaga, Ted Adams, Joe De LaCruze, John Elliott, Merrill McCormack, Roger Williams, Curly Baldwin, Budd Buster, William McCall
D: John P. McCarthy
S/SP: Zara Tazil
P: Ray Kirkwood

506. THE SINGING VAGABOND

(Republic, December 11, 1935)   52 Mins.

Gene Autry, Smiley Burnette, Ann Rutherford, Barbara Pepper, Warner Richmond, Frank LaRue, Grace Goodall, Niles Welch, Tom Brower, Robinson Neeman, Henry Rocquemore, Ray Benard (Ray Corrigan), Allan Sears, Robert Burns, Charles King, Chief Big Tree, Chief Thunder Cloud, June Thompson, Janice Thompson, Marion O'Connell, Marie Quillan, Elaine Shepherd, "Champion," Edmund Cobb, George Letz

D: Carl Pierson

S: Bill Witney

SP: Oliver Drake, Betty Burbridge

507. SWIFTY

(Diversion, December 12, 1935)   58 Mins.

Hoot Gibson, June Gale, George Hayes, Ralph Lewis, Wally Wales, Art Mix, Bob Kortman, Lafe McKee, "Starlight," Duke Lee, William Gould

D: Alan James

S: Stephen Payne

SP: Bennett Cohen

P: Walter Futter

508. THE COURAGEOUS AVENGER

(Supreme/William Steiner, December 13, 1935) 58 Mins.

Johnny Mack Brown, Helen Erikson, Warner Richmond, Edward Cassidy, Edward Parker, Frank Ball, Earl Dwire, Forrest Taylor, Robert Burns

D: Robert N. Bradbury

S/SP: Charles Francis Royal

P: A. W. Hackel

509. HEIR TO TROUBLE

(Columbia, December 17, 1935)   59 Mins.

Ken Maynard, Joan Perry, Harry Woods, Wally Wales, Martin Faust, Harry Brown, Dorothy Wolbert, Fern Emmett, Pat O'Malley, Art Mix, "Tarzan," Frank Yaconelli, Frank LaRue, Hal Price, Jim Corey, Lafe McKee, Jack Rockwell, Slim Whitaker, Roy Bucko, Buck Bucko, Jack Ward, Bud McClure, Artie Ortego

D: Spencer G. Bennet

S: Ken Maynard

SP: Nate Gatzert

P: Larry Darmour

510. BULLDOG COURAGE

(Puritan, December 30, 1935)   60 Mins.

Tim McCoy, Joan Woodbury, Karl Hackett, John Cowells, Eddie Buzzard, John Elliott, Edward Cassidy, Edmund Cobb, George Morrell, Paul Fix, Jack Rockwell, Bud Osborne

D: Sam Newfield

SP: Joseph O'Donnell, Frances Guihan

P: Sigmund Neufeld, Leslie Simmonds

511. ALIAS JOHN LAW

(Supreme/William Steiner, 1935)

Bob Steele, Roberta Gale, Buck Connors, Earl Dwire, Bob McKenzie, Steve Clark, Jack Rockwell, Roger Williams, Jack Cowell, Horace Murphy

D: Robert N. Bradbury

SP: Forbes Parkhill

P: A. W. Hackel

512. ARIZONA BAD MAN

(Kent, 1935)   58 Mins.

Reb Russell, Lois January, Edmund Cobb, Tommy Bupp, Slim Whitaker, Dick Botiller, Ben Corbett, Anne Howard, Tracy Layne, Walter James, Silver Harr, "Rebel"

D: S. Roy Luby

P: Willis Kent

513. ARIZONA TRAILS

(Superior, 1935)

Bill Patton, Edna Aslin, Denver Dixon, Ed Carey, Tom Camden

D: Alan James

S: Tom Camden

P: Victor Adamson (Denver Dixon)

514. BIG BOY RIDES AGAIN

(Beacon/First Division, 1935)

Big Boy Williams, Connie Bergen, Lafe McKee, Vic Potel, Frank Ellis, Charles K. French, Augie Gomez, Bud Osborne

D: Al Herman

P: Max and Arthur Alexander

S: William L. Nolte

515. BIG CALIBRE

(Supreme/William Steiner, 1935)

Bob Steele, Peggy Campbell, Georgia O'Dell, Bill Quinn, Earl Dwire, John Elliott, Forrest Taylor, Perry Murdock, Si Jenks, Frank Ball, Frank McCarroll, Blackie Whiteford

D: Robert N. Bradbury

S: Perry Murdock

P: A. W. Hackel

516. BLAZING GUNS

(Kent—Distributed by Marcy, 1935)

Reb Russell, Marion Shilling, Lafe McKee, Joseph Girard, Frank McCarroll, Charles "Slim" Whitaker, "Rebel"

D: Ray Heinz

SP: Forbes Parkhill

P: Willis Kent

517. BORDER VENGEANCE

(Kent—Distributed by Marcy, 1935)

Reb Russell, Mary Jane Carey, Kenneth Mac-

Donald, Ben Corbett, Hank Bell, Glenn Strange, June Bupp, Norman Feusuer, Clarence Geldert, Charles "Slim" Whitaker, Ed Phillips, Marty Joyce, Fred Burns, Pat Harmon, Bart Carre, "Rebel"
D: Ray Heinz
P: Willis Kent

518. BORN TO BATTLE
(Reliable/William Steiner, 1935)
Tom Tyler, Jean Carmen, Earl Dwire, Julian Rivero, Nelson McDowell, William Desmond, Dick Alexander, Charles King, Ralph Lewis, Ben Corbett, George Chesebro, Robert Walker, Blackie Whiteford, Jack Evans
D: Harry S. Webb
S: Oliver Drake
SP: Carl Krusada, Rose Gordon
P: Bernard B. Ray.

519. CHEYENNE TORNADO
(Kent, 1935)
Reb Russell, Victoria Vinton, Edmund Cobb, Roger Williams, Tina Menard, Dick Botiller, Ed Porter, Winton Perry, Hank Bell, Francis McDonald, Bart Carre, Lafe McKee, "Rebel," Jack Evans, Oscar Gahan, Clyde McClary
D: William O'Connor
P: Willis Kent

520. COURAGE OF THE NORTH
(Empire/Stage and Screen, 1935)
John Preston, June Love, William Desmond, Tom London, Jimmy Aubrey, James Sheridan (Sherry Tansey), Charles King, White Feather, "Dynamite" (the Wonder Horse), "Captain" (King of the Dogs)
D/P/SP: Robert Emmett (Tansey)

521. COYOTE TRAILS
(Reliable/William Steiner, 1935)
Tom Tyler, Helen Dahl, Ben Corbett, Lafe McKee, Dick Alexander, Robert Walker, Roger Williams, George Chesebro, Slim Whitaker, Jack Evans
D: B. B. Ray
S/SP: Carl Krusada, Rose Gordon
P: Bernard B. Ray

522. DANGER TRAILS
(Beacon/First Division, 1935)   55 Mins.
Big Boy Williams, Marjorie Gordon, Wally Wales, John Elliott, Ace Cain, Edmund Cobb, Steve Clark, George Chesebro
D: Bob Hill
S: Guinn "Big Boy" Williams
SP: Rock Hawley (Bob Hill)
P: Max and Arthur Alexander

523. DEFYING THE LAW
(American Pictures Corp., 1935)
Ted Wells, Edna Aslin, George Chesebro, Dick Cramer, Jimmy Aubrey, William Desmond, Bob McKenzie, Allen Greer, Doris Brook, Milburn Morante, Oscar Gahan, Herman Hack
D/P: Robert J. Horner
SP: Carl Krusada

524. DESERT MESA
(Security, 1935)
Tom Wynn (Wally West), Tonya Beauford, Franklyn Farnum, Bill Patton, Lew Meehan, Denver Dixon (Victor Adamson), William McCall, Allen Greer, Harry Keaton, Delores Booth, Horace B. Carpenter, Tex Miller
D: Alan James
P: Victor Adamson
SP: Van Johnson

525. DEVIL'S CANYON
(Sunset, 1935)
Noah Beery, Jr., William Desmond, Miami Alvarez, Pat Carlisle, Fred Church, Pat Harmon
D: Cliff Smith

526. FIGHTING CABALLERO
(Merrick/Superior, 1935)   5 Reels
Rex Lease, Dorothy Gulliver, Earl Douglas, George Chesebro, Robert Walker, Wally Wales, Milburn Morante, George Morrell, Pinky Barnes, Carl Mathews, Barney Furey, Franklyn Farnum, Marty Joyce, Paul Ellis
D: Elmer Clifton
SP: Elmer Clifton, George M. Merrick
P: Louis Weiss

527. FIVE BAD MEN
(Sunset, 1935)
Noah Beery, Jr., Buffalo Bill, Jr., Sally Darling, Wally Wales, William Desmond, Art Mix, Pete Morrison, Bill Patton, Edward Coxen, Billy Franey, Frank Yaconelli, Steve Clemente, The Five Radio Buckaroos
D: Cliff Smith

528. THE GHOST RIDER
(Argosy/Superior, 1935)   5 Reels
Rex Lease, Ann Carol, Lloyd Ingraham, Bill Patton, Bobby Nelson, William Desmond, Franklyn Farnum, Lafe McKee, Art Mix, Blackie Whiteford, Roger Williams, Ed Coxen, Denver Dixon (Victor Adamson), Blackjack Ward, Eddie Parker, John Alexander
D: Jack Levine (Jack Jevne)
S/SP: John West (Jack Jevne)
P: Louis Weiss

529. HORSES' COLLARS

(Columbia, 1935) 2 Reels

(*Three Stooges* Series)

Moe Howard, Curly Howard, Larry Fine, Dorothy Kent, Fred Kohler, Fred Kelsey

D: Clyde Bruckman

S/SP: Felix Adler

530. GUNFIRE

(Resolute, 1935)

Rex Bell, Ruth Mix, Buzz Barton, Milburn Morante, William Desmond, Theodore Lorch, Philo McCullough, Ted Adams, Lew Meehan, Jack Baston, Willie Fung, Mary Jane Irving, Fern Emmett, Howard Hickey, Chuck Morrison

D: Harry Fraser

S: "Pards in Paradise"—Eric Howard

SP: Harry C. Crist (Harry Fraser)

P: Alfred T. Mannon

531. GUN PLAY

(Beacon/First Division, 1935) 59 Min.

(Also known as *Lucky Boots*)

Big Boy Williams, Marion Shilling, Wally Wales, Frank Yaconelli, Tom London, Charles K. French, Roger Williams, Julian Rivero, Barney Beasley, Dick Botiller, Gordon Griffith, Si Jenks

D: Al Herman

S/SP: William L. Nolte

P: Arthur Alexander

532. THE IRISH GRINGO

(Keith Productions, 1935)

Pat Carlyle, William Farnum, Bryant Washburn, Elena Duran, Olin Francis, Ace Cain, Milburn Morante, Marjorie Medford, Horace B. Carpenter, Foxy Callahan, Karlyn (Karla) May, Don Orlando, Rudolf Cornell

D: William L. Thompson

533. THE JUDGEMENT BOOK

(Beaumont, 1935) 63 Mins.

Conway Tearle, Bernadine Hayes, Howard H. Lang, Richard Cramer, William Gould, Jack Pendleton, Roy Rice, James Aubrey, Ray Gallagher, Philip Keiffer, Dick Rush, Blackie Whiteford, Francis Walker, Edward Clayton, "Black King"

D: Charles Hutchinson

S: Homer King Gordon

SP: E. J. Thornton

P: Mitchell Leichter

534. KID COURAGEOUS

(Supreme/William Steiner, 1935) 5 Reels

Bob Steele, Renee Borden, Kit Guard, Arthur Loft, Jack Powell, Lafe McKee, Vane Calvert, Barry Seury, Perry Murdock, John Elliott

D/SP: Robert N. Bradbury

P: A. W. Hackel

535. THE LARAMIE KID

(Reliable/William Steiner, 1935) 5 Reels

Tom Tyler, Alberta Vaughn, Al Ferguson, Murdock McQuarrie, George Chesebro, Snub Pollard, Steve Clark

D: Harry S. Webb

S: C. C. Church

SP: Carl Krusada

P: Bernard B. Ray

536. LIGHTNING TRIGGERS

(Kent—Distributed by Marcy, 1935) 5 Reels

Reb Russell, Yvonne Pelletier, Fred Kohler, Jack Rockwell, Edmund Cobb, Lillian Castle, Lew Meehan, William McCall, Dick Botiller, Olin Francis, Artie Artego, Steve Clark, Ed Porter, song over opening credits sung by Smiley Burnette, "Rebel"

D: S. Roy Luby

P: Willis Kent

537. THE MIRACLE RIDER

(Mascot, 1935) 15 Chaps.

Tom Mix, Joan Gale, Charles Middleton, Jason Robards, Edward Hearn, Pat O'Malley, Robert Frazer, Ernie Adams, Wally Wales, Bob Kortman, Chief Standing Bear, Charles King, Tom London, Niles Welch, Edmund Cobb, George Chesebro, Jack Rockwell, Max Wagner, Stanley Price, George Burton, Lafe McKee, "Tony, Jr."

D: B. Reeves Eason, Armand Schaefer

S: Barney Sarecky, Wellyn Totman, Gerald Geraghty

SP: John Rathmell

P: Nat Levine

Chapter Titles: (1) The Vanishing Indian, (2) The Firebird Strikes, (3) The Flying Knife, (4) A Race with Death, (5) Double-Barreled Doom, (6) Thundering Hoofs, (7) The Dragnet, (8) Guerrilla Warfare, (9) The Silver Band, (10) Signal Fires, (11) A Traitor Dies, (12) Danger Rides with Death, (13) The Secret of X-94, (14) Between Two Fires, (15) Justice Rides the Plains

538. NO MAN'S RANGE

(Supreme/William Steiner, 1935) 5 Reels

Bob Steele, Roberta Gale, Buck Connors, Steve Clark, Charles K. French, Jack Rockwell, Roger Williams, Earl Dwire, Ed Cassidy, Jim Corey

D: Robert N. Bradbury

S/SP: Forbes Parkhill

P: A. W. Hackel

539. NORTH OF ARIZONA

(Reliable/William Steiner, 1935) 60 Mins.

Jack Perrin, Blanche Mehaffey, Lane Chandler, Al Bridge, Murdock McQuarrie, George Chesebro, Artie Ortego, Budd Buster, Frank Ellis, Blackie Whiteford, "Starlight"
D: Harry S. Webb
SP: Carl Krusada
P: Bernard B. Ray

540. THE PECOS KID
(Commodore, 1935)
Fred Kohler, Jr., Ruth Findlay, Roger Williams, Edward Cassidy, Wally Wales, Earl Dwire, Francis Walker, Budd Buster, Rose Plummer, Clyde McClary, Robert Walker, Jack Evans
D/P: William Berke
S: Ted Tuttle
SP: Henry Hess

541. THE PHANTOM COWBOY
(Aywon, 1935) 55 Mins.
Ted Wells, Jimmy Aubrey, Edna Aslin, George Chesebro, Richard Cramer, William Desmond, Allen Greer
D: Robert J. Horner
SP: Carl Krusada
P: Robert J. Horner

542. RAINBOW'S END
(First Division, 1935) 60 Mins.
Hoot Gibson, June Gale, Buddy Roosevelt, Oscar Apfel, Warner Richmond, Ada Ince, Stanley Blystone, John Elliott, Henry Rocquemore, Fred Gilman, Charles Hill
D: Norman Spencer
SP: Rollo Ward

543. THE RECKLESS BUCKAROO
(Crescent, 1935) 57 Mins.
Bill Cody, Bill Cody, Jr., Betty Mack, Roger Williams, Buzz Barton, Edward Cassidy, Lew Meehan, Francis Walker, Milburn Morante, Jack Nelson, Allen Greer, Budd Buster
D: Harry Fraser
S/SP: Zara Tazil
P: Ray Kirkwood

544. RIO RATTLER
(Reliable/William Steiner, 1935) 5 Reels
Tom Tyler, Marion Shilling, Eddie Gribbon, William Gould, Tom London, Slim Whitaker, Lafe McKee, Ace Cain, Frank Ellis, Jimmy Aubrey, Blackie Whiteford, Nelson McDowell
D: Franklin Shamray (B. B. Ray)
S: Bennett Cohen
SP: Carl Krusada
P: Bernard B. Ray

545. ROUGH RIDING RANGER
(Merrick/Superior, 1935) 5 Reels
Rex Lease, Bobby Nelson, Janet Chandler, Yakima Canutt, Mable Strickland, David Horsley, George Chesebro, Robert Walker, Carl Mathews, Artie Ortego, William Desmond, Allen Greer, Johnny Luther's Cowboy Band, George Morrell, Milburn Morante, "Sunday"
D: Elmer Clifton
SP: Elmer Clifton, George M. Merrick
P: George M. Merrick, Louis Weiss

546. SADDLE ACES
(Resolute, 1935) 56 Mins.
Rex Bell, Ruth Mix, Buzz Barton, Stanley Blystone, Earl Dwire, Chuck Morrison, Mary MacLaren, John Elliott, Roger Williams, Bud Osborne, Allen Greer, Chief Thunder Cloud
D: Harry Fraser
S: "Deuces Wild"—J. Kaley
SP: Harry C. Crist (Harry Fraser)
P: Alfred T. Mannon

547. THE SILENT CODE
(International/Stage and Screen, 1935) 60 Mins.
Kane Richmond, Blanche Mehaffey, "Wolfang" (a dog), J. P. McGowan, Joe Girard, Barney Furey, Pat Harmon, Ben Corbett, Carl Mathews, Ed Coxen, Bud Osborne, Clarence Davis, Ted Mapes, Douglas Ross, Rose Higgins
D: Stuart Paton
S/SP: George Morgan
P: Louis Weiss

548. THE RIDER OF THE LAW
(Supreme/William Steiner, 1935) 5 Reels
Bob Steele, Gertrude Messinger, Si Jenks, Earl Dwire, Forrest Taylor, Lloyd Ingraham, John Elliott, Sherry Tansey, Tex Palmer, Chuck Baldra
D: Robert N. Bradbury
S/SP: Jack Natteford
P: A. W. Hackel

549. SILENT VALLEY
(Reliable/William Steiner, 1935) 5 Reels
Tom Tyler, Nancy DeShon, Wally Wales, Charles King, Alan Bridge, Murdock McQuarrie, Art Miles, George Chesebro, Charles Whitaker, Jimmy Aubrey
D/P: Bernard B. Ray
SP: Carl Krusada, Rose Gordon

550. SKULL AND CROWN
(Reliable/William Steiner, 1935)
Rin-Tin-Tin, Jr., Regis Toomey, Molly O'Day, Jack Mulhall, Jack Mower, James Murray, Lois January, Tom London, John Elliott, Robert Walker

D: Elmer Clifton
S: James Oliver Curwood
SP: Bennett Cohen, Carl Krusada
P: Bernard B. Ray

551. SMOKEY SMITH
(Supreme/William Steiner, 1935)   57 Mins.
Bob Steele, Mary Kornman, George Hayes, Warner
   Richmond, Earl Dwire, Horace B. Carpenter, Tex
   Phelps, Archie Ricks
D: Robert N. Bradbury
S/SP: Robert N. Bradbury
P: A. W. Hackel

552. TEXAS JACK
(Reliable/William Steiner, 1935)   52 Mins.
Jack Perrin, Jayne Regan, Nelson McDowell, Robert
   Walker, Budd Buster, Cope Borden, Lew Meehan,
   Blackie Whiteford, Oscar Gahan, Jim Oates, Steve
   Clark, "Starlight"
D: Bernard B. Ray
SP: Carl Krusada
P: Bernard B. Ray

553. THUNDERBOLT
(Regal, 1935)
"Lobo" (the Marvel Dog), Kane Richmond, Bobby
   Nelson, Lafe McKee, Wally West, Frank Ellis,
   George Morrell, Jack Kirk, Hank Bell, Bob
   McKenzie, Frank Hagney, Barney Furey
D: Stuart Paton
S/SP: Jack T. O. Gevne (Jack Jevne)
P: Samuel S. Krellberg

554. TIMBER TERRORS
(Stage and Screen, 1935)   59 Mins.
John Preston, Marla Bratton, James Sheridan
   (Sherry Tansey), William Desmond, Tiny Skel-
   ton, Fred Parker, Harold Berquest, Tom London,
   Harry Beery, Tex Jones, "Captain" (King of the
   Dogs), "Dynamite" (the Wonder Horse)
D/P/SP: Robert Emmett (Tansey)

555. TOLL OF THE DESERT
(Commondore, 1935)   60 Mins.
Fred Kohler, Jr., Betty Mack, Tom London, Earl
   Dwire, Ted Adams, Billy Stevens, Edward Cas-
   sidy, Roger Williams, John Elliott, Ace Cain,
   George Chesebro, Blackie Whiteford, Blackjack
   Ward, Iron Eyes Cody, Herman Hack, Budd
   Buster
D: Lester Williams (William Berke)
S: Allen Hall
SP: Miller Easton
P: William Berke

556. TOMBSTONE TERROR
(Supreme/William Steiner, 1935)   58 Mins.
Bob Steele, George Hayes, Kay McCoy, Earl Dwire,
   John Elliott, Hortense Petro, Ann Howard, Nancy
   DeShon, Frank McCarroll, Artie Ortego, George
   Morrell, Herman Hack
D/SP: Robert N. Bradbury
P: A. W. Hackel

557. THE TONTO KID
(Resolute, 1935)
Rex Bell, Ruth Mix, Buzz Barton, Theodore Lorch,
   Joseph Girard, Barbara Roberts, Jack Rockwell,
   Murdock McQuarrie, Bert Lindsley, Jane Keckley,
   Stella Adams
D. Harry Fraser
S: "The Daughter of Diamond D"—Christopher B.
   Booth
SP: Harry C. Crist (Harry Fraser)
P: Alfred T. Mannon

558. TRAIL OF TERROR
(Supreme/William Steiner, 1935)   5 Reels
Bob Steele, Beth Marion, Forrest Taylor, Charles
   King, Lloyd Ingraham, Frank Lyman, Jr., Charles
   K. French, Richard Cramer, Nancy DeShon
D/SP: Robert N. Bradbury
P: A. W. Hackel

559. TRAILS OF ADVENTURE
(American, 1935)   57 Mins.
Buffalo Bill, Jr., Edna Aslin, Harry Carter, Al-
   len Holbrook, Raymond B. Wells, Belle D'Arcy,
   Shorty Hendricks
D: Jay Wilsey (Buffalo Bill, Jr.)
S/SP: Donald Kent
P: Robert J. Horner

560. TRAILS END
(Beaumont, 1935)   61 Mins.
Conway Tearle, Claudia Dell, Baby Charlene Barry,
   Fred Kohler, Ernie Adams, Pat Harmon, Victor
   Potel, Gaylord Pendleton, Stanley Blystone, Jack
   Duffy, "Black King"
D: Al Herman
S: "Trails End"—James Oliver Curwood
SP: Jack Jevne
P: Mitchell Leichter

561. TRIGGER TOM
(Reliable/William Steiner, 1935)
Tom Tyler, Al St. John, Bernadine Hayes, William
   Gould, John Elliott, Bud Osborne, Lloyd Ingra-
   ham, Wally Wales
D: Henri Samuels (Harry S. Webb)
S: "The Swimming Herd"—George Cory Franklin
SP: Tom Gibson
P   Bernard B. Ray

562. TWISTED RAILS

(Imperial, 1935)

Jack Donovan, Alice Dahl, Philo McCullough, Donald Keith, Victor Potel, Buddy Shaw, Donald Mack, Henry Rocquemore, Pat Harmon, Tom London, Ada Belle Driver, Lawrence Underwood

D: Al Herman

S/SP: L. V. Jefferson

P: Peter J. White

563. UNDERCOVER MEN

(Booth Dominions Pictures, 1935)

Charles Starrett, Adrienne Dore, Kenneth Duncan, Wheeler Oakman, Eric Clavering, Phil Brandon, Elliott Lorraine, Austin Moran, Grace Webster, Gilmore Young, Farnham Barter, Muriel Dean

D: Sam Neufield (Sam Newfield)

P: J. R. Booth, Arthur Gottlieb

Prod. Mgr: Jack Chisholm

564. VALLEY OF WANTED MEN

(Conn Pictures, 1935)   62 Mins.

Frankie Darro, Grant Withers, Dru Layron, Roy (LeRoy) Mason, Paul Fix, Russell Hopton, Walter Miller, Fred Toones, Al Bridge, William Gould, Jack Rockwell, Slim Whitaker, Irene Crane

D: Alan James

S: "All for Love"—Peter B. Kyne

SP: Barry Barringer, Forrest Barnes

P: Maurice Conn

565. WESTERN JUSTICE

(Supreme/William Steiner, 1935)

Bob Steele, Renee Bordon, Julian Rivero, Jack Cowell, Perry Murdock, Vane Calvert, Lafe McKee, Arthur Loft

D/SP: Robert N. Bradbury

P: A. W. Hackel

566. WESTERN RACKETEERS

(Aywon, 1935)

Bill Cody, Edna Aslin, Wally Wales, Ben Corbett, Budd Buster, George Chesebro, Bud Osborne, Frank Clark, Gilbert (PeeWee) Holmes, Robert Sands, Tom Dwaine, Dick Cramer, Billy Franey

D: Robert J. Horner

P: Nathan Hirsh

567. THE WHIRLWIND RIDER

(American, 1935)

Buffalo Bill, Jr., Jeanne (Genee) Boutell, Jack Long, Frank Clark, Clyde McClary

D/P: Robert J. Horner

568. WILD MUSTANG

(Ajax, 1935)   62 Mins.

Wolf Riders (Reliable / William Steiner, 1935) — Lillian Gilmore, Jack Perrin, and Lafe McKee

Harry Carey, Barbara Fritchie, Del Gordon, Cathryn Jons, Robert Kortman, George Chesebro, Dick Botiller, George Morrell, Milburn Morante, "Sonny" (the Marvel Horse), Francis Walker, Budd Buster
D: Harry Fraser
S: Monroe Talbot
SP: Weston Edwards
P: William Berke

569. WOLF RIDERS
(Reliable/William Steiner, 1935)
Jack Perrin, Lillian Gilmore, Lafe McKee, Nancy DeShon, William Gould, George Chesebro, Earl Dwire, Budd Buster, Slim Whitaker, Frank Ellis, Robert Walker, George Morrell, Blackie Whiteford, "Starlight"
D: Harry S. Webb
SP: Carl Krusada
P: Bernard B. Ray

569a. ROMANCE OF THE WEST
(Warner Bros., 1935) 2 Reels
(Technicolor)
Phil Regan, Dorothy Dare, Henry Armetta, Mary Treen, Gordon (Bill) Elliott, Joseph King
D: Ralph Staub
S/SP: Joe Traub

FILMS OF 1936

570. ACES WILD
(Commondore, January 2, 1936) 57 Mins.
Harry Carey, Gertrude Messinger, Fred Toones, Phil Dunham, Edward Cassidy, Chuck Morrison, Ted Lorch, William McCall, Roger Williams, "Sonny" (the Marvel Horse)
D: Harry Fraser
S: Monroe Talbot
P: William Berke

571. DESERT GUNS
(Beaumont, January 2, 1936) 70 Mins.
Conway Tearle, Margaret Morris, Charles K. French, Budd Buster, William Gould, Marie Werner, Kate Brinkler, Duke Lee, Roy Rice, Ray Gallagher, Art Felix, Pinky Barnes, Bull Montana, Slim Whitaker
D: Charles Hutchison
S/SP: Jacques Jaccard
P: Mitchell Leichter

572. THE OREGON TRAIL
(Republic, January 15, 1936) 59 Mins.
John Wayne, Ann Rutherford, Yakima Canutt, Joe Girard, Frank Rice, E. H. Calvert, Ben Hendricks, Harry Harvey, Fern Emmett, Jack Rutherford, Marian Ferrell, Roland Ray, Edward J. LeSaint, Octavio Girand, Gino Corrado
D: Scott Pembroke
S: Lindsley Parsons, Robert Emmett
SP: Jack Natteford, Lindsley Parsons, Robert Emmett (Tansey)
D: Paul Malvern

573. THE MYSTERIOUS AVENGER
(Columbia, January 17, 1936)
Charles Starrett, Joan Perry, Wheeler Oakman, Edward J. LeSaint, Lafe McKee, Hal Price, Charles Locher (Jon Hall), George Chesebro, Jack Rockwell, Dick Botiller, Edmund Cobb, Sons of the Pioneers (Roy Rogers, Bob Nolan, Hugh Farr, Karl Farr, Tim Spencer)
D: David Selman
S: Credited to Peter B. Kyne
S/SP: Ford Beebe

574. BLAZING JUSTICE
(Spectrum, January 19, 1936)
Bill Cody, Gertrude Messinger, Gordon Griffith, Milburn Morante, Budd Buster, Frank Yaconelli, Charles Tannen, Curley Baldwin, Buck Morgan
D: Al Herman
S/SP: Zara Tazil
P: Ray Kirkwood

575. SUNSET OF POWER
(Universal, January 22, 1936) 66 Mins.
Buck Jones, Dorothy Dix, Charles Middleton, Donald Kirk, Ben Corbett, Charles King, William Lawrence, Joe De LaCruz, Nina Campana, Eumenco Blanco, Murdock McQuarrie, Alan Sears, Monty Vandergrift, Glenn Strange, "Silver"
D: Ray Taylor
S: J. E. Grinstead
SP: Earle Snell
P: Buck Jones

576. VALLEY OF THE LAWLESS
(Supreme/William Steiner, January 25, 1936) 56 Mins.
Johnny Mack Brown, Joyce Compton, George Hayes, Dennis Meadows (Moore), Bobby Nelson, Frank Hagney, Charles King, Jack Rockwell, Frank Ball, Horace Murphy, Steve Clark, Edward Cassidy, Robert McKenzie, Forrest Taylor, George Morell, Jack Evans
D/SP: Robert N. Bradbury
P: R. W. Hackel

Valley of the Lawless (Supreme/William Steiner, 1936) — Johnny Mack Brown, Frank Ball, and Joyce Compton

577. ROARIN' GUNS
(Puritan, January 27, 1936)   59 Mins.
Tim McCoy, Rosalinda Rice, Wheeler Oakman, Rex
 Lease, Karl Hackett, John Elliott, Tommy Bupp,
 Jack Rockwell, Lew Meehan, Frank Ellis, Edward
 Cassidy, Dick Alexander, Artie Ortego, Tex
 Phelps, Al Taylor, Jack Evans
D: Sam Newfield
SP: Joseph O'Donnell
P: Sigmund Neufeld, Leslie Simmonds

578. ROSE MARIE
(MGM, January 27, 1936)   110 Mins.
Jeanette MacDonald, Nelson Eddy, James Stewart,
 Reginald Owen, Allan Jones, Gilda Gray, Alan
 Mowbray, Una O'Connor, David Niven, Robert
 Greig, Herman Bing
D: W. S. Van Dyke
SP: Francis Goodrich, Albert Hackett
P: Hunt Stromberg

579. SILVER SPURS
(Universal, January 29, 1936)   6 Reels
Buck Jones, Muriel Evans, J. P. McGowan, George
 Hayes, Dennis Moore, Robert Frazer, Bruce Lane,
 William Lawrence, Earl Askam, Charles K.
 French, Beth Marion, Kernan Cripps, "Silver"
D: Ray Taylor
S: Charles Alden Seltzer
SP: Joseph Poland
P: Buck Jones

580. ROSE OF THE RANCHO
(Paramount, January, 1936)   9 Reels
John Boles, Gladys Swarthout, Charles Bickford,
 Willie Howard, Herb Williams, Grace Bradley,
 H. B. Warner, Charlotte Granville, Don Alvarado,
 Minor Watson, Louise Carter, Bennie Baker,
 Pedro de Cordoba, Paul Harvey, Arthur Ayles-
 worth, Harry Woods, Russell Hopton
D: Marion Gering
S: From the play by Richard Walton Tully and
 David Belasco
SP: Frank Partos, Charles Brackett, Arthur Sheel-
 man, Nat Perrin
P: William LeBaron

581. SONG OF THE SADDLE
(Warner Bros., February 1, 1936)   58 Mins.
Dick Foran, Alma Lloyd, Charles Middleton, Addi-
 son Richards, Eddie Shubert, Monte Montague,
 Vic Potel, Kenneth Harlan, Myrtle Stedman,
 George Ernest, Pat West, James Farley, Julian
 Rivero, Bonita Granville, William Desmond, Bud

Osborne, Bob Kortman, Sons of the Pioneers (Roy Rogers, Bob Nolan, Tim Spencer, Hugh and Carl Farr)
D: Louis King
SP: William Jacobs
P: Bryan Foy

582. THE BOLD CABALLERO
(Republic, February 3, 1936)   69 Mins.
(MagnaColor)
Bob Livingston, Heather Angel, Sig Rumann, Ian Wolfe, Robert Warwick, Emily Fitzroy, Charles Stevens, Walter Long, Ferdinand Munier, King Martin (Chris-Pin Martin), Carlos De Valdez, John Merton, Jack Kirk, Slim Whitaker, Vinegar Roan, George Plues, Henry Morris, Chief Thunder Cloud, Pascale Perry, Jack Roberts, William Emile, Gurdial Singh
D: Wells Root
SP: Wells Root from "The Return of Zorro." Based on idea by Johnston McCulley
P: Nate Levine

583. THE KID RANGER
(Supreme/William Steiner, February 5, 1936)
   57 Mins.
Bob Steele, William Farnum, Joan Barclay, Earl Dwire, Charles King, Lafe McKee, Frank Ball, Reetsy Adams, Paul and Paulina, Buck Moulton
D: Robert N. Bradbury
S/SP: Robert N. Bradbury
P: A. W. Hackel

584. DRIFT FENCE
(Paramount, February 14, 1936)   56 Mins.
(Re-released as *Texas Desperadoes*)
Larry "Buster" Crabbe, Katherine DeMille, Tom Keene, Benny Baker, Glenn (Leif) Erickson, Stanley Andrews, Effie Ellser, Richard Carle, Jan Duggan, Irving Bacon, Walter Long, Chester Gan, Dick Alexander, Bud Fine, Jack Pennick
D: Otto Lovering
S: Zane Grey
SP: Stuart Anthony, Robert Yost
P: Harold Hurley

585. GHOST TOWN
(Commondore, February 15, 1936)   60 Mins.
Harry Carey, Ruth Findlay, Jane Novak, David Sharpe, Lee Shumway, Edward Cassidy, Roger Williams, Phil Dunham, Earl Dwire, Chuck Morrison, "Sonny" (the Marvel Horse)
D: Harry Fraser
SP: Monroe Talbot
P: William Berke

586. THE LAWLESS NINETIES
(Republic, February 15, 1936)   55 Mins.
John Wayne, Ann Rutherford, George Hayes, Harry Woods, Lane Chandler, Al Bridge, Fred Toones, Etta McDaniels, Tom Brower, Tom London, Sam Flint, Chuck Baldra, Tracy Layne, George Chesebro, Charles King, Al Taylor, Jack Rockwell, Cliff Lyons, Henry Hall, Lloyd Ingraham, Lew Meehan, Horace B. Carpenter, Sherry Tansey, Curley Dresden, Tex Palmer, Jack Kirk, Edward Hearn, Steve Clark, Philo McCullough
D: Joseph Kane
S: Joseph Poland, Scott Pembroke
SP: Joseph Poland
P: Paul Malvern

587. LUCKY TERROR
(Diversion/Grand National, February 20, 1936)
   61 Mins.
Hoot Gibson, Lona Andre, Charles Hill, George Chesebro, Bob McKenzie, Wally Wales, Art Mix, Horace Murphy, Hank Bell, Jack Rockwell, Frank Yaconelli, Charles King, Nelson McDowell, Fargo Bussey
D: Alan James
S: Roger Allman
SP: Alan James
P: Walter Futter

588. FAST BULLETS
(Reliable/William Steiner, February 24, 1936)
   57 Mins.
Tom Tyler, Rex Lease, Margaret Nearing, Al Bridge, William Gould, Robert Walker, James Aubrey, Slim Whitaker, Charles King, Lew Meehan, Nelson McDowell, Jack Evans
D: Henri Samuels (Harry S. Webb)
S: Jay J. Bryan
SP: Rose Gordon, Carl Krusada
P: Bernard B. Ray

589. RIDIN' ON
(Reliable/William Steiner, February 29, 1936)
   56 Mins.
Tom Tyler, Geraine Greear (Joan Barclay), Rex Lease, John Elliott, Earl Dwire, Bob McKenzie, Roger Williams, Slim Whitaker, Wally West, Jimmy Aubrey, Francis Walker, Dick Cramer
D: Bernard B. Ray
S: "Feud of the Jay Bar Dee"—Arthur Carhart
SP: John T. Neville
P: Bernard B. Ray

590. BORDER CABALLERO
(Puritan, March 1, 1936)   59 Mins.
Tim McCoy, Lois January, Ralph Byrd, Ted Adams, J. Frank Glendon, Earle Hodgins, John Merton, Oscar Gahan, Robert McKenzie, Frank McCarroll, George Morrell, Jack Evans, Ray Henderson, Oscar Gahan, Tex Phelps, Bill Patton

D: Sam Newfield
S: Norman S. Hall
SP: Joseph O'Donnell
P: Sigmund Neufeld, Leslie Simmonds

591. RED RIVER VALLEY

(Republic, March 2, 1936) 56 Mins.

Gene Autry, Smiley Burnette, Frances Grant, Booth Howard, Jack Kinney, Sam Flint, George Chesebro, Charles King, Eugene Jackson, Edward Hearn, Frank LaRue, Ken Cooper, Frankie Marvin, Cap Anderson (C. E. Anderson), Monty Cass, John Wilson, Lloyd Ingraham, Hank Bell, "Champion," Earl Dwire, George Morrell

D: B. Reeves Eason
S/SP: Dorrell and Stuart McGowan
P: Nat Levine

592. ROBIN HOOD OF ELDORADO

(MGM, March 4, 1936) 86 Mins.

Warner Baxter, Bruce Cabot, Margo, Ann Lanning, J. Carrol Naish, Soledad Jiminez, Edgar Kennedy, Eric Linden, Carlos DeValdez, Francis McDonald, Charles Trowbridge, Harvey Stevens, George Regas

D: William Wellman
S: Walter Noble Burns
SP: William Wellman, Joseph Calleia, Melvin Levy

593. THREE GODFATHERS

(MGM, March 4, 1936) 82 Mins.

Chester Morris, Lewis Stone, Walter Brennan, Irene Hervey, Sidney Toler, Dorothy Tree, Roger Imhoff, Robert Livingston, Willard Robertson, John Sheehan, Victor Potel, Harvey Clark, Joseph Marievsky, Helen Brown, Virginia Brissac

D: Richard Boleslawski
S: Peter B. Kyne
SP: Edward E. Paramore, Jr., Manuel Seff

594. YELLOW DUST

(RKO, March 5, 1936) 68 Mins.

Richard Dix, Leila Hyams, Moroni Olson, Jessie Ralph, Andy Clyde, Onslow Stevens, Vic Potel, Ethan Laidlaw, Ted Oliver, Art Mix

D: Wallace Fox
S: "Mother Lode"—Dan Totheroh, George O'Neill
SP: Cyril Hume, John Twist
P: Cliff Reid

595. CALL OF THE PRAIRIE

(Paramount, March 6, 1936) 65 Mins.

(*Hopalong Cassidy* Series)

William Boyd, Jimmy Ellison, Muriel Evans, George Hayes, Al Bridge, Chester Conklin, Hank Mann, Willie Fung, Howard Lang, Al Hill, John Merton, James Mason, Chill Wills and the Avalon Boys

D: Howard Bretherton

S: Clarence E. Mulford
SP: Doris Schroeder, Vernon Smith
P: Harry Sherman

596. KING OF THE PECOS

(Republic, March 9, 1936) 54 Mins.

John Wayne, Muriel Evans, Cy Kendall, Jack Clifford, J. Frank Glendon, Herbert Heywood, Arthur Aylesworth, John Beck, Mary MacLaren, Yakima Canutt, Bradley Metcalfe, Jr., Edward Hearn, Earl Dwire, Tex Palmer, Jack Kirk

D: Joseph Kane
S: Bernard McConville
SP: Bernard McConville, Dorrell and Stuart McGowan
P: Paul Malvern

597. DESERT PHANTOM

(Supreme/William Steiner, March 10, 1936) 55 Mins.

Johnny Mack Brown, Sheila Mannors, Ted Adams, Karl Hackett, Hal Price, Nelson McDowell, Charles King, Forrest Taylor, Frank Ball

D: S. Roy Luby
S: E. B. Mann
SP: Earle Snell
P: A. W. Hackel

598. SONG OF THE TRAIL

(Ambassador, March 15, 1936) 59 Mins.

Kermit Maynard, Evelyn Brent, Fuzzy Knight, George Hayes, Wheeler Oakman, Antoinette Lees (Andrea Leeds), Lee Shumway, Lynette London, Roger Williams, Ray Gallagher, Charles McMurphy, Horace Murphy, Bob McKenzie, Frank McCarroll, Artie Ortego

D: Russell Hopton
S: "Playing with Fire"—James Oliver Curwood
SP: George Sayre, Barry Barrington
P: Maurice Conn

599. RIO GRANDE ROMANCE

(Victory, March 15, 1936) 60 Mins.

Eddie Nugent, Maxine Doyle, Fuzzy Knight, Forrest Taylor, Ernie Adams, George Cleveland, Lucille Lund, Nick Stuart, Don Alvarado, George Walsh, Joyce Kay

D: Robert Hill
S: Peter B. Kyne
SP: Al Martin
P: Sam Katzman

600. CARYL OF THE MOUNTAINS

(Reliable/William Steiner, March 27, 1936) 68 Mins.

Rin-Tin-Tin, Jr., Francis X. Bushman, Jr., Lois Wild (Wilde), Joseph Swickard, Earl Dwire, Robert

Walker, George Chesebro, Jack Hendricks, Steve Clark

D: Bernard B. Ray
S: James Oliver Curwood
SP: Tom Gibson
P: Bernard B. Ray

601. DESERT GOLD

(Paramount, March 27, 1936)   58 Mins.

Larry "Buster" Crabbe, Robert Cummings, Marsha Hunt, Tom Keene, Glenn (Leif) Erickson, Monte Blue, Raymond Hatton, Walter Miller, Frank Mayo, Philip Morris

D: James Hogan
S: Zane Grey
SP: Stuart Anthony, Robert Yost
P: Harold Hurley

602. O'MALLEY OF THE MOUNTED

(Principal/20th C. Fox, March 27, 1936)   59 Mins.

George O'Brien, Irene Ware, Crauford Kent, James Bush, Victor Potel, Charles King, Stanley Fields, Tom London, Reginald Barlow, Richard Cramer, Olin Francis, Blackjack Ward

D: David Howard
S: William S. Hart
SP: Dan Jarrett, Frank Howard Clark
P: Sol Lesser

603. COMIN' ROUND THE MOUNTAIN

(Republic, March 31, 1936)   55 Mins.

Gene Autry, Ann Rutherford, Smiley Burnette, LeRoy Mason, Raymond Brown, Ken Cooper, Tracy Layne, Bob McKenzie, Laurita Puente, John Ince, Frank Lackteen, Jim Corey, Al Taylor, Steve Clark, Frank Ellis, Hank Bell, Dick Botiller, "Champion"

D: Mack V. Wright
S: Oliver Drake
SP: Oliver Drake, Dorrell and Stuart McGowan
P: Nat Levine

604. TWO IN REVOLT

(RKO, April 3, 1936)   7 Reels

John Arledge, Louise Latimer, Moroni Olson, Emmett Vogan, Harry Jans, Murray Alper, Willie Best, Max Wagner, Ethan Laidlaw, "Lightning" (a dog), "Warrior" (a horse)

D: Glenn Tyron
S: Earl Johnson, Thomas Storey
SP: Frank Howard Clark, Ferdinand Reyher, Jerry Hutchinson
S: Robert Sisk

605. OUTLAWS OF THE RANGE

(Spectrum, April 8, 1936)   59 Mins.

Bill Cody, Catherine Cotter, Bill Cody, Jr., William McCall, Wally West, Gordon Griffith, Dick Strong

D: Al Herman
S/SP: Zara Tazil
P: Roy Kirkwood

606. SUTTER'S GOLD

(Universal, April 9, 1936)   94 Mins.

Edward Arnold, Lee Tracy, Binnie Barnes, Katherine Alexander, Montague Love, Addison Richards, John Miljan, Robert Warwick, Harry Carey, Mitchell Lewis, William Janney, Ronald Cosby, Jeannie Smith, Harry Cording, Aura DeSilva, Bryant Washburn, William Ruhl, Pedro Regas, John Bliefer, William Gould, Jim Thorpe, Priscilla Lawson, Oscar Apfel, Neeley Edwards, Don Briggs, Charles Farr, Harry Stubbs, Nan Gray, Billy Gilbert, Allen Vincent, Sidney Bracey, Gaston Glass, Frank Reicher, Morgan Wallace, Russ Powell, George Irving, Al Smith

D: James Cruze
S: Blaise Cendrars, Bruno Frank
SP: Jack Kirkland, Walter Woods, George O'Neil
P: Edmund Grainger

607. THREE ON THE TRAIL

(Paramount, April 14, 1936)   67 Mins.
(*Hopalong Cassidy* Series)

William Boyd, Jimmy Ellison, Onslow Stevens, Muriel Evans, George Hayes, Claude King, William Duncan, Clara Kimball Young, Ernie Adams, Ted Adams, Lew Meehan, John St. Polis, Al Hill, Jack Rutherford, Lita Cortez, Artie Ortego, Franklyn Farnum

D: Howard Bretherton
S: Clarence E. Mulford
SP: Doris Schroeder, Vernon Smith
P: Harry Sherman

608. FEUD OF THE WEST

(Diversion, April 15, 1936)   62 Mins.

Hoot Gibson, Joan Barclay, Buzz Barton, Reed Howes, Robert Kortman, Edward Cassidy, Nelson McDowell, Lew Meehan, Bob McKenzie, Allen Greer, Roger Williams

D: Harry Fraser
Adaptation: Walton Farrar, Roger Allman
SP: Phil Dunham
P: Walter Futter

609. LIGHTNIN' BILL CARSON

(Puritan, April 15, 1936)   75 Mins.

Tim McCoy, Lois January, Rex Lease, Harry Worth, Karl Hackett, John Merton, Lafe McKee, Frank Ellis, Slim Whitaker, Edmund Cobb, Jack Rockwell, Jimmy Aubrey, Artie Ortego, Oscar Gahan

D: Sam Newfield
S: George Arthur Durlam
SP: Joseph O'Donnell
P: Sigmund Neufeld, Leslie Simmonds

610. THE COUNTRY BEYOND
(Fox, April 24, 1936) 73 Mins.
Paul Kelly, Rochelle Hudson, Robert Kent, Alan Hale, Alan Dinehart, Matt McHugh, Andrew Tombes, Paul McVey, Claudia Coleman, Holmes Herbert, "Buck," "Wolf"
D: Eugene Forde
S: James Oliver Curwood
SP: Lamar Trotti, Adele Commandini
P: Sol Wurtzel

611. ROGUE OF THE RANGE
(Supreme/William Steiner, April 25, 1936) 58 Mins.
Johnny Mack Brown, Lois January, Alden (Guy) Chase, Phyllis Hume, George Ball, Jack Rockwell, Horace Murphy, Frank Ball, Lloyd Ingraham, Fred Hoose, Forrest Taylor, George Morrell, Blackie Whiteford, Slim Whitaker, Tex Palmer, Horace B. Carpenter, Max Davidson, Art Dillard
D: S. Roy Luby
SP: Earle Snell
P: A. W. Hackel

612. ROAMIN' WILD
(Reliable/William Steiner, April 29, 1936) 58 Mins.
Tom Tyler, Max Davidson, Carol Wyndham, Al Ferguson, George Chesebro, Fred Parker, Slim Whitaker, Bud Osborne, Wally West, Earl Dwire, Lafe McKee, John Elliott, Frank Ellis, Sherry Tansey
D/P: Bernard B. Ray
SP: Robert Tansey

613. FOR THE SERVICE
(Universal, May 6, 1936) 64 Mins.
Buck Jones, Fred Kohler, Beth Marion, Frank McGlynn, Sr., Clifford Jones, Ben Corbett, Chief Thunderbird, Edward Keane, "Silver"
D: Buck Jones
S/SP: Isadore Bernstein
P: Buck Jones

614. THE MINE WITH THE IRON DOOR
(Columbia, May 6, 1936) 66 Mins.
Richard Arlen, Cecilia Parker, Henry B. Wathall, Horace Murphy, Stanley Fields, Spencer Charters, Charles Wilson, Barbara Bedford
D: David Howard
S: Harold Bell Wright
SP: Howard Swift, Dan Jarrett
P: Sol Lesser

615. LAST OF THE WARRENS
(Supreme/William Steiner, May 10, 1936) 60 Mins.
Bob Steele, Margaret Marquis, Charles King, Horace Murphy, Lafe McKee, Charles K. French, Blackie Whiteford, Steve Clark, Jim Corey
D/S/SP: Robert N. Bradbury
P: A. W. Hackel

616. THE SINGING COWBOY
(Republic, May 13, 1936) 56 Mins.
Gene Autry, Smiley Burnette, Lois Wilde, Creighton (Lon) Chaney, John Van Pelt, Earle Hodgins, Ken Cooper, Harrison Green, Wes Warner, Jack Rockwell, Tracy Layne, Fred Toones, Oscar Gahan, Frankie Marvin, Jack Kirk, Audry Davis, George Pierce, Charles McAvoy, Ann Gillis, Earl Erby, Harvey Clark, Alf James, Pat Caron, "Champion"
D: Mack V. Wright
S: Tom Gibson
SP: Dorrell and Stuart McGowan
P: Nat Levine

617. PINTO RUSTLERS
(Reliable/William Steiner, May 14, 1936) 56 Mins.
Tom Tyler, George Walsh, Al St. John, Catherine Cotter, Earl Dwire, William Gould, George Chesebro, Roger Williams, Bud Osborne, Slim Whitaker, Murdock McQuarrie, Milburn Morante, Sherry Tansey
D: Henri Samuels (Harry S. Webb)
S/SP: Robert Tansey
P: Bernard B. Ray

618. TREACHERY RIDES THE RANGE
(Warner Bros., May 15, 1936) 56 Mins.
Dick Foran, Paula Stone, Monte Blue, Craig Reynolds, Carlyle Moore, Jr., Henry Otho, Jim Thorpe, Milt Kibbee, Bud Osborne, Nick Copeland, Monte Montague, Don Barclay, Frank Bruno, Gene Alsace (Rocky Camron), Tom Wilson, Dick Botiller, Iron Eyes Cody, William Desmond, Cliff Saum, Frank McCarroll, Frank Ellis, Artie Ortego
D: Frank McDonald
SP: William Jacobs
P: Bryan Foy

619. THE COWBOY AND THE KID
(Universal, May 25, 1936) 58 Mins.
Buck Jones, Billy Burrud, Dorothy Revier, Harry Worth, Charles LeMoyne, Dick Rush, Lafe McKee, Bob McKenzie, Burr Caruth, Eddie Lee, Kernan Cripps, Oliver Eckhart, Mary Mersch, Mildred Gober, "Silver"
D: Ray Taylor
S: Buck Jones
SP: Frances Guihan
P: Buck Jones

620. THE LONELY TRAIL

(Republic, May 25, 1936) 58 Mins.

John Wayne, Ann Rutherford, Cy Kendall, Bob Kortman, Fred Toones, Etta McDaniel, Sam Flint, Dennis Meadows (Moore), Jim Toney, Yakima Canutt, Lloyd Ingraham, Bob Burns, James Marcus, Rodney Hildebrand, Eugene Jackson, Floyd Shackelford, Leon Lord, Jack Kirk, Tracy Layne, Jack Ingram, Bud Pope, Tex Phelps, Clyde Kenney, Horace B. Carpenter, Oscar Gahan, Francis Walker, Clifton Young

D: Joseph Kane
S: Bernard McConville
SP: Bernard McConville, Jack Natteford
P: Paul Malvern

621. THE CATTLE THIEF

(Columbia, May 26, 1936) 50 Mins.

Ken Maynard, Geneva Mitchell, Ward Bond, Roger Williams, Jim Marcus, Sheldon Lewis, Edward Cecil, "Tarzan," Jack Kirk, Edward Hearn, Glenn Strange, Jack King, Al Taylor, Dick Rush, Bud McClure

D: Spencer G. Bennet
S/SP: Nate Gatzert
P: Larry Darmour

622. SECRET PATROL

(Columbia, June 3, 1936) 60 Mins.

Charles Starrett, Finis Barton, J. P. McGowan, Henry Mollinson, LeStrange Millman, Arthur Kerr, Reginald Hincks, Ted Mapes, James McGrath

D: David Selman
S: Peter B. Kyne
SP: J. P. McGowan, Robert Watson

623. ACES AND EIGHTS

(Puritan, June 6, 1936) 62 Mins.

Tim McCoy, Luana Walters, Wheeler Oakman, Rex Lease, Joe Girard, John Merton, Charles Stevens, Jimmy Aubrey, Earle Hodgins, J. Frank Glendon, Tom Smith, Frank Ellis, Jack Evans

D: Sam Newfield
S/SP: George A. Durlam
P: Sigmund Neufeld, Leslie Simmonds

624. TOO MUCH BEEF

(Colony, June 6, 1936) 60 Mins.

Rex Bell, Connie Bergen, Horace Murphy, Forrest Taylor, Lloyd Ingraham, Peggy O'Connell, Vincent Dennis, George Ball, Jimmy Aubrey, Jack Cowell, Fred Burns, Steve Clark, Jack Kirk, Dennis Meadows (Dennis Moore), Frank Ellis

D: Robert Hill
S: William Colt MacDonald
SP: Rock Hawley (Robert Hill)
P: Max and Arthur Alexander

625. EVERYMAN'S LAW

(Supreme/William Steiner, June 10, 1936)
  62 Mins.

Johnny Mack Brown, Beth Marion, Frank Campeau, Roger Gray, Lloyd Ingraham, John Beck, Horace Murphy, Dick Alexander, Slim Whitaker, Edward Cassidy, Jim Corey, George Morrell, Ralph Bucko, Francis Walker

D: Albert Ray
S/SP: Earle Snell
P: A. W. Hackel

626. THE RIDING AVENGER

(Diversion, June 15, 1936) 58 Mins.

Hoot Gibson, Ruth Mix, Buzz Barton, June Gale, Stanley Blystone, Roger Williams, Francis Walker, Slim Whitaker, Budd Buster, Blackie Whiteford

D: Harry Fraser
S: "Big Bend Buckaroo"—Walton West
SP: Norman Houston
P: Walter Futter

627. WINDS OF THE WASTELAND

(Republic, June 15, 1936) 58 Mins.

John Wayne, Phyllis Fraser, Yakima Canutt, Douglas Cosgrove, Lane Chandler, Sam Flint, Lew Kelly, Bob Kortman, Edward Cassidy, Merrill McCormack, Charles Locher (Jon Hall), Jack Ingram, Joe Yrigoyen, Bud McClure, Chris Frank, Art Mix, Jack Rockwell

D: Mack Wright
SP: Joseph Poland
P: Nat Levine

628. THE LAST OUTLAW

(RKO, June 19, 1936) 62 Mins.

Harry Carey, Hoot Gibson, Tom Tyler, Henry B. Wathall, Margaret Callahan, Ray Meyer, Harry Jans, Frank M. Thomas, Russell Hopton, Frank Jenks, Maxine Jennings, Joe Sawyer, Fred Scott

D: Christy Cabanne
S: John Ford, E. Murray Campbell
SP: John Twist, Jack Townley
P: Robert Sisk

629. THE BORDER PATROLMAN

(Principal/Fox, June 20, 1936) 60 Mins.

George O'Brien, Polly Ann Young, Roy (LeRoy) Mason, Mary Doran, Smiley Burnette, Tom LondNo, William P. Carlton, Al Hill, Murdock McQuarrie, John St. Polis, Cyril Ring

D: David Howard
S/SP: Dan Jarrett, Bennett Cohen
P: Sol Lesser

630. THE LAW RIDES

(Supreme/William Steiner, June 25, 1936)
57 Mins.

Bob Steele, Harley Wood, Charles King, Buck Connors, Margaret Mann, Jack Rockwell, Norman Neilsen, Barney Furey, Ted Mapes

D: Robert N. Bradbury
S: Forbes Parkhill
SP: Al Martin
P: A. W. Hackel

631. THE ARIZONA RAIDERS

(Paramount, June 28, 1936)   54 Mins.
(Re-released as *Bad Men of Arizona*)

Larry "Buster" Crabbe, Raymond Hatton, Marsha Hunt, Jane Rhodes, Johnny Downs, Grant Withers, Don Rowan, Arthur Aylesworth, Richard Carle, Herbert Hayward, Petra Silva

D: James Hogan
S: "Raiders of Spanish Peaks"—Zane Grey
SP: Robert Yost, John Drafft
P: A. M. Botsford

632. WILDCAT TROOPER

(Ambassador, July 1, 1936)   60 Mins.

Kermit Maynard, Hobart Bosworth, Fuzzy Knight, Lois Wilde, Yakima Canutt, Eddie Phillips, Jim Thorpe, John Merton, Frank Hagney, Roger Williams, Dick Curtis, Ted Lorch, Hal Price, "Rocky"

D: Elmer Clifton
S: "The Midnight Call"—James Oliver Curwood
SP: Joseph O'Donnell
P: Maurice Conn

633. THE PHANTOM RIDER

(Universal, July 6, 1936)   15 Chaps.

Buck Jones, Marla Shelton, Diana Gibson, Joey Ray, Harry Woods, Frank LaRue, George Cooper, Eddie Gribbon, Helen Shipman, James Mason, Jim Corey, Lee Sumway, Charles LeMoyne, Clem Bevins, Cecil Weston, Matt McHugh, Jim Thorpe, Charles King, Curtis McPeters (Cactus Mack), Charles K. French, Tom London, Wally Wales, Slim Whitaker, Frank Ellis, Bob Fite, "Hi Pockets" Busse, Bill Scott, Jimmy Carroll, Hank Bell, Lafe McKee, Priscilla Lawson, Drew Stanfield, Art Mix, George Plues, Tom Carter, Scoop Martin, Fred Warren, Olin Francis, Iron Eyes Cody, Paul Regas, Eva McKenzie, Orrin Burke, George Ovey, Cliff Lyons, "Silver"

D: Ray Taylor
Original SP: George Plympton, Basil Dickey, Ella O'Neill
P: Henry MacRae
Chapter Titles: (1) Dynamite, (2) The Maddened Herd, (3) The Brink of Disaster, (4) The Phantom Rides, (5) Trapped by Outlaws, (6) Shot Down, (7) Stark Terror, (8) The Night Attack, (9) The Indian Raid, (10) Human Targets, (11) The Shaft of Doom, (12) Flaming Gold, (13) Crashing Timbers, (14) The Last Chance, (15) The Outlaw's Vengeance

634. AVENGING WATERS

(Columbia, July 8, 1936)   57 Mins.

Ken Maynard, Beth Marion, Ward Bond, John Elliott, Zella Russell, Wally Wales, Tom London, Edmund Cobb, Edward Hearn, "Tarzan," Buck Moulton, Glenn Strange, Cactus Mack, Buffalo Bill, Jr., Sterling Holloway, Jack King, Buck Bucko, Bud McClure

D: Spencer G. Bennet
S/SP: Nate Gatzert
P: Larry Darmour

635. THE LION'S DEN

(Puritan, July 8, 1936)   59 Mins.

Tim McCoy, Joan Woodbury, Don Barclay, J. Frank Glendon, John Merton, Dick Curtis, Arthur Millet, Art Felix, Jack Rockwell, Karl Hackett, Jack Evans

D: Sam Newfield
S: L. V. Jefferson
SP: John T. Neville
P: Sigmund Neufeld, Leslie Simmonds

636. WEST OF NEVADA

(Colony, July 21, 1936)   57 Mins.

Rex Bell, Joan Barclay, Al St. John, Forrest Taylor, Steve Clark, Dick Botiller, Georgia O'Dell, Frank McCarroll, Bob Woodward

D: Robert Hill
S: "Raw Gold"—Charles Kyson
SP: Rock Hawley (Robert Hill)
P: Arthur Alexander

637. HEART OF THE WEST

(Paramount, July 24, 1936)   60 Mins.
(*Hopalong Cassidy* Series)

William Boyd, Jimmy Ellison, George Hayes, Lynn Gilbert, Sidney Blackmer, Charles Martin, John Rutherford, Warner Richmond, Walter Miller, Ted Adams, Fred Kohler, Bob McKenzie, John Elliott

D: Howard Bretherton
S/SP: Doris Schroeder. Based on characters created by Clarence E. Mulford
P: Harry Sherman

638. THE CROOKED TRAIL

(Supreme/William Steiner, July 25, 1936)   60 Mins.

Johnny Mack Brown, Lucile Browne, John Merton, Ted Adams, Charles King, Dick Curtis, John Van Pelt, Edward Cassidy, Horace Murphy, Earl

Avenging Waters (Columbia, 1936) — Ward Bond and Ken Maynard

Dwire, Artie Ortego, Hal Price
D: S. Roy Luby
SP: George Plympton
P: A. W. Hackel

639. RHYTHM ON THE RANGE
(Paramount, July 31, 1936) 85 Mins.
Bing Crosby, Frances Farmer, Bob "Bazooka" Burns, Martha Raye, Samuel S. Hinds, Warren Hymer, Lucille Gleason, George E. Stone, James Burke, Clem Bevans, Leonid Kinsky, Sons of the Pioneers (Roy Rogers, Bob Nolan, Tim Spencer, Hugh and Carl Farr), Martha Sleeper
D: Norman Taurog
S: Mervin Houser
SP: Walter DeLeon, Frances Martin, John Moffitt, Sidney Salkow

640. GHOST PATROL
(Puritan, August 3, 1936) 60 Mins.
Tim McCoy, Claudia Dell, Walter Miller, Wheeler Oakman, Lloyd Ingraham, Dick Curtis, Slim Whitaker, Jim Burtis, Jack Casey, Artie Ortego, Art Dillard, Fargo Bussey
D: Sam Newfield
S: Joseph O'Donnell
SP: Wyndham Gittens
P: Sigmund Neufeld, Leslie Simmonds

641. THE IDAHO KID
(Colony, August 6, 1936) 59 Mins.
Rex Bell, Marion Shilling, David Sharpe, Lane Chandler, Charles King, Lafe McKee, Earl Dwire, Phil Dunham, Dorothy Woods, Herman Hack, Edward Cassidy, George Morrell, Jimmy Aubrey, Sherry Tansey, Dick Botiller
D: Robert Hill
S: "Idaho"—Paul Evan Lehman
SP: George Plympton
P: Arthur Alexander

642. BRAND OF THE OUTLAWS
(Supreme/William Steiner, August 15, 1936) 60 Mins.
Bob Steele, Margaret Marquis, Virginia True Boardman, Jack Rockwell, Edward Cassidy, Charles King, Frank Ball, Bud Osborne, Bob Kortman
D: Robert N. Bradbury
S/SP: Forbes Parkhill
P: A. W. Hackel

643. SANTA FE BOUND
(Reliable/William Steiner, August 15, 1936) 5 Reels
Tom Tyler, Jeanne Martel, Richard Cramer, Charles (Slim) Whitaker, Edward Cassidy, Dorothy Woods, Charles King, Lafe McKee, Earl Dwire, Wally West

D: Henri Samuels (Harry S. Webb)
S: Rose Gordon
SP: Carl Krusada
P: Bernard B. Ray

644. HEROES OF THE RANGE
(Columbia, August 18, 1936)   58 Mins.
Ken Maynard, June Gale, Harry Woods, Harry Ernest, Bob Kortman, Bud McClure, Tom London, Bud Osborne, Frank Hagney, Jack Rockwell, Lafe McKee, Wally Wales, Jay Wilsey (Buffalo Bill, Jr.), Jerome Ward, "Tarzan," Bud McClure, Bud Jamison, Bob Reeves, Jack King
D: Spencer G. Bennet
S/SP: Nate Gatzert
P: Larry Darmour

645. OH, SUSANNA!
(Republic, August 19, 1936)   59 Mins.
Gene Autry, Smiley Burnette, Frances Grant, Earle Hodgins, Donald Kirke, Booth Howard, Clara Kimball Young, Edward Piel, Sr., Frankie Marvin, Carl Stockdale, Gerald Roscoe, Roger Gray, Fred Burns, Walter James, Fred Toones, Earl Dwire, Bruce Mitchell, Jack Kirk, George Morrell, The Light Crust Doughboys, "Champion"
D: Joseph Kane
S/SP: Oliver Drake
P: Nat Levine

646. THE TEXAS RANGERS
(Paramount, August 28, 1936)   95 Mins.
Fred MacMurray, Jack Oakie, Jean Parker, Lloyd Nolan, Edward Ellis, Bennie Bartlett, Elena Martinez, Frank Shannon, George Hayes, Fred Kohler, Hank Bell
D/S: King Vidor
SP: Louis Stevens

647. THE TRAITOR
(Puritan, August 29, 1936)   56 Mins.
Tim McCoy, Frances Grant, Wally Wales, Karl Hackett, Jack Rockwell, Pedro Regas, Frank Melton, Dick Curtis, Dick Botiller, Edmund Cobb, Wally West, Tina Menard, Soledad Jiminez, J. Frank Glendon, Frank McCarroll
D: Sam Newfield
S: John Thomas Neville
SP: Joseph O'Donnell
P: Sigmund Neufeld, Leslie Simmonds

648. THE LAST OF THE MOHICANS
(United Artists, September 4, 1936)   91 Mins.
Randolph Scott, Binnie Barnes, Henry Wilcoxin, Bruce Cabot, Heather Angel, Philip Reed, Robert Barrat, Hugh Buckler, Willard Robertson, Frank McGlynn, Sr., Will Stanton, William V. Mong, Olaf Hytden Hare, Reginald Barlow, Lionel Belmore

The Idaho Kid (Colony, 1936) — Rex Bell and David Sharpe

D: George B. Seitz
S: James Fenimore Cooper
SP: Philip Dunne
P: Edward Small

649. KING OF THE ROYAL MOUNTED
(20th C. Fox, September 11, 1936)   61 Mins.
Robert Kent, Rosalind Keith, Jack Luden, Alan Dinehart, Frank McGlynn, Grady Sutton, Arthur Loft
D: Howard Bretherton
S: Zane Grey
SP: Earle Snell
P: Sol Lesser

649a. WHOOPS, I'M AN INDIAN
(Columbia, September 11, 1936)   2 Reels
(*Three Stooges* Series)
Moe Howard, Curly Howard, Larry Fine, Bud Jamison
D: Del Lord
S: Searle Kramer, Herman Boxer
SP: Clyde Bruckman

650. THE GLORY TRAIL
(Crescent, September 15, 1936)   65 Mins.
Tom Keene, Joan Barclay, James Bush, E. H. Calvert, Frank Melton, William Royle, Walter Long, Etta McDaniel, Allen Greer, William Crowell, Harvey Foster, Ann Hovey, John Lester Johnson
D: Lynn Shores
S/SP: John T. Neville
P: E. B. Derr

651. TRAILIN' WEST
(Warner Bros., September 15, 1936)   56 Mins.
Dick Foran, Paula Stone, Gordon (Bill) Elliott, Addison Richards, Robert Barratt, Joseph Crehan, Fred Lawrence, Eddie Shubert, Henry Otho, Stuart Holmes, Cliff Saum, Milt Kibbee, Carlyle Moore, Jr., Jim Thorpe, Edwin Stanley, Bud Osborne, Glenn Strange, Gene Alsace (Rocky Camron), Tom Wilson
D: Noel Smith
S: "On Secret Service"—Anthony Coldeway
P: Bryan Foy

652. RIDE 'EM COWBOY
(Universal, September 20, 1936)   59 Mins.
Buck Jones, George Cooper, Luana Walters, J. P. McGowan, William Lawrence, Joe Girard, Donald Kirke, Charles LeMoyne, Edmund Cobb, Lester Dorr, "Silver"
D: Lesley Selander
S: Buck Jones
SP: Frances Guihan
P: Buck Jones

653. THE THREE MESQUITEERS
(Republic, September 22, 1936)   61 Mins.
(*Three Mesquiteers* Series)
Bob Livingston, Ray Corrigan, Syd Saylor, Kay Hughes, J. P. McGowan, Frank Yaconelli, Al Bridge, Stanley Blystone, John Merton, Jean Marvey, Milburn Stone, Duke Yorke, Allen Connor
D: Ray Taylor
S: William Colt MacDonald
SP: Jack Natteford
P: Nat Levine

654. UNDERCOVER MAN
(Republic, September 24, 1936)   57 Mins.
Johnny Mack Brown, Suzanne Karen, Ted Adams, Lloyd Ingraham, Horace Murphy, Edward Cassidy, Frank Ball, Margaret Mann, Frank Darien, Dick Morehead, George Morrell
D: Albert Ray
S/SP: Andrew Bennison
P: A. W. Hackel

655. MEN OF THE PLAINS
(Colony, September 29, 1936)   62 Mins.
Rex Bell, Joan Barclay, George Ball, Charles King, Forrest Taylor, Roger Williams, Ed Cassidy, Lafe McKee, Jack Cowell
D: Bob Hill
S/SP: Robert Emmett (Tansey)
P: Arthur and Max Alexander

656. PHANTOM PATROL
(Ambassador, September 30, 1936)   60 Mins.
Kermit Maynard, Joan Barclay, Dick Curtis, Harry Worth, George Cleveland, Paul Fix, Julian Rivero, Eddie Phillips, Roger Williams, Lester Dorr, "Rocky"
D: Charles Hutchison
S: "Fatal Note"—James Oliver Curwood
SP: Credited to Stephen Norris (name of a character in the film)
P: Maurice Conn

657. RIDE, RANGER, RIDE
(Republic, September 30, 1936)   59 Mins.
Gene Autry, Smiley Burnette, The Tennessee Ramblers, Kay Hughes, Monte Blue, Max Terhune, George J. Lewis, Robert Homans, Chief Thunder Cloud, Frankie Marvin, Iron Eyes Cody, Sunny Chorre, Bud Pope, Nelson McDowell, Shooting Star, Arthur Singley, Greg Whitespear, Robert Thomas, "Champion"
D: Joseph Kane
S: Bernard McConville, Karen DeWolf
SP: Dorrell and Stuart McGowan
P: Nat Levine

658. ROMANCE RIDES THE RANGE

(Spectrum, September, 1936)   59 Mins.

Fred Scott, Cliff Nazarro, Marion Shilling, Buzz Barton, Bob Kortman, Ted Lorch, Frank Yaconelli, Phil Dunham, Jack Evans, William Steele, Allen Greer, "White King"

D: Harry Fraser

SP: Tom Gibson

P: Jed Buell, George H. Callaghan

659. FRONTIER JUSTICE

(Diversion, October 1, 1936)   58 Mins.

Hoot Gibson, Jane Barnes, Richard Cramer, Franklyn Farnum, Lloyd Ingraham, Joe Girard, Fred Toones, Roger Williams, George Yoeman, John Elliott, Lafe McKee, Silver Tip Baker

D: Robert McGowan

S: Colonel George B. Rodney

SP: W. Scott Darling

P: Walter Futter

660. THE GAY DESPERADO

(United Artists, October 2, 1936)   86 Mins.

Ida Lupino, Nino Martini, Leo Carrillo, Chris-Pin Martin, Paul Hurst, Mischa Auer, Frank Puglia

D: Rouben Mamoulian

S: Leo Birinski

SP: Wallace Smith

661. CAVALRY

(Republic, October 5, 1936)   63 Mins.

Bob Steele, Frances Grant, Karl Hackett, William Welch, Earl Ross, Hal Price, Ed Cassidy, Perry Murdock, Martin Turner, Pinky Barnes, Budd Buster, William Desmond, Earl Dwire, Horace B. Carpenter

D/S: Robert N. Bradbury

SP: George Plympton

P: A. W. Hackel

662. CODE OF THE RANGE

(Columbia, October 9, 1936)   55 Mins.

Charles Starrett, Mary Blake, Ed Coxen, Allan Caven, Edward Piel, Sr., Edmund Cobb, Edward J. LeSaint, Ralph McCullough, George Chesebro, Art Mix, Albert J. Smith

D: C. C. Coleman, Jr.

S: Credited to Peter B. Kyne

SP: Ford Beebe

663. HOPALONG CASSIDY RETURNS

(Paramount, October 12, 1936)   71 Mins.

(*Hopalong Cassidy* Series)

William Boyd, George Hayes, Gail Sheridan, Evelyn Brent, Stephen Morris (Morris Ankrum), William Janney, Irving Bacon, Grant Richards, John Beck, Ernie Adams, Joe Rickson, Claude Smith, Ray Whitley

D: Nate Watt

S: Clarence E. Mulford

SP: Harrison Jacobs

P: Harry Sherman

664. RIP ROARIN' BUCKAROO

(Victory, October 15, 1936)   58 Mins.

Tom Tyler, Beth Marion, Sammy Cohen, Charles King, Forrest Taylor, Dick Cramer, John Elliott

D: Robert Hill

SP: William Buchanan

P: Sam Katzman

665. DANIEL BOONE

(RKO, October 16, 1936)   77 Mins.

George O'Brien, Heather Angel, John Carradine, Ralph Forbes, Clarence Muse, George Regas, Dickie Jones, Huntley Gordon, Harry Cording, Aggie Herring, Crauford Kent, Keith Kenneth

D: David Howard

S: Edgecumb Pinchon

SP: Dan Jarrett

P: George A. Hirliman

666. THE FUGITIVE SHERIFF

(Columbia, October 20, 1936)   58 Mins.

Ken Maynard, Beth Marion, Walter Miller, Hal Price, John Elliott, Arthur Millet, Virginia True Boardman, Frank Ball, Edmund Cobb, Lafe McKee, Art Mix, William Gould, Bob Burns, Horace Murphy, Vernon Dent, Tex Palmer, Bud Osborne, Slim Whitaker, Al Taylor, Frank Ellis, Horace B. Carpenter, Oscar Gahan, Glenn Strange, Fred Burns, Lew Meehan, Blackjack Ward, Tex Cooper, "Tarzan," Roy Bucko, Buck Bucko, Art Dillard, Jack King, Bud Jamison, Bud McClure

D: Spencer G. Bennet

S/SP: Nate Gatzert

P: Larry Darmour

667. GHOST TOWN GOLD

(Republic, October 26, 1936)   55 Mins.

(*Three Mesquiteers* Series)

Bob Livingston, Ray Corrigan, Max Terhune, Kay Hughes, Yakima Canutt, Frank Hagney, LeRoy Mason, Burr Caruth, Bob Kortman, Milburn Moranti, Don Roberts, Robert Thomas, Horace Murphy, F. Herrick Herrick, Earle Hodgins, Edward Piel, Sr., Harry Harvey, Hank Worden, Bud Osborne, Bob Burns, Wally West, I. Stanford Jolley

D: Joseph Kane

S: Bernard McConville

SP: John Rathmell, Oliver Drake. Based on characters created by William Colt MacDonald

P: Nat Levine

668. REBELLION

(Crescent, October 27, 1936) 60 Mins.

Tom Keene, Rita Cansino (Hayworth), Duncan Renaldo, William Royle, Gino Corrado, Roger Gray, Robert McKenzie, Allan Cavan, Jack Ingram, Lita Cortez, Theodore Lorch, W. M. (Merrill) McCormack

D: Lynn Shores

SP: John T. Neville

P: E. B. Derr

669. END OF THE TRAIL

(Columbia, October 31, 1936) 70 Mins.

Jack Holt, Louise Henry, Douglass Dumbrille, Guinn "Big Boy" Williams, George McKay, Gene Morgan, John McGuire, Edward J. LeSaint, Frank Shannon, Erle C. Kenton, Hank Bell, Art Mix, Blackie Whiteford, Blackjack Ward, Edgar Dearing

D: Erle C. Kenton

S: "Outlaws of Palouse"—Zane Grey

SP: Harold Shumate

670. CAVALCADE OF THE WEST

(Diversion, October, 1936) 59 Mins.

Hoot Gibson, Rex Lease, Marion Shilling, Adam Goodman, Nina Guilbert, Steve Clark, Earl Dwire, Phil Dunham, Bob McKenzie, Jerry Tucker, Barry Downing, Budd Buster, Blackie Whiteford

D: Harry Fraser

S/SP: Norman Houston

P: Walter Futter

671. THE VIGILANTES ARE COMING

(Republic, October, 1936) 12 Chaps.

Robert Livingston, Kay Hughes, Guinn "Big Boy" Williams, Raymond Hatton, Fred Kohler, Robert Warwick, William Farnum, Robert Kortman, John Merton, Lloyd Ingraham, William Desmond, Yakima Canutt, Tracy Layne, Bud Pope, Steve Clemente, Bud Osborne, Philip Armenta, Ray Corrigan, Stanley Blystone, Henry Hall, John O'Brien, Joe De LaCruz, Fred Burns, Frankie Marvin, Wally West, Wes Warner, Ken Cooper, Frank Ellis, Jerome Ward, Al Taylor, Sam Garrett, Herman Hack, Jack Ingram, Jack Kirk, Jack Kinney, Pascale Perry, Vinegar Roan, Len Ward, Lloyd Saunders

D: Mack V. Wright, Ray Taylor

S: Maurice Geraghty, Winston Miller

SP: John Rathmell, Maurice Geraghty, Leslie Swabacker

P: Nat Levine

Chapter Titles: (1) The Eagle Strikes, (2) Birth of the Vigilantes, (3) Condemned by Cossacks, (4) Unholy Gold, (5) Treachery Unmasked, (6) A Tyrant's Trickery, (7) Wings of Doom, (8) A Treaty with Treason, (9) Arrow's Flight, (10) Prison of Flame, (11) A Race with Death, (12) Fremont Takes Command

672. AMBUSH VALLEY

(Reliable/William Steiner, November 1, 1936) 57 Mins.

Bob Custer, Victoria Vinton, Vane Calvert, Eddie Phillips, Wally Wales, Oscar Gahan, Ed Cassidy, Denver Dixon, Wally West, Roger Williams, John Elliott

D: Raymond Samuels (B. B. Ray)

S/SP: Bennett Cohen

P: Bernard B. Ray

673. BOSS RIDER OF GUN CREEK

(Universal, November 1, 1936) 65 Mins.

Buck Jones, Muriel Evans, Harvey Clark, Lee Phelps, Tom Chatterton, Joseph Swickard, Ernest Hillard, Mahlon Hamilton, Alphonse Ethier, Alan Sears, William Lawrence, Edward Hearn, "Silver"

D: Lesley Selander

S: E. B. Mann

SP: Frances Guihan

P: Buck Jones

674. VENGEANCE OF RANNAH

(Reliable/William Steiner, November 6, 1936) 59 Mins.

Bob Custer, Rin-Tin-Tin, Jr., John Elliott, Victoria Vinton, Roger Williams, Eddie Phillips, Edward Cassidy, Wally West, Oscar Gahan

D: Franklyn Shamray (Bernard B. Ray)

S: James Oliver Curwood

SP: Joseph O'Donnell

P: B. B. Ray

675. WILD BRIAN KENT

(Principal/RKO, November 6, 1936) 60 Mins.

Ralph Bellamy, Mae Clarke, Helen Lowell, Stanley Andrews, Lew Kelly, Eddie Chandler, Richard Alexander, Jack Duffy

D: Howard Bretherton

S: "The Re-creation of Brian Kent"—Harold Bell Wright

SP: Earle Snell, Don Swift, James Gruen

P: Sol Lesser

676. THE CALIFORNIA MAIL

(Warner Bros., November 14, 1936) 60 Mins.

Dick Foran, Linda Perry, Edmund Cobb, Tom Brower, James Farley, Gene Alsace (Rocky Camron), Glenn Strange, Bob Woodward, Wilfred Lucas, Fred Burns, Milt Kibbee, Edward Keane, Cliff Saum, Jack Kirk, Lew Meehan, Tex Palmer, Sons of the Pioneers (Roy Rogers, Bob Nolan, Tim

Spencer, Hugh Farr, Karl Farr)
D: Noel Smith
S: "The Pony Express Rider"—Harold Buckley, Roy Chanslor
SP: Harold Buckley, Roy Chanslor
P: Bryan Foy

677. NORTH OF NOME
(Columbia, November 14, 1936) 63 Mins.
Jack Holt, Evelyn Venable, Guinn "Big Boy" Williams, John Miljan, Roger Imhoe, Dorothy Appleby, Paul Hurst, Frank McGlynn, Robert Glecker, Ben Hendricks, Mike Morita, George Cleveland, Blackhawk
D: William Nigh
S: Houston Branch
SP: Albert DeMond
P: Larry Darmour

678. LAW AND LEAD
(Colony, November 15, 1936) 60 Mins.
Rex Bell, Harley Wood, Wally Wales, Lane Chandler, Earl Dwire, Soledad Jiminez, Lloyd Ingraham, Roger Williams, Karl Hackett, Edward Cassidy, Donald Reed, Lew Meehan
D: Bob Hill
S: Rock Hawley (Bob Hill)
SP: Basil Dickey
P: Arthur and Max Alexander

679. THE BIG SHOW
(Republic, November 16, 1936) 59 Mins.
Gene Autry, Smiley Burnette, Kay Hughes, Max Terhune, Sally Payne, William Newill, Charles Judels, Rex King, Harry Worth, Mary Russell, Christine Maple, Jerry Larkin, Jack O'Shea, Wedgewood Norrell, Antrim Short, June Johnson, Grace Durkin, Slim Whitaker, George Chesebro, Edward Hearn, Cliff Lyons, Tracy Layne, Jack Rockwell, Frankie Marvin, Cornelius Keefe, Martin Stevenson, Horace B. Carpenter, Helen Servis, Frances Morris, Richard Beach, Jeanne Lafayette, Art Mix, I. Stanford Jolley, Vic Lacardo, Sally Rand, The SMU 50, Sons of the Pioneers (Roy Rogers, Bob Nolan, Tim Spencer, Hugh and Karl Farr), The Light Crust Doughboys, The Beverly Hill Billies, The Jones Boys, "Champion"
D: Mack V. Wright
S/SP: Dorrell and Stuart McGowan
P: Nat Levine

680. THE COWBOY STAR
(Columbia, November 20, 1936) 56 Mins.
Charles Starrett, Iris Meredith, Si Jenks, Marc Lawrence, Edward Piel, Sr., Wally Albright, Ralph McCullough, Dick Terry, Landers Stevens, Wini-
fred Hari, Nick Copeland, Lew Meehan
D: David Selman
S: Frank Melford, Cornelius Reece
SP: Frances Guihan

681. SONG OF THE GRINGO
(Grand National, November, 22, 1936) 62 Mins.
Tex Ritter, Joan Woodbury, Fuzzy Knight, Monte Blue, Richard Adams, Warner Richmond, Martin Garralaga, Al Jennings, William Desmond, Glenn Strange, Budd Buster, Murdock McQuarrie, Ethan Laidlaw, Slim Whitaker, Edward Cassidy, Earl Dwire, Jack Kirk, Bob Burns, Forrest Taylor, Robert Fiske, "White Flash"
D: John P. McCarthy
S: John P. McCarthy, Robert Emmett (Tansey)
SP: J. P. McCarthy, Robert Emmett (Tansey), Al Jennings
P: Edward Finney

682. STAMPEDE
(Columbia, November 27, 1936) 58 Mins.
Charles Starrett, Finis Barton, J. P. McGowan, LeStrange Millman, James McGrath, Arthur Kerr, Jack Atkinson, Mike Heppell, Ted Mapes
D: Ford Beebe
S: Ford Beebe (credited to Peter B. Kyne)
SP: Robert Watson

683. THE PHANTOM OF THE RANGE
(Victory, November 28, 1936) 57 Mins.
Tom Tyler, Beth Marion, Sammy Cohen, Soledad Jiminez, Forrest Taylor, Charles King, John Elliott, Dick Cramer
D: Bob Hill
S/SP: Basil Dickey
P: Sam Katzman

684. THE UNKNOWN RANGER
(Columbia, December 1, 1936) 57 Mins.
Bob Allen, Martha Tibbets, Hal Taliaferro (Wally Wales), Harry Woods, Robert (Buzz) Henry, Edward Hearn
D: Spencer G. Bennet
SP: Nate Gatzert
P: Larry Darmour

685. ARIZONA MAHONEY
(Paramount, December 4, 1936) 58 Mins.
Larry "Buster" Crabbe, June Martel, Robert Cummings, Joe Cook, Marjorie Gateson, John Miljan, Dave Chasen, Irving Bacon, Richard Carlyle, Billie Lee, Fred Kohler, Fuzzy Knight, Si Jenks
D: James Hogan
S: "Stairs of Sand"—Zane Grey
SP: Robert Yost, Stuart Anthony

686. ROARIN' LEAD

(Republic, December 9, 1936)

(*Three Mesquiteers* Series)

Bob Livingston, Ray Corrigan, Max Terhune, Christine Maple, Hooper Atchley, Yakima Canutt, George Chesebro, Tommy Bupp, Grace Kern, Newt Kirby, George Plues, Harry Tenbrook, Pascale Perry, Beverly Luff, Kathryn Frye, Ted Frye, Lynn Kaufman, Baby Jane Keckley, The Meglin Kiddies

D: Mack V. Wright, Sam Newfield

SP: Oliver Drake, Jack Natteford. Based on characters created by William Colt MacDonald

P: Nat Levine

687. RIO GRANDE RANGER

(Columbia, December 11, 1936) 54 Mins.

Bob Allen, Iris Meredith, Hal Taliaferro (Wally Wales), Paul Sutton, Robert (Buzz) Henry, John Elliott, Tom London, Slim Whitaker, Jack Rockwell, Dick Botiller, Art Mix, Frank Ellis, Jack Ingram, Al Taylor, Jim Corey, Henry Hall, Jack C. Smith, Edward Cassidy, Ray Jones

D: Spencer G. Bennet

S: Jacques Jaccard, Ceila Jaccard

SP: Nate Gatzert

P: Larry Darmour

688. TRAIL DUST

(Paramount, December 19, 1936) 77 Mins.

(*Hopalong Cassidy* Series)

William Boyd, Jimmy Ellison, George Hayes, Gwynne Shipman, Stephen Morris (Morris Ankrum), Britt Wood, Dick Dickinson, Earl Askam, Al Bridge, John Beach, Ted Adams, Tom Halligan, Dan Wolheim, Al St. John, Harold Daniels, Kenneth Harlan, John Elliott, George Chesebro, Emmett Day, Robert Drew

D: Nate Watt

S: Clarence E. Mulford

SP: Al Martin

P: Harry Sherman

689. EMPTY SADDLES

(Universal, December 20, 1936) 67 Mins.

Buck Jones, Louise Brooks, Harvey Clark, Gertrude Astor, Frank Campeau, Niles Welch, Lloyd Ingraham, Charles Middleton, Claire Rochelle, Mary Mersh, Ruth Cherrington, Oliver Eckhart, Robert Adair, Charles LeMoyne, Ben Corbett, Buck Moulton, Earl Askam, William Lawrence, "Silver"

D: Lesley Selander

S: Cherry Wilson

SP: Frances Guihan

P: Buck Jones

690. HEADIN' FOR THE RIO GRANDE

(Grand National, December 20, 1936) 60 Mins.

Tex Ritter, Eleanor Stewart, Syd Saylor, Snub Pollard, Warner Richmond, Charles King, Earl Dwire, Forrest Taylor, William Desmond, Charles K. French, Bud Osborne, Budd Buster, Tex Palmer, Jack C. Smith, Sherry Tansey, James Mason, Bill Woods, "White Flash"

D: Robert N. Bradbury

S: Lindsley Parsons

SP: Robert Emmett (Tansey)

P: Edward Finney

691. THE OLD CORRAL

(Republic, December 21, 1936) 56 Mins.

Gene Autry, Smiley Burnette, Hope Manning, Cornelius Keefe, Sons of the Pioneers (Roy Rogers, Bob Nolan, Hugh Farr, Karl Farr, Tim Spencer), Lon Chaney, Jr., John Bradford, Milburn Morante, Abe Lefton, Merrill McCormack, Charles Sullivan, Buddy Roosevelt, Lynton Brent, Oscar and Elmer (Ed Platt and Lou Fulton), Jack Ingram, "Champion"

D: Joseph Kane

S: Bernard McConville

SP: Sherman Lowe, Joseph Poland

P: Nat Levine

692. GUNS AND GUITARS

(Republic, December 22, 1936) 56 Mins.

Gene Autry, Smiley Burnette, Dorothy Dix, Tom London, Charles King, J. P. McGowan, Earle Hodgins, Frankie Marvin, Eugene Jackson, Ken Cooper, Jack Rockwell, Harrison Greene, Pascale Perry, Bob Burns, Jack Don, Tracy Layne, Frank Stravenger, Jack Kirk, Audry Davis, Al Taylor, George Morrell, Sherry Tansey, Jack Evans, George Plues, Denver Dixon, Wes Warner, Jim Corey, "Champion"

D: Joseph Kane

S/SP: Dorrell and Stuart McGowan

P: Nat Levine

(June 22, 1936—corrected release date)

693. STORMY TRAILS

(Colony, December 23, 1936) 58 Mins.

Rex Bell, Bob Hodges, Lois Wilde, Lane Chandler, Earl Dwire, Karl Hackett, Earl Ross, Lloyd Ingraham, Murdock McQuarrie, Jimmy Aubrey, Roger Williams, Chuck Morrison, George Morrell

D: Sam Newfield

S: "Stampede"—E. B. Mann

P: Arthur and Max Alexander

694. THE PLAINSMAN

(Paramount, December 30, 1936) 115 Mins.

Gary Cooper, Jean Arthur, James Ellison, Charles

Bickford, Helen Burgess, Porter Hall, Paul Harvey, Victor Varconi, John Miljan, Frank Albertson, Frank McGlyn, Granville Bates, Purnell Pratt, Fred Kohler, George Hayes, Pat Moriarty, Charles Judels, Harry Woods, Fuzzy Knight, Anthony Quinn, Francis J. McDonald, George Ernest, George MacQuarrie, Edgar Dearing, Edwin Maxwell, Bruce Warren
D/P: Cecil B. DeMille
S: Based on book by Frank J. Wilstach
SP: Waldemar Young, Harold Lamb, Lynn Riggs

695. DODGE CITY TRAIL
(Columbia, December, 1936) 7 Reels
Charles Starrett, Donald Grayson, Marion Weldon, Russell Hicks, Si Jenks, Al Bridge, Art Mix, Ernie Adams, Lew Meehan, Hank Bell, Jack Rockwell, George Chesebro, Blackie Whiteford
D: C. C. Coleman, Jr.
SP: Harold Shumate
Adaptation: William E. Mull

696. CUSTER'S LAST STAND
(Stage and Screen, 1936) 15 Chaps.
Rex Lease, Jack Mulhall, William Farnum, Ruth Mix, Lona Andre, Reed Howes, Bobby Nelson, Dorothy Gulliver, Frank McGlynn, Jr., Helen Gibson, William Desmond, Nancy Caswell, Chief Thunder Cloud, Josef Swickard, Creighton Hale, Marty Joyce, George Chesebro, Milburn Morante, Ted Adams, George Morrell, Howling Wolf, Robert Walker, Walter James, Cactus Mack, Budd Buster, Carl Mathews, Art Ortego, Franklyn Farnum, Lafe McKee, Mabel Strickland, Allen Greer, Barney Fury, James Sheridan, Chick Davis, Ken Cooper, Big Tree, Iron Eyes Cody, Patter Poe, High Eagle, Carter Wayne, Ed Withrow
D: Elmer Clifton
SP: George A. Durlam, Eddy Graneman, Bob (William?) Lively
P: George M. Merrick
Chapter Titles: (1) Perils of the Plains, (2) Thundering Hoofs, (3) Fires of Vengeance, (4) The Ghost Dancers, (5) Trapped, (6) Human Wolves, (7) Demons of Disaster, (8) White Treachery, (9) Circle of Death, (10) Flaming Arrow, (11) Warpath, (12) Firing Squad, (13) Red Panthers, (14) Custer's Last Ride, (15) The Last Stand

697. GUN GRIT
(Atlantic, 1936) 5 Reels
Jack Perrin, Ethel Beck, David Sharpe, Roger Williams, Ralph Peters, Frank Hagney, Jimmy Aubrey, Edward Cassidy, Phil Dunham, Oscar Gahan, Earl Dwire, Horace Murphy, Baby Lester, Budd Buster, "Starlight," "Braveheart" (a dog)
D: Lester Williams (William Berke)
S: Allen Hall, Gordon Phillips
P: William Berke

698. HAIR-TRIGGER CASEY
(Atlantic, 1936) 59 Mins.
Jack Perrin, Betty Mack, Wally Wales, Fred Toones, Phil Dunham, Edward Cassidy, Robert Walker, Dennis Meadows (Moore), Vi Wong, "Starlight"
D: Harry Fraser
S/SP: Monroe Talbot
P: William Berke

699. RIDDLE RANCH
(Beaumont, 1936) 63 Mins.
David Worth, June Marlowe, Baby Charlene Barry, Julian Rivero, Richard Cramer, Snowflake (Fred Toones), Budd Buster, Arturo Feliz (Art Felix), Henry Sylvester, Ray Gallagher, "Black King" (the Horse with the Human Brain)
D: Charles Hutchison
S/SP: L. V. Jefferson
P: Mitchell Leichter

700. DESERT JUSTICE
(Atlantic, 1936) 58 Mins.
Jack Perrin, David Sharpe, Warren Hymer, Budd Buster, Dennis Meadows (Moore), Maryan Downing, Roger Williams, William Gould, Fred Toones, Earl Dwire, "Starlight," "Braveheart" (a dog)
D: Lester Williams (William Berke)
S: Allan Hall
SP: Gordon Phillips, Lewis Kingdom
P: William Berke

701. SENOR JIM
(Beaumont, 1936)
Conway Tearle, Barbara Bedford, Alberta Dugan, Fred Malatesta, Betty Mack, Bob McKenzie, Dirk Thane, Evelyn Hagara, Harrison Greene, Lloyd Brooks, Ashton and Co'ena
D: Jacques Jaccard
S/SP: "I.O.U.'s of Death"—Ceila Jaccard
P: Sam Efrus

702. SUNDOWN SAUNDERS
(Supreme/William Steiner, 1936) 59 Mins.
Bob Steele, Catherine Cotter, Earl Dwire, Milburn Morante, Ed Cassidy, Jack Rockwell, Frank Ball, Hal Price, Charles King, Horace Murphy, Edmund Cobb, Bob McKenzie, Jack Kirk, Herman Hack
D/S/SP: Robert N. Bradbury
P: A. W. Hackel

703. WILDCAT SAUNDERS

(Atlantic, 1936) 60 Mins.

Jack Perrin, Blanche Mehaffey, William Gould, Fred Toones, Roger Williams, Tom London, Edward Cassidy, Bud Osborne, Jim Corey, Earl Dwire, Dennis Moore

D: Harry Fraser

S: Miller Easton

SP: Monroe Talbot

P: William Berke

FILMS OF 1937

704. CHEYENNE RIDES AGAIN

(Victory, January 1, 1937) 56 Mins.

Tom Tyler, Lucile Browne, Creighton Chaney (Lon Chaney, Jr.), Roger Williams, Carmen LaRoux, Ed Cassidy, Ted Lorch, Bud Pope, Francis Walker, Slim Whitaker, Merrill McCormack, Wilbur McCauley

D: Robert Hill

SP: Basil Dickey

P: Sam Katzman

705. PHANTOM OF SANTA FE

(Burroughs-Tarzan Pictures, January 1, 1937) 75 Mins.

(Color)

Norman Kerry, Nena Quartero, Frank Mayo, Monte Montague, Tom O'Brien, Carmelita Geraghty, Jack Mower, Frank Ellis, Merrill McCormack

D: Jacques Jaccard

Adaptation: Charles Royal

(Originally produced in 1931)

706. GUNS OF THE PECOS

(Warner Bros.-First National, January 2, 1937) 65 Mins.

Dick Foran, Anne Nagel, Gordon (Bill) Elliott, Gordon Hart, Joseph Crehan, Eddie Acuff, Robert Middlemass, Gaby Fay (Fay Holden), Monte Montague, Milt Kibbee, Bud Osborne, Cliff Saum, Henry Othro, Bob Burns, Douglas Wood, Glenn Strange, Gene Alsace, Bob Woodward, Frank McCarroll, Jack Kirk, Ray Jones

D: Noel Smith

S: Anthony Coldeway

SP: Harold Buckley

P: Bryan Foy

707. BATTLE OF GREED

(Crescent, January 4, 1937) 65 Mins.

Tom Keene, Gwynne Shipman, James Bush, Budd Buster, Jimmy Butler, Robert Fiske, Carl Stockdale, Ray Bennett, William Worthington, Henry Rocquemore, Bobby Brown, Lloyd Ingraham

D: Harold Higgin

SP: John T. Neville

P: E. B. Derr

708. RIDERS OF THE WHISTLING SKULL

(Republic, January 4, 1937) 55 Mins.

(*Three Mesquiteers* Series)

Robert Livingston, Ray Corrigan, Max Terhune, Mary Russell, Yakima Canutt, Roger Williams, Fern Emmett, C. Montague Shaw, John Ward, George Godfrey, Frank Ellis, Earle Ross, Chief Thunder Cloud, John Van Pelt, Edward Piel, Jack Kirk, Iron Eyes Cody, Tom Steele, Wally West, Tracy Layne, Eddie Bowland, Ken Cooper

D: Mack V. Wright

S: William Colt MacDonald

SP: Oliver Drake, John Rathmell, Bernard McConville

P: Nat Levine

709. RANGER COURAGE

(Columbia, January 10, 1937) 58 Mins.

Bob Allen, Martha Tibbetts, Walter Miller, Buzz Henry, Bud Osborne, Bob Kortman, Harry Strang, William Gould, Horace Murphy, Franklyn Farnum, Jay Wilsey, Gene Alsace

D: Spencer G. Bennet

SP: Nate Gatzert

P: Larry Darmour

710. SECRET VALLEY

(Principal/20th C. Fox, January 15, 1937) 60 Mins.

Richard Arlen, Virginia Grey, Jack Mulhall, Norman Willis, Syd Saylor, Russell Hicks, Willie Fung, Maude Allen

D: Howard Bretherton

S: Harold Bell Wright

SP: Paul Franklin, Dan Jarrett, Earle Snell

P: Sol Lesser

711. THE SINGING BUCKAROO

(Spectrum, January 15, 1937) 50 Mins.

Fred Scott, William Faversham, Victoria Vinton, Cliff Nazarro, Howard Hill, Charles Kaley, Roger Williams, Dick Curtis, Lawrence LeBaron, Rosa Caprino, Pinky Barnes, Carl Mathews, Slim Carey, Augie Gomez, The Singing Buckaroos, "White King"

D/SP: Tom Gibson

P: Jed Buell, George H. Callaghan

712. GOD'S COUNTRY AND THE WOMAN

(Warner Bros., January 16, 1937)   85 Mins.
(Technicolor)

George Brent, Beverly Roberts, Barton MacLane, Robert Barrat, Alan Hale, Joseph King, El Brendel, Joseph Crehan, Addison Richards, Roscoe Ates, Billy Bevan, Vic Potel, Bert Roach, Mary Treen, Herbert Rawlinson, Harry Hayden, Pat Moriarty, Max Wagner, Susan Fleming

D: William Keighley

S: Peter Milne, Charles Belden (from James Oliver Curwood)

SP: Norman Reilly Raine

713. VALLEY OF TERROR

(Ambassador, January 20, 1937)   58 Mins.

Kermit Maynard, Harley Wood, John Merton, Jack Ingram, Dick Curtis, Roger Williams, Frank McCarroll, Hank Bell, Hal Price, Slim Whitaker, Jack Casey, George Morrell, Blackie Whiteford, Herman Hack, "Rocky"

D: Al Herman

S: James Oliver Curwood

P: Maurice Conn

714. WESTBOUND MAIL

(Columbia, January 22, 1937)   54 Mins.

Charles Starrett, Rosalind Keith, Edward Keane, Arthur Stone, Ben Weldon, Al Bridge, George Chesebro, Art Mix

D: Folmer Blangsted

S: James P. Hogan

SP: Frances Guihan

715. ARIZONA DAYS

(Grand National, January 30, 1937)   57 Mins.

Tex Ritter, Eleanor Stewart, Syd Saylor, William Faversham, Ethlind Terry, Forrest Taylor, Snub Pollard, Glenn Strange, Horace Murphy, Earl Dwire, Budd Buster, Salty Holmes, William Desmond, Tommy Bupp, Tex Palmer, "White Flash"

D: John English

S: Lindsley Parsons

SP: Sherman Lowe

P: Edward Finney

716. THE GUN RANGER

(Republic, February 9, 1937)   56 Mins.

Bob Steele, Eleanor Stewart, John Merton, Ernie Adams, Earl Dwire, Budd Buster, Frank Ball, Horace Murphy, Lew Meehan, Hal Taliaferro (Wally Wales), Horace B. Carpenter, Jack Kirk, George Morrell, Tex Palmer

D: R. N. Bradbury

S: Homer Gordon

SP: George Plympton

P: A. W. Hackel

Guns of the Pecos (Warner Bros.-First National, 1937) — Anne Nagel and Dick Foran

717. SANDFLOW

(Universal, February 14, 1937) 58 Mins.

Buck Jones, Lita Chevret, Bob Kortman, Arthur Aylesworth, Robert Terry, Enrique DeRosas, Josef Swickard, Lee Phelps, Harold Hodge, Tom Chatterton, Arthur Van Slyke, Malcolm Graham, Ben Corbett, "Silver"

D: Lesley Selander

S: Carey Wilson

SP: Frances Guihan

P: Buck Jones

718. THE GAMBLING TERROR

(Republic, February 15, 1937) 53 Mins.

Johnny Mack Brown, Iris Meredith, Charles King, Horace Murphy, Dick Curtis, Budd Buster, Ted Adams, Earl Dwire, Bobby Nelson, Frank Ellis, Lloyd Ingraham, Emma Tansey, Frank Ball, Sherry Tansey, Steve Clark, George Morrell, Art Dillard, Tex Palmer, Jack Montgomery

D: Sam Newfield

SP: George Plympton, Fred Myton

P: A. W. Hackel

719. SANTA FE RIDES

(Reliable/William Steiner, February 25, 1937) 58 Mins.

Bob Custer, Eleanor Stewart, Dave Sharpe, Lafe McKee, Snub Pollard, Nelson McDowell, Oscar Gahan, John Elliott, Roger Williams, Slim Whitaker, Ed Cassidy, The Singing Cowboys (Lloyd Perryman, Rudy Sooter, and Curley Hoag)

D: Raymond Samuels (B. B. Ray)

S: Tom Gibson

SP: Pliny Goodfriend

P: Bernard B. Ray

720. BORDERLAND

(Paramount, February 26, 1937) 82 Mins.

(*Hopalong Cassidy* Series)

William Boyd, Jimmy Ellison, George Hayes, Stephen Morris (Morris Ankrum), John Beach, George Chesebro, Nora Lane, Charlene Wyatt, Trevor Bardette, Earle Hodgins, Al Bridge, John St. Polis, Edward Cassidy, Slim Whitaker, Cliff Parkinson, Karl Hackett, Robert Walker, Frank Ellis

D: Nate Watt

S: "Bring Me His Ears"—Clarence E. Mulford

SP: Harrison Jacobs

P: Harry Sherman

721. THE SILVER TRAIL

(Reliable/William Steiner, February 27, 1937) 58 Mins.

Rex Lease, Mary Russell, Ed Cassidy, Roger Williams, Steve Clark, Slim Whitaker, Oscar Gahan,

Sherry Tansey, Tom London, Rin-Tin-Tin, Jr.

D: Raymond Samuels (B. B. Ray)

S: James Oliver Curwood

P: B. B. Ray

722. THE FEUD OF THE TRAIL

(Victory, March 1, 1937) 56 Mins.

Tom Tyler, Harlene Wood, Milburn Morante, Roger Williams, Lafe McKee, Jim Corey, Dick Alexander, Roger Williams, Vane Calvert, Slim Whitaker, Colin Chase, Francis Walker

D: Robert Hill

SP: Basil Dickey

P: Sam Katzman

723. OLD LOUISIANA

(Crescent, March 1, 1937) 64 Mins.

Tom Keene, Rita Cansino (Hayworth), Robert Fiske, Ray Bennett, Budd Buster, Allan Cavan, Will Morgan, Carlos de Valdez, Iron Eyes Cody

D: I. V. Willat

S: John T. Neville

SP: Mary Ireland

P: E. B. Derr

724. HIT THE SADDLE

(Republic, March 3, 1937) 57 Mins.

(*Three Mesquiteers* Series)

Robert Livingston, Ray Corrigan, Max Terhune, Rita Cansino (Hayworth), J. P. McGowan, Ed Cassidy, Yakima Canutt, Sammy McKim, Ed Bowland, Jack Kirk, Harry Tenbrook, George Plues, Robert Smith, Bob Burns, Russ Powell, Allan Cavan, George Morrell, Budd Buster, Kernan Cripps

D: Mack Wright

S: Oliver Drake, Maurice Geraghty

SP: Oliver Drake

P: Nat Levine

725. TRAPPED

(Columbia, March 5, 1937) 55 Mins.

Charles Starrett, Peggy Stratford, Robert Middlemass, Alan Sears, Ted Oliver, Lew Meehan, Ed Piel, Jack Rockwell, Edward J. LeSaint, Frances Sayles, Art Mix

D: Leon Barsha

S: Claude Rister

SP: John Rathmell

726. TROUBLE IN TEXAS

(Grand National, March 6, 1937) 53 Mins.

Tex Ritter, Rita Cansino (Hayworth), Earl Dwire, Yakima Canutt, Dick Palmer, Hal Price, Fred Parker, Charles King, Milburn Morante, Horace Murphy, Tex Cooper, Jack C. Smith, Shorty Miller, George Morrell, Rudy Sooter, Chick Hannon,

Oral Zumalt, Bob Crosby, Foxy Callahan, Harry Knight, Tex Sherman, Glenn Strange, The Texas Tornados, "White Flash"
D: R. N. Bradbury
SP: Robert Emmett (Tansey)
P: Edward Finney

727. LAND BEYOND THE LAW
(Warner Bros., March 13, 1937)   54 Mins.
Dick Foran, Linda Perry, Wayne Morris, Irene Franklin, Gordon Hart, Joseph King, Cy Kendall, Frank Orth, Glenn Strange, Harry Woods, Milton Kibbee, Edmund Cobb, Henry Otho, Tom Brower, Paul Panzer, Julian Rivero, Artie Ortego, Jim Corey, Bud Osborne, Wilfred Lucas, Gene Alsace, Frank McCarroll
D: B. Reeves Eason
S: Marion Jackson
SP: Luci Ward, Joseph K. Watson
P: Bryan Foy

728. PARK AVENUE LOGGER
(RKO, March 16, 1937)   67 Mins.
George O'Brien, Beatrice Roberts, Willard Robertson, Ward Bond, Bert Hanlon, Gertrude Short, Lloyd Ingraham, George Rosenor, Robert E. O'Connor, Al Baffert, Dave Wengren
D: David Howard
S: From the *Saturday Evening Post* story by Bruce Hutchinson
SP: Dan Jarrett, Ewing Scott
P: George A. Hirliman

729. LIGHTNIN' CRANDALL
(Republic, March 24, 1937)   60 Mins.
Bob Steele, Lois January, Dave O'Brien, Horace Murphy, Charles King, Ernie Adams, Earl Dwire, Frank LaRue, Lloyd Ingraham, Lew Meehan, Dick Cramer, Jack C. Smith, Sherry Tansey, Tex Palmer, Ed Carey, Art Felix
D: Sam Newfield
S: E. B. Mann
SP: Charles Francis Royal
P: A. W. Hackel

730. GIT ALONG LITTLE DOGIES
(Republic, March 27, 1937)   60 Mins.
Gene Autry, Smiley Burnette, Judith Allen, Weldon Heyburn, Maple City Four, William Farnum, Willie Fung, Carleton Young, Will and Gladys Ahern, The Cabin Kids, G. Raymond Nye, Frankie Marvin, George Morrell, Horace B. Carpenter, Rose Plummer, Earl Dwire, Lynton Brent, Jack Kirk, Al Taylor, Frank Ellis, Jack C. Smith, Murdock McQuarrie, Oscar Gahan, Monte Montague, Sam

McDaniel, Eddie Parker, Bob Burns, "Champion"
D: Joseph Kane
SP: Dorrell and Stuart McGowan
P: Joseph Kane

731. TRAIL OF VENGEANCE
(Republic, March 29, 1937)   58 Mins.
Johnny Mack Brown, Iris Meredith, Warner Richmond, Karl Hackett, Earle Hodgins, Frank LaRue, Frank Ellis, Lew Meehan, Frank Ball, Dick Curtis, Jim Corey, Horace Murphy, Dick Cramer, Steve Clark, Budd Buster, Jack C. Smith, Jack Kirk, Francis Walker, Tex Palmer
D: Sam Newfield
SP: George Plympton, Fred Myton
S: E. B. Mann
P: A. W. Hackel

732. HITTIN' THE TRAIL
(Grand National, April 3, 1937)   58 Mins.
Tex Ritter, Jerry Bergh, Tommy Bupp, Earl Dwire, Jack C. Smith, Snub Pollard, Archie Ricks, Heber Snow (Hank Worden), Charles King, Edward Cassidy, Ray Whitley and the Range Ramblers (The Phelps Brothers, Ken Card), "White Flash"
D: R. N. Bradbury
SP: Robert Emmett (Tansey)
P: Edward Finney

733. LAWLESS LAND
(Republic, April 6, 1937)   55 Mins.
Johnny Mack Brown, Louise Stanley, Horace Murphy, Ted Adams, Julian Rivero, Frank Ball, Ed Cassidy, Anita Camargo, Roger Williams, Frances Kellogg, Chiquta Hernandez Orchestra
D: Albert Ray
SP: Andrew Bennison
P: A. W. Hackel

734. TWO GUN LAW
(Columbia, April 7, 1937)   56 Mins.
Charles Starrett, Peggy Stratford, Hank Bell, Edward J. LeSaint, Charles Middleton, Alan Bridge, Lee Prather, Dick Curtis, Vic Potel, George Chesebro, Art Mix, George Morrell, Tex Cooper
D: Leon Barsha
S: Norman Sheldon
SP: John Rathmell

735. WAY OUT WEST
(MGM, April 9. 1937)   65 Mins.
Stan Laurel, Oliver Hardy, Sharon Lynne, James Finlayson, Rosina Lawrence, Stanley Fields, Vivien Oakland, Chill Wills and the Avalon Boys
D: James W. Horne
SP: Jack Jevne, Charles Rogers, James Parrott, Felix Adler

Hittin' the Trail (Grand National, 1937) — Edward Cassidy, Tex Ritter, and Heber Snow (Hank Worden)

Trouble in Texas (Grand National, 1937) — Yakima Canutt, Rita Cansino (Hayworth), and Tex Ritter

736. UNDER STRANGE FLAGS
(Crescent, April 12, 1937)   64 Mins.
Tom Keene, Luana Walters, Budd Buster, Maurice Black, Roy D'Arcy, Paul Sutton, Paul Barrett, Donald Reed, James Wolfe
D: I. V. Willat
S: John Auer
SP: Mary Ireland
P: E. B. Derr

737. MELODY OF THE PLAINS
(Spectrum, April 15,1937)   55 Mins.
Fred Scott, Louise Small, Al St. John, David Sharpe, Lafe McKee, Bud Jamison, Slim Whitaker, Hal Price, Lew Meehan, Carl Mathews, "White King," Billy Lenhart, George Morrell, George Fiske
D: Sam Newfield
SP: Bennett Cohen
P: Ray Callaghan, Jed Buell

738. HILLS OF OLD WYOMING
(Paramount, April 16, 1937)   75 Mins.
(*Hopalong Cassidy* Series)
William Boyd, George Hayes, Stephen Morris (Morris Ankrum), Russell Hayden, Gail Sheridan, Clara Kimball Young, John Beach, Earle Hodgins, George Chesebro, Steve Clemente, Paul Gustine, Leo McMahon, John Powers, James Mason, Chief John Big Tree
D: Nate Watt
S: "The Roundup"—Clarence E. Mulford
SP: Maurice Geraghty
P: Harry Sherman

739. THE OUTCASTS OF POKER FLAT
(RKO, April 16, 1937)   68 Mins.
Preston Foster, Jean Muir, Van Heflin, Virginia Weidler, Margaret Irving, Barbara Pepper, Si Jenks, Frank M. Thomas, Bradley Page, Monte Blue
D: Christy Cabanne
S: Bret Harte
P: Robert Sisk

740. LEFT HANDED LAW
(Universal, April 18, 1937)   63 Mins.
Buck Jones, Noel Francis, Frank LaRue, Lee Phelps, Matty Fain, George Regas, Robert Frazer, Lee Shumway, Nena Quartero, "Silver," Charles LeMoyne, Budd Buster, Frank Lackteen, Jim Toney, Bill Wolfe, Silver Tip Baker, Jack Evans, Jim Corey
D: Lesley Selander
S: Charles M. Martin
SP: Frances Guihan
P: Buck Jones

741. BAR Z BAD MEN
(Republic, April 22, 1937)   57 Mins.
Johnny Mack Brown, Lois January, Tom London, Ernie Adams, Dick Curtis, Jack Rockwell, Milburn Morante, Horace Murphy, Budd Buster, Frank Ball, George Morrell, Tex Palmer, Horace B. Carpenter, Art Dillard, Oscar Gahan
D: Sam Newfield
S: James P. Olson
SP: George Plympton
P: A. W. Hackel

742. ROUND-UP TIME IN TEXAS
(Republic, April 22, 1937)   58 Mins.
Gene Autry, Smiley Burnette, Maxine Doyle, The Cabin Kids, LeRoy Mason, Earle Hodgins, Buddy Williams, Dick Wessell, Cornie Anderson, Frankie Marvin, Ken Cooper, Elmer Fain, Al Ferguson, Slim Whitaker, Al Knight, Carleton Young, Jack C. Smith, Jim Corey, Jack Kirk, George Morrell
D: Joseph Kane
SP: Oliver Drake
P: Armand Schaefer

743. MYSTERY RANGE
(Victory, May 1, 1937)   56 Mins.
Tom Tyler, Jerry Bergh, Milburn Morante, Lafe McKee, Roger Williams, Dick Alexander, Jim Corey, Slim Whitaker
D: Bob Hill
SP: Basil Dickey
P: Sam Katzman

744. WHISTLING BULLETS
(Ambassador, May 3, 1937)   57 Mins.
Kermit Maynard, Harlene (Harley) Wood, Jack Ingram, Maston Williams, Bruce Mitchell, Karl Hackett, Sherry Tansey, Cliff Parkinson, Cherokee Alcorn
D: John English
S: James Oliver Curwood
SP: Joseph O'Donnell
P: Maurice Conn

745. THE TRUSTED OUTLAW
(Republic, May 4, 1937)   57 Mins.
Bob Steele, Lois January, Joan Barclay, Earl Dwire, Charles King, Dick Cramer, Hal Price, Budd Buster, Frank Ball, Oscar Gahan, George Morrell, Chick Hannon, Sherry Tansey, Clyde McClary
D: R. N. Bradbury
S: Johnston McCaulley
SP: George Plympton, Fred Myton
P: A. W. Hackel

746. CHEROKEE STRIP
(Warner Bros., May 5, 1937)   55 Mins.

Dick Foran, Jane Bryan, David Carlyle, Helen Valkis, Edmund Cobb, Gordon Hart, Joseph Crehan, Frank Faylen, Milton Kibbee, Jack Mower, Tom Brower, Walter Soderling, Tommy Bupp, Glenn Strange, Bud Osborne, Ben Corbett, Artie Ortego, Jack Kirk
D: Noel Smith
S: Ed Earl Repp
SP: Joseph K. Watson, Luci Ward
P: Bryan Foy

747. GUNSMOKE RANCH
(Republic, May 5, 1937)   56 Mins.
(*Three Mesquiteers* Series)
Robert Livingston, Ray Corrigan, Max Terhune, Kenneth Harlan, Julia Thayer (Jean Carmen), Sammy McKim, Oscar and Elmer (Lou Fulton and Ed Platt), Yakima Canutt, Burr Caruth, Allen Connor, Horace B. Carpenter, Jane Keckley, Robert Walker, Jack Ingram, Jack Kirk, Loren Riebe, Vinegar Roan, Wes Warner, Jack Padjan, Fred Toones, John Merton, Bob McKenzie, Edward Piel, Sr., Fred Burns
D: Joseph Kane
S: Oliver Drake, Jack Natteford
SP: Oliver Drake
P: Sol C. Siegel

748. IT HAPPENED OUT WEST
(20th C. Fox, May 7, 1937)   56 Mins.
Paul Kelly, Judith Allen, Johnny Arthur, LeRoy Mason, Reginald Barlow, Steve Clemente
D: Howard Bretherton
S: Harold Bell Wright
SP: Dan Jarrett
P: Sol Lesser

749. THE LAW COMMANDS
(Crescent, May 7, 1937)
Tom Keene, Lorraine Hayes (Laraine Day), Budd Buster, Mathew Betz, Robert Fiske, John Merton, Carl Stockdale, David Sharpe, Marie Stoddard, Horace B. Carpenter, Fred Burns
D: William Nigh
S/SP: Bennett Cohen
P: E. B. Derr

750. LAW OF THE RANGER
(Columbia, May 11, 1937)   57 Mins.
Bob Allen, Elaine Shepard, Hal Taliaferro, Lafe McKee, John Merton, Tom London, Lane Chandler, Slim Whitaker, Ernie Adams, Bud Osborne, Jimmy Aubrey
D: Spencer G. Bennet
S: Jesse Duffy, Joseph Levering
SP: Nate Gatzert
P: Larry Darmour

751. ROOTIN' TOOTIN' RHYTHM
(Republic, May 12, 1937)   60 Mins.
Gene Autry, Smiley Burnette, Armida, Monte Blue, Ann Pendleton, Hal Taliaferro, Charles King, Max Hoffman, Jr., Frankie Marvin, Nina Campana, Charles Mayer, Karl Hackett, Al Clauser and his Oklahoma Outlaws, Jack Rutherford, "Champion," Henry Hall, Curley Dresden, Art Davis
D: Mack Wright
S: Johnston McCulley
SP: Jack Natteford
P; Armand Schaefer

752. GUNS IN THE DARK
(Republic, May 13, 1937)   56 Mins.
Johnny Mack Brown, Claire Rochelle, Dick Curtis, Julian Madison, Ted Adams, Sherry Tansey, Slim Whitaker, Lew Meehan, Tex Palmer, Francis Walker, Frank Ellis, Budd Buster, Oscar Gahan, Merrill McCormack, Dick Cramer, Steve Clark, Syd Saylor, Jack C. Smith, Roger Williams, Jim Corey, Chick Hannon
D: Sam Newfield
S: E. B. Mann
SP: Charles Francis Royal
P: A. W. Hackel

753. BACK TO THE WOODS
(Columbia, May 14, 1937)   2 Reels
(*Three Stooges* Series)
Moe Howard, Curley Howard, Larry Fine, Bud Jamison, Vernon Dent
D: Preston Black
S: Searle Kramer
SP: Andrew Bennison

754. GUN LORDS OF STIRRUP BASIN
(Republic, May 18, 1937)   53 Mins.
Bob Steele, Louise Stanley, Karl Hackett, Ernie Adams, Frank LaRue, Frank Ball, Steve Clark, Lew Meehan, Frank Ellis, Jim Corey, Budd Buster, Lloyd Ingraham, Jack Kirk, Horace Murphy, Milburn Morante, Bobby Nelson, Tex Palmer, Emma Tansey, Horace B. Carpenter, Herman Hack
D: Sam Newfield
S: Harry Olmstead
SP: George Plympton, Fred Myton
P: A. W. Hackel

755. SING, COWBOY, SING
(Grand National, May 22, 1937)   59 Mins.
Tex Ritter, Louise Stanley, Al St. John, Karl Hackett, Charles King, Bob McKenzie, Budd Buster, Henry Snow (Hank Worden), Chick Hannon, Horace Murphy, Snub Pollard, Tex Palmer, Jack C. Smith, Oscar Gahan, Herman Hack
D: R. N. Bradbury

SP: Robert Emmett
P: Edward Finney

756. COME ON, COWBOYS
(Republic, May 24, 1937) 59 Mins.
(*Three Mesquiteers* Series)
Bob Livingston, Ray Corrigan, Max Terhune, Maxine Doyle, Willie Fung, Edward Piel, Sr., Horace Murphy, Ann Bennett, Ed Cassidy, Roger Williams, Fern Emmett, Yakima Canutt, George Burton, Merrill McCormack, Loren Riebe, Victor Allen, Al Taylor, George Plues, Milburn Morante, Carleton Young, George Morrell, Ernie Adams, Jim Corey, Jack Kirk
D: Joseph Kane
SP: Betty Burbridge
P: Sol C. Siegel

757. HOLLYWOOD COWBOY
(RKO, May 28, 1937) 64 Mins.
(Reissued as *Wings over Wyoming*)
George O'Brien, Cecilia Parker, Maude Eburne, Joe Caits, Frank Milan, Charles Middleton, Lee Shumway, Walter DePalma, William Royle, Al Hill, Frank Hagney, Al Herman, Dan Wolheim, Slim Balch, Sid Jordan, Lester Dorr, Harold Daniels
D: Ewing Scott
SP: Dan Jarrett, Ewing Scott
P: George A. Hirliman

758. RECKLESS RANGER
(Columbia, May 30, 1937) 56 Mins.
Bob Allen, Louise Small, Jack Perrin, Harry Woods, Mary MacLaren, Buddy Cox, Jack Rockwell, Jay Wilsey, Slim Whitaker, Roger Williams, Bud Osborne, Jim Corey, Tom London, Hal Price, Al Taylor, Tex Cooper, Bob McKenzie, Lane Chandler, Frank Ball, George Plues, Lafe McKee, Tex Palmer, Victor Cox, Chick Hannon
D: Spencer G. Bennet
S: Joseph Levering, Jesse Duffy
SP: Nate Gatzert
P: Larry Darmour

759. BORDER CAFE
(RKO, June 4, 1937) 69 Mins.
Harry Carey, John Beal, Armida, Walter Miller, Marjorie Lord, George Irving, Leona Roberts, J. Carrol Naish, Lee Patrick, Paul Fix, Max Wagner, Alec Craig, Dudley Clements
D: Lew Landers
S: "In the Mexican Quarter"—Thomas Gill
SP: Lionel Houser
P: Robert Sisk

760. ORPHAN OF THE PECOS
(Victory, June 5, 1937) 55 Mins.
Tom Tyler, Jeanne Martel, Lafe McKee, Forrest Taylor, Ted Lorch, Slim Whitaker, John Elliott
D: Sam Katzman
SP: Basil Dickey
P: Sam Katzman

761. THE PAINTED STALLION
(Republic, June 5, 1937) 12 Chaps.
Ray Corrigan, Hoot Gibson, LeRoy Mason, Duncan Renaldo, Sammy McKim, Hal Taliaferro, Jack Perrin, Ed Platt, Lou Fulton, Julia Thayer, Yakima Canutt, Maston Williams, Duke Taylor, Loren Riebe, George DeNormand, Gordon DeMain, Charles King, Vinegar Roan, Lafe McKee, Frank Leyva, Frankie Marvin, John Big Tree, Pascale Perry, Don Orlando, Henry Hale, Edward Piel, Sr., Horace Carpenter, Lee White, Joe Yrigoyen, Paul Lopez, Monte Montague, Gregg Star Whitespear, Ralph Bucko, Roy Bucko, Leo Dupee, Babe DeFreest, Jose Dominguez, Jack Padjan, Al Haskell, Augie Gomez
D: William Witney, Alan James, Ray Taylor
SP: Barry Shipman, Winston Miller
AP: J. Laurence Wickland
Chapter Titles: (1) Trail to Empire, (2) The Rider of the Stallion, (3) The Death Trap, (4) Avalanche, (5) Valley of Death, (6) Thundering Wheels, (7) Trail Treachery, (8) The Whispering Arrow, (9) The Fatal Message, (10) Ambush, (11) Tunnel of Terror, (12) Human Targets

762. SMOKE TREE RANGE
(Universal, June 6, 1937) 59 Mins.
Buck Jones, Muriel Evans, John Elliott, Edmund Cobb, Ben Hall, Ted Adams, Donald Kirke, Dickie Jones, Lee Phelps, Charles King, Earle Hodgins, Mable Concord, Bob Kortman, Eddie Phillips, Bob McKenzie, Slim Whitaker, "Silver"
D: Lesley Selander
S: Arthur Henry Gordon
P: Buck Jones

763. BORDER PHANTOM
(Republic, June 7, 1937) 58 Mins.
Bob Steele, Harley Wood, Don Barclay, Karl Hackett, Perry Murdock, Frank Ball, Hans Joby, Miki Morita
D: S. Roy Luby
SP: Fred Myton
P: A. W. Hackel

764. BLAZING SIXES
(Warner Bros., June 12, 1937) 55 Mins.
Dick Foran, Helen Valkis, Myra McKinney, John Merton, Glenn Strange, Kenneth Harlan, Henry

Otho, Wilfred Lucas, Milt Kibbee, Gordon Hart, Bud Osborne, Ben Corbett, Artie Ortego, Jack Mower, Gene Alsace (Rocky Camron), Frank Ellis, Cactus Mack
D: Noel Smith
S: "Miracle Mountain"—Anthony Coldeway
SP: John T. Neville
P: Bryan Foy

765. DRUMS OF DESTINY
(Crescent, June 12, 1937) 60 Mins.
Tom Keene, Edna Lawrence, Budd Buster, Rafael Bennett, Robert Fiske, Carlos de Valdez, Dave Sharpe, John Merton, Chief Flying Cloud
D: Ray Taylor
S: Roger Whatley
SP: John T. Neville, Roger Whatley
P: E. B. Derr

766. YODELIN' KID FROM PINE RIDGE
(Republic, June 14, 1937) 60 Mins.
Gene Autry, Smiley Burnette, Betty Bronson, The Tennessee Ramblers (Dick Hartman, W. J. Blair, Elmer Warren, Happy Morris, and Pappy Wolf), LeRoy Mason, Charles Middleton, Russell Simpson, Jack Dougherty, Guy Wilkerson, Frankie Marvin, Henry Hall, Fred Toones, Jack Kirk, Bob Burns, Al Taylor, George Morrell, Lew Meehan, Jim Corey, Jack Ingram, Art Dillard, Art Mix, Bud Osborne, Oscar Gahan, "Champion"
D: Joseph Kane
S: Jack Natteford
SP: Dorrell and Stuart McGowan, Jack Natteford
P: Armand Schaefer

767. TWO-FISTED SHERIFF
(Columbia, June 15, 1937) 60 Mins.
Charles Starrett, Barbara Weeks, Bruce Lane, Ed Piel, Alan Sears, Walter Downing, Ernie Adams, Claire McDowell, Frank Ellis, Robert Walker, George Chesebro, Art Mix, Al Bridge, Dick Botiller, George Morrell, Merrill McCormack, Edmund Cobb, Tex Cooper, Dick Cramer, Dick Alexander, Maston Williams, Ethan Laidlaw, Steve Clark, Wally West, Fred Burns
D: Leon Barsha
S: William Colt MacDonald
SP: Paul Perez

768. A LAWMAN IS BORN
(Republic, June 21, 1937) 58 Mins.
Johnny Mack Brown, Iris Meredith, Al St. John, Mary MacLaren, Dick Curtis, Earle Hodgins, Charles King, Frank LaRue, Steve Clark, Jack C. Smith, Sherry Tansey, Wally West, Budd Buster, Lew Meehan, Tex Palmer, Warner Richmond
D: Sam Newfield
S: Harry Olmstead

SP: George Plympton
P: A. W. Hackel

769. NORTH OF THE RIO GRANDE
(Paramount, June 28, 1937) 70 Mins.
(Hopalong Cassidy Series)
William Boyd, George Hayes, Stephen Morris (Morris Ankrum), Russell Hayden, John Beach, Bernadine Hayes, John Rutherford, Walter Long, Lee J. Cobb, Lorraine Randall, Al Ferguson, Lafe McKee
D: Nate Watt
S: "Cottonwood Gulch"—Clarence E. Mulford
SP: Joseph O'Donnell
P: Harry Sherman

770. BROTHERS OF THE WEST
(Victory, June 30, 1937) 58 Mins.
Tom Tyler, Lois Wilde, Dorothy Short, Lafe McKee, Bob Terry, Roger Williams, Jim Corey, James C. Morton, Tiny Lipson
D/P: Sam Katzman
SP: Basil Dickey

771. RANGE DEFENDERS
(Republic, June 30, 1937) 56 Mins.
(Three Mesquiteers Series)
Bob Livingston, Ray Corrigan, Max Terhune, Eleanor Stewart, Harry Woods, Yakima Canutt, Earle Hodgins, Thomas Carr, John Merton, Harrison Greene, Horace B. Carpenter, Frank Ellis, Fred Toones, Jack O'Shea, Ernie Adams, Jack Rockwell, Merrill McCormack, Curley Dresden, Jack Kirk, George Morrell, Donald Kirke, C. L. Sherwood, Milburn Morante, Al Taylor
D: Mack Wright
SP: Joseph Poland
P: Sol C. Siegel

772. THE FIGHTING TEXAN
(Ambassador, June, 1937) 59 Mins.
Kermit Maynard, Elaine Shepard, Frank LaRue, Budd Buster, Ed Cassidy, Bruce Mitchell, Murdock McQuarrie, Art Miles, Merrill McCormack, Blackie Whiteford, Wally West, John Merton, Bob Woodward, Clem Horten
D: Charles Abbott
S: James Oliver Curwood
SP: Joseph O'Donnell
P: Maurice Conn

773. WILD WEST DAYS
(Universal, June, 1937) 13 Chaps.
John Mack Brown, Lynn Gilbert, Russell Simpson, Frank Yaconelli, George Shelly, Bob Kortman, Walter Miller, Francis McDonald, Frank McGlynn, Jr., Charles Stevens, Al Bridge, Edward J. LeSaint, Bruce Mitchell, Frank Ellis, Chief Thunderbird,

Bud Osborne, Jack Clifford, Hank Bell, Lafe
McKee, Joe Girard, William Royle, Mike Morita,
Robert McClung, Sidney Bracey, Iron Eyes Cody,
Chief Thunder Cloud
D: Ford Beebe, Cliff Smith
S: "Saint Johnson"—W. R. Burnett
SP: Wyndham Gittens, Norman S. Hall, Ray
    Trampe
P: Ben Koenig, Henry MacRae
Chapter Titles: (1) Death Rides the Range, (2) The
    Redskin's Revenge, (3) The Brink of Action,
    (4) The Indians Are Coming, (5) The Leap for Life,
    (6) Death Stalks the Plains, (7) Six Gun Law,
    (8) The Gold Stampede, (9) Walls of Fire, (10) The
    Circle of Doom, (11) The Thundering Herd,
    (12) Rustlers and Redskins, (13) The Rustler's
    Roundup

774. ONE MAN JUSTICE
(Columbia, July 1, 1937)   59 Mins.
Charles Starrett, Barbara Weeks, Hal Taliaferro
    (Wally Wales), Jack Clifford, Al Bridge, Walter
    Downing, Mary Gordon, Jack Lipson, Edmund
    Cobb, Dick Curtis, Maston Williams, Harry
    Fleischman, Art Mix, Hank Bell, Steve Clark,
    Frank Ellis, Ethan Laidlaw, Eddie Laughton, Ted
    Mapes, Lew Meehan, Merrill McCormack
D: Leon Barsha
S: William Colt MacDonald (credited to Peter B.
    Kyne)
SP: Paul Perez

775. FORLORN RIVER
(Paramount, July 2, 1937)   56 Mins.
Larry "Buster" Crabbe, June Martel, John Patter-
    son, Harvey Stephen, Chester Conklin, Lew
    Kelly, Syd Saylor, William Duncan, Rafael Ben-
    nett, Ruth Warren, Lee Powell, Oscar Hendrian,
    Robert Homans, Purnell Pratt, Larry Lawrence,
    Tom Long, Merrill McCormack, Vester Pegg
D: Charles Barton
S: Zane Grey
SP: Stuart Anthony, Robert Yost

776. RIDERS OF THE ROCKIES
(Grand National, July 2, 1937)   56 Mins.
Tex Ritter, Louise Stanley, Charles King, Snub
    Pollard, Horace Murphy, Yakima Canutt, Earl
    Dwire, Martin Garralaga, Jack Rockwell, Paul
    Lopez, Heber Snow (Hank Worden), Tex Palmer,
    Clyde McClary, The Texas Tornados, "White
    Flash"
D: R. N. Bradbury
S: Lindsley Parsons
SP: Robert Emmett
P: Edward Finney

776a. GOOFS AND SADDLES
(Columbia, July 2, 1937)   2 Reels
(*Three Stooges* Series)
Moe Howard, Curly Howard, Larry Fine, Ethan
    Laidlaw, Ted Lorch, Hank Mann, Stanley Bly-
    stone, George Gray, Sam Lufkin, Hank Bell
D: Del Lord
S/SP: Felix Adler

777. ROARING TIMBER
(Columbia, July 4, 1937)   65 Mins.
Jack Holt, Grace Bradley, Ruth Donnelly, Raymond
    Hatton, Willard Robertson, J. Farrell MacDonald,
    Charles Wilson, Fred Kohler, Jr., Tom London,
    Ernest Wood, Philip Ahn, Ben Hendricks
D: Phil Rosen
S: Robert James Cosgriff
SP: Paul Franklin, Robert James Cosgriff
P: Larry Darmour

778. RAW TIMBER
(Crescent, July 6, 1937)   63 Mins.
Tom Keene, Peggy Keys, Budd Buster, Robert Fiske,
    Lee Phelps, John Rutherford, Rafael Bennett,
    Slim Whitaker
D: Ray Taylor
S: Bennett Cohen
SP: Bennett Cohen, John T. Neville
P: E. B. Derr

779. DOOMED AT SUNDOWN
(Republic, July 7, 1937)   53 Mins.
Bob Steele, Lorraine Hayes (Laraine Day), Dave
    Sharpe, Warner Richmond, Earl Dwire, Harold
    Daniels, Horace B. Carpenter, Sherry Tansey,
    Budd Buster, Jack C. Smith, Jack Kirk, Horace
    Murphy, Charles King, Lew Meehan, Jack Ingram
D: Sam Newfield
S: Fred Myton
SP: George Plympton
P: A. W. Hackel

780. EMPTY HOLSTERS
(Warner Bros., July 10, 1937)   58 Mins.
Dick Foran, Pat Wathall, Glenn Strange, Edmund
    Cobb, George Chesebro, J. P. McGowan, Milt
    Kibbee, Emmett Vogan, Earl Dwire, Jack Mower,
    Merrill McCormack, Ben Corbett, Art Mix, Artie
    Ortego
D: B. Reeves Eason
S: Ed Earl Repp
SP: John T. Neville
P: Bryan Foy

781. LOST RANCH
(Victory, July 10, 1937)   56 Mins.
Tom Tyler, Jeanne Martel, Marjorie Beebe, Howard

Bryant, Ted Lorch, Slim Whitaker, Forrest Taylor, Lafe McKee, Roger Williams
D: Sam Katzman
SP: Basil Dickey
P: Sam Katzman

782. RIDERS OF THE DAWN
(Monogram, July 14, 1937) 55 Mins.
Jack Randall, Peggy Keyes, Warner Richmond, George Cooper, James Sheridan, Earl Dwire, Lloyd Ingraham, Ed Brady, Yakima Canutt, Steve Clark, Frank Hagney, Ella McKenzie, Ed Coxen, Chick Hannon, Tim Davis, Jim Corey, Oscar Gahan, Forrest Taylor, Tex Cooper
D: R. N. Bradbury
SP: Robert Emmett
P: R. N. Bradbury

783. BOOTS OF DESTINY
(Grand National, July 16, 1937) 56 Mins.
Ken Maynard, Claudia Dell, Vince Barnett, Walter Patterson, Martin Garralaga, George Morrell, Fred Cordova, Sid D'Albrook, Ed Cassidy, Carl Mathews, Wally West, "Tarzan"
D: Arthur Rosson
SP: Philip White
P: M. K. Hoffman

784. THE CALIFORNIAN
(Principal/20th C. Fox, July 16, 1937) 58 Mins.
(Also known as *The Gentleman from California*)
Ricardo Cortez, Marjorie Weaver, Katherine DeMille, Nigel de Brulier, Morgan Wallace, Maurice Black, Helen Holmes, James Farley, George Regas, Pierre Watkin, Edward Keane, Gene Reynolds, Ann Gillis, Dick Botiller, Tom Forman, Bud Osborne, Monte Montague, William Fletcher
D: Gus Meins
SP: Gilbert Wright, Gordon Newil'
P: Sol Lesser

785. THE RED ROPE
(Republic, July 19, 1937) 56 Mins.
Bob Steele, Lois January, Horace Murphy, Charles King, Bobby Nelson, Ed Cassidy, Lew Meehan, Frank Ball, Forrest Taylor, Jack Rockwell, Karl Hackett
D: S. Roy Luby
SP: George Plympton
P: A. W. Hackel

786. WILD AND WOOLLY
(20th C. Fox, July 19, 1937) 73 Mins.
Jane Withers, Walter Brennan, Pauline Moore, Douglas Fowley, Carl "Alfalfa" Switzer, Jackie Searl, Berton Churchill, Robert Wilcox, Douglas Scott
D: Alfred Werker
AP: John Stone
SP: Lynn Root

787. RUSTLER'S VALLEY
(Paramount, July 23, 1937) 60 Mins.
(*Hopalong Cassidy* Series)
William Boyd, George Hayes, Russell Hayden, Stephen Morris (Morris Ankrum), Muriel Evans, John Beach, Lee J. Cobb, Oscar Apfel, Ted Adams, Bernadine Hayes, John St. Polis
D: Nate Watt
S: Clarence E. Mulford
SP: Harry O. Hoyt
P: Harry Sherman

788. GALLOPING DYNAMITE
(Ambassador, July, 1937)
Kermit Maynard, Ariane Allen, John Merton, John Ward, Stanley Blystone, David Sharpe, Earl Dwire, Francis Walker, Tracy Layne, Bob Burns, Allen Greer, Budd Buster
D: Harry Fraser
S: "Dawn Rider"—James Oliver Curwood
SP: Jesse Duffy, Sherman Lowe, Charles Condon
P: Maurice Conn

789. BOOTHILL BRIGADE
(Republic, August 2, 1937) 56 Mins.
Johnny Mack Brown, Claire Rochelle, Dick Curtis, Horace Murphy, Ed Cassidy, Frank LaRue, Bobby Nelson, Frank Ball, Steve Clark, Frank Ellis, Lew Meehan, Tex Palmer, Sherry Tansey, Jim Corey
D: Sam Newfield
S: Harry Olmstead
SP: George Plympton
P: A. W. Hackel

790. THE MYSTERY OF THE HOODED HORSEMEN
(Grand National, August 6, 1937) 60 Mins.
Tex Ritter, Iris Meredith, Horace Murphy, Charles King, Forrest Taylor, Earl Dwire, Joe Girard, Lafe McKee, Heber Snow (Hank Worden), Oscar Gahan, Jack C. Smith, Chick Hannon, Tex Palmer, Lynton Brent, Ray Whitley and his Range Ramblers (Ken Card, The Phelps Brothers), "White Flash"
D: Ray Taylor
SP: Edmund Kelso
P: Edward Finney

791. THE RANGERS STEP IN
(Columbia, August 8, 1937) 58 Mins.
Bob Allen, Eleanor Stewart, Jay Wilsey (Buffalo Bill, Jr.), John Merton, Hal Taliaferro (Wally Wales), Jack Ingram, Jack Rockwell, Lafe McKee, Bob

Kortman, Billy Townsend, Ray Jones, Lew Meehan, Tommy Thompson, Herman Hack, Dick Cramer, Joseph Girard, George Plues, Harry Harvey, Jr., Tex Palmer, Francis Walker, Ed Jauregi
D: Spencer G. Bennet
S: Jesse Duffy, Joseph Levering
P: Larry Darmour

792. DEVIL'S SADDLE LEGION
(Warner Bros., August 14, 1937) 57 Mins.
Dick Foran, Anne Nagel, Willard Parker, Granville Owen, Carlyle Moore, Jr., Gordon Hart, Max Hoffman, Jr., Glenn Strange, John Miller, Ernie Stanton, Frank Orth, Jack Mower, Milton Kibbee, George Chesebro, Walter Young, Charles LeMoyne, Ray Bennett, Dick Botiller, Alan Gregg, Bud Osborne, Art Mix, Artie Ortego, Ben Corbett
D: Bobby Connolly
SP: Ed Earl Repp
P: Bryan Foy

793. ROUGH RIDING RHYTHM
(Ambassador, August 15, 1937) 57 Mins.
Kermit Maynard, Beryl Wallace, Ralph Peters, Olin Francis, Curley Dresden, Betty Mack, Cliff Parkinson, Dave O'Brien, Newt Kirby, J. P. McGowan
D: J. P. McGowan
S: "Getting a Start in Life"—James Oliver Curwood
SP: Arthur Everett
P: Maurice Conn

794. HEROES OF THE ALAMO
(Sunset, August 16, 1937) 75 Mins.
(Columbia bought the film and released it as part of their own schedule in 1938)
Rex Lease, Lane Chandler, Roger Williams, Edward Piel, Earle Hodgins, Julian Rivero, Jack C. Smith, Bruce Warren, Ruth Findlay, Lee Valanios, William Costello, Marlin Hasset, Steve Clark, William McCall, Sherry Tansey, Denver Dixon, Tex Phelps, Jack Evans, Paul Ellis, George Morrell, Tex Cooper, Oscar Gahan, Ben Corbett
D: Harry Fraser
SP: Ruby Wentz
P: Anthony J. Xydias

795. PUBLIC COWBOY NO. 1
(Republic, August 23, 1937) 59 Mins.
Gene Autry, Smiley Burnette, Ann Rutherford, William Farnum, James C. Morton, Maston Williams, Arthur Loft, Frankie Marvin, House Peters, Jr., Frank LaRue, Milburn Morante, King Mojave, Hal Price, Jack Ingram, Rafael Bennett, George Plumes, Frank Ellis, James Mason, Doug

Evans, Bob Burns, "Champion"
D: Joseph Kane
S: Bernard McConville
SP: Oliver Drake
P: Sol C. Siegel

796. TRAILING TROUBLE
(Grand National/Condor, August 27, 1937) 57 Mins.
Ken Maynard, Lona Andre, Vince Barnett, Roger Williams, Grace Woods, Fred Burns, Phil Dunham, Edward Cassidy, Horace B. Carpenter, Marin Sais, Tex Palmer, "Tarzan"
D: Arthur Rosson
SP: Philip Graham White
P: M. K. Hoffman

797. WESTERN GOLD
(Principal/20th C. Fox, August 27, 1937) 56 Mins.
Smith Ballew, Heather Angel, LeRoy Mason, Ben Alexander, Otis Harlan, Vic Potel, Frank McGlynn, Horace Murphy, Tom London, Bud Osborne, Steve Clark, Howard Hickman, Al Bridge, Paul Fix, Art Lasky
D: Howard Bretherton
S: Harold Bell Wright
SP: Forrest Barnes
P: Sol Lesser

798. ROARING SIX GUNS
(Ambassador, September 1, 1937) 57 Mins.
Kermit Maynard, Mary Hayes, Sam Flint, John Merton, Budd Buster, Robert Fiske, Edward Cassidy, Curley Dresden, Dick Morehead, Slim Whitaker, Earle Hodgins, Rene Stone
D: J. P. McGowan
S: James Oliver Curwood
SP: Arthur Everett
P: Maurice Conn

799. GOD'S COUNTRY AND THE MAN
(Monogram, September 2, 1937) 56 Mins.
Tom Keene, Betty Compson, Charlotte Henry, Charles King, Billy Bletcher, Eddie Parker, Bob McKenzie, Merrill McCormack, James Sheridan (Sherry Tansey)
D: R. N. Bradbury
SP: Robert Emmett (Tansey)
P: R. N. Bradbury

800. BLACK ACES
(Universal, September 5, 1937) 59 Mins.
Buck Jones, Kay Linaker, Charles King, Bob Kortman, Fred MacKaye, William Lawrence, Robert Frazer, Raymond Brown, Bernard Phillips, Frank Campeau, Charles LeMoyne, Arthur Van Slyke, Bob McKenzie, "Silver"

D/P: Buck Jones
S: Stephen Payne
SP: Frances Guihan
P: Buck Jones

801. HEART OF THE ROCKIES

(Republic, September 6, 1937) 56 Mins.
(*Three Mesquiteers* Series)
Bob Livingston, Ray Corrigan, Max Terhune, Lynn
  Roberts, Sammy McKim, J. P. McGowan, Yakima
  Canutt, Hal Taliaferro (Wally Wales), Maston
  Williams, Guy Wilkerson, Ranny Weeks, George
  Simmons, George Pierce, Nelson McDowell,
  Herman's Mountaineers
D: Joseph Kane
S: Bernard McConville
SP: Jack Natteford, Oliver Drake
P: Sol C. Siegel

802. PRAIRIE THUNDER

(Warner Bros., September 11, 1937) 54 Mins.
Dick Foran, Ellen Clancy, Wilfred Lucas, Frank
  Orth, Frank Ellis, Yakima Canutt, Frank McCar-
  roll, Al Smith, George Chesebro, J. P. McGowan,
  John Harron, Jack Mower, Henry Otho, Art Mix,
  Iron Eyes Cody, Jim Corey, Bob Burns
D: B. Reeves Eason
SP: Ed Earl Repp
P: Bryan Foy

803. STARS OVER ARIZONA

(Monogram, September 22, 1937) 62 Mins.
Jack Randall, Kathleen Elliot, Horace Murphy, War-
  ner Richmond, Tom Herbert, Hal Price, Earl
  Dwire, Chick Hannon, Charles Romas, Shuma
  Shermatova, Jack Rockwell, Forrest Taylor, Bob
  McKenzie, Tex Palmer, Sherry Tansey
D/P: R. N. Bradbury
SP: Robert Emmett (Tansey), Ernie Adams

804. ARIZONA GUNFIGHTER

(Republic, September 24, 1937) 58 Mins.
Bob Steele, Jean Carmen, Ted Adams, Ernie Adams,
  Lew Meehan, Steve Clark, John Merton, Karl
  Hackett, A. C. Anderson, Frank Ball, Sherry Tan-
  sey, Jack Kirk, Hal Price, Budd Buster, Horace B.
  Carpenter, Tex Palmer, Archie Ricks, Allen
  Greer, Roy Bucko, Oscar Gahan, Silver Tip Baker
D: Sam Newfield
S: Harry Olmstead
SP: George Plympton
P: A. W. Hackel

805. RENFREW OF THE ROYAL MOUNTED

(Grand National, September 29, 1937) 57 Mins.
(*Renfrew* Series)
James Newill, Carol Hughes, William Royle, Her-
bert Corthell, Kenneth Harlan, Dickie Jones,
  Chief Thunder Cloud, William Austin, Donald
  Reed, Bob Terry, William Gould, David Barclay
  (Dave O'Brien), "Lightning" (a dog)
D: Al Herman
S: Laurie York Erskine
SP: Charles Logue
P: Al Herman

806. HOPALONG RIDES AGAIN

(Paramount, September 30, 1937) 65 Mins.
(*Hopalong Cassidy* Series)
William Boyd, George Hayes, Russell Hayden,
  Harry Worth, Nora Lane, William Duncan, Lois
  Wilde, Billy King, John Rutherford, Ernie Adams,
  Frank Ellis, Artie Ortego, Ben Corbett, John
  Beach, Blackjack Ward
D: Les Selander
S: Clarence E. Mulford
SP: Norman Houston
P: Harry Sherman

807. LAW FOR TOMBSTONE

(Universal, October 10, 1937) 59 Mins.
Buck Jones, Muriel Evans, Harvey Clark, Carl
  Stockdale, Earle Hodgins, Alexander Cross,
  Chuck Morrison, Mary Carney, Charles
  LeMoyne, Ben Corbett, Harold Hodge, Arthur
  Van Slyke, Ezra Paulette, Francis Walker, Bob
  Kortman, Slim Whitaker, Tom Forman, Bill
  Patton, Frank McCarroll, D. V. Tannlinger,
  Carlos Bernardo, "Silver"
D: Buck Jones, B. Reeves Eason
S: Charles M. Martin
SP: Frances Guihan
P: Buck Jones

808. BOOTS AND SADDLES

(Republic, October 11, 1937) 59 Mins.
Gene Autry, Smiley Burnette, Judith Allen, Ra
  Hould, Guy Usher, Gordon (Bill) Elliott, John
  Ward, Frankie Marvin, Chris-Pin Martin, Stan-
  ley Blystone, Bud Osborne, Merrill McCormack,
  "Champion"
D: Joseph Kane
S: Jack Natteford
SP: Oliver Drake
P: Sol C. Siegel

809. WHERE TRAILS DIVIDE

(Monogram, October 13, 1937) 60 Mins.
Tom Keene, Eleanor Stewart, Warner Richmond,
  David Sharpe, Lorraine Randall, Charles K.
  French, Steve Clark, Hal Price, Dick Cramer,
  James Sheridan (Sherry Tansey), Bud Osborne,
  Horace B. Carpenter, Wally West, James Mason,
  Forrest Taylor, Oscar Gahan

D/P: R. N. Bradbury
SP: Robert Emmett (Tansey)

810. ROLL ALONG COWBOY

(Principal/20th C. Fox, October 18, 1937)
55 Mins.
Smith Ballew, Cecilia Parker, Stanley Fiels, Gordon (Bill) Elliott, Wally Albright, Jr., Ruth Robinson, Frank Milan, Monte Montague, Bud Osborne, Harry Bernard, Budd Buster, Buster Fite and his Six Saddle Tramps, "Sheik"
D: Gus Meins
S: Zane Grey
SP: Dan Jarrett
P: Sol Lesser

811. THE TRIGGER TRIO

(Republic, October 18, 1937)   60 Mins.
(*Three Mesquiteers* Series)
Ray Corrigan, Max Terhune, Ralph Byrd, Sandra Corday, Hal Taliaferro (Wally Wales), Robert Warwick, Cornelius Keefe, Sammy McKim, Jack Ingram, Willie Fung, "Buck"
D: William Witney
S: Houston Branch, Joseph Poland
SP: Oliver Drake, Joseph Poland
P: Sol C. Siegel

812. THUNDER TRAIL

(Paramount, October 22, 1937)   58 Mins.
Gilbert Roland, Charles Bickford, Marsha Hunt, J. Carrol Naish, James Craig, Monte Blue, Barlowe Bourland, Bill Lee, Gene Reynolds, William Duncan
D: Charles Barton
S: "Arizona Ames"—Zane Grey
SP: Robert Yost, Stuart Anthony

813. RIDIN' THE LONE TRAIL

(Republic, November 1, 1937)   56 Mins.
Bob Steele, Claire Rochelle, Charles King, Ernie Adams, Lew Meehan, Julian Rivero, Steve Clark, Hal Price, Frank Ball, Jack Kirk
D: Sam Newfield
S: E. B. Mann
SP: Charles Francis Royal
P: A. W. Hackel

814. DANGER VALLEY

(Monogram, November 3, 1937)   58 Mins.
Jack Randall, Lois Wilde, Charles King, Hal Price, Frank LaRue, Chick Hannon, Earl Dwire, Jimmy Aubrey, Glenn Strange, Bud Osborne, Tex Palmer, Merrill McCormack, Oscar Gahan, Denver Dixon

The Trigger Trio (Republic, 1937) — Ray Corrigan, Max Terhune, and Ralph Byrd

SP: Robert Emmett
D/P: R. N. Bradbury

815. HOLLYWOOD ROUNDUP
(Columbia, November 6, 1937) 64 Mins.
Buck Jones, Helen Twelvetrees, Grant Withers, Shemp Howard, Dickie Jones, Eddie Kane, Monty Collins, Warren Jackson, Lester Dorr, Lee Shumway, Edward Keane, George Berlinger, Bob Woodward
D: Ewing Scott
S/SP: Joseph Hoffman, Monroe Schaff
P: L. G. Leonard

816. THE OLD WYOMING TRAIL
(Columbia, November 8, 1937) 56 Mins.
Charles Starrett, Donald Grayson, Barbara Weeks, Dick Curtis, Edward J. LeSaint, Guy Usher, George Chesebro, Edward Piel, Edward Hearn, Art Mix, Slim Whitaker, Alma Chester, Ernie Adams, Dick Botiller, Frank Ellis, Joe Yrigoyen, Charles Brinley, Fred Burns, Si Jenks, Curley Dresden, Ray Whitley, Blackie Whiteford, Tom London, Art Dillard, Ray Jones, Jerome Ward, Ed Javregi, Tex Cooper, Sons of the Pioneers (Bob Nolan, Roy Rogers, Tim Spencer, Hugh and Karl Farr)
D: Folmer Blangstead
S: J. Benton Cheney
SP: Ed Earl Repp

817. SUDDEN BILL DORN
(Universal, November 10, 1937) 60 Mins.
Buck Jones, Noel Francis, Evelyn Brent, Frank McGlynn, Harold Hodge, Ted Adams, William Lawrence, Lee Phelps
D: Ray Taylor
S: Jackson Gregory
SP: Frances Guihan
P: Buck Jones

818. THE BARRIER
(Paramount, November 12, 1937) 90 Mins.
Leo Carrillo, Jean Parker, James Ellison, Otto Kruger, J. M. Kerrigan, Robert Barrat, Andy Clyde, Sally Martin, Sara Hayden, Addison Richards, Allen Davies, Fernandez Alverado
D: Lesley Selander
S: Rex Beach
SP: Bernard Shubert, Harrison Jacobs, Mordaunt Shairp
P: Harry Sherman

819. BOSS OF LONELY VALLEY
(Universal, November 14, 1937) 59 Mins.
Buck Jones, Muriel Evans, Harvey Clark, Walter Miller, Lee Phelps, Dickie Howard, Ezra Paulette,
Matty Fain, Grace Goodall, Virginia Dabney, "Silver"
D: Ray Taylor
S: Forrest Brown
SP: Frances Guihan
P: Buck Jones

820. SPRINGTIME IN THE ROCKIES
(Republic, November 15, 1937) 60 Mins.
Gene Autry, Smiley Burnette, Polly Rowles, Ula Love, Ruth Bacon, Jane Hunt, George Chesebro, Alan Bridge, Tom London, Edward Hearn, Frankie Marvin, William Hale, Edmund Cobb, Fred Burns, Art Davis, Lew Meehan, Jack Kirk, Frank Ellis, George Letz (Montgomery), Robert Dudley, Jack Rockwell, Jimmy LeFuer's Saddle Pals, Oscar Gahan, "Champion," Victor Cox, Jim Corey
D: Joseph Kane
SP: Betty Burbridge, Gilbert Wright
P: Sol C. Siegel

821. THE LUCK OF ROARING CAMP
(Monogram, November 17, 1937) 58 Mins.
Owen Davis, Jr., Joan Woodbury, Charles Brokaw, Forrest Taylor, Bob Kortman, Charles King, Byron Foulger, Bob McKenzie, John Wallace
D: I. V. Willat
S: Bret Harte
SP: Harvey Gates
P: Scott R. Dunlap

822. THE BAD MAN OF BRIMSTONE
(MGM, November 26, 1937) 89 Mins.
Wallace Beery, Virginia Bruce, Dennis O'Keefe, Joseph Calleia, Lewis Stone, Guy Kibbee, Guinn Williams, Cliff Edwards, Noah Beery, Charley Grapewin, Arthur Hohl, John Qualen, Robert Barrat, Art Mix
D: J. Walter Reuben
SP: Maurice Rapf, J. Walter Reuben

823. TEXAS TRAIL
(Paramount, November 26, 1937) 60 Mins.
(*Hopalong Cassidy* Series)
William Boyd, George Hayes, Russell Hayden, Judith Allen, Alexander Cross, Robert Kortman, Billy King, Karl Hackett, Jack Rockwell, John Beach, Rafael Bennett, Philo McCullough, Earle Hodgins, Ben Corbett
D: David Selman
S: Clarence E. Mulford
SP: Joseph O'Donnell
P: Harry Sherman

The Bad Man of Brimstone (MGM, 1937) — Art Mix, John Qualen, Wallace Beery, Joseph Calleia, and Lewis Stone

824. COURAGE OF THE WEST

(Universal, December 5, 1937) 57 Mins.

Bob Baker, Lois January, J. Farrell MacDonald, Fuzzy Knight, Harry Woods, Carl Stockdale, Buddy Cox, Forrest Taylor, Glenn Strange, Albert Russell, Charles K. French, Thomas Monk, Oscar Gahan, Buddy Cox, Dick Cramer, Jack Montgomery, Tom London, Jack Kirk, Steve Clark

D: Joseph H. Lewis
SP: Norton S. Parker
P: Paul Malvern

825. COLORADO KID

(Republic, December 6, 1937) 56 Mins.

Bob Steele, Marion Weldon, Karl Hackett, Ernie Adams, Ted Adams, Frank LaRue, Horace Murphy, Kenne Duncan, Budd Buster, Frank Ball, John Merton, Horace B. Carpenter, Wally West

D: Sam Newfield
S: Harry Olmstead
SP: Charles Francis Royal
P: A. W. Hackel

826. WILD HORSE RODEO

(Republic, December 6, 1937) 55 Mins.

(*Three Mesquiteers* Series)

Bob Livingston, Ray Corrigan, Max Terhune, June Martel, Walter Miller, Edmund Cobb, William Gould, Jack Ingram, Fred "Snowflake" Toones, Henry Isabell, Art Dillard, Ralph Robinson, Dick Weston (Roy Rogers), Jack Kirk

D: George Sherman
S: Oliver Drake, Gilbert Wright
SP: Betty Burbridge
P: Sol C. Siegel

826a. BORN TO THE WEST

(Paramount, December 10, 1937) 59 Mins.

(Re-issued as *Hell Town*)

John Wayne, Marsha Hunt, Johnny Mack Brown, John Patterson, Monte Blue, Syd Saylor, Lucien Littlefield, Nick Lukats, James Craig, Jack Kennedy, Vester Pegg, Earl Dwire, Jim Thorpe, Jennie Boyle, Alan Ladd, Lee Prather, Jack Daley

D: Charles Barton
S: "Born to the West"—Zane Grey
SP: Stuart Anthony, Robert Yost

827. HEADIN' EAST

(Columbia, December 13, 1937)   67 Mins.

Buck Jones, Ruth Coleman, Shemp Howard, Donald
Douglas, Elaine Arden, Earle Hodgins, John Elli-
ott, Stanley Blystone, Harry Lash, Frank Faylen,
Dick Rich, Al Herman

D: Ewing Scott

S: Joseph Hoffman, Monroe Schaff

SP: Ethel La Blanche, Paul Franklin

P: L. G. Leonard

828. ROMANCE OF THE ROCKIES

(Monogram, December 15, 1937)   53 Mins.

Tom Keene, Beryl Wallace, Don Orlando, Bill Cody,
Jr., Franklyn Farnum, Earl Dwire, Russell Paul,
Steve Clark, Jim Corey, Tex Palmer, Jack C.
Smith, Blackie Whiteford, Frank Ellis

D/P: R. N. Bradbury

SP: Robert Emmett (Tansey)

829. RHYTHM WRANGLERS

(RKO, December 17, 1937)   19 Mins.

Ray Whitley, Jane Walsh, Lloyd Ingraham, Georgia
Simmons, Jack Rice, Ken Card, Willie Phelps, Norman Phelps, Earl Phelps

D: Charles Roberts

SP: Charles Roberts, Ewalt Adamson

P: Bert Gilroy

830. WELLS FARGO

(Paramount, December 31, 1937)   115 Mins.

Joel McCrea, Bob Burns, Frances Dee, Lloyd Nolan,
Henry O'Neill, Mary Nash, Ralph Morgan, John
Mack Brown, Porter Hall, Jack Clark, Clarence
Kolb, Robert Cummings, Peggy Stewart, Ber-
nard Siegel, Stanley Fields, Jane Dewey, Frank
McGlynn, Barlowe Bourland

D: Frank Lloyd

S: Stuart N. Lake

SP: Paul Schoefield, Gerald Geraghty, Frederick
Jackson

P: Frank Lloyd

831. OUTLAWS OF THE PRAIRIE

(Columbia, December, 1937)   59 Mins.

Charles Starrett, Donald Grayson, Iris Meredith,
Edward J. LeSaint, Hank Bell, Dick Curtis, Nor-
man Willis, Edmund Cobb, Art Mix, Steve Clark,
Earle Hodgins, Dick Alexander, Frank Shannon,
Fred Burns, Jack Rockwell, Jack Kirk, George
Chesebro, Charles LeMoyne, Frank Ellis, Frank
McCarroll, Curley Dresden, Vernon Dent,
George Morrell, Buel Bryant, Ray Jones, Jim
Corey, Blackie Whiteford, Lee Shumway, Bob
Burns, Sons of the Pioneers (Bob Nolan, Tim
Spencer, Pat Brady, Hugh and Karl Farr)

D: Sam Nelson

Romance of the Rockies (Monogram, 1937) — Blackie Whiteford, Tom Keene, and Frank Ellis

S: Harry Olstead
SP: Ed Earl Repp

832. THE FIGHTING DEPUTY
(Spectrum, 1937)
Fred Scott, Al St. John, Marjorie Beebe, Eddie Holden, Charles King, Frank LaRue, Lafe McKee, Phoebe Logan, Sherry Tansey, Jack C. Smith, Jack Evans, Chick Hannon, "White King"
D: Sam Newfield
S: Bennett Cohen
SP: William Lively
P: Jed Buell

833. MOONLIGHT ON THE RANGE
(Spectrum, 1937)
Fred Scott, Al St. John, Lois January, Dick Curtis, Frank LaRue, Oscar Gahan, Jimmy Aubrey, Carl Mathews, Wade Walker, William McCall, Shorty Miller, Jack Evans, Rudy Sooter, Lew Meehan, Ed Cassidy, Tex Palmer, George Morrell, Sherry Tansey, Forrest Taylor
D: Sam Newfield
S: Whitney Williams
SP: Fred Myton
P: George Callaghan, Jed Buell

834. THE ROAMING COWBOY
(Spectrum, 1937) 56 Mins.
Fred Scott, Al St. John, Lois January, Forrest Taylor, Roger Williams, Dick Cramer, Buddy Cox, Oscar Gahan, Art Miles, George Chesebro, Rudy Sooter
D: Robert Hill
SP: Fred Myton
P: Jed Buell

835. A TENDERFOOT GOES WEST
(Hoffberg, 1937)
Jack LaRue, Virginia Carroll, Russell Gleason, Ralph Byrd, Chris-Pin Martin, Si Jenks, John Merton, Joe Girard, John Ince, Ray Turner, Peewee (Glenn) Strange
D: Maurice O'Neill
P: J. H. Hoffberg

836. ZORRO RIDES AGAIN
(Republic, December, 1937) 12 Chaps.
John Carroll, Helen Christian, Reed Howes, Duncan Renaldo, Noah Beery, Richard Alexander, Robert Kortman, Paul Lopez, Jack Ingram, Roger Williams, Mona Rico, Jerry Frank, Nigel De Brulier, Edmund Cobb, Tom London, Harry Strang, George Mari, Yakima Canutt, Paul Lopez, Frank Ellis, Al Haskell, Dirk Thane, Lane Chandler, Murdock McQuarrie, Chris-Pin Martin, Frank McCarroll, Jack Kirk, Frankie Marvin, Ray Teal, Merrill McCormack, Rosa Turich, Hector Sarno, Jack Hendricks, Art Felix, Vinegar Roan, Josef Swickard, Loren Riebe, Bob Jamison, Duke Taylor, Forrest Burns, Frank Leyva, Jason Robards
D: William Witney, John English
S: Based on character created by Johnston McCulley
SP: Barry Shipman, John Rathmell, Franklyn Adreon, Ronald Davidson, Morgan B. Cox
AP: Sol C. Siegel
Chapter Titles: (1) Death from the Sky, (2) The Fatal Minute, (3) Juggernaut, (4) Unmasked!, (5) Sky Bandits, (6) The Fatal Shot, (7) Burning Embers, (8) Plunge of Peril, (9) Tunnel of Terror, (10) Trapped!, (11) Right of Way, (12) Retribution

CHAPTER 4

The Halcyon Years
1938-1941

(WHEN TRAILS WERE DOWNHILL AND SHADY)

The years 1938-1941 were peak years for the Western genre, whether one's taste ran to major Westerns, minor Westerns, serials, semi-major Westerns, pseudo Westerns, musical Westerns, comedy Westerns, or unusual Westerns. There was something for all in the 700 Western flicks released during these years, an average of 3.4 per week. Somebody had to be seeing a lot of cactus capers!

Whereas hardly any major Westerns were produced in the preceding five years, there were a slew of them in the Halcyon Years. John Ford's *Stagecoach* (United Artists, 1939) with "B" Western star John Wayne in the role of the Ringo Kid became *the* Western of the period and a classic in the genre, its fame and popularity lasting over the years. Perhaps no film exploits the visual resources of the Western landscape more brilliantly. Although some critics have suggested that Ford was only preoccupied with style and a yielder to Western myth, cinema goers seemed not to mind. Myth has always been more exciting than reality. Perhaps Ford pondered such things on his frequent trips to the bank with his deposits. *Stagecoach* has been given the credit for re-establishing the viability of the main-feature Western and beginning the renaissance which has continued more or less unabated. But in terms of production values, another classic film, *The Westerner* (United Artists, 1940), was a strong competitor. Under William Wyler's direction Gary Cooper and Walter Brennan masterfully re-created the old West in all its austerity, with Cooper building his image of the cool, taciturn, and brave, yet bashful, hero out to see justice done. The film's causticity, reminiscent of the early vehicles of Harry Carey, Roy Stewart, and William S. Hart, made the film all the more entertaining for some; for others, the unglamorous picturization of the West was non-gratifying.

Cecil B. DeMille's *Union Pacific* (Paramount, 1939), with Joel McCrea and Barbara Stanwyck, was unequaled in its majestic panorama of western railroad building. The brawling adventure was highlighted by fast-paced action and a spectacular train wreck, as well as a touching love story, and it turned out to be a blockbuster at the box office. DeMille tried for a second smash hit in 1940 with Paramount's *North West Mounted Police*, a lavishly mounted but slow-moving account of the Metis revolt of 1885 and a Texas Ranger's search for a fugitive in Canada. Against this spectacle a love conflict is generated involving a young nurse, a beautiful half-breed, and a Mountie. Audiences had mixed reactions about the film, and although it made money, it was not the success that *Union Pacific* was.

Randolph Scott scored big as Wyatt Earp in Allan Dawn's *Frontier Marshal* (Fox, 1939) and *When the Daltons Rode* (Universal, 1940), a rip-snortin' saga with a fine cast put through their paces by veteran Western director George Marshall. It was Marshall who in 1916 had discovered and developed Neal Hart, "America's Pal" of the silent Western. Both films were the kind of traditional Western that "B" aficionados could appreciate and, since Scott

North West Mounted Police (Paramount, 1940) — Gary Cooper and Madeleine Carroll

Western Union (20th C. Fox, 1941) — Randolph Scott and Virginia Gilmore

continued making this type of film, he was readily accepted by the Saturday matinee audiences as well as by the sophists who no doubt saw things in the films that escaped the "escapist." At any rate Scott's achievement in winning both audiences was one that only John Wayne was able to duplicate. Joel McCrea came close, perhaps, but never really quite made it.

The Oklahoma Kid (Warner Bros., 1939), too, was much in the "B" vein with its fast-moving story and James Cagney and Humphrey Bogart serving as the sparks to a powder-keg of action. It was pure escapist entertainment; no psychological or social messages here to bog things down. Warner Brothers made a bundle with it.

Stories of famed lawmen and outlaws of the old West were in vogue during the Halcyon Years and studios got a lot of mileage out of such films. One of the more popular yarns was *Jesse James* (Fox, 1939), a romanticized account of the old outlaw brought to the screen by director Henry King with Tyrone Power playing "Jesse" and Henry Fonda playing "Frank." The screenplay was good and the technicolor landscape beautiful. The public liked it; consequently, a sequel was in order since Frank had not been killed off in the initial film. Fritz Lang managed to evoke the spirit but not the truth of the real West in *The Return of Frank James* (Fox, 1940) by instilling the film with a revenge motif of European subtlety and shuttling to the background conventional Western characterizations. Henry Fonda again portrayed Frank, and on the basis of his masterful performance soared to new fame.

Another good Western from director Fritz Lang, though not based on a famed personage, was 20th Century-Fox's *Western Union* (1941), adapted from the Zane Grey novel. It was an especially good vehicle for Randolph Scott and character actor Barton MacLane.

Bad Men of Missouri (Warner Bros.-First National, 1941) — Dennis Morgan, Alan Baxter, Arthur Kennedy, Wayne Morris, and Walter Catlett

Equally good was Fox's *Belle Starr*, historically suspect but a fast-moving, suspenseful, well-mounted film with Gene Tierney and Randolph Scott used to good advantage in roles made to order for their talents.

Geronimo (Paramount, 1939), with Chief Thunder Cloud playing the title role, was a weak film overburdened with stock footage, but another historical outing, *Bad Men of Missouri* (Warner Bros., 1941), turned out well. It was an energetic Western in the "B" vein of fast action but with excellent production values and competent portrayals by Arthur Kennedy, Dennis Morgan, and Wayne Morris.

Metro-Goldwyn-Mayer struck out badly with *Billy the Kid* (1941), artistically if not financially. The company was attempting to capitalize on the popularity of the good bad-men Westerns in vogue at the time but made the mistake of assigning director David Miller to the task of bringing the screenplay to life. Or perhaps the mistake was in the casting. For whatever reason, Robert Taylor made a weak "Billy" and Brian Donlevy likewise was an unbelievable "Pat Garrett." The film made little more attempt to go along with historical facts than did the *Billy the Kid* series at PRC starring Bob Steele. The technicolor landscape was beautiful, but otherwise there was not a whole lot to get excited about.

On a brighter note, however, Wallace Beery, always excellent in his comedic good badman roles, measured up to expectations in the MGM films *Stand Up and Fight* (1939), *The Man from Dakota* (1940), *20-Mule Team* (1940), *Wyoming* (1940), and *The Bad Man* (1941). With Beery ranking as one of Hollywood's ten most popular stars, the MGM gloss was applied with gusto, understandable when Beery is credited for earning the big studio an estimated $50 million. Beery was that rare combination of personality and actor, a two-for-one man. Usually, audiences had to settle for one or the other.

Drums Along the Mohawk (Fox, 1939), a fringe Western directed by John Ford and starring

Dark Command (Republic, 1940) — Claire Trevor, John Wayne, and George "Gabby" Hayes

Henry Fonda, never lacked for excitement and was one of the better pictures of the period, both artistically and commercially. The story was set in Colonial times and revolved about a couple (Fonda and Claudette Colbert) trying to make a home on the early frontier.

Republic stepped into the big time with two eminent Westerns which not only made a bundle of money but which proved that the little San Fernando Valley studio could do more than just turn out the best "B" Westerns on the market. *Man of Conquest* (1939) was directed by George Nichols, Jr. and starred Richard Dix, whose interpretation of Sam Houston remained relatively faithful to history. The battle scenes were exceptionally well done, thanks to Yak Canutt and Reeves Eason. *Dark Command* (1940) is a story of Quantrill's guerrilla raiders. Raoul Walsh directed and the exceptionally fine cast includes John Wayne, Claire Trevor, Walter Pidgeon, Marjorie Main, and Roy Rogers. Yak Canutt was again around for the superb stunting, including staging the scene where the wagon and team go off a cliff into the water. Production values were again excellent, demonstrating what a studio like Republic could do in its own field of specialization. Both of these black-and-white Westerns were produced on reasonably modest budgets when compared with films such as *Union Pacific* or *Billy the Kid,* but they held their own for sheer pulse-pounding entertainment.

Universal was content to turn out snappy, fast-moving, action-full Westerns such as *Trail of the Vigilantes* (1940), an Allan Dawn film starring Franchot Tone, and *Badlands of Dakota* (1941), a Richard Dix starrer that used many character actors from "B" films in support. These and similar minor "A's" were quite palatable and quite often more entertaining than the colossal, more expensive Westerns that became overburdened with non-action elements. However, the studio had one super success in *Destry Rides Again* (1939), George Marshall's revival of the comedy or spoof Western. Better stars for his purpose could not have been found. James Stewart is a pacifist sheriff and Marlene Dietrich is the sexy dancehall girl who belts forth the unparalleled "See What the Boys in the Back Room Will Have." It was one of the few Western spoofs that have come off successfully.

At Metro-Goldwyn-Mayer star Spencer Tracy and director King Vidor both had their first experience of making a color movie when *Northwest Passage* (1940) was filmed. In the role of Robert Rogers, Tracy leads his Rogers' Rangers on a perilous expedition to defeat a murderous Indian tribe in 1759 during the French and Indian War. The public flocked to see this rousing adventure.

Errol Flynn appeared in three good Western spectacles directed by Michael Curtiz for Warner Brothers, making a surprisingly good Westerner as he adapted his dashing, swash-buckling style of adventure and engaging good humor to a new setting. The films were *Dodge City, Virginia City* (co-starred with Randolph Scott), and *Santa Fe Trail.*

Space does not permit a treatment of all of the excellent Westerns of this period, but we must at least mention a few others. At Fox, Tyrone Power scored big in *Brigham Young* (1940), a fringe Western, and *The Mark of Zorro* (1940). Both were massive productions that grossed well for the company. Shirley Temple was put into *Susanna of the Mounties* (1939), a delightful outdoor film with Randy Scott as foil for scene-stealing Shirley.

Three fairly good Westerns from Columbia were *Texas* (1941), directed by George Marshall and starring William Holden and Glenn Ford; *Arizona* (1940), directed by Wesley Ruggles and starring William Holden and Jean Arthur; and *Go West, Young Lady* (1941), directed by Frank Strayer and starring Glenn Ford and Penny Singleton.

MGM's *Honky Tonk* (1941), with Clark Gable and Lana Turner, was a profit maker, as was *The Girl of the Golden West* (1939) featuring the singing team of Nelson Eddy and Jeanette MacDonald. Paramount's *The Great Man's Lady* (1941) was a rough gem in which Joel McCrea and Barbara Stanwyck at least pleased those who like their hoss and soap oprys combined. And another film from Paramount was the underrated *Cherokee Strip* (1940) starring Richard Dix, a film reminiscent of *Cimarron* and with enough cumulative thrills to be most satisfying. *The Texans* (1938) with Randolph Scott and Joan Bennett was fine Western fare, too, although its cattle-drive story was not handled as well as it should have been by director James Hogan. RKO failed with its *Allegheny Uprising* (1939) in spite of John Wayne and Claire Trevor in the cast. Republic probably could have taken the same script and cast and made it click. United Artists did not release a lot of Westerns but those that it did generally clicked. *Kit Carson* (1940) was no exception. It was a pleasant film in spite of Jon Hall, a non-Western type, as star.

These specific films are called out simply to make the point that the Halcyon Years were a prolific period for the non-programmer Western. And in addition to the big productions there were a large number of minor "A" and non-formula "B" Westerns produced, ranging from light-hearted spoofs such as the all-black Western *Harlem Rides the Range* (Hollywood Co., Herb Jeffrey), *Buck Benny Rides Again* (Paramount, Jack Benny), and *My Little Chickadee* (Universal, W. C. Fields, Mae West) to serious dramas of the nature of *River's End* (Warner Bros., Dennis Morgan) and *The Mysterious Rider* (Paramount, Douglass Dumbrille). The interesting ones include *Wagons Westward* (Republic, Chester Morris), if for no other reason than that Buck Jones returned to the screen in a crooked sheriff role. *The Law West of Tombstone* (RKO, Harry Carey, Tim Holt), *Paniment's Bad Man* (Fox, Smith Ballew), *The Girl and the Gambler* (RKO, Leo Carrillo, Tim Holt), *Riders of the Purple Sage* (Fox, George Montgomery), *Queen of the Yukon* (Monogram, Charles Bickford), *Heart of the North* (Warner Bros., Dick Foran), and *Rangers of Fortune* (Paramount, Fred MacMurray) were good and ranked in between a common "B" and an "A" Western in quality, as did others in the film list. One could classify them as "major B's" or "minor A's."

On the serial front, a lot of dust was being stirred up at Universal with its million-dollar super serial *Riders of Death Valley* (1941), a star-studded, sepia-toned effort that would contribute some of the most enduring stock footage to later Western serials. The story was nothing exceptional, but the cast was terrific. Dick Foran, Buck Jones, Charles Bickford, and Leo Carrillo were co-billed, although Foran was actually the principal hero. In support were popular reliables Lon Chaney, Jr., Noah Beery, Jr., Guinn "Big Boy" Williams, Glenn Strange, Jack Rockwell, and Monte Blue. More routine serials were *Flaming Frontiers* (1938), *The Oregon Trail* (1939), and *Winners of the West* (1940). Columbia made three good chapter plays and one pedestrian affair, the latter being *Deadwood Dick* (1940). The good ones were Buck Jones' *White Eagle* (1941) and two starring Bill Elliott, *The Great Adventures of Wild Bill Hickok* (1938) and *Overland with Kit Carson* (1939). An enthusiastic reception was given to the two Elliott serials and Columbia quickly signed him to a contract to make feature Westerns.

Republic scored a whopping success with *The Lone Ranger* and its masked avenger motif in 1938 and the serial brought together for the first time the directorial team of William Witney, age twenty-one, and John English, an old man of twenty-nine. Together they would direct most of Republic's serials over the next fifteen years. *The Lone Ranger* became a classic among serials and was followed in 1939 by *The Lone Ranger Rides Again*. In the original serial Lee Powell had been revealed as the Lone Ranger in Chapter 15 after his four compadres had been killed off one by one (George Montgomery, Wally Wales, Bruce Bennett, and Lane Chandler). Preferring a name-actor for the second outing of the Lone Ranger, Republic chose Bob Livingston for the title role since he already had a following as a member of the Three Mesquiteers trio. The masked avenger motif was likewise used successfully in *Zorro's Fighting Legion* (1939) which itself was a follow-up to an earlier *Zorro* serial. One big advantage of the masked hero films was that Yak Canutt, Republic's ace stunt-

Riders of Death Valley (Universal, 1941) — Buck Jones, Leo Carrillo, and Dick Alexander

The Lone Ranger (Republic, 1938) — Lee Powell and Chief Thunder Cloud

man, could be filmed in close-up as he went through his stunting scenes without the audience being the wiser for it. Thus, Yak was seen on screen just about as much as the official star, yet only a few wise film buffs in the audience ever realized that it was Canutt they were cheering on to victory while the star sat on the sidelines and read a magazine or got in a little poker with the boys.

Other Republic serials of the period were *Adventures of Red Ryder* (1940), in which Donald Barry soared to Western fame; *King of the Royal Mounted* (1940), which introduced Allan Lane to the cliffhanger world and, as a result, a subsequent Western series; and *King of the Texas Rangers* (1941), with famed Texas football quarterback Slinging Sammy Baugh getting through his one and only acting experience with the help of Duncan Renaldo and Neil Hamilton.

In spite of the many colossal and outsized Westerns of the period, it was still the inelegant "B's" that kindled the most exhilaration. Even if they were all very much alike, it really made little difference. In fact, it was part of their appeal to those who frequented the Saturday matinee week after week, for they came to love the familiar faces, rhetoric, locales, story lines, and action segments of these films. One knew exactly what he was going to get for his money; it must have been enough, for the same faces could be seen in the audiences at any given theatre week after week and year after year. The faces grew older and new, younger ones appeared beside them, but the seats remained filled and the enthusiasm was sustained.

The Halcyon Years saw Gene Autry firmly entrenched as the "King of the Cowboys," ranking Number One in each of the years 1937, 1938, 1939, 1940, and 1941 in the *Motion Picture Herald*'s survey of top money-making stars. But more importantly, he ranked

Melody Ranch (Republic, 1940) — Gene Autry and "Champion"

Number Four among all Hollywood stars in popularity in 1940 and Number Six in 1941. The significant turning point in Autry's career came with *South of the Border* (Republic, 1939), a smash hit with Gene and friends cavorting below the border in a story built around the ever-popular title song. Thereafter, his films were given larger budgets and more musical content. Action was played down. *Melody Ranch* (Republic, 1940) pitted him with Ann Miller and Jimmy Durante in a musical extravaganza with a Western setting. *Down Mexico Way* (Republic, 1941) and *Sierra Sue* (Republic, 1941), Autry's fiftieth movie, packed movie houses across the nation and his fan mail zoomed to 40,000 letters a month. The world was entranced with Autry and his unique brand of Western.

Roy Rogers, too, hit the big time at Republic and in 1939, 1940, and 1941 ranked third in popularity behind Autry and William Boyd among cowboy stars. When Herbert Yates, Republic's chief, decided to give Rogers the big push as insurance in case Autry, who was making waves, decided to bolt the corral, director Joe Kane took over the directorial assignment and guided Rogers through twenty snappy, crowd-pleasing Westerns with action predominating over song-fests. In many respects these still remain the best pictures Rogers ever made. George (Gabby) Hayes played his lovable sidekick and added immensely to the enjoyment of the series.

Autry and Rogers were extremely valuable assets for Republic, but dame fortune was not through smiling on the little studio, for the *Three Mesquiteers* series, commenced in the Boom Years, continued to flourish, first with Robert Livingston, Ray Corrigan, and Max Terhune, later with John Wayne, Corrigan, and Terhune, and still later with Livingston, Bob Steele, and Rufe Davis. In addition Republic produced one series of Bob Steele Westerns and had a series with Donald Barry in progress, releasing twelve films before the end of 1941.

William Boyd remained the second most popular cowboy throughout the Halcyon

Flaming Lead (Colony, 1939) — Ethan Allen, Tom London, Ken Maynard, and Dave O'Brien

Western Caravans (Columbia, 1939) — Charles Starrett, Iris Meredith, and Dick Curtis

Years with his *Hopalong Cassidy* Westerns for Harry "Pop" Sherman at Paramount. Like George O'Brien and Gene Autry, Boyd attracted adult audiences as well as the juvenile trade and his films had longer running times and better plots than the average Western, although there was ofttimes a dearth of action. Twenty-seven *Hoppy* features were made in the Halcyon Years, most of them directed by Lesley Selander. George Hayes and Russell Hayden were featured through 1939, when Hayes dropped out of the series to support Roy Rogers at Republic. His place was ultimately taken by the capable Andy Clyde, who dated back to the slapstick comedies of the silents; and when Hayden became a star in his own right in 1941, Brad King, an uninspiring second banana, stepped into the vacated spot.

George O'Brien's RKO-Radio series of snappy, well-scripted, excellently photographed and adeptly executed Westerns kept him in fourth place in popularity until 1941, at which time he re-entered the naval service. Taking his place was Tim Holt, whose Westerns received the same fine treatment that had been heaped upon O'Brien. The result was that in his first year as a star he attained seventh ranking in popularity among all cowboy stars. Critics often praised his artistic gifts and condemned his failure to use them fully, especially after he demonstrated the depth of his acting ability in *The Magnificent Ambersons* (RKO, 1942) and *Hitler's Children* (RKO, 1943). RKO also had singing cowboy Ray Whitley who was starred in a very interesting series of musical shorts along with his Six-Bar Cowboys as well as being featured in the O'Brien and Holt films as second lead. Whitley shorts such as *Redskins and Redheads, The Musical Bandit,* and *Prairie Spooners,* each featuring gorgeous Virginia Vale as the feminine lead, give every indication that RKO goofed on two counts. Whitley had both a charisma and a voice that could have made him a leading contender among the singing cowboys and Vale was one of the most beautiful, wholesome, and talented actresses ever to grace a "B" Western. The mishandling of these personalities was a cinema crime.

Victory Pictures offered Tim McCoy in a series of eight spellbinders in 1938-1939, directed by Sam Newfield and produced by Sam Katzman, and Colony released a series of six Westerns with Ken Maynard in 1939-1940, produced by Max and Arthur Alexander. Both groups of films were old-time, straightforward shoot-em-ups emphasizing hard riding, lots of shooting, rousing fights, a chuckle or two, and the simple presence of these mighty titans of prairie fantasy. Clearly they were intended for the action fans who preferred galloping hoofs and the crack of a six-shooter to ballads, romance, and palaverin'.

Universal's contribution to programmer Westerns in the Halcyon Years was first Bob Baker and then the more popular Johnny Mack Brown. Baker's quick demise as a lead is puzzling considering his ability and voice, both of which were on a par with, if not above, that of Autry and Rogers. But the same was true of Smith Ballew at Fox, whose career was cut shorter than Baker's. The charisma may have been lacking in Ballew's case, but Baker was unmistakenly mishandled by his own studio. In 1939 he was ranked as the tenth most popular cowboy star, understandable when one views such superior productions as *Courage of the West, Singing Outlaw,* and *The Last Stand.* One thing helping the early Baker films was direction by Joseph H. Lewis, one of the best and most creative directors in the business.

Columbia's major cowboy was Charles Starrett, and the studio released thirty Westerns starring this handsome and talented saddle ace during the four-year period. The Starrett films were workmanlike jobs. He displayed genuine skill as he went about his basic task of keeping the West safe for pretty ingenues such as Iris Meredith. Starrett was no crooner, but there were musical interludes in many of his features in the form of the Sons of the Pioneers, which, for a while, included Roy Rogers. Buck Jones and Jack Luden were offered in four features each and Bill Elliott, fresh from his success in *The Great Adventures of Wild Bill Hickok,* was offered in a series of fifteen Westerns that started strong and finished

Gunman from Bodie
(Monogram, 1941)
— Buck Jones

as formula affairs, a plethora of action but a dearth of originality. As the period ended, Columbia had teamed Elliott with Tex Ritter for a group of straightforward, bang-up, fist-on-chin oaters that were bound to mesmerize the younger generation.

Monogram was vigorously trying to become an eminent force in the programmer field and offered series with Jack Randall, Tom Keene, Tim McCoy, Tex Ritter, James Newill, and the Range Busters, thrill-makers whose capacity to expedite the rate of gum-chewing or popcorn-guzzling was irrefragable. The Ritter series was especially popular and the *Range Busters* (Ray Corrigan, Max Terhune, John King) films were catching on as the period ended. Although not as polished as the *Three Mesquiteers* series and lower budgeted, the *Range Busters* trio had two of the original Mesquiteers and placed more emphasis on low-brow comedy while maintaining double-quick action. The combination gave the series a large juvenile audience, but adults generally preferred something else. George W. Weeks produced the series.

In late 1941 Monogram assembled another trio for a series to be called *The Rough Riders* and released *Arizona Bound, Gunman from Bodie,* and *Forbidden Trails* before the end of the year. Veterans Buck Jones, Tim McCoy, and Raymond Hatton comprised the trio and the three initial entries attracted considerable notice, especially *Gunman from Bodie,* one of the best Westerns the studio ever made in its long history, attributive to exceptional photography, a fine music score, a good story, and, of most importance, enthusiastic performances by the three principals. The scene of Jones milking a cow, catching the milk in his glove, and feeding a baby through a hole pinched in one of the fingers is beautiful and infinitely touching. It is typical of Jones at his best, a craftsman with an absolute command of his talent. Scott R. Dunlap, a long-time friend and former director of Jones at Fox, produced the series.

Before going with Monogram, McCoy had completed a series for PRC, directed by veteran Sam Newfield under the pseudonym Peter Stewart. The best of these, *Riders of Black Mountain,* saw McCoy reunited with old pal Rex Lease, and *The Texas Marshal* served as an introduction for yet another warbling cowtender, Art Davis.

PRC also offered a series of *Lone Rider* Westerns with George Houston and Al St. John, as well as a *Billy the Kid* series with Buster Crabbe taking over the lead in 1941 from Bob Steele who initiated the role in 1940 after completing a good group of sagebrushers for Metropolitan. Al St. John served both heroes as comedy relief.

Spectrum attempted to cash in on the singing cowboy craze with a Fred Scott series, again with Al St. John featured in the sidekick role. However, Scott did not catch on and the series died in 1940.

At Fox, Cesar Romero assumed the Cisco Kid role initially played by Warner Baxter. Thanks to the major studio polish, larger budgets, and excellent distribution setup, the series was a popular one.

And so the Halcyon Years were bonanza ones for the "B" Western, thanks to over 20,000 theatres across the U.S.A. needing low-budget films for their double-bill programs and the fact that a vast audience never tired of the same basic fare week on end. Republic, Universal, Columbia, RKO, Monogram, and even PRC made fortunes on a succession of programmer Westerns, while Paramount made a cool million or two from the *Hopalong Cassidy* series and an occasional Zane Grey story. Poverty Row studios such as Grand National, Colony, Puritan, Victory, Metropolitan, Ambassador, Steiner, and Resolute came and went, making quick profits of $40,000 to $60,000 on shoestring investments of $10,000 to $30,000 and infrequently turning out a really fine, memorable little jewel.

Some of the finest colossal Westerns in the history of the cinema had been made by the major studios and, with few exceptions, they had made money—lots of it. "Western" was anything but a dirty word in the Hollywood of the Halcyon Years. You could bank on that. And the studios did. Never had it been so easy to obtain loans on the basis of film type.

All in all, the Western utopia seemed safe and secure and its trails downhill and shady; the sun was shining brightly in the garden of happiness of Western producers.

FILMS OF 1938

837. TEX RIDES WITH THE BOY SCOUTS
(Grand National, January 2, 1938) 57 Mins.
Tex Ritter, Marjorie Reynolds, Snub Pollard, Horace Murphy, Charles King, Karl Hackett, Tommy Bupp, Tim Davis, Philip Ahn, Lynton Brent, Heber Snow (Hank Worden), Forrest Taylor, "White Flash"
D: Ray Taylor
S: Lindsley Parsons, Edmund Kelso
SP: Edmund Kelso
P: Edward Finney

838. PAROLED TO DIE
(Republic, January 11, 1938) 55 Mins.
Bob Steele, Kathleen Eliot, Karl Hackett, Horace Murphy, Steve Clark, Budd Buster, Sherry Tansey, Frank Ball, Jack C. Smith, Horace B. Carpenter
D: Sam Newfield

S: Harry Olmstead
SP: George Plympton
P: A. W. Hackel

839. WEST OF RAINBOW'S END
(Concord/Monogram, January 12, 1938) 57 Mins.
Tim McCoy, Kathleen Eliot, Walter McGrail, Frank LaRue, George Chang, Mary Carr, Ed Coxen, George Cooper, Bob Kortman, Jimmy Aubrey, Reed Howes, Ray Jones, Sherry Tansey
D: Alan James
S: Robert Emmett (Tansey)
SP: Stanley Roberts, Gennaro Rea
P: Maurice Conn

840. HAWAIIAN BUCKAROO
(Principal/20th C. Fox, January 14, 1938) 60 Mins.
Smith Ballew, Evalyn Knapp, George Regas, Pat O'Brien, Harry Woods, Benny Burt, Carl Stock-

dale, Fred Toones, Laura Treadwell
D: Ray Taylor
S/SP: Dan Jarrett
P: Sol Lesser

841. PARTNERS OF THE PLAINS

(Paramount, January 14, 1938) 68 Mins.
(*Hopalong Cassidy* Series)
William Boyd, Harvey Clark, Russell Hayden, Gwen Gaze, Hilda Plowright, John Warburton, Al Bridge, Al Hill, Earle Hodgins, John Beach, Jim Corey
D: Lesley Selander
S: Clarence E. Mulford
SP: Harrison Jacobs
P: Harry Sherman

842. THE SINGING OUTLAW

(Universal, January 23, 1938) 56 Mins.
Bob Baker, Joan Barclay, Fuzzy Knight, Carl Stockdale, Harry Woods, LeRoy Mason, Ralph Lewis, Glenn Strange, Jack Montgomery, Georgia O'Dell, Jack Rockwell, Ed Piel, Jack Kirk, Bob McKenzie, Budd Buster, Lafe McKee, Hank Worden, Art Mix, Chick Hannon, Herman Hack, Curley Gibson
D: Joseph H. Lewis

S/SP: Harry O. Hoyt
AP: Paul Malvern

843. THE PURPLE VIGILANTES

(Republic, January 24, 1938) 58 Mins.
(*Three Mesquiteers* Series)
Bob Livingston, Ray Corrigan, Max Terhune, Joan Barclay, Jack Perrin, Earle Hodgins, Earl Dwire, Frances Sayles, George Chesebro, Robert Fiske, Ernie Adams, William Gould, Harry Strang, Ed Cassidy, Frank O'Connor
D: George Sherman
SP: Betty Burbridge, Oliver Drake. Based on characters created by William Colt MacDonald
AP: Sol C. Siegel

844. THE OLD BARN DANCE

(Republic, January 29, 1938) 60 Mins.
Gene Autry, Smiley Burnette, Helen Valkis, Sammy McKim, Ivan Miller, Earl Dwire, Hooper Atchley, Ray Bennett, Carleton Young, Frankie Marvin, Earle Hodgins, Gloria Rich, Dick Weston (Roy Rogers), Denver Dixon, The Stafford Sisters, The Maple City Four, Walt Shrum and his Colorado Hillbillies, "Champion"
D: Joseph Kane

Singing Outlaw (Universal, 1938) — LeRoy Mason, Bob Baker, and Joan Barclay

SP: Bernard McConville, Charles Francis Royal
AP: Sol C. Siegel

845. WHERE THE WEST BEGINS
(Monogram, February 2, 1938)   54 Mins.
Jack Randall, Luana Walters, Fuzzy Knight, Budd
 Buster, Arthur Housman, Dick Alexander, Ralph
 Peters, Kit Guard, Ray Whitley and the Six-Bar
 Cowboys (Ken Card and the Phelps Brothers)
D: J. P. McGowan
S: Stanley Roberts
SP: Stanley Roberts, Gennaro Rea
P: Maurice Conn

846. CATTLE RAIDERS
(Columbia, February 12, 1938)   61 Mins.
Charles Starrett, Donald Grayson, Iris Meredith,
 Bob Nolan, Dick Curtis, Allen Brook, Edward J.
 LeSaint, Edmund Cobb, George Chesebro, Ed
 Coxen, Steve Clark, Art Mix, Clem Horton, Alan
 Sears, Ed Piel, Jim Thorpe, Hank Bell, Blackie
 Whiteford, Sons of the Pioneers, Jack Clifford,
 Frank Ellis, Curley Dresden, Merrill McCormack,
 George Morrell, Robert Burns, Wally West, For-
 rest Taylor, Horace B. Carpenter, James Mason
D: Sam Nelson
S: Folmer Blangsted
SP: Joseph Poland, Ed Earl Repp

847. FORBIDDEN VALLEY
(Universal, February 13, 1938)   67 Mins.
Noah Beery, Jr., Frances Robinson, Robert Barrat,
 Fred Kohler, Sr., Henry Hunter, Samuel S. Hinds,
 Alonzo Price, Stanley Andrews, Spencer Chan-
 ning, Charles Stevens, Soledad Jiminez, Margaret
 McWade, John Ridgely, James Foran
D: Wyndham Gittens
S: Stuart Hardy
SP: Wyndham Gittens
AP: Henry MacRae, Elmer Tambert

848. THE RANGERS' ROUND-UP
(Spectrum, February 15, 1938)   55 Mins.
Fred Scott, Al St. John, Christine McIntyre, Earle
 Hodgins, Steve Ryan, Karl Hackett, Robert
 Owen, Syd Chatan, Carl Mathews, Richard
 Cramer, Jimmy Aubrey, Lew Porter, Taylor
 MacPeters (Cactus Mack), Steve Clark, Sherry
 Tansey
D: Sam Newfield
S: George Plympton
SP: George Plympton
P: Jed Buell

849. GOLD IS WHERE YOU FIND IT
(Warner Bros., February 19, 1938)   90 Mins.
George Brent, Olivia de Havilland, Claude Rains,
 Margaret Lindsay, John Litel, Marcia Ralston,
 Barton MacLane, Tim Holt, Sidney Toler, Henry
 O'Neill, Willie Best, Robert McWade, George
 Hayes, Russell Simpson, Harry Davenport, Clar-
 ence Kolb, Moroni Olson, Granville Bates, Robert
 Homans, Eddie Chandler
D: Michael Curtiz
S: Clements Ripley
SP: Warren Duff, Robert Buckner
P: Hal B. Wallis

850. THE PAINTED TRAIL
(Monogram, February 23, 1938)   50 Mins.
Tom Keene, Eleanor Stewart, LeRoy Mason, Walter
 Long, Jimmy Eagles, Forrest Taylor, Harry Har-
 vey, Ernie Adams, Bud Osborne, Glenn Strange,
 Frank Campeau, Bob Kortman, Dick Cramer,
 Tom London
D: Robert Hill
SP: Robert Emmett
P: Robert Tansey

851. BORDER WOLVES
(Universal, February 25, 1938)   57 Mins.
Bob Baker, Constance Moore, Fuzzy Knight, Dickie
 Jones, Frank Campeau, Dick Dorrell, Willie Fung,
 Glenn Strange, Oscar O'Shea, Edward Cassidy,
 Jack Montgomery, Arthur Van Slyke, Frank Ellis,
 Hank Bell, Jack Kirk, Ed Brady, Jack Evans
D: Joseph H. Lewis
SP: Norton S. Parker
AP: Paul Malvern

852. CASSIDY OF BAR 20
(Paramount, February 25, 1938)   56 Mins.
(*Hopalong Cassidy* Series)
William Boyd, Frank Darien, Russell Hayden, Nora
 Lane, Robert Fiske, John Elliott, Margaret Mar-
 quis, Gertrude Hoffman, Carleton Young, Gor-
 don Hart, Edward Cassidy, Jim Toney
D: Lesley Selander
S: Clarence E. Mulford
SP: Norman Houston
P: Harry Sherman

853. FRONTIER TOWN
(Grand National, March 4, 1938)   60 Mins.
Tex Ritter, Anne Evers, Snub Pollard, Charles King,
 Horace Murphy, Karl Hackett, Lynton Brent,
 Don Marion, Edward Cassidy, Forrest Taylor,
 Jack C. Smith, Babe Lawrence, Hank Worden,
 John Elliott, Jimmy LeFieur's Saddle Pals, "White
 Flash"
D: Ray Taylor
SP: Edmund Kelso
P: Edward Finney

854. CALL THE MESQUITEERS

(Republic, March 7, 1938)   55 Mins.

(*Three Mesquiteers* Series)

Bob Livingston, Ray Corrigan, Max Terhune, Lynn Roberts, Sammy McKim, Earle Hodgins, Eddy Waller, Maston Williams, Eddie Hart, Pat Gleason, Roger Williams, Warren Jackson, Hal Price, Frank Ellis, Curley Dresden, Jack Ingram, Ralph Peters, Ethan Laidlaw, Tom Steele, Al Taylor

D: John English

S: Bernard McConville

SP: Luci Ward. Based on characters created by William Colt MacDonald

AP: William Berke

855. ROLLING CARAVANS

(Columbia, March 7, 1938)   55 Mins.

John (Jack) Luden, Eleanor Stewart, Harry Woods, Buzz Barton, Lafe McKee, Slim Whitaker, Bud Osborne, Cactus Mack, Richard Cramer, Tex Palmer, Sherry Tansey, "Tuffy" (a dog), Oscar Gahan, Curley Dresden, Jack Rockwell, Horace Murphy, Francis Walker, Franklyn Farnum

D: Joseph Levering

SP: Nate Gatzert

P: Larry Darmour

856. THUNDER IN THE DESERT

(Republic, March 7, 1938)   56 Mins.

Bob Steele, Louise Stanley, Don Barclay, Charles King, Ed Brady, Horace Murphy, Steve Clark, Lew Meehan, Ernie Adams, Dick Cramer, Budd Buster, Sherry Tansey

D: San Newfield

SP: George Plympton

P: A. W. Hackel

857. LAND OF FIGHTING MEN

(Monogram, March 11, 1938)   53 Mins.

Jack Randall, Herman Brix (Bruce Bennett), Louise Stanley, Dickie Jones, Robert Burns, Wheeler Oakman, John Merton, Lane Chandler, Rex Lease, Ernie Adams, The Colorado Hillbillies

D: Alan James

SP: Joseph O'Donnell

P: Maurice Conn

S: Stanley Roberts

858. ROSE OF THE RIO GRANDE

(Monogram, March 16, 1938)   60 Mins.

John Carroll, Movita, Antonio Moreno, Don Alvarado, Lina Basquette, George Cleveland, Duncan Renaldo, Gino Corrado, Martin Garralaga, Rosa Turich

D: William Nigh

S: Johnston McCulley

SP: Ralph Bettinson

P: George E. Kann

859. THE GIRL OF THE GOLDEN WEST

(MGM, March 18, 1938)   120 Mins.

Jeanette MacDonald, Nelson Eddy, Walter Pidgeon, Leo Carrillo, Buddy Ebsen, Leonard Penn, Priscilla Lawson, Bob Murphy, Olin Howland, Cliff Edwards, Billy Bevan, Brandon Tynan, H. B. Warner, Monte Wooley, Charles Grapewin, Noah Beery, Sr., Bill Cody, Jr., Jeanne Ellis, Ynez Seabury

D: Robert Z. Leonard

S: David Belasco

SP: Isabel Dawn, Boyce DeGaw

P: William Anthony McGuire

860. THE LONE RANGER

(Republic, March, 1938)   15 Chaps.

Lee Powell, "Silver Chief" (a horse), Chief Thunder Cloud, Lynn Roberts, Hal Taliaferro (Wally Wales), Herman Brix (Bruce Bennett), Lane Chandler, George Letz (George Montgomery), Stanley Andrews, Billy Bletcher (voice of Lone Ranger only), William Farnum, George Cleveland, John Merton, Sammy McKim, Tom London, Raphael Bennett, Maston Williams, Charles Thomas, Allan Cavan, Reed Howes, Walter James, Francis Sayles, Murdock McQuarrie, Jane Keckley, Phillip Armenta, Ted Adams, Jimmy Hollywood, Jack Kirk, Art Dillard, Millard McGowan, Frank Ellis, Carl Stockdale, Bud Osborne, Fred Burns, Inez Cody, Duke Green, Forbes Murray, Edna Lawrence, Charles King, Jack Perrin, Frank Leyva, George Mari, Charles Whitaker, Edmund Cobb, Jack Rockwell, J. W. Cody, Oscar Hancock, Buck Hires, Roy Kennedy, Al Lorenzen, Karry Mack, Frankie Marvin, Lafe McKee, Henry Olivas, Perry Pratt, Charles Williams, Wally Wilson, Ben Wright, Gunner Johnson, Bill Jones, Robert Kortman, Ralph LeFever, Ike Lewin, Elmer Napier, Post Parks, George Plues, Loren Riebe, Al Rimpau, Vinegar Roan, John Slater, George St. Leon, Burl Tatum, Al Taylor, Duke Taylor, Bobby Thompson, Blackie Whiteford, Shorty Woods, Bill Yrigoyen, Joe Yrigoyen

D: William Witney, John English

S: Fran Striker

SP: Barry Shipman, George Worthing Yates, Franklyn Adreon, Ronald Davidson, Lois Eby

AP: Sol C. Siegel

Supervisor: Robert Beche

Chapter Titles: (1) Heigh-Yo Silver, (2) Thundering Earth, (3) The Pitfall, (4) Agent of Treachery, (5) The Steaming Cauldron, (6) Red Man's Courage, (7) Wheels of Disaster, (8) Fatal Treasure, (9) The Missing Spur, (10) Flaming Fury, (11) The Silver Bullet, (12) Escape, (13) The Fatal Plunge, (14) Messenger of Doom, (15) Last of the Rangers

861. THE LAST STAND

(Universal, April 1, 1938)   56 Mins.

Bob Baker, Constance Moore, Fuzzy Knight, Earle Hodgins, Forrest Taylor, Glenn Strange, Sam Flint, Jimmy Phillips, Jack Kirk, Frank Ellis, Jack Montgomery

D: Joseph H. Lewis
S: Harry O. Hoyt
SP: Harry O. Hoyt, Norton S. Parker
AP: Paul Malvern

862. CODE OF THE RANGERS

(Monogram, April 8, 1938)   56 Mins.

Tim McCoy, Rex Lease, Judith Ford, Wheeler Oakman, Frank LaRue, Roger Williams, Kit Guard, Frank McCarroll, Jack Ingram, Loren Riebe, Budd Buster, Ed Piel, Hal Price, Zeke Clemens, Herman Hack

D: Sam Newfield
SP: Stanley Roberts
P: Maurice Conn

863. RAWHIDE

(Principal/20th C. Fox, April 8, 1938)   59 Mins.

Smith Ballew, Lou Gehrig, Evalyn Knapp, Arthur Loft, Carl Stockdale, Si Jenks, Cy Kendall, Lafe McKee, Dick Curtis, Cecil Kellogg, Slim Whitaker, Tom Forman, Cliff Parkinson, Harry Tenbrook, Lee Shumway, Ed Cassidy, Al Hill

D: Ray Taylor
S: Dan Jarrett
SP: Dan Jarrett, Jack Natteford
P: Sol Lesser

864. THE OVERLAND EXPRESS

(Columbia, April 11, 1938)   55 Mins.

Buck Jones, Marjorie Reynolds, Carlyle Moore, Maston Williams, William Arnold, Lew Kelly, Bud Osborne, Ben Taggart, Ben Corbett, Gene Alsace (Rocky Camron), Blackie Whiteford, Bob Woodward, "Silver"

D: Drew Eberson
SP: Monroe Shaff
P: L. G. Leonard

865. OUTLAWS OF SONORA

(Republic, April 14, 1938)   55 Mins.
(*Three Mesquiteers* Series)

Bob Livingston, Ray Corrigan, Max Terhune, Jack Mulhall, Otis Harlan, Jean Joyce, Stelita Peluffe, Tom London, Gloria Rich, Edwin Mordant, Ralph Peters, George Chesebro, Frank LaRue, Jack Ingram, Merrill McCormack, Curley Dresden, Jim Corey, George Cleveland, Earl Dwire, Jack Kirk

D: George Sherman
S: Betty Burbridge
SP: Betty Burbridge, Edmund Kelson. Based on characters created by William Colt MacDonald
AP: William Berke

866. CALL OF THE YUKON

(Republic, April 18, 1938)   70 Mins.

Richard Arlen, Beverly Roberts, Lyle Talbot, Ray Mala, Garry Owen, Ivan Miller, James Lono, Emory Parnell, Billy Dooley, Al St. John, Anthony Hughes, Nina Campana, "Buck"

D: B. Reeves Eason
S: "Swift Lightning"—James Oliver Curwood
SP: Gertrude Orr, William Bartlett
AP: Armand Schaefer

867. THE FEUD MAKER

(Republic, April 18, 1938)   55 Mins.

Bob Steele, Marion Weldon, Karl Hackett, Frank Ball, Budd Buster, Lew Meehan, Roger Williams, Forrest Taylor, Jack C. Smith, Steve Clark, Lloyd Ingraham, Sherry Tansey, Wally West, Tex Palmer

D: Sam Newfield
S: Harry Olmstead
SP: George Plympton
P: A. W. Hackel

868. UNDER WESTERN STARS

(Republic, April 20, 1938)   65 Mins.

Roy Rogers, Smiley Burnette, Carol Hughes, Guy Usher, Kenneth Harlan, Tom Chatterton, Alden Chase, Brandon Beach, Earl Dwire, Dick Elliott, Jack Rockwell, Frankie Marvin, Slim Whitaker, Jack Ingram, Jean Fowler, Earle Hodgins, Jack Kirk, Fred Burns, Dora Clement, Tex Cooper, Burr Caruth, Curley Dresden, The Maple City Four, Bill Wolfe, "Trigger"

D: Joseph Kane
S: Dorrell and Stuart McGowan
SP: Dorrell and Stuart McGowan, Betty Burbridge
AP: Sol C. Siegel

869. A BUCKAROO BROADCAST

(RKO, April 22, 1938)   18 Mins.

Ray Whitley, Pauline Haddon, Dick Elliott, Lloyd Ingraham, Phelps Brothers, Ken Card

D: Jean Yarbrough
SP: George Jeske, Gay Stevens

870. HEART OF ARIZONA

(Paramount, April 22, 1938)   68 Mins.
(*Hopalong Cassidy* Series)

William Boyd, George Hayes, Russell Hayden, Natalie Moorhead, John Elliott, Billy King, Dorothy Short, Lane Chandler, Alden Chase, John Beach, Leo MacMahon, Lee Phelps, Bob McKenzie

D: Lesley Selander

S: Clarence E. Mulford
SP: Norman Houston
P: Harry Sherman

871. WHIRLWIND HORSEMAN
(Grand National, April 29, 1938) 58 Mins.
Ken Maynard, Joan Barclay, Bill Griffith, Joe Girard, Kenny Dix, Roger Williams, Dave O'Brien, Walter Shumway, Budd Buster, Lew Meehan, Glenn Strange, "Tarzan"
D: Bob Hill
SP: George Plympton
P: Max and Arthur Alexander

872. CALL OF THE ROCKIES
(Columbia, April 30, 1938) 54 Mins.
Charles Starrett, Donald Grayson, Iris Meredith, Bob Nolan, Dick Curtis, Edward J. LeSaint, Edmund Cobb, Art Mix, John Tyrell, George Chesebro, Glenn Strange, Sons of the Pioneers
D: Alan James
SP: Ed Earl Repp
P: Harry Decker

873. TWO GUN JUSTICE
(Concord/Monogram, April 30, 1938) 58 Mins.
Tim McCoy, Betty Compson, John Merton, Joan Barclay, Lane Chandler, Al Bridge, Tony Paton, Alan Cavan, Harry Strang, Earl Dwire, Enid Parrish, Olin Francis, Curley Dresden, Jack Ingram
D: Alan James
S/SP: Fred Myton
P: Maurice Conn

874. KNIGHT OF THE PLAINS
(Spectrum, May 7, 1938) 57 Mins.
Fred Scott, Al St. John, Marion Weldon, Richard Cramer, John Merton, Frank LaRue, Lafe McKee, Emma Tansey, Steve Clark, Budd Buster, Carl Mathews, Jimmy Aubrey, Sherry Tansey, George Morrell, Tex Palmer, Cactus Mack, Olin Francis, Bob Burns
D: Sam Newfield
SP: Fred Myton
P: Jed Buell

875. LAW OF THE PLAINS
(Columbia, May 12, 1938) 58 Mins.
Charles Starrett, Iris Meredith, Bob Nolan, Robert Warwick, Dick Curtis, Edward J. LeSaint, Edmund Cobb, Art Mix, Jack Rockwell, George Chesebro, Jack Long, John Tyrell, Sons of the Pioneers
D: Sam Nelson
SP: Maurice Geraghty

876. GUN LAW
(RKO, May 13, 1938) 60 Mins.

George O'Brien, Rita Oehmen, Ray Whitley, Paul Everton, Ward Bond, Francis McDonald, Edward Pawley, Robert Glecker, Frank O'Connor, Hank Bell, Paul Fix, Ethan Laidlaw, Lloyd Ingraham, Robert Burns, James Mason, Ken Card, Neal Burns, Ray Jones, Herman Hack
D: David Howard
S/SP: Oliver Drake
P: Bert Gilroy

877. SONGS AND BULLETS
(Spectrum, May 15, 1938) 58 Mins.
Fred Scott, Al St. John, Alice Ardell, Charles King, Karl Hackett, Frank LaRue, Budd Buster, Dick Cramer, Carl Mathews
D: Sam Newfield
S: George Plympton
SP: Joseph O'Donnell, George Plympton
P: Jed Buell

878. SIX-SHOOTIN' SHERIFF
(Grand National, May 20, 1938) 59 Mins.
Ken Maynard, Marjorie Reynolds, Lafe McKee, Harry Harvey, Jane Keckely, Walter Long, Bob Terry, Tom London, Warner Richmond, Dick Alexander, Ben Corbett, Earl Dwire, Glenn Strange, Roger Williams, Bud Osborne, Ed Piel, Milburn Morante, Carl Mathews, Herb Holcombe, "Tarzan"
D: Harry Fraser
S: Weston Edwards (Harry Fraser)
P: Max and Arthur Alexander

879. GUNSMOKE TRAIL
(Monogram, May 27, 1938) 57 Mins.
Jack Randall, Louise Stanley, Al St. John, John Merton, Henry Rocquemore, Ted Adams, Al Bridge, Hal Price, Harry Strang, Kit Guard, Jack Ingram, Slim Whitaker, Art Dillard, Carleton Young, Sherry Tansey, George Morrell, Oscar Gahan, Blackjack Ward, Glenn Strange
D: Sam Newfield
S: Robert Emmett (Tansey)
SP: Fred Myton
P: Maurice Conn

880. PHANTOM RANGER
(Monogram, May 27, 1938) 54 Mins.
Tim McCoy, Suzanne Kaaren, John St. Polis, Karl Hackett, Charles King, Tom London, John Merton, Dick Cramer, Herb Holcombe, Harry Strang, Wally West, Horace B. Carpenter, Sherry Tansey, George Morrell, Herman Hack
D: Sam Newfield
S: Stanley Roberts
SP: Joe O'Donnell
P: Maurice Conn

881. FLAMING FRONTIERS

(Universal, May, 1938) 15 Chaps.

John Mack Brown, Eleanor Hansen, Ralph Bowman (John Archer), Charles Middleton, Chief Thunder Cloud, Horace Murphy, Charles King, James Blaine, Roy Barcroft, Charles Stevens, William Royle, John Rutherford, Eddy Waller, Edward Cassidy, Michael Slade, Karl Hackett, Iron Eyes Cody, Pat O'Brien, Earle Hodgins, J. P. McGowan, Frank Ellis, Jim Toney, Hank Bell, Horace B. Carpenter, Tom Steele, Slim Whitaker, Frank LaRue, Al Bridge, Blackjack Ward, Ferris Taylor, Jim Farley, Jim Corey, Bob Woodward, Frank Straubinger, Helen Gibson, Sunni Chorre, George Plues, Jack Saunders, Jack Roper, Bill Hazelett

D: Ray Taylor, Alan James

S: "The Tie That Binds"—Peter B. Kyne

SP: Wyndham Gittens, Paul Perez, Basil Dickey, George Plympton, Ella O'Neill

P: Henry MacRae

Chapter Titles: (1) The River Runs Red, (2) Death Rides the Wind, (3) Treachery at Eagle Pass, (4) A Night of Terror, (5) Blood and Gold, (6) Trapped by Fire, (7) A Human Target, (8) The Savage Horde, (9) Toll of the Torrent, (10) In the Claws of the Cougar, (11) The Half Breed's Revenge, (12) The Indians Are Coming, (13) The Fatal Plunge, (14) Dynamite, (15) A Duel to Death

882. WESTERN TRAILS

(Universal, June 5, 1938) 57 Mins.

Bob Baker, Marjorie Reynolds, John Ridgely, Robert Burns, Jack Kirk, Jimmy Phillips, Murdock McQuarrie, Jack Ingram, Franco Carsaro, Carlyle Moore, Jr., Jack Rockwell, Forrest Taylor, Jack Montgomery, Tex Palmer, Oscar Gahan, Herman Hack, Hank Worden

D: George Waggner

SP: Joseph West

AP: Paul Malvern

883. DESERT PATROL

(Republic, June 6, 1938) 56 Mins.

Bob Steele, Rex Lease, Marion Weldon, Ted Adams, Forrest Taylor, Budd Buster, Steve Clark, Jack Ingram, Julian Madison, Tex Palmer

D: Sam Newfield

S: Fred Myton

P: A. W. Hackel

884. RIDERS OF THE BLACK HILLS

(Republic, June 15, 1938) 55 Mins.

(*Three Mesquiteers* Series)

Bob Livingston, Ray Corrigan, Max Terhune, Ann Evers, Roscoe Ates, Maude Eburne, Frank Melton, Johnny Lang Fitzgerald, Jack Ingram, John P. Wade, Snowflake (Fred Toones), Edward Earle, Monte Montague, Ben Hall, Frank O'Connor, Tom London, Bud Osborne, Milburn Morante, Jack O'Shea, Art Dillard

D: George Sherman

S: Betty Burbridge, Bernard McConville

SP: Betty Burbridge. Based on characters created by William Colt MacDonald

AP: William Berke

885. OUTLAW EXPRESS

(Universal, June 17, 1938) 56 Mins.

Bob Baker, Cecilia Callejo, Don Barclay, LeRoy Mason, Forrest Taylor, Nina Campana, Martin Garralaga, Carleton Young, Carlyle Moore, Jr., Jack Kirk, Arthur Van Slyke, Ed Cassidy, Jack Ingram, Julian Rivero, Tex Palmer, Chief Many Treaties, Ray Jones, Bill Hazlett, Joe Dominguez, Wilbur McCauley

D: George Waggner

SP: Norton S. Parker

AP: Paul Malvern

886. STAGECOACH DAYS

(Columbia, June 20, 1938) 58 Mins.

Jack Luden, Eleanor Stewart, Harry Woods, Hal Taliaferro, Slim Whitaker, Jack Ingram, Lafe McKee, Bob Kortman, "Tuffy" (a dog), Dick Botiller, Blackjack Ward

D: Joseph Levering

SP: Nate Gatzert

P: Larry Darmour

887. BAR 20 JUSTICE

(Paramount, June 24, 1938) 70 Mins.

(*Hopalong Cassidy* Series)

William Boyd, George Hayes, Russell Hayden, Paul Sutton, Gwen Gaze, Pat O'Brien, Joseph DeStefani, William Duncan, Walter Long, John Beach, Bruce Mitchell, Frosty Royce, Jim Toney

D: Lesley Selander

S: Clarence E. Mulford

SP: Arnold Belgard, Harrison Jacobs

P: Harry Sherman

888. BORDER G-MAN

(RKO, June 24, 1938) 60 Mins.

George O'Brien, Laraine Johnson (Day), Ray Whitley, John Miljan, Rita La Roy, Edgar Dearing, William Stelling, Edward Keane, Ethan Laidlaw, Robert Burns, Hugh Sothern, Ken Card

D: David Howard

SP: Oliver Drake, Bernard McConville

P: Bert Gilroy

889. WEST OF CHEYENNE

(Columbia, June 30, 1938) 59 Mins.

Charles Starrett, Iris Meredith, Bob Nolan, Pat Brady, Dick Curtis, Edward LeSaint, Edmund Cobb, Art Mix, John Tyrell, Ernie Adams, Jack

Rockwell, Tex Cooper, Sons of the Pioneers
D: Sam Nelson
S/SP: Ed Earl Repp

890. THE GREAT ADVENTURES OF WILD BILL HICKOK

(Columbia, June 30, 1938)   15 Chaps.

Gordon Elliott (Bill Elliott), Monte Blue, Carole Wayne, Frankie Darro, Dickie Jones, Sammy McKim, Kermit Maynard, Roscoe Ates, Monte Collins, Reed Hadley, Chief Thunder Cloud, George Chesebro, Mala (Ray Mala), Walter Wills, J. P. McGowan, Eddy Waller, Alan Bridge, Slim Whitaker, Walter Miller, Lee Phelps, Robert Fiske, Earle Hodgins, Earl Dwire, Ed Brady, Ray Jones, Edmund Cobb, Art Mix, Hal Taliaferro, Blackie Whiteford

D: Mack V. Wright, Sam Nelson

SP: George Rosener, Charles Arthur Powell, George Arthur Durlam

P: Harry Webb

Chapter Titles: (1) The Law of the Gun, (2) Stampede, (3) Blazing Terror, (4) Mystery Canyon, (5) Flaming Brands, (6) The Apache Killer, (7) Prowling Wolves, (8) The Pit, (9) Ambush, (10) Savage Vengeance, (11) Burning Waters, (12) Desperation, (13) Phantom Bullets, (14) The Lure, (15) Trail's End

891. GOLD MINE IN THE SKY

(Republic, July 5, 1938)   60 Mins.

Gene Autry, Smiley Burnette, Carol Hughes, Craig Reynolds, Cupid Ainsworth, LeRoy Mason, Frankie Marvin, Robert Homans, Eddie Cherkose, Ben Corbett, Milburn Morante, Jim Corey, George Guhl, Jack Kirk, Fred Toones (Snowflake), George Letz (Montgomery), Charles King, Lew Kelly, Joe Whitehead, Matty Roubert, Anita Bolster, Earl Dwire, Maude Prickett, Al Taylor, Art Dillard, Stafford Sisters, J. L. Franks Golden West Cowboys, "Champion"

D: Joseph Kane

S: Betty Burbridge

SP: Betty Burbridge, Jack Natteford

AP: Charles E. Ford

892. MAN'S COUNTRY

(Monogram, July 7, 1938)   53 Mins.

Jack Randall, Marjorie Reynolds, Walter Long, Ralph Peters, Forrest Taylor, David Sharpe, Harry Harvey, Charles King, Bud Osborne, Dave O'Brien, Sherry Tansey, Ernie Adams

D: Robert Hill

SP: Robert Emmett (Tansey)

P: Robert Tansey

893. PANAMINT'S BAD MAN

(Principal, 20th C. Fox, July 8, 1938)   58 Mins.

Smith Ballew, Evelyn Daw, Noah Beery, Stanley Fields, Harry Woods, Pat O'Brien, Armand Wright

D: Ray Taylor

S: Edmund Kelso, Lindsley Parsons

SP: Luci Ward, Charles A. Powell

P: Sol Lesser

894. PRIDE OF THE WEST

(Paramount, July 8, 1938)   56 Mins.

(*Hopalong Cassidy* Series)

William Boyd, George Hayes, Russell Hayden, Charlotte Field, Earle Hodgins, Billy King, Kenneth Harlan, Glenn Strange, James Craig, Bruce Mitchell, Willie Fung, George Morrell, Earl Askam, Jim Toney, Horace B. Carpenter, Henry Otho

D: Lesley Selander

S: Clarence E. Mulford

SP: Nate Watt

P: Harry Sherman

895. ROLLIN' PLAINS

(Grand National, July 8, 1938)   57 Mins.

Tex Ritter, Hobart Bosworth, Harriet Bennett, Snub Pollard, Horace Murphy, Edward Cassidy, Karl Hackett, Charles King, Ernie Adams, Lynton Brent, Horace B. Carpenter, Aguie Gomez, Oscar Gahan, Hank Worden, Rudy Sooter, Carl Mathews, George Morrell, The Beverly Hillbillies, "White Flash"

D: Al Herman

SP: Lindsley Parsons, Edmund Kelso

P: Edward Finney

896. PIONEER TRAIL

(Columbia, July 15, 1938)   59 Mins.

Jack Luden, Joan Barclay, Slim Whitaker, Leon Beaumon, Hal Taliaferro, Marin Sais, Eve McKenzie, Hal Price, Dick Botiller, Tom London, Tex Palmer, "Tuffy" (a dog), Art Davis, Fred Burns, Bob McKenzie

D: Joseph Levering

S: Nate Gatzert

SP: Nate Gatzert

P: Larry Darmour

897. COWBOY FROM BROOKLYN

(Warner Bros., July 16, 1938)   80 Mins.

Dick Powell, Pat O'Brien, Priscilla Lane, Dick Foran, Ann Sheridan, Ronald Reagan, Johnnie David, Emma Dunn, Granville Bates, James Stephenson, Hobart Cavanaugh, Elizabeth Risdon, Dennis Moore, Rosella Towne, May Boley, Harry Barris, Candy Candido, Donald Briggs, Jeffrey Lynn, John Ridgely, William Davidson, Mary Field

D: Lloyd Bacon

S: "Howdy, Stranger"—Robert Sloan, Louis Peletier, Jr.

SP: Earl Baldwin
P: Hal B. Wallis

898. ON THE GREAT WHITE TRAIL
(Grand National, July 22, 1938) 58 Mins.
(*Renfrew* Series)
James Newill, Terry Walker, "Silver King," Robert Frazer, Dick Alexander, Richard Tucker, Robert Terry, Eddie Gribbon, Walter McGrail, Philo McCullough, Charles King, Juan Duval, Carl Mathews
P/D: Al Herman
S: Laurie York Erskine

898a. I'M FROM THE CITY
(RKO, July 28, 1938) 66 Mins.
Joe Penner, Richard Lane, Lorraine Kruger, Paul Guilfoyle, Kay Sutton, Ethan Laidlaw, Lafayette (Lafe) McKee, Edmund Cobb, Clyde Kinney, Katherine Sheldon
D: Ben Holmes
S: Ben Holmes
SP: Nicholas T. Barrows, Robert St. Clair, John Grey
P: William Sistrom

899. SOUTH OF ARIZONA
(Columbia, July 28, 1938) 56 Mins.

Charles Starrett, Iris Meredith, Bob Nolan, Dick Curtis, Robert Fiske, Edmund Cobb, Art Mix, Dick Botiller, Lafe McKee, Ed Coxen, Hank Bell, Hal Taliaferro, George Morrell, Steve Clark, John Tyrell, Sons of the Pioneers (Bob Nolan, Pat Brady, Hugh and Carl Farr, Lloyd Perryman)
D: Sam Nelson
SP: Bennett Cohen

900. HEROES OF THE HILLS
(Republic, August 1, 1938) 56 Mins.
(*Three Mesquiteers* Series)
Bob Livingston, Ray Corrigan, Max Terhune, Priscilla Lawson, LeRoy Mason, James Eagles, Roy Barcroft, Barry Hayes, Carleton Young, Forrest Taylor, John Wade, Maston Williams, John Beach, Jerry Frank, Roger Williams, Kit Guard, Jack Kirk, Curley Dresden
D: George Sherman
S: Stanley Roberts, Jack Natteford
SP: Betty Burbridge, Stanley Roberts. Based on characters created by William Colt MacDonald
AP: William Berke

901. THE PAINTED DESERT
(RKO, August 12, 1938) 59 Mins.
George O'Brien, Laraine Johnson (Day), Ray Whitley, Fred Kohler, Stanley Fields, Max Wagner,

Pioneer Trail (Columbia, 1938) — Wally Wales (Hal Taliaferro) seems to have the upper hand, to the consternation of hero Jack Luden and approval of ace heavy Charles "Slim" Whitaker

Harry Cording, Lee Shumway, Lloyd Ingraham, Maude Allen, William V. Mong, Lew Kelly, James Mason, Jack O'Shea, Ray Jones, Ken Card, The Phelps Brothers
D: David Howard
SP: John Rathmell, Oliver Drake
P: Bert Gilroy

902. THE TEXANS
(Paramount, August 12, 1938)   92 Mins.
Randolph Scott, Joan Bennett, May Robson, Walter Brennan, Robert Cummings, Robert Barrat, Harvey Stephens, Francis Ford, Raymond Hatton, Clarence Wilson, Jack Moore, Chris-Pin-Martin, Anna Demetrio, Richard Tucker, Ed Gargan, Otis Harlan, Spencer Charters, Archie Twitchell, William Haade, Irving Bacon, Bill Roberts, Francis MacDonald
D: James Hogan
S: "North of '36"—Emerson Hough
SP: Bertrand Millhauser, Paul Sloane, William Wister Haines
P: Lucien Hubbard

903. UTAH TRAIL
(Grand National, August 12, 1938)   56 Mins.
Tex Ritter, Horace Murphy, Snub Pollard, Adele Pearce (Pamela Blke), Dave O'Brien, Karl Hackett, Charles King, Edward Cassidy, Bud Osborne, Lynton Brent, Sherry Tansey, George Morrell, Horace B. Carpenter, Ray Jones, Oscar Gahan, Herman Hack, Chick Hannon, Rudy Sooter, "White Flash"
D: Al Herman
S: Lindsley Parsons, Edmund Kelso
SP: Edmund Kelso
P: Edward Finney

904. MAN FROM MUSIC MOUNTAIN
(Republic, August 15, 1938)   58 Mins.
Gene Autry, Smiley Burnette, Carol Hughes, Polly Jenkins and her Plowboys, Sally Payne, Ivan Miller, Al Terry, Dick Elliott, Hal Price, Cactus Mack, Edward Cassidy, Howard Chase, Lew Kelly, Frankie Marvin, Earl Dwire, Lloyd Ingraham, Lillian Drew, Al Taylor, Joe Yrigoyen, Gordon Hart, Rudy Sooter, Harry Harvey, Meredith McCormack, Chris Allen, "Champion"
D: Joseph Kane
S: Bernard McConville
SP: Betty Burbridge, Luci Ward
AP: Charles E. Ford

905. DURANGO VALLEY RAIDERS
(Republic, August 22, 1938)   55 Mins.
Bob Steele, Louise Stanley, Karl Hackett, Forrest Taylor, Ted Adams, Steve Clark, Horace Murphy, Jack Ingram, Ernie Adams, Julian Madison, Budd

Buster, Frank Ball
D: Sam Newfield
S: Harry Olmstead
SP: George Plympton
P: A. W. Hackel

906. PALS OF THE SADDLE
(Republic, August 28, 1938)   55 Mins.
(*Three Mesquiteers* Series)
John Wayne, Ray Corrigan, Max Terhune, Doreen McKay, Josef Forte, George Douglas, Frank Milan, Ted Adams, Harry Depp, Dave Weber, Don Orlando, Charles Knight, Jack Kirk, Monte Montague, Olin Francis, Curley Dresden, Art Dillard, Tex Palmer
D: George Sherman
SP: Betty Burbridge, Stanley Roberts. Based on characters created by William Colt MacDonald
AP: William Berke

907. PHANTOM GOLD
(Columbia, August 31, 1938)   56 Mins.
Jack Luden, Beth Marion, Barry Downing, Charles Whitaker, Hal Taliaferro, Art Davis, Jimmy Robinson, Jack Ingram, Buzz Barton, Marin Sais, "Tuffy" (a dog)
D: Joseph Levering
S/SP: Nate Gatzert
P: Larry Darmour

908. BILLY THE KID RETURNS
(Republic, September 4, 1938)   58 Mins.
Roy Rogers, Smiley Burnette, Mary Hart (Lynne Roberts), Fred Kohler, Sr., Morgan Wallace, Wade Boteler, Edwin Stanley, Horace Murphy, Joseph Crehan, Robert Emmett Keane, Al Taylor, George Letz (Montgomery), Chris-Pin Martin, Jim Corey, Lloyd Ingraham, Bob McKenzie, Oscar Gahan, Jack Kirk, Art Dillard, Fred Burns, Betty Roadman, Rudy Sooter, Betty Jane Haney, Patsy Lee Parsons, Ray Nichols, Ralph Dunn, "Trigger"
D: Joseph Kane
SP: Jack Natteford
AP: Charles E. Ford

909. STARLIGHT OVER TEXAS
(Monogram, September 7, 1938)   58 Mins.
Tex Ritter, Carmen LaRoux, Snub Pollard, Horace Murphy, Karl Hackett, Charles King, Martin Garralaga, George Chesebro, Carlos Villarias, Edward Cassidy, Jerry Gomez, Sherry Tansey, Bob Terry, Horace B. Carpenter, Dave O'Brien, Denver Dixon, Chick Hannon, Tex Palmer, Rosa Turich, Sebastian Damino, Fred Velasco, Stelita, Carmen Alvarez, Eduardo Chaves, The Northwesterners (Merle and Ray Scobee, Shorty Brier, Buck Rasch, and Chuck Davis), "White Flash"
D: Al Herman

S: Harry MacPherson
SP: John Rathmell
P: Edward Finney

910. THE COLORADO TRAIL
(Columbia, September 8, 1938) 55 Mins.
Charles Starrett, Iris Meredith, Edward J. LeSaint, Al Bridge, Robert Fiske, Dick Curtis, Bob Nolan, Hank Bell, Edward Piel, Sr., Edmund Cobb, Jack Clifford, Dick Botiller, Sons of the Pioneers, Stanley Brown
D: Sam Nelson
SP: Charles Francis Royal
P: Harry Decker

911. IN OLD MEXICO
(Paramount, September 9, 1938) 62 Mins.
(*Hopalong Cassidy* Series)
William Boyd, George Hayes, Russell Hayden, Betty Amann, Jane Clayton, Al Garcia, Glenn Strange, Trevor Bardette, Anna Demetrio, Tony Roux, Fred Burns, Cliff Parkinson
D: Edward D. Venturini
S: Clarence E. Mulford
SP: Harrison Jacobs
P: Harry Sherman

912. A WESTERN WELCOME
(RKO, September 9, 1938) 18 Mins.
Ray Whitley, Diana Gibson, Lloyd Ingraham, Bob McKenzie, Jack Rice, Ken Card, Phelps Brothers
D: Leslie Goodwins
SP: Charles Roberts, Leslie Goodwins

913. MEXICALI KID
(Monogram, September 14, 1938) 51 Mins.
Jack Randall, Wesley Barry, Eleanor Stewart, Ed Cassidy, Bud Osborne, George Chesebro, Ernie Adams, William von Bricken, Frank LaRue, Sherry Tansey
D: Wallace Fox
SP: Robert Emmett (Tansey)
P: Robert Tansey

914. BLACK BANDIT
(Universal, September 16, 1938) 57 Mins.
Bob Baker, Marjorie Reynolds, Hal Taliaferro, Jack Rockwell, Forrest Taylor, Glenn Strange, Arthur Van Slyke, Carleton Young, Dick Dickinson, Schuyler Standish, Rex Downing, Jack Montgomery, Tom London, Slim Whitaker, Jack Ingram, Tex Palmer
D: George Waggner
SP: Joseph West
AP: Paul Malvern

915. FRONTIER SCOUT
(Fine Arts/Grand National, September 16, 1938) 61 Mins.

George Houston, Al St. John, Beth Marion, Guy (Alden) Chase, Dave O'Brien, Jack Ingram, Slim Whitaker, Kenne Duncan, Carl Mathews, Kit Guard, Bob Woodward, Jack C. Smith, Walter Byron, Budd Buster, Mantan Moreland, Dorothy Fay, Minerva Urecal, Frank LaRue, Roger Williams, Joseph Girard
D: Sam Newfield
S/SP: Frances Guihan
P: Franklyn Warner, Maurice Conn

916. THE RENEGADE RANGER
(RKO, September 16, 1938) 60 Mins.
George O'Brien, Rita Hayworth, Tim Holt, Ray Whitley, Lucio Villegas, William Royle, Cecilia Callejo, Neal Hart, Monte Montague, Bob Kortman, Charles Stevens, James Mason, Tom London, Guy Usher, Chris-Pin Martin, Tom Steele, Ken Card
D: David Howard
S/SP: Bennett Cohen
P: Bert Gilroy

917. OVERLAND STAGE RAIDERS
(Republic, September 20, 1938) 55 Mins.
(*Three Mesquiteers* Series)
John Wayne, Ray Corrigan, Max Terhune, Louise Brooks, Anthony Marsh, Ralph Bowman (John Archer), Gordon Hart, Roy James, Olin Francis, Fern Emmett, Henry Otho, George Sherwood, Archie Hall, Frank LaRue, Yakima Canutt, Milt Kibbee, Jack Kirk, Slim Whitaker, Bud Osborne, Dirk Thane, Edwin Gaffney, Bud McClure, John Beach, Curley Dresden, Tommy Coats, George Plues
D: George Sherman
S: Bernard McConville, Edmund Kelso
SP: Luci Ward. Based on characters created by William Colt MacDonald
AP: William Berke

918. THE MYSTERIOUS RIDER
(Paramount, September 21, 1938) 73 Mins.
Douglass Dumbrille, Sidney Toler, Russell Hayden, Stanley Andrews, Weldon Heyburn, Charlotte Fields, Monte Blue, Earl Dwire, Glenn Strange, Jack Rockwell, Leo McMahon, Arch Hall, Ben Corbett, Price Mitchell, Ed Brady, Dick Alexander, Bob Kortman
D: Lesley Selander
S: Zane Grey
SP: Maurice Geraghty
P: Harry Sherman

919. THE STRANGER FROM ARIZONA
(Columbia, September 22, 1938) 54 Mins.
Buck Jones, Dorothy Fay, Hank Mann, Roy Barcroft, Hank Worden, Bob Terry, Horace Murphy,

The Renegade Ranger (RKO, 1938) — Tim Holt and Harry Carey

Budd Buster, Dot Farley, Walter Anthony, Stanley Blystone, Ralph Peters, Loren Riebe, Horace B. Carpenter, "Silver"
D: Elmer Clifton
S/SP: Monroe Shaff

920. WEST OF THE SANTA FE
(Columbia, October 3, 1938) 57 Mins.
Charles Starrett, Iris Meredith, Dick Curtis, Robert Fiske, LeRoy Mason, Bob Nolan, Hank Bell, Edmund Cobb, Clem Horton, Dick Botiller, Edward Hearn, Edward J. LeSaint, Buck Connors, Bud Osborne, Sons of the Pioneers, Blackie Whiteford, Hal Taliaferro
D: Sam Nelson
SP: Bennett Cohen

921. PRAIRIE MOON
(Republic, October 7, 1938) 58 Mins.
Gene Autry, Smiley Burnette, Shirley Deane, Tommy Ryan, Tom London, Warner Richmond, William Pawley, Walter Tetley, David Gorcey, Stanley Andrews, Peter Potter, Bud Osborne, Ray Bennett, Jack Rockwell, Merrill McCormack, Hal Price, Lew Meehan, Jack Kirk, "Champion"
D: Ralph Staub
SP: Betty Burbridge, Stanley Roberts
AP: Harry Grey

922. LIGHTNING CARSON RIDES AGAIN
(Victory, October 10, 1938) 58 Mins.
Tim McCoy, Joan Barclay, Bob Terry, Frank Wayne, Ben Corbett, Ted Adams, Karl Hackett, Forrest Taylor, Frank LaRue, James Flavin, Reed Howes, Jane Keckley
D: Sam Newfield
S/SP: Joseph O'Donnell
P: Sam Katzman

923. WHERE THE BUFFALO ROAM
(Monogram, October 12, 1938) 61 Mins.
Tex Ritter, Horace Murphy, Snub Pollard, John Merton, Dorothy Short, Richard Alexander, Karl Hackett, Dave O'Brien, Louise Massey, Bob Terry, Charles King, Blackie Whiteford, Denver Dixon, Ernie Adams, Hank Worden, Curt Massey, Ed Cassidy, Louise Massey's Westerners, "White Flash"
D: Al Herman
S/SP: Robert Emmett (Tansey)
P: Edward Finney

924. GUILTY TRAIL
(Universal, October 21, 1938) 57 Mins.
Bob Baker, Marjorie Reynolds, Hal Taliaferro, Jack Rockwell, Carleton Young, Forrest Taylor, Georgia O'Dell, Glenn Strange, Murdock McQuarrie, Tom London, Tex Palmer, Jack Kirk

D: George Waggner
SP: Joseph West
AP: Paul Malvern

925. LAW OF THE TEXAN
(Columbia, October 24, 1938) 54 Mins.
Buck Jones, Dorothy Fay, Kenneth Harlan, Don Douglas, Matty Kemp, Joe Whitehead, Forrest Taylor, Jose Tortosa, Tommy Mack, Melissa Sierra, Bob Kortman, Dave O'Brien, "Silver"
D: Elmer Clifton
S/SP: Monroe Shaff, Arthur Hoerl

926. IN EARLY ARIZONA
(Columbia, November 2, 1938) 53 Mins.
Bill Elliott, Dorothy Gulliver, Harry Woods, Jack Ingram, Franklyn Farnum, Frank Ellis, Art Davis, Charles King, Ed Cassidy, Slim Whitaker, Al Ferguson, Bud Osborne, Lester Dorr, Tom London, Kit Guard, Jack O'Shea, Frank Ball, Tex Palmer, Sherry Tansey, Dick Dorrell, Oscar Gahan, Jess Cavan, Symona Boniface, Buzz Barton
D: Joseph Levering
SP: Nate Gatzert
P: Larry Darmour

927. LAWLESS VALLEY
(RKO, November 4, 1938) 59 Mins.
George O'Brien, Kay Sutton, Chill Wills, Walter Miller, Fred Kohler, Sr., Fred Kohler, Jr., George McQuarrie, Lew Kelly, Earle Hodgins, Dot Farley, George Chesebro, Kirby Grant, Carl Stockdale, Ben Corbett, Robert McKenzie
D: David Howard
S: W. C. Tuttle
SP: Oliver Drake
P: Bert Gilroy

928. PRAIRIE JUSTICE
(Universal, November 4, 1938) 57 Mins.
Bob Baker, Dorothy Fay, Hal Taliaferro, Jack Rockwell, Carleton Young, Jack Kirk, Forrest Taylor, Glenn Strange, Tex Palmer, Slim Whitaker, Jimmy Phillips, Murdock McQuarrie
D: George Waggner
S: Joseph West
SP: Joseph West
AP: Paul Malvern

929. RHYTHM OF THE SADDLE
(Republic, November 5, 1938) 58 Mins.
Gene Autry, Smiley Burnette, Peggy Moran, Pert Kelton, LeRoy Mason, Arthur Loft, Ethan Laidlaw, Walter De Palma, Archie Hall, Eddie Hart, Eddie Acuff, Tom London, William Norton Bailey, Roger Williams, Curley Dresden, Rudy Sooter, Douglas Wright, Kelsey Sheldon, Lola Monte,

Alan Gregg, James Mason, Jack Kirk, Emmett
Vogan, "Champion"
D: George Sherman
SP: Paul Franklin
AP: Harry Grey

930. GUN PACKER

(Monogram, November 16, 1938)   51 Mins.
Jack Randall, Louise Stanley, Charles King, Bar-
lowe Bourland, Glenn Strange, Raymond Turner,
Lloyd Ingraham, Lowell Drew, Ernie Adams,
Forrest Taylor, Curley Dresden, Sherry Tansey
D: Wallace Fox
SP: Robert Emmett Tansey
P: Robert Tansey

931. COWBOY AND THE LADY

(United Artists, November 17, 1938)   91 Mins.
Gary Cooper, Merle Oberon, Patsy Kelly, Walter
Brennan, Fuzzy Knight, Mable Todd, Henry
Kolker, Harry Davenport, Emma Dunn, Walter
Walker, Berton Churchill, Charles Richman,
Frederick Vogeding
D: Henry C. Potter
S: Leo McCarey, Fred R. Adams
SP: S. N. Behrman, Sonya Levien
P: Samuel Goldwyn

932. THE LAW WEST OF TOMBSTONE

(RKO, November 18, 1938)   73 Mins.
Harry Carey, Tim Holt, Evelyn Brent, Jean Rouve-
rol, Clarence Kolb, Esther Muir, Bradley Page,
Paul Guilfoyle, Robert Moya, Allan Lane, Ward
Bond, George Irving, Monte Montague, Bob
Kortman, Kermit Maynard
D: Glenn Tyron
S: Clarence Upson Young
SP: John Twist, Clarence Upson Young
P: Cliff Reid

933. SANTA FE STAMPEDE

(Republic, November 18, 1938)   58 Mins.
(*Three Mesquiteers* Series)
John Wayne, Ray Corrigan, Max Terhune, June
Martel, LeRoy Mason, Charles King, William
Farnum, Tom London, Martin Spellman, Ferris
Taylor, Genee Hall, Walter Wills, James Cassidy,
George Chesebro, Bud Osborne, Yakima Canutt,
Dick Alexander, Nelson McDowell, Curley Dres-
den, Duke Lee, Dick Rush, Bill Wolfe
D: George Sherman
S: Luci Ward
SP: Luci Ward, Betty Burbridge
AP: William Berke

Santa Fe Stampede (Republic, 1938) — Tom London, Max Terhune, John Wayne, and Ray Corrigan

934. COME ON, RANGERS!
(Republic, November 25, 1938)   57 Mins.
Roy Rogers, Mary Hart, Raymond Hatton, J. Farrell
MacDonald, Purnell Pratt, Harry Woods, Bruce
McFarlane, Lane Chandler, Lee Powell, Chester
Gunnels, Frank McCarroll, Chick Hannon, Jack
Kirk, Al Taylor, Horace B. Carpenter, Bob Wilke,
Al Ferguson, Allan Cavan, Ben Corbett, Burr
Caruth, "Trigger"
D: Joseph Kane
SP: Gerald Geraghty, Jack Natteford
AP: Charles E. Ford

935. SIX-GUN TRAIL
(Victory, November 25, 1938)   59 Mins.
Tim McCoy, Nora Lane, Alden Chase, Ben Corbett,
Karl Hackett, Donald Gallagher, Ted Adams,
Kenne Duncan, Sherry Tansey, Bob Terry, Frank
Wayne, Hal Carey, Jimmie Aubrey, George Mor-
rell
D: Sam Newfield
SP: Joseph O'Donnell
P: Sam Katzman

936. TERROR OF TINY TOWN
(Columbia, December 1, 1938)   62 Mins.
Billy Curtis, Yvonne Moray, Little Billy, Johnny
Hembury, Billy Platt, Charles Becker, Joseph Her-
bert, Nita Krebs, Fern McDill
D: Sam Newfield
S/SP: Fred Myton
P: Jed Buell

937. WESTERN JAMBOREE
(Republic, December 2, 1938)   56 Mins.
Gene Autry, Smiley Burnette, Jean Rouveral, Esther
Muir, Frank Darien, Joe Frisco, Kermit Maynard,
Jack Perrin, Jack Ingram, Margaret Armstrong,
Harry Holman, Edward Raquello, Bentley Hewitt,
George Walcott, Ray Teal, Frank Ellis, Eddie
Dean, Davidson Clark, "Champion"
D: Ralph Staub
S: Patricia Harper
SP: Gerald Geraghty
AP: Harry Grey

938. RIO GRANDE
(Columbia, December 8, 1938)   58 Mins.
Charles Starrett, Ann Doran, Bob Nolan, Dick
Curtis, Pat Brady, Hank Bell, Art Mix, George
Chesebro, Lee Prather, Hal Taliaferro, Edward J.
LeSaint, Ed Piel, Sr., Ted Mapes, Harry Strang,
Fred Burns, Forrest Taylor, Stanley Brown,
George Morrell, Sons of the Pioneers, John Ty-
rell, Fred Evans
D: Sam Nelson
SP: Charles Francis Royal

939. HEART OF THE NORTH
(Warner Bros., December 10, 1938)   80 Mins.
(Technicolor)
Dick Foran, Gloria Dickson, Patric Knowles, Allen
Jenkins, Janet Chapman, James Stephenson, Ar-
nold Averill, Joe Sawyer, Russell Simpson, Joseph
King, Arthur Gardner, Garry Owens, Pedro De
Cordoba, Alec Hartford, Robert Homans, Ander-
son Lawlor, Bruce Carruthers, Gale Page
D: Lewis Seiler
S: William Byron Mowery

940. CALIFORNIA FRONTIER
(Columbia, December 15, 1938)   54 Mins.
Buck Jones, Carmen Bailey, Milburn Stone, Jose
Perez, Soledad Jiminez, Stanley Blystone, Carlos
Villanos, Glenn Strange, Paul Ellis, Ernie Adams,
Forrest Taylor, "Silver"
D: Elmer Clifton
SP: Monroe Shaff, Arthur Hoerl

941. THE FRONTIERSMAN
(Paramount, December 16, 1938)   74 Mins.
(Hopalong Cassidy Series)
William Boyd, George Hayes, Russell Hayden,
Evelyn Venable, William Duncan, Clara Kimball
Young, Charles (Tony) Hughes, Dickie Jones, Roy
Barcroft, Emily Fitzroy, John Beach, Blackjack
Ward, George Morrell, Jim Corey, Saint Brendan
Boys Choir
D: Lesley Selander
S: Clarence E. Mulford
SP: Norman Houston, Harrison Jacobs
P: Harry Sherman

942. GHOST TOWN RIDERS
(Universal, December 16, 1938)   54 Mins.
Bob Baker, Fay Shannon, George Cleveland, Hank
Worden, Forrest Taylor, Glenn Strange, Jack
Kirk, Martin Turner, Reed Howes, Murdock
McQuarrie, Merrill McCormack, George Morrell,
Frank Ellis, Oscar Gahan, Tex Phelps
D: George Waggner
SP: Joseph West
AP: Paul Malvern

943. PRAIRIE PAPAS
(RKO, December 16, 1938)   18 Mins.
Ray Whitley, Al St. John, Georgia Simons, Jean
Joyce, Willie Best, Lloyd Ingraham, Ken Card,
Phelps Brothers
D: Jack Townley
SP: Jack Townley, Charles Roberts

944. WILD HORSE CANYON
(Monogram, December 21, 1938)   56 Mins.
Jack Randall, Dorothy Short, Frank Yaconelli, Den-

Trigger Pals (Cinemart/Grand National, 1939) — Art Jarrett, Al St. John, and Lee Powell

Stand Up and Fight (MGM, 1939) — Wallace Beery, Robert Taylor, John Qualen (sitting at right), and unidentified players

nis Moore, Warner Richmond, Ed Cassidy, Walter Long, Charles King, Earl Douglas, Sherry Tansey, "Rusty"
D: Robert Hill
S/SP: Robert Emmett (Tansey)
P: Robert Tansey

945. RED RIVER RANGE
(Republic, December 22, 1938) 56 Mins.
(*Three Mesquiteers* Series)
John Wayne, Ray Corrigan, Max Terhune, Polly Moran, Lorna Gray (Adrian Booth), Kirby Grant, Sammy McKim, William Royle, Perry Ivans, Stanley Blyston, Lenore Bushman, Burr Caruth, Roger Williams, Earl Askam, Olin Francis, Edward Cassidy, Fred Toones, Bob McKenzie, Jack Montgomery, Al Taylor, Theodore Lorch
D: George Sherman
S: Luci Ward
SP: Luci Ward, Stanley Roberts, Betty Burbridge. Based on characters created by William Colt MacDonald
AP: William Berke

946. SHINE ON, HARVEST MOON
(Republic, December 30, 1938) 55 Mins.
Roy Rogers, Mary Hart (Lynne Roberts), Lulu Belle and Scotty, Stanley Andrews, William Farnum, Frank Jacquet, Chester Gunnels, Matty Roubert, Pat Henning, Jack Rockwell, Joe Whitehead, David Sharpe, "Trigger"
D: Joseph Kane
S/SP: Jack Natteford
AP: Charles E. Ford

947. SONGS AND SADDLES
(Roadshow Pictures/Colony, 1938) 65 Mins.
Gene Austin, Lynne Berkeley, Henry Rocquemore, Walter Willis, Charles King, Karl Hackett, Joan Brooks, Ted Claire, John Merton, Ben Corbett, Bob Terry, John Elliott, Lloyd Ingraham, Candy Hall, Coco Heimel
D: Harry Fraser
SP: Harry Fraser
P: Max and Arthur Alexander

FILMS OF 1939

948. CODE OF THE FEARLESS
(Spectrum, January 5, 1939) 56 Mins.
Fred Scott, Claire Rochelle, John Merton, Harry Harvey, Walter McGrail, Roger Williams, Carl Mathews, Frank LaRue, George Sherwood, William Woods, Gene Howard, Don Gallagher, James "Buddy" Kelly
D: Raymond K. Johnson
S: Fred Myton
P: C. C. Burr

949. WATER RUSTLERS
(Coronado/Grand National, January 6, 1939) 54 Mins.
Dorothy Page, Dave O'Brien, Vince Barnett, Ethan Allen, Stanley Price, Warner Richmond, Leonard Trainer, Merrill McCormack, Lloyd Ingraham
D: Samuel Diege
SP: Arthur Hoerl
P: Don Liegerman

949a. STAND UP AND FIGHT
(MGM, January 6, 1939) 105 Mins.
Wallace Beery, Robert Taylor, Florence Rice, Helen Broderick, Charles Bickford, Barton MacLane, Charles Grapewin, John Qualen, Robert Glecker, Clinton Rosemond, Cy Kendall, Paul Everton, Claudia Morgan, Selmer Jackson, Robert Middlemass
D: W. S. Van Dyke II
S: Forbes Parkhill
SP: James M. Cain, Jane Murfin, Harvey Fergusson
P: Mervyn LeRoy

950. SONG OF THE BUCKAROO
(Monogram, January 12, 1939) 58 Mins.
Tex Ritter, Jinx Falkenberg, Mary Ruth, Frank LaRue, Tom London, Snub Pollard, Horace Murphy, Dave O'Brien, Dorothy Fay, George Chesebro, Ernie Adams, Bob Terry, Charles King, "White Flash"
D: Al Herman
S/SP: John Rathmell
P: Edward Finney

951. THE THUNDERING WEST
(Columbia, January 12, 1939) 57 Mins.
Charles Starrett, Iris Meredith, Bob Nolan, Hal Taliaferro, Dick Curtis, Hank Bell, Edward J. LeSaint, Blackie Whiteford, Art Mix, Robert Fiske, Edmund Cobb, Ed Piel, Sr., Slim Whitaker, Steve Clark, Fred Burns, Clem Horton
D: Sam Nelson
SP: Bennett Cohen

952. HONOR OF THE WEST
(Universal, January 13, 1939) 58 Mins.
Bob Baker, Marjorie Bell (Marge Champion), Carleton Young, Jack Kirk, Tex Palmer, Frank Ellis, Reed Howes, Glenn Strange, Forrest Taylor, Murdock McQuarrie

D: George Waggner
S/SP: Joseph West
AP: Paul Malvern

953. TRIGGER PALS
(Cinemart/Grand National, January 13, 1939)
55 Mins.
Art Jarrett, Lee Powell, Al St. John, Dorothy Fay,
Charles King, Frank LaRue, Stanley Blystone,
Ted Adams, Earl Douglas, Nina Guilbert, Ethan
Allen, Ernie Adams
D: Sam Newfield
S: George Plympton, Ted Richmond
SP: George Plympton
P: Phil Krasne

954. FEUD OF THE RANGE
(Metropolitan, January 15, 1939)   56 Mins.
Bob Steele, Richard Cramer, Gertrude Messinger,
Frank LaRue, Jean Cranford, Robert Burns, Budd
Buster, Jack Ingram, Charles King, Duke Lee,
Denver Dixon, Carl Mathews
D: Harry S. Webb
SP: Carl Krusada
P: Harry S. Webb

955. FRONTIERS OF '49
(Columbia, January 19, 1939)   54 Mins.
Bill Elliott, Luana DeAlcaniz, Hal Taliaferro,
Charles King, Slim Whitaker, Al Ferguson, Jack
Walters, Octavio Giraud, Carlos Villarias, Joe
De La Cruz, Kit Guard, Bud Osborne, Jack Ingram,
Lee Shumway, Ed Cassidy, Tex Palmer, Frank Ellis
D: Joseph Levering
SP: Nate Gatzert
P: Larry Darmour

956. RIDE 'EM, COWGIRL
(Coronado/Grand National, January 19, 1939)
52 Mins.
Dorothy Page, Milton Frome, Vince Barnett, Lynn
Mayberry, Joseph Girard, Frank Ellis, Harrington
Reynolds, Merrill McCormack, Fred Berhle, Pat
Henning, Edward Gordon, Fred Cordova, Lester
Dorr, Walter Patterson, "Snowey" (a horse)
D: Samuel Diege
S/SP: Arthur Hoerl
P: George A. Hirliman, Arthur Dreifuss

957. ARIZONA LEGION
(RKO-Radio, January 20, 1939)   58 Mins.
George O'Brien, Lorraine Johnson (Day), Chill
Wills, Carlyle Moore, Jr., Edward J. LeSaint,
Harry Cording, Tom Chatterton, William Royle,
Glenn Strange, Monte Montague, Joe Rickson,
Robert Burns, John Dilson, Lafe McKee, Guy
Usher, Bob Kortman, Wilfred Lucas, James Ma-
son, Art Mix

D: David Howard
S: "The Stagecoach Stops at Pinyon Gulch"—Ber-
nard McConville
SP: Oliver Drake
P: Bert Gilroy

958. THE BRONZE BUCKAROO
(Sack Amusement Co., January 23, 1939)
Herbert Jeffrey (Herb Jeffreys), Artie Young, Rellie
Hardin, Spencer Williams, Clarence Brooks, F. E.
Miller, The Four Tunes
D: Richard Kahn
S/SP: Richard Kahn

959. DRIFTING WESTWARD
(Monogram, January 25, 1939)   58 Mins.
Jack Randall, Frank Yaconelli, Edna Duran, Stanley
Blystone, Carmen Bailey, Julian Rivero, Dave
O'Brien, Octavio Giraud, Dean Spencer, James
Sheridan (Sherry Tansey), "Rusty" (the Wonder
Horse)
D: Robert Hill
SP: Robert Emmett (Tansey)
P: Robert Tansey

960. THE LONE RANGER RIDES AGAIN
(Republic, January 25, 1939)   15 Chaps.
Robert Livingston, Chief Thunder Cloud, "Silver
Chief" (a horse), Duncan Renaldo, Billy Bletcher,
Jinx Falkenberg, Ralph Dunn, J. Farrell MacDon-
ald, Rex Lease, William Gould, Henry Otho, John
Beach, Glenn Strange, Stanley Blystone, Eddie
Parker, Al Taylor, Carleton Young, Charles
Whitaker, Bob Robinson, Ralph LeFever, Charles
Regan, Fred Schaefer, David Sharpe, Art Felix,
Chick Hannon, Eddie Dean, Bob McClung, Betty
Roadman, Duke Lee, Howard Chase, Ernie
Adams, Nelson McDowell, Walter Wills, Jack
Kirk, Fred Burns, Buddy Mason, Lew Meehan,
Wheeler Oakman, Forrest Taylor, Frank Ellis,
Herman Hack, Bill Yrigoyen, Wesley Hopper,
Bud Wolfe, Joe Yrigoyen, Duke Taylor, Forrest
Burns, George DeNormand, George Burton,
Tommy Coats, Howard Hickey, Barry Hays, Ted
Wells, Burt Dillard, Cecil Kellogg, Carl Sepulveda,
Buddy Messenger, Jerome Ward, Roger Williams,
Buddy Roosevelt, Jack Montgomery, Post Parks,
Art Dillard, Horace Carpenter, Cactus Mack, Lafe
McKee, Augie Gomez, Charles Hutchison, Monte
Montague, Griff Barnett, Joe Perez
D: William Witney, John English
SP: Franklyn Adreon, Ronald Davidson, Sol Shor,
Barry Shipman
AP: Robert Beche
Chapter Titles: (1) The Lone Ranger Returns, (2)
Masked Victory, (3) The Black Raiders Strike,
(4) The Cavern of Doom, (5) Gents of Deceit,
(6) The Trap, (7) The Lone Ranger at Bay, (8) Am-

bush, (9) Wheels of Doom, (10) The Dangerous Captive, (11) Death Below, (12) Blazing Peril, (13) Exposed, (14) Besieged, (15) Frontier Justice

961. JESSE JAMES
(20th C. Fox, January 27, 1939) 105 Mins.
(Technicolor)
Tyrone Power, Henry Fonda, Nancy Kelly, Randolph Scott, Henry Hull, Slim Summerville, J. Edward Bromberg, Brian Donlevy, John Carradine, Donald Meek, John Russell, Jane Darwell, George Chandler, Charles Tannen, Claire Dubrey, Willard Robertson, Harold Goodwin, Ernest Whitman, Eddy Waller, Paul Burns, Spencer Charters, Arthur Aylesworth, Charles Middleton, Charles Halton, Harry Tyler, Virginia Brissac, Edward J. LeSaint, John Elliott, Erville Alderson, George Breakston, Lon Chaney, Jr., Ernest Whitman, James Flavin, Harry Holman, Wylie Grant, Ethan Laidlaw, Don Douglas, George O'Hara
D: Henry King
SP: Nunnally Johnson
P: Nunnally Johnson

962. THE ARIZONA WILDCAT
(20th C. Fox, February 3, 1939) 68 Mins.
Jane Withers, Leo Carrillo, Pauline Moore, William Henry, Henry Wilcoxon, Douglas Fowley, Ethienne Girardot, Harry Woods, Rosita Harlan
D: Herbert I. Leeds
S: Frances Lyland, Albert Ray
SP: Barry Trivers, Jerry Cady
AP: John Stone

963. HOME ON THE PRAIRIE
(Republic, February 3, 1939) 58 Mins.
Gene Autry, Smiley Burnette, June Storey, Jack Mulhall, George Cleveland, Walter Miller, Gordon Hart, Hal Price, Earle Hodgins, Ethan Laidlaw, John Beach, Jack Ingram, Bob Woodward, Sherven Brothers' Rodeoliers, "Champion"
D: Jack Townley
SP: Arthur Powell, Paul Franklin
AP: Harry Grey

964. IN OLD MONTANA
(Spectrum, February 5, 1939) 61 Mins.
Fred Scott, Jean Carmen (Julia Thayer), Harry Harvey, John Merton, Walter McGrail, Wheeler Oakman, Frank LaRue, Allan Cavan, Jane Keckley, Dick Cramer, Buddy Kelly, Gene Howard, Carl Mathews, Cactus Mack
D: Raymond K. Johnson
SP: Johnson Parks, Homer King Gordon, Raymond K. Johnson
P: C. C. Burr

965. SUNDOWN ON THE PRAIRIE
(Monogram, February 8, 1939) 58 Mins.
Tex Ritter, Dorothy Fay, Horace Murphy, Hank Worden, Charles King, Dave O'Brien, Karl Hackett, Bob Terry, Frank LaRue, Edward Piel, Sr., Junita Street, Bud Osborne, "White Flash"
D: Al Herman
SP: William Nolte, Edmund Kelso
P: Edward Finney

966. TEXAS STAMPEDE
(Columbia, February 9, 1939) 57 Mins.
Charles Starrett, Iris Meredith, Fred Kohler, Jr., Bob Nolan, Lee Prather, Ray Bennett, Blackjack Ward, Hank Bell, Edmund Cobb, Edward Hearn, Ed Coxen, Ernie Adams, Blackie Whiteford, Charles Brinley, Sons of the Pioneers
D: Sam Nelson
S: "The Dawn Trail"—Forrest Sheldon
SP: Charles Francis Royal

967. THE PHANTOM STAGE
(Universal, February 10, 1939) 57 Mins.
Bob Baker, Marjorie Reynolds, George Cleveland, Forrest Taylor, Glenn Strange, Ernie Adams, Reed Howes, Murdock McQuarrie, Jack Kirk, Tex Palmer, Dick Rush
D: George Waggner
S/SP: Joseph West
AP: Paul Malvern

968. SIX-GUN RHYTHM
(Arcadia/Grand National, February 17, 1939) 55 Mins.
Tex Fletcher, Joan Barclay, Ralph Peters, Reed Howes, Malcolm "Bud" McTaggert, Ted Adams, Walter Shumway, Slim Hacker, Carl Mathews, Art Davis, Robert Frazer, Jack McHugh, Sherry Tansey, Kit Guard, Art Felix, Joe Pazen, Jack O'Shea, Cliff Parkinson, Frank Ellis, Wade Walker, Adrian Hughes
D: Sam Newfield
S/SP: Fred Myton
P: Sam Newfield

969. SUNSET TRAIL
(Paramount, February 24, 1939) 60 Mins.
(*Hopalong Cassidy* Series)
William Boyd, George Hayes, Russell Hayden, Charlotte Wynters, Jane Clayton, Robert Fiske, Glenn Strange, Kenneth Harlan, Anthony Nace, Kathryn Sheldon, Maurice Cass, Alphonse Ethler, Claudia Smith, Jack Rockwell, Tom London, Jim Toney, Fred Burns, Jerry Jerome, Jim Corey, Frank Ellis, Horace B. Carpenter
D: Lesley Selander
S: Clarence E. Mulford
P: Harry Sherman

970. CODE OF THE CACTUS

(Victory, February 25, 1939) 56 Mins.

Tim McCoy, Dorothy Short, Ben Corbett, Dave O'Brien, Alden Chase, Ted Adams, Forrest Taylor, Bob Terry, Slim Whitaker, Frank Wayne, Kermit Maynard, Art Davis, Carl Sepulveda, Carl Mathews, Lee Burns, Clyde McClary, Jack King, Rube Dalroy

D: Sam Newfield
S/SP: Edward Halperin
P: Sam Katzman

971. DEATH GOES NORTH

(Warwick/Columbia, March 1, 1939) 56 Mins.
(Filmed in Canada)

Edgar Edwards, Sheila Bromley, Dorothy Bradshaw, Jameson Thomas, Walter Byron, Arthur Kerr, James McGrath, Vivian Combe, Reginald Hincks, Rin-Tin-Tin, Jr.

D: Frank McDonald
SP: Edward R. Austin
P: Kenneth Bishop

972. ROLLIN' WESTWARD

(Monogram, March 1, 1939) 55 Mins.

Tex Ritter, Dorothy Fay, Horace Murphy, Slim Whitaker, Tom London, Herbert Cothell, Harry Harvey, Bob Terry, Hank Worden, Charles King, Estrella Novarro, "White Flash"

D: Al Herman
P: Edward Finney

973. SMOKY TRAILS

(Metropolitan, March 3, 1939) 57 Mins.

Bob Steele, Jean Carmen, Murdock McQuarrie, Jimmy Aubrey, Frank LaRue, Bruce Dane, Ted Adams, Bob Terry, Frank Wayne, George Chesebro

D: Bernard B. Ray
SP: George Plympton
P: Harry S. Webb

974. STAGECOACH

(United Artists, March 3, 1939) 96 Mins.

Claire Trevor, John Wayne, Thomas Mitchell, George Bancroft, Andy Devine, John Carradine, Louise Platt, Donald Meek, Berton Churchill, Tom Tyler, Tim Holt, Chris-Pin Martin, Elvira Rios, Bill Cody, Buddy Roosevelt, Yakima Canutt, Paul McVay, Joe Rickson, Harry Tenbrook, Jack Pennick, Kent Odell, William Hopper, Vester Pegg, Ted Lorch, Artie Ortego, Merrill McCormack, Franklyn Farnum, James Mason, Si Jenks, Robert Homans, Chief White Horse, Bryant Washburn, Walter McGrail, Francis Ford, Chief Big Tree, Marga Daighton, Florence Lake, Duke Lee, Cornelius Keefe, Nora Cecil, Lou Mason, Mary Walker, Ed Brady

D: John Ford
S: "Stage to Lordsburg"—Ernest Haycox
SP: Dudley Nichols
P: Walter Wanger

975. TWO-GUN TROUBADOR

(Spectrum, March 5, 1939) 58 Mins.

Fred Scott, Claire Rochelle, Harry Harvey, John Merton, Buddy Lenhart, Carl Mathews, Buddy Kelly, Harry Harvey, Jr., Gene Howard, William Woods, Jack Ingram, Bud Osborne, John Ward, Elias Gamboa, Cactus Mack

D: Raymond K. Johnson
S/SP: Richard L. Bare, Phil Dunham
P: C. C. Burr

976. OKLAHOMA KID

(Warner Bros., March 11, 1939) 85 Mins.

James Cagney, Humphrey Bogart, Rosemary Lane, Donald Crisp, Ward Bond, Hugh Sothern, Harvey Stephens, Charles Middleton, Edward Pawley, Trevor Bardett, John Miljan, Joe Devlin, Lew Harvey, Arthur Aylesworth, Irving Bacon, Wade Boteler, Dan Wolheim, Ray Mayer, Bob Kortman, Tex Cooper, John Harron, Stuart Holmes, Tom Chatterton, Clem Bevins, Soledad Jiminez, Jack Mower, Alan Bridge, Don Barclay, Horace Murphy, Robert Homans, George Lloyd

D: Lloyd Bacon
SP: Warren Duff, Robert Buckner, Edward E. Paramore
S: Edward E. Paramore, Wally Klein

977. ROUGH RIDERS ROUND-UP

(Republic, March 13, 1939) 58 Mins.

Roy Rogers, Mary Hart (Lynne Roberts), Raymond Hatton, Eddie Acuff, William Pawley, Dorothy Sebastian, George Meeker, Jack Rockwell, Guy Usher, George Chesebro, Glenn Strange, Duncan Renaldo, Jack Kirk, Hank Bell, Dorothy Christy, Fred Kelsey, Eddy Waller, John Merton, George Letz (Montgomery), Al Haskell, Frank Ellis, Augie Gomez, Frank McCarroll, Dan White, "Trigger"

D/AP: Joseph Kane
SP: Jack Natteford

978. LONE STAR PIONEERS

(Columbia, March 16, 1939) 56 Mins.

Bill Elliott, Dorothy Gulliver, Lee Shumway, Charles Whitaker, Charles King, Jack Ingram, Harry Harvey, Buzz Barton, Frank LaRue, David Sharpe, Frank Ellis, Budd Buster, Kit Guard, Merrill McCormack, Jack Rockwell, Tex Palmer

D: Joseph Levering
SP: Nate Gatzert
P: Larry Darmour

979. HERITAGE OF THE DESERT
(Paramount, March 17, 1939) 74 Mins.
Donald Woods, Evelyn Venable, Russell Hayden,
Robert Barrat, Sidney Toler, C. Henry Gordon,
Paul Guilfoyle, Paul Fix, Willard Robertson, Regi-
nald Barlow, John (Skins) Miller, Frankie Marvin
D: Lesley Selander
S: Zane Grey
SP: Norman Houston, Harrison Jacobs
P: Harry Sherman

980. LURE OF THE WASTELAND
(Al Lane Pictures, March 18, 1939) 55 Mins.
(Telco Color)
Grant Withers, LeRoy Mason, Marion Arnold, Snub
Pollard, Karl Hackett, Henry Rocquemore, Tom
London, Sherry Tansey
D: Harry Fraser
S/SP: Monroe Talbot
P: Al Lane

981. TRIGGER SMITH
(Monogram, March 22, 1939) 59 Mins.
Jack Randall, Joyce Bryant, Frank Yaconelli, Forrest
Taylor, Dennis Moore, Dave O'Brien, Sherry
Tansey, Ed Cassidy, Jim Corey, Reed Howes,
Warner Richmond
D: Alan James
SP: Robert Emmett
P: Robert Tansey

982. TROUBLE IN SUNDOWN
(RKO, March 24, 1939) 60 Mins.
George O'Brien, Rosalind Keith, Ray Whitley, Chill
Wills, Ward Bond, Cy Kendall, Howard Hickman,
Monte Montague, John Dilson, Otto Yamaoka,
Ken Card, Phelps Brothers, Earl Dwire, Robert
Burns
D: David Howard
S: George F. Royal (Charles Francis Royal?)
SP: Oliver Drake, Dorrell and Stuart McGowan
P: Bert Gilroy

983. MEXICALI ROSE
(Republic, March 29, 1939) 60 Mins.
Gene Autry, Smiley Burnette, Noah Beery, Luana
Walters, William Farnum, LeRoy Mason, William
Royle, Wally Albright, Kathryn Frey, Roy Bar-
croft, Dick Botiller, Vic Demourelle, John Beach,
Henry Otho, Joe Dominguez, Al Haskell, Merrill
McCormack, Fred Toones, Sherry Hall, Al Taylor,
Josef Swickard, Tom London, Jack Ingram, Ed-
die Parker, "Champion"
D: George Sherman
S: Luci Ward, Connie Lee
SP: Gerald Geraghty
AP: Harry Grey

984. NORTH OF THE YUKON
(Columbia, March 30, 1939) 64 Mins.
Charles Starrett, Linda Winters (Dorothy Coming-
gore), Bob Nolan, Lane Chandler, Paul Sutton,
Robert Fiske, Vernon Steele, Edmund Cobb, Tom
London, Dick Botiller, Kenne Duncan, Harry
Cording, Hal Taliaferro, Ed Brady, Sons of the
Pioneers
D: Sam Nelson
SP: Bennett Cohen

985. SILVER ON THE SAGE
(Paramount, March 31, 1939) 68 Mins.
(*Hopalong Cassidy* Series)
William Boyd, Russell Hayden, George Hayes, Ruth
Rogers, Stanley Ridges, Frederick Burton, Hank
Bell, Jack Rockwell, Bruce Mitchell, Ed Cassidy,
Roy Barcroft, Jim Corey, Sherry Tansey, George
Morrell, Frank O'Connor, Buzz Barton, Herman
Hack, Dick Dickinson
D: Lesley Selander
SP: Harrison Jacobs
P: Harry Sherman

986. RANCH HOUSE ROMEO
(RKO, April 7, 1939) 17 Mins.
Ray Whitley, Mary Parker, Bob McKenzie, Tom
Chatterton, Victor Wong, Ken Card, Phelps
Brothers
D: Louis Brock
SP: Gilbert Wright

987. DODGE CITY
(Warner Bros., April 8, 1939) 104 Mins.
(Technicolor)
Errol Flynn, Olivia De Havilland, Ann Sheridan,
Bruce Cabot, Frank McHugh, Alan Hale, John
Litel, Henry Travers, Henry O'Neill, Victor Jory,
William Lundigan, Guinn "Big Boy" Williams,
Bobby Watson, Gloria Holden, Douglas Fowley,
Georgia Caine, Charles Halton, Ward Bond, Cora
Witherspoon, Russell Simpson, Monte Blue
D: Michael Curtiz
SP: Robert Buckner

988. TEXAS WILDCATS
(Victory, April 10, 1939) 57 Mins.
Tim McCoy, Joan Barclay, Ben Corbett, Forrest
Taylor, Ted Adams, Dave O'Brien, Frank Ellis,
Carl Mathews, Bob Terry, Slim Whitaker, Reed
Howes, George Morrell
D: Sam Newfield
S/SP: George H. Plympton
P: Sam Katzman

989. FRONTIER PONY EXPRESS
(Republic, April 12, 1939) 58 Mins.

Roy Rogers, Mary Hart (Lynne Roberts), Raymond
Hatton, Edward Keane, Monte Blue, Donald Dill-
away, Noble Johnson, William Royle, Ethel Wales,
George Letz (Montgomery), Charles King, Bud
Osborne, Fred Burns, Jack Kirk, Bob McKenzie,
Ernie Adams, Hank Bell, Jack O'Shea, "Trigger"
D/AP: Joseph Kane
SP: Norman S. Hall

990. THE NIGHT RIDERS
(Republic, April 12, 1939)   58 Mins.
(*Three Mesquiteers* Series)
John Wayne, Ray Corrigan, Max Terhune, Ruth
Rogers, Doreen McKay, George Douglas, Tom
Tyler, Sammy McKim, Kermit Maynard, Walter
Wills, Ethan Laidlaw, Ed Piel, Sr., Tom London,
Jack Ingram, Bill Nestell, Cactus Mack, Lee Shum-
way, Hal Price, Hank Worden, Roger Williams,
Olin Francis, Francis Walker, Hugh Prosser, Jack
Kirk, Yakima Canutt, Glenn Strange, David
Sharpe, Bud Osborne, Georgia Summers
D: George Sherman
SP: Betty Burbridge, Stanley Roberts. Based on
characters created by William Colt MacDonald
AP: William Berke

991. THE LAW COMES TO TEXAS
(Columbia, April 16, 1939)   58 Mins.
Bill Elliott, Veda Ann Borg, Bud Osborne, Charles
King, Slim Whitaker, Leon Beaumon, Edmund
Cobb, Paul Everton, Lee Shumway, Frank Ellis,
Jack Ingram, Frank LaRue, David Sharpe, Forrest
Taylor, Budd Buster, Lane Chandler, Dan White,
Ben Corbett
D: Joseph Levering
SP: Nate Gatzert
P: Larry Darmour

992. MAN FROM TEXAS
(Monogram, April 19, 1939)   56 Mins.
Tex Ritter, Ruth Rogers, Hal Price, Charles B.
Wood, Kenne Duncan, Vic Demourelle, Jr.,
Roy Barcroft, Frank Wayne, Tom London, Nel-
son McDowell, Sherry Tansey, Chick Hannon,
"White Flash"
D: Al Herman
SP: Robert Emmett (Tansey)
P: Edward Finney

993. OUTLAW'S PARADISE
(Victory, April 19, 1939)   62 Mins.
Tim McCoy, Ben Corbett, Joan Barclay, Dave
O'Brien, Ted Adams, Forrest Taylor, Bob Terry,
Don Gallagher, Jack Mulhall, Carl Mathews, Jack
C. Smith, George Morrell
D: Sam Newfield
S/SP: Basil Dickey
P: Sam Katzman

994. SPOILERS OF THE RANGE
(Columbia, April 27, 1939)   57 Mins.
Charles Starrett, Iris Meredith, Dick Curtis, Ken-
neth MacDonald, Hank Bell, Bob Nolan, Edward J.
LeSaint, Forbes Murray, Art Mix, Edmund Cobb,
Edward Piel, Sr., Ethan Laidlaw, Charles Brinley,
Joe Weaver, Horace B. Carpenter, Sons of the
Pioneers
D: C. C. Coleman, Jr.
S/SP: Paul Franklin

995. THE RETURN OF THE CISCO KID
(20th C. Fox, April 28, 1939)   70 Mins.
Warner Baxter, Lynn Bari, Cesar Romero, Henry
Hull, Kane Richmond, C. Henry Gordon, Robert
Barrat, Chris-Pin Martin, Adrian Morris, Soledad
Jimenez, Harry Strang, Arthur Aylesworth, Paul
Burns, Victor Kilian, Eddy Waller, Ruth Gilette,
Ward Bond
D: Herbert I. Leeds
SP: Milton Sperling. Based on the O. Henry char-
acter
AP: Kenneth MacGowan

996. MESQUITE BUCKAROO
(Metropolitan, May 1, 1939)   55 Mins.
Bob Steele, Carolyn (Clarene) Curtis, Frank La-
Rue, Juanita Fletcher, Charles King, Gordon Rob-
erts, Ted Adams, Joe Whitehead, Ed Brady, Bruce
Dane, Snub Pollard, John Elliott, Jimmy Aubrey,
Carleton Young
D/P: Harry S. Webb
SP: George Plympton

997. BLUE MONTANA SKIES
(Republic, May 4, 1939)   56 Mins.
Gene Autry, Smiley Burnette, June Storey, Walt
Shrum and his Colorado Hillbillies, Harry Woods,
Tully Marshall, Al Bridge, Glenn Strange, Doro-
thy Granger, Edmund Cobb, Robert Winkler, Jack
Ingram, John Beach, Elmo Lincoln, Allan Cavan,
Jay Wilsey (Buffalo Bill, Jr.), Augie Gomez,
"Champion"
D: B. Reeves Eason
S: Norman S. Hall, Paul Franklin
SP: Gerald Geraghty
AP: Harry Grey

998. UNION PACIFIC
(Paramount, May 5, 1939)   125 Mins.
Barbara Stanwyck, Joel McCrea, Akim Tamiroff,
Robert Preston, Lynne Overman, Brian Donlevy,
Anthony Quinn, Evelyn Keyes, Stanley Ridges,
Regis Toomey, J. M. Kerrigan, Francis McDonald,
Julia Faye, Ruth Warren, William Haade, William
Pawley, Syd Saylor, Fuzzy Knight, Richard Lane,
Harry Woods, Joe Sawyer, Lane Chandler, Si
Jenks, Robert Barrat, Henry Kolker, Willard Rob-

ertson, Lon Chaney, Jr., Harold Goodwin, Joseph Crehan, Julia Faye, Sheila Darcy, Earl Askam, Byron Foulger, Russell Hicks, May Beatty, Stanley Andrews, Jack Richardson, Mary MacLaren, Jane Keckley, Max Davidson, Elmo Lincoln, Emory Parnell, Frank Shannon, Walter Long, Monte Blue, Maude Fealy, Edward J. LeSaint, Nestor Paiva, Ed Brady, Richard Denning, David Newell, Stanhope Wheatcroft, Noble Johnson, Mala (Ray Mala)

D/P: Cecil B. DeMille

S: Ernest Haycox

SP: Walter DeLeon, C. Gardner Sullivan, Jesse Lasky, Jr.

999. THREE TEXAS STEERS

(Republic, May 12, 1939)   59 Mins.

(*Three Mesquiteers* Series)

John Wayne, Ray Corrigan, Max Terhune, Carole Landis, David Sharpe, Roscoe Ates, Ralph Graves, Colette Lyons, Billy Curtis, Ted Adams, Stanley Blystone, Ethan Laidlaw, Lew Kelly, John Merton, Ted Mapes, Dave Willock

D: George Sherman

SP: Betty Burbridge, Stanley Roberts. Based on characters created by William Colt MacDonald

AP: William Berke

1000. MAN OF CONQUEST

(Republic, May 15, 1939)   97 Mins.

Richard Dix, Gail Patrick, Joan Fontaine, Edward Ellis, George Hayes, Victor Jory, Robert Barrat, Ralph Morgan, C. Henry Gordon, Robert Armstrong, Max Terhune, Janet Beecher, George Letz (Montgomery), Guy Wilkerson, Charles Stevens, Hal Taliaferro, Lane Chandler, Ethan Laidlaw, Edmund Cobb, Billy Benedict, Tex Cooper, Leon Ames, Ferris Taylor, Kathleen Lockhart

D: George Nichols, Jr.

S: Harold Shumate, Wells Root

SP: Wells Root, E. E. Paramore, Jr.

P: Sol C. Siegel

1001. SOUTHWARD HO!

(Republic, March 19, 1939)   57 Mins.

Roy Rogers, Mary Hart (Lynne Roberts), George Hayes, Wade Boteler, Arthur Loft, Lane Chandler, Tom London, Ed Brady, Charles Moore, Fred Burns, Frank Ellis, Jack Ingram, Frank McCarroll, Curley Dresden, Jim Corey, Rudy Bowman, George Chesebro, "Trigger"

D/AP: Joseph Kane

S: Jack Natteford, John Rathmell

SP: Gerald Geraghty

1001a. YES, WE HAVE NO BONANZA

(Columbia, May 19, 1939)   2 Reels

(*Three Stooges* Series)

Moe Howard, Larry Fine, Curly Howard, Vernon Dent, Lynton Brent, Dick Curtis

D: Del Lord

S/SP: Elwood Ullman, Searle Kramer

1002. TUMBLEWEEDS

(United Artists, December 27, 1925; Astor reissue, May 20, 1939)   89 Mins.

(Sound prologue by Hart added to the reissue version)

William S. Hart, Barbara Bedford, Lucien Littlefield, J. Gordon Russell, Richard R. Neill, Jack Murphy, Lillian Leighton, Gertrude Claire, George Marion, Captain T. E. Duncan, James Gordon, Fred Gamble, Turner Savage, Monte Collins, Al Hoxie (unbilled)

D: King Baggott

S: Hal G. Evarts

SP: C. Gardner Sullivan

P: William S. Hart

1003. WOLF CALL

(Monogram, May 22, 1939)   62 Mins.

John Carroll, Movita, Polly Ann Young, George Cleveland, Wheeler Oakman, Peter George Lynn, Guy Usher, Holmes Herbert, John Sheehan, Charles Irwin, Roger Williams, Pat O'Malley

D: George Waggner

S: Jack London

SP: Joseph West

P: Paul Malvern

1004. THE OREGON TRAIL

(Universal, May, 1939)   15 Chaps.

Johnny Mack Brown, Louise Stanley, Fuzzy Knight, Bill Cody, Jr., Edward J. LeSaint, Roy Barcroft, James Blaine, Lane Chandler, Charles King, Jack C. Smith, Forrest Taylor, Charles Stevens, Colin Kelly, Budd Buster, Frank Ellis, Tom London, Iron Eyes Cody, Jim Thorpe, Karl Hackett, Horace Murphy, Tom Steele, Helen Gibson, Jim Toney, Warner Richmond, Kenneth Harlan, George Plues, Tex Young, Chick Hannon, Cactus Mack, Frank LaRue, Lafe McKee, Tom Smith

D: Ford Beebe, Saul A. Goodkind

SP: Edmund Kelso, George Plympton, Basil Dickey, W. W. Watson

P: Henry MacRae

Chapter Titles: (1) The Renegade's Revenge, (2) The Flaming Forest, (3) The Brink of Disaster, (4) Thundering Doom, (5) Stampede, (6) Indian Vengeance, (7) Trail of Treachery, (8) Redskin's Revenge, (9) The Avalanche of Doom, (10) The Plunge of Peril, (11) Trapped in the Flames, (12) The Baited Trap, (13) Crashing Timbers, (14) Death in the Night, (15) The End of the Trail

1005. ACROSS THE PLAINS

(Monogram, June 1, 1939)   59 Mins.

Jack Randall, Frank Yaconelli, Joyce Bryant, Hal
Price, Dennis Moore, Glenn Strange, Robert
Cord, Bud Osborne, Dean Spencer, James Sheri-
dan (Sherry Tansey), Wylie Grant, "Rusty"
D: Spencer Bennet
SP: Robert Emmett (Tansey)
P: Robert Tansey

1006. SAGEBRUSH SERENADE
(RKO, June 6, 1939)   19 Mins.
Ray Whitley, Jean Joyce, Chester Conklin, Isabel
Lamar, Ed Coke, Ken Card, Phelps Brothers, Kay
Whitley
D: Charles Roberts
SP: Charles Roberts, George Jeske

1007. DOWN THE WYOMING TRAIL
(Monogram, June 14, 1939)   56 Mins.
Tex Ritter, Mary Brodel, Horace Murphy, Bobby
Lawson, Charles King, Bob Terry, Jack Ingram,
Earl Douglas, Frank LaRue, Ernie Adams, Ed
Coxen, Jean Southern, Charles Sargent, The
Northwesterners (Merle Scobee, A. J. Brier,
Wilson Rasch, Ray Scobee, and Charles Davis),
"White Flash"
D: Al Herman
S/SP: Peter Dixon, Roger Merton
P: Edward Finney

1008. RACKETEERS OF THE RANGE
(RKO, June 14, 1939)   62 Mins.
George O'Brien, Chill Wills, Marjorie Reynolds,
Gay Seabrook, Robert Fiske, Ray Whitley, John
Dilson, Monte Montague, Ben Corbett, Bud Os-
borne, Cactus Mack, Frankie Marvin, Joe Balch,
Dick Hunter, Ed Piel, Sr., Frank O'Connor, Mary
Gordon, Stanley Andrews, Wilfred Lucas, Harry
Cording, Clint Sharp, Del Maggert
D: D. Ross Lederman
S/SP: Oliver Drake
P: Bert Gilroy

1009. WESTERN CARAVANS
(Columbia, June 15, 1939)   58 Mins.
Charles Starrett, Iris Meredith, Bob Nolan, Russell
Simpson, Hal Taliaferro, Dick Curtis, Hank Bell,
Sammy McKim, Edmund Cobb, Ethan Laidlaw,
Steve Clark, Herman Hack, Charles Brinley, Sons
of the Pioneers (Bob Nolan, Pat Brady, Tim
Spencer, Hugh and Karl Farr)
D: Sam Nelson
SP: Bennett Cohen

1010. THE GIRL AND THE GAMBLER
(RKO, June 16, 1939)   63 Mins.
Leo Carrillo, Tim Holt, Steffi Duna, Donald Mac-
Bride, Chris-Pin Martin, Edward Raquello, Paul

Fix, Julian Rivero, Frank Puglia, Esther Muir, Paul
Sutton, Charles Stevens, Frank Lackteen, Henry
Rocquemore
D: Lew Landers
S: "The Blue Ribbon"—Gerald Beaumont. Based
on Willard Mack's play "The Dove"
SP: Joseph A. Fields, Clarence Upson Young
P: Cliff Reid

1010a. PEST FROM THE WEST
(Columbia, June 16, 1939)   2 Reels
Buster Keaton, Lorna Gray (Adrian Booth), Gino
Corrado, Richard Fiske, Bud Jamison, Eddie
Laughton, Ned Glass, Forbes Murray
D: Del Lord
SP: Clyde Bruckman

1011. IN OLD CALIENTE
(Republic, June 19, 1939)   57 Mins.
Roy Rogers, Mary Hart (Lynne Roberts), George
Hayes, Jack LaRue, Katherine DeMille, Frank
Puglia, Harry Woods, Paul Marion, Ethel Wales,
Merrill McCormack, "Trigger"
D/AP: Joseph Kane
SP: Norman Houston, Gerald Geraghty

1012. SUSANNAH OF THE MOUNTIES
(20th C. Fox, June 23, 1939)   78 Mins.
(Sepiatone)
Shirley Temple, Randolph Scott, Margaret Lock-
wood, Martin Good Rider, J. Farrell MacDonald,
Maurice Moscovich, Moroni Olson, Victor Jory,
Lester Matthews, Leyland Hodges, Herbert
Evans, Jack Luden, Charles Irwin, John Sutton,
Chief Big Tree
D: William A. Seiter
S: "Susannah, A Little Girl of the Mounties"—
Muriel Denison
SP: Fidel La Barba, Walter Ferris, Robert Ellis,
Helen Logan
P: Kenneth MacGowan

1013. HARLEM RIDES THE RANGE
(Hollywood Pictures, June 20, 1939)   58 Mins.
Herbert Jeffrey, Lucius Brooks, F. E. Miller, Artie
Young, Spencer Williams, Clarence Brooks, Tom
Southern, John Thomas, Wade Dumas, The Four
Tunes, Leonard Christmas
D/P: Richard C. Kahn
S/SP: Spencer Williams, Jr., F. E. Miller

1014. WYOMING OUTLAW
(Republic, June 27, 1939)   62 Mins.
(Three Mesquiteers Series)
John Wayne, Ray Corrigan, Raymond Hatton, Don-
ald Barry, Adele Pearce (Pamela Blake), LeRoy
Mason, Charles Middleton, Katherine Ken-

worthy, Elmo Lincoln, Jack Ingram, David Sharpe, Jack Kenney, Yakima Canutt, Dave O'Brien, Curley Dresden, Tommy Coats, Ralph Peters, Jack Kirk, Al Taylor, Bud McTaggert, Budd Buster, Ed Payson
D: George Sherman
S: Jack Natteford
SP: Jack Natteford, Betty Burbridge
AP: William Berke

1015. MOUNTAIN RHYTHM
(Republic, June 29, 1939)   61 Mins.
Gene Autry, Smiley Burnette, June Storey, Maude Eburne, Ferris Taylor, Walter Fenner, Jack Pennick, Hooper Atchley, Bernard Suss, Edward Cassidy, Jack Ingram, Tom London, Frankie Marvin, Roger Williams, "Champion"
D: B. Reeves Eason
S: Connie Lee
SP: Gerald Geraghty
AP: Harry Grey

1016. TIMBER STAMPEDE
(RKO, June 30, 1939)   59 Mins.
George O'Brien, Chill Wills, Marjorie Reynolds, Morgan Wallace, Guy Usher, Earl Dwire, Frank Hagney, Monte Montague, Robert Fiske, Robert Burns, William Benedict, Tom London, Elmo Lincoln, Bud Osborne, Bob Kortman, Ben Corbett, Cactus Mack, Hank Worden
D: David Howard
S: Bernard McConville, Paul Franklin
SP: Morton Grant
P: Bert Gilroy

1017. THE SINGING COWGIRL
(Coronado/Grand National, June, 1939)   59 Mins.
Dorothy Page, David O'Brien, Vince Barnett, Warner Richmond, Dorothy Short, Ed Piel, Dix Dovis, Stanley Price, Paul Barrett, Lloyd Ingraham, Ethan Allen, Ed Gordon, Merrill McCormack
D: Samuel Diege
SP: Arthur Hoerl
P: George Hirliman

1018. THE MAN FROM SUNDOWN
(Columbia, July 15, 1939)   58 Mins.
Charles Starrett, Iris Meredith, Richard Fiske, Jack Rockwell, Al Bridge, Dick Botiller, Ernie Adams, Bob Nolan, Robert Fiske, Edward Piel, Sr., Clem Horton, Forrest Dillon, Tex Cooper, Al Haskell, Edward J. LeSaint, Kit Guard, George Chesebro, Oscar Gahan, Frank Ellis, Sons of the Pioneers
D: Sam Nelson
S: Paul Franklin

1019. RENEGADE TRAIL
(Paramount, July 25, 1939)   61 Mins.
(*Hopalong Cassidy* Series)
William Boyd, George Hayes, Russell Hayden, Charlotte Wynters, Russell Hopton, Sonny Bupp, Jack Rockwell, Roy Barcroft, John Merton, Bob Kortman, Eddie Dean, The King's Men (Ken Darby, Rad Robinson, Jon Dobson, and Bud Linn)
D: Lesley Selander
SP: John Rathmell, Harrison Jacobs. Based on characters created by Clarence E. Mulford
P: Harry Sherman

1020. FRONTIER MARSHAL
(20th C. Fox, July 28, 1939)   71 Mins.
Randolph Scott, Nancy Kelly, Cesar Romero, Binnie Barnes, John Carradine, Edward Norris, Eddie Foy, Jr., Ward Bond, Lon Chaney, Jr., Tom Tyler, Joe Sawyer, Del Henderson, Harry Hayden
D: Allan Dwan
S: "Wyatt Earp, Frontier Marshal"—Stuart Lake
SP: Sam Hellman
P: Sol Wurtzel

1021. COLORADO SUNSET
(Republic, July 31, 1939)   61 Mins.
Gene Autry, Smiley Burnette, June Storey, Larry "Buster" Crabbe, Barbara Pepper, Robert Barrat, Patsy Montana, Parnell Pratt, William Farnum, Kermit Maynard, Jack Ingram, Elmo Lincoln, Frankie Marvin, Ethan Laidlaw, Fred Burns, Jack Kirk, Budd Buster, Ed Cassidy, Slim Whitaker, Murdock McQuarrie, Ralph Peters, The CBS-KMBC Texas Rangers, "Champion"
D: George Sherman
S: Luci Ward, Jack Natteford
SP: Betty Burbridge, Stanley Roberts
AP: William Berke

1022. RIDERS OF THE SAGE
(Metropolitan, August 1, 1939)   57 Mins.
Bob Steele, Claire Rochelle, Ralph Hoopers, James Whitehead, Earl Douglas, Ted Adams, Dave O'Brien, Frank LaRue, Bruce Dane, Jerry Sheldon, Reed Howes, Bud Osborne, Gordon Roberts (Carleton Young)
D/P: Harry S. Webb
S: Forrest Sheldon
SP: Carl Krusada

1023. WALL STREET COWBOY
(Republic, August 6, 1939)   66 Mins.
Roy Rogers, George Hayes, Raymond Hatton, Ann Baldwin, Pierre Watkin, Louisiana Lou, Craig Reynolds, Ivan Miller, Reginald Barlow, Adrian Morris, Jack Roper, Jack Ingram, Fred Burns, Paul Fix, George Chesebro, Ted Mapes, "Trigger"

D: Joseph Kane
S: Doris Schroeder
SP: Gerald Geraghty, Norman S. Hall
AP: Joseph Kane

1024. NEW FRONTIER
(Republic, August 10, 1939) 57 Mins.
(*Three Mesquiteers* Series)
John Wayne, Ray Corrigan, Raymond Hatton, Phyllis Isley (Jennifer Jones), Eddy Waller, Sammy McKim, LeRoy Mason, Harrison Greene, Reginald Barlow, Burr Caruth, Dave O'Brien, Hal Price, Jack Ingram, Bud Osborne, Slim Whitaker, Curley Dresden, Jody Gilbert, Cactus Mack, George Chesebro, Robert Burns, Bob Reeves, Frank Ellis, Walt LaRue, Oscar Gahan, Charles Murphy, Herman Hack, George Plues, Wilbur Mack, Bill Wolfe
D: George Sherman
SP: Betty Burbridge, Luci Ward. Based on characters created by William Colt MacDonald
AP: William Berke

1025. BAD LANDS
(RKO, August 11, 1939) 70 Mins.
Robert Barrat, Douglas Walton, Robert Coote, Noah Beery, Jr., Guinn (Big Boy) Williams, Andy Clyde, Addison Richards, Paul Hurst, Francis Ford, Francis McDonald, Jack (John) Payne
D: Lew Landers
S: Clarence Upson Young
SP: Clarence Upson Young
P: Robert Sisk

1026. IN OLD MONTEREY
(Republic, August 14, 1939) 73 Mins.
Gene Autry, Smiley Burnette, June Storey, George Hayes, The Hoosier Hot Shots, Sarie and Sallie, The Ranch Boys, Stuart Hamblen, Billy Lee, Jonathan Hale, Robert Warwick, William Hall, Eddy Conrad, Curley Dresden, Victor Cox, Ken Carson, Bob Wilke, Hal Price, Tom Steele, Jack O'Shea, Rex Lease, Edward Earle, James Mason, Fred Burns, Dan White, Frank Ellis, Jim Corey, "Champion"
D: Joseph Kane
S: Gerald Geraghty, George Sherman
SP: Gerald Geraghty, Dorrell and Stuart McGowan
AP: Armand Schaefer

1027. RIDERS OF THE FRONTIER
(Monogram, August 16, 1939) 58 Mins.
Tex Ritter, Jack Rutherford, Hal Taliaferro, Jean Joyce, Marin Sais, Mantan Moreland, Olin Francis, Roy Barcroft, Merrill McCormack, Maxine Leslie, Nolan Willis, Nelson McDowell, Charles King, Forrest Taylor, Robert Frazer, "White Flash"

D: Spencer Bennet
S/SP: Jesse Duffy, Joseph Levering
P: Edward Finney

1028. RIDERS OF BLACK RIVER
(Columbia, August 23, 1939) 59 Mins.
Charles Starrett, Iris Meredith, Bob Nolan, Dick Curtis, Stanley Brown, Edmund Cobb, Francis Sayles, Forrest Taylor, George Chesebro, Carl Sepulveda, Ethan Allen, Olin Francis, Maston Williams, Sons of the Pioneers, Clem Horton
D: Norman Deming
S: "The Revenge Rider"—Ford Beebe
SP: Bennett Cohen

1029. OKLAHOMA TERROR
(Monogram, August 25, 1939) 50 Mins.
Jack Randall, Virginia Carroll, Al St. John, Davidson Clark, Nolan Willis, Glenn Strange, Warren McCollum, Don Rowan, Brandon Beach, Tris Coffin, Ralph Peters, Slim Whitaker, "Rusty"
D: Spencer Bennet
S: Lindsley Parsons
SP: Joseph West
P: Lindsley Parsons

1030. OVERLAND WITH KIT CARSON
(Columbia, August, 1939) 15 Chaps.
Bill Elliott, Iris Meredith, Richard Fiske, Bobby Clack, James Craig, Hal Taliaferro, Trevor Bardette, LeRoy Mason, Olin Francis, Frances Sayles, Kenneth MacDonald, Dick Curtis, Dick Botiller, Ernie Adams, Flo Campbell, Joe Garcia, Stanley Brown, Hank Bell, Art Mix, John Tyrell, Lee Prather, Irene Herndon, Jack Rockwell, Edward J. LeSaint, Martin Garralaga, Iron Eyes Cody, Carl Stockdale, Eddie Foster, Francisco Moran, Arnold Clack, Del Lawrence, J. W. Cody, Robert Fiske
D: Sam Nelson, Norman Deming
SP: Morgan Cox, Joseph Poland, Ned Dandy
P: Jack Fier
Chapter Titles: (1) Doomed Men, (2) Condemned to Die, (3) Fight for Life, (4) The Ride of Terror, (5) The Path of Doom, (6) Rendezvous with Death, (7) The Killer Stallion, (8) The Devil's Nest, (9) Blazing Peril, (10) The Black Raiders, (11) Foiled, (12) The Warning, (13) Terror in the Night, (14) Crumbling Walls, (15) Unmasked

1031. THE FIGHTING RENEGADE
(Victory, September 1, 1939) 58 Mins.
Tim McCoy, Joyce Bryant, Dave O'Brien, Budd Buster, Ben Corbett, Forrest Taylor, Ted Adams, Reed Howes, John Elliott, Carl Mathews
D: Sam Newfield
S/SP: William Lively
P: Sam Katzman

Overland with Kit Carson (Columbia, 1939) — Iris Meredith, Bill Elliott, and Richard Fiske

1032. CUPID RIDES THE RANGE

(RKO, September 8, 1939) 18 Mins.

Ray Whitley, Elvira Rios, Glenn Strange, Bob McKenzie, Hank Worden, Ken Card, Phelps Brothers

D: Lou Brock

SP: Lou Brock, Charles Wright

1033. DESPERATE TRAILS

(Universal, September 8, 1939) 58 Mins.

Johnny Mack Brown, Bob Baker, Fuzzy Knight, Frances Robinson, Bill Cody, Jr., Russell Simpson, Clarence Wilson, Ed Cassidy, Charles Stevens, Horace Murphy, Ralph Dunn, Tom Smith, Fern Emmett, Anita Camargo, Al Haskell, Frank Ellis, Jack Shannon, Wilbur McCauley, Frank McCarroll, Cliff Lyons, Eddie Parker

D: Albert Ray

SP: Andrew Bennison

AP: Albert Ray

1034. RANGE WAR

(Paramount, September 8, 1939) 66 Mins.

(*Hopalong Cassidy* Series)

William Boyd, Russell Hayden, Willard Robertson, Matt Moore, Pedro De Cordoba, Betty Moran, Britt Wood, Kenneth Harlan, Francis McDonald, Earle Hodgins, Jason Robards, Stanley Price, Eddie Dean, Raphael Bennett, Glenn Strange, George Chesebro, Don Latorre

D: Lesley Selander

S: Josef Montaigue

SP: Sam Robins. Based on characters created by Clarence E. Mulford

P: Harry Sherman

1035. OUTPOST OF THE MOUNTIES

(Columbia, September 14, 1939) 63 Mins.

Charles Starrett, Iris Meredith, Stanley Brown, Kenneth MacDonald, Edmund Cobb, Bob Nolan, Lane Chandler, Dick Curtis, Albert Morin, Hal Taliaferro, Pat O'Hara, Sons of the Pioneers

D: C. C. Coleman, Jr.

SP: Paul Franklin

1036. THE ARIZONA KID

(Republic, September 29, 1939) 61 Mins.

Roy Rogers, George Hayes, Stuart Hamblen, Sally March, David Kerwin, Earl Dwire, Dorothy Sebastian, Peter Fargo, Fred Burns, Ed Cassidy, Jack Ingram, Ted Mapes, Frank McCarroll, "Trigger"

D: Joseph Kane

S: Luci Ward

SP: Luci Ward, Gerald Geraghty

AP: Joseph Kane

1037. THE ADVENTURES OF THE MASKED PHANTOM

(Equity, October 1, 1939) 60 Mins.

Monte Rawlins, Sonny LaMont, Larry Mason (Art

Davis), Betty Burgess, Dot Karroll, George Douglas, Merrill McCormack, Dick Morehead, Matty Kemp, Jack Ingram, Curley Dresden, "Boots" (a dog), "Thunder" (a horse)
D: Charles Abbott
SP: Joseph O'Donnell, Clifford Sanforth
P: B. F. Zeidman

1038. THE KANSAS TERRORS

(Republic, October 6, 1939) 57 Mins.
(*Three Mesquiteers* Series)
Bob Livingston, Raymond Hatton, Duncan Renaldo, Jacqueline Wells (Julie Bishop), Howard Hickman, George Douglas, Frank Lackteen, Myra Marsh, Yakima Canutt, Ruth Robinson, Dick Alexander, Merrill McCormack, Artie Ortego, Curley Dresden, Al Haskell
D: George Sherman
S: Luci Ward
SP: Jack Natteford, Betty Burbridge. Based on characters created by William Colt MacDonald
AP: Harry Grey

1039. OKLAHOMA FRONTIER

(Universal, October 10, 1939) 58 Mins.
Johnny Mack Brown, Bob Baker, Fuzzy Knight, Anne Gwynne, James Blaine, Bob Kortman, Charles King, Harry Tenbrook, Horace Murphy, Lloyd Ingraham, Joe De LaCruz, Anthony Warde, Al Bridge, Robert Cummings, Sr., Lane Chandler, Hank Worden, Hank Bell, Blackie Whiteford, Roy Harris (Riley Hill), George Magrill, George Chesebro, Tom Smith, The Texas Rangers
D: Ford Beebe
SP: Ford Beebe
AP: Albert Ray

1040. THE PAL FROM TEXAS

(Metropolitan, November 1, 1939) 56 Mins.
Bob Steele, Claire Rochelle, Jack Perrin, Josef Swickard, Betty Mack, Ted Adams, Carleton Young, Jack Ingram, Robert Walker
D/P: Harry S. Webb
S: Forrest Sheldon
SP: Carl Krusada

1041. LAW OF THE PAMPAS

(Paramount, November 3, 1939) 74 Mins.
(*Hopalong Cassidy* Series)
William Boyd, Sidney Toler, Steffi Duna, Russell Hayden, Sidney Blackmer, Pedro De Cordoba, Jojo La Sadio, Glenn Strange, Eddie Dean, Anna Demetrio, William Duncan, Tony Roux, Martin Garralaga, The King's Men
D: Nate Watt
SP: Harrison Jacobs. Based on characters created by Clarence E. Mulford
P: Harry Sherman

1042. MARSHAL OF MESA CITY

(RKO, November 3, 1939) 63 Mins.
George O'Brien, Virginia Vale, Leon Ames, Henry Brandon, Harry Cording, Lloyd Ingraham, Slim Whitaker, Joe McGuinn, Mary Gordon, Frank Ellis, Wilfred Lucas, Carl Stockdale, Cactus Mack, Richard Hunter, Sid Jordan
D: David Howard
SP: Jack Lait, Jr.
P: Bert Gilroy

1042a. TEACHER'S PEST

(Columbia, November 3, 1939) 2 Reels
Charley Chase, Ruth Skinner, Richard Fiske, Vernon Dent, Bud Jamison, Hank Bell, Chester Conklin, Bill Wolfe
D: Del Lord
S/SP: Elwood Ullman, Searle Kramer

1043. FIGHTING MAD

(Criterion/Monogram, November 5, 1939) 60 Mins.
(*Renfrew* Series)
James Newill, Sally Blane, Benny Rubin, Dave O'Brien, Milburn Stone, Walter Long, Warner Richmond, Ted Adams, Chief Thunder Cloud, Ole Olson, Horace Murphy
D: Sam Newfield
S: "Renfrew Rides Again"—Laurie York Erskine
SP: George Rosenor, John Rathmell
P: Philip Krasne

1044. ALLEGHENY UPRISING

(RKO, November 10, 1939) 81 Mins.
John Wayne, Claire Trevor, Brian Donlevy, George Sanders, Chill Wills, Wilfred Lucas, Robert Barrat, John Hamilton, Moroni Olson, Eddie Quillan, Ian Wolfe, Wallis Clarke, Monte Montague, Eddy Waller, Olaf Hytten, Clay Clement
D: William A. Seiter
S: Neil Swanson
SP: P. J. Wolfson
P: Pandro Berman

1045. OVERLAND MAIL

(Monogram, November 16, 1939) 51 Mins.
Jack Randall, Vince Barnett, Jean Joyce, Tristam Coffin, Glenn Strange, George Cleveland, Harry Semels, Dennis Moore, Merrill McCormack, Joe Garcia, Maxine Leslie, James Sheridan (Sherry Tansey), Hal Price, "Rusty"
D: Robert Hill
SP: Robert Emmett (Tansey)
P: Robert Tansey

1046. ROVIN' TUMBLEWEEDS

(Republic, November 16, 1939) 64 Mins.
(Also known as *Washington Cowboy*)

Gene Autry, Smiley Burnette, Mary Carlisle, Douglass Dumbrille, William Farnum, Lee "Lasses" White, Ralph Peters, Gordon Hart, Vic Potel, Sammy McKim, Jack Ingram, Reginald Barlow, Eddie Kane, Guy Usher, Horace Murphy, David Sharpe, Jack Kirk, Rose Plummer, Robert Burns, Art Mix, Horace B. Carpenter, Fred Toones, Frank Ellis, Fred Burns, Edward Cassidy, Forrest Taylor, Tom Chatterton, Crauford Kent, Maurice Costello, Charles K. French, Lee Shumway, Bud Osborne, Harry Semels, Chuck Morrison, Nora Lou Martin and the Pals of the Golden West, "Champion"
D: George Sherman
SP: Betty Burbridge, Dorrell and Stuart McGowan
AP: William Berke

1047. SAGA OF DEATH VALLEY

(Republic, November 17, 1939)   58 Mins.
Roy Rogers, George Hayes, Donald Barry, Doris Day, Frank M. Thomas, Jack Ingram, Hal Taliaferro, Lew Kelly, Fern Emmett, Tommy Baker, Buzz Buckley, Horace Murphy, Lane Chandler, Fred Burns, Jimmy Wakely, Johnny Bond, Dick Rinehart, Peter Frago, Ed Brady, Bob Thomas, Matty Roubert, Pasquel Perry, Cactus Mack, Art Dillard, Horace B. Carpenter, Hooper Atchley, Frankie Marvin, "Trigger," Art Dillard, Jess Cavan
D/AP: Joseph Kane
S: Karen DeWolf
SP: Karen DeWolf, Stuart Anthony

1048. THE FIGHTING GRINGO

(RKO, November 28, 1939)   59 Mins.
George O'Brien, Lupita Tovar, Lucio Villegas, William Royle, Glenn Strange, Slim Whitaker, LeRoy Mason, Mary Field, Martin Garralaga, Dick Botiler, Bill Cody, Cactus Mack, Chris-Pin Martin, Ben Corbett, Forrest Taylor, Hank Bell
D: David Howard
S/SP: Oliver Drake
P: Bert Gilroy

1049. CHIP OF THE FLYING U

(Universal, November 29, 1939)   55 Mins.
Johnny Mack Brown, Bob Baker, Fuzzy Knight, Doris Weston, Karl Hackett, Forrest Taylor, Anthony Warde, Henry Hall, Claire Whitney, Ferris Taylor, Cecil Kellogg, Hank Bell, Harry Tenbrook, Chester Conklin, Vic Potel, Hank Worden, Charles K. French, Al Ward, Budd Buster, Frank Ellis, Kermit Maynard, Jack Shannon, Chuck Morrison
D: Ralph Staub
S: B. M. Bower
SP: Larry Rhine, Andrew Bennison

1050. COWBOYS FROM TEXAS

(Republic, November 29, 1939)   57 Mins.
(*Three Mesquiteers* Series)
Robert Livingston, Raymond Hatton, Duncan Renaldo, Carole Landis, Charles Miller, Ivan Miller, Betty Compson, Ethan Laidlaw, Yakima Canutt, Walter Willis, Ed Cassidy, Bud Osborne, Charles King, Forbes Murray, Horace Murphy, Harry Strang, Jack Kirk, David Sharpe, Lew Meehan, Jack O'Shea
D: George Sherman
S/SP: Oliver Drake. Based on characters created by William Colt MacDonald
AP: Harry Grey

1051. FLAMING LEAD

(Colony, November, 1939)   57 Mins.
Ken Maynard, Eleanor Stewart, Dave O'Brien, Ralph Peters, Walter Long, Tom London, Carleton Young, Reed Howes, Bob Terry, Kenne Duncan, Ethan Allen, Joyce Rogers, John Merton, Carl Mathews
D: Sam Newfield
SP: Joseph O'Donnell
P: Max and Arthur Alexander

1052. EL DIABLO RIDES

(Metropolitan, December 1, 1939)   57 Mins.
Bob Steele, Claire Rochelle, Kit Guard, Carleton Young, Ted Adams, Robert Walker, Bob Robinson, Hal Carey
D: Ira Webb
SP: Carl Krusada
P: Harry S. Webb

1053. RENO

(RKO, December 1, 1939)
Richard Dix, Gail Patrick, Anita Louise, Paul Cavanaugh, Laura Hope Crews, Louis Jean Heydt, Hobart Cavanaugh, Charles Halton, Astrid Allwyn, Joyce Compton, Frank Faylen, William Haade
D: John Farrow
P: Robert Sisk
S: Ellis St. Joseph
SP: John Twist

1054. TAMING OF THE WEST

(Columbia, December 7, 1939)   55 Mins.
Bill Elliott, Iris Meredith, Dick Curtis, Dub Taylor, James Craig, Stanley Brown, Ethan Allen, Kenneth MacDonald, Victor Wong, Don Beddoe, Charles King, Hank Bell, Irene Herndon, John Tyrell, Lane Chandler, George Morrell, Bob Woodward, Art Mix, Richard Fiske
D: Norman Deming
S: Robert Lee Johnson
SP: Charles Francis Royal, Robert Lee Johnson

1055. THE LLANO KID

(Paramount, December 8, 1939) 70 Mins.

Tito Guizar, Gale Sondergaard, Alan Mowbray, Jane Clayton, Emma Dunn, Minor Watson, Chris-Pin Martin, Carlos de Valdez, Anna Demetrio, Glenn Strange, Tony Roux, Harry Worth, Eddie Dean

D: Edward Venturini

S: "Double-Dyed Deceiver"—O. Henry

SP: Wanda Tuchock

P: Harry Sherman

1056. CRASHING THRU

(Monogram, December 11, 1939) 65 Mins.

(*Renfrew* Series)

James Newill, Jean Carmen, Warren Hull, Iron Eyes Cody, Milburn Stone, Walter Byron, Stanley Blystone, Robert Frazer, Joseph Girard, Dave O'Brien, Earl Douglas, Ted Adams, Roy Barcroft

D: Elmer Clifton

S: Laurie York Erskine

SP: Sherman Lowe

P: Philip N. Krasna

1057. BANDITS AND BALLADS

(RKO, December 15, 1939) 17 Mins.

Ray Whitley, Ken Card, Phelps Brothers, Jay Novello

D: Lou Brock

SP: Hal Yates, Lou Brock

1058. SOUTH OF THE BORDER

(Republic, December 15, 1939) 71 Mins.

Gene Autry, Smiley Burnette, June Storey, Lupita Tovar, Mary Lee, Duncan Renaldo, Frank Reicher, Alan Edwards, Claire DuBrey, Dick Botiller, William Farnum, Selmer Jackson, Sheila Darcy, Rex Lease, Charles King, Reed Howes, Jack O'Shea, Slim Whitaker, Hal Price, Julian Rivero, Curley Dresden, The Checkerboard Band, "Champion," Art Wenzel

D: George Sherman

S: Dorrell and Stuart McGowan

AP: William Berke

1059. WESTBOUND STAGE

(Monogram, December 15, 1939) 56 Mins.

Tex Ritter, Nelson McDowell, Muriel Evans, Nolan Willis, Steve Clark, Tom London, Reed Howes, Frank Ellis, Chick Hannon, Kenne Duncan, Frank LaRue, Chester Gan, Hank Bell, Phil Dunham

D: Spencer Bennet

S: Robert Emmett (Tansey)

P: Edward Finney

1060. ZORRO'S FIGHTING LEGION

(Republic, December 16, 1939) 12 Chaps.

Reed Hadley, Sheila Darcy, William Corson, Leander de Cordova, Edmund Cobb, John Merton, C. Montague Shaw, Billy Bletcher, Budd Buster, Carleton Young, Guy D'Enery, Paul Marion, Joe Molina, Jim Pierce, Helen Mitchel, Charles King, Curley Dresden, Al Taylor, Joe De LaCruz, Jason Robards, Sr., Theodore Lorch, Jack O'Shea, Jerome Ward, Millard McGowan, Augie Gomez, Cactus Mack, Bud Geary, Jack Moore, George Plues, Jack Carrington, Victor Cox, Bob Wilbur, John Wallace, Burt Dillard, Jimmy Fawcett, Martin Faust, Ken Terrell, Wylie Grant, Carl Sepulveda, Eddie Cherkose, Charles Murphy, Max Marx, Buel Bryant, Norman Lane, Ralph Faulkner, Alan Gregg, Ernest Sarracino, Yakima Canutt, Reed Howes, Barry Hays, Joe McGuinn, Bill Yrigoyen, Jerry Frank, Gordon Clark, Frank Ellis, Joe Yrigoyen, Ted Mapes, Henry Wills

D: William Witney, John English

SP: Ronald Davidson, Franklyn Adreon, Morgan Cox, Sol Shor, Barney A. Sarecky

AP: Hiram S. Brown, Jr.

Chapter Titles: (1) The Golden God, (2) The Flaming "Z," (3) Descending Doom, (4) The Bridge of Peril, (5) The Decoy, (6) Zorro to the Rescue, (7) The Fugitive, (8) Flowing Death, (9) The Golden Arrow, (10) Mystery Wagon, (11) Face to Face, (12) Unmasked

1061. THE STRANGER FROM TEXAS

(Columbia, December 18, 1939) 54 Mins.

Charles Starrett, Lorna Gray (Adrian Booth), Richard Fiske, Dick Curtis, Edmund Cobb, Bob Nolan, Al Bridge, Jack Rockwell, Hal Taliaferro, Edward J. LeSaint, Buel Bryant, Art Mix, George Chesebro

D: Sam Nelson

S: "The Mysterious Avenger"—Ford Beebe

SP: Paul Franklin

1062. DAYS OF JESSE JAMES

(Republic, December 20, 1939) 63 Mins.

Roy Rogers, George Hayes, Pauline Moore, Donald Barry, Harry Woods, Arthur Loft, Wade Boteler, Ethel Wales, Scotty Beckett, Harry Worth, Glenn Strange, Olin Howlin, Monte Blue, Jack Rockwell, Fred Burns, Bud Osborne, Jack Ingram, Carl Sepulveda, Forrest Dillon, Hansel Warner, Lynton Brent, Pasquel Perry, Eddie Acuff, "Trigger"

D/AP: Joseph Kane

S: Jack Natteford

SP: Earle Snell

1063. THE GENTLEMAN FROM ARIZONA
(Monogram, December 25, 1939)   71 Mins.
(Cinecolor)
J. Farrell MacDonald, Joan Barclay, John King, Craig
    Reynolds, Ruthie Reece, Johnny Morris, Nora
    Lane, Doc Pardee
D: Earl Haley
SP: Earl Haley, Jack O'Donnell
P: Charles Goetz

1064. DESTRY RIDES AGAIN
(Universal, December 29, 1939)   94 Mins.
Marlene Dietrich, James Stewart, Charles Winnin-
    ger, Mischa Auer, Brian Donlevy, Allen Jenkins,
    Warren Hymer, Irene Hervey, Una Merkel, Tom
    Fadden, Samuel S. Hinds, Lillian Yarbro, Billy Gil-
    bert, Edmund McDonald, Virginia Brissac, Ann
    Todd, Dickie Jones, Jack Carson, Carmen D'An-
    tonio, Joe King, Harry Cording, Dick Alexander,
    Minerva Urecal, Bob McKenzie, Billy Bletcher,
    Lloyd Ingraham, Bill Cody, Jr., William Steele,
    Harry Tenbrook, Bud McClure, Alex Voloshin,
    Chief Big Tree, Loren Brown
D: George Marshall
S: Max Brand
SP: Felix Jackson, Gertrude Purcell, Harry Myers

1065. STRAIGHT SHOOTER
(Victory, 1939)   54 Mins.
Tim McCoy, Julie Sheldon, Ben Corbett, Ted

Adams, Reed Howes, Forrest Taylor, Budd Bus-
    ter, Wally West, Carl Mathews, Jack Ingram
D: Sam Newfield
SP: Joseph O'Donnell, Basil Dickey
P: Sam Katzman

1066. TRIGGER FINGERS
(Victory, 1939)   60 Mins.
Tim McCoy, Ben Corbett, Jill Martin, Joyce Bryant,
    John Elliott, Ted Adams, Ralph Peters, Bud
    McTaggert, Forrest Taylor, Kenne Duncan,
    Carleton Young, Carl Mathews
D: Sam Newfield
S: Basil Dickey
SP: Basil Dickey
P: Sam Katzman

1066a. RIDE, COWBOY, RIDE
(Warner Bros., 1939)   2 Reels
(Technicolor)
Dennis Morgan, Mavis Wrixton, George Reeves
D: George Amy
SP: Crane Wilbur

1066b. THE ROYAL RODEO
(Warner Bros., 1939)   2 Reels   (15 Min.)
(Technicolor)
John Payne, Scotty Beckett, Cliff Edwards
D: George Amy

FILMS OF 1940

1067. THE CISCO KID AND THE LADY
(20th C. Fox, January 2, 1940)   73 Mins.
(*Cisco Kid* Series)
Cesar Romero, Marjorie Weaver, Chris-Pin Mar-
    tin, George Montgomery, Robert Barrat, Vir-
    ginia Field, Harry Green, Gloria Ann White,
    John Beach, Ward Bond, J. Anthony Hughes,
    James Burke, Harry Hayden, James Flaven, Ruth
    Warren
D: Herbert Leeds
S: Stanley Rauh
SP: Frances Hyland. Based on the O. Henry charac-
    ter
AP: John Stone

1068. YUKON FLIGHT
(Criterion/Monogram, January 2, 1940)   57 Mins.
(*Renfrew* Series)
James Newill, Louise Stanley, Warren Hull, Dave
    O'Brien, William Pawley, Karl Hackett, Jack Clif-
    ford, Roy Barcroft, Bob Terry, Earl Douglas

D: Ralph Staub
S: "Renfrew Rides North"—Laurie York Erskine
SP: Edward Halperin
P: Philip N. Krasne

1069. TWO-FISTED RANGERS
(Columbia, January 4, 1940)   62 Mins.
Charles Starrett, Iris Meredith, Bob Nolan and the
    Sons of the Pioneers, Kenneth MacDonald, Hal
    Taliaferro, Dick Curtis, Bill Cody, Jr., Ethan Laid-
    law, James Craig, Bob Woodward, Francis Walker
D: Joseph H. Lewis
SP: Fred Myton

1070. LEGION OF THE LAWLESS
(RKO, January 5, 1940)   59 Mins.
George O'Brien, Virginia Vale, Herbert Heywood,
    Norman Willis, Hugh Sothern, William Bene-
    dict, Eddy Waller, Delmar Watson, Bud Osborne,
    Monte Montague, Slim Whitaker, Mary Field,
    Richard Cramer, John Dilson, Martin Garralaga,

Yukon Flight (Criterion/Monogram, 1940) — Louise Stanley, Dave O'Brien, and James Newill

Ed Piel, Lloyd Ingraham, Henry Wills, Wilfred Lucas
D: David Howard
S: Berne Giler
SP: Doris Schroeder
P: Bert Gilroy

1071. GERONIMO

(Paramount, January 12, 1940)   90 Mins.
Preston Foster, Ellen Drew, Andy Devine, William Henry, Ralph Morgan, Gene Lockhart, Marjorie Gateson, Pierre Watkin, Addison Richards, Chief Thunder Cloud, Joseph Crehan, Hank Bell, William Haade, Joe Dominguez, Stanley Andrews, Ivan Miller, Frank M. Thomas, Richard Denning
D/SP: Paul H. Sloane

1072. HEROES OF THE SADDLE

(Republic, January 12, 1940)   59 Mins.
(*Three Mesquiteers* Series)
Robert Livingston, Raymond Hatton, Duncan Renaldo, Patsy Lee Parsons, Loretta Weaver, Byron Foulger, Vince Barnett, William Royle, Jack Roper, Reed Howes, Ethel May Halls, Al Taylor, Patsy Carmichael, Kermit Maynard, Tom Hanlon, Tex Terry, Douglas Deems, Darwood Kaye, Matt McHugh, Harrison Greene
D: William Witney

SP: Jack Natteford. Based on characters created by William Colt MacDonald
AP: Harry Grey

1073. THE SAGEBRUSH FAMILY TRAILS WEST

(PDC, January 14, 1940)   60 Mins.
Bobby Clark, Earle Hodgins, Nina Guilbert, Joyce Bryant, Minerva Urecal, Archie Hall, Kenne Duncan, Forrest Taylor, Carl Mathews, Wally West, Byron Vance, Augie Gomez
D: Peter Stewart (Sam Newfield)
SP: William Lively
P: Sigmund Neufeld
(Producers Distributing Company [PDC] later became Producers Releasing Corporation [PRC])

1074. TEXAS RENEGADES

(PDC, January 17, 1940)   59 Mins.
Tim McCoy, Nora Lane, Harry Harvey, Kenne Duncan, Lee Prather, Earl Gunn, Hal Price, Joe McGuinn, Edward Cassidy
D: Peter Stewart (Sam Newfield)
SP: Joe O'Donnell
P: Sigmund Neufeld

1075. DANGER AHEAD

(Criterion/Monogram, January 22, 1940)   60 Mins.
(*Renfrew* Series)
James Newill, Dorthea Kent, Dave O'Brien, Guy

Usher, Maude Allen, Harry Depp, John Dilson, Al Shaw, Dick Rich, Bob Terry, Lester Dorr, Earl Douglas
D: Ralph Staub
SP: Edward Halperin
S: "Renfrew's Long Trail"—Laurie York Erskine
P: Philip N. Krasne

1076. PIONEER DAYS
(Monogram, January 25, 1940) 51 Mins.
Jack Randall, June Wilkins, Frank Yaconelli, Nelson McDowell, Ted Adams, Bud Osborne, Robert Walker, Glenn Strange, Jimmy Aubrey, Lafe McKee, George Chesebro, Denver Dixon, Dick Cramer
D/P: Harry S. Webb
SP: Bennett Cohen

1077. SANTA FE MARSHAL
(Paramount, January 26, 1940) 65 Mins.
(*Hopalong Cassidy* Series)
William Boyd, Russell Hayden, Marjorie Rambeau, Bernadine Hayes, Earle Hodgins, Britt Wood, Kenneth Harlan, William Pagan, George Anderson, Jack Rockwell, Eddie Dean, Fred Graham, Matt Moore, Duke Green, Billy Jones, Tex Phelps, Cliff Parkinson
D: Lesley Selander
SP: Harrison Jacobs. Based on characters created by Clarence E. Mulford
P: Harry Sherman

1078. DEATH RIDES THE RANGE
(Colony, January, 1940) 58 Mins.
Ken Maynard, Fay McKenzie, Ralph Peters, Julian Rivero, Charles King, John Elliott, William Costello, Swen Hugh Borg, Michael Vallon, Julian Madison, Kenneth Rhodes, Murdock McQuarrie, Wally West, "Tarzan," Dick Alexander, Bud Osborne
D: Sam Newfield
SP: William Lively
P: Max and Arthur Alexander

1079. MY LITTLE CHICKADEE
(Universal, February 9, 1940) 85 Mins.
Mae West, W. C. Fields, Joseph Calleia, Dick Foran, Ruth Connelly, Margaret Hamilton, Donald Meek, Fuzzy Knight, Willard Robertson, George Moran, Fay Adler, Jackie Searl, Gene Austin, Coco and Candy
D: Edward F. Cline
S: Mae West, W. C. Fields
P: Lester Cowan

1080. BULLETS AND BALLADS
(Universal, February 14, 1940) 18 Mins.

Armida, Ken Stevens, The Texas Rangers, Marilyn Kay, Caits Brothers
D: Larry Ceballos

1081. PIONEERS OF THE FRONTIER
(Columbia, February 14, 1940) 58 Mins.
Bill Elliott, Linda Winters (Dorothy Comingore), Dick Curtis, Dub Taylor, Stanley Brown, Richard Fiske, Carl Stockdale, Ralph McCullough, Lafe McKee, Al Bridge, Edmund Cobb, George Chesebro, Lynton Brent, Jack Kirk, Ralph Peters
D: Sam Nelson
SP: Fred Myton

1082. THE MAN FROM DAKOTA
(MGM, February 16, 1940) 75 Mins.
Wallace Beery, John Howard, Dolores Del Rio, Donald Meek, Robert Barrat, Addison Richards, Frederick Burton, William Haade, John Wray
D: Leslie Fenton
S: MacKinlay Kantor
SP: Lawrence Stallings
P: Edward Chodorov

1083. THE CHEYENNE KID
(Monogram, February 20, 1940) 50 Mins.
Jack Randall, Louise Stanley, Kenneth Duncan, Frank Yaconelli, Reed Howes, Charles King, George Chesebro, Forrest Taylor, Tex Palmer
D: Raymond K. Johnson
SP: Tom Gibson
P: Harry S. Webb

1084. KNIGHTS OF THE RANGE
(Paramount, February 23, 1940) 68 Mins.
Russell Hayden, Victor Jory, Jean Parker, Britt Wood, J. Farrell MacDonald, Morris Ankrum, Ethel Wales, Rad Robinson, Raphael (Ray) Bennett, Edward Cassidy, Eddie Dean, The King's Men
D: Lesley Selander
S: Zane Grey
SP: Norman Houston
P: Harry Sherman

1085. NORTHWEST PASSAGE
(MGM, February 23, 1940) 125 Mins.
Spencer Tracy, Robert Young, Walter Brennan, Ruth Hussey, Nat Pendleton, Louis Hector, Robert Barrat, Lumsden Hare, Donald McBride, Isabel Jewell, Douglas Walton, Addison Richards, Truman Bradley, Hugh Sothern, Regis Toomey, Montague Love, Lester Matthews, Andrew Pena
D: King Vidor
S: Kenneth Roberts
SP: Lawrence Stallings, Talbot Jennings
P: Hunt Stromberg

Pioneers of the Frontier (Columbia, 1940) — Bill Elliott and Dick Curtis

1086. MURDER ON THE YUKON

(Criterion/Monogram, February 25, 1940) 58 Mins.

(*Renfrew* Series)

James Newill, Polly Ann Young, Dave O'Brien, Al St. John, William Royle, Chief Thunder Cloud, Budd Buster, Karl Hackett, Snub Pollard, Kenne Duncan, Earl Douglas, Jack Clifford

D: Louis Gasnier

S: "Renfrew Rides North"—Laurie York Erskine

SP: Milton Raison

P: Philip N. Krasne

1087. WILD HORSE VALLEY

(Metropolitan, March 1, 1940) 57 Mins.

Bob Steele, Phyllis Adair, Buzz Barton, Lafe McKee, Jimmy Aubrey, Ted Adams, Bud Osborne, George Chesebro

D: Ira Webb

SP: Carl Krusada

P: Harry S. Webb

1088. RHYTHM OF THE RIO GRANDE

(Monogram, March 2, 1940) 53 Mins.

Tex Ritter, Suzan Dale, Warner Richmond, Martin Garralaga, Lloyd "Arkansas Slim" Andrews, Frank Mitchell, Glenn Strange, Tris Coffin, Mike Rodriquez, Forrest Taylor, Juan Duval, Chick Hannon, James McNally, Earl Douglas, "White Flash," Wally West

D: Al Herman

SP: Robert Emmett Tansey

P: Edward Finney

1088a. ROCKIN' THROUGH THE ROCKIES

(Columbia, March 3, 1940) 2 Reels

(*Three Stooges* Series)

Moe Howard, Curly Howard, Larry Fine, Linda Winters (Dorothy Comingore), Dorothy Appleby, Lorna Gray (Adrian Booth), Kathryn Sheldon

D: Jules White

1089. MAN FROM MONTREAL

(Universal, March 4, 1940) 60 Mins.

Richard Arlen, Andy Devine, Anne Gwynne, Kay Sutton, Jerry Marlowe, Addison Richards, Reed Hadley, Joe Sawyer, Tommy Whitten, Eddy Waller, Lane Chandler, Eddy Conrad, William Royle

D: Christy Cabanne

S: Ben Pivar

SP: Owen Francis

P: Ben Pivar

1090. BULLETS FOR RUSTLERS

(Columbia, March 5, 1940) 58 Mins.

Charles Starrett, Lorna Gray (Adrian Booth), Bob

Nolan, Dick Curtis, Jack Rockwell, Kenneth Mac-
Donald, Edward J. LeSaint, Francis Walker, Eddie
Laughton, Lee Frather, Hal Taliaferro, Sons of
the Pioneers
D: Sam Nelson
SP: John Rathmell

1091. THE SHOWDOWN

(Paramount, March 8, 1940) 65 Mins.
(*Hopalong Cassidy* Series)
William Boyd, Russell Hayden, Britt Wood, Morris
Ankrum, Jane (Jan) Clayton, Wright Kramer,
Donald Kirke, Roy Barcroft, Kermit Maynard,
Walter Shumway, Eddie Dean, The King's Men
D: Howard Bretherton
S: Jack Jungmeyer. Based on Clarence E. Mulford
characters
SP: Howard and Donald Kusel
P: Harry Sherman

1092. PIONEERS OF THE WEST

(Republic, March 12, 1940) 56 Mins.
(*Three Mesquiteers* Series)
Robert Livingston, Raymond Hatton, Duncan
Renaldo, Noah Beery, Beatrice Roberts, Lane
Chandler, George Cleveland, Hal Taliaferro,
Yakima Canutt, John Dilson, Joe McGuinn, Earl
Askam, George Chesebro, Jack Kirk, Herman
Hack, Bob Burns, Tex Terry, Chuck Baldra, Han-
sel Warner, Art Dillard, Ray Jones, Artie Ortego
D: Les Orlebeck
SP: Jack Natteford, Karen DeWolf, Gerald Ger-
aghty. Based on William Colt MacDonald char-
acters
AP: Harry Grey

1093. MOLLY CURES A COWBOY

(RKO, March 22, 1940) 17 Mins.
Ray Whitley, Lee "Lasses" White, Kathryn Adams,
Bob Burns, Hank Worden, Cactus Mack, Ken
Card
D: Jean Yarbrough
SP: Oliver Drake

1094. RANCHO GRANDE

(Republic, March 22, 1940) 68 Mins.
Gene Autry, Smiley Burnette, June Storey, Mary
Lee, Dick Hogan, Ellen Lowe, Ferris Taylor, Jo-
seph DeStefani, Roscoe Ates, Rex Lease, Ann
Baldwin, Roy Barcroft, Edna Lawrence, Jack In-
gram, Bud Osborne, Slim Whitaker, The Brewer
Kids, The Boys Choir of Saint Joseph's School,
The Pals of the Golden West, "Champion"
D: Frank McDonald
S: Pete Milne, Connie Lee
SP: Bradford Ropes, Betty Burbridge, Peter Milne
AP: William Berke

1095. VIRGINIA CITY

(Warner Bros., March 23, 1940) 121 Mins.
Errol Flynn, Miriam Hopkins, Randolph Scott,
Humphrey Bogart, Frank McHugh, Alan Hale,
Guinn (Big Boy) Williams, John Litel, Douglass
Dumbrille, Moroni Olson, Russell Hicks, Dickie
Jones, Frank Wilcox, Russell Simpson, Victor Kil-
ian, Charles Middleton
D: Michael Curtiz
SP: Robert Henry Buckner
AP: Robert Fellows

1096. GHOST VALLEY RAIDERS

(Republic, March 26, 1940) 57 Mins.
Donald Barry, Lona Andre, LeRoy Mason, Tom
London, Jack Ingram, Horace Murphy, Ralph
Peters, Curley Dresden, Yakima Canutt, John
Beach, Bud Osborne, Al Taylor, Jack Montgom-
ery, Fred Burns
D/AP: George Sherman
S: Connie Lee
SP: Bennett Cohen

1097. PHANTOM RANCHER

(Colony, March, 1940) 61 Mins.
Ken Maynard, Dorothy Short, Harry Harvey, Dave
O'Brien, Ted Adams, Tom London, John Elliott,
Reed Howes, Steve Clark, Carl Mathews, Sherry
Tansey, Wally West, George Morrell, Herman
Hack, "Tarzan"
D: Harry Fraser
SP: William Lively
P: Max and Arthur Alexander

1098. BLAZING SIX SHOOTERS

(Columbia, April 4, 1940) 61 Mins.
Charles Starrett, Iris Meredith, Dick Curtis, Bob
Nolan, Al Bridge, George Cleveland, Henry Hall,
Stanley Brown, John Tyrell, Eddie Laughton,
Francis Walker, Edmund Cobb, Bruce Bennett,
Sons of the Pioneers
D: Joseph H. Lewis
SP: Paul Franklin

1099. DARK COMMAND

(Republic, April 5, 1940) 94 Mins.
Claire Trevor, John Wayne, Walter Pidgeon, Roy
Rogers, George Hayes, Porter Hall, Marjorie
Main, Raymond Walburn, Joe Sawyer, Helen
MacKellar, J. Farrell MacDonald, Trevor Bar-
dette, Tom London, Dick Alexander, Yakima
Canutt, Hal Taliaferro, Edmund Cobb, Edward
Hearn, Ernie Adams, Jack Rockwell, Al Bridge,
Glenn Strange, Harry Woods, Harry Cording,
Frank Hagney, Dick Rich, John Dilson, Clinton
Rosemond, Budd Buster, Howard Hickman, John
Merton, Al Taylor, Mildred Gover, Jack Low,

Ferris Taylor, Edward Earle, Dick Alexander, Joe McGuinn, Harry Strang, Tex Cooper, Jack Montgomery
D: Raoul Walsh
S: W. R. Burnett
SP: F. Hugh Herbert, Grover Jones, Lionel Houser
AP: Sol C. Siegel

1100. RIDERS OF PASCO BASIN
(Universal, April 5, 1940) 56 Mins.
Johnny Mack Brown, Fuzzy Knight, Bob Baker, Frances Robinson, Frank LaRue, Arthur Loft, James Guilfoyle, Lafe McKee, Chuck Morrison, Edward Cassidy, Robert Winkler, William Gould, Ted Adams, Kermit Maynard, David Sharpe, Hank Bell, Edward Piel, John Judd, Gordon Hart, Rudy Sooter and his Californians
D: Ray Taylor
S/SP: Ford Beebe

1101. THE SINGING DUDE
(Warner Bros., April 5, 1940) 18 Mins.
(Technicolor)
Dennis Morgan, Lucille Fairbanks, Fuzzy Knight
D/SP/P: Unknown

1102. COVERED WAGON TRAILS
(Monogram, April 10, 1940) 52 Mins.
Jack Randall, Sally Cairns, David Sharpe, Lafe McKee, Budd Buster, Glenn Strange, Kenne Duncan, Hank Bell, Frank Ellis, George Chesebro, Carl Mathews, Edward Hearn, Art Mix, Jack Montgomery, Frank McCarroll
D: Raymond K. Johnson
S/SP: Tom Gibson
P: Harry S. Webb

1103. HI-YO SILVER
(Republic, April 10, 1940) 69 Mins.
(Feature edited from 1938 serial *The Lone Ranger*)
Lee Powell, Herman Brix (Bruce Bennett), Chief Thunder Cloud, Lynne Roberts, Stanley Andrews, Hal Taliaferro (Wally Wales), Lane Chandler, George Cleveland, George Letz (Montgomery), John Merton, Sammy McKim, Tom London, Raphael Bennett, Maston Williams, Raymond Hatton, Dickie Jones
(This feature version had new footage with Raymond Hatton telling the story to young Dickie Jones. Neither was in the original serial. For additional credits see the cast listing under *The Lone Ranger*)
D: William Witney, John English
SP: Barry Shipman, George Washington Yates. Based on the *Lone Ranger* radio serial
AP: Sol C. Siegel

Riders of Pasco Basin (Universal, 1940) — Bob Baker, Fuzzy Knight, and Johnny Mack Brown

Bullet Code (RKO-Radio, 1940) — Howard Hickman, Virginia Vale, George O'Brien, and Charles "Slim" Whitaker

1104. KONGA, THE WILD STALLION

(Columbia, April 10, 1940) 65 Mins.

Fred Stone, Rochelle Hudson, Richard Fiske, Eddy Waller, Robert Warwick, Don Beddoe, Carl Stockdale, George Cleveland, Burr Caruth

D: Sam Nelson

SP: Harold Shumate

P: Wallace MacDonald

1105. THE LIGHT OF WESTERN STARS

(Paramount, April 10, 1940) 67 Mins.

Russell Hayden, Victor Jory, Jo Ann Sayers, Noah Beery, Jr., J. Farrell MacDonald, Ruth Rogers, Tom Tyler, Rad Robinson, Eddie Dean, Esther Estrella, Alan Ladd

D: Lesley Selander

S: Zane Grey

SP: Norman Houston

P: Harry Sherman

1106. YOUNG BUFFALO BILL

(Republic, April 12, 1940) 59 Mins.

Roy Rogers, George Hayes, Pauline Moore, Hugh Sothern, Chief Thunder Cloud, Trevor Bardette, Julian Rivero, Gaylord Pendleton, Wade Boteler, Anna Demetrio, Estrelita Zarco, Hank Bell, William Kellogg, Iron Eyes Cody, Jack O'Shea, George Chesebro, "Trigger"

D/AP: Joseph Kane

S: Norman Houston

SP: Harrison Jacobs, Robert Yost, Gerald Geraghty

1107. VIVA CISCO KID

(20th C. Fox, April 12, 1940) 70 Mins.

(*Cisco Kid* Series)

Cesar Romero, Jean Rogers, Chris-Pin Martin, Minor Watson, Stanley Fields, Nigel de Brulier, Harold Goodwin, Francis Ford, Charles Judels

D: Norman Foster

SP: Samuel G. Engel, Hal Long. Based on the O. Henry character

P: Sol M. Wurtzel

1108. BULLET CODE

(RKO-Radio, April 12, 1940) 58 Mins.

George O'Brien, Virginia Vale, Slim Whitaker, Harry Woods, Robert Stanton (Kirby Grant), Walter Miller, William Haade, Bob Burns, Howard Hickman

D: David Howard

S: Bennett Cohen

SP: Doris Schroeder

P: Bert Gilroy

1109. COVERED WAGON DAYS

(Republic, April 22, 1940)   56 Mins.

(*Three Mesquiteers* Series)

Robert Livingston, Raymond Hatton, Duncan Renaldo, Kay Griffith, George Douglas, Ruth Robinson, Paul Marion, John Merton, Tom Chatterton, Guy D'Ennery, Tom London, Reed Howes, Dick Alexander, Art Mix, Jack Montgomery, Edward Hearn, Frank McCarroll, Jack Kirk, Al Taylor, Lee Shumway, Barry Hays, Elias Gomboa, Herman Hack, Ken Terrell, Tex Palmer

D: George Sherman

SP: Earle Snell. Based on William Colt MacDonald characters

AP: Harry Grey

1110. PALS OF THE SILVER SAGE

(Monogram, April 22, 1940)   52 Mins.

Tex Ritter, Sugar Dawn, Slim Andrews, Clarissa Curtis, Warner Richmond, Glenn Strange, Carleton Young, Joe McGuinn, Chester Gann, John Merton, Evelyn Daw, Gene Alsace, "White Flash," Harry Harvey, Fred Parker

D: Al Herman

SP: George Martin

P: Edward Finney

1111. SHOOTING HIGH

(20th C. Fox, April 26, 1940)   65 Mins.

Jane Withers, Gene Autry, Marjorie Weaver, Frank M. Thomas, Robert Lowery, Katherine (Kay) Aldridge, Hobart Cavanaugh, Jack Carson, Hamilton McFadden, Charles Middleton, Ed Brady, Tom London, Eddie Acuff, Pat O'Malley, George Chandler

D: Alfred E. Green

SP: Lou Breslow, Owen Francis

AP: John Stone

1112. PINTO CANYON

(Metropolitan, May 1, 1940)   55 Mins.

Bob Steele, Louise Stanley, Kenne Duncan, Ted Adams, Steve Clark, Budd Buster, Murdock McQuarrie, George Chesebro, Jimmy Aubrey, Carl Mathews

D: Raymond Johnson

S: Richard D. Pearsall

SP: Carl Krusada

P: Harry S. Webb

1113. THE MAN FROM TUMBLEWEEDS

(Columbia, May 2, 1940)   59 Mins.

Bill Elliott, Dub Taylor, Iris Meredith, Raphael Bennett, Francis Walker, Ernie Adams, Al Hill, Stanley Brown, Richard Fiske, Edward J. LeSaint, Don Beddoe, Eddie Laughton, John Tyrrell, Ed Cecil, Jack Lowe, Buel Bryant, Olin Francis, Jay Lawrence

Shooting High (20th C. Fox, 1940) — Gene Autry and Kay Aldridge

D: Joseph H. Lewis
SP: Charles Francis Royal

1114. MEN WITH STEEL FACES
(Times Pictures, May 2, 1940)   70 Mins.
(A feature edited from 1935's *The Phantom Empire* serial, possibly the same footage used later in 1940 for *Radio Ranch,* but the film did receive some bookings under this title. For more complete credits, see *The Phantom Empire* listing)
Gene Autry, Frankie Darro, Betsy King Ross, Dorothy Christie, Wheeler Oakman, Charles K. French, Warner Richmond, J. Frank Glendon, Smiley Burnette, Jack Carlyle, Edward Piel, William Moore
D: Otto Brower, B. Reeves Eason

1115. BUCK BENNY RIDES AGAIN
(Paramount, May 3, 1940)   82 Mins.
Jack Benny, Ellen Drew, Andy Devine, Phil Harris, Virginia Dale, Lillian Cornell, Dennis Day, Theresa Harris, Eddie (Rochester) Anderson, Kay Linaker, Ward Bond, Morris Ankrum, Charles Lane, James Burke, Merriel Abbott Dancers
D/P: Mark Sandrich
S: Arthur Stringer
SP: William Morrow, Edmund Belion

1116. 20 MULE TEAM
(MGM, May 3, 1940)   84 Mins.
Wallace Beery, Leo Carrillo, Marjorie Rambeau, Anne Baxter, Douglas Fowley, Noah Beery, Jr., Berton Churchill, Arthur Hohl, Clem Bevins, Charles Halton, Minor Watson, Oscar O'Shea, Lloyd Ingraham
D: Richard Thorpe
S: Robert C. DuSoe, Owen Atkinson
SP: Cyril Hume, E. E. Paramore, Richard Maivaum
P: J. Walter Ruben

1117. THE COWBOY FROM SUNDOWN
(Monogram, May 9, 1940)   58 Mins.
Tex Ritter, Roscoe Ates, Pauline Haddon, Carleton Young, Dave O'Brien, Patsy Moran, George Pembroke, James Farrar, Chick Hannon, Slim Andrews, Bud Osborne, Glenn Strange, "White Flash," Wally West, Sherry Tansey, Tristram Coffin
D: Spencer G. Bennet
S: Roland Lynch
SP: Roland Lynch, Robert Emmett (Tansey)
P: Edward Finney

1118. LAND OF THE SIX GUNS
(Monogram, May 9, 1940)   54 Mins.

20 Mule Team (MGM, 1940) — Majorie Rambeau and Wallace Beery

Jack Randall, Louise Stanley, Glenn Strange, Bud Osborne, Kenne Duncan, George Chesebro, Steve Clark, Frank LaRue, Carl Mathews, Jimmy Aubrey, Jack Perrin
D: Raymond K. Johnson
S/SP: Tom Gibson
P: Harry S. Webb

1119. GAUCHO SERENADE
(Republic, May 10, 1940) 66 Mins.
Gene Autry, Smiley Burnette, June Storey, Mary Lee, Duncan Renaldo, Cliff Severn, Jr., Lester Matthews, Smith Ballew, Joseph Crehan, William Ruhl, Wade Boteler, Ted Adams, Fred Burns, Julian Rivero, George Lloyd, Edward Cassidy, Joe Dominguez, Olaf Hytten, Fred Toones, Gene Morgan, Jack Kirk, Harry Strang, Hank Worden, Kernan Cripps, Jim Corey, Tom London, Walter Miller, "Champion," Wendell Niles, Fred and Mary Velasco, Frankie Marvin, Buck Bucko, The Jose Eslava Orchestra
D: Frank McDonald
S/SP: Betty Burbridge, Bradford Ropes
AP: William Berke

1120. WEST OF CARSON CITY
(Universal, May 13, 1940) 57 Mins.
Johnny Mack Brown, Bob Baker, Fuzzy Knight, Peggy Moran, Harry Woods, Robert Homans, Al Hall, Roy Barcroft, Charles King, Frank Mitchell, Edmund Cobb, Jack Roper, Ted Wells, Jack Shannon, Vic Potel, Kermit Maynard, Ernie Adams, Donald Kerr, Dick Carter, Al Bridge, The Notables Quartet
D: Ray Taylor
S: Milt Raison
SP: Milt Raison, Sherman Lowe, Jack Bernhard

1121. SWINGIN' IN THE BARN
(Universal, May 15, 1940) 19 Mins.
Texas Jim Lewis and his Lone Star Cowboys
D: Larry Ceballos

1122. THE KID FROM SANTA FE
(Monogram, May 23, 1940) 57 Mins.
Jack Randall, Clarene Curtis, Forrest Taylor, Claire Rochelle, Tom London, George Chesebro, Dave O'Brien, Jimmy Aubrey, Kenne Duncan, Carl Mathews, Steve Clark, Buzz Barton, Tex Palmer
D: Raymond K. Johnson
S: Joseph P. Murphy
SP: Carl Krusada
P: Harry S. Webb

Land of the Six Guns (Monogram, 1940) — Jack Randall, Kenne Duncan, Glenn Strange, Jack Perrin, George Chesebro, and Carl Mathews (on porch with armlock on Strange)

1123. TEXAS STAGECOACH

(Columbia, May 23, 1940) 59 Mins.

Charles Starrett, Iris Meredith, Bob Nolan, Dick Curtis, Kenneth MacDonald, Edward J. LeSaint, Harry Cording, Francis Walker, Pat Brady, George Becinita, Don Beddoe, Fred Burns, Lillian Lawrence, Eddie Laughton, George Chesebro, Sons of the Pioneers, George Morrell, Blackie Whiteford

D: Joseph H. Lewis

SP: Fred Myton

1124. ROCKY MOUNTAIN RANGERS

(Republic, May 24, 1940) 58 Mins.

(*Three Mesquiteers* Series)

Robert Livingston, Raymond Hatton, Duncan Renaldo, Rosella Towne, Sammy McKim, LeRoy Mason, Pat O'Malley, Dennis Moore, John St. Polis, Robert Blair, Burr Caruth, Jack Kirk, Hank Bell, Budd Buster

D: George Sherman

S: J. Benton Cheney

SP: Barry Shipman, Earle Snell. Based on characters created by William Colt MacDonald

AP: Harry Grey

1125. RIDERS FROM NOWHERE

(Monogram, May 30, 1940) 55 Mins.

Jack Randall, Margaret Roach, Ernie Adams, Tom London, Charles King, Nelson MacDowell, George Chesebro, Dorothy Vernon, Ted Adams, Carl Mathews, Jack Evans, Herman Hack, Archie Ricks, Ray Henderson

D: Raymond K. Johnson

S: Richard Piersall

SP: Carl Krusada

P: Harry S. Webb

1126. BADMAN FROM RED BUTTE

(Universal, May 31, 1940) 58 Mins.

Johnny Mack Brown, Fuzzy Knight, Bob Baker, Anne Gwynne, Lloyd Ingraham, Lafe McKee, Bill Cody, Jr., Buck Moulton, Roy Barcroft, Norman Willis, Earle Hodgins, James Morton, Myra McKinney, Art Mix, Texas Jim Lewis and his Lone Star Cowboys

D: Ray Taylor

SP: Sam Robins

1127. FRONTIER CRUSADER

(PRC, June 1, 1940) 62 Mins.

Tim McCoy, Dorothy Short, Lou Fulton, Karl Hackett, Ted Adams, John Merton, Forrest Taylor, Hal Price, Frank LaRue, Kenne Duncan, George Chesebro, Frank Ellis, Carl Mathews, Reed Howes, Herman Hack, Sherry Tansey, Lane Bradford, Ray Henderson

D: Peter Stewart (Sam Newfield)

S: Arthur Durlam

SP: William Lively

P: Sigmund Neufeld

1128. HIDDEN GOLD

(Paramount, June 7, 1940) 61 Mins.

(*Hopalong Cassidy* Series)

William Boyd, Russell Hayden, Minor Watson, Ruth Rogers, Britt Wood, Ethel Wales, Lee Phelps, Roy Barcroft, George Anderson, Eddie Dean, Raphael Bennett, Jack Rockwell, Walter Long, Bob Kortman, Merrill McCormack

D: Lesley Selander

SP: Jack Merseruau, Gerald Geraghty. Based on characters created by Clarence E. Mulford

P: Harry Sherman

1129. PRAIRIE LAW

(RKO, June 14, 1940) 59 Mins.

George O'Brien, Virginia Vale, Dick Hogan, Slim Whitaker, J. Farrell MacDonald, Cy Kendall, Paul Everton, Henry Hall, Monte Montague, Quen Ramsey, Bud Osborne, Frank Ellis, John Henderson

D: David Howard

S: Bernard McConville

SP: Doris Schroder, Arthur V. Jones

P: Bert Gilroy

1130. ADVENTURES OF RED RYDER

(Republic, June 15, 1940) 12 Chaps.

Donald Barry, Noah Beery, Sr., Tommy Cook, Maude Pierce Allen, Vivian Coe, Harry Worth, Hal Taliaferro, William Farnum, Robert Kortman, Carleton Young, Ray Teal, Gene Alsace, Gayne Whitman, Hooper Atchley, John Dilson, Lloyd Ingraham, Gardner James, Wheaton Chambers, Lynton Brent, Joe Yrigoyen, Joe Delacruz, Jimmy Fawcett, William Nestel, Bud Geary, James Carlisle, Augie Gomez, Max Waizman, Charles Murphy, Eddie Jauregui, Ernest Sarracino, Bob Jamison, Ray Adams, Jack Kirk, Fred Burns, Duke Green, Roy Brent, Budd Buster, Bob Burns, Curley Dresden, Chester Conklin, Walter James, Edward Hearn, Jack O'Shea, Ed Brady, Gus Shindle, Walter Stiritz, Dan White, Matty Roubert, Post Parks, Reed Howes, Al Taylor, Art Dillard, Robert Wilke, Bill Yrigoyen, Ken Terrell, Charles Thomas, Chick Hannon, Barry Hays, Bill Wilkus, Frankie McCormick, Rose Plummer, David Sharpe, Art Mix

D: William Witney, John English

SP: Franklyn Adreon, Ronald Davidson, Norman S. Hall, Barney A. Sarecky, Sol Shor

AP: Hiram S. Brown, Sr.

Chapter Titles: (1) Murder on the Santa Fe Trail,

(2) Horseman of Death, (3) Trail's End, (4) Water Rustlers, (5) Avalanche, (6) Hangman's Noose, (7) Framed, (8) Blazing Walls, (9) Records of Doom, (10) One Second to Live, (11) The Devil's Marksman, (12) Frontier Justice

1131. WAGONS WESTWARD
(Republic, June 19, 1940)   70 Mins.
Chester Morris, Anita Louise, Buck Jones, Ona Munson, George Hayes, Guinn Williams, Douglas Fowley, Edmund Cobb, Charles Stevens, Selmer Jackson, Virginia Brissac, Wayne Hull, Joe McGuinn, Trevor Bardette, John Gallaudet, Tex Cooper
D: Lew Landers
SP: Harrison Jacobs, Joseph M. Marsh
AP: Armand Schaefer

1132. CORRALLING A SCHOOL MARM
(RKO, June 19, 1940)   20 Mins.
Ray Whitley, Virginia Vale, Lee "Lasses" White, Frankie Marvin, Cactus Mack, Curley Hoag
D: Charles Roberts
SP: George Jeske

1133. WILD HORSE RANGE
(Monogram, June 25, 1940)   58 Mins.
Jack Randall, Phyllis Ruth, Frank Yaconelli, Charles King, Tom London, Marin Sais, Ralph Hoopes, Forrest Taylor, George Chesebro, Carl Mathews, Steve Clark, Ted Adams, Tex Palmer
D: Raymond K. Johnson
SP: Carl Krusada
P: Harry S. Webb

1134. THE RETURN OF WILD BILL
(Columbia, June 27, 1940)   60 Mins.
Bill Elliott, Iris Meredith, Dub Taylor, Luana Walters, George Lloyd, Edward J. LeSaint, Frank LaRue, Francis Walker, Chuck Morrison, Buel Bryant, William Kellogg, John Ince, Jack Rockwell, Jim Corey, John Merton, Donald Haines
D: Joseph H. Lewis
S: Walt Coburn
SP: Robert Lee Johnson, Fred Myton
P: Leon Barsha

1135. RIDIN' THE TRAIL
(Ziehm, Inc., June 27, 1940)   57 Mins.
Fred Scott, Iris Lancaster, Harry Harvey, Jack Ingram, John Ward, Elias Gamboa, Bud Osborne, Carl Mathews, Gene Howard, Ray Lenhart, Buddy Kelly, Denver Dixon
D: Raymond K. Johnson
SP: Phil Dunham
P: C. C. Burr

1136. LUCKY CISCO KID
(20th C. Fox, June 28, 1940)   68 Mins.
(*Cisco Kid* Series)
Cesar Romero, Mary Beth Hughes, Dana Andrews, Evelyn Venable, Chris-Pin Martin, Joe Sawyer, Dick Rush, Johnny Sheffield, Francis Ford, William Royle
D: H. Bruce Humberstone
SP: Robert Ellis, Helen Logan. Based on the character created by O. Henry
AP: John Stone

1137. ONE MAN'S LAW
(Republic, June 29, 1940)   57 Mins.
Donald Barry, Janet Waldo, George Cleveland, Dub Taylor, Rex Lease, Carleton Young, Edmund Cobb, Dick Elliott, James H. MacNamara, Robert Frazer, Edward Piel, Sr., Fred Toones, Bud Osborne, Horace B. Carpenter, Jack Kirk, Cactus Mack, Jim Corey, Curley Dresden, Roy Brent, William Kellogg, Barry Hays, Guy Usher, Matty Roubert, Jack Ingram, Charles King, Stanley Price
D/AP: George Sherman
SP: Bennett Cohen, Jack Natteford

1138. OUT WEST WITH THE PEPPERS
(Columbia, June 30, 1940)   63 Mins.
Edith Fellows, Dorothy Ann Seese, Dorothy Peterson, Charles Peck, Tommy Bond, Bobby Larson, Victor Kilian, Helen Brown, Emory Parnell, Pierre Watkin, Ronald Sinclair, Walter Soderling, Roger Gray, Hal Price
D: Charles Barton
S: Margaret Sidney
SP: Harry Rebuas

1139. LIGHTNING STRIKES WEST
(Colony, June, 1940)   56 Mins.
Ken Maynard, Claire Rochelle, Charles King, Bob Terry, Michael Vallon, Reed Howes, Dick Dickinson, George Chesebro, John Elliott, William Gould, Chick Hannon, Tex Palmer, Carl Mathews, "Tarzan"
D: Harry Fraser
S: Monroe Talbot
SP: Martha Chapin
P: Max and Arthur Alexander

1140. THE CARSON CITY KID
(Republic, July 1, 1940)   57 Mins.
Roy Rogers, George Hayes, Bob Steele, Pauline Moore, Noah Beery, Jr., Francis MacDonald, Hal Taliaferro, Arthur Loft, George Rosener, Chester Gan, Hank Bell, Ted Mapes, Jack Ingram, Jack Kirk, Jack Rockwell, Tom Smith, Art Dillard, Hal Price, Yakima Canutt, Kit Guard, Curley Dresden, Oscar Gahan, Chick Hannon, Al Taylor

D/AP: Joseph Kane
S: Joseph Kane
SP: Robert Yost, Gerald Geraghty

1141. WINNERS OF THE WEST

(Universal, July 2, 1940) 13 Chaps.

Dick Foran, Anne Nagel, James Craig, Tom Fadden, Charles Stevens, Trevor Bardette, Harry Woods, Chief Yowlachie, Edward Keane, William Desmond, Edmund Cobb, Chuck Morrison, Edgar Edwards, Jack Voglin, Roy Barcroft, Edward Cassidy

D: Ford Beebe, Ray Taylor
SP: George Plympton, Basil Dickey, Charles R. Condon
P: Henry MacRae

Chapter Titles: (1) Redskins Ride Again, (2) The Wreck at Red River Gorge, (3) The Bridge of Disaster, (4) Trapped by Redskins, (5) Death Stalks the Trail, (6) A Leap for Life, (7) Thundering Terror, (8) The Flaming Arsenal, (9) Sacrificed by Savages, (10) Under Crashing Timbers, (11) Bullets in the Dark, (12) The Battle of Blackhawk, (13) Barricades Blasted

1142. SKY BANDITS

(Criterion/Monogram, July 3, 1940) 62 Mins.

(*Renfrew* Series)

James Newill, Louise Stanley, Dave O'Brien, William Pawley, Ted Adams, Bob Terry, Dwight Frye, Joseph Stefani, Dewey Robinson, Jack Clifford, Kenne Duncan

D: Ralph Staub
SP: Edward Halperin
S: "Renfrew Rides the Sky"—Laurie York Erskine
P: Phil Goldstone

1143. THE GOLDEN TRAIL

(Monogram, July 8, 1940) 52 Mins.

Tex Ritter, "Arkansas Slim" Andrews, Warner Richmond, Patsy Moran, Ina Guest, Stanley Price, Eddie Dean, Gene Alsace, Sugar Dawn, Bill Wells, Forrest Taylor, Jack Pierce, Denver Dixon, Chuck Morrison, "White Flash," Art Mix, Tex Palmer, Chick Hannon, Frank LaRue, Sherry Tansey

D: Al Herman
SP: Roland Lynch, Roger Merton, Robert Emmett (Tansey)
P: Edward Finney

1144. STAGECOACH WAR

(Paramount, July 12, 1940) 63 Mins.

(*Hopalong Cassidy* Series)

William Boyd, Russell Hayden, Julie Carter, J. Farrell MacDonald, Rad Robinson, Eddy Waller, Frank Lackteen, Jack Rockwell, Eddie Dean, Bob Kortman, The King's Men

D: Lesley Selander

S: Norman Houston, Henry Olstea. Based on characters created by Clarence E. Mulford
SP: Norman Houston
P: Harry Sherman

1145. CAROLINA MOON

(Republic, July 15, 1940) 65 Mins.

Gene Autry, Smiley Burnette, June Storey, Mary Lee, Eddy Waller, Hardie Albright, Frank Dale, Terry Nibert, Robert Fiske, Etta McDaniel, Paul White, Fred Ritter, Ralph Sanford, Jack Kirk, Jimmie Lewis and his Texas Cowboys, "Champion"

D: Frank McDonald
S: Connie Lee
SP: Winston Miller
AP: William Berke

1146. DEADWOOD DICK

(Columbia, July 19, 1940) 15 Chaps.

Don Douglas, Lorna Gray (Adrian Booth), Harry Harvey, Marin Sais, Lane Chandler, Jack Ingram, Charles King, Ed Cassidy, Robert Fiske, Lee Shumway, Edmund Cobb, Edward Piel, Edward Hearn, Karl Hackett, Roy Barcroft, Bud Osborne, Joe Girard, Tom London, Kenne Duncan, Yakima Canutt, Fred Kelsey, Edward Cecil, Kit Guard, Al Ferguson, Constantine Romanoff, Franklyn Farnum, Charles Hamilton, Jim Corey, Eddie Featherston

D: James W. Horne
SP: Wyndham Gittens, Morgan B. Cox, George Morgan, John Cutting
P: Larry Darmour

Chapter Titles: (1) A Wild West Empire, (2) Who Is the Skull?, (3) Pirates of the Plains, (4) The Skull Baits a Trap, (5) Win, Lose, or Draw, (6) Buried Alive, (7) The Chariot of Doom, (8) The Secret of Number 10, (9) The Fatal Warning, (10) Framed for Murder, (11) The Bucket of Death, (12) A Race Against Time, (13) The Arsenal of Revolt, (14) Holding the Fort, (15) The Deadwood Express

1147. BILLY THE KID OUTLAWED

(PRC, July 20, 1940) 52 Mins.

(*Billy the Kid* Series)

Bob Steele, Al St. John, Louise Currie, Carleton Young, John Merton, Joe McGuinn, Ted Adams, Walter McGrail, Hal Price, Kenne Duncan, Reed Howes, George Chesebro, Steve Clark, Budd Buster

D: Peter Stewart (Sam Newfield)
SP: Oliver Drake
P: Sigmund Neufeld

1148. SON OF ROARING DAN

(Universal, July 26, 1940) 63 Mins.

Johnny Mack Brown, Fuzzy Knight, Nell O'Day, Jeannie Kelly, Robert Homans, Tom Chatterton, John Eldredge, Ethan Laidlaw, Lafe McKee, Dick Alexander, Eddie Polo, Bob Reeves, Chuck Morrison, Frank McCarroll, Lloyd Ingraham, Jack Shannon, Ben Taggert, Ralph Peters, Ralph Dunn, Jack Montgomery, The Texas Rangers
D: Ford Beebe
SP: Clarence Upson Young
AP: Joseph Sanford

1149. STAGE TO CHINO

(RKO, July 26, 1940)   58 Mins.
George O'Brien, Virginia Vale, Hobart Cavanaugh, Roy Barcroft, Martin Garralaga, Carl Stockdale, Harry Cording, Ethan Laidlaw, William Haade, Glenn Strange, Tom London, Pals of the Golden West
D: Edward Kelly
SP: Morton Grant, Arthur V. Jones
P: Bert Gilroy

1150. WHEN THE DALTONS RODE

(Universal, July 26, 1940)   80 Mins.
Randolph Scott, Kay Francis, Brian Donlevy, George Bancroft, Broderick Crawford, Andy Devine, Stuart Erwin, Frank Albertson, Mary Gordon, Harvey Stevens, Edgar Dearing, Quen Ramsey, Bob McKenzie, Dorothy Granger, Fay McKenzie, Walter Sodering, Mary Ainslee, Erville Alderson, Sally Payne, June Wilkins
D: George Marshall
S: "When the Daltons Rode"—Emmett Dalton, Jack Jungmeyer, Sr.
SP: Harold Shumate

1151. RAINBOW OVER THE RANGE

(Monogram, July 29, 1940)   60 Mins.
Tex Ritter, Warner Richmond, Dorothy Fay, Dennis Moore, Slim Andrews, Jim Pierce, Chuck Morrison, John Merton, Tommy Southworth, Steve Lorber, Romaine Loudermilk and his Ranch House Cowboys, "White Flash"
D: Al Herman
SP: Roland Lynch, Roger Merton, Robert Emmett
P: Edward Finney

1152. THE RANGER AND THE LADY

(Republic, July 30, 1940)   59 Mins.
Roy Rogers, George Hayes, Jacqueline Wells (Julie Bishop), Harry Woods, Henry Brandon, Noble Johnson, Si Jenks, Ted Mapes, Yakima Canutt, Chuck Baldra, Herman Hack, Chick Hannon, Art Dillard, "Trigger"
D/AP: Joseph Kane
SP: Stuart Anthony, Gerald Geraghty

1153. GUN CODE

(PRC, August 3, 1940)   54 Mins.
Tim McCoy, Inna Gest (Ina Guest), Lou Fulton, Alden Chase, Ted Adams, Dave O'Brien, Carleton Young, Robert Winkler, John Elliott, George Chesebro, Jack Richardson, Carl Mathews
D: Peter Stewart (Sam Newfield)
SP: Joseph O'Donnell
P: Sigmund Neufeld

1154. RIVER'S END

(Warner Bros., August 10, 1940)   69 Mins.
Dennis Morgan, Elizabeth Earl, George Tobias, Victor Jory, James Stephenson, Steffi Duna, Edward Pawley, John Ridgely, Frank Wilcox, David Bruce, Gilbert Emery, Stuart Robinson
D: Ray Enright
S: James Oliver Curwood
SP: Barry Trivers, Bertram Milhauser
AP: William Jacobs

1155. THE RETURN OF FRANK JAMES

(20th C. Fox, August 16, 1940)   92 Mins.
(Technicolor)
Henry Fonda, Gene Tierney, Jackie Cooper, John Carradine, J. Edward Bromberg, Donald Meek, Eddie Collins, George Barbier, Ernest Whitman, Charles Tannen, Lloyd Corrigan, Russell Hicks, Victor Kilian, Edward McWade, George Chandler, Irving Bacon, Frank Shannon, Barbara Pepper, Louis Mason, Stymie Beard, William Pawley, Frank Sully, Davidson Clark
D: Fritz Lang
SP: Sam Hellman
P: Darryl F. Zanuck
AP: Kenneth MacGowan

1156. ROLL, WAGONS, ROLL

(Monogram, August 16, 1940)   52 Mins.
Tex Ritter, Muriel Evans, Nelson McDowell, Tom London, Nolan Willis, Steve Clark, Reed Howes, Frank Ellis, Kenne Duncan, Frank LaRue, Chick Hannon, Charles King, "White Flash"
D: Al Herman
S/SP: Victor Adamson, Roger Merton, Edmund Kelso
P: Edward Finney

1157. THE TULSA KID

(Republic, August 16, 1940)   57 Mins.
Donald Barry, Luana Walters, Noah Beery, David Durand, George Douglas, Ethan Laidlaw, Stanley Blystone, John Elliott, Jack Kirk, Fred Toones, Charles Murphy, Joe De LaCruz, Charles Thomas, Art Dillard, Cactus Mack, Jimmy Wakely and his Roughriders
D/AP: George Sherman
SP: Oliver Drake, Anthony Coldeway

1158. ARIZONA FRONTIER

(Monogram, August 19, 1940) 60 Mins.

Tex Ritter, Slim Andrews, Jim Thorpe, Evelyn Finley, Frank LaRue, Tris Coffin, Gene Alsace (Rocky Camron), Dick Cramer, Jim Pierce, Hal Price, Chick Hannon, Art Wilcox and his Arizona Rangers, "White Flash"

D: Al Herman

SP: Robert Emmett (Tansey)

P: Edward Finney

1159. THE RANGE BUSTERS

(Monogram, August 22, 1940) 56 Mins.

(*Range Busters* Series)

Ray Corrigan, John King, Max Terhune, LeRoy Mason, Luana Walters, Earle Hodgins, Frank LaRue, Kermit Maynard, Bruce King, Duke (Carl) Mathews, Horace Murphy, Karl Hackett

D: S. Roy Luby

SP: John Rathmell

P: George W. Weeks

1160. THE DURANGO KID

(Columbia, August 23, 1940) 60 Mins.

Charles Starrett, Luana Walters, Bob Nolan, Kenneth MacDonald, Francis Walker, Forrest Taylor, Pat Brady, Melvin Lang, Frank LaRue, Jack Rockwell, Sons of the Pioneers, John Tyrell, Steve Clark, Ben Taggart

D: Lambert Hillyer

SP: Paul Franklin

1161. QUEEN OF THE YUKON

(Monogram, August 26, 1940) 73 Mins.

Charles Bickford, Irene Rich, Melvin Long, George Cleveland, Guy Usher, June Carlson, Dave O'Brien, Tris Coffin

D: Phil Rosen

S: Jack London

SP: Joseph West

P: Scott R. Dunlap, Paul Malvern

1162. OKLAHOMA RENEGADES

(Republic, August 29, 1940) 57 Mins.

(*Three Mesquiteers* Series)

Robert Livingston, Raymond Hatton, Duncan Renaldo, Lee "Lasses" White, Florine McKinney, Al Herman, William Ruhl, Eddie Dean, James Seay, Harold Daniels, Jack Lescoulie, Frosty Royce, Yakima Canutt

D: Nate Watt

S: Charles Condon

SP: Earl Snell, Doris Schroeder. Based on characters created by William Colt MacDonald

AP: Harry Grey

1163. KIT CARSON

(United Artists, August 30, 1940) 96 Mins.

Jon Hall, Lynn Bari, Dana Andrews, Harold Huber, Ward Bond, Renie Riano, Clayton Moore, Rowena Cook, Raymond Hatton, Harry Strang, C. Henry Gordon, Lew Merrill, Stanley Andrews, Edwin Maxwell, Peter Lynn, Charles Stevens, William Farnum

D: George B. Seitz

S: George Bruce

P: Edward Small

1164. RIDE, TENDERFOOT, RIDE

(Republic, September 6, 1940) 65 Mins.

Gene Autry, Smiley Burnette, June Storey, Mary Lee, Warren Hull, Forbes Murray, Joe McGuinn, Joe Frisco, Isabel Randolph, Herbert Clifton, Si Jenks, Mildred Shay, Cindy Walker, Patty Saks, Jack Kirk, Slim Whitaker, Fred Burns, The Pacemakers, Robert Burns, Fred Toones, Chuck Morrison, Frank O'Connors, Curley Dresden, "Champion"

D: Frank McDonald

S: Betty Burbridge, Connie Lee

SP: Winston Miller

AP: William Berke

1165. WYOMING

(MGM, September 13, 1940) 89 Mins.

Wallace Beery, Leo Carrillo, Ann Rutherford, Lee Bowman, Joseph Calleia, Bob Watson, Paul Kelly, Marjorie Main, Henry Travers, Addison Richards

D: Richard Thorpe

S: Jack Jevne

SP: Jack Jevne, Hugh Butler

P: Milton Bren

1166. COLORADO

(Republic, September 15, 1940) 57 Mins.

Roy Rogers, George Hayes, Pauline Moore, Milburn Stone, Maude Eburne, Hal Taliaferro, Vester Pegg, Fred Burns, Lloyd Ingraham, Jay Novello, Chuck Baldra, Tex Palmer, Joseph Crehan, Edward Cassidy, George Rosenor, Robert Fiske, "Trigger"

D/AP: Joseph Kane

SP: Louis Stevens, Harrison Jacobs

1167. ARIZONA GANGBUSTERS

(PRC, September 16, 1940) 57 Mins.

Tim McCoy, Pauline Haddon, Lou Fulton, Forrest Taylor, Julian Rivero, Arno Frey, Kenne Duncan, Jack Rutherford, Elizabeth LaMal, Otto Reichow, Lita Cortez, Carl Mathews, Ben Corbett, Frank Ellis, Curley Dresden

D: Peter Stewart (Sam Newfield)

SP: Joseph O'Donnell

P: Sigmund Neufeld

1168. KING OF THE ROYAL MOUNTED

(Republic, September 20, 1940)   12 Chaps.

Allan Lane, Robert Strange, Robert Kellard, Lita Conway, Herbert Rawlinson, Harry Cording, Bryant Washburn, Budd Buster, Stanley Andrews, John Davidson, John Dilson, Paul McVey, Lucien Prival, Norman Willis, Tony Paton, Ken Terrell, Charles Thomas, Bill Wilkus, Ted Mapes, Major Sam Harris, George Plues, Frank Wayne, Richard Simmons, Loren Riebe, Wallace Reid, Jr., William Justice, William Stahl, John Bagni, Earl Bunn, Curley Dresden, George DeNormand, Bud Geary, Dave Marks, Robert Wayne, William Kellogg, Tommy Coats, Alan Gregg, Denny Sullivan, Walter Low, George Ford, Bob Jamison, Dale Van Sickel, Al Taylor, Cy Slocum, Douglas Evans, Duke Taylor, Jimmy Fawcett, Duke Green, David Sharpe

D: William Witney, John English

SP: Franklyn Adreon, Norman S. Hall, Joseph Poland, Barney A. Sarecky, Sol Shor

AP: Hiram S. Brown, Jr.

Chapter Titles: (1) Man Hunt, (2) Winged Death, (3) Boomerang, (4) Devil Doctor, (5) Sabotage, (6) False Ransom, (7) Death Tunes In, (8) Satan's Cauldron, (9) Espionage, (10) Blazing Guns, (11) Master Spy, (12) Code of the Mounted

1169. RAGTIME COWBOY JOE

(Universal, September 20, 1940)   58 Mins.

Johnny Mack Brown, Fuzzy Knight, Nell O'Day, Marilyn (Lynn) Merrick, Dick Curtis, Walter Sodering, Roy Barcroft, Harry Tenbrook, George Plues, Ed Cassidy, Buck Moulton, Harold Goodwin, Wilfred Lucas, Kermit Maynard, Viola Vonn, Jack Clifford, William Gould, Bud Osborne, The Texas Rangers, Bob O'Connor, Eddie Parker, Frank McCarroll

D: Ray Taylor

SP: Sherman Lowe

AP: Joseph Sanford

1170. TRIPLE JUSTICE

(RKO, September 20, 1940)   66 Mins.

George O'Brien, Virginia Vale, Peggy Shannon, Harry Woods, Paul Fix, LeRoy Mason, Glenn Strange, Malcolm (Bud) McTaggart, Bob McKenzie, Wilfred Lucas, Herman Nolan, John Judd, Henry Rocquemore, Fern Emmett, Walter Patterson, Paul Everton, Lindeman Sisters

D: David Howard

S: Arnold Belgard, Jack Roberts

SP: Arthur V. Jones, Morton Grant

1171. UNDER TEXAS SKIES

(Republic, September 20, 1940)   57 Mins.

(*Three Mesquiteers* Series)

Robert Livingston, Bob Steele, Rufe Davis, Lois Ranson, Henry Brandon, Wade Boteler, Rex Lease, Yakima Canutt, Jack Ingram, Walter Tetley, Earle Hodgins, Curley Dresden, Jack Kirk, Ted Mapes, Vester Pegg

D: George Sherman

S: Anthony Coldeway, Betty Burbridge

SP: Anthony Coldeway, Betty Burbridge. Based on characters created by William Colt MacDonald

AP: Harry Grey

1172. THE WESTERNER

(United Artists, September 20, 1940)   100 Mins.

Gary Cooper, Walter Brennan, Fred Stone, Doris Davenport, Dana Andrews, Forrest Tucker, Chill Wills, Lillian Bond, Paul Hurst, Arthur Aylesworth, Trevor Bardette

D: William Wyler

S: Stuart Lake

SP: Jo Swerling, Niven Busch

P: Samuel Goldwyn

1173. RANGERS OF FORTUNE

(Paramount, September 27, 1940)   80 Mins.

Fred MacMurray, Patricia Morison, Betty Brewer, Albert Dekker, Gilbert Roland, Joseph Schildkraut, Dick Foran, Arthur Allen, Bernard Nedell, Brandon Tynan, Minor Watson, Rosa Turich

D: Sam Wood

S/SP: Frank Butler

P: Dale Van Every

1174. BRIGHAM YOUNG

(20th C. Fox, September 27, 1940)   114 Mins.

Tyrone Power, Linda Darnell, Dean Jagger, Brian Donlevy, Jane Darwell, John Carradine, Mary Astor, Vincent Price, Jean Rogers, Ann Todd, Willard Robertson, Moroni Olson, Stanley Andrews, Frank Thomas, Fuzzy Knight, Dickie Jones, Selmer Jackson, Frederick Jackson, Russell Simpson, Arthur Aylesworth, Chief Big Tree, Davidson Clark, Claire Du Brey, Tully Marshall, Dick Rich, Ralph Dunn, Edwin Maxwell, Edmund McDonald, George Melford

D: Henry Hathaway

S: Louis Bromfield

SP: Lamar Trotti

AP: Kenneth MacGowan

1175. BILLY THE KID IN TEXAS

(PRC, September 30, 1940)   52 Mins.

Bob Steele, Al St. John, Terry Walker, Carleton Young, Charles King, John Merton, Frank LaRue, Slim Whitaker, Curley Dresden, Tex Palmer, Chick Hannon, Merrill McCormack, Denver Dixon, Bob Woodward, Sherry Tansey, Herman Hack, Pasquel Perry

D: Peter Stewart (Sam Newfield)

SP: Joseph O'Donnell
P: Sigmund Neufeld

1176. PRAIRIE SCHOONERS
(Columbia, September 30, 1940) 58 Mins.
Bill Elliott, Evelyn Young, Dub Taylor, Kenneth Harlan, Ray Teal, Bob Burns, Netta Packer, Richard Fiske, Edmund Cobb, Jim Thorpe, George Morrell, Ned Glass, Sammy Stein, Lucien Maxwell, Merrill McCormack
D: Sam Nelson
S: George Cory Franklin
SP: Robert Lee Johnson, Fred Myton

1177. THE GAY CABALLERO
(20th C. Fox, October 4, 1940) 57 Mins.
(*Cisco Kid* Series)
Cesar Romero, Sheila Ryan, Robert Sterling, Chris-Pin Martin, Janet Beecher, Edmund McDonald, Jacqueline Dalya, Hooper Atchley, Montague Shaw, Ethan Laidlaw
D: Otto Brower
S: Walter Bullock, Albert Duffy
SP: Albert Duffy, John Larkin
AP: Walter Morosco, Ralph Dietrich

1178. WAGON TRAIN
(RKO, October 4, 1940) 62 Mins.
Tim Holt, Ray Whitley, Emmett Lynn, Martha O'Driscoll, Bud McTaggart, Cliff Clark, Ellen Lowe, Wade Crosby, Ethan Laidlaw, Monte Montague, Carl Stockdale, Bruce Dane, Glenn Strange
D: Edward Killy
S: Bernard McConville
SP: Morton Grant
P: Bert Gilroy

1179. TRAILING DOUBLE TROUBLE
(Monogram, October 10, 1940) 56 Mins.
(*Range Busters* Series)
Ray Corrigan, John King, Max Terhune, Lita Conway, Nancy Louise King, Roy Barcroft, Tom London, William Kellogg, Carl Mathews, Forrest Taylor, Kenne Duncan, Dick Cramer, Tex Felker, Jimmy Wakely and his Rough Riders
D: S. Roy Luby
S: George Plympton
SP: Oliver Drake
P: George W. Weeks

1180. FRONTIER VENGEANCE
(Republic, October 10, 1940) 57 Mins.
Donald Barry, Betty Moran, Yakima Canutt, George Offerman, Jr., Ivan Miller, Obed Packard, Cindy Walker, Kenneth MacDonald, Griff Barnett, Jack Lawrence, Matty Roubert, Fred Toones
D: Nate Watt

S: Bennett Cohen
SP: Bennett Cohen, Barry Shipman
AP: George Sherman, Eddy White

1181. CHEROKEE STRIP
(Paramount, October 11, 1940) 86 Mins.
Richard Dix, Florence Rice, William Henry, Victor Jory, Andy Clyde, Tom Tyler, George E. Stone, Morris Ankrum, Charles Trowbridge, Douglas Fowley, Addison Richards, William Haade, Ray Teal, Hal Taliaferro, Jack Rockwell, Tex Cooper
D: Lesley Selander
S: Bernard McConville
SP: Norman Houston, Bernard McConville
P: Harry Sherman

1182. WEST OF ABILENE
(Columbia, October 21, 1940) 57 Mins.
Charles Starrett, Marjorie Cooley, Bruce Bennett, Bob Nolan, Don Beddoe, William Pawley, Pat Brady, George Cleveland, Forrest Taylor, Bud Osborne, Al Bridge, Frank Ellis, Sons of the Pioneers
D: Ralph Cedar
SP: Paul Franklin

1183. YOUNG BILL HICKOK
(Republic, October 21, 1940) 59 Mins.
Roy Rogers, George Hayes, Jacqueline Wells, John Miljan, Sally Payne, Archie Twitchell, Monte Blue, Hal Taliaferro, Ethel Wales, Jack Ingram, Monte Montague, Iron Eyes Cody, Fred Burns, Frank Ellis, Slim Whitaker, Jack Kirk, Hank Bell, Henry Wills, Dick Elliott, William Desmond, John Elliott, Jack Rockwell, Bill Wolfe, Tom Smith
D/AP: Joseph Kane
SP: Olive Cooper, Norton S. Parker

1184. NORTH WEST MOUNTED POLICE
(Paramount, October 22, 1940) 125 Mins.
Gary Cooper, Madeleine Carroll, Paulette Goddard, Preston Foster, Robert Preston, George Bancroft, Lynne Overman, Akim Tamiroff, Walter Hampden, Lon Chaney, Jr., Montague Love, Francis J. McDonald, George E. Stone, Willard Robertson, Regis Toomey, Richard Denning, Douglas Kennedy, Robert Ryan, James Seay, Lane Chandler, Ralph Byrd, Eric Alden, Wallace Reid, Jr., Bud Geary, Evan Thomas, Jack Pennick, Rod Cameron, Davidson Clark, Ed Brady, Monte Blue, Mala, Jack Chapin, Chief Thunder Cloud, Harry Burns, Lou Merrill, Clara Blandick, Ynez Seabury, Eva Puig, Julia Faye, Weldon Heyburn, Phillip Terry, George Regas, Jack Luden, Soledad Jiminez, Emory Parnell, William Haade, Nestor Paiva, Donald Curtis, Jane Keckley, Noble Johnson, Norma Nelson, John Hart, Ethan Laidlaw,

The Mark of Zorro (20th C. Fox, 1940) — Tyrone Power and Basil Rathbone

Jim Pierce, Kermit Maynard, Franklyn Farnum, James Flavin
D: Cecil B. DeMille
S: "Royal Canadian Mounted Police"—R. G. Fetherstonhaugh
SP: Alan LeMay, Jesse Lasky, Jr., C. Gardner Sullivan
P: Cecil B. DeMille
AP: William H. Pine

1185. BAR BUCKAROOS
(RKO-Radio, November 8, 1940)   16 Mins.
Ray Whitley, Jane Patten, Glenn Strange, Ken Card, Mariska Aldrich, Curley Hoag
S/D: Lloyd French

1186. THE MARK OF ZORRO
(20th C. Fox, November 8, 1940)   93 Mins.
Tyrone Power, Linda Darnell, Basil Rathbone, Gale Sondergaard, Eugene Pallette, J. Edward Bromberg, Montague Love, Janet Beecher, Robert Lowery, Chris-Pin Martin, George Regas, Belle Mitchell, John Bleifer, Frank Puglia, Eugene Borden, Pedro De Cordoba, Guy D'Ennery
D: Rouben Mamoulian
S: "The Curse of Capistrano"—Johnston McCulley
SP: Garret Ford, Bess Meredith
P: Raymond Griffith

1187. RODEO DOUGH
(MGM, November 9, 1940)   10 Mins.
(Sepiatone)
Sally Payne, Mary Treen, and guest appearances by Mickey Rooney, Gene Autry, Roy Rogers, Johnny Weissmuller, Joe E. Brown, and Tom Neal
D: Sammy Lee
SP: Marion Mack
P: Louis Lewyn

1188. RIDERS OF BLACK MOUNTAIN
(PRC, November 11, 1940)   57 Mins.
Tim McCoy, Pauline Haddon, Rex Lease, Ralph Peters, Edward Piel, Sr., George Chesebro, Dirk Thane, Carl Mathews
D: Peter Stewart (Sam Newfield)
SP: Joe O'Donnell
P: Sigmund Neufeld

1189. TAKE ME BACK TO OKLAHOMA
(Monogram, November 11, 1940)   57 Mins.
Tex Ritter, Slim Andrews, Terry Walker, Karl Hackett, George Eldridge, Bob McKenzie, Olin Francis, Carleton Young, Sherry Tansey, Gene Alsace (Rocky Camron), Don Curtis, Bob Wills and his Texas Playboys, "White Flash," Tex Cooper, Rose Plummer, Chick Hannon
D: Al Herman

SP: Robert Emmett (Tansey)
P: Edward Finney

1190. THE TRAIL BLAZERS
(Republic, November 11, 1940)   58 Mins.
(*Three Mesquiteers* Series)
Robert Livingston, Bob Steele, Rufe Davis, Pauline Moore, Rex Lease, Weldon Heyburn, Carroll Nye, Tom Chatterton, Si Jenks, Mary Field, John Merton, Robert Blair, Barry Hays, Pascale Perry, Harry Strang
D: George Sherman
S: Earle Snell
SP: Barry Shipman. Based on characters created by William Colt MacDonald
AP: Harry Grey

1191. BEYOND THE SACRAMENTO
(Columbia, November 14, 1940)   58 Mins.
Bill Elliott, Evelyn Keyes, Dub Taylor, John Dilson, Bradley Page, Frank LaRue, Norman Willis, Steve Clark, Jack Clifford, Don Beddoe, Harry Bailey, Art Mix, George McKay, Bud Osborne, Blackjack Ward, Jack Low, Olin Francis, Clem Horton, Tex Cooper, Ned Glass
D: Lambert Hillyer
SP: Luci Ward

1192. THREE MEN FROM TEXAS
(Paramount, November 15, 1940)   70 Mins.
(*Hopalong Cassidy* Series)
William Boyd, Russell Hayden, Andy Clyde, Esther Estrella, Morris Ankrum, Morgan Wallace, Thornton Edwards, Davidson Clark, Dick Curtis, Glenn Strange, Neyle Marx, Robert Burns, Jim Corey, George Morrell, George Lollier, Frank McCarroll, Lucio Villegas
D: Lesley Selander
SP: Norton S. Parker. Based on characters created by Clarence E. Mulford
P: Harry Sherman

1193. MELODY RANCH
(Republic, November 15, 1940)   83 Mins.
Gene Autry, Jimmy Durante, Ann Miller, Barton MacLane, Barbara Allen, George Hayes, Jerome Cowan, Mary Lee, Horace MacMahon, Clarence Wilson, Billy Benedict, Ruth Gifford, Maxine Ardell, Veda Ann Borg, George Chandler, Jack Ingram, Horace Murphy, Lloyd Ingraham, Tom London, John Merton, Edmund Cobb, Slim Whitaker, Curley Dresden, Dick Elliott, Billy Bletcher, Art Mix, George Chesebro, Tiny Jones, Herman Hack, Jack Kirk, Merrill McCormack, Wally West, Bob Wills and the Texas Playboys, "Champion," Frankie Marvin, Carl Cotner, Tex Cooper, Herman Hack, Chick Hannon, Tom Smith

D: Joseph Santley
SP: Jack Moffitt, F. Hugh Herbert, Sid Culler, Ray
    Golden
AP: Sol C. Siegel

1194. MEXICAN SPITFIRE OUT WEST
(RKO, November 15, 1940) 76 Mins.
Lupe Velez, Leon Errol, Donald Woods, Elizabeth
    Risdon, Cecil Kellaway, Linda Hayes, Lydia Bil-
    brook, Charles Coleman, Charles Quigley, Eddie
    Dunn, Grant Withers, Tom Kennedy
D: Leslie Goodwins
S: Charles E. Roberts
SP: Charles E. Roberts, Jack Townley
P: Lee Marcus, Cliff Reid

1195. TEXAS TERRORS
(Republic, November 22, 1940) 57 Mins.
Donald Barry, Julie Duncan, Al St. John, Arthur
    Loft, Ann Pennington, Eddy Waller, William
    Ruhl, Sammy McKim, Reed Howes, Robert Fiske,
    Fred Toones, Hal Taliaferro, Edmund Cobb, Al
    Haskell, Jack Kirk, Jimmy Wakely and his Rough
    Riders, Ruth Robinson, Blackjack Ward
D/AP: George Sherman
SP: Doris Schroeder, Anthony Coldeway

1196. WEST OF PINTO BASIN
(Monogram, November 25, 1940) 60 Mins.
(*Range Busters* Series)
Ray Corrigan, John King, Max Terhune, Gwen
    Gaze, Tris Coffin, Dirk Thane, George Chesebro,
    Carl Mathews, Bud Osborne, Jack Perrin, Dick
    Cramer, Phil Dunham, Jerry Smith, Budd Buster
D: S. Roy Luby
S: Elmer Clifton
SP: Earle Snell
P: George W. Weeks

1197. LAW AND ORDER
(Universal, November 28, 1940) 57 Mins.
Johnny Mack Brown, Fuzzy Knight, Nell O'Day,
    James Craig, Harry Cording, Ethan Laidlaw, Ted
    Adams, Harry Humphrey, Jimmy Dodd, William
    Worthington, George Plues, Earle Hodgins, Rob-
    ert Fiske, Kermit Maynard, Frank McCarroll, Bob
    Kortman, Frank Ellis, Jim Corey, Lew Meehan,
    Charles King, The Notables Quartet
D: Ray Taylor
S: "Saint Johnson"—W. R. Burnette
SP: Sherman Lowe, Victor McLeod

1198. PONY POST
(Universal, December 1, 1940) 59 Mins.
Johnny Mack Brown, Fuzzy Knight, Nell O'Day,
    Lane Chandler, Edmund Cobb, Kermit Maynard,
    Dorothy Short, Tom Chatterton, Stanley Bly-
    stone, Jack Rockwell, Ray Teal, Lloyd Ingraham,

Charles King, Frank McCarroll, Iron Eyes Cody,
    Jimmy Wakely and his Rough Riders
D: Ray Taylor
S/SP: Sherman Lowe

1199. THUNDERING FRONTIER
(Columbia, December 5, 1940) 57 Mins.
Charles Starrett, Iris Meredith, Bob Nolan, Carl
    Stockdale, Fred Burns, John Dilson, Alex Callam,
    Ray Bennett, Blackie Whiteford, John Tyrell,
    Francis Walker, Pat Brady, Sons of the Pioneers
D: D. Ross Lederman
SP: Paul Franklin

1200. THE BORDER LEGION
(Republic, December 5, 1940) 58 Mins.
Roy Rogers, George Hayes, Carol Hughes, Joseph
    Sawyer, Maude Eburne, Jay Novello, Hal Talia-
    ferro, Dick Wessell, Paul Porcasi, Robert Emmett
    Keane, Ted Mapes, Fred Burns, Post Parks, Art
    Dillard, Chick Hannon, Charles Baldra
D/AP: Joseph Kane
S: Zane Grey
SP: Olive Cooper, Louis Stevens

1201. GO WEST
(MGM, December 6, 1940) 81 Mins.
Groucho, Chico, and Harpo Marx, John Carroll,
    Diana Lewis, Walter Woolf King, Robert Barrat,
    June MacCloy, George Lessey, Tully Marshall
D: Edward Buzzell
SP: Irving Brecher

1202. THE FARGO KID
(RKO, December 6, 1940) 63 Mins.
Tim Holt, Ray Whitley, Emmett Lynn, Jane Drum-
    mond, Cy Kendall, Ernie Adams, Paul Fix, Paul
    Scardon, Glenn Strange, Mary MacLaren, Dick
    Hogan, Carl Stockdale, Harry Harvey, Lee Phelps
D: Edward Killy
SP: W. C. Tuttle
P: Bert Gilroy

1203. TEXAS RANGERS RIDE AGAIN
(Paramount, December 13, 1940) 68 Mins.
John Howard, Ellen Drew, Akim Tamiroff, Brod-
    erick Crawford, May Robson, Charley Grapewin,
    John Miljan, Anthony Quinn, Tom Tyler, Donald
    Curtis, Eddie Acuff, Ruth Rogers, Robert Ryan,
    Eva Puig, Monte Blue, James Pierce, William
    Duncan, Harvey Stephens, Harold Goodwin,
    Edward Pawley, Eddie Foy, Jr., Joseph Crehan,
    Stanley Price, Charles Lane, Jack Perrin, Gordon
    Jones, Ruth Rogers, John "Skins" Miller, Henry
    Rocquemore
D: James Hogan
SP: William Lipman, Horace McCoy

1204. TRAIL OF THE VIGILANTES

(Universal, December 13, 1940) 75 Mins.

Franchot Tone, Warren William, Broderick Crawford, Andy Devine, Mischa Auer, Porter Hall, Peggy Moran, Paul Fix, Samuel S. Hinds, Charles Trowbridge, Earle Hodgins, Hank Bell, Harry Cording, Max Wagner

D: Allan Dwan

SP: Harold Shumate

1205. LONE STAR RAIDERS

(Republic, December 23, 1940) 57 Mins.

(*Three Mesquiteers* Series)

Robert Livingston, Bob Steele, Rufe Davis, June Johnson, George Douglas, Sarah Padden, John Elliott, John Merton, Rex Lease, Bud Osborne, Jack Kirk, Tom London, Hal Price

D: George Sherman

SP: Joseph March, Barry Shipman. Based on characters created by William Colt MacDonald

AP: Louis Gray

1206. ARIZONA

(Columbia, December 25, 1940) 127 Mins.

Jean Arthur, William Holden, Warren William, Porter Hall, Paul Harvey, George Chandler, Byron Foulger, Regis Toomey, Paul Lopez, Colin Tapley, Edgar Buchanan, Uvaldo Carela, Earl Crawford, Griff Barnett, Ludwig Hardt, Patrick Moriarty, Frank Darien, Syd Saylor, Wade Crosby, Frank Hill, Nina Campana, Addison Richards, Carleton Young

D/P: Wesley Ruggles

S: Clarence Buddington Kelland

SP: Claude Binyon

1207. BILLY THE KID'S GUN JUSTICE

(PRC, December 27, 1940) 57 Mins.

(*Billy the Kid* Series)

Bob Steele, Al St. John, Louise Currie, Carleton Young, Charles King, Rex Lease, Ted Adams, Kenne Duncan, Forrest Taylor, Al Ferguson, Karl Hackett, Edward Piel, Sr., Julian Rivero, Blanca Vischer

D: Peter Stewart (Sam Newfield)

SP: Oliver Drake

P: Sigmund Neufeld

1208. SANTA FE TRAIL

(Warner Bros., December 28, 1940) 110 Mins.

Errol Flynn, Olivia de Havilland, Raymond Massey, Ronald Reagan, Alan Hale, Van Heflin, Guinn "Big Boy" Williams, Gene Reynolds, Henry O'Neill, Alan Baxter, John Litel, Moroni Olson, David Bruce, Hobart Cavanaugh, Charles Brown, Joe Sawyer, Frank Wilcox, Ward Bond, Russell Simpson, Charles Middleton, Erville Alderson, Spencer Charters, Suzanne Carnahan, William Marshall, George Haywood

D: Michael Curtiz

SP: Robert Buckner

AP: Robert Fellows

P: Jack L. Warner, Hal B. Wallis

1209. BUZZY RIDES THE RANGE

(Arthur Ziehn Productions, December 30, 1940) 60 Mins.

Dave O'Brien, Claire Rochelle, Buzzy Henry, George Morrell, George Eldridge, Frank Marlo, Don Kelly

D: Richard C. Kahn

SP: E. C. Robertson

P: Dick L'Estrange

(Reissued by Elkay/Astor as *Western Terror*. The 11 x 14 set of scene cards supplied by Astor for *Western Terror* was made up entirely of scenes from *Buzzy and the Phantom Pinto*, thereby creating the confusion as to which "Buzzy" film was reissued as *Western Terror*. See 1941 entry for *Buzzy and the Phantom Pinto*)

1210. ROLLIN' HOME TO TEXAS

(Monogram, December 30, 1940) 63 Mins.

Tex Ritter, Cal Shrum, Slim Andrews, Eddie Dean, Virginia Carpenter, Harry Harvey, I. Stanford Jolley, Gene Alsace, Jack Rutherford, Minta Durfee, Walt Shrum, Charles Phillips, Olin Francis, Harold Landon, Bob Battier, Donald Kerr, Rusty Cline, Gene Haas, Tony Flores, Mack Williams, Robert Hoag, Hal Blaire, Cal Shrum's Rhythm Rangers, "White Flash"

D: Al Herman

SP: Robert Emmett (Tansey)

P: Edward Finney

1211. WILDCAT OF TUCSON

(Columbia, December 31, 1940) 59 Mins.

Bill Elliott, Evelyn Young, Stanley Brown, Dub Taylor, Kenneth MacDonald, Ben Taggart, Edmund Cobb, George Lloyd, Sammy Stein, George Chesebro, Forrest Taylor, Francis Walker, Robert Winkler, Dorothy Andre, Bert Young, Johnny Daheim, Newt Kirby, Murdock MacQuarrie

D: Lambert Hillyer

SP: Fred Myton

P: Leon Barsha

1212. PONY EXPRESS DAYS

(Warner Bros., 1940) 19 Mins.

(Technicolor)

George Reeves, David Bruce, Frank Wilcox, J. Farrell MacDonald, Joseph King, Addison Richards

D: B. Reeves Eason

SP: Charles L. Tetford

FILMS OF 1941

1213. HUDSON'S BAY
(20th C. Fox, January 3, 1941) 93 Mins.

Paul Muni, Gene Tierney, Laird Cregar, John Sutton, Virginia Field, Vincent Price, Nigel Bruce, Montague Love, Jody Gilbert, Chief Thunder Cloud, Chief John Big Tree, Ian Wolfe, Reginald Sheffield, Morton Lowry, Robert Cory

D: Irving Pichel
SP: Lamar Trotti
AP: Kenneth MacGowan

1214. TRAIL OF THE SILVER SPURS
(Monogram, January 4, 1941) 58 Mins.
(*Range Busters* Series)

Ray Corrigan, John King, Max Terhune, Dorothy Short, I. Stanford Jolley, Eddie Dean, Milburn Morante, George Chesebro, Kermit Maynard, Frank Ellis, Carl Mathews, Steve Clark

D: S. Roy Luby
S: Elmer Clifton
SP: Earle Snell
P: George W. Weeks

1215. WYOMING WILDCAT
(Republic, January 6, 1941) 56 Mins.

Don Barry, Julie Duncan, Syd Saylor, Frank M. Thomas, Dick Botiller, Edmund Cobb, Ed Brady, Edward Cassidy, George Sherwood, Ethan Laidlaw, Al Haskell, Frank Ellis, Curley Dresden, Art Dillard, Cactus Mack, Kermit Maynard, Frank O'Connor, Fred Burns

D/AP: George Sherman
S: Bennett Cohen
SP: Bennett Cohen, Anthony Coldeway

1216. BOSS OF BULLION CITY
(Universal, January 10, 1941)

Johnny Mack Brown, Fuzzy Knight, Nell O'Day, Maria Montez, Earle Hodgins, Harry Woods, Melvin Lang, Dick Alexander, Karl Hackett, George Humbert, Frank Ellis, Kermit Maynard, Tex Terry, Bob Kortman, Michael Vallon, The Guadalajara Trio

D: Ray Taylor
S: Arthur St. Claire
SP: Arthur St. Claire, Victor McLeod
AP: Will Cowan

1217. DOOMED CARAVAN
(Paramount, January 10, 1941) 62 Mins.
(*Hopalong Cassidy* Series)

William Boyd, Russell Hayden, Andy Clyde, Minna Gombell, Morris Ankrum, Georgia Hawkins, Trevor Bardette, Ray Bennett, Ed Cassidy

D: Lesley Selander
S/SP: Johnston McCulley, J. Benton Chaney. Based on characters created by William Colt MacDonald
P: Harry Sherman

1218. THE LONE RIDER RIDES ON
(PRC, January 10, 1941) 61 Mins.
(*Lone Rider* Series)

George Houston, Al St. John, Hillary Brooke, Lee Powell, Buddy Roosevelt, Al Bridge, Frank Hagney, Tom London, Karl Hackett, Forrest Taylor, Frank Ellis, Curley Dresden, Isabel LaMal, Harry Harvey, Jr., Don Forrest, Bob Kortman, Wally West, Steve Clark

D: Sam Newfield
SP: Joe O'Donnell
P: Sigmund Neufeld

1219. ROBIN HOOD OF THE PECOS
(Republic, January 14, 1941) 59 Mins.

Roy Rogers, George Hayes, Marjorie Reynolds, Sally Payne, Cy Kendall, Leigh Whipper, Eddie Acuff, Robert Strange, William Haade, Jay Novello, Roscoe Ates, Jim Corey, Chick Hannon, "Trigger"

D/AP: Joseph Kane
S: Hal Long
SP: Olive Cooper

1220. ROMANCE OF THE RIO GRANDE
(20th C. Fox, January 17, 1941) 73 Mins.
(*Cisco Kid* Series)

Cesar Romero, Patricia Morison, Lynne Roberts, Ricardo Cortez, Chris-Pin Martin, Richard Lane, Ray Bennett, Joseph McDonald

D: Herbert I. Leeds
S: "Conquistador"—Katherine Fullerton Gerould
SP: Harold Shumate, Samuel G. Engel. Based on character created by O. Henry
P: Sol Wurtzel

1221. BILLY THE KID'S RANGE WAR
(PRC, January 24, 1941) 57 Mins.
(*Billy the Kid* Series)

Bob Steele, Al St. John, Joan Barclay, Carleton Young, Rex Lease, Buddy Roosevelt, Milt Kibbee, Karl Hackett, Ted Adams, Julian Rivero, John Ince, Alden Chase, Howard Masters, Ralph Peters, Charles King, George Chesebro, Steve Clark, Tex Palmer

D: Peter Stewart (Sam Newfield)
SP: William Lively
P: Sigmund Neufeld

1222. RIDIN' ON A RAINBOW

(Republic, January 24, 1941) 79 Mins.

Gene Autry, Smiley Burnette, Mary Lee, Carol Adams, Ferris Taylor, Georgia Caine, Byron Foulger, Ralf Harolde, Jimmy Conlin, Guy Usher, Anthony Warde, Forrest Taylor, Burr Caruth, Ed Cassidy, Ben Hall, Tom London, William Mong, "Champion"

D: Lew Landers

SP: Bradford Ropes, Doris Malloy

S: Bradford Ropes

AP: Harry Grey

1223. ARKANSAS JUDGE

(Republic, January 28, 1941) 72 Mins.

Weaver Brothers and Elviry, Roy Rogers, Spring Byington, Pauline Moore, Frank M. Thomas, Veda Ann Borg, Eily Malyon, Loretta Weaver, Minerva Urecal, Harrison Greene, George Rosenor, Monte Blue, Frank Darien, Russell Hicks, Edwin Stanley

D: Frank McDonald

S: "False Witness"—Irving Stone

SP: Dorrell and Stuart McGowan

AP: Armand Schaefer

1224. PRAIRIE SPOONERS

(RKO, January 31, 1941) 13 Mins.

Ray Whitley, Virginia Vale, Jim Thorpe, Cactus Mack, Bob McKenzie, Kay Whitley, Lloyd Ingraham, Ken Card

D/SP: Harry D'Arcy

1225. WHITE EAGLE

(Columbia, January 31, 1941) 15 Chaps.

Buck Jones, Raymond Hatton, Dorothy Fay, James Craven, Chief Yowlachie, Jack Ingram, Charles King, John Merton, Roy Barcroft, Edward Hearn, Al Ferguson, J. Paul Jones, Edward Cecil, Chick Hannon, Bob Woodward, Horace B. Carpenter, Steve Clark, Merrill McCormack, Constantine Romanoff, Yakima Canutt, Kit Guard, Harry Tenbrook, Hack Richardson, Charles Hamilton, Edward Piel, Hank Bell, Lloyd Whitlock, Eddie Featherston, George Chesebro, Kenne Duncan, Bud Osborne, Edmund Cobb, Dick Cramer, Jack O'Shea, Richard Ellis, Robert Elliott, "Silver"

D: James W. Horne

S: Fred Myton. Adapted from the 1932 *White Eagle* feature

SP: Arch Heath, Morgan B. Cox, John Cutting, Lawrence Taylor

P: Larry Darmour

Chapter Titles: (1) Flaming Tepees, (2) The Jail Delivery, (3) The Dive into Quicksand, (4) The Warning Death Knife, (5) Treachery at the Stockdale, (6) The Gun-Cane Murder, (7) The Revealing Blotter, (8) Bird-Calls of Deliverance, (9) The Fake Telegram, (10) Mystic Dots and Dashes, (11) The Ear at the Window, (12) The Massacre Invitation, (13) The Framed-Up Showdown, (14) The Fake Army General, (15) Treachery Downed

1226. THE PINTO KID

(Columbia, February 5, 1941) 61 Mins.

Charles Starrett, Louise Currie, Bob Nolan, Paul Sutton, Hank Bell, Francis Walker, Ernie Adams, Jack Rockwell, Pat Brady, Roger Gray, Dick Botiller, Steve Clark, Frank Ellis, Sons of the Pioneers

D: Lambert Hillyer

SP: Fred Myton

P: Jack Fier

1227. ALONG THE RIO GRANDE

(RKO, February 7, 1941) 61 Mins.

Tim Holt, Ray Whitley, Emmett Lynn, Robert Fiske, Betty Jane Rhodes, Hal Taliaferro, Carl Stockdale, Slim Whitaker, Monte Montague, Ruth Clifford, Harry Humphrey, Ernie Adams

S: Stuart Anthony

SP: Arthur V. Jones, Morton Grant

P: Bert Gilroy

1228. THE KID'S LAST RIDE

(Monogram, February 10, 1941) 55 Mins.

(*Range Busters* Series)

Ray Corrigan, John King, Max Terhune, Luana Walters, Edwin Brian, Glenn Strange, Frank Ellis, John Elliott, George Havens, Tex Palmer, Carl Mathews, George Morrell

D: S. Roy Luby

SP: Earle Snell

P: George W. Weeks

1229. ACROSS THE SIERRAS

(Columbia, February 13, 1941) 59 Mins.

Bill Elliott, Richard Fiske, Luana Walters, Dub Taylor, Dick Curtis, LeRoy Mason, Ruth Robinson, John Dilson, Milt Kibbee, Ralph Peters, Tex Cooper, Eddie Laughton, Carl Knowles, Tom London, Edmund Cobb, Art Mix, Jim Pierce

D: D. Ross Lederman

SP: Paul Franklin

P: Leon Barsha

1230. THE PHANTOM COWBOY

(Republic, February 14, 1941) 56 Mins.

Don Barry, Virginia Carroll, Milburn Stone, Neyle Marx, Rex Lease, Nick Thompson, Bud Osborne, Ernest Wilson, Burr Caruth, Frank Ellis, Art Dillard, Jack O'Shea, Chuck Baldra

D/AP: George Sherman

SP: Doris Schroeder

1231. PRAIRIE PIONEERS
(Republic, February 16, 1941) 58 Mins.
(*Three Mesquiteers* Series)
Robert Livingston, Bob Steele, Rufe Davis, Esther Estrella, Robert Kellard, Guy D'Ennery, Davidson Clark, Jack Ingram, Kenneth MacDonald, Lee Shumway, Mary MacLaren, Yakima Canutt, Jack Kirk, Carleton Young, Wheaton Chambers, Frank Ellis, Cactus Mack, Curley Dresden, Frank McCarroll
D: Les Orlebeck
S: Karl Brown
SP: Barry Shipman. Based on characters created by William Colt MacDonald
AP: Louis Gray

1232. WESTERN UNION
(20th C. Fox, February 21, 1941) 94 Mins.
Robert Young, Randolph Scott, Dean Jagger, Virginia Gilmore, John Carradine, Slim Summerville, Chill Wills, Barton MacLane, Russell Hicks, Victor Kilian, Minor Watson, George Chandler, Chief Big Tree, Chief Thunder Cloud, Dick Rich, Harry Strange, Charles Middleton, Addison Richards, Irving Bacon
D: Fritz Lang
S: Zane Grey
SP: Robert Carson
AP: Harry Joe Brown

1233. RIDIN' THE CHEROKEE TRAIL
(Monogram, February 25, 1941) 62 Mins.
Tex Ritter, Slim Andrews, Betty Miles, Forrest Taylor, Jack Roper, Fred Burns, Bruce Nolan, Gene Alsace, Bob Card, Ed Cassidy, Hal Price, The Tennessee Ramblers, "White Flash," Chuck Baldra
D: Spencer G. Bennet
SP: Edmund Kelso
P: Edward Finney

1234. OUTLAWS OF THE PANHANDLE
(Columbia, February 27, 1941) 59 Mins.
Charles Starrett, Frances Robinson, Bob Nolan, Richard Fiske, Ray Teal, Lee Prather, Bud Osborne, Pat Brady, Steve Clark, Eddie Laughton, Jack Low, Norman Willis, Blackie Whiteford, Stanley Brown, Sons of the Pioneers
D: Sam Nelson
SP: Paul Franklin
P: Jack Fier

1235. THE LONE RIDER CROSSES THE RIO
(PRC, February 28, 1941)
(*Lone Rider* Series)
George Houston, Al St. John, Roquell Verrin, Jay Wilsey (Buffalo Bill, Jr.), Charles King, Alden Chase, Julian Rivero, Thornton Edwards, Howard Masters, Frank Ellis, Philip Turich, Frank Hagney, Curley Dresden, Sherry Tansey, Steve Clark
D: Sam Newfield
SP: William Lively
P: Sigmund Neufeld

1236. OUTLAWS OF THE RIO GRANDE
(PRC, March 7, 1941) 63 Mins.
Tim McCoy, Virginia Carpenter, Charles King, Ralph Peters, Rex Lease, Kenne Duncan, Karl Hackett, Philip Turich, Frank Ellis, Thornton Edwards, Joe Dominguez, George Chesebro, Sherry Tansey
D: Peter Stewart (Sam Newfield)
SP: George Plympton
P: Sigmund Neufeld

1237. CLIFF EDWARDS AND HIS BUCKAROOS
(Warner Bros., March 8, 1941) 10 Mins.
Cliff Edwards and a band
D: Jean Negulesco
SP: Nat Hiken

1238. BACK IN THE SADDLE
(Republic, March 14, 1941) 73 Mins.
Gene Autry, Smiley Burnette, Mary Lee, Edward Norris, Jacqueline Wells, Addison Richards, Arthur Loft, Edmund Elton, Joe McGuinn, Edmund Cobb, Robert Barron, Reed Howes, Stanley Blystone, Curley Dresden, Fred Toones, Frank Ellis, Jack O'Shea, Victor Cox, Herman Hack, Bob Burns, "Champion," Buck Bucko
D: Lew Landers
SP: Richard Murphy, Jesse Lasky, Jr.
AP: Harry Grey

1239. IN OLD COLORADO
(Paramount, March 14, 1941) 66 Mins.
(*Hopalong Cassidy* Series)
William Boyd, Russell Hayden, Andy Clyde, Margaret Hayes, Cliff Nazarro, Morris Ankrum, Sarah Padden, Stanley Andrews, Morgan Wallace, Weldon Heyburn, Glenn Strange, Eddy Waller, Philip Van Zandt, James Seay, Henry Wills, Curley Dresden
D: Howard Bretherton
SP: J. Benton Cheney, Norton S. Parker, Russell Hayden. Based on characters created by Clarence E. Mulford
P: Harry Sherman

1240. BURY ME NOT ON THE LONE PRAIRIE
(Universal, March 21, 1941) 57 Mins.
Johnny Mack Brown, Fuzzy Knight, Nell O'Day, Kathryn Adams, Lee Shumway, Frank O'Connor, Ernie Adams, Don House, Pat O'Brien, Bud Osborne, Ed Cassidy, Slim Whitaker, Kermit Maynard, William Desmond, Jack Rockwell, Bob Kort-

man, Jim Corey, Charles King, Ethan Laidlaw, Harry Cording, Frank Ellis, Jimmy Wakely's Rough Riders
D: Ray Taylor
S: Sherman Lowe
SP: Sherman Lowe, Victor McLeod
AP: Will Cowan

1241. THE BAD MAN
(MGM, March 28, 1941) 70 Mins.
Wallace Beery, Lionel Barrymore, Laraine Day, Ronald Reagan, Henry Travers, Chris-Pin Martin, Tom Conway, Chill Wills, Nydia Westman, Charles Stevens
D: Richard Thorpe
S: Porter Emerson Browne
SP: Wells Root
P: J. Walter Rubin

1242. IN OLD CHEYENNE
(Republic, March 28, 1941) 58 Mins.
Roy Rogers, George Hayes, Joan Woodbury, Sally Payne, J. Farrell MacDonald, George Rosenor, Hal Taliaferro, William Haade, Jack Kirk, Bob Woodward, Jim Corey, Cactus Mack, George Lloyd, Billy Benedict, Jack O'Shea, Edward Piel, Sr., Merrill McCormack, Ted Mapes, Fred Burns, Ben Corbett, Nick Thompson, "Trigger"
D/AP: Joseph Kane
S: John Kraft
SP: Olive Cooper

1243. NORTH FROM THE LONE STAR
(Columbia, March 31, 1941) 58 Mins.
Bill Elliott, Richard Fiske, Dorothy Fay, Dub Taylor, Arthur Loft, Jack Roper, Chuck Morrison, Claire Rochelle, Al Rhein, Edmund Cobb, Art Mix, Steve Clark, Tex Cooper, Hank Bell, Dick Botiller
D: Lambert Hillyer
SP: Charles Francis Royal
P: Leon Barsha

1244. THE ROUND UP
(Paramount, April 4, 1941) 90 Mins.
Richard Dix, Patricia Morison, Preston Foster, Don Wilson, Ruth Donnelly, Douglass Dumbrille, Jerome Cowan, Betty Brewer, Morris Ankrum, Dick Curtis, William Haade, Weldon Heyburn, Lane Chandler, Lee "Lasses" White, The King's Men
D: Lesley Selander
S: Edmund Day
SP: Harold Shumate
P: Harry Sherman

1245. PALS OF THE PECOS
(Republic, April 8, 1941) 56 Mins.
(*Three Mesquiteers* Series)

Robert Livingston, Bob Steele, Rufe Davis, June Johnson, Dennis Moore, Roy Barcroft, Pat O'Malley, Robert Frazer, John Holland, Tom London, Robert Winkler, George Chesebro, Chuck Morrison, Bud Osborne, Jack Kirk, Forrest Taylor, Frank Ellis, Eddie Dean
D: Les Orlebeck
S: Oliver Drake
SP: Oliver Drake, Herbert Delmas. Based on characters created by William Colt MacDonald
AP: Louis Gray

1246. TWO-GUN SHERIFF
(Republic, April 10, 1941) 56 Mins.
Don Barry, Lynn Merrick, Jay Novello, Fred Kohler, Jr., Lupita Tovar, Milt Kibbee, Marin Sais, Fred Toones, Dirk Thane, Archie Hall, Charles Thomas, Lee Shumway, John Merton, Carleton Young, Curley Dresden, Buck Moulton, Bud McClure, Tex Parker, Herman Nolan, George Plues
D/AP: George Sherman
S: Bennett Cohen
SP: Doris Schroeder

1247. LADY FROM CHEYENNE
(Universal, April 11, 1941) 87 Mins.
Loretta Young, Robert Preston, Edward Arnold, Frank Craven, Gladys George, Jessie Ralph, Stanley Fields, Willie Best, Samuel S. Hinds, Spencer Charters, Clare Verdera, Alan Bridge, Joseph Sawyer, Ralph Dunn, Harry Cording, Marion Martin, Gladys Blake, Sally Payne, Iris Adrian, June Wilkins, Erville Alderson, Emmett Vogan, Roger Imhoff, William Davidson, James Kirkwood, Emory Parnell
D/P: Frank Lloyd
S: Jonathan Finn, Theresa Oaks
SP: Kathryn Scola, Warren Duff

1248. REDSKINS AND REDHEADS
(RKO, April 15, 1941) 17 Mins.
Ray Whitley, Virginia Vale, Jane Kegley, Ricca Allen, Jimmy Wakely, Spade Cooley, Harry Harvey, Lloyd Ingraham, Curley Hoag, Ken Card
D/SP: Harry D'Arcy

1249. RIDE ON, VAQUERO
(20th C. Fox, April 18, 1941) 64 Mins.
(*Cisco Kid* Series)
Cesar Romero, Mary Beth Hughes, Chris-Pin Martin, Robert Lowery, Ben Carter, William Demarest, Robert Shaw, Edwin Maxwell, Paul Sutton, Don Costello, Arthur Hohl, Irving Bacon, Joan Woodbury, Paul Harvey, Dick Rich
D: Herbert I. Leeds
SP: Samuel G. Engel. Based on character created by O. Henry
P: Sol M. Wurtzel

1250. ROBBERS OF THE RANGE

(RKO, April 18, 1941) 61 Mins.

Tim Holt, Virginia Vale, Ray Whitley, Emmett Lynn, LeRoy Mason, Howard Hickman, Ernie Adams, Frank LaRue, Ray Bennett, Tom London, Ed Cassidy, Bud Osborne, George Melford, Bud McTaggart, Harry Harvey, Lloyd Ingraham

D: Edward Killy

S: Oliver Drake

SP: Morton Grant, Arthur V. Jones

P: Bert Gilroy

1251. BORDER VIGILANTES

(Paramount, April 18, 1941) 62 Mins.

(*Hopalong Cassidy* Series)

William Boyd, Russell Hayden, Andy Clyde, Victor Jory, Morris Ankrum, Frances Gifford, Ethel Wales, Tom Tyler, Hal Taliaferro, Jack Rockwell, Britt Wood, Hank Worden, Hank Bell, Edward Earle, Al Haskell, Curley Dresden, Chuck Morrison, Ted Wells

D: Derwin Abrahams

SP: J. Benton Cheney. Based on characters created by Clarence E. Mulford

P: Harry Sherman

1252. BILLY THE KID'S FIGHTING PALS

(PRC, April 18, 1941) 62 Mins.

(*Billy the Kid* Series)

Bob Steele, Al St. John, Phyllis Adair, Carleton Young, Charles King, Curley Dresden, Edward Piel, Sr., Hal Price, George Chesebro, Forrest Taylor, Budd Buster, Julian Rivero, Ray Henderson, Wally West, Art Dillard

D: Sherman Scott (Sam Newfield)

SP: George Plympton

P: Sigmund Neufeld

1253. TUMBLEDOWN RANCH IN ARIZONA

(Monogram, April 20, 1941) 60 Mins.

(*Range Busters* Series)

Ray Corrigan, John King, Max Terhune, Sheila Darcy, Marian Kirby, James Craven, Quen Ramsey, John Elliott, Jack Holmes, Steve Clark, Sam Bernard, Carl Mathews, Tex Palmer, Tex Cooper, Frank Ellis, Nick Thompson, University of Arizona Glee Club, Frank McCarroll, Chick Hannon

D: S. Roy Luby

SP: Milton Raison

P: George W. Weeks

1254. THE SINGING HILL

(Republic, April 26, 1941) 75 Mins.

Gene Autry, Smiley Burnette, Virginia Dale, Mary Lee, Spencer Charters, Gerald Oliver Smith, George Meeker, Wade Boteler, Harry Stubbs, Cactus Mack, Jack Kirk, Chuck Morrison, Monte Montague, Sam Flint, Hal Price, Fred Burns, Herman Hack, Jack O'Shea, "Champion"

D: Lew Landers

S: Jesse Lasky, Jr., Richard Murphy

SP: Olive Cooper

AP: Harry Grey

1255. BUZZY AND THE PHANTOM PINTO

(Ziehm Productions, May 1, 1941) 55 Mins.

Buzzy Henry, Dave O'Brien, Dorothy Short, George Morrell, Sven Hugo Borg, Milburn Morante, Frank Marlo, Phil Arnold

D: Richard C. Kahn

SP: E. C. Robertson

P: Dick L'Estrange

(Scenes from this film were used on the 11 x 14 scene cards for the Astor release of *Western Terror,* though that film was actually *Buzzy Rides the Range*)

1256. LAW OF THE WOLF

(Ziehm Productions, May 1, 1941) 55 Mins.

Dennis Moore, Luana Walters, George Chesebro, Steve Clark, Jack Ingram, Robert Frazer, Jimmy Aubrey, Martin Spellman, Bobby Gordon, Rin-Tin-Tin, III

D: Raymond K. Johnson

S: Tom Gibson

SP: Joseph Murphy

P: Bernard B. Ray

1257. THE RETURN OF DANIEL BOONE

(Columbia, May 7, 1941) 61 Mins.

Bill Elliott, Betty Miles, Dub Taylor, Ray Bennett, Lee Powell, Bud Osborne, Edmund Cobb, Walter Soderling, Carl Stockdale, Francis Walker, Tom Carter, Melinda Rodik, Matilda Rodik, Steve Clark, Hank Bell, Roy Butler, Art Miles, Edwin Bryant, Murdock MacQuarrie, Tex Cooper

D: Lambert Hillyer

S: Paul Franklin

SP: Paul Franklin, Joseph Hoffman

P: Leon Barsha

1258. SHERIFF OF TOMBSTONE

(Republic, May 7, 1941) 56 Mins.

Roy Rogers, George Hayes, Elyse Knox, Harry Woods, Hal Taliaferro, Jay Novello, Roy Barcroft, Jack Rockwell, Addison Richards, Sally Payne, Zeffie Tilbury, Jack Ingram, George Rosenor, Jack Kirk, Frank Ellis, Art Dillard, Herman Hack, Vester Pegg, Al Haskell, Ray Jones, Jess Cavan, "Trigger"

D/AP: Joseph Kane

S: James Webb

SP: Olive Cooper

The Pioneers (Monogram, 1941) — Red Foley and Tex Ritter

1259. THE PIONEERS

(Monogram, May 10, 1941)   58 Mins.

Tex Ritter, Red Foley and his Saddle Pals, "Arkansas Slim" Andrews, Wanda McKay, Doye O'Dell, George Chesebro, Del Lawrence, Post Park, Karl Hackett, Lynton Brent, Chick Hannon, Gene Alsace, Jack C. Smith, Chief Many Treaties, Chief Soldani, Art Dillard, "White Flash"

D: Al Herman

S: J. Fenimore Cooper

SP: Charles Alderson

P: Edward Finney

1260. SADDLEMATES

(Republic, May 16, 1941)   56 Mins.

(*Three Mesquiteers* Series)

Robert Livingston, Bob Steele, Rufe Davis, Gale Storm, Forbes Murray, Cornelius Keefe, Peter George Lynn, Marin Sais, Matty Faust, Glenn Strange, Ellen Lowe, Iron Eyes Cody, Chief Yowlachie, Bill Hazlett, Henry Wills, Major Bill Keefer

D: Les Orlebeck

S: Bernard McConville, Karen DeWolf

SP: Albert Demond, Herbert Dalmas. Based on characters created by William Colt MacDonald

AP: Louis Gray

1261. THE COWBOY AND THE BLONDE

(20th C. Fox, May 16, 1941)   68 Mins.

Mary Beth Hughes, George Montgomery, Alan Mowbray, Robert Conway, John Miljan, Richard Lane, Robert Emmett Keane, Minerva Urecal, Fuzzy Knight, George O'Hara, Monica Bannister, William Halligan

D: Ray McCarey

S: Walter Bullock, William Brent

SP: Walter Bullock

AP: Ralph Dietrich, Walter Morosco

1262. THE LONE RIDER IN GHOST TOWN

(PRC, May 16, 1941)   64 Mins.

(*Lone Rider* Series)

George Houston, Al St. John, Alaine Brandes, Budd Buster, Frank Hagney, Alden Chase, Reed Howes, Charles King, George Chesebro, Edward Piel, Sr., Archie Hall, Jay Wilsey (Buffalo Bill, Jr.), Karl Hackett, Don Forrest, Frank Ellis, Curley Dresden, Steve Clark, Byron Vance, Jack Ingram, Augie Gomez, Lane Bradford

D: Sam Newfield

SP: William Lively

P: Sigmund Neufeld

1263. DESERT BANDIT

(Republic, May 24, 1941)   56 Mins.

Don Barry, Lynn Merrick, William Haade, James Gilette, Dick Wessell, Tom Chatterton, Tom Ewelle, Robert Strange, Charles Moore, Ernie Stanton, Curley Dresden, Jim Corey, Merrill McCormack, Charles King, Jack Montgomery, Jack O'Shea, Pascale Perry

D/AP: George Sherman

S: Bennett Cohen

SP: Eliot Gibbons, Bennett Cohen

1264. SILVER STALLION

(Monogram, May 28, 1941)   57 Mins.

David Sharpe, Chief Thunder Cloud, LeRoy Mason, Janet Waldo, Fred Hoose, Thornton Edwards, Walter Long, "Thunder" (the Wonder Horse), "Captain Boots" (the Police Dog)

D/P: Edward Finney

SP: Robert Emmett (Tansey)

1265. BILLY THE KID

(MGM, May 30, 1941)   95 Mins.

Robert Taylor, Brian Donlevy, Ian Hunter, Mary Howard, Gene Lockhart, Lon Chaney, Jr., Henry O'Neill, Guinn Williams, Cy Kendall, Ted Adams, Frank Conlan, Frank Puglia, Mitchell Lewis, Dick Curtis, Grant Withers, Joe Yule, Earl Gunn, Eddie Dunn, Carl Pitti, Kermit Maynard, Ethel Griffies, Chill Wills, Olive Blakeney

D: David Miller

S: Walter Noble Burns

SP: Gene Fowler

P: Irving Asher

1266. PIRATES ON HORSEBACK

(Paramount, May 31, 1941)   69 Mins.

(*Hopalong Cassidy* Series)

William Boyd, Russell Hayden, Andy Clyde, Eleanor Stewart, Morris Ankrum, William Haade, Dennis Moore, Henry Hall, Britt Wood, Silver-Tip Baker

D: Lesley Selander

SP: Ethel La Blanche, J. Benton Cheney. Based on characters created by Clarence E. Mulford

P: Harry Sherman

1267. WRANGLER'S ROOST

(Monogram, June 4, 1941)   57 Mins.

(*Range Busters* Series)

Ray Corrigan, John King, Max Terhune, Forrest Taylor, Gwen Gaze, George Chesebro, Frank Ellis, Jack Holmes, Walter Shumway, Frank McCarroll, Carl Mathews, Hank Bell, Tex Palmer, Jim Corey, Al Haskell, Ray Jones, Horace B. Carpenter, Tex Cooper, Herman Hack, Chick Hannon

D: S. Roy Luby

S: Earle Snell

SP: John Vlahos, Robert Finkle

P: George W. Weeks

1268. MEN OF THE TIMBERLAND

(Universal, June 6, 1941)   61 Mins.

Richard Arlen, Andy Devine, Linda Hayes, Francis McDonald, Willard Robertson, Paul Burns, Gaylord Pendleton, Hardie Albright, Roy Harris (Riley Hill), John Ellis, Jack Rice

S: Paul Jarrico

D: John Rawlins

SP: Maurice Tombragel, Griffin Joy

AP: Ben Pivar

1269. CYCLONE ON HORSEBACK

(RKO, June 13, 1941)   60 Mins.

Tim Holt, Marjorie Reynolds, Ray Whitley, Lee "Lasses" White, Dennis Moore, Harry Worth, Monte Montague, John Dilson, Lew Kelly, Max Wagner, Terry Frost, Don Kelly, Slim Whitaker

D: Edward Killy

S: Tom Gibson

SP: Norton S. Parker

P: Bert Gilroy

1270. HANDS ACROSS THE ROCKIES

(Columbia, June 19, 1941)   58 Mins.

Bill Elliott, Mary Daily, Dub Taylor, Kenneth MacDonald, Frank LaRue, Donald Curtis, Tom Moray, Stanley Brown, Slim Whitaker, Harrison Greene, Art Mix, Eddy Waller, Hugh Prosser, Tex Cooper, Ethan Laidlaw, George Morrell, George Chesebro, Curley Dresden, Steve Clark, Edmund Cobb, Kathryn Bates, Eddie Laughton, Ethan Laidlaw, Buck Moulton

D: Lambert Hillyer

S: Norbert Davis

SP: Paul Franklin

1271. LAW OF THE RANGE

(Universal, June 20, 1941)   59 Mins.

Johnny Mack Brown, Fuzzy Knight, Nell O'Day, Roy Harris (Riley Hill), Pat O'Malley, Elaine Morley, Ethan Laidlaw, Al Bridge, Hal Taliaferro, Jack Rockwell, Charles King, Lucile Walker, Terry Frost, Jim Corey, Bud Osborne, Slim Whitaker, Bob Kortman, The Texas Rangers

D: Ray Taylor

AP: Will Cowan

1272. NEVADA CITY

(Republic, June 20, 1941)   58 Mins.

Roy Rogers, George Hayes, Sally Payne, Fred Kohler, Jr., George Cleveland, Billy Lee, Joseph Crehan, Pierre Watkin, Jack Ingram, Art Mix, Syd Saylor, Hank Bell, Yakima Canutt, Rex Lease,

Henry Wills, Bob Woodward, Jack Kirk, Fred Burns, "Trigger"
D/AP: Joseph Kane
SP: James R. Webb

1273. KANSAS CYCLONE
(Republic, June 24, 1941)   58 Mins.
Don Barry, Lynn Merrick, William Haade, Milton Kibbee, Harry Worth, Dorothy Sebastian, Jack Kirk, Forrest Taylor, Charles Moore, Eddie Dean, Reed Howes, Guy Usher, Edward Piel, Sr., Yakima Canutt, Cactus Mack, Bob Woodward, Tex Terry, George J. Lewis, Augie Gomez, Buddy Roosevelt, William Kellogg
D/AP: George Sherman
S: Louis Sarecky
SP: Oliver Drake, Doris Schroeder

1274. MEET ROY ROGERS
(Republic, June 24, 1941)   10 Mins.
(*Harriet Parsons* Series)
Roy Rogers, Gene Autry, Judy Canova, Bill Elliott, George "Gabby" Hayes, Billy Gilbert, Bob Baker, Roscoe Ates, Mary Lee
D/P: Harriet Parsons

1275. THE MEDICO OF PAINTED SPRINGS
(Columbia, June 26, 1941)   58 Mins.
Charles Starrett, Terry Walker, Richard Fiske, Ray Bennett, Ben Taggert, Bud Osborne, Edmund Cobb, Edith Elliott, Steve Clark, Lloyd Bridges, George Chesebro, Charles Hamilton, Jim Corey, The Simp-Phonie, "Raider"
D: Lambert Hillyer
S: James L. Rudell
SP: Winston Miller

1276. HERE COMES THE CAVALRY
(Warner Bros., June 28, 1941)   20 Mins.
(Technicolor)
William Justice
D: D. Ross Lederman
SP: Owen Crump

1277. RIDERS OF DEATH VALLEY
(Universal, July 1, 1941)   15 Chaps.
Dick Foran, Buck Jones, Leo Carrillo, Charles Bickford, Lon Chaney, Jr., Noah Beery, Jr., "Big Boy" Williams, Jeannie Kelly (Jean Brooks), Monte Blue, James Blaine, Glenn Strange, Roy Barcroft, Ethan Laidlaw, Dick Alexander, Jack Rockwell, Frank Austin, Charles Thomas, William Hall, James Guilfoyle, Ernie Adams, Edmund Cobb, William Pagan, Jack Clifford, Richard Travis, Ivar McFadden, Jerome Harte, Ruth Rickaby, Jack Perrin, Don Rowan, Bud Osborne, Slim Whitaker, Frank Brownlee, Art Miles, Ed Payson, James Farley, Alonzo Price, Ted Adams, Dick Rush, Ken

The Medico of Painted Springs (Columbia, 1941) — Charles Starrett and "Raider"

239

Nolan, Jay Michael, Gil Perkins, Duke York,
"Silver"
D: Ray Taylor, Ford Beebe
S: Oliver Drake
SP: Sherman Lowe, Basil Dickey, George Plympton, Jack Connell
P: Henry MacRae
Chapter Titles: (1) Death Marks the Trail, (2) Menacing Herd, (3) Plunge of Peril, (4) Flaming Fury, (5) Avalanche of Doom, (6) Blood and Gold, (7) Death Rides the Storm, (8) Descending Doom, (9) Death Holds the Reins, (10) Devouring Flames, (11) Fatal Blast, (12) Thundering Doom, (13) The Bridge of Disaster, (14) A Fight to the Death, (15) The Harvest of Hate

1278. GANGS OF SONORA
(Republic, July 10, 1941)   56 Mins.
(*Three Mesquiteers* Series)
Robert Livingston, Bob Steele, Rufe Davis, June Johnson, Bud McTaggart, Helen MacKellar, Robert Frazer, William Farnum, Budd Buster, Hal Price, Wally West, Bud Osborne, Bud Geary, Jack Kirk, Al Taylor, Griff Barnette, Curley Dresden, Jack Lawrence
D: John English
SP: Albert DeMond, Doris Schroeder
AP: Louis Gray

1279. BILLY THE KID IN SANTA FE
(PRC, July 11, 1941)   66 Mins.
(*Billy the Kid* Series)
Bob Steele, Al St. John, Rex Lease, Marin Sais, Dennis Moore, Karl Hackett, Steve Clark, Hal Price, Charles King, Frank Ellis, Dave O'Brien, Kenne Duncan, Curley Dresden
D: Sherman Scott (Sam Newfield)
SP: Joseph O'Donnell
P: Sigmund Neufeld

1280. THE TEXAS MARSHAL
(PRC, July 13, 1941)   58 Mins.
Tim McCoy, Art Davis and his Rhythm Riders, Kay Leslie, Karl Hackett, Edward Piel, Sr., Charles King, Dave O'Brien, Budd Buster, John Elliott, Wilson Edwards, Byron Vance, Frank Ellis
D: Peter Stewart (Sam Newfield)
SP: William Lively
P: Sigmund Neufeld

1281. SUNSET IN WYOMING
(Republic, July 15, 1941)   65 Mins.
Gene Autry, Smiley Burnette, Maris Wrixon, George Cleveland, Robert Kent, Sarah Padden, Monte Blue, Dick Elliott, John Dilson, Stanley Blystone, Eddie Dew, Fred Burns, Reed Howes, Ralph Peters, Syd Saylor, Tex Terry, Lloyd Whitlock, Herman Hack, "Champion"

D: William Morgan
S: Joe Blair
SP: Ivan Goff, Anne Morrison Chapin
AP: Harry Grey

1282. THE SON OF DAVY CROCKETT
(Columbia, July 15, 1941)   59 Mins.
Bill Elliott, Iris Meredith, Dub Taylor, Kenneth MacDonald, Richard Fiske, Eddy Waller, Donald Curtis, Paul Scardon, Edmund Cobb, Steve Clark, Harrison Greene, Lloyd Bridges, Curley Dresden, Frank Ellis, Dick Botiller, Ray Jones, Tom London, John Tyrell, Nick Thompson, Merrill McCormack, Martin Garralaga, Lew Meehan, Francis Sayles, Jack Ingram, Frank LaRue, Chuck Hamilton
D: Lambert Hillyer
SP: Lambert Hillyer
P: Leon Barsha

1283. THE SHEPHERD OF THE HILLS
(Paramount, July 18, 1941)   98 Mins.
John Wayne, Betty Field, Harry Carey, Beulah Bondi, James Barton, Samuel S. Hinds, Marjorie Main, Ward Bond, Marc Lawrence, John Qualen, Fuzzy Knight, Tom Fadden, Hank Bell, Dorothy Adams, Fern Emmett
D: Henry Hathaway
S: Harold Bell Wright
SP: Grover Jones, Stuart Anthony
P: Jack Moss

1284. RAWHIDE RANGERS
(Universal, July 18, 1941)   56 Mins.
Johnny Mack Brown, Fuzzy Knight, Nell O'Day, Kathryn Adams, Roy Harris, Harry Cording, Al Bridge, Frank Shannon, Ed Cassidy, Bob Kortman, Chester Gan, James Farley, Jack Rockwell, Frank Ellis, Fred Burns, Tex Palmer, Tex Terry, The Pickard Family, The Texas Rangers
D: Ray Taylor
SP: Ed Earl Repp
AP: Will Cowan

1285. THE MUSICAL BANDIT
(RKO, July 18, 1941)   17 Mins.
Ray Whitley, Virginia Vale, John Dilson, Lloyd Ingraham, Jane Kegley, Jack Rice, Frankie Marvin, Ken Card
D/SP: Charles Roberts

1286. ARIZONA BOUND
(Monogram, July 19, 1941)   57 Mins.
(*Rough Riders* Series)
Buck Jones, Tim McCoy, Raymond Hatton, Tris Coffin, Dennis Moore, Luana Walters, Kathryn Sheldon, Gene Alsace, Slim Whitaker, Artie Ortego, I. Stanford Jolley, Horace Murphy, Hal

Price, Jack Daley, Augie Gomez, Slim Whitaker, "Silver"
D: Spencer G. Bennet
S: Oliver Drake
SP: Jess Bowers (Adele Buffington)
P: Scott R. Dunlap

1287. HURRICANE SMITH
(Republic, July 20, 1941) 69 Mins.
Ray Middleton, Jane Wyatt, Harry Davenport, J. Edward Bromberg, Henry Brandon, Carter Johnson, Charles Trowbridge, Frank Darien, Howard Hickman, Emmett Vogan
D: Bernard Vorhaus
S: Charles G. Booth
SP: Robert Presnell
AP: Robert North

1288. WANDERERS OF THE WEST
(Monogram, July 25, 1941) 58 Mins.
Tom Keene, Betty Miles, Sugar Dawn, Slim Andrews, Tom Seidel, Stanley Price, Gene Alsace, Tom London, Fred Hoose, James Sheridan (Sherry Tansey)
D: Robert Hill
SP: Robert Emmett (Tansey)
P: Robert Tansey

1289. BAD MEN OF MISSOURI
(Warner Bros., July 26, 1941) 74 Mins.
Dennis Morgan, Jane Wyman, Wayne Morris, Arthur Kennedy, Victor Jory, Alan Baxter, Walter Catlett, Howard de Silva, Faye Emerson, Russell Simpson, Virginia Brissac, Erville Alderson, Hugh Sothern, Sam McDaniel, Dorothy Vaughn, William Gould, Robert Winkler, Ann Todd, Roscoe Ates
D: Ray Enright
S: Robert E. Kent
SP: Charles Grayson

1290. FUGITIVE VALLEY
(Monogram, July 30, 1941) 61 Mins.
(*Range Busters* Series)
Ray Corrigan, John King, Max Terhune, Julie Duncan, Glenn Strange, Bob Kortman, Ed Brady, Tom London, Reed Howes, Carl Mathews, Ed Piel, Sr., Doye O'Dell, Frank McCarroll, Elmer
D: S. Roy Luby
S: Oliver Drake
SP: John Vlahos, Robert Finkle
P: George W. Weeks

1291. THUNDER OVER THE PRAIRIE
(Columbia, July 30, 1941) 60 Mins.
Charles Starrett, Eileen O'Hearn, Cliff Edwards, Carl (Cal) Shrum and his Rhythm Rangers, Stanley Brown, Danny Mummert, David Sharpe, Joe

McGuinn, Donald Curtis, Ted Adams, Jack Rockwell, Budd Buster, Horace B. Carpenter
D: Lambert Hillyer
S: James L. Rubel
SP: Betty Burbridge
P: William Berke

1292. SIX GUN GOLD
(RKO, August 8, 1941) 57 Mins.
Tim Holt, Ray Whitley, Jan Clayton, Lee "Lasses" White, Lane Chandler, LeRoy Mason, Eddy Waller, Davidson Clark, Harry Harvey, Slim Whitaker, Jim Corey, Fern Emmett
D: David Howard
S: Tom Gibson
SP: Norton S. Parker
P: Bert Gilroy

1293. WIDE OPEN TOWN
(Paramount, August 8, 1941) 78 Mins.
(*Hopalong Cassidy* Series)
William Boyd, Russell Hayden, Andy Clyde, Evelyn Brent, Victor Jory, Morris Ankrum, Kenneth Harlan, Bernice Kay (Cara Williams), Roy Barcroft, Glenn Strange, Ed Cassidy, Jack Rockwell, Bob Kortman, George Cleveland
D: Lesley Selander
SP: Harrison Jacobs, J. Benton Cheney. Based on characters created by Clarence E. Mulford
P: Harry Sherman

1294. DYNAMITE CANYON
(Monogram, August 8, 1941) 58 Mins.
Tom Keene, Evelyn Finley, Slim Andrews, Sugar Dawn, Stanley Price, Kenne Duncan, Gene Alsace, Fred Hoose, Tom London, "Rusty"
D/P: Robert Emmett Tansey
SP: Robert Emmett, Frances Kavanaugh

1295. THE LONE RIDER IN FRONTIER FURY
(PRC, August 8, 1941)
(*Lone Rider* Series)
George Houston, Al St. John, Hillary Brooke, Karl Hackett, Ted Adams, Archie Hill, Budd Buster, Virginia Card, Edward Piel, Sr., John Elliott, Tom London, Frank Ellis, Dan White, Horace B. Carpenter, Tex Cooper, Tex Palmer, Curley Dresden, Wally West, Herman Hack
D: Sam Newfield
SP: Fred Myton
P: Sigmund Neufeld

1296. KING OF DODGE CITY
(Columbia, August 14, 1941) 59 Mins.
Bill Elliott, Tex Ritter, Judith Linden, Dub Taylor, Guy Usher, Rich Anderson, Pierce Lyden, Francis Walker, Harrison Greene, Jack Rockwell, Edmund Cobb, George Chesebro, Kenneth Harlan, Steve

Clark, Tris Coffin, Jack Ingram, Tex Cooper, Russ Powell, Frosty Royce, Ed Coxen, Lee Prather, Jay Lawrence, Ned Glass
D: Lambert Hillyer
SP: Gerald Geraghty
P: Leon Barsha

1297. THE PARSON OF PANAMINT
(Paramount, August 22, 1941) 84 Mins.
Charlie Ruggles, Ellen Drew, Phillip Terry, Joseph Schildkraut, Porter Hall, Henry Kolker, Janet Beecher, Paul Hurst, Clem Bevins, Douglas Fowley, Frank Puglia, Minor Watson, Harry Hayden, Russell Hicks, Hal Price
D: William McGann
S: Peter B. Kyne
SP: Harold Shumate, Adrian Scott
P: Harry Sherman

1298. UNDER FIESTA STARS
(Republic, August 25, 1941) 64 Mins.
Gene Autry, Smiley Burnette, Carol Hughes, Frank Darien, Joe Straugh, Jr., Pauline Drake, Ivan Miller, Sam Flint, Elias Gamboa, John Merton, Jack Kirk, Inez Palange, Curley Dresden, Hal Taliaferro, "Champion," Frankie Marvin, Pascale Perry
D: Frank McDonald
S: Karl Brown
SP: Karl Brown, Eliot Gibbons
AP: Harry Grey

1299. THE LONE RIDER AMBUSHED
(PRC, August 29, 1941) 67 Mins.
(*Lone Rider* Series)
George Houston, Al St. John, Maxine Leslie, Frank Hagney, Jack Ingram, Hal Price, Ted Adams, George Chesebro, Ralph Peters, Steve Clark, Carl Mathews, Charles King
D: Sam Newfield
SP: Oliver Drake
P: Sigmund Neufeld

1300. SADDLE MOUNTAIN ROUNDUP
(Monogram, August 29 1941) 55 Mins.
(*Range Busters* Series)
Ray Corrigan, John King, Max Terhune, Jack Mulhall, Lita Conway, Willie Fung, John Elliott, George Chesebro, Jack Holmes, Harold Goodman, Carl Mathews, Al Ferguson, Slim Whitaker, Tex Palmer, Steve Clark
D: S. Roy Luby
SP: Earle Snell, John Vlahos
P: George W. Weeks

1301. BADLANDS OF DAKOTA
(Universal, September 5, 1941) 74 Mins.
Robert Stack, Ann Rutherford, Richard Dix, Frances Farmer, Broderick Crawford, Hugh Herbert, Fuzzy Knight, Lon Chaney, Jr., Andy Devine, Addison Richards, Samuel S. Hinds, Eddie Dew, Kermit Maynard, Charles King, Hank Bell, Bradley Page, Carleton Young, Glenn Strange, Don Barclay, Emmett Vogan, Willie Fung, Edward Fielding, The Jesters (Dwight Latham, Walter Carlson, and Guy Bonham)
D: Alfred E. Greene
S: Harold Shumate
SP: Gerald Geraghty
AP: George Waggner

1302. BAD MAN OF DEADWOOD
(Republic, September 5, 1941) 61 Mins.
Roy Rogers, George Hayes, Carol Adams, Sally Payne, Henry Brandon, Herbert Rawlinson, Hal Taliaferro, Jay Novello, Horace Murphy, Monte Blue, Ralf Harolde, Jack Kirk, Yakima Canutt, Curley Dresden, Fred Burns, Lynton Brent, Lloyd Ingraham, George Lloyd, Robert Frazer, Archie Twitchell, Karl Hackett, Harry Harvey, Eddie Acuff, Tom London, Jack Rockwell, Ernie Adams, Jack O'Shea, George Morrell, Wally West, Bob Woodward, "Trigger," Pascale Perry, Horace B. Carpenter, Harrison Greene
D/AP: Joseph Kane
SP: James R. Webb

1303. MAN FROM MONTANA
(Universal, September 5, 1941) 56 Mins.
Johnny Mack Brown, Fuzzy Knight, Nell O'Day, Butch and Buddy (Billy Lenhart and Kenneth Brown), Jeanne Kelly (Jean Brooks), William Gould, James Blaine, Dick Alexander, Karl Hackett, Edmund Cobb, Frank Ellis, Kermit Maynard, Jack Shannon, Murdock McQuarrie, Charles McMurphy, Blackjack Ward, The King's Men
D: Ray Taylor
SP: Bennett Cohen
AP: Will Cowan

1304. OUTLAWS OF THE CHEROKEE TRAIL
(Republic, September 10, 1941) 56 Mins.
(*Three Mesquiteers* Series)
Bob Steele, Tom Tyler, Rufe Davis, Lois Collier, Tom Chatterton, Rex Lease, Joel Friedkin, Roy Barcroft, Philip Trent, Peggy Lynn, Bud Osborne, Chief Yowlachie, John James, Lee Shumway, Karl Hackett, Chuck Morrison, Billy Burtis, Griff Barnette, Bud Geary, Al Taylor, Henry Wills, Sarah Padden, Iron Eyes Cody, Cactus Mack
D: Les Orlebeck
SP: Albert DeMond. Based on characters created by William Colt MacDonald

1305. BELLE STARR
(20th C. Fox, September 12, 1941) 87 Mins.
Randolph Scott, Gene Tierney, Dana Andrews,

John Sheppard, Elizabeth Patterson, Chill Wills, Louise Beavers, Olin Howlin, Paul Burns, Joseph Sawyer, Joseph Downing, Howard Hickman, Charles Trowbridge, James Flavin, Charles Middleton, Clarence Muse, George Melford, Mae Marsh, Herbert Ashley, Norman Willis, Billy Wayne, George Reed, Davidson Clark, Hugh Chapman, Clinton Rosemond
D: Irvin Cummings
S: Niven Busch, Cameron Rogers
SP: Lamar Trotti
AP: Kenneth MacGowan

1306. THE APACHE KID

(Republic, September 12, 1941) 56 Mins.
Donald Barry, Lynn Merrick, Al St. John, LeRoy Mason, Robert Fiske, John Elliott, Forbes Murray, Monte Montague, Fred Toones, Charles King, Frank Brownlee, John L. "Bob" Cason, Cactus Mack, Kenne Duncan, Hal Price, Buddy Roosevelt, Buck Moulton, Tommy Coats
D/AP: George Sherman
SP: Eliot Gibbons, Richard Murphy

1306a. WESTWARD HO-HUM

(RKO, September 15, 1941) 2 Reels

Edgar Kennedy, Sally Payne, Jack Rice, Glenn Strange, Ethan Laidlaw, Ernie Adams
D: Clem Beauchamp

1307. RIDERS OF THE TIMBERLINE

(Paramount, September 17, 1941) 59 Mins.
(*Hopalong Cassidy* Series)
William Boyd, Brad King, Andy Clyde, J. Farrell MacDonald, Eleanor Stewart, Anna Q. Nilsson, Edward Keane, Hal Taliaferro, Victor Jory, Tom Tyler, Mickey Essia, Hank Bell, The Guardsman Quartet
D: Lesley Selander
SP: J. Benton Cheney. Based on characters created by Clarence E. Mulford
P: Harry Sherman

1308. PRAIRIE STRANGER

(Columbia, September 18, 1941) 58 Mins.
Charles Starrett, Cliff "Ukulele Ike" Edwards, Patti McCarty, Forbes Murray, Frank LaRue, Archie Twitchell, Francis Walker, Edmund Cobb, Jim Corey, Russ Powell, George Morrell, Lew Preston and his Ranch Hands
D: Lambert Hillyer
S: James Rubel
SP: Winston Miller
P: William Berke

Riders of the Timberline (Paramount, 1941) — William Boyd, Brad King, Andy Clyde, and Victor Jory

243

1309. DEATH VALLEY OUTLAWS
(Republic, September 26, 1941) 56 Mins.
Don Barry, Lynn Merrick, Milburn Stone, Rex
    Lease, Bob McKenzie, Karl Hackett, Jack Kirk,
    Michael Owen, Fred Toones, Bob Kortman,
    Curley Dresden, John L. "Bob" Cason, Griff Bar-
    nette, Lee Shumway, Wally West, Harry Strang,
    Reed Howes, George J. Lewis
D/AP: George Sherman
S: Don Ryan
SP: Don Ryan, Jack Lait, Jr.

1310. THE GUNMAN FROM BODIE
(Monogram, September 26, 1941) 62 Mins.
(*Rough Riders* Series)
Buck Jones, Tim McCoy, Raymond Hatton, Chris-
    tine McIntyre, David O'Brien, Robert Frazer,
    Frank LaRue, Charles King, Lynton Brent, Max
    Walzman, Gene Alsace, John Merton, Jerry Shel-
    don, Jack King, Earl Douglas, Warren Jackson,
    Billy Carro, Frederick Gee, "Silver"
D: Spencer G. Bennet
SP: Jess Bowers (Adele Buffington)
P: Scott R. Dunlap

1311. LAST OF THE DUANES
(20th C. Fox, September 26, 1941) 57 Mins.
George Montgomery, Lynne Roberts, Eve Arden,
    Francis Ford, George E. Stone, William Far-
    num, Joseph Sawyer, Truman Bradley, Russell
    Simpson, Don Costello, Harry Woods, Andrew
    Tombes
D: James Tinling
S: Zane Grey
SP: Irving Cummings, Jr., William Conselman, Jr.
P: Sol M. Wurtzel

1312. TWILIGHT ON THE TRAIL
(Paramount, September 27, 1941) 58 Mins.
(*Hopalong Cassidy* Series)
William Boyd, Andy Clyde, Brad King, Wanda
    McKay, Jack Rockwell, Norman Willis, Robert
    Kent, Tom London, Bob Kortman, Frank Austin,
    Clem Fuller, Johnny Powers, Frank Ellis, Bud Os-
    borne, The Jimmy Wakely Trio (Jimmy Wakely,
    Johnny Bond, and Dick Rinehart)
D: Howard Bretherton
SP: J. Benton Cheney, Ellen Corby, and Cecile
    Kramer. Based on characters created by Clar-
    ence E. Mulford
P: Harry Sherman

1313. STICK TO YOUR GUNS
(Paramount, September 27, 1941) 63 Mins.
(*Hopalong Cassidy* Series)
William Boyd, Andy Clyde, Brad King, Jacqueline
    (Jennifer) Holt, Dick Curtis, Weldon Heybrun,
    Henry Hall, Joe Whitehead, Bob Card, Jack C.

Smith, Homer (Herb) Holcomb, Tom London,
    Kermit Maynard, Frank Ellis, Jack Rockwell,
    Mickey Eissa, The Jimmy Wakely Trio (Jimmy
    Wakely, Johnny Bond, and Dick Rinehart)
D: Lesley Selander
SP: J. Benton Cheney. Based on characters created
    by Clarence E. Mulford
P: Harry Sherman

1314. HONKY TONK
(MGM, October 1, 1941) 105 Mins.
Clark Gable, Lana Turner, Frank Morgan, Claire
    Trevor, Marjorie Main, Albert Dekker, Henry
    O'Neill, Chill Wills, Veda Ann Borg, Douglas
    Wood, Betty Blythe, Harry Worth, Lew Harvey
D: Jack Conway
SP: Marguerite Roberts, Jack Townley
P: Pandro S. Berman

1315. BILLY THE KID WANTED
(PRC, October 4, 1941) 64 Mins.
(*Billy the Kid* Series)
Buster Crabbe, Al St. John, Dave O'Brien, Glenn
    Strange, Choti Sherwood, Charles King, Slim
    Whitaker, Howard Masters, Joe Newfield, Budd
    Buster, Frank Ellis, Curley Dresden, Wally West
D: Sherman Scott (Sam Newfield)
SP: Fred Myton
P: Sigmund Neufeld

1316. KING OF THE TEXAS RANGERS
(Republic, October 4, 1941) 12 Chaps.
Sammy Baugh, Neil Hamilton, Pauline Moore, Dun-
    can Renaldo, Charles Trowbridge, Herbert Raw-
    linson, Frank Darien, Robert O. Davis, Monte
    Blue, Stanley Blystone, Kermit Maynard, Roy
    Barcroft, Kenne Duncan, Jack Ingram, Robert
    Barron, Frank Bruno, Monte Montague, Joseph
    Forte, Lucien Prival, Paul Gustine, Henry Hall,
    William Kellogg, Richard Simmons, Alan Gregg,
    Iron Eyes Cody, Forrest Taylor, Lee Shumway,
    Ernest Sarracino, Bud Jamison, John James, Dick
    Scott, Bud Wolfe, Barry Hays, Earl Bunn, George
    Burrows, Pat O'Shea, Bert LeBaron, Jerry Jerome,
    Bobby Barber, Forrest Burns, Max Waizman,
    Charles Whitaker, Jack Chapin, Howard Hughes,
    Michael Owen, Ken Terrell, Hooper Atchley,
    Otto Reichow, Chick Hannon, Herman Hack,
    Tommy Coats, Charles Thomas, Bob Robinson,
    Edward Cassidy, Buddy Roosevelt, John Bagni,
    Eddie Dew, George Allen, Jimmy Fawcett, Al Tay-
    lor, Duke Green, Merlyn Nelson, Loren Riebe,
    David Sharpe, Cy Slocum, Tom Steele, Duke
    Taylor, Bill Wilkus, Joe Yrigoyen
D: William Witney, John English
SP: Ronald Davidson, Norman S. Hall, Joseph Po-
    land, Joseph O'Donnell, William Lively
AP: Hiram S. Brown, Jr.

Chapter Titles: (1) The Fifth Column Strikes, (2) Dead End, (3) Man Hunt, (4) Trapped, (5) Test Flight, (6) Double Danger, (7) Death Takes the Witness, (8) Counterfeit Trail, (9) Ambush, (10) Sky Raiders, (11) Trail of Death, (12) Code of the Rangers

1317. TEXAS
(Columbia, October 9, 1941) 93 Mins.
William Holden, Claire Trevor, Glenn Ford, George Bancroft, Edgar Buchanan, Don Beddoe, Andrew Tombes, Addison Richards, Edmund McDonald, Joseph Crehan, Willard Robertson, Patrick Moriarty, Edmund Cobb, Raymond Hatton
D: George Marshall
S/SP: Michael Blankfort, Lewis Meltzer
P: Samuel Bischoff

1318. THE BANDIT TRAIL
(RKO, October 10, 1941) 60 Mins.
Tim Holt, Ray Whitley, Janet Waldo, Lee "Lasses" White, Morris Ankrum , Roy Barcroft, J. Merrill Holmes, Eddy Waller, Glenn Strange, Frank Ellis, Joseph Eggerton, Guy Usher, Jack Clifford, Bud Osborne, John Merton, Bud Geary, Lew Meehan, Terry Frost, Carl Stockdale, James Farley, Al Ferguson, Armand Wright, Art Dupois, Bert LeBaron
D: Edward Killy
SP: Norton S. Parker
P: Bert Gilroy

1319. RIDERS OF THE PURPLE SAGE
(20th C. Fox, October 10, 1941) 56 Mins.
George Montgomery, Mary Howard, Robert Barrat, Lynne Roberts, Kane Richmond, Patsy Patterson, Richard Lane, Oscar O'Shea, James Gillette, Frank McGrath, LeRoy Mason
D: James Tinling
S: Zane Grey
SP: William Buckner, Robert Metzler
P: Sol M. Wurtzel

1320. TONTO BASIN OUTLAWS
(Monogram, October 10, 1941) 60 Mins.
(Range Busters Series)
Ray Corrigan, John King, Max Terhune, Jan Wiley, Tristram Coffin, Ted Mapes, Art "Dustbowl" Fowler, Carl Mathews, Reed Howes, Rex Lease, Budd Buster, Edward Piel, Sr., Tex Palmer, Hank Bell, Denver Dixon, Jim Corey
D: S. Roy Luby
S: Earle Snell
SP: John Vlahos
P: George W. Weeks

1321. DOWN MEXICO WAY
(Republic, October 15, 1941) 73 Mins.

Gene Autry, Smiley Burnette, Fay McKenzie, Harold Huber, Duncan Renaldo, Arthur Loft, Murray Alper, Joe Sawyer, Paul Fix, Julian Rivero, Eddie Dean, Thornton Edwards, Ruth Robinson, Andrew Tombes, Herrera Sisters, Sidney Blackmer, Esther Estrella, Sam Appel, Helen MacKellar, Elias Gamboa, Rico de Montez, Charles Rivero, Paquita del Rey, Jose Manero, Carmela Cansino, Reed Howes, Hank Bell, Fred Burns, Al Haskell, Jack O'Shea, Frankie Marvin, "Champion"
D: Joseph Santley
S: Dorrell and Stuart McGowan
SP: Oliver Cooper, Albert Duff
AP: Harry Grey

1322. ROARING FRONTIERS
(Columbia, October 16, 1941) 60 Mins.
Bill Elliott, Tex Ritter, Ruth Ford, Frank Mitchell, Hal Taliaferro, Bradley Page, Tris Coffin, Francis Walker, Joe McGuinn, George Chesebro, Charles Stevens, Charles King, Lew Meehan, Hank Bell, George Eldridge, Fred Burns, Ernie Adams
D: Lambert Hillyer
SP: Robert Lee Johnson
AP: Leon Barsha

1323. THE DRIFTIN' KID
(Monogram, October 17, 1941) 57 Mins.
Tom Keene, Betty Miles, Frank Yaconelli, Slim Andrews, Stanley Price, Gene Alsace (Rocky Camron), Glenn Strange, Steve Clark, Sherry Tansey, Fred Hoose, Wally West, Frank McCarroll, Lou Yaconelli
D/P: Robert Tansey
SP: Robert Emmett (Tansey), Frances Kavanaugh

1324. JESSE JAMES AT BAY
(Republic, October 17, 1941) 56 Mins.
Roy Rogers, George Hayes, Gale Storm, Sally Payne, Pierre Watkin, Hal Taliaferro, Roy Barcroft, Jack Kirk, Billy Benedict, Jack O'Shea, Rex Lease, Edward Piel, Sr., Jack Rockwell, Kit Guard, Curley Dresden, Hank Bell, Bill Wolfe, Ivan Miller, Lloyd Ingraham, Karl Hackett, Budd Buster, Fred Burns, Ray Jones, Fern Emmett, Bob Woodward, Chuck Morrison, "Trigger"
D/AP: Joseph Kane
S: Harrison Jacobs
SP: James R. Webb

1325. GAUCHOS OF ELDORADO
(Republic, October 24, 1941) 56 Mins.
(Three Mesquiteers Series)
Bob Steele, Tom Tyler, Rufe Davis, Lois Collier, Duncan Renaldo, Rosina Galli, Norman Willis, Yakima Canutt, William Ruhl, Tony Roux, Ray Bennett, Bud Geary, Edmund Cobb, Eddie Dean, John Merrill Holmes, Terry Frost, John Merton,

Virginia Farmer, Si Jenks, Ted Mapes, Bob Wood-
ward, Ray Jones, Horace B. Carpenter
D: Les Orlebeck
S: Earle Snell. Based on characters created by Wil-
liam Colt MacDonald
AP: Louis Gray

1326. THE MASKED RIDER
(Universal, October 24, 1941)   58 Mins.
Johnny Mack Brown, Fuzzy Knight, Nell O'Day,
Grant Withers, Virginia Carroll, Guy D'Ennery,
Carmela Cansino, Roy Barcroft, Dick Botiller,
Fred Cordova, Al Haskell, Rico De Montez, Rob-
ert O'Connor, Jose Cansino Dancers, The Guad-
alajara Trio
D: Ford Beebe
S: Sam Robins
SP: Sherman Lowe, Victor McLeod
AP: Will Cowan

1327. RIDING THE SUNSET TRAIL
(Monogram, October 31, 1941)   56 Mins.
Tom Keene, Betty Miles, Sugar Dawn, Frank Yaco-
nelli, Slim Andrews, Kenne Duncan, Tom Lon-
don, Tom Seidel, James Sheridan (Sherry Tan-
sey), Earl Douglas, Gene Alsace (Rocky Camron),
Fred Hoose, "Rusty"
D/P: Robert Tansey
SP: Robert Emmett, Frances Kavanaugh

1328. OUTLAWS OF THE DESERT
(Paramount, November 1, 1941)   66 Mins.
(*Hopalong Cassidy* Series)
William Boyd, Brad King, Andy Clyde, Forest Stan-
ley, Jean Phillips, Nina Guilbert, Luci Deste, Al-
bert Morin, George Woolsley, George J. Lewis,
Duncan Renaldo, Jean Del Val, Mickey Eissa,
Jamiel Hasson
D: Howard Bretherton
SP: J. Benton Cheney, Bernard McConville. Based
on characters created by Clarence E. Mulford
AP: Harry Sherman

1329. THE LONE RIDER FIGHTS BACK
(PRC, November 7, 1941)   64 Mins.
(*Lone Rider* Series)
George Houston, Al St. John, Dorothy Short, Frank
Hagney, Dennis Moore, Charles King, Frank Ellis,
Hal Price, Jack O'Shea, Merrill McCormack
D: Sam Newfield
SP: Joe O'Donnell
P: Sigmund Neufeld

1330. CALIFORNIA OR BUST
(RKO, November 11, 1941)   17 Mins.
Ray Whitley, Virginia Vale, Glenn Strange, Emmett
Lynn, Ken Card, Curly Hoag, Candy Hall
D/S: Lloyd French

1331. SIERRA SUE
(Republic, November 12, 1941)   64 Mins.
Gene Autry, Smiley Burnette, Fay McKenzie, Frank
M. Thomas, Robert Homans, Earle Hodgins, Dor-
othy Christy, Jack Kirk, Eddie Dean, Kermit May-
nard, Budd Buster, Rex Lease, Hugh Prosser,
Vince Barnett, Hal Price, Syd Saylor, Roy Butler,
Sammy Stein, Eddie Cherkose, Bob McKenzie,
Marin Sais, Bud Brown, Gene Eblen, Buel Bryant,
Ray Davis, Art Dillard, Frankie Marvin, "Cham-
pion"
D: William Morgan
SP: Earl Felton, Julian Zimet
AP: Harry Grey

1332. THE ROYAL MOUNTED PATROL
(Columbia, November 13, 1941)   59 Mins.
Charles Starrett, Russell Hayden, Wanda McKay,
Donald Curtis, Lloyd Bridges, Kermit Maynard,
Evan Thomas, Ted Adams, Harrison Greene, Ted
Mapes, George Morrell
D: Lambert Hillyer
SP: Winston Miller
P: William Berke

1333. ARIZONA CYCLONE
(Universal, November 14, 1941)   59 Mins.
Johnny Mack Brown, Fuzzy Knight, Nell O'Day,
Kathryn Adams, Dick Curtis, Herbert Rawlinson,
Buck Moulton, Jack Clifford, Kermit Maynard,
Frank Ellis, The Notables, Robert Strange, Glenn
Strange, Carl Sepulveda, Chuck Morrison
D: Joseph H. Lewis
SP: Sherman Lowe
AP: Will Cowan

1334. SECRETS OF THE WASTELAND
(Paramount, November 15, 1941)   66 Mins.
(*Hopalong Cassidy* Series)
William Boyd, Andy Clyde, Brad King, Barbara Brit-
ton, Douglas Fowley, Keith Richards, Soo Yong,
Richard Loo, Lee Tung Foo, Gordon Hart, Hal
Price, Jack Rockwell, John Rawlings, Earl Gunn,
Roland Got, Ian MacDonald
D: Derwin Abrahams
S: Bliss Lomax
SP: Gerald Geraghty. Based on characters created
by Clarence E. Mulford
P: Harry Sherman

1335. UNDERGROUND RUSTLERS
(Monogram, November 21, 1941)   56 Mins.
(*Range Busters* Series)
Ray Corrigan, John King, Max Terhune, Gwen
Gaze, Robert Blair, Forrest Taylor, Tom London,
Steve Clark, Bud Osborne, Dick Cramer, John El-
liott, Tex Palmer, Edward Piel, Sr., Carl Mathews,
Tex Cooper, Frank McCarroll

D: S. Roy Luby
S: John Rathmell
SP: Bud Tuttle, Elizabeth Beecher, John Vlahos
P: George W. Weeks

1336. A MISSOURI OUTLAW

(Republic, November 25, 1941) 58 Mins.
Don Barry, Lynn Merrick, Noah Beery, Al St. John, Paul Fix, Frank LaRue, Kenne Duncan, John Merton, Carleton Young, Frank Brownlee, Fred Toones, Karl Hackett, Lee Shumway, Ray Bennett, Bob McKenzie, Kermit Maynard, Frank McCarroll, Curley Dresden, Herman Hack
D/AP: George Sherman
SP: Doris Schroeder, Jack Lait, Jr.

1337. GO WEST, YOUNG LADY

(Columbia, November 27, 1941) 70 Mins.
Penny Singleton, Glenn Ford, Ann Miller, Charlie Ruggles, Allen Jenkins, Onslow Stevens, Edith Meiser, Bill Hazlett, Bob Wills and his Texas Playboys
D: Frank R. Strayer
SP: Richard Flournoy, Karen DeWolf
P: Robert Sparks

1338. WEST OF THE ROCKIES

(Warner Bros., November 29, 1941) 20 Mins.
William Travis, Rufe Davis, Willie Best
D: Bobby Connolly
SP: Hal Yates

1339. LONE STAR LAW MEN

(Monogram, December 5, 1941) 61 Mins.
Tom Keene, Sugar Dawn, Betty Miles, Frank Yaconelli, Glenn Strange, Charles King, Gene Alsace, James Sheridan (Sherry Tansey), Stanley Price, Fred Hoose, Franklyn Farnum, Jack Ingram, Reed Howes
D/P: Robert Tansey
SP: Robert Emmett (Tansey), Frances Kavanaugh

1340. FIGHTING BILL FARGO

(Universal, December 9, 1941) 57 Mins.
Johnny Mack Brown, Fuzzy Knight, Nell O'Day, Jeanne Kelly (Jean Brooks), Kenneth Harlan, Ted Adams, James Blaine, Al Bridge, Joseph Eggerton, Bob Kortman, Earle Hodgins, Tex Palmer, Harry Tenbrook, Kermit Maynard, Blackie Whiteford, Merrill McCormack, Bud Osborne, Eddie Dean Trio
D: Ray Taylor
S: Paul Franklin
SP: Paul Franklin, Dorcas Cochran, Arthur V. Jones
AP: Will Cowan

1341. RED RIVER VALLEY

(Republic, December 12, 1941) 62 Mins.

Roy Rogers, George Hayes, Sally Payne, Trevor Bardette, Bob Nolan, Gale Storm, Robert Homans, Hal Taliaferro, Lynton Brent, Pat Brady, Edward Piel, Sr., Dick Wessell, Jack Rockwell, Ted Mapes, Sons of the Pioneers
D/AP: Joseph Kane
SP: Malcolm Stuart Boylin

1342. DUDE COWBOY

(RKO, December 12, 1941) 59 Mins.
Tim Holt, Marjorie Reynolds, Ray Whitley, Lee "Lasses" White, Louise Currie, Helen Holmes, Eddie Kane, Eddie Dew, Byron Foulger, Tom London, Lloyd Ingraham, Glenn Strange
D: David Howard
S/SP: Morton Grant
P: Bert Gilroy

1343. BILLY THE KID'S ROUNDUP

(PRC, December 12, 1941) 58 Mins.
(*Billy the Kid* Series)
Buster Crabbe, Al St. John, Carleton Young, Joan Barclay, Glenn Strange, Charles King, Slim Whitaker, John Elliott, Dennis Moore, Kenne Duncan, Curley Dresden, Dick Cramer, Wally West, Tex Palmer, Tex Cooper, Horace B. Carpenter, Jim Mason
D: Sherman Scott (Sam Newfield)
SP: Fred Myton
P: Sigmund Neufeld

1344. WEST OF CIMARRON

(Republic, December 15, 1941) 56 Mins.
(*Three Mesquiteers* Series)
Bob Steele, Tom Tyler, Rufe Davis, Lois Collier, James Bush, Guy Usher, Hugh Prosser, Cordell Hickman, Roy Barcroft, Budd Buster, Mickey Rentschiler, John James, Bud Geary, Stanley Blystone
D: Les Orlebeck
SP: Albert DeMond, Don Ryan. Based on characters created by William Colt MacDonald
AP: Louis Gray

1345. RIDERS OF THE BADLANDS

(Columbia, December 18, 1941) 57 Mins.
Charles Starrett, Russell Hayden, Cliff Edwards, Ilene Brewer, Kay Hughes, Roy Barcroft, Rick Anderson, Edith Leach, Ethan Laidlaw, Harry Cording, Hal Price, Ted Mapes, George J. Lewis, John Cason, Edmund Cobb, Francis Walker
D: Howard Bretherton
SP: Betty Burbridge
P: William Berke

1346. ROAD AGENT

(Universal, December 19, 1941) 60 Mins.
(Reissued as *Texas Road Agent*)

Dick Foran, Leo Carrillo, Andy Devine, Anne Gwynne, Richard Davies, Ann Nagel, John Gal-laudet, Samuel S. Hinds, Morris Ankrum, Reed Hadley, Emmett Lynn, Ernie Adams, Lew Kelly
S: Sherman Lowe, Arthur St. Claire
D: Charles LaMont
SP: Morgan Cox, Arthur Strawn
AP: Ben Pivar

1347. FORBIDDEN TRAILS

(Monogram, December 26, 1941)   54 Mins.
(*Rough Riders* Series)
Buck Jones, Tim McCoy, Raymond Hatton, Tris Coffin, Charles King, Glenn Strange, Lynton Brent, Jerry Sheldon, Hal Price, Dave O'Brien, Christine McIntyre, Dick Alexander, "Silver"
D: Robert North Bradbury
SP: Jess Bowers (Adele Buffington)
S: Oliver Drake
P: Scott R. Dunlap

Forbidden Trails (Monogram, 1942) — Raymond Hatton and Tim McCoy

CHAPTER 5

The Golden Years
1942-1946

(FAMILIAR FACES AND FAST GUNS)

In the sense that the Western was still popular and profitable in the war years 1942-1946, we have labeled the period the Golden Years, a period after the peak years but before the real decline of the genre. Again, most of the nearly 500 Westerns released were of the "B" variety. There were just a handful of truly first-rate super Westerns and all of the eleven Western serials were of a rather pedestrian nature, though nevertheless winners at the box office in terms of returning a profit.

Reigning as the best of the major Westerns of the Golden Years were *They Died with Their Boots On* (Warner Bros., 1942), Raoul Walsh's whitewashed account of General George Custer leading his men to heroic deaths; *Buffalo Bill* (Fox, 1944), a highly romanticized film biography; *The Outlaw* (United Artists, 1945), the first of the "sexy" Westerns; *The Ox-Bow Incident* (Fox, 1943), one of the first of the "social" or "psychological" Westerns; *My Darling Clementine* (Fox, 1946), John Ford's masterful telling of the Wyatt Earp story; *San Antonio* (Warner Bros., 1945), a glossy production about skullduggery in the old Texas cattle town; *The Spoilers* (Universal, 1942), with its unforgettable climactic fight between John Wayne and Randolph Scott; and *The Shepherd of the Hills* (Paramount, 1942), an especial favorite for Harry Carey fans. Although the film gave a big push to the career of John Wayne, it was undoubtedly Harry Carey who was the greatest asset of this feature. His characterization of Daniel Howitt dominated this corking story, and the sharp technicolor photography and striking locations complement the drama and create a genuinely pungent insight into the lives of mountain people caught up in their own predilections and primitive passions.

Each of the aforementioned Westerns is a spectacular and lavishly mounted film, historically suspect in most cases but entertaining no less. Even though critics might have a field day commenting on the deeper meanings of these and other films of the period—their ineptitudes, artistic highlights, social implications, and such—the populace simply loved them for their majesty of story, locale, and cast. But one should remember that the world of the Western film is true to a certain historic feeling, if not to particular historic facts. Each in its own unique fashion brought to the screen some of the charm of the old West that people still longed for, regardless of the social meanings that film writers might wish to attach to each bit of action or dialogue.

The Ox-Bow Incident's message was loud and clear, a condemnation of lynch law and mob justice. And its emphasis was on character studies rather than rough and tumble action. In the Fifties and afterwards, many Westerns would explore serious themes, e.g., white prejudice against the Indian. Thus, *The Ox-Bow Incident* was an ice-breaker, as well as a coup for both star Henry Fonda and director William Wellman.

Ford's *My Darling Clementine* is about as fine a Western as one could ask for. The story is built around the personal legend of Wyatt Earp, which Ford expands into a larger Western myth using Monument Valley, his favorite locale, as his workshop. Henry Fonda again gives a magnanimous portrayal as the laconic Wyatt, "a man for his time," determined to make the West fit for decent folk.

Howard Hughes' *The Outlaw* had a brief release in 1943 before being recalled for censure problems and then later reissued. Jane Russell and her unbelievably ample bosom starred in this erotic saga of Billy the Kid, carrying Walter Huston, Jack Buetel, and Thomas Mitchell along for eye-popping sighs. Actually it wasn't a bad Western, as such, but its significant influence on the Western cinema was a growing emphasis on sex in what had once been almost a sexless genre, with the explicitness of the sex gradually growing.

John Wayne spent a major part of his time during the Golden Years winning World War II single-handed, it often seemed, but his appearances in *In Old California* (Republic, 1942), *In Old Oklahoma* (Republic, 1943), *The Spoilers* (Universal, 1942), *Tall in the Saddle* (RKO, 1944), and *Flame of the Barbary Coast* (Republic, 1945) added to his Western laurels. And Randolph Scott, too, was rapidly building his reputation as a Western star of the first magnitude with *Abilene Town* (United Artists, 1946), *The Desperadoes* (Columbia, 1943), *Badman's Territory* (RKO, 1946), and his co-starring stint with Wayne in *The Spoilers*.

The super-scale Westerns of the Golden Years were actually few in number, but "A" Westerns of a more modest nature abounded. Keeping interest in the Western alive for sophisticated audiences were a large number of gems demonstrating that a Western could be far more than a proliferation of cliche-ridden, plotless films produced for the juvenile market or the juvenile-minded and yet stay under the $1 million budget. Wallace Beery could always be depended on for a first-class performance, and he kept his record intact with *Bad Bascomb* (MGM, 1946) and *Jackass Mail* (MGM, 1942). Richard Dix, too, was an old reliable. His *Tombstone—The Town Too Tough to Die* (Paramount, 1942) was one of the better action Westerns of the year. Dix portrayed Wyatt Earp and Rex Bell was featured as his brother in a comeback attempt after several years' absence from the screen. Other good Dix Westerns were *American Empire* (United Artists, 1942), *Buckskin Frontier* (United Artists, 1943), and *The Kansan* (United Artists, 1943).

Rod Cameron, after appearing in Republic serials and Universal programmers, was being given the build-up in Universal's *Salome, Where She Danced* (1945) and *Frontier Gal* (1945), both with Yvonne De Carlo.

Gary Cooper was amusing in the comedy Western *Along Came Jones* (RKO, 1945), although the public's reception to this obvious attempt to emulate Universal's *Destry Rides Again* was not as enthusiastic as the studio had hoped. Cooper stars as an inept cowboy who drifts into a small western town with his caustic sidekick (William Demarest) and is mistaken for notorious holdup man Monte Jarrad (Dan Duryea). Since gentle Melody Jones is even unable to handle a gun, his position is precarious, but with the help of Jarrad's sympathetic girl Cherry (Loretta Young), he not only manages to stay alive, but becomes a temporary hero.

Universal was especially active with its minor "A's" featuring performers of less than super-star status—name players of the calibre of Robert Stack, Richard Dix, Dana Andrews, Leo Carrillo, and Noah Beery, Jr. These films usually boasted fine supporting casts made up of familiar faces from many "B" Westerns and were always tightly edited, fast-moving stories. Typical of these were *North to the Klondike* (1942), *Men of Texas* (1942), *Frontier Badman* (1943), *The Daltons Ride Again* (1945), and *Canyon Passage* (1946). Metro-Goldwyn-Mayer tried hard with James Craig in *Northwest Rangers* (1942), *The Omaha Trail* (1942), and *Gentle Annie* (1944), but they failed to click. The studio's *Apache Trail* (1943) with Lloyd

The Outlaw (Howard Hughes, 1943) — Jane Russell and Jack Buetel

Tombstone — The Town Too Tough to Die (Paramount, 1942) — Rex Bell, Don Castle, and Richard Dix

253

Nolan was much better. Bruce Cabot and Constance Bennett proved surprisingly good in Warner's *Wild Bill Hickok Rides,* as did Claire Trevor in *The Woman of the Town* (United Artists, 1943). *Alaska* (Monogram, 1944), based on Jack London's story "Flush of Gold," was no great shakes but it was passable and colorful in a black-and-white sort of way with a few good dramatic and action scenes. And Republic's *The Plainsman and the Lady* (1946) showed promise for William Elliott, promoted from the ranks of "B" Westerns where he had been known as "Wild Bill."

On the bread-and-butter scene, Republic dominated the "B" market in spite of the loss of Gene Autry to the armed forces for much of the period. In its corral were to be found Roy Rogers, Donald Barry, Bill Elliott, Sunset Carson, Allan Lane, Robert Livingston, Monte Hale, and the Three Mesquiteers (comprised of Bob Steele and Tom Tyler and supported at different times by comics Rufe Davis and Jimmie Dodd). Heavy guns indeed! But making the real difference in the studio's supremacy were production know-how, the finest technicians, competent contract players, and the great facilities amassed by the company in its short history. Republic was to the Western what MGM and 20th Century-Fox were to musicals. The Republic emblem meant a quality product, even though one's taste might not run to any specific cowboy under contract to the studio. At least one could count on good, sharp photography, excellent musical scores, an outstanding supporting cast generally headed by Roy Barcroft as chief villain, superb stunting by Yak Canutt, Dave Sharpe, Fred Graham, and cohorts, crisp action, beautiful locations, coherent plots, and fine sound reproduction. Such polish did much to overcome histrionic inadequacies on the part of the lead cowboy if, in fact, such inadequacies existed.

Donald Barry did himself credit in his Republic oaters, working under a number of directors. Without any particular gimmick to fall back on, the little redhead made it to the

Bordertown Trail (Republic, 1944) — Sunset Carson, Rex Lease, and Smiley Burnette

top on his own merits. His screen characterization might best be described as a combination of Lash LaRue's gruffness, Bob Steele's fighting skill, and Bill Elliott's dramatics. His Western series, for Republic, at least, came to an end in 1944 when he moved to non-Westerns.

And speaking of Elliott, he, too, made his biggest mark at Republic, coming to the studio in 1943 and completing a lively series with George "Gabby" Hayes before assuming the role of comic hero "Red Ryder." The series was popular and by 1946 Elliott was ranked second behind Roy Rogers in the *Motion Picture Herald's* poll of top money-making Western stars. As a result, Republic boosted the virile cowboy into major productions toward the end of 1946, hoping that he would prove to be another Randy Scott or John Wayne.

Allan Lane assumed the Red Ryder role after having starred in several serials and a Western series for the studio. Robert Livingston worked briefly in a *John Paul Revere* series after Eddie Dew fizzled in the role. And in 1946 Republic brought in yet another singer, Monte Hale, straight out of the cotton patches of Texas. Hale was no candidate for acting honors, but he had a certain amount of boyish charm about him and he was good looking and a fair singer. The usual Republic production finesse was given Hale's films and he seemed to be getting off to a good start as the Golden Years waned. So, too, was Sunset Carson, who got the big push in 1944—first as second banana to comic Smiley Burnette and then in his own series. Although Carson's acting was reminiscent of that of Jack Hoxie, he prospered for the same reason that Jack had. Carson was a rodeo champion and a big man who looked like a million dollars in the saddle or in a fracas. And he was good looking. As long as he didn't talk and kept on the move he fared well. It was only when he slowed down to talk that he was in trouble.

With the release of *Bells of Capistrano* (1942) Gene Autry sat out the Golden Years as a member of the Air Force until late 1946, when he returned to Republic. *Sioux City Sue*, his first post-war film, was a rather lack-luster affair with much music and little action.

Roy Rogers was king of the roost during the Golden Years and Republic pulled all stops to see that he stayed far ahead of the rest of the posse. Budgets of Rogers' films were increased beginning in 1942 and continued spiraling upward as Rogers ultimately graduated into color Westerns. Strong casts and the best Republic directors (notably Joe Kane and John English), story writers, and cameramen were assigned to the Rogers unit, and the Sons of the Pioneers were kept on as musical support. Dale Evans became his leading lady in 1944 and appeared in twenty successive Westerns with Rogers. Undoubtedly the best and most popular of all Rogers' films was *My Pal Trigger* (1946), a semi-special lengthened to seventy-nine minutes and marketed separately to his regular series. Although there was no similarity between the real West and Rogers' musicalized one, his fantasy efforts seemed to be the prescription needed by a war-weary America. And if a few serious "B" Western buffs complained at the bastardization of the genre, nobody listened. They were too busy joining in on the chorus of "Don't Fence Me In."

Universal started the Golden Years with one Western series, the exceptionally fine one of Johnny Mack Brown. There were always plenty of fights, gunplay, and vigorous riding in the Browns, and technical finesse was a cut above the average for "B" oaters. One could count on appropriate music scores, quality sound, believable action sequences, good lighting, and now and then a few running inserts and other niceties. And somehow one always felt a little more intellectual or dignified in watching a Brown vehicle than in watching most other "B's." Like Randolph Scott, Brown exuded Southern aristocracy and fine breeding, his gentlemanliness and refinement radiating from the screen. In 1943 Tex Ritter was signed to co-star with him and, when Brown left for greener pastures, Russell Hayden came in to work with Ritter in a few films before both stars were dropped. Eddie

Dew and Dennis Moore failed to pan out, too. Rod Cameron was signed on as a cowboy lead for a good series in 1944-1945 but it was discontinued when he was boosted into non-series features. And with little more than a break-even return on the Kirby Grant musical Westerns in 1945-1946, Universal lost interest in programmer Westerns on a series basis and abandoned such production.

One nice thing about Universal was that it normally did not scrimp on supporting players and extras. You could see *people* on the screen, not just one or two riders around a cheap set. And these people included such regulars as Jennifer Holt (Jack's lovely daughter), Nell O'Day, William Desmond, William Farnum, the Jimmy Wakely Trio, and Roy Barcroft. The list of names is endless. Universal always attracted competent players, and it was a significant loss to the genre when the studio decided to cease its "B" Western production—the very thing that had built the studio under Carl Laemmle.

Columbia had a Charles Starrett-Russell Hayden series going in 1942, then gave Hayden a series of his own, with Starrett once again carrying the mail in his own series. Until the mid-Forties the Starrett Westerns were of a fairly high quality, but commencing in 1945 they began slipping toward mediocrity, through no fault of the star. However, they remained popular with the juvenile audience and profitable for Columbia. It was in 1945 that Starrett assumed the role of "The Durango Kid" that he was to play for the rest of his career and which more or less gave him a new lease on stardom. Columbia terminated its Bill Elliott-Tex Ritter series in 1942 and the Russell Hayden series in 1943. After that, it was strictly Charles Starrett as Columbia's contribution to the "B" Western field for the next several years. Thanks to the profits derived from Starrett's Westerns, Harry Cohn, president of Columbia, could engage in more ambitious projects, most of which did not return as high a percent of profit on the invested dollar as did the Starrett vehicles. Starrett himself was independently wealthy, being an heir to the Starrett Tool Company fortune. However, he was extremely likable and humble and a gentleman in every sense of the word. His friendships knew no monetary bounds, easily bridging the gap from wranglers and technicians to the elite of Hollywood.

Paramount's *Hopalong Cassidy* series was carried into 1942, at which time production ceased. Thereafter, Paramount would concern itself only with non-series Westerns. United Artists picked up the *Cassidy* series for release in 1942, 1943, and 1944, then production again was terminated. Thirteen *Hoppies* were produced by Harry Sherman and released through United Artists. William Boyd and Andy Clyde appeared in all of them. Jay Kirby took over the young sidekick's role from Brad King in 1942 and was later replaced by Jimmie Rogers, son of Will. For the most part the United Artists releases were superior Westerns, with probably *Hoppy Serves a Writ* (1943), *False Colors* (1943), and *Lumberjack* (1944) ranking as the best in the distinguished series directed mainly by George Archainbaud. A quite distinguished figure, usually dressed in black and riding a snow-white horse called Topper, Boyd projected as soft-spoken and retiring, presenting more the father figure than the hard-hitting, rough-fighting stereotype Western hero—on some occasions he even came across as a genuine gentleman. A single flash of his smile and a quick burst of his hearty laughter alone were worth the price of admission to one of his films. The *Cassidy* films were usually filmed on location in more picturesque areas than the minor studios used, primarily because a good deal more money and time were spent on their production; they had well-written scripts and relatively long running times. In 1946 Boyd bought up the *Cassidy* rights, rounded up sufficient capital, and set about producing *Cassidy* Westerns for release once again through United Artists. *The Devil's Playground* and *Fool's Gold* were released in 1946 toward the close of the Golden Years. Rand

Brooks was the new sidekick to Boyd and Clyde and George Archainbaud again was directing.

It was PRC and Monogram that seriously attempted to compete with Republic in the manufacture of low-budget Westerns for the "B" market. PRC's product invariably was a shoddy one, the cheapness showing in every detail. Yet the pictures made money and were useful in filling the bottom half of a double feature "B" program when scheduled with a better quality Western from Republic, Universal, Columbia, or Monogram in the top half. Monogram's product was far superior to that of PRC in quality but, in general, did not measure up to that of Republic or the other majors. Some films, though, were exceptions, especially several in the Johnny Mack Brown and *Rough Riders* series.

PRC teamed singers Art Davis and Bill (Cowboy Rambler) Boyd with Lee Powell for a series in 1941-1942. Powell was a competent performer and had potential as an actor, whereas Davis had potential as a personality on the basis of his voice and Autry-like charisma. Boyd, a Dallas, Texas, radio singer, had little going for him. After only six entries in the series it had to be discontinued when Davis and Powell entered the military service. Powell was later killed in a Marine assault of a Japanese-held island in the South Pacific in August, 1944.

The Buster Crabbe-Al St. John series was PRC's most popular one and it was in production throughout the Golden Years. Although cheaply made, like all PRC features, these films were usually enjoyable. Crabbe and St. John made a good team and Charles King and Kermit Maynard were usually in the supporting lineup, which was a plus factor for discriminating buffs. Appeal was primarily to the rural and kiddie audience and bookings were usually restricted to second- and third-rate houses. Buster was simply not given a chance to rise above mediocrity in his PRC films. Credit is due to both Crabbe and St. John

The Kid Rides Again (PRC, 1942) — Glenn Strange, Buster Crabbe, I. Stanford Jolley, and Al "Fuzzy" St. John

for their personal popularity when evaluating the success of their Western series, for every aspect of production and story was poor. Suffice it to say that none of the films ever won an Academy Award for anything, or even an honorable mention. But they were horse operas, and their effulgence lay in the fact that Buster was tough and implacable, Al St. John was funny, the girls stayed pretty much out of the way, and the outlaws were familiar and predictable. Two of the better entries in the series were *His Brother's Ghost* (1945) in which St. John plays twin brothers, much to the consternation of Charlie King, and *Ghost of Hidden Valley* (1946), with a little different story twist.

The *Lone Rider* series was produced by PRC in 1942 with George Houston in the lead and in 1943 with Robert Livingston as star. The *Texas Rangers* series was in production until 1945 with Dave O'Brien, Jim Newill, and Guy Wilkerson comprising the trio that was supposed to compete with the Range Busters, the Three Mesquiteers, the Rough Riders, and the Trail Blazers in the trio market. Tex Ritter ultimately replaced Newill, in 1944, but it was O'Brien who carried the series throughout its twenty-one-film life span. The series was not a memorable one, but it did make money—a slight consideration of all concerned. Bob Steele's last series as a star was produced by PRC in 1945-1946 and toward the end of 1945 Eddie Dean made his debut in *Song of Old Wyoming* opposite Jennifer Holt. Filmed in cinecolor, the film introduced not only Dean (who had been around for years as a bit player) but also Al LaRue, soon to be known as Lash LaRue. Dean's chief attribute was a good singing voice, but it was apparent from the beginning that he would be no real threat to Autry or Rogers.

Brand of the Devil (PRC, 1944) — Charles King, Dave O'Brien, Jim Newill, and Kermit Maynard

Song of Old Wyoming (PRC, 1945) — Horace Murphy, Sarah Padden, and Al LaRue

Monogram's best of 1942 was the *Rough Riders* series starring Buck Jones, Tim McCoy, and Raymond Hatton, with *Ghost Town Law* probably being the best entry. It is a rather artistic, suspenseful film characteristic of some of the *Hopalong Cassidy* films and was a real showcase for Jones. Scenery and photography are effective, the story intriguing, again demonstrating what can be done on limited budgets with just a little know-how. The series' sudden demise was brought on by McCoy's entry into the armed forces at the age of fifty and Jones' death in the Boston fire. Eight films had been produced and the series had caught on big, to the delight of those who longed for the old-timers and an end to guitar-strummin' crooners. When McCoy quit, Monogram decided to star Jones in a series with Hatton as his sidekick. One film was made, *Dawn on the Great Divide.* Rex Bell, another old-timer, was featured, possibly with the idea of making him the third member of a continuing trio. Jones' death left the studio in a dilemma, compounded by the fact that the Tom Keene series terminated that year too. Negotiations began with Jack Holt to step in as replacement for Jones, but the day he was to sign a contract he received notice to report for military duty, having requested active duty several months before despite his advanced age. Johnny Mack Brown became the next choice (evidently little consideration was given to Rex Bell or Tom Keene), and he was lured away from Universal and teamed with Hatton in a long-running series that was still in production as the Golden Years ended. Brown was hardly a slouch as an actor, rider, or fighter; his Westerns were chuck full of brawls and hard riding, and were built around stories which allowed for some display of his acting talents. The first in the Brown series was *The Ghost Rider* (1943), with Johnny portraying "Nevada Jack McKenzie," a characterization he would retain until 1946 when he and Hatton abandoned the roles of McKenzie and "Sandy Hopkins," respectively, to play assorted roles. Lambert Hillyer directed nearly all of the Brown films of this period, no small factor in their success. Hillyer was one of the best directors in the business. Made at a time when movies were still popular and profitable, these little prairie gems combined fast and furious action, simple, uncomplicated stories, and the magnetism of Brown and Hatton, coupled with professional competency in both the technical and acting realms, to provide Western buffs with a truly enjoyable cinema experience. Saturday night was something to look forward to when you could throw the kids in the back seat of the family car and take off to the Bijou to see one of Johnny's films, coupled with a chapter of the latest cliffhanger and maybe a Three Stooges or Leon Errol comedy.

The *Range Busters* series, popular for several years, bit the dust in 1944. The camaraderie displayed by the trio seemed appealing to children, but it was obviously less pleasing to adults who would have preferred more straight action or romance. Another series, the *Trail Blazers,* was produced in 1943-1944, the studio hoping that old-time thrillmakers Ken Maynard and Hoot Gibson might repeat the success of the *Rough Riders.* After three entries in the series, veteran Bob Steele was signed as the third member to handle the romance and much of the action, since he was still young enough to perform adequately in both departments. Because he had always been popular, studio moguls hoped his presence would bolster the popularity of the series. Unquestionably the trio's films created nostalgic goosepimples for those old enough to remember these aces in their heyday, even though the films were quickie, $10,000 budget affairs. When Maynard quit in a contract dispute, Chief Thunder Cloud (Victor Daniels) took his place in a couple of films to complete the short-lived series. Monogram then co-starred Gibson and Steele in three more "B" Westerns before calling it quits. The magic was no longer in the old-timers or, possibly, the shoddiness of the productions, underfinanced as they were, did not allow the magic to work.

It was Johnny Mack Brown and Jimmy Wakely who carried the weight of Monogram's Western productions in 1944, 1945, and 1946. Brown had retained his popularity in spite of the musical vogue. Wakely could sing and he had a pleasant personality, that being the sum total of his qualifications as a cowboy star. It obviously was enough, as his series was a long and profitable one. Monogram also re-activated the *Cisco Kid* series in 1944 with Duncan Renaldo as the lovable bandit-turned-hero. When Renaldo took on some work for the State Department, Gilbert Roland took over the role in 1945. Although approaching the role differently, both men made an excellent Cisco. However, the series' potential was never achieved because of the usual low Monogram budgets.

RKO completed its Ray Whitley musical shorts series in 1942 and released Tim Holt features through 1943 with Whitley as second lead. Holt's entry into the Air Force left the studio without a cowboy star until his return in late 1946. Many Western connoisseurs have wondered why the studio did not let Whitley carry the saddle for them, as he would have been a "natural" for a series of his own. But RKO blew it and attempted instead to produce a series in Holt's absence with first Robert Mitchum and then James Warren, but the idea was soon abandoned when the two stars failed to match the drawing power of Holt and his streamlined assembly-line product.

There were others, of course. A small outfit called Screen Guild turned out a few films with Russell Hayden as star in 1946 and Action Pictures produced a couple of interesting ones in color with Bob Steele, who was about to reach the end of his long career as a cowboy star. A viewing of *Wildfire* and *Northwest Trail* leaves one wondering why his stardom vanished, as he was still an obviously handsome, virile cowboy.

Texas A&M football star John Kimbrough was trounced after only two Westerns at Fox, falling flat on his face as an actor. Even the Hoosier Hot Shots, a country version of

Spike Jones and his City Slickers, had their own series of Columbia musical Westerns.

Mention should at least be made of the lovely, brave heroines who carried on the traditions laid down by the prima donnas of earlier decades. There was a bevy of talented and comely cowgirls active in the Forties. Those who arose, phoenix-like, from the ashes of obscurity to make a name for themselves in the genre included Peggy Stewart, Jennifer Holt, Lynne Roberts, Nell O'Day, Helen Talbot, Christine MacIntyre, Iris Meredith, Luana Walters, and Dale Evans. Few had a chance to break out of the genre and make it as dramatic actresses, yet the charm they radiated from the screen was infectious and many a boy and man inexorably found himself concentrating more on the calico gals than on the heroics of the white-stetsoned stranger determined to ignore their natural beauty, wistful adoration, and innocent sexuality.

In the Golden Years the number of series and the number of active cowboy stars were somewhat less than in earlier periods, most of the independent companies having folded, and by the end of 1946 the "B" Western definitely was taking on a sickly hue as production costs mounted and revenues declined. Corner cutting in all aspects of production was in evidence and dark clouds were gathering over Gower Gulch. However, familiar faces and fast guns were still in command of the Western genre, and it was comforting to see virginal cowboys fighting with their backs to the wall to save the old homestead for angelical heroines set upon by assorted knaves, rogues, and brigands.

The Lone Star Vigilantes (Columbia, 1942) — Steve Clark, Bill Elliott, Tex Ritter, Lowell Drew, and Ethan Laidlaw

FILMS OF 1942

1348. THE LONE STAR VIGILANTES
(Columbia, January 1, 1942) 58 Mins.
Bill Elliott, Tex Ritter, Frank Mitchell, Virginia
  Carpenter, Luana Walters, Ethan Laidlaw, Budd
  Buster, Forrest Taylor, Gavin Gordon, Lowell
  Drew, Edmund Cobb, Rich Anderson, George
  Chesebro, Paul Mulvey, Steve Clark, Al Haskell
D: Wallace Fox
SP: Luci Ward
P: Leon Barsha
Adaptor: Milton Carter

1349. THEY DIED WITH THEIR BOOTS ON
(Warner Bros., January 1, 1942) 140 Mins.
Errol Flynn, Olivia de Havilland, Arthur Kennedy,
  Charley Grapewin, Gene Lockhart, Anthony
  Quinn, Stanley Ridges, John Litel, Walter Hamp-
  den, Sydney Greenstreet, Regis Toomey, Hattie
  McDaniel, George P. Huntley, Jr., Frank Wilcox,
  Joseph Sayer, Minor Watson
D: Raoul Walsh
SP: Wally Kline, Aeneas MacMahon

1350. TEXAS MAN HUNT
(PRC, January 2, 1942) 60 Mins.
Bill "Cowboy Rambler" Boyd, Art Davis, Lee Powell,
  Julie Duncan, Dennis Moore, Frank Hagney, Karl
  Hackett, Frank Ellis, Arno Frey, Eddie Phillips,
  Kenne Duncan
D: Peter Stewart (Sam Newfield)
SP: William Lively
P: Sigmund Neufeld

1351. ARIZONA TERROR
(Republic, January 6, 1942) 56 Mins.
Don Barry, Lynn Merrick, Al St. John, Reed Had-
  ley, Rex Lease, John Maxwell, Frank Brownlee,
  Lee Shumway, Tom London, John Merton, Fred
  Toones, Curley Dresden, Herman Hack
D/AP: George Sherman
SP: Doris Schroeder, Taylor Cavan

1352. THUNDER RIVER FEUD
(Monogram, January 9, 1942) 51 Mins.
(*Range Busters* Series)
Ray Corrigan, John King, Max Terhune, Jan Wiley,
  Jack M. Holmes, Rick Anderson, Carleton Young,
  Carl Mathews, George Chesebro, Budd Buster,
  Steve Clark, Ted Mapes, Tex Palmer, Hal Price,
  Dick Cramer
D: S. Roy Luby
S: Earle Snell
SP: John Vlahos, Earle Snell
P: George W. Weeks

1353. WEST OF TOMBSTONE
(Columbia, January 15, 1942) 59 Mins.
Charles Starrett, Russell Hayden, Cliff Edwards,
  Marcella Martin, Gordon DeMain, Clancy Cooper,
  Jack Kirk, Budd Buster, Tom London, Francis
  Walker, Ray Jones, Eddie Laughton, Lloyd Bridges,
  Ernie Adams, George Morrell
D: Howard Bretherton
SP: Maurice Geraghty
P: William Berke

1354. THE LONE RIDER AND THE BANDIT
(PRC, January 16, 1942) 54 Mins.
(*Lone Rider* Series)
George Houston, Al St. John, Dennis Moore, Vicki
  Lester, Glenn Strange, Jack Ingram, Milt Kibbee,
  Carl Sepulveda, Slim Andrews, Eddie Dean, Slim
  Whitaker, Hal Price, Kenne Duncan, Curley
  Dresden
D: Sam Newfield
SP: Steve Braxton
P: Sigmund Neufeld

1355. MAN FROM CHEYENNE
(Republic, January 16, 1942) 60 Mins.
Roy Rogers, George Hayes, Sally Payne, Gale
  Storm, Lynne Carver, William Haade, Bob Nolan,
  James Seay, Pat Brady, Jack Ingram, Jack Kirk,
  Fred Burns, Jack Rockwell, Sons of the Pioneers,
  "Trigger," Al Taylor, Chick Hannon, Art Dillard,
  Frank Brownlee
D/AP: Joseph Kane
SP: Winston Miller

1356. NORTH TO THE KLONDIKE
(Universal, January 23, 1942) 58 Mins.
Broderick Crawford, Andy Devine, Lon Chaney,
  Jr., Evelyn Ankers, Lloyd Corrigan, Willie Fung,
  Keye Luke, Stanley Andrews, Dorothy Granger,
  Monte Blue, Roy Harris (Riley Hill), Paul Dubov,
  Fred Cordova, Jeff Corey
D: Erle C. Kenton
S: William Castle. From the short story "Gold
  Hunters of the North" by Jack London
SP: Clarence Upson Young, Lou Sarecky, George
  Bricker
AP: Paul Malvern

1357. BELOW THE BORDER
(Monogram, January 30, 1942) 57 Mins.
(*Rough Riders* Series)
Buck Jones, Tim McCoy, Raymond Hatton, Linda
  Brent, Eva Puig, Charles King, Dennis Moore,
  Roy Barcroft, Ted Mapes, Bud Osborne, Merrill
  McCormack, Jack Rockwell, "Silver"

D: Howard Bretherton
SP: Jess Bowers (Adele Buffington)
P: Scott R. Dunlap

1358. CODE OF THE OUTLAW
(Republic, January 30, 1942) 57 Mins.
(*Three Mesquiteers* Series)
Bob Steele, Tom Tyler, Rufe Davis, Weldon Heyburn, Melinda Leighton, Don Curtis, John Ince, Kenne Duncan, Phil Dunham, Max Walzman, Chuck Morrison, Carleton Young, Al Taylor, Robert Frazer, Dick Alexander, Forrest Taylor, Jack Ingram, Wally West, Edward Piel, Sr., Bud Osborne, Hank Worden, Cactus Mack
D: John English
SP: Barry Shipman. Based on characters created by William Colt MacDonald
AP: Louis Gray

1359. COWBOY SERENADE
(Republic, January 30, 1942) 66 Mins.
Gene Autry, Smiley Burnette, Fay McKenzie, Cecil Cunningham, Randy Brooks, Addison Richards, Tris Coffin, Slim Andrews, Melinda Leighton, Johnny Berkes, Forrest Taylor, Hank Worden, Si Jenks, Ethan Laidlaw, Hal Price, Otto Ham, Loren Raker, Bud Wolfe, Forbes Murray, Bud Geary, Frankie Marvin, Tom London, Ken Terrell, Ralph Kirby, Ken Cooper, Rick Anderson, "Champion"
D: William Morgan
SP: Olive Cooper
AP: Harry Grey

1360. KEEP SHOOTING
(RKO, January 30, 1942 17 Mins.
Ray Whitley, Virginia Vale, Ken Card, Ester Belle, Ethan Laidlaw, Marie Mominieci, Harry Harvey, Curley Hoag, Candy Hall
D/SP: Harry D'Arcy

1361. WILD BILL HICKOK RIDES
(Warner Bros., January 31, 1942) 82 Mins.
Constance Bennett, Bruce Cabot, Warren William, Betty Brewer, Walter Catlett, Ward Bond, Howard de Silva, Frank Wilcox, Faye Emerson, Julie Bishop, Lucia Carroll, Russell Simpson, Cliff Clark, J. Farrell MacDonald, Lillian Yarbo, Trevor Bardette, Elliott Sullivan, Dick Botiller, Ray Teal
D: Ray Enright
SP: Charles Grayston, Paul Gerald Smith, Raymond Schrock

1362. VALLEY OF THE SUN
(RKO, February 6, 1942) 84 Mins.
Lucille Ball, James Craig, Sir Cedric Hardwicke, Dean Jagger, Peter Whitney, Billy Gilbert, Tom Tyler, Antonio Moreno, George Cleveland, Hank Bell, Richard Fiske

D: George Marshall
S: Clarence Budington Kelland
SP: Horace McCoy
P: Graham Baker

1363. BULLETS FOR BANDITS
(Columbia, February 12, 1942) 55 Mins.
Bill Elliott, Tex Ritter, Frank Mitchell, Dorothy Short, Forrest Taylor, Ralph Theodore, Edythe Elliott, Eddie Laughton, Joe McQuinn, Tom Moray, Art Mix, Harry Harvey, Hal Taliaferro, Ed Laughton, John Tyrrell, Bud Osborne
D: Wallace Fox
SP: Robert Lee Johnson
P: Leon Barsha
Adaptor: Milton Carter

1364. WESTERN MAIL
(Monogram, February 13, 1942)
Tom Keene, Frank Yaconelli, Jean Trent, Glenn Strange, LeRoy Mason, Fred Kohler, Jr., James Sheridan (Sherry Tansey), Gene Alsace (Rocky Camron), Karl Hackett, Tex Palmer, "Prince"
D/P: Robert Tansey
SP: Robert Emmett, Frances Kavanaugh

1365. RIDE 'EM, COWBOY
(Universal, February 13, 1942) 86 Mins.
Bud Abbott, Lou Costello, Dick Foran, Anne Gwynne, Johnny Mack Brown, The Merry Macs, Ella Fitzgerald, Douglass Dumbrille, Samuel S. Hinds, Morris Ankrum, The High Hatters, The Buckaroo Band, The Ranger Chorus, Bob Baker, Richard Lane, Chief Yowlachie
D: Arthur Lubin
S: Edmund L. Hartman
SP: True Boardman, John Grant
AP: Alex Gottlieb

1366. STAGECOACH BUCKAROO
(Universal, February 13, 1942) 58 Mins.
Johnny Mack Brown, Fuzzy Knight, Nell O'Day, Anne Nagel, Herbert Rawlinson, Glenn Strange, Ernie Adams, Henry Hall, Lloyd Ingraham, Kermit Maynard, Frank Brownlee, Jack C. Smith, Harry Tenbrook, Frank Ellis, Blackie Whiteford, Hank Bell, Ray Jones, Jim Corey, William Nestell, Carl Sepulveda, The Guardsman Quartet
D: Ray Taylor
S: "Shotgun Messenger"—Arthur St. Clair
SP: Al Martin
AP: Will Cowan

1367. SOUTH OF SANTA FE
(Republic, February 17, 1942) 56 Mins.
Roy Rogers, George Hayes, Linda Hayes, Paul Fix, Bobby Beers, Bob Nolan, Pat Brady, Arthur Loft, Charles Miller, Sam Flint, Jack Kirk, Jack Ingram,

Hank Bell, Carleton Young, Lynton Brent, Robert Strange, Henry Wills, Jack O'Shea, Merrill McCormack, "Trigger"

1367a. SHUT MY BIG MOUTH
(Columbia, February 19, 1942)   71 Mins.
Joe E. Brown, Adele Mara, Don Beddoe, Lloyd Bridges, Forrest Tucker, Earle Hodgins, Fritz Feld, Russell Simpson, Pedro De Cordoba, Joan Woodbury, Ralph Peters, Joe McGuinn, Noble Johnson, Chief Thunder Cloud
D: Charles Barton
S: Oliver Drake
SP: Oliver Drake, Karen DeWolf, Francis Martin
P: Robert Storm

1368. RAIDERS OF THE WEST
(PRC, February 20, 1942)   60 Mins.
Bill "Cowboy Rambler" Boyd, Art Davis, Lee Powell, Virginia Carroll, Rex Lease, Charles King, Glenn Strange, Slim Whitaker, Milt Kibbee, Lynton Brent, John Elliott, Eddie Dean, Curley Dresden, William Desmond, Dale Sherwood, Kenne Duncan, Bill Cody, Jr., Reed Howes, Hal Price, Fred Toones, Carl Sepulveda, Frank Ellis, John Cason
D: Peter Stewart (Sam Newfield)

SP: Oliver Drake
P: Sigmund Neufeld

1368a. CACTUS MAKES PERFECT
(Columbia, February 26, 1942)   2 Reels
(*Three Stooges* Series)
Moe Howard, Curly Howard, Larry Fine, Vernon Dent, Ernie Adams, Monte Collins
D: Del Lord

1369. RIDING THE WIND
(RKO, February 27, 1942)   60 Mins.
Tim Holt, Ray Whitley, Mary Douglas, Lee "Lasses" White, Eddie Dew, Ernie Adams, Earle Hodgins, Kate Harrington, Charles Phipps, Bud Osborne, Karl Hackett, Hank Worden, Larry Steers, Frank McCarroll, Bob Burns
D: Edward Killy
S: Bernard McConville
SP: Morton Grant, Earle Snell
P: Bert Gilroy

1370. ROCK RIVER RENEGADES
(Monogram, February 27, 1942)   56 Mins.
(*Range Busters* Series)
Ray Corrigan, John King, Max Terhune, Chris-

Shut My Big Mouth (Columbia, 1942) — Earle Hodgins, Joe E. Brown, and Fritz Feld

tine McIntyre, John Elliott, Weldon Heyburn, Kermit Maynard, Frank Ellis, Carl Mathews, Dick Cramer, Tex Palmer, Hank Bell, Budd Buster, Steve Clark
D: S. Roy Luby
S: Faith Thomas
SP: John Vlahos, Earle Snell
P: George W. Weeks

1371. BILLY THE KID TRAPPED
(PRC, February 27, 1942) 59 Mins.
(*Billy the Kid* Series)
Buster Crabbe, Al St. John, Bud McTaggart, Anne Jeffries, Glenn Strange, Walter McGrail, Ted Adams, Jack Ingram, Milt Kibbee, Eddie Phillips, Budd Buster, Jack Kinney, Jimmy Aubrey, Wally West, Bert Dillard, Kenne Duncan, George Chesebro, Carl Mathews, Dick Cramer, Ray Henderson, Curley Dresden, Augie Gomez, Horace B. Carpenter, Herman Hack, James Mason, Hank Bell, Oscar Gahan
D: Sherman Scott (Sam Newfield)
SP: Oliver Drake
P: Sigmund Neufeld

1372. ARIZONA ROUNDUP
(Monogram, March 6, 1942) 56 Mins.
Tom Keene, Hope Blackwood, Frank Yaconelli, Sugar Dawn, Jack Ingram, Steve Clark, Tom Seidel, Nick Moro, Hal Price, I. Stanford Jolley, Edward Cassidy, Tex Palmer, Gene Alsace (Rocky Camron), Fred Hoose, Horace B. Carpenter, Sherry Tansey
D/P: Robert Tansey
SP: Robert Emmett, Frances Kavanaugh

1373. STAGECOACH EXPRESS
(Republic, March 6, 1942) 57 Mins.
Don Barry, Lynn Merrick, Al St. John, Robert Kent, Emmett Lynn, Guy Kingsford, Ethan Laidlaw, Eddie Dean
D/AP: George Sherman
S: Doris Schroeder
SP: Arthur V. Jones

1374. HEART OF THE RIO GRANDE
(Republic, March 11, 1942) 70 Mins.
Gene Autry, Smiley Burnette, Fay McKenzie, Edith Fellows, Pierre Watkin, Joe Strauch, Jr., William Haade, Sarah Padden, Jean Porter, Milton Kibbee, Edmund Cobb, Jimmy Wakely Trio (Jimmy Wakely, Johnny Bond, Dick Rinehart), Budd Buster, Frank Mills, Howard Mitchell, Allan Wood, Nora Lane, Mady Lawrence, Buck Woods, Harry Deep, George Porter, Frankie Marvin, Jeannie Hebers, Kay Frye, Jane Graham, Patsy Fay Northup, Jan Lester, Gloria and Gladys Gardner, "Champion"

D: William Morgan
S: Newlin B. Wilds
SP: Lillie Hayward, Winston Miller
AP: Harry Grey

1375. RODEO RHYTHM
(PRC, March 13, 1942) 72 Mins.
Fred Scott, Pat Dunn, Loie Bridge, Patricia Redpath, Jack Cooper, Gloria Morse, H. "Doc" Hartley, Rovlene Smith, Vernon Brown, Landon Laird, John Frank, Roy Knapp's Rough Riders
D: Fred Neymeyer
P: Leo J. McCarthy

1376. LAWLESS PLAINSMEN
(Columbia, March 17, 1942) 59 Mins.
Charles Starrett, Russell Hayden, Cliff Edwards, Luana Walters, Ray Bennett, Gwen Kenyon, Frank LaRue, Stanley Brown, Nick Thompson, Eddie Laughton, Carl Mathews
D: William Berke
SP: Luci Ward
P: Jack Fier

1377. RAIDERS OF THE RANGE
(Republic, March 18, 1942) 55 Mins.
(*Three Mesquiteers* Series)
Bob Steele, Tom Tyler, Rufe Davis, Lois Collier, Frank Jacquet, Fred Kohler, Jr., Dennis Moore, Tom Chatterton, Charles Miller, Max Walzman, Hal Price, Charles Phillips, Bud Geary, Jack Ingram, Al Taylor, Chuck Morrison, Joel Friedkin, Bob Woodward, Tom Steele, Monte Montague, Ken Terrell, Dick Alexander, Cactus Mack, John Cason
D: John English
S: Albert DeMond
SP: Barry Shipman. Based on characters created by William Colt MacDonald
AP: Louis Gray

1378. LONE STAR RANGER
(20th C. Fox, March 20, 1942) 58 Mins.
John Kimbrough, Sheila Ryan, Jonathan Hale, William Farnum, Truman Bradley, George E. Stone, Russell Simpson, Dorothy Burgess, Tom Fadden, Fred Kohler, Jr., Eddy Waller, Harry Holden, George Melford, Tom London
D: James Tinling
S: Zane Grey
SP: William Conselman, Jr., George Kane, Irving Cummings, Jr.
P: Sol M. Wurtzel

1379. THE LONE RIDER IN CHEYENNE
(PRC, March 20, 1942) 59 Mins.
(*Lone Rider* Series)
George Houston, Al St. John, Dennis Moore, Ella

Neal, Roy Barcroft, Kenne Duncan, Lynton Brent, Milt Kibbee, Jack Holmes, Karl Hackett, Jack Ingram, George Chesebro
D: Sam Newfield
SP: Oliver Drake, Elizabeth Beecher
P: Sigmund Neufeld

1380. THE GREAT MAN'S LADY

(Paramount, March 21, 1942)   90 Mins.
Barbara Stanwyck, Joel McCrea, Brian Donlevy, Katherine Stevens, Thurston Hall, Lloyd Corrigan, Etta McDaniel, Frank M. Thomas, William B. Davidson, Lillian Yarbo, Helen Lynd, Mary Treen, Lucien Littlefield, John Hamilton, Fred Toones, Damian O'Flynn, Charles Lane, George Chandler, Milton Parsons, Anna Q. Nilsson, G. P. Huntley
D: William A. Wellman
S: Adela Rogers St. John, Seena Owen. Based on a short story by Vina Delmar
SP: W. L. River
P: William A. Wellman

1381. JESSE JAMES, JR.

(Republic, March 25, 1942)   56 Mins.
Don Barry, Lynn Merrick, Al St. John, Douglas Walton, Bob Kortman, Karl Hackett, Lee Shumway, Stanley Blystone, Jack Kirk, George Chesebro, Frank Brownlee, Forbes Murray, Jim Corey, Kermit Maynard, Ken Cooper, Tommy Coats
D/AP: George Sherman
S: Richard Murphy
SP: Richard Murphy, Taylor Cavan, Doris Schroeder

1382. SUNDOWN JIM

(20th C. Fox, March 27, 1942)   63 Mins.
John Kimbrough, Virginia Gilmore, Arlean Whelan, Moroni Olson, Paul Hurst, Joe Sawyer, Don Costello, Tom Fadden, Frank McGrath, LeRoy Mason, James Bush, Lane Chandler, Charles Tanner, Cliff Edwards, Paul Sutton, Eddy Waller
D: James Tinling
S: Ernest Haycox
SP: Robert F. Metzler, William Bruckner
P: Sol M. Wurtzel

1383. GHOST TOWN LAW

(Monogram, March 27, 1942)   62 Mins.
(*Rough Riders* Series)
Buck Jones, Tim McCoy, Raymond Hatton, Virginia Carpenter, Murdock McQuarrie, Charles King, Howard Masters, Ben Corbett, Tom London, "Silver"
D: Howard Bretherton
SP: Jess Bowers (Adele Buffington)
P: Scott R. Dunlap

1384. SUNSET ON THE DESERT

(Republic, April 1, 1942)   54 Mins.
Roy Rogers, George Hayes, Lynne Carver, Frank M. Thomas, Bob Nolan, Beryl Wallace, Glenn Strange, Douglas Fowley, Fred Burns, Roy Barcroft, Henry Wills, Forrest Taylor, Bob Woodward, Edward Cassidy, Pat Brady, Cactus Mack, Sons of the Pioneers, "Trigger"
D/AP: Joseph Kane
SP: Gerald Geraghty

1385. WHERE TRAILS END

(Monogram, April 1, 1942)   58 Mins.
Tom Keene, Joan Curtis, Frank Yaconelli, Charles King, Donald Stewart, Steve Clark, William Vaughn, Horace B. Carpenter, Nick Moro, Gene Alsace (Rocky Camron), Fred Hoose, James Sheridan (Sherry Tansey), Steve Clensos, Tex Palmer, Tom Seidel, Chick Hannon, "Prince"
D/P: Robert Tansey
SP: Robert Emmett (Tansey), Frances Kavanaugh

1386. NORTH OF THE ROCKIES

(Columbia, April 2, 1942)   60 Mins.
Bill Elliott, Tex Ritter, Frank Mitchell, Shirley Patterson, Larry Parks, John Miljan, Ian MacDonald, Lloyd Bridges, Gertrude Hoffman, Earl Gunn, Boyd Irwin, Art Dillard, Dave Harper, Francis Sayles
D: Lambert Hillyer
SP: Herbert Dalmas
P: Leon Barsha
Adaptor: Norman Deming

1387. THE SPOILERS

(Universal, April 10, 1942)   87 Mins.
Marlene Dietrich, Randolph Scott, John Wayne, Margaret Lindsay, Harry Carey, Richard Barthelmess, William Farnum, George Cleveland, Samuel S. Hinds, Russell Simpson, Marietta Canty, Jack Norton, Ray Bennett, Forrest Taylor, Art Miles, Charles McMurphy, Charles Halton, Bud Osborne, Robert W. Service
D: Ray Enright
S: Rex Beach
SP: Tom Reed
P: Frank Lloyd

1388. DUDES ARE PRETTY PEOPLE

(United Artists, April 14, 1942)   46 Mins.
Jimmy Rogers, Noah Beery, Jr., Marjorie Woodworth, Paul Hurst, Marjorie Gateson, Russell Gleason, Grady Sutton, Bob Gregory, Frank Moran
D: Hal Roach, Jr.
S: Donald Hough
SP: Louis Kaye
P: Hal Roach

1389. THE GIRL FROM ALASKA

(Republic, April 16, 1942)   75 Mins.

Ray Middleton, Jean Parker, Jerome Cowan, Robert Barrat, Ray Mala, Francis McDonald, Raymond Hatton, Milton Parsons, Nestor Paiva

D: Nick Grinde

S: "The Golden Portage"—Robert Ormond Case

SP: Edward T. Lowe, Robert Ormond Case

P: Armand Schaefer

1390. LAND OF THE OPEN RANGE

(RKO, April 17, 1942)   60 Mins.

Tim Holt, Ray Whitley, Janet Waldo, Lee "Lasses" White, Hobart Cavanaugh, Lee Bonnell, Roy Barcroft, John Elliott, Frank Ellis, Tom London, J. Merrill Holmes

D: Edward Killy

S: "Homesteads of Hate"—Lee Bond

SP: Morton Grant

P: Bert Gilroy

1391. DOWN RIO GRANDE WAY

(Columbia, April 23, 1942)   57 Mins.

Charles Starrett, Russell Hayden, Britt Wood, Rose Anne Stevens, Norman Willis, Davidson Clark, Edmund Cobb, Budd Buster, Joseph Eggenton, Paul Newlin, Betty Roadman, William Desmond, Jim Corey, Tom Smith, Steve Clark, Forrest Taylor, Edward Piel, Sr., John Cason, Art Mix, Kermit Maynard, Frank McCarroll

D: William Berke

SP: Paul Franklin

P: Jack Fier

1392. CACTUS CAPERS

(RKO, April 23, 1942)   17 Mins.

Ray Whitley, Virginia Vale, Emmett Lynn, Ken Card, Spade Cooley

D: Charles Roberts

SP: Max Bercutt

1393. WESTWARD HO

(Republic, April 24, 1942)   56 Mins.

(*Three Mesquiteers* Series)

Bob Steele, Tom Tyler, Rufe Davis, Evelyn Brent, Donald Curtis, Lois Collier, Emmett Lynn, John James, Tom Seidel, Jack Kirk, Kenne Duncan, Milton Kibbee, Edmund Cobb, Monte Montague, Al Taylor, Bud Osborne, Jack Montgomery, Horace B. Carpenter, John L. Cason, Jack O'Shea, Ray Jones, Tex Palmer, Curley Dresden, Budd Buster

D: John English

S: Morton Grant

SP: Morton Grant, Doris Schroeder. Based on characters created by William Colt MacDonald

P: Louis Gray

1394. BOOT HILL BANDITS

(Monogram, April 24, 1942)   58 Mins.

(*Range Busters* Series)

Ray Corrigan, John King, Max Terhune, Jean Brooks (Jeanne Kelly), John Merton, Glenn Strange, I. Stanford Jolley, Steve Clark, Dick Cramer, George Chesebro, Budd Buster, Milburn Morante, Jimmy Aubrey, Charles King, Carl Mathews, Tex Palmer, Merrill McCormack

D: S. Roy Luby

SP: Arthur Durlam

P: George W. Weeks

1395. ROLLING DOWN THE GREAT DIVIDE

(PRC, April 24, 1942)   59 Mins.

Bill "Cowboy Rambler" Boyd, Art Davis, Lee Powell, Wanda McKay, Glenn Strange, Karl Hackett, J. Merrill Holmes, Ted Adams, Jack Ingram, John Elliott, George Chesebro, Horace B. Carpenter, Jack Roper, Curley Dresden, Dennis Moore, Tex Palmer

D: Peter Stewart (Sam Newfield)

SP: George Milton

P: Sigmund Neufeld

1396. HOME IN WYOMIN'

(Republic, April 29, 1942)   67 Mins.

Gene Autry, Smiley Burnette, Faye McKenzie, Olin Howlin, Chick Chandler, Joe Strauch, Jr., Forrest Taylor, James Seay, George Douglas, Charles Lane, Hal Price, Bud Geary, Ken Cooper, Jean Porter, James McNamara, Kermit Maynard, Roy Butler, Billy Benedict, Cyril Ring, Spade Cooley, Ted Mapes, Jack Kirk, William Kellogg, Betty Farrington, Rex Lease, Tom Hanlon, Lee Shumway, "Champion"

D: William Morgan

S: Stuart Palmer

SP: Robert Tasker, M. Coates Webster

AP: Harry Grey

1397. YUKON PATROL

(Republic, April 30, 1942)

(Feature version of the serial *King of the Royal Mounted*)

Allan Lane, Robert Strange, Robert Kellard, Lita Conway, Herbert Rawlinson, Harry Cording, Bryant Washburn, Budd Buster, Stanley Andrews, John Davidson, John Dilson, Paul McVey, Lucien Prival, Norman Willis, Tony Paton, Ken Terrell, Charles Thomas, Bill Wilkus, Ted Mapes, Major Sam Harris, George Plues, Frank Wayne, Richard Simmons, Loren Riebe, Wallace Reid, Jr., William Justice, William Stahl, John Bagni, Earl Bunn, Curley Dresden, George DeNormand, Bud Geary, Dave Marks, Robert Wayne, William Kellogg, Tommy Coats, Dale Van Sickel, David Sharpe, Duke Taylor, Bob Jamison, Al Taylor, Douglas Evans

Boot Hill Bandits (Monogram, 1942) — Richard Cramer, Ray Corrigan, Steve Clark, Herman Hack, Jimmy Aubrey, and unidentified player

D: William Witney, John English
SP: Franklyn Adreon, Norman S. Hall, Joseph Poland, Barney A. Sarecky, Sol Shor
AP: Hiram S. Brown, Jr.

1398. BILLY THE KID'S SMOKING GUNS
(PRC, May 1, 1942)   58 Mins.
(*Billy the Kid* Series)
Buster Crabbe, Al St. John, Dave O'Brien, Joan Barclay, John Merton, Milt Kibbee, Ted Adams, Karl Hackett, Frank Ellis, Slim Whitaker, Budd Buster, Joel Newfield, Bert Dillard
D: Sherman Scott (Sam Newfield)
SP: George Milton (George Sayre/Milton Raison)
P: Sigmund Neufeld

1399. THE DEVIL'S TRAIL
(Columbia, May 14, 1942)   61 Mins.
Bill Elliott, Tex Ritter, Eileen O'Hearn, Frank Mitchell, Noah Beery, Art Mix, Ruth Ford, Joel Friedkin, Joe McGuinn, Edmund Cobb, Tris Coffin, Paul Newland, Steve Clark, Sarah Padden, Bud Osborne, Stanley Brown, Buck Moulton
D: Lambert Hillyer
S: "The Town in Hell's Backyard"—Robert Lee Johnson
SP: Leon Barsha

1400. ROMANCE ON THE RANGE
(Republic, May 18, 1942)   63 Mins.
Roy Rogers, George Hayes, Sally Payne, Linda Hayes, Bob Nolan and the Sons of the Pioneers, Edward Pawley, Hal Taliaferro, Harry Woods, Glenn Strange, Roy Barcroft, Jack Kirk, Pat Brady, Jack O'Shea, Dick Wessell, Dick Alexander, "Trigger"
D/AP: Joseph Kane
SP: J. Benton Cheney

1401. DOWN TEXAS WAY
(Monogram, May 22, 1942)   57 Mins.
(*Rough Riders* Series)
Buck Jones, Tim McCoy, Raymond Hatton, Luana Walters, Dave O'Brien, Glenn Strange, Lois Austin, Harry Woods, Tom London, Kansas Moehring, Jack Daley, "Silver"
D: Howard Bretherton
SP: Jess Bowers (Adele Buffington)
P: Scott R. Dunlap

1402. PERILS OF THE ROYAL MOUNTED
(Columbia, May 24, 1942)   15 Chaps.
Robert Stevens (Robert Kellard), Nell O'Day, Herbert Rawlinson, Kermit Maynard, Kenneth MacDonald, John Elliott, Nick Thompson, Art Miles,

Richard Fiske, Richard Vallin, Forrest Taylor, George Chesebro, Jack Ingram, Iron Eyes Cody
D: James W. Horne
SP: Basil Dickey, Scott Littleton, Jesse A. Duffy, Louis Heifetz
P: Larry Darmour
Chapter Titles: (1) The Totem Talks, (2) The Night Raiders, (3) The Water God's Revenge, (4) Beware, The Vigilantes, (5) The Masked Mountie, (6) Underwater Gold, (7) Bridge to the Sky, (8) Lost in the Mine, (9) Into the Trap, (10) Betrayed by Law, (11) Blazing Beacon, (12) The Mountie's Last Chance, (13) Painted White Man, (14) Burned at the Stake, (15) The Mountie Gets His Man

1403. STARDUST ON THE SAGE
(Republic, May 25, 1942)   65 Mins.
Gene Autry, Smiley Burnette, Bill Henry, Edith Fellows, Louise Currie, George Ernest, Emmett Vogan, Vince Barnett, Betty Farrington, Roy Barcroft, Tom London, Rex Lease, Frank Ellis, Edward Cassidy, Fred Burns, Frank LaRue, Franklyn Farnum, Edmund Cobb, Jerry Jerome, Merrill McCormack, Bert LeBaron, Monte Montague, George DeNormand, Bill Jamison, Jimmy Fox, George Sherwood, William Nestell, Frank O'Connor, Griff Barnett, Frankie Marvin, Lee Shumway, "Champion"
D: William Morgan
S: Dorrell and Stuart McGowan
SP: Betty Burbridge
AP: Harry Grey

1404. CYCLONE KID
(Republic, May 31, 1942)   57 Mins.
Don Barry, Lynn Merrick, John James, Slim Andrews, Rex Lease, Alex Callan, Joel Friedkin, Monte Montague, Joe McGuinn, Frank LaRue, Edmund Cobb, Budd Buster, Hal Price, Jack Rockwell, Al Taylor, Jack O'Shea, Curley Dresden, Bob Woodward, Joe Cody, Rose Plummer
D/AP: George Sherman
SP: Richard Murphy

1405. PIERRE OF THE PLAINS
(MGM, June 1, 1942)   57 Mins.
John Carroll, Ruth Hussey, Bruce Cabot, Paul Brown, Reginald Owen, Henry Travers, Evelyn Ankers, Pat McVey, Charles Stevens, Sheldon Leonard, Lois Ransom, Frederick Worlock
D: George B. Seitz
S: Edgar Selwyn
SP: Lawrence Kimble
P: Edgar Selwyn

1406. COME ON, DANGER!
(RKO, June 5, 1942)   58 Mins.

Tim Holt, Frances Neal, Ray Whitley, Lee "Lasses" White, Karl Hackett, Bud McTaggart, Glenn Strange, Evelyn Dickson, Davidson Clark, John Elliott, Slim Whitaker, Kate Harrington, Henry Rocquemore
D: Edward Killy
S: Bennett Cohen
SP: Norton S. Parker
P: Bert Gilroy

1407. TEXAS JUSTICE
(PRC, June 5, 1942)   58 Mins.
(Lone Rider Series)
George Houston, Al St. John, Dennis Moore, Wanda McKay, Claire Rochelle, Archie Hall, Slim Whitaker, Edward Piel, Sr., Karl Hackett, Julian Rivero, Curley Dresden, Dirk Thane, Horace B. Carpenter, Steve Clark, Frank Ellis, Merrill McCormack, Ray Jones
D: Sam Newfield
SP: Steve Braxton (Sam Robins)
P: Sigmund Neufeld

1408. IN OLD CALIFORNIA
(Republic, June 11, 1942)   88 Mins.
John Wayne, Binnie Barnes, Albert Dekker, Helen Parrish, Patsy Kelly, Edgar Kennedy, Dick Purcell, Harry Shannon, Charles Halton, Emmett Lynn, Bob McKenzie, Milt Kibbee, Paul Sutton, Anne O'Neal, Hooper Atchley, Pearl Early, Ruth Robinson, Frank Jacquet, Jack O'Shea, Jack Kirk, Lynne Carver, James Morton, Horace B. Carpenter, Olin Howlin, Chester Conklin, Ralph Peters, Forrest Taylor, Dick Alexander, Donald Curtis, George Lloyd, Stanley Blystone, Slim Whitaker, Frank Ellis, Frank Hagney, Bud Osborne, Ed Brady, Wade Crosby, Guy Usher, Minerva Urecal, Martin Garralaga, Rex Lease, Karl Hackett, Art Mix, Robert Homans, Merrill McCormack, Frank McGlynn
D: William McGann
S: J. Robert Bren, Gladys Atwater
SP: Gertrude Purcess, Frances Hyland
AP: Robert North

1409. TEXAS TROUBLE SHOOTERS
(Monogram, June 12, 1942)   55 Mins.
(Range Busters Series)
Ray Corrigan, John King, Max Terhune, Julie Duncan, Glenn Strange, Roy Harris (Riley Hill), Kermit Maynard, Eddie Phillips, Frank Ellis, Ted Mapes, Steve Clark, Gertrude Hoffman, Jack Holmes, Dick Cramer, Carl Mathews
D: S. Roy Luby
S: Elizabeth Beecher
SP: Arthur Hoerl
P: S. Roy Luby

Come On, Danger!
(RKO-Radio, 1942)
— Lee "Lasses"
White, Ray Whitley, and Tim Holt

1410. TOMBSTONE—THE TOWN TOO TOUGH TO DIE

(Paramount, June 13, 1942) 79 Mins.

Richard Dix, Kent Taylor, Edgar Buchanan, Frances Gifford, Don Castle, Clem Bevins, Victor Jory, Rex Bell, Chris-Pin Martin, Jack Rockwell, Charles Stevens, Hal Taliaferro, Wallis Clark, James Ferrara, Paul Sutton, Dick Curtis, Harvey Stephens, Charles Middleton, Don Curtis, Beryl Wallace

D: William McGann

S: Dean Franklin, Charles Beisner

SP: Albert Shelby LeVino, Edward E. Paramore

P: Harry Sherman

1411. THE PHANTOM PLAINSMEN

(Republic, June 16, 1942) 65 Mins.

(*Three Mesquiteers* Series)

Bob Steele, Tom Tyler, Rufe Davis, Lois Collier, Robert O. Davis, Charles Miller, Alex Callam, Monte Montague, Henry Roland, Richard Crane, Jack Kirk, Edward Cassidy, Vince Barnett, Lloyd Ingraham, Al Taylor, Bud Geary, Herman Hack

D: John English

S: Robert Yost

SP: Robert Yost, Barry Shipman. Based on characters created by William Colt MacDonald

AP: Louis Gray

1412. RIDERS OF THE NORTHLAND

(Columbia, June 18, 1942) 58 Mins.

Charles Starrett, Russell Hayden, Cliff Edwards, Shirley Patterson, Lloyd Bridges, Bobby Larson, Kenneth MacDonald, Paul Sutton, Robert O. Davis, Joe McGuinn, Francis Walker, George Filtz, Blackjack Ward, Dick Jensen

D: William Berke

SP: Paul Franklin

P: Jack Fier

1413. JACKASS MAIL

(MGM, July 1, 1942) 80 Mins.

Wallace Beery, Marjorie Main, J. Carrol Naish, Darryl Hickman, William Haade, Dick Curtis, Robert Cavanaugh, Joe Yule, Esther Howard

D: Norman Z. McLeod

S: C. Gardner Sullivan

SP: Lawrence Hazard

P: John W. Considine, Jr.

1414. SONS OF THE PIONEERS

(Republic, July 2, 1942) 61 Mins.

Roy Rogers, George Hayes, Maris Wrixon, Sons of the Pioneers, Forrest Taylor, Hal Taliaferro, Minerva Urecal, Bradley Page, Jack O'Shea, Frank Ellis, Tom London, Bob Woodward, Fern Emmett, Chester Conklin, Ken Cooper, Karl Hackett, Fred Burns, "Trigger"

D/AP: Joseph Kane
S: Mauri Grashin, Robert T. Shannon
SP: M. Coates Webster, Mauri Grashin, Robert T. Shannon

1415. MEN OF TEXAS
(Universal, July 3, 1942)   87 Mins.
Robert Stack, Broderick Crawford, Jackie Cooper, Ann Gwynne, Ralph Bellamy, Jane Darwell, Leo Carrillo, John Litel, William Farnum, Janet Beecher, Kay Linaker, J. Frank Hamilton, Joseph Crehan, Addison Richards
D: Ray Enright
SP: Harold Shumate, Richard Brooks
AP: George Waggner

1416. TUMBLEWEED TRAIL
(PRC, July 10, 1942)   57 Mins.
Bill "Cowboy Rambler" Boyd, Art Davis, Lee Powell, Marjorie Manners, Jack Rockwell, Charles King, Karl Hackett, George Chesebro, Frank Hagney, Reed Howes, Curley Dresden, George Morrell, Jack Montgomery, Art Dillard, Steve Clark, Dan White, Augie Gomez
D: Peter Stewart (Sam Newfield)
SP: Fred Myton
P: Sigmund Neufeld

1417. RANGE RHYTHM
(RKO, July 12, 1942)   17 Mins.
Ray Whitley, Virginia Vale, Lee White, Robert Kent, Frankie Marvin, Ken Card
D/SP: Charles Roberts
S: Max Bercutt

1418. PRAIRIE GUNSMOKE
(Columbia, July 16, 1942)   56 Mins.
Bill Elliott, Tex Ritter, Frank Mitchell, Virginia Carroll, Hal Price, Tris Coffin, Joe McGuinn, Frosty Royce, Rick Anderson, Art Mix, Francis Walker, Ray Jones, Ted Mapes, Glenn Strange, Steve Clark
D: Lambert Hillyer
SP: Fred Myton
S: Jack Ganzhorn
P: Leon Barsha

1419. THUNDERING HOOFS
(RKO, July 24, 1942)   61 Mins.
Tim Holt, Luana Walters, Ray Whitley, Lee "Lasses" White, Fred Scott, Archie Twitchell, Gordon De-Main, Charles Phipps, Monte Montague, Joe Bernard, Frank Fanning, Frank Ellis, Bob Kortman, Lloyd Ingraham
D: Lesley Selander
SP: Paul Franklin
P: Bert Gilroy

1420. THE SOMBRERO KID
(Republic, July 31, 1942)   56 Mins.
Don Barry, Lynn Merrick, Robert Homans, John James, Joel Friedkin, Rand Brooks, Stuart Hamblen, Bob McKenzie, Lloyd "Slim" Andrews, Anne O'Neal, Kenne Duncan, I. Stanford Jolley, Bud Geary, Frank Brownlee, William Nestell, Hank Bell, Curley Dresden, Jack O'Shea, Pascale Perry, Griff Barnett, Chick Hannon, Merrill McCormack, Edward Cassidy
D/AP: George Sherman
SP: Norman S. Hall

1421. THE SILVER BULLET
(Universal, August 5, 1942)   56 Mins.
Johnny Mack Brown, Fuzzy Knight, Jennifer Holt, William Farnum, Rex Lease, LeRoy Mason, Grace Lenard, Claire Whitney, Slim Whitaker, Michael Vallon, Merrill McCormack, Harry Holman, Lloyd Ingraham, Hank Bell, William Desmond, James Farley, Pals of the Golden West (with Nora Lou Martin)
D: Joseph H. Lewis
SP: Elizabeth Beecher
S: Oliver Drake
AP: Will Cowan

1422. BAD MEN OF THE HILLS
(Columbia, August 13, 1942)   58 Mins.
Charles Starrett, Russell Hayden, Cliff Edwards, Luana Walters, Al Bridge, Guy Usher, Joel Friedkin, Norma Jean Wooters, John Shay, Dick Botiller, Art Mix, Jack Ingram, Ben Corbett, Carl Sepulveda, John Cason, Frank Ellis
D: William Berke
SP: Luci Ward
P: Jack Fier

1423. VENGEANCE OF THE WEST
(Columbia, August 16, 1942)   60 Mins.
Bill Elliott, Tex Ritter, Frank Mitchell, Adele Mara, Dick Curtis, Robert Fiske, Eva Puig, Jose Tortosa, Guy Wilkerson, Ted Mapes, Edmund Cobb, Ed Laughton, Stanley Brown, John Tyrrell, Steve Clark
D: Lambert Hillyer
S: Jack Townley
SP: Luci Ward
P: Leon Barsha

1424. CALL OF THE CANYON
(Republic, August 17, 1942)   71 Mins.
Gene Autry, Smiley Burnette, Ruth Terry, Joe Strauch, Jr., Thurston Hall, Cliff Nazarro, Dorthea Kent, Bob Nolan, Pat Brady, Edmund McDonald, Marc Lawrence, John Holland, Eddy Waller, Budd Buster, Frank Jacquet, Lorin Raker, Johnny Duncan, Broderick O'Farrell, Ray Bennett, Carey

Harrison, Anthony Marsh, Fred Santley, Frank Ward, Freddie Walburn, Earle Hodgins, John Harmon, Red Knight, Al Taylor, Jimmy Lucas, Edna Johnson, Frankie Marvin, Charles Flynn, Bob Burns, Charles Williams, Sons of the Pioneers, Joy Barton, "Champion"
D: Joseph Santley
S: Olive Cooper, Maurice Raff
SP: Olive Cooper
P: Harry Grey

1425. BOSS OF HANGTOWN MESA
(Universal, August 21, 1942) 58 Mins.
Johnny Mack Brown, Fuzzy Knight, Helen Deverell, William Farnum, Rex Lease, Hugh Prosser, Michael Vallon, Robert Barron, Henry Hall, Jack C. Smith, Fred Kohler, Jr., Mickey Simpson, Frank Hagney, The Pals of the Golden West
D: Joseph H. Lewis
SP: Oliver Drake
P: Will Cowan

1426. LAW AND ORDER
(PRC, August 21, 1942) 56 Mins.
(*Billy the Kid* Series)
Buster Crabbe, Al St. John, Tex (Dave) O'Brien, Sarah Padden, Wanda McKay, Charles King, Hal Price, John Merton, Kenne Duncan, Ted Adams, Budd Buster, Kermit Maynard
D: Sherman Scott (Sam Newfield)
SP: Sam Robins
P: Sigmund Neufeld

1427. RIDERS OF THE WEST
(Monogram, August 21, 1942) 58 Mins.
(*Rough Riders* Series)
Buck Jones, Tim McCoy, Raymond Hatton, Sarah Padden, Dennis Moore, Harry Woods, Christine McIntyre, Walter McGrail, Harry Frazer, Bud Osborne, Charles King, Lee Phelps, Kermit Maynard, Milburn Morante, Edward Piel, Sr., Lynton Brent, J. Merrill Holmes, George Morrell, Tom London, "Silver"
D: Howard Bretherton
SP: Jess Bowers (Adele Buffington)
P: Scott R. Dunlap

1428. THE OMAHA TRAIL
(MGM, September 1, 1942) 64 Mins.
James Craig, Pamela Blake, Dean Jagger, Edward Ellis, Chill Wills, Donald Meek, Howard de Silva, Henry Morgan, Morris Ankrum, Kermit Maynard
D: Edward Buzzell
S: Jesse Lasky, Jr.
SP: Jesse Lasky, Jr., Hugh Butler
P: Jack Chertok

1429. ARIZONA STAGECOACH
(Monogram, September 4, 1942) 58 Mins.
(*Range Busters* Series)
Ray Corrigan, John King, Max Terhune, Nell O'Day, Kermit Maynard, Charles King, Carl Mathews, Slim Whitaker, Slim Harvey, Steve Clark, Frank Ellis, Roy Harris (Riley Hill), Jack Ingram, Stanley Price, Forrest Taylor, Dick Cramer, Eddie Dean
D: S. Roy Luby
S: Oliver Drake
SP: Arthur Hoerl
P: George W. Weeks

1430. PRAIRIE PALS
(PRC, September 4, 1942)
Bill "Cowboy Rambler" Boyd, Art Davis, Lee Powell, Charles King, Esther Estrella, John Merton, J. Merrill Holmes, Kermit Maynard, I. Stanford Jolley, Karl Hackett, Bob Burns, Al St. John, Al Taylor, Art Dillard, Curley Dresden, Frank McCarroll, Bill Patton, Carl Mathews, Frank Ellis, Jack Kinney, Morgan Flowers
D: Peter Stewart (Sam Newfield)
SP: Patricia Harper
P: Sigmund Neufeld

1431. SUNSET SERENADE
(Republic, September 14, 1942) 58 Mins.
Roy Rogers, George Hayes, Helen Parrish, Onslow Stevens, Joan Woodbury, Frank M. Thomas, Bob Nolan and the Sons of the Pioneers, Roy Barcroft, Jack Kirk, Dick Wessell, Rex Lease, Jack Ingram, Fred Burns, Budd Buster, Jack Rockwell, "Trigger"
D/AP: Joseph Kane
S: Robert Yost
SP: Earl Felton

1432. BELLS OF CAPISTRANO
(Republic, September 15, 1942) 73 Mins.
Gene Autry, Smiley Burnette, Virginia Grey, Lucien Littlefield, Morgan Conway, Claire DuBrey, Charles Cane, Joe Strauch, Jr., Marla Shelton, Tris Coffin, Jay Novello, Al Bridge, Terrisita Osta, Eddie Acuff, Jack O'Shea, Julian Rivero, William Forrest, Bill Telaak, Ken Christy, Dick Wessell, Ed Jauregui, Guy Usher, Ralph Peters, Joe McGuinn, Howard Hickman, William Kellogg, Carla Ramos, Fernando Ramos, Peggy Satterlee, Ray Jones, "Champion," Frankie Marvin
D: William Morgan
SP: Lawrence Kimble
AP: Harry Grey

1433. KING OF THE STALLIONS
(Monogram, September 18, 1942) 63 Mins.

Prairie Pals (PRC, 1942) — John Merton, Kermit Maynard, Bill "Cowboy Rambler" Boyd, and Art Davis

Shadows on the Sage (Republic, 1942) — Tom Tyler, Cheryl Walker, and Bob Steele

273

Chief Thunder Cloud, Chief Yowlachie, Dave O'Brien, Barbara Felker, Sally Cairns, Rick Vallin, Ted Adams, Gordon DeMain (G. D. Woods), Forrest Taylor, Joe Cody, Bill Wilkerson, Chief Many Treaties, George Sky Eagle, Charles Brunner, Iron Eyes Cody, Willow Bird

D/P: Edward Finney

SP: Sherman Lowe, Arthur St. Clair

1434. SHADOWS ON THE SAGE

(Republic, September 24, 1942) 58 Mins.

(*Three Mesquiteers* Series)

Bob Steele, Tom Tyler, Jimmie Dodd, Cheryl Walker, Harry Holman, Yakima Canutt, Tom London, Bryant Washburn, Griff Barnette, Freddie Mercer, Rex Lease, Curley Dresden, Eddie Dew, Horace B. Carpenter, Frank Brownlee, John Cason, Pascale Perry

D: Les Orlebeck

SP: J. Benton Cheney. Based on characters created by William Colt MacDonald

AP: Louis Gray

1435. BANDIT RANGER

(RKO, September 25, 1942)

Tim Holt, Cliff Edwards, Joan Barclay, Kenneth Harlan, LeRoy Mason, Glenn Strange, Jack Rockwell, Frank Ellis, Bob Kortman, Bud Geary, Dennis Moore, Russell Wade, Ernie Adams, Lloyd Ingraham, Tom London

D: Lesley Selander

SP: Bennett Cohen, Morton Grant

P: Bert Gilroy

1436. DEEP IN THE HEART OF TEXAS

(Universal, September 25, 1942) 62 Mins.

Johnny Mack Brown, Tex Ritter, Fuzzy Knight, Jennifer Holt, William Farnum, Jimmy Wakely Trio (Jimmy Wakely, Johnny Bond, Scotty Harrell), Harry Woods, Kenneth Harlan, Pat O'Malley, Roy Brent, Edmund Cobb, Earle Hodgins, Budd Buster, Frank Ellis, Tom Smith, Ray Jones, Eddie Polo

D: Elmer Clifton

S: Oliver Drake

SP: Grace Norton

AP: Oliver Drake

1437. OVERLAND TO DEADWOOD

(Columbia, September 25, 1942) 59 Mins.

Charles Starrett, Russell Hayden, Leslie Brooks, Cliff Edwards, Norman Willis, Francis Walker, Lynton Brent, Matt Willis, June Pickrell, Gordon DeMain, Art Mix, Herman Hack, Bud Osborne, Bud Geary

D: William Berke

SP: Paul Franklin

P: Jack Fier

1438. SIN TOWN

(Universal, September 25, 1942) 75 Mins.

Constance Bennett, Broderick Crawford, Patric Knowles, Anne Gwynne, Leo Carrillo, Andy Devine, Ward Bond, Arthur Aylesworth, Ralf Harolde, Charles Wagenheim, Billy Wayne, Hobart Bosworth, Bryant Washburn, Jack Mulhall

S: Ray Enright

SP: W. Scott Darling, Gerald Geraghty, Richard Brooks

P: George Waggner

1439. OVERLAND MAIL

(Universal, September 27, 1942) 15 Chaps.

Lon Chaney, Jr., Helen Parrish, Don Terry, Noah Beery, Jr., Bob Baker, Noah Beery, Sr., Tom Chatterton, Charles Stevens, Robert Barron, Harry Cording, Marguerite De La Motte, Ben Taggart, Jack Rockwell, Roy Harris (Riley Hill), Carleton Young, Ethan Laidlaw, Jack Clifford, Chief Thunder Cloud, Chief Many Treaties

D: Ford Beebe, John Rawlins

S: Johnston McCulley

SP: Paul Huston

P: Henry MacRae

Chapter Titles: (1) A Race with Disaster, (2) Flaming Havoc!, (3) The Menacing Herd, (4) The Bridge of Disaster, (5) Hurled to the Depths, (6) Death at the Stake, (7) The Path of Peril, (8) Imprisoned in Flames, (9) Hidden Danger, (10) Blazing Wagons, (11) The Trail of Terror, (12) In the Claws of the Cougar, (13) The Frenzied Mob, (14) The Toll of Treachery, (15) The Mail Goes Through

1440. BORDER ROUNDUP

(PRC, September 18, 1942) 57 Mins.

(*Lone Rider* Series)

George Houston, Al St. John, Dennis Moore, Patricia Knox, John Elliott, Charles King, I. Stanford Jolley, Edward Piel, Sr., Jimmy Aubrey, Dale Sherwood, Nick Thompson, Frank Ellis, Curley Dresden, Lynton Brent

D: Sam Newfield

P: Sigmund Neufeld

1441. ALONG THE SUNDOWN TRAIL

(PRC, October 1, 1942)

Bill (Cowboy Rambler) Boyd, Art Davis, Lee Powell, Julie Duncan, Kermit Maynard, Charles King, Howard Masters, Karl Hackett, John Merton, Jack Ingram, Ted Adams, Herman Hack, Frank Ellis, Jack Holmes, Reed Howes, Al St. John, Augie Gomez, Art Dillard, Al Taylor, Tex Palmer, Curley Dresden, Steve Clark, Hal Price, Jimmy Aubrey, Roy Bucko, Buck Bucko

D: Peter Stewart (Sam Newfield)

SP: Arthur St. Clair

P: Sigmund Neufeld

1442. RIDING THROUGH NEVADA

(Columbia, October 2, 1942)

Charles Starrett, Shirley Patterson, Arthur Hunnicutt, Jimmie Davis and his Rainbow Ramblers, Clancy Cooper, Davidson Clark, Minerva Urecal, Edmund Cobb, Ethan Laidlaw, Kermit Maynard, Art Mix, Stanley Brown

D: William Berke

SP: Gerald Geraghty

P: Jack Fier

1443. SHERIFF OF SAGE VALLEY

(PRC, October 2, 1942)   60 Mins.

(*Billy the Kid* Series)

Buster Crabbe, Al St. John, Tex (Dave) O'Brien, Maxine Leslie, Charles King, John Merton, Kermit Maynard, Hal Price, Curley Dresden, Jack Kirk, Lynton Brent

D: Sherman Scott (Sam Newfield)

SP: Milton Raison, George W. Sayre

P: Sigmund Neufeld

1444. WEST OF THE LAW

(Monogram, October 2, 1942)   60 Mins.

(*Rough Riders* Series)

Buck Jones, Tim McCoy, Raymond Hatton, Evelyn Cook, Milburn Morante, Harry Woods, Roy Barcroft, Bud McTaggart, George DeNormand, Jack Daley, Bud Osborne, Lynton Brent, "Silver"

D: Howard Bretherton

SP: Jess Bowers (Adele Buffington)

P: Scott R. Dunlap

1445. KING OF THE MOUNTIES

(Republic, October 10, 1942)   12 Chaps.

Allan Lane, Gilbert Emery, Russell Hicks, Peggy Drake, George Irving, Abner Biberman, William Vaughn, Nestor Paiva, Bradley Page, Douglass Dumbrille, William Bakewell, Duncan Renaldo, Francis Ford, Jay Novello, Anthony Warde, Norman Nesbitt, John Hiestand, Allen Jung, Paul Fung, Arvon Dale, Ken Terrell, John Roy, Bud Weiser, Duke Taylor, Frank Wayne, Pete Katchenaro, Harry Cording, Carleton Young, Tom Steele, Kam Tong, Earl Bunn, Hal Taliaferro, Duke Green, Stanley Price, Tommy Coats, Duke Taylor, Duke Green, Bob Jamison, Jack Kenney, Sam Serrano, King Kong, Joe Chambers, Forrest Taylor, David Sharpe

D: William Witney

SP: Taylor Caven, Ronald Davidson, William Lively, Joseph O'Donnell, Joseph Poland

AP: W. J. O'Sullivan

S: Zane Grey

Chapter Titles: (1) Phantom Invaders, (2) Road to Death, (3) Human Target, (4) Railroad Saboteurs, (5) Suicide Dive, (6) Blazing Barrier, (7) Perilous

West of the Law (Monogram, 1942) — Roy Barcroft, Tim McCoy, Harry Woods, and Buck Jones

Plunge, (8) Electrocuted, (9) Reign of Terror, (10) The Flying Coffin, (11) Deliberate Murder, (12) On to Victory

1446. THE LONE PRAIRIE

(Columbia, October 15, 1942) 58 Mins.
Russell Hayden, Dub Taylor, Bob Wills and his Texas Playboys, Lucille Lambert, John Merton, John Maxwell, Jack Kirk, Edmund Cobb, Ernie Adams, Kermit Maynard
D: William Berke
S: Ed Earl Repp, J. Benton Cheney
SP: Fred Mynton
P: Leon Barsha

1447. TEXAS TO BATAAN

(Monogram, October 16, 1942) 56 Mins.
(*Range Busters* Series)
John King, David Sharpe, Max Terhune, Marjorie Manners, Budd Buster, Kenne Duncan, Escolastico Baucin, Frank Ellis, Carl Mathews, Guy Kingsford, Steve Clark, Al Ferguson, Tom Steele, Tex Palmer
D: Robert Tansey
SP: Arthur Hoerl
P: George W. Weeks

1448. UNDERCOVER MAN

(United Artists, October 23, 1942) 68 Mins.
(*Hopalong Cassidy* Series)
William Boyd, Andy Clyde, Jay Kirby, Antonio Moreno, Nora Lane, Chris-Pin Martin, Esther Estrella, John Vosper, Eva Puig, Alan Baldwin, Jack Rockwell, Bennett George, Tony Roux, Pierce Lyden, Ted Wells, Martin Garralaga, Joe Dominguez, Earle Hodgins, Frank Ellis
D: Lesley Selander
SP: J. Benton Cheney. Based on characters created by Clarence E. Mulford
P: Harry Sherman
(First in this series to be distributed by United Artists, but a Paramount pressbook and advertising posters were prepared and issued on this film. Authors have examples of both)

1449. OUTLAWS OF PINE RIDGE

(Republic, October 27, 1942) 56 Mins.
Don Barry, Lynn Merrick, Noah Beery, Emmett Lynn, Clayton Moore, Donald Kirke, Forrest Taylor, Stanley Price, Francis Ford, Wheaton Chambers, George J. Lewis, Roy Brent, Ken Terrell, Al Taylor, Tex Terry, Jack O'Shea, Cactus Mack, Tom Steele, Horace B. Carpenter, Duke Green, Duke Taylor, Jess Cavin
D: William Witney
SP: Norman S. Hall
AP: Eddy White

1450. SILVER QUEEN

(United Artists, November 13, 1942) 80 Mins.
George Brent, Priscilla Lane, Bruce Cabot, Lynne Overman, Eugene Pallette, Janet Beecher, Guinn (Big Boy) Williams
D: Lloyd Bacon
SP: Bernard Schulbert, Cecile Kramer
P: Harry Sherman

1451. LITTLE JOE THE WRANGLER

(Universal, November 13, 1942) 64 Mins.
Johnny Mack Brown, Tex Ritter, Fuzzy Knight, Jennifer Holt, Hal Taliaferro, Glenn Strange, Florine McKinney, James Craven, Ethan Laidlaw, Jimmy Wakely Trio (Jimmy Wakely, Johnny Bond, Scotty Harrell)
D: Lewis Collins
S: Sherman Lowe
SP: Sherman Lowe, Elizabeth Beecher
AP: Oliver Drake

1452. VALLEY OF HUNTED MEN

(Republic, November 13, 1942) 60 Mins.
(*Three Mesquiteers* Series)
Bob Steele, Tom Tyler, Jimmie Dodd, Anna Marie Stewart, Edward Van Sloan, Roland Varno, Edythe Elliott, Arno Frey, Richard French, Robert Stevenson, George Neiss, Duke Aldon, Budd Buster, Hal Price, Billy Benedict, Charles Flynn, Rand Brooks, Kenne Duncan, Jack Kirk
D: John English
S: Charles Tetford
SP: Albert DeMond, Morton Grant. Based on characters created by William Colt MacDonald
AP: Louis Gray

1453. HEART OF THE GOLDEN WEST

(Republic, November 16, 1942) 65 Mins.
Roy Rogers, Smiley Burnette, George Hayes, Ruth Terry, Bob Nolan and the Sons of the Pioneers, Walter Catlett, Paul Harvey, Edmund McDonald, Leigh Whipper, Hal Taliaferro, Cactus Mack, Hank Bell, Fred Burns, Carl Mathews, Horace B. Carpenter, Frank McCarroll, Art Dillard, Hall Johnson Choir, "Trigger"
D/AP: Joseph Kane
SP: Earl Felton

1454. THE MYSTERIOUS RIDER

(PRC, November 20, 1942) 56 Mins.
(*Billy the Kid* Series)
Buster Crabbe, Al St. John, Caroline Burke, John Merton, Kermit Maynard, Jack Ingram, Slim Whitaker, Ted Adams, Guy Wilkerson, Edwin Brien, Frank Ellis
D: Sam Newfield
SP: Steve Braxton (Sam Robins)
P: Sigmund Neufeld

Northwest Rangers (MGM, 1942) — Granite-jawed Jack Holt gives advice to youngsters Darryl Hickman and Drew Roddy

Trail Riders (Monogram, 1942) — Max Terhune, David Sharpe, John King, and Steve Clark

1455. PIRATES OF THE PRAIRIE

(RKO, November 20, 1942)   57 Mins.

Tim Holt, Cliff Edwards, Nell O'Day, John Elliott, Roy Barcroft, Karl Hackett, Dick Cramer, Edward Cassidy, Eddie Dew, Merrill McCormack, Reed Howes, Charles King, Bud Geary, Lee Shumway, Russell Wade, Ben Corbett, Frank McCarroll, Artie Ortego, George Morrell

D: Howard Bretherton

SP: Doris Schroeder, J. Benton Cheney

P: Bert Gilroy

1456. OUTLAWS OF BOULDER PASS

(PRC, November 28, 1942)

(*Lone Rider* Series)

George Houston, Al St. John, Dennis Moore, Marjorie Manners, Charles King, I. Stanford Jolley, Karl Hackett, Ted Adams, Kenne Duncan, Frank Ellis, Steve Clark, Jimmy Aubrey, Budd Buster

D: Sam Newfield

SP: Steve Braxton

P: Sigmund Neufeld

1457. NORTHWEST RANGERS

(MGM, December 1, 1942)   64 Mins.

James Craig, William Lundigan, Patricia Dane, John Carradine, Jack Holt, Keenan Wynn, Grant Withers, Darryl Hickman, Drew Roddy

D: Joe Newman

S: Arthur Caesar

SP: Gordon Kahn

P: Samuel Marx

1458. PARDON MY GUN

(Columbia, December 1, 1942)   56 Mins.

Charles Starrett, Alma Carroll, Arthur Hunnicutt, Texas Jim Lewis and his Lone Star Cowboys, Noah Beery, Dick Curtis, Lloyd Bridges, Ted Mapes, Dave Harper, Roger Gray, Jack Kirk, Art Mix, George Morrell, Joel Friedkin, Guy Usher, Denver Dixon

D: William Berke

S/SP: Wyndham Gittens

P: Jack Fier

1459. TRAIL RIDERS

(Monogram, December 4, 1942)   55 Mins.

(*Range Busters* Series)

John King, David Sharpe, Max Terhune, Evelyn Finley, Forrest Taylor, Lynton Brent, Charles King, Kermit Maynard, John Curtis, Steve Clark, Kenne Duncan, Frank LaRue, Bud Osborne, Tex Palmer, Dick Cramer, Frank Ellis

D: Robert Tansey

SP: Frances Kavanaugh

P: George W. Weeks

1460. AMERICAN EMPIRE

(United Artists, December 11, 1942)

Richard Dix, Leo Carrillo, Preston Foster, Frances Gifford, Guinn (Big Boy) Williams, Robert Barrat, Jack LaRue, Cliff Edwards, Guy Rodin, Chris-Pin Martin, Richard Webb, William Farnum, Etta McDaniel, Hal Taliaferro, Tom London

D: William McGann

SP: J. Robert Bren, Gladys Atwater, Ben Grauman Kohn

P: Harry Sherman

1461. THE OLD CHISHOLM TRAIL

(Universal, December 11, 1942)   61 Mins.

Johnny Mack Brown, Tex Ritter, Fuzzy Knight, Jennifer Holt, Mary Correll, Earle Hodgins, Roy Barcroft, Edmund Cobb, Budd Buster, Jimmy Wakely Trio (Jimmy Wakely, Johnny Bond, Scotty Harrell)

D: Elmer Clifton

SP: Elmer Clifton

AP: Oliver Drake

1462. OVERLAND STAGECOACH

(PRC, December 11, 1942)

(*Lone Rider* Series)

Bob Livingston, Al St. John, Smoky (Dennis) Moore, Julie Duncan, Glenn Strange, Charles King, Art Mix, Budd Buster, Ted Adams, Julian Rivero, John Elliott, Tex Cooper

D: Sam Newfield

SP: Steve Braxton

P: Sigmund Neufeld

1463. A TORNADO IN THE SADDLE

(Columbia, December 15, 1942)   59 Mins.

Russell Hayden, Dub Taylor, Alma Carroll, Bob Wills and his Texas Playboys, Tris Coffin, Don Curtis, Jack Baxley, Leon McAulfie, Hailey Higgins, Tex Cooper, John Merton, Ted Mapes, Blackie Whiteford, Art Mix, Carl Sepulveda, Rube Dalroy, Jack Kirk, Jack Evans, George Morrell

D: William Berke

SP: Charles Francis Royal

P: Leon Barsha

1464. THE VALLEY OF VANISHING MEN

(Columbia, December 17, 1942)   15 Chaps.

Bill Elliott, Slim Summerville, Carmen Morales, Kenneth MacDonald, Jack Ingram, George Chesebro, John Shay, Tom London, Julian Rivero, Roy Barcroft, I. Stanford Jolley, Ted Mapes, Lane Chandler, Ernie Adams, Michael Vallon, Robert Fiske, Davidson Clark, Lane Bradford, Blackie Whiteford, Chief Thunder Cloud

D: Spencer G. Bennet

SP: Harry Fraser, Lewis Clay, George Gray
P: Larry Darmour
Chapter Titles: (1) Trouble in Canyon City, (2) The Mystery of the Ghost Town, (3) Danger Walks by Night, (4) Hillside Horror, (5) Guns in the Night, (6) The Bottomless Well, (7) The Man in the Gold Mask, (8) When the Devil Drives, (9) The Traitor's Shroud, (10) Death Strikes at Seven, (11) Satan in the Saddle, (12) The Mine of Missing Men, (13) Danger on Dome Rock, (14) The Door That Has No Key, (15) Empire's End

1465. DAWN ON THE GREAT DIVIDE
(Monogram, December 18, 1942) 63 Mins.
Buck Jones, Mona Barrie, Raymond Hatton, Rex Bell, Robert Lowery, Harry Woods, Christine McIntyre, Betty Blythe, Robert Frazer, Tris Coffin, Jan Wiley, Roy Barcroft, Dennis Moore, Steve Clark, Reed Howes, Bud Osborne, I. Stanford Jolley, Artie Ortego, George Morrell, Milburn Morante, Ray Jones, "Silver"
D: Howard Bretherton
SP: Jess Bowers (Adele Buffington)
P: Scott R. Dunlap

1466. THE RANGERS TAKE OVER
(PRC, December 25, 1942) 60 Mins.
(*Texas Rangers* Series)
Dave (Tex) O'Brien, Jim Newill, Iris Meredith, Guy Wilkerson, Cal Shrum's Rhythm Rangers, Forrest Taylor, I. Stanford Jolley, Charles King, Carl Mathews, Harry Harvey, Lynton Brent, Bud Osborne
D: Al Herman
SP: Elmer Clifton
P: Alfred Stern, Arthur Alexander

1467. SUNDOWN KID
(Republic, December 28, 1942) 57 Mins.
Don Barry, Ian Keith, Helen MacKellar, Linda Johnson, Emmett Lynn, Wade Crosby, Bob Kortman, Ted Adams, Kenne Duncan, Bud Geary, Fern Emmett, Kenneth Harlan, Jack Ingram, Jack Rockwell, Joe McGuinn, Cactus Mack
D: Elmer Clifton
SP: Norman S. Hall
AP: Eddy White

1468. RIDIN' DOWN THE CANYON
(Republic, December 30, 1942) 55 Mins.
Roy Rogers, George Hayes, Bob Nolan and the Sons of the Pioneers (Pat Brady, Hugh and Earl Farr, Tim Spencer, and Lloyd Perryman), Dee "Buzzy" Henry, Linda Hayes, Addison Richards, Lorna Gray (Adrian Booth), Olin Howlin, James Seay, Hal Taliaferro, Forrest Taylor, Roy Barcroft, Art Mix, Art Dillard, "Champion"
D: Joseph Kane
S: Robert Williams, Norman Houston
SP: Albert DeMond
AP: Harry Grey

FILMS OF 1943

1469. TWO FISTED JUSTICE
(Monogram, January 8, 1943) 61 Mins.
(*Range Busters* Series)
John King, David Sharpe, Max Terhune, Gwen Gaze, Joel Davis, John Elliott, Charles King, George Chesebro, Frank Ellis, Cecil Weston, Hal Price, Carl Mathews, Lynton Brent, Kermit Maynard, Dick Cramer, Tex Palmer, John Curtis
D: Robert Tansey
SP: William L. Nolte
P: George W. Weeks

1470. THUNDERING TRAILS
(Republic, January 25, 1943) 56 Mins.
(*Three Mesquiteers* Series)
Bob Steele, Tom Tyler, Jimmie Dodd, Nell O'Day, Sam Flint, Karl Hackett, Charles Miller, John James, Forrest Taylor, Ed Cassidy, Forbes Murray, Reed Howes, Bud Geary, Budd Buster, Vince Barnett, Lane Bradford, Cactus Mack, Edwin Parker, Al Taylor, Art Mix, Jack O'Shea
D: John English
SP: Norman S. Hall, Robert Yost. Based on characters created by William Colt MacDonald
AP: Louis Gray

1471. THE KID RIDES AGAIN
(PRC, January 27, 1943) 60 Mins.
(*Billy the Kid* Series)
Buster Crabbe, Al St. John, Iris Meredith, Glenn Strange, Charles King, I. Stanford Jolley, Edward Piel, Ted Adams, Karl Hackett, Kenne Duncan, Curley Dresden, Snub Pollard, John Merton, Slim Whitaker
D: Sherman Scott (Sam Newfield)
P: Sigmund Neufeld
SP: Fred Myton

1472. CALABOOSE
(United Artists, January 29, 1943) 45 Mins.
Jimmy Rogers, Noah Beery, Jr., Mary Brian, Bill

Henry, Paul Hurst, Marc Lawrence, William Davidson, Jean Porter, Iris Adrian, Sarah Edwards
D: Hal Roach, Jr.
S: Donald Hough
SP: Arnold Belgard
P: Glenn Tyron

1473. FIGHTING FRONTIER
(RKO-Radio, January 29, 1943) 57 Mins.
Tim Holt, Cliff Edwards, Ann Summers, Eddie Dew, William Gould, Davidson Clark, Slim Whitaker, Tom London, Monte Montague, Jack Rockwell, Bud Osborne, Russell Wade
D: Lambert Hillyer
S: Bernard McConville
SP: J. Benton Cheney, Norton S. Parker
P: Bert Gilroy

1474. THE FIGHTING BUCKAROO
(Columbia, February 1, 1943) 58 Mins.
Charles Starrett, Arthur Hunnicutt, Kay Harris, Stanley Brown, Wheeler Oakman, Forrest Taylor, Robert Stevens, Norma Jean Wooters, Roy Butler, Lane Bradford, Ernest Tubb with Johnny Luther's Ranch Boys
D: William Berke
SP: Luci Ward
P: Jack Fier

1475. TENTING TONIGHT ON THE OLD CAMP GROUND
(Universal, February 5, 1943) 58 Mins.
Johnny Mack Brown, Tex Ritter, Fuzzy Knight, Jennifer Holt, Jimmy Wakely Trio (Jimmy Wakely, Johnny Bond, and Scotty Harrell), John Elliott, Earle Hodgins, Rex Lease, Lane Chandler, Hank Worden, Al Bridge, Dennis Moore, Tom London, Bud Osborne, Reed Howes, Lynton Brent, George Plues, Ray Jones, George Eldridge
D: Lewis Collins
S: Harry Fraser
SP: Elizabeth Beecher
AP: Oliver Drake

1476. DEAD MAN'S GULCH
(Republic, February 12, 1943) 56 Mins.
Don Barry, Lynn Merrick, Clancy Cooper, Emmett Lynn, Rex Lease, Bud McTaggart, John Vosper, Jack Rockwell, Pierce Lyden, Lee Shumway, Al Taylor, Robert Frazer, Robert Fiske, Charlie Sullivan, Frank Brownlee
D: John English
S: Norman S. Hall
SP: Norman S. Hall, Robert Williams
P: Eddy White

1477. WILD HORSE RUSTLERS
(PRC, February 12, 1943)
(*Lone Rider* Series)

Bob Livingston, Al St. John, Linda Johnson, Lane Chandler, Stanley Price, Frank Ellis, Karl Hackett, Jimmy Aubrey, Kansas Moehring, Silver Harr
D: Sam Newfield
SP: Joe O'Donnell
P: Sigmund Neufeld

1478. RIDERS OF THE NORTHWEST MOUNTED
(Columbia, February 15, 1943)
Russell Hayden, Dub Taylor, Adele Mara, Bob Wills and the Texas Playboys, Dick Curtis, Richard Bailey, Jack Ingram, Leon McAuliffe, Vernon Steele
D: William Berke
SP: Fred Myton
P: Leon Barsha

1479. HAUNTED RANCH
(Monogram, February 19, 1943) 57 Mins.
(*Range Busters* Series)
John King, David Sharpe, Max Terhune, Rex Lease, Julie Duncan, Bud Osborne, Budd Buster, Steve Clark, Glenn Strange, Tex Palmer, Charles King, Fred Toones, Carl Mathews, Jimmy Aubrey, Hank Bell, Augie Gomez, Jim Corey
D: Robert Tansey
S: Arthur Hoerl
SP: Elizabeth Beecher
P: George W. Weeks

1480. THE OUTLAW
(Howard Hughes Productions, February, 1943) 123 Mins.
Jack Buetel, Jane Russell, Thomas Mitchell, Walter Houston, Mimi Aguglia, Joe Sawyer, Gene Rizzi
D: Howard Hughes (Howard Hawks withdrew shortly after production began)
SP: Jules Furtham
P: Howard Hughes
(20th Century-Fox was originally the intended distributor in 1941, and issued advertising materials and a pressbook on this film. Fox and Hughes split. Hughes put the film in San Francisco's Geary Theatre for a World Premiere in early February of 1943 and then withdrew it from distribution. United Artists released it on initial release. RKO-Radio had it on later reissues. See entry for February 8, 1946)

1481. CARSON CITY CYCLONE
(Republic, March 3, 1943) 55 Mins.
Don Barry, Lynn Merrick, Noah Beery, Emmett Lynn, Bryant Washburn, Stuart Hamblen, Roy Barcroft, Bud Osborne, Jack Kirk, Bud Geary, Curley Dresden, Tom London, Frank Ellis, Horace B. Carpenter, Edward Cassidy, Reed Howes,

Jack O'Shea, Tom Steele, Frank McCarroll, Roy Brent, Pascale Perry
D: Howard Bretherton
SP: Norman S. Hall
AP: Eddy White

1482. BAD MEN OF THUNDER GAP
(PRC, March 5, 1943) 57 Mins.
(*Texas Rangers* Series)
Dave (Tex) O'Brien, Jim Newill, Guy Wilkerson, Janet Shaw, Jack Ingram, Charles King, Michael Vallon, Lucille Vance, Tom London, I. Stanford Jolley, Bud Osborne, Jimmy Aubrey, Artie Ortego, Cal Shrum and his Rhythm Rangers (Robert Hoag, Don Weston, Rusty Cline, Art Wenzel)
D: Al Herman
SP: Elmer Clifton
P: Alfred Stern, Arthur Alexander

1483. IDAHO
(Republic, March 10, 1943) 70 Mins.
Roy Rogers, Smiley Burnette, Bob Nolan and the Sons of the Pioneers, Virginia Grey, Harry J. Shannon, Ona Munson, Dick Purcell, The Robert Mitchell Boychoir, Onslow Stevens, Arthur Hohl, Hal Taliaferro, Rex Lease, Tom London, Jack Ingram, James Bush, "Trigger"
D: Joseph Kane
AP: Joseph Kane
SP: Roy Chanslor, Olive Cooper

1484. THE BLOCKED TRAIL
(Republic, March 12, 1943) 58 Mins.
(*Three Mesquiteers* Series)
Bob Steele, Tom Tyler, Jimmie Dodd, Helen Deverall, George J. Lewis, Walter Sodering, Charles Miller, Kermit Maynard, Pierce Lyden, Carl Mathews, Hal Price, Budd Buster, Earle Hodgins, Bud Osborne, Al Taylor, Art Dillard, Bud Geary
D: Elmer Clifton
SP: John K. Butler, Jacquin Frank. Based on characters created by William Colt MacDonald
AP: Louis Gray

1485. HOPPY SERVES A WRIT
(United Artists, March 12, 1943) 67 Mins.
(*Hopalong Cassidy* Series)
William Boyd, Andy Clyde, Jay Kirby, Victor Jory, George Reeves, Jan Christy, Forbes Murray, Robert Mitchum, Earle Hodgins, Hal Taliaferro, Roy Barcroft, Byron Foulger, Ben Corbett, Art Mix
D: George Archainbaud
SP: Gerald Geraghty. Based on characters created by Clarence E. Mulford
P: Harry Sherman

1486. LAND OF HUNTED MEN
(Monogram, March 26, 1943) 58 Mins.
(*Range Busters* Series)
Ray Corrigan, Dennis Moore, Max Terhune, Phyllis Adair, Charles King, John Merton, Ted Mapes, Frank McCarroll, Forrest Taylor, Steve Clark, Fred Toones, Carl Sepulveda
D: S. Roy Luby
S: William Nolte
SP: Elizabeth Beecher
P: George W. Weeks

1487. FUGITIVE OF THE PLAINS
(PRC, April 1, 1943) 57 Mins.
(*Billy the Kid* Series)
Buster Crabbe, Al St. John, Maxine Leslie, Kermit Maynard, Jack Ingram, Karl Hackett, Hal Price, Budd Buster, Artie Ortego, Carl Sepulveda
D: Sam Newfield
SP: George Sayre
P: Sigmund Neufeld

1488. BORDER PATROL
(United Artists, April 2, 1943) 60 Mins.
(*Hopalong Cassidy* Series)
William Boyd, Andy Clyde, Jay Kirby, Claudia Drake, Russell Simpson, Duncan Renaldo, Cliff Parkinson, George Reeves, Robert Mitchum, Pierce Lyden, Merrill McCormack
D: Lesley Selander
SP: Michael Wilson. Based on characters created by Clarence E. Mulford
P: Harry Sherman

1489. THE GHOST RIDER
(Monogram, April 2, 1943) 58 Mins.
Johnny Mack Brown, Raymond Hatton, Beverly Boyd, Tom Seidel, Bud Osborne, Milburn Morante, Harry Woods, Edmund Cobb, Charles King, Artie Ortego, George DeNormand, Jack Daley, George Morrell
D: Wallace Fox
SP: Jess Bowers (Adele Buffington)
P: Scott R. Dunlap

1490. SAGEBRUSH LAW
(RKO-Radio, April 2, 1943)
Tim Holt, Cliff Edwards, Joan Barclay, John Elliott, Ed Cassidy, Karl Hackett, Roy Barcroft, Ernie Adams, John Merton, Bud McTaggart, Edmund Cobb, Otto Hoffman, Cactus Mack, Ben Corbett, Frank McCarroll, Bob McKenzie, Merrill Rodin, Dick Rush
D: Sam Nelson
SP: Bennett Cohen
P: Bert Gilroy

Border Patrol (United Artists, 1943) — William Boyd, Andy Clyde, and Jay Kirby

1491. KING OF THE COWBOYS
(Republic, April 9, 1943)   67 Mins.
Roy Rogers, Smiley Burnette, Peggy Moran, Bob Nolan and the Sons of the Pioneers, Gerald Mohr, Dorthea Kent, Lloyd Corrigan, James Bush, Russell Hicks, Irving Bacon, Stuart Hamblen, Emmett Vogan, Eddie Dean, Forrest Taylor, Dick Wessell, Jack Kirk, Edward Earle, Yakima Canutt, Charles King, Jack O'Shea, "Trigger"
D: Joseph Kane
S: Hal Long
SP: Olive Cooper, J. Benton Chaney
AP: Harry Grey

1492. MY FRIEND FLICKA
(TCF, April 10, 1943)   90 Mins.
(Technicolor)
Roddy McDowall, Preston Foster, Rita Johnson, James Bell, Jeff Corey, Diana Hale, Arthur Loft, Jimmy Aubrey
D: Harold Shumate
S: Mary O'Hara
SP: Lillie Hayward, Frances Edwards Faragoh
P: Ralph Dietrich

1493. SANTA FE SCOUTS
(Republic, April 16, 1943)   57 Mins.
(*Three Mesquiteers* Series)
Bob Steele, Tom Tyler, Jimmie Dodd, Lois Collier, John James, Tom Chatterton, Elizabeth Valentine, Tom London, Budd Buster, Jack Ingram, Kermit Maynard, Rex Lease, Ed Cassidy, Yakima Canutt, Jack Kirk, Curley Dresden, Reed Howes, Bud Geary, Carl Sepulveda, Al Taylor, Kenne Duncan
D: Howard Bretherton
SP: Morton Grant, Betty Burbridge. Based on characters created by William Colt MacDonald
AP: Louis Gray

1494. WILD HORSE STAMPEDE
(Monogram, April 16, 1943)   59 Mins.
(*Trail Blazers* Series)
Ken Maynard, Hoot Gibson, Betty Miles, Bob Baker, Ian Keith, Si Jenks, Donald Stewart, John Bridges, Glenn Strange, Reed Howes, Kenneth Harlan, Tom London, Tex Palmer, Forrest Taylor, I. Stanford Jolley, Kenne Duncan, Bob McKenzie, Chick Hannon

D: Alan James
S: Frances Kavanaugh
SP: Elizabeth Beecher
P: Robert Tansey

1495. DAREDEVILS OF THE WEST
(Republic, April 17, 1943)   12 Chaps.
Allan Lane, Kay Aldridge, Eddie Acuff, William Haade, Robert Frazer, Ted Adams, George J. Lewis, Stanley Andrews, Jack Rockwell, Charles Miller, John Hamilton, Budd Buster, Kenneth Harlan, Kenne Duncan, Rex Lease, Chief Thunder Cloud, Duke Green, Eddie Parker, Ray Jones, Joe Yrigoyen, Bill Yrigoyen, Many Treaties, Tom Steele, Jack O'Shea, George Magrill, Earl Bunn, Pierce Lyden, George Plues, Al Taylor, Ralph Bucko, Edmund Cobb, Frank McCarroll, Augie Gomez, Harry Smith, Crane Whitley, Tom London, George Pembroke, Allen Pomeroy, Edward Cassidy, Herbert Rawlinson, Tex Cooper, Babe Defreest, George Sky Eagle, Charles Soldani, George Sowards, Bryan Topetchy
D: John English
SP: Ronald Davidson, Basil Dickey, Joseph O'Donnell, Joseph Poland, William Lively
AP: W. J. O'Sullivan
Chapter Titles: (1) Valley of Death, (2) Flaming Prison, (3) The Killer Strikes, (4) Tunnel of Terror, (5) Fiery Tomb, (6) Redskin Raiders, (7) Perilous Pursuit, (8) Dance of Doom, (9) Terror Trail, (10) Suicide Showdown, (11) Cavern of Cremation, (12) Frontier Justice

1496. SADDLES AND SAGEBRUSH
(Columbia, April 27, 1943)
Russell Hayden, Dub Taylor, Bob Wills and the Texas Playboys, Ann Savage, William Wright, Frank LaRue, Wheeler Oakman, Edmund Cobb, Jack Ingram, Joe McGuinn, Ray Jones, Art Mix, Blackie Whiteford, Ben Corbett, Bob Burns
D: William Berke
SP: Ed Earl Repp
P: Leon Barsha

1497. CHEYENNE ROUNDUP
(Universal, April 29, 1943)   59 Mins.
Johnny Mack Brown, Fuzzy Knight, Tex Ritter, Jennifer Holt, Jimmy Wakely Trio (Jimmy Wakely, Johnny Bond, Scotty Harrell), Harry Woods, Roy Barcroft, Robert Barron, Budd Buster, Gil Patric, Carl Mathews, Kermit Maynard, William Desmond, Kenne Duncan
D: Ray Taylor
S: Elmer Clifton
SP: Elmer Clifton, Bernard McConville

1498. CALLING WILD BILL ELLIOTT
(Republic, April 30, 1943)   55 Mins.
Bill Elliott, George Hayes, Anne Jeffreys, Herbert Heyes, "Buzzy" Dee Henry, Fred Kohler, Jr., Roy Barcroft, Charles King, Frank Hagney, Bud Geary, Lynton Brent, Frank McCarroll, Eve March, Burr Caruth, Forbes Murray, Ted Mapes, Cliff Parkinson, Herman Hack, Yakima Canutt
D: Spencer Bennet
S: Luci Ward
SP: Anthony Coldeway
AP: Harry Grey

1499. DEATH RIDES THE PLAINS
(PRC, May 7, 1943)
(*Lone Rider* Series)
Bob Livingston, Al St. John, Nica Doret, Ray Bennett, I. Stanford Jolley, Kermit Maynard, George Chesebro, John Elliott, Slim Whitaker, Karl Hackett, Frank Ellis, Ted Mapes, Dan White, Jimmy Aubrey
D: Sam Newfield
S: Patricia Harper
SP: Joe O'Donnell
P: Sigmund Neufeld

1500. THE OX-BOW INCIDENT
(20th C. Fox, May 10, 1943)   75 Mins.
Henry Fonda, Dana Andrews, Mary Beth Hughes, Anthony Quinn, William Eythe, Henry (Harry) Morgan, Jane Darwell, Matt Briggs, Harry Davenport, Frank Conroy, Marc Lawrence, Paul Hurst, Victor Kilian, Chris-Pin Martin, Ted North, George Meeker, Almira Sessions, Margaret Hamilton, Dick Rich, Francis Ford, Stanley Andrews, William Benedict, Rondo Hatton, Paul Burns, Leigh Whipper, George Chandler, George Lloyd
D: William Wellman
S: Walter Van Tilburg Clark
SP/P: Lamar Trotti

1501. WEST OF TEXAS
(PRC, May 10, 1943)
(*Texas Rangers* Series)
(Reissued as *Shootin' Irons*)
Dave O'Brien, Jim Newill, Guy Wilkerson, Frances Gladwin, Madilyn Hare, Robert Barron, Tom London, Jack Rockwell, Jack Ingram, Art Fowler
D/SP: Oliver Drake
P: Alfred Stern, Arthur Alexander

1502. BUCKSKIN FRONTIER
(United Artists, May 14, 1943)   74 Mins.
Richard Dix, Jane Wyatt, Albert Dekker, Lee J.

Cobb, Victor Jory, Lola Lane, Max Baer, Joe
Sawyer, George Reeves, Henry Allen, Francis
McDonald, Bill Nestell
D: Lesley Selander
SP: Norman Houston
S: Harry Sinclair Drango
P: Harry Sherman

1503. WESTERN CYCLONE

(PRC, May 14, 1943)   56 Mins.
(*Billy the Kid* Series)
Buster Crabbe, Al St. John, Marjorie Manners, Karl
Hackett, Milt Kibbee, Kermit Maynard, Glenn
Strange, Charles King, Hal Price, Frank Ellis,
Frank McCarroll, Artie Ortego, Herman Hack, Al
Haskell
D: Sam Newfield
SP: Patricia Harper
P: Sigmund Neufeld

1504. DAYS OF OLD CHEYENNE

(Republic, May 15, 1943)   56 Mins.
Don Barry, Lynn Merrick, William Haade, Emmett
Lynn, Herbert Rawlinson, Charles Miller, Wil-
liam Ruhl, Harry McKim, Bob Kortman, Nolan
Leary, Kenne Duncan, Edwin Parker, Bob Reeves,
Art Dillard
D: Elmer Clifton
SP: Norman S. Hall
AP: Eddy White

1505. THE AVENGING RIDER

(RKO-Radio, May 21, 1943)   55 Mins.
Tim Holt, Cliff Edwards, Ann Summers, David-
son Clark, Norman Willis, Karl Hackett, Earle
Hodgins, Ed Cassidy, Kenne Duncan, Bud
McTaggert, Bud Osborne, Bob Kortman, Guy
Usher, Lloyd Ingraham, David Sharpe
D: Sam Nelson
S: Harry O. Hoyt
SP: Morton Grant
P: Bert Gilroy

1506. PRAIRIE CHICKENS

(United Artists, Hal Roach, May 21, 1943)
46 Mins.
Jimmy Rogers, Noah Beery, Jr., Joe Sawyer, Mar-
jorie Woodworth, Rosemary LaPlanche, Ray-
mond Hatton, Jack Norton, Mary Ann Deighton,
Ed Gargan, Frank Faylen, Dudley Dickerson
D: Hal Roach, Jr.
SP: Arnold Belgarde, Earle Snell
S: Donald Hough
P: Fred Guoil

1507. RIDERS OF THE RIO GRANDE

(Republic, May 21, 1943)   55 Mins.
(*Three Mesquiteers* Series)
Bob Steele, Tom Tyler, Jimmie Dodd, Lorraine Mil-
ler, Edward Van Sloan, Rick Vallin, Harry Worth,
Roy Barcroft, Charles King, Jack Ingram, John
James, Jack O'Shea, Henry Hall, Bud Osborne
D: Howard Bretherton
SP: Albert DeMond. Based on characters created by
William Colt MacDonald
AP: Louis Gray

1508. THE DESPERADOES

(Columbia, May 25, 1943)   85 Mins.
(Technicolor)
Randolph Scott, Glenn Ford, Claire Trevor, Edgar
Buchanan, Guinn (Big Boy) Williams, Evelyn
Keyes, Raymond Walburn, Porter Hall, Joan
Woodbury, Bernard Nedell, Irving Beacon, Glenn
Strange, Ethan Laidlaw, Slim Whitaker, Edward
Pawley, Chester Clute, Bill Wolfe, Francis Ford,
Tom Smith, Jack Kinney, Silver Harr
D: Charles Vidor
S: Max Brand
SP: Robert Carson
P: Harry Joe Brown

1509. LAW OF THE NORTHWEST

(Columbia, May 27, 1943)   57 Mins.
Charles Starrett, Shirley Patterson, Arthur Hunni-
cutt, Stanley Brown, Davidson Clark, Don Curtis,
Douglas Levitt, Reginald Barlow, Douglas Drake
D: William Berke
SP: Luci Ward
P: Jack Fier

1510. THE LEATHER BURNERS

(United Artists, May 28, 1943)   58 Mins.
(*Hopalong Cassidy* Series)
William Boyd, Andy Clyde, Jay Kirby, Victor Jory,
George Reeves, Shelley Spencer, George Givot,
Bobby Larson, Hal Taliaferro, Forbes Murray,
Bob Mitchum, Bob Kortman, Herman Hack
D: Joseph E. Henabery
S: Bliss Lomax
SP: Jo Pagano. Based on characters created by
Clarence E. Mulford
P: Harry Sherman

1511. COWBOY COMMANDOS

(Monogram, June 4, 1943)   55 Mins.
(*Range Busters* Series)
Ray Corrigan, Dennis Moore, Max Terhune, Evelyn
Finley, Johnny Bond, Budd Buster, John Merton,
Edna Bennett, Steve Clark, Bud Osborne, Frank

Ellis, Hank Bell, Denver Dixon, Artie Ortego, Ray Jones, Augie Gomez, George Chesebro, Carl Sepulveda
D: S. Roy Luby
SP: Elizabeth Beecher
P: George W. Weeks

1512. RAIDERS OF SAN JOAQUIN
(Universal, June 4, 1943)   60 Mins.
Johnny Mack Brown, Tex Ritter, Fuzzy Knight, Jennifer Holt, Jimmy Wakely Trio (Jimmy Wakely, Johnny Bond, and Scotty Harrell), Henry Hall, Joseph Bernard, George Eldridge, Henry Rocquemore, Carl Sepulveda, John Elliott, Michael Vallon, Jack O'Shea, Jack Ingram, Robert Thompson, Scoop Martin, Roy Brent, Budd Buster, Earle Hodgins, Slim Whitaker
D: Lewis Collins
S: Patricia Harper
SP: Elmer Clifton, Morgan Cox
AP: Oliver Drake

1513. THE MAN FROM THUNDER RIVER
(Republic, June 11, 1943)   57 Mins.
Bill Elliott, George Hayes, Anne Jeffreys, Ian Keith, John James, Georgia Cooper, Jack Ingram, Eddie

Lee, Charles King, Bud Geary, Jack Rockwell, Ed Cassidy, Roy Brent, Al Taylor, Al Bridge, Edmund Cobb, Robert Barron, Jack O'Shea, Curley Dresden, Frank McCarroll
D: John English
SP: J. Benton Cheney
AP: Harry Grey

1514. SONG OF TEXAS
(Republic, June 14, 1943)   69 Mins.
Roy Rogers, Sheila Ryan, Barton MacLane, Harry Shannon, Pat Brady, Arline Judge, Bob Nolan and the Sons of the Pioneers, William Haade, Hal Taliaferro, Yakima Canutt, Tom London, Forrest Taylor, Eve March, Alex Nehera Dancers, "Trigger"
D: Joseph Kane
SP: Winston Miller
AP: Harry Grey

1515. BORDER BUCKAROOS
(PRC, June 15, 1943)   60 Mins.
(*Texas Rangers* Series)
Dave O'Brien, Jim Newil!, Guy Wilkerson, Christine McIntyre, Eleanor Counts, Jack Ingram, Ethan Laidlaw, Charles King, Michael Vallon, Kenne

The Man from Thunder River (Republic, 1943) — Bill Elliott, Roy Brent, Jack Rockwell, Anne Jeffreys, Georgia Cooper, John James, and Al Taylor

285

Duncan, Reed Howes, Kermit Maynard, Bud Osborne
D: Oliver Drake
SP: Oliver Drake
P: Alfred Stern, Arthur Alexander

1516. COLT COMRADES

(United Artists, June 18, 1943) 67 Mins.

(*Hopalong Cassidy* Series)

William Boyd, Andy Clyde, Jay Kirby, George Reeves, Gayle Lord, Earle Hodgins, Victor Jory, Douglas Fowley, Herbert Rawlinson, Bob Mitchum
D: Lesley Selander
SP: Michael Wilson. Based on characters created by Clarence E. Mulford
P: Harry Sherman

1517. WOLVES OF THE RANGE

(PRC, June 21, 1943)

(*Lone Rider* Series)

Bob Livingston, Al St. John, Frances Gladwin, I. Stanford Jolley, Karl Hackett, Ed Cassidy, Jack Ingram, Kenne Duncan, Budd Buster, Robert Hill, Slim Whitaker, Jack Holmes, Roy Bucko
D: Sam Newfield
SP: Joe O'Donnell
P: Sigmund Neufeld

1518. FRONTIER FURY

(Columbia, June 24, 1943) 55 Mins.

Charles Starrett, Arthur Hunnicutt, Roma Aldrich, Clancy Cooper, I. Stanford Jolley, Edmund Cobb, Bruce Bennett, Ted Mapes, Bill Wilkerson, Stanley Brown, Joel Friedkin, Frank LaRue, Lew Meehan, Chief Yowlachie, Johnny Bond, Jimmy Davis and his Singing Buckaroos
D: William Berke
SP: Betty Burbridge
P: Jack Fier

1519. FUGITIVE FROM SONORA

(Republic, July 1, 1943) 56 Mins.

Don Barry, Lynn Merrick, Wally Vernon, Harry Cording, Ethan Laidlaw, Frank McCarroll, Pierce Lyden, Gary Bruce, Kenne Duncan, Tommy Coats, Karl Hackett, Charlie Sullivan, Slim Whitaker, Art Dillard, Ray Jones
D: Howard Bretherton
SP: Norman S. Hall
P: Eddy White

1520. THE STRANGER FROM PECOS

(Monogram, July 16, 1943) 55 Mins.

Johnny Mack Brown, Raymond Hatton, Kirby Grant, Christine McIntyre, Steve Clark, Sam Flint, Roy Barcroft, Robert Frazer, Edmund Cobb,

Charles King, Bud Osborne, Artie Ortego, Tom London, Kermit Maynard, Milburn Morante, Lynton Brent, Carol Henry, George Morrell
D: Lambert Hillyer
SP: Jess Bowers (Adele Buffington)
P: Scott R. Dunlap

1521. RED RIVER ROBIN HOOD

(RKO-Radio, July 23, 1943)

Tim Holt, Cliff Edwards, Barbara Moffett, Eddie Dew, Otto Hoffman, Russell Wade, Tom London, Earle Hodgins, Bud McTaggart, Reed Howes, Kenne Duncan, David Sharpe, Bob McKenzie, Jack Rockwell, Jack Montgomery
D: Lesley Selander
S: Whitney J. Stanton
SP: Bennett Cohen
P: Bert Gilroy

1522. ROBIN HOOD OF THE RANGE

(Columbia, July 29, 1943) 57 Mins.

Charles Starrett, Arthur Hunnicutt, Kay Harris, Jimmy Wakely Trio, Stanley Brown, Kenneth MacDonald, Douglas Drake, Bud Osborne, Edward Piel, Sr., Frank LaRue, Frank McCarroll, Ray Jones, Johnny Bond, Merrill McCormack
D: William Berke
SP: Betty Burbridge
P: Jack Fier

1523. FRONTIER BADMAN

(Universal, August 6, 1943) 77 Mins.

Robert Paige, Diana Barrymore, Leo Carrillo, Andy Devine, Noah Beery, Jr., Anne Gwynne, Tex Ritter, Thomas Gomez, William Farnum, Lon Chaney, Jr., Robert Homans, Arthur Loft, Tom Fadden, Frank Lackteen
D: William McGann (and Ford Beebe uncredited)
SP: Gerald Geraghty, Morgan Cox
AP: Ford Beebe

1524. THE LAW RIDES AGAIN

(Monogram, August 6, 1943) 58 Mins.

(*Trail Blazers* Series)

Ken Maynard, Hoot Gibson, Betty Miles, Jack LaRue, Chief Thunder Cloud, Hank Bell, Bryant Washburn, Emmett Lynn, Kenneth Harlan, John Bridges, Fred Hoose, Charles Murray, Jr., Chief Many Treaties, John Merton
D: Alan James
SP: Frances Kavanaugh
P: Robert Tansey

1525. THE LONE STAR TRAIL

(Universal, August 6, 1943) 58 Mins.

Johnny Mack Brown, Tex Ritter, Fuzzy Knight, Jennifer Holt, Earle Hodgins, Jack Ingram, Bob

Mitchum, George Eldridge, Michael Vallon, Ethan Laidlaw, Harry Strang, Fred Graham, William Desmond, Henry Rocquemore, Denver Dixon, Eddie Parker, Jimmy Wakely Trio (Jimmy Wakely, Johnny Bond, Scotty Harrell), Billy Engle, Carl Mathews, Bob Reeves, Tom Steele
D: Ray Taylor
S: Victor Halperin
SP: Oliver Drake
AP: Oliver Drake

1526. FIGHTING VALLEY
(PRC, August 8, 1943)   58 Mins.
(*Texas Rangers* Series)
Dave O'Brien, Jim Newill, Guy Wilkerson, Patti McCarty, John Merton, Robert Rice, Stanley Price, Mary MacLaren, John Elliott, Charles King, Dan White, Carl Mathews, Curley Dresden, Jimmy Aubrey, Jess Cavin
D: Oliver Drake
SP: Oliver Drake
P: Alfred Stern, Arthur Alexander

1527. SILVER SPURS
(Republic, August 12, 1943)   65 Mins.
Roy Rogers, Smiley Burnette, John Carradine, Phyllis Brooks, Jerome Cowan, Joyce Compton, Bob Nolan and the Sons of the Pioneers, Hal Taliaferro, Jack Kirk, Kermit Maynard, Dick Wessell, Forrest Taylor, Byron Foulger, Charles Wilson, Pat Brady, Jack O'Shea, Slim Whitaker, Arthur Loft, Eddy Waller, Tom London, Bud Osborne, Fred Burns, Henry Wills, "Trigger"
D: Joseph Kane
SP: John K. Butler, J. Benton Cheney
AP: Harry Grey

1528. BLACK HILLS EXPRESS
(Republic, August 15, 1943)   56 Mins.
Don Barry, Wally Vernon, Ariel Heath, George J. Lewis, William Halligan, Hooper Atchley, Charles Miller, Pierce Lyden, Jack Rockwell, LeRoy Mason, Milt Kibbee, Wheaton Chambers, Marshall Reed, Curley Dresden, Ray Jones, Frank Ellis, Al Taylor, Bob Kortman, Carl Sepulveda
D: John English
S: Fred Myton
SP: Norman Hall
P: Eddy White

1529. CATTLE STAMPEDE
(PRC, August 16, 1943)   60 Mins.
(*Billy the Kid* Series)
Buster Crabbe, Al St. John, Frances Gladwin, Charles King, Ed Cassidy, Hansel Warner, Ray Bennett, Frank Ellis, Steve Clark, Roy Brent, John Elliott, Budd Buster, Hank Bell, Tex Cooper, Ted

Adams, Frank McCarroll, Ray Jones, Rose Plummer, George Morrell
D: Sam Newfield
SP: Joe O'Donnell
P: Sigmund Neufeld

1530. A LADY TAKES A CHANCE
(RKO-Radio, August 19, 1943)   86 Mins.
Jean Arthur, John Wayne, Charles Winninger, Phil Silvers, Mary Field, Don Costello, John Philliber, Grady Sutton, Grant Withers, Hans Conreid, Peggy Carroll, Ariel Heath, Sugar Geise, John Blair, Tom Fadden, Eddy Waller, Nina Quartero, Alex Melesh, Paul Scott, Charles D. Brown, Butch and Buddy, The Three Peppers
D: William Seiter
S: Jo Swerling
SP: Robert Audrey
P: Frank Ross

1531. THE RENEGADE
(PRC, August 25, 1943)
(*Billy the Kid* Series)
Buster Crabbe, Al St. John, Lois Ransom, Karl Hackett, Ray Bennett, Frank Hagney, Jack Rockwell, Tom London, George Chesebro, Jimmy Aubrey, Carl Sepulveda, Dan White, Wally West
D: Sam Newfield
S: George Milton (George Sayre/Milton Raison)
SP: Joe O'Donnell
P: Sigmund Neufeld

1532. BLACK MARKET RUSTLERS
(Monogram, August 27, 1943)   58 Mins.
(*Range Busters* Series)
Ray Corrigan, John King, Max Terhune, Evelyn Finley, Steve Clark, Glenn Strange, Carl Sepulveda, George Chesebro, Hank Worden, Frank Ellis, John Merton, Frosty Royce, Hal Price, Stanley Price, Wally West, Carl Mathews, Tex Cooper, Claire McDowell, Foxy Callahan
D: S. Roy Luby
SP: Patricia Harper
P: George W. Weeks

1533. LAW OF THE SADDLE
(PRC, August 28, 1943)   59 Mins.
(*Lone Rider* Series)
Bob Livingston, Al St. John, Betty Miles, Lane Chandler, John Elliott, Reed Howes, Curley Dresden, Al Ferguson, Frank Ellis, Frank Hagney, Jimmy Aubrey
D: Melville De Lay
SP: Fred Myton
P: Sigmund Neufeld

1534. APACHE TRAIL
(MGM, September 1, 1943) 66 Mins.
Lloyd Nolan, Donna Reed, William Lundigan, Ann Ayars, Connie Gilchrist, Chill Wills, Miles Mander, Gloria Holden, Ray Teal, Grant Withers, Fuzzy Knight, Trevor Bardette, Tito Renaldo, Frank M. Thomas, George Watts
D: Richard Thorpe
S: Ernest Haycox
SP: Maurice Geraghty
P: Samuel Marx

1535. SIX GUN GOSPEL
(Monogram, September 3, 1943) 59 Mins.
Johnny Mack Brown, Raymond Hatton, Inna Gest, Eddie Dew, Roy Barcroft, Kenneth MacDonald, Edmund Cobb, Milburn Morante, Artie Ortego, L. W. (Lynton) Brent, Bud Osborne, Kernan Cripps, Jack Daley, Mary MacLaren
D: Lambert Hillyer
SP: Ed Earl Repp, Jess Bowers (Adele Buffington)
P: Scott R. Dunlap

1536. BLAZING FRONTIER
(PRC, September 4, 1943) 59 Mins.
(*Billy the Kid* Series)
Buster Crabbe, Al St. John, Marjorie Manners, Milt Kibbee, I. Stanford Jolley, Kermit Maynard, Frank Hagney, George Chesebro, Frank Ellis, Hank Bell, Jimmy Aubrey
D: Sam Newfield
SP: Patricia Harper
P: Sigmund Neufeld

1537. TRAIL OF TERROR
(PRC, September 7, 1943) 63 Mins.
(*Texas Rangers* Series)
Dave O'Brien, Jim Newill, Guy Wilkerson, Patricia Knox, Jack Ingram, I. Stanford Jolley, Budd Buster, Kenne Duncan, Frank Ellis, Robert Hill, Dan White, Jimmy Aubrey, Rose Plummer, Torn Smith, Artie Ortego
D/SP: Oliver Drake
P: Alfred Stern, Arthur Alexander

1538. THE KANSAN
(United Artists, September 10, 1943) 79 Mins.
Richard Dix, Jane Wyatt, Victor Jory, Albert Dekker, Eugene Pallette, Robert Armstrong, Clem Bevans, Rod Cameron, Francis McDonald, Willie Best, Glenn Strange, Douglas Fowley, Jack Norton, Eddy Waller, Ray Bennett, Sam Flint, Merrill McCormack
D: George Archainbaud
S: Frank Gruber
SP: Harold Shumate
P: Harry Sherman

1539. HAIL TO THE RANGERS
(Columbia, September 16, 1943) 57 Mins.
Charles Starrett, Arthur Hunnicutt, Leota Atcher, Robert Atcher, Norman Willis, Lloyd Bridges, Ted Adams, Ernie Adams, Tom London, Davidson Clark, Jack Kirk, Edmund Cobb, Budd Buster, Art Mix, Eddie Laughton, Dick Botiller
D: William Berke
SP: Gerald Geraghty
P: Jack Fier

1540. BEYOND THE LAST FRONTIER
(Republic, September 18, 1943) 57 Mins.
(*John Paul Revere* Series)
Eddie Dew, Smiley Burnette, Lorraine Miller, Bob Mitchum, Harry Woods, Kermit Maynard, Ernie Adams, Richard Cramer, Charles Miller, Jack Kirk, Wheaton Chambers, Jack Rockwell, Cactus Mack, Al Taylor, Art Dillard, Frank O'Connor, Tom Steele, Henry Wills, Curley Dresden
D: Howard Bretherton
SP: John K. Butler, Morton Grant
AP: Louis Gray

1541. ARIZONA TRAIL
(Universal, September 24, 1943)
Tex Ritter, Fuzzy Knight, Dennis Moore, Janet Shaw, Johnny Bond and his Red River Valley Boys, Jack Ingram, Erville Alderson, Joseph Greene, Glenn Strange, Dan White, Art Fowler, Bill Wolfe, Roy Brent, Ray Jones
D: Vernon Keays
SP: William Lively
AP: Oliver Drake

1542. DEATH VALLEY MANHUNT
(Republic, September 25, 1943) 55 Mins.
Bill Elliott, George Hayes, Anne Jeffries, Weldon Heyburn, Herbert Heyes, Davidson Clark, Pierce Lyden, Charles Murray, Jr., Jack Kirk, Eddie Phillips, Al Taylor, Bud Geary, Marshall Reed, Edward Keane, Curley Dresden
D: John English
S: Fred Myton, Eddy White
SP: Norman Hall, Anthony Coldeway
AP: Eddy White

1543. RAIDERS OF RED GAP
(PRC, September 30, 1943)
(*Lone Rider* Series)
Bob Livingston, Al St. John, Myrna Dell, Ed Cassidy, Charles King, Slim Whitaker, Kermit Maynard, Roy Brent, Frank Ellis, George Chesebro, Bud Osborne, Jimmy Aubrey, Merrill McCormack, George Morrell, Wally West, Reed Howes
D: Sam Newfield
SP: Joe O'Donnell
P: Sigmund Neufeld

Raiders of Red Gap (PRC, 1943) — Charles King (on table), Frank Ellis, Bob Livingston, Slim Whitaker, and Al "Fuzzy" St. John

1544. BAR 20

(United Artists, October 1, 1943)   54 Mins.
(*Hopalong Cassidy* Series)
William Boyd, Andy Clyde, Dustin Farnum, George Reeves, Victor Jory, Douglas Fowley, Betty Blythe, Bob Mitchum, Francis McDonald, Earle Hodgins, Buck Bucko
D: Lesley Selander
SP: Morton Grant, Norman Houston, Michael Wilson. Based on characters created by Clarence E. Mulford
P: Harry Sherman

1545. BORDERTOWN GUNFIGHTERS

(Republic, October 1, 1943)   55 Mins.
Bill Elliott, George Hayes, Anne Jeffreys, Ian Keith, Harry Woods, Roy Barcroft, Bud Geary, Karl Hackett, Carl Sepulveda, Charles King, Edward Keane, Frank McCarroll, Wheaton Chambers, Ken Terrell, Bill Wolfe, Rose Plummer, Al Haskell, Foxy Callahan, Neal Hart, Frosty Royce, Buck Bucko, Marshall Reed, Jim Massey
D: Howard Bretherton
S: Norman S. Hall
AP: Eddy White

1546. BLAZING GUNS

(Monogram, October 8, 1943)   55 Mins.
(*Trail Blazers* Series)
Ken Maynard, Hoot Gibson, Kay Forrester, LeRoy Mason, Roy Brent, Lloyd Ingraham, Charles King, Weldon Heyburn, Dan White, Frank Ellis, Kenne Duncan, Emmett Lynn
D: Robert Tansey
SP: Frances Kavanaugh
P: Robert Tansey

1547. OUTLAWS OF STAMPEDE PASS

(Monogram, October 15, 1943)   58 Mins.
Johnny Mack Brown, Raymond Hatton, Ellen Hall, Harry Woods, Milburn Morante, Edmund Cobb, Sam Flint, Jon Dawson, Charles King, Mauritz Hugo, Art Mix, Cactus Mack, Artie Ortego, Eddie Burns, Bill Wolfe, Hal Price, Dan White, Kansas Moehring, Tex Cooper
D: Wallace Fox
S: Johnston McCulley
SP: Jess Bowers (Adele Buffington)
P: Scott R. Dunlap

1548. THE MAN FROM THE RIO GRANDE

(Republic, October 18, 1943)   57 Mins.
Don Barry, Wally Vernon, Nancy Gay, Twinkle Watts, Kirk Alyn, Roy Barcroft, Harry Cording, Paul Scardon, LeRoy Mason, Earle Hodgins, Ken Terrell, Robert Homans, Tom London, Bud Geary, Kenne Duncan, Kansas Moehring, Jack Kirk, Jack O'Shea
D: Howard Bretherton

SP: Norman S. Hall
P: Eddy White

1549. THE RETURN OF THE RANGERS
(PRC, October 26, 1943) 60 Mins.
(*Texas Rangers* Series)
Dave O'Brien, Jim Newill, Guy Wilkerson, Nell
O'Day, Glenn Strange, Emmett Lynn, I. Stanford
Jolley, Robert Barron, Henry Hall, Harry Harvey,
Dick Alexander, Charles King
D: Elmer Clifton
SP: Elmer Clifton
P: Arthur Alexander

1550. WAGON TRACKS WEST
(Republic, October 28, 1943) 55 Mins.
Bill Elliott, George Hayes, Tom Tyler, Anne Jeff-
reys, Rick Vallin, Robert Frazer, Roy Barcroft,
Charles Miller, Tom London, Cliff Lyons, Jack
Rockwell, Kenne Duncan, Minerva Urecal, Hal
Price, William Nestell, Frank Ellis, Hank Bell, Jack
O'Shea, Ray Jones, Jack Ingram, Curley Dresden,
Frank McCarroll, Marshall Reed, Ben Corbett,
Jack Montgomery, Tom Steele, J. W. Cody, Roy
Butler

D: Howard Bretherton
SP: William Lively
AP: Louis Gray

1551. BULLETS AND SADDLES
(Monogram, October 29, 1943) 54 Mins.
(*Range Busters* Series)
Ray Corrigan, Dennis Moore, Max Terhune, Julie
Duncan, Budd Buster, Rose Plummer, Forrest
Taylor, Glenn Strange, Steve Clark, John Merton,
Edward Cassidy, Joe Garcia, Silver Harr, Carl
Mathews
D: Anthony Marshall
S: Arthur Hoerl
SP: Elizabeth Beecher
P: George W. Weeks

1552. MAN FROM MUSIC MOUNTAIN
(Republic, October 30, 1943) 71 Mins.
Roy Rogers, Bob Nolan, and the Sons of the Pio-
neers, Ruth Terry, Ann Gillis, Paul Kelly, Pat
Brady, Paul Harvey, George Cleveland, Renie
Riano, Hank Bell, Jay Novello, Hal Taliaferro,
I. Stanford Jolley, Jack O'Shea, Tom Smith,
Charles Morton, "Trigger"

Man from Music Mountain (Republic, 1943) — Ann Gillis, "Trigger," Roy Rogers, and Ruth Terry

D: Joseph Kane
SP: J. Benton Cheney, Bradford Ropes
AP: Harry Grey

1553. SILVER CITY RAIDERS
(Columbia, November 4, 1943) 55 Mins.
Russell Hayden, Dub Taylor, Alma Carroll, Bob
  Wills and the Texas Playboys, Edmund Cobb, Jack
  Ingram, Art Mix, Luther Wills, Paul Sutton, Jack
  Rockwell, John Tyrell, Merrill McCormack,
  George Morrell, Horace B. Carpenter, Tex
  Palmer
D: William Berke
SP: Ed Earl Repp
P: Leon Barsha

1554. DEVIL RIDERS
(PRC, November 5, 1943)
(*Billy Carson* Series)
Buster Crabbe, Al St. John, Patty McCarthy, Kermit
  Maynard, Charles Merton, Frank LaRue, Jack In-
  gram, George Chesebro, Ed Cassidy, Al Ferguson,
  Frank Ellis, Bert Dillard, Bud Osborne, Artie Or-
  tego, Herman Hack, Roy Bucko, Buck Bucko
D: Sam Newfield
SP: Joe O'Donnell
P: Sigmund Neufeld

1555. FALSE COLORS
(United Artists, November 5, 1943) 65 Mins.
(*Hopalong Cassidy* Series)
William Boyd, Andy Clyde, Jimmy Rogers, Claudia
  Drake, Robert Mitchum, Douglass Dumbrille,
  Roy Barcroft, Glenn Strange, Pierce Lyden, Earle
  Hodgins, Sam Flint, Tom Seidel, Tom London,
  George Morrell, Dan White, Elmer Jerome, Ray
  Jones, Bob Burns, Tom Smith
D: George Archainbaud
SP: Bennett Cohen. Based on characters created by
  William Colt MacDonald
P: Harry Sherman

1556. FRONTIER LAW
(Universal, November 15, 1943) 59 Mins.
Russell Hayden, Fuzzy Knight, Jennifer Holt, Den-
  nis Moore, Jack Ingram, Hal Taliaferro, George
  Eldridge, I. Stanford Jolley, Frank LaRue, James
  Farley, Michael Vallon, Tex Cooper, Johnny Bond
  and his Red River Valley Boys (Paul Sells, Wesley
  Tuttle, and Jimmie Dean)
D/SP: Elmer Clifton
AP: Oliver Drake

1556a. PHONY EXPRESS
(Columbia, November 18, 1943) 2 Reels
(*Three Stooges* Series)
Moe Howard, Curly Howard, Larry Fine, Shirley

Patterson, Chester Conklin, Snub Pollard, Bud
  Jamison
D: Del Lord

1557. BOSS OF RAWHIDE
(PRC, November 20, 1943) 57 Mins.
(*Texas Rangers* Series)
Dave O'Brien, Jim Newill, Guy Wilkerson, Nell
  O'Day, Edward Cassidy, Jack Ingram, Billy Blet-
  cher, Charles King, George Chesebro, Robert
  Hill, Dan White, Lucille Vance, Bob Kortman
D/SP: Elmer Clifton
P: Alfred Stern

1558. OVERLAND MAIL ROBBERY
(Republic, November 20, 1943) 56 Mins.
Bill Elliott, George Hayes, Anne Jeffreys, Weldon
  Heyburn, Nancy Gay, Kirk Alyn, Roy Barcroft,
  Bud Geary, Tom London, Peter Michael, Alice
  Fleming, Jack Kirk, Kenne Duncan, Jack Rockwell,
  Frank McCarroll, Jack O'Shea, LeRoy Mason,
  Hank Bell, Cactus Mack, Ray Jones, Tom Steele,
  Frank Ellis, Maxine Doyle, Diane Henry
D: John English
S: Robert Yost
SP: Bob Williams, Robert Yost
AP: Louis Gray

1559. DEERSLAYER
(Republic, November 22, 1943) 67 Mins.
Bruce Kellogg, Jean Parker, Larry Parks, Warren
  Ashe, Wanda McKay, Yvonne De Carlo, Addi-
  son Richards, Johnny Michaels, Phil Van Zandt,
  Clancy Cooper, Trevor Bardette, Robert War-
  wick, Chief Many Treaties, Princess Whynemah,
  William Edmund
D: Lew Landers
S: James Fenimore Cooper
SP: P. S. Harrison, E. B. Derr
P: E. B. Derr

1560. CANYON CITY
(Republic, November 24, 1943)
Don Barry, Wally Bernon, Helen Talbot, Twinkle
  Watts, LeRoy Mason, Pierce Lyden, Forbes Mur-
  ray, Edward Piel, Sr., Eddie Gribbon, Tom Lon-
  don, Morgan Conway, Emmett Vogan, Stanley
  Andrews, Roy Barcroft, Jack Kirk, Kenne Dun-
  can, Bud Geary, Bud Osborne, Hank Worden
D: Spencer Bennet
SP: Robert Yost
AP: Eddy White

1561. THE TEXAS KID
(Monogram, November 26, 1943) 59 Mins.
Johnny Mack Brown, Raymond Hatton, Shirley Pat-
  terson, Marshall Reed, Kermit Maynard, Edmund

Cobb, Robert Fiske, Stanley Price, Lynton Brent, Bud Osborne, John Judd, Charles King, Cyrus Ring, George J. Lewis
D: Lambert Hillyer
S: Lynton Brent
SP: Jess Bowers (Adele Buffington)
P: Scott R. Dunlap

1562. DEATH VALLEY RANGERS
(Monogram, December 3, 1943) 59 Mins.
(*Trail Blazers* Series)
Ken Maynard, Hoot Gibson, Bob Steele, Linda Brent, Kenneth Harlan, Bob Allen, Charles King, George Chesebro, John Bridges, Al Ferguson, Steve Clark, Wally West, Glenn Strange, Forrest Taylor, Lee Roberts, Weldon Heyburn, Karl Hackett
D: Robert Tansey
SP: Robert Emmett, Frances Kavanaugh, Elizabeth Beecher
P: Robert Tansey

1563. RIDERS OF THE DEADLINE
(United Artists, December 3, 1943) 60 Mins.
(*Hopalong Cassidy* Series)
William Boyd, Andy Clyde, Jimmy Rogers, Richard Crane, William Halligan, Frances Woodward, Tony Ward (Anthony Warde), Bob Mitchum, Jim Bannon, Hugh Prosser, Herbert Rawlinson, Monte Montana, Earle Hodgins, Bill Beckford, Pierce Lyden, Art Felix, Roy Bucko, Cliff Parkinson
D: Lesley Selander
SP: Bennett Cohen. Based on characters created by Clarence E. Mulford
P: Harry Sherman

1564. WAR OF THE WILDCATS
(Republic, December 6, 1943) 102 Mins.
(Title was changed to *In Old Oklahoma* after initial release)
John Wayne, Martha Scott, Albert Dekker, George Hayes, Marjorie Rambeau, Dale Evans, Grant Withers, Sidney Blackmer, Paul Fix, Cecil Cunningham, Irving Bacon, Byron Foulger, Anne O'Neill, Richard Graham, Lane Chandler, Robert Warwick, Harry Shannon, Arthur Loft, Stanley Andrews, Harry Woods, Bud Geary, LeRoy Mason, Will Wright, Fred Graham, Tom London, Edward Gargan, Kenne Duncan, Hooper Atchley, Emmett Vogan, Wade Crosby, George Chandler, Curley Dresden, Roy Barcroft, Jack Kirk, Slim Whitaker, Dick Rich, Yakima Canutt, Shirley Rickert, Oril Taller, Linda Scott, Juanita Colteaux, Jess Cavan, Charles Agnew, Pat Hogan, Bonnie Jean Harley, Pearl Early, Linda Brent, Rhonda Fleming

D: Albert S. Rogell
S: "War of the Wildcats"—Thomson Burtis
SP: Ethel Hill, Eleanor Griffin
AP: Robert North

1565. KLONDIKE KATE
(Columbia, December 16, 1943)
Ann Savage, Tom Neal, Glenda Farrell, Constance Worth, Sheldon Leonard, Lester Allen, George Cleveland, George McKay, Dan Seymour
D: William Castle
S/SP: Houston Branch, M. Coates Webster
P: Irving Briskin

1566. LOST CANYON
(United Artists, December 18, 1943) 61 Mins.
(*Hopalong Cassidy* Series)
William Boyd, Andy Clyde, Jay Kirby, Lola Lane, Douglas Fowley, Herbert Rawlinson, Guy Usher, Karl Hackett, Hugh Prosser, Keith Richards, Herman Hack, Merrill McCormack, George Morrell
D: Lesley Selander
S: Clarence E. Mulford
SP: Harry O. Hoyt
P: Harry Sherman

1567. COWBOY IN THE CLOUDS
(Columbia, December 23, 1943)
Charles Starrett, Dub Taylor, Julie Duncan, Jimmy Wakely, Hal Taliaferro, Charles King, Lane Chandler, Davidson Clark, Dick Curtis, Ed Cassidy, Ted Mapes, John Tyrell, Paul Zarema
D: Benjamin Kline
SP: Elizabeth Beecher
P: Jack Fier

1568. CALIFORNIA JOE
(Republic, December 29, 1943)
Don Barry, Helen Talbot, Wally Vernon, Twinkle Watts, Terry Frost, Brian O'Hara, Edward Earle, LeRoy Mason, Charles King, Pierce Lyden, Edmund Cobb, Karl Hackett, Bob Kortman, Edward Keane, Tom London, Jack O'Shea, Bob Wilke
D: Spencer Bennet
SP: Norman S. Hall
P: Eddy White

1569. RAIDERS OF SUNSET PASS
(Republic, December 30, 1943) 57 Mins.
(*John Paul Revere* Series)
Eddie Dew, Smiley Burnette, Jennifer Holt, Roy Barcroft, Charles Miller, LeRoy Mason, Maxine Doyle, Mozelle Cravens, Nancy Worth, Kenne Duncan, Jack Kirk, Jack Rockwell, Hank Bell, Budd Buster, Jack Ingram, Frank McCarroll, Fred Burns, Al Taylor
D: John English

Raiders of Sunset Pass
(Republic, 1943) —
Eddie Dew, Jennifer Holt, Smiley
Burnette, and
Charles Miller

SP: John K. Butler
AP: Louis Gray

1570. THE WOMAN OF THE TOWN

(United Artists, December 31, 1943)   90 Mins.

Claire Trevor, Albert Dekker, Barry Sullivan, Henry Hull, Marion Martin, Porter Hall, Percy Kilbride, Beryl Wallace, Arthur Hohl, Clem Bevins, Teddi Sherman, George Cleveland, Russell Hicks, Herbert Rawlinson, Marlene Mains, Dorothy Granger, Dewey Robinson, Wade Crosby, Hal Taliaferro, Glenn Strange, Charley Foy, Claire Whitney, Russell Simpson, Eula Gay, Frances Morris

D: George Archainbaud
SP: Aeneas MacKenzie
P: Harry Sherman

1570a. OKLAHOMA OUTLAWS

(Warner Bros., 1943)   20 Mins.

Robert Shayne, Juanita Stark, Warner Anderson, Erville Alderson, Addison Richards, Charles Middleton

D: B. Reeves Eason
SP: Ed Earl Repp
P: Gordon Hollingshead

1570b. WAGON WHEELS WEST

(Warner Bros., 1943)   20 Mins.

Robert Shayne, Nina Foch, Charles Middleton, Addison Richards

D: B. Reeves Eason
SP: Ed Earl Repp
P: Gordon Hollingshead

FILMS OF 1944

1571. GUNSMOKE MESA

(PRC, January 3, 1944)   59 Mins.

(*Texas Rangers* Series)

Dave O'Brien, Jim Newill, Patti McCarty, Guy Wilkerson, Jack Ingram, Kermit Maynard, Robert Barron, Dick Alexander, Michael Vallon, Roy Brent, Jack Rockwell

D: Harry Fraser

SP: Elmer Clifton
P: Arthur Alexander

1572. HANDS ACROSS THE BORDER

(Republic, January 5, 1944)   73 Mins.

Roy Rogers, Bob Nolan and the Sons of the Pioneers, Ruth Terry, Guinn (Big Boy) Williams,

Onslow Stevens, Mary Treen, Joseph Crehan, Duncan Renaldo, Frederick Burton, LeRoy Mason, Larry Steers, Julian Rivero, Janet Martin, The Wiere Brothers, Roy Barcroft, Kenne Duncan, Jack Kirk, Jack O'Shea, Curley Dresden, "Trigger"
D: Joseph Kane
SP: Bradford Ropes, J. Benton Cheney
AP: Harry Grey

1573. PRIDE OF THE PLAINS

(Republic, January 5, 1944)   56 Mins.
(*John Paul Revere* Series)
Robert Livingston, Smiley Burnette, Nancy Gay, Steven Barclay, Kenneth MacDonald, Charles Miller, Kenne Duncan, Jack Kirk, Bud Geary, Yakima Canutt, Budd Buster, Bud Osborne
D: Wallace Fox
S: Oliver Drake
SP: John K. Butler, Bob Williams
AP: Louis Gray

1574. GUN TO GUN

(Warner Bros., January 8, 1944)   20 Mins.
(*Santa Fe Trail* Series)
(Technicolor)

Robert Shayne, Lupita Tovar, Pedro De Cordoba, Harry Woods, Tom Tyler, Anita Camargo, Roy Bucko, Julian Rivero, Jack Kinney
D: D. Ross Lederman

1575. WESTWARD BOUND

(Monogram, January 17, 1944)   54 Mins.
(*Trail Blazers* Series)
Ken Maynard, Hoot Gibson, Bob Steele, Betty Miles, John Bridges, Harry Woods, Karl Hackett, Weldon Heyburn, Hal Price, Roy Brent, Frank Ellis, Curley Dresden, Dan White, Al Ferguson
D/P: Robert Tansey
SP: Frances Kavanaugh

1576. MARSHAL OF GUNSMOKE

(Universal, January 21, 1944)   58 Mins.
Tex Ritter, Russell Hayden, Fuzzy Knight, Jennifer Holt, Harry Woods, Herbert Rawlinson, Ethan Laidlaw, Ray Bennett, Michael Vallon, Ernie Adams, Slim Whitaker, George Chesebro, James Farley, William Desmond, Dan White, Roy Brent, Bud Osborne, Johnny Bond and his Red River Valley Boys

Gun to Gun (Warner Bros., 1944) — Roy Bucko, Harry Woods, Tom Tyler, Anita Camargo, Jack Kinney, Robert Shayne, and Pedro De Cordoba

D: Vernon Keyes
SP: William Lively
AP: Oliver Drake

1577. RAIDERS OF THE BORDER
(Monogram, January 31, 1944) 58 Mins.
Johnny Mack Brown, Raymond Hatton, Ellen Hall, Craig Woods, Stanley Price, Ray Bennett, Edmund Cobb, Lynton Brent, Dick Alexander, Kermit Maynard, Ernie Adams
D: John P. McCarthy
S: Johnston McCulley
SP: Jess Bowers (Adele Buffington)
P: Scott R. Dunlap

1578. THE VIGILANTES RIDE
(Columbia, February 3, 1944) 56 Mins.
Russell Hayden, Dub Taylor, Shirley Patterson, Bob Wills and the Texas Playboys, Jack Rockwell, Tris Coffin, Bob Kortman, Dick Botiller, Jack Kirk, Stanley Brown, Blackie Whiteford
D: William Berke
SP: Ed Earl Repp
P: Leon Barsha

1579. COWBOY CANTEEN
(Columbia, February 8, 1944) 72 Mins.
Charles Starrett, Jane Frazee, Vera Vague (Barbara Jo Allen), Tex Ritter, Guinn "Big Boy" Williams, The Mills Brothers, Jimmy Wakely and his Saddle Pals, Chickie and Buck, Roy Acuff and his Smokey Mountain Boys and Girls, The Tailor Maids, Dub Taylor, Max Terhune, Emmett Lynn, Edythe Elliott, Jeff Donnell, Dick Curtis
D: Lew Landers
SP: Paul Gangelin, Felix Adler
P: Jack Fier

1580. OUTLAW ROUNDUP
(PRC, February 10, 1944) 55 Mins.
(*Texas Rangers* Series)
Dave O'Brien, Jim Newill, Guy Wilkerson, Helen Chapman, Jack Ingram, Reed Howes, I. Stanford Jolley, Charles King, Bud Osborne, Frank Ellis, Budd Buster, Frank McCarroll, Jimmy Aubrey
D: Harry Fraser
SP: Elmer Clifton
P: Alfred Stern

1581. TEXAS MASQUERADE
(United Artists, February 18, 1944) 59 Mins.
(*Hopalong Cassidy* Series)
William Boyd, Andy Clyde, Jimmy Rogers, Mady Correll, Don Costello, Russell Simpson, Nelson Leigh, Francis McDonald, J. Farrell MacDonald, June Pickerell, John Merton, Pierce Lyden, Robert McKenzie, Bill Hunter, Keith Richards, George Morrell

D: George Archainbaud
SP: Norman Houston. Based on characters created by Clarence E. Mulford
P: Harry Sherman

1582. ARIZONA WHIRLWIND
(Monogram, February 21, 1944) 59 Mins.
(*Trail Blazers* Series)
Ken Maynard, Hoot Gibson, Bob Steele, Ian Keith, Myrna Dell, Donald Stewart, Charles King, Karl Hackett, George Chesebro, Dan White, Charles Murray, Jr., Frank Ellis, Chief Soldani, Willow Bird
D: Robert Tansey
SP: Frances Kavanaugh
P: Robert Tansey

1583. BENEATH WESTERN SKIES
(Republic, March 3, 1944) 56 Mins.
(*John Paul Revere* Series)
Robert Livingston, Smiley Burnette, Effie Laird, Joe Strauch, Jr., LeRoy Mason, Kenne Duncan, Bud Geary, Jack Kirk, Charles Dorety, Charles Miller, Tom London, Frank Jacquet, Jack Ingram, John James, Budd Buster, Bob Wilke, Tom Steele, Herman Hack, Carl Sepulveda
D: Spencer Bennet
S: Albert DeMond
SP: Albert DeMond, Bob Williams
AP: Louis Gray

1584. FRONTIER OUTLAWS
(PRC, March 4, 1944) 56 Mins.
(*Billy Carson* Series)
Buster Crabbe, Al St. John, Frances Gladwin, Marin Sais, Charles King, Jack Ingram, Kermit Maynard, Edward Cassidy, Emmett Lynn, Budd Buster, Frank Ellis
D: Sam Newfield
SP: Joe O'Donnell
P: Sigmund Neufeld

1585. OKLAHOMA RAIDERS
(Universal, March 17, 1944) 57 Mins.
Tex Ritter, Fuzzy Knight, Jennifer Holt, Dennis Moore, Jack Ingram, George Eldridge, Johnny Bond and his Red River Valley Boys, John Elliott, Slim Whitaker, I. Stanford Jolley, Dick Alexander, Herbert Rawlinson, Ethan Laidlaw, Stephen Keyes, Lane Chandler, Frank Ellis, William Desmond, Bob Baker
D: Lewis Collins
SP: Betty Burbridge
AP: Oliver Drake

1586. MOJAVE FIREBRAND
(Republic, March 19, 1944) 55 Mins.
Bill Elliott, George Hayes, Anne Jeffreys, LeRoy

Mason, Jack Ingram, Harry McKim, Karl Hackett, Forrest Taylor, Hal Price, Marshall Reed, Kenne Duncan, Bud Geary, Jack Kirk, Fred Graham, Tom London, Frank Ellis, Tom Steele, Bob Burns, Jess Cavan, Art Dillard, Bud Osborne, Larry Steers
D: Spencer G. Bennet
SP: Norman S. Hall
AP: Eddy White

1587. SUNDOWN VALLEY

(Columbia, March 23, 1944)   55 Mins.
Charles Starrett, Bud Taylor, Jeanne Bates, Jimmy Wakely, Clancy Cooper, Jesse Arnold, Wheeler Oakman, Jack Ingram, Forrest Taylor, Joel Friedkin, Grace Lenard, Eddie Laughton, The Tennessee Ramblers
D: Ben Kline
SP: Luci Ward
P: Jack Fier

1588. THUNDERING GUN SLINGERS

(PRC, March 25, 1944)   59 Mins.
(*Billy Carson* Series)
Buster Crabbe, Al St. John, Frances Gladwin, Karl Hackett, Charles King, Kermit Maynard, Jack Ingram, Budd Buster, George Chesebro
D: Sam Newfield
SP: Fred Myton
P: Sigmund Neufeld

1589. PARTNERS OF THE TRAIL

(Monogram, March 28, 1944)   57 Mins.
Johnny Mack Brown, Raymond Hatton, Christine McIntyre, Craig Woods, Robert Frazer, Harry L. (Hal) Price, Jack Ingram, Lynton Brent, Ben Corbett, Steve Clark, Marshall Reed, Lloyd Ingraham, Ted Mapes
D: Lambert Hillyer
SP: Frank Young
P: Scott R. Dunlap

1590. GUNS OF THE LAW

(PRC, March 31, 1944)   55 Mins.
(*Texas Rangers* Series)
Dave O'Brien, Jim Newill, Guy Wilkerson, Budd Buster, Charles King, Jack Ingram, Robert Kortman, Robert Barron, Frank McCarroll, Bud Osborne
D/SP: Elmer Clifton
P: Arthur Alexander

1591. BUFFALO BILL

(20th C. Fox, April 1, 1944)   90 Mins.
Joel McCrea, Maureen O'Hara, Linda Darnell, Thomas Mitchell, Edgar Buchanan, Anthony Quinn, Moroni Olson, Frank Fenton, Matt Briggs, George Lessey, Frank Orth, George Chandler, Chief Thunder Cloud, Sidney Blackmer, Edwin Stanley, Nick Thompson, Chief Many Treaties, John Dilson, Evelyn Beresford, William Haade, Merrill Rodin, Talzumbia Dupea
D: William A. Wellman
S: Frank Winch
SP: Aeneas MacKenzie, Clemente Ripley, Cecile Kramer
P: Harry Sherman

1592. HIDDEN VALLEY OUTLAWS

(Republic, April 2, 1944)
Bill Elliott, George Hayes, Anne Jeffreys, Roy Barcroft, Kenne Duncan, John James, Charles Miller, Fred Toones, Budd Buster, Tom London, LeRoy Mason, Earle Hodgins, Yakima Canutt, Jack Kirk, Tom Steele, Bud Geary, Frank McCarroll, Edward Cassidy, Bob Wilke, Charles Morton, Cactus Mack, Forbes Murray, Frank O'Connor
D: Howard Bretherton
S: John K. Butler
SP: John K. Butler, Bob Williams
AP: Louis Gray

1593. THE LARAMIE TRAIL

(Republic, April 3, 1944)   55 Mins.
Robert Livingston, Smiley Burnette, Linda Brent, Emmett Lynn, John James, George J. Lewis, Leander de Cordova, Slim Whitaker, Bud Osborne, Bud Geary, Roy Barcroft, Kenne Duncan, Marshall Reed
D: John English
S: "Mystery at Spanish Hacienda"—Jackson Gregory
SP: J. Benton Chaney
AP: Louis Gray

1594. OUTLAWS OF SANTA FE

(Republic, April 4, 1944)   56 Mins.
Donald Barry, Helen Talbot, Wally Vernon, Twinkle Watts, Charles Morton, Herbert Heyes, Bud Geary, LeRoy Mason, Kenne Duncan, Nolan Leary, Walter Soderling, Edmund Cobb, Frank McCarroll, Bob Kortman, Emmett Lynn, Ernie Adams, Jack Kirk, Pierce Lyden, Forrest Taylor, Bob Burns, Jack O'Shea, Fred Graham
D: Howard Bretherton
SP: Norman S. Hall
AP: Eddy White

1595. OUTLAW TRAIL

(Monogram, April 18, 1944)   53 Mins.
(*Trail Blazers* Series)
Hoot Gibson, Bob Steele, Chief Thunder Cloud, Jennifer Holt, Cy Kendall, Rocky Camron, George Eldridge, Charles King, Hal Price, John Bridges,

Outlaw Trail (Monogram, 1944) — Hoot Gibson, Bob Steele, Jennifer Holt, and Rocky Camron

Bud Osborne, Jim Thorpe, Frank Ellis, Al Ferguson, Warner Richmond, Tex Palmer
D/P: Robert Tansey
S: Alvin J. Neitz (Alan James)
SP: Frances Kavanaugh

1596. WYOMING HURRICANE
(Columbia, April 20, 1944) 58 Mins.
Russell Hayden, Dub Taylor, Alma Carroll, Bob Wills and his Texas Playboys, Paul Sutton, Hal Price, Tristram Coffin, Benny Petti, Robert Kortman
D: William Berke
SP: Fred Myton
P: Leon Barsha

1597. LAW MEN
(Monogram, April 25, 1944) 58 Mins.
Johnny Mack Brown, Raymond Hatton, Jan Wiley, Kirby Grant, Robert Frazer, Edmund Cobb, Art Fowler, Hal Price, Marshall Reed, Isabel Withers, Ted Mapes, Steve Clark, Bud Osborne, Ben Corbett, Jack Rockwell, George Morrell, Ray Jones
D: Lambert Hillyer
SP: Glenn Tyron
P: Charles J. Bigelow

1598. THE PINTO BANDIT
(PRC, April 27, 1944) 56 Mins.
(*Texas Rangers* Series)
Dave O'Brien, Jim Newill, Guy Wilkerson, Mady Lawrence, James Martin, Jack Ingram, Edward Cassidy, Budd Buster, Karl Hackett, Robert Kortman, Charles King, Jimmy Aubrey
D/SP: Elmer Clifton
P: Alfred Stern

1599. LUMBERJACK
(United Artists, April 28, 1944) 65 Mins.
(*Hopalong Cassidy* Series)
William Boyd, Andy Clyde, Jimmy Rogers, Douglass Dumbrille, Ellen Hall, Francis McDonald, Herbert Rawlinson, Ethel Wales, John Whitney, Hal Taliaferro, Henry Wills, Charles Morton, Frances Morris, Jack Rockwell, Bob Burns, Hank Worden, Earle Hodgins, Pierce Lyden
D: Lesley Selander
SP: Norman Houston, Barry Shipman. Based on characters created by Clarence E. Mulford
P: Harry Sherman

1600. VALLEY OF VENGEANCE
(PRC, May 5, 1944) 56 Mins.
(*Billy Carson* Series)

297

Buster Crabbe, Al St. John, Evelyn Finley, Edward Cassidy, Nora Bush, Donald Mayo, David Polonsky, Glenn Strange, Charles King, Jack Ingram, John Merton, Lynton Brent, Bud Osborne, Steve Clark, Budd Buster
D: Sam Newfield
SP: Joe O'Donnell
P: Sigmund Neufeld

1601. THE COWBOY AND THE SENORITA
(Republic, May 12, 1944)   78 Mins.
Roy Rogers, Mary Lee, Dale Evans, John Hubbard, Guinn "Big Boy" Williams, Fuzzy Knight, Dorothy Christy, Lucien Littlefield, Hal Taliaferro, Jack Kirk, Jack O'Shea, Jane Beebe, Ben Rochelle, Bob Nolan and the Sons of the Pioneers, Rex Lease, Lynton Brent, Julian Rivero, Bob Wilke, Wally West, Tito and Corinne Valdes, "Trigger"
D: Joseph Kane
S: Bradford Ropes
SP: Gordon Kahn
AP: Harry Grey

1602. TUCSON RAIDERS
(Republic, May 14, 1944)   55 Mins.
Bill Elliott, George Hayes, Bobby Blake, Alice Fleming, Ruth Lee, Peggy Stewart, LeRoy Mason, Stanley Andrews, John Whitney, Bud Geary, Karl Hackett, Tom Steele, Tom Chatterton, Edward Cassidy, Edward Howard, Fred Graham, Frank McCarroll, Marshall Reed, Stanley Andrews, Frank Pershing, and the voices of Roy Barcroft, Kenne Duncan, Tom London, and Jack Kirk
D: Spencer G. Bennet
S: Jack (Joe?) O'Donnell
SP: Anthony Coldeway
AP: Eddy White

1603. RIDING WEST
(Columbia, May 18, 1944)   58 Mins.
(Filmed in 1943)
Charles Starrett, Arthur Hunnicutt, Shirley Patterson, Clancy Cooper, Steve Clark, Wheeler Oakman, Blackie Whiteford, Bill Wilkerson, Johnny Bond, Ernest Tubb
D: William Berke
SP: Luci Ward
P: Jack Fier

1604. BOSS OF BOOMTOWN
(Universal, May 22, 1944)   58 Mins.
Rod Cameron, Fuzzy Knight, Tom Tyler, Vivian Austin (Vivian Coe), Ray Whitley, Jack Ingram, Robert Barron, Marie Austin, Max Wagner, Sam Flint, Dick Alexander, Forrest Taylor, Tex Cooper, Hank Bell, Ray Jones, Ray Whitley's Bar-6 Cowboys
D: Ray Taylor
SP: William Lively
AP: Oliver Drake

1604a. TRIAL BY TRIGGER
(Warner Bros., May 27, 1944)   20 Mins.
(Technicolor)
Robert Shayne, Cheryl Walker, Warner Anderson, Ralph Dunn, Henry Sharp
D: William McGann
SP: Gordon Hollingshead
P: Gordon Hollingshead

1605. MYSTERY MAN
(United Artists, May 31, 1944)   58 Mins.
(*Hopalong Cassidy* Series)
William Boyd, Andy Clyde, Jimmy Rogers, Don Costello, Eleanor Stewart, Francis McDonald, Forrest Taylor, Jack Rockwell, Bill Hunter, John Merton, Pierce Lyden, Bob Burns, Ozie Waters, Art Mix, Hank Bell, Bob Baker, George Morrell
D: George Archainbaud
SP: J. Benton Cheney. Based on characters created by Clarence E. Mulford
P: Harry Sherman

1606. WELLS FARGO DAYS
(Warner Bros., May, 1944)   20 Mins.
(Cinecolor)
Dennis Moore, Louise Stanley, Karl Hackett, Edward Cassidy, Lafe McKee, Eva McKenzie
D: Mack V. Wright
S: Stuart N. Lake

1607. SPOOK TOWN
(PRC, June 3, 1944)   59 Mins.
(*Texas Rangers* Series)
Dave O'Brien, Jim Newill, Guy Wilkerson, Mady Lawrence, Dick Curtis, Harry Harvey, Edward Cassidy, Charles King, Robert Barron, Dick Alexander, John Cason
D/SP: Elmer Clifton
P: Arthur Alexander

1608. SONORA STAGECOACH
(Monogram, June 10, 1944)   61 Mins.
(*Trail Blazers* Series)
Hoot Gibson, Bob Steele, Chief Thunder Cloud, Rocky Camron, Betty Miles, Glenn Strange, George Eldridge, Karl Hackett, Henry Hall, Charles King, Bud Osborne, Charles Murray, Jr., John Bridges, Al Ferguson, Forrest Taylor, Frank Ellis, Hal Price, Rodd Redwing, John Cason, Horace B. Carpenter
D/P: Robert Tansey
SP: Frances Kavanaugh

1609. THE DRIFTER

(PRC, June 14, 1944) 62 Mins.

(*Billy Carson* Series)

Buster Crabbe, Al St. John, Carol Parker, Kermit Maynard, Jack Ingram, Roy Brent, George Chesebro, Ray Bennett, Jimmy Aubrey, Slim Whitaker, Wally West

D: Sam Newfield

SP: Patricia Harper

P: Sigmund Neufeld

1610. THE LAST HORSEMAN

(Columbia, June 22, 1944)

Russell Hayden, Dub Taylor, Ann Savage, Bob Wills and his Texas Playboys, John Maxwell, Frank LaRue, Nick Thompson, Ted Mapes, Forrest Taylor, Curley Dresden

D: William Berke

SP: Ed Earl Repp

P: Leon Barsha

1611. FORTY THIEVES

(United Artists, June 23, 1944) 60 Mins.

(*Hopalong Cassidy* Series)

William Boyd, Andy Clyde, Jimmy Rogers, Louise Currie, Douglass Dumbrille, Kirk Alyn, Herbert Rawlinson, Robert Frazer, Glenn Strange, Jack Rockwell, Bob Kortman, Hal Taliaferro

D: Lesley Selander

SP: Michael Wilson, Bernie Kamins. Based on characters created by Clarence E. Mulford.

P: Harry Sherman

1612. YELLOW ROSE OF TEXAS

(Republic, June 24, 1944) 69 Mins.

Roy Rogers, Dale Evans, George Cleveland, Harry Shannon, Grant Withers, Bob Nolan and the Sons of the Pioneers, William Haade, Weldon Heyburn, Hal Taliaferro, Tom London, Dick Botiller, Janet Martin, Don Kay Reynolds, Bob Wilke, Jack O'Shea, Rex Lease, Emmett Vogan, John Dilson, "Trigger"

D: Joseph Kane

SP: Jack Townley

AP: Harry Grey

1613. RANGE LAW

(Monogram, June 24, 1944) 57 Mins.

Johnny Mack Brown, Raymond Hatton, Sarah Padden, Ellen Hall, Lloyd Ingraham, Marshall Reed, Steve Clark, Jack Ingram, Hugh Prosser, Stanley Price, Art Fowler, Harry (Hal) Price, Ben Corbett, Bud Osborne, Tex Palmer, George Morrell, Lynton Brent, Forrest Taylor, Horace B. Carpenter

D: Lambert Hillyer

SP: Frank H. Young

P: Charles J. Bigelow

1614. MARSHAL OF RENO

(Republic, July 2, 1944) 54 Mins.

(*Red Ryder* Series)

Bill Elliott, George Hayes, Bobby Blake, Alice Fleming, Herbert Rawlinson, Tom London, Jay Kirby, Charles King, Jack Kirk, Kenne Duncan, LeRoy Mason, Bob Wilke, Fred Burns, Tom Steele, Edmund Cobb, Fred Graham, Blake Edwards, Hal Price, Bud Geary, Jack O'Shea, Al Taylor, Marshall Reed, Tom Chatterton, Carl Sepulveda, Ken Terrell, Horace B. Carpenter, Charles Sullivan, Roy Barcroft (voice only)

D: Wallace Grissell

S: Anthony Coldeway, Taylor Cavan

SP: Anthony Coldeway

AP: Louis Gray

1615. TRIGGER TRAIL

(Universal, July 7, 1944) 59 Mins.

Rod Cameron, Fuzzy Knight, Eddie Dew, Vivian Austin, Ray Whitley and his Bar-6 Cowboys (Ezra Paulette, Lem Giles, and Charley Quirt), Lane Chandler, George Eldridge, Buzzy Henry, Davidson Clark, Michael Vallon, Dick Alexander, Jack Rockwell, Budd Buster, Bud Osborne, Ray Jones, Jack Ingram, Artie Ortego

D: Lewis Collins

SP: Ed Earl Repp, Patricia Harper

AP: Oliver Drake

1616. CALL OF THE ROCKIES

(Republic, July 14, 1944)

Smiley Burnette, Sunset Carson, Ellen Hall, Frank Jacquet, Harry Woods, Kirk Alyn, Charles Williams, Jack Kirk, Tom London, Bob Kortman, Edmund Cobb, Jack O'Shea, Rex Lease, Frank McCarroll, Herman Hack, Bill Nestell, Charles B. Williams

D: Lesley Selander

SP: Bob Williams

AP: Louis Gray

1617. TWILIGHT ON THE PRAIRIE

(Universal, July 14, 1944) 62 Mins.

Johnny Downs, Vivian Austin, Leon Errol, Connie Haines, Eddie Quillan, Jack Teagarden Orchestra, Milburn Stone, Jimmie Dodd, Olin Howlin, Perc Launders, Dennis Moore, Ralph Peters, Foy Willing

D: Jean Yarbrough

S: Warren Wilson

SP: Clyde Bruckman

AP: Warren Wilson

1618. SILVER CITY KID

(Republic, July 20, 1944) 55 Mins.

Allan Lane, Peggy Stewart, Wally Vernon, Twin-

kle Watts, Frank Jacquet, Harry Woods, Glenn Strange, Lane Chandler, Bud Geary, Tom London, Tom Steele, Jack Kirk, Sam Flint, Frank McCarroll, Hal Price, Edward Piel, Sr., Fred Graham, Frank O'Connor, Horace Carpenter
D: John English
S: Bennett Cohen
SP: Taylor Cavan
AP: Stephen Auer

1619. FUZZY SETTLES DOWN

(PRC, July 25, 1944) 60 Mins.

(*Billy Carson* Series)

Buster Crabbe, Al St. John, Patti McCarthy, Charles King, John Merton, Frank McCarroll, Hal Price, John Elliott, Edward Cassidy, Robert Hill, Ted Mapes, Tex Palmer
D: Sam Newfield
SP: Louise Rousseau
P: Sigmund Neufeld

1620. RAIDERS OF GHOST CITY

(Universal, July 25, 1944) 13 Chaps.

Dennis Moore, Wanda McKay, Lionel Atwill, Virginia Christine, Regis Toomey, Joe Sawyer, Edmund Cobb, Eddy Waller, Emmett Vogan, Addison Richards, Charles Wagenheim, Jack Ingram, Jack Rockwell, Ernie Adams, George Eldridge, Gene Garrick, Chief Thunder Cloud, Herman Hack, Chick Hannon
D: Ray Taylor, Lewis Collins
SP: Luci Ward, Morgan Cox
P: Morgan Cox, Ray Taylor
Chapter Titles: (1) Murder by Accident, (2) Flaming Treachery, (3) Death Rides Double, (4) Ghost City Terror, (5) The Fatal Lariat, (6) Water Rising, (7) Bullet Avalanche, (8) Death Laughs Last, (9) Cold Steel, (10) Showdown, (11) The Trail to Torture, (12) Calling All Buckboards, (13) Golden Vengeance

1621. THE UTAH KID

(Monogram, July 26, 1944) 55 Mins.

Hoot Gibson, Bob Steele, Beatrice Gray, Evelyn Eaton, Ralph Lewis, Mike Letz, Mauritz Hugo, Jamesson Shade, Dan White, George Morrell, Bud Osborne
D: Vernon Keyes
SP: Victor Hammond
P: William Strobach

1622. MARKED TRAILS

(Monogram, July 29, 1944) 58 Mins.

Hoot Gibson, Bob Steele, Veda Ann Borg, Ralph Lewis, Mauritz Hugo, Steve Clark, Charles Stevens, Lynton Brent, Bud Osborne, George Morrell, Allen B. Sewell, Ben Corbett

D: J. P. McCarthy
SP: J. P. McCarthy, Victor Hammond
P: William Strobach

1623. BRAND OF THE DEVIL

(PRC, July 30, 1944) 57 Mins.

(*Texas Rangers* Series)

Dave O'Brien, Jim Newill, Guy Wilkerson, Ellen Hall, I. Stanford Jolley, Charles King, Reed Howes, Kermit Maynard, Budd Buster, Karl Hackett, Ed Cassidy
D: Harry Fraser
SP: Elmer Clifton
P: Arthur Alexander

1624. SONG OF NEVADA

(Republic, August 5, 1944) 75 Mins.

Roy Rogers, Dale Evans, Mary Lee, Bob Nolan and the Sons of the Pioneers, Lloyd Corrigan, Thurston Hall, John Eldredge, Forrest Taylor, George Meeker, Emmett Vogan, LeRoy Mason, William Davidson, Kenne Duncan, Si Jenks, Frank McCarroll, Henry Wills, Jack O'Shea, Helen Talbot, "Trigger"
D: Joseph Kane
SP: Gordon Kahn, Oliver Cooper
AP: Harry Grey

1625. WEST OF THE RIO GRANDE

(Monogram, August 5, 1944) 57 Mins.

Johnny Mack Brown, Raymond Hatton, Dennis Moore, Christine McIntyre, Lloyd Ingraham, Kenneth MacDonald, Frank LaRue, Art Fowler, Hugh Prosser, Edmund Cobb, Steve Clark, Jack Rockwell, Hal Price, John Merton, Bob Kortman, Bud Osborne, Pierce Lyden, Lynton Brent
D: Lambert Hillyer
S/SP: Betty Burbridge
P: Charles J. Bigelow

1626. BORDERTOWN TRAIL

(Republic, August 11, 1944) 55 Mins.

Smiley Burnette, Sunset Carson, Ellen Lowe, Weldon Heyburn, Addison Richards, Frances McDonald, Jack Luden, Rex Lease, John James, Jack Kirk, Henry Wills, Cliff Parkinson, Neal Hart, Chick Hannon, Jack O'Shea, Bob Wilke
D: Lesley Selander
SP: Bob Williams, Jesse Duffy
AP: Louis Gray

1627. THE SAN ANTONIO KID

(Republic, August 16, 1944) 59 Mins.

(*Red Ryder* Series)

Bill Elliott, Bobby Blake, Alice Fleming, Linda Stirling, Tom London, Earle Hodgins, Glenn Strange, Duncan Renaldo, LeRoy Mason, Jack Kirk, Bob

Wilke, Cliff Parkinson, Jack O'Shea, Tex Terry, Bob Woodward, Herman Hack, Henry Wills, Tom Steele, Joe Garcia, Billy Vincent, Bud Geary
D: Howard Bretherton
SP: Norman S. Hall
AP: Stephen Auer

1628. TRAIL TO GUNSIGHT
(Universal, August 18, 1944)   58 Mins.
Eddie Dew, Fuzzy Knight, Maris Wrixon, Lyle Talbot, Glenn Strange, Marie Austin, Ray Whitley and his Bar-6 Cowboys (Ezra Paulette, Len Giles, and Charley Quirt), Buzzy Henry, Sarah Padden, Ray Bennett, Charles Morton, Forrest Taylor, Terry Frost, Jack Clifford, Henry Wills
D: Vernon Keyes
S: Jay Karth
SP: Bennett Cohen, Patricia Harper
AP: Oliver Drake

1629. SWING IN THE SADDLE
(Columbia, August 31, 1944)
Jane Frazee, Guinn "Big Boy" Williams, Slim Summerville, Sally Bliss, Mary Treen, Red River Dave, Carole Mathews, Byron Foulger, Hoosier Hot Shots, King (Nat) Cole Trio, Jimmy Wakely and his Oklahoma Cowboys, Cousin Emmy
D: Lew Landers
SP: Elizabeth Beecher, Morton Grant, Bradford Ropes
P: Jack Fier

1630. BOB WILLS AND HIS TEXAS PLAYBOYS
(Warner Bros., September 2, 1944)   10 Mins.
Bob Wills and his Texas Playboys, narration by James Bloodworth
D: LeRoy Prinz

1631. RUSTLERS' HIDEOUT
(PRC, September 2, 1944)   60 Mins.
(*Billy Carson* Series)
Buster Crabbe, Al St. John, Patti McCarty, Charles King, John Merton, Lane Chandler, Terry Frost, Hal Price, Al Ferguson, Frank McCarroll, Edward Cassidy, Bud Osborne
D: Sam Newfield
SP: Joe O'Donnell
P: Sigmund Neufeld

1632. MOONLIGHT AND CACTUS
(Universal, September 8, 1944)   60 Mins.
Andrews Sisters, Leo Carrillo, Elyse Knox, Tom Seidel, Eddie Quillan, Shemp Howard, Tom Kennedy, Murray Alper, Frank Lackteen, Minerva Urecal, Mitch Ayers Orchestra
D: Edward F. Cline
P: Frank Gross

1633. SAN FERNANDO VALLEY
(Republic, September 15, 1944)   74 Mins.
Roy Rogers, Dale Evans, Jean Porter, Andrew Tombes, Bob Nolan and the Sons of the Pioneers, Edward Gargan, Dot Farley, LeRoy Mason, Charles Smith, Pierce Lyden, Maxine Doyle, Helen Talbot, Pat Starling, Kay Forrester, Marguerite Blount, Mary Kenyon, Hank Bell, Vernon and Draper, Morell Trio, "Trigger"
D: John English
SP: Dorrell and Stuart McGowan
AP: Eddy White

1634. STAGECOACH TO MONTEREY
(Republic, September 15, 1944)   55 Mins.
Allan Lane, Peggy Stewart, Wally Vernon, Twinkle Watts, Tom London, Roy Barcroft, LeRoy Mason, Kenne Duncan, Bud Geary, Carl Sepulveda, Jack O'Shea, Jack Kirk, Fred Graham, Henry Wills, Cactus Mack
D: Lesley Selander
SP: Norman S. Hall
AP: Stephen Auer

1635. LAND OF THE OUTLAWS
(Monogram, September 16, 1944)   56 Mins.
Johnny Mack Brown, Raymond Hatton, Stephen Keyes, Nan Holliday, Hugh Prosser, Charles King, John Merton, Steve Clark, Art Fowler, Tom Quinn, Ray Elder, Chick Hannon, Bob Cason, Kansas Moehring, Ben Corbett, George Morrell
D: Lambert Hillyer
SP: Joe O'Donnell
P: Charles J. Bigelow

1636. GANGSTERS OF THE FRONTIER
(PRC, September 21, 1944)   56 Mins.
(*Texas Rangers* Series)
Tex Ritter, Dave O'Brien, Guy Wilkerson, Patti McCarty, Betty Miles, Harry Harvey, I. Stanford Jolley, Charles King, Marshall Reed, Clarke Stevens
D/SP: Elmer Clifton
P: Arthur Alexander

1637. COWBOY FROM LONESOME RIVER
(Columbia, September 21, 1944)   55 Mins.
Charles Starrett, Vi Athens, Dub Taylor, Jimmy Wakely, Kenneth MacDonald, Ozie Waters, Arthur Wenzel, Shelby Atkinson, Foy Willing, Al Sloey, Craig Woods, Ian Keith, John Tyrell, Bud Geary, Steve Clark, Jack Rockwell
D: Ben Kline
SP: Luci Ward
P: Jack Fier

1638. TRIGGER LAW
(Monogram, September 30, 1944) 56 Mins.
Hoot Gibson, Bob Steele, Beatrice Gray, Ralph Lewis, Edward Cassidy, Jack Ingram, George Eldridge, Pierce Lyden, Lane Chandler, Bud Osborne, George Morrell
D: Vernon Keyes
SP: Victor Hammond
P: Charles J. Bigelow

1639. CHEYENNE WILDCAT
(Republic, September 30, 1944) 56 Mins.
(*Red Ryder* Series)
Bill Elliott, Bobby Blake, Alice Fleming, Peggy Stewart, Francis McDonald, Roy Barcroft, Tom London, Tom Chatterton, Kenne Duncan, Bud Geary, Jack Kirk, Sam Burton, Bud Osborne, Bob Wilke, Rex Lease, Tom Steele, Charles Morton, Forrest Taylor, Franklyn Farnum, Wee Willie Keeler, Universal Jack, Tom Smith, Rudy Bowman, Horace B. Carpenter, Frank Ellis, Steve Clark, Bob Burns, Jack O'Shea
D: Lesley Selander
SP: Randall Faye
AP: Louis Gray

1640. CODE OF THE PRAIRIE
(Republic, October 6, 1944) 56 Mins.
Smiley Burnette, Sunset Carson, Peggy Stewart, Weldon Heyburn, Tom Chatterton, Roy Barcroft, Bud Geary, Tom London, Jack Kirk, Tom Steele, Bob Wilke, Frank Ellis, Rex Lease, Henry Wills, Ken Terrell, Charles King, Nolan Leary, Hank Bell, Karl Hackett, Horace B. Carpenter, Jack O'Shea
D: Spencer Bennet
S: Albert DeMond
SP: Albert DeMond, Anthony Coldeway
AP: Louis Gray

1641. THE SINGING SHERIFF
(Universal, October 9, 1944) 63 Mins.
Bob Crosby, Fay McKenzie, Fuzzy Knight, Iris Adrian, Samuel S. Hinds, Andrew Tombes, Joe Sawyer, Edward Norris, Walter Sande, Doodles Weaver, Pat Starling, Louis Da Pron, Spade Cooley Orchestra
D: Leslie Goodwins
S: John Gray
SP: Henry Blankford, Eugene Conrad
AP: Bernard W. Burton

1642. BLACK ARROW
(Columbia, October 20, 1944) 15 Chaps.
Robert Scott, Adele Jergens, Robert Williams, Kenneth MacDonald, Charles Middleton, Martin Garralaga, George J. Lewis, Nick Thompson, George Navarro, I. Stanford Jolley, Harry Harvey, John Laurenz, Dan White, Eddie Parker, Stanley Price, Ted Mapes, Chief Thunder Cloud, Iron Eyes Cody
D: Lew Landers
SP: Sherman Lowe, Jack Stanley, Leighton Brill, Royal K. Cole
P: Rudolph C. Flothow
Chapter Titles: (1) A City of Gold, (2) Signal of Fear, (3) The Seal of Doom, (4) Terror of the Badlands, (5) The Secret of the Vault, (6) Appointment with Death, (7) The Chamber of Horror, (8) The Vanishing Dagger, (9) Escape from Death, (10) The Gold Cache, (11) The Curse of the Killer, (12) Test by Torture, (13) The Sign of Evil, (14) An Indian's Revenge, (15) Black Arrow Triumphs

1642a. GIRL RUSH
(RKO, October 25, 1944) 65 Mins.
Wally Brown, Alan Carney, Frances Langford, Vera Vague (Barbara Jo Allen), Robert Mitchum, Paul Hurst, Patti Brill, Sarah Padden, Cy Kendall, John Merton, Bud Osborne, Ernie Adams, Ken Terrell, Michael Vallon, Kernan Cripps, Wheaton Chambers, Byron Foulger, Dale Van Sickel, Elaine Riley, Chili Williams, Rita Corday, Virginia Belmont, Daun Kennedy, Rosemary LaPlanche, Lee Phelps, Bert LeBaron
D: Gordon Douglas
S: Laszlo Vadnay, Aladar Laszio
SP: Robert E. Kent
P: John Auer

1643. WILD HORSE PHANTOM
(PRC, October 28, 1944) 56 Mins.
(*Billy Carson* Series)
Buster Crabbe, Al St. John, Elaine Morey, Kermit Maynard, Budd Buster, Hal Price, Robert Meredith, Frank Ellis, Frank McCarroll, Bob Cason, John Elliott
D: Sam Newfield
SP: George Milton
P: Sigmund Neufeld

1644. LAW OF THE VALLEY
(Monogram, November 4, 1944) 52 Mins.
Johnny Mack Brown, Raymond Hatton, Lynne Carver, Edmund Cobb, Charles King, Kirk Barton, Tom Quinn, Marshall Reed, Hal Price, George DeNormand, Steve Clark, George Morrell, Charles McMurphy
D: Howard Bretherton
SP: Joe O'Donnell
P: Charles J. Bigelow

1645. LIGHTS OF OLD SANTA FE
(Republic, November 6, 1944) 76 Mins.

Roy Rogers, George Hayes, Dale Evans, Bob Nolan and the Sons of the Pioneers, Lloyd Corrigan, Richard Powers (Tom Keene), Claire DuBrey, Arthur Loft, Roy Barcroft, Lucien Littlefield, Sam Flint, "Trigger," Jack Kirk
D: Frank McDonald
SP: Gordon Kahn, Bob Williams
AP: Harry Grey

1646. SHERIFF OF SUNDOWN
(Republic, November 7, 1944)
Allan Lane, Linda Stirling, Max Terhune, Twinkle Watts, Duncan Renaldo, Roy Barcroft, Herbert Rawlinson, Bud Geary, Jack Kirk, Tom London, Bob Wilke, Kenne Duncan, Herman Hack, Jack O'Shea, Carl Sepulveda, Rex Lease, Nolan Leary, Horace B. Carpenter, Cactus Mack
D: Lesley Selander
SP: Norman S. Hall
AP: Stephen Auer

1647. CYCLONE PRAIRIE RANGERS
(Columbia, November 9, 1944) 56 Mins.
Charles Starrett, Dub Taylor, Constance Worth, Jimmy Davis, Jimmy Wakely and his Saddle Pals, Foy Willing, Clancy Cooper, Bob Fiske, Ray Bennett, I. Stanford Jolley, Edmund Cobb, Forrest Taylor, Paul Zaremba, Eddie Phillips, John Tyrell, Ted Mapes

D: Ben Kline
SP: Elizabeth Beecher
P: Jack Fier

1648. DEAD OR ALIVE
(PRC, November 9, 1944) 56 Mins.
(*Texas Rangers* Series)
Tex Ritter, Dave O'Brien, Marjorie Clements, Guy Wilkerson, Charles King, Rebel Randall, Ray Bennett, Bud Osborne, Henry Hall, Ted Mapes, Reed Howes
D: Elmer Clifton
SP: Harry Fraser
P: Arthur Alexander

1649. RIDERS OF THE SANTA FE
(Universal, November 10, 1944) 60 Mins.
Rod Cameron, Fuzzy Knight, Eddie Dew, Jennifer Holt, Ray Whitley and his Bar-6 Cowboys, Lane Chandler, Earle Hodgins, George Douglas, Dick Alexander, Budd Buster, Ida Moore, Al Ferguson, Ray Jones, Henry Wills
D: Wallace Fox
SP: Ande Lamb
AP: Oliver Drake

1650. VIGILANTES OF DODGE CITY
(Republic, November 15, 1944) 54 Mins.
(*Red Ryder* Series)

Riders of the Santa Fe (Universal, 1944)— Budd Buster, Fuzzy Knight, and Rod Cameron

Bill Elliott, Bobby Blake, Alice Fleming, Linda Stirling, LeRoy Mason, Hal Taliaferro, Tom London, Stephen Barclay, Bud Geary, Kenne Duncan, Bob Wilke, Horace B. Carpenter, Stanley Andrews
D: Wallace Grissell
S: Norman S. Hall
SP: Norman S. Hall, Anthony Coldeway
AP: Stephen Auer

1651. GHOST GUNS
(Monogram, November 17, 1944) 60 Mins.
Johnny Mack Brown, Raymond Hatton, Evelyn Finley, Sarah Padden, Riley Hill, Ernie Adams, Jack Ingram, Tom Quinn, Frank LaRue, John Merton, Bob Cason, Marshall Reed, Steve Clark, George Morrell
D: Lambert Hillyer
S: Bennett Cohen
SP: Frank H. Young
P: Charles J. Bigelow

1652. ALASKA
(Monogram, November 18, 1944) 76 Mins.
Kent Taylor, Margaret Lindsay, John Carradine, Dean Jagger, Nils Asther, Iris Adrian, George Cleveland, Lee "Lasses" White, Dewey Robinson, John Rogers, Jack Norton, John Maxwell, Warren Jackson, Dick Scott, Glenn Strange, Tex Cooper
D: George Archainbaud
S: "Flush of Gold"—Jack London
SP: George Wallace Sayre, Malcolm Stuart Boylan, Harrison Orkow
P: Lindsay Parsons

1653. FIREBRANDS OF ARIZONA
(Republic, December 1, 1944) 55 Mins.
Smiley Burnette, Sunset Carson, Peggy Stewart, Earle Hodgins, Roy Barcroft, Rex Lease, Tom London, Jack Kirk, Bud Geary, Bob Wilke, LeRoy Mason, Charles Morton, Fred Toones, Pierce Lyden, Frank Ellis, Frank McCarroll, Budd Buster, Bob Burns, Jack O'Shea, Hank Bell, Jess Cavin
D: Lesley Selander
SP: Randall Faye
AP: Louis Gray

1654. HARMONY TRAIL
(Mattox Productions, December 1, 1944) 57 Mins.
(Released in 1947 by Astor Pictures as *White Stallion*)
Ken Maynard, Eddie Dean, Max Terhune, Rocky Camron, Ruth Roman, Glenn Strange, Bob McKenzie, Charles King, Bud Osborne, Al Ferguson, Dan White, Fred Gildart, Jerry Shields, Hal Price, John Bridges
D: Robert Emmett (Tansey)
S: Frank Simpson
SP: Frances Kavanaugh
P: Walt Mattox

1655. NEVADA
(RKO, December 1, 1944) 62 Mins.
Robert Mitchum, Anne Jeffreys, Nancy Gates, Craig Reynolds, Guinn "Big Boy" Williams, Richard Martin, Harry Woods, Edmund Glover, Alan Ward, Harry McKim, Wheaton Chambers, Philip Morris, Emmett Lynn, Bryant Washburn, Larry Wheat, Jack Overman, George DeNormand, Virginia Belmont, Russell Hopton
D: Edward Killy
S: Zane Grey
SP: Norman Houston
P: Sid Rogell, Herman Schlom

1656. TALL IN THE SADDLE
(RKO, December 1, 1944) 87 Mins.
John Wayne, Ella Raines, George Hayes, Ward Bond, Audrey Long, Don Douglas, Elizabeth Risdon, Paul Fix, Russell Wade, Raymond Hatton, Emory Parnell, Harry Woods, Wheaton Chambers, Frank Puglia, Bob McKenzie, William Desmond, Russell Simpson
D: Edwin L. Marin
S: Gordon Ray Young
SP: Michael Hogan, Paul Fix
P: Robert Fellows

1657. SONG OF THE RANGE
(Monogram, December 1, 1944) 55 Mins.
Jimmy Wakely, Dennis Moore, Lee "Lasses" White, Kay Forrester, Pierre Watkin, George Eldridge, Hugh Prosser, Steve Clark, Edmund Cobb, Bud Osborne, Ken Terrell, Carl Mathews, Carl Sepulveda, The Sunshine Girls, Johnny Bond and his Red River Valley Boys
D: Wallace Fox
SP: Betty Burbridge
P: Phil N. Krasne

1658. SWING, COWBOY, SWING
(Three Crown, December 1, 1944)
(Released in 1949 by Astor Pictures as *Bad Man from Big Bend*)
Cal Shrum, Max Terhune, Alta Lee, Walt Shrum, Don Weston, I. Stanford Jolley, Ann Roberts, Frank Ellis, Edward Cassidy, Ted Adams, Phil Dunham, Tom Hubbard, Robert Hoag, Rusty Cline, Jeanne Akers, Chuck Peters, Shorty Woodward, Ace Dehne, Judy Barnes, Cal Shrum's Rhythm Rangers, Walt Shrum's Colorado Hillbillies
D: Elmer Clifton
S: Elmer Clifton
P: Birger E. Williamson

1659. BELLE OF THE YUKON
(International/RKO, December 6, 1944) 84 Mins.
Randolph Scott, Gypsy Rose Lee, Dinah Shore,

Bob Burns, Charles Winninger, William Marshall, Guinn "Big Boy" Williams, Robert Armstrong, Florence Bates, Edward Fielding, Wanda McKay, Charles Soldani
D/P: William A. Seiter
S: Houston Branch
SP: James Edward Grant

1660. OATH OF VENGEANCE
(PRC, December 9, 1944) 57 Mins.
(*Billy Carson* Series)
Buster Crabbe, Al St. John, Mady Lawrence, Jack Ingram, Charles King, Marin Sais, Karl Hackett, Kermit Maynard, Hal Price, Frank Ellis, Budd Buster, Jimmy Aubrey
D: Sam Newfield
SP: Fred Myton
P: Sigmund Neufeld

1661. THE OLD TEXAS TRAIL
(Universal, December 15, 1944) 60 Mins.
Rod Cameron, Fuzzy Knight, Eddie Dew, Marjorie Clements, Edmund Cobb, Virginia Christine, Ray Whitley and his Bar-6 Cowboys, Joseph J. Greene, George Eldridge, Jack Clifford, Dick Purcell, Harry Strang, Ray Jones, Merle Travis, William Desmond, George Turner (role credited to Terry Frost), Art Fowler, Henry Wills, Terry Frost
D: Lewis Collins
SP: William Lively
AP: Oliver Drake

1662. ZORRO'S BLACK WHIP
(Republic, December 16, 1944) 12 Chaps.
George J. Lewis, Linda Stirling, Lucien Littlefield, Francis McDonald, Hal Taliaferro, John Merton, John Hamilton, Tom Chatterton, Tom London, Jack Kirk, Jay Kirby, Si Jenks, Stanley Price, Tom Steele, Duke Green, Dale Van Sickel, Cliff Lyons, Roy Brent, Bill Yrigoyen, Forrest Taylor, Fred Graham, Marshall Reed, Augie Gomez, Carl Sepulveda, Horace Carpenter, Herman Hack, Carey Loftin, Cliff Parkinson, Ken Terrell, Duke Taylor, Vinegar Roan, Roy Brent, Babe DeFreest
D: Spencer G. Bennet, Wallace Grissell
SP: Basil Dickey, Jesse Duffey, Grant Nelson, Joseph Poland
AP: Ronald Davidson
Chapter Titles: (1) The Masked Avenger, (2) Tomb of Terror, (3) Mob Murder, (4) Detour to Death, (5) Take Off That Mask!, (6) Fatal Gold, (7) Wolf Pack, (8) The Invisible Victim, (9) Avalanche, (10) Fangs of Doom, (11) Flaming Juggernaut, (12) Trail of Tyranny

1663. GENTLE ANNIE
(MGM, December 20, 1944) 80 Mins.
James Craig, Donna Reed, Marjorie Main, Henry

(Harry) Morgan, Paul Langton, Barton MacLane, John Philliber, Morris Ankrum
D: Andrew Martin
S: MacKinlay Kantor
SP: Lawrence Hazard
P: Robert Sisk

1664. THE WHISPERING SKULL
(PRC, December 20, 1944)
(*Texas Rangers* Series)
Dave O'Brien, Tex Ritter, Guy Wilkerson, Denny Burke, I. Stanford Jolley, Henry Hall, George Morrell, Edward Cassidy, Bob Kortman, Wen Wright
D: Elmer Clifton
SP: Harry Fraser
P: Arthur Alexander

1665. SADDLE LEATHER LAW
(Columbia, December 21, 1944)
Charles Starrett, Dub Taylor, Vi Athens, Lloyd Bridges, Reed Howes, Robert Kortman, Ted French, Frank LaRue, Edward Cassidy, Steve Clark, Nolan Leary, Budd Buster, Joseph Eggenton, Jimmy Wakely, Salty Holmes, Ted Adams, Frank O'Connor, Franklyn Farnum
D: Ben Kline
SP: Elizabeth Beecher
P: Jack Fier

1666. THE BIG BONANZA
(Republic, December 30, 1944) 68 Mins.
Richard Arlen, Robert Livingston, Jane Frazee, George Hayes, Lynne Roberts, Bobby Driscoll, J. M. Kerrigan, Russell Simpson, Frank Reicher, Cordell Hickman, Howard Soo Hoo, Roy Barcroft, Fred Kohler, Jr., Monte Hale, Charles King, Jack Rockwell, Henry Wills, Fred Graham, Dan White, Bob Wilke
D: George Archainbaud
S: Robert Presnell, Leonard Praskins
SP: Dorrell and Stuart McGowan, Paul Gengelin
AP: Eddy White

1667. SHERIFF OF LAS VEGAS
(Republic, December 31, 1944) 55 Mins.
(*Red Ryder* Series)
Bill Elliott, Bobby Blake, Alice Fleming, Peggy Stewart, Selmer Jackson, William Haade, Jay Kirby, John Hamilton, Kenne Duncan, Bud Geary, Jack Kirk, Dickie Dillon, Frank McCarroll, Freddie Chapman
D: Lesley Selander
SP: Norman S. Hall
AP: Stephen Auer

1667a. ROARING GUNS
(Warner Bros., 1944) 20 Mins.

Robert Shayne, Virginia Patton, Stephen Richards,
Charles Arnt, Norman Willis, Russell Simpson
D: Jean Negulesco
S: Clements Ripley
SP: Ed Earl Repp
P: Gordon Hollingshead

1667b. LUCKY COWBOY
(Paramount, 1944)   2 Reels
Eddie Dew, Julie Gibson, Frank Hagney, Bernard
Nedell, LeRoy Mason, Syd Saylor
D: Josef Berne

FILMS OF 1945

1668. THE NAVAJO TRAIL
(Monogram, January 5, 1945)   60 Mins.
Johnny Mack Brown, Raymond Hatton, Jennifer
Holt, Riley Hill, Edmund Cobb, Charles King, Ray
Bennett, Bud Osborne, Tom Quinn, Edward Cas-
sidy, John Carpenter
D: Howard Bretherton
S: Frank Young
SP: Jess Bowers (Adele Buffington)
P: Charles J. Bigelow

1669. UNDER WESTERN SKIES
(Universal, January 19, 1945)   57 Mins.
Martha O'Driscoll, Noah Beery, Jr., Leo Carrillo,
Leon Errol, Irving Bacon, Ian Keith, Jennifer Holt,
Edna May Wonacott, Earle Hodgins, Shaw and
Lee, Dorothy Granger, Jack Rice
D: Jean Yarbrough
S: Stanley Roberts
SP: Stanley Roberts, Clyde Bruckman
P: Warren Wilson

1670. THE TOPEKA TERROR
(Republic, January 26, 1945)   55 Mins.
Allan Lane, Linda Stirling, Roy Barcroft, Earle
Hodgins, Twinkle Watts, Bud Geary, Frank Jac-
quet, Jack Kirk, Tom London, Eve Novak, Hank
Bell, Bob Wilke, Monte Hale, Jess Cavan, Fred
Graham
D: Howard Bretherton
S: Patricia Harper
SP: Patricia Harper, Norman S. Hall
AP: Stephen Auer

1671. HIS BROTHER'S GHOST
(PRC, February 3, 1945)   54 Mins.
(*Billy Carson* Series)
Buster Crabbe, Al St. John, Charles King, Karl
Hackett, Archie Hall, Roy Brent, Bud Osborne,
Bob Cason, Frank McCarroll, George Morrell
D: Sam Newfield
SP: George Plympton
P: Sigmund Neufeld

1672. MARKED FOR MURDER
(PRC, February 8, 1945)   58 Mins.
(*Texas Rangers* Series)
Tex Ritter, Dave O'Brien, Guy Wilkerson, Marilyn

McConnell, Henry Hall, Edward Cassidy, Charles
King, Jack Ingram, Bob Kortman, Wen Wright,
The Milo Twins, Kermit Maynard
D/SP: Elmer Clifton
P: Arthur Alexander

1673. SING ME A SONG OF TEXAS
(Columbia, February 8, 1945)   66 Mins.
Tom Tyler, Rosemary Lane, Hal McIntyre and his
Orchestra, The Hoosier Hotshots, Guinn "Big
Boy" Williams, Slim Summerville, Carole Mat-
thews, Noah Beery, Sr., Pinky Tomlin, Marie
Austin, Foy Willing and his Riders of the Purple
Sage
D: Vernon Keays
SP: J. Benton Cheney, Elizabeth Beecher
P: Colbert Clark

1674. GREAT STAGECOACH ROBBERY
(Republic, February 15, 1945)   56 Mins.
(*Red Ryder* Series)
Bill Elliott, Bobby Blake, Alice Fleming, Francis
McDonald, Don Costello, Sylvia Arslan, Bud
Geary, Leon Tyler, Freddie Chapman, Henry
Wills, Hank Bell, Bob Wilke, John James, Tom
London, Dickie Dillon, Bobby Dillon, Raymond
ZeBrack, Patsy May, Chris Wren, Horace Car-
penter, Grace Cunard, Frederick Howard
D: Lesley Selander
SP: Randall Faye
AP: Louis Gray

1675. THE CISCO KID RETURNS
(Monogram, February 16, 1945)   64 Mins.
(*Cisco Kid* Series)
Duncan Renaldo, Martin Garralaga, Cecilia Callejo,
Roger Pryor, Anthony Warde, Fritz Leiber, Vicky
Lane, Jan Wiley, Sharon Smith, Cy Kendall, Eva
Puig, Bud Osborne, Bob Duncan, Elmer Napier,
Carl Mathews, Jerry Fields, Neyle Marx, Cedric
Stevens, Walter Clinton
D: John P. McCarthy
SP: Betty Burbridge
P: Philip N. Krasne

1676. GUN SMOKE
(Monogram, February 16, 1945)   57 Mins.
Johnny Mack Brown, Raymond Hatton, Jennifer

Holt, Riley Hill, Frank Ellis, Ray Bennett, Marshall Reed, Steve Clark, Bob Cason, Elmer Napier, Roy Butler, Wen Wright, Demas Sotello, Kansas Moehring, Louis Hart, Chick Hannon
D: Howard Bretherton
SP: Frank Young
P: Charles E. Bigelow

1677. FRISCO SAL

(Universal, February 23, 1945)   94 Mins.
Susanna Foster, Turhan Bey, Alan Curtis, Andy Devine, Thomas Gomez, Collette Lyons, Samuel S. Hinds, Fuzzy Knight, Billy Green, Ernie Adams, George Lloyd, Bert Fiske
D: George Waggner
SP: Curt Siodmak, Gerald Geraghty
P: George Waggner

1678. SHERIFF OF CIMARRON

(Republic, February 28, 1945)
Sunset Carson, Linda Stirling, Olin Howlin, Riley Hill, Jack Kirk, Jack Ingram, Bob Wilke, Edward Cassidy, George Chesebro, Dickie Dillon, Tom London, Jack O'Shea, Sylvia Arslan, Henry Wills, Hal Price, Carol Henry
D: Yakima Canutt
SP: Bennett Cohen
AP: Thomas Carr

1679. ROUGH RIDIN' JUSTICE

(Columbia, March 14, 1945)   58 Mins.
Charles Starrett, Dub Taylor, Betty Jane Graham, Jimmy Wakeley and his Oklahoma Cowboys, Wheeler Oakman, Jack Ingram, Forrest Taylor, Jack Rockwell, Edmund Cobb, Dan White, Bob Kortman, George Chesebro, Robert Ross, Carl Sepulveda, Butch and Buddy
D: Derwin Abrahams
SP: Elizabeth Beecher
P: Jack Fier

1680. UTAH

(Republic, March 21, 1945)   78 Mins.
Roy Rogers, George Hayes, Dale Evans, Peggy Stewart, Beverly Loyd, Grant Withers, Jill Browning, Vivien Oakland, Hal Taliaferro, Jack Rutherford, Emmett Vogan, Edward Cassidy, Ralph Colby, Bob Nolan and the Sons of the Pioneers, "Trigger"
D: John English
S: Gilbert Wright, Betty Burbridge
SP: Jack Townley, John K. Butler
AP: Donald H. Brown

1680a. PISTOL PACKIN' NITWITS

(Columbia, April 4, 1945)   2 Reels
Harry Langdon, El Brendel, Christine McIntyre,

Dick Curtis, Tex Cooper, Brad King, Victor Cox, Heinie Conklin, Vernon Dent
D: Harry Edwards

1681. STRANGER FROM SANTA FE

(Monogram, April 15, 1945)   57 Mins.
Johnny Mack Brown, Raymond Hatton, Beatrice Gray, Jo Ann Curtis, Jack Ingram, Bud Osborne, Jimmie Martin, Steve Clark, Hal Price, John Merton, Tom Quinn, Ray Elder, Eddie Parker, Louis Hart, Jack Rockwell
D: Lambert Hillyer
SP: Frank Young
P: Charles J. Bigelow

1682. ROCKIN' IN THE ROCKIES

(Columbia, April 17, 1945)   63 Mins.
Mary Beth Hughes, Jay Kirby, Gladys Blake, The Three Stooges (Moe Howard, Jerry Howard, and Larry Fine), Jack Clifford, Forrest Taylor, Tim Ryan, Vernon Dent, The Hoosier Hotshots, The Cappy Barra Boys, Spade Cooley
D: Vernon Keays
S: Louise Rousseau, Gail Davenport
SP: J. Benton Cheney, John Gray
P: Colbert Clark

1683. SHADOWS OF DEATH

(PRC, April 19, 1945)   60 Mins.
(*Billy Carson* Series)
Buster Crabbe, Al St. John, Donna Dax, Charles King, Karl Hackett, Edward Piel, Sr., Bob Cason, Frank Ellis, Frank McCarroll
D: Sam Newfield
SP: Fred Myton
P: Sigmund Neufeld

1684. RETURN OF THE DURANGO KID

(Columbia, April 19, 1945)   58 Mins.
(*Durango Kid* Series)
Charles Starrett, Tex Harding, Jean Stevens, John Calvert, Betty Roadman, Hal Price, Dick Botiller, Britt Wood, Ray Bennett, Paul Conrad, Steve Clark, Carl Sepulveda, Elmo Lincoln, Ted Mapes, Herman Hack, The Jesters
D: Derwin Abrahams
SP: J. Benton Cheney
P: Colbert Clark

1685. CORPUS CHRISTI BANDITS

(Republic, April 20, 1945)   55 Mins.
Allan Lane, Helen Talbot, Twinkle Watts, Tom London, Francis McDonald, Jack Kirk, Roy Barcroft, Kenne Duncan, Bob Wilke, Ruth Lee, Edward Cassidy, Emmett Vogan, Dickie Dillon, Freddie Chapman, Shelby Bacon, Neal Hart, Horace B. Carpenter, Hal Price, Frank Ellis, Frank McCarroll, Henry Wills

D: Wallace Grissell
SP: Norman S. Hall
AP: Stephen Auer

1686. BEYOND THE PECOS
(Universal, April 27, 1945)   58 Mins.
Rod Cameron, Eddie Dew, Fuzzy Knight, Jennifer
    Holt, Ray Whitley, Eugene Stutenroth (Gene
    Roth), Robert Homans, Jack Ingram, Frank Jac-
    quet, Henry Wills, Jack Rockwell, Jim Thorpe,
    Dan White, Al Ferguson, Forrest Taylor, Herman
    Hack, Artie Ortego, William Desmond, Ray Whit-
    ley's Bar-6 Cowboys
D: Lambert Hillyer
S: Jay Karth
SP: Bennett Cohen
AP: Oliver Drake

1687. SALOME, WHERE SHE DANCED
(Universal, April 27, 1945)   90 Mins.
(Technicolor)
Yvonne De Carlo, Rod Cameron, David Bruce,
    Walter Slezak, Albert Dekker, Marjorie Rambeau,
    J. Edward Bromberg, Abner Biberman, John Litel,
    Kent Katch, Arthur Hohl, Will Wright, Matt
    McHugh
D: Charles Lamont
S: Michael Phillips
SP: Laurence Stalling
AP: Alexander Golitzen

1688. ENEMY OF THE LAW
(PRC, May 7, 1945)   59 Mins.
(*Texas Rangers* Series)
Tex Ritter, Dave O'Brien, Guy Wilkerson, Kay
    Hughes, Jack Ingram, Charles King, Frank Ellis,
    Kermit Maynard, Henry Hall, Karl Hackett,
    Edward Cassidy, Ben Corbett
D/SP: Harry Fraser
P: Arthur Alexander

1689. IN OLD NEW MEXICO
(Monogram, May 15, 1945)   62 Mins.
(*Cisco Kid* Series)
Duncan Renaldo, Martin Garralaga, Gwen Kenyon,
    Norman Willis, Lee "Lasses" White, Pedro De
    Cordoba, Frank Jacquet, Bud Osborne, Artie Or-
    tego, Aurora Roche, Edward Earle, Donna Dax,
    John Lawrence, Richard Gordon, James Farley,
    Car-Bert Dancers
D: Phil Rosen
SP: Betty Burbridge
P: Philip Krasne

1690. BOTH BARRELS BLAZING
(Columbia, May 17, 1945)   57 Mins.
(*Durango Kid* Series)

Charles Starrett, Tex Harding, Dub Taylor, Pat
    Parrish, Emmett Lynn, Alan Bridge, Dan White,
    Edward Howard, The Jesters, Jack Rockwell,
    Charles King, Robert Barron, Mauritz Hugo
D: Derwin Abrahams
SP: William Lively
AP: Colbert Clark

1691. LONE TEXAS RANGER
(Republic, May 20, 1945)   56 Mins.
(*Red Ryder* Series)
Bill Elliott, Bobby Blake, Alice Fleming, Roy Bar-
    croft, Helen Talbot, Jack McClendon, Rex Lease,
    Tom Chatterton, Jack Kirk, Nelson McDowell,
    Larry Olson, Dale Van Sickel, Frank O'Connor,
    Bob Wilke, Bud Geary, Budd Buster, Hal Price,
    Horace B. Carpenter, Nolan Leary, Tom Steele,
    LeRoy Mason (voice only), Earl Dobbins, Larry
    Olsen, Nolan Leary, Frank O'Connor, Bill
    Stevens
D: Spencer Bennet
SP: Bob Williams
AP: Louis Gray

1692. FLAME OF THE BARBARY COAST
(Republic, May 28, 1945)   91 Mins.
John Wayne, Ann Dvorak, Joseph Schildkraut, Wil-
    liam Frawley, Virginia Grey, Russell Hicks, Jack
    Norton, Paul Fix, Manart Kippen, Eve Lynne,
    Marc Lawrence, Butterfly McQueen, Rex Lease,
    Hank Bell, Al Murphy
D/AP: Joseph Kane
SP: Borden Chase

1693. RENEGADES OF THE RIO GRANDE
(Universal, June 1, 1945)   57 Mins.
Rod Cameron, Fuzzy Knight, Jennifer Holt, Eddie
    Dew, Glenn Strange, Ray Whitley, Ethan Laid-
    law, Edmund Cobb, Dick Alexander, Iris Clive,
    John James, Jack Casey, Hal Hart, Dick Botiller,
    Percy Carson, Ray Whitley's Bar-6 Cowboys
D: Howard Bretherton
SP: Ande Lamb
AP: Oliver Drake

1694. SANTA FE SADDLEMATES
(Republic, June 2, 1945)   56 Mins.
Sunset Carson, Linda Stirling, Olin Howlin, Roy
    Barcroft, Rex Lease, Bud Geary, Kenne Duncan,
    George Chesebro, Bob Wilke, Forbes Murray,
    Henry Wills, Frank Jacquet, Josh (John) Carpen-
    ter, Edmund Cobb, Nolan Leary, Fred Graham,
    George Magril, Jack O'Shea, Carol Henry, Billy
    Vincent
D/AP: Thomas Carr
SP: Bennett Cohen

1695. SPRINGTIME IN TEXAS

(Monogram, June 2, 1945) 55 Mins.

Jimmy Wakely, Dennis Moore, Lee "Lasses" White, Marie Harmon, Rex Lease, Pearl Early, Horace Murphy, I. Stanford Jolley, Hal Taliaferro, Budd Buster, Roy Butler, Johnny Bond, Lloyd Ingraham, The Callahan Brothers and their Blue Ridge Mountain Folks

D/P: Oliver Drake

SP: Frances Kavanaugh

1696. RHYTHM ROUND-UP

(Columbia, June 7, 1945) 66 Mins.

Ken Curtis, Cheryl Walker, Hoosier Hotshots, Guinn "Big Boy" Williams, Raymond Hatton, Victor Potel, The Pied Pipers, Bob Wills and his Texas Playboys, Eddie Bruce, Arthur Loft, Walter Baldwin, Vera Lewis

D: Vernon Keays

S: Louise Rousseau

SP: Charles Marion

P: Colbert Clark

1697. GANGSTER'S DEN

(PRC, June 14, 1945) 55 Mins.

(*Billy Carson* Series)

Buster Crabbe, Al St. John, Sidney Logan, Charles King, Emmett Lynn, Kermit Maynard, Edward Cassidy, I. Stanford Jolley, George Chesebro, Karl Hackett, Michael Owen, Bob Cason, Wally West

D: Sam Newfield

SP: George Plympton

P: Sigmund Neufeld

1698. WEST OF THE PECOS

(RKO, June 18, 1945) 68 Mins.

Robert Mitchum, Barbara Hale, Richard Martin, Thurston Hall, Rita Corday, Russell Hopton, Bill Williams, Bruce Edwards, Harry Woods, Perc Launders, Bryant Washburn, Philip Morris, Martin Garralaga, Ethan Laidlaw, Larry Wheat

D: Edward Killy

S: Zane Grey

SP: Norman Houston

P: Herman Schlom

1699. BELLS OF ROSARITA

(Republic, June 19, 1945) 68 Mins.

Roy Rogers, George Hayes, Dale Evans, Adele Mara, Grant Withers, Janet Martin, Syd Saylor, Addison Richards, Edward Cassidy, Roy Barcroft, Kenne Duncan, Rex Lease, Earle Hodgins, Bob Wilke, Ted Adams, Wally West, Bob Nolan and the Sons of the Pioneers, Robert Mitchell Boychoir, "Trigger," and guest stars Bill Elliott, Allan Lane, Don Barry, Robert Livingston, Sunset Carson, Poodles Hanneford, Helen Talbot,

Charles Sullivan, Hank Bell, Forbes Murray, Eddie Kane, Tom London, Marin Sais, Rosemond James, Marian Kerrigan, Sam Ash, Craig Lawrence, Barbara Elliott, Mary McCarty, Tom Plank, George Barton

D: Frank McDonald

SP: Jack Townley

AP: Eddy White

1700. ALONG CAME JONES

(International/RKO, June 23, 1945) 90 Mins.

Gary Cooper, Loretta Young, Dan Duryea, William Demarest, Frank Sully, Russell Simpson, Arthur Loft, Willard Robertson, Don Costello, Ray Teal, Lane Chandler

D: Stuart Heisler

S: Alan LeMay

SP: Nunnally Johnson

P: Gary Cooper

1701. FLAME OF THE WEST

(Monogram, June 25, 1945) 70 Mins.

Johnny Mack Brown, Joan Woodbury, Raymond Hatton, Douglass Dumbrille, Lynne Carver, Harry Woods, Riley Hill, Jack Ingram, John Merton, Tom Quinn, Jack Rockwell, Ted Mapes, Bob Duncan, Pierce Lyden, Frank McCarroll, Ray Bennett, Steve Clark, Bud Osborne, Hal Price, Bob Cason, Eddie Parker, Horace B. Carpenter

D: Lambert Hillyer

S: Bennett Foster

SP: Adele Buffington

P: Scott R. Dunlap

1702. TRAIL OF KIT CARSON

(Republic, July 11, 1945) 57 Mins.

Allan Lane, Helen Talbot, Tom London, Twinkle Watts, Roy Barcroft, Kenne Duncan, Jack Kirk, Bud Geary, Tom Dugan, George Chesebro, Bob Wilke, Freddie Chapman, Dickie Dillon, Herman Hack, John Carpenter, Henry Wills, Tom Steele

D: Lesley Selander

SP: Albert DeMond, Jack Natteford

AP: Stephen Auer

1703. OREGON TRAIL

(Republic, July 14, 1945) 55 Mins.

Sunset Carson, Peggy Stewart, Frank Jacquet, Si Jenks, John Merton, Mary Carr, Earle Hodgins, Tom London, Kenne Duncan, Bud Geary, Lee Shumway, Steve Winston, Henry Wills, Cactus Mack, Tex Terry, Bud Osborne (scene with Monte Hale and Rex Lease edited out of release print)

D: Thomas Carr

S: Frank Gruber

SP: Betty Burbridge

AP: Bennett Cohen

1704. WILDFIRE

(Action Pictures, July 18, 1945) 57 Mins.
(Cinecolor)

Bob Steele, Sterling Holloway, John Miljan, William Farnum, Virginia Maples, Eddie Dean, Sarah Padden, Wee Willie Davis, Rocky Camron, Al Ferguson, Francis Ford, Frank Ellis, Hal Price
D: Robert Tansey
S: W. C. Tuttle
SP: Frances Kavanaugh
P: William B. David

1705. THREE IN THE SADDLE

(PRC, July 26, 1945) 61 Mins.
(*Texas Rangers* Series)

Dave O'Brien, Tex Ritter, Guy Wilkerson, Lorraine Miller, Charles King, Edward Howard, Edward Cassidy, Bud Osborne, Frank Ellis
D: Harry Fraser
SP: Elmer Clifton
P: Arthur Alexander

1706. THE MAN FROM OKLAHOMA

(Republic, August 1, 1945) 68 Mins.

Roy Rogers, Dale Evans, George Hayes, Bob Nolan and the Sons of the Pioneers, Roger Pryor, Arthur Loft, Maude Eburne, Sam Flint, Si Jenks, June Bryde, Elaine Lange, Charles Soldani, Edmund Cobb, George Sherwood, Eddie Kane, George Chandler, Wally West, Tex Terry, Bob Wilke, Bobbie Priest, Dorothy Bailer, Rosamond James, Melva Anstead, Beverly Reedy, Geraldine Farnum, "Trigger"
D: Frank McDonald
SP: John K. Butler
AP: Louis Gray

1707. SADDLE SERENADE

(Monogram, August 11, 1945) 57 Mins.

Jimmy Wakely, Lee "Lasses" White, John James, Nancy Brinkman, Alan Foster, Jack Ingram, Claire James, Pat Gleason, Kay Deslys, Roy Butler, Elmer Napier, Frank McCarroll, Jack Hendricks, Bob Duncan, Dee Cooper, Jack Spears, Foy Willing and his Riders of the Purple Sage
D/P: Oliver Drake
SP: Frances Kavanaugh

1708. RUSTLERS OF THE BADLANDS

(Columbia, August 16, 1945) 55 Mins.
(*Durango Kid* Series)

Charles Starrett, Tex Harding, Dub Taylor, Sally Bliss, George Eldridge, Edward Howard, Ray Bennett, Ted Mapes, Karl Hackett, James Nelson, Frank McCarroll, Carl Sepulveda, Steve Clark, Al Trace and his Silly Symphonists
D: Derwin Abrahams
S: Richard Hill Wilkinson

SP: J. Benton Cheney
P: Colbert Clark

1709. STAGECOACH OUTLAWS

(PRC, August 17, 1945) 55 Mins.
(*Billy Carson* Series)

Buster Crabbe, Al St. John, Frances Gladwin, Kermit Maynard, Ed Cassidy, I. Stanford Jolley, Bob Cason, Bob Kortman, Steve Clark, George Chesebro, Hank Bell
D: Sam Newfield
SP: Fred Myton
P: Sigmund Neufeld

1710. FRONTIER FUGITIVES

(PRC, September 1, 1945) 53 Mins.
(*Texas Rangers* Series)

Dave O'Brien, Tex Ritter, Lorraine Miller, Guy Wilkerson, I. Stanford Jolley, Jack Ingram, Frank Ellis, Jack Hendricks, Charles King, Karl Hackett, Budd Buster
D: Harry Fraser
SP: Elmer Clifton
P: Arthur Alexander

1711. SPADE COOLEY, KING OF WESTERN SWING

(Warner Bros., September 1, 1945) 10 Mins.
Spade Cooley and his Band
D: Jack Scholl
P: Gordon Hollingshead

1712. PHANTOM OF THE PLAINS

(Republic, September 7, 1945) 56 Mins.
(*Red Ryder* Series)

Bill Elliott, Bobby Blake, Alice Fleming, Ian Keith, William Haade, Virginia Christine, Bud Geary, Henry Hall, Fred Graham, Jack Kirk, Jack Rockwell, Tom London, Earle Hodgins, Rose Plummer
D: Lesley Selander
SP: Earle Snell, Charles Kenyon
AP: R. G. Springsteen

1713. SOUTH OF THE RIO GRANDE

(Monogram, September 8, 1945) 62 Mins.
(*Cisco Kid* Series)

Duncan Renaldo, Martin Garralaga, Armida, George J. Lewis, Lillian Molieri, Francis McDonald, Charles Stevens, Pedro Regas, Soledad Jiminez, Tito Renaldo, The Guadalajara Trio
D: Lambert Hillyer
S: Johnston McCulley
SP: Victor Hammond, Ralph Bettinson
P: Philip N. Krasne

1714. BANDITS OF THE BADLANDS

(Republic, September 14, 1945) 55 Mins.
Sunset Carson, Peggy Stewart, Si Jenks, Monte

Hale, John Merton, Forrest Taylor, Wade Crosby, Jack Ingram, Fred Graham, Alan Ward, Bob Wilke, Tex Terry, Jack O'Shea, Jack Kirk, Horace B. Carpenter, Charles Stevens, Charlie Sullivan, Henry Wills, Marshall Reed
D: Thomas Carr
SP: Doris Schroeder
AP: Bennett Cohen

1715. BLAZING THE WESTERN TRAIL
(Columbia, September 18, 1945) 60 Mins.
(*Durango Kid* Series)
Charles Starrett, Tex Harding, Dub Taylor, Carole Matthews, Alan Bridge, Nolan Leary, Virginia Sale, Steve Clark, Mauritz Hugo, Ethan Laidlaw, Edmund Cobb, Frank LaRue, Forrest Taylor, Francis Walker, Nolan Leary, Bob Wills and his Texas Playboys
D: Vernon Keays
SP: J. Benton Cheney
AP: Colbert Clark

1716. OUTLAWS OF THE ROCKIES
(Columbia, September 18, 1945) 55 Mins.
(*Durango Kid* Series)
Charles Starrett, Tex Harding, Dub Taylor, Carole Matthews, Philip Van Zandt, I. Stanford Jolley, George Chesebro, Steve Clark, Jack Rockwell, Carolina Cotton, Spade Cooley
D: Ray Nazarro
SP: J. Benton Cheney
AP: Colbert Clark

1717. RIDERS OF THE DAWN
(Monogram, September 22, 1945) 58 Mins.
Jimmy Wakely, Lee "Lasses" White, John James, Phyllis Adair, Sarah Padden, Horace Murphy, Jack Baxley, Bob Shelton, Dad Pickard, Arthur Smith, Eddie Taylor, Brooks Temple, Bill Hammond, Michael Joseph Ward, Wesley Tuttle and his Texas Stars
D: Oliver Drake
SP: Louis Rousseau
P: Charles J. Bigelow

1718. SONG OF THE PRAIRIE
(September 27, 1945) 62 Mins.
Ken Curtis, June Storey, Guinn "Big Boy" Williams, Jeff Donnell, Andy Clyde, Grady Sutton, Robert Williams, John Tyrell, Deuce Spriggins, Dick Curtis, Thurston Hall, Carolina Cotton, The Hoosier Hotshots, The Town Criers
D: Ray Nazzaro
SP: J. Benton Cheney
P: Colbert Clark

1719. BAD MEN OF THE BORDER
(Universal, September 28, 1945) 56 Mins.
Kirby Grant, Fuzzy Knight, Armida, John Eldredge, Barbara Sears, Francis McDonald, Soledad Jiminez, Edward Howard, Edmund Cobb, Pierce Lyden, Gene Stutenroth (Gene Roth), Roy Brent, Glenn Strange, Ethan Laidlaw, Charles Stevens
D: Wallace Fox
S/SP: Adele Buffington
AP: Wallace Fox

1720. SUNSET IN EL DORADO
(Republic, September 29, 1945) 65 Mins.
Roy Rogers, George Hayes, Dale Evans, Hardie Albright, Margaret Dumont, Roy Barcroft, Tom London, Stanley Price, Bob Wilke, Ed Cassidy, Dorothy Granger, Bob Nolan and the Sons of the Pioneers, Edmund Cobb, Hank Bell, Jack Kirk, Gino Corrado, Frank Ellis, Tex Cooper, Bert Morehouse, Joe McGuinn, Tex Terry, Bud Osborne, "Trigger"
D: Frank McDonald
S: Leon Abrams
SP: John K. Butler
AP: Louis Gray

1721. MARSHAL OF LAREDO
(Republic, October 7, 1945) 56 Mins.
(*Red Ryder* Series)
Bill Elliott, Bobby Blake, Alice Fleming, Peggy Stewart, Roy Barcroft, Tom London, George Carleton, Wheaton Chambers, Tom Chatterton, George Chesebro, Don Costello, Bud Geary, Robert Grady, Sarah Padden, Jack O'Shea, Lane Bradford, Ken Terrell, Dorothy Granger, Dick Scott
D: R. G. Springsteen
SP: Bob Williams
AP: Sidney Picker

1722. BORDER BADMEN
(PRC, October 10, 1945) 59 Mins.
(*Billy Carson* Series)
Buster Crabbe, Al St. John, Lorraine Miller, Charles King, Ray Bennett, Archie Hall, Budd Buster, Marilyn Gladstone, Marin Sais, Bud Osborne, Bob Kortman
D: Sam Newfield
SP: George Milton
P: Sigmund Neufeld

1723. SENORITA FROM THE WEST
(Universal, October 12, 1945) 63 Mins.
Allan Jones, Bonita Granville, Jess Barker, Olin Howlin, Danny Mummert, Emmett Vogan, Oscar O'Shea, Fuzzy Knight, George Cleveland, Renny McEvoy, Bob Merrill, Billy Nelson, Jack Clifford, Spade Cooley Orchestra
D: Frank Strayer

SP: Howard Dimsdale
P: Philip Cahn

1724. FLAMING BULLETS
(PRC, October 15, 1945)   55 Mins.
(*Texas Rangers* Series)
Tex Ritter, Dave O'Brien, Guy Wilkerson, Patricia Knox, Charles King, Bud Osborne, I. Stanford Jolley, Bob Duncan, Kermit Maynard, Dick Alexander, Dan White
D/SP: Harry Fraser
P: Arthur Alexander

1725. WANDERER OF THE WASTELAND
(RKO, October 18, 1945)   67 Mins.
James Warren, Richard Martin, Audrey Long, Robert Barrat, Robert Clarke, Harry Woods, Minerva Urecal, Harry D. Brown, Tommy Cook, Harry McKim, Jason Robards, Sr.
D: Edward Killy, Wallace Grissell
S: Zane Grey
SP: Norman Houston
P: Herman Schlom

1726. CODE OF THE LAWLESS
(Universal, October 19, 1945)   57 Mins.
Kirby Grant, Fuzzy Knight, Poni (Jane) Adams, Charles Miller, Rex Lease, Barbara Sears, Hugh Prosser, Bob McKenzie, Blackie Whiteford, Edmund Cobb, Budd Buster, Edward Howard, Stanley Andrews, Pierce Lyden, Roy Brent, Fred Graham, Brick Sullivan
D: Wallace Fox
SP: Patricia Harper
AP: Wallace Fox

1727. DON'T FENCE ME IN
(Republic, October 20, 1945)   71 Mins.
Roy Rogers, Dale Evans, George Hayes, Bob Nolan and the Sons of the Pioneers, Robert Livingston, Moroni Olson, Marc Lawrence, Lucille Gleason, Andrew Tombes, Paul Harvey, Douglas Fowley, Stephen Barclay, Edgar Dearing, Helen Talbot, "Trigger"
D: John English
SP: Dorrell and Stuart McGowan, John K. Butler
AP: Donald H. Brown

1728. THE LOST TRAIL
(Monogram, October 20, 1945)   53 Mins.
Johnny Mack Brown, Raymond Hatton, Jennifer Holt, Kenneth MacDonald, Riley Hill, Lynton Brent, John Ince, John Bridges, Eddie Parker, Frank McCarroll, Dick Dickinson, Milburn Morante, Frank LaRue, Steve Clark, George Morrell, Carl Mathews, Victor Cox, Cal Shrum and his Rhythm Rangers
D: Lambert Hillyer

SP: Jess Bowers (Adele Buffington)
P: Charles J. Bigelow

1729. THE ROYAL MOUNTED RIDES AGAIN
(Universal, October 23, 1945)   13 Chaps.
Bill Kennedy, Daun Kennedy, George Dolenz, Milburn Stone, Paul E. Burns, Robert Armstrong, Danny Morton, Addison Richards, Tom Fadden, Joseph Haworth, Helen Bennett, Joseph Crehan, Selmer Jackson, Daral Hudson, George Lloyd, George Eldridge
D: Ray Taylor, Lewis D. Collins
SP: Joseph O'Donnell, Harold C. Wire
P: Morgan Cox
Chapter Titles: (1) Canaska Gold, (2) The Avalanche Trap, (3) River on Fire, (4) Skyline Target, (5) Murder Toboggan, (6) Ore Car Accident, (7) Buckboard Runaway, (8) Thundering Water, (9) Dead Men for Decoys, (10) Derringer Death, (11) Night Trail Danger, (12) Twenty Dollars Doublecross, (13) Flaming Showdown

1730. FIGHTING BILL CARSON
(PRC, October 31, 1945)   51 Mins.
(*Billy Carson* Series)
Buster Crabbe, Al St. John, Kay Hughes, I. Stanford Jolley, Kermit Maynard, John L. "Bob" Cason, Budd Buster, Bud Osborne, Charles King
D: Sam Newfield
S: Louise Rousseau
SP: Louise Rousseau
P: Sigmund Neufeld

1731. ROUGH RIDERS OF CHEYENNE
(Republic, November 1, 1945)   56 Mins.
Sunset Carson, Peggy Stewart, Mira McKinney, Monte Hale, Wade Crosby, Kenne Duncan, Michael Sloane, Tom London, Eddy Waller, Jack O'Shea, Bob Wilke, Tex Terry, Jack Rockwell, Jack Luden, Rex Lease, Hank Bell, Henry Wills, Cactus Mack, Artie Ortego
D: Thomas Carr
SP: Elizabeth Beecher
AP: Bennett Cohen

1732. PRAIRIE RUSTLERS
(PRC, November 7, 1945)   56 Mins.
(*Billy Carson* Series)
Buster Crabbe, Al St. John, Evelyn Finley, Karl Hackett, Bud Osborne, Marin Sais, I. Stanford Jolley, Kermit Maynard, Herman Hack, George Morrell, Tex Cooper, Dorothy Vernon
D: Sam Newfield
S/SP: Fred Myton
P: Sigmund Neufeld

1733. SONG OF OLD WYOMING

(PRC, November 12, 1945)   65 Mins.
(Cinecolor)

Eddie Dean, Jennifer Holt, Sarah Padden, Al "Lash" LaRue, Emmett Lynn, Ray Elder, John Carpenter, Ian Keith, Robert Barron, Horace Murphy, Pete Natchenaro, Rocky Camron, Bill Bovett, Richard Cramer, Steve Clark

D/P: Robert Emmett (Tansey)
SP: Frances Kavanaugh

1734. COLORADO PIONEERS

(Republic, November 14, 1945)   57 Mins.
(*Red Ryder* Series)

Bill Elliott, Bobby Blake, Alice Fleming, Roy Barcroft, Bud Geary, Billy Cummings, Freddie Chapman, Frank Jacquet, Tom London, Monte Hale, Buckwheat Thomas, George Chesebro, Emmett Vogan, Tom Chatterton, Edward Cassidy, Fred Graham, Cliff Parkinson, Horace B. Carpenter, Bill Wolfe, Jess Cavin, Howard Mitchell, Jack Rockwell, George Morrell, Jack Kirk, Gary Armstrong, Bobby Anderson, Roger Williams, Richard Lydon, Robert Goldschmidt, Romey Foley

D: R. G. Springsteen
S: Peter Whitehead

SP: Earle Snell
AP: Sidney Picker

1735. LAWLESS EMPIRE

(Columbia, November 15, 1945)   58 Mins.
(*Durango Kid* Series)

Charles Starrett, Tex Harding, Dub Taylor, Mildred Law, Johnny Walsh, John Calvert, Ethan Laidlaw, Forrest Taylor, Jack Rockwell, George Chesebro, Boyd Stockman, Lloyd Ingraham, Jessie Arnold, Tom Chatterton, Ray Jones, Bob Wills and the Texas Playboys

D: Vernon Keays
S: Elizabeth Beecher
SP: Bennett Cohen
AP: Colbert Clark

1736. THE NAVAJO KID

(PRC, November 21, 1945)   59 Mins.

Bob Steele, Syd Saylor, Edward Cassidy, Caren Marsh, Stanley Blystone, Edward Howard, Charles King, Bud Osborne, Budd Buster, Henry Hall, Gertrude Glorie, Bert Dillard, Rex Rossi

D/SP: Harry Fraser
P: Arthur Alexander

Lawless Empire (Columbia, 1945) — Dub "Cannonball" Taylor, Charles Starrett, and Bob Wills

1737. THE DALTONS RIDE AGAIN

(Universal, November 23, 1945) 72 Mins.

Alan Curtis, Lon Chaney, Jr., Kent Taylor, Noah Beery, Jr., Martha O'Driscoll, Thomas Gomez, Milburn Stone, Jess Barker, John Litel, Walter Sande, Douglass Dumbrille, Virginia Brissac, Ruth Lee

D: Ray Taylor

SP: Roy Chanslor, Paul Gangelin

P: Howard Welsch

1738. FRONTIER FEUD

(Monogram, November 24, 1945) 54 Mins.

Johnny Mack Brown, Raymond Hatton, Christine McIntyre, Dennis Moore, Jack Ingram, Eddie Parker, Frank LaRue, Steve Clark, Jack Rockwell, Mary MacLaren, Edmund Cobb, Lloyd Ingraham, Ted Mapes, Stanley Price, Terry Frost, Dan White, Ray Jones, Charles King, Lynton Brent

D: Lambert Hillyer

S: Charles N. Heckelmann

SP: Jess Bowers (Adele Buffington)

P: Charles J. Bigelow

1739. NORTHWEST TRAIL

(Action Pictures/Lippert, November 30, 1945)
(Cinecolor)

Bob Steele, John Litel, Joan Woodbury, Madge Bellamy, George Meeker, Ian Keith, Raymond Hatton, Poodles Hanaford, John Hamilton, Charles Middleton, Grace Hanaford, Bill Hammond, Bud Osborne, Al Ferguson, Bob Duncan, Josh (John) Carpenter

D: Derwin Abrahams

SP: Harvey Gates, L. J. Swabacher

P: William B. David, Max M. King

1740. TRAIL TO VENGEANCE

(Universal, November 30, 1945) 58 Mins.

Kirby Grant, Fuzzy Knight, Poni (Jane) Adams, Tom Fadden, Frank Jacquet, Walter Baldwin, John Kelly, Stanley Andrews, Beatrice Gray, Roy Brent, Pierce Lyden, Dan White, Carey Loftin

D/AP: Wallace Fox

SP: Robert Williams

1741. FRONTIER DAYS

(Warner Bros., 1945) 20 Mins.
(Technicolor)

Robert Shayne, Dorothy Malone, Rory Mallison

D: Jack Scholl

1742. LONESOME TRAIL

(Monogram, December 8, 1945) 57 Mins.

Jimmy Wakely, Lee "Lasses" White, John James, Iris Clive, Horace Murphy, Lorraine Miller, Eddie Majors, Zon Murray, Roy Butler, Jasper Palmer, Frank McCarroll, Arthur Smith

D/S/P: Oliver Drake

SP: Louise Rousseau

1743. THE CHEROKEE FLASH

(Republic, December 13, 1945) 55 Mins.

Sunset Carson, Linda Stirling, Tom London, Roy Barcroft, John Merton, Bud Geary, Frank Jacquet, Fred Graham, Joe McGuinn, Pierce Lyden, James Lynn, Bud Osborne, Edmund Cobb, Herman Hack, Bill Wolfe, Hank Bell, Chick Hannon, Roy Bucko, Buck Bucko

D: Thomas Carr

SP: Betty Burbridge

AP: Bennett Cohen

1744. ALONG THE NAVAJO TRAIL

(Republic, December 15, 1945) 66 Mins.

Roy Rogers, George Hayes, Dale Evans, Estelita Rodriguez, Douglas Fowley, Nestor Paiva, Sam Flint, Emmett Vogan, Roy Barcroft, David Cota, Bob Nolan, Pat Brady, Edward Cassidy, Poppy Del Vando, Rosemond James, Tex Terry, Budd Buster, Sons of the Pioneers, "Trigger"

D: Frank McDonald

S: William Colt MacDonald

SP: Gerald Geraghty

AP: Eddy White

1745. TEXAS PANHANDLE

(Columbia, December 20, 1945) 57 Mins.
(*Durango Kid* Series)

Charles Starrett, Tex Harding, Dub Taylor, Nanette Parks, Carolina Cotton, Forrest Taylor, Edward Howard, Ted Mapes, George Chesebro, William Gould, Jack Kirk, Budd Buster, Tex Palmer, Hugh Hooker, Spade Cooley

D: Ray Nazarro

SP: Ed Earl Repp

P: Colbert Clark

1746. FRONTIER GAL

(Universal, December 21, 1945) 84 Mins.
(Technicolor)

Yvonne De Carlo, Rod Cameron, Andy Devine, Fuzzy Knight, Sheldon Leonard, Andrew Tombes, Clara Blandick, Beverly Simmons, Frank Lackteen, Claire Carleton, Eddie Dunn, Harold Goodwin, Jack Overman, Jan Wiley, Rex Lease, Jack Ingram, George Eldridge, Joseph Haworth, Lloyd Ingraham, Joseph Bernard, Douglas Carter, Paul Bratti, Edward Howard, Joan Fulton, Jean Trent, Kerry Vaughn, Karen Randle

D: Charles Lamont

SP: Michael Fessier, Ernest Pagano

1747. WAGON WHEELS WESTWARD
(Republic, December 21, 1945) 56 Mins.
(*Red Ryder* Series)
Bill Elliott, Bobby Blake, Alice Fleming, Linda Stirling, Roy Barcroft, Emmett Lynn, Jay Kirby, Dick Curtis, George J. Lewis, Bud Geary, Tom London, Kenne Duncan, George Chesebro, Tom Chatterton, Frank Ellis, Bob McKenzie, Jack Kirk
D: R. G. Springsteen
S: Gerald Geraghty
SP: Earle Snell
AP: Sidney Picker

1748. DAKOTA
(Republic, December 25, 1945) 82 Mins.
John Wayne, Vera Ralston, Walter Brennan, Ward Bond, Ona Munson, Hugo Haas, Mike Mazurki, Olive Blakeney, Nicodemus Stewart, Paul Fix, Grant Withers, Robert Livingston, Olin Howlin, Pierre Watkin, Robert Barrat, Jonathan Hale, Bobby Blake, Paul Hurst, Eddy Waller, Sarah Padden, Jack LaRue, George Cleveland, Roy Barcroft, Selmer Jackson, Claire DuBrey
D/AP: Joseph Kane
S: Carl Foreman
SP: Howard Estabrook, Lawrence Hazard

1749. SAN ANTONIO
(Warner Bros., December 29, 1945) 111 Mins.
(Technicolor)
Errol Flynn, Alexis Smith, S. Z. "Cuddles" Sakall, Victor Francen, Florence Bates, John Litel, Paul Kelly, Robert Shayne, John Alvin, Monte Blue, Robert Barrat, Pedro De Cordoba, Tom Tyler, Chris-Pin Martin, Charles Stevens, Poodles Hanaford, Doodles Weaver, Dan White, Ray Spikes, Hap Winters, Harry Cording, Chalky Williams, Wallis Clark, Bill Steele, Allen Smith, Howard Hill, Arnold Kent
D: David Butler
SP: Alan LeMay, W. R. Burnette
P: Robert Buckner

1749a. LAW OF THE BADLANDS
(Warner Bros., 1945) 20 Mins.
Robert Shayne, Warren Douglas, Angela Greene, Trevor Bardette, Norman Willis
D: Jack Scholl
SP: Jack Scholl
P: Gordon Hollingshead

FILMS OF 1946

1750. THE HARVEY GIRLS
(MGM, January 2, 1946) 101 Mins.
(Technicolor)
Judy Garland, John Hodiak, Ray Bolger, Angela Lansbury, Preston Foster, Virginia O'Brien, Kenny Baker, Marjorie Main, Chill Wills, Selena Royle, Cyd Charisse, Ruth Brady, Jack Lambert, Edward Earle, Morris Ankrum, William "Bill" Phillips, Ben Carter, Norman Leavitt, Horace (Stephen) McNally
D: George Sidney
S: Samuel Hopkins Adams, Eleanore Griffin, William Rankin
SP: Edmund Beloin, Nathaniel Curtis
P: Arthur Freed

1750a. LIGHTNING RAIDERS
(PRC, January 7, 1946) 61 Mins.
(*Billy Carson* Series)
Buster Crabbe, Al St. John, Mady Lawrence, Ray Brent, Henry Hall, Steve Darrell, Marin Sais, Al Ferguson, Karl Hackett, I. Stanford Jolley
D: Sam Newfield
SP: Elmer Clifton
P: Sigmund Neufeld

1751. ABILENE TOWN
(United Artists, January 11, 1946) 89 Mins.
Randolph Scott, Ann Dvorak, Edgar Buchanan, Rhonda Fleming, Lloyd Bridges, Helen Boyce, Howard Freeman, Richard Hale, Jack Lambert, Hank Patterson, Dick Curtis, Eddy Waller
D: Edwin L. Marin
S: "Trail Town"—Ernest Haycox
SP: Harold Shumate
P: Jules Levey

1752. BORDER BANDITS
(Monogram, January 12, 1946) 58 Mins.
Johnny Mack Brown, Raymond Hatton, Riley Hill, Rosa Del Rosario, John Merton, Tom Quinn, Frank LaRue, Steve Clark, Charles Stevens, Lucio Villegas, Bud Osborne, Pat R. McGee, I. Stanford Jolley, Ray Jones, Terry Frost, Julia Vilirea
D: Lambert Hillyer
SP: Frank Young
P: Charles J. Bigelow

1753. GUN TOWN
(Universal, January 18, 1946) 57 Mins.
Kirby Grant, Fuzzy Knight, Lyle Talbot, Claire

Carleton, Louise Currie, Dan White, Ray Bennett, Earle Hodgins, George Morrell, Tex Cooper, Merrill McCormack
D/P: Wallace Fox
SP: William Lively

1754. THE SCARLET HORSEMAN
(Universal, January 22, 1946)   13 Chaps.
Peter Cookson, Janet Shaw, Paul Guilfoyle, Virginia Christine, Victoria Horne, Danny Morton, Fred Coby, Jack Ingram, Edward Howard, Ralph Lewis, Edmund Cobb, Cy Kendall, Harold Goodwin
D: Ray Taylor, Lewis D. Collins
SP: Joseph O'Donnell, Patricia Harper, Tom Gibson
P: Morgan Cox
Chapter Titles: (1) Scarlet for a Champion, (2) Dry Grass Danger, (3) Railroad Rescue, (4) Staked Plains Stampede, (5) Death Shifts Passengers, (6) Stop That Stage, (7) Blunderbuss Broadside, (8) Scarlet Doublecross, (9) Doom Beyond the Door, (10) The Edge of Danger, (11) Comanche Avalanche, (12) Staked Plains Massacre, (13) Scarlet Showdown

1755. THE PHANTOM RIDER
(Republic, January 26, 1946)   12 Chaps.
Robert Kent, Peggy Stewart, LeRoy Mason, George J. Lewis, Kenne Duncan, Hal Taliaferro, Chief Thunder Cloud, Tom London, Roy Barcroft, Monte Hale, John Hamilton, Hugh Prosser, Jack Kirk, Rex Lease, Tommy Coats, Joe Yrigoyen, Bill Yrigoyen, Jack O'Shea, Walt LaRue, Cliff Parkinson, Carl Sepulveda, Art Dillard, Bud Bailey, George Carleton, Dale Van Sickel, Tom Steele, George Chesebro, Wayne Burson, Cliff Lyons, Post Parks, Fred Graham, Bob Duncan, Augie Gomez, Robert Wilke, John Roy, Cactus Mack, Eddie Parker, Ted Mapes, Duke Taylor, Hal Price, James Linn, Tex Cooper, Henry Wills
D: Spencer G. Bennet, Fred Brannon
SP: Albert DeMond, Basil Dickey, Jesse Duffy, Lynn Perkins, Barney Sarecky
AP: Ronald Davidson
Chapter Titles: (1) The Avenging Spirit, (2) Flaming Ambush, (3) Hoofs of Doom, (4) Murder Masquerade, (5) Flying Fury, (6) Blazing Peril, (7) Gauntlet of Guns, (8) Behind the Mask, (9) The Captive Chief, (10) Beasts at Bay, (11) The Death House, (12) The Last Stand

1756. DRIFTING ALONG
(Monogram, January 26, 1946)   60 Mins.
Johnny Mack Brown, Lynne Carver, Raymond Hatton, Douglas Fowley, Smith Ballew, Milburn Morante, Thornton Edwards, Steve Clark, Marshall Reed, Jack Rockwell, Lynton Brent, Terry Frost, Leonard St. Leo, Ted Mapes, Curt Barrett and the Trailsmen
D: Derwin Abrahams
SP: Adele Buffington
P: Scott R. Dunlap

1757. FOOL'S GOLD
(United Artists, January 31, 1946)   63 Mins.
(*Hopalong Cassidy* Series)
William Boyd, Andy Clyde, Rand Brooks, Robert Emmett Keane, Jane Randolph, Stephen Barclay, Forbes Murray, Harry Cording, Earle Hodgins, Wee Willie Davis, Ben Corbett, Fred Toones, Bob Bentley, Glen Gallagher
D: George Archainbaud
SP: Doris Schroeder
P: Lewis J. Rachmil

1758. FRONTIER GUNLAW
(Columbia, January 31, 1946)   60 Mins.
(*Durango Kid* Series)
Charles Starrett, Tex Harding, Dub Taylor, Jean Stevens, Al Trace, and his Silly Symphonists, Weldon Heyburn, Jack Rockwell, Frank LaRue, John Elliott, Bob Kortman, Stanley Price
D: Derwin Abrahams
S: Victor McLeod
SP: Bennett Cohen
P: Colbert Clark

1759. SIX GUN MAN
(PRC, February 1, 1946)   57 Mins.
Bob Steele, Syd Saylor, Jean Carlin, I. Stanford Jolley, Brooke Temple, Bud Osborne, Budd Buster, Jimmie Martin, Stanley Blystone, Roy Brent, Steve Clark, Dorothy Whitmore, Ray Jones
D/SP: Harry Fraser
P: Arthur Alexander

1760. CALIFORNIA GOLD RUSH
(Republic, February 4, 1946)   51 Mins.
(*Red Ryder* Series)
Bill Elliott, Bobby Blake, Alice Fleming, Peggy Stewart, Russell Simpson, Dick Curtis, Joel Friedkin, Kenne Duncan, Monte Hale, Tom London, Wen Wright, Dickie Dillon, Jack Kirk, Mary Arden, Budd Buster, Bud Osborne, Neal Hart, Frank Ellis, Jim Mitchell, Herman Hack, Freddie Chapman, Jess Cavan, Pascale Perry, Silver Harr
D: R. G. Springsteen
SP: Bob Williams
P: Sidney Picker

1761. BAD BASCOMB
(MGM, February 8, 1946)   112 Mins.
Wallace Beery, Margaret O'Brien, Marjorie Main, J. Carrol Naish, Frances Rafferty, Marshall Thompson, Russell Simpson, Warner Anderson, Don Curtis, Connie Gilchrist, Sara Haden, Renie Riano, Jane Green, Henry O'Neill, Frank Darien

D: S. Sylvan Simon
S: D. A. Loxley
SP: William Lipman, Grant Garrett

1762. DAYS OF BUFFALO BILL

(Republic, February 8, 1946) 56 Mins.
Sunset Carson, Peggy Stewart, Tom London, James
  Craven, Rex Lease, Edmund Cobb, Eddie Parker,
  Michael Sloane, Jay Kirby, George Chesebro, Ed-
  ward Cassidy, Frank O'Connor, Jess Cavan
D: Thomas Carr
SP: William Lively, Doris Schroeder
AP: Bennett Cohen

1763. THE OUTLAW

(RKO, February 8, 1946) 123 Mins.
(A reissue of the film originally released in 1943 by
  United Artists and recalled shortly afterwards be-
  cause of censorship problems)
Jack Buetel, Jane Russell, Thomas Mitchell, Walter
  Huston, Mimi Aguglia, Joe Sawyer, Gene Rizzi
D: Howard Hughes, Howard Hawks
SP: Jules Furthman
P: Howard Hughes

1764. ROARING RANGERS

(Columbia, February 14, 1946) 55 Mins.
(Durango Kid Series)
Charles Starrett, Smiley Burnette, Adelle Roberts,
  Jack Rockwell, Edward Cassidy, Mickey Kuhn,
  Edmund Cobb, Ted Mapes, Gerald Mackey, Bob
  Wilke, Herman Hack, Merle Travis and his
  Bronco Busters
D: Ray Nazarro
SP: Barry Shipman
P: Colbert Clark

1765. MOON OVER MONTANA

(Monogram, February 16, 1946) 56 Mins.
Jimmy Wakely, Lee "Lasses" White, Jennifer Holt,
  Woody Woodell and his Riding Rangers, Jack
  Ingram, Louise Arthur, Stanley Blystone, Brad
  Slavin, Terry Frost, Eddie Majors, Bob Duncan,
  Arthur Smith, John Elliott, Ray Jones, Denver
  Dixon
D/S/P: Oliver Drake
SP: Louise Rousseau, Ande Lamb

1766. AMBUSH TRAIL

(PRC, February 17, 1946) 60 Mins.
Bob Steele, Syd Saylor, Lorraine Miller, I. Stanford
  Jolley, Charles King, Bob Cason, Budd Buster,
  Kermit Maynard, Frank Ellis, Edward Cassidy,
  Roy Brent
D: Harry Fraser
SP: Elmer Clifton
P: Arthur Alexander

1767. THE HAUNTED MINE

(Monogram, March 2, 1946) 51 Mins.
Johnny Mack Brown, Raymond Hatton, Linda John-
  son, Ray Bennett, Riley Hill, Claire Whitney, John
  Merton, Marshall Reed, Terry Frost, Lynton
  Brent, Leonard St. Leo, Frank LaRue, Ray Jones
D: Derwin Abrahams
SP: Frank Young
P: Charles E. Bigelow

1768. SONG OF ARIZONA

(Republic, March 9, 1946) 68 Mins.
Roy Rogers, George Hayes, Dale Evans, Bob Nolan
  and the Sons of the Pioneers, Lyle Talbot, Tommy
  Cook, Johnny Calkins, Sarah Edwards, Tommy
  Ivo, Michael Chapin, Dick Curtis, Edmund Cobb,
  Tom Quinn, Kid Chissell, Robert Mitchell Boy-
  choir, "Trigger"
D: Frank McDonald
SP: M. Coates Webster
AP: Eddy White

1769. THROW A SADDLE ON A STAR

(Columbia, March 14, 1946) 60 Mins.
Ken Curtis, Jeff Donnell, Adelle Roberts, Guinn
  "Big Boy" Williams, Andy Clyde, Emmett Lynn,
  Frank Sully, Robert Stevens, Eddie Bruce, Earl
  Duane, Jack Parker, Foy Willing and the Riders
  of the Purple Sage, The Dinning Sisters, The
  Hoosier Hot Shots
D: Ray Nazarro
SP: J. Benton Cheney
P: Colbert Clark

1770. ROMANCE OF THE WEST

(PRC, March 20, 1946) 58 Mins.
(Cinecolor)
Eddie Dean, Joan Barton, Emmett Lynn, Forrest
  Taylor, Robert McKenzie, Jerry Jerome, Stanley
  Price, Chief Thunder Cloud, Don Kay Reynolds,
  Rocky Camron, Lee Roberts, Lottie Harrison,
  Don Williams, Jack Richardson, Matty Roubert,
  Forbes Murray, Jack O'Shea, Tex Cooper, Grace
  Christy, Jerry Riggio
D/P: Robert Emmett (Tansey)
SP: Frances Kavanaugh

1771. GUNNING FOR VENGEANCE

(Columbia, March 21, 1946) 56 Mins.
(Durango Kid Series)
Charles Starrett, Smiley Burnette, Marjean Neville,
  Robert Kortman, George Chesebro, Frank La-
  Rue, Lane Chandler, Phyliss Adair, Robert Wil-
  liams, Jack Kirk, John Tyrell, Curt Barrett and the
  Trailsmen
D: Ray Nazarro
S: Louise Rousseau

SP: Ed Earl Repp
P: Colbert Clark

1772. GENTLEMEN WITH GUNS

(PRC, March 27, 1946) 52 Mins.
(*Billy Carson* Series)
Buster Crabbe, Al St. John, Patricia Knox, Steve
  Darrell, George Chesebro, Karl Hackett, Budd
  Buster, Frank Ellis, George Morrell
D: Sam Newfield
SP: Fred Myton
P: Sigmund Neufeld

1773. THE GAY CAVALIER

(Monogram, March 30, 1946) 65 Mins.
(*Cisco Kid* Series)
Gilbert Roland, Martin Garralaga, Nacho Galindo,
  Ramsey Ames, Helen Gerald, Drew Allen, Tris
  Coffin, Iris Flores, Gabriel Peralta, Pierre Andre,
  Iris Bocigon, John Merton, Frank LaRue, Ray Ben-
  nett, Artie Ortego
D: William Nigh
SP: Charles S. Belden
P: Scott R. Dunlap

1774. THE VIRGINIAN

(Paramount, April 5, 1946) 90 Mins.
Joel McCrea, Brian Donlevy, Sonny Tufts, Barbara
Britton, Fay Bainter, Tom Tully, Henry O'Neill,
  Bill Edwards, William Frawley, Paul Guilfoyle,
  Marc Lawrence, Vince Barnett, Al Bridge, Martin
  Garralaga, Nana Bryant
D: Stuart Gilmore
S: Owen Wister
SP: Frances Goodrich, Albert Hackett, Edward E.
  Paramore, Jr.
P: Paul Jones

1775. THUNDER TOWN

(PRC, April 12, 1946) 57 Mins.
Bob Steele, Syd Saylor, Ellen Hall, Bud Geary,
  Charles King, Edward Howard, Steve Clark, Bud
  Osborne, Jimmy Aubrey, Pascale Perry
D: Harry Fraser
SP: James Oliver
P: Arthur Alexander

1776. GOD'S COUNTRY

(Action Pictures/Screen Guild, April 15, 1946)
  64 Mins.   (Cinecolor)
Robert Lowery, Helen Gilbert, William Farnum,
  Buster Keaton, Si Jenks, Stanley Andrews, Al Fer-
  guson, "Ace" (a dog)
D: Robert Tansey
S: James Oliver Curwood
SP: Frances Kavanaugh
P: William B. David

Thunder Town (PRC, 1946) — Syd Saylor, Bob Steele, Ellen Hall, and Bud Geary

1777. ALIAS BILLY THE KID
(Republic, April 17, 1946)   56 Mins.

Sunset Carson, Peggy Stewart, Tom London, Roy Barcroft, Russ Whiteman, Tom Chatterton, Tex Terry, Pierce Lyden, James R. Linn, Stanley Price, Edward Cassidy, Steve Clark

D: Thomas Carr
S: Norman Sheldon
SP: Betty Burbridge, Earle Snell
AP: Bennett Cohen

1778. HOME ON THE RANGE
(Republic, April 18, 1946)   55 Mins.
(Magnacolor)

Monte Hale, Adrian Booth, Bob Nolan and the Sons of the Pioneers, Tom Chatterton, Bobby Blake, LeRoy Mason, Roy Barcroft, Kenne Duncan, Budd Buster, Jack Kirk, John Hamilton

D: R. G. Springsteen
S: Betty Burbridge, Bernard McConville
SP: Betty Burbridge
AP: Louis Gray

1779. THE CARAVAN TRAIL
(PRC, April 20, 1946)   57 Mins.
(Cinecolor)

Eddie Dean, Emmett Lynn, Al "Lash" LaRue, Jean Carlin, Robert Malcolm, Charles King, Robert Barron, Forrest Taylor, Bob Duncan, Jack O'Shea, Terry Frost, George Chesebro, Bud Osborne, Lee Roberts, Wylie Grant, Lee Bennett, Lloyd Ingraham

D/P: Robert Emmett (Tansey)
SP: Frances Kavanaugh

1780. WEST OF THE ALAMO
(Monogram, April 20, 1946)   58 Mins.

Jimmy Wakely, Lee "Lasses" White, Ray Whitley, Iris Clive, Jack Ingram, Early Cantrell, Betty Lou Head, Budd Buster, Eddie Majors, Rod Holton, Billy Dix, Arthur Smith, Ted French, Steven Keys, Ray Jones, Rudy Bowman

D/P: Oliver Drake
SP: Louise Rousseau

1781. BADMAN'S TERRITORY
(RKO, April 22, 1946)   98 Mins.

Randolph Scott, Ann Richards, George Hayes, Lawrence Tierney, Tom Tyler, John Halloran, Phil Warren, Steve Brodie, William Moss, James Warren, Isabel Jewell, Morgan Conway, Nestor Paiva, Chief Thunder Cloud, Ray Collins, Virginia Sale, Andrew Tombes, Harry Holman, Richard Hale, Emory Parnell, Ethan Laidlaw, Kermit Maynard, Bud Osborne, Chuck Hamilton

D: Tim Whelan
SP: Jack Natteford, Luci Ward
P: Nat Holt

1782. GALLOPING THUNDER
(Columbia, April 25, 1946)   54 Mins.
(*Durango Kid* Series)

Charles Starrett, Smiley Burnette, Adelle Roberts, Richard Bailey, Kermit Maynard, Edmund Cobb, Ray Bennett, Curt Barrett, John Merton, Nolan Leary, Budd Buster, Forrest Taylor, Merle Travis and his Bronco Busters

D: Ray Nazarro
SP: Ed Earl Repp
P: Colbert Clark

1782a. THREE TROUBLEDOERS
(Columbia, April 25, 1946)   2 Reels
(*Three Stooges* Series)

Moe Howard, Larry Fine, Curly Howard, Christine McIntyre, Dick Curtis, Hank Bell, Steve Clark, Bud Fine, Joe Garcia, Blackie Whiteford, Ethan Laidlaw

D: Edward Bernds

1783. KING OF THE FOREST RANGERS
(Republic, April 27, 1946)   12 Chaps.

Larry Thompson, Helen Talbot, Stuart Hamblen, Anthony Warde, LeRoy Mason, Scott Elliott, Tom London, Walter Soderling, Bud Geary, Harry Strang, Ernie Adams, Eddie Parker, Jack Kirk, Tom Steele, Dale Van Sickel, Stanley Blystone, Marin Sais, Buddy Roosevelt, Scott Elliott, Robert Wilke, Sam Ash, Carey Loftin, Sailor Vincent, Jay Kirby, Joe Yrigoyen, Nick Warick, Ken Terrell, Bud Wolfe, Wheaton Chambers, James Martin, Rex Lease, Charles Sullivan, David Sharpe

D: Spencer Bennet, Fred Brannon
SP: Albert DeMond, Basil Dickey, Jesse Duffy, Lynn Perkins
AP: Ronald Davidson
Chapter Titles: (1) The Mystery of the Towers, (2) Shattered Evidence, (3) Terror by Night, (4) Deluge of Destruction, (5) Pursuit into Peril, (6) Brink of Doom, (7) Design for Murder, (8) The Flying Coffin, (9) S.O.S. Ranger, (10) The Death Detector, (11) The Flaming Pit, (12) Tower of Vengeance

1784. UNDER ARIZONA SKIES
(Monogram, April 27, 1946)   59 Mins.

Johnny Mack Brown, Raymond Hatton, Reno Blair (Browne), Riley Hill, Tris Coffin, Reed Howes, Ted Adams, Ray Bennett, Frank LaRue, Steve Clark, Jack Rockwell, Bud Geary, Ted Mapes, Kermit Maynard, Ray Jones, Smith Ballew and the Sons of the Sage

D: Lambert Hillyer
SP: J. Benton Cheney
P: Scott R. Dunlap

1785. TERRORS ON HORSEBACK
(PRC, May 1, 1946) 55 Mins.
(*Billy Carson* Series)
Buster Crabbe, Al St. John, Patti McCarty, I. Stanford Jolley, Kermit Maynard, Henry Hall, Karl Hackett, Marin Sais, Budd Buster, Steve Darrell, Steve Clark, Bud Osborne, Al Ferguson, George Chesebro, Frank Ellis, Jack Kirk, Lane Bradford
D: Sam Newfield
SP: George Milton
P: Sigmund Neufeld

1786. RAINBOW OVER TEXAS
(Republic, May 9, 1946) 65 Mins.
Roy Rogers, George Hayes, Dale Evans, Bob Nolan and the Sons of the Pioneers, Sheldon Leonard, Robert Emmett Keane, Gerald Oliver Smith, Minerva Urecal, George J. Lewis, Kenne Duncan, Pierce Lyden, Dick Elliott, Jo Ann Dean, Bud Osborne, George Chesebro, "Trigger"
D: Frank McDonald
S: Max Brand
SP: Gerald Geraghty
AP: Eddy White

1787. SUN VALLEY CYCLONE
(Republic, May 10, 1946) 56 Mins.
(*Red Ryder* Series)
Bill Elliott, Bobby Blake, Alice Fleming, Roy Barcroft, Monte Hale, Kenne Duncan, Eddy Waller, Tom London, Edmund Cobb, Edward Cassidy, George Chesebro, Rex Lease, Hal Price, Jack Kirk, Frank O'Connor, Jack Sparks
D: R. G. Springsteen
SP: Earle Snell
AP: Sidney Picker

1788. THAT TEXAS JAMBOREE
(Columbia, May 16, 1946) 59 Mins.
The Hoosier Hot Shots, Ken Curtis, Jeff Donnell, Andy Clyde, Guinn "Big Boy" Williams, Robert Stevens, The Dinning Sisters, Deuce Spriggins and his Band, The Plainsmen, Carolina Cotton, Nolan Leary, Claire Carleton, George Chesebro, Kenneth MacDonald, Curt Barrett, Dick Elliott
D: Ray Nazarro
SP: J. Benton Cheney
P: Colbert Clark

1789. THE EL PASO KID
(Republic, May 22, 1946) 54 Mins.
Sunset Carson, Marie Harmon, Hank Patterson, Edmund Cobb, Robert Filmer, Wheaton Chambers, John Carpenter, Tex Terry, Zon Murray, Bob Wilke, Edward Cassidy, Post Park, Charlie Sullivan
D: Thomas Carr
SP: Norman Sheldon
AP: Bennett Cohen

1790. TWO-FISTED STRANGER
(Columbia, May 30, 1946) 50 Mins.
(*Durango Kid* Series)
Charles Starrett, Smiley Burnette, Doris Houck, Charles Murray, Lane Chandler, Ted Mapes, George Chesebro, Jack Rockwell, Herman Hack, I. Stanford Jolley, Edmund Cobb, Davidson Clark, Maudie Prickett, Zeke Clements
D: Ray Nazarro
S: Peter Whitehead
SP: Robert Lee Johnson
P: Colbert Clark

1791. IN OLD SACRAMENTO
(Republic, May 31, 1946) 89 Mins.
William (Bill) Elliott, Constance Moore, Hank Daniels, Ruth Donnelly, Eugene Pallette, Lionel Stander, Jack LaRue, Grant Withers, Bobby Blake, Charles Judels, Paul Hurst, Victoria Horne, Dick Wessel, Hal Taliaferro, Jack O'Shea, H. T. Tsiang, Marshall Reed, Wade Crosby, Eddy Waller, William Haade, Boyd Irwin, Lucien Littlefield, Ethel Wales, Elaine Lange, William B. Davidson, Ellen Corby, Fred Burns
D/AP: Joseph Kane
S: Jerome Odlum
SP: Frances Lyland, Frank Gruber
(Re-released as *Flame of Sacramento*)

1792. GHOST OF HIDDEN VALLEY
(PRC, June 5, 1946) 56 Mins.
(*Billy Carson* Series)
Buster Crabbe, Al St. John, Jean Carlin, John Meredith, Charles King, Karl Hackett, Jimmy Aubrey, John L. "Bob" Cason, Silver Harr, Zon Murray, George Morrell, Bert Dillard, Cecil Trenton
D: Sam Newfield
SP: Ellen Coyle
P: Sigmund Neufeld

1793. THE GENTLEMAN FROM TEXAS
(Monogram, June 8, 1946) 55 Mins.
Johnny Mack Brown, Raymond Hatton, Claudia Drake, Reno Blair (Browne), Christine McIntyre, Curt Barrett and the Trailsmen, Tris Coffin, Marshall Reed, Terry Frost, Jack Rockwell, Steve Clark, Pierce Lyden, Wally West, Artie Ortego, Bill Wolfe, Ted Adams, Lynton Brent, Frank LaRue
D: Lambert Hillyer
SP: J. Benton Cheney
P: Scott R. Dunlap

1794. THE RENEGADES

(Columbia, June 13, 1946)   87 Mins.

(Technicolor)

Evelyn Keyes, Willard Parker, Larry Parks, Edgar Buchanan, Jim Bannon, Forrest Tucker, Ludwig Donath, Frank Sully, Willard Robertson, Paul E. Burns, Eddy Waller, Francis Ford, Virginia Brissac, Vernon Dent, Addison Richards, Hermine Stereir

D: George Marshall

S: Harold Shumate

SP: Melvin Levy, Francis Edwards Faragoh

P: Michel Kraike

1795. MAN FROM RAINBOW VALLEY

(Republic, June 15, 1946)   56 Mins.

(Magnacolor)

Monte Hale, Adrian Booth, Jo Ann Marlowe, Ferris Taylor, Emmett Lynn, Tom London, Bud Geary, Kenne Duncan, Doyle O'Dell, Bert Roach, The Sagebrush Serenaders (Enright Busse, John Scott, and Frank Wilder)

D: R. G. Springsteen

SP: Betty Burbridge

AP: Louis Gray

1796. SOUTH OF MONTEREY

(Monogram, June 15, 1946)   63 Mins.

(Cisco Kid Series)

Gilbert Roland, Martin Garralaga, Frank Yaconelli, Marjorie Riordan, Iris Flores, George J. Lewis, Harry Woods, Terry Frost, Wheaton Chambers, Rose Turich

D: William Nigh

SP: Charles Belden

P: Scott R. Dunlap

1797. TRAIL TO MEXICO

(Monogram, June 29, 1946)   56 Mins.

Jimmy Wakely, Lee "Lasses" White, Julian Rivero, Delores Castelli, Dora Del Rio, Terry Frost, Forrest Matthews, Brad Slaven, Alex Montoya, Jonathan McCall, Juan Duval, Arthur Smith, Cactus Mack, Wheaton Chambers, Dee Cooper, Billy Dix, The Saddle Pals, The Guadalajara Trio

D/SP/P: Oliver Drake

1798. COLORADO SERENADE

(PRC, June 30, 1946)   68 Mins.

(Cinecolor)

Eddie Dean, Roscoe Ates, David Sharpe, Mary Kenyon, Forrest Taylor, Dennis Moore, Abigail Adams, Warner Richmond, Lee Bennett, Robert McKenzie, Bob Duncan, Charles King, Bud Osborne

D/P: Robert Emmett Tansey

SP: Frances Kavanaugh

1799. MY PAL TRIGGER

(Republic, July 10, 1946)   79 Mins.

Roy Rogers, George Hayes, Dale Evans, Jack Holt, Bob Nolan and the Sons of the Pioneers, LeRoy Mason, Roy Barcroft, Sam Flint, Kenne Duncan, Ralph Sanford, Francis McDonald, Harlan Briggs, William Haade, Alan Bridge, Paul E. Burns, Frank Reicher, Fred Graham, Ted Mapes, "Trigger"

D: Frank McDonald

S: Paul Gangelin

SP: Jack Townley, John K. Butler

AP: Armand Schaefer

1800. THE DESERT HORSEMAN

(Columbia, July 11, 1946)   57 Mins.

(Durango Kid Series)

Charles Starrett, Smiley Burnette, Adelle Roberts, Richard Bailey, John Merton, George Morgan, Tommy Coats, Jack Kirk, Bud Osborne, Riley Hill, Walt Shrum and his Colorado Hillbillies

D: Ray Nazarro

SP: Sherman Lowe

P: Colbert Clark

1801. PRAIRIE BADMEN

(PRC, July 17, 1946)   55 Mins.

(Billy Carson Series)

Buster Crabbe, Al St. John, Patricia Knox, Charles King, Edward Cassidy, Kermit Maynard, John L. Cason, Steve Clark, Frank Ellis, Budd Buster

D: Sam Newfield

SP: Fred Myton

P: Sigmund Neufeld

1802. COWBOY BLUES

(Columbia, July 18, 1946)   62 Mins.

Ken Curtis, Jeff Donnell, Guy Kibbee, The Hoosier Hotshots, Guinn "Big Boy" Williams, Peg LaCentra (Radio's "Mrs. Uppington"), Robert Scott, The Town Criers, Deuce Spriggins and his Band, Carolina Cotton, The Plainsmen, Alan Bridge, Jack Rockwell, Forbes Murray, Vernon Dent, Coulter Irwin

D: Ray Nazarro

SP: J. Benton Cheney

P: Colbert Clark

1803. SUNSET PASS

(RKO, July 18, 1946)   59 Mins.

James Warren, Nan Leslie, Jane Greer, Steve Brodie, John Laurenz, Robert Clarke, Harry Woods, Harry Harvey

D: William Berke

S: Zane Grey

SP: Norman Houston

P: Herman Schlom

1804. RED RIVER RENEGADES
(Republic, July 23, 1946)   55 Mins.
Sunset Carson, Peggy Stewart, Bruce Langley, Tom London, LeRoy Mason, Kenne Duncan, Ted Adams, Edmund Cobb, Jack Rockwell, Tex Terry
D: Thomas Carr
SP: Norman S. Hall
P: Bennett Cohen

1804a. CANYON PASSAGE
(Universal, July 26, 1946)   90 Mins.
(Technicolor)
Dana Andrews, Brian Donlevy, Susan Hayward, Patricia Roc, Ward Bond, Andy Devine, Rose Hobart, Halliwell Hobbes, Lloyd Bridges, Stanley Ridges, Dorothy Peterson, Vic Cutler, Fay Holden, Tad Devine, Dennis Devine, Hoagy Carmichael
D: Jacques Tourneur
S: Ernest Haycox
SP: Ernest Pascal
P: Walter Wanger

1805. CONQUEST OF CHEYENNE
(Republic, July 29, 1946)   55 Mins.
(*Red Ryder* Series)
Bill Elliott, Peggy Stewart, Bobby Blake, Alice Fleming, Jay Kirby, Milton Kibbee, Tom London, Emmett Lynn, Kenne Duncan, George Sherwood, Frank McCarroll, Jack Kirk, Tom Chatterton, Ted Mapes, Jack Rockwell
D: R. G. Springsteen
S: Bert Horswell, Joseph Poland
SP: Earle Snell
AP: Sidney Picker

1805a. BOY'S RANCH
(MGM, July, 1946)   97 Mins.
Jackie "Butch" Jenkins, James Craig, Skippy Homeier, Dorothy Patrick, Ray Collins, Darryl Hickman, Sharon McManus, Minor Watson, Geraldine Wall, Arthur Space, Robert Emmett O'Connor, Moroni Olsen
D: Roy Rowland
SP: William Ludwig
P: Robert Sisk

1806. RUSTLER'S ROUNDUP
(Universal, August 9, 1946)   57 Mins.
Kirby Grant, Fuzzy Knight, Jane Adams, Earle Hodgins, Charles Miller, Mauritz Hugo, Eddy Waller, Roy Brent, Frank Marlo, Edmund Cobb, Ethan Laidlaw, Steve Clark, Hank Bell, Bud Osborne, Rex Lease, Budd Buster, George Morrell, Artie Ortego, Kermit Maynard
D: Wallace Fox
S: Sherman Lowe, Victor McLeod

SP: Jack Natteford
P: Wallace Fox

1807. WILD BEAUTY
(Universal, August 9, 1946)   61 Mins.
Don Porter, Lois Collier, Jacqueline de Wit, Robert Wilcox, George Cleveland, Dick Curtis, Eva Puig, Buzz Henry, Pierce Lyden, Roy Brent, Isabel Withers, Hank Patterson
D/P: Wallace Fox
SP: Adele Buffington

1808. DEATH VALLEY
(Screen Guild/Golden Gate, August 15, 1946)   72 Mins.
Robert Lowery, Nat Pendleton, Helen Gilbert, Sterling Holloway, Barbara Reed, Russell Simpson
D: Lew Landers
P: William B. David

1809. HEADING WEST
(Columbia, August 15, 1946)   54 Mins.
(*Durango Kid* Series)
Charles Starrett, Smiley Burnette, Doris Houch, Norman Willis, Nolan Leary, Bud Geary, Frank McCarroll, John Merton, Tom Chatterton, Hal Taliaferro, Stanley Price, Tommy Coats, Hank Penny and his Plantation Boys
D: Ray Nazarro
SP: Ed Earl Repp
P: Colbert Clark

1810. LAWLESS BREED
(Universal, August 16, 1946)   58 Mins.
Kirby Grant, Fuzzy Knight, Jane Adams, Harry Brown, Dick Curtis, Charles King, Karl Hackett, Hank Worden, Claudia Drake, Ernie Adams, Harry Wilson, Artie Ortego
D: Wallace Fox
SP: Robert Williams
AP: Wallace Fox

1811. OVERLAND RIDERS
(PRC, August 21, 1946)   55 Mins.
(*Billy Carson* Series)
Buster Crabbe, Al St. John, Patti McCarty, Slim Whitaker, Bud Osborne, Jack O'Shea, Frank Ellis, Al Ferguson, John L. "Bob" Cason, George Chesebro, Lane Bradford, Wally West
D: Sam Newfield
SP: Ellen Coyle
P: Sigmund Neufeld

1812. UNDER NEVADA SKIES
(Republic, August 26, 1946)   69 Mins.
Roy Rogers, George Hayes, Dale Evans, Bob Nolan and the Sons of the Pioneers, Douglass Dum-

brille, Leyland Hodgson, Tris Coffin, Rudolph Anders, LeRoy Mason, Peter George Lynn, George J. Lewis, Iron Eyes Cody, "Trigger"
D: Frank McDonald
SP: Paul Gengelin, J. Benton Cheney
AP: Eddy White

1813. GUNMAN'S CODE
(Universal, August 30, 1946)   57 Mins.
Kirby Grant, Fuzzy Knight, Jane Adams, Danny Morton, Bernard Thomas, Karl Hackett, Charles Miller, Frank McCarroll, Jack Montgomery, Artie Ortego, Dan White
D: Wallace Fox
S: Arthur St. Claire, Sherman Lowe
SP: William Lively
AP: Wallace Fox

1814. RIO GRANDE RAIDERS
(Republic, September 9, 1946)   56 Mins.
Sunset Carson, Linda Stirling, Bob Steele, Tom London, Tris Coffin, Edmund Cobb, Jack O'Shea, Tex Terry, Kenne Duncan, Al Taylor, Fred Burns, Roy Bucko, Blackie Whiteford
D: Thomas Carr
SP: Norton S. Parker
AP: Bennett Cohen

1815. ROLL ON, TEXAS MOON
(Republic, September 12, 1946)   68 Mins.
Roy Rogers, George Hayes, Dale Evans, Bob Nolan and the Sons of the Pioneers, Dennis Hoey, Elizabeth Risdon, Francis McDonald, Edward Keane, Kenne Duncan, Tom London, Harry Strang, Edward Cassidy, Lee Shumway, Steve Darrell, Pierce Lyden, "Trigger"
D: William Witney
S: Jean Murray
SP: Paul Gangelin, Mauri Grashin
AP: Eddy White

1816. SINGING ON THE TRAIL
(Columbia, September 12, 1946)   60 Mins.
Ken Curtis, Jeff Donnell, Guy Kibbee, Dusty Anderson, The Hoosier Hot Shots, Guinn "Big Boy" Williams, Ian Keith, Matt Willis, Sam Flint, Joe Haworth, Jody Gilbert, Eddy Waller, The Plainsmen, Carolina Cotton, Four Chicks and Chuck
D: Ray Nazarro
SP: J. Benton Cheney
P: Colbert Clark

1817. TRIGGER FINGERS
(Monogram, September 21, 1946)   56 Mins.
Johnny Mack Brown, Raymond Hatton, Jennifer

Trigger Fingers (Monogram, 1946) — Jennifer Holt, Johnny Mack Brown, and Raymond Hatton

Holt, Riley Hill, Steve Clark, Eddie Parker, Pierce Lyden, Ted Adams, Cactus Mack, Edward Cassidy, Ray Jones, George Morrell, Frank McCarroll
D: Lambert Hillyer
SP: Frank H. Young
P: Charles J. Bigelow

1818. OUTLAW OF THE PLAINS
(PRC, September 22, 1946)   56 Mins.
(*Billy Carson* Series)
Buster Crabbe, Al St. John, Patti McCarty, Charles King, Karl Hackett, Jack O'Shea, John L. "Bob" Cason, Bud Osborne, Budd Buster, Roy Brent, Charles "Slim" Whitaker
D: Sam Newfield
SP: Elmer Clifton
P: Sigmund Neufeld

1819. SHERIFF OF REDWOOD VALLEY
(Republic, September 29, 1946)   54 Mins.
(*Red Ryder* Series)
Bill Elliott, Bobby Blake, Alice Fleming, Bob Steele, Peggy Stewart, Arthur Loft, James Craven, Tom London, Kenne Duncan, Bud Geary, John Wayne Wright, Tom Chatterton, Budd Buster, Frank McCarroll, Frank Linn
D: R. G. Springsteen
SP: Earle Snell
AP: Sidney Picker

1820. DRIFTIN' RIVER
(PRC, October 1, 1946)   59 Mins.
Eddie Dean, Roscoe Ates, Shirley Patterson, William Fawcett, Lee Bennett, Dennis Moore, Bob Callahan, Lottie Harrison, Forrest Taylor, Don Murphy, Lee Roberts, Wyley Grant, Marion Carney, The Sunshine Boys (M. H. Richman, J. O. Smith, A. L. Smith, and Edward F. Wallace), "Flash"
D/P: Robert Emmett Tansey
SP: Frances Kavanaugh

1821. FRONTIER FROLIC
(Universal, October 9, 1946)   15 Mins.
Bob Wills and his Texas Playboys
D: Lewis D. Collins
P: Will Cowan

1822. 'NEATH CANADIAN SKIES
(Screen Guild/Golden Gate, October 15, 1946)   40 Mins.
Russell Hayden, Inez Cooper, Douglas Fowley, Cliff Nazarro, I. Stanford Jolley, Kermit Maynard, Jack Mulhall, Dick Alexander, Pat Hurst, Gil Patrick, Boyd Stockman, Jimmie Martin
D: B. Reeves Eason
S: James Oliver Curwood

SP: Arthur V. Jones
P: William B. David

1823. SHADOWS ON THE RANGE
(Monogram, October 16, 1946)   58 Mins.
Johnny Mack Brown, Raymond Hatton, Jan Bryant, Marshall Reed, John Merton, Jack Perrin, Steve Clark, Terry Frost, Cactus Mack, Pierce Lyden, Ted Adams, Lane Bradford
D: Lambert Hillyer
SP: Jess Bowers (Adele Buffington)
P: Scott R. Dunlap

1824. LANDRUSH
(Columbia, October 18, 1946)   53 Mins.
(*Durango Kid* Series)
Charles Starrett, Smiley Burnette, Doris Houck, Emmett Lynn, Bud Geary, Stephen Barclay, Robert Kortman, George Chesebro, Bud Osborne, Ozie Waters and his Colorado Rangers
D: Vernon Keays
S/SP: Michael Simmons
P: Colbert Clark

1825. TUMBLEWEED TRAIL
(PRC, October 28, 1946)   57 Mins.
Eddie Dean, Roscoe Ates, Shirley Patterson, Johnny McGovern, Bob Duncan, Ted Adams, Kermit Maynard, William Fawcett, Carl Mathews, Matty Roubert, Lee Roberts, Frank Ellis, The Sunshine Boys (M. H. Richman, J. O. Smith, A. L. Smith, Edward F. Wallace), "Flash"
D/P: Robert Emmett Tansey
SP: Frances Kavanaugh

1826. HOME IN OKLAHOMA
(Republic, November 8, 1946)   72 Mins.
Roy Rogers, George Hayes, Dale Evans, Carol Hughes, Bob Nolan and the Sons of the Pioneers, George Meeker, Lanny Rees, Ruby Dandridge, George Lloyd, Arthur Space, Frank Reicher, George Carleton, "Trigger"
D: William Witney
SP: Gerald Geraghty
P: Eddy White

1827. BEAUTY AND THE BANDIT
(Monogram, November 9, 1946)   77 Mins.
(*Cisco Kid* Series)
Gilbert Roland, Martin Garralaga, Frank Yaconelli, Ramsay Ames, Vida Aldana, George J. Lewis, William Gould, Dimas Sotello, Felipe Turich, Glenn Strange, Alex Montoya, Artie Ortego
D: William Nigh
SP: Charles Belden
P: Scott R. Dunlap

Tumbleweed Trail (PRC, 1946) — Ted Adams, Frank Ellis, Shirley Patterson, and Eddie Dean

1828. THE PLAINSMAN AND THE LADY

(Republic, November 11, 1946)   87 Mins.

William Elliott, Vera Ralston, Gail Patrick, Joseph Schildkraut, Andy Clyde, Donald Barry, Raymond Walburn, Hal Taliaferro, Reinhold Schunzel, Russell Hicks, William B. Davidson, Paul Hurst, Charles Judels, Byron Foulger, Jack Lambert, Stuart Hamblen, Noble Johnson, Eva Puig, Eddy Waller, Henry Wills, Iron Eyes Cody, Lola and Fernando, Rex Lease, Pierre Watkin, Charles Morton, Martin Garralaga, Joseph Crehan, Roy Barcroft, Hank Bell, Jack O'Shea, Carl Sepulveda, Chuck Roberson, David Williams, Eddie Parks

D/AP: Joseph Kane

S: Michael Uris, Ralph Spence

SP: Richard Wormser

1829. THE DEVIL'S PLAYGROUND

(United Artists, November 15, 1946)   62 Mins.

William Boyd, Andy Clyde, Rand Brooks, Elaine Riley, Robert Elliott, Joseph J. Green, Francis McDonald, Ned Young, Earle Hodgins, George Eldridge, Everett Shields, John George, Glenn Strange

D: George Archainbaud

P: Lewis J. Rachmil

1830. NORTH OF THE BORDER

(Screen Guild/Golden Gate, November 15, 1946)   40 Mins.

Russell Hayden, Lyle Talbot, Inez Cooper, Anthony Warde, Guy Beach, Jack Mulhall, I. Stanford Jolley, Dick Alexander, Douglas Fowley, Artie Ortego

D: B. Reeves Eason

S: James Oliver Curwood

SP: Arthur V. Jones

P: William B. David

1831. SANTA FE UPRISING

(Republic, November 15, 1946)   55 Mins.

(*Red Ryder* Series)

Allan Lane, Bobby Blake, Martha Wentworth, Barton MacLane, Jack LaRue, Tom London, Dick Curtis, Forrest Taylor, Emmett Lynn, Hank Patterson, Edmund Cobb, Pat Michaels, Kenne Duncan, Edythe Elliott, Frank Ellis, Art Dillard, Lee Reynolds, Forrest Burns

D: R. G. Springsteen

SP: Earle Snell

P: Sidney Picker

1832. SILVER RANGE

(Monogram, November 16, 1946)   53 Mins.

Johnny Mack Brown, Raymond Hatton, Jan Bryant, I. Stanford Jolley, Terry Frost, Eddie Parker, Ted Adams, Frank LaRue, Cactus Mack, Lane Bradford, Dee Cooper, Billy Dix, Bill Willmering, George Morrel

D: Lambert Hillyer

SP: J. Benton Cheney

P: Charles J. Bigelow

1833. STARS OVER TEXAS

(PRC, November 18, 1946)   57 Mins.

Eddie Dean, Roscoe Ates, Shirley Patterson, Lee Bennett, Lee Roberts, Kermit Maynard, Jack O'Shea, Hal Smith, Matty Roubert, Carl Mathews, William Fawcett, The Sunshine Boys, "Flash"

D/P: Robert Emmett Tansey

SP: Frances Kavanaugh

1834. SIOUX CITY SUE

(Republic, November 21, 1946)   69 Mins.

Gene Autry, Lynne Roberts, Sterling Holloway, Cass County Boys, Richard Lane, Ralph Sanford, Ken Lundy, Helen Wallace, Pierre Watkin, Edwin Wills, Minerva Urecal, Frank Marlowe, LeRoy Mason, Harry Cheshire, George Carleton, Sam Flint, Michael Hughes, Tex Terry, Tris Coffin, Frankie Marvin, Forrest Burns, Tommy Coats, "Champion"

D: Frank McDonald

SP: Olive Cooper

AP: Armand Schaefer

1835. TERROR TRAIL

(Columbia, November 21, 1946)   55 Mins.

(*Durango Kid* Series)

Charles Starrett, Smiley Burnette, Barbara Pepper, Lane Chandler, Zon Murray, Elvin Eric Field, Tommy Coats, George Chesebro, Robert Barron, Budd Buster, Bill Clark, Ted Mapes, Ozie Waters and his Colorado Rangers

D: Ray Nazarro

S/SP: Ed Earl Repp

P: Colbert Clark

1836. SONG OF THE SIERRAS

(Monogram, November 28, 1946)   58 Mins.

Jimmy Wakely, Lee "Lasses" White, Jean Carlin, Jack Baxley, Iris Clive, Zon Murray, Budd Buster, Bob Duncan, Brad Slaven, Jonathan Black, Jasper Palmer, Billy Dix, Ben Corbett, Ray Jones, Carl Sepulveda, Wesley Tuttle and his Texas Stars

D/S/P: Oliver Drake

SP: Elmer Clifton

1837. WILD WEST

(PRC, December 1, 1946)   73 Mins.

(Cinecolor)

Eddie Dean, Roscoe Ates, Al LaRue, Robert "Buzzy" Henry, Sarah Padden, Louise Currie, Jean Carlin, Lee Bennett, Terry Frost, Warner Richmond, Lee Roberts, Bob Allen, Chief Yowlachie, Bob Duncan, Frank Pharr, John Bridges, Al Ferguson, Bud Osborne, "Flash"

D/P: Robert Emmett Tansey

SP: Frances Kavanaugh

1838. MY DARLING CLEMENTINE

(20th C. Fox, December 3, 1946)   97 Mins.

Henry Fonda, Victor Mature, Linda Darnell, Walter Brennan, Tim Holt, Cathy Downs, Ward Bond, Alan Mowbray, John Ireland, Roy Roberts, Jane Darwell, Grant Withers, J. Farrell MacDonald, Don Garner, Francis Ford, Ben Hall, Arthur Walsh, Jack Pennick, Louis Mercier, Mickey Simpson, Fred Libby, Harry Woods, Charles Stevens, Russell Simpson, Hank Bell

D: John Ford

S: Sam Hellman from the book "Wyatt Earp, Frontier Marshal" by Stuart Lake

SP: Samuel G. Engel, Winston Miller

AD: William Eckhardt

P: Samuel G. Engel

1839. TUMBLEWEED TEMPOS

(Universal, December 4, 1946)   15 Mins.

Spade Cooley and Orchestra

D/P: Will Cowan

1840. OUT CALIFORNIA WAY

(Republic, December 5, 1946)   67 Mins.

(Trucolor)

Monte Hale, Adrian Booth, Bobby Blake, John Dehner, Nolan Leary, Fred Graham, Tom London, Jimmy Starr, Edward Keane, Bob Wilke, Brooks Benedict, St. Luke's Choristers, Foy Willing and the Riders of the Purple Sage, and guest stars Roy Rogers, Allan Lane, Dale Evans, Donald Barry, and "Trigger"

D: Lesley Selander

S: Barry Shipman

SP: Betty Burbridge

AP: Louis Gray

1841. THE FIGHTING FRONTIERSMAN

(Columbia, December 10, 1946)   61 Mins.

(*Durango Kid* Series)

Charles Starrett, Smiley Burnette, Helen Mowery, Emmett Lynn, Robert W. Filmer, George Chesebro, Zon Murray, Jim Diehl, Maudie Prickett, Russell Meeker, Frank Ellis, Ernie Adams, Frank

LaRue, Jacques J. O'Mahoney (Jock Mahoney), Hank Newman and the Georgia Crackers
D: Derwin Abrahams
SP: Ed Earl Repp
P: Colbert Clark

1842. LONE STAR MOONLIGHT
(Columbia, December 12, 1946) 67 Mins.
Ken Curtis, Joan Barton, Guy Kibbee, The Hoosier Hotshots, Robert Stevens, Claudia Drake, Arthur Loft, Vernon Dent, Sam Flint, The Smart Set, Merle Travis Trio, Judy Clark and her Rhythm Cowgirls
D: Ray Nazarro
SP: Louise Rousseau
P: Colbert Clark

1843. HELDORADO
(Republic, December 15, 1946) 70 Mins.
Roy Rogers, George Hayes, Dale Evans, Bob Nolan and the Sons of the Pioneers, LeRoy Mason, Paul Harvey, Rex Lease, Barry Mitchell, John Bagni, John Phillips, James Taggert, Steve Darrell, Doye O'Dell, Charles Williams, Eddie Acuff, Clayton Moore, "Trigger"
D: William Witney
SP: Gerald Geraghty, Julian Zimet
AP: Eddy White

1844. STAGECOACH TO DENVER
(Republic, December 23, 1946) 56 Mins.
(*Red Ryder* Series)
Allan Lane, Bobby Blake, Martha Wentworth, Peggy Stewart, Roy Barcroft, Emmett Lynn, Ted Adams, Edmund Cobb, Tom Chatterton, Bobbie Hyatt, George Chesebro, Edward Cassidy, Wheaton Chambers, Forrest Taylor, Britt Wood, Tom London, Stanley Price
D: R. G. Springsteen
SP: Earle Snell
AP: Sidney Picker

1845. RENEGADE GIRL
(Affiliated/Screen Guild, December 25, 1946) 65 Mins.
Alan Curtis, Ann Savage, Edward Brophy, Russell Wade, Jack Holt, Ray Corrigan, John King, Chief Thunder Cloud, Edmund Cobb, Claudia Drake, Dick Curtis, Nick Thompson, James Martin, Harry Cording
D/P: William Berke
SP: Edwin K. Westrate

1846. SINGIN' IN THE CORN
(Columbia, December 26, 1946) 65 Mins.
Judy Canova, Allen Jenkins, Guinn "Big Boy" Williams, Alan Bridge, Charles Halton, Robert Dudley, Nick Thompson, Frances Rey, George Chesebro, Ethan Laidlaw, The Singing Indian Braves
D: Del Lord
SP: Richard Weil
P: Ted Richmond

CHAPTER 6

The Resurgent Years
1947-1952

(A NEW DAWN OVER THE WESTERN RANGE)

The late Forties and early Fifties represented a resurgence in popularity of the large-scale Western. Whereas the "B" was in its old age and dying, the "A" was reaching a new degree of maturity and acceptance. Although the resurgence had started a year or two before, old reliables John Wayne, Joel McCrea, and Randolph Scott paved the way for its further escalation in 1947 with *Angel and the Badman* (Republic, Wayne), *Trail Street* (RKO, Scott), *The Gunfighters* (Columbia, Scott), and *Ramrod* (United Artists, McCrea). William Elliott, a recent promotee into the "A" ranks, was presented in two Republic specials, *Wyoming* and *The Fabulous Texan*. And then there were George Montgomery in *Belle Starr's Daughter* (Fox) and Rod Cameron in *Pirates of Monterey* (Universal). Although these weren't great Westerns—or maybe even superior ones—they nevertheless were the forerunners of great Westerns to come and contributed to the resurgence by simply making money and stimulating studios to gamble more heavily on the expensive Western.

The real blockbuster Westerns of the period came in 1948. One such film was David Selznick's *Duel in the Sun*, directed by King Vidor and with an impressive cast headed by Joseph Cotten, Gregory Peck, and Jennifer Jones. Sometimes referred to as "Lust in the Dust," the popular film was a masterpiece of passions and family conflicts set against a Western backdrop, culminating in the two lovers—Peck and Jones—shooting each other to death. There were too many sexual shenanigans, but they assured its box-office success. One redeeming quality was its mass action scenes which were vividly done.

An even more impressive film, and one qualifying for classic recognition, was *Red River* (United Artists, 1948), Howard Hawks' sympathetic and psychological portrait of a self-made cowman and his tribulations along the Chisholm Trail as he challenges the elements, outlaws, and his own adopted son. It has the authentic tang of the outdoors and is full of manginess and man and beast. John Wayne, as the aging "Thomas Dunson," gained much stature as an actor in this, his best Western since *Stagecoach* (United Artists, 1939). "B" buffs could take delight in the supporting cast, which included venerable Harry Carey, Tom Tyler, Lane Chandler, and Hal Taliaferro.

Bret Harte's theme of the wastrel sacrificing himself for the waif-heroine is transformed into sacrifice for a baby by three bank robbers in John Ford's *Three Godfathers* (MGM, 1948). The ritual of sacrifice and redemption is acted out in the American West using Christian symbols and parables by John Wayne, Harry Carey, Jr., and Pedro Armendariz. And there was something in the situation of the little waif sheltered and loved by three outlaws on the run that overbalanced the bathos and sentimentalism. John Ford dedicated the film "To the memory of Harry Carey—bright star of the early western sky," Carey, his first star and close friend, having died in 1947.

Treasure of the Sierra Madre (Warner Bros., 1948), was a fringe Western set in Mexico in 1920 with director John Huston exacting the best performances of their respective careers

Pirates of Monterey
(Universal, 1947)—
Maria Montez and
Rod Cameron

*Treasure of the Sierra
Madre* (Warner
Bros., 1948) —
Humphrey Bogart
and Tim Holt

from veterans Tim Holt, Humphrey Bogart, and Walter Huston in a story of gold lust, bandits, and crumbling moral fibre.

Few Westerns were superior in entertainment value to John Ford's cavalry trilogy, a compelling fusion of myth and history. *Fort Apache* (RKO, 1948) was the first. As Captain Kirby York, John Wayne is in excellent form as the knowledgeable Indian fighter suppressed by arrogant Colonel Owen Thursday, played by Henry Fonda. Lusty songs and robust comedy abound, and the action is exciting and heroic to a degree rare in Ford films. In *She Wore a Yellow Ribbon* (RKO, 1949), considered by most critics as the best of the trilogy, Wayne is an aging cavalry officer on his last mission before retirement, bent on maintaining the tradition of honor of the cavalry to the very last. Particularly symbolic of Ford's image of the West as both harsh and congenial is Nathan Brittles' (Wayne) watering of the Cyclamen plants around his wife's grave. And the music score was irresistible. *Rio Grande* (Republic, 1950) again finds Wayne an aged cavalry officer, this time with an estranged wife and a son who winds up in his command. The decision to pursue Indians into Mexico is patently played against a backdrop of cavalry ritual.

Wayne had by this time come into his own as a giant among Hollywood's great. In 1949 he ranked Number Four in the *Motion Picture Herald*'s ranking of top money-making stars. (This was the listing of stars other than the "B" Western category.) In both 1950 and 1951 he was Hollywood's top-ranking star, dropping to third position in 1953. Yakima Canutt's protege had stirred up a lot of dust in twenty years, finally fighting his way to the top of the heap.

Randolph Scott had been vying with Wayne (and we might say also with Autry and Rogers) as the screen's favorite cowboy performer. During the early years of the Resurgent Years he made *Trail Street* (RKO, 1947), playing Bat Masterson, the marshal hired to clean up Liberal, Kansas. This was followed by the successful *The Gunfighters* (Columbia, 1947), his last Zane Grey story. *Albuquerque* (Paramount, 1948) had Scott portraying a Texas Ranger turned freight-line operator accused of a gold shipment robbery. *Return of the Bad Men* (RKO, 1948) was the kind of action Western that appealed to "B" aficionados and was a box-office winner. Scott is a marshal who matches wits and gunfire with just about every outlaw in the West, including Billy the Kid, the Doolins, the Daltons, the Youngers, and the Sundance Kid. In *Coroner Creek* (Columbia, 1948) Scott avenges the death of his fiancee at the hands of George Macready, a prelude film to many such "avenger" Westerns in the Fifties.

In 1949 Scott formed an association with Nat Holt, who produced *Canadian Pacific* (Fox, 1949), *Fighting Man of the Plains* (Fox, 1949), and *The Cariboo Trail* (Fox, 1950), all money-makers that helped put Scott at the top in star popularity. His *The Walking Hills* (Columbia, 1949) had him on the run from the law and searching for a lost wagon train in the shifting sands of Death Valley. In *The Doolins of Oklahoma* (Columbia, 1949) he tries to go straight but is killed off along with his brothers by a nasty sheriff. Scott likewise formed an association with Harry Joe Brown in 1949 and they produced, with Scott starring in, a series of Westerns for Columbia release that made Western cinema history in terms of the fabulous success of the films, each of which would be classified as a traditional action Western but with strong plots that often made Scott the loner seeking revenge for injustices done him or his loved ones. Those released during the Resurgent Years were *The Nevadan* (Columbia, 1950), *Man in the Saddle* (Columbia, 1951), *Santa Fe* (Columbia, 1951), and *Hangman's Knot* (Columbia, 1952). *His Man in the Saddle* anticipated Gary Cooper's *High Noon* with an over-the-credits and throughout-the-action title song sung by Tennessee Ernie Ford and utilized a whopping good script, while *Hangman's Knot* was one of Hollywood's first ventures into the extremely violent Western. In addition to these, Scott starred in such

Hangman's Knot (Columbia, 1952) — Donna Reed and Randolph Scott

outstanding Westerns as *Colt 45* (Warner Bros., 1950), *Sugarfoot* (Warner Bros., 1951), *Fort Worth* (Warner Bros., 1951), and *The Man Behind the Gun* (Warner Bros., 1952). During the Resurgent Years he made nineteen money-making sagas of the West which critics found little fault with. No one, including Wayne, was as believable a Westerner as Scott, and the more his craggy face became wrinkled and weatherbeaten, the more believable he was. Young and old alike enjoyed the Scott Westerns and going to see the latest Scott flick became almost a ritual in the sense that two decades before "B" fans would go to see Buck Jones or Ken Maynard. The title, the story, the director, and the rest of the cast mattered little—one knew that Scott in a Western was good for an enjoyable evening at the movies. The only thing questionable was whether the popcorn would be good or not. In 1950 Scott was the tenth-ranking star in popularity of all Hollywood stars; in 1951, he was eighth in popularity; and in 1952 he was again in tenth position. He was the only exclusively Western star in the Top Ten, since Wayne had made many non-Westerns.

Ramrod (United Artists, 1947) and *Four Faces West* (United Artists, 1948), both produced by Harry Sherman, projected star Joel McCrea further along the Western genre's trail of no return, clinching his recognition as a Westerner of the magnitude of Wayne and Scott. He would never again make a non-Western—out of choice, not necessity. *Ramrod* depicted the violence of a range war, while *Four Faces West* was a tale of a fleeing outlaw. Carefully selected supporting casts coupled with superior screenplays and good photography and enhanced by McCrea's soft-spoken charm made these medium-budget, artistic Westerns entertaining, although they returned but a small profit. *South of St. Louis* (Warner Bros., 1949) was a better and likewise more profitable film, with a surprisingly good, meaty performance by Bob Steele. The story concerns rival ranchers, McCrea and Zachary Scott, fighting over land and for Dorothy Malone. In Raoul Walsh's *Colorado Territory* (Warner

Bros., 1949), one of the so-called "psychological" Westerns, McCrea is on the lam from the law and involved with two women, Virginia Mayo and Dorothy Malone. There is an inevitable shoot-out in this Western remake of Humphrey Bogart's *High Sierra.*

McCrea's dignified demeanor and regulated voice made him a natural for roles calling for an amiable, at-peace-with-the-world cowpoke who could galvanize to action when he finally reached the boiling point. In this respect he was much like his idol, Hoot Gibson, only without the comedy element. *Saddle Tramp* (Universal, 1950) was typical of this characterization, as McCrea is an itinerant cowboy who hates to work and who tries to avoid trouble but who finds himself caring for four orphaned children in the middle of a range war. As an ex-gunfighter turned parson, McCrea lends rustic charm to *Stars in My Crown* (Warner Bros., 1950), an off-beat Western recounting the trying experiences of a soft-spoken minister who matches wits with the Ku Klux Klan, befriends a young doctor and a freed slave, and hunts down the cause of a plague he is suspected of carrying. It was a medium-budget effort directed by Jacques Tourneur. Other Westerns helping to make McCrea a leading Western star were *The Outriders* (MGM, 1950), *Frenchie* (Universal, 1950), *Cattle Drive* (Universal, 1951), and a fringe one, *The San Francisco Story* (Warner Bros., 1952).

Three Westerns that established James Stewart as a son of the West were *Winchester '73* (Universal, 1950), *Broken Arrow* (Fox, 1950), and *Bend of the River* (Universal, 1952). *Winchester '73* was a traditional Western with the usual amount of action and a fine story built around the famous rifle. Anthony Mann directed this first of a series of superb Westerns that emphasized violent situations and loners in pursuit of revenge or redemption. *Broken Arrow* presented the Indian in a sympathetic role and was one of the first of a long list of "conscience" films dealing with a multitude of social and moral problems. Delmer Daves directed his one great masterpiece. *Bend of the River,* with Anthony Mann again at the helm, was a psychological Western showing, as had early William S. Hart films, the good and bad of the hero. Many of Mann's heroes behave as if they must punish themselves for sins committed in the past, e.g., *Devil's Doorway* (1950), *The Furies* (1950), and *The Naked Spur* (1952), the latter again with Stewart in the lead as a bounty hunter with a conscience.

Three cowboys deserving of special mention for their medium-budget thrillers of the Resurgent Years are Rod Cameron, William Elliott, and George Montgomery, all closely tied to the Western genre for much of their careers. Each star's films were generally a big step down in quality from those of McCrea, Scott, or Wayne but were nevertheless semi-lavish flicks that seldom failed to please those audiences that preferred mild romance, suspenseful drama, numerous showdowns, frequent knuckle-on-chin encounters, and eyeball-to-eyeball blasts of gunfire in escapism, pure and simple.

Both Cameron and Elliott made their best Westerns at Republic and Monogram/Allied Artists during the Resurgent Years, appearing in slickly made, basically "pure" Westerns in terms of plot and tradition. The stories had merit and the productions were basically solid. Cameron's *Brimstone* (Republic, 1949), *Stampede* (Monogram, 1949), *Wagons West* (Monogram, 1952), *Cavalry Scout* (Monogram, 1951), *Fort Osage* (Monogram, 1952), and similar films satisfied that vast audience who liked simple action films a grade or two above the "B" product. There was little female dalliance in the Cameron vehicles. The tall, rugged hero got on with the job at hand, aptly demonstrating his agility and scrapping prowess. The fast tempo maintained throughout the reels and the pleasing personality of Cameron undoubtedly sufficed to put over his Westerns in this era.

Elliott's *Hellfire* (Republic, 1949), *The Gallant Legion* (Republic, 1948), and *The Savage Horde* (Republic, 1950) were better in terms of excitement and over-all production quality than the Cameron films. The last-mentioned one, for example, is a direct action proposition from start to finish. There is no mincing of intentions, no hesitation, no indecision. From the first scene to the last, there is something doing—an interesting something at that. The whole blooming film is made up of scenes and situations wherein Elliott is at his best. When he switched to Monogram/Allied Artists, Elliott's films were made on smaller budgets but his characterizations became more austere and the stories more mature. *The Longhorn, Fargo, Waco, Kansas Territory, The Maverick,* and *Vengeance Trail,* all for Allied Artists and released in 1952, were well-made medium-budget cowboy thrillers several quality steps above the average "B" product. Six reels of continuous "where men are men" stuff might best characterize Elliott's films, and his hero was sometimes less than virtuous in that he drank, smoked, and beat the hell out of the badmen while holding a gun on them. Violence was more evident and bloodier than in the Westerns Elliott had made for Columbia and Republic.

George Montgomery was somewhat similar to both Cameron and Elliott as a hero. Between 1948 and 1958 he appeared almost exclusively in Westerns that generally pleased and were well made, although not creating any particular stir in film circles. Probably his best in the Resurgent Years were *The Texas Rangers* (Columbia, 1951), made more enjoyable by the presence of Gale Storm and Noah Beery, Jr., *Dakota Lil* (Fox, 1950), co-starring Rod Cameron and directed by Lesley Selander, and *Cripple Creek* (Columbia, 1952), directed by veteran Ray Nazarro. The wide-awake wits and ready fists of Montgomery would generally nonplus the villains, with the little thread of a story strengthened with the usual swift riding and heroics. Such agility and scrapping prowess was apparently enough for the insatiable appetite of the neighborhood theatre-goer.

A lot of "pretty boys in chaps" were playing at being cowboys during the Resurgent Years as large-scale Westerns came into vogue. Take for instance Clark Gable, whose *Across the Wide Missouri* (MGM, 1951) was a colossal and profitable Western with a lot of money behind it. Tyrone Power was not nearly so successful with *Rawhide* (Fox, 1951) as he had been earlier with *The Mark of Zorro* and *Jesse James.* Raoul Walsh's *Along the Great Divide* (Warner Bros., 1951), with he-man Kirk Douglas, was moderately successful, as was his *Distant Drums* (Warner Bros., 1951) with Gary Cooper, who, of course, was thought of as a cowboy by movie audiences. Alan Ladd tried with *Whispering Smith* (Paramount, 1949) and *Branded* (Paramount, 1951), Van Heflin with *Tomahawk* (Universal, 1951), Edmond O'Brien with *Warpath* (Paramount, 1951), Robert Taylor with *Ambush* (MGM, 1950) and *Westward the Women* (MGM, 1952), Ray Milland with *Copper Canyon* (Paramount, 1950), Joseph Cotten with *Two Flags West* (Fox, 1950), Errol Flynn with *Silver River* (Warner Bros., 1948), Lloyd Bridges with *Little Big Horn* (Lippert, 1951), Ronald Reagan with *The Last Outpost* (Paramount, 1951), Dennis Morgan with *Raton Pass* (Warner Bros., 1951), Dick Powell with *Station West* (RKO, 1948), *ad infinitum.* Whether these fellows were convincing as Westerners is debatable; what isn't is the fact that stuntmen had a field day performing the heroics, which in some cases were nothing more than simply swinging up into a saddle. These "dude" Westerns provided a modest to good return on investment and further stimulated a proliferation of Westerns of moderate merit, unencumbered with eroticism, sadism, neuroses, or subtle social messages. Unknown at the time, these traditional "A" Westerns, like the lowly "B's," were making a last-ditch fight for survival against forces that would soon infiltrate and change the Western perceptibly.

Unconquered (Paramount, 1948) was a mammoth 2½-hour historical epic set in the year 1853, staged by Cecil B. DeMille and starring Gary Cooper and Paulette Goddard. It had its good moments (which included Miss Goddard in the inevitable DeMille bathtub scene) but was overshadowed by the even greater Westerns of the era. Glenn Ford and William Holden gave a good account of themselves in *The Man from Colorado* (Columbia, 1948), a technicolor film that offered little that was new in plot but which had its better moments from both action and scenic standpoints. Ford made a convincing Westerner (e.g., *Lust for Gold* [Columbia, 1949] and *The Redhead and the Cowboy* [Paramount, 1951]) but did not spend enough time in the genre to become associated with it to the extent that McCrea, Scott, Cameron, and others did.

The Gunfighter (Fox, 1950) was one of the first films to use the motif of a famous gunman being constantly hunted by those unknown, often sadistic misfits, out to make a name for themselves. Henry King gave us a gunfighter who was not bigger than life, *a la* Bill Elliott or John Wayne, but a real man possessing the same feelings that lesser men held. The film attempts to deromanticize the gunfighter figure, who does not like the life he must lead, but who leads it because it is his life. Gregory Peck, the tired gunfighter who ponders the nebulousness of his life, is shot down by a young punk plunging down the same death's-end road.

Equally good was a lower-budget, black-and-white Western directed by John Ford. *Wagonmaster* (RKO, 1950) is a film very rich in nostalgia and underscored by comedy, with Ford extracting the best in performances from his cast headed by Ben Johnson, Harry Carey, Jr., Joanne Dru, and Ward Bond. Johnson and Carey are horse traders hired by Mormons to lead them over unfamiliar country. And with such a plot thread, Ford weaves a magnificently artistic and entertaining film loaded with double-barreled action in a rugged and romantic setting where love is fraught with danger. It was Ford's mythical West at its best.

Unquestionably the Western which shook the movie world as no Western in twenty or thirty years had was Fred Zinnemann's *High Noon* (United Artists, 1952), starring Gary Cooper as sheriff Will Kane, who has to serve society on his wedding day. The tension builds slowly to the climactic gun battle, and Tex Ritter's rendition of the Oscar-winning title song, used throughout as a musical motif, is soul-stirring. Cooper survives only because his pacifist wife (Grace Kelly) compromises her belief to help in his defense. In the end, disgusted with those he protected, Cooper contemptuously throws down his badge and walks callously away. Cooper deservedly received an Oscar for his performance and the Western genre suddenly became a mecca for producers who had shunned it before. *High Noon* was the impetus for Western production for the next ten years, aided by some lesser—though still great—Western sagas.

In 1952 the professional rodeo cowboy got some deserved, or ill-deserved, publicity, depending upon one's opinion of rodeo cowboys, in two films. *The Lusty Men* (RKO, 1952) is a vivid, harsh, and dynamic demonstration of the activities of the professional cowboy, with Robert Mitchum playing a former world champion bronc rider out to train a newcomer, Arthur Kennedy, and to seduce his wife, Susan Hayward. And *Bronc Buster* (Universal, 1952), too, is concerned with the rodeo circuit of today and the relationship between a "has been" and a novice. Again, a woman causes friction. Budd Boetticher directed and Scott Brady, John Lund, and Joyce Holden were featured. *Rodeo* (Monogram, 1952) was another film about rodeo cowboys but was a low-budget film quickly forgotten.

Reference has already been made to *Broken Arrow* (Fox, 1949), a film in which Indians were presented as a proud, dignified race of warriors with their own culture, code of honor, and justifiable hatred of the white man. It was a sympathetic portrayal of Cochise, played by Jeff Chandler, and further stimulated a flood of pro-Indian films. In 1950 came *Devil's Doorway* (MGM) with Robert Taylor as an educated Shoshoni who seeks justice for his people against marauding sheep raiders. In 1951 the plot of *Pony Soldier* (Fox) revolves about the U.S. government's mistreatment of starving Canadian Cree Indians hunting buffalo in the U.S., based on an actual happening. *Slaughter Trail* (RKO, 1951) depicts the injustice done Navahos when the murder of members of their tribe goes unpunished. *The Savage* (Paramount, 1952) is a sympathetic treatment of a white adopted into the Sioux who becomes a chief and then must decide between blood and love when war breaks out with whites. Charlton Heston starred. Howard Hawks' *The Big Sky* (RKO, 1952) was also pro-Indian, attempting to show that white culture degraded Indian morality. And there were others besides these that were sympathetic to the Indian.

In the late Forties production standards, generally speaking, slipped noticeably in programmers as costs rose and the market shrank; the illness besetting the genre was showing. The sale to television in 1950 of a vast quantity of Westerns from the Thirties and Forties inexorably did the "B" in. It was the beginning of a continuing practice and a blow from which the "B" Western never recovered. Studios found it impossible to compete with the superior Westerns made in the Boom and Golden Years. Cost cutting became a passion as producers attempted to serve diminishing theatrical markets. Not only was television creating havoc but rural America was moving to the city.

By 1947 most of the former big-name Western stars were dead or in retirement, leaving the field to a different and less exciting breed of cowboy star who, for the most part, leaned more toward the drugstore variety than he did the cinema trailblazers who had won their spurs on the range years before as robust actors who did not hesitate at chances to create real thrills for audiences. Monte Hale, Jimmy Wakely, Allan Lane, Eddie Dean, Tex Williams, the Hoosier Hot Shots, James Ellison, and Kirby Grant were passive heroes in comparison to the Big Guns of the recent past—Buck Jones, Tim McCoy, Hoot Gibson, George O'Brien, Ken Maynard, Bob Steele, and Tom Tyler. But unlike the old-

Six Gun Serenade (Monogram, 1947) — Jimmy Wakely and Pierce Lyden

time stars who catered to both an adult and juvenile audience, the contemporary cowboy's following was mainly a juvenile, less critical one that had no basis of comparison. In this the audience was fortunate.

The ineluctable decline of the "B" Western, however, did not affect the Roy Rogers or Tim Holt series at Republic and RKO respectively. Both series maintained quality production values until they were terminated in 1952. Both cowboys managed to turn out their best Westerns during the late Forties and early Fifties, thanks to Republic and RKO adhering to a high degree of integrity for their series in the declining days of the programmer when neither studio's fortune was exactly sanguine. Luckily, neither series was subjected to the economy measures foisted on most series—shorter scripts; fewer camera set-ups; inept music scores; a dearth of actors, livestock, and sets; and such other cost-cutting steps as could be devised.

Director William Witney, of serial fame, took over the Rogers films and injected them with action and some semblance of realism, while softening the musical content. Trucolor added box-office allure to some of them. *Springtime in the Rockies* (1947), *Eyes of Texas* (1948), *Bells of Coronado* (1950), *Trail of Robin Hood* (1950), *Heart of the Rockies* (1951), and his last, *Pals of the Golden West* (1951), were very good films for Rogers and showed the seasoned performer to good advantage. Republic, however, chose to drop the series in 1951 and to sell its library of Roy Rogers Westerns to television for a handsome profit. Rogers fought the sale but lost his case and his job. He subsequently went into television himself.

Tim Holt jumped to third position behind Rogers and Autry in 1951 with *Saddle Legion*, *Pistol Harvest*, *Gunplay*, *Hot Lead*, and *Overland Telegraph* released that year. He also made a non-Western, *His Kind of Woman*, with Jane Russell and Robert Mitchum. In 1952 his series came to an end with *Trail Guide*, *Road Agent*, *Target*, and *Desert Passage*. Developing gradually as the star had matured, Holt's screen character was a likeable one but he was quite often tight-lipped and this taciturnity left much of the dialogue as well as comedy to Richard Martin, whose good-natured jesting reflected that of an over-aged and temporarily reformed juvenile delinquent. Tim's romantic interludes with his leading ladies were business-like and not particularly convincing, as he always seemed anxious to get on with the work at hand. But to those in the audience, it all seemed natural enough. It was easy for youth to identify with a hero who preferred action to romance and one looked forward to seeing this cowboy roamin' the hills again with his accustomed dash. Except for a pair of thin leather gloves, our hero also avoided the fancy clothes worn by other Western stars and was quite often seen wearing unfashionable denims, or at least a plain shirt with striped trousers, which added to the realism.

The Rex Allen series, though not on a par with that of Rogers or Holt, was benefited by the Allen personality and legitimate Western heritage. It, too, was produced by Republic and maintained fairly high production standards. It was still in production as the Resurgent Years ended.

But the best "B" series of the Resurgent Years and perhaps the best of any period was that of Gene Autry at Columbia, beginning in 1947 and lasting into 1953. Most of the films were directed by John English and supervised by Armand Schaefer and were produced by Gene himself. With running times averaging seventy minutes and relatively lavish budgets in comparison with those of any other series Western, Autry's Columbia releases could almost be considered minor "A's." Although *The Last Roundup* (1947), *The Strawberry Roan* (1948), *Loaded Pistols* (1948), and *The Big Sombrero* (1949), the first four, were probably the best, all entries in the long-running series exceeded the average "B" Western in production accoutrements. The films were shot in picturesque locales, used plenty of extras when they were needed, included many name performers in the supporting casts, con-

Utah Wagon Train
(Republic, 1951) —
Rex Allen and Bud-
dy Ebsen

tained more action in general than many of Gene's pre-war Republic outings, maintained a good balance between musical interludes, drama, and thrills, and were well scripted, competently directed, and tightly photographed and edited.

Autry made thirty feature Westerns during the Resurgent Years, four for Republic and twenty-six for Columbia release. Ironically, his series was one of the best ever made, yet was done as the "B" genre was dying. The Autry charisma was still evident as he continued to gallop off into sunsets with prettier-than-ever maidens while other screen cowpokes slipped, jumped, or were pushed into an abyss of oblivion as night, with little warning, settled on their careers.

William Boyd's final series of *Hopalong Cassidy* films were sickly imitations of the former *Hoppies*. The twelve Cassidys produced from 1946-1948 were directed by George Archainbaud and featured Andy Clyde and Rand Brooks, a decided improvement over Jimmy Rogers and Jay Kirby. As with so many series, the first few were good and then quality plummeted disastrously, with talk replacing action, a malady increasingly apparent as the series went on. Too, the scripts were written so as to call for modest sets and a minimum of actors.

Kirby Grant and "Chinook," a dog, did journeyman's chores in a Northwest Mountie series at Monogram that usually was strong on supporting casts if not in scripting and production finesse. The series debuted with *Trail of the Yukon* (1949).

A Western action-melodrama series with plenty of heroism and villainy and capably sustained dramatic tensions that offered exciting entertainment for the average "B" fan was that of Donald Barry. After a hiatus as a Western lead, Barry once again climbed into the saddle for a Robert L. Lippert series in 1950-1951 which sported at least novel spin-off stories of more popular "A" Westerns and were a cut above the average "B" in spite of budget stringency.

At Universal country-and-western bandleader Tex Williams was given the lead in a series of featurettes quite similar to the old Ray Whitley musical shorts at RKO. But, unfortunately, Williams did not have the Whitley charm, voice, or acting ability. However, the films were sturdily produced and Williams acquired a modest coterie of fans, the result being a group of fifteen films running between twenty and twenty-five minutes in length. Later, as with the *Wild Bill Hickok* television series in the Fifties, the shorts were grouped together in twos or threes to form a feature presentation for theatrical release.

Allan Lane became Republic's chief blood-and-thunder actioneer of low-budget, non-musical Westerns with Bill Elliott's boost into the "A" ranks, proving adequate for the assignment albeit less picturesque than Elliott. Lane's screen personality was a lukewarm one and he was a little too fastidious and humorless; these traits aside, he carried his roles well and they added up to a good, sound, blood-red series replete with action if not romance.

As movies entered the Resurgent Years, the combination of Johnny Mack Brown and Raymond Hatton, under the direction of Lambert Hillyer, was still making money for Monogram. Made at a time when movies were still popular and profitable, these little Westerns combined fast and furious action, simple, uncomplicated stories, and the magnetism of Brown and Hatton, coupled with professional competency in both the technical and acting realms to provide a truly enjoyable hour of entertainment. Audiences could always count on lots of action and a generous number of old familiar faces in each film—nameless faces to most, but, to dyed-in-the-wool "B" buffs, the faces had names such as Charles King, Bud Osborne, Harry Woods, Tris Coffin, Kermit Maynard, Jack Rockwell, George Chesebro, Ted Adams, I. Stanford Jolley, and Marshall Reed.

Hatton left the series in 1948 to be replaced by Max Terhune who appeared with Brown in eight features. Brown did one special in 1949, *Stampede,* playing second lead to Rod Cameron and Gale Storm in Allied Artists' (a name change for Monogram) minor "A" shot in sepiatone. By 1950 Johnny was showing his age and putting on weight, yet his features were still popular. Beginning with *West of Wyoming* (1950) Brown made the remainder of his films without the aid of a comedy sidekick, something few cowboys did. Lambert Hillyer, who directed thirty-three Browns, performed his last directorial assignment on *Trail's End* (1949). Thereafter, the Brown vehicles were mostly directed by Ray Taylor, Wallace Fox, Lewis Collins, or Derwin Abrahams. In 1950 and 1951 Johnny made twelve programmers and one special, *Short Grass,* another Allied Artists film with Rod Cameron. Brown completed four films in 1952, the last, *Canyon Ambush,* released on October 12. With its release Monogram stopped production of Westerns on a series basis. Johnny had lasted almost to the end of the "B" era.

Charles Starrett no doubt deserved some sort of medal for meritorious and continuous service on behalf of Columbia Pictures, completing forty-eight *Durango Kid* features during the Resurgent Years to bring his total Westerns for Columbia to 129. Lovable comic Smiley Burnette appeared as second lead in all of the Starrett films made after 1946 and was so popular that he, too, appeared in the Top Ten Cowboys rankings for thirteen consecutive years, 1940 through 1952. *The Kid from Broken Gun,* released on August 19, 1952, was Starrett's last Western, his seventeen-year tenure as Columbia's saddle ace coming to a close, leaving Columbia with only the Gene Autry series in the way of programmer Westerns. In many of the last Starrett features the studio used scenes from films made five to ten years before, editing them in with new footage, thus saving some on costs of sky-rocketing labor and production expenses, likewise reducing shooting schedules from three weeks in the Thirties to five and six days in the Fifties. With the exception of 1943 (Charles took a brief "walk" during the year in a contract dispute), Starrett had been continuously

Junction City (Columbia, 1952) — Jock Mahoney, Charles Starrett, and Smiley Burnette

ranked in the Top Ten Cowboy Stars poll since 1937, achieving his highest ranking in 1951 when he garnered the Number Four position behind Rogers, Autry, and Holt.

When PRC went out of business in 1948, Lash LaRue and Al St. John quickly found work for an outfit called Western Adventure Productions in a series produced by Ron Ormond and directed by Ray Taylor. Later the releases were credited to White-Houck and directed by Ron Ormond. *King of the Bullwhip* (1949) interestingly foreshadowed the hard times to come for "B" feature players in that six former stars played supporting roles in a cheapie Western for union wages. Besides LaRue and St. John as co-stars, the film boasted Michael Whalen, Anne Gwynne, Jack Holt, Tom Neal, Dennis Moore, and George J. Lewis, $50,000 worth of talent for probably $1,000.

LaRue was a whip-cracking, obstreperous, black-garbed, sulky, gangster-looking, tough-talking poor physical specimen who never should have been cast as a lead. His success was a quirk. He was so unbelievably bad as an actor that people were drawn to him either in sympathy or in disbelief that such a cowboy could be filling the screen once occupied by Buck Jones, Ken Maynard, and George O'Brien. Perhaps audiences came to see the outrageously funny buffoon that shuffled and fumbled his way through each film and who shared co-starring honors—Al St. John, a bewhiskered, lovable, scene-stealing little guy who was consistently picking fights for his partner to finish. St. John, a holdover from the Keystone Kops days when he starred in numerous two-reelers, became one of Western filmdom's most popular sidekicks in spite of almost exclusive work in the cheapies of PRC and similar independents. As "Fuzzy Q. Jones" he found a place in the hearts of "B" devotees and stayed there, truly a comic as much fun to watch in the quiet darkness of a movie theatre as Emmett Kelly in the center ring of Ringling Brothers. And Jennifer Holt sometimes graced the LaRue-St. John films, her beauty and charm adding greatly to an enjoyment of the goings-on, although one suspects that she sometimes wondered what these fellows were doing in the type of film that her father and brother loved so dearly. But as one of the better-known actresses who made "B" Westerns in the Forties, Jennifer never traded on the family name. Her own talent, beauty, and personality carried her through thirty-eight Western programmers and two serials as feminine lead before becoming a television headliner in her own award-winning children's series.

Another whip-cracker, Whip Wilson, was in about the same predicament as LaRue when it came to acting and his series, too, was undistinguished except for the comedy relief handled by Andy Clyde, another real old pro from the silent days of pantomime. Although the series was no more popular than that of LaRue, it was better produced and one could count on Monogram's using a lot of favorite character actors in the various films.

The decline of Western serials paralleled the decline of "B" Westerns generally. Of thirteen Western cliffhangers, eight were made by Republic and five by Columbia. None was memorable and all reflected the cheapness and swiftness with which they were created. Those of Columbia, especially, were spasmodically thrown together by producer Sam Katzman with every dollar-cutting gimmick imaginable employed. Even as fine a director as Spencer Bennet could not save them from mediocrity. Nevertheless, they filled a need and pleased the juvenile market they were designed for. Interestingly, Columbia seemed to take a tongue-in-cheek attitude toward their serials of the post-World War II era, giving them an individuality through a deliberate stress on artificial speed, derisive and sarcastic end-of-chapter narrations, and ludicrous story-lines. The serials made by Republic, however, received more overall attention and were somewhat better. Republic's scripts were generally more coherent than Columbia's and the studio attached more importance to its serial product than did Columbia, which was not dependent on the chapterplay as a major source of income. The Republic serials, as in earlier days, were enhanced by excellent miniature work by the Lydecker brothers, good sound equipment and photography, better screenplays, casts which were competent to meet the exigencies of fast-paced action films, superb editing coupled with a vault of exclusive stock footage, and, not the least important factor, a kind of mechanical artistry honed to perfection through years of polishing.

The Resurgent Years had been good years for Westerns and the outlook for the genre was a favorable one. True, the "B" feature was dying and the serial along with it, but their places were being filled with larger-scale Westerns more acceptable to a wider audience. The forces destined to change the cinema West could not be retarded for long; the breakthrough was in progress and bigger and better cinematic tales of the old West were on the horizon as the Capricious Years (1953-1957) settled over the genre.

FILMS OF 1947

1847. RIDING THE CALIFORNIA TRAIL
(Monogram, January 11, 1947)   59 Mins.
(*Cisco Kid* Series)
Gilbert Roland, Martin Garralaga, Frank Yaconelli, Teala Loring, Inez Cooper, Ted Hecht, Marcelle Granville, Eve Whitney, Frank Marlowe, Alex Montoya, Rose Turich, Julia Kent, Gerald Echevirria
D: William Nigh
S/SP: Clarence Upson Young
P: Scott R. Dunlap

1848. ANGEL AND THE BADMAN

(Republic, January 15, 1947)   100 Mins.

John Wayne, Gail Russell, Harry Carey, Bruce Cabot, Irene Rich, Lee Dixon, Stephen Grant, Tom Powers, Paul Hurst, Olin Howlin, John Halloran, Joan Barton, Craig Woods, Marshall Reed

D: James Edward Grant

S/SP: James Edward Grant

P: John Wayne

1849. WILD COUNTRY

(PRC, January 17, 1947)   55 Mins.

Eddie Dean, Roscoe Ates, Peggy Wynn, Douglas Fowley, I. Stanford Jolley, Steve Clark, Henry Hall, Lee Roberts, Forrest Matthews, William Fawcett, Charles Jordan, Richard Cramer, Gus Taute, The Sunshine Boys, "Flash"

D: Ray Taylor

SP: Arthur E. Orloff

P: Jerry Thomas

1850. RAIDERS OF THE SOUTH

(Monogram, January 18, 1947)   55 Mins.

Johnny Mack Brown, Evelyn Brent, Raymond Hatton, Reno Blair, Marshall Reed, John Hamilton, John Merton, Eddie Parker, Frank LaRue, Ted Adams, Pierce Lyden, Cactus Mack, George Morrell, Ray Jones, Artie Ortego, Curt Barrett and the Trailsmen, Billy Dix, Dee Cooper

D: Lambert Hillyer

SP: J. Benton Cheney

P: Scott R. Dunlap

1851. SON OF ZORRO

(Republic, January 18, 1947)   13 Chaps.

George Turner, Peggy Stewart, Roy Barcroft, Edward Cassidy, Ernie Adams, Stanley Price, Edmund Cobb, Ken Terrell, Wheaton Chambers, Fred Graham, Eddie Parker, Si Jenks, Jack O'Shea, Jack Kirk, Tom Steele, Dale Van Sickel, Mike Frankovich, Jack Kirk, Pierce Lyden, Rocky Shahan, Ted Adams, Gil Perkins, Tex Terry, Tom London, Art Dillard, Joe Phillips, George Bell, Duke Taylor, Charles King, Post Parks, Cactus Mack, Bud Wolfe, Newton House, Frank O'Connor, Ted Mapes, Al Ferguson, Tommy Ryan, Carl Sepulveda, Herman Hack, George Chesebro, John Dahiem, Howard Mitchell, Doc Adams, Ralph Bucko, Joe Balch, Tommy Coats, Frank Ellis, Silver Harr, Pascale Perry, Roy Bucko

D: Spencer Bennet, Fred C. Brannon

SP: Franklyn Adreon, Basil Dickey, Jesse Duffy, Sol Shor

AP: Ronald Davidson

Chapter Titles: (1) Outlaw Country, (2) The Deadly Millstone, (3) Fugitive from Injustice, (4) Buried Alive, (5) Water Trap, (6) Volley of Death, (7) The Fatal Records, (8) Third Degree, (9) Shoot to Kill, (10) Den of the Beast, (11) The Devil's Trap, (12) Blazing Walls, (13) Checkmate

1852. TRAIL TO SAN ANTONE

(Republic, January 25, 1947)   67 Mins.

Gene Autry, Peggy Stewart, Sterling Holloway, William Henry, John Duncan, Tris Coffin, Dorothy Vaughn, Edward Keane, Ralph Peters, The Cass County Boys, "Champion"

D: John English

SP: Luci Ward, Jack Natteford

AP: Armand Schaefer

1853. SOUTH OF THE CHISHOLM TRAIL

(Columbia, January 30, 1947)   58 Mins.

(*Durango Kid* Series)

Charles Starrett, Smiley Burnette, Nancy Saunders, Frank Sully, Jim Diehl, Jack Ingram, George Chesebro, Frank LaRue, Jacques O'Mahoney (Jock Mahoney), Eddie Parker, Kit Guard, Ray Elder, Hank Newman and his Georgia Crackers

D: Derwin Abrahams

S/SP: Michael Simmons

P: Colbert Clark

1854. LAST FRONTIER UPRISING

(Republic, February 1, 1947)   67 Mins.

(Trucolor)

Monte Hale, Adrian Booth, James Taggert, Roy Barcroft, Philip Van Zandt, Edmund Cobb, John Ince, Frank O'Conner, Bob Blair, Doye O'Dell, Foy Willing and the Riders of the Purple Sage

D: Lesley Selander

S: Jerome Odlum

SP: Harvey Gates

AP: Louis Gray

1855. CODE OF THE WEST

(RKO-Radio, February 2, 1947)   57 Mins.

James Warren, Debra Alden, John Laurenz, Robert Clarke, Steve Brodie, Rita Lynn, Carol Forman, Harry Woods, Raymond Burr, Harry Harvey, Phil Warren, Emmett Lynn

D: William Berke

S: Zane Grey

SP: Norman Houston

P: Herman Schlom

1856. RAINBOW OVER THE ROCKIES

(Monogram, February 8, 1947)   54 Mins.

Jimmy Wakely, Lee "Lasses" White, Dennis Moore, Pat Starling, Wesley Tuttle and his Texas Stars, Jack Baxley, Budd Buster, Zon Murray, Billy Dix, Jasper Palmer, Carl Sepulveda, Bob Gilbert

D: Oliver Drake

S: Oliver Drake

SP: Elmer Clifton

P: Oliver Drake

1857. OVER THE SANTA FE TRAIL
(Columbia, February 13, 1947)   63 Mins.
The Hoosier Hot Shots (Hezzie, Ken, Gil, and
   Gabe), Ken Curtis, Jennifer Holt, Guy Kibbee,
   Guinn "Big Boy" Williams, The DeCastro Sisters,
   Art West and his Sunset Riders, Noel Neill,
   Holmes Herbert, George Chesebro, Jim Diehl,
   Frank LaRue, Steve Clark, Julian Rivero, Nolan
   Leary, Bud Osborne
D: Ray Nazarro
S: Eileen Gary
SP: Louise Rousseau
P: Colbert Clark

1858. APACHE ROSE
(Republic, February 15, 1947)   75 Mins.
(Trucolor)
Roy Rogers, Dale Evans, Olin Howlin, Bob Nolan
   and the Sons of the Pioneers, George Meeker,
   John Laurenz, Russ Vincent, Minerva Urecal,
   LeRoy Mason, Donna DeMario, Terry Frost,
   Conchita Lemus, Tex Terry, "Trigger"
D: William Witney
SP: Gerald Geraghty
AP: Eddy White

1859. VIGILANTES OF BOOMTOWN
(Republic, February 15, 1947)   56 Mins.
(*Red Ryder* Series)
Allan Lane, Bobby Blake, Martha Wentworth, Roy
   Barcroft, Peggy Stewart, George Turner, Eddie
   Lou Simms, George Chesebro, Bobby Barber,
   George Lloyd, Ted Adams, John Dehner, Earle
   Hodgins, Harlan Briggs, Budd Buster, Jack
   O'Shea, Tom Steele
D: R. G. Springsteen
SP: Earle Snell
AP: Sidney Picker

1860. VALLEY OF FEAR
(Monogram, February 15, 1947)   54 Mins.
Johnny Mack Brown, Raymond Hatton, Christine
   McIntyre, Tris Coffin, Edward Cassidy, Eddie
   Parker, Edward Piel, Sr., Ted Adams, Pierce
   Lyden, Steve Darrell, Cactus Mack, Budd Buster,
   Gary Garrett, Robert O'Byrne, Matty Roubert
D: Lambert Hillyer
SP: J. Benton Cheney
P: Charles J. Bigelow

1861. TRAIL STREET
(RKO-Radio, February 19, 1947)   84 Mins.
Randolph Scott, Robert Ryan, Anne Jeffreys,
   George Hayes, Madge Meredith, Steve Brodie,
   Billy House, Virginia Sale, Harry Woods, Phil
   Warren, Harry Harvey, Jason Robards, Sr., For-
   rest Taylor, Kit Guard, Stanley Andrews, Sarah
   Padden, Frank McGlynn, Jr., Ernie Adams, Roy
   Butler, Jessie Arnold, Guy Beach, Warren Jack-
   son, Billy Vincent, Frank Austin, Betty Hill, Larry
   McGrath, Chris Willowbird
D: Ray Enright
S: William Corcoran
SP: Norman Houston, Gene Lewis
P: Nat Holt

1862. LAW OF THE LASH
(PRC, February 28, 1947)   53 Mins.
"Lash" LaRue, Al St. John, Mary Scott, Lee Roberts,
   Jack O'Shea, John Elliott, Charles King, Carl
   Mathews, Matty Roubert, Slim Whitaker, Ted
   French, Dick Cramer, Brad Slaven
D: Ray Taylor
SP: William L. Nolte
P: Jerry Thomas

1863. THE BELLS OF SAN FERNANDO
(Hillcrest/Screen Guild, March 1, 1947)   74 Mins.
Donald Woods, Gloria Warren, Shirley O'Hara,
   Byron Foulger, Paul Newlan, Anthony Warde,
   Monte Blue, Claire DuBrey, David Leonard, Gor-
   don Clark, Gilbert Galvan, Felipe Turich
D: Terry Morse
S/SP: Jack DeWitt, Renault Duncan (Duncan
   Renaldo)
P: Duncan Renaldo

1864. THE LONE HAND TEXAN
(Columbia, March 6, 1947)   54 Mins.
(*Durango Kid* Series)
Charles Starrett, Smiley Burnette, Mary Newton,
   Fred Sears, Mustard and Gravy, Maude Prickett,
   George Chesebro, Robert Stevens, Bob Cason,
   Jim Diehl, George Russell, Jasper Weldon, Ernest
   Stokes
D: Ray Nazarro
SP: Ed Earl Repp
P: Colbert Clark

1865. GUNSMOKE
(Standard Pictures/Astor, March 8, 1947)
Nick Stuart, Carol Forman, Robert Garden, Craig
   Lawrence, Marie Harmon, Clark Bush, Lee
   "Stormy" Weather, Smokey Joe LaDue, Curley
   Fletcher, Larraine Jensen, Danny Dowling, Lee
   Carling, Charlie Quirk, Bill Jones
D: Fred King
SP: Reg Browne
P: Fred Walker
(Distributed in the Southwest and Southeast by
   Astor as *Gunsmoke Killers*)

1866. RANGE BEYOND THE BLUE

(PRC, March 17, 1947)   53 Mins.

Eddie Dean, Roscoe Ates, Helen Mowery, Bob Duncan, Ted Adams, Bill Hammond, George Turner, Ted French, Brad Slavin, Steve Clark, The Sunshine Boys, "Flash"

D: Ray Taylor

SP: Patricia Harper

P: Jerry Thomas

1867. JESSE JAMES RIDES AGAIN

(Republic, March 21, 1947)   13 Chaps.

Clayton Moore, Linda Stirling, Roy Barcroft, John Compton, Tristram Coffin, Tom London, Holly Bane, Edmund Cobb, Gene Strutenroth, Fred Graham, LeRoy Mason, Edward Cassidy, Dave Anderson, Eddie Parker, Tom Steele, Dale Van Sickel, Robert Blair, Ted Mapes, Tex Terry, Gil Perkins, Tex Palmer, Casey MacGregor, Emmett Lynn, Charles Morton, Watson Downs, Duke Taylor, Monte Montague, Lee Shumway, Carey Loftin, Loren Riebe, Frank Marlowe, Herman Hack, Chuck Roberson, Carl Sepulveda, Ken Terrell, Bert LeBaron, Pascale Perry, Nellie Walker, Chester Conklin, Tommy Coats, George Chesebro, Bud Wolfe, Tom Chatterton, Charles King, Robert Riordan, Howard Mitchell, Richard Alexander, Keith Richards, Victor Cox, Helen Griffith, Don Summers

D: Fred C. Brannon, Thomas Carr

SP: Franklyn Adreon, Basil Dickey, Jesse Duffy, Sol Shor

AP: Mike Frankovitch

Chapter Titles: (1) The Black Raiders, (2) Signal for Action, (3) The Stacked Deck, (4) Concealed Evidence, (5) The Corpse of Jesse James, (6) The Traitor, (7) Talk or Die, (8) Boomerang, (9) The Captured Raider, (10) The Revealing Torch, (11) The Spy, (12) Black Gold, (13) Deadline at Midnight

1868. WEST OF DODGE CITY

(Columbia, March 27, 1947)   57 Mins.

(*Durango Kid* Series)

Charles Starrett, Smiley Burnette, Nancy Saunders, Fred Sears, Glenn Stuart, I. Stanford Jolley, George Chesebro, Bob Wilke, Nolan Leary, Steve Clark, Zon Murray, Marshall Reed, Mustard and Gravy

D: Ray Nazarro

SP: Bert Horswell

P: Colbert Clark

1869. UNEXPECTED GUEST

(United Artists, March 28, 1947)   61 Mins.

(*Hopalong Cassidy* Series)

William Boyd, Rand Brooks, Andy Clyde, Una O'Connor, Patricia Tate, Ian Wolfe, John Parrish, Earle Hodgins, Bob Williams, Ned Young, Joel Friedkin

D: George Archainbaud

SP: Ande Lamb

P: Lewis J. Rachmil

1870. TRAILING DANGER

(Monogram, March 29, 1947)   58 Mins.

Johnny Mack Brown, Raymond Hatton, Peggy Wynne, Marshall Reed, Patrick Desmond, Steve Darrell, Eddie Parker, Bonnie Jean Parker, Ernie Adams, Bud Osborne, Cactus Mack, Kansas Moehring, Gary Garrett, Dee Cooper, Jack Hendricks, Artie Ortego

D: Lambert Hillyer

SP: J. Benton Cheney

P: Barney Sarecky

1871. KING OF THE WILD HORSES

(Columbia, March 29, 1947)   79 Mins.

Preston Foster, Gail Patrick, Bill Sheffield, Guinn "Big Boy" Williams, Buzz Henry, Charles Kemper, Patti Brady, John Kellogg, Ruth Warren, Louis Faust

D: George Archainbaud

S: Ted Thomas

SP: Brenda Weisberg

P: Ted Richmond

1872. THE MICHIGAN KID

(Universal, March, 1947)   69 Mins.

John Hall, Rita Johnson, Victor McLaglen, Andy Devine, William Ching, Milburn Stone, Leonard East, Byron Foulger, Stanley Andrews, William Brooks, Joan Fulton, Ray Teal, Guy Wilkerson, Eddy Waller, Karl Hackett, Tom Quinn, Bert LeBaron, Edmund Cobb

D: Ray Taylor

S: Suggested by Rex Beach's "Michigan Kid"

SP: Roy Chanslor

P: Howard Welsch

1873. HOMESTEADERS OF PARADISE VALLEY

(Republic, April 1, 1947)   59 Mins.

(*Red Ryder* Series)

Allan Lane, Bobby Blake, Martha Wentworth, Ann Todd, Gene Stutenroth, John James, Mauritz Hugo, Emmett Vogan, Milton Kibbee, Tom London, Edythe Elliott, George Chesebro, Edward Cassidy, Jack Kirk, Herman Hack

D: R. G. Springsteen

SP: Earle Snell

P: Sidney Picker

Homesteaders of Paradise Valley (Republic, 1947) — Allan Lane, Bobby Blake, Jack Kirk, and Edythe Elliott

1874. TWILIGHT ON THE RIO GRANDE

(Republic, April 1, 1947) 71 Mins.

Gene Autry, Sterling Holloway, Adele Mara, Bob Steele, Charles Evans, Martin Garralaga, Howard J. Negley, George J. Lewis, Nacho Galindo, Tex Terry, George Magril, Bob Burns, Enrique Acosta, Frankie Marvin, Barry Norton, Gil Perkins, Nina Campana, Kenne Duncan, Tom London, Alberto Morin, Keith Richards, Anna Camargo, Donna Martell, Jack O'Shea, Steve Soldi, Bud Osborne, Frank McCarroll, Bob Wilke, Alex Montoya, Connie Menard, Joaquin Elizondo, The Cass County Boys, "Champion, Jr."

D: Frank McDonald
SP: Dorrell and Stuart McGowan
AP: Armand Schaefer

1875. WEST TO GLORY

(PRC, April 12, 1947) 56 Mins.

Eddie Dean, Roscoe Ates, Delores Castle, Gregg Barton, Jimmie Martin, Zon Murray, Alex Montoya, Casey MacGregor, Billy Hammond, Ted French, Carl Mathews, Harry Vehar, The Sunshine Boys

D: Ray Taylor
SP: Elmer Clifton, Robert Churchill
P: Jerry Thomas

1875a. MY PAL RINGEYE

(Columbia, April 12, 1947) 10 Mins.

(*Screen Snapshots* Series)

Smiley Burnette, "Ringeye" (a horse), Eddie Dean, Jeff Donnell, Texas Jim Lewis, Ken Curtis, Curly Turford, Lee "Lasses" White

D/P: Ralph Staub

1876. BELLS OF SAN ANGELO

(Republic, April 15, 1947)

(Trucolor)

Roy Rogers, Dale Evans, Andy Devine, John McGuire, Olaf Hytten, David Sharpe, Fritz Leiber, Hank Patterson, Fred Toones, Eddie Acuff, Dale Van Sickel, Bob Nolan and the Sons of the Pioneers, "Trigger," Silver Harr, Buck Bucko

D: William Witney
S: Paul Gangelin
SP: Sloan Nibley
AP: Eddy White

1877. SIX GUN SERENADE

(Monogram, April 15, 1947) 54 Mins.

Jimmy Wakely, Lee "Lasses" White, Jimmie Martin, Steve Clark, Pierce Lyden, Bud Osborne,

Rivers Lewis, Arthur Smith, Stanley Ellison, Chick Hannon, Kay Morley, Cactus Mack
D: Ford Beebe
SP: Bennett Cohen
P: Barney Sarecky

1878. BUFFALO BILL RIDES AGAIN
(Jack Schwartz Productions, April 19, 1947) 59 Mins.
Richard Arlen, Jennifer Holt, Lee Shumway, Gil Patrick, Edward Cassidy, Edmund Cobb, Ted Adams, Shooting Star, Charles Stevens, Chief Many Treaties, John Dexter, Holly Bane, Frank McCarroll, Carl Mathews, Clark Stevens, George Sherwood, Fred Graham, Paula Hill, Philip Arnold, Tom Leffingwell, Frank O'Connor, Fred Fox, Dorothy Curtis
D: Bernard B. Ray
S/SP: Barney Sarecky, Fran Gilbert
P: Jack Schwarz

1879. LAW OF THE CANYON
(Columbia, April 24, 1947) 55 Mins.
(*Durango Kid* Series)
Charles Starrett, Smiley Burnette, Nancy Saunders, Buzz Henry, Fred Sears, George Chesebro, Edmund Cobb, Zon Murray, Jack Kirk, Bob Wilke, Frank Marlo, Texas Jim Lewis and his Lone Star Cowboys
D: Ray Nazarro
SP: Eileen Gary
P: Colbert Clark

1880. LAND OF THE LAWLESS
(Monogram, April 26, 1947) 54 Mins.
Johnny Mack Brown, Raymond Hatton, Christine McIntyre, Tris Coffin, June Harrison, Marshall Reed, I. Stanford Jolley, Steve Clark, Edmund Cobb, Roy Butler, Cactus Mack, Gary Garrett, Carl Sepulveda, Victor Cox
D: Lambert Hillyer
SP: J. Benton Cheney
P: Barney Sarecky

1881. RAMROD
(Enterprise/United Artists, May 2, 1947) 94 Mins.
Joel McCrea, Veronica Lake, Ian McDonald, Charlie Ruggles, Preston Foster, Arleen Whelan, Lloyd Bridges, Donald Crisp, Rose Higgens, Chic York, Sarah Padden, Don DeFore, Nestor Paiva, Cliff Parkinson, Trevor Bardette, John Powers, Ward Wood, Hal Taliaferro, Wally Cassell, Ray Teal, Jeff Corey
D: Andre de Toth
S: Luke Short
SP: Jack Moffitt, Graham Baker, Cecile Kramer
P: Harry Sherman

1882. OREGON TRAIL SCOUTS
(Republic, May 5, 1947) 58 Mins.
(*Red Ryder* Series)
Allan Lane, Bobby Blake, Martha Wentworth, Roy Barcroft, Emmett Lynn, Edmund Cobb, Earle Hodgins, Edward Cassidy, Frank Lackteen, Billy Cummings, Jack Kirk, Jack O'Shea, Chief Yowlachie
D: R. G. Springsteen
SP: Earle Snell
P: Sidney Picker

1883. THE ADVENTURES OF DON COYOTE
(Comet/United Artists, May 9, 1947) 65 Mins.
(Cinecolor)
Frances Rafferty, Richard Martin, Marc Cramer, Val Carlo, Bennie Bartlett, Frank Fenton, Byron Foulger, Eddie Parker, Pierce Lyden, Frank McCarroll
D: Reginald LeBorg
S: Bob Williams
SP: Bob Williams, Ralph Cohn
P: Buddy Rogers, Ralph Cohn

1884. BORDER FEUD
(PRC, May 10, 1947) 55 Mins.
Lash LaRue, Al St. John, Gloria Marlen, Bob Duncan, Brad Slaven, Kenneth Farrell, Casey MacGregor, Mikel Conrad, Ed Cassidy, Ian Keith, Bud Osborne, Frank Ellis, Dick Cramer
D: Ray Taylor
SP: Joseph O'Donnell, Patricia Harper
P: Jerry Thomas

1885. THE VIGILANTE
(Columbia, May 22, 1947) 15 Chaps.
Ralph Byrd, Ramsay Ames, Lyle Talbot, George Offerman, Jr., Robert Barron, Frank Marlo, Hugh Prosser, Jack Ingram, Eddie Parker, George Chesebro, Bill Brauer, Frank Ellis, Edmund Cobb, Terry Frost
D: Wallace Fox
S: Based on "The Vigilante" feature in *Action Comics*
SP: George Plympton, Lewis Clay, Arthur Hoerl

P: Sam Katzman

Chapter Titles: (1) the Vigilante Rides Again, (2) Mystery of the White Horses, (3) Double Peril, (4) Desperate Flight, (5) In the Gorilla's Cage, (6) Battling the Unknown, (7) Midnight Rendezvous, (8) Blasted to Eternity, (9) The Fatal Flood, (10) Danger Ahead, (11) X-1 Closes In, (12) Death Rides the Rails, (13) The Trap That Failed, (14) Closing In, (15) The Secret of the Skyroom

1886. DANGEROUS VENTURE

(United Artists, May 23, 1947)   59 Mins.

(*Hopalong Cassidy* Series)

William Boyd, Andy Clyde, Rand Brooks, Fritz Leiber, Douglas Evan, Elaine Riley, Harry Cording, Betty Alexander, Francis McDonald, Neyle Morrow, Patricia Tate, Bob Faust

D: George Archainbaud

SP: Doris Schroeder

P: Lewis J. Rachmil

1887. THE LAW COMES TO GUNSIGHT

(Monogram, May 24, 1947)   56 Mins.

Johnny Mack Brown, Raymond Hatton, Reno Blair (Browne), Lanny Rees, Zon Murray, Frank La-Rue, Ernie Adams, Kermit Maynard, Ted Adams, Gary Garrett, Lee Roberts, Willard Willingham, Artie Ortego

D: Lambert Hillyer

SP: J. Benton Cheney

P: Barney Sarecky

1888. PRAIRIE RAIDERS

(Columbia, May 29, 1947)   54 Mins.

(*Durango Kid* Series)

Charles Starrett, Smiley Burnette, Nancy Saunders, Robert Scott, Hugh Prosser, Lane Bradford, Ray Bennett, Doug Coppin, Steve Clark, Tommy Coats, Frank LaRue, Bob Cason, Ozie Waters and his Colorado Rangers

D: Derwin Abrahams

SP: Ed Earl Repp

P: Colbert Clark

1889. SONG OF THE WASTELAND

(Monogram, May 31, 1947)   56 Mins.

Jimmy Wakely, Lee "Lasses" White, Holly Bane, Dottye Brown, John James, Henry Hall, Marshall Reed, Gary Garrett, Ted Adams, Pierce Lyden, George Chesebro, Chester Conklin, John Car-penter, The Saddle Pals (Johnny Bond, Dick Rinehart, and Rivers Lewis), Jesse Ashlock, Cotton Thompson, Ray Jones

D: Thomas Carr

SP: J. Benton Cheney

P: Barney Sarecky

1890. SADDLE PALS

(Republic, June 6, 1947)   72 Mins.

Gene Autry, Lynne Roberts, Sterling Holloway, Irving Bacon, Damian O'Flynn, Charles Arnt, Jean Van, Tom London, Charles Williams, Francis McDonald, Edward Gargan, Carl Sepulveda, George Chandler, Paul E. Burns, Joel Friedkin, LeRoy Mason, Larry Steers, Edward Keane, Maurice Cass, Nolan Leary, Minerva Urecal, John S. Roberts, James Carlisle, Sam Ash, Frank O'Connor, Neal Hart, Frank Henry, Edward Piel, Sr., Bob Burns, Joe Yrigoyen, Johnny Day, The Cass County Boys, "Champion, Jr."

D: Lesley Selander

S: Dorrell and Stuart McGowan

SP: Bob Williams, Jerry Sackheim

AP: Sidney Picker

1890a. GAS HOUSE KIDS GO WEST

(PRC, June 12, 1947)   61 Mins.

Carl "Alfalfa" Switzer, Bennie Bartlett, Rudy Wissler, Tommy Bond, Emory Parnell, Chili Williams, Vince Barnett, William Wright, Lela Bliss, Ronn Marvin, Ray Dolciame

D: William Beaudine

S: Sam Baerwitz

SP: Robert E. Kent, Robert A. MacGowan, Eugene Conrad

P: Sam Baerwitz

1891. THUNDER MOUNTAIN

(RKO, June 15, 1947)   60 Mins.

Tim Holt, Martha Hyer, Richard Martin, Steve Brodie, Richard Powers (Tom Keene), Virginia Owen, Harry Woods, Jason Robards, Sr., Robert Clarke, Harry Harvey

D: Lew Landers

S: Zane Grey

SP: Norman Houston

P: Herman Schlom

1892. HOLLYWOOD BARN DANCE

(Screen Guild, June 21, 1947)   72 Mins.

Ernest Tubb, Lori Nelson, Helen Boyce, Earle Hod-

Thunder Mountain (RKO-Radio, 1947) — Jason Robards, Harry Harvey, Sr., Martha Hyer, and Tim Holt

gins, Frank McGlynn, Phil Arnold, Larry Reed, Red Harron, Anne Kundi, Betty Mudge, Cy Rino, Frank Bristow, Albin Robeling, Dotti Hackett, Pat Combs, Jack Guthrie, Philharmonic Trio
D: B. B. Ray
S: B. B. Ray
SP: Dorothea Knox Martin
P: Jack Schwarz

1893. SWING THE WESTERN WAY
(Columbia, June 26, 1947)   66 Mins.
The Hoosier Hot Shots, Jack Leonard, Mary Dugan, Thurston Hall, Regina Wallace, Johnny Bond, The Crew Chiefs, Tris Coffin, Sam Flint, Ralph Littlefield, George Lloyd, Eddie Acuff, Lane Bradford, Lyn Craft, Rube Schaefer, Earl Brown, George Dockstader, Jerry Wald and his Orchestra
D: Derwin Abrahams
S: Bert Horswell
SP: Barry Shipman
P: Colbert Clark

1894. CODE OF THE SADDLE
(Monogram, June 28, 1947)   53 Mins.
Johnny Mack Brown, Raymond Hatton, Riley Hill, Kay Morley, William Norton Bailey, Zon Murray, Ted Adams, Bud Osborne, Kenne Duncan, Jr., Gary Garrett, Curley Gibson, Jack Hendricks,

Boyd Stockman, Bob McElroy, Ray Jones, Chick Hannon
D: Thomas Carr
SP: Eliot Biggons
P: Barney Sarecky

1895. PIONEER JUSTICE
(PRC, June 28, 1947)   56 Mins.
Lash LaRue, Al St. John, Jennifer Holt, William Fawcett, Jack Ingram, Dee Cooper, Lane Bradford, Henry Hall, Steve Drake, Bob Woodward, Terry Frost, Wally West, Slim Whitaker
D: Ray Taylor
SP: Adrian Page
P: Jerry Thomas

1896. THE GUNFIGHTERS
(Columbia, July 1, 1947)   87 Mins.
(Cinecolor)
Randolph Scott, Barbara Britton, Dorothy Hart, Bruce Cabot, Charley Grapewin, Steven Geray, Forrest Tucker, Charles Kemper, Grant Withers, John Miles, Griff Barnett
D: George Waggner
S: "Twin Sombreros"—Zane Grey
SP: Alan LeMay
P: Harry Joe Brown

1897. THE MARAUDERS
(United Artists, July 1, 1947)   63 Mins.
(*Hopalong Cassidy* Series)
William Boyd, Andy Clyde, Rand Brooks, Ian Wolfe, Dorinda Clifton, Mary Newton, Harry Cording, Earle Hodgins, Richard Bailey, Dick Alexander, Herman Hack
D: George Archainbaud
SP: Charles Belden
P: Lewis J. Rachmil

1898. RUSTLERS OF DEVIL'S CANYON
(Republic, July 1, 1947)   58 Mins.
(*Red Ryder* Series)
Allan Lane, Bobby Blake, Martha Wentworth, Peggy Stewart, Arthur Space, Emmett Lynn, Roy Barcroft, Tom London, Harry Carr, Pierce Lyden, Forrest Taylor, Bob Burns
D: R. G. Springsteen
SP: Earle Snell
AP: Sidney Picker

1899. THE STRANGER FROM PONCA CITY
(Columbia, July 3, 1947)   56 Mins.
(*Durango Kid* Series)
Charles Starrett, Smiley Burnette, Virginia Hunter, Paul Campbell, Jim Diehl, Forrest Taylor, Ted Mapes, Jacques O'Mahoney (Jock Mahoney), Tom McDonough, John Carpenter, Texas Jim Lewis and his Lone Star Cowboys
D: Derwin Abrahams
SP: Ed Earl Repp
P: Colbert Clark

1900. SPRINGTIME IN THE SIERRAS
(Republic, July 15, 1947)   75 Mins.
(Trucolor)
Roy Rogers, Jane Frazee, Andy Devine, Stephanie Bachelor, Hal Landon, Harry V. Cheshire, Roy Barcroft, Chester Conklin, Hank Patterson, Whitey Christy, Pascale Perry, Bob Woodward, Bob Nolan and the Sons of the Pioneers, "Trigger"
D: William Witney
SP: Sloan Nibley
AP: Eddy White

1901. ROBIN HOOD OF TEXAS
(Republic, July 15, 1947)   71 Mins.
Gene Autry, Sterling Holloway, Lynne Roberts, Adele Mara, James Cardwell, John Kellogg, Ray Walker, Michael Branden, Paul Bryar, James Flavin, Dorothy Vaughn, Stanley Andrews, Alan
Bridge, Hank Patterson, Edmund Cobb, Lester Dorr, William Norton Bailey, Irene Mack, Opal Taylor, Eve Novak, Norma Brown, Frankie Marvin, Billy Wilkerson, Duke Greene, Ken Terrell, Joe Yrigoyen, The Cass County Boys, "Champion, Jr."
D: Lesley Selander
SP: John Butler, Earle Snell
AP: Sidney Picker

1902. FLASHING GUNS
(Monogram, July 16, 1947)   59 Mins.
Johnny Mack Brown, Raymond Hatton, Jan Bryant, Douglas Evans, James E. Logan, Ted Adams, Edmund Cobb, Norman Jolley, Ken Adams, Gary Garrett, Ray Jones, Jack O'Shea, Steve Clark, Frank LaRue, Jack Rockwell, Riley Hill, Bob Woodward
D: Lambert Hillyer
SP: Frank H. Young
P: Barney Sarecky

1903. HOPPY'S HOLIDAY
(United Artists, July 18, 1947)   60 Mins.
(*Hopalong Cassidy* Series)
William Boyd, Andy Clyde, Rand Brooks, Mary Ware, Andrew Tombes, Leonard Penn, Jeff Corey, Donald Kirke, Holly Bane, Gil Patrick, Frank Henry
D: George Archainbaud
S: Ellen Corby, Cecile Kramer
SP: J. Benton Cheney, Bennett Cohen, Ande Lamb
P: Lewis J. Rachmil

1904. GHOST TOWN RENEGADES
(PRC, July 26, 1947)   57 Mins.
Lash LaRue, Al St. John, Jennifer Holt, Jack Ingram, Terry Frost, Steve Clark, Lee Roberts, Lane Bradford, Henry Hall, William Fawcett, Mason Wynn, Dee Cooper
D: Ray Taylor
SP: Patricia Harper
P: Jerry Thomas

1905. WYOMING
(Republic, July 28, 1947)   84 Mins.
William Elliott, Vera Ralston, John Carroll, George Hayes, Albert Dekker, Virginia Grey, Mme. Maria Ouspenskaya, Grant Withers, Harry Woods, Minna Gombell, Dick Curtis, Roy Bar-

croft, Trevor Bardette, Paul Harvey, Louise Kane, Tom London, George Chesebro, Linda Green, Jack O'Shea, Tex Cooper, Charles Middleton, Eddy Waller, Olin Howlin, Eddie Acuff, Rex Lease, Glenn Strange, Charles Morton, Marshall Reed, Charles King, Tex Terry, Dale Fink, Ed Piel, Jr., James Archuletta, David Williams, Lee Shumway, Roque Ybarra
D: Joseph Kane
SP: Lawrence Hazard, Gerald Geraghty
AP: Joseph Kane
Second Unit D: Yakima Canutt

1906. THE VIGILANTES RETURN
(Universal, July, 1947) 67 Mins.
Jon Hall, Margaret Lindsay, Andy Devine, Paula Drew, Robert Wilcox, Jack Lambert, Jonathan Hale, Arthur Hohl, Wallace Scott, Lane Chandler, Joan Fulton, John Hart, Monte Montague, Bob Wilke
D: Ray Taylor
SP: Roy Chanslor
P: Howard Welsch

1907. LAST OF THE REDMEN
(Columbia, August 1, 1947) 77 Mins.
(Vitacolor)
Jon Hall, Michael O'Shea, Evelyn Ankers, Julie Bishop, Buster Crabbe, Rick Vallin, Buzz Henry, Guy Hedlund, Frederick Worlock, Emmett Vogan, Chief Many Treaties
D: George Sherman
S: "Last of the Mohicans"—James Fenimore Cooper
SP: Herbert Dalmas, George Plympton
P: Sam Katzman

1908. UNDER THE TONTO RIM
(RKO, August 1, 1947) 61 Mins.
Tim Holt, Nan Leslie, Richard Martin, Richard Powers (Tom Keene), Carol Forman, Tony Barrett, Harry Harvey, Jason Robards, Sr., Lex Barker, Robert Clarke, Jay Norris, Steve Savage, Herman Hack
D: Lew Landers
S: Zane Grey
SP: Norman Houston
P: Herman Schlom

1909. RIDERS OF THE LONE STAR
(Columbia, August 14, 1947) 55 Mins.
(Durango Kid Series)

Charles Starrett, Smiley Burnette, Virginia Hunter, Steve Darrell, Edmund Cobb, Mark Dennis, Lane Bradford, Ted Mapes, George Chesebro, Peter Perkins, Eddie Parker, Curly Williams and his Georgia Peach Pickers
D: Derwin Abrahams
SP: Barry Shipman
P: Colbert Clark

1910. MARSHAL OF CRIPPLE CREEK
(Republic, August 15, 1947) 58 Min.
(Red Ryder Series)
Allan Lane, Bobby Blake, Martha Wentworth, Trevor Bardette, Tom London, Roy Barcroft, Gene Stutenroth, William Self, Helen Wallace
D: R. G. Springsteen
SP: Earle Snell
AP: Sidney Picker

1910a. THE RED STALLION
(Eagle Lion, August 16, 1947) 81 Mins.
(Cinecolor)
Robert Paige, Noreen Nash, Ted Donaldson, Jane Darwell, Ray Collins, Guy Kibbee, Willie Best, Robert Bice, Pierre Watkin, Bill Carledge, "Big Red" (a horse), "Daisy" (a dog)
D: Lesley Selander
SP: Robert E. Kent, Crane Wilbur
P: Ben Stoloff

1910b. SMOKY RIVER SERENADE
(Columbia, August 21, 1947) 67 Mins.
Paul Campbell, Ruth Terry, Hoosier Hotshots, Billy Williams, Virginia Hunter, Paul E. Burns, Russell Hicks, Emmett Vogan, Carolina Cotton, Cottonseed Clark, The Boyd Triplets
D: Derwin Abrahams
S/SP: Barry Shipman
P: Colbert Clark

1911. TEX WILLIAMS AND HIS WESTERN CARAVAN
(Universal, August 27, 1947) 15 Mins.
Tex Williams and his Western Caravan Band (including Deuce Spriggins and Smokey Rogers)
D/P: Will Cowan

1912. ALONG THE OREGON TRAIL
(Republic, August 30, 1947) 64 Mins.
(Trucolor)

Monte Hale, Adrian Booth, Max Terhune, Clayton Moore, Roy Barcroft, Will Wright, Wade Crosby, LeRoy Mason, Tom London, Forrest Taylor, Kermit Maynard, Foy Willing and the Riders of the Purple Sage
D: R. G. Springsteen
SP: Earle Snell
AP: Melville Tucker

1913. ROBIN HOOD OF MONTEREY
(Monogram, September 6, 1947)   55 Mins.
(*Cisco Kid* Series)
Gilbert Roland, Chris-Pin Martin, Evelyn Brent, Jack LaRue, Pedro De Cordoba, Donna DeMario, Travis Kent, Thornton Edwards, Nestor Paiva, Ernie Adams, Julian Rivero, Alex Montoya, Fred Cordova, Felipe Turich
D: Christy Cabanne
SP: Bennett R. Cohen
P: Jeffrey Bernard

1914. HEAVEN ONLY KNOWS
(United Artists, September 12, 1947)
(Title changed to *Montana Mike* during initial release period)
Robert Cummings, Brian Donlevy, Marjorie Reynolds, Jorja Cartright, Bill Goodwin, John Litel, Stuart Erwin, Gerald Mohr, Edgar Kennedy, Lurene Tuttle, Peter Miles, Will Orleans
D: Albert S. Rogell
S: Aubrey Wisberg
SP: Ernest Haycox, Art Arthur, Rowland Leigh
P: Seymour Nebenzal

1915. STAGE TO MESA CITY
(PRC, September 13, 1947)   56 Mins.
Lash LaRue, Al St. John, Jennifer Holt, George Chesebro, Brad Slavin, Marshall Reed, Terry Frost, Carl Mathews, Bob Woodward, Steve Clark, Frank Ellis, Lee Morgan, Dee Cooper, Wally West, Russell Arms
D: Ray Taylor
SP: Joseph Poland
P: Jerry Thomas

1916. THE WILD FRONTIER
(Republic, October 1, 1947)   59 Mins.
(First in *Rocky Lane* series)
Allan Lane, Jack Holt, Eddy Waller, Pierre Watkin, John James, Roy Barcroft, Budd Buster, Wheaton Chambers, Tom London, Sam Flint, Ted Mapes, Bob Burns, Art Dillard, Silver Harr, Bud McClure
D: Philip Ford

Robin Hood of Monterey (Monogram, 1947) — Gilbert Roland and Chris-Pin Martin

SP: Albert DeMond
AP: Gordon Kay

1917. RIDIN' DOWN THE TRAIL
(Monogram, October 4, 1947)   53 Mins.
Jimmy Wakely, Dub Taylor, Beverly Jons, Douglas Fowley, John James, Doug Aylesworth, Charles King, Matthew B. Slaven (Brad Slaven), Kermit Maynard, Harry Carr, Milburn Morante, Ted French, Post Park, Dick Rinehart, Don Weston, Jesse Ashlock, Stanley Ellison, Wayne Burson
D: Howard Bretherton
SP/P: Bennett Cohen

1918. BLACK HILLS
(PRC-Eagle Lion, October 10, 1947)   60 Mins.
Eddie Dean, Roscoe Ates, Shirley Patterson, Terry Frost, Steve Drake, Nina Bara, William Fawcett, Lane Bradford, Lee Morgan, George Chesebro, Steve Crane, Bud Osborne, Carl Mathews, Eddie Parker, Andy Parker and the Plainsmen, "White Cloud"
D: Ray Taylor
SP: Joseph Poland
P: Jerry Thomas

1919. RETURN OF THE LASH
(PRC, October 11, 1947)   55 Mins.
Lash LaRue, Al St. John, Mary Maynard, Brad Slaven, George Chesebro, George DeNormand, Lee Morgan, Lane Bradford, John Gibson, Dee Cooper, Carl Mathews, Bud Osborne, Slim Whitaker, Kermit Maynard, Frank Ellis, Bob Woodward
D: Ray Taylor
SP: Joseph O'Donnell
P: Jerry Thomas

1920. BUCKAROO FROM POWDER RIVER
(Columbia, October 14, 1947)   55 Mins.
(*Durango Kid* Series)
Charles Starrett, Smiley Burnette, Eve Miller, Forrest Taylor, Paul Campbell, Doug Coppin, Phillip Morris, Casey MacGregor, Ted Adams, Ethan Laidlaw, Frank McCarroll, The Cass County Boys, Kermit Maynard
D: Ray Nazarro
SP: Norman S. Hall
P: Colbert Clark

1921. ON THE OLD SPANISH TRAIL
(Republic, October 15, 1947)   75 Mins.

(Trucolor)
Roy Rogers, Jane Frazee, Andy Devine, Tito Guizar, Estelita Rodriguez, Bob Nolan and the Sons of the Pioneers, Charles McGraw, Fred Graham, Steve Darrell, Marshall Reed, Wheaton Chambers, "Trigger"
D: William Witney
S: Gerald Geraghty
SP: Sloan Nibley
AP: Eddy White

1922. PRAIRIE EXPRESS
(Monogram, October 25, 1947)   55 Mins.
Johnny Mack Brown, Raymond Hatton, Virginia Belmont, Marshall Reed, William Ruhl, Robert Winkler, Frank LaRue, Ted Adams, Steve Darrell, Ken Adams, Gary Garrett, Hank Worden, Bob McElroy, Carl Mathews, Boyd Stockman, Jack Gibson, Steve Clark, Artie Ortego, I. Stanford Jolley, Jack Hendricks
D: Lambert Hillyer
SP: Anthony Coldeway, J. Benton Cheney
P: Barney Sarecky

1922a. THE WISTFUL WIDOW OF WAGON GAP
(Universal-International, October, 1947)   78 Mins.
Bud Abbott, Lou Costello, Marjorie Main, Audrey Young, George Cleveland, Gordon Jones, William Ching, Peter Thompson, Olin Howlin, Bill Clauson, Billy O'Leary, Pamela Wells, Jimmie Bates, Paul Dunn, Diane Florentine, Rex Lease, Glenn Strange, Edmund Cobb, Wade Crosby, Forbes Murray, Charles King, Murray Leonard, Emmett Lynn, Iris Adrian, Lee "Lasses" White, George Lewis, Dewey Robinson, Jack Shutta, Harry Evans, Mickey Simpson, Frank Marlo, Ethan Laidlaw
D: Charles Barton
S: D. D. Beauchamp, William Bowers
SP: Frederic I. Rinaldo, John Grant
P: Robert Arthur

1923. THE LAST ROUND-UP
(Columbia, November 5, 1947)   77 Mins.
Gene Autry, Jean Heather, Ralph Morgan, Carol Thurston, Mark Daniels, Bobby Blake, Russ Vincent, Shug Fisher, Trevor Bardette, Lee Bennett, John Halloran, Sandy Saunders, Roy Gordon, Silverheels Smith, Frances Rey, Bob Cason, Dale Van Sickle, Billy Wilkinson, Ed Piel, Sr., George Carleton, Don Kay Reynolds, Nolan Leary, Ted Adams, Jack Baxley, Steve Clark, Chuck Ham-

ilton, Bud Osborne, Frankie Marvin, Kernan
Cripps, Jose Alvarado, J. W. Cody, Iron Eyes
Cody, Blackie Whiteford, Robert Walker, Vir-
ginia Carroll, Arline Archuletta, Louis Crosby,
Brian O'Hara, Rodd Redwing, Alex Montoya, The
Texas Rangers, "Champion, Jr."
D: John English
S: Jack Townley
SP: Jack Townley, Earle Snell
P: Armand Schaefer

1924. KING OF THE BANDITS
(Monogram, November 8, 1947) 66 Mins.
(*Cisco Kid* Series)
Gilbert Roland, Angela Greene, Chris-Pin Martin,
Anthony Warde, Laura Treadwell, William Blake-
well, Rory Mallison, Pat Golden, Cathy Carter,
Boyd Irwin, Antonio Filauri, Jasper Palmer, Bill
Cabanne, Jack O'Shea
D: Christy Cabanne
S: Christy Cabanne
SP: Bennett Cohen, Gilbert Roland

1925. THE FABULOUS TEXAN
(Republic, November 9, 1947) 95 Mins.
William (Bill) Elliott, John Carroll, Catherine
McLeod, Andy Devine, Albert Dekker, Ruth Don-
nelly, Jim Davis, Russell Simpson, George Beban,
Jr., James Brown, John Miles, Robert Coleman,
Tommy Kelly, Johnny Sands, Harry Davenport,
Robert Barrat, Douglass Dumbrille, Reed Hadley,
Roy Barcroft, Frank Ferguson, Glenn Strange,
Selmar Jackson, Harry V. Cheshire, John Ham-
ilton, Harry Woods, Karl Hackett, Ed Cas-
sidy, Pierre Watkin, Tristram Coffin, Stanley
Andrews, Olin Howlin, Kenneth MacDonald,
Edythe Elliott, Crane Whitley, Jack Ingram, Ted
Mapes, Pierce Lyden, Al Ferguson, Ethan Laidlaw,
Franklyn Farnum, Ray Teal
D: Edward Ludwig
S: Hal Long
SP: Lawrence Hazard, Horace McCoy
AP: Edmund Grainger

1926. LAST DAYS OF BOOT HILL
(Columbia, November 11, 1947) 56 Mins.
(*Durango Kid* Series)
Charles Starrett, Smiley Burnette, Virginia Hunter,
Paul Campbell, Mary Newton, Bill Free, J. Court-
land Lytton, Bob Wilke, Alan Bridge
D: Ray Nazarro
SP: Norman S. Hall
P: Colbert Clark

1927. BELLE STARR'S DAUGHTER
(Alson Production/20th C. Fox, November 15, 1947)
  85 Mins.
George Montgomery, Rod Cameron, Ruth Roman,
Wallace Ford, Charles Kemper, William Phipps,
Edith King, Chris-Pin Martin, Jack Lambert, Paul
Libby, J. Farrell MacDonald, Charles Jewell
D: Lesley Selander
S/SP: W. R. Burnette
P: Edward L. Alperson

1928. THE FIGHTING VIGILANTES
(PRC, November 15, 1947) 51 Mins.
Lash LaRue, Al St. John, Jennifer Holt, George
Chesebro, Steve Clark, Lee Morgan, Marshall
Reed, Carl Mathews, Russell Arms, John Elliott,
Felice Richmond, John Elliott
D: Ray Taylor
SP: Robert Churchill
P: Jerry Thomas

1929. WILD HORSE MESA
(RKO, November 21, 1947) 60 Mins.
Tim Holt, Nan Leslie, Richard Martin, Richard
Powers (Tom Keene), Jason Robards, Sr., Tony
Barrett, Harry Woods, William Gould, Robert
Bray, Richard Foote, Frank Yaconelli
D: Wallace Grissell
S: Zane Grey
SP: Norman Houston
P: Herman Schlom

1929a. BOWERY BUCKAROOS
(Monogram, November 22, 1947) 66 Mins.
(*Bowery Boys* Series)
Leo Gorcey, Huntz Hall, Billy Jordan, Billy Benedict,
David Gorcey, Julie Briggs, Bernard Gorcey, Jack
Norman (Norman Willis), Minerva Urecal
D: William Beaudine
SP: Tim Ryan, Edmond Seward
P: Jan Grippo

1930. SHADOW VALLEY
(PRC-Eagle Lion, November 29, 1947) 58 Mins.
Eddie Dean, Roscoe Ates, Jennifer Holt, George
Chesebro, Eddie Parker, Lee Morgan, Lane Brad-
ford, Carl Mathews, Budd Buster, Forrest Taylor,
Andy Parker and the Plainsmen, "White Cloud"
D: Ray Taylor
SP: Arthur Sherman
P: Jerry Thomas

1931. THE MAN FROM TEXAS
(Eagle Lion, November 29, 1947) 71 Mins.
James Craig, Lynn Bari, Johnny Johnston, Sara All-
good, Una Merkel, Harry Davenport, Vic Cutler,

Cheyenne Takes Over (PRC, 1947) — Nancy Gates, Al "Fuzzy" St. John, and Al "Lash" La-Rue

Reed Hadley, Clancy Cooper, Bert Conway, King Donovan
D: Leigh Jason

1932. CHEYENNE TAKES OVER
(PRC, December 13, 1947) 58 Mins.
Lash LaRue, Al St. John, Nancy Gates, George Chesebro, Lee Morgan, John Merton, Steve Clark, Bob Woodward, Marshall Reed, Budd Buster, Carl Mathews, Dee Cooper, Brad Slaven, Hank Bell
D: Ray Taylor
SP: Arthur E. Orloff
P: Jerry Thomas

1933. WHERE THE NORTH BEGINS
(Screen Guild, December 13, 1947) 40 Mins.
Russell Hayden, Jennifer Holt, Tris Coffin, Denver Pyle, Stephen Barclay, Artie Ortego, Keith Richards, Anthony Warde, Frank Hagney, J. W. Cody, Chief Willow Bird
D: Howard Bretherton
S: Carl Hittleman, Harold Kline
SP: Betty Burbridge, Les Swabacker
P: Carl Hittleman

1934. BANDITS OF DARK CANYON
(Republic, December 15, 1947) 59 Mins.
Allan Lane, Bob Steele, Eddy Waller, Roy Barcroft,

John Hamilton, Linda Johnson, Gregory Marshall, Francis Ford, Eddie Acuff, LeRoy Mason, Jack Norman, "Black Jack"
D: Phillip Ford
SP: Bob Williams
AP: Gordon Kay

1935. UNDER COLORADO SKIES
(Republic, December 15, 1947) 65 Mins.
(Trucolor)
Monte Hale, Adrian Booth, Paul Hurst, William Haade, John Alvin, LeRoy Mason, Tom London, Steve Darrell, Gene Evans, Ted Adams, Steve Raines, Hank Patterson, Foy Willing and the Riders of the Purple Sage
D: R. G. Springsteen
SP: Louise Rousseau
AP: Melville Tucker

1936. GUN TALK
(Monogram, December 20, 1947) 57 Mins.
Johnny Mack Brown, Raymond Hatton, Christine McIntyre, Douglas Evans, Geneva Gray, Wheaton Chambers, Frank LaRue, Ted Adams, Carl Mathews, Zon Murray, Cactus Mack, Carol Henry, Bill Hale, Boyd Stockman, Roy Butler, Bob McElroy
D: Lambert Hillyer

SP: J. Benton Cheney
P: Barney Sarecky

1937. TRAIL OF THE MOUNTIES
(Screen Guild, December 20, 1947) 42 Mins.
Russell Hayden, Jennifer Holt, Emmett Lynn, Terry Frost, Harry Cording, Charles Bedell, Zon Murray, Pedro Regas, Frank Lackteen, Britt Wood, Felice Raymond
D: Howard Bretherton
S: Leslie Schwabacher
SP: Elizabeth (Betty) Burbridge
P: Carl Hittleman

1938. FIGHT OF THE WILD STALLIONS
(Universal-International, December 24, 1947) 20 Mins.
(Documentary)
Narration by Ben Grauer
P: Thomas Mead

1939. THE PRAIRIE
(Screen Guild, December 27, 1947) 80 Mins.
Lenore Aubert, Alan Baxter, Russ Vincent, Jack Mitchum, Charles Evans, Edna Holland, Chief Thunder Cloud, Fred Colby, Bill Murphy, David Gerber, Don Lynch, George Morrell, Chief Yowlachie, Jay Silverheels, Beth Taylor, Frank Hemingway (commentator)
D: Frank Wishbar
S: James Fenimore Cooper
SP: Arthur St. Claire
P: Edward Finney

1940. PIRATES OF MONTEREY
(Universal-International, December, 1947) 77 Mins.
(Technicolor)
Maria Montez, Rod Cameron, Mikhail Rasumny, Philip Reed, Gilbert Roland, Gale Sondergaard, Tamara Shayne, Robert Warwick, Michael Raffeto, Neyle Morrow, Victor Varconi, Charles Wagenheim, George J. Lewis, Joe Bernard, George Navarro, Victor Romito, Don Driggers, George Magrill
D: Alfred Werker
S: Edward T. Lowe, Bradford Ropes
SP: Sam Hellman, Margaret Buell Wilder
P: Paul Malvern

FILMS OF 1948

1941. SIX GUN LAW
(Columbia, January 4, 1948) 54 Mins.
(*Durango Kid* Series)
Charles Starrett, Smiley Burnette, Nancy Saunders, Paul Campbell, Hugh Prosser, George Chesebro, Billy Dix, Bob Wilke, Bob Cason, Ethan Laidlaw, Pierce Lyden, Bud Osborne, Budd Buster, Curly Clements and his Rodeo Rangers
D: Ray Nazarro
SP: Barry Shipman
P: Colbert Clark

1942. THE GAY RANCHERO
(Republic, January 10, 1948) 72 Mins.
(Trucolor)
Roy Rogers, Tito Guizar, Jane Frazee, Andy Devine, Estelita Rodriguez, George Meeker, LeRoy Mason, Dennis Moore, Keith Richards, Betty Gagnon, Robert Rose, Ken Terrell, Bob Nolan and the Sons of the Pioneers, "Trigger"
D: William Witney
SP: Sloan Nibley
AP: Eddy White

1943. SONG OF THE DRIFTER
(Monogram, January 17, 1948) 53 Mins.
Jimmy Wakely, Dub Taylor, Mildred Coles, Patsy Moran, William Ruhl, Marshall Reed, Frank LaRue, Carl Mathews, Jimmie Martin, Steve Clark, Wheaton Chambers, Bud Osborne, Bob Woodward, Gary Garrett, Arthur Smith, Dick Rinehart, Cliffie Stone, Wayne Burson, Homer Bill Callahan
D: Lambert Hillyer
SP: Frank Young
P: Louis Gray

1944. CHECK YOUR GUNS
(PRC-Eagle Lion, January 24, 1948) 55 Mins.
Eddie Dean, Roscoe Ates, Nancy Gates, George Chesebro, I. Stanford Jolley, Mikel Conrad, Lane Bradford, Terry Frost, Mason Wynn, Dee Cooper, William Fawcett, Ted Adams, Budd Buster, Wally West, Andy Parker and the Plainsmen, "White Cloud"
D: Ray Taylor
SP: Joseph O'Donnell
P: Jerry Thomas

1944a. TREASURE OF THE SIERRA MADRE
(Warner Bros.-First National, January 24, 1948) 126 Mins.
Humphrey Bogart, Walter Huston, Tim Holt, Bruce Bennett, Barton MacLane, Alfonso Bedoya, A. Soto Rangel, Manuel Donde, Jose Torvay, Margarito Luna, Jacqueline Dalya, Bobby Blake, John Huston, Jack Holt
D: John Huston

P: Henry Blanke
SP: John Huston. Based on the novel by B. Traven

1945. OVERLAND TRAILS

(Monogram, January 31, 1948) 58 Mins.

Johnny Mack Brown, Raymond Hatton, Virginia Belmont, Bill Kennedy, Virginia Carroll, Holly Bane, Ted Adams, Steve Darrell, Sonny Rees, Carl Mathews, Milburn Morante, Bob Woodward, Boyd Stockman, George Peters, Tom London, Pierce Lyden, Roy Butler, Post Park, Marshall Reed, Artie Ortego
D: Lambert Hillyer
SP: Jess Bowers (Adele Buffington)
P: Barney Sarecky

1946. PANHANDLE

(Allied Artists, February 1, 1948) 85 Mins.
(Sepiatone)

Rod Cameron, Cathy Downs, Reed Hadley, Anne Gwynne, Blake Edwards, Dick Crockett, Charles Judels, Alex Gerry, Francis McDonald, J. Farrell MacDonald, Henry Hall, Stanley Andrews, Jeff York, James Harrison, Charles LaTorre, Frank Dae, Bud Osborne
D: Lesley Selander
SP/P: John C. Champion, Blake Edwards

1947. HIDDEN VALLEY DAYS

(Universal-International, Feburary 5, 1948)
27 Mins.

Red River Dave, Peggy Perron, Kenne Duncan, Curley Williams, The Texas Tophands
D/P: William Forest Crouch
SP: Charles W. Curran

1948. WESTERN HERITAGE

(RKO, February 7, 1948) 61 Mins.

Tim Holt, Nan Leslie, Richard Martin, Lois Andrews, Tony Barrett, Walter Reed, Harry Woods, Richard Powers (Tom Keene), Jason Robards, Sr., Robert Bray, Perc Launders, Emmett Lynn
D: Wallace Grissell
SP: Norman Houston
P: Herman Schlom

1949. FIGHTING MUSTANG

(Yucca Pictures/Astor, February 10, 1948)
56 Mins.

Sunset Carson, Patricia Starling, Al Terry, Lee Roberts, Forrest Matthews, Polly McKay, William Val, Felice Raymond, Bob Curtis, Stephen Keyes, Joe Hiser, Al Ferguson, Hugh Hooker, Tex Wilson, Don Gray, Dale Harrison
D: Oliver Drake
SP: Rita Ross
P: Walt Mattox

1950. PHANTOM VALLEY

(Columbia, February 19, 1948) 53 Mins.
(*Durango Kid* Series)

Charles Starrett, Smiley Burnette, Virginia Hunter, Sam Flint, Fred Sears, Joel Friedkin, Zon Murray, Robert Filmer, Mikel Conrad, Teddy Infuhr, Jerry Jerome, Ozie Walters and his Colorado Rangers
D: Ray Nazarro
SP: J. Benton Cheney
P: Colbert Clark

1951. ALBUQUERQUE

(Paramount, February 20, 1948) 90 Mins.
(Cinecolor)

Randolph Scott, Barbara Britton, George Hayes, Russell Hayden, Lon Chaney, Jr., Catherine Craig, George Cleveland, Irving Bacon, Bernard Nedell, Karolyn Grimes, Russell Simpson, Jody Gilbert, Dan White, Walter Baldwin, John Halloran
D: Ray Enright
S: Luke Short
SP: Gene Lewis, Clarence Upson Young

1952. RELENTLESS

(Columbia, February 20, 1948) 93 Mins.
(Technicolor)

Robert Young, Marguerite Chapman, Willard Parker, Akim Tamiroff, Barton MacLane, Mike Mazurki, Robert Barrat, Clem Bevins, Frank Fenton, Hank Patterson, Paul E. Burns, Emmett Lynn, Will Wright
D: George Sherman
S: Kenneth Perkins
SP: Winston Miller
P: Eugene B. Rodney

1953. TORNADO RANGE

(PRC, February 21, 1948) 56 Mins.

Eddie Dean, Roscoe Ates, Jennifer Holt, George Chesebro, Brad Slavin, Marshall Reed, Terry Frost, Lane Bradford, Russell Arms, Steve Clark, Hank Bell, Jack Hendricks, Ray Jones, Andy Parker and the Plainsmen (Paul Smith, George Bamby, Earl Murphy, and Charles Morgan), "Copper"
D: Ray Taylor
SP: William Lively
P: Jerry Thomas

1954. OKLAHOMA BADLANDS

(Republic, February 22, 1948) 59 Mins.

Allan Lane, Eddy Waller, Mildred Coles, Roy Barcroft, Gene Stutenroth, Earle Hodgins, Dale Van Sickle, Jay Kirby, Claire Whitney, Terry Frost, Hank Patterson, House Peters, Jr., Jack Kirk, Bob Woodward
D: Yakima Canutt

SP: Bob Williams
AP: Gordon Kay

1955. POWDER RIVER GUNFIRE
(Universal-International, February 26, 1948)
   24 Mins.
Kenne Duncan, Paula Raymond, Don Douglas, Dick
   Thomas, The Santa Fe Rangers
D: Harold James Moore
SP: Irwin Winehouse

1956. DEADLINE
(Yucca Pictures/Astor, March 12, 1948)   57 Mins.
Sunset Carson, Pat Starling, Lee Roberts, Stephen
   Keyes, Frank Ellis, Forrest Matthews, Al Terry,
   Pat Gleason, Bob Curtis, Phil Arnold, Joe Hiser,
   Don Gray, Buck Monroe, Al Wyatt
D/SP: Oliver Drake
P: Walt Mattox, Oliver Drake

1957. THE WESTWARD TRAIL
(PRC, March 13, 1948)   56 Mins.
Eddie Dean, Roscoe Ates, Phyllis Planchard, Ei-
   leen Hardin, Steve Drake, Bob Duncan, Carl
   Mathews, Lee Morgan, Bob Woodward, Budd
   Buster, Charles "Slim" Whitaker, Frank Ellis,
   Andy Parker and the Plainsmen, "Copper"
D: Ray Taylor
SP: Robert Alan Miller
P: Jerry Thomas

1958. SILENT CONFLICT
(United Artists, March 19, 1948)   51 Mins.
(*Hopalong Cassidy* Series)
William Boyd, Andy Clyde, Rand Brooks, Virginia
   Belmont, Earle Hodgins, James Harrison, Forbes
   Murray, John Butler, Herbert Rawlinson, Dick
   Alexander, Don Haggerty
D: George Archainbaud
SP: Charles Earl Belden
P: Lewis Rachmil

1959. ADVENTURES IN SILVERADO
(Columbia, March 25, 1948)   75 Mins.
William Bishop, Gloria Henry, Edgar Buchanan,
   Forrest Tucker, Edgar Barrier, Irving Bacon, Jo-
   seph Crehan, Paul E. Burns, Patti Brady, Fred
   Sears, Joe Wong, Charles Cane, Eddy Waller,
   Netta Packer, Trevor Bardette
D: Phil Karlson
S: "Silverado Squatters"—Robert Louis Stevenson
SP: Kenneth Gamet, Tom Kilpatrick, Jo Pagano
P: Ted Richmond, Robert Cohn

1960. WEST OF SONORA
(Columbia, March 25, 1948)   52 Mins.
(*Durango Kid* Series)
Charles Starrett, Smiley Burnette, Steve Darrell,

George Chesebro, Anita Castle, Hal Taliaferro,
   Bob Wilke, Emmett Lynn, Lynn Farr, Lloyd In-
   graham, The Sunshine Boys
D: Ray Nazarro
SP: Barry Shipman
P: Colbert Clark

1961. OKLAHOMA BLUES
(Monogram, March 28, 1948)   56 Mins.
Jimmy Wakely, Dub Taylor, Virginia Belmont,
   I. Stanford Jolley, Zon Murray, George J. Lewis,
   Steve Clark, Frank LaRue, J. C. Lytton, Milburn
   Morante, Charles King, Bob Woodward
D: Lambert Hillyer
SP: Bennett Cohen
P: Louis Gray

1962. SONG OF IDAHO
(Columbia, March 30, 1948)   69 Mins.
Kirby Grant, The Hoosier Hot Shots, June Vincent,
   Tommy Ivo, Dorothy Vaughn, Emory Parnell,
   Eddie Acuff, Maude Prickett, The Starlighters,
   The Sunshine Boys, The Sunshine Girls
D: Ray Nazarro
SP: Barry Shipman
P: Colbert Clark

1963. DUEL IN THE SUN
(Selznick, March, 1948)   134 Mins.
(Technicolor)
Jennifer Jones, Joseph Cotten, Gregory Peck, Lio-
   nel Barrymore, Herbert Marshall, Lillian Gish,
   Walter Huston, Charles Bickford, Harry Carey,
   Tilly Losch, Joan Tetzel, Sidney Blackmer, Francis
   McDonald, Victor Kilian, Griff Barnett, Butterfly
   McQueen, Frank Cordell, Scott McKay, Dan
   White, Otto Kruger, Steve Dunhill, Lane Chand-
   ler, Lloyd Shaw, Thomas Dillon, Robert McKen-
   zie, Charles Dingle
D: King Vidor
S: Niven Busch
SP: Oliver H. P. Garrett
P: David O. Selznick

1964. CALIFORNIA FIREBRAND
(Republic, April 1, 1948)   63 Mins.
(Trucolor)
Monte Hale, Adrian Booth, Paul Hurst, Alice Tyrell,
   Tris Coffin, LeRoy Mason, Douglas Evans, Sarah
   Edwards, Dan Sheridan, Duke York, Lanny Rees,
   Foy Willing and the Riders of the Purple Sage
D: Philip Ford
SP: J. Benton Cheney, John K. Butler

1965. ECHO RANCH
(Universal-International, April 1, 1948)   25 Mins.
Red River Dave, Diane Hart, Kenne Duncan, Curley
   Williams, The Texas Tophands

D/P: William Forest Crouch
SP: Charles W. Curran

1966. TEX GRANGER
(Columbia, April 1, 1948)   15 Chaps.
Robert Kellard, Peggy Stewart, Buzz Henry, Smith Ballew, Jack Ingram, I. Stanford Jolley, Terry Frost, Jim Diehl, Britt Wood, Bill Brauer, William Fawcett
D: Derwin Abrahams
S: Based on the feature in *Calling All Boys* and *Tex Granger* comics
SP: Arthur Hoerl, Lewis Clay, Harry Fraser, Royal K. Cole
P: Sam Katzman
Chapter Titles: (1) Tex Finds Trouble, (2) Rider of Mystery Mesa, (3) Dead or Alive, (4) Dangerous Trails, (5) Renegade Pass, (6) A Crooked Deal, (7) The Rider Unmasked, (8) Mystery of the Silver Ghost, (9) The Rider Trapped, (10) Midnight Ambush, (11) Renegade Roundup, (12) Carson's Last Draw, (13) Blaze Takes Over, (14) Riding Wild, (15) The Rider Meets Blaze

1967. THE HAWK OF POWDER RIVER
(Eagle Lion, April 10, 1948)   54 Mins.
Eddie Dean, Jennifer Holt, Roscoe Ates, June Carlson, Eddie Parker, Terry Frost, Lane Bradford, Carl Mathews, Ted French, Steve Clark, Tex Palmer, Charles King, Marshall Reed, Andy Parker and the Plainsmen, "White Cloud"
D: Ray Taylor
SP: George Smity
P: Jerry Thomas

1968. CROSSED TRAILS
(Monogram, April 11, 1948)   53 Mins.
Johnny Mack Brown, Raymond Hatton, Lynne Carver, Douglas Evans, Kathy Frye, Zon Murray, Mary MacLaren, Ted Adams, Steve Clark, Frank LaRue, Milburn Morante, Robert D. (Bob) Woodward, Pierce Lyden, Henry Hall, Hugh Murray, Bud Osborne, Artie Ortego, Boyd Stockman
D: Lambert Hillyer
SP: Colt Remington (probably Adele Buffington)
P: Louis Gray

1969. THE BOLD FRONTIERSMAN
(Republic, April 15, 1948)   60 Mins.
Allan Lane, Eddy Waller, Roy Barcroft, Fred Graham, John Alvin, Francis McDonald, Edward Cassidy, Edmund Cobb, Harold Goodwin, Jack Kirk, Ken Terrell, Marshall Reed, Al Murphy, "Black Jack"
D: Philip Ford
SP: Bob Williams
AP: Gordon Kay

1970. GREEN GRASS OF WYOMING
(20th C. Fox, April 20, 1948)   89 Mins.
(Technicolor)
Peggy Cummings, Charles Coburn, Robert Arthur, Lloyd Nolan, Burl Ives, Geraldine Wall, Robert Adler, Will Wright, Herbert Heywood, Richard Garrick, Charles Hart, Charles Tannen
D: Louis King
S: Mary O'Hara
SP: Martin Berkeley
P: Robert Bassler

1971. DANGERS OF THE CANADIAN MOUNTED
(Republic, April 24, 1948)   12 Chaps.
Jim Bannon, Virginia Belmont, Anthony Warde, Dorothy Granger, Dale Van Sickel, Tom Steele, I. Stanford Jolley, Phil Warren, Lee Morgan, James Dale, Ted Adams, John Crawford, Jack Clifford, Eddie Parker, Frank O'Connor, James Carlisle, Ken Terrell, Eddie Phillips, Robert Wilke, Carey Loftin, Marshall Reed, House Peters, Jr., Tom McDonough, Holly Bane, Paul Gustine, Ted Mapes, Charles Regan, Jack Kirk, Al Taylor, Harry Cording, Bud Wolfe, Arvon Dale, Roy Bucko, David Sharpe
D: Yakima Canutt, Fred Brannon
SP: Franklyn Adreon, Basil Dickey, Sol Shor, Robert G. Walker
SP: Mike Frankovitch
Chapter Titles: (1) Legend of Genghis Khan, (2) Key to the Legend, (3) Ghost Town, (4) Terror in the Sky, (5) Pursuit, (6) Stolen Cargo, (7) The Fatal Shot, (8) Fatal Testimony, (9) The Prisoner Spy, (10) The Secret Meeting, (11) Secret of the Altar, (12) Liquid Jewels

1972. IN OLD LOS ANGELES
(Republic, April 25, 1948)   88 Mins.
(Re-released as *California Outpost*)
William (Bill) Elliott, John Carroll, Catherine McLeod, Joseph Schildkraut, Andy Devine, Estelita Rodriguez, Virginia Brissac, Grant Withers, Tito Renaldo, Roy Barcroft, Henry Brandon, Julian Rivero, Earle Hodgins, Augi Gomez
D: Joseph Kane
S: Clements Riley
SP: Clements Riley, Gerald Adams
P: Joseph Kane

1973. THE RANGERS RIDE
(Monogram, April 26, 1948)   56 Mins.
Jimmy Wakely, Dub Taylor, Virginia Belmont, Riley Hill, Marshall Reed, Steve Clark, Pierce Lyden, Jim Diehl, Milburn Morante, Cactus Mack, Bud Osborne, Bob Woodward, Carol Henry, Boyd Stockman, Jack Sparks, Arthur Smith, Louis W.

Armstrong, Don Weston
D: Derwin Abrahams
SP: Basil Dickey
P: Louis Gray

1974. THE DEAD DON'T DREAM
(United Artists, April 30, 1948)   68 Mins.
(*Hopalong Cassidy* Series)
William Boyd, Andy Clyde, Rand Brooks, Mary
Ware, Francis McDonald, John Parrish, Leonard
Penn, Dick Alexander, Bob Gabriel, Stanley An-
drews, Forbes Murray, Don Haggerty
D: George Archainbaud
SP: Frances Rosenwald
P: Lewis J. Rachmil

1975. BLACK BART
(Universal-International, April, 1948)   88 Mins.
(Technicolor)
Yvonne De Carlo, Dan Duryea, Jeffrey Lynn, Percy
Kilbride, Lloyd Gough, Frank Lovejoy, John
McIntyre, Don Beddoe, Ray Walker, Soledad Jimi-
nez, Eddy C. Waller, Anne O'Neal, Chief Many
Treaties
D: George Sherman
S: Luci Ward, Jack Natteford
SP: Luci Ward, Jack Natteford, William Bowers
P: Leonard Goldstein

1976. UNCONQUERED
(Paramount, April, 1948)   147 Mins.
(Technicolor)
Gary Cooper, Paulette Goddard, Howard De Silva,
Boris Karloff, Cecil Kellaway, Ward Bond, Kath-
erine DeMille, Henry Wilcoxon, Sir C. Aubrey
Smith, Victor Varconi, Porter Hall, Mike Ma-
zurki, Richard Gaines, Virginia Campbell, Gavin
Muir, Alan Napier, Nan Sunderland, Marc Law-
rence, Jane Nigh, Robert Warwick, Lloyd Bridges,
Oliver Thorndike, Russ Conklin, John Mylong,
Raymond Hatton, Julia Faye, Jeff York, Dick Alex-
ander, John Miljan, Jay Silverheels, Lex Barker,
Byron Foulger, Frank Wilcox, Clarence Muse,
Boyd Irwin, Hope Landin, Richard Reeves, Noble
Johnson, James Horne, Ottola Nesmith, Fred
Kohler, Jr., Greta Granstedt, William Haade, Jeff
Corey, Mike Killian, Lane Chandler, Francis Ford,
Francis J. McDonald
D/P: Cecil B. DeMille
S: Neil H. Swanson
SP: Charles Bennett, Frederick M. Frank, Jesse
Lasky, Jr.

1977. UNDER CALIFORNIA STARS
(Republic, May 1, 1948)   70 Mins.
(Trucolor)
Roy Rogers, Jane Frazee, Andy Devine, Michael

Chapin, Wade Crosby, George Lloyd, House
Peters, Jr., Steve Clark, Joseph Carro, Paul
Powers, John Wald, Bob Nolan and the Sons of the
Pioneers, "Trigger"
D: William Witney
SP: Sloan Nibley, Paul Gangelin
AP: Eddy White

1978. GUNS OF HATE
(RKO, May 13, 1948)   62 Mins.
Tim Holt, Nan Leslie, Richard Martin, Steve Brodie,
Myrna Dell, Tony Barrett, Jim Nolan, Jason Ro-
bards, Sr., Robert Bray, Marilyn Mercer
D: Lesley Selander
S: Ed Earl Repp
SP: Norman Houston, Ed Earl Repp
P: Herman Schlom

1979. CARSON CITY RAIDERS
(Republic, May 13, 1948)   60 Mins.
Allan Lane, Eddy Waller, Frank Reicher, Beverly
Jons, Hal Landon, Steve Darrell, Harold Goodwin,
Dale Van Sickel, Tom Chatterton, Edmund Cobb,
Holly Bane, Bob Wilke, Herman Hack
D: Yakima Canutt
SP: Earle Snell
P: Gordon Kay

1980. WHIRLWIND RAIDERS
(Columbia, May 13, 1948)   54 Mins.
(*Durango Kid* Series)
Charles Starrett, Smiley Burnette, Fred Sears,
Nancy Saunders, Don Kay Reynolds, Jack Ingram,
Philip Morris, Patrick Hurst, Eddie Parker, Lynn
Farr, Arthur Loft, Doye O'Dell and the Radio
Rangers
D: Vernon Keays
SP: Norman S. Hall
P: Colbert Clark

1981. FRONTIER AGENT
(Monogram, May 16, 1948)   56 Mins.
Johnny Mack Brown, Raymond Hatton, Reno Blair,
Kenneth MacDonald, Dennis Moore, Riley Hill,
Frank LaRue, Ted Adams, Virginia Carroll, Wil-
liam Ruhl, Kansas Moehring, Bill Hale, Lane
Bradford, Bob Woodward, Boyd Stockman
D: Lambert Hillyer
SP: J. Benton Cheney
P: Barney Sarecky

1982. THE ARIZONA RANGER
(RKO, May 18, 1948)   63 Mins.
Tim Holt, Jack Holt, Nan Leslie, Richard Martin,
Steve Brodie, Paul Hurst, Jim Nolan, Robert Bray,
Richard Benedict, William Phipps, Harry Harvey
D: John Rawlins

SP: Norman Houston
P: Herman Schlom

1983. SILVER RIVER
(Warner Bros., May 20, 1948)   110 Mins.
Errol Flynn, Ann Sheridan, Thomas Mitchell, Bruce
  Bennett, Tom D'Andrea, Barton MacLane, Monte
  Blue, Jonathan Hale, Alan Bridge, Arthur Space,
  Art Baker, Joseph Crehan
D: Raoul Walsh
S: Stephen Longstreet
SP: Stephen Longstreet, Harriet Frank, Jr.

1984. THE GALLANT LEGION
(Republic, May 24, 1948)   88 Mins.
William (Bill) Elliott, Adrian Booth, Joseph Schild-
  kraut, Bruce Cabot, Andy Devine, Jack Holt,
  Grant Withers, Adele Mara, James Brown, Hal
  Landon, Max Terry, Lester Sharpe, Hal Talia-
  ferro, Russell Hicks, Herbert Rawlinson, Mar-
  shall Reed, Steve Drake, Harry Woods, Roy Bar-
  croft, Bud Osborne, Hank Bell, Jack Ingram,
  George Chesebro, Rex Lease, Noble Johnson,
  Emmett Vogan, John Hamilton, Trevor Bardette,
  Gene Stutenroth, Ferris Taylor, Iron Eyes Cody,
  Kermit Maynard, Jack Kirk, Merrill McCormack,
  Augie Gomez, Cactus Mack, Fred Kohler, Glenn
  Strange, Tex Terry, Joseph Crehan, Peter Perkins
D/AP: Joseph Kane
S: John K. Butler, Gerald Geraghty
SP: Gerald Adams

1985. THE DUDE GOES WEST
(King Bros./Allied Artists, May 30, 1948)
  86 Mins.
Eddie Albert, Gale Storm, James Gleason, Gilbert
  Roland, Binnie Barnes, Barton MacLane, Douglas
  Fowley, Tom Tyler, Harry Hayden, Chief Yow-
  lachie, Sarah Padden, Catherine Doucet, Edward
  Gargan, Frank Yaconelli, Olin Howlin, Charles
  Williams, Francis Pierlot, Dick Elliott, Lee "Lasses"
  White, Si Jenks, George Meeker, Ben Welden
D: Kurt Neumann
SP: Richard Sale, Mary Loos
P: Frank and Maurice King

1986. RANGE RENEGADES
(Monogram, June 6, 1948)   54 Mins.
Jimmy Wakely, Dub Taylor, Jennifer Holt, Dennis
  Moore, Riley Hill, John James, Frank LaRue, Steve
  Clark, Milburn Morante, Bob Woodward, Carl
  Mathews, Roy Garrett, Don Weston, Agapito
  Martinez, Arthur Smith
D: Lambert Hillyer
SP: Ronald Davidson, William Lively
P: Louis Gray

1987. SINISTER JOURNEY
(United Artists, June 11, 1948)   59 Mins.
(Hopalong Cassidy Series)
William Boyd, Andy Clyde, Rand Brooks, Elaine
  Riley, John Kellogg, Don Haggerty, Stanley An-
  drews, Harry Strang, Herbert Rawlinson, John
  Butler, Will Orleans, Wayne Treadway
D: George Archainbaud
SP: Doris Schroeder
P: Lewis J. Rachmil

1988. THE TIMBER TRAIL
(Republic, une 15, 1948)   67 Mins.
(Trucolor)
Monte Hale, Lynne Roberts, James Burke, Roy Bar-
  croft, Francis Ford, Robert Emmett Keane, Steve
  Darrell, Fred Graham, Wade Crosby, Eddie Acuff,
  Foy Willing and the Riders of the Purple Sage
D: Phillip Ford
SP: Bob Williams
AP: Melville Tucker

1989. THE TIOGA KID
(PRC, June 17, 1948)   54 Mins.
Eddie Dean, Roscoe Ates, Jennifer Holt, Dennis
  Moore, Lee Bennett, William Fawcett, Eddie Par-
  ker, Bob Woodward, Louis J. Corbett, Terry Frost,
  Tex Palmer, Andy Parker and the Plainsmen,
  "Flash"
D: Ray Taylor
SP: Ed Earl Repp
P: Jerry Thomas

1990. TRIGGERMAN
(Monogram, June 20, 1948)   56 Mins.
Johnny Mack Brown, Raymond Hatton, Virginia
  Carroll, Bill Kennedy, Marshall Reed, Forrest
  Matthews, Bob Woodward, Dee Cooper
D: Howard Bretherton
SP: Ronald Davidson
P: Barney Sarecky

1991. WESTERN WHOOPEE
(Universal-International, June 23, 1948)   15 Mins.
Tex Williams, Patricia Alphin, Smokey Rogers, Judy
  Clark, Jimmie Dodd
D/P: Will Cowan

1992. ADVENTURES OF FRANK AND
    JESSE JAMES
(Republic, June 24, 1948)   13 Chaps.
Clayton Moore, Steve Darrell, Noel Neill, George J.
  Lewis, Stanley Andrews, John Crawford, Sam
  Flint, House Peters, Jr., Dale Van Sickel, Tom
  Steele, James Dale, I. Stanford Jolley, Gene Stu-
  tenroth, Lane Bradford, George Chesebro, Jack
  Kirk, Steve Clark, Duke Taylor, Carey Loftin,

Duke Green, Frank Ellis, Roy Bucko, Art Dillard, Ralph Bucko, Victor Cox, Fred Graham, Guy Teague, Frank O'Connor, Joe Yrigoyen, Augie Gomez, Eddie Parker, Bud Osborne, Bud Wolfe, Rosa Turich, David Sharpe, Bob Reeves, Ken Terrell, Joe Phillips

D: Fred Brannon, Yakima Canutt

SP: Franklyn Adreon, Sol Shor, Basil Dickey

AP: Franklyn Adreon

Chapter Titles: (1) Agent of Treachery, (2) The Hidden Witness, (3) The Lost Tunnel, (4) Blades of Death, (5) Roaring Wheels, (6) Passage to Danger, (7) The Secret Code, (8) Doomed Cargo, (9) The Eyes of the Law, (10) The Stolen Body, (11) Suspicion, (12) Talk or Die!, (13) Unmasked

1993. RIVER LADY

(Universal-International, June, 1948)   78 Mins.

Yvonne De Carlo, Rod Cameron, Dan Duryea, Helena Carter, Lloyd Gough, John McIntyre, Florence Bates, Jack Lambert, Esther Somers, Anita Turner, Edmund Cobb, Dewey Robinson, Eddy Waller, Milton Kibbee, Billy Wayne, Jimmy Ames, Edward Earle

D: George Sherman

S: Houston Branch, Frank Waters

SP: D. D. Beauchamp, William Bowers

P: Leonard Goldstein

1994. BLAZING ACROSS THE PECOS

(Columbia, July 1, 1948)   56 Mins.

(*Durango Kid* Series)

Charles Starrett, Smiley Burnette, Patricia White, Chief Thunder Cloud, Paul Campbell, Charles Wilson, Thomas Jackson, Pat O'Malley, Jock Mahoney, Frank McCarroll, Pierce Lyden, Paul Conrad, Jack Ingram, Red Arnall and the Western Aces

D: Ray Nazarro

SP: Norman S. Hall

P: Colbert Clark

1995. CORONER CREEK

(Columbia, July 1, 1948)   90 Mins.

(Cinecolor)

Randolph Scott, Marguerite Chapman, George Macready, Sally Eilers, Edgar Buchanan, Barbara Reed, Wallace Ford, Forrest Tucker, William Bishop, Joe Sawyer, Russell Simpson, Douglas Fowley, Lee Bennett, Forrest Taylor, Phil Shumaker, Warren Jackson

D: Ray Enright

S: Luke Short

SP: Kenneth Gamet

P: Harry Joe Brown

1996. THUNDERHOOF

(Columbia July 8, 1948)   77 Mins.

Preston Foster, Mary Stuart, William Bishop, "Thunderhoof" (complete cast)

D: Phil Karlson

SP: Hal Smith

P: Ted Richmond

1997. COWBOY CAVALIER

(Monogram, July 11, 1948)   57 Mins.

Jimmy Wakely, Dub Taylor, Jan Bryant, Douglas Evans, Claire Whitney, William Ruhl, Steve Clark, Milburn Morante, Bud Osborne, Carol Henry, Bob Woodward, Louis Armstrong, Don Weston

D: Derwin Abrahams

SP: Ronald Davidson, J. Benton Cheney

P: Louis Gray

1998. EYES OF TEXAS

(Republic, July 15, 1948)   70 Mins.

(Trucolor)

Roy Rogers, Lynne Roberts, Andy Devine, Nana Bryant, Roy Barcroft, Danny Morton, Francis Ford, Pascale Perry, Stanley Blystone, Bob Nolan and the Sons of the Pioneers, "Trigger"

D: William Witney

SP: Sloan Nibley

AP: Eddy White

1999. RETURN OF THE BADMEN

(RKO, July 17, 1948)   96 Mins.

Randolph Scott, Robert Ryan, Anne Jeffreys, George Hayes, Jacqueline White, Richard Powers (Tom Keene), Tom Tyler, Steve Brodie, Robert Bray, Lex Barker, Walter Reed, Michael Harvey, Dan White, Robert Armstrong, Lew Harvey, Gary Gray, Walter Baldwin, Minna Gombell, Warren Jackson, Robert Clarke, Jason Robards, Sr., Ernie Adams, Bud Osborne, Forrest Taylor, Lane Chandler, Charles Stevens, Kenneth MacDonald, Earle Hodgins, Harry Shannon, Larry McGrath, Billy Vincent, Brandon Beach, Ida Moore, John Hamilton, Charles McAvoy

D: Ray Enright

SP: Charles O'Neal, Jack Natteford, Luci Ward

P: Nat Holt

2000. BACK TRAIL

(Monogram, July 18, 1948)   57 Mins.

Johnny Mack Brown, Raymond Hatton, Mildred Coles, Marshall Reed, James Horne, Snub Pollard, Ted Adams, Pierce Lyden, George Holmes, Bob Woodward, Carol Henry, William Norton Bailey, George Morrell

D: Christy Cabanne

SP: J. Benton Cheney

P: Barney Sarecky

2001. MARSHAL OF AMARILLO

(Republic, July 25, 1948)   60 Mins.

Allan Lane, Eddy Waller, Mildred Coles, Clayton Moore, Roy Barcroft, Trevor Bardette, Minerva Urecal, Denver Pyle, Charles Williams, Tom Chatterton, Peter Perkins, Tom London, Lynn Castile, "Black Jack"
D: Philip Ford
SP: Bob Williams
AP: Gordon Kay

2002. NORTHWEST STAMPEDE

(Eagle Lion, July 28, 1948)   79 Mins.
(Cinecolor)

James Craig, Joan Leslie, Jack Oakie, Chill Wills, Victor Kilian, Stanley Andrews, Ray Bennett, Lane Chandler, Harry Shannon, Kermit Maynard
D: Albert S. Rogell
S: "Wild Horse Roundup"—*Saturday Evening Post* article by Jean Muir
SP: Art Arthur, Lillian Hayward
P: Albert S. Rogell

2003. RANGE JUSTICE

(Monogram, August 7, 1948)   57 Mins.

Johnny Mack Brown, Max Terhune, Felice Ingersoll, Fred Kohler, Jr., Tris Coffin, Riley Hill, Sarah Padden, Eddie Parker, Kenne Duncan, Myron Healey, Bill Hale, Bill Potter, Bob Woodward
D: Ray Taylor
SP: Ronald Davidson
P: Barney Sarecky

2004. TRAIL TO LAREDO

(Columbia, August 12, 1948)   54 Mins.
(*Durango Kid* Series)

Charles Starrett, Smiley Burnette, Jim Bannon, Virginia Maxey, Tommy Ivo, Ethan Laidlaw, Hugh Prosser, Mira McKinney, John Merton, George Chesebro, The Cass County Boys
D: Ray Nazarro
SP: Barry Shipman
P: Colbert Clark

2005. THE FIGHTING RANGER

(Monogram, August 15, 1948)   57 Mins.

Johnny Mack Brown, Raymond Hatton, Christine Larson, Marshall Reed, Eddie Parker, Charlie Hughes, I. Stanford Jolley, Milburn Morante, Steve Clark, Bob Woodward, Peter Perkins
D: Lambert Hillyer
SP: Ronald Davidson
P: Barney Sarecky

2006. THE STRAWBERRY ROAN

(Columbia, August 15, 1948)   79 Mins.
(Cinecolor)

Gene Autry, Gloria Henry, Jack Holt, Dick Jones, Pat Buttram, Rufe Davis, Eddy Waller, John McGuire, Rodd Harper, Jack Ingram, Eddie Parker, Ted Mapes, Sam Flint, "Champion, Jr."
D: John English
SP: Dwight Cummings, Dorothy Yost
P: Armand Schaefer

2007. PARTNERS OF THE SUNSET

(Monogram, August 22, 1948)   53 Mins.

Jimmy Wakely, Dub Taylor, Christine Larson, Steve Darrell, Marshall Reed, Jay Kirby, Leonard Penn, J. C. Lytton, Bob Woodward, Carl Mathews, Carl Sepulveda, Agapito Martinez, Don Weston, Arthur Smith
D: Lambert Hillyer
SP: J. Benton Cheney
P: Louis Gray

2008. SILVER TRAILS

(Monogram, August 22, 1948)   53 Mins.

Jimmy Wakely, Dub Taylor, Whip Wilson, Christine Larson, George J. Lewis, Pierce Lyden, William Norton Bailey, Fred Edwards, Robert Strange, Bob Woodward, Bud Osborne, Consuelo Asnis
D: Christy Cabanne
SP: J. Benton Cheney
P: Louis Gray

2009. NIGHT TIME IN NEVADA

(Republic, September 5, 1948)   67 Mins.
(Trucolor)

Roy Rogers, Andy Devine, Adele Mara, Grant Withers, Marie Harmond (Harmon), Joseph Crehan, George Carleton, Holly Bane, Steve Darrell, Hank Patterson, Jim Nolan, Bob Nolan and the Sons of the Pioneers, "Trigger"
D: William Witney
SP: Sloan Nibley
AP: Eddy White

2010. DEAD MAN'S GOLD

(Western Adventure/Screen Guild, September 10, 1948)   60 Mins.

Lash LaRue, Al St. John, Peggy Stewart, John (Bob) Cason, Terry Frost, Lane Bradford, Pierce Lyden, Stephen Keyes, Cliff Taylor, Marshall Reed, Britt Wood, Bob Woodward
D: Ray Taylor
SP: Ron Ormond, Ira Webb
P: Ron Ormond

2011. FALSE PARADISE

(United Artists, September 10, 1948)   60 Mins.

(*Hopalong Cassidy* Series)

William Boyd, Andy Clyde, Rand Brooks, Elaine Riley, Joel Friedkin, Cliff Clark, Kenneth Mac-Donald, Don Haggerty, Dick Alexander, William Norton Bailey, Zon Murray, George Eldridge
D: George Archainbaud
SP: Harrison Jacobs, Doris Schroeder
P: Lewis J. Rachmil

2012. SUNSET CARSON RIDES AGAIN

(Yucca Pictures/Astor, September 10, 1948)
Sunset Carson, Pat Starling, Al Terry, Dan White, Pat Gleason, Bob Cason, Steven Keyes, Ron Ormond, Bob Curtis, Joe Hiser, William Val, Forrest Matthews, Don Gray, Dale Harrison, The Rodeo Revelers
D: Oliver Drake
SP: Elmer Clifton
P: Walt Mattox

2013. DESPERADOES OF DODGE CITY

(Republic, September 15, 1948)   60 Mins.
Allan Lane, Eddy Waller, Mildred Coles, Roy Barcroft, Tris Coffin, William Phipps, James Craven, John Hamilton, Edward Cassidy, House Peters, Jr., Dale Van Sickel, Peggy Wynne, Ted Mapes
D: Philip Ford
SP: Bob Williams
AP: Gordon Kay

2014. SON OF GOD'S COUNTRY

(Republic, September 15, 1948)   60 Mins.
Monte Hale, Pamela Blake, Paul Hurst, Jim Nolan, Jay Kirby, Steve Darrell, Francis McDonald, Jason Robards, Sr., Fred Graham, Herman Hack
D: R. G. Springsteen
SP: Paul Gangelin
AP: Melville Tucker

2015. SUNDOWN RIDERS

(Film Enterprises, September 15, 1948)   56 Mins.
Andy Clyde, Jay Kirby, Russell Wade, Evelyn Finley, Marshall Reed, Jack Ingram, Steve Clark, Hal Price, Ted Mapes, Bud Osborne, Ted Wells, Jack Shannon, Henry Wills, Cliff Parkinson, George Fuller, Elmer Napier, Cactus Mack, Emily Crittenden, Chief Many Treaties
D: Lambert Hillyer
SP: Rodney J. Graham
P: H. V. George
(Filmed in 1944 in 16mm and intended for rental outside the regular theatrical market. Unreleased until above date when Film Enterprises, a small, short-lived Denver company, made some blown-up 35mm prints available to the independent distributors)

2016. BLACK EAGLE

(Columbia, September 16, 1948)   76 Mins.
William Bishop, Virginia Patton, Gordon Jones, James Bell, Trevor Bardette, Will Wright, Edmund McDonald, Paul E. Burns, Harry V. Cheshire, Al Eben, Ted Mapes, Richard Talmadge
D: Robert Gordon
S: "The Passing of Black Eagle"—O. Henry
SP: Edward Huebsch, Hal Smith
P: Robert Cohn

2017. RED RIVER

(Monterey/United Artists, September 17, 1948)   125 Mins.
John Wayne, Montgomery Clift, Joanne Dru, Walter Brennan, Coleen Gray, John Ireland, Noah Beery, Jr., Chief Yowlachie, Harry Carey, Sr., Harry Carey, Jr., Mickey Kuhn, Paul Fix, Hank Worden, Ivan Parry, Hal Taliaferro, Paul Fiero, Billy Self, Ray Hyke, Glenn Strange, Tom Tyler, Dan White, Lane Chandler, Lee Phelps, George Lloyd, Shelley Winters
D: Howard Hawks
S: "The Chisholm Trail" (also titled "Red River")—Borden Chase
SP: Borden Chase, Charles Schnee
P: Howard Hawks

2018. SINGING SPURS

(Columbia, September 23, 1948)   62 Mins.
The Hoosier Hot Shots, Kirby Grant, Patricia Knox, Lee Patrick, Jay Silverheels, Dick Elliott, Billy Wilderson, Fred Sears, Chester Clute, Marion Colby, Red Enger, Riley Hill, The Shamrock Cowboys
D: Ray Nazarro
SP: Barry Shipman
P: Colbert Clark

2019. THE DENVER KID

(Republic, October 1, 1948)   60 Mins.
Allan Lane, Eddy Waller, William Henry, Douglas Fowley, Rory Mallison, George Lloyd, George Meeker, Emmett Vogan, Hank Patterson, Bruce Edwards, Peggy Wynne, Tom Steele, Carole Gallagher, "Black Jack"
D: Philip Ford
SP: Bob Williams
AP: Gordon Kay

2020. RACHEL AND THE STRANGER

(RKO, October 2, 1948)   93 Mins.
Loretta Young, William Holden, Robert Mitchum, Gary Gray, Tom Tully, Sara Hayden, Frank Ferguson, Walter Baldwin, Regina Wallace

D: Norman Foster
P: Richard H. Berger
SP: Waldo Salt. From the story "Rachel" by Howard Fast

2021. THE SHERIFF OF MEDICINE BOW
(Monogram, October 3, 1948)   55 Mins.
Johnny Mack Brown, Raymond Hatton, Max Terhune, Evelyn Finley, Bill Kennedy, George J. Lewis, Frank LaRue, Peter Perkins, Carol Henry, Bob Woodward, Ted Adams
D: Lambert Hillyer
SP: J. Benton Cheney
P: Barney Sarecky

2022. STRANGE GAMBLE
(United Artists, October 8, 1948)   62 Mins.
(Last in the *Hopalong Cassidy* series)
William Boyd, Andy Clyde, Rand Brooks, Elaine Riley, Francis McDonald, Paul Fix, William Leicester, Joan Barton, James Craven, Joel Friedkin, Herbert Rawlinson, Robert Williams, Albert Morin, Lee Tung Foo
D: George Archainbaud
SP: J. Benton Cheney, Bennett Cohen, Ande Lamb
P: Lewis J. Rachmil

2023. EL DORADO PASS
(Columbia, October 14, 1948)   56 Mins.
(*Durango Kid* Series)
Charles Starrett, Smiley Burnette, Elena Verdugo, Steve Darrell, Ted Mapes, Rory Mallison, Blackie Whiteford, Shorty Thompson and his Saddle Rockin' Rhythm
D: Ray Nazarro
SP: Earle Snell
P: Colbert Clark

2024. MARK OF THE LASH
(Western Adventure/Screen Guild,
   October 15, 1948)   60 Mins.
Lash LaRue, Al St. John, Suzi Crandall, Marshall Reed, John Cason, Jimmy Martin, Tom London, Lee Roberts, Steve Darrell, Jack Hendricks, Cliff Taylor, Harry Cody, Britt Wood
D: Ray Taylor
SP: Ron Ormond, Ira Webb
P: Ron Ormond

2025. STATION WEST
(RKO, October 16, 1948)   92 Mins.
Dick Powell, Jane Greer, Agnes Moorehead, Burl Ives, Tom Powers, Gordon Oliver, Steve Brodie, Guinn "Big Boy" Williams, Raymond Burr, Regis Toomey, Michael Steele, Olin Howlin, John Berkes, Dan White, John Kellogg, Charles Middleton, John Doucette, Suzi Crandall

D: Sidney Lanfield
S: Luke Short
SP: Frank Fenton, Winston Miller

2026. THE UNTAMED BREED
(Columbia, October 21, 1948)   79 Mins.
(Cinecolor)
Sonny Tufts, Barbara Britton, George Hayes, Edgar Buchanan, William Bishop, George E. Stone, Joe Sawyer, Gordon Jones, James Kirkwood, Harry Tyler, Virginia Brissac, Reed Howes
D: Charles Lamont
S: Eli Colter
SP: Tom Reed
P: Harry Joe Brown

2027. OUTLAW BRAND
(Monogram, October 28, 1948)   58 Mins.
Jimmy Wakely, Dub Taylor, Kay Morley, Christine Larson, John James, Bud Osborne, Nolan Leary, Eddie Majors, Tom Chatterton, Boyd Stockman, Leonard Penn, Frank McCarroll, Jay Kirby, Ray Whitley, John James, Dick Rinehart
D: Lambert Hillyer
SP: J. Benton Cheney
P: Louis Gray

2028. GRAND CANYON TRAIL
(Republic, November 5, 1948)   67 Mins.
(Trucolor)
Roy Rogers, Andy Devine, Jane Frazee, Robert Livingston, Roy Barcroft, Charles Coleman, Emmett Lynn, Ken Terrell, James Finlayson, Tommy Coats, Zon Murray, Foy Willing and the Riders of the Purple Sage, "Trigger"
D: William Witney
SP: Gerald Geraghty
AP: Eddy White

2029. SUNDOWN IN SANTA FE
(Republic, November 5, 1948)   60 Mins.
Allan Lane, Eddy Waller, Roy Barcroft, Trevor Bardette, Jean Dean, Rand Brooks, Russell Simpson, Lane Bradford, B. G. Norman, Minerva Urecal, Joseph Crehan, Kenne Duncan, Bob Wilke, "Black Jack"
D: R. G. Springsteen
SP: Norman S. Hall
AP: Melville Tucker

2030. GUNNING FOR JUSTICE
(Monogram, November 7, 1948)   55 Mins.
Johnny Mack Brown, Raymond Hatton, Max Terhune, Evelyn Finley, I. Stanford Jolley, House Peters, Jr., Bill Potter, Ted Adams, Bud Osborne, Dan White, Bob Woodward, Carol Henry, Boyd Stockman, Dee Cooper, Artie Ortego

D: Ray Taylor
SP: J. Benton Cheney
P: Barney Sarecky

2031. BLOOD ON THE MOON

(RKO-Radio, November 9, 1948)   88 Mins.
Robert Mitchum, Barbara Bel Geddes, Robert Preston, Walter Brennan, Phyllis Thaxter, Frank Faylen, Tom Tully, Charles McGraw, Tom Tyler, Richard Powers (Tom Keene), Clifton Young, George Cooper, Bud Osborne, Zon Murray, Robert Bray, Ben Corbett, Harry Carey, Jr., Chris-Pin Martin, Al Ferguson, Iron Eyes Cody, Ruth Brennan, Erville Aldesron, Joe Devlin, Al Murphy, Robert Malcolm
D: Robert Wise
S: Luke Short
SP: Harold Shumate, Luke Short
P: Sid Rogell

2032. THUNDER IN THE PINES

(Lippert/Screen Guild, November 11, 1948)
   62 Mins.
(Sepiatone)
George Reeves, Ralph Byrd, Greg McClure, Michael Whalen, Denise Darcel, Marion Martin, Lyle Talbot, Vince Barnett, Roscoe Ates, Tom Kennedy
D: Robert Edwards
P: William Stephens

2033. COURTIN' TROUBLE

(Monogram, November 21, 1948)   56 Mins.
Jimmy Wakely, Dub Taylor, Virginia Belmont, Leonard Penn, Marshall Reed, Steve Clark, House Peters, Jr., Frank LaRue, William Norton Bailey, Bud Osborne, Bill Hale, Bob Woodward, Carol Henry, Bill Potter, Don Weston, Louis Armstrong, Arthur Smith
D: Ford Beebe
SP: Ronald Davidson
P: Louis Gray

2034. RENEGADES OF SONORA

(Republic, November 24, 1948)   60 Mins.
Allan Lane, Eddy Waller, William Henry, Douglas Fowley, Roy Barcroft, Frank Fenton, Mauritz Hugo, George J. Lewis, Holly Bane, Dale Van Sickel, Marshall Reed, House Peters, Jr., Art Dillard, "Black Jack"
D: R. G. Springsteen
SP: M. Coates Webster
AP: Gordon Kay

2035. THE PLUNDERERS

(Republic, December 1, 1948)   87 Mins.
(Trucolor)
Rod Cameron, Ilona Massey, Adrian Booth, Forrest Tucker, George Cleveland, Grant Withers, Taylor Holmes, Paul Fix, Francis Ford, James Flavin, Maude Eburne, Russell Hicks, Mary Ruth Wade, Louis R. Faust, Hank Bell, Rex Lease
D: Joseph Kane
S: James Edward Grant
SP: Gerald Geraghty, Gerald Adams
AP: Joseph Kane

2036. THREE GODFATHERS

(Argosy/MGM, December 1, 1948)   106 Mins.
(Technicolor)
John Wayne, Pedro Armendariz, Harry Carey, Jr., Ward Bond, Mae Marsh, Mildred Natwick, Jane Darwell, Guy Kibbee, Dorothy Ford, Ben Johnson, Charles Halton, Hank Worden, Jack Pennick, Fred Libby, Michael Dugan, Don Summers, Francis Ford, Gertrude Astor, Eva Novak, Ruth Clifford, Emilia Grace Yelda, Cliff Lyons, Frank McGrath, Richard Hageman
D: John Ford
S: Peter B. Kyne
SP: Laurence Stallings, Frank S. Nugent
P: John Ford, Merian C. Cooper

2037. QUICK ON THE TRIGGER

(Columbia, December 2, 1948)   55 Mins.
(*Durango Kid* Series)
Charles Starrett, Smiley Burnette, Lyle Talbot, Helen Parrish, George Eldridge, Ted Adams, Alan Bridge, Russell Arms, Budd Buster, Tex Cooper, Blackie Whiteford, The Sunshine Boys
D: Ray Nazarro
SP: Elmer Clifton
P: Colbert Clark

2038. INDIAN AGENT

(RKO, December 11, 1948)   63 Mins.
Tim Holt, Noah Beery, Jr., Richard Martin, Nan Leslie, Lee "Lasses" White, Richard Powers (Tom Keene), Harry Woods, Claudia Drake, Robert Bray, Bud Osborne, Iron Eyes Cody
D: Lesley Selander
SP: Norman Houston
P: Herman Schlom

2039. HIDDEN DANGER

(Monogram, December 12, 1948)   55 Mins.
Johnny Mack Brown, Raymond Hatton, Max Terhune, Christine Larson, Myron Healey, Marshall Reed, Kenne Duncan, Steve Clark, Edmund Cobb, Milburn Morante, Carol Henry, Bill Hale, Bob Woodward, Boyd Stockman, Bill Potter
D: Ray Taylor
SP: J. Benton Cheney, Eliot Gibbons
P: Barney Sarecky

2040. THE VALIANT HOMBRE
(United Artists, December 15, 1948) 60 Mins.
(*Cisco Kid* Series)
Duncan Renaldo, Leo Carrillo, John Litel, Barbara
Billingsley, Lee "Lasses" White, Stanley Andrews,
Frank Ellis, Herman Hack, Ralph Peters, "Daisy"
(the Wonder Dog)
D: Wallace Fox
SP: Adele Buffington
P: Phillip N. Krasne

2041. SMOKY MOUNTAIN MELODY
(Columbia, December 16, 1948) 61 Mins.
Roy Acuff, Guinn "Big Boy" Williams, Russell Arms,
Sybil Merritt, Jason Robards, Sr., Harry V.
"Pappy" Cheshire, Fred Sears, Trevor Bardette,
Carolina Cotton, Tommy Ivo, Jock Mahoney,
Lonnie Wilson, John Elliott, Ralph Littlefield, Sam
Flint, Eddie Acuff, Jack Ellis, Heinie Conklin, Olin
Howlin, Peter Kirby, Jimmy Riddle, Joe Zinkan,
Tommy Magness, The Smoky Mountain Boys
D: Ray Nazarro
SP: Barry Shipman
P: Colbert Clark

2042. FRONTIER REVENGE
(Western Adventure/Screen Guild,
    December 17, 1948) 55 Mins.
Lash LaRue, Al St. John, Jim Bannon, Peggy
Stewart, Ray Bennett, Sarah Padden, Jimmie
Martin, Jack Hendricks, Lee Morgan, Sandy San-
ders, Billy Dix, Cliff Taylor, Steve Raines, Bud
Osborne, George Chesebro, Forrest Matthews,
Kermit Maynard
D/SP: Ray Taylor
P: Ron Ormond

2043. THE PALEFACE
(Paramount, December 24, 1948) 91 Mins.
(Technicolor)
Bob Hope, Jane Russell, Robert Armstrong, Iris
Adrian, Robert Watson, Jack Searl, Joseph Vitale,
Charles Trowbridge, Clem Bevins, Jeff York,
Stanley Andrews, Wade Crosby, Chief Yow-
lachie, Iron Eyes Cody, John Maxwell, Tom Ken-
nedy, Henry Brandon, Francis McDonald, Frank
Hagney, Skelton Knaggs, Olin Howlin, George
Chandler, Nestor Paiva, Carl Andre, Ted Mapes,
Kermit Maynard
D: Norman Z. McLeod
SP: Edmund Hartmann, Frank Tashlin, Jack Rose
P: Robert L. Welch

2044. LAST OF THE WILD HORSES
(Lippert/Screen Guild, December 27, 1948)
(Sepiatone)
James Ellison, Mary Beth Hughes, Jane Frazee,
Douglass Dumbrille, James Millican, Reed Had-
ley, Olin Howlin, Grady Sutton, William Haade,
Stanley Andrews, Rory Mallison
SP: Jack Harvey
P: Robert L. Lippert, Carl Hittleman

2045. GUN SMUGGLERS
(RKO, December 28, 1948) 61 Mins.
Tim Holt, Richard Martin, Martha Hyer, Gary
Gray, Paul Hurst, Douglas Fowley, Robert War-
wick, Don Haggerty, Frank Sully, Robert Bray
D: Frank McDonald
SP: Norman Houston
P: Herman Schlom

2046. THE FAR FRONTIER
(Republic, December 29, 1948) 67 Mins.
(Trucolor)
Roy Rogers, Gail Davis, Andy Devine, Francis Ford,
Roy Barcroft, Clayton Moore, Robert Strange,
Holly Bane, Lane Bradford, John Bagni, Clarence
Straight, Edmund Cobb, Tom London, Foy Will-
ing and the Riders of the Purple Sage, "Trigger"
D: William Witney
SP: Sloan Nibley
AP: Eddy White

2047. THE MAN FROM COLORADO
(Columbia, December, 1948) 99 Mins.
(Technicolor)
Glenn Ford, William Holden, Ellen Drew, Ray Col-
lins, Edgar Buchanan, Jerome Courtland, James
Millican, Jim Bannon, Bill Phillips, Denver Pyle,
James Bush, Mikel Conrad, David Clarke, Ian
MacDonald, Clarence Chase, Stanley Andrews,
Myron Healey, Craig Reynolds, David York
D: Henry Levin
S: Borden Chase
SP: Robert D. Andrews, Ben Maddow
P: Jules Schermer

2048. YELLOW SKY
(20th C. Fox, December, 1948) 98 Mins.
Gregory Peck, Anne Baxter, Richard Widmark,
Robert Arthur, John Russell, Henry (Harry) Mor-
gan, James Barton, Charles Kemper, Robert
Adler, Harry Carter, Victor Kilian, Paul Hurst,
Hank Worden, Jay Silverheels, William Gould,
Norman Leavitt, Chief Yowlachie
D: William A. Wellman
S: W. R. Burnett
SP/P: Lamar Trotti

FILMS OF 1949

2049. SIX GUN MUSIC

(Universal-International, January 6, 1949)
25 Mins.
Tex Williams, Lina Romay, Smokey Rogers, Deuce
Spriggins, Patricia Alphia
D: Nate Watt
SP: Luci Ward
P: Will Cowan

2050. OUTLAW COUNTRY

(Western Adventure/Screen Guild,
January 7, 1949) 66 Mins.
Lash LaRue, Al St. John, Nancy Saunders, Dan
White, House Peters, Jr., Steve Dunhill, Lee Rob-
erts, Ted Adams, John Merton, Dee Cooper,
Sandy Sanders, Jack O'Shea, Bob Duncan
D: Ray Taylor
SP: Ron Ormond, Ira Webb
P: Ron Ormond

2051. CRASHING THRU

(Monogram, January 9, 1949) 58 Mins.
Whip Wilson, Andy Clyde, Christine Larson, Kenne
Duncan, Tris Coffin, Virginia Carroll, Steve Dar-
rell, Jack Richardson, Jan Bryant, Bob Woodward,
Tom Quinn, Dee Cooper, George J. Lewis, Boyd
Stockman
D: Ray Taylor
SP: Adele Buffington
P: Barney Sarecky

2052. BAD MEN OF TOMBSTONE

(Allied Artists, January 22, 1949) 75 Mins.
Barry Sullivan, Marjorie Reynolds, Broderick Craw-
ford, Fortunio Bonanova, Guinn "Big Boy" Wil-
liams, John Kellogg, Mary Newton, Louis Jean
Heydt, Virginia Carroll, Dick Wessell, Claire
Carleton, Ted Hecht, Harry Cording, Lucien
Littlefield, Harry Hayden, William Yip, Olin
Howlin, Robert Barrat, Julie Gibson, Joseph
Crehan, Ted Mapes, Rory Mallison, Ted French,
Douglas Fowley, Dennis Hoey, Morris Ankrum,
Tom Fadden, Dick Foote, Billy Gray, Gerald
Courtemarche, Bonnie Lou Donaldson
D: Kurt Neumann
S: "Last of the Badmen"—Jay Monaghan
P: Maurice and Frank King

2053. SHERIFF OF WICHITA

(Republic, January 22, 1949) 60 Mins.
Allan Lane, Eddy Waller, Roy Barcroft, Lyn Wilde,
Clayton Moore, Eugene Roth, Trevor Bardette,
House Peters, Jr., Earle Hodgins, Edmund Cobb,
John Hamilton, Steve Raines, Jack O'Shea, Dick
Curtis, Lane Bradford, "Black Jack"
D: R. G. Springsteen
SP: Bob Williams
AP: Gordon Kay

2054. SHADOWS OF THE WEST

(Monogram, January 24, 1949) 59 Mins.
Whip Wilson, Andy Clyde, Riley Hill, Reno Browne,
Bill Kennedy, Pierce Lyden, Keith Richards, Wil-
liam H. Ruhl, Ted Adams, Lee Phelps, Bert Hamil-
ton, Bud Osborne, Donald Kerr, Billy Hammond,
Clem Fuller, Carol Henry, Bob Woodward, Ed-
mund Glover, Dee Cooper, Curt Barrett, Red
Egner
D: Ray Taylor
SP: Adele Buffington
P: Barney Sarecky

2055. GUN RUNNER

(Monogram, January 30, 1949) 54 Mins.
Jimmy Wakely, Dub Taylor, Noel Neill, Mae Clarke,
Kenne Duncan, Steve Clark, Marshall Reed, Ted
Adams, Bud Osborne, Carol Henry, Bob Wood-
ward, Clem Fuller, Ray Jones, Ray Whitley
D: Lambert Hillyer
SP: J. Benton Cheney
P: Louis Gray

2056. LOADED PISTOLS

(Columbia, January, 1949) 79 Mins.
Gene Autry, Barbara Britton, Chill Wills, Jack Holt,
Russell Arms, Robert Shayne, Fred Kohler, Jr.,
Vince Barnett, Leon Weaver, Clem Bevins, Sandy
Sanders, Budd Buster, John R. McKee, Stanley
Blystone, Hank Bell, Felice Raymond, Dick Alex-
ander, Frank O'Connor, Reed Howes, William
Sundholm, Snub Pollard, Heinie Conklin, "Cham-
pion, Jr."
D: John English
SP: Dwight Cummings, Dorothy Yost
P: Armand Schaefer

2057. RIDE, RYDER, RIDE

(Equity/Eagle Lion, February 1, 1949) 60 Mins.
(*Red Ryder* Series) (Cinecolor)
Jim Bannon, Don Kay Reynolds, Emmett Lynn,
Peggy Stewart, Gaylord Pendleton, Jack O'Shea,
Jean Budinger, Marin Sais, Stanley Blystone, Wil-
liam Fawcett, Billy Hammond, Edwin Max, Steve
Clark
D: Lewis D. Collins
SP: Paul Franklin
P: Jerry Thomas

2058. CHALLENGE OF THE RANGE
(Columbia, February 3, 1949)   54 Mins.
(*Durango Kid* Series)
Charles Starrett, Smiley Burnette, Paula Raymond, Billy Halop, Steve Darrell, Henry Hall, Robert Filman, George Chesebro, Frank McCarroll, John (Bob) Cason, John McKay, The Sunshine Boys
D: Ray Nazarro
SP: Ed Earl Repp
P: Colbert Clark

2059. BROTHERS IN THE SADDLE
(RKO, February 8, 1949)   60 Mins.
Tim Holt, Richard Martin, Steve Brodie, Virginia Cox, Carol Forman, Richard Powers (Tom Keene), Stanley Andrews, Robert Bray, Francis McDonald, Emmett Vogan, Monte Montague
D: Lesley Selander
SP: Norman Houston
P: Herman Schlom

2060. CHEYENNE COWBOY
(Universal-International, February 10, 1949)   25 Mins.
Tex Williams, Lina Romay, Smokey Rogers, Deuce Spriggins, Cactus Soldi, Stanley Andrews
D: Nate Watt
SP: Luci Ward
P: Will Cowan

2061. DAUGHTER OF THE WEST
(Film Classics, February 15, 1949)   77 Mins.
(Cinecolor)
Martha Vickers, Philip Reed, Donald Woods, Marion Carney, Anthony Barr, James J. Griffith, Tommy Cook, Luz Alba, Pedro De Cordoba, William Farnum, Milton Kibbee, Helen Servis
D: Harold Daniels
S: Robert E. Callahan
SP: Irving R. Franklyn, Raymond L. Schrock
P: Martin Mooney

2062. WHISPERING SMITH
(Paramount, February 15, 1949)   88 Mins.
(Technicolor)
Alan Ladd, Robert Preston, Brenda Marshall, Donald Crisp, William Demarest, Fay Holden, Murvyn Vye, Frank Faylen, John Eldredge, Robert Wood, J. Farrell MacDonald, Will Wright, Don Barclay, Eddy Waller, Ashley Cowan, Jimmy Dundee, Ray Teal, Bob Kortman
D: Leslie Fenton
S: Frank H. Spearman
SP: Frank Butler, Karl Kamb

2063. LAW OF THE WEST
(Monogram, February 20, 1949)   54 Mins.
Johnny Mack Brown, Max Terhune, Gerry Patter-
son, Bill Kennedy, Jack Ingram, Riley Hill, Eddie Parker, Marshall Reed, Kenne Duncan, Jack Harrison, Bud Osborne, Steve Clark, Bob Woodward, Frank Ellis
D: Ray Taylor
SP: J. Benton Cheney
P: Barney Sarecky

2064. I SHOT JESSE JAMES
(Lippert/Screen Guild, February 26, 1949)   81 Mins.
John Ireland, Preston Foster, Barbara Britton, J. Edward Bromberg, Victor Kilian, Barbara Woodell, Tom Tyler, Reed Hadley, Tommy Noonan, Byron Foulger, Eddie Dunn, Jeni Le Gon, Robin Short
D/SP: Samuel Fuller
S: Homer Croy
P: Robert L. Lippert, Carl Hittleman

2065. RUSTLERS
(RKO, March 1, 1949)   61 Mins.
Tim Holt, Martha Hyer, Richard Martin, Lois Andrews, Steve Brodie, Francis McDonald, Harry Shannon, Addison Richards, Frank Fenton, Robert Bray, Don Haggerty, Monte Montague, Stanley Blystone, Pat Patterson, Mike Jeffers, Tom Lloyd, George Ross, Art Souvern, Bob Robinson
D: Lesley Selander
SP: Jack Natteford, Luci Ward
P: Herman Schlom

2066. GUN LAW JUSTICE
(Monogram, March 13, 1949)   55 Mins.
Jimmy Wakely, Dub Taylor, Jane Adams, John James, Lee Phelps, Myron Healey, I. Stanford Jolley, Bud Osborne, Edmund Cobb, Carol Henry, Tom Chatterton, Bob Curtis, Zon Murray, Eddie Majors, Ray Jones, Herman Hack, Merrill McCormack, George Morrell, Ray Whitley
D: Lambert Hillyer
SP: Basil Dickey
P: Louis Gray

2067. TREACHERY RIDES THE TRAIL
(Warner Bros., March 19, 1949)   10 Mins.
Narration by Art Gilmore; juvenile cast
D: Charles Moore

2068. WEST OF LARAMIE
(Universal-International, March 24, 1949)   23 Mins.
Tex Williams, Smokey Rogers, Deuce Spriggins, Pat Hall, Patricia Alphin
D/P: Will Cowan

2069. RIMFIRE
(Lippert/Screen Guild, March 25, 1949)   64 Mins.
James Millican, Mary Beth Hughes, Henry Hull,

Reed Hadley, Fuzzy Knight, Chris-Pin Martin, Glenn Strange, Dick Alexander, George Cleveland, John Cason, Ray Bennett, Margia Dean, I. Stanford Jolley, Victor Kilian, Jason Robards, Sr., Don Harvey, Lee Roberts, Stanley Price
D: B. Reeves Eason
SP: Arthur St. Clair, Frank Wisbar
P: Ron Ormond

2070. DEATH VALLEY GUNFIGHTER

(Republic, March 29, 1949) 60 Mins.
Allan Lane, Gail Davis, Eddy Waller, Jim Nolan, William Henry, Harry Harvey, Mauritz Hugo, George Chesebro, Forrest Taylor, George Lloyd, Lane Bradford
D: R. G. Springsteen
SP: Bob Williams
AP: Gordon Day

2071. THE BIG SOMBRERO

(Columbia, March, 1949) 82 Mins.
(Cinecolor)
Gene Autry, Elena Verdugo, Stephen Dunne, George J. Lewis, Vera Marshe, William Edmunds, Martin Garralaga, Gene Stutenroth, Neyle Morrow, Bob Cason, Pierce Lyden, Rian Valente, Antonio Filauri, Sam Bernard, Jasper Palmer, Jose Alvarado, Robert Espinosa, Cosmo Sardo, Alex Montoya, Jose Portugal, Joe Kirk, Artie Ortego, Joe Dominguez, "Champion, Jr."
D: Frank McDonald
SP: Olive Cooper
P: Armand Schaefer

2072. THE WALKING HILLS

(Columbia, March, 1949) 78 Mins.
Randolph Scott, Ella Raines, William Bishop, Edgar Buchanan, Arthur Kennedy, John Ireland, Jerome Courtland, Josh White, Russell Collins, Charles Stevens, Houseley Stevenson, Reed Howes
D: John Sturges
S/SP: Alan LeMay
P: Harry Joe Brown

2073. SON OF BILLY THE KID

(Western Adventure/Screen Guild, April 2, 1949) 65 Mins.
Lash LaRue, Al St. John, Marion Colby, June Carr, George Baxter, Terry Frost, John James, House Peters, Jr., Clarke Stevens, Bob Duncan, Cliff Taylor, William Perrott, Felipe Turich, Rosa Turich, Jerry Riggio, Eileen Dixon, Fraser McMinn, I. Stanford Jolley, Bud Osborne
D: Ray Taylor
SP: Ron Ormond, Ira Webb
P: Ron Ormond

2074. TRAIL'S END

(Monogram, April 3, 1949) 57 Mins.
Johnny Mack Brown, Max Terhune, Kay Morley, Douglas Evans, Zon Murray, Myron Healey, Keith Richards, George Chesebro, William Norton Bailey, Carol Henry, Boyd Stockman, Eddie Majors
D: Lambert Hillyer
SP: J. Benton Cheney
P: Barney Sarecky

2075. PRINCE OF THE PLAINS

(Republic, April 8, 1949) 60 Mins.
Monte Hale, Paul Hurst, Shirley Davis, Roy Barcroft, Rory Mallison, Harry Lauter, Lane Bradford, George Carleton
D: Philip Ford
SP: Louise Rousseau, Albert DeMond
AP: Melville Tucker

2076. HOME IN SAN ANTONE

(Columbia, April 15, 1949) 62 Mins.
Roy Acuff, Jacqueline Thomas, Bill Edwards, George Cleveland, William Frawley, Dorothy Vaughn, Ivan Triesault, Matt Willis, Sam Flint, Fred Sears, Doye O'Dell, The Smoky Mountain Boys, The Modernaires, Lloyd Corrigan
D: Ray Nazarro
SP: Barry Shipman
P: Colbert Clark

2076a. CACTUS CUT-UP

(RKO, April 15, 1949) 2 Reels
Leon Errol, Dorothy Granger, Noel Neill, Ralph Peters, Roland Morris
D: Charles Roberts

2077. SON OF A BADMAN

(Western Adventure/Screen Guild, April 16, 1949) 64 Mins.
Lash LaRue, Al St. John, Michael Whalen, Noel Neill, Zon Murray, Jack Ingram, Steve Raines, Chuck (Bob) Cason, Don Harvey, Frank Lackteen, Francis McDonald, Edna Holland, William Norton Bailey, Sandy Sanders, Doye O'Dell
D: Ray Taylor
SP: Ron Ormond, Ira Webb
P: Ron Ormond

2078. THE LAST BANDIT

(Republic, April 23, 1949) 80 Mins.
(Trucolor)
William (Bill) Elliott, Andy Devine, Jack Holt, Forrest Tucker, Adrian Booth, Grant Withers, Minna Gombell, Virginia Brissac, Louis Faust, Stanley Andrews, Martin Garralaga, Joseph Crehan, Charles Middleton, Rex Lease, Emmett Lynn,

Eugene Roth, George Chesebro, Hank Bell, Jack O'Shea, Tex Terry, Steve Clark
D: Joseph Kane
S: Luci Ward, Jack Natteford
SP: Thomas Williamson
AP: Joseph Kane

2079. SUSANNA PASS
(Republic, April 29, 1949) 67 Mins.
Roy Rogers, Dale Evans, Estelita Rodriguez, Martin Garralaga, Robert Emmett Keane, Lucien Littlefield, Douglas Fowley, David Sharpe, Robert Bice, Foy Willing and the Riders of the Purple Sage, "Trigger"
D: William Witney
SP: Sloan Nibley, John K. Butler
AP: Eddy White

2080. STAMPEDE
(Allied Artists, May 1, 1949) 76 Mins.
Rod Cameron, Johnny Mack Brown, Gale Storm, Don Castle, Don Curtis, John Miljan, Jonathan Hale, John Eldredge, Kenne Duncan, Tim Ryan, Steve Clark, Bob Woodward, Duke York, Artie Ortego, Neal Hart
D: Lesley Selander
SP: John C. Champion, Blake Edwards
P: Scott R. Dunlap, John C. Champion, Blake Edwards

2081. FRONTIER MARSHAL
(Republic, May 2, 1949) 59 Mins.
Allan Lane, Gail Davis, Eddy Waller, Clayton Moore, Roy Barcroft, Robert Emmett Keane, Marshall Reed, Francis Ford, Claire Whitney, Harry Lauter, Tom London, George Lloyd, "Black Jack"
D: Fred C. Brannon
SP: Bob Williams
AP: Gordon Kay

2082. RED STALLION IN THE ROCKIES
(Eagle Lion, May 2, 1949) 85 Mins.
(Cinecolor)
Arthur Franz, Jean Heather, Jim Davis, Ray Collins, Wallace Ford, Leatrice Joy, James Kirkwood, "Dynamite"
D: Ralph Murphy
S: Tom Teed
SP: Francis Rosenwald
P: Aubrey Schenck

2083. LAW OF THE GOLDEN WEST
(Republic, May 9, 1949) 60 Mins.
Monte Hale, Paul Hurst, Gail Davis, Roy Barcroft, John Holland, Scott Elliott, Lane Bradford, Harold Goodwin, John Hamilton
D: Philip Ford

SP: Norman S. Hall
AP: Melville Tucker

2084. THE GAY AMIGO
(United Artists, May 13, 1949) 60 Mins.
(Cisco Kid Series)
Duncan Renaldo, Leo Carrillo, Armida, Joe Sawyer, Clayton Moore, Fred Kohler, Jr., Walter Baldwin, Kenneth MacDonald, George DeNormand, Fred Crane, Helen Servis, Bud Osborne, Sam Flint, Beverly Jons
D: Wallace Fox
SP: Doris Schroeder
P: Philip N. Krasne

2085. ACROSS THE RIO GRANDE
(Monogram, May 15, 1949)
Jimmy Wakely, Dub Taylor, Reno Browne, Riley Hill, Dennis Moore, Kenne Duncan, Ted Adams, Myron Healey, Bud Osborne, Polly Burgin (Polly Bergen), Bob Curtis, Carol Henry, Boyd Stockman, William Norton Bailey, Bill Potter, Bob Woodward
D: Oliver Drake
SP: Ronald Davidson
P: Louis Gray

2086. RIDERS OF THE PONY EXPRESS
(Kayson/Screencraft, May 15, 1949) 60 Mins.
(Color)
Ken Curtis, Shug Fisher, Cathy Douglas, Billy Benedict, Eddie McLean, Truman Van Dyke, John Dehner, Lou Marcelle, Rodd Redwing
D/SP: Michael Salle
P: Richard Kay, D. A. Anderson

2087. LARAMIE
(Columbia, May 19, 1949) 55 Mins.
(Durango Kid Series)
Charles Starrett, Smiley Burnette, Fred Sears, Tommy Ivo, Marjorie Stapp, Elton Britt, Bob Wilke, George Lloyd, Myron Healey, Shooting Star, Jay Silverheels, Ethan Laidlaw, Bob Cason
D: Ray Nazarro
SP: Barry Shipman
P: Colbert Clark

2088. RIDERS OF THE WHISTLING PINES
(Columbia, May, 1949) 70 Mins.
Gene Autry, Patricia White, Jimmy Lloyd, Douglass Dumbrille, Damian O'Flynn, Clayton Moore, Britt Wood, Harry Cheshire, Leon Weaver, Lois Bridge, Jerry Scroggings, Fred Martin, Bert Dodson, Roy Gordon, Jason Robards, Sr., Len Torrey, Lane Chandler, Lynn Farr, Al Thompson, Emmett Vogan, Virginia Carroll, Nolan Leary, Steve

Benton, The Cass County Boys, The Pinagores, "Champion, Jr."
D: John English
SP: Jack Townley
P: Armand Schaefer

2089. STREETS OF LAREDO
(Paramount, May 27, 1949) 92 Mins.
(Technicolor)
William Holden, William Bendix, MacDonald Carey, Mona Freeman, Stanley Ridges, Alfonso Bedoya, Ray Teal, Clem Bevins, James Bell, Dick Foote, Joe Dominguez, Grandon Rhodes, Perry Ivans
D: Leslie Fenton
S: Louis Stevens, Elizabeth Hill, King Vidor
SP: Charles Marquis Warren
P: Robert Fellows
(A remake of *The Texas Rangers*)

2090. STAGECOACH KID
(RKO, June 1, 1949) 60 Mins.
Tim Holt, Richard Martin, Jeff Donnell, Joe Sawyer, Thurston Hall, Carol Hughes, Robert Bray, Robert B. Williams, Kenneth MacDonald, Harry Harvey
D: Lew Landers
SP: Norman Houston
P: Herman Schlom

2091. THE BLAZING TRAIL
(Columbia, June 5, 1949) 56 Mins.
(*Durango Kid* Series)
Charles Starrett, Smiley Burnette, Marjorie Stapp, Jock Mahoney, Trevor Bardette, Fred Sears, Steve Darrell, Steve Pendleton, Robert Malcolm, John (Bob) Cason, Hank Penny, Slim Duncan, Frank McCarroll, John Merton, Merrill McCormack
D: Ray Nazarro
SP: Barry Shipman
P: Colbert Clark

2092. OUTCASTS OF THE TRAIL
(Republic, June 8, 1949) 60 Mins.
Monte Hale, Jeff Donnell, Paul Hurst, Roy Barcroft, John Gallaudet, Milt Parsons, Tommy Ivo, Minerva Urecal, Ted Mapes, George Lloyd, Steve Darrell, Tom Steele
D: Philip Ford
SP: Oliver Cooper
AP: Melville Tucker

2093. COLORADO TERRITORY
(Warner Bros., June 11, 1949) 94 Mins.
Joel McCrea, Virginia Mayo, Dorothy Malone, Henry Hull, John Archer, James Mitchell, Morris Ankrum, Basil Ruysdael, Frank Puglia, Ian Wolfe,

Harry Woods, Houseley Stevenson, Victor Kilian, Oliver Blake
D: Raoul Walsh
SP: John Twist, Edmund H. North

2094. THE DARING CABALLERO
(United Artists, June 14, 1949) 60 Mins.
(*Cisco Kid* Series)
Duncan Renaldo, Leo Carrillo, Kippee Valez, Charles Halton, Pedro De Cordoba, Stephen Chase, David Leonard, Edmund Cobb, Frank Jacquet, Mickey Little
D: Wallace Fox
S: Frances Kavanaugh
SP: Betty Burbridge
AP: Philip N. Krasne

2095. STALLION CANYON
(Kanab/Astor, June 15, 1949) 72 Mins.
(Trucolor)
Ken Curtis, Caroline Cotton, Shug Fisher, Forrest Taylor, Ted Adams, Billy Hammond, Roy Butler, Alice Richey, L. H. Larsen, E. N. (Dick) Hammer, Clark Veater, D. C. Swapp, Gail Bailey, Bud Gates, Bob Brandon
D: Harry Fraser
SP: Hy Heath

2096. WEST OF ELDORADO
(Monogram, June 15, 1949) 56 Mins.
Johnny Mack Brown, Max Terhune, Reno Browne, Milburn Morante, Teddy Infuhr, Terry Frost, Marshall Reed, Boyd Stockman, Kenne Duncan, Bud Osborne, William Norton Bailey, Artie Ortego, Bill Potter, Bob Woodward
D: Ray Taylor
SP: Adele Buffington
P: Barney Sarecky

2097. HELLFIRE
(Republic, June 26, 1949) 90 Mins.
(Trucolor)
William (Bill) Elliott, Marie Windsor, Forrest Tucker, Jim Davis, H. B. Warner, Grant Withers, Paul Fix, Emory Parnell, Esther Howard, Jody Gilbert, Louis Faust, Harry Woods, Denver Pyle, Trevor Bardette, Dewey Robinson, Harry Tyler, Roy Barcroft, Hank Worden, Ken MacDonald, Paula Hill, Dewey Robinson, Eva Novak, Dick Alexander, Louis R. Faust, Edward Keane, Elizabeth Marshall, Keenan Elliott
D: R. G. Springsteen
S/SP: Dorrell and Stuart McGowan
Exec. P: Dorrell and Stuart McGowan
P: William J. O'Sullivan

Outcasts of the Trail (Republic, 1949) — Roy Barcroft and Jeff Donnell

The Daring Caballero (United Artists, 1949) — Duncan Renaldo as "The Cisco Kid"

2098. LUST FOR GOLD
(Columbia, June, 1949) 90 Mins.
Ida Lupino, Glenn Ford, Gig Young, William Prince, Edgar Buchanan, Will Geer, Paul Ford, Jay Silverheels, Eddy Waller, Will Wright, Virginia Mullen, Antonio Moreno, Myrna Dell, Tom Tyler, Elspeth Dudgeon, Paul Burns, Hayden Rorke
D: S. Sylvan Simon
S: "Thunder God's Gold"—Barry Storm
SP: Ted Sherdeman, Richard English
P: S. Sylvan Simon

2099. TROUBLE AT MELODY MESA
(Three Crown/Astor, July 1, 1949) 60 Mins.
Brad King, Cal Shrum, Lorraine Michie, I. Stanford Jolley, Walt Shrum, Alta Lee, Jimmie Shrum, Carl Sepulveda, Stacey Alexander, Pappy Hoag, Ace Dehner, Shorty Woodward, Sue Gamboa, Rusty Cline, Dusty Taylor, Jack Gress, Frank Bertoldi, Lefty Walker
D: W. M. Connell
SP: Ned Dandy
P: Biryer E. Williamson
(Filmed in 1944 along with that year's *Swing, Cowboy, Swing* but never released until above date)

2100. BRAND OF FEAR
(Monogram, July 10, 1949) 56 Mins.
Jimmy Wakely, Dub Taylor, Gail Davis, Tom London, Marshall Reed, William Ruhl, William Norton Bailey, Boyd Stockman, Joe Galbrath, Dee Cooper, Frank McCarroll, Holly Bane, Bob Curtis, Myron Healey, Bob Woodward, Denver Dixon, Ray Jones, Ray Whitley
D: Oliver Drake
SP: Basil Dickey
P: Louis Gray

2101. THE WYOMING BANDIT
(Republic, July 15, 1949) 60 Mins.
Allan Lane, Eddy Waller, Trevor Bardette, Victor Kilian, Rand Brooks, Reed Hadley, Harold Goodwin, Lane Bradford, Bob Wilke, John Hamilton, Edmund Cobb, William Haade, "Black Jack"
D: Philip Ford
SP: M. Coates Webster
AP: Gordon Kay

2102. LAW OF THE BARBARY COAST
(Columbia, July 21, 1949) 65 Mins.
Gloria Henry, Stephen Dunne, Adele Jergens, Robert Shayne, Stefan Schnabel, Edwin Max, Ross Ford, J. Farrell MacDonald
D: Lew Landers
SP: Robert Libott, Frank Burt
P: Wallace MacDonald

2103. SOUTH OF RIO
(Republic, July 27, 1949) 60 Mins.
Monte Hale, Kay Christopher, Paul Hurst, Roy Barcroft, Douglas Kennedy, Don Haggerty, Rory Mallison, Lane Bradford, Emmett Vogan, Myron Healey, Tom London
D: Philip Ford
SP: Norman S. Hall
AP: Melville Tucker

2104. SPADE COOLEY AND HIS ORCHESTRA
(Universal-International, July 27, 1949) 15 Mins.
Spade Cooley and his Western Caravan, Karel's Adagio Four, Les Anderson, The Pickard Family, Bill Roberts
D/P: Will Cowan

2105. SILVER BUTTE
(Universal-International, July 28, 1949) 27 Mins.
Tex Williams, Smokey Rogers, Deuce Spriggins, Barbara Payton, Joe Granby, Lane Bradford
D/P: Will Cowan
SP: Sherman Lowe, Victor McLeod

2106. TRAIL OF THE YUKON
(Monogram, July 31, 1949) 69 Mins.
Kirby Grant, Suzanne Dalbert, Bill Edwards, Iris Adrian, Dan Seymour, William Forrest, Anthony Warde, Maynard Holmes, Peter Mamakos, Jay Silverheels, Guy Beach, Stanley Andrews, Dick Elliott, Bill Kennedy, Harrison Hearne, Burt Wenland, Alan Bridge, Wally Walker, "Chinook" (the Wonder Dog)
D: William X. Crowley
S: "The Gold Hunters"—James Oliver Curwood
SP: Oliver Drake
P: Lindsley Parsons

2107. MOUNTAIN RHYTHM
(Astor, July, 1949) 10 Mins.
Georgia Slim, The Texas Roundup Boys
(No other credits available)

2108. RIM OF THE CANYON
(Columbia, July, 1949) 70 Mins.
Gene Autry, Nan Leslie, Thurston Hall, Clem Bevins, Walter Sande, Jock Mahoney, Francis McDonald, Alan Hale, Jr., Amelita Ward, John R. McKee, Denver Pyle, Bobby Clark, Boyd Stockman, Sandy Sanders, Lynn Farr, Rory Mallison, Frankie Marvin, "Champion, Jr."
D: John English
S: "Phantom 45's Talk Loud"—Joseph Chadwick, *Western Aces* magazine
SP: John K. Butler
P: Armand Schaefer

2109. SATURDAY NIGHT SQUARE DANCE

(Astor, July, 1949) 10 Mins.
Jim Boyd and the Men of the West
(No other credits available)

2110. GHOST OF ZORRO

(Republic, August 6, 1949) 12 Chaps.
Clayton Moore, Pamela Blake, Roy Barcroft, George J. Lewis, Gene Stutenroth, John Crawford, I. Stanford Jolley, Steve Clark, Steve Darrell, Dale Van Sickel, Tom Steele, Alex Montoya, Marshall Reed, Frank O'Connor, Jack O'Shea, Holly Bane, Bob Reeves, John Daheim, Eddie Parker, Post Parks, Stanley Blystone, Joe Yrigoyen, George Chesebro, Charles King, Roger Creed, Ken Terrell, Robert Wilke, Roy Bucko, Art Dillard, Frank Ellis, Bob Robinson
D: Fred C. Brannon
SP: Royal Cole, William Lively, Sol Shor
AP: Franklyn Adreon (sometimes spelled "Franklin")
Chapter Titles: (1) Bandit Territory, (2) Forged Orders, (3) Robber's Agent, (4) Victims of Vengeance, (5) Gun Trap, (6) Deadline at Midnight, (7) Tower of Disaster, (8) Mob Justice, (9) Money Lure, (10) Message of Death, (11) Runaway Stagecoach, (12) Trail of Blood

2111. SOUTH OF DEATH VALLEY

(Columbia, August 8, 1949) 54 Mins.
(*Durango Kid* Series)
Charles Starrett, Smiley Burnette, Gail Davis, Clayton Moore, Fred Sears, Lee Roberts, Richard Emory, Jason Robards, Sr., Tommy Duncan and his Western All Stars
D: Ray Nazarro
SP: Earle Snell
P: Colbert Clark

2112. BRIMSTONE

(Republic, August 15, 1949) 90 Mins.
Rod Cameron, Adrian Booth, Walter Brennan, Forrest Tucker, Jack Holt, Jim Davis, James Brown, Guinn "Big Boy" Williams, Charlita, Hal Taliaferro
D: Joseph Kane
S: Norman S. Hall
SP: Thames Williams
AP: Joseph Kane

2113. MASKED RAIDERS

(RKO, August 15, 1949) 60 Mins.
Tim Holt, Richard Martin, Marjorie Lord, Gary Gray, Frank Wilcox, Charles Arnt, Tom Tyler, Harry Woods, Houseley Stevenson, Clayton Moore, Bill George
D: Lesley Selander

SP: Norman Houston
P: Herman Schlom

2114. HAUNTED TRAILS

(Monogram, August 21, 1949) 58 Mins.
Whip Wilson, Andy Clyde, Reno Browne, Dennis Moore, I. Stanford Jolley, William Ruhl, John Merton, Mary Gordon, Steve Clark, Myron Healey, Milburn Morante, Eddie Majors, Bud Osborne, Ted Adams, Lynton Brent, Bill Potter, Jason Robards, Sr., Carl Mathews, Thornton Edwards, Chuck Roberson
D: Lambert Hillyer
SP: Adele Buffington
P: Eddie Davis

2115. ROLL, THUNDER, ROLL

(Equity/Eagle Lion, August 27, 1949) 60 Mins.
(*Red Ryder* Series) (Cinecolor)
Jim Bannon, Don Kay Reynolds, Emmett Lynn, Marin Sais, Glenn Strange, Nancy Gates, I. Stanford Jolley, Lee Morgan, Lane Bradford, Steve Pendleton, Charles Stevens, William Fawcett, Dorothy Latta, Joe Green, Rocky Shahan, Carol Henry, George Chesebro, Jack O'Shea
D: Lewis D. Collins
SP: Paul Franklin
P: Jerry Thomas

2116. BANDIT KING OF TEXAS

(Republic, August 29, 1949) 60 Mins.
Alan Lane, Eddy Waller, Helen Stanley, Jim Nolan, Harry Lauter, Robert Bice, John Hamilton, Lane Bradford, George Lloyd, Steve Clark, I. Stanford Jolley, Danni Nolan, Richard Emory
D: Fred C. Brannon
SP: Olive Cooper
AP: Gordon Kay

2117. A COWBOY'S HOLIDAY

(Astor, August, 1949) 10 Mins.
Art Davis and his Rhythm Riders
(No other credits available)

2118. DOWN DAKOTA WAY

(Republic, September 9, 1949) 67 Mins.
(Trucolor)
Roy Rogers, Dale Evans, Pat Brady, Monte Montana, Elizabeth Risdon, Byron Barr, James Cardwell, Roy Barcroft, Emmett Vogan, Foy Willing and the Riders of the Purple Sage, "Trigger"
D: William Witney
SP: John K. Butler, Sloan Nibley
AP: Eddy White

2119. THE MYSTERIOUS DESPERADO
(RKO, September 10, 1949) 61 Mins.
Tim Holt, Richard Martin, Movita, Edward Norris,
Frank Wilcox, William Tannen, Robert Livingston, Robert B. Williams, Kenneth MacDonald,
Frank Lackteen
D: Lesley Selander
SP: Norman Houston
P: Herman Schlom

2120. THE COWBOY AND THE INDIANS
(Columbia, September 15, 1949) 70 Mins.
Gene Autry, Sheila Ryan, Frank Richards, Hank
Patterson, Jay Silverheels, Claudia Drake, George
Nokes, Charles Stevens, Alex Frazer, Frank Lackteen, Chief Yowlachie, Lee Roberts, Nolan Leary,
Maudie Prickett, Harry Macklin, Charles Quigley, Gilbert Alonzo, Roy Gordon, Jose Alvarado,
Ray Beltram, Felipe Gomez, Iron Eyes Cody,
Shooting Star, Romere Darling, "Champion, Jr."
D: John English
SP: Dwight Cummings, Dorothy Yost
P: Armand Schaefer

2121. THE GIRL FROM GUNSIGHT
(Universal-International, September 15, 1949)
24 Mins.
Tex Williams, Donna Martell, Smokey Rogers,
Deuce Spriggins, Myron Healey
D/P: Will Cowan

2122. ROARING WESTWARD
(Monogram, September 15, 1949) 58 Mins.
Jimmy Wakely, Dub Taylor, Lois Hall, Dennis
Moore, Jack Ingram, Claire Whitney, Kenne Duncan, Buddy Swan, Holly Bane, Marshall Reed,
Nolan Leary, Bud Osborne, Bob Woodward, Al
Haskell, Tom Smith, Denver Dixon
D: Oliver Drake
SP: Ronald Davidson
P: Louis Gray

2123. DUDE RANCH HARMONY
(Astor, September, 1949) 10 Mins.
Dewey Groom and his Texans
(No other credits available)

2124. THE TALENTED TRAMPS
(Astor, September, 1949) 10 Mins.
Billy Gray, Robert Larry, Sons of Texas
(No other credits available)

2125. JEEP-HERDERS
(Astor, October 1, 1949) 46 Mins.
John Day, June Carlson, Pat Michaels, Steve Clark,
Ashley Cowan
D: Richard Talmadge

2126. SAN ANTONE AMBUSH
(Republic, October 1, 1949) 60 Mins.
Monte Hale, Bette Daniels, Paul Hurst, Roy Barcroft, James Cardwell, Trevor Bardette, Lane
Bradford, Tommy Coats, Tom London, Edmund
Cobb, Carl Sepulveda
D: Philip Ford
SP: Norman S. Hall
AP: Melville Tucker

2127. TRAILIN' WEST
(Warner Bros., October 1, 1949) 20 Mins.
(Technicolor)
Chill Wills, Elaine Riley, Earle Hodgins, Jack Elam,
John Spelvin
D: George Templeton
S/SP: Alan LeMay
P: Alan LeMay

2128. SATAN'S CRADLE
(United Artists, October 7, 1949) 60 Mins.
(*Cisco Kid* Series)
Duncan Renaldo, Leo Carrillo, Ann Savage, Douglas Fowley, Byron Foulger, Buck Bailey, George
DeNormand, Wesley Hudman, Claire Carleton
D: Ford Beebe
SP: Jack (J. Benton) Cheney
P: Philip N. Krasne

2129. WESTERN RENEGADES
(Monogram, October 9, 1949) 56 Mins.
Johnny Mack Brown, Max Terhune, Jane Adams,
Hugh Prosser, Constance Worth, Riley Hill, Marshall Reed, Steve Clark, Terry Frost, William
Ruhl, Myron Healey, John Merton, Marshall
Bradford, Milburn Morante, Chuck Roberson,
Lane Bradford, Bill Potter, James Harrison, Dee
Cooper
D: Wallace Fox
SP: Adele Buffington
P: Eddie Davis

2130. THE FIGHTING REDHEAD
(Equity/Eagle Lion, October 12, 1949) 55 Mins.
(*Red Ryder* Series)
(Cinecolor)
Jim Bannon, Don Kay Reynolds, Emmett Lynn,
Marin Sais, Peggy Stewart, John Hart, Lane Bradford, Forrest Taylor, Lee Roberts, Bob Duncan,
Sandy Sanders, Billy Hammond, Ray Jones
D: Lewis D. Collins
SP: Paul Franklin, Jerry Thomas
P: Jerry Thomas

2131. NAVAJO TRAIL RAIDERS
(Republic, October 15, 1949) 60 Mins.
Allan Lane, Eddy Waller, Barbara Bestar, Robert

Emmett Keane, Hal Landon, Dick Curtis, Dennis Moore, Ted Adams, Forrest Taylor, Marshall Reed, Steve Clark, Chick Hannon
D: R. G. Springsteen
SP: M. Coates Webster
AP: Gordon Kay

2132. BANDITS OF ELDORADO
(Columbia, October 20, 1949)   56 Mins.
(*Durango Kid* Series)
Charles Starrett, Smiley Burnette, George J. Lewis, Fred Sears, John Dehner, Clayton Moore, Jock Mahoney, John Doucette, Max Wagner, Henry Kulky, Mustard and Gravy
D: Ray Nazarro
SP: Barry Shipman
P: Colbert Clark

2133. THE DALTON GANG
(Lippert, October 21, 1949)   58 Mins.
Don Barry, Robert Lowery, James Millican, Betty Adams (Julie Adams), Byron Foulger, J. Farrell MacDonald, Greg McClure, George J. Lewis, Marshall Reed, Ray Bennett, Lee Roberts, Cliff Taylor, Cactus Mack, Dick Curtis, Stanley Price
D/SP: Ford Beebe
P: Ron Ormond

2134. SHE WORE A YELLOW RIBBON
(Argosy/RKO, October 22, 1949)   104 Mins.
(Technicolor)
John Wayne, Joanne Dru, John Agar, Ben Johnson, Harry Carey, Jr., Victor McLaglen, Mildred Natwick, George O'Brien, Arthur Shields, Harry Woods, Chief John Big Tree, Noble Johnson, Cliff Lyons, Tom Tyler, Mike Dugan, Mickey Simpson, Frank McGrath, Don Summer, Fred Libby, Jack Pennick, Billy Jones, Bill Goettinger (William Steele), Fred Graham, Fred Kennedy, Rudy Bowman, Post Parks, Ray Hyke, Lee Bradley, Francis Ford, Paul Fix, Fred Graham, Dan White
D: John Ford
S: James Warner Bellah
SP: Frank Nugent, Laurence Stallings
P: John Ford, Merian C. Cooper

2135. THE PECOS PISTOL
(Universal-International, October 27, 1949)
   26 Mins.
Tex Williams, Smokey Rogers, Deuce Spriggins, Barbara Payton, William Cassady, Forrest Taylor, George Lloyd, Monte Montague, Harry Calkin, Terry Frost
D/P: Will Cowan

2136. DEPUTY MARSHAL
(Lippert, October 28, 1949)   60 Mins.
Jon Hall, Frances Langford, Dick Foran, Julie Bishop, Joe Sawyer, Russell Hayden, Clem Bevins, Vince Barnett, Mary Gordon, Kenne Duncan, Stanley Blystone, Roy Butler, Wheaton Chambers, Forrest Taylor, Tom Greenway, Ted Adams
D/SP: William Berke
P: Robert L. Lippert

2137. THE WOLF HUNTERS
(Monogram, October 30, 1949)   70 Mins.
Kirby Grant, Jan Clayton, Edward Norris, Helen Parrish, Charles Lang, Ted Hecht, Luther Crockett, Elizabeth Root, "Chinook" (the Wonder Dog)
D: Oscar (Budd) Boetticher
S: James Oliver Curwood
SP: W. Scott Darling
P: Lindsley Parsons

2138. RIDERS IN THE SKY
(Columbia, November 1, 1949)   70 Mins.
Gene Autry, Gloria Henry, Pat Buttram, Mary Beth Hughes, Robert Livingston, Steve Darrell, Alan Hale, Jr., Tom London, Hank Patterson, Ben Welden, Dennis Moore, Joe Forte, Kenne Duncan, Frank Jacquet, Roy Gordon, Loi Bridge, Boyd Stockman, Vernon Johns, Pat O'Malley, John Parrish, Kermit Maynard, Bud Osborne, Lynton Brent, Isobel Withers, Sandy Sanders, Denver Dixon, Robert Walker, "Champion, Jr."
D: John English
S: Herbert A. Woodbury
SP: Gerald Geraghty
P: Armand Schaefer

2139. APACHE CHIEF
(Lippert, November 4, 1949)   60 Mins.
Alan Curtis, Tom Neal, Russell Hayden, Carol Thurston, Fuzzy Knight, Francis McDonald, Trevor Bardette, Ted Hecht, Allan Wells
D: Frank McDonald
SP: Gerald Green, Leonard Picker
P: Leonard Picker

2140. RANGER OF CHEROKEE STRIP
(Republic, November 4, 1949)   60 Mins.
Monte Hale, Paul Hurst, Alice Talton, Roy Barcroft, Douglas Kennedy, George Meeker, Monte Blue, Frank Fenton, Neyle Morrow, Lane Bradford
D: Philip Ford
SP: Bob Williams
AP: Melville Tucker

2141. DESERT VIGILANTE
(Columbia, November 8, 1949)
(*Durango Kid* Series)
Charles Starrett, Smiley Burnette, Peggy Stewart,

Tris Coffin, George Chesebro, Jack Ingram, Mary Newton, Paul Campbell, Ted Mapes, I. Stanford Jolley, The Georgia Crackers
D: Fred F. Sears
SP: Earle Snell
P: Colbert Clark

2142. SQUARE DANCE JUBILEE

(Lippert, November 11, 1949) 79 Mins.
Donald Barry, Wally Vernon, Mary Beth Hughes, Max Terhune, Britt Wood, Thurston Hall, Tom Tyler, John Eldredge, Spade Cooley, Chester Clute, Tom Kennedy, Clarke Stevens, Lee Roberts, Marshall Reed, Slim Gault, Cliff Taylor, Hazel Nilsen, Ralph Moody, Alex Montoya, Hal King, Cowboy Uopas, Johnny Downs, The Broome Brothers, Smiley and Kitty, Hermit the Hermit, Ray Vaughn, The Tumbleweed Tumblers, The Elder Lovelies, Claude Casey, Buddy McDowell, Dana Gibson, Charles Cirillo, Dot Remey, Les Gotcher
D: Paul Landres
S: William L. Nolte
SP: Ron Ormond, Dan Ullman
P: Ron Ormond

2143. RIDERS OF THE DUSK

(Monogram, November 13, 1949) 57 Mins.
Whip Wilson, Andy Clyde, Reno Browne (Blair), Tris Coffin, Marshall Reed, Myron Healey, John Merton, Holly Bane, Lee Roberts, Dee Cooper, Thornton Edwards, Ray Jones
D: Lambert Hillyer
SP: Jess Bowers (Adele Buffington), Robert Tansey
P: Eddie Davis

2144. THE GOLDEN STALLION

(Republic, November 15, 1949) 67 Mins.
Roy Rogers, Dale Evans, Pat Brady, Estelita Rodriguez, Chester Conklin, Douglas Evans, Greg McClure, Frank Fenton, Dale Van Sickel, Clarence Straight, Karl Hackett, Foy Willing and the Riders of the Purple Sage, "Trigger"
D: William Witney
SP: Sloan Nibley
AP: Eddy White

2145. TOUGH ASSIGNMENT

(Donald Barry Productions/Lippert, November 15, 1949) 61 Mins.
Don Barry, Marjorie Steele, Steve Brodie, Marc Lawrence, Sid Melton, Ben Welden, Iris Adrian, Michael Whalen, Fred Kohler, Jr., Dewey Robinson, Frank Richards, John Cason, J. Farrell MacDonald
D: William Beaudine
P: Carl K. Hittleman

2146. COYOTE CANYON

(Universal-International, November 17, 1949) 24 Mins.
Tex Williams, Donna Martell, Deuce Spriggins, Smokey Rogers, George Eldridge, Judd Holdren, Leslie Kimmell, Jim Hayward, Bob Wilke, Jess Fargo
D/P: Will Cowan
S: Norton S. Parker
SP: Joseph O'Donnell

2147. CALL OF THE FOREST

(Lippert, November 18, 1949) 74 Mins.
Robert Lowery, Ken Curtis, Martha Sherrill, Chief Thunder Cloud, Charles Hughes
D: John Link
P: Edward Finney

2148. HORSEMEN OF THE SIERRAS

(Columbia, November 22, 1949) 56 Mins.
(Durango Kid Series)
Charles Starrett, Smiley Burnette, T. Texas Tyler, Lois Hall, Tommy Ivo, John Dehner, Jason Robards, Sr., Dan Sheridan, Jock Mahoney, George Chesebro
D: Fred F. Sears
SP: Barry Shipman
P: Colbert Clark

2149. PIONEER MARSHAL

(Republic, November 24, 1949) 60 Mins.
Monte Hale, Nan Leslie, Paul Hurst, Roy Barcroft, Damian O'Flynn, Myron Healey, Ray Walker, John Hamilton, Clarence Straight, Robert Williams
D: Philip Ford
SP: Bob Williams
AP: Melville Tucker

2150. RENEGADES OF THE SAGE

(Columbia, November 24, 1949) 56 Mins.
(Durango Kid Series)
Charles Starrett, Smiley Burnette, Leslie Banning, Trevor Bardette, Douglas Fowley, Jock O'Mahoney, Fred Sears, Jerry Hunt, George Chesebro, Frank McCarroll, Selmer Jackson
D: Ray Nazarro
S/SP: Earle Snell
P: Colbert Clark

2151. POWDER RIVER RUSTLERS

(Republic, November 25, 1949) 60 Mins.
Allan Lane, Eddy Waller, Gerry Ganzer, Roy Barcroft, Francis McDonald, Cliff Clark, Douglas Evans, Bruce Edwards, Clarence Straight, Ted Jacques, Tom Monroe, Stanley Blystone, Eddie Parker, Herman Hack, "Black Jack"
D: Philip Ford

SP: Richard Wormser
AP: Gordon Kay

2152. LAWLESS CODE
(Monogram, December 4, 1949) 58 Mins.
Jimmy Wakely, Dub Taylor, Ellen Hall, Tris Coffin,
Riley Hill, Kenne Duncan, Terry Frost, Myron
Healey, Beatrice Maude, Steve Clark, Bud Os-
borne, Bob Curtis, Carl Deacon Moore, Frank
McCarroll, Michael Royal
D: Oliver Drake
SP: Basil Dickey
P: Louis Gray

2153. COWBOY AND THE PRIZEFIGHTER
(Equity/Eagle Lion, December 15, 1949)
59 Mins.
(*Red Ryder* Series) (Cinecolor)
Jim Bannon, Don Kay Reynolds, Emmett Lynn,
Marin Sais, Lou Nova, Don Haggerty, Karen
Randle, John Hart, Marshall Reed, Forrest Taylor,
Lane Bradford, Bud Osborne, Steve Clark, Ray
Jones
D: Lewis D. Collins
SP/P: Jerry Thomas

2154. RED DESERT
(Lippert, December 17, 1949) 60 Mins.
Donald Barry, Tom Neal, Jack Holt, Margia Dean,
Byron Foulger, Joseph Crehan, John Cason, Tom
London, Holly Bane, Hank Bell, George Slocum
D: Ford Beebe
S: Daniel B. Ullman
SP: Daniel B. Ullman, Ron Ormond
P: Ron Ormond

2155. SOUTH OF SANTA FE
(Universal-International, December 22, 1949)
25 Mins.
Tex Williams, Smokey Rogers, Deuce Spriggins,
Donna Martell, William Tannen, Kenneth Mac-
Donald, Ethan Laidlaw, Harry Calkin
D/P: Will Cowan
S: Norton S. Parker
SP: Joseph O'Donnell

2156. MRS. MIKE
(Nassour-Hartford/United Artists,
December 23, 1949) 99 Mins.
Dick Powell, Evelyn Keyes, J. M. Kerrigan, Angela
Clarke, John Miljan, Nan Boardman, Will Wright,
Frances Morris, Joel Nester, Jean Inness, Chief
Yowlachie, Fred Aldrich, Clarence Straight, Gary
Lee Jackson, Romere Darling, Archie Leonard,
James Fairfax, Robin Camp, Donald Pietro, Janet
Sackett, Judith Sackett
D: Louis King
S: Benedict and Nancy Freedman
SP: Alfred Lewis, DeWitt Bodeen
P: Samuel Bischoff

2157. RANGE LAND
(Monogram, December 25, 1949) 56 Mins.
Whip Wilson, Andy Clyde, Reno Browne (Blair),
Reed Howes, Kenne Duncan, Kermit Maynard,
Steve Clark, Stanley Blystone, Leonard Penn,
John Cason, William M. Griffith, Michael Dugan,
Carol Henry
D: Lambert Hillyer
SP: Adele Buffington
P: Eddie Davis

2158. FIGHTING MAN OF THE PLAINS
(20th C. Fox, December, 1949) 94 Mins.
(Cinecolor)
Randolph Scott, Bill Williams, Victor Jory, Jane
Nigh, Dale Robertson, Douglas Kennedy, Joan
Taylor, Barry Kroeger, Rhys Williams, Barry
Kelly, James Todd, James Millican, Burk Symon,
Herbert Rawlinson, J. Farrell MacDonald, Harry
Cheshire, James Griffith, Tony Hughes
D: Edwin L. Marin
S/SP: Frank Gruber
P: Nat Holt

2159. PRETTY WOMEN
(Sack Amusement Enterprises, December, 1949)
10 Mins.
Red River Dave
(No other credits available)

2160. RIO GRANDE
(Lautem Productions/Astor, 1949) 56 Mins.
Sunset Carson, Evohn Keyes, Lee Morgan, Bobby
Clark (Bobby Clack), Bob Deats, Henry Garcia,
Walter Calmback, Jr., Maria Louisa Marulanda,
Curley Rucker, Don Gray, Houston Teehee,
Frank Lawyer, Carmen Grasso, Neil Levang,
Morry Levang
D: Norman Sheldon
S/SP: Norman Sheldon
P: Charles Lautem

FILMS OF 1950

2161. PUNCHY COWPUNCHERS
(Columbia, January 5, 1950)   2 Reels
(*Three Stooges* Series)
Moe Howard, Shemp Howard, Larry Fine, Jacques O'Mahoney (Jock Mahoney), Christine McIntyre, Dick Wessel, Kenneth MacDonald, Vernon Dent, Emil Sitka
D: Edward Bernds

2161a. DAVY CROCKETT, INDIAN SCOUT
(United Artists, January 6, 1950)   71 Mins.
George Montgomery, Ellen Drew, Philip Reed, Noah Beery, Jr., Paul Wilkerson, John Hamilton, Vera Marshe, Jimmy Moss, Chief Thunder Cloud, Kenneth Duncan, Ray Teal
D: Lew Landers
S: Ford Beebe
SP: Richard Schayer
P: Edward Small

2162. BELLS OF CORONADO
(Republic, January 8, 1950)   67 Mins.
(Trucolor)
Roy Rogers, Dale Evans, Pat Brady, Grant Withers, Leo Cleary, Clifton Young, Robert Bice, Stuart Randall, John Hamilton, Edmund Cobb, Eddie Lee, Rex Lease, Lane Bradford, Foy Willing and the Riders of the Purple Sage, "Trigger"
D: William Witney
SP: Sloan Nibley
AP: Eddy White

2163. RED ROCK OUTLAW
(Friedgen, January 10, 1950)   56 Mins.
Bob Gilbert, Lee "Lasses" White, Ione Nixon, Forrest Matthews, Virginia Jackson, Wanda Cantlon
D/SP: Elmer S. Pond (probably Elmer Clifton)
P: Raymond Friedgen
(Probably filmed after *The Kid from Gower Gulch* in 1947)

2164. SONS OF NEW MEXICO
(Columbia, January 14, 1950)   71 Mins.
(Sepiatone)
Gene Autry, Gail Davis, Robert Armstrong, Dick Jones, Frankie Darro, Clayton Moore, Irving Bacon, Russell Arms, Marie Blake, Sandy Sanders, Roy Gordon, Frankie Marvin, Paul Raymond, Pierce Lyden, Kenne Duncan, Harry Mackin, Bobby Clark, Gaylord Pendleton, Billy Lechner, "Champion, Jr."
D: John English
SP: Paul Gangelin
P: Armand Schaefer

2165. BATTLING MARSHAL
(Astor, January 15, 1950)   55 Mins.
(Filmed in 1947)
Sunset Carson, Pat Starling, Forrest Matthews, Al Terry, Lee Roberts, A. J. Baxley, Richard Bartell, Bob Curtis, Pat Gleason, Stephen Keyes, Don Gray, Dale Carson, William Val, Buck Buckley, Joe Hiser
D: Oliver Drake
SP: Rose Kreves
P: Walt Mattox

2166. THE KID FROM GOWER GULCH
(Friedgen, January 15, 1950)   56 Mins.
Spade Cooley, Bob Gilbert, Wanda Cantlon, Billy Dix, Jack Baxley, Joe Hiser, William Val
D: Oliver Drake
P: Raymond Friedgen
SP: Elmer S. Pond (Elmer Clifton)
(Probably filmed around 1947. Distributed by Astor in some locales)

2167. THE JAMES BROTHERS OF MISSOURI
(Republic, January 21, 1950)   12 Chaps.
Keith Richards, Robert Bice, Noel Neill, Roy Barcroft, Patricia Knox, Lane Bradford, Gene Stutenroth, John Hamilton, Edmund Cobb, Hank Patterson, Dale Van Sickel, Tom Steele, Lee Roberts, Frank O'Connor, Marshall Reed, Wade Ray, Nolan Leary, David Sharpe, Art Dillard, Duke Green, John Crawford, Jim Rinehart, May Morgan, Post Parks, Duke Taylor, Al Ferguson, Cactus Mack, Joe Phillips, Tommy Coats, Bert LeBaron, Ken Terrell, Ted Hubert, Robert Wilke, Ray Morgan, Hank Patterson, Ralph Bucko, Forrest Burns, Helen Griffith, Herman Hack, Chick Hannon, Chuck Roberson, Bud Wolfe, Frosty Royce, Rocky Shahan
D: Fred C. Brannon
SP: Royal Cole, William Lively, Sol Shor
AP: Franklyn Adreon (sometimes spelled Franklin)
Chapter Titles: (1) Frontier Renegades, (2) Racing Peril, (3) Danger Road, (4) Murder at Midnight, (5) Road to Oblivion, (6) Missouri Manhunt, (7) Hangman's Noose, (8) Coffin on Wheels, (9) Dead Man's Return, (10) Galloping Gunslingers, (11) The Haunting Past, (12) Fugitive Code

2168. THE RAWHIDE TRAIL
(Allied Artists, January 26, 1950)
Rex (Rhodes) Reason, Nancy Gates, Richard Erdman, Rusty Lane, Frank Chase, Ann Doran, Rob-

ert Knapp, Sam Buffington, Jana Davi, Richard
Warren, William Murphy, Al Wyatt
D: Robert Gordon
SP: Alexander Wells
P: Earle Lyon

2169. MONTANA
(Warner Bros., January 28, 1950) 76 Mins.
(Technicolor)
Errol Flynn, Alexis Smith, S. Z. "Cuddles" Sakall,
Douglas Kennedy, Ian MacDonald, James Brown,
Charles Irwin, Paul E. Burns, Tudor Owen, Les-
ter Matthews, Nacho Galindo, Lane Chandler,
Monte Blue, Billy Vincent, Warren Jackson
D: Ray Enright
S: Ernest Haycox
SP: James R. Webb, Borden Chase, Charles O'Neal
P: William Jacobs

2170. FENCE RIDERS
(Monogram, January 29, 1950) 57 Mins.
Whip Wilson, Andy Clyde, Reno Browne, Riley
Hill, Myron Healey, Ed Cassidy, Terry Frost,
Frank McCarroll, George DeNormand, Holly
Bane, John Merton, Buck Bailey
D: Wallace Fox
SP: Eliot Gibbons
P: Wallace Fox

2171. DAKOTA LIL
(20th C. Fox, February 1, 1950) 88 Mins.
(Cinecolor)
George Montgomery, Marie Windsor, Rod Cam-
eron, John Emery, Wallace Ford, Jack Lambert,
Larry Johns, Marian Martin, James Flavin, J. Far-
rell MacDonald
D: Leslie Selander
S: Frank Gruber
SP: Maurice Geraghty
P: Edward L. Alperson

2172. THE SUNDOWNERS
(LeMay-Templeton/Eagle Lion, February 1, 1950)
83 Mins.
(Technicolor)
Robert Preston, John Barrymore, Jr., Robert Ster-
ling, Chill Wills, Cathy Downs, John Litel, Jack
Elam, Don Haggerty, Stanley Price, Dave Kash-
ner
D: George Templeton
SP: Alan LeMay
P: Alan LeMay, George Templeton

2173. TRAIL OF THE RUSTLERS
(Columbia, February 2, 1950) 55 Mins.
(*Durango Kid* Series)
Charles Starrett, Smiley Burnette, Gail Davis,

Tommy Ivo, Myron Healey, Don Harvey, Mira
McKinney, Chuck Roberson, Gene Roth, Blackie
Whiteford, Eddie Cletro and his Roundup Boys
D: Ray Nazarro
SP: Victor Arthur
P: Colbert Clark

2174. GUNMEN OF ABILENE
(Republic, February 6, 1950) 60 Mins.
Allan Lane, Eddy Waller, Roy Barcroft, Donna Ham-
ilton, Peter Brocco, Selmer Jackson, Duncan Rich-
ardson, Arthur Walsh, Don Harvey, Don Dilla-
way, George Chesebro, Steve Clark
D: Fred C. Brannon
SP: M. Coates Webster
AP: Gordon Kay

2175. THE FARGO PHANTOM
(Universal-International, February 9, 1950)
25 Mins.
Tex Williams, Deuce Spriggins, Smokey Rogers,
Shirlee Allard, Forrest Taylor, Stark Bishop,
Monte Montague, Chuck Hayward, Ray Jones,
Robert O'Neill
D/P: Will Cowan
SP: Joseph O'Donnell

2176. RIDERS OF THE RANGE
(RKO, February 11, 1950) 60 Mins.
Tim Holt, Richard Martin, Jacqueline White, Reed
Hadley, Robert Barrat, Tom Tyler, Robert Clarke,
William Tannen
D: Lesley Selander
SP: Norman Houston
P: Herman Schlom

2177. WEST OF WYOMING
(Monogram, February 19, 1950) 57 Mins.
Johnny Mack Brown, Gail Davis, Milburn Morante,
Myron Healey, Dennis Moore, Stanley Andrews,
Mary Gordon, Carl Mathews, Paul Cramer, John
Merton, Mike Ragan (Holly Bane), Steve Clark,
Frank McCarroll, Bud Osborne
D: Wallace Fox
SP: Adele Buffington
P: Eddie Davis

2178. THE SILVER BANDIT
(Friedgen, February 20, 1950) 54 Mins.
Spade Cooley, Bob Gilbert, Virginia Jackson, Richard
Elliott, Billy Dix, Jene Gray
D: Elmer Clifton
P: Raymond Friedgen
SP: Elmer S. Pond (Elmer Clifton)

2179. MULE TRAIN

(Columbia, February 22, 1950)   70 Mins.

(Sepiatone)

Gene Autry, Pat Buttram, Sheila Ryan, Robert Livingston, Frank Jacquet, Vince Barnett, Syd Saylor, Sandy Sanders, Gregg Barton, Kenne Duncan, Roy Gordon, Stanley Andrews, Robert Hilton, Bob Wilke, John Miljan, Robert Carson, Pat O'Malley, Eddie Parker, George Morrell, John R. McKee, George Slocum, Frank O'Connor, Norman Leavitt, "Champion, Jr."

D: John English

S: Alan James

SP: Gerald Geraghty

P: Armand Schaefer

2180. THE GIRL FROM SAN LORENZO

(United Artists, February 24, 1950)   59 Mins.

(Last entry in the *Cisco Kid* series)

Duncan Renaldo, Leo Carrillo, Jane Adams, David Sharpe, Leonard Penn, Lee Phelps, Edmund Cobb, Bill Lester, Wes Hudman, Byron Foulger, Don Harvey

D: Derwin Abrahams

SP: Ford Beebe

P: Philip N. Krasne

2181. THE DALTONS' WOMEN

(Western Adventure/Howco, February 25, 1950)   80 Mins.

Lash LaRue, Al St. John, Jack Holt, Tom Neal, Pamela Blake, Jacqueline Fontaine, Raymond Hatton, Lyle Talbot, Tom Tyler, J. Farrell MacDonald, Terry Frost, Stanley Price, Bud Osborne, Cliff Taylor, Buff Brown, Clarke Stevens, Lee Bennett, Jimmie Martin, Archie Twitchell

D: Thomas Carr

SP: Ron Ormond, Maurice Tombragel

P: Ron Ormond

2182. SINGING GUNS

(Palomar/Republic, February 28, 1950)   91 Mins.

(Trucolor)

Vaughn Monroe, Ella Raines, Walter Brennan, Ward Bond, Jeff Corey, Barry Kelly, Harry Shannon, Tom Fadden, Ralph Dunn

D: R. G. Springsteen

S: Max Brand

SP: Dorral and Stuart McGowan

AP: Melville Tucker, Abe Lyman

2183. THE NEVADAN

(Columbia, February, 1950)   81 Mins.

(Cinecolor)

Randolph Scott, Dorothy Malone, Forrest Tucker, Frank Faylen, George Macready, Charles Kemper, Jeff Corey, Tom Powers, Jock O'Mahoney, Stanley Andrews, James Kirkwood, Kate Drain Lawson, Olin Howlin, Louis Mason

D: Gordon Douglas

SP: George W. George, George F. Slavin, Rowland Brown

P: Harry Joe Brown

2184. THE BARON OF ARIZONA

(Deputy Corp./Lippert, March 4, 1950)   97 Mins.

Vincent Price, Ellen Drew, Beulah Bondi, Vladimir Sokoloff, Reed Hadley, Robert Barrat, Robin Short, Barbara Woodell, Tina Rome, Margia Dean, Edward Keane, Gene Roth, Karen Kester, Joseph Green, Fred Kohler, Jr., Tris Coffin, Angelo Rosito, I. Stanford Jolley, Terry Frost, Zachary Yaconelli, Adolfo Ornelas, Wheaton Chambers, Robert O'Neil, Stephen Harrison

D/SP: Samuel Fuller

P: Carl K. Hittleman

2185. YOUNG DANIEL BOONE

(Monogram, March 5, 1950)   71 Mins.

(Cinecolor)

David Bruce, Kristine Miller, Damian O'Flynn, Don Beddoe, Mary Treen, John Mylong, William Roy, Stanley Logan, Herbert Naish, Nipo T. Strongheart, Richard Foote, Stephen S. Harrison

D: Reginald LeBorg

SP: Clint Johnson, Reginald LeBorg

P: James S. Burkett

2186. OVER THE BORDER

(Monogram, March 12, 1950)   58 Mins.

Johnny Mack Brown, Wendy Waldron, Myron Healey, Pierre Watkin, Frank Jacquet, Marshall Reed, House Peters, Jr., Milburn Morante, Mike Ragan (Holly Bane), Hank Bell, George DeNormand, Bud Osborne, Herman Hack, Buck Bailey, George Sowards, Carol Henry, Ray Jones, Frank McCarroll, Artie Ortego, Bob Woodward

D/P: Wallace Fox

SP: J. Benton Cheney

2187. DYNAMITE PASS

(RKO, March 15, 1950)   61 Mins.

Tim Holt, Richard Martin, Lynne Roberts, Regis Toomey, Robert Shayne, Don Harvey, Cleo Moore, John Dehner, Don Haggerty, Ross Elliott, Denver Pyle

D: Lew Landers

SP: Norman Houston

P: Herman Schlom

2188. THE PALOMINO

(Columbia, March 18, 1950)   73 Mins.

(Technicolor)

Jerome Courtland, Beverly Tyler, Joseph Calleia,

Roy Roberts, Gordon Jones, Robert Osterloh, Tom Trout, Harry Garcia, Trevor Bardette, Juan Duval
D: Ray Nazzaro
SP: Tom Kilpatrick
P: Robert Cohn

2189. THE KID FROM TEXAS

(Universal-International, March 19, 1950) 78 Mins.
(Technicolor)
Audie Murphy, Gale Storm, Albert Dekker, Shepperd Strudwick, Will Geer, William Talman, Martin Garralaga, Robert Barrat, Walter Sande, Frank Wilcox, Dennis Hoey, Ray Teal, Don Haggerty, Paul Ford, Zon Murray
D: Kurt Newmann
S: Robert Hardy Andrews
SP: Robert Hardy Andrews, Karl Lamb
P: Paul Short

2190. TWILIGHT IN THE SIERRAS

(Republic, March 22, 1950) 67 Mins.
(Trucolor)
Roy Rogers, Dale Evans, Estelita Rodriguez, Pat Brady, Russ Vincent, George Meeker, Fred Kohler, Jr., Edward Keane, House Peters, Jr., Pierce Lyden, Don Frost, Joseph Carro, William Lester, Bob Burns, Bob Wilke, Foy Willing and the Riders of the Purple Sage, "Trigger"
D: William Witney
SP: Sloan Nibley
AP: Eddy White

2191. THE FIGHTING STALLION

(Eagle Lion, March 23, 1950) 63 Mins.
(Cinecolor)
Bill Edwards, Doris Merrick, Forrest Taylor, Rocky Camron (Gene Alsace), John Carpenter, Maria Hart, Don Harvey, Bob Cason, W. M. (Merrill) McCormack, Concha Ybarra
D: Robert Tansey
S: George Slavin
SP: Frances Kavanaugh
P: Jack Schwarz, Robert Tansey

2192. HOSTILE COUNTRY

(Lippert, March 24, 1950) 60 Mins.
Jimmy Ellison, Russell Hayden, Fuzzy Knight, Raymond Hatton, Betty (Julie) Adams, Tom Tyler, Dennis Moore, George J. Lewis, John Cason, Stanley Price, Stephen Carr, George Chesebro, Bud Osborne, Jimmie Martin, Judith Webster, Jimmy Van Horn, Cliff Taylor, Ray Jones, I. Stanford Jolley, George Sowards, J. Farrell MacDonald
D: Thomas Carr
SP: Maurice Tombragel, Robert Lippert
P: Ron Ormond

2193. CODE OF THE SILVER SAGE

(Republic, March 25, 1950) 60 Mins.
Allan Lane, Eddy Waller, Roy Barcroft, Kay Christopher, Rex Lease, Lane Bradford, William Ruhl, Richard Emory, Forrest Taylor, Kenne Duncan, Hank Patterson, John Butler
D: Fred Brannon
SP: Arthur E. Orloff
AP: Gordon Ray

2194. GOLD STRIKE

(Universal-International, March 30, 1950) 25 Mins.
Tex Williams, Deuce Spriggins, Smokey Rogers, Shirlee Allard, Jack Ingram, Fred Kohler, Jr., Bob Anderson, James Linn
D/P: Will Cowan
SP: Joseph O'Donnell

2195. THE VANISHING WESTERNER

(Republic, March 31, 1950) 60 Mins.
Monte Hale, Paul Hurst, Aline Towne, Roy Barcroft, Arthur Space, Richard Anderson, William Phipps, Don Haggerty, Dick Curtis, Rand Brooks, Edmund Cobb, Harold Goodwin
D: Philip Ford
SP: Bob Williams
AP: Melville Tucker

2196. THE ARIZONA COWBOY

(Republic, April 1, 1950) 67 Mins.
Rex Allen, Teala Loring, Gordon Jones, Minerva Urecal, James Cardwell, Roy Barcroft, Stanley Andrews, Harry Cheshire, Edmund Cobb, Joseph Crehan, Steve Darrell, Douglas Evans, John Elliott, Chris-Pin Martin, Frank Reicher, George Lloyd, Lane Bradford
D: R. G. Springsteen
SP: Bradford Ropes
AP: Franklin Adreon

2197. BARRICADE

(Warner Bros., April 1, 1950) 75 Mins.
Dane Clark, Raymond Massey, Ruth Roman, Robert Douglas, Morgan Farley, Walter Loy, George Stern, Robert Griffin, Frank Marlowe, Tony Martinez
D: Peter Godfrey
S/SP: William Sackheim
P: Saul Elkins

2198. WYOMING MAIL

(Universal-International, April 1, 1950) 87 Mins.
(Technicolor)
Stephen McNally, Alexis Smith, Howard DeSilva, Ed Begley, Don Riss, Roy Roberts, Whit Bissell, James Arness, Richard Jaeckel, Frankie Darro, Gene Evans, Frank Fenton

D: Reginald LeBorg
S: Robert Hardy Andrews
SP: Harry Essex, Leonard Lee
P: Aubrey Schenck

2199. CODY OF THE PONY EXPRESS

(Columbia, April 6, 1950)   15 Chaps.

Jock O'Mahoney, Dickie Moore, Peggy Stewart, William Fawcett, Tom London, Helena Dare, George J. Lewis, Pierce Lyden, Jack Ingram, Rick Vallin, Frank Ellis, Ross Elliott, Ben Corbett, Rusty Westcoatt
D: Spencer G. Bennet
SP: David Matthews, Lewis Clay, Charles Condon
S: George Plympton, Joseph F. Poland
P: Sam Katzman
Chapter Titles: (1) Cody Carries the Mail, (2) Captured by Indians, (3) Cody Saves a Life, (4) Cody Follows a Trail, (5) Cody to the Rescue, (6) The Fatal Arrow, (7) Cody Gets His Man, (8) Revenge Raiders, (9) Frontier Law, (10) Cody Tempts Fate, (11) Trouble at Silver Gap, (12) Cody Comes Through, (13) Marshal of Nugget City, (14) Unseen Danger, (15) Cody's Last Ride

2200. GUNSLINGERS

(Monogram, April 9, 1950)   55 Mins.

Whip Wilson, Andy Clyde, Reno Browne, Dennis Moore, Riley Hill, Sarah Padden, Hank Bell, Bill Kennedy, Steve Clark, George Chesebro, Carl Mathews, Frank McCarroll, Reed Howes, Carol Henry, George DeNormand
D/P: Wallace Fox
SP: Adele Buffington

2201. OUTCASTS OF BLACK MESA

(Columbia, April 13, 1950)   54 Mins.
(*Durango Kid* Series)

Charles Starrett, Smiley Burnette, Martha Hyer, Richard Bailey, Stanley Andrews, William Haade, Lane Chandler, Chuck Roberson, Ozie Waters
D: Ray Nazarro
S: Elmer Clifton
SP: Barry Shipman
P: Colbert Clark

2202. WAGONMASTER

(Argosy/RKO, April 19, 1950)   86 Mins.

Ben Johnson, Harry Carey, Jr., Joanne Dru, Ward Bond, Charles Kemper, Alan Mobray, Jane Darwell, Ruth Clifford, Russell Simpson, Kathleen O'Malley, James Arness, Movita Castaneda, Fred Libby, Mickey Simpson, Hank Worden, Francis Ford, Jim Thorpe, Cliff Lyons, Don Summers
D: John Ford
SP: Frank Nugent, Patrick Ford
P: John Ford, Merian C. Cooper
Second Unit D: Cliff Lyons

2203. THE CAPTURE

(RKO, April 21, 1950)   81 Mins.

Lew Ayres, Teresa Wright, Victor Jory, Jacqueline White, Jimmy Hunt, Barry Kelly, Duncan Rinaldo, William Bakewell, Milton Parsons, Frank Matts, Felipe Turich, Edwin Rand
D: John Sturges
S/SP: Niven Busch
P: Niven Busch

2204. MARSHAL OF HELDORADO

(Lippert, April 21, 1950)   53 Mins.

Jimmy Ellison, Russell Hayden, Raymond Hatton, Fuzzy Knight, Betty (Julie) Adams, Tom Tyler, George J. Lewis, John Cason, Stanley Price, Stephen Carr, Dennis Moore, George Chesebro, Jimmie Martin, Cliff Taylor, Ned Roberts, Jack Hendricks, Wally West, James Van Horn, Jack Geddes, Bud Osborne, Carl Mathews
D: Thomas Carr
SP: Ron Ormond, Maurice Tombragel
P: Ron Ormond, Murray Lerner

2205. THE OUTRIDERS

(MGM, April 21, 1950)   93 Mins.
(Technicolor)

Joel McCrea, Arlene Dahl, Barry Sullivan, Claude Jarman, Jr., James Whitmore, Ramon Novarro, Jeff Corey, Ted De Corsia, Martin Garralaga
D: Roy Rowland
S/SP: Irving Ravetch
P: Richard Goldstone

2206. STORM OVER WYOMING

(RKO, April 22, 1950)   60 Mins.

Tim Holt, Richard Martin, Noreen Nash, Richard Powers (Tom Keene), Betty Underwood, Kenneth MacDonald, Leo MacMahon, Bill Kennedy, Holly Bane, Richard Kean, Don Haggerty
D: Lesley Selander
SP: Ed Earl Repp
P: Herman Schlom

2207. JIGGS AND MAGGIE OUT WEST

(Monogram, April 23, 1950)   66 Mins.

Joe Yule, Renie Riano, George McManus, Tim Ryan, Jim Bannon, Riley Hill, Pat Goldin, June Harrison, Terry McGinnis
D: William Beaudine
SP: Barney Gerard, Adele Buffington
P: Barney Gerard

2208. SIX GUN MESA

(Monogram, April 30, 1950)   56 Mins.

Johnny Mack Brown, Milburn Morante, Gail Davis, Holly Bane, Steve Clark, Carl Mathews, Bud Osborne, Leonard Penn, George DeNormand, Riley

Hill, Marshall Reed, Stanley Blystone, Frank Jacquet, Artie Ortego, Merrill McCormack
D: Wallace Fox
SP: Adele Buffington
P: Eddie Davis

2209. COMANCHE TERRITORY
(Universal-International, May 1, 1950)   76 Mins.
(Technicolor)
Maureen O'Hara, MacDonald Carey, Will Geer, Charles Drake, Pedro De Cordoba, Ian MacDonald, Rick Vallin, Parley Baer, James Best, Edmund Cobb, Glenn Strange
D: George Sherman
S: Lewis Meltzer
SP: Oscar Brodney, Lewis Meltzer
P: Leonard Goldstein

2210. SALT LAKE RAIDERS
(Republic, May 1, 1950)   60 Mins.
Allan Lane, Eddy Waller, Roy Barcroft, Martha Hyer, Byron Foulger, Myron Healey, Clifton Young, Stanley Andrews, Rory Mallison, Kenneth MacDonald, George Chesebro
D: Fred C. Brannon
SP: M. Coates Webster
AP: Gordon Kay

2211. TICKET TO TOMAHAWK
(20th C. Fox, May 1, 1950)   90 Mins.
Dan Dailey, Anne Baxter, Rory Calhoun, Walter Brennan, Charles Kemper, Connie Gilchrist, Arthur Hunnicutt, Will Wright, Chief Yowlachie, Victor Sen Yung, Mauritz Hugo, Raymond Greenleaf, Harry Carter, Harry Seymour, Robert Adler, Chief Thunder Cloud, Marion Marshall, Joyce McKenzie, Marilyn Monroe
D: Richard Sale
S/SP: Mary Loos, Richard Sale
P: Robert Bassler

2212. PRAIRIE PIRATES
(Universal-International, May 5, 1950)   23 Mins.
Tex Williams, Smokey Rogers, Deuce Spriggins, Patricia Hall, William Haade
D/P: Will Cowan
SP: Sherman Lowe

2213. PANCHO VILLA RETURNS
(Hispano Continental Films, May 11, 1950)   95 Mins.
(Filmed in Mexico)
Leo Carrillo, Esther Fernandez, Rodolfo Acosta, Jeanette Comber, Rafael Alcayde, Jorge Trevino, Eduardo Gonzales Pliego
D/SP/P: Miguel Contreras Torres

2214. STARS IN MY CROWN
(MGM, May 11, 1950)   89 Mins.
Joel McCrea, Ellen Drew, Dean Stockwell, Alan Hale, James Mitchell, Lewis Stone, Amanda Blake, Juano Hernandez, Charles Kemper, Connie Gilchrist, Ed Begley, Jack Lambert, Arthur Hunnicutt
D: Jacques Tourneur
S: Joe David Brown
SP: Margaret Fitts
P: William H. Wright

2215. COLORADO RANGER
(Lippert, May 12, 1950)   59 Mins.
Jimmy "Shamrock" Ellison, Russell "Lucky" Hayden, Fuzzy Knight, Raymond Hatton, Betty (Julie) Adams, George J. Lewis, Tom Tyler, John Cason, Stanley Price, Stephen Carr, Dennis Moore, George Chesebro, Bud Osborne, Jimmie Martin, Gene Roth, I. Stanford Jolley, Joseph Richards
D: Thomas Carr
SP: Ron Ormond, Maurice Tombragel
P: Ron Ormond, Murray Lerner

2216. ROCK ISLAND TRAIL
(Republic, May 18, 1950)   90 Mins.
Forrest Tucker, Adele Mara, Adrian Booth, Bruce Cabot, Chill Wills, Jeff Corey, Grant Withers, Barbara Fuller, Roy Barcroft, Pierre Watkin, Valentine Perkins, Jimmy Hunt, Olin Howlin, Sam Flint, John Holland, Kate Drain Lawson, Emory Parnell, Billy Wilkerson, Dick Elliott
D: Joseph Kane
S: "A Yankee Dared"—Frank J. Nevins
SP: James Edward Grant
AP: Paul Malvern

2217. COW TOWN
(Columbia, May 19, 1950)   70 Mins.
(Sepiatone)
Gene Autry, Gail Davis, Harry Shannon, Jock O'Mahoney, Clark Burroughs, Harry Harvey, Steve Darrell, Sandy Sanders, Ralph Sanford, Bud Osborne, Robert Hilton, Ted Mapes, Chuck Roberson, House Peters, Jr., Walt LaRue, Herman Hack, Ken Cooper, Victor Cox, Holly Bane, Felice Raymond, Frank McCarroll, Pat O'Malley, Blackie Whiteford, Frankie Marvin, "Champion, Jr."
D: John English
SP: Gerald Geraghty
P: Armand Schaefer

2218. THE SAVAGE HORDE
(Republic, May 22, 1950)   90 Mins.
William (Bill) Elliott, Adrian Booth, Grant Withers, Barbara Fuller, Noah Beery, Jr., Jim Davis, Douglass Dumbrille, Bob Steele, Will Wright, Roy Bar-

Colorado Ranger (Lippert, 1950) — Russell Hayden, Stephen Chase, Raymond Hatton, Jimmy Ellison, and Stanley Price

croft, Earle Hodgins, Stuart Hamblen, Hal Taliaferro, Lloyd Ingraham, Marshall Reed, Crane Whitley, Charles Stevens, James Flavin, Edward Cassidy, Kermit Maynard, George Chesebro, Jack O'Shea, Monte Montague, Bud Osborne, Reed Howes

D: Joseph Kane
S: Thames Williamson, Gerald Geraghty
SP: Kenneth Gamet
AP: Joseph Kane

2219. ANNIE GET YOUR GUN

(MGM, May 23, 1950)   107 Mins.
(Technicolor)
Betty Hutton, Howard Keel, Lewis Colborn, Edward Arnold, Keenan Wynn, J. Carroll Naish, Benay Venuta
D: George Sidney
S: Dorothy Fields, Herbert Fields
SP: Sidney Shelton
P: Arthur Freed

2220. COLT 45

(Warner Bros., May 27, 1950)   70 Mins.
(Technicolor)
Randolph Scott, Zachary Scott, Ruth Roman, Lloyd

Bridges, Alan Hale, Ian MacDonald, Chief Thunder Cloud, Walter Coy, Luther Crockett, Charles Evans, Buddy Roosevelt, Hal Taliaferro, Art Miles, Barry Reagan, Howard Negley, Aurora Navarro, Paul Newland, Franklyn Farnum, Ed Piel, Sr., Jack Watt, Carl Andre, Royden Clark, Clyde Hudkins, Jr., Leroy Johnson, Ben Corbett, Kansas Moehring, Warren Fisk, Forrest R. Colee, Artie Ortego, Richard Brehm, Dick Hudkins, Leo McMahon, Bob Burrows, William Steele
D: Edward L. Marin
S/SP: Thomas Blackburn
P: Saul Elkins

2221. THE EAGLE AND THE HAWK

(Paramount, May 30, 1950)   104 Mins.
(Technicolor)
John Payne, Rhonda Fleming, Dennis O'Keefe, Thomas Gomez, Fred Clark, Frank Faylen, Walter Reed, Margaret Martin
D: Lewis R. Foster
S: "A Mission to General Houston"—Jess Arnold
SP: Geoffrey Homes, Lewis R. Foster
P: William H. Pine, William G. Thomas

2222. ROAR OF THE IRON HORSE

(Columbia, May 31, 1950)   15 Chaps.

Jock O'Mahoney, Virginia Herrick, William Fawcett, Hal Landon, Jack Ingram, Mickey Simpson, George Eldridge, Myron Healey, Rusty Westcoatt, Frank Ellis, Pierce Lyden, Dick Curtis, Hugh Prosser, Rick Vallin, Bud Osborne

D: Spencer G. Bennet, Thomas Carr

SP: George Plympton, Sherman Lowe, Royal K. Cole

P: Sam Katzman

Chapter Titles: (1) Indian Attack, (2) Captured by Redskins, (3) Trapped by Outlaws, (4) In the Baron's Stronghold, (5) A Ride for Life, (6) White Indians, (7) Flames of Fate, (8) Midnight Marauders, (9) Raid on the Pay Train, (10) Trapped on a Trestle, (11) Redskin's Revenge, (12) Plunge of Peril, (13) The Law Takes Over, (14) When Killers Meet, (15) The End of the Trail

2223. CURTAIN CALL AT CACTUS CREEK

(Universal-International, June 1, 1950)   86 Mins. (Technicolor)

Donald O'Connor, Gale Storm, Vincent Price, Walter Brennan, Eve Arden, Chick Chandler, Joe Sawyer, Harry Shannon, Rex Lease, I. Stanford Jolley

D: Charles Lamont

S: Stanley Roberts, Howard Dimsdale

SP: Howard Dimsdale

P: Robert Arthur

2224. HILLS OF OKLAHOMA

(Republic, June 1, 1950)   67 Mins.

Rex Allen, Fuzzy Knight, Elizabeth Fraser, Elizabeth Risdon, Roscoe Ates, Robert Karnes, Rex Lease, Robert Emmett Keane, Trevor Bardette, Lee Phelps, Edmund Cobb, Ted Adams, Lane Bradford, Michael Carr, Johnny Downs, "Koko"

D: R. G. Springsteen

SP: Olive Cooper, Victor Arthur

AP: Franklin Adreon

2225. SIERRA

(Universal-International, June 1, 1950)   83 Mins. (Technicolor)

Audie Murphy, Wanda Hendrix, Dean Jagger, Burl Ives, Richard Rober, Anthony Caruso, Houseley Stevenson, Elliott Reid, Griff Barnett, Elizabeth Risdon, Roy Roberts, Gregg Martell, Sara Allgood, Jim Arness, Ted Jordan, I. Stanford Jolley, Jack Ingram

D: Alfred E. Greene

S: Stuart Hardy

SP: Edna Anhalt

P: Michel Kraike

2226. TEXAS DYNAMO

(Columbia, June 1, 1950)   54 Mins.

(*Durango Kid* Series)

Charles Starrett, Smiley Burnette, Lois Hall, Jock O'Mahoney, Slim Duncan, John Dehner, George Chesebro, Marshall Reed, Lane Bradford, Fred Sears, Emil Sitka, Greg Barton

D: Ray Nazarro

SP: Barry Shipman

P: Colbert Clark

2227. WEST OF THE BRAZOS

(Lippert, June 2, 1950)   58 Mins.

Jimmy Ellison, Russell Hayden, Raymond Hatton, Fuzzy Knight, Betty (Julie) Adams, Tom Tyler, Stanley Price, Dennis Moore, George J. Lewis, John Cason, Bud Osborne, George Chesebro, Judith Webster, Gene Roth, Jimmie Martin, Stephan Carr

D: Thomas Carr

SP: Ron Ormond, Maurice Tombragel

P: Ron Ormond, Murray Lerner

2228. RIDER FROM TUCSON

(RKO, June 7, 1950)   60 Mins.

Tim Holt, Richard Martin, Elaine Riley, Douglas Fowley, Veda Ann Borg, Robert Shayne, William Phipps, Harry Tyler, Marshall Reed, Stuart Randall, Luther Crockett, Dorothy Vaughn

D: Lesley Selander

SP: Ed Earl Repp

P: Herman Schlom

2229. CROOKED RIVER

(Lippert, June 9, 1950)   55 Mins.

Jimmy Ellison, Russell Hayden, Fuzzy Knight, Raymond Hatton, Betty (Julie) Adams, Tom Tyler, George J. Lewis, John Cason, Stanley Price, Stephen Carr, Dennis Moore, George Chesebro, Bud Osborne, Jimmie Martin, Cliff Taylor, Helen Gibson, Carl Mathews, George Sowards, Scoop Martin, Joe Phillips

D: Thomas Carr

SP: Ron Ormond, Maurice Tombragel

P: Ron Ormond, Murray Lerner

2230. THE IROQUOIS TRAIL

(United Artists, June 16, 1950)   85 Mins.

George Montgomery, Brenda Marshall, Glenn Langan, Reginald Denny, Monte Blue, Sheldon Leonard, Paul Cavanaugh, Holmes Herbert, Dan O'Herlihy, Don Gerner, Marcel Gourmet, Arthur Little, Jr., Esther Somers, John Doucette

D: Phil Karlson

S: James Fenimore Cooper

SP: Richard Schayer

P: Edward Small, Bernard Small

The Iroquois Trail (United Artists, 1950) — Brenda Marshall and George Montgomery

2231. RETURN OF THE FRONTIERSMAN

(Warner Bros., June 24, 1950)   74 Mins.
(Technicolor)

Gordon MacRae, Jack Holt, Rory Calhoun, Julie London, Fred Clark, Edwin Rand, Raymond Bond, Britt Wood, Matt McHugh
D: Richard Bare
S/SP: Edna Anhalt
P: Saul Elkins

2232. COVERED WAGON RAID

(Republic, June 30, 1950)   60 Mins.

Allan Lane, Eddy Waller, Alex Gerry, Lyn Thomas, Byron Barr, Dick Curtis, Pierce Lyden, Sherry Jackson, Rex Lease, Lester Dorr, Lee Roberts, Wee Willie Keeler, Marshall Reed, "Black Jack"
D: R. G. Springsteen
SP: M. Coates Webster
AP: Gordon Kay

2233. FAST ON THE DRAW

(Lippert, June 30, 1950)   55 Mins.

Jimmy Ellison, Russell Hayden, Raymond Hatton, Fuzzy Knight, Betty (Julie) Adams, Tom Tyler, George J. Lewis, John Cason, Dennis Moore, Judith Webster, Bud Osborne, Helen Gibson, Cliff Taylor, Stanley Price, Jimmy Van Horn, Bud Hooker, Ray Jones, I. Stanford Jolley
D: Thomas Carr
SP: Maurice Tombragel, Ron Ormond
P: Ron Ormond

2234. TRIGGER, JR.

(Republic, June 30, 1950)   68 Mins.
(Trucolor)

Roy Rogers, Dale Evans, Pat Brady, Gordon Jones, Grant Withers, Peter Miles, George Cleveland, Frank Fenton, I. Stanford Jolley, Stanley Andrews, The Raynor Lehr Circus, Foy Willing and the Riders of the Purple Sage, "Trigger," "Trigger, Jr."
D: William Witney
SP: Gerald Geraghty
AP: Eddy White

2235. BEYOND THE PURPLE HILLS

(Columbia, July 1, 1950)   70 Mins.
(Sepiatone)

Gene Autry, Pat Buttram, Jo Dennison, Don Beddoe, James Millican, Don Kay Reynolds, Hugh O'Brian, Bob Wilke, Roy Gordon, Harry Harvey, Gregg Barton, Ralph Peters, Frank Ellis, John Cliff, Sandy Sanders, Merrill McCormack, Tex Terry, Fenton Jones, Maudie Prickett, Pat O'Malley, Herman Hack, Cliff Barnett, Frank O'Connor, Frankie Marvin, Bobby Clark, Boyd Stock-

man, Lynton Brent, Victor Cox, Jerry Ambler,
"Champion, Jr."
D: John English
SP: Norman S. Hall
P: Armand Schaefer

2236. THE GUNFIGHTER
(20th C. Fox, July 1, 1950) 84 Mins.
Gregory Peck, Helen Westcott, Millard Mitchell,
Jean Parker, Karl Malden, Skip Homeier, An-
thony Ross, Verna Felton, Ellen Corby, Richard
Jaeckel, Alan Hale, Jr., David Clark, John Pickard,
B. G. Norman, Angela Clarke, Cliff Clark, Jean
Inness, Eddie Ehrhart, Albert Morin, Kenneth
Tobey, Michael Branden, Eddie Parkes, Ferris
Taylor, Hank Patterson, Mae Marsh, Credda Za-
jak, Anne Whitfield, Kim Spaulding, Harry Shan-
non, Houseley Stevenson, James Millican, William
Vedder, Ed Mundy
D: Henry King
S: William Bowers, Andre de Toth
SP: William Bowers, William Sellers
P: Nunnally Johnson

2237. ARIZONA TERRITORY
(Monogram, July 2, 1950) 56 Mins.
Whip Wilson, Andy Clyde, Nancy Saunders, Den-
nis Moore, John Merton, Carl Mathews, Carol
Henry, Bud Osborne, Frank Austin, Ted Adams
D: Wallace Fox
SP: Adele Buffington
P: Vincent Fennelly

2238. CACTUS CARAVAN
(Universal-International, July 6, 1950) 26 Mins.
Tex Williams, Smokey Rogers, Deuce Spriggins,
Leslie Banning, Tris Coffin, Marshall Reed, Frank-
lin Parker, Steve Clark
D/P: Will Cowan
SP: Joseph O'Donnell

2239. WINCHESTER '73
(Universal-International, July 12, 1950) 92 Mins.
James Stewart, Shelley Winters, Dan Duryea, Ste-
phen McNally, Millard Mitchell, Charles Drake,
John McIntyre, Will Geer, Jay C. Flippen, Rock
Hudson, John Alexander, Steve Brodie, James
Millican, Abner Biberman, Tony Curtis, James
Best
D: Anthony Mann
SP: Robert L. Richards, Borden Chase
P: Aaron Rosenberg

2240. SNOW DOG
(Monogram, July 16, 1950) 63 Mins.
Kirby Grant, Elena Verdugo, Rick Vallin, Milburn
Stone, Richard Karlan, Jane Adrian, Hal Gerard,
Richard Avonde, Duke York, Guy Zanette, "Chi-
nook" (the Wonder Dog)
D: Frank McDonald
S: "Tentacles of the North"—James Oliver Cur-
wood
SP: William Raynor
P: Lindsley Parsons

2241. THE OLD FRONTIER
(Republic, July 29, 1950) 60 Mins.
Monte Hale, Paul Hurst, Claudia Barrett, William
Henry, Tris Coffin, William Haade, Victor Kilian,
Lane Bradford, Denver Pyle, Almira Sessions,
Tom London
D: Philip Ford
SP: Bob Williams
AP: Melville Tucker

2242. TALES OF THE WEST #1
(Universal-International, July 30, 1950) 55 Mins.
(A two-story feature made up of the shorts *South of
Santa Fe* [1949] and *Cactus Caravan* [1950])
Tex Williams, Smokey Rogers, Deuce Spriggins,
Leslie Banning, Tris Coffin, Marshall Reed,
Franklin Parker, Steve Clark, Donna Martell, Wil-
liam Tannen, Kenneth MacDonald, Ethan Laid-
law, Harry Calkin
D/P: Will Cowan
SP: Joseph O'Donnell

2243. BROKEN ARROW
(20th C. Fox, August 1, 1950) 93 Mins.
(Technicolor)
James Stewart, Jeff Chandler, Debra Paget, Basil
Ruysdael, Will Geer, Joyce McKenzie, Arthur
Hunnicutt, Raymond Branley, Jay Silverheels,
Argentina Brunetti, Jack Lee, Robert Adler, Harry
Carter, Robert Griffin, Bill Wilkerson, Mickey
Kuhn, Chris Willow Bird, J. W. Cody, John War
Eagle, Charles Soldani, Iron Eyes Cody, Robert
Foster Dovey, John Marston, Edwin Rand, John
Doucette
D: Delmer Daves
S: "Blood Brother"—Elliott Arnold
SP: Michael Blankfort
P: Julian Blaustein

2244. THE CARIBOO TRAIL
(20th C. Fox, August 1, 1950) 81 Mins.
(Cinecolor)
Randolph Scott, George Hayes, Bill Williams, Karin
Booth, Victor Jory, Douglas Kennedy, Jim Davis,
Dale Robertson, Mary Stuart, James Griffith, Lee
Tung Foo, Tony Hughes, Mary Kent, Ray Hyke,
Kansas Moehring, Dorothy Adams, Jerry Root,
Cliff Clark, Fred Libby, Tom Montore, Michael
Barret

D: Edwin L. Marin
S: John Rhodes Sturdy
SP: Frank Gruber
P: Nat Holt

2245. STREETS OF GHOST TOWN

(Columbia, August 3, 1950)   54 Mins.
(Durango Kid Series)
Charles Starrett, Smiley Burnette, George Chesebro, Mary Ellen Kay, Stanley Andrews, Frank Fenton, John Cason, Don Kay Reynolds, Jack Ingram, Ozie Waters and his Colorado Rangers
D: Ray Nazarro
SP: Barry Shipman
P: Colbert Clark

2246. VIGILANTE HIDEOUT

(Republic, August 6, 1950)   60 Mins.
Allan Lane, Eddy Waller, Roy Barcroft, Virginia Herrick, Cliff Clark, Don Haggerty, Paul Campbell, Guy Teague, Art Dillard, Chick Hannon, Bob Woodward, "Black Jack"
D: Fred C. Brannon
SP: Richard Wormser
AP: Gordon Kay

2247. I KILLED GERONIMO

(Eagle Lion Classics, August 8, 1950)   62 Mins.
James Ellison, Virginia Herrick, Chief Thunder Cloud, Smith Ballew, Dennis Moore, Luther Crockett, Jean Andren, Ted Adams, Myron Healey
D: John Hoffman
S/SP: Sam Neuman, Nat Tanchuck
P: Jack Schwarz

2248. GUNFIRE

(Lippert, August 11, 1950)   59 Mins.
Don Barry, Robert Lowery, Wally Vernon, Pamela Blake, Claude Stroud, Leonard Penn, Gaylord Pendleton, Tommy Farrell, Dean Reisner, Paul Jordan, Steve Conti, Robert Anderson, Gil Pelman, James Adrian, William Norton Bailey
D/P: William Berke
SP: William Berke, Victor West

2249. THE SHOWDOWN

(Republic, August 15, 1950)   86 Mins.
Bill Elliott, Walter Brennan, Marie Windsor, Henry (Harry) Morgan, Rhys Williams, Jim Davis, William Ching, Nacho Galindo, Leif Erickson, Henry Rowland, Charles Stevens, Victor Kilian, Yakima Canutt, Guy Teague, William Steele, Jack Sparks
D/SP: Dorrell and Stuart McGowan
S: *Esquire* magazine story by Richard Wormser and Dan Gordon
P: William J. O'Sullivan, William Elliott

2250. SILVER RAIDERS

(Monogram, August 20, 1950)   55 Mins.
Whip Wilson, Andy Clyde, Virginia Herrick, Leonard Penn, Patricia Rios, Dennis Moore, Kermit Maynard, Reed Howes, Riley Hill, Marshall Reed, George DeNormand
D: Wallace Fox
SP: Dan Ullman
P: Vincent M. Fennelly

2251. THE FURIES

(Paramount, August 21, 1950)   109 Mins.
Barbara Stanwyck, Walter Huston, Wendell Corey, Gilbert Roland, Judith Anderson, Thomas Gomez, Beulah Bondi, Albert Dekker, John Bromfield, Wallace Ford, Blanche Yurka, Louis Jean Heydt, Frank Ferguson, Movita, Myrna Dell, Charles Evans, Craig Kelly
D: Anthony Mann
S: Niven Busch
SP: Charles Schnee
P: Hal B. Wallis

2252. I SHOT BILLY THE KID

(Lippert, August 25, 1950)   57 Mins.
Don Barry, Robert Lowery, Wally Vernon, Tom Neal, Judith Allen, Wendy Lee, Barbara Woodell, Dick Lane, Sid Nelson, Archie Twitchell, John Merton, Claude Stroud, Henry Marud, Bill Kennedy
D/P: William Berke
SP: Ford Beebe, Orville Hampton

2253. TALES OF THE WEST #2

(Universal-International, August 30, 1950)
   50 Mins.
(A two-story feature made up of the shorts *Coyote Canyon* [1949] and *The Fargo Phantom* [1950])
Tex Williams, Deuce Spriggins, Smokey Rogers, Shirlee Allard, Forrest Taylor, Stark Bishop, Monte Montague, Chuck Hayward, Ray Jones, Robert O'Neill, Donna Martell, George Eldridge, Judd Holdren, Leslie Kimmell, Jim Hayward, Bob Wilke, Jess Fargo
D/P: Will Cowan
SP: Joseph O'Donnell

2254. HIGH LONESOME

(Eagle Lion Classics, September 1, 1950)   81 Mins.
(Technicolor)
John Barrymore, Jr., Chill Wills, Lois Butler, Kristine Miller, Basil Ruysdael, Jack Elam, John Archer
D: Alan LeMay
S/SP: Alan LeMay
P: George Templeton

2255. SADDLE TRAMP

(Universal-International, September 1, 1950)
77 Mins.

(Technicolor)

Joel McCrea, Wanda Hendrix, John Russell, John McIntyre, Jeannette Nolan, Russell Simpson, Ed Begley, Jimmy Hunt, Antonio Moreno, John Midgeley, Walter Coy, Paul Piceroni

D: Hugo Fregonese

S/SP: Harold Shumate

P: Leonard Goldstein

2256. THE RETURN OF JESSE JAMES

(Lippert, September 8, 1950)   73 Mins.

John Ireland, Ann Dvorak, Henry Hull, Reed Hadley, Hugh O'Brian, Carleton Young, Barbara Woodell, Margia Dean, Sid Melton, Victor Kilian, Byron Foulger, Sam Flint, Robin Short, Paul Maxen

D: Arthur Hilton

S/P: Carl K. Hittleman

SP: Jack Natteford

2257. ACROSS THE BADLANDS

(Columbia, September 15, 1950)   55 Mins.

(*Durango Kid* Series)

Charles Starrett, Smiley Burnette, Helen Mowery, Stanley Andrews, Bob Wilke, Dick Elliott, Hugh Prosser, Robert W. Cavendish, Charles Evans, Paul Campbell, Dick Alexander, Harmonica Bill

D: Fred F. Sears

SP: Barry Shipman

P: Colbert Clark

2258. DEVIL'S DOORWAY

(MGM, September 15, 1950)   84 Mins.

Robert Taylor, Louis Calhern, Paula Raymond, Marshall Thompson, James Mitchell, Edgar Buchanan, Rhys Williams, Spring Byington, James Millican, Bruce Cowling, Fritz Leiber, Chief Big Tree

D: Anthony Mann

S/SP: Guy Trosper

P: Nicholas Nayfack

2259. BORDER TREASURE

(RKO, September 16, 1950)   60 Mins.

Tim Holt, Jane Nigh, Richard Martin, John Doucette, House Peters, Jr., Inez Cooper, Julian Rivero, Kenneth MacDonald, Vince Barnett, Robert Payton, David Leonard, Tom Monroe

D: George Archainbaud

SP: Norman Houston

P: Herman Schlom

2260. TRAIN TO TOMBSTONE

(Lippert, September 16, 1950)   56 Mins.

Don Barry, Robert Lowery, Tom Neal, Wally Vernon, Judith Allen, Minna Phillips, Barbara Stanley, Nan Leslie, Claude Stroud, Bill Kennedy

D/S/P: William Berke

SP: Victor West, Orville Hampton

2261. LAW OF THE PANHANDLE

(Monogram, September 17, 1950)   55 Mins.

Johnny Mack Brown, Jane Adams, Riley Hill, Marshall Reed, Myron Healey, Ted Adams, Lee Roberts, Kermit Maynard, Carol Henry, Milburn Morante, Bob Duncan, Boyd Stockman, George DeNormand, Tex Palmer, Ray Jones

D: Lewis Collins

SP: Joseph Poland

P: Jerry Thomas

2262. REDWOOD FOREST TRAIL

(Republic, September 18, 1950)   67 Mins.

Rex Allen, Jeff Donnell, Carl "Alfalfa" Switzer, Jane Darwell, Marten Lamont, Pierre Watkin, Jimmy Ogg, Dick Jones, John Cason, Jimmy Grasher, Bob Larson, Robert W. Wood, Jack Larson, Ted Fries, Joseph Granby, Robert Burns, "Koko"

D: Philip Ford

SP: Bradford Ropes

2263. SUNSET IN THE WEST

(Republic, September 25, 1950)   67 Mins.

(Trucolor)

Roy Rogers, Estelita Rodriguez, Penny Edwards, Gordon Jones, Will Wright, Pierre Watkin, Charles LaTorre, William J. Tannen, Gaylord Pendleton, Paul E. Burns, Dorothy Ann White, Foy Willing and the Riders of the Purple Sage, "Trigger"

D: William Witney

SP: Gerald Geraghty

AP: Eddy White

2264. INDIAN TERRITORY

(Columbia, September 30, 1950)   70 Mins.

(Sepiatone)

Gene Autry, Pat Buttram, Gail Davis, Kirby Grant, James Griffith, Philip Van Zandt, Pat Collins, Roy Gordon, Charles Stevens, Robert Carson, Chief Thunder Cloud, Chief Yowlachie, Frank Lackteen, Boyd Stockman, Sandy Sanders, Frank Ellis, Frankie Marvin, John R. McKee, Bert Dodson, Nick Rodman, Wesley Hudman, Robert Hilton, Roy Butler, Kenne Duncan, Chief Thundersky, "Champion, Jr."

D: John English

SP: Norman S. Hall

P: Armand Schaefer

2265. FANCY PANTS

(Paramount, September, 1950)   92 Mins.

(Technicolor)

Bob Hope, Lucille Ball, Bruce Cabot, Jack Kirkwood,

Indian Territory (Columbia, 1950) — Gene Autry, Charles Stevens, and Pat Buttram

Lea Penman, Hugo French, Eric Blore, Joseph Vitale, John Anderson

D: George Marshall
S: Harry Leon Wilson
SP: Edmund Hartman, Robert O'Brien
P: Robert Welch

2266. FRISCO TORNADO

(Republic, October 1, 1950)   60 Mins.

Allan Lane, Eddy Waller, Martha Hyer, Stephen Chase, Ross Ford, Mauritz Hugo, Lane Bradford, Hal Price, Rex Lease, George Chesebro, Edmund Cobb, Bud Geary, "Black Jack"

D: R. G. Springsteen
SP: M. Coates Webster
P: Gordon Kay

2267. READY TO RIDE

(Universal-International, October 5, 1950)   25 Mins.

Tex Williams, Smokey Rogers, Deuce Spriggins, Donna Martell, Ann Pearce, Felipe Turich, Harry Lauter, Holly Bane, Edmund Cobb, Harry Vijar

D/P: Will Cowan
SP: Joseph O'Donnell

2268. BORDER RANGERS

(Lippert, October 6, 1950)   57 Mins.

Don Barry, Robert Lowery, Wally Vernon, Pamela Blake, Lyle Talbot, Claude Stroud, Ezelle Poule, Bill Kennedy, Paul Jordon, Alyn Lockwood, John Merton, Tom Monroe, George Keymas, Tom Kennedy, Eric Norden, Bud Osborne

D: William Berke
SP: Victor West, William Berke
P: William Berke, Murray Lerner

2269. COPPER CANYON

(Paramount, October 6, 1950)   83 Mins.
(Technicolor)

Ray Milland, Hedy Lamarr, Macdonald Carey, Mona Freeman, Harry Carey, Jr., Frank Faylen, Hope Emerson, Taylor Holmes, Peggy Knudsen, James Burke, Percy Helton, Philip Van Zandt, Francis Pierlot, Erno Verebes, Paul Lees, Robert Watson, Georgia Backus, Ian Wolfe, Bob Kortman

D: John Farrow
S: John English
SP: Jonathan Latimer
P: Mel Epstein

2270. CHEROKEE UPRISING

(Monogram, October 8, 1950)   55 Mins.

Whip Wilson, Andy Clyde, Lois Hall, Iron Eyes Cody, Sam Flint, Forrest Taylor, Marshall Reed, Chief Yowlachie, Lee Roberts, Stanley Price, Lyle Talbot, Edith Mills

D: Lewis Collins
SP: Dan Ullman
P: Vincent M. Fennelly

2271. RIO GRANDE PATROL

(RKO, October 21, 1950)   60 Mins.

Tim Holt, Richard Martin, Jane Nigh, Douglas Fowley, Cleo Moore, Tom Tyler, Rick Vallin, John Holland, Larry Johns, Harry Harvey, Forrest Burns

D: Lesley Selander
SP: Norman Houston
P: Herman Schlom

2272. RUSTLERS ON HORSEBACK

(Republic, October 23, 1950)   60 Mins.

Allan Lane, Eddy Waller, Roy Barcroft, Claudia Barrett, John Eldredge, George Nader, Forrest Taylor, John Cason, Stuart Randall, Douglas Evans, Tom Monroe, "Black Jack"

D: Fred C. Brannon
SP: Richard Wormser
AP: Gordon Kay

2273. TALES OF THE WEST #3

(Universal-International, October 30, 1950)

(A two-story feature made up of the shorts *Rustlers' Ransom* [1950] and *Gold Strike* [1950])

Tex Williams, Duece Spriggins, Smokey Rogers, Shirlee Allard, Jack Ingram, Fred Kohler, Jr., Bob Anderson, James Linn

D/P: Will Cowan
SP: Joseph O'Donnell

2274. RAIDERS OF TOMAHAWK CREEK

(Columbia, October, 1950)   55 Mins.

(*Durango Kid* Series)

Charles Starrett, Smiley Burnette, Edgar Dearing, Kay Buckley, Billy Kimbley, Paul Marion, Paul McGuire, Bill Hale, Ted Mapes, Lee Morgan

D: Fred F. Sears
S: Robert Schaefer
SP: Barry Shipman
P: Colbert Clark

2275. TWO FLAGS WEST

(20th C. Fox, November 1, 1950)   92 Mins.

Joseph Cotten, Linda Darnell, Jeff Chandler, Cornel Wilde, Dale Robertson, Jay C. Flippen, Noah Beery, Jr., Harry Von Zell, John Sands, Arthur Hunnicutt, Jack Lee, Robert Adler, Harry Carter, Ferris Taylor, Sally Corner, Everett Glass, Mar-

Frisco Tornado (Republic, 1950) — Allan "Rocky" Lane, Ross Ford, and Eddy Waller

394

jorie Bennett, Lee MacGregor, Roy Gordon, Aurora Castillo, Stanley Andrews, Don Garner
D: Robert Wise
S: Frank S. Nugent, Curtis Kenyon
SP/P: Casey Robinson

2276. BORDER OUTLAWS

(United International/Eagle Lion,
  November 2, 1950) 59 Mins.
Spade Cooley, Maria Hart, Bill Edwards, Bill Kennedy, George Slocum, John Laurenz, Douglas Wood, Bud Osborne, John Carpenter, Metzetti Brothers (including Richard Talmadge)
D: Richard Talmadge
SP: Arthur Hoerl
P: Jack Schwarz, Richard Talmadge

2277. ROCKY MOUNTAIN

(Warner Bros., November 11, 1950) 83 Mins.
Errol Flynn, Patrice Wymore, Scott Forbes, Guinn "Big Boy" Williams, Dick Jones, Howard Petrie, Slim Pickens, Chubby Johnson, Buzz Henry, Sheb Wooley, Peter Coe, Rush Williams, Steve Dunhill, Alex Sharpe, Yakima Canutt, Nakai Snez
D: William Keighley
S: Alan LeMay
SP: Winston Miller, Alan LeMay

2278. NORTH OF THE GREAT DIVIDE

(Republic, November 15, 1950) 67 Mins.
(Trucolor)
Roy Rogers, Penny Edwards, Gordon Jones, Roy Barcroft, Jack Lambert, Douglas Evans, Keith Richards, Noble Johnson, Iron Eyes Cody, Foy Willing and the Riders of the Purple Sage, "Trigger"
D: William Witney
SP: Eric Taylor
AP: Eddy White

2279. RIO GRANDE

(Argosy/Republic, November 15, 1950) 105 Mins.
John Wayne, Maureen O'Hara, Claude Jarman, Jr., Ben Johnson, Harry Carey, Jr., Chill Wills, J. Carrol Naish, Victor McLaglen, Grant Withers, Peter Ortiz, Steve Pendleton, Karolyn Grimes, Pat Wayne, Alberto Morin, Stan Jones, Fred Kennedy, Sons of the Pioneers (Ken Curtis, Hugh Farr, Karl Farr, Lloyd Perryman, Shug Fisher, Tommy Doss), Chuck Roberson, Jack Pennick, Cliff Lyons
D: John Ford
Second-Unit D: Cliff Lyons
S: James Warner Bellah
SP: James Kevin McGuinness
P: John Ford, Merian C. Cooper

2280. ROGUE RIVER

(Ventura Pictures/Eagle Lion, November 15, 1950)
  84 Mins.
(Cinecolor)
Rory Calhoun, Peter Graves, Frank Felton, Ralph Sanford, George Stern, Ellye Marshall, Roy Engel, Jane Liddell, Robert Rose, Stephen Roberts, Duke York
D: John Rawlins
SP: Louis Lantz
P: Frank Melford

2281. UNDER MEXICALI STARS

(Republic, November 20, 1950) 67 Mins.
Rex Allen, Dorothy Patrick, Roy Barcroft, Buddy Ebsen, Percy Helton, Walter Coy, Steve Darrell, Alberto Morin, Ray Walker, Frank Ferguson, Stanley Andrews, Robert Bice, "Koko"
D: George Blair
SP:Bob Williams
AP: Melville Tucker

2282. THE TEXAN MEETS CALAMITY JANE

(Columbia, November 15, 1950) 71 Mins.
(Cinecolor)
Evelyn Ankers, James Ellison, Lee "Lasses" White, Ruth Whitney, Jack Ingram, Frank Pharr, Sally Weidman, Rudy de Saxe, Ferrell Lester, Paul Barney, Ronald Marriott, Walter Strand, Hugh Hooker, Bill Orisman, Lou W. Pierce, Elmer Herzberg, Ray Jones
D/SP/P: Ande Lamb

2283. THE BLAZING SUN

(Columbia, November 20, 1950) 70 Mins.
(Sepiatone)
Gene Autry, Pat Buttram, Lynne Roberts, Anne Gwynne, Edward Norris, Kenne Duncan, Alan Hale, Jr., Gregg Barton, Steve Darrell, Tom London, Sandy Sanders, Frankie Marvin, Bob Woodward, Boyd Stockman, Lewis Martin, Virginia Carroll, Sam Flint, Chris Allen, Charles Coleman, Pat O'Malley, Almira Sessions, Nolan Leary, "Champion, Jr."
D: John English
SP: Jack Townley
P: Armand Schaefer

2284. KANSAS RAIDERS

(Universal-International, November 20, 1950)
  80 Mins.
(Technicolor)
Audie Murphy, Brian Donlevy, Marguerite Chapman, Scott Brady, Tony Curtis, Richard Arlen, Richard Long, James Best, John Kellogg, Dewey Martin, George Chandler, Charles Delaney, Richard Egan, David Wolfe

D: Ray Enright
SP: Robert L. Richards
P: Ted Richmond

2285. THE MISSOURIANS

(Republic, November 25, 1950)   60 Mins.
Monte Hale, Paul Hurst, Roy Barcroft, Lyn Thomas,
Howard J. Negley, Robert Neil, Lane Bradford,
John Hamilton, Sarah Padden, Charles Williams,
Perry Ivans
D: George Blair
SP: Arthur E. Orloff
AP: Melville Tucker

2286. OUTLAW GOLD

(Monogram, November 26, 1950)   56 Mins.
Johnny Mack Brown, Jane Adams, Myron Healey,
Milburn Morante, Marshall Reed, Hugh Prosser,
Carol Henry, Bud Osborne, George DeNormand,
Frank Jacquet, Carl Mathews, Ray Jones, Steve
Clark, Bob Woodward, Merrill McCormack
D: Wallace Fox
SP: Jack Lewis
P: Vincent M. Fennelly

2287. OUTLAWS OF TEXAS

(Monogram, December 10, 1950)   56 Mins.
Whip Wilson, Andy Clyde, Phyllis Coates, Terry
Frost, Tommy Farrell, Zon Murray, George De-
Normand, Steve Carr, Stanley Price
D: Thomas Carr
SP: Dan Ullman
P: Vincent M. Fennelly

2288. LIGHTNING GUNS

(Columbia, December 10, 1950)   55 Mins.
(*Durango Kid* Series)
Charles Starrett, Smiley Burnette, Gloria Henry,
William Norton Bailey, Edgar Dearing, Raymond
Bond, Jock O'Mahoney, Chuck Roberson, Frank
Griffin, Joel Friedkin, George Chesebro, Merrill
McCormack
D: Fred Sears
SP: Victor Arthur
P: Colbert Clark

2289. CALIFORNIA PASSAGE

(Republic, December 15, 1950)   90 Mins.
Forrest Tucker, Adele Mara, Estelita Rodriguez, Jim
Davis, Peter Miles, Charles Kemper, Bill Williams,
Rhys Williams, Paul Fix, Francis McDonald, Eddy
Waller, Charles Stevens, Iron Eyes Cody, Alan
Bridge, Ruth Brennan
D: Joseph Kane
SP: James Edward Grant
AP: Joseph Kane

2290. TRAIL OF ROBIN HOOD

(Republic, December 15, 1950)   67 Mins.
(Trucolor)
Roy Rogers, Penny Edwards, Gordon Jones, Jack
Holt, Emory Parnell, Clifton Young, James Magill,
Carol Nugent, George Chesebro, Edward Cas-
sidy, Foy Willing and the Riders of the Purple
Sage, "Trigger" and guest stars Tom Tyler, Ker-
mit Maynard, Ray Corrigan, Tom Keene, Monte
Hale, Rex Allen, Allan Lane, William Farnum
D: William Witney
SP: Gerald Geraghty
AP: Eddy White

2291. CALL OF THE KLONDIKE

(Monogram, December 17, 1950)   67 Mins.
Kirby Grant, Anne Gwynne, Lynne Roberts, Tom
Neal, Russell Simpson, Marc Krah, Paul Bryar,
Pat Gleason, Duke York, "Chinook" (the Won-
der Dog)
D: Frank McDonald
S: James Oliver Curwood
SP: Charles Lang
P: Lindsley Parsons, William F. Broidy

2292. BANDIT QUEEN

(Lippert, December 22, 1950)   70 Mins.
Barbara Britton, Willard Parker, Philip Reed, Barton
MacLane, Martin Garralaga, John Merton, Jack
Ingram, Victor Kilian, Thurston Hall, Anna De-
metrio, Paul Martin, Pepe Hern, Lalo Rios, Jack
Perrin, Cecile Weston, Carl Pitti, Hugh Hooker,
Mike Conrad, Elias Gamboa, Chuck Roberson,
Trina Varela, Nancy Laurenz, Minna Philips,
Margia Dean, Felipe Turich, Joe Dominguez, Roy
Butler
D: William Berke
S: Victor West
SP: Victor West, Budd Lesser
P: William Berke, Murray Lerner

2293. DESPERADOES OF THE WEST

(Republic, December 23, 1950)   12 Chaps.
Richard Powers (Tom Keene), Judy Clark, Roy Bar-
croft, I. Stanford Jolley, Lee Phelps, Lee Roberts,
Cliff Clark, Edmund Cobb, Hank Patterson, Dale
Van Sickel, Tom Steele, Sandy Sanders, John
Cason, Guy Teague, Bud Osborne, Stanley Bly-
stone, Chuck Hayward, Bert LeBaron, Frank
O'Connor, George Chesebro, Art Dillard, Holly
Bane, Duke Taylor, Cactus Mack, Ken Cooper,
Dennis Moore, Steve Clark, Chick Hannon, Mau-
ritz Hugo, Jack Harden, Ace Hudkins, Al Taylor,
Bob Reeves, Tom McDonough, Eddie Parker,
John Daheim, Paul Gustine, Fred Kohler, Jr.,
Ralph Bucko, Harold Goodwin, Jack Ingram, Jim
Rinehart, Billy Dix, Ray Morgan, Wayne Burson,
Augie Gomez, Merrill McCormack, Joe Phillips

D: Fred C. Brannon
SP: Ronald Davidson
AP: Franklin Adreon (sometimes spelled Franklyn)
Chapter Titles: (1) Tower of Jeopardy, (2) Perilous Barrier, (3) Flaming Cargo, (4) Trail of Terror, (5) Plunder Cave, (6) Six-Gun Hijacker, (7) The Powder Keg, (8) Desperate Venture, (9) Stagecoach to Eternity, (10) Hidden Desperado, (11) Open Warfare, (12) Desperate Gamble

2294. SHORT GRASS

(Allied Artists, December 24, 1950) 82 Mins.
Rod Cameron, Cathy Downs, Johnny Mack Brown, Raymond Walburn, Alan Hale, Jr., Morris Ankrum, Jonathan Hale, Harry Woods, Marlo Dwyer, Riley Hill, Jeff York, Stanley Andrews, Jack Ingram, Myron Healey, Tris Coffin, Rory Mallison, Felipe Turich, George J. Lewis, Lee Tung Foo, Kermit Maynard
D: Lesley Selander
S/SP: Tom W. Blackburn
P: Scott R. Dunlap

2295. FRONTIER OUTPOST

(Columbia, December 29, 1950) 55 Mins.
(*Durango Kid* Series)
Charles Starrett, Smiley Burnette, Lois Hall, Steve Darrell, Fred Sears, Bob Wilke, Paul Campbell, Jock Mahoney, Bud Osborne, Chuck Roberson, Pierre Watkin, Dick Wessell, Hank Penny, Slim Duncan
D: Ray Nazarro
SP: Barry Shipman
P: Colbert Clark

2296. DALLAS

(Warner Bros., December 30, 1950) 94 Mins.
(Technicolor)
Gary Cooper, Ruth Roman, Steve Cochran, Raymond Massey, Barbara Payton, Leif Erickson, Antonio Moreno, Jerome Cowan, Reed Hadley, Gil Donaldson, Zon Murray, Will Wright, Monte Blue, Byron Keith, Jose Dominguez, Steve Dunhill
D: Stuart Heisler
SP: John Twist
P: Anthony Veiller

FILMS OF 1951

2297. FRENCHIE

(Universal-International, January 1, 1951) 81 Mins.
(Technicolor)
Joel McCrea, Shelley Winters, Paul Kelly, Elsa Lanchester, Marie Windsor, John Russell, John Emery, George Cleveland, Regis Toomey, Paul E. Burns, Frank Ferguson, Vincent Renno, Larry Dobkin, Lucille Barkley
D: Louis King
S/SP: Oscar Brodney
P: Michel Kraike

2298. STAGE TO TUCSON

(Columbia, January 1, 1951) 82 Mins.
(Technicolor)
Rod Cameron, Wayne Morris, Kay Buckley, Sally Eilers, Carl Benton Reid, Roy Roberts, Harry Bellaver, Douglas Fowley, John Pickard, Olin Howlin, Boyd Stockman, John Sheehan, Reed Howes, James Kirkwood
D: Ralph Murphy
S: Frank Bonham
SP: Bob Williams, Frank Burt, Robert Libott
P: Harry Joe Brown

2299. SIERRA PASSAGE

(Monogram, January 7, 1951) 81 Mins.
Wayne Morris, Lola Albright, Lloyd Corrigan, Alan Hale, Jr., Roland Winters, Jim Bannon, Billy Gray, Paul McGuire, Richard Karlan, George Eldridge
D: Frank McDonald
SP: Tom W. Blackburn, Warren D. Wandberg, Sam Rosca
P: Lindsley Parsons

2300. THREE DESPERATE MEN

(Lippert, January 12, 1951) 71 Mins.
Preston Foster, Jim Davis, Virginia Grey, Ross Latimer, Monte Blue, Sid Melton, Rory Mallison, John Brown, Margaret Seddon, House Peters, Jr., Joel Newfield, Lee Bennett, Steve Belmont, Carol Henry, Kermit Maynard, Bert Dillard, Gene Randall, Milton Kibbee, William N. Bailey
D: Sam Newfield
S/SP: Orville Hampton
P: Sigmund Neufeld

2301. COLORADO AMBUSH

(Monogram, January 14, 1951) 51 Mins.
Johnny Mack Brown, Myron Healey, Lois Hall, Tommy Farrell, Christie McIntyre, Lee Roberts,

Marshall Bradford, Lyle Talbot, Joe McGuinn, John Hart, Roy Butler, George DeNormand
D: Lewis Collins
SP: Myron Healey
P: Vincent M. Fennelly

2302. PRAIRIE ROUNDUP
(Columbia, January 15, 1951)   55 Mins.
Charles Starrett, Smiley Burnette, Mary Castle, Frank Fenton, Lane Chandler, Frank Sully, Paul Campbell, Forrest Taylor, Don Harvey, George Baxter, John Cason, Al Wyatt, Glenn Thompson, Ace Richman, Alan Sears, The Sunshine Boys
D: Fred F. Sears
SP: Joseph O'Donnell
P: Colbert Clark

2303. BELLE LE GRANDE
(Republic, January 27, 1951)   90 Mins.
Vera Ralston, John Carroll, William Ching, Muriel Lawrence, Hope Emerson, John Qualen, Henry (Harry) Morgan, Stephen Chase, Charles Cane
D: Allan Dwan
S: Peter B. Kyne
SP: D. D. Beauchamp
P: Herbert J. Yates

2304. GENE AUTRY AND THE MOUNTIES
(Columbia, January 30, 1951)   70 Mins.
(Sepiatone)
Gene Autry, Pat Buttram, Elena Verdugo, Carleton Young, Richard Emory, Herbert Rawlinson, Trevor Bardette, Francis McDonald, Jim Frasher, Gregg Barton, House Peters, Jr., Jody Gilbert, Nolan Leary, Boyd Stockman, Bruce Carruthers, Robert Hilton, Teddy Infuhr, Billy Gray, John R. McKee, Roy Butler, Steven Elliott, Chris Allen, "Champion, Jr."
D: John English
SP: Norman S. Hall
P: Armand Schaefer

2305. ROUGH RIDERS OF DURANGO
(Republic, January 30, 1951)   60 Mins.
Allan Lane, Walter Baldwin, Aline Towne, Steve Darrell, Ross Ford, Denver Pyle, Stuart Randall, Hap Price, Tom London, Russ Whiteman, Dale Van Sickel, Bob Burns, "Black Jack"
D: Fred C. Brannon
SP: M. Coates Webster
AP: Gordon Kay

2306. TALES OF THE WEST #4
(Universal-International, January 30, 1951)   54 Mins.
(A two-story feature made up of the shorts *Western Courage* [1950] and *Ready to Ride* [1950])
Tex Williams, Smokey Rogers, Deuce Spriggins,

Donna Martell, Ann Pearce, Felipe Turich, Harry Lauter, Holly Bane, Edmund Cobb, Harry Vijar
D/P: Will Cowan
SP: Joseph O'Donnell

2307. KING OF THE BULLWHIP
(Western Adventure, February 1, 1951)   59 Mins.
Lash LaRue, Al St. John, Jack Holt, Tom Neal, Anne Gwynne, Michael Whalen, Willis Houck, George J. Lewis, Dennis Moore, Cliff Taylor, Frank Jacquet, Tex Cooper, Hugh Hooker, Jimmie Martin, Roy Butler
D/P: Ron Ormond
SP: Jack Lewis, Ira Webb

2308. TOMAHAWK
(Universal-International, February 1, 1951)   82 Mins.
(Technicolor)
Van Heflin, Yvonne De Carlo, Preston Foster, Jack Oakie, Tom Tully, Susan Cabot, Alex Nicol, John War Eagle, Rock Hudson, Arthur Space, Russell Conway, Ann Doran, Stuart Randall
D: George Sherman
SP: Silvia Richards, Maurice Geraghty
P: Leonard Goldstein

2309. SPOILERS OF THE PLAINS
(Republic, February 2, 1951)   68 Mins.
Roy Rogers, Penny Edwards, Gordon Jones, Grant Withers, Fred Kohler, Jr., William Forrest, Don Haggerty, House Peters, Jr., George Meeker, Keith Richards, Foy Willing and the Riders of the Purple Sage, "Trigger"
D: William Witney
SP: Sloan Nibley
AP: Eddy White

2310. ABILENE TRAIL
(Monogram, February 4, 1951)   54 Mins.
Whip Wilson, Andy Clyde, Tommy Farrell, Steve Clark, Noel Neill, Dennis Moore, Marshall Reed, Lee Roberts, Milburn Morante, Ted Adams, Bill Kennedy, Stanley Price, Lyle Talbot
D: Lewis Collins
SP: Harry Fraser
P: Vincent M. Fennelly

2311. VENGEANCE VALLEY
(MGM, February 16, 1951)   83 Mins.
(Technicolor)
Burt Lancaster, Robert Walker, Joanne Dru, Sally Forrest, John Ireland, Ted de Corsia, Carleton Carpenter, Ray Collins, Hugh O'Brian, Will Wright, Grace Mills, James Hayward, James Harrison, Stanley Andrews, Glenn Strange, Bob Wilke, Al Ferguson, Monte Montague, Dan

White, Paul E. Burns, John R. McKee, Tom Fadden, Roy Butler, Margaret Bert, Norman Leavitt, Harvey Dunn
D: Richard Thorpe
S: Luke Short
SP: Irving Ravetch
P: Nicholas Nayfack

2312. THE GREAT MISSOURI RAID
(Paramount, February 22, 1951) 83 Mins.
(Technicolor)
Wendell Corey, MacDonald Carey, Ellen Drew, Ward Bond, Bruce Bennett, Bill Williams, Anne Revere, Edgar Buchanan, Lois Chastland, Louis Jean Heydt, Barry Kelly, James Millican, Guy Wilkerson, Ethan Laidlaw, Tom Tyler, Paul Fix, James Griffith, Whit Bissell, Steve Pendleton, Paul Lees, Bob Brey, Alan Wells
D: Gordon Douglas
S/SP: Frank Gruber
P: Nat Holt

2313. RIDIN' THE OUTLAW TRAIL
(Columbia, February 23, 1951) 56 Mins.
(*Durango Kid* Series)
Charles Starrett, Smiley Burnette, Sunny Vickers, Jim Bannon, Edgar Dearing, Peter Thompson, Lee Morgan, Chuck Roberson, Ethan Laidlaw, Pee Wee King and his Golden West Cowboys
D: Fred F. Sears
SP: Victor Arthur
P: Colbert Clark

2314. LAW OF THE BADLANDS
(RKO, February 24, 1951) 60 Mins.
Tim Holt, Richard Martin, Joan Dixon, Robert Livingston, Leonard Penn, Harry Woods, Larry Johns, Robert Bray, Kenneth MacDonald, John Cliff, Sam Lufkin, Danny Sands, Art Felix, Booger McCarthy
D: Lesley Selander
SP: Ed Earl Repp
P: Herman Schlom

2315. NIGHT RIDERS OF MONTANA
(Republic, February 28, 1951) 60 Mins.
Allan Lane, Chubby Johnson, Claudia Barrett, Roy Barcroft, Arthur Space, Myron Healey, Mort Thompson, Marshall Reed, Lane Bradford, Lester Dorr, Ted Adams, George Chesebro, Don Harvey, Zon Murray
D: Fred C. Brannon
SP: M. Coates Webster
AP: Gordon Kay

2316. AL JENNINGS OF OKLAHOMA
(Columbia, March 1, 1951) 79 Mins.
(Technicolor)
Dan Duryea, Gale Storm, Dick Foran, Gloria Henry, Guinn "Big Boy" Williams, Raymond Greenleaf, Stanley Andrews, James Millican, Harry Shannon, Helen Brown, Robert Phillips, John Dehner, Charles Meredith
D: Ray Nazarro
S: Al Jennings, Will Irwin
SP: George Bricker
P: Rudolph C. Flothow

2317. THE REDHEAD AND THE COWBOY
(Paramount, March 1, 1951) 82 Mins.
Glenn Ford, Edmond O'Brien, Rhonda Fleming, Alan Reed, Morris Ankrum, Edith Evanson, Perry Ivans, Janine Perreau, Douglas Spencer, Ray Teal, Ralph Byrd, King Donovan, Tom Moore
D: Leslie Fenton
S: Charles Marquis Warren
SP: Jonathan Latimer, Liam O'Brien
P: Irving Asher

2318. SILVER CITY BONANZA
(Republic, March 1, 1951) 67 Mins.
Rex Allen, Buddy Ebsen, Mary Ellen Kay, Billy Kimbley, Alix Ebsen, Bill Kennedy, Gregg Barton, Clem Bevins, Frank Jenks, Hank Patterson, Harry Lauter, Harry Harvey, "Koko"
D: George Blair
SP: Bob Williams
AP: Melville Tucker

2319. SUGARFOOT
(Warner Bros., March 3, 1951) 80 Mins.
(Technicolor)
Randolph Scott, Adele Jergens, Raymond Massey, S. Z. Sakall, Robert Warwick, Hugh Sanders, Hope Landin, Hank Worden, Gene Evans, Arthur Hunnicutt, Edward Hearn, John Hamilton, Cliff Clark, Kenneth MacDonald, Dan White, Paul Newland, Philo McCullough
D: Edwin L. Marin
S: Clarence Buddington Kelland
SP: Russell Hughes
P: Saul Elkins

2320. OH SUSANNA
(Republic, March 3, 1951) 90 Mins.
(Trucolor)
Rod Cameron, Adrian Booth, Forrest Tucker, Chill Wills, William Ching, Jim Davis, Wally Cassell, Douglas Kennedy, James Lydon, William Haade, John Compton, James Flavin, Charles Stevens, Alan Bridge, Marion Randolph, Marshall Reed, John Pickard, Ruth Brennan, Louise Kane

D/AP: Joseph Kane
SP: Charles Marquis Warren

2321. MAN FROM SONORA
(Monogram, March 11, 1951) 54 Mins.
Johnny Mack Brown, Phyllis Coates, Lyle Talbot,
    House Peters, Jr., Lee Roberts, John Merton,
    Stanley Price, Dennis Moore, Ray Jones, Pierce
    Lyden, Sam Flint, George DeNormand
D: Lewis Collins
SP: Maurice Tombragel
P: Vincent M. Fennelly

2322. MY OUTLAW BROTHER
(Eagle Lion Classics, March 15, 1951) 82 Mins.
Mickey Rooney, Wanda Hendrix, Robert Preston,
    Robert Stack, Carlos Muzquiz, Jose Tervay, Fer-
    nando Waggner, Felipe Flores, Hilda Moreno
D: Elliott Nugent
S: "South of the Rio Grande"—Max Brand
SP: Gene Fowler, Jr., Albert L. Levitt
P: Benedict Bogeaus

2323. FORT SAVAGE RAIDERS
(Columbia, March 15, 1951) 54 Mins.
(*Durango Kid* Series)
Charles Starrett, Smiley Burnette, John Dehner,
    Trevor Bardette, Peter Thompson, Fred Sears,
    John Cason, Frank Griffin, Sam Flint, Dusty
    Walker
D: Ray Nazarro
SP: Barry Shipman
P: Colbert Clark

2324. TEXANS NEVER CRY
(Columbia, March 15, 1951) 70 Mins.
(Sepiatone)
Gene Autry, Pat Buttram, Mary Castle, Gail Davis,
    Russell Hayden, Richard Powers (Tom Keene),
    Don Harvey, Roy Gordon, Michael Ragan (Holly
    Bane), Frank Fenton, Sandy Sanders, John R.
    McKee, Harry McKim, Minerva Urecal, Richard
    Flato, I. Stanford Jolley, Duke York, Roy Cutler,
    "Champion, Jr."
D: Frank McDonald
SP: Norman S. Hall
P: Armand Schaefer

2325. HEART OF THE ROCKIES
(Republic, March 30, 1951) 67 Mins.
Roy Rogers, Penny Edwards, Gordon Jones, Ralph
    Morgan, Fred Graham, Mira McKinney, Robert
    "Buzz" Henry, William Gould, Pete Hern, Rand
    Brooks, Foy Willing and the Riders of the Purple
    Sage, "Trigger"
D: William Witney
SP: Eric Taylor
AP: Eddy White

2326. THE BATTLE OF APACHE PASS
(Universal-International, April 1, 1951) 85 Mins.
(Technicolor)
John Lund, Jeff Chandler, Beverly Tyler, Susan
    Cabot, Bruce Cowling, John Hudson, James Best,
    Regis Toomey, Richard Egan, Hugh O'Brian,
    Palmer Lee, William Reynolds, Jay Silverheels,
    Tommy Cook, Jack Elam, Richard Garland, Jack
    Ingram, John Baer, Paul Smith
D: George Sherman
S/SP: Gerald Drayson Adams
P: Leonard Goldstein

2327. SANTA FE
(Columbia, April 1, 1951) 89 Mins.
(Technicolor)
Randolph Scott, Janis Carter, Jerome Courtland,
    Peter Thompson, John Archer, Warner Ander-
    son, Roy Roberts, Billy House, Olin Howlin, Al-
    lene Roberts, Jock O'Mahoney, Harry Cording,
    Sven Hugo Borg, Frank Ferguson, Irving Pichel,
    Harry Tyler, Chief Thunder Cloud, Paul E. Burns,
    Reed Howes, Charles Meredith, Paul Stanton,
    Richard Cramer, William Haade, Francis McDon-
    ald, Frank O'Connor, Harry Tenbrook, James
    Mason, Guy Wilkerson, Frank Hagney, William
    Tannen, James Kirkwood, Stanley Blystone, Ed-
    gar Dearing, Al Kunde, Art Loeb, Blackie White-
    ford, Bud Fine, Richard Fortune, Lane Chandler,
    Charles Evans, Chuck Hamilton, George Sher-
    wood, Louis Mason, Roy Butler, Ralph Sanford,
    William McCormack
D: Irving Pichel
S: Louis Stevens from the novel by James Marshall
SP: Kenneth Hamet
P: Harry Joe Brown

2328. BADMAN'S GOLD
(Eagle Lion Classics, April 3, 1951) 56 Mins.
Johnny Carpenter, Alyn Lockwood, Emmett Lynn,
    Verne Teters, Troy Terrell, Kenne Duncan, Jack
    Daly, "Daish" (a dog)
D/P: Robert Tansey
SP: Robert Emmett (Tansey), Alyn Lockwood

2329. WANTED DEAD OR ALIVE
(Frontier Pictures/Monogram, April 3, 1951)
    59 Mins.
Whip Wilson, Fuzzy Knight, Jim Bannon, Christine
    McIntyre, Leonard Penn, Lane Bradford, Zon
    Murray, Marshall Reed, Stanley Price, Ray Jones,
    Jack O' Shea
D: Thomas Carr
SP: Clint Johnson
P: Vincent M. Fennelly

2330. RATON PASS

(Warner Bros., April 7, 1951)   84 Mins.

Dennis Morgan, Patricia Neal, Steve Cochran, Scott Forbes, Dorothy Hart, Basil Ruysdael, Louis J. Heydt, Roland Winters, James Burke, Elvira Curci, Carlos Conde, John Crawford, Rudolpho Hoyos, Jr.

D: Edwin L. Marin

S: Tom W. Blackburn

SP: Tom W. Blackburn, James R. Webb

2331. SADDLE LEGION

(RKO, April 7, 1951)   61 Mins.

Tim Holt, Dorothy Malone, Richard Martin, Robert Livingston, James Rush, Maurita Hugo, Cliff Clark, George J. Lewis, Dick Foote, Bob Wilke, Stanley Andrews, Movita Casteneda

D: Lesley Selander

SP: Ed Earl Repp

P: Herman Schlom

2332. THUNDER IN GOD'S COUNTRY

(Republic, April 8, 1951)   67 Mins.

Rex Allen, Mary Ellen Kay, Buddy Ebsen, Ian MacDonald, Paul Harvey, Harry Lauter, John Doucette, Harry Cheshire, John Ridgely, Frank Ferguson, Wilson Wood, "Koko"

D: George Blair

SP: Arthur E. Orloff

AP: Melville Tucker

2333. CANYON RAIDERS

(Monogram, April 8, 1951)   54 Mins.

Whip Wilson, Fuzzy Knight, Jim Bannon, Phyllis Coates, I. Stanford Jolley, Barbara Woodell, Marshall Reed, Riley Hill, Bill Kennedy

D: Lewis Collins

SP: Jay Gilgore

P: Vincent M. Fennelly

2333a. SO YOU WANT TO BE A COWBOY

(Warner Bros., April 14, 1951)   1 Reel

George O'Hanlon, Phyllis Coates

D: Richard L. Bare

2334. ONLY THE VALIANT

(Warner Bros., April 21, 1951)   105 Mins.

Gregory Peck, Barbara Payton, Ward Bond, Gig Young, Lon Chaney, Jr., Neville Brand, Jeff Corey, Warner Anderson, Steve Brodie, Dan Riss, Terry Kilburn, Herbert Heyes, Art Baker, Hugh Sanders, Michael Ansara, Nana Bryant

D: Gordon Douglas

S: Charles Marquis Warren

SP: Edmund H. North, Harry Brown

P: William Cagney

Canyon Raiders (Monogram, 1951) — Fuzzy Knight, Riley Hill, Whip Wilson, and Jim Bannon

2335. SKIPALONG ROSENBLOOM

(Eagle Lion Classics/United Artists,
April 30, 1951) 72 Mins.

Maxie Rosenbloom, Max Baer, Jackie Coogan,
Fuzzy Knight, Hillary Brooke, Jacqueline Fon-
taine, Raymond Hatton, Ray Walker, Sam Lee, Al
Shaw, Joseph Greene, Dewey Robinson, Whitey
Haupt, Carl Mathews, Artie Ortego

D: Sam Newfield
S: Eddie Forman
SP: Dean Reisner, Eddie Forman
P: Wally Kline

(Reissued in 1953 as *The Square Shooter*)

2336. WHIRLWIND

(Columbia, April, 1951) 70 Mins.
(Sepiatone)

Gene Autry, Smiley Burnette, Gail Davis, Thurston
Hall, Harry Lauter, Dick Curtis, Harry Harvey,
Gregg Barton, Tommy Ivo, Kenne Duncan, Al
Wyatt, Gary Goodwin, Pat O'Malley, Bud Os-
borne, Boyd Stockman, Frankie Marvin, Stan
Jones, Leon DeVoe, "Champion, Jr."

D: John English
SP: Norman S. Hall
P: Armand Schaefer

2337. BUCKAROO SHERIFF OF TEXAS

(Republic, May 1, 1951) 60 Mins.
(*Rough Ridin' Kids* Series)

Michael Chapin, Eilene Janssen, James Bell, Hugh
O'Brian, Steve Pendleton, Tris Coffin, William
Haade, Alice Kelly, Selmer Jackson, Edward Cas-
sidy, George Taylor, Steve Dunhill, Billy Dix,
Eddie Dunn

D: Philip Ford
SP: Arthur E. Orloff
AP: Rudy Ralston

2338. THE LAST OUTPOST

(Paramount, May 1, 1951) 89 Mins.
(Technicolor)

Ronald Reagan, Rhonda Fleming, Bruce Bennett,
Bill Williams, Noah Beery, Jr., Peter Hanson,
Hugh Beaumont, Lloyd Corrigan, John Ridgley,
Charles Evans, James Burke, John War Eagle,
Richard Crane, Ewing Mitchell

D: Lewis R. Foster
S: David Lang
SP: Geoffrey Holmes, George Worthington Yates,
Winston Miller
P: William H. Pine, William C. Thomas

2339. RAWHIDE

(20th C. Fox, May 1, 1951) 86 Mins.
Tyrone Power, Susan Hayward, Hugh Marlowe,
Dean Jagger, Edgar Buchanan, Jack Elam, George

Tobias, Jeff Corey, James Millican, Louis Jean
Heydt, William Haade, Milton R. Corey, Ken
Tobey

D: Henry Hathaway
S/SP: Dudley Nichols
P: Samuel G. Engel

2340. BLAZING BULLETS

(Frontier Pictures/Monogram, May 6, 1951)
51 Mins.

Johnny Mack Brown, Lois Hall, House Peters, Jr.,
Stanley Price, Dennis Moore, Edmund Cobb, Mil-
burn Morante, Forrest Taylor, Edward Cassidy,
George DeNormand, Carl Mathews

D: Wallace Fox
SP: George Daniels
P: Vincent M. Fennelly

2341. CAVALRY SCOUT

(Monogram, May 13, 1951) 78 Mins.
(Cinecolor)

Rod Cameron, Audrey Long, Jim Davis, James Millican, James Arness, John Doucette, William Phillips, Stephen Chase, Rory Mallison, Eddy Waller,
Paul Bryar

D: Lesley Selander
SP: Dan Ullman, Thomas Blackburn
P: Walter Mirisch

2342. WELLS FARGO GUNMASTER

(Republic, May 15, 1951) 60 Mins.

Allan Lane, Chubby Johnson, Mary Ellen Kay,
Michael Chapin, Roy Barcroft, Walter Reed, Stu-
art Randall, William Bakewell, George Meeker,
Anne O'Neal, James Craven, Forrest Taylor, Lee
Roberts, "Black Jack"

D: Philip Ford
SP: M. Coates Webster
AP: Gordon Kay

2343. IN OLD AMARILLO

(Republic, May 15, 1951) 67 Mins.

Roy Rogers, Estelita Rodriguez, Penny Edwards,
Pinky Lee, Roy Barcroft, Pierre Watkin, Ken
Howell, Elizabeth Risdon, William Holmes, Ker-
mit Maynard, Alan Bridge, Roy Rogers Riders,
"Trigger"

D: William Witney
SP: Sloan Nibley
AP: Eddy White

2344. NEW MEXICO

(United Artists, May 24, 1951) 76 Mins.
(AnscoColor)

Lew Ayres, Marilyn Maxwell, Andy Devine, Robert
Hutton, Raymond Burr, Jeff Corey, Lloyd Corrigan, Verna Felton, Ted de Corsia, John Hoyt,

Ronald Buka, Robert Osterloh, Ian MacDonald, William Tannen, Arthur Lowe, Jr.
D: Irving Reiss
S/SP: Max Trell
P: Irving Allen

2345. NEVADA BADMEN
(Frontier Pictures/Monogram, May 27, 1951)
58 Mins.
Whip Wilson, Fuzzy Knight, Jim Bannon, Phyllis Coates, I. Stanford Jolley, Marshall Reed, Riley Hill, Lee Roberts, Pierce Lyden, Bill Kennedy, Bud Osborne, Stanley Price, Artie Ortego, Carl Mathews
D: Lewis Collins
SP: Joseph O'Donnell
P: Vincent M. Fennelly

2346. SNAKE RIVER DESPERADOES
(Columbia, May 30, 1951)   54 Mins.
(*Durango Kid* Series)
Charles Starrett, Smiley Burnette, Don Reynolds, Tommy Ivo, Monte Blue, Boyd (Red) Morgan, George Chesebro, John Pickard, Charles Horvath, Sam Flint, Duke York
D: Fred F. Sears
SP: Barry Shipman
P: Colbert Clark

2347. WHEN THE REDSKINS RODE
(Columbia, May 30, 1951)   78 Mins.
(Super Cinecolor)
Jon Hall, Mary Castle, James Seay, Sherry Morland, Pedro De Cordoba, John Dehner, Lewis Russell, William Bakewell, Gregory Gay, Rusty Westcott, Milton Kibbee, Rick Vallin
D: Lew Landers
SP: Robert E. Kent
P: Sam Katzman

2348. APACHE DRUMS
(Universal-International, June 1, 1951)   75 Mins.
(Technicolor)
Stephen McNally, Coleen Gray, Willard Parker, Arthur Shields, James Griffith, Armando Silvestre, Georgia Backus, Clarence Muse, James Best, Ruthelma Stevens, Chinto Gusman, Ray Bennett
D: Hugo Fregonese
S: David Chandler
P: Val Lewton

2349. THE TEXAS RANGERS
(Columbia, June 1, 1951)   74 Mins.
(Super Cinecolor)
George Montgomery, Gale Storm, Jerome Courtland, Noah Beery, Jr., John Litel, William Bishop,

Douglas Kennedy, John Dehner, Ian MacDonald, John Doucette, Jock O'Mahoney, Joseph Fallon, Myron Healey, Julian Rivero, Trevor Bardette, Stanley Andrews, Edward Earle
D: Phil Karlson
S: Frank Gruber
SP: Richard Schayer
P: Edward Small

2350. ALONG THE GREAT DIVIDE
(Warner Bros., June 2, 1951)   88 Mins.
Kirk Douglas, Virginia Mayo, John Agar, Walter Brennan, Ray Teal, Hugh Sanders, Morris Ankrum, James Anderson, Charles Meredith
D: Raoul Walsh
S: Walter Doniger
SP: Walter Doniger, Lewis Meltzer
P: Anthony Veiller

2351. GUNPLAY
(RKO, June 7, 1951)   69 Mins.
Tim Holt, Joan Dixon, Richard Martin, Harper Carter, Mauritz Hugo, Robert Bice, Marshall Reed, Jack Hill, Robert Wilke, Leo MacMahon, Cornelius O'Keefe
D: Lesley Selander
SP: Ed Earl Repp
P: Herman Schlom

2352. BEST OF THE BADMEN
(RKO, June 9, 1951)   84 Mins.
(Technicolor)
Robert Ryan, Claire Trevor, Jack Buetel, Robert Preston, Walter Brennan, Bruce Cabot, John Archer, Lawrence Tierney, Barton MacLane, Tom Tyler, Bob Wilke, John Cliff, Lee MacGregor, Emmett Lynn, Carleton Young, Byron Foulger, William Tannen, Harry Woods, Everett Glass
D: William D. Russell
S: Robert Hardy Andrews
SP: Robert Hardy Andrews, John Twist
P: Herman Schlom

2353. LITTLE BIG HORN
(Lippert, June 18, 1951)   86 Mins.
Lloyd Bridges, Marie Windsor, John Ireland, Reed Hadley, Jim Davis, Wally Cassell, Hugh O'Brian, Sheb Wooley, King Donovan, Rodd Redwing, Richard Emory, John Pickard, Robert Sherwood, Larry Stewart, Richard Paxton, Barbara Woodell, Ted Avery, Anne Warren
D: Charles Marquis Warren
SP: Charles Marquis Warren, Harold Shumate
P: Carl K. Hittleman

2354. SILVER CANYON

(Columbia, June 20, 1951)   70 Mins.

(Sepiatone)

Gene Autry, Pat Buttram, Gail Davis, Jim Davis, Bob Steele, Edgar Dearing, Dick Alexander, Terry Frost, Peter Mamakos, Steve Clark, Stanley Andrews, Duke York, Eugene Borden, Bobby Clark, Frankie Marvin, Boyd Stockman, Sandy Sanders, Kenne Duncan, Bill Hale, Jack O'Shea, Frank Matts, Stanley Blystone, John Merton, Jack Pepper, Pat O'Malley, Martin Wilkins, Jim Magill, John R. McKee, "Champion, Jr."

D: John English

S: Alan James

SP: Gerald Geraghty

P: Armand Schaefer

2355. MONTANA DESPERADO

(Frontier Pictures/Monogram, June 24, 1951)   51 Mins.

Johnny Mack Brown, Virginia Herrick, Myron Healey, Marshall Reed, Steve Clark, Edmund Cobb, Lee Roberts, Carl Mathews, Ben Corbett

D: Wallace Fox

SP: Dan Ullman

P: Vincent M. Fennelly

2356. THE DAKOTA KID

(Republic, July 1, 1951)   60 Mins.

(*Rough Ridin' Kids* Series)

Michael Chapin, Eilene Janssen, James Bell, Danny Morton, Margaret Field, Robert Shayne, Roy Barcroft, Mauritz Hugo, House Peters, Jr., Lee Bennett, Michael Ragan (Holly Bane)

D: Philip Ford

SP: William Lively

AP: Rudy Ralston

2357. PASSAGE WEST

(Paramount, July 1, 1951)   80 Mins.

(Technicolor)

John Payne, Dennis O'Keefe, Arlene Whelan, Frank Faylen, Mary Anderson, Peter Hanson, Richard Rober, Griff Barnett, Dooley Wilson, Mary Field, Richard Travis, Mary Beth Hughes, Arthur Hunnicutt, Lillian Bronson, Ilka Gruning, Estelle Carr, Susan Whitney, Paul Fierro

D: Lewis R. Foster

S: Nedrick Young

SP: Lewis R. Foster

P: William Pine, William Thomas

2358. YUKON MANHUNT

(Monogram, July 8, 1951)   63 Mins.

Kirby Grant, Gail Davis, Margaret Field, Rand Brooks, Nelson Leigh, John Doucette, Paul McGuire, "Chinook" (a dog)

D: Frank McDonald

S: James Oliver Curwood

SP: Bill Raynor

P: Lindsley Parsons

2359. FORT WORTH

(Warner Bros., July 14, 1951)   80 Mins.

(Technicolor)

Randolph Scott, David Brian, Phyllis Thaxter, Helena Carter, Dick Jones, Ray Teal, Lawrence Tolan, Paul Picerni, Emerson Treacy, Bob Steele, Dick Jones, Walter Sande, Chubby Johnson

D: Edwin L. Marin

S/SP: John Twist

P: Anthony Veiller

2360. STAGECOACH DRIVER

(Frontier Pictures/Monogram, July 15, 1951)   52 Mins.

Whip Wilson, Fuzzy Knight, Jim Bannon, Gloria Winters, Lane Bradford, Barbara Allen, John Hart, Leonard Penn, Stanley Price, Marshall Reed, George DeNormand

D: Lewis Collins

SP: Joseph O'Donnell

P: Vincent M. Fennelly

2361. RODEO KING AND THE SENORITA

(Republic, July 15, 1951)   67 Mins.

Rex Allen, Mary Ellen Kay, Buddy Ebsen, Roy Barcroft, Tris Coffin, Bonnie DeSimone, Don Beddoe, Jonathan Hale, Harry Harvey, Rory Mallison, Joe Forte, Buff Brady, "Koko"

D: Philip Ford

SP: John K. Butler

AP: Melville Tucker

2362. BONANZA TOWN

(Columbia, July 26, 1951)   56 Mins.

(*Durango Kid* Series)

Charles Starrett, Smiley Burnette, Fred F. Sears, Luther Crockett, Myron Healey, Charles Hovarth, Ted Jordon, Al Wyatt, Marshall Reed, Vernon Dent, Slim Duncan

D: Fred F. Sears

SP: Barry Shipman, Bart Horswell

P: Colbert Clark

2363. CATTLE DRIVE

(Universal-International, August 1, 1951)   77 Mins.

(Technicolor)

Joel McCrea, Dean Stockwell, Chill Wills, Leon Ames, Henry Brandon, Howard Petrie, Bob Steele, Griff Barnett

D: Kurt Neumann

SP: Jack Natteford, Lillie Hayward

P: Aaron Rosenberg

2364. MARK OF THE RENEGADE

(Universal-International, August 1, 1951)
81 Mins.

Ricardo Montalban, Cyd Charisse, J. Carroll Naish, Gilbert Roland, Andrea King, Antonio Moreno, George Backus, Robert Warwick, Armando Silvestre, Bridget Carr, Alberto Morin, Dave Wolfe

D: Hugo Fregonese
S: Johnston McCulley
SP: Louis Solomon, Robert Hardy Andrews
P: Jack Cross

2365. THE SECRET OF CONVICT LAKE

(20th C. Fox, August 1, 1951)   83 Mins.

Glenn Ford, Gene Tierney, Ethel Barrymore, Zachary Scott, Ann Doran, Barbara Bates, Cyril Cusack, Richard Hylton, Helen Westcott, Jeanette Nolan, Ruth Donnelly, Harry Carter, Jack Lambert, Mary Carroll, Houseley Stevenson, Charles Flynn, David Post, Max Wagner, Raymond Greenleaf, William Leicester, Frances Enfield, Bernard Szold, Ray Teal, Tom London

D: Michael Gordon
S: Anna Hunger, Jack Pollexfen
SP: Oscar Paul, Victor Trivas
P: Frank P. Rosenberg

2366. THE THUNDERING TRAIL

(Western Adventure, August 1, 1951)

Lash LaRue, Al St. John, Sally Anglim, Archie Twitchell, Ray Bennett, Reed Howes, Bud Osborne, John Cason, Clarke Stevens, Jimmie Martin, Mary Lou Webb, Sue Hussey, Ray Broome, Cliff Taylor

D/P: Ron Ormond
SP: Alexander White

2367. WARPATH

(Paramount, August 1, 1951)   95 Mins.
(Technicolor)

Edmond O'Brien, Dean Jagger, Forrest Tucker, Harry Carey, Jr., Polly Bergen, James Millican, Wallace Ford, Paul Fix, Louis Jean Heydt, Paul Lees, Walter Sande, Charles Dayton, Robert Bray, Douglas Spencer, James Burke, Chief Yowlachie, John Mansfield, Monte Blue, Frank Ferguson, Cliff Clark, Paul Burns, Charles Stevens, John Hart

D: Byron Haskin
S/SP: Frank Gruber
P: Nat Holt

2368. CYCLONE FURY

(Columbia, August 19, 1951)   54 Mins.
(*Durango Kid* Series)

Charles Starrett, Smiley Burnette, Fred F. Sears, Clayton Moore, Bob Wilke, Louis Lettieri, George Chesebro, Frank O'Connor, Merle Travis and his Bronco Busters

D: Ray Nazarro
SP: Barry Shipman, Ed Earl Repp
P: Colbert Clark

2369. OKLAHOMA JUSTICE

(Monogram, August 19, 1951)

Johnny Mack Brown, James Ellison, Phyllis Coates, Barbara Allen, Kenne Duncan, Lane Bradford, Marshall Reed, Zon Murray, Stanley Price, I. Stanford Jolley, Bruce Edwards, Richard Avonde, Carl Mathews, Edward Cassidy, Lyle Talbot, George DeNormand

D: Lewis Collins
SP: Joseph O'Donnell
P: Vincent M. Fennelly

2370. FORT DODGE STAMPEDE

(Republic, August 24, 1951)   60 Mins.

Allan Lane, Chubby Johnson, Mary Ellen Kay, Roy Barcroft, Trevor Bardette, Bruce Edwards, Wesley Hudman, William Forrest, Chuck Roberson, Rory Mallison, Jack Ingram, Kermit Maynard, Frank O'Connor, "Black Jack"

D/AP: Harry Keller
SP: Richard Wormser

2371. PISTOL HARVEST

(RKO, August 30, 1951)   60 Mins.

Tim Holt, Richard Martin, Joan Dixon, Guy Edward Hearn, Mauritz Hugo, Robert Clarke, William (Billy) Griffith, Lee Phelps, Bob Wilke, Joan Freeman, Harper Carter, F. Herrick

D: Lesley Selander
SP: Norman Houston
P: Herman Schlom

2372. DON DAREDEVIL RIDES AGAIN

(Republic, September 1, 1951)   12 Chaps.

Ken Curtis, Aline Towne, Roy Barcroft, Lane Bradford, Robert Einer, John Cason, I. Stanford Jolley, Hank Patterson, Lee Phelps, Sandy Sanders, Guy Teague, Tom Steele, Mike Ragan, Cactus Mack, Art Dillard, Joe Phillips, Roy Bucko, Bud Osborne, Saul Gorss, Gene Stutenroth, James Magill, David Sharpe, Charles Horvath, Frank McCarroll, Dale Van Sickel, Jack Ingram, George Lloyd, Jack Harden, Carey Loftin, Art Dillard, Carlie Taylor, Forrest Taylor, Bert LeBaron, James Linn, Gene Christopher, Tony DeMario, Don Harvey, Frank Meredith, Tex Terry, Bob Reeves, Chick Hannon, Herman Hack

D: Fred D. Brannon
SP: Ronald Davidson
AP: Franklin Adreon (sometimes spelled Franklyn)
Chapter Titles: (1) Return of the Don, (2) Double

405

Death, (3) Hidden Danger, (4) Retreat to Destruction, (5) Cold Steel, (6) The Flaming Juggernaut, (7) Claim Jumper, (8) Perilous Combat, (9) Hostage of Destiny, (10) Marked for Murder, (11) The Captive Witness, (12) Flames of Vengeance

2372a. MERRY MAVERICKS

(Columbia, September 6, 1951)   2 Reels
(*Three Stooges* Series)
Moe Howard, Shemp Howard, Larry Fine, Mary Martin, Paul Campbell, Dan Harvey
D: Edward Bernds

2373. GOLD RAIDERS

(Schwarz/United Artists, September 14, 1951)
   56 Mins.
George O'Brien, The Three Stooges (Moe Howard, Shemp Howard, and Larry Fine), Sheila Ryan, Clem Bevins, Monte Blue, Lyle Talbot, John Merton, Al Baffert, Hugh Hooker, Bill Ward, Fuzzy Knight, Dick Crockett, Roy Canada
D: Edward Bernds
SP: Elwood Ullman (Daniel E. Ullman), William Lively
P: Jack Schwarz

2374. ARIZONA MANHUNT

(Republic, September 15, 1951)   60 Mins.
(*Rough Ridin' Kids* Series)
Michael Chapin, Eilene Janssen, James Bell, Lucille Barkley, Roy Barcroft, Hazel Shaw, John Baer, Harry Harvey, Stuart Randall, Ted Cooper
D: Fred C. Brannon
SP: William Lively
AP: Rudy Ralston

2375. BORDER FENCE

(Astor, September 15, 1951)   89 Mins.
Walt Wayne, Lee Morgan, Mary Nord, Steve Raines, Harry Garcia, LeRoy (Shug) Fisher, Frank Savage, Charles Clark, Frank Miller, Alvin Franke, Chester Scott, Jr., Ray Young, Jerry O'Dell and his Band
D: Norman Sheldo (Sheldon), H. W. Kier
SP: Norman Sheldo
P: H. W. Kier

2376. THE RED BADGE OF COURAGE

(MGM, September 28, 1951)   69 Mins.
Audie Murphy, Bill Mauldin, John Dierkes, Royal Dano, Arthur Hunnicutt, Tim Durant, Douglas Dick, Robert Easton Burke, Andy Devine, Smith Ballew
D: John Huston
S: Stephen Crane
SP: John Huston
Adaptor: Albert Band
P: Gottfried Reinhardt

2377. HILLS OF UTAH

(Columbia, September 30, 1951)   70 Mins.
(Sepiatone)
Gene Autry, Pat Buttram, Elaine Riley, Onslow Stevens, Denver Pyle, Donna Martell, William Fawcett, Harry Lauter, Tom London, Kenne Duncan, Sandy Sanders, Teddy Infuhr, Lee Morgan, Boyd Stockman, Billy Griffith, Tommy Ivo, Bob Woodward, Stanley Price, "Champion, Jr."
D: John English
S: Les Savage, Jr.
SP: Gerald Geraghty
P: Armand Schaefer

2378. HOT LEAD

(RKO, October 1, 1951)   60 Mins.
Tim Holt, Richard Martin, Joan Dixon, Ross Elliott, John Dehner, Paul Marion, Lee MacGregor, Stanley Andrews, Paul E. Burns, Bob Wilke, Kenneth MacDonald
D: Stuart Gilmore
SP: William Lively
P: Herman Schlom

2379. THE LADY FROM TEXAS

(Universal-International, October 1, 1951)
   77 Mins.
(Technicolor)
Howard Duff, Mona Freeman, Josephine Hull, Gene Lockhart, Craig Stevens, Ed Begley, Barbara Knudson, Lane Bradford, Chris-Pin Martin, Kenneth Patterson, Jay C. Flippen
D: Joseph Pevney
S: Harold Shumate
SP: Gerald Drayson Adams, Connie Lee Bennett
P: Leonard Goldstein

2380. WHISTLING HILLS

(Frontier Pictures/Monogram, October 7, 1951)
   58 Mins.
Johnny Mack Brown, Jimmy Ellison, Noel Neill, Lee Roberts, Pamela Duncan, I. Stanford Jolley, Marshall Reed, Bud Osborne, Pierce Lyden, Frank Ellis, Ray Jones, Merrill McCormack
D: Derwin Abrahams
SP: Fred Myton
P: Vincent M. Fennelly

2381. DRUMS IN THE DEEP SOUTH

(King Bros./RKO, October 15, 1951)   87 Mins.
(Super Cinecolor)
James Craig, Barbara Payton, Guy Madison, Barton MacLane, Craig Stevens, Tom Fadden, Robert Osterloh, Taylor Holmes, Robert Easton, Lewis Martin, Peter Brocco, Dan White, Louis Jean Heydt
D: William Cameron Menzies
S: Hollister Noble

SP: Philip Yordan, Sidney Harmon
P: Maurice King, Frank King

2382. SLAUGHTER TRAIL
(RKO, October 15, 1951)   78 Mins.
(Cinecolor)
Brian Donlevy, Gig Young, Virginia Grey, Andy Devine, Robert Hutton, Terry Wilkerson, Lew Bedell, Myron Healey, Ken Kountik, Eddie Parker, Ralph Peters, Rick Roman, Lois Hall, Robin Fletcher, Fenton Jones
D: Irving Allen
SP: Sid Kuller
P: Irving Allen

2383. SOUTH OF CALIENTE
(Republic, October 15, 1951)   67 Mins.
Roy Rogers, Dale Evans, Pinky Lee, Douglas Fowley, Pat Brady, Charlita, Rick Roman, Leonard Penn, Willie Best, Frank Richards, Lillian Molieri, George J. Lewis, Marguerite McGill, Roy Rogers Riders, "Trigger"
D: William Witney
SP: Eric Taylor
AP: Eddy White

2384. UTAH WAGON TRAIN
(Republic, October 15, 1951)   67 Mins.
Rex Allen, Penny Edwards, Buddy Ebsen, Roy Barcroft, Sarah Padden, Grant Withers, Arthur Space, Edwin Rand, Robert Karnes, William Holmes, Stanley Andrews, Frank Jenks, "Koko"
D: Philip Ford
SP: John K. Butler
AP: Melville Tucker

2385. HONEYCHILE
(Republic, October 21, 1951)   90 Mins.
(Trucolor)
Judy Canova, Eddie Foy, Jr., Alan Hale, Walter Catlett, Claire Carleton, Karolyn Grimes, Brad Morrow, Roy Barcroft, Leonid Kinskey, Fuzzy Knight, Gus Schilling, Irving Bacon, Roscoe Ates, Ida Moore, Sarah Edwards, Emory Parnell, Dick Elliott, Dick Wessel
D: R. G. Springsteen
S/SP: Jack Townley, Charles E. Roberts
AP: Sidney Picker

2386. ACROSS THE WIDE MISSOURI
(MGM, October 23, 1951)   78 Mins.
(Technicolor)
Clark Gable, Ricardo Montalban, John Hodiac, Adolphe Menjou, Maria Elena Marques, J. Carroll Naish, Jack Holt, Alan Napier, George Chandler, Richard Anderson, Douglas Fowley, Russell Simpson, Frankie Darro
D: William Wellman

S: Talbot Jennings, Frank Cavett
SP: Talbot Jennings
P: Robert Sisk

2387. THE KID FROM AMARILLO
(Columbia, October 30, 1951)   56 Mins.
(*Durango Kid* Series)
Charles Starrett, Smiley Burnette, Harry Lauter, Fred Sears, Don Megowan, Scott Lee, Guy Teague, Charles Evans, George J. Lewis, Henry Kulky, George Chesebro, Jerry Scroggins and the Cass County Boys
D: Ray Nazarro
SP: Barry Shipman
P: Colbert Clark

2388. CAVE OF OUTLAWS
(Universal-International, November 1, 1951)
   75 Mins.
(Technicolor)
MacDonald Carey, Alexis Smith, Edgar Buchanan, Victor Jory, Hugh O'Brian, Houseley Stevenson, Charles Horvarth, Jimmy Van Horn, Tim Graham, Clem Fuller
D: William Castle
SP: Elizabeth Wilson
P: Leonard Goldstein

2389. THE VANISHING OUTPOST
(Western Adventure, November 1, 1951)
Lash LaRue, Al St. John, Riley Hill, Sue Hussey, Bud Osborne, Sharon Hall, Clarke Stevens, Lee Morgan, Ted Adams, Ray Broome, Cliff Taylor, Archie Twitchell, Johnny Paul
D/P: Ron Ormond
SP: Alexander White

2390. LAWLESS COWBOYS
(Monogram, November 7, 1951)   58 Mins.
Whip Wilson, Fuzzy Knight, Jim Bannon, Pamela Duncan, Lee Roberts, Lane Bradford, I. Stanford Jolley, Bruce Edwards, Marshall Reed, Ace Malloy, Stanley Price, Richard Emory
D: Lewis Collins
SP: Maurice Tombragel
P: Vincent M. Fennelly

2391. FORT DEFIANCE
(United Artists, November 9, 1951)   81 Mins.
(Cinecolor)
Dane Clark, Ben Johnson, Peter Graves, Tracey Roberts, George Cleveland, Ralph Sanford, Iron Eyes Cody, Dennis Moore, Craig Woods, Dick Elliott
D: John Rawlins
SP: Louis Lantz
P: Frank Melford

2392. DESERT OF LOST MEN

(Republic, November 19, 1951)   54 Mins.

Allan Lane, Irving Bacon, Mary Ellen Kay, Roy Barcroft, Ross Elliott, Cliff Clark, Boyd "Red" Morgan, Leo Cleary, Kenneth MacDonald, Steve Pendleton, Herman Hack, "Black Jack"

D/AP: Harry Keller

SP: M. Coates Webster

2393. VALLEY OF FIRE

(Columbia, November 20, 1951)   70 Mins.
(Sepiatone)

Gene Autry, Pat Buttram, Gail Davis, Russell Hayden, Christine Larsen, Harry Lauter, Bud Osborne, Terry Frost, Barbara Stanley, Riley Hill, Duke York, Teddy Infuhr, Marjorie Liszt, Victor Sen Young, Gregg Barton, Sandy Sanders, Fred Sherman, James Magill, Frankie Marvin, Pat O'Malley, Wade Crosby, William Fawcett, Syd Saylor, John Miller, "Champion, Jr."

D: John English

S: Gerald Geraghty

SP: Earle Snell

P: Armand Schaefer

2394. THE LONGHORN

(Monogram, November 25, 1951)   70 Mins.
(Sepiatone)

Wild Bill Elliott, Myron Healey, Phyllis Coates, John Hart, Marshall Reed, William Fawcett, Lee Roberts, Carol Henry, Zon Murray, Steve Clark, Marshall Bradford, Herman Hack, Carl Mathews, Lane Bradford

D: Lewis Collins

SP: Dan Ullman

P: Vincent M. Fennelly

2395. SILVER CITY

(Paramount, December 1, 1951)   90 Mins.
(Technicolor)

Edmond O'Brien, Yvonne De Carlo, Richard Arlen, Barry Fitzgerald, Gladys George, Laura Elliott, Edgar Buchanan, Michael Moore, John Dierkes

D: Byron Haskins

S: Luke Short

SP: Frank Gruber

P: Nat Holt

2396. MAN IN THE SADDLE

(Scott-Brown/Columbia, December 2, 1951)
   87 Mins.
(Technicolor)

Randolph Scott, Joan Leslie, Ellen Drew, Alexander Knox, Richard Rober, John Russell, Alfonso Bedoya, Guinn "Big Boy" Williams, Clem Bevins, Cameron Mitchell, Richard Crane, Frank Sully, George Lloyd, James Kirkwood, Frank Hagney, Don Beddoe, Tennessee Ernie Ford

D: Andre de Toth

S: Ernest Haycox

SP: Kenneth Gamet

P: Harry Joe Brown

2397. TEXAS LAWMEN

(Frontier Pictures/Monogram, December 2, 1951)
   54 Mins.

Johnny Mack Brown, Jimmy Ellison, I. Stanford Jolley, Lee Roberts, Terry Frost, Marshall Reed, John Hart, Lyle Talbot, Pierce Lyden, Stanley Price

D: Lewis Collins

SP: Joseph Poland

P: Vincent M. Fennelly

2398. NORTHWEST TERRITORY

(Monogram, December 9, 1951)   61 Mins.

Kirby Grant, Gloria Saunders, Warren Douglas, Pat Mitchell, Tris Coffin, John Crawford, Duke York, Don Harvey, Sam Flint, "Chinook"

D: Frank McDonald

S: James Oliver Curwood

SP: Bill Raynor

P: Lindsley Parsons

2399. OVERLAND TELEGRAPH

(RKO, December 15, 1951)   60 Mins.

Tim Holt, Richard Martin, Gail Davis, George Nader, Mari Blanchard, Hugh Beaumont, Bob Wilke, Fred Graham, Robert Bray, Cliff Clark, Russell Hicks

D: Lesley Selander

SP: Adele Buffington

P: Herman Schlom

2400. PALS OF THE GOLDEN WEST

(Republic, December 15, 1951)   68 Mins.

Roy Rogers, Dale Evans, Estelita Rodriguez, Pinky Lee, Roy Barcroft, Anthony Caruso, Edwardo Jimenez, Ken Terrell, Emmett Vogan, Maurice Jara, Roy Rogers Riders, "Trigger"

D: William Witney

S: Sloan Nibley

SP: Robert DeMond, Eric Taylor

AP: Eddy White

2401. PECOS RIVER

(Columbia, December 15, 1951)   54 Mins.
(*Durango Kid* Series)

Charles Starrett, Smiley Burnette, Jack (Jock) Mahoney, Dolores Sidener, Steve Darrell, Edgar Dearing, Frank Jenks, Paul Campbell, Zon Murray, Maudie Prickett, Eddie Featherstone, Harmonica Bill

D: Fred F. Sears

SP: Barry Shipman

P: Colbert Clark

2402. CALLAWAY WENT THATAWAY

(MGM, December 18, 1951)   81 Mins.

Fred MacMurray, Dorothy McGuire, Howard Keel, Jesse White, Fay Roope, Natalie Schafer, Douglas Kennedy, Elizabeth Fraser, Johnny Indirsano, Stan Freberg, Don Haggerty

D: Norman Panama, Melvin Frank

S/SP: Norman Panama, Melvin Frank

P: Norman Panama, Melvin Frank

2403. DISTANT DRUMS

(United States Pictures/Warner Bros., December 29, 1951)   101 Mins.

(Technicolor)

Gary Cooper, Mari Aldon, Richard Webb, Ray Teal, Arthur Hunnicutt, Robert Barrat, Clancy Cooper

D: Raoul Walsh

S: Niven Busch

SP: Niven Busch, Martin Racklin

P: Milton Sperling

2404. STAGE TO BLUE RIVER

(Frontier Pictures/Monogram, December 30, 1951)   55 Mins.

Whip Wilson, Fuzzy Knight, Phyllis Coates, Lee Roberts, John Hart, Lane Bradford, Pierce Lyden, Terry Frost, I. Stanford Jolley, William Fawcett, Steve Clark, Stanley Price, Bud Osborne

D: Lewis Collins

SP: Joseph Poland

P: Vincent M. Fennelly

2405. BRANDED

(Paramount, 1951)   95 Mins.

Alan Ladd, Mona Freeman, Charles Bickford, Robert Keith, Joseph Callem, Peter Hansen, Tom Tully, John Berkes, Milburn Stone, Martin Garralaga, Edward Clark, John Butler

D: Rudolph Mate

S: Evan Evans

SP: Sidney Boehm, Cyril Hume

P: Mel Epstein

FILMS OF 1952

2406. THE BLACK LASH

(Western Adventure, January 2, 1952)

Lash LaRue, Al St. John, Peggy Stewart, Kermit Maynard, Ray Bennett, Byron Keith, Jimmie Martin, John (Bob) Cason, Clarke Stevens, Bud Osborne, Roy Butler, Larry Barton

D/P: Ron Ormond

SP: Kathy McKeel

2407. THE CIMARRON KID

(Universal-International, January 2, 1952)   84 Mins.

(Technicolor)

Audie Murphy, Yvette Dugay, Beverly Tyler, John Hudson, James Best, Leif Erickson, Noah Beery, Jr., John Hubbard, Hugh O'Brian

D: Budd Boetticher

SP: Lewis Stevens

P: Ted Richmond

2408. INDIAN UPRISING

(Columbia, January 2, 1952)   75 Mins.

(Super Cinecolor)

George Montgomery, Audrey Long, Carl Benton Reid, Eugene Iglesias, Jo Baer, Joe Sawyer, Robert Dover, Eddy Waller, Douglas Kennedy, Robert Shayne, Miguel Inclan, Hugh Sanders, John Call, Robert Griffin, Hank Patterson, Fay Roope, Peter Thompson

D: Ray Nazarro

SP: Kenneth Gamet, Richard Schayler

P: Edward Small

2409. THE BUSHWACKERS

(Broder/Realart, January 8, 1952)   70 Mins.

John Ireland, Wayne Morris, Lawrence Tierney, Dorothy Malone, Lon Chaney, Jr., Myrna Dell, Frank Marlowe, Bill Holmes, Jack Elam, Bob Wood, Kit Guard, Charles Trowbridge, Stuart Randall, George Lynn, Gordon Wynne, Gabriel Conrad, Norman Leavitt, Eddie Parks, Evelyn Bispham, John Anthony Ireland, Bob Broder, Jack Hardin, Venise Grove, Ted Jordon

D: Rod Amateau

SP: Rod Amateau, Thomas Gries

P: Larry Filney, Jack Broder

2410. WESTWARD THE WOMEN

(MGM, January 11, 1952)   116 Mins.

Robert Taylor, Denise Darcel, John McIntire, Julie Bishop, Hope Emerson, Marilyn Erskine, Lenore Lonergan, Henry Nakamura, Beverly Dennis, Renata Vanni, Bruce Cowling, George Chandler, Guido Martufi

D: William A. Wellman

S: Frank Capra

SP: Charles Schnee

P: Dore Schary

2411. THE OLD WEST

(Columbia, January 15, 1952)   61 Mins.

(Sepiatone)

Gene Autry, Gail Davis, Pat Buttram, Lyle Talbot, Louis Jean Heydt, House Peters, Sr., House Peters, Jr., Dick Jones, Kathy Johnson, Don Har-

vey, Dee Pollack, Raymond L. Morgan, James Craven, Tom London, Frank Marvin, Syd Saylor, Bob Woodward, Buddy Roosevelt, Tex Terry, Pat O'Malley, Bobby Clark, Robert Hilton, John Merton, Frank Ellis
D: George Archainbaud
SP: Gerald Geraghty
P: Armand Schaefer

2412. CAPTIVE OF BILLY THE KID
(Republic, January 22, 1952)   54 Mins.
Allan Lane, Penny Edwards, Grant Withers, Clem Bevins, Roy Barcroft, Mauritz Hugo, Gary Goodwin, Frank McCarroll, Richard Emory, "Black Jack"
D: Fred C. Brannon
SP: M. Coates Webster, Richard Wormser
AP: Harry Keller

2413. SMOKY CANYON
(Columbia, January 22, 1952)   55 Mins.
(*Durango Kid* Series)
Charles Starrett, Smiley Burnette, Jack (Jock) Mahoney, Dani Sue Nolan, Tris Coffin, Larry Hudson, Chris Alcaide, Sandy Sanders, Forrest Taylor, Charles Stevens, LeRoy Johnson
D: Fred F. Sears
SP: Barry Shipman
P: Colbert Clark

2414. TEXAS CITY
(Monogram, January 27, 1952)
Johnny Mack Brown, Jimmy Ellison, Lois Hall, Lyle Talbot, Terry Frost, Marshall Reed, Lorna Thayer, Lane Bradford, Pierce Lyden, John Hart, Bud Osborne, Stanley Price
D: Lewis Collins
SP: Joseph Poland
P: Vincent M. Fennelly

2415. FLAMING FEATHER
(Paramount, February 1, 1952)   78 Mins.
(Technicolor)
Sterling Hayden, Forrest Tucker, Arleen Whelan, Barbara Rush, Victor Jory, Richard Arlen, Edgar Buchanan, Carol Thurston, Ian MacDonald, George Cleveland, Bob Kortman, Ethan Laidlaw, Don Dunning, Paul Burns, Ray Teal, Nacho Galindo, Frank Lackteen, Gene Lewis, Larry McGrath, Herman Newlin, Bryan Hightower, Donald Kerr
D: Ray Enright
S: Gerald Drayson Adams
SP: Gerald Drayson Adams, Frank Gruber
P: Nat Holt

2416. THE FRONTIER PHANTOM
(Western Adventure, February 1, 1952)   56 Mins.
Lash LaRue, Al St. John, Archie Twitchell, Clarke Stevens, Virginia Herrick, Bud Osborne, Cliff Taylor, Kenne Duncan, George Chesebro, Sandy Sanders, Buck Garret, Jack O'Shea, Frank Ellis
D/P: Ron Ormond
SP: Maurice Tombragel, June Carr

2417. NIGHT RAIDERS
(Monogram, February 3, 1952)
Whip Wilson, Fuzzy Knight, Lois Hall, Tommy Farrell, Terry Frost, Lane Bradford, Marshall Reed, Steve Clark, Iron Eyes Cody, Boyd Stockman, Ed Cassidy, Carol Henry, Forrest Taylor, Roy Butler, Stanley Price
D: Howard Bretherton
SP: Maurice Tombragel
P: Vincent M. Fennelly

2418. BUFFALO BILL IN TOMAHAWK TERRITORY
(Schwarz Productions/United Artists, February 8, 1952)   66 Mins.
Clayton Moore, Slim Andrews, Rodd Redwing, Chief Yowlachie, Chief Thunder Cloud, Charlie Hughes, Sharon Dexter, Eddie Phillips, Tom Hubbard, Helena Dare, Charles Harvey
D: B. B. Ray
S/SP: Sam Neuman, Nat Tanchuck
P: Edward Finney, B. B. Ray

2419. COLORADO SUNDOWN
(Republic, February 8, 1952)   67 Mins.
Rex Allen, Mary Ellen Kay, Slim Pickens, June Vincent, Fred Graham, John Daheim, Louise Beavers, Chester Clute, Clarence Straight, The Republic Rhythm Riders, "Koko"
D: William Witney
SP: Eric Taylor, William Lively
AP: Eddy White

2420. LONE STAR
(MGM, February 8, 1952)   94 Mins.
Clark Gable, Ava Gardner, Broderick Crawford, Lionel Barrymore, Beulah Bondi, Ed Begley, James Burke, William Farnum, Lowell Gilmore, Lucius Cook, Ralph Reed, Rick Roman, Victor Sutherland, Jonathan Cott, Charles Kane, Nacho Galindo, Trevor Bardette, Harry Woods, Dudley Sadler, Emmett Lynn, Rex Bell
D: Vincent Sherman
S/SP: Borden Chase
P: Z. Wayne Griffin

2421. FORT OSAGE

(Monogram, February 10, 1952)   72 Mins.
(Cinecolor)

Rod Cameron, Jane Nigh, Morris Ankrum, Douglas Kennedy, John Ridgely, William Phipps, I. Stanford Jolley, Dorothy Adams, Francis McDonald, Myron Healey, Lane Bradford, Iron Eyes Cody, Barbara Woodell, Russ Conway

D: Lesley Selander
S/SP: Dan Ullman
P: Walter Mirisch

2422. TRAIL GUIDE

(RKO, February 15, 1952)   60 Mins.

Tim Holt, Richard Martin, Linda Douglas, Frank Wilcox, Robert Sherwood, John Pickard, Kenneth MacDonald, Wendy Waldron, Patricia Wright, Tom London, Mauritz Hugo

D: Lesley Selander
SP: William Lively
P: Herman Schlom

2423. BEND OF THE RIVER

(Universal-International, February 15, 1952)
   91 Mins.
(Technicolor)

James Stewart, Arthur Kennedy, Julia Adams, Rock Hudson, Jay C. Flippen, Stepin Fetchit, Lori Nelson, Henry (Harry) Morgan, Chubby Johnson, Howard Petrie, Frances Bavier, Jack Lambert, Royal Dano, Cliff Lyons

D: Anthony Mann
S: Bill Bulick
P: Aaron Rosenberg

2424. WACO

(Monogram, February 24, 1952)   68 Mins.
(Sepiatone)

Bill Elliott, Pamela Blake, I. Stanford Jolley, Rand Brooks, Richard Avonde, Stanley Andrews, Paul Pierce, Lane Bradford, Pierce Lyden, Terry Frost, Stanley Price, Michael Whelan, Ray Bennett, House Peters, Jr., Richard Paxton, Ray Jones, Edward Cassidy, Russ Whiteman, Ray Bennett

D: Lewis Collins
SP: Dan Ullman
P: Vincent M. Fennelly

2425. THE HAWK OF WILD RIVER

(Columbia, February 28, 1952)   54 Mins.
(*Durango Kid* Series)

Charles Starrett, Smiley Burnette, Jack (Jock) Mahoney, Clayton Moore, Edwin Parker, Jim Diehl, Lane Chandler, Syd Saylor, John Cason, LeRoy Johnson, Jack Carry, Sam Flint, Donna Hall

D: Fred F. Sears
SP: Howard J. Green
P: Colbert Clark

2426. THE LAST MUSKETEER

(Republic, March 1, 1952)   67 Mins.

Rex Allen, Mary Ellen Kay, Slim Pickens, James Anderson, Boyd "Red" Morgan, Monte Montague, Michael Hall, Alan Bridge, Stan Jones, The Republic Rhythm Riders, "Koko"

D: William Witney
SP: Arthur E. Orloff
AP: Eddy White

2427. RANCHO NOTORIOUS

(RKO-Fidelity, March 1, 1952)   70 Mins.
(Technicolor)

Marlene Dietrich, Arthur Kennedy, Mel Ferrer, Gloria Henry, William Frawley, Lisa Ferraday, John Raven, Jack Elam, George Reeves, Frank Ferguson, Francis McDonald, Dan Seymour, John Kellogg, Rodd Redwing, Stuart Randall, Roger Anderson, I. Stanford Jolley, Felipe Turich, John Doucette, Jose Dominguez, William Lee

D: Fritz Lang
S: Sylvia Richards
SP: Daniel Taradash
P: Howard Welsh

2428. RETURN OF THE TEXAN

(20th C. Fox, March 1, 1952)   88 Mins.

Dale Robertson, Joanne Dru, Walter Brennan, Richard Boone, Tom Tully, Robert Horton, Helen Westcott, Lannie Thomas, Dennis Ross, Robert Adler, Kathryn Sheldon, Aileen Carlyle, Linda Green, Brad Mora

D: Delmer Daves
S: Fred Gipson
SP: Dudley Nichols
P: Frank P. Rosenberg

2429. TREASURE OF LOST CANYON

(Universal-International, March 1, 1952)   81 Mins.
(Technicolor)

William Powell, Julia Adams, Rosemary DeCamp, Charles Drake, Chubby Johnson, Henry Hull, Jimmy Ivo, John Doucette, Marvin Press, Frank Wilcox

D: Ted Tetzlaff
S: "The Treasure of Franchard"—Robert Louis Stevenson
SP: Brainerd Duffield, Emerson Crocker
P: Leonard Goldstein

2430. VIVA ZAPATA!
(20th C. Fox, March 1, 1952)   113 Mins.
Marlon Brando, Jean Peters, Anthony Quinn, Joseph Wiseman, Arnold Moss, Alan Reed, Margo, Harold Gordon, Lon Gilbert, Mildred Dunnock, Frank Silvera, Nina Valero, Florenz Ames, Bernie Gozier, Frank de Kova, Fay Roope
D: Elia Kazan
S/SP: John Steinbeck
P: Darryl F. Zanuck

2431. BUGLES IN THE AFTERNOON
(Warner Bros., March 8, 1952)   85 Mins.
(Technicolor)
Ray Milland, Helena Carter, Hugh Marlowe, Forrest Tucker, Barton MacLane, George Reeves, James Millican, Gertrude Michael, Stuart Randall, William "Bill" Phillips, Sheb Wooley, John Pickard
D: Roy Rowland
S: Ernest Haycox
SP: Geoffrey Homes, Harry Brown
P: William Cagney

2432. RODEO
(Monogram, March 9, 1952)   70 Mins.
(Cinecolor)
Jane Nigh, John Archer, Wallace Ford, Gary Gray, Frances Rafferty, Sarah Hayden, Frank Ferguson, Myron Healey, Fuzzy Knight, Robert Karnes, Jim Bannon, I. Stanford Jolley
D: William Beaudine
SP: Charles R. Marion
P: Walter Mirisch

2433. NIGHT STAGE TO GALVESTON
(Columbia, March 18, 1952)   60 Mins.
(Sepiatone)
Gene Autry, Pat Buttram, Virginia Huston, Thurston Hall, Judy Nugent, Robert Livingston, Harry Cording, Robert Bice, Frank Sully, Clayton Moore, Frank Rawls, Steve Clark, Harry Lauter, Robert Peyton, Lois Austin, Kathleen O'Malley, Riley Hill, Dick Alexander, Boyd Stockman, Bob Woodward, Sandy Sanders, Ben Welden, Gary Goodwin, "Champion, Jr."
D: George Archainbaud
SP: Norman S. Hall
P: Armand Schaefer

2434. LEADVILLE GUNSLINGER
(Republic, March 22, 1952)   54 Mins.
Allan Lane, Eddy Waller, Grant Withers, Elaine Riley, Roy Barcroft, Richard Crane, I. Stanford Jolley, Kenneth MacDonald, Mickey Simpson, Ed Hinton, Art Dillard, Wesley Hudman, "Black Jack"
D/AP: Harry Keller
SP: M. Coates Webster

2435. OKLAHOMA ANNIE
(Republic, March 24, 1952)   90 Mins.
Judy Canova, John Russell, Grant Withers, Roy Barcroft, Emmett Lynn, Frank Ferguson, Minerva Urecal, Houseley Stevenson, Almira Sessions, Allen Jenkins
D: R. G. Springsteen
SP: Jack Townley
AP: Sidney Picker

2436. THE WILD NORTH
(MGM, March 28, 1952)   97 Mins.
(AnscoColor)
Stewart Granger, Wendell Corey, Cyd Charisse, Howard Petrie, Morgan Farley, J. M. Kerrigan, Houseley Stevenson, Lewis Martin, John War Eagle, Ray Teal, Clancy Cooper
D: Andrew Marton
S/SP: Frank Fenton
P: Stephen Ames

2437. THE BIG TREES
(Warner Bros., March 29, 1952)   89 Mins.
(Technicolor)
Kirk Douglas, Eve Miller, Patrice Wymore, Edgar Buchanan, John Archer, Alan Hale, Jr., Roy Roberts, Charles Meredith, Harry Cording, Ellen Corby, Iris Adrian, Lillian Bond, Kay Marlow, William Challee
D: Felix Feist
S: Kenneth Earl
SP: John Twist, James R. Webb
P: Louis F. Edelman

2438. ROAD AGENT
(RKO, March 29, 1952)   60 Mins.
Tim Holt, Richard Martin, Noreen Nash, Mauritz Hugo, Dorothy Patrick, Bob Wilke, Tom Tyler, Guy Edward Hearn, William Tannen, Sam Flint, Forbes Murray, Stanley Blystone, Tom Kennedy
D: Lesley Selander
SP: Norman Houston
P: Herman Schlom

2439. MAN FROM THE BLACK HILLS
(Monogram, March 30, 1952)   51 Mins.
Johnny Mack Brown, Jimmy Ellison, Rand Brooks, Lane Bradford, I. Stanford Jolley, Stanley Andrews, Denver Pyle, Ray Bennett, Robert Bray, Florence Lake, Stanley Price, Joel Allen, Bud Osborne, Merrill McCormack, Roy Bucko, Ralph Bucko
D: Thomas Carr
SP: Joseph O'Donnell
P: Vincent M. Fennelly

Man from the Black Hills (Monogram, 1952) — Rand Brooks, Lane Bradford, I. Stanford Jolley, Jimmy Ellison, and Johnny Mack Brown

2440. ROSE OF CIMARRON

(Alco/20th C. Fox, April 1, 1952)   72 Mins.
(Natural Color)
Jack Buetel, Mala Powers, Bill Williams, Jim Davis,
   Dick Curtis, Lane Bradford, William Phipps, Bob
   Steele, Alex Gerry, Lillian Bronson, Art Smith,
   Monte Blue, Argentina Brunetti, John Doucette
D: Harry Keller
SP: Maurice Geraghty
P: Edward L. Alperson

2441. THE GUNMAN

(Silvermine/Monogram, April 13, 1952)   52 Mins.
Whip Wilson, Fuzzy Knight, Phyllis Coates, Rand
   Brooks, Terry Frost, Lane Bradford, I. Stanford
   Jolley, Gregg Barton, Russ Whiteman, Richard
   Avonde, Robert Bray
D: Lewis Collins
SP: Fred Myton
P: Vincent M. Fennelly

2442. BORDER SADDLEMATES

(Republic, April 15, 1952)   67 Mins.
Rex Allen, Mary Ellen Kay, Slim Pickens, Roy Bar-
   croft, Forrest Taylor, Jimmy Moss, Zon Murray,
   Keith McConnell, Mark Hanna, Bud Osborne,
   The Republic Rhythm Riders, "Koko"
D: William Witney
SP: Albert DeMond
AP: Eddy White

2443. WILD HORSE AMBUSH

(Republic, April 15, 1952)   54 Mins.
(*Rough Ridin' Kids* Series)
Michael Chapin, Eilene Janssen, James Bell, Richard
   Avonde, Roy Barcroft, Julian Rivero, Movita,
   Drake Smith, Scott Lee, Alex Montoya, John
   Daheim, Ted Cooper, Wayne Burson
D: Fred C. Brannon
SP: William Lively
AP: Rudy Ralston

2444. THE LION AND THE HORSE

(Warner Bros., April 19, 1952)   83 Mins.
(WarnerColor)
Steve Cochran, Ray Teal, Bob Steele, Harry An-
   trim, George O'Hanlon, Sherry Jackson, William
   Fawcett, House Peters, Jr., Lane Chandler, Lee
   Roberts
D: Louis King
S/SP: Crane Wilbur
P: Bryan Foy

2445. TARGET
(RKO, April 20, 1952)   61 Mins.
Tim Holt, Richard Martin, Linda Douglas, Walter
  Reed, Harry Harvey, John Hamilton, Lane Brad-
  ford, Riley Hill, Mike Ragan
D: Stuart Gilmore
SP: Norman Houston
P: Herman Schlom

2446. LARAMIE MOUNTAINS
(Columbia, April 20, 1952)   54 Mins.
(*Durango Kid* Series)
Charles Starrett, Smiley Burnette, Jack (Jock) Ma-
  honey, Fred Sears, Marshall Reed, Rory Mallison,
  Zon Murray, John War Eagle, Bob Wilke
D: Ray Nazarro
SP: Barry Shipman
P: Colbert Clark

2447. WILD STALLION
(Monogram, April 27, 1952)   70 Mins.
(Cinecolor)
Ben Johnson, Edgar Buchanan, Martha Hyer, Hay-
  den Rorke, Hugh Beaumont, Orley Lindgren,
  Don Haggerty, Susan Odin
D: Lewis Collins
SP: Dan Ullman
P: Walter Mirisch

2448. BRONCO BUSTER
(Universal-International, May 1, 1952)   80 Mins.
(Technicolor)
John Lund, Scott Brady, Joyce Holden, Chill Wills,
  Don Haggerty, Dan Poore, Bill Williams, Casey
  Tibbs, Pete Crump, Manuel Enos
D: Budd Boetticher
SP: Horace McCoy, Lillie Hayward
P: Ted Richmond

2449. THE HALF-BREED
(RKO, May 4, 1952)   81 Mins.
(Technicolor)
Robert Young, Janis Carter, Jack Buetel, Barton
  MacLane, Reed Hadley, Porter Hall, Connie Gil-
  christ, Sammy White, Damian O'Flynn, Frank
  Wilcox, Judy Walsh, Tom Monroe, Lee Mac-
  Gregor, Charles Delaney, Caleen Calder, Mari-
  etta Elliott, Jeane Cochran, Betty Leonard, Shirley
  Whitney, Mary Menzies, Shelah Hackett
D: Stuart Gilmore
S: Robert Hardy Andrews
SP: Harold Shumate, Richard Wormser
P: Herman Schlom

2450. KANSAS TERRITORY
(Monogram, May 4, 1952)   65 Mins.
(Sepiatone)
Bill Elliott, Peggy Stewart, House Peters, Jr., Fuzzy

Knight, Lane Bradford, I. Stanford Jolley, Lyle
  Talbot, Stanley Andrews, Marshall Reed, Terry
  Frost, John Hart, William Fawcett, Lee Roberts,
  Ted Adams, Pierce Lyden
D: Lewis Collins
SP: Dan Ullman
P: Vincent M. Fennelly

2451. THE OUTCASTS OF POKER FLATS
(20th C. Fox, May 4, 1952)   81 Mins.
Anne Baxter, Dale Robertson, Miriam Hopkins,
  Cameron Mitchell, Craig Hill, Barbara Bates, Bill
  Lynn, Dick Rich, Tom Greenway, Russ Conway,
  John Midgely, Harry T. Shannon, Harry Harvey,
  Jr.
D: Joseph M. Newman
S: Bret Harte
SP: Edmund H. North
P: Julian Blaustein

2452. DESERT PURSUIT
(Monogram, May 11, 1952)   71 Mins.
Wayne Morris, Virginia Grey, Anthony Caruso,
  George Tobias, Emmett Lynn, Gloria Talbot,
  Frank Lackteen, John Doucette, Billy Wilkerson,
  Robert Bice
D: George Blair
S: "Starlight Canyon"—Kenneth Perkins
SP: W. Scott Darling
P: Lindsley Parsons

2453. THE SAN FRANCISCO STORY
(Warner Bros., May 17, 1952)   80 Mins.
Joel McCrea, Yvonne De Carlo, Richard Erdmann,
  Onslow Stevens, Florence Bates, Sidney Black-
  mer, John Raven, O. Z. Whitehead, Ralph Dumke,
  Robert Foulk, Lane Chandler, Trevor Bardette,
  John Doucette, Peter Virgo, Frank Hagney, Tor
  Johnson, Fred Graham
D: Robert Parrish
S: Richard Summers
SP: D. D. Beauchamp
P: Howard Welsch

2454. BLACK HILLS AMBUSH
(Republic, May 20, 1952)   54 Mins.
Allan Lane, Eddy Waller, Leslye Banning, Roy Bar-
  croft, Michael Hall, John Vosper, Edward Cassidy,
  John Cason, Wesley Hudman, Michael Barton,
  "Black Jack"
D/AP: Harry Keller
SP: M. Coates Webster, Ronald Davidson

2455. THE FIGHTER
(United Artists, May 25, 1952)   78 Mins.
Richard Conte, Vanessa Brown, Lee J. Cobb, Frank
  Silvera, Roberta Haynes, Hugh Sanders, Claire

Apache Country (Columbia, 1952) — Gene Autry, Iron Eyes Cody, and Pat Buttram

Denver and Rio Grande (Paramount, 1952) — Sterling Hayden

Carleton, Martin Garralaga, Argentina Brunetti, Rodolfo Hoyos, Jr., Margaret Padilla, Paul Fierro
D: Herbert Kline
SP: Aben Kandel, Herbert Kline
P: Alex Gottlieb

2456. APACHE COUNTRY
(Columbia, May 30, 1952) 62 Mins.
(Sepiatone)
Gene Autry, Pat Buttram, Carolina Cotton, Harry Lauter, Mary Scott, Sidney Mason, Francis X. Bushman, Gregg Barton, Tom London, Byron Foulger, Frank Matts, Mickey Simpson, Iron Eyes Cody, Tony Whitecloud's Jemez Indians, Cass County Boys, "Champion, Jr."
D: George Archainbaud
SP: Norman S. Hall
P: Armand Schaefer

2457. DESERT PASSAGE
(RKO, May 30, 1952) 60 Mins.
Tim Holt, Richard Martin, Joan Dixon, Walter Reed, Clayton Moore, Dorothy Patrick, John Dehner, Lane Bradford, Denver Pyle, Francis McDonald
D: Lesley Selander
SP: Norman Houston
P: Herman Schlom

2458. BRAVE WARRIOR
(Columbia, June 1, 1952) 73 Mins.
(Technicolor)
Jon Hall, Christine Larson, Jay Silverheels, Michael Ansara, Harry Cording, James Seay, George Eldridge, Leslie Denison, Rory Mallison, Rusty Westcoatt, Bert Davidson, William P. Wilkerson, Gilbert V. Perkins
D: Spencer G. Bennet
SP: Robert E. Kent
P: Sam Katzman

2459. DENVER AND RIO GRANDE
(Paramount, June 1, 1952) 89 Mins.
(Technicolor)
Edmond O'Brien, Sterling Hayden, Dean Jagger, Laura Elliott, Lyle Bettger, J. Carroll Naish, Zasu Pitts, Tom Powers, Robert Barrat, Paul Fix, Don Haggerty, James Burke
D: Byron Haskin
S/SP: Frank Gruber
P: Nat Holt

2460. MONTANA TERRITORY
(Columbia, June 1, 1952) 64 Mins.
(Technicolor)
Lon McCallister, Wanda Hendrix, Preston Foster, Hugh Sanders, Jack Elam, Clayton Moore, Robert Griffin, Myron Healey, Eddy Waller, George Rus-

sell, Ethan Laidlaw, Frank Matts, Ruth Warren, Trevor Bardette, George Chesebro
D: Ray Nazarro
SP: Barry Shipman
P: Colbert Clark

2461. OUTLAW WOMEN
(Howco Productions, June 2, 1952) 75 Mins.
(Cinecolor)
Marie Windsor, Richard Rober, Allan Nixon, Carla Balenda, Jacqueline Fontaine, Jackie Coogan, Maria Hart, Billy House, Richard Avonde, Leonard Penn, Lyle Talbot, Brad Johnson
D: Samuel Newfield
SP: Orville Hampton
P: Ron Ormond

2462. CARSON CITY
(Warner Bros., June 14, 1952) 87 Mins.
(WarnerColor)
Randolph Scott, Lucille Norman, Raymond Massey, Richard Webb, James Millican, Larry Keating, George Cleveland, William Haade, Thurston Hall, Vince Barnett, Don Beddoe, Jack Woody, James Smith, Guy Tongue, Carle Andre, Marlin Nelson, Clyde Hudkins, Sarah Edwards, Iris Adrian, Edmund Cobb, Zon Murray, House Peters, Jr., Pierce Lyden, Kenneth MacDonald
D: Andre de Toth
S: Sloan Nibley
SP: Sloan Nibley, Winston Miller
P: David Weisbart

2463. GOLD FEVER
(Monogram, June 15, 1952) 63 Mins.
John Calvert, Ralph Morgan, Ann Cornell, Gene Roth, Tom Kennedy, Judd Holdren, Danny Rense, Bobby Graham, George Morrell
D: Leslie Goodwins
SP: Edgar B. Anderson, Jr., Cliff Lancaster
P: John Calvert

2464. THE ROUGH, TOUGH WEST
(Columbia, June 15, 1952) 54 Mins.
(*Durango Kid* Series)
Charles Starrett, Smiley Burnett, Jack (Jock) Mahoney, Carolina Cotton, Marshall Reed, Fred Sears, Bert Arnold, Tommy Ivo, Boyd Morgan, Pee Wee King and his Band, Valeria Fisher
D: Ray Nazarro
SP: Barry Shipman
P: Colbert Clark

2465. CALIFORNIA CONQUEST
(Columbia, July 1, 1952) 79 Mins.
(Technicolor)
Cornel Wilde, Teresa Wright, Alfonso Bedoya, Lisa

Ferraday, Eugene Iglesias, John Dehner, Ivan Lebedeff, Tito Renaldo, Renzo Cesana, Baynes Barron, Rico Alaniz, William P. Wilkerson, Alex Montoya, Hank Patterson, George Eldridge
D: Lew Landers
SP: Robert E. Kent
P: Sam Katzman

2466. CRIPPLE CREEK
(Resolute/Columbia, July 1, 1952) 78 Mins.
(Technicolor)
George Montgomery, Karin Booth, Jerome Courtland, William Bishop, Richard Egan, Don Porter, John Dehner, Roy Roberts, George Cleveland, Byron Foulger, Robert Bice, Grandon Rhodes, Zon Murray, Peter Brocco, Cliff Clark, Robert G. Armstrong, Harry Cording, Chris Alcaide
D: Ray Nazarro
SP: Richard Schayer

2467. WAGONS WEST
(Monogram, July 6, 1952) 70 Mins.
(Cinecolor)
Rod Cameron, Noah Beery, Jr., Peggie Castle, Michael Chapin, Henry Brandon, Sarah Hayden, Frank Ferguson, Anne Kimbell, Wheaton Chambers, Riley Hill, Effie Laird, I. Stanford Jolley, Harry Tyler, Almira Sessions
D: Ford Beebe
SP: Dan Ullman
P: Vincent M. Fennelly

2468. JUNCTION CITY
(Columbia, July 12, 1952) 54 Mins.
(*Durango Kid* Series)
Charles Starrett, Smiley Burnette, Jack (Jock) Mahoney, Kathleen Case, John Dehner, Steve Darrell, George Chesebro, Anita Castle, Mary Newton, Robert Bice, Hal Price, Hal Taliaferro, Chris Alcaide, Bob Woodward, Frank Ellis
D: Ray Nazarro
SP: Barry Shipman
P: Colbert Clark

2469. DEAD MAN'S TRAIL
(Frontier Pictures/Monogram, July 20, 1952) 59 Mins.
Johnny Mack Brown, Jimmy Ellison, Barbara Allen, Lane Bradford, I. Stanford Jolley, Terry Frost, Gregg Barton, Dale Van Sickel, Richard Avonde, Stanley Price
D: Lewis Collins
SP: Joseph Poland
P: Vincent M. Fennelly

2470. THUNDERING CARAVANS
(Republic, July 20, 1952) 54 Mins.
Allan Lane, Eddy Waller, Mona Knox, Roy Barcroft, Isabel Randolph, Richard Crane, Bill Henry, Edward Clark, Pierre Watkin, Stanley Andrews, Boyd Morgan, "Black Jack"
D: Harry Keller
SP: M. Coates Webster
AP: Rudy Ralston

2471. BARBED WIRE
(Columbia, July 25, 1952) 61 Mins.
(Sepiatone)
Gene Autry, Pat Buttram, Anne James, William Fawcett, Leonard Penn, Michael Vallon, Terry Frost, Clayton Moore, Edwin Parker, Sandy Sanders, Stuart Whitman, Zon Murray, Frankie Marvin, Alan Bridge, Victor Cox, Bobby Clark, Pat O'Malley, Bud Osborne, Bob Woodward, Wesley Hudman, Duke York, Harry Harvey, "Champion, Jr."
D: George Archainbaud
SP: Gerald Geraghty
P: Armand Schaefer

2472. OLD OKLAHOMA PLAINS
(Republic, July 25, 1952) 60 Mins.
Rex Allen, Slim Pickens, Elaine Edwards, Roy Barcroft, John Crawford, Joel Marston, Russell Hicks, Fred Graham, Stephen Chase, The Republic Rhythm Riders, "Koko"
D: William Witney
SP: Milton Raison
AP: Eddy White

2473. HIGH NOON
(United Artists, July 30, 1952) 85 Mins.
Gary Cooper, Thomas Mitchell, Lloyd Bridges, Katy Jurado, Grace Kelly, Otto Kruger, Lon Chaney, Jr., Henry (Harry) Morgan, Ian MacDonald, Eve McVeagh, Harry Shannon, Lee Van Cleef, Bob Wilke, Sheb Wooley, Tom London, Ted Stanhope, Larry Blake, William Phillips, Jeanne Blackford, James Millican, Cliff Clark, Ralph Reed, William Newill, Lucien Priva, Guy Beach, Howland Chamberlin, Morgan Farley, Virginia Christine, Virginia Farmer
D: Fred Zinnemann
SP: Carl Foreman
P: Stanley Kramer
(Theme song sung by Tex Ritter)

2474. THE BIG SKY
(Winchester/RKO, August 1, 1952) 122 Mins.
Kirk Douglas, Dewey Martin, Elizabeth Threatt, Arthur Hunnicutt, Buddy Baer, Steven Geray, Hank Worden, Jim Davis, Henri Letondal, Robert

Hunter, Booth Coleman, Paul Frees, Frank de Kova, Guy Wilkerson, Fred Graham, Cactus Mack, Frank Lackteen, George Wallace, Don Beddoe, Viola Vonn, Nolan Leary, Cliff Clark, Eugene Borden, Max Wagner
S: "The Big Sky"—A. B. Guthrie, Jr.
SP: Dudley Nichols
P: Howard Hawks

2475. THE DUEL AT SILVER CREEK
(Universal-International, August 1, 1952) 77 Mins.
(Technicolor)
Audie Murphy, Faith Domergue, Stephen McNally, Susan Cabot, Gerald Mohr, Eugene Iglesias, Walter Sande, Lee Marvin, George Eldridge
D: Don Siegel
SP: Gerald Drayson Adams, Joseph Hoffman
P: Leonard Goldstein

2476. SON OF PALEFACE
(Paramount, August 1, 1952) 95 Mins.
(Technicolor)
Bob Hope, Jane Russell, Roy Rogers, Bill Williams, Lloyd Corrigan, Paul E. Burns, Douglass Dumbrille, Iron Eyes Cody, Harry Von Zell, Wee Willie Davis, Charley Cooley
D: Frank Tashlin
SP: Frank Tashlin, Robert L. Welch, Joseph Quillan
P: Robert L. Welch

2477. MONTANA INCIDENT
(Monogram, August 10, 1952) 54 Mins.
Whip Wilson, Rand Brooks, Noel Neill, Peggy Stewart, Hugh Prosser, William Fawcett, Terry Frost, Marshall Reed, Lyle Talbot, Russ Whiteman, Barbara Woodell, Bruce Edwards, Stanley Price
D: Lewis Collins
SP: Dan Ullman
P: Vincent M. Fennelly

2478. THE KID FROM BROKEN GUN
(Columbia, August 15, 1952) 56 Mins.
(Durango Kid Series)
Charles Starrett, Smiley Burnette, Jack (Jock) Mahoney, Angela Stevens, Tris Coffin, Myron Healey, Pat O'Malley, Helen Mowery, Chris Alcaide, John Cason, Mauritz Hugo, Edgar Dearing, Eddie Parker
D: Fred F. Sears
SP: Ed Earl Repp, Barry Shipman
P: Colbert Clark

2479. YUKON GOLD
(Monogram, August 31, 1952) 62 Mins.
Kirby Grant, Martha Hyer, Harry Lauter, Philip

Van Zandt, Frances Charles, Mauritz Hugo, James Parnell, Sam Flint, I. Stanford Jolley, "Chinook" (a dog)
D: Frank McDonald
S: James Oliver Curwood
SP: Bill Raynor
P: William F. Broidy

2480. LOST IN ALASKA
(Universal-International, August, 1952) 76 Mins.
Bud Abbott, Lou Costello, Mitzi Green, Tom Ewell, Bruce Cabot, Minerva Urecal, Emory Parnell, Michael Ross, Rex Lease, Jack Ingram, Joe Kirk, Howard Negley, Maudie Pricket, Billy Wayne, Paul Newlan, Julia Montoya, Iron Eyes Cody, Fred Aldrich, Donald Kerr, George Barton, Bobby Barber
D: Jean Yarbrough
SP: Leonard Stern, Martin A. Ragaway
P: Howard Christie

2481. UNTAMED FRONTIER
(Universal-International, September 1, 1952) 75 Mins.
(Technicolor)
Joseph Cotten, Shelley Winters, Scott Brady, Minor Watson, Susan Ball, Katherine Emery, Antonio Moreno, Douglas Spencer, John Alexander, Richard Garland, Lee Van Cleef, Robert Anderson, Fess Parker
D: Hugo Fregonese
S: Houston Branch, Eugenia Night
SP: Gerald Drayson Adams, John and Gwen Bagni
P: Leonard Goldstein

2482. HELLGATE
(Lippert, September 5, 1952) 87 Mins.
Sterling Hayden, Joan Leslie, Ward Bond, James Arness, Peter Coe, John Pickard, Robert Wilke, Lyle James, Richard Emory, Richard Paxton, William R. Hamel, Marshall Bradford, Sheb Wooley, Rory Mallison, Pat Coleman, Timothy Carey, Kyle Anderson, Rodd Redwing, Stanley Price
D/SP: Charles Marquis Warren
P: John C. Champion

2483. WOMAN OF THE NORTH COUNTRY
(Republic, September 5, 1952) 92 Mins.
(Trucolor)
Ruth Hussey, Rod Cameron, John Agar, Gale Storm, J. Carroll Naish, Jim Davis, Jay C. Flippen, Taylor Holmes, Barry Kelley, Grant Withers, Stephen Bekassy, Howard Petrie, Hank Worden, Virginia Brissac
D/AP: Joseph Kane
S: Charles Marquis Warren
SP: Norman Reilly Raine

2484. FARGO

(Silvermine/Monogram, September 7, 1952)
69 Mins.
(Sepiatone)

Bill Elliott, Phyllis Coates, Myron Healey, Fuzzy Knight, Jack Ingram, Arthur Space, Bob Wilke, Terry Frost, Robert Bray, Tim Ryan, Florence Lake, Stanley Andrews, Richard Reeves, Gene Roth

D: Lewis Collins
SP: Joseph Poland, Jack DeWitt
P: Vincent M. Fennelly

2485. WAGON TEAM

(Columbia, September 30, 1952)   61 Mins.
(Sepiatone)

Gene Autry, Pat Buttram, Gail Davis, Dick Jones, Harry Harvey, Gordon Jones, Henry Rowland, George J. Lewis, John Cason, Gregg Barton, Carlo Tricoli, Pierce Lyden, Syd Saylor, Sandy Sanders, Cass County Boys (Jerry Scroggins, Fred Martin, and Fred Dodson), "Champion, Jr."

D: George Archainbaud
SP: Gerald Geraghty
P: Armand Schaefer

2486. HORIZONS WEST

(Universal-International, October 1, 1952)
87 Mins.
(Technicolor)

Robert Ryan, Julia Adams, Rock Hudson, John McIntire, Judith Braun, Raymond Burr, Frances Bavier, Dennis Weaver, Rodolfo Acosta, James Arness, Tom Powers, John Hubbard, Walter Reed, Tom Monroe, Douglas Fowley, Raymond Greenleaf, Buddy Roosevelt, Forbes Murray, Dan White, Robert Bice, Mae Clarke, Alberto Morin, Eddie Parker, Monte Montague, Forbes Murray, John Harmon, Peter Mamakos, Paulette Turner

D: Budd Boetticher
S/SP: Louis Stevens
P: Albert J. Cohen

2487. THE LUSTY MEN

(Wald-Krasna/RKO, October 1, 1952)   113 Mins.

Susan Hayward, Robert Mitchum, Arthur Kennedy, Arthur Hunnicutt, Frank Faylen, Walter Coy, Carol Nugent, Maria Hart, Lorna Thayer, Burt Mustin, Karen King, Jimmy Dodd, Riley Hill, Lane Chandler, Glenn Strange, Dennis Moore, Robert Bray, Sheb Wooley, Marshall Reed, Paul E. Burns, George Wallace, Lane Bradford, Eleanor Todd, George Sherwood

D: Nicholas Ray
S: Claude Stanush
SP: Horace McCoy, David Sortort
P: Jerry Wald

2488. DESPERADOES' OUTPOST

(Republic, October 8, 1952)   54 Mins.

Allan Lane, Eddy Waller, Roy Barcroft, Myron Healey, Lyle Talbot, Claudia Barrett, Lee Roberts, Lane Bradford, Ed Cassidy, Slim Duncan, Zon Murray, Charles Evans

D: Philip Ford
SP: Albert DeMond, Arthur E. Orloff
AP: Rudy Ralston

2489. TOUGHEST MAN IN ARIZONA

(Republic, October 10, 1952)   90 Mins.
(Trucolor)

Vaughn Monroe, Joan Leslie, Walter Brennan, Victor Jory, Jean Parker, Harry Morgan, Ian MacDonald, Diana Christian, Bobby Hyatt, Charlita, Nadene Ashdown, Francis Ford, Paul Hurst, John Doucette

D: R. G. Springsteen
SP: John K. Butler
AP: Sidney Picker

2490. CANYON AMBUSH

(Silvermine/Monogram, October 12, 1952)
53 Mins.

Johnny Mack Brown, Phyllis Coates, Lee Roberts, DennisMoore, Denver Pyle, Pierce Lyden, Hugh Prosser, Marshall Reed, Stanley Price, Bill Koontz, Frank Ellis, Russ Whiteman, Carol Henry, George DeNormand

D: Lewis Collins
SP: Joseph Poland
P: Vincent M. Fennelly

2491. APACHE WAR SMOKE

(MGM, October 17, 1952)   67 Mins.

Gilbert Roland, Glenda Farrell, Robert Horton, Barbara Ruick, Gene Lockhart, Henry (Harry) Morgan, Patricia Tiernan, Hank Worden, Myron Healey, Emmett Lynn, Argentina Brunetti, Bobby Blake, Douglass Dumbrille

D: Harold Kress
S: Ernest Haycox
SP: Jerry Davis
P: Hayes Goetz

2492. SOUTH PACIFIC TRAIL

(Republic, October 20, 1952)   60 Mins.

Rex Allen, Estelita Rodriguez, Slim Pickens, Nestor Paiva, Roy Barcroft, Douglas Evans, Joe McGuinn, Forrest Taylor, The Republic Rhythm Riders (Michael Barton, Darol Rice, George Bamby, Slim Duncan, and Buddy Dooley), "Koko"

D: William Witney
SP: Arthur Orloff
AP: Eddy White

2493. SPRINGFIELD RIFLE

(Warner Bros., October 25, 1952)   93 Mins.

(WarnerColor)

Gary Cooper, Phyllis Thaxter, David Brian, Paul Kelly, Philip Carey, Lon Chaney, Jr., James Millican, Guinn "Big Boy" Williams, Alan Hale, Jr., Wilton Graff, Richard Hale, James Brown, Vince Barnett, Poodles Hanaford, Jack Woody, Jerry O'Sullivan, William Fawcett, Ned Young, Martin Milner

D: Andre de Toth

S: Sloan Nibley

SP: Charles Marquis Warren, Frank Davis

P: Louis F. Edelman

2494. THE RAIDERS

(Universal-International, November 1, 1952)   80 Mins.

(Technicolor)

Richard Conte, Viveca Lindfors, Barbara Britton, Hugh O'Brian, Richard Martin, Palmer Lee, William Reynolds, William Bishop, Morris Ankrum, Dennis Weaver, Margaret Field, John Kellogg, Lane Bradford, Riley Hill, Neyle Morrow, Carlos Rivero, George J. Lewis, Francis McDonald

D: Lesley Selander

SP: Polly James, Lillie Hayward

P: William Alland

2495. THE SAVAGE

(Paramount, November 1, 1952)   95 Mins.

(Technicolor)

Charlton Heston, Susan Morrow, Peter Hanson, Joan Taylor, Richard Rober, Orley Lindgren, Larry Tolan, Howard Negley, Frank Richards, Milburn Stone, Ian MacDonald, Don Porter, Ted de Corsia

D: George Marshall

S: "The Renegade"—L. L. Foreman

SP: Sidney Boehm

P: Mel Epstein

2496. BEHIND SOUTHERN LINES

(Monogram, November 2, 1952)   51 Mins.

(*Wild Bill Hickok* Series)

Guy Madison, Andy Devine, Rand Brooks, Murray Alper, Jonathan Hale, Orley Lindgren, Milburn Stone, Robert Shayne, Lee Phelps, Bill Meade, Duke York

D: Thomas Carr

SP: Melvin Levy, Maurice Tombragel

P: Wesley E. Barry

(Compiled from the television episodes "Behind Southern Lines" and "The Silver Mine Protection Story")

2497. THE GHOST OF CROSSBONES CANYON

(Monogram, November 2, 1952)   56 Mins.

(*Wild Bill Hickok* Series)

Guy Madison, Andy Devine, Betty Davison, John Doucette, Russell Simpson

D: Frank McDonald

SP: Maurice Tombragel

P: Wesley Barry

2498. TRAIL OF THE ARROW

(Monogram, November 2, 1952)   54 Mins.

(*Wild Bill Hickok* Series)

Guy Madison, Andy Devine, Wendy Waldron, Raymond Hatton, Terry Frost, Jack Reynolds, Steve Pendleton, Neyle Morrow

D: Thomas Carr

SP: Maurice Tombragel

P: Wesley E. Barry

(Compiled from the television episodes "The Indian Bureau Story" and one other unknown title)

2499. THE YELLOW HAIRED KID

(Monogram, November 2, 1952)   72 Mins.

(*Wild Bill Hickok* Series)

Guy Madison, Andy Devine, Alan Hale, Jr., Marcia Mae Jones, Alice Rolph, David Bruce, William Phipps, Riley Hill, Tommy Ivo, Emory Parnell

D: Frank McDonald

SP: Dwight Babcock, Maurice Tombragel

P: Wesley E. Barry

(Compiled from the television episodes "The Yellow-Haired Kid" and "Johnny Deuce")

2500. SON OF GERONIMO

(Columbia, November 6, 1952)   15 Chaps.

Clay (Clayton) Moore, Rodd Redwing, Tommy Farrell, Eileen Rowe, Bud Osborne, John Crawford, Marshall Reed, Zon Murray, Rick Vallin, Lyle Talbot, Chief Yowlachie, Wally West, Frank Matta, Sandy Sanders, Bob Cason

D: Spencer G. Bennet

SP: Arthur Hoerl, Royal K. Cole, George H. Plympton

P: Sam Katzman

Chapter Titles: (1) War of Vengeance, (2) Running the Gauntlet, (3) Stampede, (4) Apache Allies, (5) Indian Ambush, (6) Trapped by Fire, (7) A Sinister Scheme, (8) Prisoners of Porico, (9) On the Warpath, (10) The Fight at Crystal Springs, (11) A Midnight Marauder, (12) Trapped in a Flaming Tepee, (13) Jim Scott Tempts Fate, (14) A Trap for Geronimo, (15) Peace Treaty

2501. WYOMING ROUNDUP

(Monogram, November 9, 1952)   53 Mins.

Whip Wilson, Phyllis Coates, Tommy Farrell, Henry

Rowland, House Peters, Jr., I. Stanford Jolley, Richard Emory, Bob Wilke, Stanley Price
D: Thomas Carr
SP: Dan Ullman
P: Vincent M. Fennelly

2502. MONTANA BELLE
(RKO, November 11, 1952)   81 Mins.
(Trucolor)
Jane Russell, George Brent, Scott Brady, Forrest Tucker, Andy Devine, Jack Lambert, John Litel, Ray Teal, Rory Mallison, Roy Barcroft, Holly Bane, Ned Davenport, Dick Elliott, Eugene Roth, Stanley Andrews
D: Allan Dwan
S: M. Coates Webster, Howard Welsch
SP: Horace McCoy, Norman S. Hall
AP: Robert Peters
P: Howard Welsch

2503. PONY SOLDIER
(20th C. Fox, November 11, 1952)   82 Mins.
(Technicolor)
Tyrone Power, Cameron Mitchell, Thomas Gomez, Penny Edwards, Robert Horton, Anthony Numken, Adeline De Walt Reynolds, Howard Petrie, Stuart Randall, Richard Shackelford, James Hayward, Muriel Landers, Frank de Kova, Louis Heminger, Grady Calloway, Nipo T. Strongheart, John War Eagle, Chief Brightfire Thundersky
D: Joseph M. Newman
S: Garnett Weston
SP: John D. Higgins
P: Samuel G. Engel

2504. THE BRIDE COMES TO YELLOW SKY
(RKO, November 14, 1952)   45 Mins.
(Coupled with James Mason in Joseph Conrad's story "The Secret Sharer," this was the second half of *Face to Face*)
Robert Preston, Marjorie Steele, Minor Watson, Dan Seymour, Olive Carey, James Agee
D: Bretaigne Windust
S: Stephen Crane
SP: James Agee
P: Huntington Hartford

2505. HANGMAN'S KNOT
(Scott-Brown/Columbia, November 15, 1952)   84 Mins.
(Technicolor)
Randolph Scott, Donna Reed, Claude Jarman, Jr., Frank Faylen, Glenn Langan, Richard Denning, Lee Marvin, Jeanette Nolan, Clem Bevins, Ray Teal, Guinn "Big Boy" Williams, Monte Blue, John Call, Reed Howes, Edward Earle, Post Park, Frank Hagney, Frank Yaconelli

D/SP: Roy Huggins
P: Harry Joe Brown

2506. THE IRON MISTRESS
(Warner Bros., November 22, 1952)   110 Mins.
(Technicolor)
Alan Ladd, Virginia Mayo, Joseph Calleia, Phyllis Kirk, Alf Ejellin, Douglas Dick, Anthony Caruso, Ned Young, Don Beddoe, Robert Emhardt, Richard Carlyle, Jay Novello, George J. Lewis, Daria Massey
D: Gordon Douglas
S: Paul I. Wellman
SP: James M. Webb
P: Henry Blanke

2507. THE BATTLES OF CHIEF PONTIAC
(Jack Broder Prod./Realart, November 30, 1952)   72 Mins.
Lex Barker, Lon Chaney, Helen Westcott, Barry Kroeger, Roy Roberts, Larry Chance, Katherine Warren
D: Felix Feist
SP: Jack De Witt
P: Irving Starr

2508. BLUE CANADIAN ROCKIES
(Columbia, November 30, 1952)   58 Mins.
(Sepiatone)
Gene Autry, Pat Buttram, Gail Davis, Caroline Cotton, Russ Ford, Tom London, Mauritz Hugo, Don Beddoe, Gene Roth, John Merton, David Garcia, Bob Woodward, W. C. "Billy" Wilkerson, The Cass County Boys, "Champion, Jr."
D: George Archainbaud
SP: Gerald Geraghty
P: Armand Schaefer

2509. CATTLE TOWN
(Warner Bros., December 6, 1952)   71 Mins.
Dennis Morgan, Philip Carey, Rita Moreno, Paul Picerni, Amanda Blake, George O'Hanlon, Ray Teal, Jay Novello, Bob Wilke, Sheb Wooley, Charles Meredith, Merv Griffin, A. Guy Teague, Boyd Morgan, Jack Kenney
D: Noel Smith
SP: Tom Blackburn
P: Bryan Foy

2510. SKY FULL OF MOON
(MGM, December 12, 1952)   73 Mins.
Carleton Carpenter, Jan Sterling, Keenan Wynn, Robert Burton, Elaine Stewart, Emmett Lynn, Douglass Dumbrille, Sheb Wooley, Jonathan Cott
D/SP: Norman Foster
P: Sidney Franklin, Jr.

2511. THE MAVERICK

(Silvermine/Allied Artists, December 14, 1952)
71 Mins.
(Sepiatone)

Bill Elliott, Phyllis Coates, Myron Healey, Richard Reeves, Terry Frost, Rand Brooks, Russell Hicks, Robert Bray, Florence Lake, Gregg Barton, Denver Pyle, Robert Wilke, Eugene Roth, Joel Allen

D: Thomas Carr
SP: Sid Theil
P: Vincent M. Fennelly

2512. HIAWATHA

(Allied Artists, December 28, 1952) 80 Mins.
(Cinecolor)

Vincent Edwards, Yvette Dugay, Keith Larsen, Morris Ankrum, Gene Iglesias, Ian MacDonald, Stuart Randall, Katherine Emery, Stephen Chase, Armando Silvestre, Michael Tolan, Richard Bartlett, Michael Granger, Robert Bice, Gene Peterson, Henry Corden

D: Kurt Neumann
S: Based on the poem by Henry Wadsworth Longfellow
SP: Arthur Strawn, Dan Ullman
P: Walter Mirisch

2513. SCORCHING FURY

(Fraser Productions, 1952) 68 Mins.

Richard Devon, William Leslie, Peggy Nelson, Sherwood Price, Audrey Dineen, Rory Mallison, Eddie McClean, Allen Windsor, Twyla Paxton, Phyllis Coates, Charles Morton

D: Rick Freers
SP/P: Unknown

Cattle Town (Warner Bros., 1952) — Dennis Morgan and George O'Hanlon

CHAPTER 7

The Capricious Years 1953-1957

(TANGLED TRAILS)

In the Fifties old stereotypes of roles and role limitations for both men and women started falling away. Some critics have referred to the period as that time when the Western grew up and became serious. The decade brought the psychological Western, a cinematic attempt to talk out our historical neuroses and psychoses. And this "palaver therapy" in Westerns continued into the Sixties, despite the fact that it was not especially popular, owing to its emphasis on talk at the expense of action. The "serious," "adult," "psychological," or "mature" (take your pick of monikers) Westerns of the Fifties had in common a jaundiced view of various elements of the Western myth and the traditional Western of bygone days. However, many "A" Westerns of the Capricious Years (1953-1957), so called for the Western's changing nature and unpredictability, catered to the action requirements of "B" buffs while attracting general audiences on the basis of cast, technicolor, and running time. Universal and Allied Artists in particular tried with some success to appeal to both audiences with this type of product. Sporadic non-series, non-formula "B" Westerns continued to be made by several companies who found that such films still turned a profit through judicious marketing. A lot of small theatres still preferred the "B" product, sometimes using two such films on a double bill, or using one in combination with an "A," or, in smaller towns, using one as the single attraction. Although the genre was splintered as producers and directors followed diverse interests in putting together their products, the astute fan could still pick his way along tangled trails to reach familiar valleys of refuge if he did not want to explore new ranges.

The Capricious Years saw Randolph Scott unofficially crowned "King of the Range," his accomplished acting, distinctive and dignified voice, and demeanor carrying conviction. His weather-beaten countenance looked authentically Western and advancing age only enhanced the image of authenticity. Too, the sense of reality was always present in his films. Budd Boetticher directed several of the better Scott vehicles, notably *Seven Men from Now* (Warner Bros., 1956), *The Tall T* (Columbia, 1957), and *Decision at Sundown* (Columbia, 1957), and the idea of man's struggle with himself and his hostile environment is at work in these films. Scott is the true individual of the old West, a man who confronts his destiny directly as he sees it. Scott's hero is a man who acts little out of revenge or a lust for power; much like the old Hart, he is simply a man who comes to realize in the movie that a man should do what is "right." Basically, the Scott Westerns are traditional action affairs with a few added ingredients, and they proved to be popular and profitable.

The Scott-Harry Joe Brown co-production company filmed *The Stranger Wore a Gun* (Columbia, 1953), *Ten Wanted Men* (Columbia, 1955), *A Lawless Street* (Columbia, 1955), *Seventh Cavalry* (Columbia, 1956), *The Tall T* (Columbia, 1957), and *Decision at Sundown* (Columbia, 1957), with Scott starred. It is difficult to pick one over the others as being

The Tall T (Columbia, 1957) — Randolph Scott and Arthur Hunnicutt

superior. They all are direct action propositions from start to finish and possess quite a little pathos and heart appeal as well as physical punches. At Warner Brothers, Scott appeared in several excellent Westerns reeking with realism and the customary amount of rough-riding and gunplay. The films were extremely well made and the plots generally exerted a certain sentimental pressure in the hero's behalf, creating sympathy and straight human appeal. One of the best of these, *Seven Men from Now* (Warner Bros., 1956), was produced by John Wayne's Batjac Productions and originally meant for Wayne himself. Scott plays a former sheriff who tracks down seven men who killed his wife while robbing a Wells Fargo office. The story has refreshing novelty in treatment and boasts an imposing cast. A plot interestingly presented and intelligently acted and directed, aided by superior sound, photography, and scenic beauty, makes this film a memorable contribution to Western cinemania.

All of Scott's films after 1949, with the lone exception of *Shootout at Medicine Bend* (Warner Bros., 1957), were in color. RKO's *Rage at Dawn* (1955) was the only one not released through either Columbia or Warner Brothers during the Capricious Years.

Both *Seventh Cavalry* (Columbia, 1956) and *The Tall T* (Columbia, 1957) are classical Westerns and among Scott's all-time greatest hits. Joseph H. Lewis was at the helm of *Seventh Cavalry* and put his "B" training with Bob Baker and Johnny Mack Brown to good use as he kept the suspense high and the action moving. Scott portrays an officer in Custer's command who escaped the tragedy at the Little Big Horn and conducts an investigation which reveals politicians were actually responsible for the massacre. Budd Boetticher might have been lacking in the experience which Lewis had going for him but was still able to manipulate the ingredients in just the right way to create a masterful film in *The Tall T*, which centers around Scott and Maureen O'Sullivan being held captive by desperadoes on the Scott ranch.

Joel McCrea and George Montgomery were easily the second and third most popular performers who consistently made Westerns during the Capricious Years and their combined total of twenty-four films was quite satisfying. Though not as serious or grandiose as many others, the McCrea and Montgomery films were bread-and-butter oaters a considerable cut above the programmer "B's" that had been abandoned. Undistinguished they might have been; cheap they were not. Although the usually strong supporting casts and color photography helped to raise the McCrea and Montgomery vehicles out of the "ho-hum" category, it was the stars themselves that made the real difference in the sustained interest their movies had. Too, they were content with modest success and the tried-and-proven formula that had served Westerns since *The Great Train Robbery*. Content with their adeptness in providing a pleasant evening's entertainment, they left to others the task of creating classics that would live on in the memory for decades. And so it was that a lot of former "B" devotees, with nowhere else much to go, picked their way along tangled trails with these old reliables.

McCrea's role of Wyatt Earp in *Wichita* (Allied Artists, 1955), yet another old-fashioned shoot-em-up about the famed peace officer, is helped along by sensuous Vera Miles and a fine cast; as a different kind of lawman in *Stranger on Horseback* (United Artists, 1955), McCrea is a tight-lipped judge who is forced to kill in order to set justice straight and bring a murderer to trial; *The Oklahoman* (Allied Artists, 1957) is a more restrained Western centering around McCrea's attempts to help an outcast Indian protect his rights; while *Black Horse Canyon* (Universal, 1954) is a diverting, gentle Western about a rebellious black stallion and those who recapture him. Montgomery's best of the period were probably *Gun Belt* (United Artists, 1953), the story of a notorious outlaw trying to go straight; *Robber's Roost* (United Artists, 1955), a zippy Zane Grey yarn about outlaw gangs; and *Black Patch* (Warner Bros., 1957), his own production about a lawman out to clear his name.

William Elliott's Western career came to a close in the Capricious Years with six medium-budget products from Allied Artists. These stark little sagas, despite plot developments not unfamiliar, were pleasing and fast-moving, though sometimes harsh, and noteworthy for the Elliott characterizations modeled somewhat after William S. Hart's good badman hero of the silent era. His heroes were not afraid to act like adults scared for their lives; if he felt he needed to draw first and bang someone over the head, he did.

Audie Murphy, working strictly at Universal, turned out a product similar to that of George Montgomery and Joel McCrea, although generally it was not quite as good. First, Murphy was not the actor that Montgomery and McCrea were; second, the screenplays were not as good. However, the Murphy films were delightful at viewing time even if they were not the kind that would make life-long impressions on the viewer. Two of his better ones were *Destry* (Universal, 1955) and *Walk the Proud Land* (Universal, 1956). *Destry*, of course, was a remake of the 1939 James Stewart classic about a tenderfoot out to tame a town and its celebrated dancehall girl. The latter film told the true-life story of Indian agent John Philip Clum, a hero of the Southwest who, with the Apache force he has trained, forces the surrender of the notorious warrior outlaw Geronimo.

The Western from the Capricious Years that immediately achieved classic status is *Shane* (Paramount, 1953), a film that evokes the pastoral mood of the Western as contrasted with sudden eruptions and violence. Director George Stevens was at the helm in this nostalgic vision of the West, while Alan Ladd played the saviour-like hero who takes up the cause of the farmers against the cruel ranchers and their hired gun, Jack Palance. Critics have written realms of copy relative to *Shane*'s sociological and psychological messages, and it has been the model for a number of Westerns made subsequently.

The Capricious Years were lean ones for John Wayne fans, as the star made only two

Jesse James' Women (United Artists, 1954) — Peggy Castle and Donald Barry

Westerns. *Hondo* (Warner Bros., 1954) was filmed in 3-D and technicolor and has Wayne befriending a woman and her son and saving white settlers from massacre by Indians. It is not unlike *Shane* in that Wayne's Hondo is an ex-gunfighter who shows up at the woman's (Geraldine Page) ranch and helps her to keep it going. The story is a strong one and the characterizations are believable.

The Searchers (Warner Bros., 1956) is a melancholic yet enthralling film that is stupefying in its beauty. Director John Ford had the selective sense of a painter; he knew how to compose his scenes, or, rather, how to record those scenes which have been most perfectly composed by nature. John Wayne is the outsider on a five-year quest of revenge and rescue, and in his performance as Ethan Edwards, a man tormented for years with the poignancy of lost love and burdened with an error of judgment in being away from those he loves when he is needed, he has given what surely must be one of his best screen characterizations, if not the greatest. The film proved Wayne capable of expressing and conveying the feeling of inner torment. The moment that he resists shooting his niece because of her wishing to live with an Indian buck is one of the greatest moments in Western cinema.

In a spin-off from *High Noon, 3:10 to Yuma* (Columbia, 1957) is an intriguing film. Glenn Ford and Van Heflin, as outlaw and reluctant lawman respectively, pack a lot of wallop in this story of the tired gunman being escorted back to a Yuma prison by a courageous but frightened rancher. Heflin, *a la* Cooper in *High Noon,* is the hero alone among those intent on killing him. In this instance, however, badman Ford evidences a streak of humanity in the end when he saves Heflin's life by jumping aboard a train with him rather than see Heflin shot by his outlaw cronies.

Jubal (Columbia, 1956) is typical of a number of Westerns of the period in its emphasis on sexual lust rather than the older traditional staples associated with such films. Glenn

Ford, Ernest Borgnine, Rod Steiger, Valerie French, and Felicia Farr pant their way through this erotic tale. *The King and Four Queens* (United Artists, 1956), too, allowed for sexual emphasis, with Clark Gable and Eleanor Parker heading up the cast. Raoul Walsh directed. Just previous to this one, Walsh had directed Gable and Jane Russell in *The Tall Men* (Fox, 1955), the biggest production in the history of 20th Century-Fox to that time. Jane Russell in bloomers was not exactly playing down sex. And smaller-scale Westerns of the "B" calibre also capitalized on sex, as, for example, Donald Barry's *Jesse James' Women* (United Artists, 1954).

Racial matters continued to generate a lot of interest and, naturally, the emphasis was on the Indian, who blossomed into a misunderstood, mistreated, sensitive, and intelligent human being from his previous status symbolized in the cliche, "The only good Indian is a dead Indian." *Broken Lance* (Fox, 1954), *Arrowhead* (Paramount, 1953), *Walk the Proud Land* (Universal, 1956), *Chief Crazy Horse* (Universal, 1955), *The Vanishing American* (Republic, 1955), and other dramas of the era cast the Indian in a favorable light and the white man as the villain.

Musical Westerns had a brief fling with such vehicles as *Calamity Jane* (Warner Bros., 1953), *Seven Brides for Seven Brothers* (MGM, 1954), *Rose Marie* (MGM, 1954), *Red Garters* (Paramount, 1954), and *Oklahoma* (Todd-AO, 1956), but perhaps the least said about these the better.

National guilt feelings were focused on in John Sturges' contemporary Western, *Bad Day at Black Rock* (MGM, 1955). Spencer Tracy, a one-armed war veteran, arrives in Black Rock to deliver a medal belonging to a dead Japanese-American soldier, only to find that the town has killed the boy's father in a wave of anti-Japanese hatred during the war. The suspenseful film revolves about Tracy's overcoming of the bigoted villains. In the final showdown, he defeats a rifle-armed Robert Ryan with, ironically, an improvised bomb.

Cowboy life was explored in *Cowboy* (Lippert, 1954), a semi-documentary film contrasting the present-day cowboy with his old-time predecessor, poignantly emphasizing the function of cowboys as against cowboy fiction.

Allan Dwan directed three suspenseful Westerns in the mid-Fifties that added to his reputation in the genre. *Silver Lode* (RKO, 1954) is the story of a violent three hours in a Western community in the 1870's when the entire town is drawn into one man's determined fight to clear himself of a murder charge brought against him on his wedding day, while *Tennessee's Partner* (RKO, 1955) is based on Bret Harte's timeless story of two men becoming fast friends after one saves the other from being shot in the back. John Payne starred in both features. *Cattle Queen of Montana* (RKO, 1954) had as its chief asset Barbara Stanwyck, but the story of territorial Montana in the 1880's is a good one. Dwan, of course, had been directing Westerns as early as 1911 for the American Film Company, where he made innumerable one-reelers, many of them with Pete Morrison and J. Warren Kerrigan, and he knew how to exact the most from his story and his cast.

Space does not allow a discussion, or even mention, of most of the period's great Western cinematic experiences, but the number of deluxe Westerns produced is evidence enough that the genre was still popular, despite numerous changes in its makeup and emphasis. The major Westerns were fairly straightforward vehicles with no real social or moral axes to grind; they were meant to entertain in the old-fashioned way and the Western myth and hero, as well as other traditional elements, were yet much in evidence. Still riding the range were heroes with pure, unselfish motivations and unshattered psyches, and on occasion a hero and heroine could still be seen riding into the sunset at the fade-out. And more often than not, one could figure out whom he was supposed to be cheering for without resorting to a film critic's analysis of the movie. Filmmakers put in busy, exhausting days to grind out the many commercial successes of the period, aided in part by the innovations of CinemaScope, three dimension, and varied color processes. It was a high point for the sustained production and popularity of colossal Westerns and big-name stars dabbled in the genre with some regularity and considerable success.

On the "B" scene, series Westerns were in the last death throes, jerking and sputtering in the dust as they ran out of steam and lost their audience to television and increased sophistication. At least the Gene Autry series at Columbia ended on a high note, with Gene producing and starring in six quality Westerns in 1953. George Archainbaud directed the group and Smiley Burnette, Gene's original sidekick, was featured in each film. *Last of the Pony Riders*, released in November, 1953, and filmed in Sepiatone, was Autry's last theatrical release; thereafter, the multi-millionaire cowboy would go on making millions—part of them in television, first with his own "Gene Autry Show," then with other shows produced by his Flying A Productions. To his credit the Autry features remained top-grade films right through the last one released. Nearly all of his Columbia features had strong plots and excellent production values. And throughout his long movie career he adhered to a strict on-screen moral code which, under today's guidelines, would guarantee each of his films a "G" rating.

Republic struggled through 1953 before throwing in the towel regarding series Westerns. The Allan Lane series ceased after four releases in 1953, whereas Rex Allen made six features, the last one, *Phantom Stallion*, released on February 4, 1954. It was a sad day for "B" Western aficionados when the once great little studio shut down forever its production of both "B" Westerns and serials. In a short while, the studio itself would shut down and its facilities would be sold to television interests.

Over at Allied Artists (Monogram), management had been more competent and that studio, which had never been able to match the quality of the Republic product, survived the demise of the "B" Western and plunged into the production of medium-budget "A" Westerns with Joel McCrea, George Montgomery, Bill Elliott, and Rod Cameron headlining their beefed-up product. But in 1953 the little studio was still competing in the programmer market with a Kirby Grant Northwest Mountie series, which petered out early in 1954, and a Wayne Morris Western series which lasted on into 1954. Morris was not a cowboy. He had spent sixteen years as a dramatic actor prior to strapping on a six-shooter as a cowboy hero. But he managed admirably, in spite of a protruding beer-belly, and the films were entertaining, a cut above the average, and, for lack of something better, an acceptable finish to the series Western after a fifty-year stand. The film *Two Guns and a Badge*, released September 12, 1954, is generally credited with being the last "B" Western released in this country as part of a series. Many "B's" would subsequently be made, but not as part of a block of Westerns starring a single personality; the "B's" henceforth would be isolated, non-series ones.

Take, for example, two Buster Crabbe films. After an absence from Westerns for nine years Crabbe was back in the saddle as star of United Artists' *Gun Brothers* (1956). Crabbe is good as an ex-cavalryman fighting an outlaw gang of which his brother, played by Neville Brand, is a member. In 1957 came *The Lawless Eighties* for Republic, a fair, slow-moving Western revolving about a gunfighter who protects a circuit rider beaten up by thugs.

John Carpenter (and here we pause for the reader to soliloquize, "Who?!") was one of the last cowboys to try something approaching a "B" series, having gotten off to an inauspicious beginning with *Badman's Gold* for Robert Tansey in 1951. In 1953 came *Son of the Renegade* (United Artists), in 1954 *The Lawless Rider* (United Artists), and in 1955 *Outlaw Treasure* (American). Having contemplated the former drawing power of the Carpenter name, he changed it for the latter film to John Forbes. But in 1956 he was back as John

Outlaw Treasure (Amco, 1956) — Frank "Red" Carpenter and John Forbes (John Carpenter)

Carpenter in *I Killed Wild Bill Hickok* (Wheeler). Mercifully, it was the last film in Carpenter's attempts to create a new "B" hero. A Buck Jones or Gene Autry, he was not. Supporting casts in these "indies" were good, but the films were sadly lacking in production finesse.

Another independent produced by Ken Murray and sold to United Artists was *The Marshal's Daughter* (1953), a nostalgic and entertaining Western starring Hoot Gibson as an old sheriff who calls on cronies Johnny Mack Brown, Jimmy Wakely, Preston Foster, and Buddy Baer for help in the pinch. Ken Murray and Laurie Anders were co-starred and the comedic Western came off pleasantly. The mildly spoofing reminders of the Western aficionado's naivete and innocence were refreshing and there was even a flashback to some silent footage of Hoot as he reminisces about his prowess as a younger man. It was really Miss Anders, however, who stole the film, leaving us to wonder why this vivacious young lady did not go on to make a name for herself in movies.

Clayton Moore, long a serial star and supporting player in Westerns, hit the jackpot as television's "The Lone Ranger." As a result of the popularity of that series, a full-length motion picture was made with Clayton as the masked ranger and Jay Silverheels as Tonto. *The Lone Ranger* was released by Warner Brothers (1956), filmed in WarnerColor, and produced by Jack Wrather. An interesting sidelight is that Lane Chandler, one of the original five rangers in the Republic serial classic *The Lone Ranger* (1938), had a small part in the Warner Brothers feature as a character called "Whitebeard."

Only six Western serials were made during the Capricious Years, none of them memorable. *Perils of the Wilderness*, released by Columbia in 1956, has the distinction of being the last American serial made. It starred Dennis Moore, a featured player in Westerns for years. Fittingly, two old-timers who had appeared in some of the earliest sound serials were on hand for the demise of the genre, Rex Lease and Kermit Maynard both having minor roles in the last of the cliffhangers. Another era had ended, and its passing was nostalgically painful.

The Capricious Years were good years in terms of the number of quality Westerns made, the revenues received, and the innovative and creative aspects of production. Although traditional action Westerns rooted in the "B" formula predominated, there was a trend toward more serious, adult-oriented Westerns embodying less action, fewer real heroes, more pathos, more sex, more violence, and more schizophrenic Westerners. (Luckily, the horses seemed as stable as ever, *Cat Ballou* having not yet popularized the drunken horse!) As the period came to a close, Westerns, along with movies in general, had again slumped in popularity, and the outlook was for lean years ahead and a reduced number of Westerns. The tangled trails taken by the genre seemed to be carrying the Western cinema nearer to the perilous plunge into the dangerous depths of cynicism from which few traditional heroes in white hats would emerge.

FILMS OF 1953

2514. THE PATHFINDER
(Columbia, January 1, 1953)   78 Mins.
(Technicolor)
George Montgomery, Helena Carter, Jay Silver-heels, Walter Kingsford, Rodd Redwing, Stephen Bekassy, Elena Verdugo, Bruce Lester, Chief Yowlachie, Ed Coch, Jr., Ross Conklin, Vi Ingraham, Adele St. Maur
D: Sidney Salkow
S: James Fenimore Cooper
SP: Robert E. Kent
P: Sam Katzman

2515. THE REDHEAD FROM WYOMING
(Universal-International, January 1, 1953)
  80 Mins.
(Technicolor)
Maureen O'Hara, Alex Nicol, Robert Strauss, Jeanne Cooper, William Bishop, Alexander Scourby, Palmer Lee, Jack Kelly, Claudette Thornton, Ray Bennett, Joe Bailey, Rush Williams, Dennis Weaver, David Alpert, Joe Bassett, Stacey Harris, Betty Allen, Larry Hudson
D: Lee Sholem
SP: Polly James, Herb Meadow
P: Leonard Goldstein

2516. RIDE THE MAN DOWN
(Republic, January 1, 1953)   90 Mins.
(Trucolor)
Brian Donlevy, Rod Cameron, Ella Raines, Forrest Tucker, Barbara Britton, Chill Wills, J. Carroll Naish, Jim Davis, Taylor Holmes, James Bell, Paul Fix, Al Caudebec, Roydon Clark, Roy Barcroft, Douglas Kennedy, Chris-Pin Martin, Jack LaRue, Claire Carleton

D/AP: Joseph Kane
S: From the *Saturday Evening Post* story by Luke Short
SP: Mary McCall, Jr.

2517. STAR OF TEXAS
(Westwood/Allied Artists, January 11, 1953)
  68 Mins.
Wayne Morris, Paul Fix, Frank Ferguson, Rick Vallin, Jack Larson, James Flavin, William Fawcett, Robert Bice, Mickey Simpson, George Wallace, John Crawford, Stanley Price, Lyle Talbot
D: Thomas Carr
SP: Dan Ullman
P: Vincent M. Fennelly

2518. FANGS OF THE ARTIC
(Monogram, January 18, 1953)   62 Mins.
Kirby Grant, Lorna Hansen, Warren Douglas, Leonard Penn, Richard Avonde, Robert Sherman, John Close, Phil Tead, Roy Gordon, Kit Carson, "Chinook" (a dog)
D: Rex Bailey
S: James Oliver Curwood
SP: Bill Raynor, Warren Douglas
P: Lindsley Parsons

2519. WINNING OF THE WEST
(Columbia, January 20, 1953)   57 Mins.
(Sepiatone)
Gene Autry, Smiley Burnette, Gail Davis, Richard Crane, Robert Livingston, House Peters, Jr., Gregg Barton, William Fawcett, Ewing Mitchell, Rodd Redwing, George Chesebro, Frank Jacquet, Charles Delaney, Charles Soldani, Eddie Parker, Terry Frost, James Kirkwood, Boyd Morgan, Bob Woodward, "Champion, Jr."

D: George Archainbaud
SP: Norman S. Hall
P: Armand Schaefer

S: William Alland
SP: Bernard Gordon
P: Raoul Walsh

2520. THE MAN BEHIND THE GUN
(Warner Bros., January 31, 1953) 82 Mins.
(Technicolor)
Randolph Scott, Patrice Wymore, Dick Wesson, Philip Carey, Lina Romay, Roy Roberts, Morris Ankrum, Katherine Warren, Alan Hale, Jr., Douglas Fowley, Tony Caruso, Clancy Cooper, Robert Cabal, James Brown, Reed Howes, Rory Mallinson, John Logan, Vickie Raaf, Lee Morgan, Ray Spiker, Edward Hearn, Terry Frost, Charles Horvath, Art Millian, Rex Lease, Jack Parker, James Bellah, Billy Vincent, Albert Morin, Edward Colemans, Herbert Deans
D: Felix Feist
S: Forest Buckner
SP: John Twist
P: Robert Sisk

2520a. THE LAWLESS BREED
(Universal-International, January, 1953)
83 Mins.
Rock Hudson, Julia Adams, Mary Castle, John McIntire, Hugh O'Brian, Dennis Weaver, Forrest Lewis, Lee Van Cleef, Tom Fadden, Race Gentry
D: Raoul Walsh

2521. LAST OF THE COMANCHES
(Columbia, February 1, 1953) 85 Mins.
(Technicolor)
Broderick Crawford, Barbara Hale, Johnny Stewart, Lloyd Bridges, Mickey Shaughnessy, George Mathews, Hugh Sanders, Ric Roman, Chubby Johnson, Martin Milner, Milton Parsons, Jack Woody, John War Eagle, Carleton Young, William Andrews
D: Andre de Toth
SP: Kenneth Gamet
P: Buddy Adler

2522. MARSHAL OF CEDAR ROCK
(Republic, February 1, 1953) 54 Mins.
Allan Lane, Eddy Waller, Phyllis Coates, Roy Barcroft, Bill Henry, Robert Shayne, John Crawford, John Hamilton, Kenneth MacDonald, Herbert Lytton, "Black Jack"
D: Harry Keller
S: M. Coates Webster
SP: Albert DeMond
AP: Rudy Ralston

Last of the Comanches (Columbia, 1953) — Barbara Hale and Broderick Crawford

2523. THE SILVER WHIP

(20th C. Fox, February 1, 1953)   73 Mins.

Dale Robertson, Rory Calhoun, Robert Wagner, Kathleen Crowley, James Millican, Lola Albright, J. M. Kerrigan, John Kellogg, Harry Carter, Ian MacDonald, Robert Adler, Clancy Cooper, Burt Mustin, Dan White, Paul Wexler, Charles Watts, Jack Rice, Bobby Diamond, Cameron Grant

D: Harmon Jones

S: Jack Schaefer

SP: Jesse L. Lasky, Jr.

P: Robert Bassler, Michael Abel

2524. THE NAKED SPUR

(MGM, February 6, 1953)   91 Mins.
(Technicolor)

James Stewart, Janet Leigh, Ralph Meeker, Robert Ryan, Millard Mitchell

D: Anthony Mann

SP: Sam Rolfe, Harold Jack Bloom

P: William H. Wright

2525. THE COMMAND

(Warner Bros., February 13, 1953)   88 Mins.
(Cinemascope)   (WarnerColor)

Guy Madison, Joan Weldon, James Whitmore, Carl Benton Reid, Harvey Lembeck, Ray Teal, Bob Nichols, Don Shelton, Gregg Barton, Boyd (Red) Morgan, Zachary Yaconelli, Renata Vanni, Tom Monroe

D: David Butler

S: "The White Invader"—James Warner Bellah

SP: Russell Hughes, Samuel Fuller

P: David Weisbart

2526. KANSAS PACIFIC

(Allied Artists, February 22, 1953)   73 Mins.
(Cinecolor)

Sterling Hayden, Eve Miller, Barton MacLane, Harry Shannon, Reed Hadley, Tom Fadden, Douglas Fowley, Bob Keys, Irving Bacon, Myron Healey, James Griffith, Clayton Moore, Jonathan Hale

D: Ray Nazarro

SP: Dan Ullman

P: Walter Wanger

2527. OLD OVERLAND TRAIL

(Republic, February 25, 1953)   60 Mins.

Rex Allen, Slim Pickens, Roy Barcroft, Virginia Hall, Gil Herman, Wade Crosby, Leonard Nimoy, Zon Murray, Harry Harvey, The Republic Rhythm Riders, "Koko"

D: William Witney

SP: Milt Raison

AP: Eddy White

2528. GUNSMOKE

(Universal-International, March 1, 1953)   79 Mins.
(Technicolor)

Audie Murphy, Susan Cabot, Paul Kelly, Charles Drake, Mary Castle, Jack Kelly, Jesse White, William Reynolds, Chubby Johnson, Al Haskell, Edmund Cobb, Bill Radovich, Donald Randolph, James F. Stone, Clem Fuller, Jimmy Van Horn

D: Nathan Juran

SP: D. D. Beauchamp

P: Aaron Rosenberg

2529. RIDE CLEAR OF DIABLO

(Universal-International, March 1, 1953)   80 Mins.
(Technicolor)

Audie Murphy, Dan Duryea, Susan Cabot, Abbe Lane, Russell Johnson, Paul Birch, William Pullen, Jack Elam, Lane Bradford, Mike Regan, Denver Pyle

D: Jesse Hibbs

S: Ellis Marcus

SP: George Zuckerman

P: John W. Rogers

2530. THE WOMAN THEY ALMOST LYNCHED

(Republic, March 20, 1953)   90 Mins.

John Lund, Brian Donlevy, Joan Leslie, Audrey Totter, Ben Cooper, James Brown, Nina Varela, Ellen Corby, Fern Hall, Minerva Urecal, Jim Davis, Reed Hadley, Ann Savage, Virginia Christine, Marilyn Lindsey, Nacho Galindo, Richard Simmons, Gordon Jones, Frank Ferguson, Post Park, Tom McDonough, Ted Ryan, Richard Crane, Carl Pitti, Joe Yrigoyen, Jimmie Hawkins, James Kirkwood, Paul Livermore

D: Allan Dwan

S: From the *Saturday Evening Post* story by Michael Fessier

SP: Steve Fischer

2531. THE HOMESTEADERS

(Allied Artists, March 22, 1953)   62 Mins.
(Sepiatone)

Bill Elliott, Robert Lowery, Emmett Lynn, George Wallace, Buzz Henry, Stanley Price, Rick Vallin, William Fawcett, James Seay, Tom Monroe, Barbara Allen, Ray Walker

D: Lewis Collins

SP: Sol Theil, Milton Raison

P: Vincent M. Fennelly

2532. ON TOP OF OLD SMOKY

(Columbia, March 25, 1953)   59 Mins.
(Sepiatone)

Gene Autry, Smiley Burnette, Gail Davis, Grandon Rhodes, Sheila Ryan, Kenne Duncan, Robert Bice, Zon Murray, Fred S. Martin, Jerry Scroggins, Bert Dodson, Pat O'Malley, "Champion, Jr."

D: George Archainbaud
SP: Gerald Geraghty
P: Armand Schaefer

2533. SON OF THE RENEGADE
(Schwarz/United Artists, March 27, 1953)
57 Mins.
John Carpenter, Lori Irving, Joan McKellan, Valley Keene, Jack Ingram, Verne Teters, Bill Goonz, Ted Smile, Bill Ward, Roy Canada, Whitney Hughes, Lennie Smith, Ewing Brown, Freddie Carson, Perry Lennon, Jack Wilson, Pat McGeehan (narrator)
D: Reg Brown
SP/P: John Carpenter

2534. FORT VENGEANCE
(Allied Artists, March 29, 1953)   75 Mins.
(Cinecolor)
James Craig, Rita Moreno, Keith Larsen, Reginald Denny, Charles Irwin, Morris Ankrum, Guy Kingsford, Michael Grainger, Patrick Whyte, Paul Marion, Emory Parnell
D: Lesley Selander
S/SP: Dan Ullman
P: Walter Wanger

2535. BORN TO THE SADDLE
(Astor, March, 1953)   73 Mins.
(Trucolor)
Chuck Courtney, Donald Woods, Leif Erickson, Karen Morley, Rand Brooks, Glenn Strange, Dolores Priest, Bob Anderson, Lucille Thompson, Fred Kohler, Jr., Dan White, Milton Kibbee, Boyd Davis
D: William Beaudine
S: "Quarter Horse"—Gordon Young
SP: Adele Buffington
P: Hall Shelton

2536. JACK McCALL, DESPERADO
(Columbia, April 1, 1953)   76 Mins.
(Technicolor)
George Montgomery, Angela Stevens, Douglas Kennedy, James Seay, Eugene Iglesias, William Tannen, Jay Silverheels, John Hamilton, Selmer Jackson, Stanley Blystone, Gene Roth, Alva Lacy, Joe McGuinn
D: Sidney Salkow
S: David Chandler
SP: John O'Dea
P: Sam Katzman

2537. THE MARKSMAN
(Westwood/Allied Artists, April 12, 1953)
62 Mins.
Wayne Morris, Elena Verdugo, Frank Ferguson, Rick Vallin, I. Stanford Jolley, Tom Powers, Rob-ert Bice, Stanley Price, Russ Whiteman, Brad Johnson, William Fawcett, Jack Rice, Tim Ryan
D: Lewis Collins
SP: Dan Ullman
P: Vincent Fennelly

2538. COW COUNTRY
(Allied Artists, April 26, 1953)   82 Mins.
Edmond O'Brien, Helen Westcott, Robert Lowery, Barton MacLane, Peggie Castle, Robert Barrat, James Millican, Don Beddoe, Robert Wilke, Raymond Hatton, Chuck Courtney, Steve Clark, Rory Mallison, Marshall Reed, Brett Houston, Tom Tyler, Sam Flint, Jack Ingram, George J. Lewis
D: Lesley Selander
S: Adele Buffington
SP: Tom W. Blackburn
P: Scott R. Dunlap

2539. AMBUSH AT TOMAHAWK GAP
(Columbia, May 1, 1953)   73 Mins.
(Technicolor)
John Hodiak, John Derell, David Brian, Maria Elena Marques, Ray Teal, John Qualen, Otto Hullett, Percy Helton, Trevor Bardette, John Doucette
D: Fred Sears
S/SP: David Lang
P: Wallace MacDonald

2540. FORT TI
(Columbia, May 1, 1953)   73 Mins.
(Technicolor)   (3-D)
George Montgomery, Joan Vohs, Irving Bacon, James Seay, Ben Astar, Phyllis Fowler, Howard Petrie, Cicely Browne, Lester Matthews, George Dee, Louis Merrill
D: William Castle
S/SP: Robert E. Kent
P: Sam Katzman

2541. LAW AND ORDER
(Universal-International, May 1, 1953)   80 Mins.
(Technicolor)
Ronald Reagan, Dorothy Malone, Preston Foster, Alex Nicol, Ruth Hampton, Dennis Weaver, Chubby Johnson, Barry Kelly
D: Nathan Juran
S: "Saint Johnson"—W. R. Burnett
SP: John and Gwen Bagni, D. D. Beauchamp
P: John W. Rogers

2542. THE LONE HAND
(Universal-International, May 1, 1953)   80 Mins.
(Technicolor)
Joel McCrea, Barbara Hale, Alex Nicol, Charles Drake, Jimmy Hunt, James Arness, Wesley Morgan, Roy Roberts

D: George Sherman
SP: Joseph Hoffman
P: Howard Christie

2543. PONY EXPRESS
(Paramount, May 1, 1953) 101 Mins.
(Technicolor)
Charlton Heston, Rhonda Fleming, Jan Sterling,
Forrest Tucker, Michael Moore, Porter Hall,
Richard Shannon, Henry Brandon, Stuart Randall, Lewis Martin, Pat Hogan, Eric Alden, Howard
Joslin, LeRoy Johnson, Jimmy H. Burke, Robert J.
Miles, Robert Scott, Bob Templeton, Willard Willingham, John Mansfield, Frank Wilcox
D: Jerry Hopper
S: Frank Gruber
SP: Charles Marquis Warren
P: Nat Holt

2544. IRON MOUNTAIN TRAIL
(Republic, May 8, 1953) 54 Mins.
Rex Allen, Slim Pickens, Nan Leslie, Grant Withers,
Roy Barcroft, Alan Bridge, Forrest Taylor, George
Lloyd, John Hamilton, "Koko"
D: William Witney
SP: Gerald Geraghty
AP: Eddy White

2545. REBEL CITY
(Silvermine/Allied Artists, May 10, 1953) 62 Mins.
(Sepiatone)
Bill Elliott, Marjorie Lord, Robert Kent, Ray Walker,
Henry Rowland, Keith Richards, I. Stanford Jolley, Denver Pyle, Otto Waldis, John Crawford,
Stanley Price, Michael Vallon, Bill Walker
D: Thomas Carr
SP: Sid Theil
P: Vincent M. Fennelly

2546. SAVAGE FRONTIER
(Republic, May 15, 1953) 54 Mins.
Allan Lane, Eddy Waller, Bob Steele, Dorothy Patrick, Roy Barcroft, Richard Avonde, Bill Phipps,
Jimmy Hawkins, Lane Bradford, John Cason,
Kenneth MacDonald, Bill Henry, Gerry Flash,
"Black Jack"
D: Harry Keller
SP: Dwight Babcock, Gerald Geraghty
AP: Rudy Ralston

2547. GOLDTOWN GHOST RAIDERS
(Columbia, May 30, 1953) 59 Mins.
(Sepiatone)
Gene Autry, Smiley Burnette, Gail Davis, Kirk
Rile, Carleton Young, Neyle Morrow, Denver
Pyle, Steve Conte, John Doucette, "Champion,
Jr."

D: George Archainbaud
SP: Gerald Geraghty
P: Armand Schaefer

2548. COLUMN SOUTH
(Universal-International, June 1, 1953) 84 Mins.
(Technicolor)
Audie Murphy, Joan Evans, Robert Sterling, Ray
Collins, Palmer Lee, Ralph Moody, Dennis Weaver,
Johnny Downs, Russell Johnson, Bob Steele, Jack
Kelly, Raymond Montgomery, Richard Garland,
James Best, Ed Rand
D: Frederick de Cordova
S/SP: William Sackheim
P: Ted Richmond

2549. POWDER RIVER
(20th C. Fox, June 8, 1953) 78 Mins.
(Technicolor)
Rory Calhoun, Corinne Calvet, Cameron Mitchell,
Penny Edwards, Carl Betz, John Dehner, Raymond Greenleaf, Victor Sutherland, Ethan Laidlaw, Bob Wilke, Harry Carter, Robert Adler, Post
Park, Richard Garrick, Archer MacDonald, Frank
Ferguson, Henry Kulky, Walter Sande, Zon Murray, Ray Bennett, Harry Hines
D: Louis King
S: Sam Hellman
SP: Geoffrey Homes
P: Andre Hakim

2550. TAKE ME TO TOWN
(Universal-International, June 8, 1953) 81 Mins.
(Technicolor)
Ann Sheridan, Sterling Hayden, Philip Reed, Lee
Patrick, Lee Aaker, Phyllis Stanley, Larry Gates,
Forrest Lewis, Harvey Grant, Dusty Henley, Ann
Tyrell, Dorothy Neumann, Robert Anderson,
Lane Chandler, Frank Sully
D: Douglas Sirk
S/SP: Richard Morris
P: Ross Hunter, Leonard Goldstein

2551. ARENA
(MGM, June 12, 1953) 83 Mins.
(Technicolor) (3-D)
Gig Young, Jean Hagen, Polly Bergen, Henry (Harry)
Morgan, Barbara Lawrence, Robert Horton, Lee
Aaker, Lee Van Cleef, Marilee Phelps, Jim Hayward, George Wallace, Stuart Randall, Morris
Ankrum
D: Richard Fleischer
S/P: Arthur M. Lowe, Jr.
SP: Harold Jack Bloom

2552. THE MARSHAL'S DAUGHTER

(United Artists, June 26, 1953) 71 Mins.

Hoot Gibson, Laurie Anders, Harry Lauter, Ken Murray, Robert Bray, Bob Duncan, Forrest Taylor, Tom London, Bruce Norman, Cecil Elliott, Bettie Lou Walters, Francis Ford, Julian Upton, Ted Jordan, Lee Phelps, and guest stars Preston Foster, Johnny Mack Brown, Jimmy Wakely, and Buddy Baer

D: William Berke

SP: Bob Duncan

P: Ken Murray

2553. SON OF BELLE STARR

(Allied Artists, June 28, 1953) 70 Mins.

(Cinecolor)

Keith Larsen, Dona Drake, Peggy Castle, Regis Toomey, James Seay, Myron Healey, Frank Puglia, Robert Keys, I. Stanford Jolley, Paul McGuire, Lane Bradford, Mike Ragan (Holly Bane), Joe Dominguez, Alex Montoya

D: Frank McDonald

S: Jack DeWitt

SP: D. D. Beauchamp, William Raynor

P: Peter Scully

2554. THE VANQUISHED

(Paramount, June, 1953) 84 Mins.

(Technicolor)

John Payne, Jan Sterling, Coleen Gray, Lyle Bettger, Willard Parker, Roy Gordon, John Dierkes, Charles Evans, Ellen Corby

D: Edward Ludwig

S: Karl Brown

SP: Winston Miller, Frank Moss, Lewis R. Foster

P: William H. Pine, William C. Thomas

2555. THE LAST POSSE

(Columbia, July 1, 1953) 73 Mins.

Broderick Crawford, John Derek, Charles Bickford, Wanda Hendrix, Warner Anderson, Henry Hull, Will Wright, Tom Powers, Raymond Greenleaf, James Kirkwood, Eddy Waller, Skip Homeier, James Bell, Guy Wilkerson, Mira McKinney, Helen Wallace, Harry Hayden, Monte Blue

D: Alfred Werker

S: Seymour and Connie Lee Bennett

SP: Seymour and Connie Lee Bennett, Kenneth Gamet

P: Harry Joe Brown

2556. CANADIAN MOUNTIES VS. ATOMIC INVADERS

(Republic, July 8, 1953) 12 Chaps.

Bill Henry, Susan Morrow, Arthur Space, Dale Van Sickel, Pierre Watkin, Mike Ragan, Stanley Andrews, Harry Lauter, Hank Patterson, Edmund Cobb, Gayle Kellogg, Tom Steele, Jean Wright, Jeane Wood, Bob Reeves, Joe Yrigoyen, Carey Loftin, Duane Thorsen, Fred Graham, Drew Cahil, William Fawcett, Kenner Kemp, Gordon Armitage, George DeNormand, Paul Palmer, Earl Bunn, Jimmy Fawcett, David Sharpe, Bob Jamison, Duke Taylor

D/AP: Franklin Adreon

SP: Ronald Davidson

Chapter Titles: (1) Arctic Intrigue, (2) Murder or Accident?, (3) Fangs of Death, (4) Underground Inferno, (5) Pursuit to Destruction, (6) The Boat Trap, (7) Flame Versus Gun, (8) Highway of Horror, (9) Doomed Cargo, (10) Human Quarry, (11) Mechanical Homicide, (12) Cavern of Revenge

2557. THE CHARGE AT FEATHER RIVER

(Warner Bros., July 11, 1953) 96 Mins.

(WarnerColor) (3-D)

Guy Madison, Frank Lovejoy, Helen Westcott, Vera Miles, Dick Wesson, Onslow Stevens, Steve Brodie, Ron Hagerthy, Fay Roope, Neville Brand, Henry Kulky, Lane Chandler, Fred Carson, James Brown, Ben Corbett, Ralph Brooke, Carl Andre, Fred Kennedy, Dub Taylor, John Damler, David Alpert

D: Gordon Douglas

SP: James R. Webb

P: David Weisbart

2558. NORTHERN PATROL

(Monogram, July 12, 1953) 63 Mins.

Kirby Grant, Marion Carr, Emmett Lynn, Bill Phipps, Claudia Drake, Frank Sully, Dale Van Sickel, Gloria Talbot, Richard Walsh, Frank Lackteen, "Chinook" (a dog)

D: Rex Bailey

S: James Oliver Curwood

SP: Warren Douglas

P: Lindsley Parsons

2559. THE GREAT JESSE JAMES RAID

(Lippert, July 17, 1953) 73 Mins.

(AnscoColor)

Willard Parker, Barbara Payton, Tom Neal, Wallace Ford, James Anderson, Jim Bannon, Richard Cutting, Barbara Woodell, Marin Sais, Earle Hodgins, Tom Walker, Joan Arnold, Helene Hayden, Steve Pendleton, Bob Griffin, Robin Moore, Ed Russell, Rory Mallison

D: Reginald Le Borg

SP: Richard Landau

P: Robert L. Lippert, Jr.

2560. THE GREAT SIOUX UPRISING

(Universal-International, July 17, 1953)   80 Mins.

(Technicolor)

Jeff Chandler, Faith Domergue, Lyle Bettger, Peter Whitney, John War Eagle, Stephen Chase, Stacey Harris, Walter Sande, Clem Fuller, Glenn Strange, Ray Bennett, Charles Arnt, Rosa Rey

D: Lloyd Bacon

SP: Melvin Levy, J. Robert Bren, Gladys Atwater

P: Albert J. Cohen, Leonard Goldstein

2561. RIDE, VAQUERO!

(MGM, July 17, 1953)   90 Mins.

(AnscoColor)

Robert Taylor, Ava Gardner, Howard Keel, Anthony Quinn, Kurt Kasznar, Ted de Corsia, Charlita, Jack Elam, Walter Baldwin, Joe Dominguez, Frank McGrath, Charles Stevens, Rex Lease, Tom Greenway

D: John Farrow

SP: Frank Fenton

P: Stephen Ames

2562. GUN BELT

(Global/United Artists, July 24, 1953)   77 Mins.

(Technicolor)

George Montgomery, Tab Hunter, Helen Westcott, John Dehner, William Bishop, Jack Elam, Joe Haworth, Hugh Sanders, Willis Bouchey, James Millican, Bruce Cowling, Boyd Stockman, Douglas Kennedy, Boyd Morgan, William Phillips, Chuck Roberson

D: Ray Nazarro

S: Arthur E. Orloff

SP: Richard Schayer, Jack DeWitt

2563. HANNAH LEE

(Broder/Realart, July 30, 1953)   79 Mins.

(Pathé Color)

Joanne Dru, MacDonald Carey, John Ireland, Stuart Randall, Frank Ferguson, Ralph Dumke, Peter Ireland, Don Haggerty, Tom Powers, Tris Coffin, Harold Kennedy, Alex Pope, Ruth Whitney, Kay Riehl, Dean Gromer, Norman Leavitt

D: John Ireland, Lee Garmes

S: Mackinlay Kantor

SP: John Ireland, Lee Garmes

P: Jerry Thomas

(Also released in 3-D as *Outlaw Territory*)

2564. PACK TRAIN

(Columbia, July 30, 1953)   57 Mins.

(Sepiatone)

Gene Autry, Smiley Burnette, Gail Davis, Kenne Duncan, Sheila Ryan, Tom London, Harry Lauter, Melinda Plowman, B. G. Norman, Louise Lorimer, Frankie Marvin, Norman E. Westcoatt, Tex Terry, Wesley Hudman, Kermit Maynard, Frank

Ellis, Frank O'Connor, Dick Alexander, Jill Zeller, Herman Hack

D: George Archainbaud

SP: Norman S. Hall

P: Armand Schaefer

2565. ARROWHEAD

(Paramount, August 1, 1953)   105 Mins.

(Technicolor)

Charlton Heston, Jack Palance, Katy Jurado, Brian Keith, Mary Sinclair, Milburn Stone, Richard Shannon, Lewis Martin, Frank de Kova, Robert Wilke, Peter Coe, Kyle James, John Pickard, Pat Hogan, Chick Hannon, Mike Ragan, Judith Ames, Richard Paxton, Frank Cordell, James Burke

D/SP: Charles Marquis Warren

S: W. R. Burnett

P: Nat Holt

2566. THE MAN FROM THE ALAMO

(Universal-International, August 1, 1953)   79 Mins.

(Technicolor)

Glenn Ford, Julia Adams, Chill Wills, Victor Jory, Hugh O'Brian, Jeanne Cooper, Butch Cavell, John Day, Dan Poore, Myra Marsh, George Eldridge, Howard Negley

D: Budd Boetticher

SP: Niven Busch, Oliver Crawford

P: Aaron Rosenberg

2567. SHANE

(Paramount, August 1, 1953)   118 Mins.

(Technicolor)

Alan Ladd, Jean Arthur, Van Heflin, Brandon De Wilde, Jack Palance, Ben Johnson, Edgar Buchanan, Emile Meyer, Elisha Cook, Jr., Douglas Spencer, John Dierkes, Ellen Corby, Paul McVey, John Miller, Edith Evanson, Leonard Strong, Ray Spiker, Janice Carroll, Martin Mason, Helen Brown, Nancy Kulp

D/P: George Stevens

S: Jack Schaefer

SP: A. B. Guthrie, Jr., Jack Sher

2568. DOWN LAREDO WAY

(Republic, August 5, 1953)   54 Mins.

Rex Allen, Slim Pickens, Dona Drake, Marjorie Lord, Roy Barcroft, Judy Nugent, Percy Helton, Clayton Moore, Zon Murray, "Koko"

D: William Witney

SP: Gerald Geraghty

AP: Rudy Ralston

2569. BANDITS OF THE WEST

(Republic, August 8, 1953)   54 Mins.

Allan Lane, Eddy Waller, Cathy Downs, Roy Bar-

croft, Trevor Bardette, Ray Montgomery, Byron Foulger, Harry Harvey, Robert Bice, "Black Jack"
D: Harry Keller
SP: Gerald Geraghty
AP: Rudy Ralston

2570. TOPEKA
(Westwood/Allied Artists, August 9, 1953) 69 Mins.
(Sepiatone)
Bill Elliott, Phyllis Coates, Fuzzy Knight, Rick Vallin, John James, Denver Pyle, Dick Crockett, Harry Lauter, Dale Van Sickel, Ted Mapes, Henry Rowland, Edward Clark
D: Thomas Carr
SP: Milt Raison
P: Vincent M. Fennelly

2571. DEVIL'S CANYON
(RKO, August 15, 1953) 92 Mins.
(Technicolor) (3-D)
Virginia Mayo, Dale Robertson, Stephen McNally, Arthur Hunnicutt, Robert Keith, Jay C. Flippen, George J. Lewis, Whit Bissell, Morris Ankrum, James Bell, William Phillips, Earl Holliman, Irving Bacon
D: Alfred Werker
SP: Frederick Hazlitt Brennan, Harry Essex
P: Edmund Grainger

2572. THE STRANGER WORE A GUN
(Columbia, August 15, 1953) 83 Mins.
(Technicolor) (3-D)
Randolph Scott, Claire Trevor, Joan Weldon, George Macready, Alfonso Bedoya, Lee Marvin, Ernest Borgnine, Pierre Watkin, Joseph Vitale, Clem Bevins, Roscoe Ates, Paul Maxey, Frank Scannell, Reed Howes, Edward Earle, Guy Wilkerson, Mary Newton, Mary Lou Holloway, Franklyn Farnum, Barry Brooks, Tap Canutt, Al Haskell, Frank Hagney, Frank Ellis, Francis McDonald, Phil Tully, Al Hill, Harry Mendoza, Terry Frost, Diana Dawson, Richard Benjamin, Herbert Rawlinson, Britt Wood, Harry Seymour, James Millican, Jack Woody, Rayford Barnes, Rudy Germaine, Edith Evanson, Guy Teague
D: Andre de Toth
S: "Yankee Gold"—John Cunningham
SP: Kenneth Gamet
P: Harry Joe Brown, Randolph Scott

2573. WAR PAINT
(K-B/United Artists, August 28, 1953) 89 Mins.
(Pathe Color)
Robert Stack, Joan Taylor, Charles McGraw, Peter Graves, Keith Larsen, William Pullen, Richard Cutting, Douglas Kennedy, Walter Reed, Charles Nolte, James Parnell, Paul Richards, John Doucette, Robert Wilke
D: Lesley Selander
SP: Richard Alan Simmons, Martin Berkeley
P: Howard W. Koch

2574. CITY OF BADMEN
(20th C. Fox, September 1, 1953) 82 Mins.
(Technicolor)
Jeanne Crain, Dale Robertson, Richard Boone, Lloyd Bridges, Carole Mathews, Carl Betz, Whitfield Connor, Hugh Sanders, Rodolfo Acosta, Pasqual Garcia Pena, Harry Carter, Robert Adler, John Doucette, Alan Dexter, Don Haggerty, Leo Gordon, Gil Perkins, John Day, James Best, Richard Cutting, Douglas Evans, Kit Carson, Tom McDonough, Charles R. Smith, Harry Hines, Barbara Fuller, Harry Brown, Harris Brown, Jane Easton, Anthony Jochim, Leo Curley, George Melford, George Selk (Budd Buster), Charles Tannen, Gordon Nelson
D: Harmon Jones
SP: George W. George, George F. Slavin
P: Leonard Goldstein

2575. CONQUEST OF COCHISE
(Columbia, September 1, 1953) 70 Mins.
(Technicolor)
John Hodiak, Robert Stack, Joy Page, Rico Alaniz, Fortunio Bonanova, Edward Colemans, Alex Montoya, Stephen Ritch, Carlo Thurston, Rodd Redwing, Robert E. Griffin, Joseph Waring
D: William Castle
S: DeVallon Scott
SP: Arthur Lewis, DeVallon Scott
P: Sam Katzman

2576. THE STAND AT APACHE RIVER
(Universal-International, September 1, 1953) 77 Mins.
(Technicolor)
Stephen McNally, Julia Adams, Hugh Marlowe, Jack Kelly, Hugh O'Brian, Russell Johnson, Edgar Barrier, Jaclynne Greene, Forrest Lewis
D: Lee Sholem
S: "Apache Landing"—Robert J. Hogan
SP: Arthur Ross
P: William Alland

2577. EL PASO STAMPEDE
(Republic, September 8, 1953) 54 Mins.
Allan Lane, Eddy Waller, Phyllis Coates, Stephen Chase, Roy Barcroft, Edward Clark, Tom Monroe, Stanley Andrews, William Tannen, John Hamilton, "Black Jack"
D: Harry Keller
SP: Arthur Orloff
AP: Rudy Ralston

A Bullet Is Waiting
(Columbia, 1954)
— Jean Simmons
and Rory Calhoun

2578. THE MOONLIGHTER
(Warner Bros., September 19, 1953)   77 Mins.
(3-D)
Barbara Stanwyck, Fred MacMurray, Ward Bond, William Ching, John Dierkes, Morris Ankrum, Jack Elam, Charles Halton, Norman Leavitt, Sam Flint, Myra Marsh
D: Roy Rowland
S/SP: Niven Busch
P: Joseph Bernhard

2579. THE FIGHTING LAWMAN
(Westwood/Allied Artists, September 20, 1953)   71 Mins.
Wayne Morris, Virginia Grey, John Kellogg, Harry Lauter, John Pickard, Rick Vallin, Myron Healey, Dick Rich
D: Thomas Carr
SP: Dan Ullman
P: Vincent M. Fennelly

2580. WINGS OF THE HAWK
(Universal-International, September 20, 1953)   77 Mins.
Van Heflin, Julia Adams, Abbe Lane, George Dolenz, Antonio Moreno, Noah Beery, Jr., Pedro Gonzales-Gonzales, Paul Fierro, Mario Siletti, Rico Alaniz, John Daheim, Rodolfo Acosta, Nancy Westbrook, Ricardo Alba
D: Budd Boetticher
S: Gerald Drayson Adams
SP: James E. Moser
P: Aaron Rosenberg

2581. SAGINAW TRAIL
(Columbia, September 20, 1953)   56 Mins.
(Sepiatone)
Gene Autry, Smiley Burnette, Connie Marshall, Eugene Borden, Ralph Reed, Henry Blair, Myron Healey, Mickey Simpson, John War Eagle, Rodd Redwing, Billy Wilkerson, Gregg Barton, John Parrish, John Merton, Charlie Hayes, "Champion, Jr."
D: George Archainbaud
SP: Dorothy Yost, Dwight Cummings
P: Armand Schaefer

2582. SHADOWS OF TOMBSTONE
(Republic, September 28, 1953)   54 Mins.
Rex Allen, Slim Pickens, Jeanne Cooper, Roy Barcroft, Emory Parnell, Ric Roman, Richard Avonde, Julian Rivero, "Koko"
D: William Witney
SP: Gerald Geraghty
AP: Rudy Ralston

2582a. A BULLET IS WAITING

(Columbia, September, 1954)   82 Mins.
(Technicolor)

Jean Simmons, Rory Calhoun, Stephen McNally,
  Brian Aherne

D: John Farrow
P: Howard Welsch
S: Thames Williamson
SP: Thames Williamson, Casey Robinson

2583. OUTLAW TERRITORY

(Broder/Realart, October 12, 1953)   75 Mins.
(Pathe Color)

MacDonald Carey, Joanne Dru, John Ireland, Stuart
  Randall, Frank Ferguson, Ralph Dumke, Peter
  Ireland, Don Haggerty, Tom Powers, Tris Coffin,
  Harold Kennedy, Alex Pope, Ruth Whitney, Kay
  Riehl, Dean Gromer, Norman Leavitt

D/SP: John Ireland, Lee Garmes
S: Mackinlay Kantor
P: Jerry Thomas
(Also released in 3-D as *Hannah Lee*)

2584. THOSE REDHEADS FROM SEATTLE

(Paramount, October, 1953)   90 Mins.
(Technicolor) (3-D)

Rhonda Fleming, Gene Barry, Agnes Moorehead,
  Guy Mitchell, Teresa Brewer, Cynthia Bell, Kay
  Bell, Bill Pullen, John Kellogg, Frank Wilcox, Jean
  Parker, Roscoe Ates, Michael Ross, Walter Reed,
  Ed Rand

D: Lewis R. Foster
SP: Lewis R. Foster, Geoffrey Homes, George
  Worthing Yates
P: William H. Pine, William C. Thomas

2585. GUN FURY

(Columbia, November 1, 1953)   83 Mins.
(Technicolor) (3-D)

Rock Hudson, Donna Reed, Phil Carey, Roberta
  Haynes, Leo Gordon, Lee Marvin, Neville Brand,
  Ray Thomas, Robert Herron, Phil Rawlins, For-
  rest Lewis, John Cason, Don Carlos, Pat Hogan,
  Mel Welles, Post Park

D: Raoul Walsh
S: "Ten Against Caesar"—Kathleen B. George,
  Robert A. Granger
SP: Irving Wallace, Roy Huggins
P: Lewis J. Rachmil

2586. JACK SLADE

(Allied Artists, November 8, 1953)   90 Mins.

Mark Stevens, Dorothy Malone, Barton MacLane,
  John Litel, Paul Langton, Harry Shannon, John
  Harmon, Jim Bannon, Lee Van Cleef, David May,
  Ron Hargrave

D: Harold Schuster

SP: Warren Douglas
P: Lindsley Parsons

2587. SHARK RIVER

(United Artists, November 13, 1953)   80 Mins.
(Color Corp. of America)

Steve Cochran, Carole Matthews, Steve Warren,
  Robert Cunningham, Spencer Fox, Ruth Foreman

D/P: John Rawlins
SP: Joseph Carpenter, Lewis Meltzer

2588. CALAMITY JANE

(Warner Bros., November 14, 1953)   101 Mins.
(Technicolor)

Doris Day, Howard Keel, Allyn McLerie, Philip
  Carey, Dick Wesson, Paul Harvey, Chubby Johnson, Gale Robbins

D: David Butler
SP: James O'Hanlon
P: William Jacobs

2589. BORDER CITY RUSTLERS

(Newhall/Allied Artists, November 15, 1953)
  54 Mins.
(*Wild Bill Hickok* Series)

Guy Madison, Andy Devine, Gloria Talbot, Isabel
  Randolph, George J. Lewis, George Eldridge,
  Steve Pendleton, Murray Alper, Robert Bice, Don
  Turner

D: Frank McDonald
SP: Bill Raynor
P: Wesley Barry
(Compiled from the television episodes "Border
City" and one other, title unknown)

2590. SECRET OF OUTLAW FLATS

(Newhall/Allied Artists, November 15, 1953)
  54 Mins.
(*Wild Bill Hickok* Series)

Guy Madison, Andy Devine, Kristine Miller, Rich-
  ard Avonde, Jane Adams, Bobby Jordan, Tris
  Coffin, Wade Crosby, John Crawford, Bill Hale,
  Ed Clark, William Haade, Len Green, Reed Howes

D: Frank McDonald
SP: Bill Raynor
P: Wesley E. Barry
(Compiled from the television episodes "Outlaw
Flats" and "Silver Stage Holdup")

2591. SIX-GUN DECISION

(Newhall/Allied Artists, November 15, 1953)
  54 Mins.
(*Wild Bill Hickok* Series)

Guy Madison, Andy Devine, Don Haydon, Gloria
  Saunders, Fred Kohler, Jr., Peggy Stewart, Lyle
  Talbot, Zon Murray, Mike Vallon, Park Mac-
  Gregor, Fred Hoose, Robert Bice, Tom Steele

Vigilante Terror (Allied Artists, 1953) — Myron Healey, Henry Rowland, and Bill Elliott

D: Frank McDonald
SP: Bill Raynor
P: Wesley E. Barry
(Compiled from the television episodes "Border City Election" and "Pony Express Vs. Telegraph")

2592. TWO-GUN MARSHAL
(Newhall/United Artists, November 15, 1953) 52 Mins.
(*Wild Bill Hickok* Series)
Guy Madison, Andy Devine, Carole Mathews, Frankie Darro, Raymond Hatton, Sara Hayden, Pamela Duncan, Minerva Urecal, Michael Vallon, Richard Tyler, Alan Foster, Francis McDonald, Elizabeth Harrower, Irene Martin, George Meader
D: Frank McDonald
SP: Maurice Tombragel, Bill Raynor
P: Wesley Barry
(Compiled from the television episodes "Papa Antinelli" and "The Slocum Family")

2593. VIGILANTE TERROR
(Westwood/Allied Artists, November 15, 1953) 70 Mins.
Bill Elliott, Mary Ellen Kay, Myron Healey, Fuzzy Knight, I. Stanford Jolley, Henry Rowland, George Wallace, Zon Murray, Richard Avonde, Michael Colgan, Denver Pyle, Robert Bray, Al Haskell, John James
D: Lewis Collins
SP: Sid Theil
P: Vincent M. Fennelly

2594. CAPTAIN JOHN SMITH AND POCAHONTAS
(United Artists, November 20, 1953) 75 Mins.
(Pathe Color)
Anthony Dexter, Jody Lawrence, Alan Hale, Jr., Robert Clarke, Stuart Randall, James Seay, Philip Van Zandt, Shepard Menken, Douglass Dumbrille, Anthony Eustral, Henry Rowland, Eric Colmar, Francesco di Scaffa
D: Lew Landers
SP: Aubrey Wisberg, Jack Pollexfen
P: Aubrey Wisberg

2595. HONDO
(Warner Bros., November 27, 1953) 83 Mins.
(WarnerColor) (3-D)
John Wayne, Geraldine Page, Ward Bond, Michael Pate, James Arness, Rodolfo Acosta, Leo Gordon, Tim Irish, Lee Aaker, Paul Fix, Rayford Barnes
D: John Farrow

442

S: Louis L'Amour
SP: James Edward Grant
P: Robert Fellows

2596. BACK TO GOD'S COUNTRY

(Universal-International, November 30, 1953)
  78 Mins.
(Technicolor)
Rock Hudson, Marcia Henderson, Steve Cochran,
  Hugh O'Brian, Chubby Johnson, Tudor Owen,
  Arthur Space, John Cliff
D: Joseph Penney
S: James Oliver Curwood
SP: Tom Reed
P: Howard Christie

2597. LAST OF THE PONY RIDERS

(Columbia, November 30, 1953) 59 Mins.
(Sepiatone)
Gene Autry, Smiley Burnette, Kathleen Case, Dick
  Jones, Howard Wright, Arthur Space, Gregg Bar-
  ton, Buzz Henry, Harry Mackin, Harry Hines,
  "Champion, Jr."
D: George Archainbaud
SP: Ruth Woodman
P: Armand Schaefer

2598. THE NEBRASKAN

(Columbia, December 1, 1953) 68 Mins.
(Technicolor) (3-D)
Phil Carey, Roberta Haynes, Wallace Ford, Richard
  Webb, Lee Van Cleef, Maurice Jara, Regis Toomey,
  Jay Silverheels, Pat Hogan, Dennis Weaver, Boyd
  "Red" Morgan
D: Fred Sears
S: David Lang
SP: David Lang, Martin Berkeley
P: Wallace MacDonald

2599. TUMBLEWEED

(Universal-International, December 1, 1953)
  80 Mins.
(Technicolor)
Audie Murphy, Lori Nelson, Chill Wills, K. T. Ste-
  vens, Russell Johnson, Madge Meredith, Roy
  Roberts, Ralph Moody, Ross Elliott, Eugene Ig-
  lesias, I. Stanford Jolley, Lee Van Cleef
D: Nathan Juran
S: "Three Were Renegades"—Kenneth Perkins

SP: John Meredyth Lucas
P: Ross Hunter

2600. ESCAPE FROM FORT BRAVO

(MGM, December 4, 1953) 98 Mins.
(AnscoColor)
William Holden, Eleanor Parker, John Forsythe, Wil-
  liam Demarest, William Campbell, John Lupton,
  Richard Anderson, Polly Bergen, Carl Benton
  Reid
D: John Sturges
S: Philip Rock, Michael Pate
SP: Frank Fenton
P: Nicholas Nayfack

2601. THUNDER OVER THE PLAINS

(Warner Bros., December 12, 1953) 82 Mins.
(WarnerColor)
Randolph Scott, Lex Barker, Phyllis Kirk, Charles
  McGraw, Henry Hull, Elisha Cook, Jr., Hugh San-
  ders, Lane Chandler, James Brown, Fess Parker,
  Richard Benjamin, Mark Dana, Jack Woody, Tre-
  vor Bardette, Frank Matts, Steve Darrell, Earle
  Hodgins, John Carson, Monte Montague, Carl
  Andre, Charles Horvath, John McKee, Gail Rob-
  inson, Boyd Morgan, Gayle Kellogg
D: Andre de Toth
SP: Russell Hughes
P: David Weisbart

2602. RED RIVER SHORE

(Republic, December 15, 1953) 54 Mins.
Rex Allen, Slim Pickens, Lyn Thomas, Bill Phipps,
  Douglas Fowle, Trevor Bardette, William Haade,
  Emmett Vogan, John Cason, Rayford Barnes,
  "Koko"
D: Harry Keller
SP: Arthur Orloff, Gerald Geraghty
AP: Rudy Ralston

2603. TEXAS BAD MAN

(Westwood/Allied Artists, December 20, 1953)
  62 Mins.
Wayne Morris, Frank Ferguson, Elaine Riley, Sheb
  Wooley, Denver Pyle, Myron Healey, Mort Mills,
  Nelson Leigh
D: Lewis Collins
SP: Joseph F. Poland
P: Vincent M. Fennelly

FILMS OF 1954

2604. BORDER RIVER

(Universal-International, January 2, 1954)
  81 Mins.
(Technicolor)
Joel McCrea, Yvonne De Carlo, Pedro Armendariz,
  Howard Petrie, Erika Nordin, Alfonso Bedoya,

Ivan Triesault, George J. Lewis, Lane Chandler,
  Charles Hovarth, Nacho Galindo
D: George Sherman
S: Louis Stevens
SP: William Sackheim, Louis Stevens
P: Albert J. Cohen

2604a. WAR ARROW

(Universal-International, January 2, 1954)
78 Mins.

(Technicolor)

Jeff Chandler, Maureen O'Hara, Suzan Ball, John McIntire, Charles Drake, Dennis Weaver, Noah Beery, Jr., Henry Brandon, Steve Wyman, Jim Bannon, Jay Silverheels

D: George Sherman
S: John Michael Hayes
P: John Rogers

2605. YUKON VENGEANCE

(Allied Artists, January 17, 1954)   68 Mins.

Kirby Grant, Monte Hale, Mary Ellen Kay, Henry Kulky, Carol Thurston, Park MacGregor, Fred Gabourie, Billy Wilkerson, Marshall Bradford

D: William Beaudine
S: James Oliver Curwood
SP: Bill Raynor
P: William F. Broidy

2606. TAZA, SON OF COCHISE

(Universal-International, February 1, 1954)
79 Mins.

(Technicolor) (3-D)

Rock Hudson, Barbara Rush, Gregg Palmer, Bart Roberts, Morris Ankrum, Gene Iglesias, Richard Cutting, Robert Kurton, Ian MacDonald, Joe Sawyer, Brad Johnson, Lance Fuller

D: Douglas Sirk
S: Gerald Drayson Adams
SP: George Zuckerman
P: Ross Hunter

2607. THREE YOUNG TEXANS

(20th C. Fox, February 1, 1954)   78 Mins.

(Technicolor)

Mitzi Gaynor, Jeffrey Hunter, Keefe Brasselle, Harvey Stephens, Dan Riss, Michael Ansara, Aaron Spelling, Morris Ankrum, Frank Wilcox, Helen Wallace, John Harmon, Alex Montoya

D: Henry Levin
S: William MacLeod Raine
SP: Gerald Drayson Adams
P: Leonard Goldstein

2608. PHANTOM STALLION

(Republic, February 10, 1954)   54 Mins.

Rex Allen, Slim Pickens, Carla Balenda, Harry Shannon, Don Haggerty, Peter Price, Rosa Turich, Zon Murray, "Koko"

D: Harry Keller
SP: Gerald Geraghty
AP: Rudy Ralston

2609. BITTER CREEK

(Westwood/Allied Artists, February 21, 1954)
74 Mins.

Bill Elliott, Carleton Young, Beverly Garland, Veda Ann Borg, Claude Akins, Jim Hayward, John Harmon, John Pickard, Forrest Taylor, Mike Ragan, Dan Mummert, Zon Murray, John Larch, Jane Easton, Florence Lake, Earle Hodgins, Joe Devlin

D: Thomas Carr
SP: George Waggner
P: Vincent M. Fennelly

2610. THE BOY FROM OKLAHOMA

(Warner Bros., February 27, 1954)   88 Mins.

(WarnerColor)

Will Rogers, Jr., Nancy Olson, Lon Chaney, Jr., Anthony Caruso, Wallace Ford, Clem Bevins, Merv Griffin, Louis Jean Heydt, Sheb Wooley, Slim Pickens, Tyler McDuff, Skippy Torgensen, James Griffith, Charles Watts

D: Michael Curtiz
S: Michael Fessier
SP: Frank Davis, Winston Miller
P: David Weisbart

2611. OVERLAND PACIFIC

(Reliance/United Artists, February 27, 1954)
73 Mins.

(Color by Color Corp. of America)

Jack (Jock) Mahoney, Peggie Castle, Adele Jergens, William Bishop, Walter Sande, Chubby Johnson, Pat Hogan, Chris Alcaide, Phil Chambers, George Eldredge, Dick Rich, House Peters, Jr.

D: Fred F. Sears
S: Frederic Louis Fox
SP: J. Robert Bren, Gladys Atwater, Martin Goldsmith

2612. PAL AND GALS

(Columbia, February, 1954)   2 Reels

(*Three Stooges* Series)

Moe Howard, Shemp Howard, Larry Fine, Christine McIntyre, George Chesebro, Norman Willis, Heinie Conklin, Vernon Dent

D: Jules White

2613. BATTLE OF ROGUE RIVER

(Columbia, March 1, 1954)   71 Mins.

(Technicolor)

George Montgomery, Richard Denning, Martha Hyer, John Crawford, Emory Parnell, Michael Granger, Freeman Morse, Bill Bryant, Charles Evans, Lee Roberts, Frank Sully, Steve Ritch, Bill Hale, Wesley Hudman, Jimmy Lloyd, Willis Bouchy

D: William Castle
S/SP: Douglas Heyes
P: Sam Katzman

2614. RED GARTERS
(Paramount, March 1, 1954) 90 Mins.
(Technicolor)
Rosemary Clooney, Jack Carson, Guy Mitchell, Pat
    Crowley, Joanne Gilbert, Gene Barry, Cass Daley,
    Frank Faylen, Reginald Owen, Buddy Ebsen,
    Richard Hale
D: George Marshall
SP: Michael Fessier
P: Pat Duggan

2615. RIVER OF NO RETURN
(20th C. Fox, March 1, 1954) 91 Mins.
(Technicolor)
Robert Mitchum, Marilyn Monroe, Rory Calhoun,
    Tommy Rettig, Murvyn Vye, Will Wright, Doug-
    las Spencer, Ed Hinton, Don Beddoe, Clair Andre,
    Jack Mather, Edmund Cobb, Jarma Lewis, Hal
    Baylor, Barbara Nichols, Fay Morley, John
    Doucette, Arthur Shields, Geneva Gray, Larry
    Chance, Paul Newlan, Hal Baylor
D: Otto Preminger
S: Louis Lantz
SP: Frank Fenton
P: Stanley Rubin

2616. ROSE MARIE
(MGM, March 19, 1954) 104 Mins.
(Eastman Color) (Cinemascope)
Ann Blyth, Howard Keel, Fernando Lamas, Bert
    Lahr, Marjorie Main, Joan Taylor, Ray Collins,
    Chief Yowlachie
D: Mervyn LeRoy
S: From the operetta by Otto A. Harbach and
    Oscar Hammerstein II
SP: Ronald Miller, George Froeschel
P: Mervyn LeRoy

2617. SASKATCHEWAN
(Universal-International, March 30, 1954)
    87 Mins.
(Technicolor)
Alan Ladd, Shelley Winters, Robert Douglas, J. Car-
    roll Naish, Hugh O'Brian, Richard Long, Jay
    Silverheels, Antonio Moreno, Lowell Gilmore,
    George J. Lewis, Frank Chase, John Cason, Henry
    Wills
D: Raoul Walsh
S/SP: Gil Doud
P: Aaron Rosenberg

2618. RACING BLOOD
(20th C. Fox, March, 1954) 76 Mins.

(Super Cinecolor)
Bill Williams, Jean Porter, Jimmy Boyd, George
    Cleveland, John Eldredge, Sam Flint, Fred Kohler,
    Jr., George Steele, Bobby Johnson, Fred Kelsey,
    Frankie Darro
D/P: Wesley Barry
SP: Sam Roeca, Wesley Barry

2619. JESSE JAMES VS. THE DALTONS
(Columbia, April 1, 1954) 65 Mins.
(Technicolor) (3-D)
Brett King, Barbara Lawrence, James Griffith, Bill
    Phillips, John Cliff, Rory Mallison, William Tan-
    nen, Richard Garland, Nelson Leigh, Raymond
    Largay
D: William Castle
S: Edwin Westrate
SP: Robert E. Kent, Samuel Newman
P: Sam Katzman

2620. GYPSY COLT
(MGM, April 2, 1954) 72 Mins.
(AnscoColor)
Donna Corcoran, Ward Bond, Frances Dee, Larry
    Keating, Lee Van Cleef, Bobby Hyatt, Nacho Ga-
    lindo, Rodolfo Hoyos, Jr., Joe Dominguez, Jester
    Hairston, Peggy Maley
D: Andrew Marton
S: Eric Knight
SP: Martin Berkeley
P: William Grady, Jr., Sidney Franklin

2621. FANGS OF THE WILD
(Lippert, April 2, 1954) 71 Mins.
Charles Chaplin, Jr., Onslow Stevens, Margie Dean,
    Freddie Ridgeway, Phil Tead, Robert Stevenson,
    "Buck" (a dog)
D: William Claxton
SP: Orville Hampton, William Claxton
P: Robert L. Lippert, Jr.

2622. RAILS INTO LARAMIE
(Universal-International, April 2, 1954) 81 Mins.
(Technicolor)
John Payne, Mari Blanchard, Dan Duryea, Joyce
    McKenzie, Barton MacLane, Harry Shannnon,
    Ralph Dumke, Lee Van Cleef, Myron Healey,
    James Griffith, Alexander Campbell, George
    Cleveland, Charles Horvath, Stephen Chase
D: Jesse Hibbs
SP: D. D. Beauchamp, Joseph Hoffman
P: Ted Richmond

2623. RIDING SHOTGUN
(Warner Bros., April 10, 1954) 75 Mins.
(WarnerColor)
Randolph Scott, Wayne Morris, Joan Weldon, Joe

Sawyer, James Millican, Charles Buchinsky (Bronson), James Bell, Fritz Field, Richard Garrick, Victor Perrin, John Baer, William Johnstone, Kem Dibbs, Alvin Freeman, Edward Coch, Jr., Eva Lewis, Lonnie Pierce, Mary Lou Holloway, Boyd Morgan, Richard Benjamin, Jay Lawrence, George Ross, Ray Bennett, Jack Kenney, Jack Woody, Allegra Varron, Frosty Royse, Jimmy Mohley, Ruth Whitney, Bud Osborne, Budd Buster, Buddy Roosevelt, Dub Taylor, Joe Brockman, Harry Hines, Clem Fuller, Opan Evard, Morgan Brown, Bob Stephenson
D: Andre de Toth
S: Kenneth Perkins
SP: Tom Blackburn
P: Ted Sherdeman

2624. UNTAMED HEIRESS
(Republic, April 12, 1954)   70 Mins.
Judy Canova, Donald Barry, Taylor Holmes, George Cleveland, Chick Chandler, Jack Kruschen, Hugh Sanders, Douglas Fowley, William Haade, Ellen Corby
D: Charles Lamont
S: Jack Townley
SP: Barry Shipman
AP: Sidney Picker

2625. GUNFIGHTERS OF THE NORTHWEST
(Columbia, April 15, 1954)   15 Chaps.
Jack (Jock) Mahoney, Phyllis Coates, Clayton Moore, Don Harvey, Marshall Reed, Rodd Redwing, Lyle Talbot, Tommy Farrell, Lee Roberts, Terry Frost, Joe Allen, Jr., Gregg Barton, Chief Yowlachie, Pierce Lyden
D: Spencer G. Bennet
SP: Arthur Hoerl, Royal K. Cole, George H. Plympton
P: Sam Katzman
Chapter Titles: (1) A Trap for the Mounties, (2) Indian War Drums, (3) Between Two Fires, (4) Midnight Raiders, (5) Running the Gauntlet, (6) Mounties at Bay, (7) Plunge of Peril, (8) Killer at Large, (9) The Fighting Mounties, (10) The Sergeant Gets His Man, (11) The Fugitive Escapes, (12) Stolen Gold, (13) Perils of the Mounted Police, (14) Surprise Attack, (15) Trail's End

2626. ARROW IN THE DUST
(Allied Artists, April 25, 1954)   80 Mins.
(Technicolor)
Sterling Hayden, Coleen Gray, Keith Larsen, Tom Tully, Jimmy Wakely, Tudor Owen, Lee Van Cleef, John Pickard, Carleton Young
D: Lesley Selander
S: L. L. Foreman
SP: Don Martin
P: Hayes Goetz

2627. THE LONE GUN
(Superior/United Artists, April 25, 1954)   73 Mins.
(Color by Color Corp. of America)
George Montgomery, Dorothy Malone, Frank Faylen, Neville Brand, Skip Homeier, Douglas Kennedy, Robert Wilke, Fay Roope, Douglas Fowley
D: Ray Nazarro
S: L. L. Foreman
SP: Don Martin, Richard Schayer

2628. SOUTHWEST PASSAGE
(Small/United Artists, April 25, 1954)   82 Mins.
(Pathe Color)   (3-D)
John Ireland, Joanne Dru, Rod Cameron, Guinn Williams, John Dehner, Mark Hanna, Darryl Hickman, Stuart Randall, Morris Ankrum, Kenneth MacDonald, Stanley Andrews
D: Ray Nazarro
SP: Harry Essex
P: Edward Small

2629. MASSACRE CANYON
(Columbia, May 1, 1954)   66 Mins.
(Sepiatone)
Phil Carey, Audrey Totter, Douglas Kennedy, Jeff Donnell, Guinn Williams, Charlita, Ross Elliott, Ralph Dumke, Mel Welles, Chris Alcaide, Steve Ritch, John Pickard, James Flavin, Bill Hale
D: Fred F. Sears
S/SP: David Lang
P: Wallace MacDonald

2630. THE SIEGE AT RED RIVER
(Panoramic Productions/20th C. Fox, May 1, 1954)   86 Mins.
(Technicolor)
Van Johnson, Joanne Dru, Richard Boone, Milburn Stone, Jeff Morrow, Craig Hill, Rico Alanix, Robert Burton, Pilar Del Rey, Ferris Taylor
D: Rudolph Mate
S: J. Robert Bren, Gladys Atwater
SP: Sydney Boehm
P: Leonard Goldstein

2631. THE FORTY-NINERS
(Westwood/Allied Artists, May 9, 1954)   71 Mins.
Bill Elliott, Virginia Grey, Henry (Harry) Morgan, John Doucette, Lane Bradford, I. Stanford Jolley, Denver Pyle, Gregg Barton, Ralph Sanford, Harry Lauter, Earle Hodgins
D: Thomas Carr
SP: Dan Ullman
P: Vincent M. Fennelly

2632. JUBILEE TRAIL
(Republic, May 15, 1954)   103 Mins.
(Trucolor)
Vera Ralston, Joan Leslie, Forrest Tucker, John Rus-

sell, Ray Middleton, Pat O'Brien, Buddy Baer, Jim Davis, Barton MacLane, Richard Webb, James Millican, Nina Varela, Martin Garralaga, Charles Stevens, Jack Elam
D/AP: Joseph Kane
S: Gwen Bristow
SP: Bruce Manning

2633. THE YELLOW TOMAHAWK
(Bel-Air/United Artists, May 20, 1954)   82 Mins.
(Color by Color Corp. of America)
Rory Calhoun, Peggie Castle, Noah Beery, Jr., Warner Anderson, Peter Graves, Lee Van Cleef, Rita Moreno, Walter Reed, Dan Riss, Adam Williams, Ned Glass
D: Lesley Selander
SP: Richard Alan Simmons
P: Howard W. Koch

2634. THE COWBOY
(Lippert, May 28, 1954)   69 Mins.
(Documentary)   (Eastman Color)
Narrated by Tex Ritter, William Conrad, and John Dehner
D: Elmo Williams
SP: Lorraine Williams
P: Larry Dobkin

2635. BLACK HORSE CANYON
(Universal-International, June 1, 1954)   82 Mins.
(Technicolor)
Joel McCrea, Mari Blanchard, Murvyn Vye, Irving Bacon, Ewing Mitchell, John Pickard, Pilar Del Rey, William J. Williams, Henry Wills, Race Gentry
D: Jesse Hibbs
S: "The Wild Horses"—Les Savage, Jr.
SP: Geoffrey Homes
P: John W. Rogers

2636. DRUMS ACROSS THE RIVER
(Universal-International, June 1, 1954)   78 Mins.
(Technicolor)
Audie Murphy, Lisa Gaye, Lyle Bettger, Walter Brennan, Mara Corday, Hugh O'Brian, Jay Silverheels, Regis Toomey, Morris Ankrum, James Anderson, George Wallace, Bob Steele, Lane Bradford, Emile Meyer, Gregg Barton, Howard McNear, Ken Terrell
D: Nathan Juran
SP: John K. Butler
P: Melville Tucker

2637. SILVER LODE
(RKO, June 19, 1954)   80 Mins.
(Technicolor)
John Payne, Lizabeth Scott, Dan Duryea, Dolores Moran, Emile Meyer, Robert Warwick, John Hudson, Harry Carey, Jr., Stuart Whitman, Alan Hale,

Jr., Frank Sully, Morris Ankrum, Hugh Sanders, Florence Auer, Roy Jordon
D: Allan Dwan
S/SP: Karen DeWolf
P: Benedict Bogeaus

2637a. CORRAL CUTIES
(Universal-International, June 20, 1954)   15 Mins.
Tennessee Ernie Ford, Molly Bee
D/P: Will Cowan

2638. THE DESPERADO
(Silvermine/Allied Artists, June 20, 1954)   81 Mins.
Wayne Morris, James Lydon, Beverly Garland, Rayford Barnes, Dabbs Greer, Lee Van Cleef, Nestor Paiva, Roy Barcroft, John Dierkes, Richard Shackleton, I. Stanford Jolley, Charles Garland, Florence Lake
D: Thomas Carr
S: Clifton Adams
SP: Geoffrey Homes
P: Vincent M. Fennelly

2639. APACHE
(United Artists, July 1, 1954)   91 Mins.
(Technicolor)
Burt Lancaster, Jean Peters, John McIntyre, Charles Buchinsky (Bronson), John Dehner, Paul Guilfoyle, Ian MacDonald, Walter Sande, Morris Ankrum, Monte Blue
D: Robert Aldrich
S: Paul I. Wellman
SP: James R. Webb
P: Harold Hecht

2640. THE LAWLESS RIDER
(United Artists, July 1, 1954)   62 Mins.
John Carpenter, Rose Bascom, Frankie Darro, Douglass Dumbrille, Frank "Red" Carpenter, Noel Neill, Kenne Duncan, Weldon Bascom, Bud Osborne, Lon Roberson, Bill Coontz, Bill Chaney, Roy Canada, Tap Canutt, Hank Caldwell and his Saddle Kings
D: Yakima Canutt
S/SP: John Carpenter
P: Alex Gordon, John Carpenter

2641. MAN WITH THE STEEL WHIP
(Republic, July 19, 1954)   12 Chaps.
Richard Simmons, Barbara Bestar, Dale Van Sickel, Lane Bradford, Mauritz Hugo, Roy Barcroft, Pat Hogan, Stuart Randall, Edmund Cobb, I. Stanford Jolley, Guy Teague, Alan Wells, Tom Steele, Art Dillard, Chuck Hayward, Charles Stevens, Jerry Brown, Harry Harvey, Bob Clark, Charles Sullivan, Robert Henry, Tom Monroe, Chris Mitchell, Gregg Barton, Tex Terry, Walt LaRue, George Eldridge, Herman Hack

D/AP: Franklin Adreon (sometimes spelled Franklyn)

SP: Donald Davidson

Chapter Titles: (1) The Spirit Rider, (2) Savage Fury, (3) Mask of El Latigo, (4) The Murder Cave, (5) The Stone Guillotine, (6) Flame and Battle, (7) Double Ambush, (8) The Blazing Barrier, (9) The Silent Informer, (10) Window of Death, (11) The Fatal Masquerade, (12) Redskin Raiders

2642. GARDEN OF EVIL

(20th C. Fox, July, 1954)   100 Mins.

(Technicolor) (CinemaScope) (Filmed in Mexico)

Gary Cooper, Susan Hayward, Richard Widmark, Hugh Marlowe, Cameron Mitchell, Rita Moreno, Victor Manuel Mendoza, Fernando Wagner, Arturo Soto Rangel, Manuel Donde, Antonio Bribiesca

D: Henry Hathaway

S: Fred Freiberger, William Tunberg

SP: Frank Fenton

P: Charles Brackett

2643. THE GAMBLER FROM NATCHEZ

(20th C. Fox, July, 1954)   88 Mins.

(Technicolor)

Dale Robertson, Debra Paget, Thomas Gomez, Lisa

Daniels, Kevin McCarthy, Douglas Dick, John Wengraf, Donald Randolph, Henri Letondal, Jay Novello, Woody Strode, Peter Mamakos

D: Henry Levin

S: Gerald Drayson Adams

SP: Gerald Drayson Adams, Irving Wallace

P: Leonard Goldstein

2644. THE OUTLAW STALLION

(Columbia, July, 1954)   64 Mins.

(Technicolor)

Phil Carey, Dorothy Patrick, Billy Gray, Roy Roberts, Gordon Jones, Trevor Bardette, Morris Ankrum, Chris Alcaide, Robert Anderson, Harry Harvey, Guy Teague

D: Fred F. Sears

S/SP: David Lang

P: Wallace MacDonald

2645. BROKEN LANCE

(20th C. Fox, August 1, 1954)   96 Mins.

(DeLuxe Color) (CinemaScope)

Spencer Tracy, Robert Wagner, Jean Peters, Richard Widmark, Katy Jurado, Hugh O'Brian, Edward Franz, Earl Holliman, E. G. Marshall, Carl Benton Reid, Philip Ober, Robert Burton, Robert Adler, Robert Grandlin, Harry Carter, Nacho Galindo,

The Law vs. Billy the Kid (Columbia, 1954) — Scott Brady and James Griffith

Julian Rivero, Edmund Cobb, Russell Simpson, King Donovan, George E. Stone, Jack Mather, Paul Kruger, John Eppers
D: Edward Dmytryk
S: Philip Yordan
SP: Richard Murphy
P: Sol C. Siegel

2646. THE LAW VS. BILLY THE KID

(Columbia, August 1, 1954)   73 Mins.
(Technicolor)
Scott Brady, Betta St. John, James Griffith, Alan Hale, Jr., Paul Cavanaugh, William Phillips, Benny Rubin, Steve Darrell, George Berkeley, William Tannen, Martin Garralaga, Richard Cutting, John Cliff, Otis Garth, Frank Sully, William Fawcett, Robert Griffin
D: William Castle
SP: John T. Williams
P: Sam Katzman

2647. THE RAID

(20th C. Fox, August 1, 1954)   83 Mins.
(Technicolor)
Van Heflin, Anne Bancroft, Richard Boone, Lee Marvin, Tommy Rettig, Peter Graves, Douglas Spencer, Paul Cavanaugh, Will Wright, James Best, John Dierkes, Helen Ford, Harry Hines, Simon Scott, Claude Akins
D: Hugo Fregonese
SP: Sidney Boehm
P: Leonard Goldstein

2648. THE OUTCAST

(Republic, August 15, 1954)   90 Mins.
(Trucolor)
John Derek, Joan Evans, Jim Davis, Catherine McLeod, Ben Cooper, Taylor Holmes, Nana Bryant, Slim Pickens, Frank Ferguson, James Millican, Bob Steele, Nacho Galindo, Harry Carey, Jr., Robert "Buzz" Henry, Nicholas Coster
D: William Witney
S: From *Esquire* magazine by Todhunter Ballard
SP: John K. Butler, Richard Wormser
AP: William J. O'Sullivan

2649. JOHNNY GUITAR

(Republic, August 23, 1954)   110 Mins.
(Trucolor)
Joan Crawford, Sterling Hayden, Scott Brady, Mercedes McCambridge, Ward Bond, Ben Cooper, Ernest Borgnine, John Carradine, Royal Dano, Frank Ferguson, Paul Fix, Rhys Williams, Ian MacDonald
D: Nicholas Ray
SP: Philip Yordan
P: Herbert J. Yates

2650. THE BLACK DAKOTAS

(Columbia, September 1, 1954)   65 Mins.
(Technicolor)
Gary Merrill, Wanda Hendrix, John Bromfield, Noah Beery, Jr., Fay Roope, Howard Wendell, Robert Simon, James Griffith, Richard Webb, John War Eagle, Peter Whitney, Jay Silverheels, George Keymas, Robert Griffin, Clayton Moore, Chris Alcaide, Frank Wilcox
D: Ray Nazarro
S: Roy Buffum
SP: Roy Buffum, DeVallon Scott
P: Wallace MacDonald

2651. DAWN AT SOCORRO

(Universal-International, September 1, 1954)   80 Mins.
(Technicolor)
Rory Calhoun, Piper Laurie, David Brian, Kathleen Hughes, Alex Nicol, Edgar Buchanan, Mara Corday, Skip Homeier, Roy Roberts, James Millican, Lee Van Cleef, Stanley Andrews, Richard Garland, Scott Lee, Paul Brinegar, Philo McCullough, Forrest Taylor
D: George Sherman
SP: George Zuckerman
P: William Alland

2652. JESSE JAMES' WOMEN

(United Artists, September 1, 1954)   83 Mins.
(Technicolor)
Don Barry, Jack Buetel, Peggie Castle, Lita Baron, Joyce Rhed, Betty Brueck, Laura Lee, Sam Keller
D: Donald Barry
SP: D. D. Beauchamp
P: Lloyd Royal, T. V. Garraway

2653. TWO GUNS AND A BADGE

(Westwood/Allied Artists, September 12, 1954)   69 Mins.
(Credited by numerous sources as the last film released in a regular "B" Western series)
Wayne Morris, Morris Ankrum, Beverly Garland, Roy Barcroft, William Phipps, Damian O'Flynn, I. Stanford Jolley, Bob Wilke, Chuck Courtney, John Pickard, Henry Rowland, Gregg Barton
D: Lewis Collins
SP: Dan Ullman
P: Vincent M. Fennelly

2654. THUNDER PASS

(Lippert, September 20, 1954)   76 Mins.
Dane Clark, Dorothy Patrick, Andy Devine, Raymond Burr, John Carradine, Mary Ellen Kay, Raymond Hatton, Nestor Paiva, Charles Fredericks, Tom Hubbard
D: Frank McDonald

S: George Van Marter
SP: Tom Hubbard, Fred Eggers
P: A. Robert Nunes

2655. THE BOUNTY HUNTER
(Transcona/Warner Bros., September 25, 1954)
79 Mins.
(WarnerColor)
Randolph Scott, Dolores Dorn, Marie Windsor, Howard Petrie, Harry Antrim, Robert Keys, Ernest Borgnine, Dub Taylor, Tyler McDuff, Archie Twitchell, Paul Picerni, Phil Chambers, Mary Lou Holloway, Katherine Marlowe, Dorothy Seese, Hope Miller, Guy Teague, Charles Delaney, Gail Robinson, Vincent Perry, Wanda Barbour, Fess Parker, Shirley Whitney
D: Andre de Toth
SP: Winston Miller
P: Sam Bischoff

2656. THREE HOURS TO KILL
(Columbia, October 1, 1954) 77 Mins.
(Technicolor)
Dana Andrews, Donna Reed, Dianne Foster, Stephen Elliott, Richard Coogan, Laurence Hugo, James Westerfield, Richard Webb, Carolyn Jones, Charlotte Fletcher, Whit Bissell, Felipe Turich, Arthur Fox, Francis McDonald
D: Alfred Werker
S: Alex Gottlieb
SP: Richard Alan Simmons, Roy Huggins, Maxwell Shane
P: Harry Joe Brown

2657. PASSION
(RKO, October 6, 1954) 84 Mins.
(Technicolor)
Cornel Wilde, Yvonne De Carlo, Raymond Burr, Lon Chaney, Jr., Rodolfo Acosta, John Qualen, Anthony Caruso, Frank de Kova, Peter Coe, John Dierkes, Richard Hale, Rozene Kemper, Belle Mitchell, Alex Montoya, Zon Murray, Rosa Turich, Stuart Whitman, James Kirkwood, Robert Warwick
D: Allan Dwan
SP: Beatrice A. Dresher, Miguel Padilla, Josef Leytes
S: Howard Estabrook
P: Benedict Bogeaus

2658. SITTING BULL
(United Artists, October 6, 1954) 105 Mins.
(Eastman Color) (CinemaScope)
(Filmed in Mexico)
Dale Robertson, Mary Murphy, J. Carroll Naish, Iron Eyes Cody, John Litel, William Hopper, Douglas Kennedy, William Tannen, Joel Fluellen, John Hamilton, Tom Brown Henry, Felix Gonzales, Al Wyatt
D: Sidney Salkow
SP: Jack DeWitt, Sidney Salkow
P: W. R. Frank, Tele-Voz, S.A.

2658a. SHOT IN THE FRONTIER
(Columbia, October 7, 1954) 2 Reels
(*Three Stooges* Series)
Moe Howard, Larry Fine, Shemp Howard
D: Jules White

2659. FOUR GUNS TO THE BORDER
(Universal-International, November 1, 1954)
82 Mins.
(Technicolor)
Rory Calhoun, Coleen Miller, George Nader, Walter Brennan, Nina Foch, John McIntire, Charles Drake, Jay Silverheels, Nestor Paiva, Mary Field, Bob Herron, Bob Hoy, Reg Parton
D: Richard Carlson
S: Louis L'Amour
SP: George Van Marter, Franklin Coen
P: William Alland

2660. THE OUTLAW'S DAUGHTER
(Regal Films/20th C. Fox, November 1, 1954)
75 Mins.
(Color by Color Corp. of America)
Jim Davis, Kelly Ryan, Bill Williams, George Cleveland, Elisha Cook, Jr., Guinn "Big Boy" Williams, Sara Hayden, Nelson Leigh, George Barrows
D/P: Wesley Barry
SP: Sam Roeca

2661. RICOCHET ROMANCE
(Universal-International, November 1, 1954)
80 Mins.
Marjorie Main, Chill Wills, Pedro Gonzales-Gonzales, Alfonso Bedoya, Rudy Vallee, Ruth Hamilton, Benay Venuta, Judith Ames, Darryl Hickman, Lee Aaker, Irene Ryan, Philip Tonge, Philip Chambers, Charles Watts, Marjorie Bennett
D: Charles Lamont
SP: Kay Lenard
P: Robert Arthur, Richard Wilson

2662. RIDING WITH BUFFALO BILL
(Columbia, November 11, 1954) 15 Chaps.
Marshall Reed, Rick Vallin, Joanne Rio, Shirley Whitney, Jack Ingram, William Fawcett, Gregg Barton, Ed Coch, Steve Ritch, Pierce Lyden, Michael Fox, Lee Roberts, John Truex, Zon Murray, Al Cantor
D: Spencer G. Bennet
SP: George H. Plympton
P: Sam Katzman
Chapter Titles: (1) The Ridin' Terror from St. Joe,

(2) Law of the Six Guns, (3) Raiders from Ghost Town, (4) Cody to the Rescue, (5) Midnight Marauders, (6) Under the Avalanche, (7) Night Attack, (8) Trapped in the Power Shack, (9) Into an Outlaw Trap, (10) Blast to Oblivion, (11) The Depths of the Earth, (12) The Ridin' Terror, (13) Trapped in the Apache Mine, (14) Railroad Wreckers, (15) Law Comes to the West

2663. DRUM BEAT
(Warner Bros., November 13, 1954)   111 Mins.
(WarnerColor)   (CinemaScope)
Alan Ladd, Audrey Dalton, Marisa Pavan, Robert Keith, Rodolfo Acosta, Charles Bronson, Warner Anderson, Elisha Cook, Jr., Anthony Caruso, Richard Gaines, Edgar Stehli, Hayden Rorke, Frank de Kova, Isabel Jewell, Perry Lopez, Willis Bouchey, George J. Lewis, Frank Ferguson, Peggy Converse
D/SP: Delmer Daves
P: Alan Ladd

2664. CATTLE QUEEN OF MONTANA
(RKO, November 18, 1954)   88 Mins.
(Technicolor)
Barbara Stanwyck, Ronald Reagan, Gene Evans, Lance Fuller, Anthony Caruso, Jack Ingram, Yvette Dugay, Morris Ankrum, Chubby Johnson, Myron Healey, Rodd Redwing
D: Allan Dwan
S: Thomas Blackburn
SP: Howard Estabrook, Robert Blees
P: Benedict Bogeaus

2665. TRACK OF THE CAT
(Warner Bros., November 27, 1954)   102 Mins.
(WarnerColor)   (CinemaScope)
Robert Mitchum, Teresa Wright, Diana Lynn, Tab Hunter, Beulah Bondi, Philip Tonge, William Hopper, Carl "Alfalfa" Switzer
D: William W. Wellman
S: Walter Van Tilburg Clark
SP: A. I. Besserides
P: John Wayne, Robert Fellows

2666. THEY RODE WEST
(Columbia, December 1, 1954)   84 Mins.
(Technicolor)
Robert Francis, Donna Reed, May Wynn, Phil Carey, Onslow Stevens, Peggy Converse, Roy Roberts, Jack Kelly, Stuart Randall, Eugene Iglesias, Frank de Kova, John War Eagle, Ralph Dumke, Julia Montoya, James Best, George Kenyas, Maurice Jara
D: Phil Karlson
S: Leo Katcher
SP: DeVallon Scott, Frank Nugent
P: Lewis J. Rachmil

2667. THE YELLOW MOUNTAIN
(Universal-International, December 1, 1954)
   78 Mins.
(Technicolor)
Lex Barker, Mala Powers, Howard Duff, William Demarest, John McIntire, Leo Gordon, Hal K. Dawson, Dayton Lummis
D: Jesse Hibbs
S: Harold Channing Wire
SP: George Zuckerman, Russell Hughes, Robert Blees
P: Ross Hunter

2668. HELL'S OUTPOST
(Republic, December 15, 1954)   90 Mins.
Rod Cameron, Joan Leslie, John Russell, Chill Wills, Jim Davis, Kristine Miller, Ben Cooper, Taylor Holmes, Barton MacLane, Ruth Lee, Arthur Q. Bryan, Oliver Blake
D/AP: Joseph Kane
S: "Silver Rock"—Luke Short
SP: Kenneth Gamet

2669. VERA CRUZ
(Hecht-Lancaster/United Artists,
   December 20, 1954)   94 Mins.
(Technicolor)   (SuperScope)   (Filmed in Mexico)
Gary Cooper, Burt Lancaster, Denise Darcel, Cesar Romero, Sarita Monteil, George Macready, Ernest Borgnine, Morris Ankrum, James McCallion, Jack Lambert, Henry Brandon, Charles Buchinsky (Bronson), Jack Elam, James Seay, Archie Savage, Charles Horvath, Juan Garcia
D: Robert Aldrich
S: Borden Chase
SP: Roland Kibbee, James R. Webb
P: James Hill

2670. MARSHALS IN DISGUISE
(Newhall/Allied Artists, December 26, 1954)
(*Wild Bill Hickok* Series)
Guy Madison, Andy Devine, Norma Eberhardt, Leonard Penn, Tris Coffin, Fred Kelsey, John Merton, Pat Mitchell, Ric Vallon, Bill Hale, David Sharpe, Don Turner, Anthony Sydes, Guy Beach, John Eldredge, James Bush, Bud Osborne
D: Frank McDonald
SP: Bill Raynor, Maurice Tombragel
P: Wesley Barry
(Compiled from the television episodes "The Lost Indian Mine" and "Civilian Clothes")

2671. OUTLAW'S SON
(Newhall/Allied Artists, December 26, 1954)
(*Wild Bill Hickok* Series)
Guy Madison, Andy Devine, Anne Kimball
D: Frank McDonald
SP: Maurice Tombragel

P: Wesley E. Barry
(Compiled from two television episodes, titles unknown)

2672. TROUBLE ON THE TRAIL
(Newhall/Allied Artists, December 26, 1954)
(*Wild Bill Hickok* Series)
Guy Madison, Andy Devine
D: Frank McDonald
SP: Maurice Tombragel
P: Wesley E. Barry

(Compiled from two television episodes, titles unknown)

2673. THE TWO GUN TEACHER
(Newhall/Allied Artists, December 26, 1954)
(*Wild Bill Hickok* Series)
Guy Madison, Andy Devine
D: Frank McDonald
SP: Maurice Tombragel
P: Wesley E. Barry
(Compiled from two television episodes, titles unknown)

FILMS OF 1955

2674. BAD DAY AT BLACK ROCK
(MGM, January 1, 1955)   81 Mins.
(Eastman Color)   (CinemaScope)
Spencer Tracy, Robert Ryan, Anne Francis, Dean Jagger, Walter Brennan, John Ericson, Ernest Borgnine, Lee Marvin, Russell Collins, Walter Sande
D: John Sturges
S: Howard Breslin

SP: Millard Kaufman, Don McGuire
P: Dore Schary

2675. DESTRY
(Universal-International, January 1, 1955)
95 Mins.
(Technicolor)
Audie Murphy, Mari Blanchard, Lyle Bettger, Lori Nelson, Thomas Mitchell, Edgar Buchanan, Wal-

The Violent Men (Columbia, 1955) — Edward G. Robinson, Barbara Stanwyck, Brian Keith, and Glenn Ford

lace Ford, Mary Wickes, Alan Hale, Jr., Lee Aaker, Trevor Bardette, Walter Baldwin
D: George Marshall
S: Max Brand
SP: Felix Jackson, Edmund H. North, D. D. Beauchamp

2676. MASTERSON OF KANSAS
(Columbia, January 1, 1955)   73 Mins.
(Technicolor)
George Montgomery, Nancy Gates, James Griffith, Jean Willes, Benny Rubin, William Henry, David Bruce, Bruce Cowling, Gregg Barton, Donald Murphy, Sandy Sanders, Gregg Martell, Jay Silverheels, John Maxwell, Wesley Hudman, Leonard Geer
D: William Castle
S/SP: Douglas Heyes
P: Sam Katzman

2677. THE VIOLENT MEN
(Columbia, January 1, 1955)   96 Mins.
(Technicolor)   (CinemaScope)
Glenn Ford, Barbara Stanwyck, Edward G. Robinson, Dianne Foster, Brian Keith, May Wynn, Warner Anderson, Basil Ruysdael, Lita Milan, Richard Jaeckel, James Westerfield, Jack Kelly, Willis Bouchey, Harry Shannon, Peter Hanson, Don C. Harvey, Robo Bechi, Carl Andre, James Anderson, Katherine Warren, Tom Browne Henry, Bill Phills
D: Rudolph Mate
S: Donald Hamilton
SP: Harry Kleiner
P: Lewis J. Rachmil

2678. THE AMERICANO
(RKO, January 15, 1955)   85 Mins.
(Technicolor)   (Filmed in Brazil)
Glenn Ford, Frank Lovejoy, Cesar Romero, Ursula Theiss, Abbe Lane, Rodolfo Hoyos, Jr., Salvador Baguez, Tom Powers, Dan White, Frank Marlowe
D: William Castle
S: Leslie T. White
SP: Guy Trosper
P: Robert Stillman

2679. TREASURE OF RUBY HILLS
(Allied Artists, January 23, 1955)   71 Mins.
Zachary Scott, Carole Mathews, Barton MacLane, Dick Foran, Lola Albright, Lee Van Cleef, Raymond Hatton, Gordon Jones, Steve Darrell, Charles Fredericks, Stanley Andrews, James Alexander, Rick Vallin
D: Frank McDonald
S: Louis L'Amour

SP: Tom Hubbard, Fred Eggers
P: William F. Broidy

2680. CAROLINA CANNONBALL
(Republic, January 28, 1955)   74 Mins.
Judy Canova, Andy Clyde, Ross Elliott, Sig Ruman, Leon Askin, Jack Kruschen, Frank Wilcox, Roy Barcroft
D: Charles Lamont
S: Frank Gill, Jr.
SP: Barry Shipman
AP: Sidney Picker

2681. THE FAR COUNTRY
(Universal-International, February 1, 1955)   97 Mins.
(Technicolor)
James Stewart, Ruth Roman, Corinne Calvet, Walter Brennan, John McIntire, Jay C. Flippen, Henry (Harry) Morgan, Steve Brodie, Royal Dano, Gregg Barton, Chubby Johnson, Eddy C. Walker, Robert Foulk, Eugene Borden, Allan Ray
D: Anthony Mann
S/SP: Borden Chase
P: Aaron Rosenberg

2682. TEN WANTED MEN
(Scott-Brown, Columbia, February 1, 1955)   80 Mins.
(Technicolor)
Randolph Scott, Jocelyn Brando, Richard Boone, Alfonso Bedoya, Donna Martell, Skip Homeier, Clem Bevins, Leo Gordon, Minor Watson, Lester Matthews, Tom Powers, Dennis Weaver, Lee Van Cleef, Louis Jean Heydt, Kathleen Crowley, Boyd "Red" Morgan, Denver Pyle, Francis McDonald, Pat Collins, Paul Maxey, Jack Perrin, Julian Rivero, Carlos Vera, Edna Holland, Reed Howes, Terry Frost, Franklyn Farnum, George Boyce
D: Bruce Humberstone
S: Irving Ravetch, Harriet Frank, Jr.
SP: Kenneth Gamet
P: Harry Joe Brown

2683. MANY RIVERS TO CROSS
(MGM, February 4, 1955)   92 Mins.
(Eastman Color)   (CinemaScope)
Robert Taylor, Eleanor Parker, Victor McLaglen, Jeff Richards, Russ Tamblyn, James Arness, Alan Hale, Jr., John Hudson, Rhys Williams, Josephine Hutchinson, Sig Ruman, Rosemary DeCamp, Russell Johnson, Ralph Moody, Abel Fernandez
D: Roy Rowland
SP: Harry Brown, Guy Trosper
P: Jack Cummings

2684. WHITE FEATHER

(Panoramic/20th C. Fox, February 4, 1955)
  102 Mins.

(Technicolor) (CinemaScope)

Robert Wagner, John Lund, Debra Paget, Jeffrey
  Hunter, Eduard Franz, Noah Beery, Jr., Virginia
  Leith, Emile Meyer, Hugh O'Brian, Milburn Stone

D: Robert Webb

S: John Prebble

SP: Delmer Daves, Leo Townsend

P: Robert L. Jacks, Leonard Goldstein

2685. TIMBERJACK

(Republic, February 18, 1955) 92 Mins.

(Trucolor)

Sterling Hayden, Vera Ralston, David Brian,
  Adolphe Menjou, Hoagy Carmichael, Chill Wills,
  Jim Davis, Howard Petrie, Ian MacDonald, Elisha
  Cook, Karl Davis, Wally Cassell, Tex Terry,
  George Marshall

D: Joseph Kane

S: Dan Cushman

SP: Allen Rivkin

P: Herbert J. Yates

2686. CANYON CROSSROADS

(Joyce-Werker/United Artists, February, 1955)
  83 Mins.

Richard Basehart, Phyllis Kirk, Stephen Elliott, Russell Collins, Charles Waggenheim, Richard Hale,
  Alan Wells, Tommy Cook, William Pullen

D: Alfred Werker

SP: Emmet Murphy, Leonard Heideman

P: William Joyce

2687. SMOKE SIGNAL

(Universal-International, March 1, 1955) 88 Mins.

(Technicolor)

Dana Andrews, Piper Laurie, Rex Reason, William
  Talman, Milburn Stone, Peter Cow, Douglas
  Spencer, Gordon Jones, William Schallert, Bill
  Phipps, Bob Wilke, Pat Hogan, Peter Coe

D: Jerry Hopper

S/SP: George F. Slavin, George W. George

P: Howard Christie

2688. YELLOWNECK

(Empire/Republic, March 22, 1955) 83 Mins.

(Trucolor)

Lin McCarthy, Stephen Courtleigh, Barry Kroger,
  Harold Gordon, Bill Mason

D/S: R. John Hugh

SP: Nat S. Linden

P: Harlow G. Frederick

2689. STRANGER ON HORSEBACK

(United Artists, March 23, 1955) 66 Mins.

(AnscoColor) (Filmed in Mexico)

Joel McCrea, Miroslava, Kevin McCarthy, John
  McIntire, Nancy Gates, John Carradine, Emile
  Meyer, Robert Cornthwaite, James Bell, Jaclynne
  Greene, Walter Baldwin

D: Jacques Tourneur

S: Louis L'Amour

SP: Herb Meadow, Don Martin

P: Robert Goldstein

2690. THE SILVER STAR

(Lippert, March 25, 1955) 73 Mins.

Edgar Buchanan, Marie Windsor, Lon Chaney, Jr.,
  Earle Lyon, Richard Bartlett, Barton MacLane,
  Morris Ankrum, Edith Evanson, Steve Rowland,
  Michael Whalen, voice of Jimmy Wakely

D: Richard Bartlett

S/SP: Richard Bartlett, Ian MacDonald

P: Earle Lyon

2691. RAGE AT DAWN

(RKO, March 26, 1955) 87 Mins.

(Technicolor)

Randolph Scott, Forrest Tucker, Mala Powers,
  J. Carroll Naish, Edgar Buchanan, Myron Healey,
  Howard Petrie, Ray Teal, William Forrest, Denver
  Pyle, Trevor Bardette, Kenneth Tobey, Chubby
  Johnson, Richard Garland, Ralph Moody, Guy
  Prescott, Mike Ragan, Phil Chambers

D: Tim Whelan

S: Frank Gruber

SP: Horace McCoy

P: Nat Holt

(Briefly released under the title *Seven Bad Men*)

2692. SEVEN ANGRY MEN

(Allied Artists, March 27, 1955) 90 Mins.

Raymond Massey, Debra Paget, Jeffrey Hunter,
  Larry Pennell, Leo Gordon, John Smith, James
  Best, Dennis Weaver, Guy Williams, Tom Irish,
  James Anderson, James Edwards, John Pickard,
  Smoki Whitfield, Jack Lomas, Robert Simon,
  Dabbs Greer, Ann Tyrell, Robert Osterloh

D: Charles Marquis Warren

SP: Daniel B. Ullman

P: Vincent M. Fennelly

2693. WYOMING RENEGADES

(Columbia, March 27, 1955) 73 Mins.

(Technicolor)

Phil Carey, Martha Hyer, Gene Evans, William
  Bishop, Douglas Kennedy, Roy Roberts, Don
  Beddoe, Aaron Spelling, George Keymas, Harry
  Harvey, Mel Welles, Henry Rowland, Boyd Stock-
  man, A. Guy Teague, Bob Woodward, Don C.
  Harvey, John (Bob) Cason, Don Carlos

D: Fred F. Sears

S/SP: David Lang
P: Wallace MacDonald

2694. CHIEF CRAZY HORSE
(Universal-International, April 1, 1955) 86 Mins.
(Technicolor) (CinemaScope)
Victor Mature, Suzan Ball, John Lund, Ray Danton, Keith Larsen, Paul Guilfoyle, David Janssen, Robert Warwick, James Millican, Morris Ankrum, Stuart Randall, Robert Simon, James Westerfield, Donald Randolph, Dennis Weaver, John Peters
D: George Sherman
S: Gerald Drayson Adams
SP: Franklin Coen, Gerald Drayson Adams
P: William Alland

2695. MAN WITHOUT A STAR
(Universal-International, April 1, 1955) 89 Mins.
(Technicolor)
Kirk Douglas, Jeanne Craine, Claire Trevor, William Campbell, Jay C. Flippen, Myrna Hansen, Mara Corday, Eddy C. Waller, Richard Boone, Frank Chase, Roy Barcroft, Millicent Patrick, Casey MacGregor, Jack Ingram, Ewing Mitchell, George Wallace, William Challee, Sheb Wooley, William Phillips, James Hayward, Malcolm Atterbury, Paul Birch, Myron Healey, Mark Hanna, Lee Roberts
D: King Vidor
S: Dee Linford
SP: Borden Chase, D. D. Beauchamp
P: Aaron Rosenberg

2696. RUN FOR COVER
(Paramount, April 1, 1955) 93 Mins.
(Technicolor) (VistaVision)
James Cagney, Viveca Lindfors, John Derek, Jean Hersholt, Grant Withers, Jack Lambert, Ernest Borgnine, Irving Bacon, Trevor Bardette, Ray Teal, John Miljan, Denver Pyle, Emerson Treacy, Gus Schilling, Phil Chambers, Harold Kennedy, Joe Haworth, Henry Wills
D: Nicholas Ray
SP: Winston Miller
P: William H. Pine, William C. Thomas

2697. FIVE GUNS WEST
(American Releasing Corp., April 15, 1955)
79 Mins.
(Pathe Color)
John Lund, Dorothy Malone, Touch (Mike) Connors, Jonathan Haze, Paul Birch, James Stone, Bob Campbell, Jack Ingram, Larry Thor
D/P: Roger Corman
SP: R. Wright Campbell

2698. SHOTGUN
(Allied Artists, April 24, 1955) 80 Mins.
(Technicolor)
Sterling Hayden, Yvonne De Carlo, Zachary Scott, Guy Prescott, Robert Wilke, Angela Green, Paul Marion, John Pickard, Ralph Sanford, Rory Mallison, Fiona Hale, Ward Wood, Lane Chandler, Al Wyatt, Harry Harvey
D: Lesley Selander
SP: Clark E. Reynolds, Rory Calhoun, John C. Champion
P: John C. Champion

2699. STRANGE LADY IN TOWN
(Warner Bros., April 30, 1955) 112 Mins.
(WarnerColor) (CinemaScope)
Greer Garson, Dana Andrews, Cameron Mitchell, Lois Smith, Walter Hampden, Pedro Gonzales-Gonzales, Joan Camden, Jose Torvay, Adele Jergens, Bob Wilke, Frank de Kova, Russell Johnson, Gregory Walcott, Douglas Kennedy, Ralph Moody, Nick Adams, Jack Williams, The Trianas
D/P: Mervyn LeRoy
S/SP: Frank Butler

2700. SEMINOLE UPRISING
(Columbia, May 1, 1955) 74 Mins.
(Technicolor)
George Montgomery, Karin Booth, William Fawcett, Steve Ritch, Ed Hinton, John Pickard, Jim Maloney, Rory Mallison, Howard Wright, Russ Conklin, Jonni Paris, Joanne Rio, Richard Cutting, Paul McGuire, Kenneth MacDonald, Rube Schafer, Edward Coch
D: Earl Bellamy
S: "Bugle's Wake"—Curt Brandon
SP: Robert E. Kent
P: Sam Katzman

2701. TIMBER COUNTRY TROUBLE
(Newhall/Allied Artists, May 8, 1955)
(*Wild Bill Hickok* Series)
Guy Madison, Andy Devine, Frances Charles, Kenne Duncan, George Barrows
D: Frank McDonald
SP: Maurice Tombragel
P: Wesley E. Barry
(Compiled from two television episodes, titles unknown)

2702. THE MATCH-MAKING MARSHAL
(Newhall/Allied Artists, May 8, 1955)
(*Wild Bill Hickok* Series)
Guy Madison, Andy Devine
D: Frank McDonald
SP: Unknown
P: Wesley E. Barry
(Compiled from two television episodes, titles unknown)

2703. THE TITLED TENDERFOOT
(Newhall/Allied Artists, May 8, 1955)
(*Wild Bill Hickok* Series)
Guy Madison, Andy Devine, Jeanne Cagney,
    Clayton Moore, Hal Gerald, James Bell, Jack Rey-
    nolds, Dick Cavendish, Dick Elliott, Gerald Smith,
    Parke MacGregor, Russ Whiteman, I. Stanford
    Jolley, Guy Teague, Marshall Reed
D: Frank McDonald
SP: Maurice Tombragel
P: Wesley E. Barry
(Compiled from the television episodes "The Trap-
    per Story" and "A Joke on Sir Anthony")

2704. PHANTOM TRAILS
(Newhall/Allied Artists, May 8, 1955)
(*Wild Bill Hickok* Series)
Guy Madison, Andy Devine
D: Frank McDonald
SP: Unknown
P: Wesley E. Barry
(Compiled from two television episodes, titles un-
    known)

2705. SANTA FE PASSAGE
(Republic, May 12, 1955)   90 Mins.
(Trucolor)
John Payne, Faith Domergue, Rod Cameron, Slim
    Pickens, Irene Tedrow, George Keymas, Leo Gor-
    don, Anthony Caruso
D: William Witney
SP: Lillie Hayward
S: Clay Fisher in *Esquire* magazine
AP: Sidney Picker

2706. OUTLAW TREASURE
(American Releasing Corp., May 15, 1955)
    67 Mins.
John Forbes (John Carpenter), Frank "Red" Carpen-
    ter, Adele Jergens, Glenn Langan, Hal Baylor,
    Michael Whelan, Frank Jenks, Harry Lauter
D: Oliver Drake
SP/P: John Carpenter

2707. THE MARAUDERS
(MGM, May 20, 1955)   80 Mins.
(Eastman Color)
Dan Duryea, Jeff Richards, Keenan Wynn, Jurma
    Lewis, John Hudson, Harry Shannon, David Kas-
    day, James Anderson, Richard Lupino, Peter Ma-
    makos, Mort Mills, John Damler, Michael Dugan,
    Ken Carlton
D: Gerald Mayer
S: Alan Margus
SP: Jack Leonard, Earl Felton
P: Arthur M. Lowe, Jr.

2708. ROBBER'S ROOST
(United Artists, May 30, 1955)   82 Mins.
(DeLuxe Color)
George Montgomery, Richard Boone, Sylvia Find-
    ley, Bruce Bennett, Peter Graves, Warren Ste-
    vens, Tony Romano, William Hopper, Leo Gor-
    don, Stanley Clements, Joe Bassett, Leonard Geer,
    Al Wyatt, Boyd Morgan
D: Sidney Salkow
S: Zane Grey
SP: John O'Dea, Sidney Salkow, Maurice Geraghty
P: Robert Goldstein, Leonard Goldstein

**2709. DAVY CROCKETT, KING OF THE
            WILD FRONTIER**
(Buena Vista, June 1, 1955)   95 Mins.
(Technicolor)
Fess Parker, Buddy Ebsen, Basil Ruysdael, Hans
    Conried, William Bakewell, Ken Tobey, Pat Ho-
    gan, Helene Stanley, Nick Cravet, Don Megowan,
    Mike Mazurki, Jeff Thompson, Henry Joyner,
    Benjamin Hornbuckle, Hal Youngblood, Jim Mad-
    dox, Robert Booth, Eugene Brindel, Ray White-
    tree, Col. Campbell Brown
D: Norman Foster
SP: Tom Blackburn
P: Bill Walsh

2710. THE FAR HORIZONS
(Paramount, June 1, 1955)   108 Mins.
(Technicolor) (VistaVision)
Fred MacMurray, Charlton Heston, Donna Reed,
    Barbara Hale, William Demarest, Alan Reed,
    Eduardo Noriega, Larry Pennell, Herbert Heyes,
    Lester Matthews, Argentina Brunetti, Julia Mon-
    toya, Ralph Moody, Helen Wallace, Walter Reed,
    Bill Phipps, Tom Monroe, LeRoy Johnson, Joe
    Canutt, Bob Herron, Al Wyatt, Bill Wallace, Fran
    Bennett, Vernon Rich, Bill Walker, Margarita
    Martin
D: Rudolph Mate
S: "Sacajaewa of the Shoshones"—Della Gould
    Emmons
SP: Winston Miller, Edmund H. North
P: William H. Pine, William C. Thomas

2711. THE MAN FROM BITTER RIDGE
(Universal-International, June 1, 1955)   80 Mins.
(Eastman Color)
Lex Barker, Mara Corday, Stephen McNally, Trevor
    Bardette, John Dehner, Myron Healey, Warren
    Stevens, Richard Garland, Jennings Miles, John
    Cliff, Ray Teal, John Harmon
D: Jack Arnold
S: William MacLeod Raine
SP: Lawrence Roman, Teddi Sherman
P: Howard Pine

2712. THE ROAD TO DENVER

(Republic, June 16, 1955)   90 Mins.

(Trucolor)

John Payne, Mona Freeman, Lee J. Cobb, Ray Middleton, Skip Homeier, Andy Clyde, Lee Van Cleef, Karl Davis, Glenn Strange, Buzz Henry, Dan White, Robert Burton, Anne Carroll, Tex Terry

D: Joseph Kane

S: *Saturday Evening Post* short story by Bill Gullick

SP: Horace McCoy, Allen Rivkin

P: Herbert J. Yates

2713. TALL MAN RIDING

(Warner Bros., June 18, 1955)   83 Mins.

(WarnerColor)

Randolph Scott, Dorothy Malone, Peggie Castle, William Ching, John Baragrey, Robert Barrat, John Dehner, Paul Richards, Lane Chandler, Mickey Simpson, Joe Bassett, Charles Watts, Russ Conway, Mike Ragan, Carl Andre, John Logan, Guy Hearn, Bill Faucett, Nolan Leary, Phil Rich, Eva Novak, Buddy Roosevelt, Jack Henderson, Bob Peoples, William Bailey, Patrick Henry, Joe Brooks, Vernon Rich, Bob Stephenson, Dub Taylor, Roger Creed

D: Lesley Selander

S: Norman A. Fox

SP: Joseph Hoffman

P: David Weisbart

2714. WEBB PIERCE AND HIS WANDERIN' BOYS

(Universal-International, June 20, 1955)   16 Mins.

Webb Pierce and Band, Hank Penny, Sue Thompson, Marion Colby, Red Sovine

D/P: Will Cowan

2715. THE LONESOME TRAIL

(Lippert, July 1, 1955)   73 Mins.

Wayne Morris, John Agar, Margia Dean, Edgar Buchanan, Adele Jergens, Earle Lyon, Ian MacDonald, Douglas Fowley, Richard Bartlett, Betty Blythe

D: Richard Bartlett

S: "Silent Beckoning"—Gordon D. Shirreffs

SP: Richard Bartlett, Ian MacDonald

P: Earle Lyon

2716. WICHITA

(Allied Artists, July 3, 1955)   81 Mins.

(Technicolor)   (CinemaScope)

Joel McCrea, Vera Miles, Lloyd Bridges, Wallace Ford, Edgar Buchanan, Peter Graves, Keith Larsen, Carl Benton Reid, John Smith, Walter Coy, Walter Sande, Robert J. Wilke, Rayford Barnes, Jack Elam, Mae Clarke, Gene Wesson, voice of Tex Ritter

D: Jacques Tourneur

S/SP: Daniel B. Ullman

P: Walter Mirisch

2717. LAY THAT RIFLE DOWN

(Republic, July 7, 1955)   71 Mins.

Judy Canova, Robert Lowery, Jil Jarmyn, Jacqueline de Witt, Richard Deacon, Robert Burton, James Bell, Leon Tyler, Tweeny Canova

D: Charles Lamont

SP: Barry Shipman

AP: Sidney Picker

2718. THE KENTUCKIAN

(Hecht-Lancaster/United Artists, August 1, 1955)   104 Mins.

(Technicolor)   (CinemaScope)

Burt Lancaster, Dianne Foster, Diana Lynn, John McIntire, Una Merkel, Walter Matthau, John Carradine, Ronald MacDonald, John Litel, Rhys Williams, Edward Norris, Lee Erickson, Clem Bevins, Lisa Ferraday, Douglas Spencer, Whip Wilson

D: Burt Lancaster

S: "The Gabriel Horn"—Felix Holt

SP: A. B. Guthrie, Jr.

P: Harold Hecht

2719. THE MAN FROM LARAMIE

(Columbia, August 1, 1955)   104 Mins.

(Technicolor)   (CinemaScope)

James Stewart, Arthur Kennedy, Donald Crisp, Cathy O'Donnell, Alex Nicol, Aline MacMahon, Wallace Ford, Jack Elam, John War Eagle, James Millican, Gregg Barton, Boyd Stockman, Frank de Kova

D: Anthony Mann

S: Thomas T. Flynn in *Saturday Evening Post*

SP: Philip Yordan, Frank Burt

P: William Goetz

2719a. THE LAST COMMAND

(Republic, August 3, 1955)   110 Mins.

(Trucolor)

Sterling Hayden, Anna Maria Alberghetti, Richard Carlson, Arthur Hunnicutt, Ernest Borgnine, J. Carroll Naish, Ben Cooper, John Russell, Virginia Grey, Jim Davis, Eduard Franz, Otto Kruger, Russell Simpson, Roy Roberts, Slim Pickens, Hugh Sanders

D: Frank Lloyd

S: Sy Bartlett

SP: Warren Duff

AP: Frank Lloyd

2720. APACHE AMBUSH

(Columbia, September 1, 1955)   68 Mins.

Bill Williams, Richard Jaeckel, Alex Montoya, Mo-

vita, Adelle August, Tex Ritter, Ray "Crash" Corrigan, Ray Teal, Don Harvey, James Griffith, James Flavin, George Chandler, Forrest Lewis, George Keymas, Victor Milan, Harry Lauter, Bill Hale, Robert Foulk
D: Fred F. Sears
S/SP: David Lang
P: Wallace MacDonald

2721. THE GUN THAT WON THE WEST
(Columbia, September 1, 1955)   71 Mins.
(Technicolor)
Dennis Morgan, Paula Raymond, Richard Denning, Chris O'Brien, Robert Bice, Michael Morgan, Roy Gordon, Howard Wright, Richard Cutting, Howard Negley, Kenneth MacDonald
D: William Castle
SP: James R. Gordon
P: Sam Katzman

2722. APACHE WOMAN
(Golden State/American Releasing Corp., September 15, 1955)   83 Mins.
(Pathe Color)
Lloyd Bridges, Joan Taylor, Lance Fuller, Morgan Jones, Paul Birch, Lou Place, Paul Dubov, Jonathan Hale, Gene Marlow, Dick Miller, Chester Conklin, Jean Howell
D: Roger Corman
S/SP: Lou Rusoff
P: Roger Corman, Alex Gordon

2723. TENNESSEE'S PARTNER
(RKO-Radio, September 21, 1955)   86 Mins.
(Technicolor)   (SuperScope)
John Payne, Ronald Reagan, Rhonda Fleming, Coleen Gray, Tony Caruso, Morris Ankrum, Leo Gordon, Chubby Johnson, Myron Healey, Joe Devlin, John Mansfield
D: Allan Dwan
S: Bret Harte
SP: Milton Krims, D. D. Beauchamp, Gram Baker, Teddi Sherman
P: Benedict Bogeaus

2724. COUNT THREE AND PRAY
(Columbia, October 3, 1955)   102 Mins.
(Technicolor)   (CinemaScope)
Van Heflin, Joanne Woodward, Phil Carey, Raymond Burr, Allison Hayes, Myron Healey, Nancy Kulp, James Griffith, Richard Webb, Robert Burton, John Cason, Jean Wilkes, Steve Raines
D: George Sherman
S: "Calico Pony"—Herb Meadows
SP: Herb Meadows
P: Ted Richmond

2725. KISS OF FIRE
(Universal-International, October 3, 1955)
   87 Mins.
(Technicolor)
Jack Palance, Barbara Rush, Rex Reason, Martha Hyer, Alan Reed, Leslie Bradley, Larry Dobkin, Pat Hogan, Henry Rowland, Bernie Gozier, Joseph Waring
D: Joseph M. Newman
S: "The Rose and the Flame"—Jonreed Lauritzen
SP: Franklin Coen, Richard Collins
P: Samuel Marx

2726. FORT YUMA
(Bel-Air/United Artists, October 6, 1955)   78 Mins.
(Technicolor)
Peter Graves, Jean Vohs, Joan Taylor, Abel Fernandez, James Lilburn, Abel Hernandez, Stanley Clements, John Picard, Addison Richards, John Hudson, Bill Phipps
D: Lesley Selander
S/SP: Danny Arnold
P: Howard W. Koch

2727. THE TALL MEN
(20th C. Fox, October 6, 1955)   121 Mins.
(DeLuxe Color)   (CinemaScope)
Clark Gable, Jane Russell, Robert Ryan, Cameron Mitchell, Juan Garcia, Harry Shannon, Emile Meyer, Steve Darrell, Will Wright, Robert Adler, J. Lewis Smith, Russell Simpson, Mae Marsh, Gertrude Graner, Tom Wilson, Tom Fadden, Dan White, Argentina Brunetti, Doris Kemper, Carl Harbaugh, Post Park
D: Raoul Walsh
S: Clay Fisher
SP: Sidney Boehm, Frank Nugent
P: William A. Bacher, William B. Hawks

2728. THE RETURN OF JACK SLADE
(Allied Artists, October 9, 1955)   79 Mins.
(SuperScope)
John Ericson, Mari Blanchard, Neville Brand, Casey Adams, Jon Shepodd, Howard Petrie, John Dennis, Angie Dickinson, Donna Drew, Mike Ross, Lyla Graham, Alan Wells, Raymond Bailey
D: Harold Schuster
SP: Warren Douglas
P: Lindsley Parsons

2729. THE TWINKLE IN GOD'S EYE
(Republic, October 13, 1955)   73 Mins.
Mickey Rooney, Coleen Gray, Hugh O'Brian, Joey Forman, Don Barry, Touch (Mike) Connors, Jil Jarmyn, Kem Dibbs, Tony Garcen, Raymond Hatton, Ruta Lee
D: George Blair

SP: P. J. Wolfson
AP: Maurice Duke

2730. OKLAHOMA!
(Magna Corp., October 15, 1955) 145 Mins.
(Todd-AO) (Eastman Color)
Gordon MacRae, Shirley Jones, Gloria Grahame, Gene Nelson, Charlotte Greenwood, Eddie Albert, James Whitmore, Rod Steiger, Barbara Lawrence, Jay C. Flippen, Roy Barcroft, James Mitchell, Bambi Lynn, Jennie Workman, Virginia Bosler, Kelly Brown, Marc Platt, Evelyn Taylor, Jane Fisher
D: Fred Zinnemann
S: From Rodgers & Hammerstein's musical of a play by Lynn Riggs
SP: Sonya Levien, William Ludwig
P: Arthur Hornblow, Jr.

2731. A MAN ALONE
(Republic, October 17, 1955) 96 Mins.
(Trucolor)
Ray Milland, Mary Murphy, Ward Bond, Raymond Burr, Arthur Space, Lee Van Cleef, Alan Hale, Jr., Douglas Spencer, Thomas B. Henry, Grandon Rhodes, Martin Garralaga, Howard J. Negley, Kim Spalding
D: Ray Milland
S: Mort Briskin
SP: John Tucker Battle
P: Herbert J. Yates

2732. THE TREASURE OF PANCHO VILLA
(RKO, October 19, 1955) 92 Mins.
(Technicolor) (SuperScope) (Filmed in Mexico)
Rory Calhoun, Shelley Winters, Gilbert Roland, Joseph Calleia, Fanny Schiller, Tony Carvajal, Carlos Mosquiz, Pasquel Pena
D: George Sherman
S: J. Robert Bren, Gladys Atwater
SP: Niven Busch
P: Edmund Grainger

2733. MAN WITH THE GUN
(United Artists, November 1, 1955) 83 Mins.
Robert Mitchum, Jan Sterling, Karen Sharpe, Henry Hull, Emile Meyer, John Lupton, Barbara Lawrence, Ted de Corsia, Leo Gordon, James Westerfield, Joe Barry, Florenz Ames, Robert Osterloh, Jay Adler, Angie Dickinson, Strafford Repp, Thom Conroy, Maudie Prickett
D: Richard Wilson
SP: N. B. Stone, Jr., Richard Wilson
P: Samuel Goldwyn, Jr.

2734. THE NAKED DAWN
(Universal-International, November 1, 1955)
82 Mins.
(Technicolor) (Filmed in Mexico)
Arthur Kennedy, Betta St. John, Eugene Iglesias, Charlita, Roy Engel
D: Edgar G. Ulmer
SP: Nina and Herman Schneider
AP: James O. Radford

2735. THE VANISHING AMERICAN
(Republic, November 17, 1955) 90 Mins.
Scott Brady, Audrey Totter, Forrest Tucker, Gene Lockhart, Jim Davis, John Dierkes, Gloria Castillo, Julian Rivero, Lee Van Cleef, George Keymas, Charles Stevens, Jay Silverheels, James Millican, Glenn Strange
D: Joseph Kane
S: Zane Grey
SP: Alan LeMay
P: Herbert J. Yates

2736. TEXAS LADY
(RKO, November 23, 1955) 85 Mins.
(Technicolor) (SuperScope)
Claudette Colbert, Barry Sullivan, Gregory Walcott, Ray Collins, Walter Sande, James Bell, Horace McMahon, John Litel, Douglas Fowley, Don Haggerty, Celia Lovsky
D: Tim Whelan
S/SP: Horace McCoy
P: Nat Holt

2737. LAST OF THE DESPERADOS
(Associated, December 1, 1955) 70 Mins.
James Craig, Jim Davis, Barton MacLane, Margia Dean, Donna Martell, Myrna Dell, Bob Steele, Stanley Clements
D: Sam Newfield
SP: Orville Hampton
P: Sigmund Neufeld

2738. TOP GUN
(Fame Pictures/United Artists, December 15, 1955) 73 Mins.
Sterling Hayden, William Bishop, Karen Booth, James Millican, Regis Toomey, Hugh Sanders, John Dehner, Rod Taylor, Denver Pyle, William "Bill" Phillips, Dick Reeves
D: Ray Nazarro
S: Steve Fisher
SP: Richard Schayer, Steve Fisher

2739. THE INDIAN FIGHTER
(Bryna/United Artists, December 15, 1955) 88 Mins.
(Eastman Color) (CinemaScope)
Kirk Douglas, Elsa Martinelli, Walter Abel, Walter Matthau, Diana Douglas, Eduard Franz, Lon

A Lawless Street (Scott-Brown/Columbia, 1955) — Angela Lansbury and Randolph Scott

Chaney, Jr., Alan Hale, Jr., Elisha Cook, Jr., Michael Winkelman, Harry Landers, William Phipps, Buzz Henry, Ray Teal, Frank Cady, Hank Worden, Lane Chandler
D: Andre de Toth
S: Ben Kadish
SP: Frank Davis, Ben Hecht
P: William Schorr

2740. A LAWLESS STREET

(Scott-Brown/Columbia, December 15, 1955) 78 Mins.
(Technicolor)
Randolph Scott, Angela Lansbury, Warner Anderson, Jean Parker, Wallace Ford, John Emery, James Bell, Ruth Donnelly, Michael Pate, Don Megowan, Jeanette Nolan, Peter Ortiz, Don Carlos, Frank Hagney, Charles Williams, Frank Ferguson, Harry Tyler, Harry Antrim, Jay Lawrence, Reed Howes, Guy Teague, Hal K. Dawson, Pat Collins, Frank Scannell, Stanley Blystone, Barry Brooks, Edwin Chandler
D: Joseph H. Lewis
S: "Marshal of Medicine Bend"—Brad Ward
SP: Kenneth Gamet
P: Harry Joe Brown, Randolph Scott

2741. AT GUNPOINT

(Allied Artists, December 25, 1955) 81 Mins.
(Technicolor) (CinemaScope)
Fred MacMurray, Dorothy Malone, Walter Brennan, Tommy Rettig, John Qualen, Irving Bacon, Skip Homeier, Whit Bissell, Jack Lambert, John Pickard, Harry Shannon, James Lilburn, Frank Ferguson
D: Alfred Werker
S/SP: Daniel B. Ullman
P: Vincent M. Fennelly

2742. THE LAST FRONTIER

(Columbia, 1955) 97 Mins.
Victor Mature, James Whitmore, Robert Preston, Guy Madison, Anne Bancroft, Peter Whitney, Pat Hogan, Russell Collins, Manuel Donde, Guy Williams, Mickey Kuhn, William Calles
D: Anthony Mann
S: Richard Emery Roberts
SP: Philip Yordan, Russell S. Hughes
P: William Fadiman

2742a. FURY IN PARADISE

(Filmmakers, 1955) 77 Mins.
(Eastman Color) (Filmed in Mexico)

Peter Thompson, Rea Iturbi, Edward Norlega, Felipe Nolan, Jose Espinosa, Fran Schiller, Carlos Rivas, Claud Brooks

D: George Bruce
S/SP: George Bruce
P: Alfonso Sanchez-Tello

FILMS OF 1956

2743. THE SPOILERS
(Universal-International, January 2, 1956)
84 Mins.
(Technicolor)
Anne Baxter, Jeff Chandler, Rory Calhoun, Ray Danton, Barbara Britton, John McIntire, Carl Benton Reid, Wallace Ford, Raymond Walburn, Dayton Lummis, Willis Bouchey, Roy Barcroft, Ruth Donnelly, Forrest Lewis
D: Jesse Hibbs
S: Rex Beach
SP: Oscar Brodney, Charles Hoffman
P: Ross Hunter

2744. PERILS OF THE WILDERNESS
(Columbia, January 6, 1956)   15 Chaps.
Dennis Moore, Richard Emory, Eve Anderson, Kenneth MacDonald, Rick Vallin, John Elliott, Don Harvey, Terry Frost, Al Ferguson, Bud Osborne, Rex Lease, Pierce Lyden, John Mitchum, Lee Roberts, Stanley Price, Ed Coch, Kermit Maynard
D: Spencer G. Bennet
SP: George H. Plympton
P: Sam Katzman
Chapter Titles: (1) The Voice from the Sky, (2) The Mystery Plane, (3) The Mine of Menace, (4) Ambush for a Mountie, (5) Laramie's Desperate Chance, (6) Trapped in the Flaming Forest, (7) Out of the Trap, (8) Laramie Rides Alone, (9) Menace of the Medicine Man, (10) Midnight Marauders, (11) The Falls of Fate, (12) Rescue from the Rapids, (13) Little Bear Pays a Debt, (14) The Mystery Plane Flies Again, (15) Laramie Gets His Man

2744a. DIG THAT URANIUM
(Allied Artists, January 8, 1956)   61 Mins.
(*Bowery Boys* Series)
Leo Gorcey, Huntz Hall, Bernard Gorcey, Mary

Beth Hughes, Raymond Hatton, Harry Lauter, Myron Healey, Richard Powers (Tom Keene), Paul Fierro, David Condon, Bennie Bartlett, Carl "Alfalfa" Switzer
D: Edward Bernds
SP: Ellwood Ullman, Bert Lawrence
P: Edward Bernds

2745. HIDDEN GUNS
(Republic, January 30, 1956) 66 Mins.
Richard Arlen, Bruce Bennett, John Carradine, Faron Young, Lloyd Corrigan, Angie Dickinson, Damian O'Flynn, Irving Bacon, Tom Hubbard, Ron Kennedy, Bill Ward, Raymond L. Morgan, Edmund Cobb, Ben Welden, Guinn "Big Boy" Williams, Gordon Terry, Bill Coontz, Michael Darrin
D: Al Gannaway
S/SP: Sam Roeca, Al Gannaway
P: Al Gannaway, C. J. Ver Halen, Jr.

2746. FURY AT GUNSIGHT PASS
(Columbia, February 15, 1956) 68 Mins.
David Brian, Neville Brand, Richard Long, Lisa Davis, Kathleen Warren, Percy Helton, Morris Ankrum, Addison Richards, Joe Forte, Wally Vernon, Paul E. Burns, Frank Fenton, James Anderson, George Keymas, Robert Anderson, Frank Coby, John Lehmann, Guy Teague
D: Fred F. Sears
S/SP: David Lang
P: Wallace MacDonald

2747. THE LAST HUNT
(MGM, February 24, 1956) 108 Mins.
(Eastman Color) (CinemaScope)
Robert Taylor, Stewart Granger, Lloyd Nolan, Debra Paget, Russ Tamblyn, Constance Ford, Joe DeSantis, Ainslie Pryor, Ralph Moody, Fred Graham
D/SP: Richard Brooks
P: Dore Schary

2748. THE LONE RANGER
(Wrather/Warner Bros., February 25, 1956)
86 Mins.
(WarnerColor)
Clayton Moore, Jay Silverheels, Lyle Bettger, Bonita Granville, Perry Lopez, Robert Wilke, John Pickard, Beverly Washburn, Michael Ansara, Frank de Kova, Charles Meredith, Mickey Simpson, Zon Murray, Lane Chandler
D: Stuart Heisler
SP: Herb Meadow. Based on "The Lone Ranger Legend"
P: Willis Goldbeck

2749. THE WILD DAKOTAS
(Associated, February 28, 1956) 73 Mins.
Bill Williams, Coleen Gray, Jim Davis, John Litel, Dick Jones, John Miljan, Lisa Montell, I. Stanford Jolley, Wally Brown, Bill Dix, Iron Eyes Cody
D: Sam Newfield
SP: Thomas W. Blackburn
P: Sigmund Neufeld

2750. GHOST TOWN
(Bel-Air/United Artists, March 1, 1956) 75 Mins.
Kent Taylor, John Smith, Marian Carr, John Doucette, William "Bill" Phillips, Serena Sande, Joel Ashley, Gilman H. Rankin, Edward Hashim, Gary Murray
D: Allen Miner
S/SP: Jameson Brewer
P: Howard Koch

2751. RED SUNDOWN
(Universal-International, March 1, 1956) 82 Mins.
(Technicolor)
Rory Calhoun, Martha Hyer, Dean Jagger, Robert Middleton, James Millican, Lita Baron, Grant Williams, Trevor Bardette, David Kasday, Stevie Wootton, Leo Gordon, Steve Darrell
D: Jack Arnold
S: Martin Berkeley
P: Albert Zugsmith

2752. THE SEARCHERS
(C. V. Whitney/Warner Bros., March 13, 1956)
119 Mins.
(Technicolor) (VistaVision)
John Wayne, Jeffrey Hunter, Vera Miles, Ward Bond, Natalie Wood, John Qualen, Olive Carey, Henry Brandon, Ken Curtis, Harry Carey, Jr., Antonio Moreno, Hank Worden, Lana Wood, Walter Coy, Dorothy Jordan, Pippa Scott, Pat Wayne, Beulah Archuletta, Jack Pennick, Peter Mamakos, Chuck Roberson, Nacho Galindo, Robert Lyden, Chief Thunder Cloud, Cliff Lyons
D: John Ford
S: Alan LeMay
SP: Frank S. Nugent
P: Merian C. Cooper, C. V. Whitney
AP: Patrick Ford

2753. COMANCHE
(United Artists, March 25, 1956) 87 Mins.
(DeLuxe Color) (CinemaScope)
(Filmed in Mexico)
Dana Andrews, Kent Smith, Nestor Paiva, Linda Cristal, Henry Brandon, John Litel, Reed Sherman, Stacy Harris, Lowell Gilmore, Mike Mazurki
D: George Sherman
SP/P: Carl Krueger

2754. BACKLASH
(Universal-International, April 1, 1956) 84 Mins.
(Technicolor)
Richard Widmark, Donna Reed, William Campbell, John McIntyre, Barton MacLane, Edward C. Platt, Harry Morgan, Bob Wilke, Reg Parton, Robert Foulk, Roy Roberts
D: John Sturges
SP: Borden Chase
P: Aaron Rosenberg

2755. BLACKJACK KETCHUM, DESPERADO
(Clover/Columbia, April 1, 1956) 76 Mins.
Howard Duff, Victor Jory, Maggie Mahoney, Angela Stevens, David Orrick, William Tannen, Ken Christy, Martin Garralaga, Robert Roark, Don C. Harvey, Pat O'Malley, Jack Littlefield, Sidney Mason, Ralph Sanford, George Edward Mather, Charles Wagenheim, Wes Hudman
D: Earl Bellamy
S: Louis L'Amour
SP: Luci Ward, Jack Natteford
P: Sam Katzman

2756. MOHAWK
(20th C. Fox, April 1, 1956) 79 Mins.
(Eastman Color)
Scott Brady, Rita Gam, Neville Brand, Lori Nelson, Allison Hayes, John Hoyt, Vera Vague (Barbara Jo Allen), Rhys Williams, Ted de Corsia, Mae Clarke, John Hudson, Tommy Cook, Michael Granger, James Lilburn, Chabon Jadi
D: Kurt Neumann
S/SP: Maurice Geraghty, Milton Krims
P: Edward L. Alperson

2757. STRANGER AT MY DOOR
(Republic, April 6, 1956) 85 Mins.
MacDonald Carey, Patricia Medina, Skip Homeier, Stephen Wootton, Louis Jean Heydt, Howard Wright, Slim Pickens, Fred Sherman, Malcolm Atterbury
D: William Witney
S/SP: Barry Shipman
SP: Sidney Picker

2758. TRIBUTE TO A BADMAN
(MGM, April 13, 1956) 95 Mins.
(Eastman Color) (CinemaScope)
James Cagney, Don Dubbins, Stephen McNally, Irene Papas, Vic Morrow, James Griffith, Onslow Stevens, James Bell, Jeanette Nolan, Chubby Johnson, Royal Dano, Lee Van Cleef, Peter Chong, Buddy Roosevelt, Bud Osborne, Dennis Moore, Tom London, Tony Hughes, Roy Engel, John Halloran, Billy Dix, Clint Sharp

D: Robert Wise
S: Jack Schaefer
SP: Michael Blankfort
P: Sam Zimbalist

2759. THE BROKEN STAR
(Bel-Air/United Artists, April 25, 1956) 82 Mins.
Howard Duff, Lita Baron, Bill Williams, Henry Calvin, Douglas Fowley, Addison Richards, Joel Ashby, John Pickard, William Phillips, Dorothy Adams, Joe Dominguez
D: Lesley Selander
S/SP: John C. Higgins
P: Aubrey Schenck

2760. A DAY OF FURY
(Universal-International, May 1, 1956) 78 Mins.
(Technicolor)
Dale Robertson, Mara Corday, Jock Mahoney, Carl Benton Reid, Jan Merlin, John Dehner, Dayton Lummis, Sidney Mason, Dee Carroll, Sheila Bromley, Harry Tyler, Helen Kleeb
D: Harmon Jones
SP: James Edmiston, Oscar Brodney
P: Robert Arthur

2761. JUBAL
(Columbia, May 1, 1956) 101 Mins.
(Technicolor) (CinemaScope)
Glenn Ford, Ernest Borgnine, Rod Steiger, Valerie French, Felicia Farr, Basil Ruysdael, Noah Beery, Jr., Charles Bronson, John Dierkes, Jack Elam, Robert Burton, Robert Knapp, Juney Ellis, Don C. Harvey, Guy Wilkerson, Larry Hudson, Mike Lawrence, Robert "Buzz" Henry
D: Delmer Daves
S: "Jubal Troop"—Paul I. Wellman
SP: Russell S. Hughes, Delmer Daves
P: William Fadiman

2762. QUINCANNON, FRONTIER SCOUT
(Bel-Air/United Artists, May 1, 1956) 83 Mins.
(DeLuxe Color)
Tony Martin, Peggie Castle, John Bromfield, John Smith, Ron Randell, John Doucette, Morris Ankrum, Peter Mamakos, Ed Hashim
D: Lesley Selander
SP: John C. Higgins, Don Martin
P: Howard W. Koch

2763. THE MAVERICK QUEEN
(Republic, May 3, 1956) 92 Mins.
(Trucolor) (Naturama)
Barbara Stanwyck, Barry Sullivan, Scott Brady, Mary Murphy, Wallace Ford, Howard Petrie, Jim Davis, Emile Meyer, Walter Sande, George

Keymas, John Doucette, Taylor Holmes, Pierre Watkin
D: Joseph Kane
S: Zane Grey
SP: Kenneth Gamet, DeVallon Scott
AP: Joseph Kane

2764. THE THREE OUTLAWS

(Associate Film Releasing Corp., May 13, 1956) 74 Mins.
(SuperScope)
Neville Brand, Alan Hale, Jr., Bruce Bennett, Jose Gonzales, Jeanne Carmen, Rudolfo Hoyos, Robert Tafur, Lillian Molderi, Robert Christopher, Vincent Padula, Henry Escalante, Bill Henry
D: Sam Newfield
SP: Orville Hampton
P: Sigmund Neufeld

2765. GREAT DAY IN THE MORNING

(RKO, May 16, 1956) 92 Mins.
(Technicolor) (SuperScope)
Virginia Mayo, Robert Stack, Ruth Roman, Alex Nicol, Raymond Burr, Leo Gordon, Donald McDonald, Regis Toomey, Peter Whitney, Dan White
D: Jacques Tourneur
S: Robert Hardy Andrews
SP: Lesser Samuels
P: Edmund Grainger

2766. THE PROUD ONES

(20th C. Fox, May 27, 1956) 94 Mins.
(DeLuxe Color) (CinemaScope)
Robert Ryan, Virginia Mayo, Jeffrey Hunter, Robert Middleton, Walter Brennan, Arthur O'Connell, Ken Clark, Rodolfo Acosta, George Matthews, Fay Roope, Edward Platt, Whit Bissell, Richard Deacon, Frank Gerstle, Charles Tannen, Lois Ray, Jack Low, Ken Terrell, Harrison Lewis, Ed Mundy, Jackie Coogan, Juanita Close, Stan Jolley, Steve Darrell, Paul Burns
D: Robert D. Webb
S: Verne Athanas
SP: Edward North, Joseph Petracca
P: Robert L. Jacks

2767. MASSACRE

(Lippert, 20th C. Fox, June 1, 1956) 76 Mins.
(AnscoColor)
Dane Clark, James Craig, Marta Roth, Miguel Torruco, Jamie Fernandez, Ferrusquilla, Enrique Zambrano, Jose Munoz
D: Louis King
S: Fred Freiberger, William Tunberg
SP: D. D. Beauchamp
P: Robert L. Lippert, Jr., Olallo Rubio, Jr.

2768. STAR IN THE DUST

(Universal-International, June 1, 1956) 80 Mins.
(Technicolor)
John Agar, Mamie Van Doren, Richard Boone, Leif Erickson, Coleen Gray, James Gleason, Randy Stuart, Terry Gilkyson
D: Charles Haas
S: Lee Leighton
SP: Oscar Brodney
P: Albert Zugsmith

2769. THE OKLAHOMA WOMAN

(Sunset/American Releasing Corp., June 15, 1956) 80 Mins.
(SuperScope)
Richard Denning, Peggie Castle, Cathy Downs, Tudor Owen, Martin Kingsley, Touch (Mike) Connors, Jonathan Haze, Richard Miller, Tom Dillon, Edmund Cobb
D/P: Roger Corman
SP: Lou Rusoff

2770. GUNSLINGER

(American Releasing Corp., June 15, 1956) 83 Mins.
(Pathe Color)
John Ireland, Beverly Garland, Allison Hayes, Martin Kingsley, Jonathan Haze, Chris Alcaide, Richard Miller, Bruno De Sota, Margaret Campbell, William Schallert, Aaron Saxon, Chris Miller
D/P: Roger Corman
SP: Mark Hanna, Charles B. Griffith

2771. I KILLED WILD BILL HICKOK

(Wheeler Company Productions, June 16, 1956) 63 Mins.
John Forbes (John Carpenter), Helen Westcott, Tom Brown, Frank Carpenter, I. Stanford Jolley, Virginia Gibson, Denver Pyle, R. J. Thomas, Roy DeLar, Phil Barton, Bill Mims, Billy Dean, Lee Sheldon
D: Richard Talmadge
S/SP/P: John Carpenter

2772. THE NAKED HILLS

(Allied Artists, June 17, 1956) 73 Mins.
(Pathe Color)
David Wayne, Keenan Wynn, James Barton, Jim Backus, Marcia Henderson, Denver Pyle, Myrna Dell, Lewis Russell, Frank Fenton, Fuzzy Knight, Jim Hayward, Chris Olsen, Steve Terrell
D/SP/P: Josef Shaftel
S: Helen S. Bilkie

2773. THE GREAT LOCOMOTIVE CHASE

(Buena Vista/Disney, June 20, 1956) 85 Mins.
(Technicolor)
Fess Parker, Jeffrey Hunter, Jeff York, John Lupton, Eddie Firestone, Kenneth Tobey, Don Megowan, Claude Jarman, Jr., Harry Carey, Jr., Lennie Geer, George Robotham, Stan Jones, Marc Hamilton, John Wiley, Slim Pickens, Morgan Woodward, Harvey Hester
D: Francis D. Lyon
SP/P: Lawrence Edward Watkin

2774. SECRET OF TREASURE MOUNTAIN

(Columbia, June 25, 1956) 68 Mins.
Valerie French, Raymond Burr, William Prince, Lance Fuller, Susan Cummings, Pat Hogan, Reginald Sheffield, Rodolfo Hoyos, Paul McGuire, Tom Hubbard, Boyd Stockman
D: Seymour Freidman
S/SP: David Lang
P: Wallace MacDonald

2775. THE FIRST TEXAN

(Allied Artists, June 29, 1956) 82 Mins.
(Technicolor) (CinemaScope)
Joel McCrea, Felicia Farr, Jeff Morrow, Wallace Ford, Abraham Sofaer, Jody McCrea, Chubby Johnson, Dayton Lummis, Rodolfo Hoyos, William Hopper, Roy Roberts, David Silva, Frank Puglia, James Griffith, Nelson Leigh
D: Byron Haskin
S/SP: Daniel B. Ullman
P: Walter Mirisch

2776. THE RAWHIDE YEARS

(Universal-International, July 1, 1956) 85 Mins.
(Technicolor)
Tony Curtis, Colleen Miller, Arthur Kennedy, William Demarest, William Gargan, Peter Van Eyck, Minor Watson, Donald Randolph, Chubby Johnson, James Anderson, Bob Wilke, Trevor Bardette, Robert Foulk, Leigh Snowden, Don Beddoe
D: Rudolph Mate
S: Norman A. Fox
SP: Earl Felton, Robert Presnell, Jr., D. D. Beauchamp
P: Stanley Rubin

2777. JOHNNY CONCHO

(United Artists, July 1, 1956) 84 Mins.
Frank Sinatra, Keenan Wynn, William Conrad, Phyllis Kirk, Wallace Ford, Dorothy Adams, Christopher Dark, Howard Petrie, Harry Bartell, Dan Russ, Willis Bouchey, Robert Osterloh, Jean Byron, Leo Gordon, Claude Akins, John Qualen, Wilfred Knapp, Ben Wright, Joe Bassett
D: Don McGuire
P: Frank Sinatra
SP: David Harmon, Don McGuire

2778. FRONTIER WOMAN

(Top Pictures Corp., July 4, 1956) 80 Mins.
(Eastman Color) (VistaRama)
Cindy Carson, Lance Fuller, Ann Kelly, James Clayton, Rance Howard, Curtis Dorsett, Mario Galento, Geneva Rush, Dan Jones, Pete Cunningham, Sam Keller, Pearl River Reservation Indians
D: Ron Ormond
SP: Paul Peil
P: Lloyd Royal, Tom Garraway

2779. THE FASTEST GUN ALIVE

(MGM, July 6, 1956) 92 Mins.
Glenn Ford, Jeanne Crain, Broderick Crawford, Russ Tamblyn, Allyn Joslin, Leif Erickson, John Dehner, Noah Beery, Jr., J. M. Kerrigan, Rhys Williams, Virginia Gregg, Chubby Johnson, John Doucette, William Phillips, Chris Olsen, Paul Birch, Florenz Ames, Joseph Sweeney
D: Russell Rouse
S: "The Last Notch"—Frank D. Gilroy
SP: Frank D. Gilroy, Russell Rouse
P: Clarence Greene

2780. DAVY CROCKETT AND THE RIVER PIRATES

(Buena Vista, July 17, 1956) 81 Mins.
(Technicolor)
Fess Parker, Buddy Ebsen, Jeff York, Ken Tobey, Irvin Ashkanezy, Paul Newlan, Troy Melton, Dick Crockett
D: Norman Foster
SP: Tom B. Blackburn, Norman Foster
P: Bill Walsh

2781. DAKOTA INCIDENT

(Republic, July 23, 1956) 88 Mins.
(Trucolor)
Linda Darnell, Dale Robertson, John Lund, Ward Bond, Regis Toomey, Skip Homeier, Irving Bacon, John Doucette, Whit Bissell, William Fawcett, Malcolm Atterbury, Diane Du Bois, Charles Horvath
D: Lewis R. Foster
SP: Frederick Louis Fox
AP: Michael Baird

2782. REBEL IN TOWN

(Bel-Air/United Artists, July 30, 1956) 78 Mins.
John Payne, Ruth Roman, J. Carroll Naish, Ben Cooper, John Smith, James Griffith, Mary Adams, Bobby Clark, Mimi Gibson, Ben Johnson, Sterling Franck, Joel Ashley
D: Alfred Werker

S/SP: Danny Arnold
P: Aubrey Schenck

2783. KENTUCKY RIFLE
(Howco, July, 1956)   82 Mins.
(Pathe Color)
Chill Wills, Lance Fuller, Cathy Downs, Jess Barker, Jeanne Cagney, Sterling Holloway, Henry Hull, John Pickard, John Alvin, I. Stanford Jolley, Rory Mallison, George Keymas, Clyde Houck, Alice Rolph
D/P: Carl K. Hittleman
SP: Carl K. Hittleman, Lee J. Hewitt

2784. PARDNERS
(Paramount, August 1, 1956)   88 Mins.
(Technicolor)   (VistaVision)
Dean Martin, Jerry Lewis, Lori Nelson, Jeff Morrow, Jackie Loughery, John Baragrey, Agnes Moorehead, Lon Chaney, Jr., Milton Frome, Richard Aherne, Lee Van Cleef, Stuart Randall, Scott Douglas, Jack Elam, Bob Steele, Mickey Finn, Douglas Spencer, Philip Tonge
D: Norman Taurog
S: Marvin J. Houser
SP: Sidney Sheldon, Jerry Davis
P: Paul Jones

2785. BLAZING THE OVERLAND TRAIL
(Columbia, August 4, 1956)   15 Chaps.
Lee Roberts, Dennis Moore, Norma Brooks, Gregg Barton, Don Harvey, Lee Morgan, Ed Coch, Pierce Lyden, Reed Howes, Kermit Maynard, Al Ferguson, Pete Kellett
D: Spencer Gordon Bennet
SP: George H. Plympton
P: Sam Katzman
Chapter Titles: (1) Gun Emperor of the West, (2) Riding the Danger Trail, (3) The Black Raiders, (4) Into the Flames, (5) Trapped in a Runaway Wagon, (6) Rifles for Redskins, (7) Midnight Attack, (8) Blast at Gunstock Pass, (9) War at the Wagon Camp, (10) Buffalo Stampede, (11) Into the Fiery Blast, (12) Cave-In, (13) Bugle Call, (14) Blazing Peril, (15) Raiders Unmasked

2786. SEVEN MEN FROM NOW
(Batjac/Warner Bros., August 4, 1956)   78 Mins.
(WarnerColor)
Randolph Scott, Gail Russell, Lee Marvin, Walter Reed, John Larch, Donald Barry, Fred Graham, John Barradino, John Phillips, Chuck Roberson, Steve Mitchell, Pamela Duncan, Stuart Whitman
D: Budd Boetticher
S/SP: Burt Kennedy
P: Andrew V. McLaglen, Robert E. Morrison

2787. THUNDER OVER ARIZONA
(Republic, August 4, 1956)   70 Mins.
(Trucolor)
Skip Homeier, Kristine Miller, George Macready, Wallace Ford, Jack Elam, Nacho Galindo, Gregory Walcott, George Keymas, John Doucette, John Compton, Bob Swain, Julian Rivero, Francis McDonald
D/AP: Joseph Kane
SP: Sloan Nibley

2788. CANYON RIVER
(Allied Artists, August 5, 1956)   80 Mins.
(DeLuxe Color)   (CinemaScope)
George Montgomery, Peter Graves, Marcia Henderson, Richard Eyer, Walter Sande, Robert Wilke, Alan Hale, John Harmon, Jack Lambert, William Fawcett
D: Harmon Jones
S/SP: Daniel F. Ullman
P: Scott R. Dunlap

2789. THE YOUNG GUNS
(Allied Artists, August 12, 1956)   84 Mins.
Russ Tamblyn, Gloria Talbott, Perry Lopez, Scott Marlowe, Wright King, Walter Coy, Chubby Johnson, Myron Healey, James Goodwin, Rayford Barnes, I. Stanford Jolley
D: Albert Band
SP: Louis Garfinkle
P: Richard Heermance

2790. THE FIRST TRAVELING SALESLADY
(RKO, August 15, 1956)   92 Mins.
(Technicolor)
Ginger Rogers, Barry Nelson, Carol Channing, David Brian, James Arness, Clint Eastwood, Robert Simon, Frank Wilcox, Dan White, Harry Cheshire, John Eldredge, Robert Hinkle, Jack Rice, Kate Drain Lawson, Edward Cassidy, Fred Essler
D/P: Arthur Lubin
SP: Stephen Longstreet, Devery Freeman

2791. THE BEAST OF HOLLOW MOUNTAIN
(Nassour/United Artists, August 25, 1956)   79 Mins.
(DeLuxe Color)   (CinemaScope)
(Filmed in Mexico)
Guy Madison, Patricia Medina, Eduardo Noriega, Carlos Rivas, Marjo Navarro, Pascual Garcia Pena, Margarito Luna, Lupe Carriles
D: Edward Nassour
S: Willis O'Brien
SP: Robert Hill
P: William and Edward Nassour

2792. BANDIDO

(United Artists, September 1, 1956)   92 Mins.
(DeLuxe Color)   (CinemaScope)
(Filmed in Mexico)
Robert Mitchum, Ursula Thiess, Gilbert Roland,
  Zachary Scott, Rodolfo Acosta, Henry Brandon,
  Douglas Fowley, Jose I. Torvay, Victor Junco,
  Alfonso Sanchez Tello, Arturo Manrique
D: Richard Fleischer
S/SP: Earl Felton
P: Robert L. Jacks

2793. THE BURNING HILLS

(Warner Bros., September 1, 1956)   94 Mins.
(Technicolor)   (CinemaScope)
Tab Hunter, Natalie Wood, Skip Homeier, Eduard
  Franz, Earl Holliman, Claude Akins, Ray Teal,
  Frank Puglia, Hal Baylor, Tyler MacDuff, Rayford
  Barnes, Tony Terry
D: Stuart Heisler
S: Louis L'Amour
SP: Irving Wallace
P: Richard Whorf

2794. RAW EDGE

(Universal-International, September 1, 1956)
  76 Mins.
(Technicolor)
Rory Calhoun, Yvonne De Carlo, Mara Corday,
  Rex Reason, Neville Brand, Emile Meyer, Herbert
  Rudley, Bob Wilke
D: John Sherwood
SP: Harry Essox, Robert Hill
P: Albert Zugsmith

2795. WALK THE PROUD LAND

(Universal-International, September 1, 1956)
  88 Mins.
(Technicolor)   (CinemaScope)
Audie Murphy, Anne Bancroft, Pat Crowley,
  Charles Drake, Tommy Rall, Jay Silverheels, Rob-
  ert Warwick, Victor Millan, Eugene Mazzola,
  Anthony Caruso, Morris Ankrum, Addison Rich-
  ards, Ainslie Pryor
D: Jesse Hibbs
S: Woodworth Clum
SP: Gil Doud, Jack Sher
P: Aaron Rosenberg

2795a. FRONTIER GAMBLER

(Associated Releasing Corp.,
  September 1, 1956)   70 Mins.
John Bromfield, Coleen Gray, Kent Taylor, Jim
  Davis, Margia Dean, Veda Ann Borg, Tracey Rob-
  erts, Stanley Andrews, Roy Engel, Nadene Ash-
  down, Frank Sully, Pierce Lyden, Ewing Brown,
  Rick Vallin, John Merton, Helen Jay
D: Sam Newfield
SP: Orville Hampton
P: Sigmund Neufeld

2796. GUN BROTHERS

(United Artists, September 15, 1956)   79 Mins.
Buster Crabbe, Ann Robinson, Neville Brand, Mi-
  chael Ansara, Walter Sande, Lita Milan, James
  Seay, Roy Barcroft, Slim Pickens, Dorothy Ford
D: Sidney Salkow
S/SP: Gerald Drayson Adams

2797. THE LAST WAGON

(20th C. Fox, September 15, 1956)   99 Mins.
(DeLuxe Color)   (CinemaScope)
Richard Widmark, Felicia Farr, Susan Kohner,
  Tommy Rettig, Stephanie Griffin, Ray Stricklyn,
  Nick Adams, Carl Benton Reid, Douglas Kennedy,
  George Matthews, James Drury, Ken Clark, Tim-
  othy Carey, Juney Ellis, George Ross
D: Delmer Daves
S: Gwen Bagni Gielgud
SP: James Edward Grant, Delmer Daves, Gwen
  Bagni Gielgud
P: William B. Hawks

2798. FLESH AND THE SPUR

(American-International, September 25, 1956)
  80 Mins.
(Pathe Color)
John Agar, Marla English, Touch (Mike) Connors,
  Raymond Hatton, Maria Monay, Joyce Meadows,
  Kenne Duncan, Frank Lackteen, Mel Gaines, Mi-
  chael Harris, Eddie Kafafain, Dick Alexander,
  Kermit Maynard, Bud Osborne, Buddy Roosevelt
D: Edward L. Cahn
SP: Charles B. Griffith, Mark Hanna
P: Alex Gordon

2799. PILLARS OF THE SKY

(Universal-International, October 1, 1956)
  95 Mins.
(Technicolor)   (CinemaScope)
Jeff Chandler, Dorothy Malone, Ward Bond, Keith
  Andes, Lee Marvin, Sidney Chaplin, Willis Bou-
  chey, Michael Ansara, Olive Carey, Charles Hor-
  vath, Orlando Rodriguez, Glen Kramer, Floyd
  Simmons, Pat Hogan, Felix Noriego, Paul Smith,
  Martin Milner, Robert Ellis, Ralph J. Votrian,
  Walter Coy, Alberto Morin, Richard Hale, Frank
  de Kova, Terry Wilson, Gilbert Conner
D: George Marshall
S: "Frontier Fury"—Will Henry
SP: Sam Rolfe
P: Robert Arthur

2800. SHOWDOWN AT ABILENE

(Universal-International, October 1, 1956)
80 Mins.
(Technicolor)
Jock Mahoney, Martha Hyer, Lyle Bettger, David Janssen, Grant Williams, Ted de Corsia, Harry Harvey, Dayton Lummis, John Maxwell, Richard Cutting, Robert Anderson, Lane Bradford
D: Charles Haas
SP: Berne Biler
P: Howard Christie

2801. TENSION AT TABLE ROCK

(RKO, October 3, 1956) 93 Mins.
(Technicolor)
Richard Egan, Dorothy Malone, Cameron Mitchell, Billy Chapin, Royal Dano, Edward Andrews, John Dehner, DeForrest Kelly, Angie Dickinson, Joe DeSantis
D: Charles Marquis Warren
S: "Bitter Sage"—Frank Gruber
SP: Winston Miller
P: Sam Wiesenthal

2802. DANIEL BOONE, TRAIL BLAZER

(Republic, October 5, 1956) 76 Mins.
(Trucolor) (Filmed in Mexico)
Bruce Bennett, Lon Chaney, Jr., Faron Young, Kem Dibbs, Damian O'Flynn, Jacqueline Evans, Nancy Rodman, Freddy Fernandez, Carol Kelly, Eduardo Noriega, Fred Kohler, Jr., Gordon Mills, Lee Morgan, Claude Brook, Joe Quinley
D: Albert C. Gannaway, Ismael Rodriguez
SP: Tom Hubbard, Jess Patrick
P: Albert C. Gannaway

2803. YAQUI DRUMS

(Allied Artists, October 14, 1956) 71 Mins.
Rod Cameron, Mary Castle, J. Carroll Naish, Roy Roberts, Robert Hutt, Denver Pyle, Keith Richards, Ray Walker, Donald Kerr, G. Pat Collins, John Merrick, Paul Fierro, Fred Gabourie, Saul Gorss
D: Jean Yarbrough
S: Paul Peil
SP: Jo Pagano, D. D. Beauchamp
P: William F. Broidy

2804. TWO-GUN LADY

(Associated Film Releasing Corp., October 15, 1956)
70 Mins.
Peggie Castle, William Talman, Marie Windsor, Earle Lyon, Joe Besser, Robert Lowery, Barbara Turner, Ian MacDonald, Norman Jolley
D/P: Richard H. Bartlett
SP: Norman Jolley

2805. STAGECOACH TO FURY

(Regal/20th C. Fox, October 20, 1956) 76 Mins.
(RegalScope)
Forrest Tucker, Mari Blanchard, Wallace Ford, Rodolfo Hoyos, Paul Fix, Rico Alaniz, Wright King, Margia Dean, Ian MacDonald
D: William Claxton
S: Earle Lyon, Eric Nordon
SP: Eric Nordon
P: Earle Lyon

2806. MAN FROM DEL RIO

(United Artists, October 30, 1956) 82 Mins.
Anthony Quinn, Katy Jurado, Peter Whitney, Douglas Fowley, John Larch, Whitt Bissell, Douglas Spencer, Guinn "Big Boy" Williams, Marc Hamilton, Adrienne Marden, Barry Atwater, Carl Thayler
D: Harry Horner
S/SP: Richard Carr
P: Robert L. Jacks

2807. THE DESPERADOS ARE IN TOWN

(Regal/20th C. Fox, November 1, 1956) 73 Mins.
(RegalScope)
Robert Arthur, Kathy Nolan, Rhys Williams, Rhodes (Rex) Reason, Dave O'Brien, Kelly Thordsen, Mae Clarke, Robert Osterloh
D/P: Kurt Neumann
S: "The Outlaws Are in Town"—*Saturday Evening Post* story by Bennett Foster
SP: Earle Snell, Kurt Neumann

2808. THE NAKED GUN

(Associated Film Releasing Company,
November 1, 1956) 69 Mins.
Willard Parker, Mara Corday, Barton MacLane, Billy House, Veda Ann Borg, Morris Ankrum, Chick Chandler, Bill Phillips, Tom Brown, Timothy Carey, X. Brands, Steve Raines, Jim Hayward, Rick Vallin, Elene Di Vinci, Jody McCrea, Tony McCoy, Bill Ward, Merry Ogden, Helen Jay, Doris Simons
D: Edward Dew
S/SP: Ron Ormond, Jack Lewis
P: Ron Ormond

2809. THE WHITE SQUAW

(Columbia, November 1, 1956) 73 Mins.
David Brian, May Wynn, William Bishop, Nancy Hale, William Leslie, Myron Healey, Robert C. Ross, Frank de Kova, George Keymas, Roy Roberts, Grant Withers, Wally Vernon, Paul Birch, Neyle Morrow, Guy Teague
D: Ray Nazarro

S: Larabie Sutter
SP: Les Savage, Jr.
P: Wallace MacDonald

2810. LOVE ME TENDER

(20th C. Fox, November 15, 1956) 89 Mins.
(CinemaScope)
Richard Egan, Debra Paget, Elvis Presley, Robert Middleton, William Campbell, Neville Brand, Mildred Dunnock, Bruce Bennett, James Drury, Russ Conway, Ken Clark, Barry Coe, L. Q. Jones, Paul E. Burns, Jerry Sheldon
D: Robert D. Webb
SP: Robert Buckner
P: David Weisbart

2811. GUN THE MAN DOWN

(United Artists, November 15, 1956) 78 Mins.
James Arness, Angie Dickinson, Robert Wilke, Emile Meyer, Don Megowan, Michael Emmett, Harry Carey, Jr.
D: Andrew V. McLaglen
S: Sam C. Freedle
SP: Burt Kennedy
P: Robert E. Morrison

2812. FRIENDLY PERSUASION

(United Artists, November 25, 1956) 140 Mins.
(DeLuxe Color)
Gary Cooper, Dorothy McGuire, Marjorie Main, Anthony Perkins, Richard Eyer, Phyllis Love, Robert Middleton, Mark Richman, Walter Catlett, Richard Hale, Joel Fluellen, Theodore Newton, John Smith, Mary Carr, Edna Skinner, Marjorie Durant, Frances Farwell, Russell Simpson, Charles Halton, Everett Glass
D: William Wyler
S: Jessamyn West
P: William Wyler, Robert Wyler

2813. THE PEACEMAKER

(United Artists, November 30, 1956) 82 Mins.
James Mitchell, Rosemarie Bowe, Jan Merlin, Jess Barker, Hugh Sanders, Herbert Patterson, Dorothy Patrick, Taylor Holmes, Robert Armstrong, Philip Tonge, David McMahon, Wheaton Chambers, Jack Holland, Nancy Evans, Harry Shannon
D: Ted Post
S: Richard Poole
SP: Hal Richards, Jay Ingram
P: Hal R. Makelim

2814. GIANT

(Warner Bros., November 24, 1956) 201 Mins.
(WarnerColor)
Elizabeth Taylor, Rock Hudson, James Dean, Carol Baker, Chill Wills, Jane Withers, Mercedes McCambridge, Sal Mineo, Dennis Hopper, Judith Evelyn, Paul Fix, Rod Taylor, Earl Holliman, Robert Nichols, Alexander Scourby, Fran Bennett, Charles Watts, Eliza Cardenas, Carolyn Craig, Monte Hale, Mary Ann Edwards, Sheb Wooley, Victor Millan, Mickey Simpson, Pilar del Rey, Maurice Java, Ray Whitley, Noreen Nash, Tina Menard, Max Terhune
D: George Stevens
S: Edna Ferber
SP: Fred Guiol, Ivan Moffat
P: George Stevens

2815. REPRISAL!

(Columbia, November 30, 1956) 74 Mins.
(Technicolor)
Guy Madison, Felicia Farr, Kathryn Grant, Michael Pate, Edward Platt, Otto Mulett, Wayne Mallory, Robert Burton, Ralph Moody, Frank de Kova, Paul McGuire, Don Rhodes, Philip Breedlove, Malcolm Atterbury, Eve McVeagh, Victor Zamudia, Pete Kellett, Jack Lomas, Addison Richards, John Zaremba
D: George Sherman
S: Arthur Gordon
SP: David P. Harmon, Raphael Hayes, David Dortort
P: Lewis J. Rachmil

2816. RUNNING TARGET

(Canyon/United Artists, November, 1956) 82 Mins.
(DeLuxe Color)
Doris Dowling, Arthur Franz, Richard Reeves, Myron Healey, James Parnell, Charles Delaney, James Anderson, Gene Roth, Frank Richards
D: Marvin R. Weinstein
S: Steve Frazee
SP: Marvin Weinstein, Jack Couffer, Conrad Hall
P: Jack C. Couffer

2817. 7TH CAVALRY

(Scott-Brown/Columbia, December, 1956) 75 Mins.
(Technicolor)
Randolph Scott, Barbara Hale, Jay C. Flippen, Jeanette Nolan, Frank Faylen, Lee Gordon, Denver Pyle, Harry Carey, Jr., Michael Pate, Donald Curtis, Frank Wilcox, Pat Hogan, Russell Hicks, Peter Ortiz, William Leslie, Jack Parker, Edward F. Stidder, Al Wyatt
D: Joseph H. Lewis
S: Glendon F. Swarthout
SP: Peter Packer
P: Harry Joe Brown

2818. THE BLACK WHIP

(Regal/20th C. Fox, December, 1956)   77 Mins.
(RegalScope)

Hugh Marlowe, Coleen Gray, Richard Gilden, Angie Dickinson, Strother Martin, Paul Richards, Charles Gray, William R. Hamel, Patrick O'Moore, Dorothy Schuyler, Sheb Wooley, John Pickard, Adele Mara, Harry Landers, Howard Culver, Rush Williams

D: Charles Marquis Warren
S/SP: Orville Hampton
P: Robert Stabler

2819. THE BRASS LEGEND

(United Artists, December, 1956)   79 Mins.

Hugh O'Brian, Nancy Gates, Raymond Burr, Reba Tassell, Donald MacDonald, Robert Burton, Eddie Firestone, Willard Sage, Stacy Harris, Norman Leavitt, Dennis Cross, Russell Simpson, Michael Garrett, Jack Farmer

D: Gerd Oswald
S: George Zuckerman, Jess Arnold
SP: Don Martin
P: Robert Goldstein

2820. THE KING AND FOUR QUEENS

(Russ-Field-Gabco/United Artists, December, 1956)   86 Mins.
(DeLuxe Color)   (CinemaScope)

Clark Gable, Eleanor Parker, Jo Van Fleet, Jean Willes, Barbara Nichols, Sara Shane, Roy Roberts, Arthur Shields, Jay C. Flippen

D: Raoul Walsh
S: Margaret Fitts
SP: Margaret Fitts, Richard Alan Simmons
P: David Hempstead

2821. HOLLYWOOD BRONC BUSTERS

(Columbia, 1956)   9 Mins.
(*Screen Snapshot* Series)

Jack Lemmon, Ralph Staub; Film clips featuring Gene Autry, Roy Rogers, Tom Mix, William Boyd, William S. Hart, Buck Jones, Hoot Gibson, Charles Starrett

D/P: Ralph Staub

FILMS OF 1957

2822. DRANGO

(Earlmar Productions/United Artists, January 2, 1957)   96 Mins.

Jeff Chandler, Joanne Dru, Julie London, Ronald Howard, Donald Crisp, John Lupton, Morris Ankrum, Helen Wallace, Walter Sande, Parley Barr, Amzie Strickland, Charles Horvath, Barney Phillips, David Stollery, Mimi Gibson, Paul Lukather, Damian O'Flynn, Edith Evanson, Phil Chambers, David Saber, Chuck Webster, Katherine Warren, Chubby Johnson, Milburn Stone, Anthony Jochim, Maura Murphy

D: Hall Bartlett, Jules Bricken
SP/P: Hall Bartlett

2823. THREE VIOLENT PEOPLE

(Paramount, January 2, 1957)   100 Mins.
(Technicolor)   (VistaVision)

Charlton Heston, Anne Baxter, Gilbert Roland, Tom Tryon, Forrest Tucker, Bruce Bennett, Elaine Stritch, Barton MacLane, Peter Hansen, John Harmon, Ross Bagdasarian, Bobby Blake, Jameel Farah, Leo Castillo, Don Devlin, Raymond Greenleaf, Roy Engel, Argentina Brunetti

D: Rudolph Mate
S: Leonard Praskins, Barney Slater
SP: James Edward Grant
P: Hugh Brown

2824. THE QUIET GUN

(Regal Films/20th C. Fox, January 10, 1957)   77 Mins.
(RegalScope)

Forrest Tucker, Mara Corday, Jim Davis, Kathleen Crowley, Lee Van Cleef, Tom Brown, Lewis Martin, Hank Worden, Gerald Milton, Everett Glass, Edith Evanson

D: William Claxton
SP: Eric Norden
P: Earle Lyon

2825. THE HALLIDAY BRAND

(United Artists, January 12, 1957)   77 Mins.

Joseph Cotten, Viveca Lindfors, Betsy Blake, Ward Bond, Bill Williams, Jay C. Flippen, Christopher Dark, Jeanette Nolan, Glenn Strange, John Dierkes, I. Stanford Jolley, John Ayres, Robin Short, Jay Lawrence, George Lynn, John Halloran, Michael Hinn

D: Joseph H. Lewis
SP: George W. George, George S. Slavin
P: Collier Young

2826. DUEL AT APACHE WELLS

(Republic, January 25, 1957)   70 Mins.
(Naturama)

Anna Marie Alberghetti, Ben Cooper, Jim Davis,

Harry Shannon, Francis McDonald, Bob Steele, Frank Puglia, Argentina Brunetti, Ian MacDonald, John Dierkes, Ric Roman
D: Joseph Kane
SP: Bob Williams
P: Joseph Kane

2827. TOMAHAWK TRAIL
(Bel-Air/United Artists, February 1, 1957) 60 Mins.
Chuck Connors, John Smith, Susan Cummings, Lisa Montell, George Neise, Robert Knapp, Eddie Little, Frederick Ford, Dean Stanton
D: Robert Parry
SP: David Chandler
P: Howard Koch

2828. UTAH BLAINE
(Columbia, February 1, 1957) 75 Mins.
Rory Calhoun, Susan Cummings, Max Baer, Angela Stevens, Paul Langton, George Keymas, Ray Teal, Gene Roth, Norman Fredric, Ken Christy, Steve Darrell, Terry Frost, Dennis Moore, Jack Ingram
D: Fred F. Sears
SP: Robert E. Kent, James B. Gordon
P: Sam Katzman

2829. THE TRUE STORY OF JESSE JAMES
(20th C. Fox, February 15, 1957) 93 Mins.
(DeLuxe Color) (CinemaScope)
Robert Wagner, Jeffrey Hunter, Hope Lange, Agnes Moorehead, Alan Hale, Alan Baxter, John Carradine, Rachel Stephens, Barney Phillips, Barry Atwater, Biff Elliott, Chubby Johnson, Frank Gorshin, John Doucette, Robert Adler, Clancy Cooper, Sumner Williams, Tom Greenway, Mike Steen, Aaron Saxon, Marian Seldes, Anthony Ray, Clegg Hoyt, Tom Pittman, Louis Zito, Carl Thayler, Mark Hickman, Adam Marshall, Frank Overton, Joseph De Reda, J. Frederick Albeck, Kellogg Junge, Jr.
D: Nicholas Ray
SP: Walter Newman. Based on a screenplay by Nunnally Johnson
P: Herbert B. Swope, Jr.

2830. LAST OF THE BADMEN
(Allied Artists, February 17, 1957) 80 Mins.
(DeLuxe Color) (CinemaScope)
George Montgomery, Keith Larsen, James Best, Douglas Kennedy, Robert Foulk, Tom Greenway, Meg Randall, Willis Bouchey, Michael Ansara, Addison Richards, John Doucette, John Damler, Harlan Warde
D: Paul Landres
S: Daniel B. Ullman

SP: Daniel B. Ullman, David Chandler
P: Vincent M. Fennelly

2831. THE BIG LAND
(Warner Bros., February 23, 1957) 93 Mins.
(WarnerColor)
Alan Ladd, Virginia Mayo, Edmond O'Brien, Anthony Caruso, Julie Bishop, John Qualen, Don Castle, David Ladd, Jack Wrather, Jr., George J. Lewis, James Anderson, Don Kelly, Charles Watts
D: Gordon Douglas
S: Frank Gruber
SP: David Dortort, Martin Rackin
AP: George C. Bertholon

2832. THE RAINMAKER
(Paramount, February, 1957) 121 Mins.
(Technicolor)
Burt Lancaster, Katharine Hepburn, Wendell Corey, Lloyd Bridges, Earl Holliman, Cameron Prud'homme, Wallace Ford, Yvonne Lime, Dottie Bee Baker, Dan White
D: Joseph Anthony
SP: N. Richard Nash. Based on his play
P: Hal B. Wallis

2833. GUN FOR A COWARD
(Universal-International, March 1, 1957) 88 Mins.
(Eastman Color) (Cinemascope)
Fred MacMurray, Jeffrey Hunter, Janice Rule, Chill Wills, Dean Stockwell, Josephine Hutchinson, Betty Lynn, Iron Eyes Cody, Robert Hoy, Jane Howard, Marjorie Stapp, John Leach, Paul Birch, Bob Steele, Francis Morris
D: Abner Biberman
SP: H. Wright Campbell
P: William Alland

2834. REVOLT AT FORT LARAMIE
(Bel-Air/United Artists, March 1, 1957) 73 Mins.
(DeLuxe Color)
John Dehner, Gregg Palmer, Frances Helm, Don Gordon, Robert Keys, William (Bill) Phillips, Cain Mason, Robert Knapp, Eddie Little, Dean Stanton, Bill Barker, Clay Randolph, Kenne Duncan
D: Lesley Selander
SP: Robert C. Dennis
P: Aubrey Schenck

2835. THE STORM RIDER
(Regal Films/20th C. Fox, March 1, 1957) 70 Mins.
(RegalScope)
Scott Brady, Mala Powers, Bill Williams, John Goddard, William Fawcett, Roy Engel, George Keymas, Olin Howlin, Hank Patterson, James Dob-

son, John Close, Jim Hayward, Rocky Shahan,
Frank Richards, Rick Vallin
D: Edward Bernds
S: L. L. Foreman
SP: Edward Bernds, Don Martin
P: Bernard Glasser

2836. HELL'S CROSSROADS

(Republic, March 8, 1957)   73 Mins.
(Naturama)
Stephen McNally, Peggie Castle, Robert Vaughn,
Barton MacLane, Harry Shannon, Henry Bran-
don, Douglas Kennedy, Grant Withers, Myron
Healey, Frank Wilcox, Jean Howell, Morris Ank-
rum
D: Franklin Adreon
S: John K. Butler
SP: John K. Butler, Barry Shipman
AP: Michael Baird

2837. FURY AT SHOWDOWN

(Goldstein Productions/United Artists,
   April 1, 1957)   75 Min.
John Derek, John Smith, Carolyn Craig, Nick
Adams, Gage Clarke, Robert E. Griffin, Malcolm
Atterbury, Rusty Lane, Sidney Smith, Frances
Morris, Tyler McDuff, Robert Adler, Norman
Leavitt, Ken Christy, Tom McKee
D: Gerd Oswald
S: Lucas Todd
SP: Jason James
P: John Beck

2838. THE GUNS OF FORT PETTICOAT

(Universal-International, April 1, 1957)   82 Mins.
(Technicolor)
Audie Murphy, Kathryn Grant, Hope Emerson, Jeff
Donnell, Jeanette Nolan, Sean McClory, James
Griffith, Dorothy Crider, Madge Meredith, Er-
nestine Wade, Peggy Maley, Isobel Elson, Patricia
Livingston, Kim Charney, Ray Teal, Nestor Paiva,
Ainslie Pryor, Charles Horvath
D: George Marshall
S: C. William Harrison
SP: Walter Doniger
P: Harry Joe Brown

2839. THE IRON SHERIFF

(Grand Productions/United Artists, April 1, 1957)
   73 Mins.
Sterling Hayden, Constance Ford, John Dehner,
Kent Taylor, Darryl Hickman, Walter Sande,
Frank Ferguson, King Donovan, Mort Mills, Peter
Miller, Kathy Nolan
D: Sidney Salkow
SP: Seeleg Lester
P: Jerome C. Robinson

2840. THE PHANTOM STAGECOACH

(Columbia, April 1, 1957)   79 Mins.
William Bishop, Kathleen Crowley, Richard Webb,
Hugh Sanders, John Doucette, Frank Ferguson,
Ray Teal, Percy Helton, Maudie Prickett, Lane
Bradford, John Lehmann, Eddy Waller, Robert
Anderson
D: Ray Nazarro
SP: David Lang
P: Wallace MacDonald

2841. THE TALL T

(Columbia, April 1, 1957)   78 Mins.
(Technicolor)
Randolph Scott, Richard Boone, Maureen O'Sulli-
van, Arthur Hunnicutt, Skip Homeier, Henry
Silva, John Hubbard, Robert Burton, Robert An-
derson, Fred E. Sherman, Chris Olsen
D: Budd Boetticher
S: Elmore Leonard
SP: Burt Kennedy
P: Harry Joe Brown, Randolph Scott

2842. WAR DRUMS

(Bel-Air/United Artists, April 1, 1957)   75 Mins.
(DeLuxe Color)
Lex Barker, Ben Johnson, Joan Taylor, Larry Chance,
Richard Cutting, James Parnell, John Pickard,
John Colicos, Tom Monroe, Jil Jarmyn, Jeanne
Carmen, Mauritz Hugo, Ward Ellis, Fred Sher-
man, Paul Fierro, Alex Montoya, Stuart Whit-
man, Barbara Perry, Jack Hupp, Red Morgan,
Monie Freeman
D: Reginald Le Borg
SP: Gerald Drayson Adams
P: Howard W. Koch

2843. DRAGOON WELLS MASSACRE

(Allied Artists, April 28, 1957)   88 Mins.
(DeLuxe Color)   (CinemaScope)
Barry Sullivan, Dennis O'Keefe, Mona Freeman,
Katy Jurado, Jack Elam, Sebastian Cabot, Casey
Adams, Trevor Bardette, Jon Shepodd, Hank
Worden, Warren Douglas, Judy Stranges, Alma
Beltran, John War Eagle
D: Harold Schuster
SP: Oliver Drake
SP: Warren Douglas
P: Lindsley Parsons

2844. OUTLAW QUEEN

(Globe Releasing Corp., April 28, 1957)   70 Mins.
Andrea King, Harry James, Robert Clarke, Jim

Harakas, Andy Ladas, Kenne Duncan, I. Stanford Jolley, William Murphy, Vince Barnett, Hal Peary, John Heldring
D: Herbert Greene
SP: Pete La Roche
P: Ronnie Ashcroft

2845. BADLANDS OF MONTANA

(20th C. Fox, May 1, 1957) 75 Mins.
(RegalScope)
Rex Reason, Margia Dean, Beverly Garland, Keith Larsen, Emile Meyer, William Phipps, Stanley Farrar, Rankin Mansfield, John Pickard, Ralph Peters, Paul Newlan, Russell Bender, Robert Cunningham, Jack Kruschen
D: Daniel B. Ullman
SP: Daniel B. Ullman
P: Daniel B. Ullman, Herbert E. Mendelson

2846. GUN DUEL IN DURANGO

(Peerless/United Artists, May 1, 1957) 73 Mins.
George Montgomery, Ann Robinson, Steve Brodie, Bobby Clark, Frank Ferguson, Donald Barry, Henry Rowland, Denver Pyle, Mary Treen, Al Wyatt, Red Morgan, Joe Yrigoyen
D: Sidney Salkow
SP: Louis Stevens
P: Robert E. Kent

2847. THE RIDE BACK

(The Associates and Aldrich Co./United Artists, May 1, 1957) 79 Mins.
(Sepiatone)
Anthony Quinn, William Conrad, George Trevino, Lita Milan, Victor Millan, Ellen Hope Monroe, Joe Dominguez, Louis Towers
D: Allen H. Miner
SP: Antony Ellis
P: William Conrad

2848. SIERRA STRANGER

(Columbia, May 1, 1957) 74 Mins.
Howard Duff, Gloria McGhee, Dick Foran, John Hoyt, Barton MacLane, George E. Stone, Ed Kemmer, Robert Foulk, Eve McVeagh, Henry Kulky, Byron Foulger
D: Lee Sholem
S/SP: Richard J. Dorso
P: Norman T. Herman

2849. SHOOT-OUT AT MEDICINE BEND

(Warner Bros., May 4, 1957) 87 Mins.
Randolph Scott, James Craig, Angie Dickinson, Dani Crayne, James Garner, Gordon Jones, Trevor Bardette, Don Beddoe, Myron Healey, John Alderson, Harry Harvey, Sr., Robert Warwick, Howard Negley, Marshall Bradford, Ann Foran,

Daryn Hinton, Dickie Bellis, Edward Hinton, Lane Bradford, Francis Morris, Robert Lynn, Sam Flint, Philip Van Zandt, Guy Wilkerson, Syd Saylor, Harry Rowland, Marjorie Bennett, Jesslyn Fay, Marjorie Stapp, Nancy Kulp, George Meader, Rory Mallinson, Dee Carroll, Gerald Charlebois, Dale Van Sickel, Gil Perkins, Harry Lauter, George Russ, Carol Henry, George Pembroke, Tom Monroe, John Roy, Buddy Roosevelt, George Bell
D: Richard L. Bare
SP: John Tucker Battle, D. D. Beauchamp
P: Richard Whorf

2850. THE OKLAHOMAN

(Allied Artists, May 19, 1957) 81 Mins.
(DeLuxe Color) (CinemaScope)
Joel McCrea, Barbara Hale, Brad Dexter, Gloria Talbott, Michael Pate, Verna Felton, Douglas Dick, Anthony Caruso, Esther Dale, Adam Williams, Ray Teal, Peter Votrian, John Pickard, Mimi Gibson, I. Stanford Jolley, Jody Williams
D: Francis D. Lyon
S/SP: Daniel B. Ullman
P: Walter Mirisch

2851. GUNFIGHT AT THE O.K. CORRAL

(Paramount, May 20, 1957) 122 Mins.
(Technicolor) (VistaVision)
Burt Lancaster, Kirk Douglas, Rhonda Fleming, Jo Van Fleet, John Ireland, Lyle Bettger, Frank Faylen, Earl Holliman, Ted de Corsia, Dennis Hopper, Whit Bissell, George Mathews, John Hudson, DeForest Kelley, Martin Milner, Kenneth Tobey, Lee Van Cleef, Joan Camden, Olive Carey, Brian Hutton, Nelson Leigh, Jack Elam, Don Castle, Dennis Moore, Ethan Laidlaw, William N. Bailey, Dorothy Abbott, Morgan Lane, Harry Mendoza, Roger Creed, Gregg Martell
D: John Sturges
S: From an article by George Scullin
SP: Leon Uris
P: Hal B. Wallis

2852. THE BADGE OF MARSHAL BRENNAN

(Allied Artists, May 26, 1957) 74 Mins.
Jim Davis, Arleen Whelan, Louis Jean Heydt, Lee Van Cleff, Carl Smith, Douglas Fowley, Larry Dobkin, Harry Lauter, Marty Robbins
D: Albert C. Gannaway
SP: Thomas G. Hubbard
P: Albert C. Gannaway

2853. THE LONELY MAN

(Paramount, June 1, 1957) 87 Mins.
(VistaVision)
Jack Palance, Anthony Perkins, Neville Brand, Rob-

ert Middleton, Elaine Aiken, Elisha Cook, Jr., Claude Akins, Lee Van Cleef, Harry Shannon, James Bell, Adam Williams, Denver Pyle, John Doucette, Paul Newlan, Elaine Aiken
D: Henry Levin
SP: Harry Essex
P: Pat Duggan

2854. THE RESTLESS BREED

(Alperson/20th C. Fox, June 1, 1957) 86 Mins.
(Eastman Color)
Scott Brady, Anne Bancroft, Jay C. Flippen, Jim Davis, Rhys Williams, Leo Gordon, Scott Marlowe, Eddy Waller, Harry Cheshire, Myron Healey, Gerald Milton, Dennis King, Jr., James Flavin, Gregg Hoyt, Marilyn Winston, Billy Miller, Evelyn Rudie, Marty Cariosa
D: Allan Dwan
SP: Steve Fisher
P: Edward L. Alperson

2855. TROOPER HOOK

(United Artists, June 1, 1957) 81 Mins.
Joel McCrea, Barbara Stanwyck, Earl Holleman, Edward Andrews, John Dehner, Susan Kohner, Royal Dano, Terry Lawrence, Celia Lovsky, Rodolfo Acosta, Stanley Adams, Pat O'Moore, Jeanne Bates, Rush Williams, Dick Shannon, D. J. Thompson, Sheb Wooley, Cyril Delevanti
D: Charles Marquis Warren
S: Jack Schaefer
SP: Charles Marquis Warren
P: Sol Baer Fielding

2856. THE BUCKSKIN LADY

(United Artists, July 1, 1957) 66 Mins.
Patricia Medina, Richard Denning, Gerald Mohr, Henry Hull, Hank Worden, Robin Short, Richard Reeves, Dorothy Adams, Frank Sully, George Cisar, Louis Lettieri, Byron Foulger, John Dierkes
D: Carl K. Hittleman
S: Francis S. Chase, Jr.
SP: David Lang, Carl Hittleman
P: Carl K. Hittleman, D. Jersey Grut

2857. LAST STAGECOACH WEST

(Ventura/Republic, July 15, 1957) 67 Mins.
(Naturama)
Jim Davis, Mary Castle, Victor Jory, Lee Van Cleef, Grant Withers, Roy Barcroft, John Alderson, Glenn Strange, Francis McDonald, Willis Bouchey, Lewis Martin, Tris Coffin
D: Joseph Kane
SP: Barry Shipman
AP: Rudy Ralston

2858. APACHE WARRIOR

(Regal Films/20th C. Fox, July 20, 1957) 73 Mins.
(RegalScope)
Keith Larsen, Jim Davis, Rodolfo Acosta, John Miljan, Eddie Little, Michael Carr, George Keymas, Lane Bradford, Eugenia Paul, Damian O'Flynn, Dehl Berti, Nick Thompson, Ray Kellogg, Allan Nixon, Karl Davis, Dick Carlile, Vance Howard, Mark Sheeler, Walter Kray, Boyd Stockman
D: Elmo Williams
S: Carroll Young, Kurt Neumann
SP: Kurt Neumann, Eric Norden
P: Plato Skouras

2859. OUTLAW'S SON

(Bel-Air/United Artists, July 20, 1957) 87 Mins.
Dane Clark, Ben Cooper, Lori Nelson, Ellen Drew, Charles Watts, Cecile Rogers, Joseph "Bucko" Stafford, Eddie Foy III, John Pickard, Robert Knapp, Les Mitchel, Guy Prescott, George Pembroke, Jeff Daley, Wendy Stuart, Anna Marie Nanasi, James Parnell
D: Lesley Selander
S: "Gambling Man"—Clifton Adams
SP: Richard Alan Simmons
P: Aubrey Schenck

2860. NIGHT PASSAGE

(Universal-International, August 1, 1957)
90 Mins.
(Technicolor) (Technirama)
James Stewart, Audie Murphy, Dan Duryea, Dianne Foster, Elaine Stewart, Brandon de Wilde, Jay C. Flippen, Herbert Anderson, Robert J. (Bob) Wilke, Hugh Beaumont, Boyd Stockman, Olive Carey, Harold Hart, Polly Burson, Patsy Novak, Jack Elam, Tommy Cook, Paul Fix, James Flavin, Donald Curtis, Ellen Corby, John Day, Kenny Williams, Frank Chase, Harold Goodwin, Henry Wills, Chuck Roberson, Willard Willingham, Ted Mapes
D: James Neilson
SP: Bordon Chase
P: Aaron Rosenberg

2861. GUN GLORY

(MGM, August 16, 1957) 89 Mins.
(Metrocolor) (CinemaScope)
Stewart Granger, Rhonda Fleming, Chill Wills, Steve Rowland, James Gregory, Jacques Aubuchon, Arch Johnson, voice of Burl Ives
D: Roy Rowland
S: "Man of the West"—Philip Yordan
SP: William Ludwig
P: Nicholas Nayfack

2862. VALERIE

(United Artists, August, 1957) 84 Mins.

Sterling Hayden, Anita Ekberg, Anthony Steel, Peter Walker, John Wengraf, Iphigenie Castiglioni, Jerry Barclay, Robert Adler, Tom McKee, Gage Clarke

D: Gerd Oswald

SP: Leonard Heideman, Emmett Murphy

P: Hal R. Makelim

2863. GUNSIGHT RIDGE

(United Artists, September 1, 1957) 85 Mins.

Joel McCrea, Mark Stevens, Joan Weldon, Darlene Fields, Addison Richards, Carolyn Craig, Robert Griffin, Slim Pickens, I. Stanford Jolley, George Chandler, Herb Vigran, Cindy Robbins, Jody McCrea, Martin Garralaga

D: Francis D. Lyon

SP: Talbot and Elizabeth Jennings

P: Robert Bassler

2864. FORTY GUNS

(Globe Enterprises/20th C. Fox, September 1, 1957) 79 Mins.

(CinemaScope)

Barbara Stanwyck, Barry Sullivan, Dean Jagger, John Ericson, Gene Barry, Robert Dix, "Jidge" Carroll, Paul Dubov, Gerald Milton, Ziva Rodann, Hank Worden, Sandra Wirth, Neyle Morrow, Chuck Roberson, Chuck Hayward, Eve Brent

D/SP/P: Samuel Fuller

2865. JOE DAKOTA

(Universal-International, September 1, 1957)

(Eastman Color)

Jock Mahoney, Luana Patten, Charles McGraw, Barbara Lawrence, Claude Akins, Lee Van Cleef, Anthony Caruso, Paul Birch, George Dunn, Steve Darrell, Rita Lynn, Gregg Barton, Jeane Wood, Junie Ellis

D: Richard Bartlett

SP: William Talman, Norman Jolley

P: Howard Christie

2866. THE PARSON AND THE OUTLAW

(Columbia, September 1, 1957) 71 Mins.

(Technicolor)

Anthony Dexter, Sonny Tufts, Marie Windsor, Charles "Buddy" Rogers, Jean Parker, Robert Lowery, Madalyn Trahey, Bob Steele

D: Oliver Drake

SP: Oliver Drake, John Mantley

P: Robert Gilbert, Charles Rogers

2867. RUN OF THE ARROW

(RKO, September 1, 1957) 85 Mins.

(Technicolor)

Rod Steiger, Sarita Montiel, Brian Keith, Ralph Meeker, Jay C. Flippen, Colonel Tim McCoy, Frank de Kova, Stuart Randall, Charles Bronson, Olive Carey, H. M. Wynant, Neyle Morrow, Frank Warner, Billy Miller, Chuck Hayward, Chuck Roberson

D/SP/P: Samuel Fuller

2868. 3:10 TO YUMA

(Columbia, September 1, 1957) 92 Mins.

Glenn Ford, Van Heflin, Felicia Farr, Leora Dana, Henry Jones, Richard Jaeckel, Robert Emhardt, Sheridan Comerate, George Mitchell, Robert Ellenstein, Ford Rainey

D: Delmer Daves

S: Elmore Leonard

SP: Haisten Wells

P: David Heilweil

2869. PAWNEE

(Republic, September 7, 1957) 80 Mins.

(Trucolor)

George Montgomery, Bill Williams, Lola Albright, Francis McDonald, Robert E. Griffin, Dabbs Greer, Kathleen Freeman, Charlotte Austin, Ralph Moody, Anne Barton, Raymond Hatton, Charles Horvath, Robert Nash

D/SP: George Waggner

P: Jack J. Gross, Philip N. Krasne

2870. THE DEERSLAYER

(20th C. Fox, September 10, 1957) 78 Mins.

(DeLuxe Color) (CinemaScope)

Lex Barker, Rita Moreno, Forrest Tucker, Cathy O'Donnell, Jay C. Flippen, Carlos Rivas, John Halloran, Joseph Vitale, Rocky Shahan, Paul Schumacker, George Robotham, Carol Henry

D/SP/P: Kurt Neumann

S: James Fenimore Cooper

2871. BLACK PATCH

(Montgomery Productions/Warner Bros., September 14, 1957)

George Montgomery, Diane Brewster, Tom Pittman, Leo Gordon, House Peters, Jr., Lynn Cartwright, George Trevino, Sebastian Cabot, Peter Brocco, Ted Jacques, Strother Martin, Gil Rankin

D/P: Allen H. Miner

SP: Leo Gordon

2872. COPPER SKY

(Regal Films/20th C. Fox, September 20, 1957) 77 Mins.

(RegalScope)

Jeff Morrow, Coleen Gray, Paul Brinegar, William R. Hamel, Jack M. Lomas, Strother Martin, John Pickard, Patrick O'Moore, Rocky Shahan, Bill McGraw, Jerry Oddo, Rush Williams, Rodd Redwing

D: Charles Marquis Warren
S: Robert Stabler
SP: Eric Norden
P: Robert Stabler, Charles Marquis Warren

2873. THE HIRED GUN
(Rorvic/MGM, September 20, 1957)   63 Mins.
(CinemaScope)
Rory Calhoun, Anne Francis, Vince Edwards, John Litel, Chuck Connors, Robert Burton, Salvadore Baques, Guinn "Big Boy" Williams, Regis Parton
D: Ray Nazarro
S: Buckley Angell
SP: David Lang, Buckley Angell
P: Rory Calhoun, Victor M. Orsatti

2874. NAKED IN THE SUN
(Empire/Allied Artists, September 29, 1957)   78 Mins.
(Eastman Color)
James Craig, Lita Milan, Barton MacLane, Robert Wark, Jim Boles, Tony Hunter, Douglas Wilson, Bill Armstrong, Dennis Cross, Peter Dearing, Tony Morris, Mike Recco
D/P: R. John Hugh
SP: John Cresswell

2875. DOMINO KID
(Rorvic/Columbia, October 1, 1957)   74 Mins.
Rory Calhoun, Kristine Miller, Andrew Duggan, Yvette Dugay, Peter Whitney, Eugene Iglesias, Robert Burton, Bart Bradley, James Griffith, Roy Barcroft, Denver Pyle, Ray Corrigan, William Christensen, Don Orlando
D: Ray Nazarro
S: Rory Calhoun
SP: Kenneth Gamet
P: Rory Calhoun, Victor M. Orsatti

2876. QUANTEZ
(Universal-International, October 1, 1957)   80 Mins.
(Eastman Color)   (CinemaScope)
Fred MacMurray, Dorothy Malone, James Barton, Sidney Chaplin, John Gavin, John Larch, Michael Ansara
D: Harry Keller
SP: H. Wright Campbell
P: Gordon Kay

2877. HELL CANYON OUTLAWS
(Zukor/Republic, October 6, 1957)   72 Mins.
Dale Robertson, Brian Keith, Rossana Rory, Dick

Kallman, Don Megowan, Mike Lane, Buddy Baer, Charles Fredericks, Alexander Lockwood, James Nusser, James Maloney, William Pullen, George Ross, George Pembroke, Vincent Padula, Tom Hubbard
D: Paul Landres
SP: Allan Kaufman, Max Glandbard
P: T. Frank Woods

2878. THE PERSUADER
(World-Wide/Allied Artists, October 13, 1957)   72 Mins.
William Talman, James Craig, Kristine Miller, Darryl Hickman, Georgia Lee, Alvy Moore, Rhoda Williams, Gregory Walcott, Paul Engle, Jason Johnson, Nolan Leary, John Milford, Frank Richards
D/P: Dick Ross
SP: Curtis Kenyon

2879. GUN BATTLE AT MONTEREY
(Allied Artists, October 27, 1957)   67 Mins.
Sterling Hayden, Pamela Duncan, Ted de Corsia, Mary Beth Hughes, Lee Van Cleef, Charles Cane, Pat Comiskey, Byron Foulger, Mauritz Hugo, I. Stanford Jolley, Fred Sherman, George Baxter, Michael Vallon, John Dalmer
D: Carl K. Hittleman, Sidney A. Franklin, Jr.
SP: Jack Leonard, Lawrence Resner
P: Carl K. Hittleman

2880. RAIDERS OF OLD CALIFORNIA
(Republic, November 1, 1957)   72 Mins.
Jim Davis, Arleen Whelan, Faron Young, Marty Robbins, Lee Van Cleef, Louis Jean Heydt, Harry Lauter, Douglas Fowley, Larry Dobkin, Bill Coontz, Don Diamond, Ric Vallin, Tom Hubbard
D/P: Albert C. Gannaway
SP: Sam Roeca, Thomas C. Hubbard

2881. SLIM CARTER
(Universal-International, November 1, 1957)   82 Mins.
(Eastman Color)
Jock Mahoney, Julie Adams, Tim Hovey, William Hopper, Ben Johnson, Joanna Moore, Walter Reed, Maggie Mahoney, Roxanne Arlen, Jim Healy, Bill Williams, Barbara Hale
D: Richard Bartlett
S: David Bramson, Mary C. McCall, Jr.
SP: Montgomery Pittman
P: Howie Horwitz

2882. THE TIN STAR
(Paramount, November 1, 1957)   93 Mins.
Henry Fonda, Anthony Perkins, Betsy Palmer, Michel Ray, Neville Brand, John McIntyre, Mary Webster, Peter Baldwin, Lee Van Cleef, Richard

Shannon, Russell Simpson, Frank Cady, James Bell, Mickey Finn, Howard Petrie, Frank Cordell, Hal K. Dawson, Tim Sullivan, Jack Kennedy
D: Anthony Mann
S: Barney Slater, Joel Kane
SP: Dudley Nichols
P: William Perlberg, George Seaton

2883. DECISION AT SUNDOWN

(Columbia, November 10, 1957) 77 Mins.
(Technicolor)
Randolph Scott, John Carroll, Karen Steele, Valerie French, Noah Beery, Jr., John Archer, Andrew Duggan, James Westerfield, John Litel, Ray Teal, Vaughn Taylor, Richard Deacon, H. M. Wynant, Guy Wilkerson
D: Budd Boetticher
SP: Charles Lang, Jr.
P: Harry Joe Brown, Randolph Scott

2884. THE TALL STRANGER

(Allied Artists, November 17, 1957) 81 Mins.
(DeLuxe Color) (CinemaScope)
Joel McCrea, Virginia Mayo, Barry Kelley, Michael Ansara, Whit Bissell, James Dobson, George Neise, Adam Kennedy, Michael Pate, Leo Gordon, Ray Teal, Philip Phillips, Robert Foulk, Jennifer Lea, George J. Lewis, Guy Prescott, Ralph Reed
D: Thomas Carr
S: Louis L'Amour
SP: Christopher Knopf
P: Walter Mirisch, Richard Heermance

2885. RIDE OUT FOR REVENGE

(Bryna Productions/United Artists, November 1957) 78 Mins.
Rory Calhoun, Gloria Grahame, Lloyd Bridges, Joanne Gilbert, Frank de Kova, Vince Edwards, Michael Winkelman, Richard Shannon, Cyril Delevanti, John Merrick
D/SP/P: Norman Retchin

2886. THE HARD MAN

(Romson/Columbia, December 1, 1957) 80 Mins.
(Technicolor)
Guy Madison, Valerie French, Lorne Greene, Barry Atwater, Robert Burton, Rudy Bond, Trevor Bardette, Renata Vanni, Rickie Sorenson, Frank Richards, Myron Healey, Robert B. Williams
D: George Sherman
S/SP: Leo Katcher
P: Helen Ainsworth

2887. RIDE A VIOLENT MILE

(Regal Films/20th C. Fox, December 1, 1957) 80 Mins.
(RegalScope)
John Agar, Penny Edwards, John Pickard, Richard Shannon, Charles Gray, Bing Russell, Helen Wallace, Richard Gilden, Sheb Wooley, Patrick O'Moore, Rush Williams, Roberto Contreas, Eve Novak, Mary Townsend, Dorothy Schuyler, Rocky Shahan, Norman B. Cram, Karl R. MacDonald
D/S/P: Charles Marquis Warren
SP: Eric Norden

2888. GUNFIRE AT INDIAN GAP

(Republic, December 13, 1957) 70 Mins.
(Naturama) (Scope Process)
Vera Ralston, Anthony George, George Macready, Barry Kelley, John Doucette, George Keymas, Chubby Johnson, Glenn Strange, Dan White, Steve Warren, Chuck Hicks
D: Joseph Kane
SP: Barry Shipman
AP: Rudy Ralston

2889. THE DALTON GIRLS

(Bel-Air/United Artists, December 15, 1957) 71 Mins.
Merry Anders, Lisa Davis, Penny Edwards, Sue George, John Russell, Ed Hinton, Glenn Dixon, Johnny Western, Malcolm Atterbury, Douglas Henderson, Kevin Enright, Al Wyatt, Red Morgan, H. E. Willmerling, E. C. MacGregor, David Swapp
D: Reginald Le Borg
S: Herbert Purdom
SP: Maurice Tombragel
P: Howard W. Koch

2890. LEGEND OF THE LOST

(Batjac-Hagging/United Artists, December 17, 1957) 109 Mins.
(Technicolor) (Technirama)
John Wayne, Sophia Loren, Rossano Brazzi, Kurt Kasznar, Sonia Moser, Angela Portaluri, Ibrahim El Hadish
D: Henry Hathaway
SP: Robert Presnell, Jr., Ben Hecht
P: Henry Hathaway
(Although not a Western, this film has certain Western elements, e.g., expedition on horses into the desert, and is included for that reason)

2891. WESTWARD HO THE WAGONS!

(Disney/Buena Vista, December 25, 1957) 90 Mins.
(Technicolor)
Fess Parker, Jeff York, Kathleen Crowley, Karen Pendleton, David Stollery, Leslie Bradley, George Reeves, Sebastian Cabot
D: William Beaudine
SP: Tom Blackburn
P: Walt Disney

CHAPTER 8

The Evolving Years 1958-1962

(WHEN WHITE AND BLACK BLENDED INTO GREY)

The period 1958-1962 represents a time when the unglamorous or "realistic" Westerner came into his own and traditional heroes in white hats diminished in number. The trend, still in progress today, would see the likes of Randolph Scott, Joel McCrea, and Audie Murphy, every inch heroes, gradually give way to the anti-heroes, Yul Brynner, Lee Marvin, Clint Eastwood, *et al.* Fortunately, the Evolving Years still had a few "traditionalists" of the old school that kids could idolize and believe in and place on the same pedestal as motherhood, pumpkin pie at Thanksgiving, and Santa Claus. But more and more heroes were depicted as not necessarily heroic and the civilized were no longer necessarily civilized.

Filmmakers wrought havoc with the Western myth savoured and nourished for fifty years. On the cynical and practical level, they knew they had to pay the bills; consequently, they kept an eye on the box office and on that which seemed to excite an audience. It did not take much observation to conclude that sex and violence, in that order, are proven stimulants; thus, both became standard ingredients in Westerns. And so it was that the traditional Western myth and the anti-myth co-existed, and elements of both were usually present in the films of the era.

Probably the most expensive Western of the period was *The Alamo* (United Artists, 1959), running three hours and nineteen minutes in length. Although producer-director-star John Wayne intended it to be the definitive story of the heroism at the Alamo and envisioned it as one of the great epics of the genre, the film failed on both counts. As a history of the fall of the Alamo, it is probably less accurate than *Heroes of the Alamo* (Columbia, 1937), a low-budget film starring Rex Lease and Lane Chandler. And as an epic it is only so in terms of size, scope, length, and budget—not in terms of being a film that will be remembered for decades by those who view it. The film is reputed to have cost $6.5 million to make. On first issue it fell far short of recouping production costs, but subsequent reissues and television rentals have put it into the black financially. Wayne, however, sold his interests in the film before the profits were realized.

As director and star Wayne does a creditable job, and the second-unit work of Cliff Lyons has to be commended too. The battle scenes are terrific. Wayne makes a good Davy Crockett and Richard Widmark is acceptable as Jim Bowie, but Laurence Harvey is pathetically weak as Colonel Travis and one can only wonder why Wayne chose the Englishman for such an important role. After almost losing his shirt on this venture, Wayne went back to making less pretentious but more enjoyable and profitable Westerns.

Besides *The Alamo*, Wayne, back in the genre after only two Westerns in the years 1953-1957, completed five other Westerns in the Evolving Years to re-establish himself as the screen's foremost Westerner. *Rio Bravo* (Warner Bros., 1959) is an exceptionally fine film presenting both John Wayne and director Howard Hawks at their best. Suspense and action are maintained throughout as old indefectible Duke goes about his task of cleaning out a nest of varmints, aided by Dean Martin, Angie Dickinson, Walter Brennan, Ricky Nelson, and Ward Bond. The psychological ingredients are not built on as they might have been under Sam Peckinpah or Henry Mann, but the picture is more entertaining for it. Wayne intended the film as a rebuttal of *High Noon*, which he felt was unrealistic in that Westerners who had survived untold hardships would not be buffaloed by a few scroungy badmen. Thus, in *Rio Bravo,* the sheriff has more help than he bargained for.

Wayne's reputation as an action-adventure star was given added lustre under the tutelage of John Ford in *The Horse Soldiers* (United Artists, 1959), an attempt at another cavalry picture and a film some critics have called their weakest collaboration. But be that as it may, the film is worthy of praise for its pictorial quality alone if nothing else. Ford's former star and long-time friend, Hoot Gibson, was cast in a supporting role while William Holden shared co-billing with Wayne. Constance Towers is the Southern woman with whom Union officer Wayne falls in love. The final scene shows him riding off with her headscarf as a souvenir while Ford's favorite "Ann Rutledge" theme generates a musical sense of bittersweet poignancy.

In *North to Alaska* (Fox, 1960) producer-director Henry Hathaway has but one purpose—to entertain, approaching the objective in a lighthearted, comedic fashion. The film has two splendid mass brawls handled in silent comedy style and Wayne is amusing in his by now familiar role of the man's man experiencing pangs of unrequited love. With a virility and an enthusiasm that belie his age, he adeptly combines fast adventure with mild comedy, while his impeccable sense of structure is ever present. His wry humor is germane to the narrative and a dynamic element in it.

In *The Comancheros* (Fox, 1961), Wayne has begun to accept his age and leaves the heavy romance to younger folks, concentrating on mild comedy and the crisp action which is his *raison d'etre.* Old friends Bob Steele and Big Boy Williams add a nostalgic twinge to the proceedings and Lee Marvin is superb as a hard-drinking, eagle-eyed, half-scalped "Tully Crow."

The Man Who Shot Liberty Valance (Paramount, 1962) was in many ways Wayne's best picture of the Evolving Years—certainly better than the many times more costly *The Alamo.* John Ford directed this black-and-white film, the lack of color capturing more of the essence of the austere West. The theme is classic; its treatment is classic; the atmosphere is classic. In the story the hero's fate is to serve as midwife to a society that forgets its past and looks for leadership to one who makes his way by living a lie. John Wayne's role of Tom Doniphon recalls an individualism which seems to no longer exist in the complexities of modern life. As film critic Allen Eyles in his book *John Wayne and the Movies* has so aptly stated, "The clash between the West of fact and the West of legend is central to the film . . . it shapes up as one of Ford's most heartfelt and moving pictures. No other film has so poignantly confronted the real West of slow and difficult progress with the colourful West of legend. No other film has so hauntingly conveyed the transition between the old and new West in making Wayne's Tom Doniphon both the instrument and victim of its evolution." Wayne is the hero doggedly clinging to old ways who loses his girl Hallie (Vera Miles) out of his great love for her and his own code of ethics. Hallie's beauty, her exquisite charm, and her haunting face were such as to wreck Doniphon's life thereafter and propel Ranse Stoddard (James Stewart) into national prominence. Director Ford managed to bring to the screen both an atmosphere and a Wayne performance reminiscent in a small, wispy way of what Robert N. Bradbury had been able to do with Wayne at Lonestar/Monogram in 1934-1935, and the manner of the telling makes this old story of the love triangle seem new.

Ride the High Country (MGM, 1962) — Randolph Scott and Joel McCrea

In a similar vein Sam Peckinpah's *Ride the High Country* (MGM, 1962) presents a character in Steve Judd (Joel McCrea) not unlike Ford's Tom Doniphon (Wayne), an old lawman who has lived past his prime and who struggles to maintain his code of honor. But, along with his old friend, Gil Westrum (Randolph Scott), he finds himself out of step in the new West he had helped to effect. The film is a poignant re-creation of the old West's values as an aging pair of former lawmen hook up to protect a gold shipment and a girl. One of the most poetic Westerns ever made, it is undoubtedly Peckinpah's best Western to date. The ties between two old Westerners caught up in a West they do not like and torn between doing what is right and serving their own self-interest makes for a compelling story. The final scene depicting the death of Judd suggests the passing nature of the whole Western myth and is magnified by the colorful sunset ending—a masterful stroke of direction. The film, a real sleeper, caught on big and grossed heavily at the box office as well as scoring artistically. No one was as surprised as the Metro-Goldwyn-Mayer moguls, who considered the medium-budget Western just another oater.

Sadly, *Ride the High Country* was Scott's farewell film. Upon its completion he retired from the screen to pursue other business interests. If any Western star could be said to have carried on the Bill Hart tradition, it was Randolph Scott. His vehicles were marked by simplicity in dress and carefully selected locations which emphasized the dramatic mood of the moment, resulting in a feeling of the austere reality that permeated the Hart Westerns. Prior to this "last hooray," Scott and director Budd Boetticher had continued their winning streak of fine Westerns with *Buchanan Rides Alone* (Columbia, 1958), *Ride Lonesome* (Columbia, 1959), *Westbound* (Warner Bros., 1959), and *Comanche Station* (Columbia, 1960). The Columbia releases were co-produced by Scott and Harry Joe Brown. *Westbound*, besides being a first-rate action saga, is notable for "B" buffs in that Buddy Roosevelt, Jack Perrin, and

The Magnificent Seven (United Artists, 1960) — Yul Brynner

484

Kermit Maynard were in the supporting cast. All three, of course, were top headliners in the silent and early sound era. Perhaps the central theme in the Scott vehicles is his sage "Some things a man can't ride around" and, having said it, he is projected into troubles his righteous spirit tells him must be faced. "He must live the way a man should."

Commercially, one of the most successful Westerns of the Evolving Years was *The Magnificent Seven* (Mirisch-Alpha, 1960), a box-office extravaganza with gunfighters Yul Brynner, Steve McQueen, Charles Bronson, and cohorts tangling with Eli Wallach and his Mexican bandits who are terrorizing a village of farmers. The settling down of seven egotistical specialists into a functioning fighting force is masterfully detailed by director John Sturges. In the boisterous story the gunmen help the peasants because they have nothing better to do, nothing to love, nothing to look forward to, the odds are a challenge, and there is a chance to use their guns once more before civilization closes in on them and relegates them to menial tasks as store clerks or ranch hands. The accuracy of the exteriors, interiors, costumes, and accessories is refreshing and the picture is staged with the right kind of settings, and exceedingly beautiful photographic and lighting effects. As a result, the picture lifts the spectator from his seat and transports him to the wilds of Mexico, so realistic is the atmosphere.

Cowboy (Columbia, 1958) avoids the well-trod trails of movie Westerns merely by staying on the little-known paths of the real West and presents a historical image of the cowboy and an accurate definition of the cow country. Glenn Ford and Jack Lemmon as the tough cowboy and tenderfoot, respectively, are convincing performers and the film is a delightful experience in semi-realism.

Gary Cooper's last traditional Western (a semi-Western, *They Came to Cordura* [Columbia, 1959], was released the following year) was Anthony Mann's *Man of the West* (United Artists, 1958). Violence and sex are accentuated in keeping with the promiscuity of the times, but Cooper's hero is rather straight-laced. The film is a fitting end to Cooper's Western career.

Lonely Are the Brave (Universal, 1962), like *The Man Who Shot Liberty Valance* and *Ride the High Country*, is based on a feeling of loss for the vanishing West. Jack Burns (Kirk Douglas), a jail escapee, attempts to elude a motorized posse as he tries to make his way over a mountain to safety, having rejected the customary pursuit of material things for a life as a drifter and personal freedom. He carries a guitar and sings folksy ballads of the old West, *a la* Tex Ritter. The movie hammers home the fact that one must conform in modern society or be beaten down. Ultimately, the hero and his steed "Whiskey" are struck down by the new horse of the West, a truck—and, ironically, one filled with porcelain toilets!

In another poignant Western starring Douglas he falls in love with his own daughter by his former mistress and then purposely gets himself killed by Rock Hudson in a duel after finding out that Carol Lynley is his daughter. The movie was *The Last Sunset*.

Paul Newman proved mildly inept in *The Left Handed Gun* (Warner Bros., 1958), a poorly accepted, poorly directed, farcical account of New Mexico's third-rate, neurotic badman, and Marlon Brando's *One-Eyed Jacks*, which he also directed, is another *Billy the Kid* yarn which did only ho-hum business in spite of Brando's lavish over-budget spending on it. Perhaps the significance of this latter film is summed up in film writer John Baxter's words: "Few Westerns have realized so successfully the potential for psychological and psychosexual comment that exists in this most powerful of American art forms."

Deserved mention goes to *No Name on the Bullet* (Universal, 1959), a suspense-filled psychological study of a hired gunman's impact on a frontier town and those who, because of guilty consciences, wonder who his intended victim is.

A delightfully entertaining respite from violence, sex, and sordid shenanigans is *The Sheepman* (Columbia, 1958), in which director George Marshall has adroitly handled one of the fiercest of Western issues in a charmingly humorous fashion, highlighted by fine performances from Glenn Ford and Shirley MacLaine.

Two other John Ford films deserve mention as being among the better Westerns of the period. *Sergeant Rutledge* (Warner Bros., 1960) relies on a strong story rather than a name cast for its pulling punch, although the characters are notably well presented by the surprisingly fine cast of able if not renowned players. The film's underlying theme is racism and the story concerns the efforts of Lieutenant Tom Cantrell (Jeffrey Hunter) in defending Sergeant Braxton Rutledge (Woody Strode), a black, against a charge of rape and murder.

In *Two Rode Together* (Columbia, 1961) Ford has masterfully unfolded a tale of search similar to *The Searchers* in its circular form. James Stewart is the pessimistic, uncommitted mercenary, whereas Richard Widmark is the taintless cavalry officer who would ride into hell and pummel the devil in his own bailiwick if ordered to do so. It is a cynical film, reflecting Ford's growing languidness with values he once held in high esteem, but he has gotten the most from his players and handled every scene effectively. The film was well conceived, well written, carefully executed, and extremely well acted.

Henry Hathaway's *From Hell to Texas* (Fox, 1958) was an artistic success but a dismal flop commercially. All the pieces were there to make a great Western—an excellent story; a good director; a fine cast; excellent photography, sound, and music—yet the pieces failed to jell and the public ho-hummed the film into an early shelving.

William Wyler's *The Big Country* (United Artists, 1958) created a lot of stir and was one of the more grandiose Westerns of the period, its commercial success practically assured by its cast, scope, theme, and publicity campaign. Critics panned it as insipid and action fans felt somewhat cheated in the absence of hairbreadth escapes and last-stand shootouts, but it proved to be enjoyable film fare to the rank-and-file movie patrons and the coffers of United Artists swelled with the profits from this epic film.

There were other Westerns of more than passing interest that deserved an "A" for effort, such as Clark Gable's *The Misfits* (United Artists, 1961), Robert Taylor's *The Law and Jake Wade* (MGM, 1958), Jeff Chandler's *The Plunderers* (Allied Artists, 1960), Richard Boone's *A Thunder of Drums* (MGM, 1961), and Glenn Ford's *Cimarron* (MGM, 1960). But it was those films already referred to that constitute the more significant efforts of the period.

For those aficionados swearing allegiance to the series Westerns of the Thirties and Forties and whose taste ran to low-budget, non-precedent shattering, white-hat-versus-black-hat shoot-em-ups, a little discreet shopping around at neighborhood theatres and drive-ins could uncover some gems chuck full of familiar people with whom a Western buff could feel comfortable. For instance, Buster Crabbe could be seen in *The Lawless Eighties* (Republic, 1958) and *Gunfighters of Abilene* (United Artists, 1960), both films relying heavily on the Crabbe name to offset mediocre productions. Unforgettable is the scene in *Gunfighters of Abilene* where Buster's gun hangs in the holster as he attempts to draw it and Barton MacLane, obviously perturbed and not sure whether the camera is still running or not, delivers his line that went something like "I know you're fast, Tanner . . ." Probably even PRC would not have let that scene stay in the release print, but aside from that one scene that should have been edited out the film was acceptable.

Most of the old-timers were not so fortunate as to be cast in the leading role of a Western in the Evolving Years but former "B" aces such as Guinn Williams, Kermit Maynard, Lane Chandler, Donald Barry, and Allan Lane occasionally added nostalgic value to

Gunfighters of Abilene (United Artists, 1960) — Judith Ames, Buster Crabbe, and unidentified players

Westerns of the period. One of the most frequently seen was Bob Steele, the "little giant of Westerns" whose career dated back to the early Twenties. And in *Once upon a Horse,* the Rowan and Martin spoof, Bob shared the company of Tom Keene, Bob Livingston, and Kermit Maynard in cameo guest appearances. Myron Healey, Dub Taylor, I. Stanford Jolley, George J. Lewis, and other Western character actors from the "B" days popped up in many productions of the Evolving Years.

Gone were Charles Starrett, Johnny Mack Brown, Tom Tyler, Tim Holt, and Roy Rogers, but in their places were other stars making a larger-scale traditional-type Western on enlarged budgets that permitted color, longer running times, name players, location shooting, and a general finesse lacking in the low-budget "B's," although certainly not qualifying as auspicious Westerns. Audie Murphy's popularity was undebauched as he rode, fought, and loved through such gritty, fervid sagebrushers as *Posse from Hell* (Universal, 1961), *Hell Bent for Leather* (Universal, 1960), *Six Black Horses* (Universal, 1962), and *Seven Ways from Sundown* (Universal, 1961), to mention only a few of his rather entrancing little Westerns. And Jim Davis, James Brown, George Montgomery, and Rory Calhoun were making the same type of minor "A's," emphasizing old-time thrills and spills rather than sex and gory violence.

On a larger scale but below the colossal level were Joel McCrea's Westerns, noteworthy as clean, highly entertaining, easily forgotten little gems (with the exception of *Ride the High Country)* that adhered to the spirit of the Western myth. *The Gunfight at Dodge City* (United Artists, 1959), *Cattle Empire* (Fox, 1959), and *Fort Massacre* (United Artists, 1958) each did much to appease the longing of action fans for something akin to what they had lost in the passing of the series "B." McCrea's basic characterization of the simple, easy-going fellow who prizes his independence was still in evidence in these titillating horse-and-dust flicks devoid of the plethora of sex and explicit blood-letting to be found elsewhere.

By 1962 the number of Westerns of any quality being produced was somewhat curtailed in comparison to former periods. Only twenty-three Westerns were released in 1961 and sixteen in 1962, small numbers indeed when compared to the hundreds turned out annually in the Boom Years. Western filmdom was suddenly in the doldrums again and the virtuous hero and his white charger so familiar to traditionalists were taking on a decidedly grey color when silhouetted against the darkening bluffs of societal mores and the cynical Sixties. White hats and black hats were merging into grey.

FILMS OF 1958

2892. ESCAPE FROM RED ROCK
(Regal Films/TCF, January 2, 1958)   75 Mins.
(RegalScope)
Brian Donlevy, Elaine Janssen, Gary Murray, Jay C. Flippen, William Phipps, Richard Healey, Nesdon Booth, Rick Vallin, Dan White
D/SP: Edward Bernds
P: Bernard Glaser

2893. GUN FEVER
(United Artists, January 2, 1958) 81 Mins.
Mark Stevens, John Lupton, Larry Storch, Jana Davi, Aaron Saxon, Jerry Barclay, Norman Frederic, Clegg Hoyt, Jean Inness, Russell Thorson, Michael Himm, Iron Eyes Cody, Eddie Little, Cyril Delavanti, John Godard, Vic Smith, Robert Stevenson, William Erwin, David Bond, George Selk
D: Mark Stevens
S: Harry S. Franklin, Julius Evans
SP: Stanley H. Silverman
P: Harry Jackson, Sam Weston

2894. OREGON PASSAGE
(Allied Artists, January 12, 1958)   82 Mins.
(DeLuxe Color) (CinemaScope)
John Ericson, Lola Albright, Toni Gerry, Edward Platt, Judith Ames, H. M. Wynant, Jon Shepodd, Walter Barnes, Paul Fierro, Harvey Stephens
D: Paul Landres
S: Gordon D. Shirreffs
SP: Jack DeWitt
P: Lindsley Parsons

2895. RETURN TO WARBOW
(Columbia, January 27, 1958)   67 Mins.
(Technicolor)
Phil Carey, Catherine McLeod, Andrew Duggan, William Leslie, Robert J. Wilke, James Griffith, Jay Silverheels, Chris Olsen, Francis de Sales, Harry Lauter, Paul Picerni, Joe Forte

D: Ray Nazarro
S/SP: Les Savage, Jr.
P: Wallace MacDonald

2896. OLD YELLER
(Buena Vista, January, 1958)   83 Mins.
(Technicolor)
Fess Parker, Dorothy McGuire, Tommy Kirk, Kevin Corcoran, Jeff York, Chuck Connors, Beverly Washburn
D: Robert Stevenson
S: Fred Gipson
SP: Fred Gipson, William Tunberg
P: Walt Disney

2897. FORT BOWIE
(United Atists, February 1, 1958)   80 Mins.
Ben Johnson, Jan Harrison, Kent Taylor, Jana Davi, Larry Chance, J. Ian Douglas, Peter Mamakos, Jerry Frank, Barbara Parry, Ed Hinton, Johnny Western
D: Howard W. Koch
SP: Maurice Tombragel
P: Aubrey Schenck

2898. FORT DOBBS
(Warner Bros., February 8, 1958)   90 Mins.
Clint Walker, Virginia Mayo, Brian Keith, Richard Eyer, Russ Conway, Michael Dante
D: Gordon Douglas
SP: Burt Kennedy, George W. George
P: Martin Rackin

2899. MAN FROM GOD'S COUNTRY
(Allied Artists, February 9, 1958)   70 Mins.
(DeLuxe Color) (CinemaScope)
George Montgomery, Randy Stuart, James Griffith, House Peters, Jr., Susan Cummings, Kim Charney, Frank Wilcox, Gregg Barton, Philip Terry, Al Wyatt

D: Paul Landres
SP: George Waggner
P: Scott R. Dunlap

2900. AMBUSH AT CIMARRON PASS
(Regal Films/TCF, March 1, 1958)   87 Mins.
(RegalScope)
Scott Brady, Margia Dean, Clint Eastwood, Irving Bacon, Frank Gerstle, Dirk London, Baynes Barron, Ken Mayer, Keith Richards, William Vaughn, John Damler, John Merrick
D: Jodie Copelan
S: Robert A. Reeds, Robert E. Woods
SP: Richard G. Taylor, John K. Butler
P: Herbert E. Mendelson

2901. COWBOY
(Columbia, March 1, 1958)   92 Mins.
(Technicolor)
Glenn Ford, Jack Lemmon, Anna Kashfi, Brian Donlevy, Dick York, Victor Manuel Mendoza, Richard Jaeckel, King Donovan, Vaughn Taylor, Donald Randolph, James Westerfield, Buzz Henry, Eugene Iglesias, Frank de Kova
D: Delmer Daves
S: "My Reminiscences as a Cowboy"—Frank Harris
P: Julian Blaustein

2902. THE MISSOURI TRAVELER
(Buena Vista, March 1, 1958)   103 Mins.
(Technicolor)
Brandon de Wilde, Lee Marvin, Gary Merrill, Mary Hosford, Paul Ford, Ken Curtis, Cal Tinney, Frank Cady, Mary Field, Kathleen Freeman, Will Wright, Tom Tiner, Billy Bryant, Barry Curtis, Eddie Little, Rodney Bell, Helen Brown, Billy Newill, Roy Jensen, Earle Hodgins
D: Jerry Hopper
S: John Burress
SP: Norman Shannon Hall
P: Patrick Ford, Lowell J. Farrell

2903. SEVEN GUNS TO MESA
(Allied Artists, March 16, 1958)   69 Mins.
Charles Quinlivan, Lola Albright, James Griffith, Jay Adler, John Cliff, Burt Nelson, John Merrick, Charles Keane, Jack Carr, Don Sullivan, Rush Williams, Neil Grant, Reed Howes, Mauritz Hugo, Harvey Russell
D: Edward Dein
S: Myles Wilder
SP: Myles Wilder, Edward and Mildred Dein
P: William F. Broidy

2904. SADDLE THE WIND
(MGM, March 21, 1958)   84 Mins.
(Metrocolor)   (CinemaScope)
Robert Taylor, Julie London, John Cassavetes, Donald Crisp, Charles McGraw, Royal Dano, Richard Erdman, Douglas Spencer, Ray Teal
D: Robert Parrish
S: Rod Serling
SP: Thomas Thompson
P: Armand Deutsch

2905. COLE YOUNGER, GUNFIGHTER
(Allied Artists, March 30, 1958)   78 Mins.
(DeLuxe Color)   (CinemaScope)
Frank Lovejoy, James Best, Abby Dalton, Jan Merlin, Douglas Spencer, Ainslie Pryor, Frank Ferguson, Myron Healey, George Keymas, Dan Sheridan, John Mitchum
D: R. G. Springsteen
S: Clifton Adams
SP: Daniel Mainwaring
P: Ben Schwald

2906. BLOOD ARROW
(Emirau/Regal Films, April 1, 1958)
(RegalScope)
Scott Brady, Paul Richards, Phyllis Coates, Don Haggerty, Rocky Shahan, Des Slatterty, Bill McGraw, Patrick O'Moore, Jeanne Bates, Richard Gilden, John Dierkes, Diana Darrin
D: Charles Marquis Warren
SP: Fred Freiberger
P: Robert Stabler

2907. DAY OF THE BAD MAN
(Universal-International, April 1, 1958)   81 Mins.
(Eastman Color)   (CinemaScope)
Fred MacMurray, Joan Weldon, John Ericson, Robert Middleton, Marie Windsor, Edgar Buchanan, Eduard Franz, Skip Homeier, Peggy Converse, Robert Foulk, Ann Doran, Lee Van Cleef, Eddy Waller, Christopher Dark, Don Haggerty, Chris Alcaide
D: Harry Keller
S: John M. Cunningham
SP: Lawrence Roman
P: Gordon Kay

2908. CATTLE EMPIRE
(20th C. Fox, April 15, 1958)   83 Mins.
(DeLuxe Color)   (CinemaScope)
Joel McCrea, Gloria Talbott, Don Haggerty, Phyllis Coates, Bing Russell, Paul Brinegar, Hal K. Dawson, Duane Gray, Richard Shannon, Charles Gray, Patrick O'Moore, Bill McGraw, Jack Lomas, Steve Raines, Rocky Shahan, Nesdon Booth, Bill Hale, Ronald Foster, Howard B. Culver, Edward Jauregui, Ted Smile
D: Charles Marquis Warren
S: Daniel B. Ullman

SP: Endre Bohem, Eric Norden
P: Robert Stabler

2909. QUANTRILL'S RAIDERS
(Allied Artists, April 27, 1958) 71 Mins.
(DeLuxe Color) (CinemaScope)
Steve Cochran, Diane Brewster, Leo Gordon, Gale
  Robbins, Will Wright, Kim Charney, Myron Hea-
  ley, Robert Foulk, Glenn Strange, Lane Chandler,
  Guy Prescott, Thomas B. Henry
D: Edward Bernds
SP: Polly James
P: Ben Schwalb

2910. FORT MASSACRE
(Mirisch Company/United Artists, May 1, 1958)
  80 Mins.
(DeLuxe Color) (CinemaScope)
Joel McCrea, Forrest Tucker, Susan Cabot, John
  Russell, Anthony Caruso, Bob Osterloh, Denver
  Pyle, George N. Neise, Rayford Barnes, Guy
  Prescott, Larry Chance, Irving Bacon, Claire
  Carleton, Francis McDonald, Walter Kray
D: Joseph M. Newman
SP: Martin N. Goldsmith
P: Walter M. Mirisch

2911. SHOWDOWN AT BOOT HILL
(Regal Films/20th C. Fox, May 1, 1958) 72 Mins.
Charles Bronson, Robert Hutton, John Carradine,
  Carole Matthews, Paul Maxey, Thomas B. Henry,
  William Stevens, Martin Smith, Joe McGuinn,
  George Douglas, Michael Mason, George Pem-
  broke, Argentini Brunetti, Ed Wright, Stacey
  Marshall, Shirle Haven, Fintan Meyler, Dan
  Simmons, Barbara Woodell, Norman Leavitt,
  Tony Douglas, Jose Gonzales-Gonzales
D: Gene Fowler, Jr.
SP: Louis Vitters
P: Harold E. Knox

2912. TOUGHEST GUN IN TOMBSTONE
(United Artists, May 1, 1958) 72 Mins.
George Montgomery, Beverly Tyler, Don Beddoe,
  Jim Davis, Scott Morrow, Harry Lauter, Charles
  Wagenheim, Jack Kenney, John Merrick, Al Wy-
  att, Joey Ray, Gerald Milton, Lane Bradford,
  Gregg Barton, Hank Worden, Tex Terry, Charles
  Hayes, Kathleen Mulqueen, Rodolfo Hoyos, Alex
  Montoya, Rico Alaniz, Jack Carr, William Forrest,
  Harry Strang, Mary Newton
D: Earl Bellamy
SP: Orville Hampton
P: Robert E. Kent

2913. THE SHEEPMAN
(MGM, May 16, 1958) 85 Mins.

(Metrocolor) (CinemaScope)
Glenn Ford, Shirley MacLaine, Leslie Neilsen,
  Mickey Shaughnessy, Edgar Buchanan, Willis
  Bouchey, Pernell Roberts, Slim Pickens, Buzz
  Henry, Pedro Gonzales-Gonzales
D: George Marshall
SP: William Bowers, James Edward Grant
P: Edmund Grainger

2914. THE LEFT HANDED GUN
(Warner Bros., May 17, 1958) 102 Mins.
Paul Newman, Lita Milan, John Dehner, Hurd Hat-
  field, James Congdon, James Best, Colin Keith-
  Johnston, John Dierkes, Bob Anderson, Wally
  Brown, Ainslie Pryor, Martin Garralaga, Denver
  Pyle, Paul Smith, Nestor Paiva
D: Arthur Penn
SP: Leslie Stevens
P: Fred Coe

2915. SNOWFIRE
(Allied Artists, May 18, 1958) 73 Mins.
(Eastman Color)
Don Megowan, Molly McGowan, Claire Kelly, John
  Cason, Michael Vallon, Melody McGowan
D/SP/P: Dorrell and Stuart McGowan

2916. BULLWHIP
(Allied Artists, May 25, 1958) 80 Mins.
(DeLuxe Color) (CinemaScope)
Guy Madison, Rhonda Fleming, James Griffith, Don
  Beddoe, Peter Adams, Dan Sheridan, Burt Nel-
  son, Al Terry, Tim Graham, Hank Worden, Wayne
  Mallory, Barbara Woodell, Rhys Williams, Don
  Shelton, Jack Reynolds, Frank Griffin, J. W. Cody,
  Jack Carr, Rick Vallin, Saul Gorss
D: Harmon Jones
SP: Adele Buffington
P: William F. Broidy

2917. MAN OR GUN
(Republic, May 30, 1958) 79 Mins.
(Naturama)
MacDonald Carey, Audrey Totter, James Craig,
  James Gleason, Warren Stevens, Harry Shannon,
  Jil Jarmyn, Robert Burton, Ken Lynch, Karl Davis,
  Julian Burton, Carl York, Harry Keekas, Mel
  Gaines, Ron McNeil
D: Albert C. Gannaway
SP: Vance Skarstedt, James C. Cassity
P: Albert C. Gannaway

2918. THE LAWLESS EIGHTIES
(Ventura/Republic, May 31, 1958) 70 Mins.
Buster Crabbe, John Smith, Marilyn Saris, Ted de
  Corsia, Anthony Caruso, John Doucette, Frank
  Ferguson, Sheila Bromley, Walter Reed, Buzz

The Left Handed Gun (Warner Bros., 1958) — Paul Newman

The Lone Ranger and the Lost City of Gold (United Artists, 1958) — Jay Silverheels, Clayton Moore, and unidentified player

491

Henry, Will J. White, Bob Swan
D: Joseph Kane
S: "Brother Van"—Alson Jesse Smith
SP: Kenneth Gamet
AP: Rudy Ralston

2919. FROM HELL TO TEXAS
(20th C. Fox, June 1, 1958)   100 Mins.
(DeLuxe Color)   (CinemaScope)
Don Murray, Diane Varsi, Chill Wills, Dennis Hopper, R. G. Armstrong, Jay C. Flippen, Margo, John Larch, Ken Scott, Rodolfo Acosta, Salvador Baguez, Harry Carey, Jr., Jerry Oddo, Jose Torvay, Malcolm Atterbury
D: Henry Hathaway
S: "The Hell-Bent Kid"—Charles O. Locke
SP: Robert Buckner, Wendell Mayes

2920. THE PROUD REBEL
(Buena Vista, June 1, 1958)   103 Mins.
(Technicolor)
Alan Ladd, Olivia de Havilland, David Ladd, Dean Jagger, Dean Stanton, Thomas Pittman, Cecil Kellaway, James Westerfield, Henry Hull, Eli Mintz, John Carradine
D: Michael Curtiz
S: James Edward Grant
SP: Joe Petracca, Lillie Hayward
P: Samuel Goldwyn, Jr.

2921. THE LONE RANGER AND
THE LOST CITY OF GOLD
(United Artists, June 15, 1958)   80 Mins.
(Eastman Color)
Clayton Moore, Jay Silverheels, Douglas Kennedy, Charles Watts, Noreen Nash, Lisa Montell, Ralph Moody, Norman Frederic, John Miljan, Maurice Jara, Bill Henry, Lane Bradford, Belle Mitchell
D: Lesley Selander
SP: Robert Schaefer, Eric Freiwald
P: Sherman A. Harris, Jack Wrather

2922. THE LAW AND JAKE WADE
(MGM, June 20, 1958)   86 Mins.
(Metrocolor)   (CinemaScope)
Robert Taylor, Richard Widmark, Patricia Owens, Robert Middleton, Henry Silva, DeForest Kelley, Burt Douglas, Eddie Firestone
D: John Sturges
SP: William Bowers
P: William Hawks

2923. THE BRAVADOS
(TCR, July 27, 1958)   98 Mins.
(DeLuxe Color)   (CinemaScope)
(Filmed in Mexico)
Gregory Peck, Joan Collins, Stephen Boyd, Albert

Salmi, Henry Silva, Kathleen Gallant, Barry Coe, George Voscovec, Herbert Rudley, Lee Van Cleef, Andrew Duggan, Ken Scott, Gene Evans, Ninos Cantores, Jack Mather, Joe De Rita, Robert Adler, Jason Wingreen, Robert Griffin, Jacqueline Evans, Ada Carrasco, Ninos Cantores De Morelia Choral Group
D: Henry King
SP: Philip Yordan
P: Herbert B. Swope, Jr.

2924. GUNMAN'S WALK
(Columbia, July 27, 1958)   97 Mins.
(Technicolor)   (CinemaScope)
Van Heflin, Tab Hunter, Kathryn Grant, James Darren, Mickey Shaughnessy, Robert F. Simon, Edward Platt, Ray Teal, Paul Birch, Michael Granger, Will Wright, Chief Blue Eagle, Bert Convy, Paul E. Burns, Paul Bryar, Everett Glass, Dorothy Adams
D: Phil Karlson
S: Ric Hardman
SP: Frank Nugent
P: Fred Kohlmar

2925. THE LAST OF THE FAST GUNS
(Universal-International, July 27, 1958)   82 Mins.
(Eastman Color)   (CinemaScope)
Jock Mahoney, Gilbert Roland, Linda Cristal, Eduard Franz, Lorne Greene, Carl Benton Reid, Edward C. Platt, Eduardo Noriega, Jorge Trevino, Rafael Alcayde, Lee Morgan, Milton Bernstein, Stillman Segar, Jose Chavez Thowe, Francisco Reyguera, Richard Cutting, Ralph Neff
D: George Sherman
SP: David P. Harmon
P: Howard Christie

2926. SIERRA BARON
(20th C. Fox, July 30, 1958)   80 Mins.
(DeLuxe Color)   (CinemaScope)
(Filmed in Mexico)
Brian Keith, Rick Jason, Rita Gam, Mala Powers, Allan Lewis, Pedro Calvan, Fernando Wagner, Steve Brodie, Carlos Muzquiz, Lee Morgan, Jose Espinoza, Enrique Lucero, Alberto Mariscal, Lynne Ehrlich, Michael Schmidt, Tommy Riste, Reed Howes, Robin Glattley, Enrique Inigo, Faith Perry, Doris Contreras, Marc Lambert, Stillam Segar, Alicia del Lago, Jose Trowe, Armando Saenz, Ricardo Adalid, Roy Fletcher, John Courier, Mark Zachary, Paul Arnett, Bob Janis
D: James B. Clark
S: Thomas Wakefield Blackburn
SP: Houston Branch
P: Plato A. Skouras

2927. THE LIGHT IN THE FOREST
(Buena Vista, July, 1958)   93 Mins.
(Technicolor)
Fess Parker, Wendell Corey, Joanne Dru, James MacArthur, Carol Lynley, Jessica Tandy, John McIntire, Joseph Calleia, Rafael Campos, Frank Ferguson, Norman Frederic, Marian Seldes, Sam Buffington, Stephen Bekassy
D: Herschel Daugherty
S: Conrad Richter
SP: Lawrence Edward Watkin
P: Walt Disney

2928. WOLF DOG
(Regal Films/TCF, July, 1958)   61 Mins.
Jim Davis, Allison Hayes, Tony Brown, Austin Willis, Don Garrard, Juan Root, B. Braithwaite, Lloyd Chester, Jay MacDonald
D/P: Sam Newfield
SP: Louis Stevens

2929. THE BADLANDERS
(Arcola Pictures Corp./MGM, August 1, 1958)   85 Mins.
(Metrocolor)   (CinemaScope)
Alan Ladd, Ernest Borgnine, Katy Jurado, Claire Kelly, Kent Smith, Nehemiah Persoff, Anthony Caruso, Robert Emhardt, Adam Williams, Ford Rainey, John Day
D: Delmer Daves
S: W. R. Burnett
SP: Richard Collins
P: Aaron Rosenberg

2930. BUCHANAN RIDES ALONE
(Columbia, August 1, 1958)   78 Mins.
(Technicolor)
Randolph Scott, Craig Stevens, Barry Kelley, Tol Avery, Peter Whitney, Manual Rojab, William Leslie, Don C. Harvey, L. Q. Jones, Robert Anderson, Joe De Santis, Jennifer Holden, Nacho Galindo, Roy Jenson, Frank Scannell, Barbara James, Al Wyatt, Terry Frost, Riley Hill, Leo Ogletree, Jim B. Leon
D: Budd Boetticher
S: Charles Lang, Jr. From Jonal Wood's novel "The Name's Buchanan"
P: Harry Joe Brown, Randolph Scott

2931. FLAMING FRONTIER
(Regal Films/20th C. Fox, August 1, 1958)   70 Mins.
(RegalScope)   (Filmed in Canada)
Bruce Bennett, Don Garrard, Jim Davis, Paisley Maxwell, Cecil Linder, Peter Humphreys, Ben Lennick, Larry Sloway, Bill Walsh, Larry Mann, Mike Fitzgerald, Bob Vanstone, Shane Rimmer, Charles Kehoe, Jeffrey Alexander, Brandon Dillon, Daryl Masters, Allen Chrysler, Dave Wright, Elizabeth Beattie
D/P: Sam Newfield
SP: Louis Stevens

2932. WILD HERITAGE
(Universal-International, August 1, 1958)   78 Mins.
(Eastman Color)   (CinemaScope)
Will Rogers, Jr., Maureen O'Sullivan, Rod McKuen, Casey Tibbs, Judy Meredith, George Winslow, Gigi Perreau, Troy Donahue, Gary Gray, Jeanette Nolan, Paul Birch, Stephen Ellsworth, John Beradino, Phil Harvey, Lawrence Dobkin, Stephen Ellsworth, Ingrid Gonde, Guy Wilkerson, Christopher Dark
D: Charles Haas
S: Steve Frazee
SP: Paul King, Joseph Stone
P: John E. Horton

2933. BADMAN'S COUNTRY
(Peerless/Warner Bros., August 2, 1958)   68 Mins.
George Montgomery, Neville Brand, Buster Crabbe, Karin Booth, Gregory Walcott, Malcolm Atterbury, Russell Johnson, Richard Devon, Morris Ankrum, Dan Riss, Lewis Martin, Steve Drexel, Fred Graham, John Harmon, Al Wyatt, Fred Krone, William Bryant, Jack Kinney, Tim Sullivan, LeRoy Johnson, Jack Carol
D: Fred F. Sears
SP: Orville Hampton
P: Robert E. Kent

2934. THE BIG COUNTRY
(World Wide/United Artists, August 15, 1958)   156 Mins.
(Technicolor)   (Technirama)
Gregory Peck, Jean Simmons, Carroll Baker, Charlton Heston, Burl Ives, Charles Bickford, Alfonso Bedoya, Chuck Connors, Chuck Hayward, Bubb Brady, Jim Burk
D: William Wyler
SP: James R. Webb, Sy Bartlett, Robert Wilder
P: Gregory Peck, William Wyler

2935. THE FIEND WHO WALKED THE WEST
(TCF, August 22, 1958)   100 Mins.
(CinemaScope)
Hugh O'Brian, Robert Evans, Dolores Michaels, Linda Cristal, Stephen McNally, Edward Andrews, Ron Ely, Ken Scott, Emile Meyer, Gregory Morton, Shari Lee Bernath, Georgia Simmons
D: Gordon Douglas
S: Eleazar Lipsky
SP: Harry Brown, Philip Yordan
P: Herbert B. Swope, Jr.

2936. APACHE TERRITORY

(Rorvic/Columbia, September, 1958) 75 Mins.

Rory Calhoun, Barbara Bates, John Dehner, Carolyn Craig, Thomas Pittman, Leo Gordon, Myron Healey, Francis de Sales, Frank de Kova, Reg Parton, Bob Woodward, Fred Krone

D: Ray Nazarro

S: Louis L'Amour

SP: Charles R. Marion, George W. George

P: Rory Calhoun, Victor M. Orsatti

2937. ONCE UPON A HORSE

(Universal-International, September, 1958) 85 Mins.

(CinemaScope)

Dan Rowan, Dick Martin, Martha Hyer, Leif Erickson, Nina Talbot, James Gleason, John McGiver, David Burns, Dick Ryan, Max Baer, Buddy Baer, Steve Pendleton, Sydney Chatton, Paul Anderson, and guest stars Tom Keene, Bob Livingston, Kermit Maynard, and Bob Steele

D/SP/P: Hal Kanter

S: Henry Gregor Felsen

2938. RIDE A CROOKED TRAIL

(Universal-International, September, 1958) 87 Mins.

(Eastman Color) (CinemaScope)

Audie Murphy, Gia Scala, Walter Matthau, Henry Silva, Joanna Moore, Eddie Little, Mary Field, Leo Gordon, Mort Mills, Frank Chase, Bill Walker

D: Jesse Hibbs

S: Borden Chase

SP: George Bruce

P: Howard Pine

2939. TERROR IN A TEXAS TOWN

(United Artists, September, 1958) 80 Mins.

Sterling Hayden, Sebastian Cabot, Carol Kelly, Eugene Martin, Ned Young, Victor Millan, Ann Verela, Sheb Wooley, Fred Kohler, Jr., Steve Mitchell, Marilee Earle, Jamie Russell, Tyler McVey, Ted Stanhope, Gil Lamb, Frank Ferguson, Hank Patterson

D: Joseph H. Lewis

SP: Ben L. Perry

P: Frank N. Seltzer

2940. MAN OF THE WEST

(United Artists, October, 1958) 100 Mins.

(DeLuxe Color) (CinemaScope)

Gary Cooper, Julie London, Lee J. Cobb, Arthur O'Connell, Jack Lord, John Dehner, Royal Dano, Robert Wilke, Jack Williams, Guy Wilkerson, Chuck Roberson, Frank Ferguson, Emory Parnell

D: Anthony Mann

S: Will C. Brown

SP: Reginald Rose

P: Walter Mirisch

2941. VILLA!

(20th C. Fox, October, 1958) 72 Mins.

(DeLuxe Color) (CinemaScope)

(Filmed in Mexico)

Brian Keith, Cesar Romero, Margia Dean, Rodolfo Hoyos, Carlos Muzquiz, Marie Navarro, Ben Wright

D: James B. Clark

SP: Louis Vittes

P: Plato A. Skouras

2942. TEN DAYS TO TULARA

(United Artists, November, 1958) 77 Mins.

(Filmed in Mexico)

Sterling Hayden, Grace Raynor, Rodolfo Hoyos, Carlos Muzquiz, Tony Caravajal, Juan Garcia, Rafael Alcayde, Felix Gonzales, Jose Pulido, Major M. Badager, Milton Bernstein, Barry Grail, Paco Arenas

D: George Sherman

SP: Laurence Mascott

P: George Sherman, Clarence Eurist

2943. FRONTIER GUN

(Regal Films/20th C. Fox, December 1, 1958) 70 Mins.

(RegalScope)

John Agar, Joyce Meadows, Barton MacLane, Robert Strauss, Morris Ankrum, James Griffith, Lyn Thomas, Leslie Bradley, Doodles Weaver, Mike Ragan (Holly Bane), Tom Daly, Sammy Ogg, Claire DuBrey, George Brand

D: Paul Landres

SP: Stephen Kandel

P: Richard Lyons

2944. GUNSMOKE IN TUCSON

(Allied Artists, December 7, 1958) 79 Mins.

(DeLuxe Color) (CinemaScope)

Mark Stevens, Forrest Tucker, Gale Robbins, Vaughn Taylor, John Ward, Kevin Hagen, Bill Henry, Richard Reeves, John Cliff, Gail Kobe, George Keymas, Zon Murray, Paul Engle, Anthony Sydes

D: Thomas Carr

S: Paul Leslie Peil

SP: Paul Leslie Peil, Robert Joseph

P: Herbert Kaufman

2945. TONKA

(Buena Vista/Disney, December, 1958) 97 Mins.

(Technicolor)

Sal Mineo, Phil Carey, Jerome Courtland, Rafael Campos, Joy Page, H. N. Wynant, Britt Lomond, Herbert Rudley, Sidney Smith, John War Eagle, Gregg Martell, Slim Pickens, Buzz Henry

D: Lewis Foster
S: "Comanche"—David Appel
SP: Lewis R. Foster, Lillie Hayward
P: James Pratt

FILMS OF 1959

2946. MONEY, WOMEN AND GUNS

(Universal-International, January 2, 1959)
80 Mins.
(Eastman Color) (CinemaScope)
Jock Mahoney, Kim Hunter, Tim Hovey, Gene Evans, Jeffrey Stone, Lon Chaney, Jr., William Campbell, Tom Drake, James Gleason, Judy Meredith, Philip Terry
D: Richard Bartlett
SP: Montgomery Pittman
P: Howie Horowitz

2947. THE SHERIFF OF FRACTURED JAW

(TCF, January 2, 1959) 103 Mins.
(DeLuxe Color) (CinemaScope)
(Made in England)
Kenneth More, Jayne Mansfield, Henry Hull, William Campbell, Bruce Cabot, Robert Morley, Donald Squire, David Horne, Eynon Evans
D: Raoul Walsh
S: Jacob Hay
SP: Arthur Dales
P: Daniel M. Angel

2948. GOOD DAY FOR A HANGING

(Columbia, January 10, 1959) 85 Mins.
(Eastman Color)
Fred MacMurray, Maggie Hayes, Robert Vaughn, Joan Blackman, James Drury, Wendell Holmes, Edmon Ryan, Stacy Harris, Kathryn Card, Emile Meyer, Bing Russell, Russell Thorson, Denver Pyle, Phil Chambers, Howard McVear, Rusty Swope, Harry Lauter, Greg Barton, Michael Garth
D: Nathan Juran
SP: Daniel B. Ullman
P: Charles H. Schneer

2949. ZORRO RIDES AGAIN

(Republic, January 16, 1959) 68 Mins.
(Feature version of the 1937 serial)
John Carroll, Helen Christian, Reed Howes, Duncan Renaldo, Noah Beery, Richard Alexander, Robert Kortman, Paul Lopez, Jack Ingram, Roger Williams, Mona Rico, Jerry Frank, Yakima Canutt, Edmund Cobb, Tom London, Harry Strang (See 1937 listing for additional cast)
D: William Witney, John English
S: Based on the character created by Johnston McCulley
SP: Barry Shipman, John Rathmell, Franklyn Adreon, Ronald Davidson, Morgan B. Cox
AP: Sol C. Siegel

2950. ESCORT WEST

(Romina/United Artists, January 23, 1959)
75 Mins.
(CinemaScope)
Victor Mature, Elaine Stewart, Faith Domergue, Reba Waters, Noah Beery, Jr., Leo Gordon, Rex Ingram, John Hubbard, Harry Carey, Jr., Slim Pickens, Roy Barcroft, William Ching
D: Francis D. Lyon
S: Steven Hayes
SP: Lee Gordon, Fred Hartsook
P: Robert E. Morrison, Nate H. Edwards

2951. PLUNDERERS OF PAINTED FLATS

(Republic, January 23, 1959) 77 Mins.
(Naturama)
Corinne Calvet, John Carroll, Skip Homeier, George Macready, Edmund Lowe, Bea Benaderet, Madge Kennedy, Joe Besser, Allan Lurie, Candy Candido, Ricky Allen, Herb Vigran, Bob Kline, Burt Topper, William Foster, Lee Redman, Roy Gordon, Wade Lane, David Waldor, John Kidd
D: Albert C. Gannaway
SP: Phil Shuken, John Greene
P: Albert C. Gannaway

2952. NO NAME ON THE BULLET

(Universal-International, February 1, 1959)
77 Mins.
(Eastman Color)
Audie Murphy, Charles Drake, Joan Evans, Virginia Grey, Warren Stevens, R. G. Armstrong, Willis Bouchey, Edgar Stehli, Simon Scott, Karl Swanson, Whit Bissell, Charles Watts
D: Jack Arnold
S: Howard Amacker
SP: Gene L. Coon
P: Howard Christie

2953. THESE THOUSAND HILLS

(TCF, February 1, 1959) 96 Mins.
(DeLuxe Color) (CinemaScope)

Ride Lonesome (Columbia, 1959) — Randolph Scott, Lee Marvin, and Donna Reed

Don Murray, Richard Egan, Lee Remick, Patricia Owens, Stuart Whitman, Albert Dekker, Harold J. Stone, Royal Dano, Jean Willes, Douglas Fowley, Fuzzy Knight, Robert Adler, Barbara Morrison, Ned Wever, song by Randy Sparks
D: Richard Fleischer
S: A. B. Guthrie, Jr.
SP: Alfred Hayes
P: David Weisbart

2954. RIDE LONESOME
(Columbia, February 15, 1959)   75 Mins.
(Eastman Color)   (CinemaScope)
Randolph Scott, Karen Steele, Pernell Roberts, James Best, Lee Van Cleef, James Coburn, Duke Johnson, Boyd Stockman, Roy Jenson, Boyd "Red" Morgan, Bennie Dobbins, Lee Marvin, Donna Reed
D: Budd Boetticher
SP: Burt Kennedy
P: Harry Joe Brown, Randolph Scott

2955. THE HANGING TREE
(Warner Bros., February 21, 1959)   106 Mins.
(Technicolor)
Gary Cooper, Maria Schell, Karl Malden, George

C. Scott, Karl Swenson, Virginia Gregg, John Dierkes, King Donovan, Ben Piazza
D: Delmer Daves
S: Dorothy M. Johnson
SP: Wendell Mayes, Halsted Wells
P: Martin Jurow, Richard Shepherd

2956. GUNMEN FROM LAREDO
(Columbia, March 1, 1959)   67 Mins.
(Columbia Color)
Robert Knapp, Jana Davi, Walter Coy, Paul Birch, Don C. Harvey, Clarence Straight, Jerry Barclay, Ron Hayes, Charles Horvath, Jean Moorehead, X. Brands, Harry Antrim
D: Wallace MacDonald
SP: Clark E. Reynolds
P: Wallace MacDonald

2957. LONE TEXAN
(20th C. Fox, March 1, 1959)   70 Mins.
(RegalScope)
Willard Parker, Grant Williams, Audrey Dalton, Douglas Kennedy, June Blair, Dabbs Greer, Barbara Heller
D: Paul Landres
S: James Landis

SP: James Landis, Jack Thomas
P: Jack Leewood

2958. MUSTANG

(United Artists, March 15, 1959)   73 Mins.
Jack Buetel, Madalyn Trahey, Steve Keyes, Milt Swift, Autum Moon
D: Peter Stephens
SP: Tom Gries
P: Robert Arnell

2959. ALIAS JESSE JAMES

(United Artists, April 2, 1959)   92 Mins.
(DeLuxe Color)
Bob Hope, Rhonda Fleming, Wendell Corey, Jim Davis, Gloria Talbot, Will Wright, Mary Young
D: Norman McLeod
S: Robert St. Aubrey, Bert Lawrence
SP: D. D. Beauchamp, William Bowers
P: Jack Hope

2960. RIO BRAVO

(Armada/Warner Bros., April 4, 1959)   141 Mins.
(Technicolor)
John Wayne, Dean Martin, Ricky Nelson, Angie Dickinson, Walter Brennan, Ward Bond, John Russell, Pedro Gonzales-Gonzales, Estelita Rodriguez, Claude Akins, Malcolm Atterbury, Harry Carey, Jr., Bob Steele, Bing Russell, Myron Healey, Eugene Iglesias, Fred Graham, Tom Monroe, Riley Hill
D: Howard Hawks
S: B. H. McCampbell
SP: Leigh Brackett, Jules Furthman
P: Howard Hawks

2961. WARLOCK

(20th C. Fox, April 15, 1959)   121 Mins.
(Technicolor)   (CinemaScope)
Richard Widmark, Henry Fonda, Anthony Quinn, Dorothy Malone, Dolores Michaels, Wallace Ford, Tom Drake, Richard Arlen, DeForest Kelley, Regis Toomey, Vaughn Taylor, Don Beddoe, Whit Bissell, Bartlett Robinson, J. Anthony Hughes, Donald Barry, Frank Gorshin, Ian Mac-Donald, Stan Kamber, Paul Comi, L. Q. Jones, Mickey Simpson, Robert Osterloh, James Philbrook, David Garcia, Robert Adler
D/P: Edward Dmytryk
SP: Robert Alan Arthur

2962. WESTBOUND

(Warner Bros., April 25, 1959)   96 Mins.
(WarnerColor)
Randolph Scott, Virginia Mayo, Karen Steele, Michael Dante, Andrew Duggan, Michael Pate, Wally Brown, John Day, Walter Barnes, Fred Sherman, Mack Williams, Ed Prentiss, Rory Mallinson, Rudi Dana, Tom Monroe, Jack Perrin, Buddy Roosevelt, Kermit Maynard, May Boss, William A. Green, Jack E. Henderson, Felice Richmond, Creighton Hale, Gertrude Keeler, Walter Reed, Jack C. Williams, Gerald Roberts, John Hudkins, Don Happy, Bobby Herron, Fred Stromscoe
D: Budd Boetticher
S: Berne Giler, Albert Shelby LeVino
SP: Berne Giler
P: Henry Blanke

2963. FACE OF A FUGITIVE

(Columbia, May 1, 1959)   81 Mins.
(Eastman Color)
Fred MacMurray, Lin McCarthy, Dorothy Green, Alan Baxter, Myrna Fahey, James Coburn, Francis de Sales, Gina Gillespie, Ron Hayes, Paul E. Burns, Buzz Henry, John Milford, James Gavin, Hal K. Dawson, Stanley Farrar, Rankin Mansfield, Harrison Lewis
D: Paul Wendkos
S: "Long Gone"—Peter Dawson
SP: David T. Chantler, Daniel B. Ullman
P: David Heilwell

2964. THE SAD HORSE

(20th C. Fox, May 1, 1959)   78 Mins.
(DeLuxe Color)
David Ladd, Chill Wills, Rex Reason, Patrice Wymore, Gregg Palmer
D: James B. Clark
S: Zoe Atkins
SP: Charles Hoffman
P: Richard E. Lyons

2965. THUNDER IN THE SUN

(Paramount, May 1, 1959)   81 Mins.
(Eastman Color)
Susan Hayward, Jeff Chandler, Jacques Bergerac, Blanche Yurka, Carl Esmond, Fortunio Bonanova, Felix Locher
D: Russell Rouse
S: Guy Trosper, James Hill
SP: Russell Rouse
P: Clarence Greene

2966. THE WILD AND THE INNOCENT

(Universal-International, May 1, 1959)   84 Mins.
(Eastman Color)
Audie Murphy, Joanne Dru, Gilbert Roland, Jim Backus, Sandra Dee, George Mitchell, Peter Brack, Strother Martin, Wesley Marie Tackett, Betty Harford, Mel Leonard, Lillian Adams, Val Benedict
D: Jack Shor
SP/P: Sy Gomberg

The Gunfight at Dodge City (Mirisch/United Artists, 1959) — Joel McCrea and Julia Adams

2967. THE YOUNG LAND

(Columbia, May 1, 1959)   89 Mins.

(Technicolor)

Pat Wayne, Yvonne Craig, Dennis Hopper, Dan O'Herlihy, Roberto de la Madrid, Cliff Ketchum, Ken Curtis, Pedro Gonzales-Gonzales, Edward Sweeney, Miguel Camacho, Randy Sparks

D: Ted Tetzlaff

SP: Norman Shannon Hall

P: Patrick Ford, C. V. Whitney

2968. BORN RECKLESS

(Warner Bros., May 9, 1959)   79 Mins.

Mamie Van Doren, Jeff Richards, Arthur Hunnicutt, Carol Ohmart, Tom Duggan, Tex Williams, Donald Barry, Nacho Galindo, Orlando Rodriguez

D: Howard Koch

S: Richard Landau

SP: Richard Landau, Aubrey Schenck

P: Aubrey Schenck

2969. THE GUNFIGHT AT DODGE CITY

(Mirisch/United Artists, May 16, 1959)   81 Mins.

(DeLuxe Color)   (CinemaScope)

Joel McCrea, Julia Adams, John McIntire, Nancy Gates, Richard Anderson, Jim Westerfield, Walter Coy, Don Haggerty, Wright King, Harry Lauter, Myron Healey, Mauritz Hugo, Henry Kulky

D: Joseph M. Newman

SP: Daniel B. Ullman, Martin M. Goldsmith

P: Walter Mirisch

2970. KING OF THE WILD STALLIONS

(Allied Artists, May 17, 1959)   75 Mins.

(DeLuxe Color)   (CinemaScope)

George Montgomery, Diane Brewster, Edgar Buchanan, Emile Meyer, Jerry Hartleben, Byron Foulger, Denver Pyle, Dan Sheridan, Rory Mallison

D: R. G. Springsteen

SP: Ford Beebe

P: Ben Schwalb

2971. THE HORSE SOLDIERS

(Mirisch Company/United Artists, June 12, 1959)   119 Mins.

(DeLuxe Color)

John Wayne, William Holden, Constance Towers, Althea Gibson, Hoot Gibson, Anna Lee, Russell

Simpson, Stan Jones, Carleton Young, Basil Ruysdael, Willis Bouchey, Ken Curtis, O. Z. Whitehead, Judson Pratt, Denver Pyle, Strother Martin, Hank Worden, Walter Reed, Jack Pennick, Fred Graham, Chuck Hayward, Charles Seel, Stuart Holmes, Major Sam Harris, Richard Cutting, Bing Russell, William Leslie, Ron Haggerty
D: John Ford
S: Harold Sinclair
SP: John Lee Mahin, Martin Rackin
P: John Lee Mahin, Martin Rackin

2972. THE HANGMAN

(Paramount, June 17, 1959) 86 Mins.
Robert Taylor, Fess Parker, Tina Louise, Jack Lord, Shirley Harmer, Mickey Shaughnessey, Gene Evans
D: Michael Curtiz
SP: Dudley Nichols
P: Frank Freeman, Jr.

2973. GHOST OF ZORRO

(Republic, June 30, 1959) 69 Mins.
(Feature version of 1949 serial)
Clayton Moore, Pamela Blake, Roy Barcroft, George J. Lewis, I. Stanford Jolley, Steve Clark, Marshall Reed, Jack O'Shea, Steve Darrell, John Crawford (See 1949 credits for further cast players)
D: Fred C. Brannon
SP: Royal Cole, William Lively, Sol Shor
AP: Franklyn Adreon

2974. LEGEND OF TOM DOOLEY

(Columbia, July 24, 1959) 79 Mins.
Michael Landon, Jo Morrow, Jack Hogan, Richard Rust, Dee Pollack, Ken Lynch, Howard Wright, Ralph Moody, John Cliff
D: Ted Post
SP/P: Stan Shpetner

2975. CAST A LONG SHADOW

(Mirisch/United Artists, July 27, 1959) 82 Mins.
Audie Murphy, Terry Moore, John Dehner, James Best, Rita Flynn, Denver Pyle, Ann Doran, Stach B. Harris, Robert Foulk, Wright King
D: Thomas Carr
S: Wayne D. Overholser
SP: Martin G. Goldsmith, John McGreevey
P: Walter Mirisch

2976. THE MIRACLE OF THE HILLS

(20th C. Fox, July 27, 1959) 73 Mins.
(CinemaScope)
Rex Reason, Theona Bryant, Jay North, Gilbert Smith, Tracy Stratford, Gene Roth, I. Stanford Jolley, Gene Collins, Kelton Garwood, Paul Wexler, Kenneth Mayer, June Vincent, Pat O'Hara,
Tom Daly, Cecil Elliott, Charles Arnt, Claire Carleton, Nan Leslie, Betty Lou Gerson, Vince Townsend, Jr.
D: Paul Landres
SP: Charles Hoffman
P: Richard E. Lyons (Earle Lyons)

2977. LAST TRAIN FROM GUN HILL

(Paramount, July 27, 1959) 94 Mins.
(Technicolor) (VistaVision)
Kirk Douglas, Anthony Quinn, Carolyn Jones, Earl Holliman, Brad Dexter, Brian Hutton, Ziva Rodann, Bing Russell, Val Avery, Walter Sande
D: John Sturges
S: Les Crutchfield
SP: James Poe
P: Hal Wallis

2978. DAY OF THE OUTLAW

(United Artists, July 27, 1959) 90 Mins.
Robert Ryan, Burl Ives, Tina Louise, Alan Marshall, Nehemiah Persoff, Venetia Stevenson, Donald Elson, Helen Westcott, Robert Cornthwaite, Jack Lambert, Lance Fuller, Frank de Kova, Paul Wexler, Jack Woody, David Nelson, Arthur Space, William Schallert, Michael McGreevy, Dabbs Greer, Betty Jones Moreland, Elisha Cook, Jr., Dan Sheridan, George Ross
D: Andre de Toth
SP: Philip Yordan
P: Sidney Harmon

2979. THE OREGON TRAIL

(20th C. Fox, September 1, 1959) 86 Mins.
(DeLuxe Color) (CinemaScope)
Fred MacMurray, William Bishop, Nina Shipman, Gloria Talbot, Henry Hull, John Carradine, Addison Richards, Lumsden Hare, Ollie O'Toole, Elizabeth Patterson, James Bell, C. N. Fowler, Tex Terry, John Dierkes, John Sanford, Ed Wright, Oscar Beregi, Avo Ojala
D: Gene Fowler, Jr.
SP: Gene Fowler, Jr., Louis Vittes
P: Richard Einfeld

2980. YELLOWSTONE KELLY

(Warner Bros., September 5, 1959) 91 Mins.
(Technicolor)
Clint Walker, Edward Byrnes, John Russell, Ray Danton, Claude Akins, Rhodes (Rex) Reason, Andra Martin, Gary Vinson, Warren Oates
D: Gordon Douglas
S: Clay Fisher
SP: Burt Kennedy

2981. THE WONDERFUL COUNTRY
(DRM Productions/United Artists, October 8, 1959)
96 Mins.
(Technicolor)
Robert Mitchum, Julie London, Gary Merrill, Pedro Armendariz, Jack Oakie, Albert Dekker, Charles McGraw, Leroy "Satchel" Paige, Victor Mendoza, Tom Lea
D: Robert Parrish
S: Tom Lea
SP: Robert Ardrey
P: Chester Erskine

2982. THE JAYHAWKERS
(Paramount, October 15, 1959)   100 Mins.
(Technicolor)
Jeff Chandler, Fess Parker, Nicole Maurey, Henry Silva, Herbert Rudley, Jimmy Carter, Shari Lee Bernath, Leo Gordon
D: Melvin Frank
SP: Melvin Frank, Joseph Petracca, Frank Fenton, A. I. Bezzerides
P: Norman Panama, Melvin Frank

2983. THE SAGA OF HEMP BROWN
(Universal-International, October, 1959)   80 Mins.
(Eastman Color)
Rory Calhoun, Beverly Garland, John Lorch, Russell Johnson, Fortunio Bonanova, Allan Lane, Trevor Bardette, Morris Ankrum, Addison Richards, Victor Sen Yung, Theodore Newton, Francis McDonald
D: Richard Carlson
S: Bernard Girard
SP: Bob Williams
P: Gordon Kay

2984. THEY CAME TO CORDURA
(Columbia, October, 1959)   123 Mins.
(Eastman Color)   (CinemaScope)
Gary Cooper, Rita Hayworth, Van Heflin, Tab Hunter, Richard Conte, Michael Callan, Dick York, Robert Keith, Cesar Romero, Jim Bannon, Edward Platt, Maurice Jara, Sam Buffington, Arthur Hanson
D: Robert Rossen
S: Glendon Swarthout
SP: Ivan Moffat, Robert Rossen
P: William Goetz

They Came to Cordura
(Columbia,   1959)
— Rita Hayworth
and Gary Cooper

FILMS OF 1960

[Films are listed in order of release. This is the beginning of the period when most films carried no national release date. From this point on the release order was determined by the month the producer/distributor made the film available combined with the numbers assigned by National Screen Service.]

2985. GUNFIGHTERS OF ABILENE

(United Artists, January, 1960)   67 Mins.
Buster Crabbe, Barton MacLane, Judith Ames, Russell Thorson, Lee Farr, Eugenia Paul, Jan Arvan, Richard Devon, Arthur Space, Kenneth MacDonald, Richard Cutting, Hank Patterson, Reed Howes
D: Edward L. Cahn
SP: Orville Hampton
P: Robert E. Kent

2986. FOUR FAST GUNS

(Universal-International, February, 1960)   72 Mins.
(CinemaScope)
James Craig, Martha Vickers, Edgar Buchanan, Brett Halsey, Paul Richards, Blu Wright, Richard Martin, John Swift, Paul Raymond
D: William J. Hole, Jr.
SP: James Edmiston, Dallas Gaultois
P: William J. Hole, Jr.

2987. HELL BENT FOR LEATHER

(Universal-International, February, 1960)   82 Mins.
(Eastman Color)   (CinemaScope)
Audie Murphy, Felicia Farr, Stephen McNally, Robert Middleton, Rad Fulton, Jan Merlin, Herbert Rudley, Malcolm Atterbury, Joseph Ruskin, Allan Lane, John Qualen, Eddie Little Sky, Steve Gravers, Beau Gentry, Bob Steele
D: George Sherman
S: Ray Hogan
SP: Christopher Knopf
P: Gordon Kay

2988. OKLAHOMA TERRITORY

(United Artists, March, 1960)   67 Mins.
Bill Williams, Gloria Talbott, Ted de Corsia, Grant Richards, Walter Sande, X. Brands, Walter Baldwin, Grandon Rhodes
D: Edward L. Cahn
SP: Orville Hampton
P: Robert E. Kent

2989. COMANCHE STATION

(Columbia, March, 1960)   74 Mins.
(Eastman Color)   (CinemaScope)
Randolph Scott, Nancy Gates, Claude Akins, Skip Homeier, Richard Rust, Rand Brooks, Dyke Johnson, Foster Hood, Joe Molina, Vince St. Cyr, Paul Holland
D: Budd Boetticher
SP: Burt Kennedy
P: Harry Joe Brown, Budd Boetticher

2990. GUNS OF THE TIMBERLAND

(Warner Bros., March 5, 1960)   91 Mins.
(Technicolor)
Alan Ladd, Jeanne Crain, Gilbert Roland, Frankie Avalon, Lyle Bettger, Noah Beery, Jr., Verna Felton, Alana Ladd, Regis Toomey, Johnny Seven, George Selk, Paul E. Burns, Henry Kulky
D: Robert D. Webb
S: Louis L'Amour
SP: Joseph Petracca
P: Aaron Spelling

2991. HELLER IN PINK TIGHTS

(Paramount, March, 1960)   100 Mins.
(Technicolor)
Sophia Loren, Anthony Quinn, Margaret O'Brien, Steve Forrest, Eileen Heckart, Edmund Lowe, Ramon Navarro
D: George Cukor
S: "Heller with a Gun"—Louis L'Amour
SP: Dudley Nichols, Walter Bernstein
P: Carlo Ponti, Marcello Girosi

2992. 13 FIGHTING MEN

(20th C. Fox, April, 1960)   69 Mins.
(CinemaScope)
Grant Williams, Brad Dexter, Carole Matthews, Robert Dix, Richard Garland, Rayford Barnes, John Erwin, Richard Crane, Rex Holman, Bob Palmer, Mauritz Hugo, Dick Monohan, Ted Knight, Fred Kohler, Jr., Stephen Ferry, I. Stanford Jolley, Walter Reed, John Merrick, Mark Hickman, Ford Dunhill, Brad Harris, Earl Holmes, Bill Browne, Jerry Mobley
D: Harry Gerstad
SP: Robert Hammer, Jack Thomas
P: Jack Leewood

2993. THE UNFORGIVEN

(United Artists, April, 1960)   125 Mins.
(Technicolor)   (PanaVision)
Burt Lancaster, Audrey Hepburn, Audie Murphy, John Saxon, Charles Bickford, Lillian Gish, Albert

Salmi, Joseph Wiseman, Kipp Hamilton, Arnold Merritt, Carlos Riva, Doug McClure
D: John Huston
S: Alan LeMay
SP: Ben Maddow
P: James Hill

2994. NOOSE FOR A GUNMAN
(United Artists, May, 1960) 69 Mins.
Jim Davis, Lyn Thomas, Ted de Corsia, Walter Sande, Barton MacLane, Harry Carey, Jr., Lane Chandler, John Hart, Leo Gordon, William Tannen, Jan Arvan, Bob Tetrick, William Remick, Kermit Maynard, William Challee, Cecil Weston
D: Edward L. Cahn
SP: Robert B. Gordon
P: Robert E. Kent

2995. SERGEANT RUTLEDGE
(Warner Bros., May 18, 1960) 111 Mins.
(Technicolor)
Jeffrey Hunter, Constance Towers, Billie Burke, Woodie Strode, Juano Hernandez, Willis Bouchey, Carleton Young, Judson Pratt, Bill Henry, Walter Reed, Chuck Hayward, Mae Marsh, Fred Libby, Toby Richards, Jan Style, Cliff Lyons, Charles Seel, Shug Fisher, Jack Pennick, Hank Worden, Chuck Roberson, Eva Novak, Estelle Winwood
D: John Ford
SP: James Warner Bellah, Willis Goldbeck
P: Willis Goldbeck, Patrick Ford

2996. THE SIGN OF ZORRO
(Buena Vista, June, 1960) 91 Mins.
Guy Williams, Henry Calvin, Gene Sheldon, Romney Brent, Britt Lomond, George J. Lewis, Tony Russo, Jan Arvan, Than Wyenn, Lisa Gaye, John Dehner
D: Norman Foster, Lewis R. Foster
S: Johnston McCulley
SP: Norman Foster, Bob Wehling, Lowell S. Hawley, John Meredyth Lucas
P: William H. Anderson
(Assembled from Episodes 1-13 of the television series)

2997. WALK LIKE A DRAGON
(Paramount, June, 1960) 95 Mins.
Jack Lord, Nobu McCarthy, James Shigeta, Mel Torme, Josephine Hutchinson, Rudolfo Acosta, Benson Fong, Michael Pate, Lilyan Chauvin, Don Kennedy, Donald Barry, Natalie Trundy
D: James Clavell
SP: James Clavell, Daniel Mainwaring
P: James Clavell

2998. YOUNG JESSE JAMES
(20th C. Fox, August, 1960) 73 Mins.
(CinemaScope)
Ray Stricklyn, Willard Parker, Merry Anders, Robert Dix, Emile Meyer, Jacklyn O'Neill, Leslie Bradley, Norman Leavitt, Lee Kindall
D: William Claxton
SP: Orville H. Hampton, Jerry Sackheim
P: Jack Leewood

2999. FOR THE LOVE OF MIKE
(20th C. Fox, August, 1960) 84 Mins.
(DeLuxe Color) (CinemaScope)
Richard Basehart, Stu Erwin, Arthur Shields, Armando Silvestre, Elsa Cardenas, Michael Steckler, Rex Allen, Danny Bravo
D/P: George Sherman
SP: D. D. Beauchamp

3000. ONE FOOT IN HELL
(20th C. Fox, August, 1960) 90 Mins.
(DeLuxe Color) (CinemaScope)
Alan Ladd, Don Murray, Dan O'Herlihy, Dolores Michaels, Barry Cox, Larry Gates, Karl Swenson, John Alexander, Rachel Stephens, Henry Norell, Harry Carter, Ann Morriss
D: James B. Clark
S/SP: Aaron Spelling
P: Sidney Boehm

3001. FIVE BOLD WOMEN
(Citation, August, 1960) 82 Mins.
(Eastman Color)
Jeff Morrow, Merry Anders, Jim Ross, Guinn "Big Boy" Williams, Irish McCalla, Kathy Marlowe, Lucita Blain, Dee Carroll, Robert Caffey, George Kramer
D: Jorge Lopez-Portillo
S/SP: Mortimer Braus, Jack Pollexfen
P: Jim Ross, Glenn H. McCarthy

3002. SEVEN WAYS FROM SUNDOWN
(Universal-International, September, 1960) 86 Mins.
(Eastman Color)
Audie Murphy, Barry Sullivan, Venetia Stevenson, John McIntire, Kenneth Tobie, Mary Field, Teddy Rooney, Suzanne Lloyd, Ken Lynch, Wade Ramsey, Don Collier, Jack Kruschen, Claudia Barrett, Don Haggerty, Robert Burton, Fred Graham, Dale Van Sickel
S/SP: Clair Huffaker
P: Gordon Kay
D: Harry Keller

Seven Ways from Sundown (Universal-International, 1960) — Audie Murphy and John McIntire

3003. WALK TALL
(20th C. Fox,-September, 1960) 60 Mins.
(DeLuxe Color) (CinemaScope)
Willard Parker, Joyce Meadows, Kent Taylor
D/P: Maury Dexter

3004. THE MAGNIFICENT SEVEN
(United Artists, October, 1960) 126 Mins.
(DeLuxe Color) (CinemaScope)
Yul Brynner, Eli Wallach, Steve McQueen, Horst Buchholz, Charles Bronson, Robert Vaughn, Brad Dexter, James Coburn, Vladimir Sokoloff, Rosenda Monterosa, Jorge Martinez de Hoyos
D: John Sturges
SP: William Roberts
P: John Sturges, Walter Mirisch

3005. THE ALAMO
(United Artists, October 24, 1960) 190 Mins.
(Technicolor) (Todd-AO)
John Wayne, Richard Widmark, Laurence Harvey, Richard Boone, Carlos Arruza, Frankie Avalon, Patrick Wayne, Linda Cristal, Joan O'Brien, Chill Wills, Joseph Calleia, Ken Curtis, Hank Worden, Denver Pyle, Aissa Wayne, Julian Trevino, Jester Hairston, Veda Ann Borg, Olive Carey, Wesley Lau, Tom Hennesy, Cy Malis, Carol Baxter, John Dierkes, Bill Henry, Rojelio Estrada, Guinn "Big Boy" Williams, Fred Graham, Le Jeanne Guye, Bill Daniel, Chuck Roberson, Ruben Padilla, Red Morgan
D/P: John Wayne
SP: James Edward Grant

3006. TEN WHO DARED
(Buena Vista, November, 1960) 92 Mins.
(Technicolor)
Brian Keith, John Beal, James Drury, R. G. Armstrong, L. Q. Jones, David Stollery, Ben Johnson, Dan Sheridan, Stan Jones, David Frankham
D: William Beaudine
S: Major John Wesley Powell
SP: Lawrence Edward Watkin
P: Walt Disney

3007. DALTON THAT GOT AWAY
(Dalton Film Co., November 2, 1960) 69 Mins.
Michael Connors, Elsie Cardenas (Elsa Cardenas), Carlos Rivas, Felix Moreno, Zachary Milton, Stilman Segar, George Russell, Reed Howes, Francisco Reynolds, Quinton Bulnes, Sam Murphy, Arlene King
D: Jimmy Salvador
S/SP: E. L. Erwin
P: Henri A. Lube

3008. NORTH TO ALASKA
(20th C. Fox, November 7, 1960)   122 Mins.
(DeLuxe Color)   (CinemaScope)
John Wayne, Stewart Granger, Ernie Kovaks, Fabian, Capucine, Mickey Shaughnessy, Karl Swenson, Jr., Joe Sawyer, Kathleen Freeman, John Qualen, Stanley Adams, Stephen Courtleigh, Douglas Dick, Jerry O'Sullivan, Ollie O'Toole, Tudor Owen, Lilyan Chauvin, Marcel Hillaire, Richard Deacon, James Griffith, Max Hellinger, Richard Collier, Fortune Gordien, Roy Jensen, Charles Seel, Esther Dale, Rayford Barnes, Fred Graham, Alan Carney, Peter Bourne, Tom Dillon, Arlene Harris, Paul Maxey, Oscar Beregi, Johnny Lee, Kermit Maynard, Pamela Raymond, Maurice Delamore, Patty Wharton
D/P: Henry Hathaway
SP: John Lee Mahin, Martin Rackin, Claude Binyon
S: Laszlo Fodor (from an idea by John Kafka)

3009. THE PLUNDERERS
(Allied Artists, November, 1960)   94 Mins.
Jeff Chandler, John Saxon, Dolores Hart, Marsha Hunt, Jay C. Flippen, Ray Stricklyn, James Westerfield, Dee Pollack, Roger Torrey, Harvey Stephens, Vaughn Taylor, Joseph Hamilton, Ray Farrell, William Challee, Ken Patterson, Ella Ethridge
D: Joseph Pevney
SP: Bob Barbash
P: Lindsley Parsons

3010. CIMARRON
(MGM, December 8, 1960)   147 Mins.
(Metrocolor)   (CinemaScope)
Glenn Ford, Maria Schell, Anne Baxter, Arthur O'Connell, Russ Tamblyn, Mercedes McCambridge, Vic Morrow, Robert Keith, Charles McGraw, Henry (Harry) Morgan, David Opatoshu, Aline MacMahon, Lili Darvas, Edgar Buchanan, Mary Wickes, Royal Dano, L. Q. Jones, George Brenlin, Vladimir Sokoloff, Ivan Tissault, John Cason, Dawn Little Sky, Eddie Little Sky
D: Anthony Mann
S: Edna Ferber
SP: Arnold Schulman
P: Edmund Grainger

3011. FLAMING STAR
(20th C. Fox, December, 1960)   101 Mins.
(DeLuxe Color)   (CinemaScope)
Elvis Presley, Barbara Eden, Steve Forrest, Dolores Del Rio, John McIntire, Rudolfo Acosta, Karl Swensen, Ford Rainey, Richard Jaeckel, Anne Benton, L. Q. Jones, Douglas Dick, Tom Reese
D: Don Siegel
S: Clair Huffaker
SP: Clair Huffaker, Nunnally Johnson
P: David Weisbart

3012. ZORRO THE AVENGER
(Walt Disney/Buena Vista, 1960)   97 Mins.
Guy Williams, Henry Calvin, Gene Sheldon, Don Diamond, George J. Lewis, Jay Novello, Ralph Clanton, Henry Rowland, Michael Pate, Charles Korvin
D: Charles Barton
SP: Lowell S. Hawley, Bob Wehling. Based on the *Zorro* stories by Johnston McCulley
P: William H. Anderson
(Assembled from Episodes 27-39 of the television series)

FILMS OF 1961

3013. FIVE GUNS TO TOMBSTONE
(United Artists, January 7, 1961)   71 Mins.
James Brown, John Wilder, Walter Coy, Robert Karnes, Joe Haworth, Quent Sondergaard, Boyd Morgan, Jon Locke, Della Sherman, Gregg Palmer, Willis Bouchey, John Eldredge, Jeff DeBenning, Brad Trumbull, Willis Robards, Jerry Todd, Boyd Stockman, Al Wyatt, Bob Woodward
D: Edward L. Chan
S: Arthur Orloff
SP: Richard Schayer
P: Robert E. Kent

3014. THE LONG ROPE
(20th C. Fox, February, 1961)   61 Mins.
(CinemaScope)
Hugh Marlowe, Alan Hale, Jr., Robert Wilke, John Alonzo, Lisa Montell, Madaleine Holmes, David Renard, Jeffrey Morris, Chris Robinson
D: William Witney
SP: Robert Hamner
P: Margia Dean

3015. THE MISFITS
(United Artists, February 4, 1961)   124 Mins.
Clark Gable, Marilyn Monroe, Montgomery Clift, Thelma Ritter, Eli Wallach, James Barton, Estelle Winwood, Kevin McCarthy, Dennis Shaw, Philip Mitchell, Walter Ramage, Peggy Barton, J. Lewis Smith, Marietta Tree, Bobby LaSalle, Ryall Bowker, Ralph Roberts, Rex Bell
D: John Huston
SP: Arthur Miller
P: Frank E. Taylor

3016. GOLD OF THE SEVEN SAINTS

(Warner Bros., February 18, 1961) 88 Mins.
(WarnerScope)

Clint Walker, Roger Moore, Leticia Roman, Robert Middleton, Chill Wills, Gene Evans, Roberto Contreras, Jack C. Williams, Art Stewart

D: Gordon Douglas
S: Steve Frazee
SP: Leigh Brackett, Leonard Freeman
P: Leonard Freeman

3017. THE CANADIANS

(20th C. Fox, February, 1961) 85 Mins.
(DeLuxe Color) (CinemaScope)
(Filmed in Canada)

Robert Ryan, John Dehner, Torin Thatcher, Burt Metcalfe, John Sutton, Jack Creley, Scott Peters, Richard Alden, Terese Stratas

D/SP: Burt Kennedy
P: Herman E. Webber

3018. FRONTIER UPRISING

(United Artists, March, 1961) 60 Mins.

Jim Davis, Nancy Hadley, Ken Mayer, Nestor Paiva, Don O'Kelly, Stuart Randall, David Renard, John Marshall, Eugene Iglesias, Renata Vanni, Tudor Owen, Addison Richards, Herman Rudin, Jan Arvan, Norman Pabst, Allen Ray, Dina Caesar, Sid Kane, Barbara Mansell

D: Edward L. Cahn
S: George Bruce
SP: Owen Harris
P: Robert E. Kent

3019. TOMBOY AND THE CHAMP

(Universal-International, April, 1961) 92 Mins.
(Eastman Color)

Candy Moore, Ben Johnson, Jesse White, Jess Kilpatrick, Christine Smith, Paul Bernath, Norman Sherry, John Carpenter, Wally Phillips, Ralph Fischer, Larry Hickie, Rex Allen, Casey Tibbs, Jerry Naill

D: Francis D. Lyon
S: Tommy Reynolds, William Lightfoot
SP: Virginia M. Cooke
P: Tommy Reynolds, William Lightfoot

3020. ONE-EYED JACKS

(Paramount, May, 1961) 141 Mins.
(Technicolor) (VistaVision) (Filmed in Mexico)

Marlon Brando, Karl Malden, Pina Pellicer, Katy Jurado, Ben Johnson, Slim Pickens, Larry Duncan, Sam Gilman, Timothy Carey, Miriam Colon, Elisha Cook, Jr., Rudolph Acosta, Ray Teal, John Dierkes, Margarita Cordova, Hank Worden, Nina Martinez

D: Marlon Brando
S: "The Authentic Death of Hendry Jones"— Charles Neider
SP: Guy Trosper, Calder Willingham
P: Frank P. Rosenberg

3021. POSSE FROM HELL

(Universal-International, May, 1961) 89 Mins.
(Eastman Color)

Audie Murphy, John Saxon, Zohra Lampert, Vic Morrow, Robert Keith, Ward Ramsey, Rudolph Acosta, Royal Dano, Frank Overton, James Bell, Paul Carr, Lee Van Cleef, Ray Teal, Forrest Lewis, Charles Horvath, Harry Lauter, Henry Wills, Stuart Randall, Allan Lane

D: Herbert Coleman
S/SP: Clair Huffaker
P: Gordon Kay

3022. THE GAMBLER WORE A GUN

(United Artists, May, 1961) 66 Mins.

Jim Davis, Mark Allen, Addison Richards, Merry Anders, Don Dorrell, Robert Anderson, Keith Richards, John Craig, Charles Cane, Joe McGuinn, Morgan Shaan, Boyd "Red" Morgan, Boyd Stockman, Jack Kenney, Eden Hartford, Brad Trumbull

D: Edward L. Cahn
S: L. L. Foreman
SP: Owen Harris
P: Robert E. Kent

3023. GUN FIGHT

(United Artists, May, 1961) 68 Mins.

James Brown, Joan Staley, Gregg Palmer, Ron Soble, Ken Mayer, Charles Cooper, Walter Coy, James Parnell, Connie Buck, Kate Murtah, Andy Albin, Jon Locke, Morgan Shaan, Monte Burkhart, David Donaldson, John Damler, Robert Nash, Jack Kenney, Frank Watkins, Frank Eldredge, Gene Coogan, Bill Koontz, Boyd Stockman, Bob Woodward

D: Edward L. Cahn
S: Gerald Drayson Adams
SP: Gerald Drayson Adams, Richard Schayer
P: Robert E. Kent

3024. OLE REX

(Universal-International, May, 1961) 80 Mins.
(Eastman Color)

"Rex," Billy Hughes, William Foster, Robert Hinkle, Whitey Hughes, William Hughes, Richard McCarty, Red Bray, Robert Marlow, Jr., Dale Terry, Jim Cochran, Charles E. King (not the Charles King of "B" Western fame)

D/SP: Robert Hinkle
S: Jack Specht
P: Robert Hinkle, Charles E. King

3025. THE DEADLY COMPANIONS
(Pathe-American, June 6, 1961) 90 Mins.
(Pathe Color) (PanaVision)
Maureen O'Hara, Brian Keith, Steve Cochran, Chill Wills, Strother Martin, Will Wright, Jim O'Hara, Peter O'Crotty, Billy Vaughn, Robert Sheldon, John Hamilton, Hank Gobble, Buck Sharpe
D: Sam Peckinpah
S/SP: A. S. Fleischman
P: Charles S. Fitzsimmons

3026. HALF WAY TO HELL
(Victor Adamson Production, June, 1961)
(Parts filmed in Mexico)
Lyle Felice
(No other information available on this film)

3027. THE LAST GUNFIGHTER
(Brenner, June 30, 1961) 56 Mins.
Don Borisenko, Tass Tory, Jay Shannon, Michael Zenon, Ken James, Gordon Clark, James Beggs, Art Jenoff, Buddy Ferens, Jim Peddie, Ed Holmes, Bill William, James Barron, Mike Conway, Spud Abbot, Al Waxman, Bert Hilckman, Garrick Hagon
D/P/S: Lindsay Shonteff
AP: James Beggs

3028. THE LAST SUNSET
(Universal-International, July, 1961) 112 Mins.
(Eastman Color) (Filmed in Mexico)
Rock Hudson, Kirk Douglas, Dorothy Malone, Joseph Cotten, Carol Lynley, Neville Brand, Regis Toomey, Rad Fulton, Adam Williams, Jack Elam, John Shay, Margarito De Luna, Jose Torvay
D: Robert Aldrich
S: "Sundown at Crazy Horse"—Howard Rigsby
SP: Dalton Trumbo
P: Eugene Frenke, Edward Lewis

3029. TWO RODE TOGETHER
(Columbia, July, 1961) 109 Mins.
(Eastman Color)
James Stewart, Richard Widmark, Shirley Jones, Linda Cristal, Andy Devine, John McIntire, Paul Birch, Willis Bouchey, Henry Brandon, Harry Carey, Jr., Olive Carey, Ken Curtis, Chet Douglas, Annelle Hayes, David Kent, Anna Lee, Jeanette Nolan, John Qualen, Ford Rainey, Woody Strode, O. Z. Whitehead, Cliff Lyons, Mae Marsh, Frank Baker, Ruth Clifford, Ted Knight, Major Sam Harris, Jack Pennick, Chuck Roberson, Dan Borzage, Bill Henry, Chuck Hayward, Edward Brophy
D: John Ford
S: Will Cook
SP: Frank Nugent
P: Stan Shpetner

3030. BUFFALO GUN
(Globe, July, 1961) 72 Mins.
(Actually made in 1958)
Webb Pierce, Marty Robbins, Carl Smith, Wayne Morris, Donald Barry, Mary Ellen Kay, Douglsa Fowley, Harry Lauter, Edward Crandall, Bill Coontz, Eddie Little, Charles Solandi
D: Albert C. Gannaway
SP: A. R. Milton
P: A. R. Milton

3031. ——
3032. A THUNDER OF DRUMS
(MGM, September 21, 1961) 97 Mins.
(Metrocolor) (CinemaScope)
Richard Boone, George Hamilton, Luana Patten, Arthur O'Connell, Charles Bronson, James Douglas, Richard Chamberlain, Carole Wells, Tommy Marihugh, Irene Tedrow, Slim Pickens, Clem Harvey, Duane Eddy
D: Joseph M. Newman
SP: James Warner Bellah
P: Robert J. Enders

3033. THE COMANCHEROS
(20th C. Fox, October 30, 1961) 107 Mins.
(DeLuxe Color) (CinemaScope)
John Wayne, Stuart Whitman, Ina Balin, Nehemiah Persoff, Lee Marvin, Michael Ansara, Pat Wayne, Bruce Cabot, Joan O'Brien, Jack Elam, Edgar Buchanan, Henry Daniell, Richard Devon, Steve Baylor, John Dierkes, Roger Mobley, Bob Steele, Luisa Triana, Iphigenie Castiglioni, Aissa Wayne, George J. Lewis, Greg Palmer, Don Brodie, Jon Lormer, Phil Arnold, Alan Carney, Dennis Cole
D: Michael Curtiz
S: Paul I. Wellman
SP: James Edward Grant, Clair Huffaker
P: George Sherman

3034. THE PURPLE HILLS
(20th C. Fox, November, 1961) 60 Mins.
(DeLuxe Color) (CinemaScope)
Gene Nelson, Joanna Barnes, Kent Taylor, Russ Bender, Jerry Summers, Danny Zapien, Jack Carr, Medford Salway, Jack Riggs
D/P: Maury Dexter
S: Edith Cash Pearl, Russ Bender

3035. GUN STREET
(United Artists, November, 1961) 67 Mins.
James Brown, Jean Willes, John Clark, Ned Flory, John Pickard, Peggy Stewart, Sandra Stone, Warren Kemmerling, Nesdon Booth, Herb Armstrong, Renny McEvoy
D: Edward L. Cahn
SP: Sam C. Freedle
P: Robert E. Kent

3036. THE SECOND TIME AROUND
(20th C. Fox, December, 1961) 99 Mins.
(DeLuxe Color) (CinemaScope)
Debbie Reynolds, Steve Forrest, Andy Griffith, Juliet Prowse, Thelma Ritter, Ken Scott, Isobel Elsom, Rudolph Acosta, Timothy Carey, Tom Greenway, Eleanor Stratford, Jimmy Garrett, Lisa Pons, Nicky Blair
D: Vincent Sherman
S: "Star in the West"—Richard Emery Roberts
SP: Oscar Saul, Cecil Dan Hansen
P: Jack Cunningham

FILMS OF 1962

3037. SERGEANTS 3
(United Artists, February, 1962) 112 Mins.
(Technicolor) (PanaVision)
Frank Sinatra, Dean Martin, Sammy Davis, Jr., Peter Lawford, Joey Bishop, Henry Silva, Ruta Lee, Buddy Lester, Philip Crosby, Dennis Crosby, Lindsay Crosby, Hank Henry, Richard Simmons, Michael Pate, Armand Alzamora, Richard Hale, Mickey Finn, Sonny King, Eddie Little Sky, Rodd Redwing, James Waters, Madge Blake, Dorothy Abbott, Walter Merrill
D: John Sturges
SP: W. R. Burnette
P: Howard W. Koch

3038. THE BROKEN LAND
(20th C. Fox, April, 1962) 60 Mins.
(DeLuxe Color) (CinemaScope)
Kent Taylor, Dianna Darrin, Jody McCrea, Robert Sampson, Jack Nicholson, Gary Sneed, Don Orlando, Helen Joseph, H. Tom Cain, Bud Pollard
D: John Bushelman
SP: Edward Lasko
P: Leonard A. Schwartz

3039. THE MAN WHO SHOT LIBERTY VALANCE
(Paramount, April 11, 1962) 123 Mins.
John Wayne, James Stewart, Vera Miles, Lee Marvin, Edmond O'Brien, Andy Devine, Woody Strode, John Qualen, Jeanette Nolan, Lee Van Cleef, Strother Martin, Ken Murray, Buddy Roosevelt, John Carradine, Willis Bouchey, Carleton Young, Denver Pyle, Robert F. Simon, O. Z. Whitehead, Paul Birch, Jack Pennick, Anna Lee, Charles Seel, Shug Fisher, Earle Hodgins, Stuart Holmes, Dorothy Phillips, Gertrude Astor, Eva Novak, Slim Talbot, Montie Montana, Bill Henry, John B. Whiteford, Helen Gibson, Major Sam Harris
D: John Ford
SP: James Warner Bellah, Willis Goldbeck
P: Willis Goldbeck

3040. RIDE THE HIGH COUNTRY
(MGM, May, 1962) 94 Mins.
(Metrocolor) (CinemaScope)
Randolph Scott, Joel McCrea, Mariette Hartley, Ronald Starr, Edgar Buchanan, R. G. Armstrong, John Anderson, L. Q. Jones, Warren Oates, James Drury, John Davis Chandler, Jenie Jackson
D: Sam Peckinpah
SP: N. B. Stone, Jr.
P: Richard E. Lyons

3041. GERONIMO
(United Artists, May, 1962) 101 Mins.
(Technicolor) (PanaVision) (Filmed in Mexico)
Chuck Connors, Kamala Devi, Ross Martin, Pat Conway, Adam West, Enid James, Larry Dobkin, Denver Pyle, Armando Silvestre, John Anderson, Armanda Ames, Mario Navarro, Eduardo Noriega, Nancy Rodman, Joe Higgins, Robert Hughes, James Burk, Bill Hughes
D: Arnold Laven
S: Arnold Laven, Pat Fielder
SP: Pat Fielder
P: Arnold Laven

3042. RIDER ON A DEAD HORSE
(Allied Artists, May 27, 1962) 72 Mins.
John Vivyan, Bruce Gordon, Kevin Hagen, Lisa Lu, Charls Lampkin
D: Herbert L. Strock
S: James Edmiston
SP: Stephen Longstreet
P: Kenneth Altrose

3043. SIX BLACK HORSES
(Universal-International, June, 1962) 80 Mins.
(Eastman Color)
Audie Murphy, Dan Duryea, Joan O'Brien, George Wallace, Roy Barcroft, Bob Steele, Henry Wills, Phil Chambers, Charles Regis, Dale Van Sickel
D: Harry Keller
SP: Burt Kennedy
P: Gordon Kay

3044. SHOOT OUT AT BIG SAG
(Parallel, June, 1962) 64 Mins.
Walter Brennan, Leif Erickson, Luana Patten, Chris Robinson, Constance Ford, Virginia Gregg, Les Tremayne, Don O'Kelly, Andy Brennan, William Foster, Robert Beecher, Lennie Geer
D/SP: Roger Kay

P: Walter A. Brennan, Jr.
S: "Barb Wire"—Walt Coburn

3045. NIGHT RIDER
(Parallel, June, 1962)   22 Mins.
Johnny Cash, Eddie Dean, Dick Jones, Johnny Western, Merle Travis, Gordon Terry, Wesley Tuttle, Karen Downes, Whitey Hughes
D: Michael Hinn
S: Helen Diller
P: Michael Hinn

3046. LONELY ARE THE BRAVE
(Universal-International, June, 1962)   107 Mins.
(PanaVision)
Kirk Douglas, Gena Rowlands, Walter Matthau, Michael Kane, Carroll O'Connor, William Schallert, George Kennedy, Karl Swenson, Bill Mims, Martin Garralaga, Lalo Rios
D: David Miller
S: "Brave Cowboy"—Edward Abbey
SP: Dalton Trumbo
P: Edward Lewis

3047. THE WILD WESTERNERS
(Columbia, June, 1962)   70 Mins.
(Eastman Color)
James Philbrook, Nancy Kovack, Duane Eddy, Guy Mitchell, Hugh Sanders, Elizabeth MacRae, Marshall Reed, Nestor Paiva, Harry Lauter, Bob Steele, Lisa Burkert, Terry Frost, Hans Wedemeyer, Don Harvey, Elizabeth Harrower, Francis Osborne, Tim Sullivan, Pierce Lyden, Joe McGuinn, Charles Horvath, Marjorie Stapp
D: Oscar Rudolph
SP: Gerald Drayson Adams
P: Sam Katzman

3048. TERROR AT BLACK FALLS
(Beckman, June, 1962)   72 Mins.
House Peters, Jr., John Alonso, Sandra Knight, Peter Mamakos, Gary Gray, Jim Bysel, I. Stanford Jolley, Marshall Bradford, William Erwin, Jim Hayward
D: Robert C. Sarafian
S/SP: Not credited in pressbook or reviews
P: Robert C. Sarafian

3049. THE FIREBRAND
(20th C. Fox, August, 1962)   63 Mins.
(CinemaScope)
Valentin De Vargas, Kent Taylor, Lisa Montell, Joe Raciti, Chubby Johnson, Barbara Mansell, Allen Jaffe, Troy Melton, Fred Krone, Sid Haig, Felix Locher, Jerry Summers
D: Maury Dexter
SP: Harry Spalding
P: Maury Dexter

3050. THE LEGEND OF LOBO
(Buena Vista, November, 1962)   67 Mins.
(Technicolor)
Told in song and story by Rex Allen and the Sons of the Pioneers
D: James Algar
S: Ernest Thompson-Seton
SP: Dwight Hauser, James Algar
P: A Walt Disney Presentation

3051. STAGECOACH TO DANCER'S ROCK
(Universal-International, November, 1962)   72 Mins.
Warren Stevens, Martin Landau, Jody Lawrence, Judy Dan, Del Moore, Don Wilbanks, Bob Anderson, Rand Brooks, Gene Roth, Charles Tannen, Mike Ragan, Mauritz Hugo, Tim Bolton, Milan Smith, Alicia Li, Cherrylene Lee
D/P: Earl Bellamy
S/SP: Kenneth Darling

CHAPTER 9

The Clouded Years
1963-1967

(UNFAMILIAR RIDERS AND OVERGROWN TRAILS)

Whereas in the Westerns of earlier days the hero would clean up a town and ride into the horizon a virtuous figure clothed in the gratitude of the ingenue's sparkling eyes and handshake, ready to return should his services again be needed in the defense of righteousness, it was not so in the Sixties. Sadly, true heroes were often lacking; when they did exist, they likely as not got their stuffin' kicked out, leaving them as orphans of the storm when the dust of greed and turmoil settled over the cinematic landscape. One theme evident in most contemporary Westerns of the period we have chosen to call the Clouded Years (1963-1967) is that of conflict of the past and present. Producers with no love of the traditional Western or no desire of perpetuating the myths surrounding it used the Western formula to condemn modern society's shortcomings. Examples are to be found in *Hud, A Time for Killing, Hour of the Gun, Invitation to a Gunfighter,* and *The Outrage.* Those who clung to the old-fashioned individualism school continued to churn out the more traditional Westerns, best exemplified in the movies of John Wayne and Audie Murphy.

The films of the Sixties have had read into them by film writers values and meanings probably never intended. Seemingly, to produce a film for the mere purpose of entertaining was unforgivable. Nearly every major Western myth was saddled with social significance of some sort, and John Wayne was criticized for making old-fashioned escapist films. Superfluous sex and sadistic brutality were well in evidence. Often an outlaw was not merely shot in a gunfight, *a la* Rex Bell beating Slim Whitaker to the draw, but was literally disemboweled in living color in a prolonged sequence played for shock. And the virginal hero's courageous "Aw shucks, Miss Molly, you're pretty as a prairie flower" has evolved into explicit sex with all the sounds, sighs, grunts, panting, and visual documentation possible. Certainly many leading characters in modern Westerns differ from the older archetype in both their moral makeup and their attitudes of the social order. The tendency for several years had been for Westerns to take an openly critical and pessimistic look at the West they once championed. This critical attitude would become even more pronounced in later years.

The communal belief in the past and future that nurtured the classic Western was sorely missing during the Sixties, the belief in a unifying heritage and a common cause last felt during World War II a generation before. The Western had experienced both its birth and renaissance during periods of intense national pride, confidence, energetic spirit, and faith in the future. Having somewhat lost this mood because of the difficult moral, ecological, political, and sociological problems of the Sixties, the Western film which had spoken for the unifying spirit began to disappear as well. The trend during the Clouded Years was away from heroes of any kind.

Gone for the most part were the character actors who graced hundreds of "B" Westerns throughout the Twenties, Thirties, Forties, and into the Fifties—men like Charlie

How the West Was Won (MGM, 1963) — James Stewart and Carrol Baker

King, Tom London, Lafe McKee, Hank Bell, Fred Kohler, and Edmund Cobb. Type-cast they were, but audiences associated them with Westerns and felt comfortable in watching any film in which they filled up the background. Their presence added immeasurably to the atmosphere of a Western, far more than that of modern-day character actors who have not been so typed. Indeed, the stock players of the Thirties and Forties accounted for as much of the pleasure in seeing a Saturday afternoon shoot-em-up as did the name stars, and their passing has been sorely missed and their places in the hearts of Western followers unfilled.

Several good Westerns emerged from the Clouded Years. Undoubtedly the most expensive, over-plotted, over-elaborate, and lengthy one was *How the West Was Won* (MGM, 1963). The film's thesis is too broad and vague, and its several separate stories do not clearly develop its thesis in a consistent manner and never achieve believability. Although meant to be the definitive Western, its failure in this regard is overwhelming and complete. But as a sterling film with majestic locales, superb, well-staged stunting and action sequences, and superior performances by a galaxy of stars, it is imposing enough. As one of the most ambitious exercises in the cinerama process, the film is only partially successful in bringing to the screen the story of Western expansion as originally told in text and illustrations in *Life* magazine. Directors John Ford, George Marshall, and Henry Hathaway and a slew of seasoned performers did their best with the segmented script, and it might be added that two of the better episodes are those featuring James Stewart and John Wayne.

Cheyenne Autumn (Warner Bros., 1964) has been described as John Ford's apology to the Indians he presented so badly in his earlier films. Possibly. At any rate the Cheyenne is here treated with a great deal of respect, although told from the white man's view rather than the Indian's. It is the story of the American Indian caught up in politics and

512

bureaucracy and of the flight of the Cheyenne from their reservation in Oklahoma to the Yellowstone Country. The story, one of pathos and defeat, is beautifully told by a master story-teller. It was the final Western for both director Ford and George O'Brien, his former star and personal friend who had a supporting role in the film.

For John Wayne, at least, the old-time escapist action Western devoid of any especial social messages or significance was still capable of creating lines at the box office. He had four winners during the period. *McLintock* (United Artists, 1963) was a smash hit, with Wayne reunited with Maureen O'Hara. Drama, comedy, and photographic spectacle constituted a triple alliance. The story moves along conventional but well-defined lines that give the star many effective moments in a character skillfully adapted to his personality. The highlight of the film is the spectacular mud fight that involved practically half of the cast.

The Sons of Katie Elder (Paramount, 1965) is the kind of traditional Western that made and kept Duke Wayne a star. Made as pure escapism and not to sermonize, it is one of the Duke's more enjoyable of many enjoyable outings. Again he is the loner, as in so many films before, though temporarily allied with his younger brothers to avenge the suffering of their recently deceased mother. Wayne is a gunman, noble, mother-loving, and middle-aged. Martha Hyer as the friend of Katie Elder adds the slight romantic touch, and one is compelled to fall madly in love with her while bemoaning the stupidity which allows Wayne to ride away from such a caressable and comely creature. The film was great box office, doing a landslide business as the public expressed its vulnerability to a nostalgic Western in the old vein with the one and only Wayne. Somehow the nostalgia and the reverence for the last of the Western heroes had taken the young too, and the long lines at ticket windows were again to see a man, not a story.

In *El Dorado* (Paramount, 1967) Wayne is once more a gunfighter, beset with physical problems, who salvages and shapes alcoholic sheriff Robert Mitchum into a man again and divests the community of a greedy landowner and his cutthroats. Wayne is still the hero and incorruptible, but he is no longer self-sufficient and invulnerable. The action and suspense are plentiful, while the original strength of the story is increased and accentuated, made more human and more appealing, by the delicate touch of Wayne.

A reversion to good, non-psychological Western entertainment as only Wayne could present it was to be found in *The War Wagon* (Universal, 1967). True, critics rated it "routine Wayne fare that is easily forgotten." Perhaps that was the blessing it needed, for this fast-paced comedic action Western easily proved popular at the box office.

These Wayne features were traditional in concept and stayed clear of pornography or anything bordering on it. The emphasis on solid action and clean stories persisted in keeping the old-timer on top, even though critics had been trying to write him off as a fluke for years. No doubt about it, one major factor in his success has been the fact that the kids of the Thirties who idolized him in the serials and the programmer Westerns have grown up and become fathers and grandfathers while retaining their loyalty to "one of their own." In this sense Wayne has been amply rewarded for his lean years at Mascot, Lonestar, and Republic.

In the lighter vein, *Cat Ballou* (Columbia, 1965) was a surprise smash hit with an Academy Award-winning performance by Lee Marvin playing a double role as a boozer hero and his outlaw brother. His hero is the very opposite of the courageous hero of countless "B" Westerns and his horse is no Tarzan or Rebel or Silver, either. The film is hilariously funny. Jane Fonda is on hand to supply (with considerable technical assistance from the cameraman) an adequate amount of sensuality and sexuality for the titillation of the carnal-minded, but it is Marvin and his stupefied horse that steal the show. Equally funny was *The Hallelujah Trail* (United Artists, 1965) with Burt Lancaster and Brian Keith in the forefront of the slapstick Western revolving about a wagon train of booze.

The Rounders (MGM, 1965) is a beguiling, thoroughly enjoyable spoof of a too true look at cowboys as they really are. A hilarious film, it is a good example of cowboy humor, with two aging horse wranglers, Glenn Ford and Henry Fonda, trying to make a living busting broncs for a rascally old reprobate who keeps them in debt to him. Other Westerns in the comedic or tongue-in-cheek vein included *Four for Texas* (Warner Bros., 1964), *Mail Order Bride* (MGM, 1964), *The Unsinkable Molly Brown* (MGM, 1964), *Texas Across the River* (Universal, 1966), *The Adventures of Bullwhip Griffin* (Buena Vista, 1967), and *Waterhole #3* (Paramount, 1967).

Bars, bedrooms, women, foul language, hard-drinking, and a pink Cadillac convertible are hardly what one associates with the idealized image of the cowboy, but they are there in *Hud* (Paramount, 1963), set in modern northwest Texas with Paul Newman cast as the cynical, self-centered yet appealing "Hud." The film is like *Shane* in that the core of the action exists in the mind of a sensitive young man who must decide if he will strive to be like Hud, a flashy, egotistical, appealing heel, or strive for the nobility and moral values, albeit a less exciting life, of his grandfather. The story is by Larry McMurtry and it is about the desolate Texas country. Newman is the archetypal cowboy caught up in a changing world. It was about as far from the type of Western made by Ken Maynard and Wally Wales as one could imagine, but it was a popular and profitable drama with general audiences who preferred not to be caught up in the dust clouds of real Westerns.

By 1967 Wyatt Earp is no longer a defender of the law; rather, he hides under the law to satisfy his near-psychotic lust for violent revenge in *Hour of the Gun* (United Artists, 1967). James Garner plays Earp and John Sturges directs. One commendable thing about the film is the rather accurate retelling of the gunfight at the O.K. Corral.

Sam Peckinpah adds to his credentials, as do actors Charlton Heston and Richard Harris, with *Major Dundee* (Columbia, 1965), a tangy film that smoothly balances the poetry and realism of the West. Peckinpah concentrates on the human conflicts in the story of a Northern officer and Confederate prisoners united to fight Indian renegades. A key motif woven through the fabric of the film with great skill is that of the complex interaction of Indian and white man, and both are shown to be savages.

Bullet for a Badman (Universal, 1964) is one of the better Audie Murphy yarns, this one about a Texas Ranger turned bank robber who escapes with the loot and a vow to kill his former Ranger friend who has married his ex-wife. The action is fast and furious and old-timer Bob Steele has a good role, endorsement enough for any film. Murphy's films were about the closest thing to the old shoot-em-ups of the "B" era as one was likely to find, his acting was definitely improving, and he was respected by Western buffs for the fact that he was exclusively a cowboy in an era when practically every male Hollywood star was trying his spurs in at least one cactus and cayuse characterization. But horses, high-heeled boots, six-shooters, neck scarfs, big hats, and a swagger do not a cowboy make, and it was a little difficult to accept in the role of a Western hero such Hollywood personalities as Frank Sinatra, Troy Donahue, Yul Brynner, Paul Newman, Russ Tamblyn, Robert Taylor, Steve McQueen, Marlon Brando, Bobby Darin, or Dean Martin. Thus Murphy, making Westerns on a consistent basis, was a welcome relief for the Western-starved fan.

A couple of nostalgic "last hurrah" technicolor Westerns of the "B" type produced by Alex Gordon and directed by Spencer G. Bennet were among the more entertaining films of the period because of the exciting casts they sported. *The Bounty Killer* (Embassy, 1965) is a low-key, adult Western minus a happy ending. It features Rod Cameron, Dan Duryea, Buster Crabbe, Richard Arlen, Johnny Mack Brown, Bob Steele, Fuzzy Knight, I. Stanford

Bullet for a Badman (Universal, 1964) — Audie Murphy and Darren Mc-Gavin

Requiem for a Gunfighter (Embassy, 1965) — Rod Cameron

Jolley, Frank Lackteen, Audrey Dalton, and Tom Kennedy. Even the screen's first cowboy, Bronco Billy Anderson, is seen after an absence of forty-five years from movie-making. The other film, *Requiem for a Gunfighter* (Embassy, 1965), has Tim McCoy, Bob Steele, Johnny Mack Brown, Rod Cameron, Lane Chandler, Raymond Hatton, Eddie Cobb, Frank Lackteen, Dick Alexander, and Dale Van Sickel in yet another tribute to old-time Westerns of the Saturday matinee type. Any true lover of "B" Westerns worth his salt would have to sit through these at least a couple of times to completely savor the nostalgia.

We'll mention just one more film, *Shenandoah* (Universal, 1965). A non-cynical, semi-Western, it was one of the better films of the Clouded Years. James Stewart heads up the cast of this beautiful story of a frontier family and a father's search for his young son taken captive during the Civil War.

The Clouded Years yielded few memorable Westerns other than those few just mentioned. Things were rather quiet on the cinema range. There were really no significant trends, just a gradual blending of white and black to produce heroes who were earthy and human. The traditional heroes in white hats had been mostly deflowered in favor of more lascivious defenders of the range. The European Westerns began to make their impact on American audiences and to some extent their terse, violent, pseudo-realistic style would serve as models for American Westerns.

Stories reflected the relaxed censorship of the Sixties, with the result that on occasion it was not certain whether the heroine was being saved *from* a fate worse than death or *for* such a fate. More Westerns were played tongue-in-cheek, while a few were over-serious. The middle-of-the-trail entries fared best.

As the Clouded Years ended it was obvious that more cynical years were in the offing and that the entrancement of the traditional Western was in further jeopardy. A few blockbusters were needed to stimulate interest in the genre once more.

FILMS OF 1963

3052. YOUNG GUNS OF TEXAS
(20th C. Fox, January, 1963)   78 Mins.
(DeLuxe Color)   (CinemaScope)
James Mitchum, Alana Ladd, Jody McCrea, Chill Wills, Gary Conway, Barbara Mansell, Robert Lowery, Troy Melton, Fred Krone, Alex Sharpe, Robert Hinkle, Will Wills
D: Maury Dexter
SP: Harry Cross
P: Maury Dexter

3053. HOW THE WEST WAS WON
(MGM, February 20, 1963)   165 Mins.
(Technicolor)   (Cinerama)
Carroll Baker, Lee J. Cobb, Henry Fonda, Carolyn Jones, Karl Malden, Gregory Peck, George Peppard, Robert Preston, Debbie Reynolds, James Stewart, Eli Wallach, John Wayne, Richard Widmark, Brigid Bazlen, Walter Brennan, David Brian, Andy Devine, Raymond Massey, Agnes Moorehead, Henry (Harry) Morgan, Thelma Ritter, Mickey Shaughnessey, Russ Tamblyn, Rodolfo Acosta, Dean Stanton, Lee Van Cleef, Kim Charney, Bryan Russell, Karl Swenson, Jack Lambert, Christopher Dark, Jay C. Flippen, Gene Roth, Barry Harvey, Jamie Ross, Joe Sawyer, James Griffith, Clinton Sundberg, Walter Burke, John Lorch, Mark Allen, Edward J. McKinley, Craig Duncan, Charles Briggs, Boyd "Red" Morgan, Chuck Roberson
D: John Ford, Henry Hathaway, George Marshall
SP: James R. Webb
P: Bernard Smith
(Above date was U.S. premiere date. The world premiere was in London, England on November 1, 1962)

3054. CALIFORNIA
(American International, March 17, 1963)   86 Mins.
Jock Mahoney, Faith Domergue, Michael Pate, Susan Seaforth, Rodolfo Hoyos, Penny Santon, Jimmy Murphy, Nestor Paiva, Roberto Contreras, Felix Locher, Charles Horvath
D/P: Hamil Petroff
SP: James West

3055. HUD

(Paramount, May, 1963) 112 Mins.

(PanaVision)

Paul Newman, Melvyn Douglas, Patricia Neal, Brandon de Wilde, John Ashley, Whit Bissell, Crahan Denton, Val Avery, Shelton Allman, Pitt Herbert, Peter Brooks, Curt Conway, Yvette Vickers, George Petrie, David Kent, Frank Killmond

D: Martin Ritt

S: "Horseman, Pass By"—Larry McMurty

SP: Irving Ravetch, Harriet Frank, Jr.

P: Martin Ritt, Irving Ravetch

3056. SHOWDOWN

(Universal, May, 1963) 79 Mins.

Audie Murphy, Kathleen Crowley, Charles Drake, Harold J. Stone, Skip Homeier, L. Q. Jones, Strother Martin, Charles Horvath, John McKee, Henry Wills, Joe Haworth, Kevin Brodie, Carol Thurston, Dabbs Greer

D: R. G. Springsteen

SP: Bronson Howitzer

P: Gordon Kay

3057. CATTLE KING

(MGM, June, 1963) 88 Mins.

(Eastman Color)

Robert Taylor, Joan Caulfield, Robert Loggia, Robert Middleton, Larry Gates, Malcolm Atterbury, William Windom, Virginia Christine, Ray Teal, Richard Devon, Robert Ivers, Maggie Pierce, Woodrow Pelfrey, Richard Tretter, John Mitchum

D: Tay Garnett

SP: Thomas Thompson

P: Nat Holt

3058. SAVAGE SAM

(Buena Vista, June, 1963) 103 Mins.

(Technicolor)

Brian Keith, Tommy Kirk, Kevin Corcoran, Dewey Martin, Jeff York, Marta Kristen, Rafael Campos, Slim Pickens, Rodolfo Acosta, Pat Hogan, Dean Federicks, Brad Weston, Royal Dano

D: Norman Tokar

S/SP: Fred Gipson

P: A Walt Disney Presentation

3059. THE GUN HAWK

(Allied Artists, August 28, 1963) 92 Mins.

(DeLuxe Color)

Rory Calhoun, Rod Cameron, Ruta Lee, Rod Lauren, Morgan Woodward, Robert J. (Bob) Wilke, John Litel, Rodolfo Hoyos, Lane Bradford, Glenn Stensel, Joan Connors, Ron Whalen, Lee Bradley

D: Edward Ludwig

S: Richard Bernstein, Max Steeber

SP: Jo Heims

P: Richard Bernstein

3060. GUNFIGHT AT COMANCHE CREEK

(Allied Artists, November 6, 1963) 91 Mins.

(DeLuxe Color) (PanaVision)

Audie Murphy, Ben Cooper, Coleen Miller, DeForest Kelley, Jan Merlin, John Hubbard, Damian O'Flynn, Susan Seaforth

D: Frank McDonald

SP: Edward Bernds

P: Ben Schwalb

3061. McLINTOCK

(Batjac/United Artists, November 13, 1963) 127 Mins.

(Technicolor) (PanaVision)

John Wayne, Maureen O'Hara, Yvonne De Carlo, Patrick Wayne, Stefanie Powers, Jack Kruschen, Chill Wills, Jerry Van Dyke, Edgar Buchanan, Bruce Cabot, Perry Lopez, Michael Pate, Strother Martin, Gordon Jones, Robert Lowery, Ed Faulkner, H. W. Gim, Aissa Wayne, Chuck Roberson, Hal Needham, Pedro Gonzales, Jr., Hank Worden, Ralph Volkie, Dan Borzage, John Stanley, Karl Noven, Mari Blanchard, Leo Gordon, Bob Steele, John Hamilton

D: Andrew V. McLaglen

SP: James Edward Grant

P: Michael Wayne

3062. BULLET FOR BILLY THE KID

(Assoc. Distrs. Productions, November, 1963) 61 Mins.

(Eastman Color)

Gaston Sands, Steve Brodie, Lloyd Nelson, Marla Blaine, Richard McIntyre, Gilbert Cramer, Rita Mace, Peter Gillon

SP: Raymond Obon

P: Alfred Ripstein, Jerry Warren

D: Rafael Baledon

FILMS OF 1964

3063. FOUR FOR TEXAS
(Warner Bros., January 4, 1964) 124 Mins.
(Technicolor)
Frank Sinatra, Dean Martin, Anita Ekberg, Ursula Andress, Charles Bronson, Victor Buono, Edric Connor, Nick Dennis, Richard Jaeckel, Mike Mazurki, Wesley Addy, Marjorie Bennett, Jack Elam, Fritz Field, Percy Helton, Jonathan Hale, Jack Lambert, Paul Langton, Teddy Buckner and his All Stars, The Three Stooges, Bob Steele, Virginia Christine, Ellen Corby, Ralph Volkie
D: Richard Thorpe
SP: Allan Weiss
P: Hal Wallis

3064. THE MAN FROM GALVESTON
(Warner Bros., January 11, 1964) 57 Mins.
Jeffrey Hunter, Preston Foster, James Coburn, Joanna Moore, Edward Andrews, Kevin Hagen, Martin West, Ed Nelson, Karl Swenson, Grace Lee Whitley, Claude Stroud, Sherwood Price, Arthur Malet, Marjorie Bennett
D: William Conrad
SP: Dean Riesner, Michael Zagor
P: Jack Webb, Michael Meshekoff

3065. MAIL ORDER BRIDE
(MGM, February, 1964) 85 Mins.
(Metrocolor) (PanaVision)
Buddy Ebsen, Keir Dullea, Lois Nettleton, Warren Oates, Barbara Luna, Paul Fix, Marie Windsor, Denver Pyle, Bill Smith, Kathleen Freeman, Abigail Shelton, Jimmy Mathews
D: Burt Kennedy
S: Van Cort
SP: Burt Kennedy
P: Richard E. Lyons

3066. BALLAD OF A GUNFIGHTER
(Parade, March, 1964) 84 Mins.
(Eastman Color)
Marty Robbins, Joyce Redd, Bob Barron, Nestor Paiva, Michael Davis, Laurette Luez, Charlie Aldrich, Paul McDonald, Cynthia Goodwins, Claud Aldrich, Gene Davis, Tommy Cloud, Rick Arnold, Chuck Balis, "Traveler" (a horse)
D/SP/P: Bill Ward

3067. HE RIDES TALL
(Universal, April, 1964) 84 Mins.
Tony Young, Dan Duryea, Jo Morrow, Madlyn Rhue, R. G. Armstrong, Joel Fluellen, Carl Reindel, Mickey Simpson, George Murdock, Michael Carr, George Petrie

D: R. G. Springsteen
S: Charles W. Irwin
SP: Charles W. Irwin, Robert Creighton Williams
P: Gordon Kay

3068. ADVANCE TO THE REAR
(MGM, April, 1964) 97 Mins.
(PanaVision)
Glenn Ford, Stella Stevens, Melvyn Douglas, Jim Backus, Joan Blondell, Andrew Prine, Jesse Pearson, Alan Hale, Jr., James Griffith, Whit Bissell, Michael Pate
D: George Marshall
S: Jack Schaefer. Suggested by "Company of Cowards" by William Chamberlain
SP: Samuel A. Peeples
P: Ted Richmond

3069. THE QUICK GUN
(Columbia, April, 1964) 88 Mins.
(Technicolor) (TechniScope)
Audie Murphy, Merry Anders, James Best, Ted de Corsia, Walter Sande, Rex Holman, Charles Meredith, Frank Ferguson, Mort Mills, Gregg Palmer, Frank Gerstle, Stephen Roberts, Paul Bryar, Raymond Hatton, William Fawcett
D: Sidney Salkow
S: "The Fastest Gun"—Steve Fisher
SP: Robert E. Kent
P: Grant Whytock

3070. LAW OF THE LAWLESS
(Paramount, May, 1964) 87 Mins.
(Technicolor) (TechniScope)
Dale Robertson, Yvonne De Carlo, William Bendix, Bruce Cabot, Barton MacLane, John Agar, Richard Arlen, Jody McCrea, Kent Taylor, Bill Williams, Rod Lauren, George Chandler, Lon Chaney, Jr., Donald Barry, Roy Jenson, Jerry Summers, Reg Parton, Alex Sharpe
D: William F. Claxton
SP: Steve Fisher
P: A. C. Lyles

3071. THE RAIDERS
(Universal, May, 1964) 75 Mins.
(Eastman Color)
Brian Keith, Robert Culp, Judi Meredith, James McMullan, Alfred Ryder, Simon Oakland, Ben Cooper, Trevor Bardette, Harry Carey, Jr., Richard Cutting, Addison Richards, Cliff Osmond, Paul Birch, Richard Deacon, Michael Burns
D: Herschel Daugherty
SP: Gene L. Coon
P: Howard Christie

3072. A DISTANT TRUMPET

(Warner Bros., May 30, 1964)   117 Mins.

(Technicolor)   (PanaVision)

Troy Donahue, Suzanne Pleshette, Diane McBain,
  James Gregory, William Reynolds, Claude Akins,
  Kent Smith, Judson Pratt, Bartlett Robinson,
  Bobby Bare, Larry Ward, Richard X. Slattery,
  Mary Patton, Russell Johnson, Lane Bradford

D: Raoul Walsh

S: P. Horgan

SP: John Twist, Richard Fielder, Albert Beich

P: William H. Wright

3073. STAGE TO THUNDER ROCK

(Paramount, June, 1964)   82 Mins.

(Technicolor)   (TechniScope)

Barry Sullivan, Marilyn Maxwell, Scott Brady, Lon
  Chaney, Jr., John Agar, Wanda Hendrix, Anne
  Seymour, Allan Jones, Ralph Taeger, Laurel Good-
  win, Robert Strauss, Robert Lowery, Argentina
  Brunetti, Rex Bell, Jr., Suzanne Cupito, Wayne
  Peters, Keenan Wynn

D: William F. Claxton

SP: Charles Wallace

P: A. C. Lyles

3074. THE UNSINKABLE MOLLY BROWN

(MGM, July, 1964)   128 Mins.

(Metrocolor)   (PanaVision)

Debbie Reynolds, Harve Presnell, Ed Begley, Jack
  Kruschen, Hermione Baddeley, Vassili Lam-
  brinos, Fred Essler, Harvey Lembeck, Kathryn
  Card, Hayden Rorke, Harry Holcombe, Amy
  Douglass, George Mitchell, Martita Hunt,
  Vaughn Taylor, Antony Eustrel, Audrey Christie,
  Grover Dale, Brendan Dillon, Maria Karnilova,
  Gus Trikonis, Lauren Gilbert

D: Charles Walters

S: Richard Morris

SP: Helen Deutsch

P: Lawrence Weingarten

3075. VENGEANCE

(BadAxe Prod./Crown International Pictures,
  April, 1964)   79 Mins.

William Thourlby, Melora Conway, Owen Pavitt,
  Ed Cook, Byrd Holland, John Bliss, Larry Gerst,
  Gordon Wynn, Donald Cook, James Cavanaugh,
  Tiger Joe Marsh

D: Dene Hilyard

SP/S: Alex Sharp, Ed Erwin

P: William Thourlby

3076. BULLET FOR A BADMAN

(Universal, September, 1964)   80 Mins.

(Eastman Color)

Audie Murphy, Darren McGavin, Ruta Lee, Beverly
  Owen, Skip Homeier, George Tobias, Alan Hale,
Jr., Berkeley Harris, Edward C. Platt, Kevin Tate,
  CeCe Whitney, Mort Mills, Buff Brady, Bob
  Steele

D: R. G. Springsteen

S: Marvin H. Albert

SP: Mary and Willard Willingham

P: Gordon Kay

3077. APACHE RIFLES

(20th C. Fox, October, 1964)   92 Mins.

(DeLuxe Color)

Audie Murphy, Michael Dante, Linda Lawson, L. Q.
  Jones, Ken Lynch, John Archer, Charles Watts,
  Howard Wright, Peter Hansen, Robert Karnes,
  Hugh Sanders, Sydney Smith, S. John Launer,
  Robert B. Williams

D: William H. Witney

S: Kenneth Gamet, Richard Schayer

SP: Charles B. Smith

P: Grant Whytock

3078. BLOOD ON THE ARROW

(Allied Artists, October, 1964)   91 Mins.

(DeLuxe Color)

Dale Robertson, Martha Hyer, Wendell Corey,
  Dandy Curran, Paul Mantee, Ted de Corsia,
  Elisha Cook, Jr., John Matthews, Tom Reese,
  Bloyce Wright, Michael Hammond, Leland Wain-
  scott

D: Sidney Salkow

S: Robert E. Kent, Mark Hanna

SP: Robert E. Kent

P: Leon Fromkess

3079. THE OUTRAGE

(MGM, November, 1964)   97 Mins.

(PanaVision)

Paul Newman, Laurence Harvey, Claire Bloom,
  Edward G. Robinson, William Shatner, Howard
  De Silva, Albert Salmi, Thomas Chalmers, Paul
  Fix

D: Martin Ritt

S: Fay and Michael Kanin. From "Rashomon" by
  Ryunoshuka Akutagawa

SP: Michael Kanin

P: Ronald Rubin

3080. INVITATION TO A GUNFIGHTER

(United Artists, November, 1964)   92 Mins.

(DeLuxe Color)

Yul Brynner, Janice Rule, Brad Dexter, Alfred
  Ryder, Mike Kellin, George Segal, Clifford David,
  Pat Hingle, Bert Freed, Curt Conway, Clifton
  James, Clarke Gordon, Arthur Peterson, Strother
  Martin

D: Richard Wilson

S: Hal Goodman, Larry Klein

SP: Elizabeth and Richard Wilson
P: Richard Wilson

3081. RIO CONCHOS
(20th C. Fox, November, 1964)   107 Mins.
(DeLuxe Color) (CinemaScope)
Richard Boone, Stuart Whitman, Tony Franciosa,
  Wende Wagner, Warner Anderson, Jim Brown,
  Rodolfo Acosta, Barry Kelly, Vito Scotti, House
  Peters, Jr., Kevin Hagen, Edmond O'Brien
D: Gordon Douglas
S: "Guns of the Rio Conchos"—Clair Huffaker
SP: Joseph Landon, Clair Huffaker
P: David Weisbart

3082. NAVAJO RUN
(American International, November 25, 1964)
  75 Mins.
Johnny Seven, Warren Kemmerling, Virginia Vin-
  cent, Ron Soble
D: Johnny Seven
SP: Jo Heims

P: Johnny Seven
AP: Edward J. Forsyth

3083. CHEYENNE AUTUMN
(Warner Bros., December 19, 1964)   160 Mins.
(Technicolor)   (Super PanaVision 70)
James Stewart, Richard Widmark, Carroll Baker,
  Ricardo Montalban, Karl Malden, Sal Mineo,
  Dolores Del Rio, Gilbert Roland, Arthur Kennedy,
  Patrick Wayne, Elizabeth Allen, John Carradine,
  Mike Mazurki, George O'Brien, Sean McClory,
  Judson Pratt, Carmen D'Antonio, Ken Curtis,
  Victor Jory, Edward G. Robinson, Walter Bald-
  win, Shug Fisher, Nancy Hsueh, Chuck Rober-
  son, Harry Carey, Jr., Ben Johnson, Jimmy O'Hara,
  Chuck Hayward, Lee Bradley, Frank Bradley,
  Walter Reed, Willis Bouchey, Carleton Young,
  Denver Pyle, John Qualen, Dan Borzage, Na-
  nomba "Moonbeam" Morton, Dean Smith, David
  H. Miller, Bing Russell
D: John Ford
S: Mari Sandoz
SP: Joseph R. Webb
P: Bernard Smith

FILMS OF 1965

3084. THE OUTLAWS IS COMING!
(Columbia, January 1, 1965)   89 Mins.
The Three Stooges, Adam West, Nancy Kovack,
  Mort Mills, Don Lamond, Rex Holman, Emil
  Sitka, Henry Gibson, Murray Alper, Tiny Brauer,
  Joe Bolton, Bill Camfield, Hal Fryar, Johnny
  Ginger, Wayne Mack, Edward T. McDonnell,
  Bruce Sedley, Paul Shannon, Sally Starr
D: Norman Maurer
S: Norman Maurer
SP: Elwood Ullman
P: Norman Maurer

3085. TAGGART
(Universal, February 1, 1965)   85 Mins.
(Color)
Tony Young, Dan Duryea, Dick Foran, Elsa Car-
  denas, John Hale, Emile Meyer, David Carradine,
  Peter Duryea, Tom Reese, Ray Teal, Claudia Bar-
  rett, Stuart Randall, Harry Carey, Jr., Bill Henry,
  Sarah Selby, George Murdock, Arthur Space, Bob
  Steele
D: R. G. Springsteen
S: Louis L'Amour
SP: Robert Creighton Williams
P: Gordon Kay

3086. YOUNG FURY
(Paramount, February 1, 1965)   80 Mins.
(Technicolor)   (TechniScope)
Rory Calhoun, Virginia Mayo, Lon Chaney, John
  Agar, Richard Arlen, Linda Foster, Merry Anders,
  Joan Huntington, Jody McCrea, Rex Bell, Jr., Bill
  Wellman, Jr., Reg Parton, Preston Pierce, Robert
  Biheller, Marc Cavell, Jay Ripley, Kevin O'Neal,
  Jerry Summers, Fred Alexander, Dal Jenkins, Wil-
  liam Bendix
D: Chris Nyby
SP: Steve Fisher
P: A. C. Lyles

3087. THE ROUNDERS
(MGM, March 1, 1965)   85 Mins.
(Metrocolor)   (PanaVision)
Glenn Ford, Henry Fonda, Sue Ann Langdon, Hope
  Holiday, Chill Wills, Edgar Buchanan, Kathleen
  Freeman, Denver Pyle, Joan Freeman, Barton
  MacLane, Doodles Weaver, Allegra Varron, Casey
  Tibbs
D: Burt Kennedy
S: Max Evans
SP: Burt Kennedy
P: Richard E. Lyons

3088. WAR PARTY

(20th C. Fox, March 1, 1965)   72 Mins.

Michael T. Mikler, Davey Davison, Donald Barry, Laurie Mack, Dennis Robertson, Charles Horvath, Guy Wilkerson, Michael Carr, Fred Krone

D: Lesley Selander

SP: George Williams, William Marks

P: Hal Klein

3089. MAJOR DUNDEE

(Columbia, April 1, 1965)   134 Mins.

(Eastman Color)   (PanaVision)

(Filmed in Mexico)

Charlton Heston, Richard Harris, Jim Hutton, James Coburn, Michael Anderson, Jr., Senta Berger, Mario Adorf, Brock Peters, Warren Oates, Ben Johnson, R. G. Armstrong, L. Q. Jones, Slim Pickens, Karl Swenson, Michael Pate, John Davis Chandler, Dub Taylor, Albert Carter, Jose Carlos Ruiz, Aurora Clavell, Regonia Palacious, Enrique Lucero, Francisco Reyguera

D: Sam Peckinpah

S: Harry Julian Fink

SP: Harry Julian Fink, Oscar Paul, Sam Peckinpah

P: Jerry Bresler

3090. THE MAN FROM BUTTON WILLOW

(United Screen Arts, April 3, 1965)   84 Mins.

(Eastman Color)   (Animated cartoon feature)

Features the voices of: Dale Robertson, Edgar Buchanan, Howard Keel, Barbara Jean Wong, Hershel Bernardi, Ross Martin, Verna Felton, Cliff Edwards

D/SP: David Detiege

P: Phyllis Bounds Detiege

3091. INDIAN PAINT

(Tejas Productions/Eagle American Films/Crown International Pictures, April 8, 1965)   91 Mins.

(Eastman Color)

Johnny Crawford, Jay Silverheels, Pat Hogan, Robert Crawford, Jr., George J. Lewis, Joan Hollmark, Bill Blackwell, Robert Crawford, Sr., Al Doney, Cinda Siler, Suzanne Goodman, Marshall Jones, Warren L. Dodge

D/S: Norman Foster

P: Gene Goree

3092. FORT COURAGEOUS

(20th C. Fox, May 1, 1965)   72 Mins.

Fred Beir, Donald Barry, Hanna Landy, Harry Lauter, Walter Reed, Joseph Partridge, Michael Carr, Fred Krone, George Sawaya, Cheryl MacDonald

D: Lesley Selander

SP: Richard Landau

P: Hal Klein

3093. BLACK SPURS

(Paramount, June 1, 1965)   81 Mins.

(Technicolor)   (TechniScope)

Rory Calhoun, Terry Moore, Linda Darnell, Scott Brady, Lon Chaney, Bruce Cabot, Richard Arlen, Patricia Owens, James Best, Jerome Courtland, DeForest Kelley, James Brown, Joe Hoover, Manuel Padilla, Sandra Giles, Sally Nichols, Rusty Allen, Jean Baird, Chuck Roberson

D: R. G. Springsteen

SP: Steve Fisher

P: A. C. Lyles

3094. CONVICT STAGE

(20th C. Fox, June 2, 1965)   71 Mins.

Harry Lauter, Donald Barry, Jodi Mitchell, Hanna Landy, Joseph Partridge, Eric Matthews, Walter Reed, George Sawaya, Michael Carr, Fred Krone, Karl MacDonald

D: Lesley Selander

S: Donald Barry

SP: Daniel Mainwaring

P: Hal Klein

3095. TICKLE ME

(Allied Artists, June 30, 1965)   90 Mins.

(DeLuxe Color)   (PanaVision)

Elvis Presley, Jocelyn Lane, Julie Adams, Jack Mullaney, Merry Anders, Connie Gilchrist, Edward Faulkner, Bill Williams, Louis Elias, John Dennis, Laurie Burton

D: Norman Taurog

S/SP: Elwood Ullman, Edward Bernds

P: Ben Schwald

3096. THE HALLELUJAH TRAIL

(United Artists, June 30, 1965)   156 Mins.

(Technicolor)   (Ultra PanaVision)

Burt Lancaster, Lee Remick, Jim Hutton, Pamela Tiffin, Donald Pleasence, Brian Keith, Martin Landau, John Anderson, Tom Stern, Robert J. Wilke, Jerry Gatlin, Larry Doran, Dub Taylor, James Burk

D: John Sturges

S: "The Hallelujah Trail"—Bill Gulick

SP: John Gay

P: John Sturges

3097. DEADWOOD '76

(Fairway, June 30, 1965)   100 Mins.

(Technicolor)   (TechniScope)

Arch Hall, Jr., Jack Lester, Melissa Morgan, William Watters, Robert Dix, LaDonna Cottier, Richard S. Cowl, David Reed, Rex Marlow, Gordon Schwenk, John Bryant, Barbara Moore, Ray Zachary, Willard Willingham, Harold Bizzy, Red

Black Spurs (Paramount, 1965) — Rory Calhoun gets the drop on a badman

Morgan, John Cardos, Little Jack Little, Bobby Means, Ray Vegas
D: James Landis
SP: Arch Hall, Jr., William Watters (Arch Hall, Sr.)
S: William Watters (Arch Hall, Sr.)
P: Nicholas Merriwether (Arch Hall, Sr.)

3098. REQUIEM FOR A GUNFIGHTER
(Embassy, June 30, 1965)   91 Mins.
(Technicolor)   (TechniScope)
Rod Cameron, Stephen McNally, Mike Mazurki, Olive Sturgess, Tim McCoy, Johnny Mack Brown, Bob Steele, Lane Chandler, Raymond Hatton, Chet Douglas, Dick Jones, Chris Hughes, Rand Brooks, Dale Van Sickel, Frank Lackteen, Zon Murray, Ronn Delanor, Edmund Cobb, Margo Williams, Doris Spiegel, Dick Alexander, Fred Carson, Red Morgan
D: Spencer G. Bennet
S: Evans W. Cornell, Guy J. Tedesco
SP: R. Alexander
P: Alex Gordon

3099. CAT BALLOU
(Columbia, July 1, 1965)   96 Mins.
(Eastman Color)
Jane Fonda, Lee Marvin, Michael Callan, Dwayne Hickman, Nat "King" Cole, Stubby Kaye, Tom Nardini, John Marly, Reginald Denny, Jay C. Flippen, Arthur Hunnicutt, Bruce Cabot, Burt Mustin, Paul Gilbert
D: Elliott Silverstein
S: Roy Chanslor
SP: Walter Newman, Frank R. Pierson
P: Harold Hecht

3100. THE SONS OF KATIE ELDER
(Paramount, July 1, 1965)   122 Mins.
(Technicolor)   (PanaVision)   (Filmed in Mexico)
John Wayne, Dean Martin, Martha Hyer, Michael Anderson, Jr., Earl Holliman, Jeremy Slate, James Gregory, Paul Fix, George Kennedy, Dennis Hopper, Sheldon Allman, John Litel, John Doucette, James Westerfield, Rhys Williams, John Qualen, Rodolfo Acosta, Strother Martin, Percy Helton, Karl Swenson
D: Henry Hathaway
S: Talbot Jennings
SP: William H. Wright, Allan Weiss, Harry Essex
P: Hal Wallis

3101. THE GLORY GUYS
(United Artists, July 7, 1965)   112 Mins.

The Hallelujah Trail (United Artists, 1965) — Burt Lancaster, Lee Remick, and unidentified player

(Technicolor) (TechniScope) (Filmed in Mexico)

Tom Tryon, Harve Presnell, Michael Anderson, Jr., Senta Berger, James Caan, Andrew Duggan, Slim Pickens, Peter Breck, Jeanne Cooper, Laurel Goodwin, Adam Williams, Erik Holland, Robert McQueeney, Wayne Rogers, William Meigs, Alice Backes

D: Arnold Laven

S: "The Dice of God"—Hoffman Birney

SP: Sam Peckinpah

P: Arnold Laven, Arthur Gardner, Jules Levy

3102. THE BOUNTY KILLER

(Embassy, July 31, 1965) 92 Mins.

(Technicolor) (TechniScope)

Dan Duryea, Rod Cameron, Audrey Dalton, Richard Arlen, Buster Crabbe, Fuzzy Knight, Johnny Mack Brown, Bob Steele, Bronco Billy Anderson, Peter Duryea, Eddie Quillan, Norman Willis, Edmund Cobb, I. Stanford Jolley, Frank Lackteen, Dan White, Grady Sutton, Emory Parnell, Duane Ament, Red Morgan, John Reach, Dolores Domasin, Dudley Ross, Ronn Delanor, Tom Kennedy

D: Spencer G. Bennet

SP: R. Alexander, Leo Gordon

P: Alex Gordon

3103. ARIZONA RAIDERS

(Columbia, August 1, 1965) 88 Mins.

(Technicolor) (TechniScope)

Audie Murphy, Michael Dante, Ben Cooper, Buster Crabbe, Gloria Talbott, Red Morgan, Ray Stricklyn, George Keymas, Fred Krone, Willard Willingham, Fred Graham

D: William Witney

S: Frank Gruber, Richard Schayer

SP: Alex Gottlieb, Mary and Willard Willingham

P: Grant Whytock

3104. SHENANDOAH

(Universal, August 1, 1965) 105 Mins.

(Technicolor)

James Stewart, Doug McClure, Glenn Corbett, Patrick Wayne, Rosemary Forsyth, Philip Alford, Katherine Ross, Charles Robinson, James McMullan, Tim McIntyre, Eugene Jackson, Jr., Paul Fix, Denver Pyle, George Kennedy, James Best, Tom Simcox, Berkeley Harris, Harry Carey, Jr., Kevin Hagen, Dabbs Greer, Strother Martin, Kelly Thordsen

D: Andrew V. McLaglen

SP: James Lee Barrett

P: Robert Arthur

3105. THE GREAT SIOUX MASSACRE
(Columbia, September 1, 1965) 91 Mins.
(Pathe Color) (CinemaScope)
Joseph Cotten, Darren McGavin, Philip Carey, Julie Sommars, Nancy Kovack, John Matthews, Michael Pate, Don Haggerty, Frank Ferguson, Stacy Harris, Iron Eyes Cody, House Peters, Jr., John Napier, William Tannen, Blair Davis, Louise Serpa
D: Sidney Salkow
S: Sidney Salkow, Marvin Gluck
SP: Fred C. Dobbs (Marvin Gluck)
P: Leon Fromkess

3106. THE REWARD
(20th C. Fox, October 1, 1965) 92 Mins.
(DeLuxe Color) (CinemaScope)
Max von Sydow, Yvette Mimieux, Efrem Zimbalist, Jr., Gilbert Roland, Emilio Fernandez, Nino Castelnuovo, Henry Silva, Rodolfo Acosta, Julian Rivero
D: Serge Bourguignon
S: Michael Barrett
SP: Serge Bourguignon, Oscar Millard
P: Aaron Rosenberg

3107. TOWN TAMER
(Paramount, November 1, 1965) 89 Mins.
(Technicolor) (TechniScope)
Dana Andrews, Terry Moore, Pat O'Brien, Lon Chaney, Bruce Cabot, Lyle Bettger, Coleen Gray, Richard Arlen, Barton MacLane, Richard Jaeckel, Philip Carey, DeForest Kelley, Sonny Tufts, Roger Torres, James Brown, Richard Webb, Jeanne Cagney, Donald Barry, Bob Steele
D: Lesley Selander
S/SP: Frank Gruber
P: A. C. Lyles

FILMS OF 1966

3108. APACHE UPRISING
(Paramount, January, 1966) 90 Mins.
(Technicolor) (TechniScope)
Rory Calhoun, Corinne Calvet, John Russell, Lon Chaney, Jr., Gene Evans, Richard Arlen, Robert H. Harris, Arthur Hunnicutt, DeForest Kelley, George Chandler, Johnny Mack Brown, Jean Parker, Abel Fernandez, Don Barry, Robert Carricart, Paul Daniel
D: R. G. Springsteen
SP: Harry Sanford
P: A. C. Lyles

3109. THE RARE BREED
(Universal, February, 1966) 97 Mins.
(Technicolor) (PanaVision)
James Stewart, Maureen O'Hara, Brian Keith, Juliet Mills, Don Galloway, David Brian, Jack Elam, Ben Johnson, Harry Carey, Jr., Perry Lopez
D: Andrew V. McLaglen
SP: Ric Hardman
P: William Alland

3110. JOHNNY RENO
(Paramount, March, 1966) 83 Mins.
(Technicolor) (TechniScope)
Dana Andrews, Jane Russell, Lon Chaney, Jr., John Agar, Lyle Bettger, Tom Drake, Richard Arlen, Robert Lowery, Tracy Olsen, Paul Daniel, Dale Van Sickel
D: R. G. Springsteen

S: Steven Fisher, A. C. Lyles
SP: Steve Fisher
P: A. C. Lyles

3111. BILLY THE KID VS. DRACULA
(Embassy, April, 1966) 72 Mins.
(Pathe Color)
Chuck Courtney, John Carradine, Melinda Plowman, Virginia Christine, Walter Janovitz, Bing Russell, Lennie Geer, Roy Barcroft, Olive Carey, Hannie Landman, Marjorie Bennett, William Forrest, George Cisar, Charlita, Harry Carey, Jr., Richard Reeves, Max Kleven, Jack Williams, William Chailee
D: William Beaudine
S/SP: Carl K. Hittleman
P: Carroll Case

**3112. JESSE JAMES VS.
FRANKENSTEIN'S DAUGHTER**
(Embassy, April, 1966) 82 Mins.
(Pathe Color)
John Lupton, Cal Bolder, Narda Onyx, Steven Geray, Felipe Turich, Rosa Turich, Jim Davis, Raymond Barnes, William Fawcett, Page Slattery, Nestor Paiva, Dan White, Roger Creed, Fred Stromsoe, Mark Norton
D: William Beaudine
S/SP: Carl K. Hittleman
P: Carroll Case

3113. THE NIGHT OF THE GRIZZLY

(Paramount, May, 1966) 103 Mins.

(Technicolor) (TechniScope)

Clint Walker, Martha Hyer, Keenan Wynn, Nancy Kulp, Kevin Brodie, Ellen Corby, Jack Elam, Ron Ely, Med Flory, Leo Gordan, Don Haggerty, Sammy Jackson, Victoria Paige Meyerink, Candy Moore, Regis Toomey

D: Joseph Pevney

SP: Warren Douglas

P: Burt Dunne

3114. DUEL AT DIABLO

(United Artists, May, 1966) 103 Mins.

(DeLuxe Color)

James Garner, Sidney Poitier, Bibi Andersson, Dennis Weaver, Bill Travers, William Redfield, John Hoyt, John Crawford, John Hubbard, Kevin Coughlin, Jay Ripley, Jeff Cooper, Ralph Bahnsen, Bobby Crawford

D: Ralph Nelson

S: "Apache Rising"—Marvin H. Albert

SP: Marvin H. Albert, Michel M. Grilikhes

P: Ralph Nelson, Fred Engel

3115. GUNPOINT

(Universal, May, 1966) 86 Mins.

(Technicolor)

Audie Murphy, Joan Staley, Warren Stevens, Edgar Buchanan, Denver Pyle, David Macklin, Royal Dano, Nick Dennis

D: Earl Bellamy

SP: Mary and Willard Willingham

P: Gordon Kay

3116. A BIG HAND FOR THE LITTLE LADY

(Warner Bros., June 11, 1966) 95 Mins.

(Technicolor)

Henry Fonda, Joanne Woodward, Jason Robards, Charles Bickford, Burgess Meredith, Kevin McCarthy, Robert Middleton, John Qualen, James Kenney, Allen Collins, Jim Boles, Gerald Michenaud, Virginia Gregg, Chester Conklin, Mae Clarke, Ned Glass, James Griffith, Noah Keen, Paul Ford

D: Fielder Cook

SP: Sidney Carroll

P: Fielder Cook

3117. STAGECOACH

(20th C. Fox, June, 1966) 114 Mins.

(DeLuxe Color) (CinemaScope)

Ann-Margret, Red Buttons, Michael Connors, Alex Cord, Bing Crosby, Robert Cummings, Van Heflin, Slim Pickens, Stefanie Powers, Keenan Wynn, Brad Weston, Joseph Hoover

D: Gordon Douglas

S: "Stage to Lordsburg"—Ernest Haycox

SP: Joseph Landon. From the screenplay by Dudley Nichols

P: Martin Rackin

3118. . . . AND NOW MIGUEL

(Universal, June, 1966) 95 Mins.

(Technicolor) (TechniScope)

Guy Stockwell, Pat Cardi, Michael Ansara, Clu Gulager, Joe De Santis, Pilar Del Ray, Peter Robbins, Buck Taylor, Edmund Hashim, Emma Tyson, Richard Brehm

D: James B. Clark

S: Joseph Krumgold

SP: Ted Sherdeman, Jane Klove

P: Robert B. Radnitz

3119. NEVADA SMITH

(Paramount, July, 1966) 128 Mins.

(Color) (PanaVision)

Steve McQueen, Karl Malden, Brian Keith, Arthur Kennedy, Suzanne Pleshette, Raf Vallone, Janet Margolin, Howard De Silva, Pat Hingle, Martin Landau, Paul Fix, Gene Evans, Josephine Hutchinson, John Doucette, Val Avery, Sheldon Allman, Lyle Bettger, Burt Freed, David McLean, Steve Mitchell, Ric Roman, John Litel, Ted de Corsia

D: Henry Hathaway

S/SP: John Michael Hayes. From Harold Robbins' "The Carpetbaggers"

P: Joseph E. Levine, Henry Hathaway

3120. INCIDENT AT PHANTOM HILL

(Universal, July, 1966) 88 Mins.

(Technicolor)

Robert Fuller, Jocelyn Lane, Dan Duryea, Claude Akins, Noah Beery, Jr., Lindon Chiles, Tom Simcox, Paul Fix

D: Earl Bellamy

SP: Frank Nugent

P: Harry Tatelman

3121. WACO

(Paramount, September, 1966) 85 Mins.

(Technicolor) (TechniScope)

Howard Keel, Jane Russell, Brian Donlevy, Wendell Corey, Terry Moore, John Smith, John Agar, Gene Evans, Richard Arlen, Ben Cooper, Tracy Olsen, DeForest Kelley, Anne Seymour, Robert Lowery, Willard Parker, Jeff Richards, Reg Parton, Fuzzy Knight

D: R. G. Springsteen

S: "Emporia"—Harry Sanford, Max Lamb

SP: Steve Fisher

P: A. C. Lyles

3122. SMOKY

(20th C. Fox, September, 1966)   103 Mins.

(DeLuxe Color)

Fess Parker, Diana Hyland, Katy Jurado, Hoyt Axton, Robert Wilke, Armando Silvestre, Jose Hector Galindo, Jorge Martinez de Hoyos, Ted White, Chuck Roberson, Robert Terhune, Jack Williams

D: George Sherman

S: Will James

SP: Howard Medford. Based on the screenplay by Lillie Hayward, Dwight Cummings, and Dorothy Yost

P: Aaron Rosenberg

3123. THE PLAINSMAN

(Universal, September, 1966)   92 Mins.

(Color)

Don Murray, Guy Stockwell, Abby Dalton, Bradford Dillman, Henry Silva, Simon Oakland, Leslie Nielsen, Edward Binns, Michael Evans, Percy Rodriguez, Terry Wilson, Walter Berke, Emily Banks

D: David Lowell

SP: Michael Blankfort

P: Richard E. Lyons, Jack Leewood

3124. ALVAREZ KELLY

(Columbia, October, 1966)   116 Mins.

(Pathe Color)   (PanaVision)

William Holden, Richard Widmark, Janice Rule, Patrick O'Neal, Victoria Shaw, Roger C. Carmel, Richard Rust, Arthur Franz, Donald Barry, Duke Hobbie, Harry Carey, Jr., Howard Caine, Mauritz Hugo, G. B. Atwater, Robert Morgan, Stephanie Hill, Paul Lukather, Indus Arthur, Clint Ritchie

D: Edward Dmytryck

S: Franklin Coen

SP: Franklin Coen, Elliott Arnold

P: Sol C. Siegel

3125. THE APPALOOSA

(Universal, October, 1966)   98 Mins.

(Technicolor)   (TechniScope)

Marlon Brando, Anjanette Comer, John Saxon, Emilio Fernandez, Alex Montoya, Miriam Colon, Rafael Campos, Frank Silvera, Larry Mann, Argentina Brunetti

D: Sidney J. Furie

S: Robert McLeod

SP: James Bridges, Roland Kibbee

P: Alan Miller

3126. TEXAS ACROSS THE RIVER

(Universal, November, 1966)   101 Mins.

(Technicolor)   (TechniScope)

Dean Martin, Alain Delon, Joey Bishop, Rosemary Forsyth, Tina Marquand, Peter Graves, Andrew Prine, Stuart Anderson, Michael Ansara, George Wallace, Roy Barcroft, John Harmon, Dick Farnsworth, Linden Chiles

D: Michael Gordon

SP: Wells Root, Harold Green, Ben Starr

P: Harry Keller

3127. THE PROFESSIONALS

(Columbia, November, 1966)   117 Mins.

(Technicolor)   (TechniScope)

Burt Lancaster, Lee Marvin, Robert Ryan, Jack Palance, Claudia Cardinale, Ralph Bellamy, Woody Strode, Joe De Santis, Rafael Bertrand, Jorge Martinez de Hoyos, Marie Gomez, Jose Chavez, Carlos Romero, Vaughn Taylor

D: Richard Brooks

S: "A Mule for the Marquesa"—Frank O'Rourke

SP: Richard Brooks

FILMS OF 1967

3128. RED TOMAHAWK

(Paramount, January, 1967)   82 Mins.

(Technicolor)

Howard Keel, Joan Caulfield, Broderick Crawford, Scott Brady, Wendell Corey, Richard Arlen, Tom Drake, Tracy Olsen, Ben Cooper, Donald Barry, Reg Parton, Gerald Jann, Roy Jensen, Dan White, Henry Wills, Saul Gorss

D: R. G. Springsteen

S: Steve Fisher, Andrew Craddock

SP: Steve Fisher

P: A. C. Lyles

3129. THE ADVENTURES OF BULLWHIP GRIFFIN

(Buena Vista, March, 1967)   110 Mins.

(Technicolor)

Roddy McDowall, Suzanne Pleshette, Karl Malden, Harry Guardino, Richard Haydn, Hermione Baddeley, Brian Russell, Liam Redmond, Cecil Kellaway, Jody Baker, Mike Mazurki, Alan Carney, Parley Baer, Arthur Hunnicutt, Dub Taylor, Pedro Gonzales-Gonzales

D: James Neilson

S: "By the Great Horn Spoon"—Sid Fleischman

SP: Lowell S. Hawley
P: A Walt Disney Presentation

3130. HOMBRE
(20th C. Fox, April, 1967)   110 Mins.
(DeLuxe Color)   (PanaVision)
Paul Newman, Fredric March, Richard Boone, Diane Cilento, Cameron Mitchell, Barbara Rush, Peter Lazer, Margaret Blye, Martin Balsam, Skip Ward, Frank Silvera, David Canary, Val Avery, Larry Ward
D: Martin Ritt
S: Elmore Leonard
SP: Irving Ravetch, Harriet Frank, Jr.
P: Martin Ritt, Irving Ravetch

3131. WELCOME TO HARD TIMES
(MGM, May, 1967)   105 Mins.
(Metrocolor)
Henry Fonda, Janice Rule, Keenan Wynn, Janis Paige, John Anderson, Warren Oates, Fay Spain, Edgar Buchanan, Aldo Ray, Denver Pyle, Michael O'Shea, Arlene Golonka, Lon Chaney, Jr., Royal Dano, Alan Baxter, Paul Birch, Dan Ferrone, Paul Fix, Elisha Cook, Jr., Kalen Liu, Ann McCrea
D/SP: Burt Kennedy

S: E. L. Doctorow
P: Max E. Youngstein, David Karr

3132. 40 GUNS TO APACHE PASS
(Admiral/Columbia, May, 1967)   95 Mins.
(Eastman Color)
Audie Murphy, Michael Burns, Kenneth Tobey, Laraine Stephens, Robert Brubaker, Michael Blodgett, Michael Keep, Kay Stewart, Kenneth MacDonald, Byron Morrow, Willard Willingham, Ted Gehring, James Beck
D: William Witney
SP: Willard Willingham, Mary Willingham

3133. CHUKA
(Paramount, May, 1967)   91 Mins.
(Pathe Color)
Rod Taylor, Ernest Borgnine, John Mills, Luciana Paluzzi, James Whitmore, Angela Dorian, Louis Hayward, Michael Cole, Hugh Reill, Barry O'Hara, Joseph Sirola, Marco Antonio, Gerald York, Herlinda del Carmen, Lucky Carson
D: Gordon Douglas
S/SP: Richard Jessup
P: Rod Taylor, Jack Jason

Hombre (20th C. Fox, 1967) — Fredric March, Peter Lazer, Margaret Blye, Paul Newman, Martin Balsam, and Diane Cilento

3134. GUNFIGHT IN ABILENE
(Universal, May, 1967) 86 Mins.
(Technicolor) (TechniScope)
Bobby Darin, Emily Banks, Leslie Nielsen, Donnelly Rhodes, Don Galloway, Frank McGrath, Michael Sarrazin, Barbara Werle, Johnny Seven, William Phipps, William Mims, Robert Sorrells, Don Dubbins, James McCallion, Bryan O'Byrne
D: William Hale
S: Clarence Upson Young
SP: Berne Giler, John D. F. Black
P: Howard Christie

3135. THE WAY WEST
(United Artists, May 24, 1967) 122 Mins.
(DeLuxe Color) (PanaVision)
Kirk Douglas, Robert Mitchum, Richard Widmark, Lola Albright, Michael Witney, Stubby Kaye, Sally Field, Katherine Justice, Michael McGreevey, Connie Sawyer, Harry Carey, Jr., Elizabeth Fraser, William Lundigan, Anne Barton, Roy Barcroft, Eve McVeagh, Jack Elam, Hal Lynch, Timothy Scott, John Mitchum, Roy Glenn, Patric Knowles, Nick Cravat, Gary Morris
D: Andrew V. McLaglen
S: A. B. Guthrie, Jr.
SP: Ben Maddow, Mitch Lindemann
P: Harold Hecht

3136. THE WAR WAGON
(Marvin Schwartz/Batjac/Universal, June, 1967) 101 Mins.
(Technicolor) (PanaVision) (Filmed in Mexico)
John Wayne, Kirk Douglas, Howard Keel, Robert Walker, Jr., Keenan Wynn, Bruce Cabot, Valora Noland, Gene Evans, Joanna Barnes, Terry Wilson, Don Collier, Bruce Dern, Sheb Wooley, Ann McCrea, Emilio Fernandez, Frank McGrath, Chuck Roberson, Red Morgan, Hal Needham, Marco Antonio, Perla Walter, Miko Mayama Midori, Margarite Luna, Jose Trinidad Villa
D: Burt Kennedy
S: "Badman"—Clair Huffaker
SP: Clair Huffaker
P: Marvin Schwartz

3137. EL DORADO
(Laurel/Paramount, July, 1967) 126 Mins.
(Technicolor)
John Wayne, Robert Mitchum, James Caan, Charlene Holt, Paul Fix, Arthur Hunnicutt, Michele Carey, R. G. Armstrong, Edward Asner, Christopher George, Marina Ghane, John Gabriel, Robert Rothwell, Robert Donner, Adam Roarke, Victoria George, Jim Davis, Anne Newman, Diane Strom, Johnny Crawford, Olaf Weighorst, Chuck Courtney, Anthony Rogers, Bill Henry, Nacho Galindo, John Mitchum
D: Howard Hawks
S: "The Stars in Their Crowns"—Harry Brown
SP: Leigh Brackett
P: Howard Hawks

3138. RIDE TO HANGMAN'S TREE
(Universal, July, 1967) 90 Mins.
(Technicolor)
Jack Lord, James Farentino, Don Galloway, Melodie Johnson, Richard Anderson, Robert Yuro, Ed Peck, Paul Reed, Richard Cutting, Bing Russell, Virginia Capers, Robert Sorrells, Robert Cornthwaite, Fabian Dean
D: Al Rafkin
S: Luci Ward, Jack Natteford
SP: Luci Ward, Jack Natteford, William Bowers
P: Howard Christie

3139. THE FASTEST GUITAR ALIVE
(MGM, September, 1967) 85 Mins.
(Technicolor)
Roy Orbison, Sammy Jackson, Maggie Pierce, Joan Freeman, Lyle Bettger, John Doucette, Patricia Donohue, Ben Cooper, Douglas Kennedy, Len Hendry, Iron Eyes Cody, Sam the Sham, Wilda Taylor, Victoria Carroll, Maria Korda, Poupee Gamin
D: Michael Moore
SP: Robert E. Kent
P: Sam Katzman

3140. FORT UTAH
(Paramount, September, 1967) 83 Mins.
(Technicolor) (TechniScope)
John Ireland, Virginia Mayo, Scott Brady, John Russell, Robert Strauss, James Craig, Richard Arlen, Jim Davis, Donald Barry, Harry Lauter, Red Morgan, Reg Parton, Eric Cody
D: Lesley Selander
SP: Steve Fisher, Andrew Craddock
P: A. C. Lyles

3140a. HONDO AND THE APACHES
(Batjac/Fenady/MGM, September, 1967) 85 Mins.
(Metrocolor)
Ralph Taeger, Michael Rennie, John Smith, Gary Clark, Buddy Foster, Victor Lundin, Steve Mario, William Bryant, Kathie Browne, Gary Merrill, Noah Beery, Jr., Randy Boone, Michael Pate, Jim Davis, John Pickard
D: Lee H. Katzin
SP: Andrew J. Fenady. From the screenplay for "Hondo" by James E. Grant and based on the story "The Gift of Cochise" by Louis L'Amour
P: Andrew J. Fenady

3141. THE LAST CHALLENGE

(MGM, October, 1967)   105 Mins.

(Metrocolor) (PanaVision)

Glenn Ford, Angie Dickinson, Chad Everett, Gary Merrill, Jack Elam, Delphi Lawrence, Royal Dano, Kevin Hagen, Florence Sundstrom, Marian Collier, Robert Sorrells, John Milford, Frank McGrath

D/P: Richard Thorpe

S: "Pistolero's Progress"—John Sherry

SP: John Sherry, Robert Emmett Ginna

3142. HOUR OF THE GUN

(United Artists, October 4, 1967)   100 Mins.

(DeLuxe Color) (PanaVision)

James Garner, Jason Robards, Robert Ryan, Albert Salmi, Charles Aidman, Steve Ihnat, Michael Tolan, Frank Converse, Sam McIville, Austin Willis, Richard Bull, Larry Gates, Karl Swenson, Bill Fletcher, Robert Phillips, William Schallert, Jon Voight, Lonny Chapman, Monte Markham, William Windom, Edward Anhalt, Walter Gregg, David Perna, Jim Sheppard, Jorge Russell

D: John Sturges

SP: Edward Anhalt

P: John Sturges

3143. ROUGH NIGHT IN JERICHO

(Universal, October, 1967)   104 Mins.

(Technicolor) (TechniScope)

Dean Martin, Jean Simmons, George Peppard, John McIntire, Slim Pickens, Don Galloway, Brad Weston, Richard O'Brien, Carol Anderson, Steve Sandor, Warren Vanders, John Napier

D: Arnold Laven

S: "The Man in Black"—Marvin H. Albert

SP: Sidney Boehm, Marvin H. Albert

P: Martin Rackin

3144. A TIME FOR KILLING

(Columbia, November, 1967)   88 Mins.

(Pathe Color) (PanaVision)

Glenn Ford, Inger Stevens, Paul Peterson, Timothy Carey, Kenneth Tobey, Richard X. Slattery, Harrison J. Gord, Kay E. Kuter, Dick Miller, Emile Meyer, Marshall Reed, George Hamilton, Max Baer, Todd Armstrong, Duke Hobbie, Dean Stanton, James Davidson, Charlie Briggs, Craig Curtis, Jay Ripley

D: Phil Karlson

Hour of the Gun (United Artists, 1967) — James Garner, Jason Robards (center), and unidentified players

529

S: Nelson and Shirley Wolford
SP: Halsted Welles
P: Harry Joe Brown

3145. WATERHOLE #3
(Paramount, November, 1967)   95 Mins.
(Technicolor)   (TechniScope)
James Coburn, Carroll O'Connor, Margaret Blye, Claude Akins, Timothy Carey, Bruce Dern, Joan Blondell, James Whitmore, Harry Davis, Roy Jensen, Robert Cornthwaite, Jim Boles, Steve Whittaker, Ted Markland, Robert Crosse, Jay Ose, Buzz Henry
D: William Graham

SP: Joseph T. Steck, R. R. Young
P: Joseph T. Steck

3146. HOSTILE GUNS
(Paramount, December, 1967)   91 Mins.
(Technicolor)   (TechniScope)
George Montgomery, Yvonne De Carlo, Tab Hunter, Brian Donlevy, John Russell, Leo Gordon, Robert Emhardt, Pedro Gonzales-Gonzales, James Craig, Richard Arlen, Emile Meyer, Donald Barry, Fuzzy Knight, William Fawcett, Joe Brown, Reg Parton, Eric Cody, Read Morgan
D: R. G. Springsteen
S: Sloan Nibley, James Edward Grant
SP: Steve Fisher
P: A. C. Lyles

CHAPTER 10

The Cynical Years
1968-1972

(NOW AND THEN A GLINT OF WHITE ON A SULLEN SEA)

During the Cynical Years of 1968-1972 Westerns began to explore the legends that surround familiar Western figures, tearing down the folk-hero images that had been built up in earlier-day films. For example, *Little Big Man* (National General, 1971) is hardly an endorsement of General George Custer, and William H. Bonney is truthfully depicted as a punk killer by Michael Pollard in *Dirty Little Billy* (Columbia, 1972), a characterization quite different from the sympathetic versions of *Billy the Kid* in 1930 and 1941 and the "hero" series by Bob Steele and Buster Crabbe in the Forties. There seemed an undeniable desire to tell the truth, to bring to the knowledge of millions of Americans what it was all about, to "expose" the life and times of the old West in frankest terms. The Western became a fount of vigorous social comment, carefully analyzing the flaws in American society. The anti-Westerns made their appearance, notable examples being *The Wild Bunch* (Warner Bros., 1969), *McCabe and Mrs. Miller* (Warner Bros., 1971), *The Culpepper Cattle Company* (Fox, 1972), and *The Great Northfield, Minnesota Raid* (Universal, 1972), the purpose evidently to counter the traditional Western's glorification of the American West, the cowboy, heroism, and social progress and to show the West as it really was—dirty and violent. This critical and pessimistic view of the West once championed was by no means unanimous—and let us be thankful for small blessings—but there was a sufficient number of such films to constitute a trend.

The most financially successful Western of the period, and of any period, was *Butch Cassidy and the Sundance Kid* (Fox, 1969), grossing over $30 million. Its success was in part the result of the comic approach which was in vogue and which had made *Cat Ballou, Four for Texas, The Hallelujah Trail*, and *The Rounders* popular films previously. Nearly fifty years before Hoot Gibson and Pete Morrison had laid the foundation for comic Westerns in which the hero was totally at the mercy of events swirling about him. However, Gibson's and Morrison's heroes were true-blue, red-blooded, morally uncorrupted cowboys who just happened into humorous situations. The heroes of these latter-day films were, to say the least, morally suspect, and usually they differed from the older archetype, too, in their attitude toward society. *Butch Cassidy and the Sundance Kid* is a rather exhilarating *tour de force* with Paul Newman and Robert Redford presented as a pair of happy-go-lucky outlaws who, venturing forth against the mighty Union Pacific Railroad, find themselves unable to elude their fate as doomed anachronisms from a past era. Less fearsome than the corporate villains who crush them, they are depicted as childlike figures who drift along in a world of fantasy. Director George Roy Hill, with the help of his stars Newman, Redford, and Katherine Ross, pulled off the surprise hit Western of the century, and the excursions into sepia for sequences suggestive of the 1890's is technically outstanding. The characters and dialogue are played with tongue-in-cheek but the film does present a rather factual account of the last days of these holdovers from a West that no longer is.

Butch Cassidy and the Sundance Kid (20th C. Fox, 1969) — Paul Newman, Katherine Ross, and Robert Redford

The Wild Bunch (Warner Bros., 1969) — Ben Johnson, William Holden, Ernest Borgnine, Warren Oates, and unidentified players

In a similar vein, *Will Penny* (Paramount, 1968) gives us not an outlaw but a tired cowhand (Charlton Heston) forced to take on menial work. And *Monte Walsh* (National General, 1970) is the story of two cowboys (Lee Marvin, Jack Palance) down on their luck in a modern world they don't empathize with.

Paul Newman is effective in the off-beat comedy *The Life and Times of Judge Roy Bean* (National General, 1972), a happy blend of myth and realism brought about by a good screenplay and able cast.

One of the bloodiest and most violent Westerns ever made is *The Wild Bunch* (Warner Bros., 1969), a deeply cynical film that brings out the innate violence and greed of man, although there is a complexity to its cynicism that makes it both an unsettling and very rewarding cinema experience. Its blood-letting, though repulsive, is, nevertheless, an entrancing cinematic accomplishment and the film scored big at the box office. The complexity of its cynicism distinguishes it and lifts it above the others of its breed. Sam Peckinpah, with his montage techniques, fluctuating fast and slow motion, and other camera illusions, is at his best when focusing on that time in our history when the old West was evolving into the new West. In the story, the Wild Bunch is an unsuccessful, disoriented, and frustrated group of crooks, led by William Holden, who hire out to a small-time Mexican revolutionary for one last job before retirement. The Bunch comes to an end in an especially bloody finale.

Billy Jack (Warner Bros., 1971) at times becomes a rebuttal to the traditional Western and is steeped in the Seventies' sense of the times. It is an austere endeavor in which the filmmaker manipulates the conventions of his genre to express himself through the public language, thereby perhaps manipulating the viewer into revised sympathies, refined reactions, and even a change in view. However, the characters are mixed-up people and the film generates little enthusiasm for traditional psychological/sociological drama in a modern Western setting.

Ralph Nelson's *Soldier Blue* (Avco Embassy, 1970), with Candice Bergen, clumsily rejects the heroic U.S. Cavalry image of the John Ford Westerns and turns the Cavalry into bestial murderers in a reconstruction of the infamous Sand Creek Massacre. The film's purpose, apparently, is to generate sympathy for the Indian and to cause guilt-feelings in whites for the Indian wars. Soldier Blue is thrown into chains for criticizing the leader of a massacre that results in the killing of a tribe's women and children, obviously a reference to the My Lai incident of the Vietnam conflict.

Another film depicting Indian culture as more honorable and dignified than the white man's is *Little Big Man* (National General, 1971), a film already mentioned. General Custer is depicted as a madman in this one, and he fares little better in *Custer of the West* (Cinerama, 1968). In *A Man Called Horse* (National General, 1970), Richard Harris plays an Englishman captured by the Sioux. As he gradually wins acceptance among the tribe and weds an Indian girl, he comes to understand the noble ways of his captors. And in *Ulzana's Raid* (Universal, 1972) the Apache is presented sympathetically. *The Scalphunters* (United Artists, 1968), while an entertaining action Western, is a serious statement about the relationships between blacks, whites, and Indians, and in *Jeremiah Johnson* (Warner Bros., 1972) mountain man Johnson is torn between civilization and nature, between the white settlers' attempts to defeat nature and the Indians' determination to live with it. In the end his decision is to live in conformity with nature.

J. W. Coop (Columbia, 1972), *The Honkers* (United Artists, 1972), and *Junior Bonner* (Cinerama, 1972) are contemporary rodeo films that allow spectactors an inside view of the rodeo world and its cowboys. Cliff Robertson gives a good performance in *J. W. Coop* as an ex-con on the comeback trail after a decade in jail, as does James Coburn who plays the

Junior Bonner (Cinerama Releasing, 1972) — Steve McQueen

drunken, lecherous "has been" who is out to take what he can in *The Honkers*. The rodeo itself was intended to be a metaphor for life with its many victories and spills. And Steve McQueen is *Junior Bonner*, a worldly-wise loser with a "hangdog look" and a hitch in his get-along so typical of rodeo cowboys, in a story that focuses on the trials and tribulations of two generations of rodeo cowboys.

John Wayne parodies himself in Henry Hathaway's *True Grit* (Paramount, 1969) and wins an Academy Award for his portrayal of a fat, old, one-eyed lawman. No thanks to Glen Campbell's acting ineptness, the film became one of the highest grossing Westerns in screen history and, if it was needed, rejuvenated Wayne's career. The role of cantankerous, whiskey-guzzling "Rooster" Cogburn was a natural for Wayne, who played it for all it was worth. For director Hathaway, the film suggested that his previous but financially disappointing exceptional Western *From Hell to Texas* (Fox, 1958) was no fluke.

Two noteworthy films honed in on the simple subject of cowboyin', putting the punchers back on the range where they belong. *The Culpepper Cattle Company* (Fox, 1972) deglamourizes the West and shows the life of a cowboy to be anything but romantic or exciting. As cowboy historian Ramon Adams has written, "There was little romance in getting up at four o'clock in the mornin', eatin' dust behind a trail herd, swimmin' muddy and turbulent rivers, or in doctorin' screw worms, pullin' stupid cows from bog hones, sweatin' in the heat of summer and freezin' in the cold of winter." This was the message interwoven throughout the fabric of the film as the cowboy's life is pictured as dirty, unglamourous, unrewarding, fraught with danger, and sometimes violent. It was not nearly as successful as the second of the two "cowboy" films.

Though *The Cowboys* (Warner Bros., 1972) is awash in sentimentality, it largely avoids mawkishness by means of many warm and humorous touches in the screenplay and the glowing performances of the principals. Few films of recent years have as realistically presented the harshness and frustrations of ranching and the trail drive to the railheads as does this one, although it arouses reactions among critics for its violence. But, except for the excesses of the climax, the film is relatively non-violent and far more palatable from this standpoint than films such as *The Wild Bunch* and the spaghetti Westerns of Clint Eastwood and confreres. It emerges as a mammoth spectacle with brilliantly staged action sequences. Wayne plays rancher Will Anderson who takes to the trail with eleven young boys as trail hands, teaching them about "cowboyin'" as they go along. When he is killed by outlaws, the boys kill the rustlers and deliver the cattle to market. As one critic put it, "*The Cowboys* is meant as a message of hope for lovers of old Westerns. And it is that—a gritty, pungent film in which Wayne passes along the legacy of the Western hero."

The Cynical Years were good ones for John Wayne, despite the fact that he made a less cynical, more traditional type Western than was then in vogue. *The Undefeated* (Fox, 1969) is a run-of-the-mill Wayne vehicle which, interpreted, means that it is still superior Western entertainment, and it does have its good moments. But those good moments are mainly in the action scenes and two or three dramatic sequences dominated by Wayne. Director Andrew V. McLaglen failed to make things click in this one, although his work on other Wayne features has been exceptional. *Rio Lobo* (Cinema Center, 1970) was Wayne's weakest Western in a number of years, even though directed by Howard Hawks, who, more than Wayne, has to accept responsibility for the film's faults. A weak script by Burton Wohl and Leigh Brackett and a mediocre supporting cast compounded Hawks' poor direction. Wayne and Jack Elam have a few good moments and these, together with Yak Canutt's second-unit work, save the insipid film from utter disaster.

In Wayne's remaining two films of the period he is back in his old stride in good stories adapted to his image and personality, clinging to the basic traditional Western formula so successful for him in yesteryears. In his own inimitable way Wayne has prevented the spirit if not the body of the Saturday matinee shoot-em-up from fading away and a pleasurable vicarious experience is afforded by viewing his range thrillers. Take *Chisum* (Warner Bros., 1970), a story of the Lincoln County range wars. Wayne is once again the portrait of heroic masculinity in a straight-from-the-shoulder approach to chicanery in the old West. His role as a cattle king is perfectly engaging and the film is extraordinarily fascinating, although no doubt its entrancement is more easily discernible to Wayne buffs and tradition lovers than to others. But being guilty on both counts, the authors' proclivity is to rate it as one of the better Westerns of the period. The remaining film, *Big Jake* (National General, 1971), reunites Wayne with Maureen O'Hara, again an ex-wife who needs his assistance, in saving their grandson from kidnappers. Traditional ways, as manifested in Wayne's behavior, win out over progress, as represented by the motorized Texas Rangers. *Big Jake* stirs up a lot of the excitement that Saturday matinee audiences used to experience and react to with shrills, hand-and-foot clapping, and unrestrained whoops-and-hollers. Maybe it was because George Sherman was again directing Wayne and applying some of the old "B" techniques to the film. Sherman had directed Wayne in eight *Three Mesquiteers* features at Republic thirty years before and knew how to pace a film. The star and director should have gotten together more often over the years.

Characteristic of the Cynical Years was a diversity in screenplays as evidenced by a number of Westerns somewhat original in story and execution. *Death of a Gunfighter* (Uni-

Chisum (Warner Bros., 1970) — Forrest Tucker, Bruce Cabot, and John Wayne.

versal, 1969) is the story of a gunfighter, this time a marshal, whose knowledge of the deeds and misdeeds of the inhabitants of the community has kept him in office but whose strict execution of his job has created enemies. He is forced to defend himself and his new bride (Lena Horne) against the whole town. No mention is made in the story of the fact that Lena is a Negro. But *Buck and the Preacher* (Columbia, 1972) features black heroes in the persons of Sidney Poitier and Harry Belafonte, the first major Western to do so. *Man and Boy* (Levitt-Pickman, 1972), *Soul Soldier* (Hirschman Northern, 1971), *The Legend of Nigger Charley* (Paramount, 1972), and *Black Rodeo* (Cinerama, 1972), a documentary on the black rodeo riders, have all provided black awareness in the Western genre, and blacks have played prominent, serious parts in "white" Westerns, as for example, Roscoe Lee Brown in *The Cowboys*. Blacks have come far since the days when Fred "Snowflake" Toones might be used for a little comedy routine. Not only did blacks and Indians receive overdue recognition in Westerns but so did Mexicans, as in, for example, *Valdez Is Coming* (United Artists, 1971) in which Burt Lancaster has the title role as the revenge seeker whose repertoire of tricks is seemingly limitless.

Women's liberation comes to the West in *Hannie Caulder* (Paramount, 1972) as Raquel Welch is trained and unleashed as a skillful gunfightress. Naturally her opponents never had a chance, as the topography of her anatomy distracted their concentration. Man's relationship to God and his fellow man is explored in a non-violent, romantic film directed by Sam Peckinpah and titled *The Ballad of Cable Hogue* (Warner Bros., 1970). *Wild Rovers* (MGM, 1972) emphasizes the idealized comradeship of two saddle partners, William Holden and Ryan O'Neal, who turn to robbing banks and abducting women hostages as they attempt to escape to a better life in Mexico. Blake Edwards' direction is masterful and Holden's performance its usual perfection. And another story of two drifting cowboys, *The Hired Hand* (Universal, 1971), is a simple, almost old-fashioned love story which, at its best, reveals the greater value placed on human life than is ordinarily found in the traditional Western. There is less violence; more gentle and tender moments prevail.

But violence is back aplenty in *Hang 'Em High* (United Artists, 1968) starring Clint Eastwood and made in much the same vein as his Italian Westerns for Sergio Leone. The film is violent, but the story of a hanged man who survives to become a deputy marshal charged with bringing in the men who hanged him is a good one, made more so by the excellent cast that includes Bob Steele, Ben Johnson, Bruce Dern, Ed Begley, and Inger Stevens. The film cost under $2 million to make and has grossed over $11 million, reason enough for Eastwood to try again with a film titled *High Plains Drifter* (Universal, 1972) which he directed and in which he is once again smoking cheroots as the "Man with No Name." This time he is out to protect the residents of a guilt-ridden town from three gunmen just out of jail and literally turns the town into a raging hell as the story builds to a fiery climax. It did only modest business worldwide, the pulling power of this type of innovative Western having waned by the time of the film's release.

As further proof that Westerns have never been limited to a mere handful of formulae, we mention such films as *McCabe and Mrs. Miller* (Warner Bros., 1971), a lyrical re-creation of the Washington frontier of 1903 with, we might add, striking color photography by cinematographer Vilmos Zsigmond. A most interesting aspect of the film is its demythologizing of the Western hero and heroine, as well as the individual twist which it gives to a number of other stock characters of the traditional Western. Not understanding or appreciating the subtlety which appeals to film critics, audiences weren't especially impressed by the movie. Robert Altman directed. And merely representative of the many cynical films purporting to show the West as it really was are *One Hundred Rifles* (Fox, 1969), about Mexican revolutionaries and an American capitalist; *Villa Rides* (Paramount, 1968), with Villa again presented as a bandit without redeeming qualities; *Bandolero* (Fox, 1968), with James Stewart playing an aged gunfighter on a rescue mission; *Five Card Stud* (Paramount, 1968), with Robert Mitchum as the spiritually suspect preacher-undertaker; *A Gunfight* (Paramount, 1971), a unique story with Kirk Douglas and Johnny Cash cast as down-and-outers who agree to a shoot-out for money; *There Was a Crooked Man* (Warner Bros., 1970), with Kirk Douglas and Henry Fonda in a new twist on the good badman vs. honest sheriff theme; *Pocket Money* (National General, 1972), a dismal south-of-the-border story of two American bums; *Paint Your Wagon* (Paramount, 1969), in which Jean Seberg courageously and untiringly serves both Lee Marvin and Clint Eastwood as wife; and *Tell Them Willie Boy Is Here* (Universal, 1970), a complex, often brilliant film that uses hostility toward the Indian to mirror the primitivism and inequities of the American culture. Watching these and other such films, one is apt to wonder if the producers haven't gone as far in one direction as "B" producers did in another one and if the truth about the old West and its inhabitants didn't lie somewhere between these so-called "myth" and "realism" films.

Cynicism was rampant but Western filmdom was not adrift in a completely dark, brooding, foreboding sea. *Heaven with a Gun* (MGM, 1969), *Firecreek* (Warner Bros., 1968), *Arizona Bushwackers* (Paramount, 1968), and *The Gatling Gun* (Ellman, 1972) were representative of the more tradition-bound Westerns with honorable or semi-honorable heroes, while *The Shakiest Gun in the West* (Universal, 1968), *The Great Bank Robbery* (Warner Bros., 1969), *The Cheyenne Social Club* (National General, 1970), and *The Cockeyed Cowboys of Calico County* (Universal, 1970) provided good, healthy belly laughs appropriate for any era. Thus, there was now and then a glint of white on a sullen sea, holding promise of smoother sailing once the storm of cynicism was ridden out.

FILMS OF 1968

3147. FIRECREEK
(Warner Bros.-7 Arts, February, 1968) 104 Mins.
(Technicolor) (PanaVision)
James Stewart, Henry Fonda, Gary Lockwood, Dean Jagger, Ed Begley, Jay C. Flippen, Jack Elam, James Best, Barbara Luna, Jacqueline Scott, Brooke Bundy, J. Robert Porter, Morgan Woodward, John Qualen, Louise Latham, Athena Lord, Harry "Slim" Duncan, Inger Stevens
D: Vincent McEveety
SP: Calvin Clements
P: Philip Leacock

3148. THE BALLAD OF JOSIE
(Universal, February, 1968) 102 Mins.
(Technicolor) (TechniScope)
Doris Day, Peter Graves, George Kennedy, Andy Devine, William Talman, David Hartman, Guy Raymond, Audrie Christian, Karen Jensen, Elizabeth Fraser
D: Andrew V. McLaglen
SP: Harold Swanton
P: Norman MacDonnell

3149. ARIZONA BUSHWACKERS
(Paramount, March, 1968) 86 Mins.
(Technicolor) (TechniScope)
Howard Keel, Yvonne De Carlo, John Ireland, Marilyn Maxwell, Scott Brady, Brian Donlevy, Barton MacLane, James Craig, Roy Roberts, Reg Parton, Montie Montana, Eric Cody
D: Lesley Selander
S: Steve Fisher, Andrew Craddock
SP: Steve Fisher
P: A. C. Lyles

3150. WILL PENNY
(Paramount, March, 1968) 109 Mins.
(Technicolor)
Charlton Heston, Joan Hackett, Donald Pleasence, Lee Majors, Bruce Dern, Ben Johnson, Slim Pickens, Clifton James, Anthony Zerbe, Roy Jenson, G. D. Spradlin, Quentin Dean, William Schallert, Lydia Clarke, Robert Luster, Cal Jenkins, Matt Clark, Luke Askew
D: Tom Gries
SP: Tom Gries
P: Fred Engel, Walter Seltzer

540

Will Penny (Paramount, 1968) — Charlton Heston and Joan Hackett

3151. DAY OF THE EVIL GUN

(MGM, March, 1968) 95 Mins.

(Metrocolor) (PanaVision) (Filmed in Mexico)

Glenn Ford, Arthur Kennedy, Dean Jagger, John Anderson, Paul Fix, Nico Minardos, Dean Stanton, Pilar Pellicer, Parley Baer, Royal Dano, Ross Elliott, Barbara Babcock, James Griffith

D: Jerry Thorpe

S: Charles Marquis Warren

SP: Charles Marquis Warren, Eric Bercovici

P: Jerry Thorpe

3152. THE DEVIL'S MISTRESS

(Emerson/W-G-W, March, 1968) 66 Mins.

(Eastman Color) (Filmed in New Mexico)

Joan Stapleton, Robert Gregory, Forest Westmoreland, Douglas Warren, Oren Williams, Arthur Resley

D/SP: Orville Wanzer

P: Wes Moreland

3153. GUNS FOR SAN SEBASTIAN

(MGM, April, 1968) 111 Mins.

(Metrocolor) (Franscope) (Filmed in Mexico)

Anthony Quinn, Anjanette Comer, Charles Bronson, Sam Jaffe, Silvia Pinal, Jorge Martinez de Hoyos, Jaime Fernandez, Rosa Forman, Jorge Russek, Leon Askin, Jose Chavez, Ivan Desny, Fernand Gravey, Pedro Armendariz, Jr., Aurora Clavel

D: Henri Verneuil

S: "A Wall for San Sebastian"—William Barby Faherty

SP: James R. Webb

P: Jacques Bar

3154. THE SCALPHUNTERS

(United Artists, April, 1968) 102 Mins.

(DeLuxe Color) (PanaVision) (Filmed in Mexico)

Burt Lancaster, Shelley Winters, Telly Savalas, Ossie Davis, Armando Sylvestre, Dan Vadis, Dabney Coleman, Paul Picerni, Nick Cravat, Tony Epper, Chuck Roberson, John Epper, Jack Williams, Augela Rodriguez, Amelia Rivera, Alicia De Lago

D: Sidney Pollack

S/SP: William Norton

P: Jules Levy, Arthur Gardner, Arnold Laven

3155. BUCKSKIN

(Paramount, May, 1968) 97 Mins.

(Pathe Color)

Barry Sullivan, Joan Caulfield, Wendell Corey, Lon Chaney, John Russell, Barbara Hale, Barton MacLane, Bill Williams, Richard Arlen, Leo Gordon, Gerald Michenaud, George Chandler, Aki Aleong, Michael Larrain, Craig Littler, James X. Mitchell, Emile Meyer

D: Michael Moore

SP: Steve Fisher

P: A. C. Lyles

3156. BLUE

(Paramount, May, 1968) 113 Mins.

(Technicolor) (Panavision)

Terence Stamp, Joanna Pettet, Karl Malden, Ricardo Montalban, Anthony Costello, Joe De Santis, James Westerfield, Stathis Giallelis, Carlos East, Sara Vardi, Robert Lipton, Kevin Corcoran, Ivalou Redd, Dorothy Konrad, Helen Kleeb, Michael Bell

D: Silvio Narizzano

S: Ronald M. Cohen

SP: Meade Roberts, Ronald M. Cohen

P: Judd Bernard, Irwin Winkler

3157. THE SHAKIEST GUN IN THE WEST

(Universal, May, 1968) 101 Mins.

(Technicolor)

Don Knotts, Barbara Rhodes, Jackie Coogan, Donald Barry, Ruth McDevitt, Frank McGrath, Terry Wilson, Carl Ballantine, Pat Morita, Robert Yuro, Herbert Voland, Fay DeWitt, Dub Taylor, Hope Summers, Dick Wilson, Vaughn Taylor, Ed Peck, Ed Faulkner, Arthur Space, Gregory Mullavey

D: Alan Rafkin

SP: Jim Fritzell, Everett Greenbaum. From the screenplay by Edmund Hartman and Frank Tashlin

P: Edward J. Montagne

3158. THREE GUNS FOR TEXAS

(Universal, June, 1968) 99 Mins.

(Technicolor)

Neville Brand, Peter Brown, William Smith, Martin Milner, Philip Carey, Albert Salmi, Cliff Osmond, Michael Conrad, John Abbott, Richard Devon, Ralph Manza, Dub Taylor, Shelley Morrison

D: David Lowell Rich, Paul Stanley, Earl Bellamy

SP: John D. F. Black

P: Richard Irving

3159. JOURNEY TO SHILOH

(Universal, June, 1968) 101 Mins.

(Technicolor)

James Caan, Michael Sarrazin, Brenda Scott, Don Stroud, Paul Petersen, Michael Burns, Michael Vincent, Harrison Ford, John Doucette, Noah Beery, Jr., Tisha Sterling, James Gammon, Brian Avery, Clark Gordon, Robert Pine, Sean Kennedy, Wesley Lau, Chet Stratton, Bing Russell, Lane Bradford, Rex Ingram, Myron Healey, Eileen Wesson, Albert Popwell

D: William Hale

S: Will Henry
SP: Gene Coon
P: Howard Christie

3160. BANDOLERO!
(20th C. Fox, July, 1968) 106 Mins.
(DeLuxe Color) (PanaVision)
James Stewart, Dean Martin, Raquel Welch, George
  Kennedy, Andrew Prine, Will Geer, Clint Ritchie,
  Denver Pyle, Tom Heaton, Rudy Diaz, Sean
  McClory, Harry Carey, Jr., Donald Barry, Guy
  Raymond, Perry Lopez, Jack (Jock) Mahoney,
  Dub Taylor, Big John Hamilton, Bob Adler, John
  Mitchum, Joseph Patrick Crenshaw, Roy Barcroft
D: Andrew V. McLaglen
S: Stanley L. Hough
SP: James Lee Barrett
P: Robert L. Jacks

3161. HANG 'EM HIGH
(United Artists, August, 1968) 114 Mins.
(DeLuxe Color)
Clint Eastwood, Inger Stevens, Ed Begley, Pat
  Hingle, Arlene Golonka
D: Ted Post (Sergio Leone)
SP: Leonard Freeman, Mel Goldberg
P: Leonard Freeman

3162. 5 CARD STUD
(Paramount, August, 1968) 102 Mins.
(Technicolor)
Dean Martin, Robert Mitchum, Inger Stevens,
  Roddy McDowell, Katherine Justice, John Ander-
  son, Ruth Springford, Denver Pyle, Yaphet Kotto,
  Ted de Corsia, Bill Fletcher, Roy Jensen, Robert
  Hoy, George Robotham, Louise Lorimer, Don

Collier, Chuck Hayward, Jerry Gatlin, Whit Bis-
  sell, Boyd Morgan
D: Henry Hathaway
S: Ray Gauldern
SP: Marguerite Roberts
P: Hal B. Wallis

3163. BORN TO BUCK
(Casey Tibbs, Inc., September, 1968)
Documentary with Casey Tibbs; narrated by Henry
  Fonda and Rex Allen
(Production credits unavailable)

3164. COOGAN'S BLUFF
(Universal, November, 1968) 100 Mins.
(Technicolor)
Clint Eastwood, Lee J. Cobb, Susan Clark, Tisha
  Sterling, Don Stroud, Betty Field, Tom Tully,
  Melodie Johnson, James Edwards, Rudy Diaz,
  David F. Doyle, Louise Zorich, Meg Myles, Mar-
  jorie Bennett, Seymour Cassell, John Coe
D: Don Siegel
S: Herman Miller
SP: Herman Miller, Dean Riesner, Howard Rod-
  man
P: Richard E. Lyons, Don Siegel

3165. THE LAST REBEL
(Sterling World, 1968) 83 Mins.
(Eastman Color) (Filmed in Mexico)
Carlos Thompson, Ariadne Welter, Rudolph Acosta,
  Charles Fawcett, Lee Morgan
D/P: Miguel Contreras Torres
SP: Not credited

FILMS OF 1969

3166. THE STALKING MOON
(National General, January, 1969) 109 Mins.
(Technicolor) (PanaVision)
Gregory Peck, Eva Marie Saint, Robert Forster,
  Nolan Clay, Russell Thorson, Frank Silvera,
  Lonny Chapman, Lou Frizell, Henry Beckman,
  Charles Tyner, Richard Bull, Sandy Wyeth, Joa-
  quin Martinez, Red Morgan
D: Robert Mulligan
S: Theodore V. Olsen
SP: Wendell Mayes, Alvin Sargent
P: Alan J. Pakula

3167. MARK OF THE GUN
(Emerson, February, 1969) 85 Mins.

Ross Hagan, Brad Thomas, Chris Carter, Wallace J.
  Campodanio, Erick Lindberg
(No other information available)

3168. MORE DEAD THAN ALIVE
(United Artists, February, 1969) 101 Mins.
(DeLuxe Color)
Clint Walker, Vincent Price, Anne Francis, Mike
  Henry, Beverly Powers
D: Robert Sparr
P: Hal Klein, Aubrey Schneck

3169. HEAVEN WITH A GUN
(MGM, April, 1969) 101 Mins.

MacKenna's Gold (Columbia, 1969)— Camilla Sparv and Gregory Peck

Death of a Gunfighter (Universal, 1969) — Richard Widmark and Lena Horne

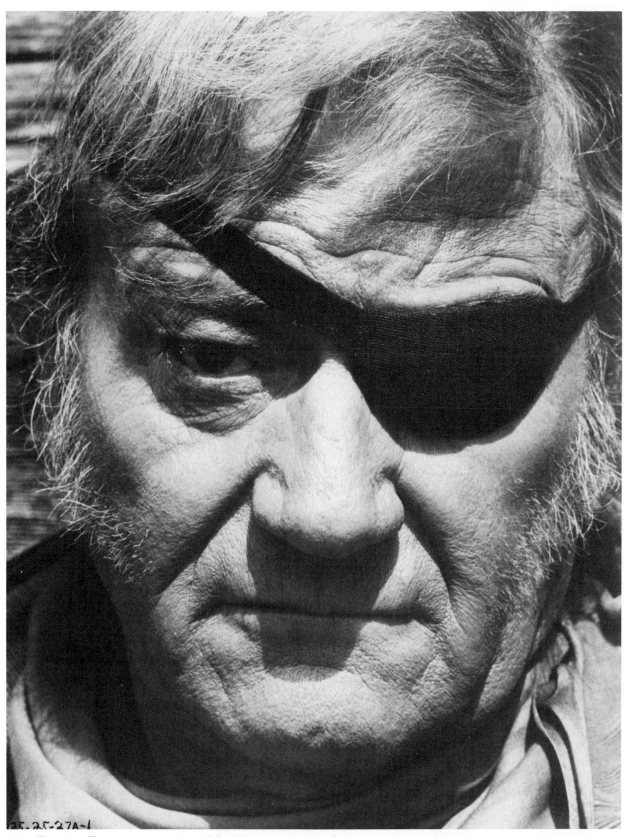

True Grit (Paramount, 1969) — John Wayne in his Academy Award-winning role as "Rooster Cogburn"

(Metrocolor)   (PanaVision)

Glenn Ford, Carolyn Jones, Barbara Hershey, John Anderson, David Carradine, J. D. Cannon, Noah Beery, Jr., Harry Townes, William Bryant, Virginia Gregg, James Griffith, Roger Perry, Claude Woolman, Ed Bakey, Barbara Babcock, James Chandler, Angelique Pettyjohn, Jessica James, Bee Tompkins, Bill Catching, Al Wyatt, Ed McCready, Miss Eddie Crispell, Barbara Dombre

D: Lee H. Katzin
SP: Richard Carr
P: Frank and Maurice King

3170. SAM WHISKEY

(United Artists, April, 1969)   96 Mins.
(DeLuxe Color)

Burt Reynolds, Clint Walker, Ossie Davis, Angie Dickinson, Rick Davis, Del Reeves, William Schallert

D: Arnold Laven
S/SP: William W. Norton
P: Jules Levy, Arthur Gardner, Arnold Laven

3171. SMITH!

(Buena Vista, April, 1969)   102 Mins.
(Technicolor)

Glenn Ford, Nancy Olson, Dean Jagger, Keenan Wynn, Warren Oates, Chief Dan George

D: Michael O'Herlihy
P: Bill Anderson

3172. SUPPORT YOUR LOCAL SHERIFF

(Cherokee/United Artists, April, 1969)   92 Mins.
(DeLuxe Color)

James Garner, Joan Hackett, Walter Brennan, Harry Morgan, Jack Elam, Bruce Dern, Henry Jones, Walter Burke, Dick Peabody, Gene Evans

D: Burt Kennedy
S/SP: William Bowers
P: William Bowers

3173. CHARRO!

(National General, April, 1969)   98 Mins.
(Technicolor)   (PanaVision)

Elvis Presley, Ina Balin, Victor French, Barbara Werle, Solomon Sturges, Paul Brinegar, James Sikking, Harry Landers, Tony Young, James Almanzar, Charles H. Gray, Rodd Redwing, Garry Walberg, Duane Grey, J. Edward McKinley, John Pickard, Robert Luster, Christa Lang, Robert Karnes, Lynn Kellogg

D: Charles Marquis Warren
S: Frederic Louis Fox
SP/P: Charles Marquis Warren

3174. A MAN CALLED GANNON

(Universal, May, 1969)   105 Mins.
(Technicolor)   (TechniScope)

Tony Franciosa, Michael Sarrazin, Judi West, Susan Oliver, John Anderson

D: James Goldstone
S: "Man Without a Star"—Dee Lindford
SP: Gene Kearney, Borden Chase, and D. D. Beauchamp
P: Howard Christie

3175. BACKTRACK

(Universal, May, 1969)   97 Mins.
(Technicolor)

James Drury, Rhonda Fleming, Neville Brand, Ida Lupino, Fernando Lamas, Philip Carey

D: Earl Bellamy
P: David J. O'Connell

3176. MacKENNA'S GOLD

(Columbia, June, 1969)   128 mins.
(Technicolor)   (Super PanaVision)

Gregory Peck, Omar Sharif, Telly Savalas, Camilla Sparv, Keenan Wynn, Julie Newmar, Ted Cassidy, Eduardo Cianelli, Dick Peabody, Rudy Diaz, Robert Phillips, Shelly Morrison, J. Robert Porter, John Garfield, Jr., Pepe Callahan, Madeline Taylor Holmes, Duke Hobbie and "The Gentlemen from Hadleyburg," Lee J. Cobb, Raymond Massey, Burgess Meredith, Anthony Quayle, Edward G. Robinson, Eli Wallach, narration by Victor Jory

D: J. Lee Thompson
S: Will Henry
SP: Carl Foreman
P: Carl Foreman, Dimitri Tiomkin

3177. TRUE GRIT

(Paramount, June, 1969)   128 Mins.
(Technicolor)

John Wayne, Glen Campbell, Kim Darby, Jeremy Slate, Robert Duvall, Strother Martin, Dennis Hopper, Alfred Ryder, Jeff Corey, Ron Soble, John Fiedler, James Westerfield, Edith Atwater, Carlos Rivas, John Doucette, Donald Woods, Isabel Boniface, John Pickard, H. W. Gim, Ken Renard, Elizabeth Harrower, Kenneth Becker, Myron Healey, Hank Worden, Guy Wilkerson, Red Morgan, Robin Morse

D: Henry Hathaway
S: Charles Portis
SP: Marguerite Roberts
P: Hal Wallis

3178. DEATH OF A GUNFIGHTER

(Universal, June, 1969)   94 Mins.
(Technicolor)

Richard Widmark, Lena Horne, Carroll O'Connor,

The Great Bank Robbery (Warner Bros.-7 Arts, 1969) — Clint Walker, Kim Novak, and Zero Mostel

David Opatoshu, Kent Smith, Jacqueline Scott, Morgan Woodward, Larry Gates, Dub Taylor, John Saxon

D: Allen Smithee
S: Lewis B. Patten
SP: Joseph Calvelli
P: Richard E. Lyons

3179. THE WILD BUNCH

(Warner Bros., July, 1969) 140 Mins.
(Technicolor) (PanaVision) (Filmed in Mexico)
William Holden, Ernest Borgnine, Robert Ryan, Edmond O'Brien, Warren Oates, Jaime Sanchez, Ben Johnson, Emilio Fernandez, Strother Martin, L. Q. Jones, Albert Dekker, Bo Hopkins, Dub Taylor, Jorge Russek, Alfonso Arau, Chano Urueta, Sonia Amelio, Aurora Clavel, Elsa Cardenas

D: Sam Peckinpah
S: Walton Green, Roy N. Sickner
SP: Walton Green, Sam Peckinpah
P: Phil Feldman

3180. THE GREAT BANK ROBBERY

(Warner Bros.-7 Arts, July, 1969) 98 Mins.
(Technicolor) (PanaVision)
Zero Mostel, Kim Novak, Clint Walker, Claude Akins, Akim Tamiroff, Larry Storch, John Anderson, Sam Jaffe, Mako, Elisha Cook, Ruth Warrick, John Fiedler, John Larch, Peter Whitney, Norman Alden, Bob Steele

D: Hy Averback
S: Frank O'Rourke
SP: William Peter Blatty
P: Malcolm Stuart

3181. THIS SAVAGE LAND

(Universal, July, 1969) 97 Mins.
(Technicolor)
George C. Scott, Barry Sullivan, Kathryn Hays, Glenn Corbett, John Drew Barrymore, Brenda Scott, Andrew Prine

D: Vincent McEveety
SP: Richard Fielder
P: Norman MacDonnell

3182. YOUNG BILLY YOUNG

(United Artists, September, 1969) 88 Mins.
(DeLuxe Color)
Robert Mitchum, Angie Dickinson, Robert Walker (Jr.), David Carradine, Jack Kelly, John Anderson, Paul Fix, Willis Bouchey, Parley Baer, Bob Anderson, Rodolfo Acosta, Deana Martin

D: Burt Kennedy
S: "Who Rides with Wyatt?"—Will Henry

SP: Burt Kennedy
P: Max Youngstein

3183. BUTCH CASSIDY AND THE SUNDANCE KID
(20th C. Fox, October, 1969)   110 Mins.
(DeLuxe Color)   (PanaVision)
Paul Newman, Robert Redford, Katherine Ross, Strother Martin, Henry Jones, Jeff Corey, George Furth, Cloris Leachman, Ted Cassidy, Kenneth Mars, Donnelly Rhodes, Jody Gilbert, Timothy Scott, Don Keefer, Charles Dierkop, Francisco Cordova, Nelson Olmstead, Paul Bryar, Sam Elliott, Charles Akins, Eric Sinclair
D: George Roy Hill
SP: William Goldman
P: John Foreman

3184. THE GOOD GUYS AND THE BAD GUYS
(Warner Bros.-7 Arts, October, 1969)   91 Mins.
(Technicolor)   (PanaVision)
Robert Mitchum, George Kennedy, David Carradine, Tina Louise, Douglas V. Fowley, Lois Nettleton, John Davis Chandler, John Carradine, Martin Balsam, Marie Windsor, Dick Peabody, Kathleen Freeman, Jimmy Murphy, Garrett Lewis, Nick Dennis
D: Burt Kennedy
SP: Ronald M. Cohen, Dennis Shryack
P: Ronald M. Cohen, Dennis Shryack

3185. PAINT YOUR WAGON
(Paramount, October, 1969)   166 Mins.
(Technicolor)   (PanaVision)

Lee Marvin, Clint Eastwood, Jean Seberg, Harve Presnell, Ray Walston, Tom Ligon, Alan Dexter, William O'Connell, Ben Baker, Alan Baxter, Paula Trueman, Robert Easton, Geoffrey Morgan, H. B. Haggerty, Terry Jenkins, Karl Bruck, John Mitchum, Sue Casey, Eddie Little Sky, Harvey Parry, H. W. Gim, William Mims, Roy Jenson, Pat Hawley, The Nitty Gritty Dirty Band
D: Joshua Logan
S: Based on the play "Paint Your Wagon"
SP: Alan Jay Lerner
P: Alan Jay Lerner

3186. THE UNDEFEATED
(20th C. Fox, November 27, 1969)   119 Mins.
(DeLuxe Color)   (PanaVision)
(Partly filmed in Mexico)
John Wayne, Rock Hudson, Antonio Aguilar, Roman Gabriel, Marian McCargo, Lee Meriwether, Merlin Olsen, Melissa Newman, Bruce Cabot, Michael Vincent, Ben Johnson, Edward Faulkner, Harry Carey, Jr., Paul Fix, Royal Dano, Richard Mulligan, Carlos Rivas, John Agar, Guy Raymond, Don Collier, Big John Hamilton, Dub Taylor, Henry Beckman, Victor Junco, Robert Bonner, Pedro Armendariz, Jr., James Dobson, Rudy Diaz, Richard Angarola, James McEachin, Gregg Palmer, Juan Garcia, Liel Martin, Bob Gravage, Chuck Roberson

D: Andrew V. McLaglen
S: Stanley L. Hough
SP: James Lee Barrett
P: Robert L. Jacks

FILMS OF 1970

3187. TELL THEM WILLIE BOY IS HERE
(Universal, January, 1970)   96 Mins.
(Technicolor)   (PanaVision)
Robert Redford, Katherine Ross, Robert Blake, Susan Clark, Barry Sullivan, John Vernon, Charles Aidman, Charles McGraw, Shelly Novack, Robert Lipton
D: Abraham Polonsky
S: "Willie Boy"—Harry Lawton
SP: Abraham Polonsky
P: Philip A. Waxman

3188. FIVE BLOODY GRAVES
(Independent-International, February, 1970)   88 Mins.
(Technicolor)   (TechniScope)
Robert Dix, Scott Brady, Jim Davis, John Carradine, Paula Raymond, John Cardos, Tara Ashton,

Kent Osborne, Vicki Volante, Denver Dixon (Victor Adamson), Ray Young, Julie Edwards, Fred Meyers, Maria Polo, Gene Raymond
D: Al Adamson
S/SP: Robert Dix
P: Al Adamson

3189. CAIN'S WAY
(M.D.A. Associates, Inc., March, 1970)   95 Mins.
(Eastman Color)
John Carradine, Scott Brady, Robert Dix, Don Epperson, Adair Jamison, Darwin Joston, Bruce Kimbale, Teresa Thaw
D: Kent Osborne
SP: Wilton Denmark
P: Kent Osborne
(Title changed to *Cain's Cut-Throats* with running time edited down to 81 minutes, and released by Fanfare in 1971)

3190. THE BALLAD OF CABLE HOGUE

(Warner Bros., March, 1970)   120 Min.
(Technicolor)
Jason Robards, Stella Stevens, David Warner, Strother Martin, Slim Pickens, L. Q. Jones, Peter Whitney, R. G. Armstrong, Gene Evans, William Mims, Kathleen Freeman, Susan O'Connell, Vaughn Taylor, Max Evans, James Anderson, Felix Nelson
D: Sam Peckinpah
SP: John Crawford, Edmund Penny
P: Sam Peckinpah

3191. KING OF THE GRIZZLIES

(Buena Vista, April, 1970)   93 Mins.
(Technicolor)   (Filmed in Canada)
John Yesno, Chris Wiggins, Hugh Webster, Jack Van Evera
D: Ron Kelly
S: "The Biography of a Grizzly"—Ernest Thompson Seton
SP: Jack Speirs
P: Winston Hibler

3192. A MAN CALLED HORSE

(National General, May, 1970)   114 Mins.
(Technicolor)   (PanaVision)   (Filmed in Mexico)
Richard Harris, Dame Judith Anderson, Jean Gascon, Manu Tupou, Corinna Tsopei, Dub Taylor,
William Jordan, James Gammon, Edward Little Sky, Lina Marin, Tamara Garina, Michael Baseleon, Manuel Padilla, Iron Eyes Cody, Richard Fools Bull, Ben Eagleman, Terry Leonard
D: Elliott Silverstein
S: Dorothy M. Johnson
SP: Jack DeWitt
P: Sandy Howard

3193. THE COCKEYED COWBOYS OF CALICO COUNTY

(Universal, May, 1970)   97 Mins.
(Technicolor)
Dan Blocker, Nanette Fabray, Jim Backus, Wally Cox, Mickey Rooney, Jack Elam, Henry Jones, Stubby Kaye, Noah Beery, Jr., Marge Champion, Donald Barry, Jack Cassidy
D: Tony Leader
SP/P: Ranald MacDougall

3194. BARQUERO

(United Artists, May, 1970)   108 Mins.
(DeLuxe Color)
Lee Van Cleef, Warren Oates, Kerwin Mathews, Mariette Hartley, Marie Gomez, Armando Silvestre, John Davis Chandler, Craig Littler, Ed Bakey, Richard Lapp, Harry Lauter, Brad Weston,

The Cheyenne Social Club (National General, 1970) — Henry Fonda and James Stewart

Forrest Tucker
D: Gordon Douglas
SP: George Schenck, William Marks
P: Hal Klein

3195. THE CHEYENNE SOCIAL CLUB
(National General, June, 1970) 103 Mins.
(Technicolor) (PanaVision)
James Stewart, Henry Fonda, Shirley Jones, Sue
Ane Langdon, Elaine Devry, Robert Middleton,
Arch Johnson, Dabbs Greer, Jackie Russell, Jackie
Joseph, Sharon De Bord, Richard Collier, Charles
Tyner, Jean Willes, Robert J. Wilke, Carl Reindel,
J. Pat O'Malley, Jason Wingreen, John Dehner,
Hal Baylor, Charlotte Stewart, Alberto Morin,
Myron Healey, Warren Kammerling, Dick John-
stone, Phil Mead, Hi Roberts, Ed Pennybacker,
Red Morgan, Dean Smith, Bill Hicks, Bill Davis,
Walt Davis, John Welty, Beverly Ann Adams
Moore
D/P: Gene Kelly
SP: James Lee Barrett

3196. EL CONDOR
(National General, June, 1970) 102 Mins.
(Technicolor)
Jim Brown, Lee Van Cleef, Patrick O'Neal, Mariana
Hill, Iron Eyes Cody, Imogen Hassall, Elisha Cook,
Jr., Gustavo Rojo, Florencio Amarilla, Julio Pena,
Angel Del Pozo, Patricio Santiago, John Clark,
Raul Mendoza Castro, Rafael Albaicin, George
Ross, Ricardo Palacios, Charles Stalnaker, Carlos
Bravo, Dale Van Husen, Peter Lenahan, Art Lar-
kin, Per Barclay
D: John Gullermin
S: Steven Carabatsos
SP: Larry Cohen, Steven Carabatsos
P: Andre de Toth

3197. TWO MULES FOR SISTER SARA
(Universal, July, 1970) 105 Mins.
(Technicolor) (PanaVision) (Filmed in Mexico)
Clint Eastwood, Shirley MacLaine, Manolo Fabre-
gas, Armando Silvestre, John Kelly, Enrique Lu-
cero, David Estuardo, Ada Carrasco, Pancho Cor-
doba, Jose Chavez
D: Don Siegel
S: Budd Boetticher
SP: Albert Maltz
P: Martin Rackin, Carroll Case

3198. CHISUM
(Warner Bros. July, 1970) 111 Mins.
(Technicolor) (PanaVision) (Filmed in Mexico)
John Wayne, Forrest Tucker, Christopher George,
Ben Johnson, Glenn Corbett, Andrew Prine,

Bruce Cabot, Patric Knowles, Richard Jaeckel,
Lynda Day (George), Geoffrey Deuel, Pamela
McMyler, John Agar, Lloyd Battista, Ray Teal,
Robert Donner, Edward Faulkner, Ron Soble,
John Mitchum, Alan Baxter, Glenn Langan, Al-
berto Morin, William Bryant, Pedro Armendariz,
Jr., Chuck Roberson, Hank Worden, Ralph Volkie
D/SP: Andrew V. McLaglen
P: Andrew J. Fenady

3199. THE McMASTERS
(Chevron, August, 1970) 90 Mins.
(Color by Movielab)
Burl Ives, Brock Peters, David Carradine, Nancy
Kwan, Jack Palance, John Carradine, L. Q. Jones,
R. G. Armstrong, Dane Clark, Frank Raiter, Alan
Vint, Marian Brash, Neil Davis, Paul Eichenberg,
Richard Alden, Lonnie Samuel, Albert Hockmeis-
ter, Rev. David Strong, Dumas Slade, Joan How-
ard, William Kiernan, Jose Naranjo, Leo Dillen-
schneider, Richard Martinez, Joseph Duran, Bill
Alexander, Frank Nanoia, David Welty
D: Alf Kjellin
SP: Harold Jacob Smith
P: Monroe Sachson

3200. MACHO CALLAHAN
(Avco Embassy, August, 1970) 99 Mins.
(Color by Movielab) (PanaVision)
(Filmed in Mexico)
David Janssen, Jean Seberg, Lee J. Cobb, James
Booth, Pedro Armendariz, Jr., David Carradine,
Anne Revere, Richard Anderson, Matt Clarke,
Richard Evans
D: Bernard Kowalski
SP: Cliff Gould
P: Martin C. Schute, Bernard Kowalski

3201. SOLDIER BLUE
(Avco Embassy, August, 1970) 112 Mins.
(Technicolor) (PanaVision)
Candice Bergen, Peter Strauss, Donald Pleasence,
Bob Carraway, Mort Mills, Jorge Rivero, Dana
Elcar, John Anderson, Martin West, Jorge Russek,
Marco Antonio Arzate
D: Ralph Nelson
S: "Arrow in the Sun"—Theodore V. Olsen
SP: John Gay

3202. CRY BLOOD, APACHE
(Golden Eagle, September, 1970) 82 Mins.
(Eastman Color)
Jody McCrea, Dan Kemp, Jack Starrett, Don Hen-
ley, Rick Nervick, Robert Tessier, Carolyn Stellar,
Marie Gahva; special guest star Joel McCrea
D: Jack Starrett
S: Harold Roberts

SP: Sean MacGregor
P: Jody McCrea

3203. MONTE WALSH

(National General, October, 1970) 98 Mins.

(Technicolor) (PanaVision)

Lee Marvin, Jeanne Moreau, Jack Palance, Mitch Ryan, Jim Davis, Bear Hudkins, Ray Guth, John McKee, Michael Conrad, Tom Heaton, G. D. Spradlin, Ted Gehring, Bo Hopkins, Matt Clark, Billy Bush, Allyn Ann McLerie, John McLiam, LeRoy Johnson, Eric Christmas, Charles Tyner, Dick Farnsworth, Fred Waugh, Jack Colvin, William Graeff, Jr., John Carter, Guy Wilkerson, Roy Barcroft

D: William A. Fraker
S: Jack Schaefer
SP: Lukas Heller, David Z. Goodman
P: Hal Landers, Bobby Roberts

3204. DIRTY DINGUS MAGEE

(MGM, November, 1970) 91 Mins.

(Metrocolor) (PanaVision)

Frank Sinatra, George Kennedy, Anne Jackson, Lois Nettleton, Jack Elam, Michele Carey, John Dehner, Henry Jones, Harry Carey, Jr., Paul Fix, Donald Barry, Mike Wagner, Terry Wilson, David Burk, David Cass, Tom Fadden, Mae Old Coyote, Lillian Hogan, Florence Real Bird, Ina Bad Bear, Marya Christian, Mina Martinez, Sheila Foster, Irene Kelly, Diane Sayer, Jean London, Gayle Rogers, Timothy Blake, Lisa Todd, Maray Ayres, Carol Anderson

D: Burt Kennedy
S: "The Ballad of Dingus Magee"—David Markson
SP: Tom Waldman, Frank Waldman, Joseph Heller
P: Burt Kennedy

3205. FLAP

(Warner Bros., November, 1970) 105 Mins.

(Technicolor) (PanaVision)

Anthony Quinn, Claude Akins, Tony Bill, Shelley Winters, Victor Jory, Don Collier, Victor French, Rudolfo Acosta, Susana Miranda, Anthony Caruso, William Mims, Rudy Diaz, Pedro Regas, John War Eagle, J. Edward McKinley, Robert Cleaves

D: Carol Reed
S: "Nobody Loves a Drunken Indian"—Clair Huffaker
SP: Clair Huffaker
P: Jerry Adler

3206. THERE WAS A CROOKED MAN

(Warner Bros., December, 1970) 126 Mins.

(Technicolor) (PanaVision)

Kirk Douglas, Henry Fonda, Hume Cronyn, War-

ren Oates, Burgess Meredith, Arthur O'Connell, Martin Gabel, Lee Grant, John Randolph, Michael Blodgett, Claudia McNeil, Alan Hale, Victor French, Jeanne Cooper, C. K. Yang, Bert Freed, Gene Evans, Pamela Hensley, Barbara Rhodes

D: Joseph L. Mankiewicz
S/SP: David Newman, Robert Benton
P: Joseph L. Mankiewicz

3207. THE RED, WHITE AND BLACK

(Hirschman Northern, December 16, 1970) 97 Mins.

(Eastman Color)

Robert Doqui, Issac Fields, Barbara Hale, Rafer Johnson, Lincoln Kilpatrick, Isabel Sanford, Otis Taylor, Steve Drexel, Robert Dix, Cesar Romero, James Michelle, Bobby Clark, Byrd Holland, Bill Collins, John Fox, Russ Nannarello, Jr., Bernard Brown, Clarence Comas, Donald Diggs, Jeff Everett, Cal Fields, Perry Fluker, Noah Hobson, Earl Humphrey, DeVaughn LaBon, Rod Law, John Nettles, Jim Pace, Eric Richmond, John Ramsey, Charles Wells, Paul Wheaton, Dave White

D: John Cardos
SP: Marlene Weed
P: James M. Northern, Stuart Z. Hirschman
(Film played from December 16 through December 24, 1970 at Pix Theatre, Los Angeles. Was not shown again until it was released as *Soul Soldiers* by Fanfare on December 25, 1971. Running time had been cut to 81 minutes, new ads said Metrocolor, and Rafer Johnson was top billed)

3208. RIO LOBO

(National General, December, 1970) 114 Mins.

(Technicolor) (Partly filmed in Mexico)

John Wayne, Jorge Rivero, Jennifer O'Neill, Jack Elam, Christopher Mitchum, Victor French, Susana Dosamantes, David Huddleston, Mike Henry, Bill Williams, Jim Davis, Sherry Lansing, Dean Smith, Robert Donner, George Plimpton, Edward Faulkner, Peter Jason, Robert Rothwell, Bob Steele, Chuck Courtney, Red Morgan, Hank Worden, Chuck Roberson

D: Howard Hawks
S: Burton Wohl
SP: Burton Wohl, Leigh Brackett
P: Howard Hawks
SP: Sean MacGregor
P: Jody McCrea

FILMS OF 1971

3209. LITTLE BIG MAN
(National General, February, 1971)   150 Mins.
(Technicolor)   (PanaVision)
(Partly filmed in Canada)
Dustin Hoffman, Faye Dunaway, Martin Balsam, Richard Mulligan, Chief Dan George, Jeff Corey, Amy Eccles, Kelly Jean Peters, Carol Androsky, Robert Little Star, Cal Bellini, Ruben Moreno, Steve Shemayne, William Hickey, James Anderson, Jess Vint, Alan Oppenheimer, Thayer David, Philip Kenneally, Jack Bannon, Ray Dimas, Alan Howard, Jack Mullaney, Steve Miranda, Lou Cutell, M. Emmet Walsh, Emily Cho, Cecelia Kootenay, Linda Dyer, Dessie Bad Bear, Len George, Norman Nathan, Helen Verbit, Bert Conway, Earl Rosell, Ken Mayer, Bud Cokes, Rory O'Brien, Tracy Hetchner
D: Arthur Penn
S: Thomas Berger
SP: Calder Willingham
P: Stuart Millar

3210. THE WILD COUNTRY
(Buena Vista, February, 1971)   100 Mins.
(Technicolor)
Steve Forrest, Jack Elam, Ronny Howard, Frank de Kova, Vera Miles, Morgan Woodward, Clint Howard, Dub Taylor, Woodrow Chambliss, Karl Swenson, Mills Watson
D: Robert Totten
S: "Little Britches"—Ralph Moody
SP: Calvin Clements, Jr., Paul Moody
P: Ron Miller

3211. ZACHARIAH
(Cinerama Releasing Corp., February, 1971)
   92 Mins.
(Metrocolor)   (Partly filmed in Mexico)
John Rubinstein, Pat Quinn, Don Johnson, Country Joe and the Fish, Elvin Jones, Doug Kershaw, William Challee, Robert Ball, Dick Van Patten, The James Gang, White Lightnin', The New York Rock Ensemble
D/P: George Englund
SP: Joe Massot

3212. THE SHOOTING
(Jack H. Harris Enterprises, February 25, 1971)
   82 Mins.
(DeLuxe Color)
Jack Nicholson, Millie Perkins, Warren Oates, Will Hutchins, B. J. Merholz, Guy El Tsosie, Charles Eastman

D: Monte Hellman
SP: Adrien Joyce
P: Jack Nicholson, Monte Hellman
(Filmed in 1966, played television, then had theatrical release following the popularity of *Easy Rider*)

3213. SUPPORT YOUR LOCAL GUNFIGHTER
(United Artists, May, 1971)   92 Mins.
(DeLuxe Color)
James Garner, Suzanne Pleshette, Jack Elam, Joan Blondell, Harry Morgan, Marie Windsor, Henry Jones, John Dehner, Chuck Connors, Dub Taylor, Kathleen Freeman, Willis Bouchey, Walter Burke, Gene Evans, Dick Haymes, John Daheim (Day), Ellen Corby, Ben Cooper, Grady Sutton, Pedro Gonzales-Gonzales, Roy Glenn
D: Burt Kennedy
SP: James Edward Grant
P: William Finnegan

3214. BILLY JACK
(Warner Bros., May, 1971)   112 Mins.
(Technicolor)
Tom Laughlin, Delores Taylor, Clark Howat, Bert Freed, Julie Webb, Ken Tobey, Victor Izay, Debbie Schock, Stan Rice, Teresa Kelly, Katy Moffatt, Susan Foster, Paul Bruce, Lynn Baker, Susan Sosa, David Roya, Gwen Smith, John McClune, Cissie Colpitts
D: T. C. Frank (Delores Taylor)
SP: Frank and Teresa Christina
P: Mary Rose Solti

3215. SHOOT OUT
(Universal, June, 1971)   94 Mins.
(Technicolor)
Gregory Peck, Pat Quinn, Robert F. Lyons, Susan Tyrell, Jeff Corey, James Gregory, Rita Gam, Dawn Lyn, Pepe Serna, John Chandler, Paul Fix, Arthur Hunnicutt, Nicholas Beauvy
D: Henry Hathaway
S: "The Lone Cowboy"—Will James
SP: Marguerite Roberts
P: Hal B. Wallis

3216. BIG JAKE
(National General, June, 1971)   110 Mins.
(Technicolor)   (PanaVision)   (Filmed in Mexico)
John Wayne, Richard Boone, Maureen O'Hara, Patrick Wayne, Chris Mitchum, Bobby Vinton, Bruce Cabot, Glenn Corbett, Harry Carey, Jr., John Doucette, Jim Davis, John Agar, Gregg

Palmer, Robert Warner, Jim Burke, Dean Smith, John Ethan Wayne, Virginia Capers, William Walker, Jerry Gatlin, Tom Hennessy, Don Epperson, Everett Creach, Jeff Wingfield, Hank Worden
D: George Sherman
S/SP: Harry Julian Fink, R. M. Fink
P: Michael Wayne

3217. WILD ROVERS
(MGM, June, 1971) 109 Mins.
(Metrocolor) (PanaVision)
William Holden, Ryan O'Neal, Karl Malden, Lynn Carlin, Tom Skerritt, Joe Don Baker, James Olson, Leora Dana, Moses Gunn, Victor French, Rachel Roberts, Sam Gilman, Charles Gray, William Bryant, Jack Garner, Caitlin Wyles, Mary Jackson, William Lucking, Ed Bakey, Ted Gehring, Alan Carney, Ed Long, Lee DeBroux, Hal Lynch, Boyd "Red" Morgan, Bennie Dobbins, Bob Beck, Geoffrey Edwards, Studs Tanney, Bruno DeSota, Dick Crockett
D/SP: Blake Edwards
P: Blake Edwards, Ken Wales

3218. A GUNFIGHT
(Paramount, June, 1971) 90 Mins.
(Technicolor)
Kirk Douglas, Johnny Cash, Jane Alexander, Raf Vallone, Karen Black, Eric Douglas, Philip Mead, John Wallwork, Dana Elcar, Bob Wilke, George LeBow, Don Cavasos, Keith Carradine
D: Lamont Johnson
SP: Harold Jack
P: A. Ronald Lubin, Harold Jack Bloom

3219. ONE MORE TRAIN TO ROB
(Universal, June, 1971) 108 Mins.
(Technicolor)
George Peppard, Diana Muldaur, John Vernon, France Nuyen, Steve Sandor, Soon-Taik Oh, Richard Loo, C. K. Yang, John Doucette, Robert Donner, George Chandler, Pamela McMyler, Merlin Olsen, Phil Olsen
D: Andrew V. McLaglen
S: William Roberts
SP: Don Tait, Dick Nelson
P: Robert Arthur

3220. MACHISMO—40 GRAVES FOR 40 GUNS
(Boxoffice International, July, 1971) 94 Mins.
(Color by Movielab)
Robert Padilla, Stanley Adams, Rita Rogers, Sue Bernard, Bruce Gordon, Kid Chissel, Dirk Peno, Frederico Gomez, Louis Ojena, Leslie York, Nancy Caroline, Royal Dano, Chuey Franco, Jose Jasd, Liberty Angelo, Mike Robelo, Patti Heider, Lilian Chauvin, Sean Kenney, Joseph Tornatore, Gary

Kent, James Lemp, Gary Graver, Randy Starr, Biff Maynard, Harry Novak, Terry Woolman, Frisco Estes, David Scheinder, Richard Paradise, Robert Gerald, Hank Adams, Ray Lester
D: Paul Hunt
SP: Ron Garcia, Paul Hunt
P: Harry Novak

3221. SCANDALOUS JOHN
(Buena Vista, July, 1971) 113 Mins.
(Technicolor) (PanaVision)
Brian Keith, Alfonso Arau, Michele Carey, Rick Lenz, Harry Morgan, Simon Oakland, Bill Williams, Christopher Dark, Fran Ryan, Bruce Glover, Richard Hale, James Lydon, John Ritter, Iris Adrian, Larry D. Mann, Jack Raine, Booth Colman, Edward Faulkner, Bill Zuckert, John Zaremba, Robert Padilla, Alex Tinne, Ben Baker, Paul Koslo, William O'Connell, Sam Edwards
D: Robert Butler
S: Richard Gardner
SP: Bill Walsh, Don DaGradi
P: Bill Walsh

3222. McCABE AND MRS. MILLER
(Warner Bros., July, 1971) 115 Mins.
(Technicolor) (PanaVision) (Filmed in Canada)
Warren Beatty, Julie Christie, Rene Auberjonois, Hugh Naughton, Shelley Duvall, Michael Murphy, John Schuck, Corey Fischer, Keith Carradine, William Devane, Anthony Holland, Bert Remsen, Jace Vander Veen, Carey Lee McKenzie, Elizabeth Murphy, Jackie Crossland
D: Robert Altman
S: "McCabe"—Edmund Naughton
SP: Robert Altman, Brian McKay
P: David Foster, Mitchell Brower

3223. RIDE IN THE WHIRLWIND
(Jack H. Harris Enterprises, July, 1971) 82 Mins.
(Deluxe Color)
Jack Nicholson, Millie Perkins, Rupert Crosse, Cameron Mitchell, Katherine Squire, George Mitchell, (Harry) Dean Stanton
D: Monte Hellman
SP: Jack Nicholson
P: Monte Hellman, Jack Nicholson
(1966 film that played on television prior to theatre release)

3224. A TOWN CALLED HELL
(Scotia, July 28, 1971) 95 Mins.
(Technicolor) (Franscope)
Robert Shaw, Stella Stevens, Martin Landau, Telly Savalas, Michael Craig, Fernando Rey, Al Lettieri, Dudley Sutton, Aldo Sambrell
D: Robert Parrish

SP: Richard Aubrey
P: S. Benjamin Fisz

3225. THE HIRED HAND
(Universal, August, 1971)   93 Mins.
(Technicolor)
Peter Fonda, Warren Oates, Verna Bloom, Robert Pratt, Severn Darden, Ted Markland, Own Orr, Gray Johnson, Rita Rogers, Al Hopson, Megan Denver
D: Peter Fonda
SP: Alan Sharp
P: William Hayward

3226. LAWMAN
(United Artists, September, 1971)   99 Mins.
(Deluxe Color)   (Filmed in Mexico)
Burt Lancaster, Robert Ryan, Lee J. Cobb, Sheree North, Joseph Wiseman, Robert Duvall, Albert Salmi, J. D. Cannon, John McGiver, Richard Jordan, John Beck, Walter Brooke
D: Richard Winner
SP: Gerald Wilson
P: Michael Winner

3227. THE FEMALE BUNCH
(Dalia Productions, September, 1971)   86 Mins.
(Color)
Russ Tamblyn, Jenifer Bishop, Lon Chaney, Jr., Nesa Renet, Jeoffrey Land, Regina Carroll, Al-lesha Lee, Don Epperson, John Cardos, Jackie Taylor, William Bonner, Bobby Clark
D: Al Adamson, John Cardos
S: Raphael Nussbaum
SP: Jale Lockwood, Brent Nimrod
P: Raphael Nussbaum

3228. SKIN GAME
(Warner Bros., October, 1971)   102 Mins.
(Technicolor)   (PanaVision)
James Garner, Lou Gossett, Susan Clark, Brenda Sykes, Edward Asner, Andrew Duggan, Henry Jones, Neva Patterson, Parley Baer, George Tyne, Royal Dano, Pat O'Malley, Joel Fluellen, Napoleon Whiting, Juanita Moore, Cort Clark
D: Paul Bogart
S: Richard Alan Simmons
SP: Pierre Marton
P: Harry Keller

3229. THE ANIMALS
(Levitt-Pickman, October, 1971)   86 Mins.
(Color)
Henry Silva, Keenan Wynn, Michele Carey
D: Ron Joy
SP: Unavailable
P: Richard Bakalyan

3230. MAN AND BOY
(Levitt-Pickman, November, 1971)   98 Mins.
(Color)
Bill Cosby, Gloria Foster, Leif Erickson, George Spell, Douglas Turner Ward, John Anderson, Henry Silva, Dub Taylor, Shelley Morrison, Yaphet Kotto
D: E. W. Swackhamer
SP: Harry Essex, Oscar Saul
P: Marvin Miller

3231. SOMETHING BIG
(National General, December, 1971)   108 Mins.
(Technicolor)   (Filmed in Mexico)
Dean Martin, Brian Keith, Honor Blackman, Carol White, Ben Johnson, Albert Salmi, Don Knight, Joyce Van Patten, Denver Pyle, Merlin Olsen, Robert Donner, Harry Carey, Jr., Judi Meredith, Ed Faulkner, Paul Fix, Armand Alzamora, David Huddleston, Bob Steele, Shirlenna Manchur, Jose Angel Espinosa, Juan Garcia, Robert Gravage, Chuck Hicks, John Kelly, Enrique Lucerno, Lupe Amador
D/P: Andrew V. McLaglen
S/SP: James Lee Barrett

3232. POWDERKEG
(Filmways, 1971)
(Color)
Rod Taylor, Dennis Cole, Fernando Lamas, John McIntire, Luciana Paluzzi, Michael Ansara, Tisha Sterling, Reni Santoni, Melodie Johnson, William Bryant, Joe De Santis, Jay Novello, Roy Jensen, William D. Gordon, Todd Martin, Duane Grey, Charles Gray, Maurice Jara, Jim Brown, Val De Vargas, Francisco Ortega, Patrick Whyte, Michael Carr
D/SP/P: Douglas Heyes

FILMS OF 1972

3233. J. W. COOP
(Columbia, January, 1972)   113 Mins.
(Eastman Color)
Cliff Robertson, Geraldine Page, Cristina Ferrare, R. G. Armstrong, John Crawford, R. L. Armstrong, Wade Crosby, Marjorie Durant Dye, Paul Harper, Son Hooker, Richard Kennedy, Bruce Kirby, Larry Mahan, Mary-Robin Redd, Larry Clapman
D/P: Cliff Robertson
SP: Cliff Robertson, Gary Cartwright, Edwin "Bud" Shrake

3234. THE COWBOYS
(Warner Bros., February, 1972)   128 Mins.
(Technicolor)   (PanaVision 70)
John Wayne, Roscoe Lee Browne, Bruce Dern, A. Martinez, Alfred Barker, Jr., Nicolas Beauvy, Steve Benedict, Robert Carradine, Norman Howell, Jr., Stephen Hudis, Sean Kelly, Clay O'Brien, Sam O'Brien, Mike Pyeatt, Colleen Dewhurst, Slim Pickens, Lonny Chapman, Sarah Cunningham, Charles Tyner, Allyn Ann McLerie, Wallace Brooks, Jim Burk, Larry Finley, Maggie Costain, Matt Clark, Jerry Gatlin, Walter Scott, Dick Farnsworth, Charise Cullin, Collette Poeppel, Margaret Kelly, Larry Randles, Norman Hiwell, Joe Yrigoyen, Tap Canutt, Chuck Courtney
D: Mark Rydell
S: William Dale Jennings
SP: Irving Ravetch, Harriet Frank, Jr., William Dale Jennings
P: Mark Rydell

3235. POCKET MONEY
(National General, February, 1972)
(Technicolor)
Paul Newman, Lee Marvin, Strother Martin, Christine Belford, Kelly Jean Peters, Fred Graham, Wayne Rogers, Hector Elizondo, R. Camargo, Gregg Sierra, Wynn Pearce, John Verros, Mickey Gilbert, Terry Malick
D: Stuart Rosenberg
S: "Jim Kane"—J. P. S. Brown
SP: Terry Malick
P: John Foreman

3236. THE HONKERS
(United Artists, March, 1972)   103 Mins.
(DeLuxe Color)
James Coburn, Lois Nettleton, Slim Pickens, Anne Archer, Richard Anderson, Joan Huntington, Jim Davis, Ramon Bieri, Ted Eccles, Mitchell Ryan, Wayne McLaren, John Harmon, Richard O'Brien, Pitt Herbert, Larry Mahan, Chuck Henson, Larry McKinney, Jerry Gatlin, Buzz Henning, Wayne McClellan, Chris Howell
D: Steve Ihnat
SP: Steve Ihnat, Stephen Lodge
P: Arthur Gardner, Jules Levy

3237. JOURNEY THROUGH ROSEBUD
(G.S.F., April, 1972)   93 Mins.
(Color by Movielab)   (PanaVision)
Robert Forster, Kristoffer Tabori, Victoria Racimo, Eddie Little Sky, Roy Jenson, Wright King, Larry Pennell, Robert Cornwaithe, Steve Shemayne, Beau Little Sky, Lynn Burnette, Nancy White Horse, Robert Wagner, and the People of the Rosebud Sioux Indian Reservation
D: Tom Gries
SP: Albert Ruben
P: David Gil

3238. SQUARES
(Pleaeau/International, April 12, 1972)   92 Mins.
(Metrocolor)
Andrew Prine, Gilmer McCormack, Robert Easton, Harriet Medin, Jack Mather, Dean Smith, Tom Hennessy, Tom Basham, William Wintersole, Patricia Sauers, Sam Christopher
D: Patrick Murphy
SP: Mary Ann Saxon
P: Patrick Murphy

3239. THE CULPEPPER CATTLE COMPANY
(20th C. Fox, April, 1972)   92 Mins.
(DeLuxe Color)
Gary Grimes, Billy "Green" Bush, Luke Askew, Bo Hopkins, Geoffrey Lewis, Wayne Sutherlin, John McLiam, Matt Clark, Raymond Guth, Anthony James, Charles Martin Smith, Larry Finley, Bob Morgan, Jan Burrell, Gregory Sierra
D/S: Dick Richards
SP: Eric Bercovici, Gregory Prentiss
P: Paul A. Helmick

3240. THE GREAT NORTHFIELD, MINNESOTA RAID
(Universal, April, 1972)   91 Mins.
(Technicolor)
Cliff Robertson, Robert Duvall, Luke Askew, R. G. Armstrong, Dana Elcar, Donald Moffat, John Pearce, Matt Clark, Wayne Sutherlin, Robert H. Harris, Jack Manning, Elisha Cook, Royal Dano, Mary-Robin Redd, Bill Callaway, Craig Curtis, Barry Brown
D/SP: Philip Kaufman
P: Jennings Lang

3241. BUCK AND THE PREACHER

(Columbia, May, 1972) 102 Mins.

(Color) (Filmed in Mexico)

Sidney Poitier, Harry Belafonte, Ruby Dee, Cameron Mitchell, Denny Miller, Nita Talbot, John Kelly, Tony Brubaker, Bobby Johnson, James McEachin, Lynn Hamilton, Clarence Muse, Ken Menard, Pamela Jones, Dennis Hines, Enrique Lucero, Julie Robinson

D: Sidney Poitier

S: Ernest Kinoy, Drake Walker

SP: Ernest Kinoy

P: Joel Glickman

3242. THE LEGEND OF NIGGER CHARLIE

(Paramount, May, 1972) 100 Mins.

(Color by TVC)

Fred Williamson, D'Urville Martin, Don Pedro Colley, Gertrude Jeanette, Marcia McBroom, Alan Gifford, John Ryan, Will Hussung, Mill Moor, Thomas Anderson, Jerry Gatlin, Tricia O'Neil, Doug Rowe, Keith Prentice, Tom Pemberton, Joe Santos, Fred Lerner

D: Martin Goldman

S: James Bellah

SP: Martin Goldman, Larry G. Spangler

P: Larry G. Spangler

3243. BLACK RODEO

(Cinerama Releasing Corp., June, 1972) 87 Mins.

(Color)

Muhammad Ali, Woody Strode, Bud Bramwell, Cleo Hearn, Skeets Richardson, Rocky Watson, Nelson Jackson, James Thomas, Moses Fields, Cornell Fields, Alfred Peet, Nat Purefoy, Gordon Hayes, Sandy Goodman, Joanne Eason, Lisa Bramwell, Betsy Bramwell, Dorothy Wright, Sandra Young

D/P: Jeff Kanew

SP: Jeff Kanew

3244. THE GATLING GUN

(Ellman Enterprises, June, 1972) 93 Mins.

(Technicolor) (TechniScope)

Guy Stockwell, Woody Strode, Barbara Luna, Robert Fuller, Patrick Wayne, Pat Buttram, John Carradine, Phil Harris, July Jordan, Carlos Rivas

D: Robert Gordon

SP: Joseph Van Winkle, Mark Hanna

P: Oscar Nichols

3245. JUNIOR BONNER

(Cinerama Releasing Corp., June, 1972) 100 Mins.

(Color by Movielab) (Todd-AO)

Steve McQueen, Robert Preston, Ida Lupino, Ben Johnson, Joe Don Baker, Barbara Leigh, Mary Murphy, Bill McKinney, Sandra Deel, Donald "Red" Barry, Dub Taylor, Charles Gray, Matthew Peckinpah, Sundown Spencer, Rita Garrison

D: Sam Peckinpah

SP: Jed Rosebrook

P: Joe Wizan

3246. THE REVENGERS

(National General, June, 1972) 110 Mins.

(DeLuxe Color) (PanaVision) (Filmed in Mexico)

William Holden, Ernest Borgnine, Susan Hayward, Woody Strode, Roger Hanin, Rene Koldehoff, Jorge Luke, Jorge Martinez de Hoyos, Arthur Hunnicutt, Warren Vanders, Larry Pennell, John Kelly, Scott Holden, James Daughton, Lorraine Chanel, Raul Prieto

D: Daniel Mann

S: Steven W. Carabatsos

SP: Wendell Mayes

P: Martin Rackin

3247. JOE KIDD

(Universal, July, 1972) 88 Mins.

(Technicolor) (PanaVision)

Clint Eastwood, Robert Duvall, John Saxon, Don Stroud, Stella Garcia, James Wainwright, Paul Koslo, Gregory Walcott, Dick Van Patten, Lynne Marta, John Carter, Pepe Hern

D: John Sturges

SP: Elmore Leonard

P: Sidney Beckerman

3248. DISCIPLES OF DEATH

(A.I.D. Variety, July, 1972) 75 Mins.

(Eastman Color)

Josh Bryant, Irene Kelly, Dave Cass, John Martin, Carl Bensen, Linda Rascoe, Norris Domingue, Wanda Wilson, Ed Geldert, Robert John Allen, Willie Gonzales, Happy Shahan

D: Frank Q. Dobbs

SP: David Cass, Frank Q. Dobbs

P: Michael F. Cusack

3249. THE MAGNIFICENT SEVEN RIDE!

(United Artists, August, 1972) 100 Mins.

(DeLuxe Color)

Lee Van Cleef, Stefanie Powers, Mariette Hartley, Michael Callan, Luke Askew, Pedro Armendariz, Jr., William Lucking, James B. Sikking, Melissa Murphy, Darrell Larson, Ed Lauter, Carolyn Conwell, Jason Wingreen, Allyn Ann McLerie, Elizabeth Thompson, Ralph Waite

D: George McCowan

SP: Arthur Rowe

P: William A. Calihan

3250. WHEN THE LEGENDS DIE

(20th C. Fox, August, 1972) 106 Mins.

(DeLuxe Color)

The Great Northfield, Minnesota Raid (Columbia, 1972) — Cliff Robertson

557

Richard Widmark, Frederic Forrest, Luana Anders, Vito Scotti, Herbert Nelson, John War Eagle, John Gruber, Garry Walberg, Jack Mullaney, Malcolm Curley, Roy Engel, Rex Holman, Mal Gallagher, Tillman Box, Sondra Pratt, Verne Muehlstedt, Evan Stevens, John Renworth, Rhoda Stevens, Mel Flock, Joyce Davis, Bennett Thompson, Bart Brower
D: Stuart Miller
S: Hal Borland
SP: Robert Dozier
P: Stuart Miller

3251. TRAP ON COUGAR MOUNTAIN

(Sun International, September, 1972) 94 Mins.
(Technicolor) (PanaVision)
Keith Larsen, Karen Steele, Eric Larsen
D/SP/P: Keith Larsen

3252. BAD COMPANY

(Paramount, October, 1972) 93 Mins.
(Technicolor)
Jeff Bridges, Barry Brown, Jim Davis, David Huddleston, John Savage, Jerry Houser, Damon Cofer, Joshua Hill Lewis, Geoffrey Lewis, Raymond Guth, Edward Lauter, John Quade, Jean Allison, Ned Wertimer, Charles Tyner, Ted Gehring, Claudia Bryar, John Byrd, Monika Henreid, Todd Martin
D: Robert Benton
SP: David Newman, Robert Benton
P: Stanley R. Jaffe

3253. DIRTY LITTLE BILLY

(Columbia, November, 1972) 93 Mins.
(Color)
Michael J. Pollard, Lee Purcell, Richard Evans, Charles Aidman, Dran Hamilton, William Sage, Josip Elic, Mills Watson, Alex Wilson
D: Stan Dragoti
SP: Charles Moses, Stan Dragoti
P: Jack L. Warner

3254. ULZANA'S RAID

(Universal, November, 1972) 103 Mins.
(Technicolor)
Burt Lancaster, Bruce Davison, Richard Jaeckel, Jorge Luke, Joaquin Martinez, Lloyd Bochner, Karl Swenson, Douglass Watson, Dran Hamilton, John Pearce, Gladys Holland, Margaret Fairchild, Aimee Eccles, Richard Bull, Otto Reichow, Dean Smith

D: Robert Aldrich
SP: Alan Sharp
P: Carter DeHaven

3255. JORY

(Avco Embassy, November, 1972) 97 Mins.
(Color by Movielab) (Filmed in Mexico)
John Marley, B. J. Thomas, Bobby Benson, Brad Dexter, Claudio Brook, Patricia Aspillaga, Todd Martin, Ben Baker, Carlos Cortes, Linda Purl, Anne Lockhart, Betty Sheridan, Ted Markland, Quintin Bulnes, John Kelly, Eduardo Lopez Rojas
D: Jorge Fons
S: Milton R. Bass
SP: Gerald Herman, Robert Irving
P: Howard G. Minsky

3256. THE LIFE AND TIMES OF JUDGE ROY BEAN

(National General, December, 1972) 120 Mins.
(Technicolor) (PanaVision)
Paul Newman, Jacqueline Bisset, Tab Hunter, John Huston, Ava Gardner, Stacy Keach, Roddy McDowall, Anthony Perkins, Victoria Principal, Anthony Zerbe, Ned Beatty, Roy Jenson, LeRoy Johnson, Matt Clark, Dean Smith, Bill McKinney, Fred Krone, Jack Colvin, David Sharpe, John Hudkins, Gary Combs, Fred Brookfield, Ben Dobbins, Dick Farnsworth, Terry Leonard, Margo Epper, Jeannie Epper, Stephanie Epper, Barbara Carr, Dolores Clark, Lee Meza, Neil Summers, Howard Morton, Billy Pearson, Stan Barrett, Don Starr, Alfred G. Bosnos
D: John Huston
SP: John Milius
P: John Foreman

3257. JEREMIAH JOHNSON

(Warner Bros., December, 1972) 108 Mins.
(Technicolor) (PanaVision)
Robert Redford, Will Geer, Stefan Gierasch, Allyn Ann McLerie, Charles Tyner, Delle Bolton, Josh Albee, Joaquin Martinez, Paul Benedict, Matt Clark, Richard Angarola, Jack Colvin
D: Sidney Pollack
S: "Mountain Man"—novel by Vardis Fisher; "Crow Killer"—story by Raymond W. Thorp and Robert Bunker
SP: John Milius, Edward Anhalt
P: Joe Wizan

Dirty Little Billy (Columbia, 1972) — Michael Pollard and unidentified player

The Life and Times of Judge Roy Bean (National General, 1972) — Paul Newman

CHAPTER 11

The Restless Years
1973-1977

(SHADOWY VALLEYS AND AN AGED LONE RIDER)

Whereas the Cynical Years (1968-1972) saw an exploration of the legends surrounding Western history (or the film versions) and its personalities, subsequent years did not bring about any noticeable escalation of this openly critical and pessimistic look at the West once championed by Western films. Some filmmakers, of course, were still bent on exposing myths and "telling the true story," but others were taking a less cynical stance. Restlessness seems to best characterize the years 1973-1977; and though not a great number of Westerns were made, an interesting assortment of them did emerge.

John Wayne was still Hollywood's figurehead, a big box-office draw and the most exciting cowboy around despite nearly fifty years in the saddle. Both *Cahill, United States Marshal* (Warner Bros., 1973) and *The Train Robbers* (Warner Bros., 1973) can be classified as standard Wayne heroics in the style of *Big Jake, Chisum,* and a score of others, with Wayne simply playing Wayne—or at least that is what a number of film critics would have us believe. Maybe that in itself is worth the price of admission. Millions of moviegoers seemed to think so. Actually, it is asinine to believe that Wayne, or any other actor, could climb to the top in such a competitive profession and stay there for decades simply on the basis of "being himself" or, as Wayne puts it, "reacting." The man is a consummate actor so gifted as to appear not to be acting at all. Both *Cahill, United States Marshal* and *The Train Robbers* were entertaining and commercially successful, leaving the musings of critics as somewhat academic. It's easier to knock success than it is to match it, thereby leaving many openings for the less gifted. The public seems determined to hang onto this last of the rip-snortin', old-time Saturday matinee and cliffhanger stars as long as possible—Wayne indeed may outlast his public—keeping its link with the glorious past and Wayne's weatherbeaten countenance forever a fresco in the Western skyline.

Rooster Cogburn (Universal, 1975) is, of course, a sequel to *True Grit* (Paramount, 1969). My co-author and I disagree as to whether it is a better film, but we both agree that the absence of Glen Campbell in the sequel is a plus factor. Actress Martha Hyer (wife of the producer Hal Wallis), writing under the name of "Martin Julien," provided a good screenplay, with or without a nod of thanks to *The African Queen.*

While its track record has so far dictated otherwise, Wayne's last film to date, *The Shootist* (Paramount, 1976), should be near the top of any list of the great Westerns, and certainly ranks with *Stagecoach, She Wore a Yellow Ribbon,* and *The Searchers* on a strictly Wayne list. The film shows us a man with irrepressible sincerity for his art—a man whose power of emotion, sincerity, and love of craft are as great as they were in those he long ago chose to emulate, Harry Carey and Buck Jones. Feeling that those who search for austerity in its purest form need not—nay, can not—go past *Cripple Creek Bar-Room,* it is a film of slick austerity about an aging gunfighter dying with cancer who chooses his own way of dying

—a shootout with those who would win coveted recognition in out-gunning him. It could well serve as a perfect and graceful farewell to Westerns should Wayne choose not to make others.

Nostalgia aside, one of the more pleasant events of the period was the return of Roy Rogers to theatrical Westerns after an absence from the screen of twenty-four years. *Macintosh and T.J.* (Penland, 1976) stars Rogers as a middle-age ranchhand in the Texas of 1975. It plows no new ground, and, aside from the fact the director didn't have to cut to a full-face closeup every seven minutes for a transition to a commercial break, it is little more than made-for-television fare. For certain, it stands no chance of being "rediscovered" in a decade or so as a "minor classic." At that, it is far better than most of what the decade has seen so far.

In *The Trial of Billy Jack* (Warner Bros., 1974), the Laughlins have once again proved they have no peers at manipulating an audience's emotions, albeit at the same time causing a paralysis of the brain. As in its predecessor, *Trial* achieves the seemingly impossible feat of causing the conservatives (its audience) to applaud the liberals (ol' Billy Jack and them). Or was it the other way around? Either way, it boggles the mind. There's no horsey virtuosity or pioneer women in poke bonnets in this one, which combines the optimism of the traditional Western opus with a criticism of current culture. Audience acceptance has been only lukewarm.

Sam Peckinpah's *Pat Garrett and Billy the Kid* (MGM, 1973) puts Billy and his period of New Mexico history in a slightly different perspective than previous films have done and is rich in characterization. Structure and composition of the film are outstanding; both interiors and exteriors are superb in authenticity, detail, and photography; the story is good; and the supporting cast is excellent. The film's major drawback is the slightly weak performance of the star, Kris Kristofferson.

Arthur Penn's *The Missouri Breaks* (United Artists, 1976) and Robert Altman's *Buffalo Bill and the Indians, or Sitting Bull's History Lesson* (United Artists, 1976) seem to be two examples of what Steinbeck's "Preacher Casey" had in mind when he opined that something seemed to be going on out there. Penn, whose *Bonnie and Clyde* (a non-Western) comes closer to capturing the spirit and heart of the West and its people than do all but a few of the over 3,000 entries in this book, paired Marlon Brando and Jack Nicholson in a story that would have been called "The Regulator and the Rustlers" in Bill Hart's day. Other than proving that the Godfather would come out second in one-on-one against "J. J. Giddings," it served mostly to show that Harry Dean Stanton should have been given hazard pay for exposing his talents to Nicholson's one-note exercise and Brando's self-indulgence. Giant talents all, but the biorhythm charts of Penn, Brando, and Nicholson must have taken a nose-dive here.

Much better, granted a minority opinion, was Altman's *Buffalo Bill and the Indians*. In style and speed it owed a debt to Howard Hawks' *His Girl Friday* in addition to being yet another chapter in Altman's "keep-up-with-me-if-you-can" direction. The speed comes to a grinding halt toward the end when Newman, as Buffalo Bill, spends a couple of days in a "what's-it-all-about, Alfie?" discussion with Sitting Bull, who may or may not have been present and, either way, didn't seem to much care. But the film has its moments, especially when Joel Gray and the vastly underrated Kevin McCarthy are on hand to show the difference between "actors" and "personalities," which may have been Altman's point all along.

Richard Brooks' *Bite the Bullet* (Columbia, 1975) is most appreciated by his band of small but knowledgeable followers. The film concerns a marathon horse race across the West with a couple of sub-plots thrown in to take up the slack periods while the racers are

The Shootist (Paramount, 1976) — John Wayne and James Stewart

Pat Garrett & Billy the Kid (MGM, 1973) — Kris Kristofferson, R. G. Armstrong, and James Coburn

565

Buffalo Bill and the Indians, or Sitting Bull's History Lesson (United Artists, 1976) — Burt Lancaster and Paul Newman

resting and the dust settling. Major drawbacks are that the Ben Johnson character cashes in his chips early in the game and James Coburn is around from gun to gun.

The Master Gunfighter (Taylor-Laughlin, 1975) has a premise as superficial and as unrealistic as all the films with fast guns as the theme, with the added drawback of not having a Gregory Peck or Kirk Douglas on hand. Clint Eastwood's *High Plains Drifter* (Universal, 1973) has one of the genre's all-time great titles and little else, which does put it one up on his *The Outlaw Josey Wales* (Warner Bros., 1976). Both films carry the smell of spaghetti.

Breakheart Pass (United Artists, 1976) is both a Western and a mystery, and fails to pass muster on either count if one overlooks great photography and stunning scenery; in this instance, one had better not. Starred is Charles Bronson, whose *White Buffalo* (United Artists, 1977) is most notable as the film Slim Pickens calls "the only one in which I was better looking than the star."

Comedy fared well during the period, in quantity and popularity if not in quality. In *Blazing Saddles* (Warner Bros., 1974) Mel Brooks stretches familiar conventions and situations to their ultimate fantastic limits . . . and beyond. Brooks may have been saying that the Western myth is an artificial and even ridiculous creation without meaning in today's America, but that seems a bit heavy for Brooks. It appears more likely that Mel Brooks was the first producer of the decade to realize that all the great comedy to be found in the films of the Thirties and Forties and the silent movies had never been seen by today's television generation—for golden oldies, they get reruns of "Kojak"—so it all might appear new and funny. It did. *The Duchess and the Dirtwater Fox* (Fox, 1976) and *The Great Scout and Cathouse Thursday* (American International, 1976) followed, only to offer proof that Melvin Frank and Don Taylor didn't have as good memories as Mel Brooks. Buena Vista's *The Apple Dumpling Gang* (1975) served to show that a "G" rating was no guarantee of taste or style, though nothing with Tim Conway can be a complete waste of time. *The Brothers O'Toole* (American National, 1973) had audiences disappearing under their seats with laughter. It is slapstick all the way and calculated to keep everyone in stitches for most of its running time, as John Astin demonstrates his rare talent for pantomiming every nuance of expression and delivers ludicrously funny dialogue with aplomb. Another funny spoof is *The Wackiest Wagon Train in the West* (Topar, 1976) with Bob Denver heading the shenanigans. *Hearts of the West* (MGM, 1975) is more palatable, being a thoroughly delightful comedy about the making of "B" Westerns in the Thirties.

The Great American Cowboy (American National, 1974) won the 1974 Academy Award as best documentary film. It bristles with authenticity of feeling as it lyrically, violently, and thoughtfully examines the world of the rodeo cowboy and stresses the struggle between two stars, Larry Mahan and Phil Lyne, for the World's Championship.

In a spin-off from *The Cowboys* (Warner Bros., 1972), *The Spikes Gang* (United Artists, 1974) stars Lee Marvin as a bank robber nursed back to health by a gang of boys after he has been shot up. He makes outlaws out of the boys and in the end they are all killed.

Fred Williamson practically monopolized the black Western market with *The Soul of Nigger Charley* (Paramount, 1973), *Boss Nigger* (Dimension, 1974), *Adios Amigo* (Atlas, 1975), and *Joshua* (Lone Star, 1977). Our pick as best of the bunch and one of the better black Westerns made to date is *Boss Nigger*, in which Fred is a bounty hunter out to collect a debt.

Several other films of the period are notable in the sense that they, in the aggregate, have fine casting, well-done action shots, good plot lines, excellent photography, good first- and second-unit direction, appropriate costuming, good lighting, fine music scores,

Posse (Paramount, 1975) — Kirk Douglas

567

and, most importantly, believable acting based on the exigencies of the drama. Thus, without laying claim to pontifical authority or impeccable wiseness, we suggest that merit is present in *Posse* (Paramount, 1975), *Kino, the Padre on Horseback* (Key International, 1977), *The Man Who Loved Cat Dancing* (MGM, 1973), *The Deadly Trackers* (Warner Bros., 1973), *Zandy's Bride* (Warner Bros., 1974), *The Return of a Man Called Horse* (United Artists, 1976), *The Life and Times of Grizzly Adams* (Sun, 1975), and *The Last Hard Man* (Fox, 1976).

The films pointed out in this chapter clearly prove the continued international popularity of the Western and demonstrate its versatility in story and execution. The genre has come a long way since the days when conflict, *per se*, was required to motivate the plot and the "weenie" or gimmick around which the plot revolved was a lost gold mine, water rights, land boundaries, rivalry between stagecoach and railroad, between two railroads, between two stagecoach lines, between cattlemen and farmers or cattlemen and sheepherders or cattlemen and homesteaders, or between settlers and Indians. Producers have discovered that there are more than a handful of basic dramatic plots and that the hero does not necessarily have to be a government agent working undercover to ferret out in picture #1 a crooked sheriff, in picture #2 a crooked saloon owner, in picture #3 a crooked Indian commissioner, and so forth.

The outstanding and expensive Westerns produced during the Restless Years together with the revenues from them suggest a definite resurgence in the genre. Big money and big names are being drawn again to the cinematic range responsible for many a "fatted cow." There's still gold in "them thur hills" once ridden by Tom Mix and Bronco Billy Anderson; obviously, the extraction of it will require different techniques. There are still new valleys to discover, new trails to ride, new sunsets to enthrall the young at heart. Producers, directors, writers, and actors are scurrying into those hills looking for the gold still buried there.

The shadowy valleys are less dark and the aged, lone rider standing his ground in a last ditch fight on behalf of the classical Western is now silhouetted against the rising sun of a new day showing promise of support for his cause.

FILMS OF 1973

3258. MOLLY AND LAWLESS JOHN
(Producers Distributing Corp., January, 1973)
98 Mins.
(DeLuxe Color)
Vera Miles, Sam Elliott, Clu Gulager, John Anderson, Cynthia Myers, Charles A. Pinney, Robert Westmoreland, Melinda Chavaria, Pasqualita Baca, George LeBow, Dave Burleson, Grady Hill, Dick Bullock, Terry Kingsley-Smith
D: Gary Nelson
SP: Terry Kingsley-Smith
P: Dennis Durney

3259. THE TRAIN ROBBERS
(Warner Bros., February, 1973)   92 Mins.
(Technicolor)   (PanaVision)   (Filmed in Mexico)
John Wayne, Ann-Margret, Rod Taylor, Ben Johnson, Chris George, Bobby Vinton, Jerry Gatlin, Richardo Montalban

D/SP: Burt Kennedy
P: Michael Wayne

3260. HIGH PLAINS DRIFTER
(Universal, April, 1973)   105 Mins.
(Technicolor)   (PanaVision)
Clint Eastwood, Verna Bloom, Mariana Hill, Mitchell Ryan, Jack Ging, Stefan Gierasch, Ted Hartley, Bill Curtis, Geoffrey Lewis
D: Clint Eastwood
SP: Ernest Tidyman
P: Robert Daley

3261. KID BLUE
(20th C. Fox, May, 1973)   100 Mins.
(DeLuxe Color)   (PanaVision)   (Filmed in Mexico)
Dennis Hopper, Warren Oates, Peter Boyle, Ben Johnson, Lee Purcell, Janice Rule, Ralph Waite, Clifton James, Jose Torvay, Mary Jackson, Jay

The Train Robbers (Warner Bros., 1973) — John Wayne and Ann-Margret

Varela, Claude Ennis Starrett, Jr., Warren Finnerty, Owen Orr, Richard Rust, Howard Hessman, Emmet Walsh, Henry Smith, Bobby Hall, Melvin Stewart, Eddy Donno
D: James Frawley
S/SP: Edwin "Bud" Shrake
P: Marvin Schwartz

3262. PAT GARRETT AND BILLY THE KID
(MGM, May, 1973) 106 Mins.
(Metrocolor) (PanaVision) (Filmed in Mexico)
James Coburn, Kris Kristofferson, Richard Jaeckel, Katy Jurado, Chill Wills, Jason Robards, Bob Dylan, R. G. Armstrong, Luke Askew, John Beck, Richard Bright, Matt Clark, Rita Coolidge, Jack Dodson, Jack Elam, Emilio Fernandez, Paul Fix, L. Q. Jones, Slim Pickens, Jorge Russek, Charlie Martin Smith, Harry Dean Stanton, Claudia Bryar, John Chandler, Mike Mikler, Aurora Clavel, Rutayna Alda, Walter Kelley, Rudy Wurlitzer, Elisha Cook, Jr., Gene Evans, Donnie Fritts, Dub Taylor, Don Levy
D: Sam Peckinpah
SP: Rudolph Wurlitzer
P: Gordon Carroll

3263. GUNS OF A STRANGER
(Universal, May, 1973) 91 Mins.
(Technicolor)
Marty Robbins, Chill Wills, Dovie Beams, Steve Tackett, William Foster, Shug Fisher, Tom Hartman, Charley Aldridge, Ronny Robbins, Melody Hinkle
D: Robert Hinkle
SP: Charles W. Aldridge
P: Robert Hinkle

3264. THE BROTHERS O'TOOLE
(American National Enterprises, May 16, 1973)
(Color by C.I.F.)
John Astin, Steve Carlson, Pat Carroll, Hans Conreid, Richard Erdman, Allyn Joslyn, Richard Jury, Lee Meriwether, Jesse White, Leon Inge
D: Richard Erdman
S: Tim Kelly
SP: Tim Kelly, Marion Hargrove
P: Charles E. Sellier, Jr.

3265. THE SOUL OF NIGGER CHARLEY
(Paramount, May, 1973) 109 Mins.
(Color by Movielab) (PanaVision)
Fred Williamson, D'Urville Martin, Denise Nicholas, Pedro Armendariz, Jr., Kirk Calloway, George Allen, Kevin Hagen, Michael Cameron, Johnny Greenwood, James Garbo, Nai Bonet, Robert Minor, Fred Lerner, Joe Henderson, Dick Farnsworth, Tony Brubaker, Boyd "Red" Morgan, Al Hussan, Ed Hice, Henry Wills, Phil Avenetti
D/S: Larry G. Spangler
SP: Harold Stone
P: Larry G. Spangler

3266. CAHILL, UNITED STATES MARSHAL
(Warner Bros., June, 1973) 103 Mins.
(Technicolor) (PanaVision) (Filmed in Mexico)
John Wayne, George Kennedy, Gary Grimes, Neville Brand, Clay O'Brien, Marie Windsor, Morgan Paull, Dan Vadis, Royal Dano, Scott Walker, Denver Pyle, Jackie Coogan, Rayford Barnes, Dan Kemp, Harry Carey, Jr., Walter Barnes, Paul Fix, Pepper Martin, Vance Davis, Chuck Roberson, Ken Wolger, Hank Worden, James Nusser, Murray MacLeod, Hunter Von Leer
D: Andrew V. McLaglen
S: Barney Slater
SP: Harry Julian Fink, Rita M. Fink
P: Michael Wayne

3267. ONE LITTLE INDIAN
(Buena Vista, June, 1973) 90 Mins.
(Technicolor)
James Garner, Vera Miles, Pat Hingle, Morgan Woodward, John Doucette, Clay O'Brien, Robert Pine, Bruce Glover, Ken Swofford, Jay Silverheels, Andrew Prine, Jodie Foster, Walter Brooke, Rudy Diaz, John Flynn, Tim Simcox, Lois Red Elk, Hal Baylor, Terry Wilson, Paul Sorenson, Boyd "Red" Morgan, Jim Davis
D: Bernard McEveety
SP: Harry Spalding
P: Winston Hibler

3268. SHOWDOWN
(Universal, July, 1973) 99 Mins.
(Technicolor) (Todd-AO 35)
Rock Hudson, Dean Martin, Susan Clark, Donald Moffat, John McLiam, Charles Baca, Jackson Kane, Ben Zeller, John Richard Gill, Philip L. Mead, Rolly Gardenheir
D/P: George Seaton
S: Hank Fine
SP: Theodore Taylor

3269. THE MAN WHO LOVED CAT DANCING
(MGM, July, 1973) 114 Mins.
(Metrocolor) (PanaVision)
Burt Reynolds, Sarah Miles, Lee J. Cobb, Jack Warden, George Hamilton, Bo Hopkins, Robert Donner, Sandy Kevin, Larry Littlebird, Nancy Malone, Jay Silverheels, Jay Varela, Owen Bush, Larry Finley, Sutero Garcia, Jr.
D: Richard C. Sarafian
S: Marilyn Durham

The Soul of Nigger Charley (Paramount, 1973) — Fred Williamson

Cahill, United States Marshal (Warner Bros., 1973) — John Wayne

SP: Eleanor Perry
P: Martin Poll, Eleanor Perry

3270. RUNNING WILD

(Golden Circle, August 15, 1973)   104 Mins.
(Eastman Color)

Lloyd Bridges, Dina Merrill, Pat Hingle, Morgan Woodward, Gilbert Roland, Fred Betts, Slavio Martinez

D/P: Robert McChaon
S/SP: Robert McChaon

3271. SANTEE

(Crown Productions, September, 1973)   93 Mins.
(Color)

Glenn Ford, Michael Burns, Dana Wynter, Jay Silverheels, Harry Townes, John Larch, Robert Wilke, Bob Donner, Taylor Lacher, Lindsay Crosby, Charles Courtney, X. Brand, John Hart, Russ McCubbin, Robert Mellard, Boyd "Red" Morgan, Ben Zeller, Brad Merhege

D: Gary Nelson
S: Brand Bell
SP: Tom Blackburn
P: Deno Paoli, Edward Platt

3272. THE DEADLY TRACKERS

(Warner Bros., November, 1973)   110 Mins.
(Technicolor)   (Filmed in Mexico)

Richard Harris, Rod Taylor, Al Lettieri, Neville Brand, William Smith, Paul Benjamin, Pedro Armendariz, Jr., Kelly Jean Peters, Sean Marshall, Red Morgan, Joan Swift, William Bryant, Ray Moyer, Armando Acosta, Federico Gonzales, John Kennedy

D: Barry Shear
S: "Riata"—Samuel Fuller
SP: Lukas Heller
P: Fouad Said

3273. A KNIFE FOR THE LADIES

(Bryanston, 1973)
(Color by Movielab)

Jack Elam, Ruth Roman, Jeff Cooper, John Kellogg, Joe Santos, Gene Evans, Diana Ewing, Jon Spangler, Derek Sanderson, Fred Biletnikoff

D: Larry G. Spangler
SP: George Arthur Bloom
P: Larry G. Spangler, Stan Jolley

(This film was completed in 1973, but no record of it had been released as of July, 1977)

FILMS OF 1974

3274. BLAZING SADDLES

(Warner Bros., February, 1974)   94 Mins.
(Technicolor)   (PanaVision)

Cleavon Little, Gene Wilder, Slim Pickens, David Huddleston, Liam Dunn, Alex Karras, John Hillerman, George Furth, Claude Ennis Starrett, Jr., Mel Brooks, Harvey Korman, Madeline Kahn, Carol Arthur, Charles McGregor, Robyn Hilton, Dom DeLuise, Richard Collier, Don Megowan, Karl Lukas, Burton Gilliam, Count Basie, Harvey Parry, Tom Steele

D: Mel Brooks
S: Andrew Bergman
SP: Mel Brooks, Norman Steinberg, Andrew Bergman, Richard Pryor, Alan Unger
P: Michael Hertzberg

3275. LOVIN' MOLLY

(Columbia, March, 1974)   98 Mins.
(Color)

Anthony Perkins, Beau Bridges, Blythe Danner, Edward Binns, Susan Sarandon, Conrad Fowkes, Claude Transverse, John Henry Faulk

D: Sidney Lumet
S: "Leaving Cheyenne"—Larry McMurtry
SP/P: Stephen Friedman

3276. THE SPIKES GANG

(United Artists, April, 1974)   96 Mins.
(DeLuxe Color)

Lee Marvin, Gary Grimes, Ron Howard, Charlie Martin Smith, Arthur Hunnicutt, Noah Beery, Marc Smith, Don Fellows, Elliott Sullivan, Robert Beatty, Ralph Brown, Bill Curran, Ricardo Palacious, David Thomson, Bert Conway, Adolfo Thous, Allen E. Russell, Frances O'Flynn

D: Richard Fleischer
SP: Irving Ravetch, Harriet Frank, Jr.
P: Walter Mirisch

3277. THOMASINE AND BUSHROD

(Columbia, April, 1974)   95 Mins.
(Color)

Max Julien, Vonetta McGee, George Murdock, Glynn Turman, Juanita Moore, Joel Fluellen, Jackson D. Kane, Bud Conlan, Kip Allen, Ben Zeller, Herb Robins, Harry Luck, Jason Bernard

D: Gordon Parks, Jr.
SP: Max Julien
P: Harvey Bernhard, Max Julien

The Spikes Gang (United Artists, 1974) — Lee Marvin, Gary Grimes, and Ron Howard

3278. THE GREAT AMERICAN COWBOY

(American National Enterprises, June 19, 1974)
90 Mins.
(DeLuxe Color)
Larry Mahan, Phil Lyne, Joel McCrea
D/P: Keith Merrill
SP: Douglas Kent Hall

3279. ZANDY'S BRIDE

(Warner Bros., July, 1974) 116 Mins.
(Technicolor) (PanaVision)
Gene Hackman, Liv Ullman, Eileen Heckart, Harry
Dean Stanton, Joe Santos, Frank Cady, Sam Bot-
toms, Susan Tyrell, Bob Simpson, Fabian Gregory
Cordova, Don Wilbanks, Vivian Gordon, Alf Kjel-
lin
D: Jan Troell
S: "The Stranger"—Lillian Bos Ross
SP: Marc Norman
P: Harvey Matofsky

3280. THE CASTAWAY COWBOY

(Buena Vista, August, 1974) 91 Mins.
(Technicolor)
James Garner, Vera Miles, Robert Culp, Eric Shea,
Gregory Sierra, Shug Fisher, Elizabeth Smith,

Manu Tupou, Nephi Hannemann, Lito Capina,
Ralph Hanalei, Kahana, Lee Wood, Luis Delgado,
Buddy Joe Hooker, Patrick Sullivan Burke
D: Bernard McEveety
S: Don Tait, Richard Bluel, Hugh Benson
SP: Don Tait
P: Ron Miller, Winston Hibler

3281. FACE TO THE WIND

(Warner Bros., August, 1974) 93 Mins.
(DeLuxe Color) (PanaVision)
Cliff Potts, Xochitl, Harry Dean Stanton, Don Wil-
banks, Woodrow Chambliss, James Gammon,
William Carstens, Roy Jensen, Richard Breeding
D: William A. Graham
SP: David Markson
P: Harvey Matofsky

3282. THE LEGEND OF EARL DURAND

(Howco Productions, November, 1974) 110 Mins.
(Color by C.F.I.)
Peter Haskell, Slim Pickens, Keenan Wynn, Martin
Sheen, Anthony Caruso, Albert Salmi, Phil Lopp,
Hal Bokar, Ivy Bethune, Carl Kennerson, J. H.
Richardson, Luana Jackman, Johnny Patterson,
Gregory Patterson, Howard Wright, Joan How-

ard, Robert Drake, Fred Peterson, Gibb Stepp, Sis Pilcher, Harry Woolman, Billy Rowe, Kelly Wilson
D/P: John D. Patterson
SP: J. Frank James

3283. THE TRIAL OF BILLY JACK
(Taylor-Laughlin Productions, November 13, 1974) 170 Mins.
(Metrocolor) (PanaVision)
Delores Taylor, Tom Laughlin, Victor Izay, Teresa Laughlin, William Wellman, Jr., Russell Lane, Michelle Wilson, Geo Anne Sosa, Lynn Baker, Riley Hill, Sparky Stanley, Gus Greymountain, Sacheen Littlefeather, Michael Bolland, Jack Stanley, Bong Soo Han, Rolling Thunder, Sandra Ego, Trinidad Hopkins
D: Frank Laughlin
SP: Frank and Teresa Christina
P: Joe Cramer
(Note: Taylor-Laughlin distributed the film from November 13, 1974 through December 24, 1974. Warner Brothers took over distribution on December 25, 1974)

3284. BOSS NIGGER
(Dimension Productions, December, 1974) 87 Mins.
(DeLuxe Color) (Todd-AO 35)
Fred Williamson, D'Urville Martin, William Smith,
Barbara Leigh, R. G. Armstrong, Don "Red" Barry, Carmen Hayworth, Ben Zeller
D: Jack Arnold
SP: Fred Williamson
P: Jack Arnold, Fred Williamson

3285. SEVEN ALONE
(Doty-Dayton Productions, December 20, 1974) 97 Mins.
(Color)
Dewey Martin, Aldo Ray, Ann Collings, Dean Smith, Stewart Petersen, James Griffith, Dehl Berti, Bea Morris
D: Earl Bellamy
S: "On to Oregon"—Honor Morrow
SP: Eleanor Lamb, Douglas C. Stewart
P: Lyman D. Dayton

3286. SAVAGE RED—OUTLAW WHITE
(Avco Embassy, December, 1974)
(Color)
Robert Padilla, Malilia St. Duval, Richard Rust, Steven Oliver, David Eastman, Rockne Tarkington, Michael Green, Doodles Weaver
D: Paul Hunt
SP: Steve Fisher
P: Paul Norbert

FILMS OF 1975

3287. THE LIFE AND TIMES OF GRIZZLY ADAMS
(Sun Classic, January, 1975) 93 Mins.
(DeLuxe Color)
Dan Haggerty, Don Shanks, Marjorie Harper, Lisa Jones
D: Richard Friedenberg
SP: Larry Dobkin
P: Charles E. Sellier, Jr.

3288. RANCHO DELUXE
(United Artists, April, 1975) 93 Mins.
(DeLuxe Color)
Jeff Bridges, Sam Waterston, Elizabeth Ashley, Charlene Dallas, Clifton James, Slim Pickens, Harry Dean Stanton, Richard Bright, Patti D'Arbanville, Maggie Wellman, Bert Conway, Anthony Palmer
D: Frank Perry
SP: Thomas McGuane
P: Elliott Kastner

3289. JESSI'S GIRLS
(Manson Productions, April, 1975) 86 Mins.
(Color)
Sondra Currie, Geoffrey Land, Ben Frank, Regina Carroll, Jennifer Bishop, Ellen Stern, Joe Cortese, Jon Shank, Biff Yeager, Gavin Murrell, Rigg Kennedy, William Hammer, Hugh Warden, Joe Arrowsmith, John Durren, Rod Cameron
D: Al Adamson
SP: Budd Donnelly
P: Michael F. Goldman, Al Adamson

3290. SMOKE IN THE WIND
(Gamalex Productions, April, 1975)
(Color)
John Ashley, John Russell, Myron Healey, Walter Brennan, Susan Houston, Linda Weld, Henry Kingi, Adair Jameson, Dan White, Lorna Thayer, Billy Hughes, Jr., Bill Foster, Jack Horton, Bill McKenzie
D: Joseph Kane
S/SP: Eric Allen
P: Robert "Whitey" Hughes, Bill Hughes

Bite the Bullet (Columbia, 1975) — Ben Johnson

3291. POSSE

(Paramount, May, 1975)   94 Mins.

(Technicolor)   (PanaVision)

Kirk Douglas, Bruce Dern, Bo Hopkins, James Stacy, Alfonso Arau, David Canary, Luke Askew, Beth Brickell, Katherine Woodville, Mark Roberts, Dick O'Neill, Bill Burton, Louie Elias, Gus Greymountain, Allan Warnick

D: Kirk Douglas

S: Christopher Knopf

SP: William Roberts, Christopher Knopf

P: Kirk Douglas

3292. WINTERHAWK

(Howco Productions, June 4, 1975)   99 Mins.

(Technicolor)   (TechniScope)

Michael Dante, Leif Erickson, Woody Strode, Denver Pyle, Elisha Cook, Jr., L. Q. Jones, Arthur Hunnicutt, Dawn Wells, Chuck Pierce, Jr., Sacheen Littlefeather, Dennis Finple, Seamon Glass, Jimmy Clem, Ace Powell

D/SP/P: Charles B. Pierce

3293. PURSUIT

(Key International, June, 1975)   86 Mins.

(DeLuxe Color)

Ray Danton, DeWitt Lee, Troy Nabors, Diane Taylor, Eva Kovacs, Jason Clark

D: Thomas Quillen

S/SP: DeWitt Lee, Jack Lee

P: Vern Piehl

3294. BLAZING STEWARDESSES

(Independent International, June, 1975)   85 Mins.

(Metrocolor)

Yvonne De Carlo, Bob Livingston, Don "Red" Barry, Harry Ritz, Jimmy Ritz, Geoffrey Land, Connie Hoffman, Regina Carroll, T. A. King, Lon Bradshaw, Jerry Mills, Nicole Riddell, Sheldon Lee, Carol Bilger, John Shank

D: Al Adamson

S/P: Samuel M. Sherman

SP: Samuel M. Sherman, John R. D'Amato

3295. STARBIRD AND SWEET WILLIAM

(Howco Productions, June, 1975)   90 Mins.

(Eastman Color)

A. Martinez, Louise Fitch, Don Haggerty, Ancil Cook, Skip Homeier, Skeeter Vaughn, Monika Ramirez, Roger Bear, Caesar Ramirez

D: Jack B. Hively

SP: Axel Gruenberg

P: Dick Alexander

3296. BITE THE BULLET
(Columbia, July, 1975)   131 Mins.
(Color)   (Panavision)
Gene Hackman, Candice Bergen, James Coburn, Ben Johnson, Ian Bannen, Jan-Michael Vincent, John McLiam, Dabney Coleman, Jerry Gatlin, Mario Arteaga, Robert Donner, Robert Hoy, Paul Stewart, Jean Willes, Sally Kirkland, Walter Scott, Jr., Bill Burton, Buddy Van Horn
D/S/SP/P: Richard Brooks

3297. THE APPLE DUMPLING GANG
(Buena Vista, July, 1975)   100 Mins.
(Technicolor)
Bill Bixby, Susan Clark, Don Knotts, Tim Conway, David Wayne, Slim Pickens, Harry Morgan, Clay O'Brien, Brad Savage, Stacy Manning, Iris Adrian
D: Norman Tokar
S: Jack M. Bickham
SP: Don Tait
P: Bill Anderson

3298. DAN CANDY'S LAW
(Cinerama Rel. Corp./American International, July, 1975)   95 Mins.
(Color)   (Filmed in Canada)
Donald Sutherland, Chief Dan George, Jean Duceppe, Francine Rocette, Kevin McCarthy, Gordon Tootoosis
D: Claude Fournier
SP: George Malko
P: Marie Jose-Raymond

3299. MY NAME IS LEGEND
(Film Center, July, 1975)   88 Mins.
(Color by Alexander)
Duke Kelly, Tom Kirk, Stan Foster, Kerry Smith, Rand Porter, Curley Montana, Scott Kelly, Roberta Eaton, Bill Lear, Jerry Stark, Randy Parker, Terry Christgau
D/SP/P: Duke Kelly

3300. THE MASTER GUNFIGHTER
(Taylor-Laughlin Productions, October 3, 1975)   121 Mins.
(Metrocolor)   (PanaVision)
Tom Laughlin, Ron O'Neal, Lincoln Kilpatrick, Geo Anne Sosa, Barbara Carrera, Victor Campos, Hector Elias, Michael Lane, Patti Clifton
D: Frank Laughlin
SP: Harold Lapland
P: Philip Parslow

3301. ROOSTER COGBURN (And the Lady)
(Universal, October 17, 1975)   107 Mins.
(Technicolor)   (PanaVision)
John Wayne, Katharine Hepburn, Anthony Zerbe, Richard Jordan, John McIntire, Paul Koslo, Strother Martin, Jack Colvin, Jon Lormer, Richard Romancito, Lane Smith, Warren Vanders, Jerry Gatlin, Mickey Gilbert, Chuck Hayward, Gary McLarty
D: Stuart Millar
S/SP: Martin Julien (Martha Hyer). Based on the character "Rooster Cogburn" from the novel "True Grit" by Charles Portis
P: Hal B. Wallis

3302. POSSE FROM HEAVEN
(P. M. Films, October 24, 1975)   87 Mins.
(Eastman Color)
Fanne Foxe, Todd Compton, Sherry Bain, Ward Wood, Rod Roddy, Dick Burch, Robert Perkin
D: Philip Pine
SP: Ward Wood, Philip Pine
P: Ward Wood, Philip Pine

3303. HEARTS OF THE WEST
(MGM/United Artists, October, 1975)   102 Mins.
(Metrocolor)
Jeff Bridges, Andy Griffith, Donald Pleasence, Blythe Danner, Alan Arkin, Richard B. Shull, Herbert Edelman, Alex Rocco, Frank Cady, Anthony James, Burton Gilliam, Matt Clark, Candy Azzara, Thayer David, Wayne Storm, Marie Windsor
D: Howard Zieff
SP: Rob Thompson
P: Tony Bill

3304. SUNDANCE CASSIDY AND BUTCH THE KID
(Film Ventures, December, 1975)   95 Mins.
(Color)
John Wade, Karen Blake, Robert Neuman
D: Arthur Pitt
(Title changed to *Sundance and the Kid*, approximately March, 1976)

3305. AGAINST A CROOKED SKY
(Doty-Dayton, December 12, 1975)   100 Mins.
(Color)   (Todd AO-35)
Richard Boone, Stewart Petersen, Henry Wilcoxon, Clint Richie, Shannon Farnon, Jewel Branch, Brenda Venus, Geoffrey Land, Gordon Hanson, Vincent St. Cyr, Rich Wheeler, Margaret Willey
D: Earl Bellamy
SP: Eleanor Lamd, Douglas Stewart
P: Lyman Dayton

3306. ADIOS AMIGO
(Atlas Productions, December 25, 1975)   87 Mins.
(Eastman Color)   (PanaVision)
Fred Williamson, Richard Pryor, James Brown, Robert Phillips, Mike Henry, Suhaila Farhat, Victoria Jee, Lynne Jackson, Heidi Dobbs, Liz Treadwell, Joy Lober, Thalmus Rasulala
D/SP/P: Fred Williamson

Breakheart Pass (United Artists, 1976) — Charles Bronson and Jill Ireland

FILMS OF 1976

**3307. THE ADVENTURES OF
FRONTIER FREMONT**

(Sun Classic, January 14, 1976)   85 Mins.

Dan Haggerty, Denver Pyle, Tony Mirrati, Norman
Goodman

D: Richard Friedenberg

S: Richard Friedenberg, Charles E. Sellier, Jr., David O'Malley

SP: David O'Malley

P: Charles E. Sellier, Jr.

3308. MACINTOSH AND T. J.

(Penland Productions, February 5, 1976)   96 Mins.
(Technicolor)

Roy Rogers, Clay O'Brien, Billy Green Bush, Andrew Robinson, Joan Hackett, James Hampton,
Walter Barnes, Dean Smith, Larry Mahan

D: Marvin Chomsky

SP: Paul Savage

P: Tim Penland

(Film had playdates in mid-central and mid-western
U.S. in the fall of 1975, but officially premiered on
February 5, 1976 in Lubbock, Texas at the Winchester Theatre)

3309. BREAKHEART PASS

(United Artists, February, 1976)   95 Mins.
(Color)

Charles Bronson, Ben Johnson, Richard Crenna,
Jill Ireland, Charles Durning, Ed Lauter, David
Huddleston, Roy Jenson, Casey Tibbs, Archie
Moore, Joe Kapp, Read Morgan, Robert Rothwell,
Rayford Barnes, Scott Newman, Eldon Burke,
William McKinney, Eddie Little Sky, Robert Tessier, Doug Atkins

D: Tom Gries

S: Alistair MacLean

P: Jerry Gershwin

3310. THE WINDS OF AUTUMN

(Howco Productions, February 25, 1976)
(Technicolor)   (PanaVision)

Jack Elam, Jeanette Nolan, Andrew Prine, Dub Taylor, Chuck Pierce, Jr., Earl E. Smith, Belinda
Palmer, Jimmy Clem

D/P: Charles B. Pierce

SP: Earl E. Smith

The Missouri Breaks (United Artists, 1976) — Marlon Brando and Jack Nicholson

3311. MUSTANG COUNTRY
(Universal, March 19, 1976) 79 Mins.
(Technicolor) (Filmed in Canada)
Joel McCrea, Robert Fuller, Patrick Wayne, Nika
  Mina
D/SP/P: John Champion

3312. SECRET OF NAVAJO CAVE
(Key International, April 19, 1976) 87 Mins.
(Eastman Color)
Rex Allen, Holger Kasper, Steven Benally, Jr.,
  Johnny Guerro, and members of the Navajo
  Nation
D/SP/P: James T. Flocker

**3313. THE DUCHESS AND THE
        DIRTWATER FOX**
(20th C. Fox, April, 1976) 103 Mins.
(DeLuxe Color) (PanaVision)
George Segal, Goldie Hawn, Conrad Janis, Thayer
  David, Jennifer Lee, Sid Gould, Pat Ast, E. J.
  Andre, Dick Farnsworth, Clifford Turknett, Har-
  lan Knudson, Jean Favre, Bill McLaughlin, Rich-
  ard Jamison, Barbara Ulrich, John Alderson, Jim
  Frank, Georgine Rozman, Kathy Christopher,
  Ellen Stern, Pater Rachback, Jerry Taft, Prentis
  Rowe, Ronald Colizzo, June Constable, Vern
  Porter, Roy Jenson, Bob Roy, Bennie Dobbins,
  Walter Scott, Jerry Gatlin
D/P: Melvin Frank
S: Barry Sandler
SP: Melvin Frank, Barry Sandler, Jack Rose

3314. THE MISSOURI BREAKS
(United Artists, May 19, 1976) 126 Mins.
(DeLuxe Color)
Marlon Brando, Jack Nicholson, Randy Quaid, Kath-
  leen Lloyd, Frederic Forrest, Harry Dean Stanton,
  John McLiam, John Ryan, Sam Gilman, Steve
  Franken, Richard Bradford, James Greene, Luana
  Anders, Danny Goldman, Hunter Van Leer, Vir-
  gil Frye, R. L. Armstrong, Dan Ades, Dorothy
  Neumann, Charles Wagenheim, Vern Chandler
D: Arthur Penn
SP: Thomas McGuane
P: Elliott Kastner, Robert M. Sherman

3315. HAWMPS!
(Mulberry Square, May 20, 1976) 126 Mins.
(Color by C.F.I.)
James Hampton, Christopher Connelly, Slim
  Pickens, Denver Pyle, Gene Conforti, Mimi May-
  nard, Jack Elam, Lee deBroux, Herb Vigran, Jesse
  Davis, Frank Inn, Mike Travis, Larry Swartz,
  Tiny Wells, Dick Drake, Henry Kendrick, Don
  Starr, Cynthia Smith, Roy Gunzburg, Rex Jans-
  sen, Catherine Hearne, Larry Strawbridge, James

Weie, Alvin Wright, Lee Tiplitsky, Joey Camp,
  Perry Martin, Richard Lundin, Charles Starkey
D: Joe Camp
S: William Bickley, Michael Warren, Joe Camp
SP: William Bickley, Michael Warren
P: Joe Camp, Ben Vaughn

3316. THE LAST HARD MEN
(20th C. Fox, June, 1976) 98 Mins.
(DeLuxe Color) (PanaVision)
Charlton Heston, James Coburn, Barbara Hershey,
  Chris Mitchum, Jorge Rivero, Michael Parks,
  Larry Wilcox, Morgan Paul, Thalmus Rasulala,
  Bob Donner, John Quade
D: Andrew V. McLaglen
S: "Gun Down"—Brian Garfield
SP: Guerdon Trueblood
P: Russell Thacher, Walter Seltzer

**3317. THE GREAT SCOUT AND
        CATHOUSE THURSDAY**
(American International, June 23, 1976) 102 Mins.
Lee Marvin, Oliver Reed, Robert Culp, Elizabeth
  Ashley, Strother Martin, Sylvia Miles, Kay Lenz,
  Howard Platt, Jac Zacha, Phaedra, Leticia Robles,
  Luz Maria Pena, Erika Carlson, C. C. Charity,
  Ana Verdugo
D: Don Taylor
SP: Richard Shapiro
P: Jules Buck, David Korda

**3318. BUFFALO BILL AND THE INDIANS,
        OR SITTING BULL'S HISTORY LESSON**
(United Artists, July, 1976) 123 Mins.
(Color) (PanaVision) (Filmed in Canada)
Paul Newman, Burt Lancaster, Joel Grey, Kevin
  McCarthy, Harvey Keitel, Allan Nicholls, Geral-
  dine Chaplin, John Considine, Robert Doqui, Mike
  Kaplan, Bert Remsen, Bonnie Leaders, Noelle
  Rogers, Evelyn Lear, Denver Pyle, Frank Ka-
  quitts, Will Sampson, Ken Krossa, Fred N. Larsen,
  Jerry and Joy Duce, Alex Green and Gary Mac-
  Kenzie, Humphrey Gratz, Pat McCormick,
  Shelley Duvall
D/P: Robert Altman
SP: Alan Rudolph, Robert Altman

3319. THE OUTLAW JOSEY WALES
(Warner Bros., July, 1976) 136 Mins.
(Ad credits read color by DeLuxe; film credits read
  Technicolor) (PanaVision)
Clint Eastwood, Chief Dan George, Sondra Locke,
  Bill McKinney, John Vernon, Paula Trueman,
  Sam Bottoms, Geraldine Keams, Woodrow Par-
  frey, Joyce Jameson, Sheb Wooley, Royal Dano,
  Matt Clark, John Verros, Will Sampson, William
  O'Connell, John Quade

The Last Hard Men
(20th C. Fox, 1976)
— Charlton Heston
and James Coburn

D: Clint Eastwood
S: "Gone to Texas"—Forrest Carter
SP: Phil Kaufman, Sonia Chernus
P: Robert Daley

3320. THE SHOOTIST

(Paramount, July, 1976)   100 Mins.
(Technicolor)
John Wayne, Lauren Bacall, Ron Howard, James
    Stewart, Richard Boone, Hugh O'Brian, Bill
    McKinney, Harry Morgan, John Carradine,
    Sheree North, Richard Lenz, Scatman Crothers,
    Gregg Palmer, Alfred Dennis, Dick Winslow,
    Melody Thomas, Kathleen O'Malley
D: Don Siegel
S: Glen Swarthout
SP: Miles Hood Swarthout, Scott Hale
P: M. J. Frankovich

3321. TREASURE OF MATECUMBE

(Buena Vista, July, 1976)   117 Mins.
(Technicolor)
Robert Foxworth, Joan Hackett, Peter Ustinov,
    Vic Morrow, Jane Wyatt, Virginia Vincent, Don
    Knight, Robert Doqui, Dub Taylor, Johnny
    Doran, Billy Attmore, Mills Watson, Val De Var-
    gas, Dick Van Patten

D: Vincent McEveety
S: "A Journey to Matecumbe"—Robert Lewis Tay-
    lor
SP: Don Tait
P: Bill Anderson

3322. THE WACKIEST WAGON TRAIN
IN THE WEST

(Topar, August, 1976)   86 Mins.
(Color)
Bob Denver, Forrest Tucker, Jeannine Riley, Lori
    Saunders, Ivor Francis, Lynn Wood, Bill Cort
SP: Sherwood Schwartz, Elroy Schwartz, Brad
    Radnitz, Howard Ostroff, Sherwood Friedman
P: Elroy Schwartz

3323. SHADOW OF THE HAWK

(Columbia, August, 1976)   92 Mins.
(Eastman Color)   (PanaVision)
(Filmed in Canada)
Jan-Michael Vincent, Marilyn Hassett, Chief Dan
    George, Pia Shandel, Marianne Jones, Jacques
    Hubert
D: George McGowan
SP: Norman Thaddeus Vane, Herbert J. Wright
P: John Kemeny

3324. THE RETURN OF A MAN CALLED HORSE

(United Artists, August, 1976) 129 Mins.
(DeLuxe Color) (PanaVision)
(Filmed in Mexico, England, and U.S.A.)
Richard Harris, Gale Sondergaard, Geoffrey Lewis,
    Bill Lucking, Jorge Luke, Claudio Brook, Enrique
    Lucero, Jorge Russek, Ana DeSade, Pedro Da-
    mien, Humberto Lopez-Pineda, Patricia Reyes,
    Regino Herrerra, Rigobert Rico, Albert Mariscal
D: Irvin Kershner
SP: Jack DeWitt. Based on "A Man Called Horse" by
    Dorothy M. Johnson
P: Terry Morse, Jr.

3325. FROM NOON TILL THREE

(United Artists, October, 1976) 99 Mins.
(Technicolor) (PanaVision)
Charles Bronson, Jill Ireland, Douglas V. Fowley,
    Stan Haze, Damon Douglas, Betty Cole, Hector
    Morales, Sonny Jones, Howard Brunner, Don
    "Red" Barry
D/S/SP: Frank D. Gilroy
P: M. J. Frankovich, William Self

**3326. THE LIFE AND LEGEND OF
        BUFFALO JONES**

(Starfire, November, 1976)
(Color)
Rick Guinn, John Freeman, George Sager, Rich
    Scheeland
P: John Fabian, Dick Robinson
(Four-walled by the producer in Roswell, New
    Mexico, Lubbock, Texas, and Davenport, Iowa in
    November, 1976. Chances are good, based on a
    viewing, that those three cities saved the rest of
    the country from a similar fate)

3327. JOE PANTHER

(Artists Creation, November, 1976) 110 Mins.
(Color)
Brian Keith, Ricardo Montalban, Ray Tracey, A.
    Martinez, Cliff Osmond, Alan Feinstein, Lois Red
    Elk
D: Paul Krasny
SP: Based on the novels of Paul Krasny
P: Stewart H. Beveridge

3328. PONY EXPRESS RIDER

(Doty-Dayton, November 19, 1976) 100 Mins.
(DeLuxe Color)
Stewart Petersen, Henry Wilcoxon, Buck Taylor,
    Maureen McCormack, Ken Curtis, Joan Caul-

field, Slim Pickens, Dub Taylor, Ace Reis, Jack
    Elam
D: Robert Totten
SP: Dan Greer, Hal Harrison, Jr., Robert Totten
P: Dan Greer, Hal Harrison, Jr.

3329. ACROSS THE GREAT DIVIDE

(Pacific International, December 20, 1976)
(Color by C.F.I.) (Partly filmed in Canada)
Robert Logan, George "Buck" Flower, Heather
    Rattray, Mark Hall
D/SP: Stewart Raffill
P: Arthur R. Dubs

3330. BAKER'S HAWK

(Doty-Dayton, December 22, 1976) 105 Mins.
(DeLuxe Color)
Clint Walker, Burl Ives, Diane Baker, Lee H. Mont-
    gomery, Alan Young, Taylor Lacher, Bruce M.
    Fischer
D: Lyman D. Dayton
S: "Baker's Hawk"—Jack Bickham
SP: Dan Greer, Hal Harrison, Jr.
P: Lyman D. Dayton

3331. GUARDIAN OF THE WILDERNESS

(Sunn Classic, December, 1976) 152 Mins.
(Color)
Denver Pyle, John Dehner, Ken Berry, Cheryl Mil-
    ler, Ford Rainey, Cliff Osmond, Norman Fell,
    Jack Kruschen, Don Shanks, Melissa Jones, Brett
    Palmer, Hyde Clayton, Prentiss Rowe, Coleman
    Creel, Tom Carlin, Michael G. Kavanagh, Lynn
    Lehman, Earl Benton, Michael Rudd
D: David O'Malley
S/P: Charles E. Sellier, Jr.
SP: Casey Conlon
(Producing company changed its name from Sun
    Classic to Sunn Classic; 152 minute running time
    may be a transposition of 125 minutes. The time
    comes from a review and just doesn't ring true for
    this type of production)

3332. GONE WITH THE WEST

(Cougar Productions, February 11, 1976)
James Caan and Stefanie Powers
(This film is purposely listed last. It had a world
    premiere on February 11, 1976 in Tucson, Ari-
    zona but as of July, 1977 nothing more has been
    heard of it and the film is no longer being carried
    in Cougar's 1977 releasing schedule)

FILMS OF 1977

3333. JOSHUA
(Lone Star Productions, March, 1977)   90 Mins.
(Color)
Fred Williamson, Isela Vega, Calvin Bartlett, Brenda
    Venus
D/SP/P: Larry Spangler

3334. THE WHITE BUFFALO
(United Artists, May, 1977)   97 Mins.
(Color)
Charles Bronson, Jack Warden, Will Sampson, Kim
    Novak, Clint Walker, Stuart Whitman, Slim
    Pickens, Cara Williams, John Carradine
D: J. Lee Thompson
S/SP: Richard Sale
P: Pancho Kohner

3335. KINO, THE PADRE ON HORSEBACK
(Key International, June 8, 1977)   116 Mins.
(Color)
Richard Egan, Ricardo Montalban, John Ireland,
    Cesar Romero, Joe Campanella, Stephen McNally,
    Anthony Caruso, Rory Calhoun, Keenan Wynn,
    Aldo Ray, Michael Ansara, John Russell, Joe Pe-
    trullo, Victor Jory, William Dozier, Tris Coffin,
    Henry Brandon, Danny Zapien
D: Ken Kennedy
SP: Ken Kennedy
P: Arthur E. Coates

3336. THE GREAT GUNDOWN
(Sun Productions, August 4, 1977)   95 Mins.
(Technicolor)
Robert Padilla, Malia St. Duval, Richard Rust,
    Steven Oliver, David Eastman, Stanley Adams,
    Rockne Tarkington, Michael Christian, Owen
    Orr, Michael Green

D: Paul Hunt
SP: Steve Fisher
S: Robert Padilla
P: Paul Norbert

3337. WISHBONE CUTTER
(Howco Productions, August, 1977)   114 Mins.
(Technicolor)   (PanaVision)
Joe Don Baker, Sondra Locke, Ted Neeley, Joy
    Houck, Jr., Slim Pickens, Dennis Fimple, John
    Chandler, Linda Dano
D/SP/P: Earl E. Smith
(August release was changed to October due to new
    ad campaign)

3338. THE WEST IS STILL WILD/ MULEFEATHERS
(B.A.M. Productions—a 1975 film tentatively
    scheduled for release in 1977)
Rory Calhoun, Richard Webb, Angela Richardson,
    Doodles Weaver, Noble "Kid" Chissell, Nicholas
    Worth, Arthur Roberts, Cathy Carribu, Ted Leh-
    man, Dee Cooper, Nedra Volz, Pat Crenshaw,
    Dorinda Carey, Kenneth Smedberg, Frank Otter-
    man, Ken Johnson, Ruth Vinson
D/S/SP: Don Von Mizener
P: Robert F. Slatzer

3339. GRAYEAGLE
(American International, December 23, 1977)
(Color)
Ben Johnson, Alex Cord, Lana Wood, Iron Eyes
    Cody, Jack Elam, Paul Fix, Jacob Daniels
D: Charles B. Pierce
S/SP: Charles B. Pierce
P: Charles B. Pierce

CHAPTER 12

The Continental Westerns 1962-1977

(ANYONE FOR SPAGHETTI, TORTILLAS, OR SAUERKRAUT
—MAYBE SPRINKLED WITH A LITTLE RICE?)

Since the fantastic success of Sergio Leone's *A Fistful of Dollars* (United Artists, 1967), continental Westerns have commanded considerable attention, if not respect, from those who once passed them off as unimportant, amoral, amateurish, and noisy films. Cinecitta (the studios of Rome) had actually produced about twenty-five oaters prior to *A Fistful of Dollars*, so that the film's reputation as the first Italian Western is somewhat akin to the actor who labors in the vineyard of filmdom for thirty years to suddenly discover that he has become an "overnight" success or "new" find.

But *A Fistful of Dollars* was a first of sorts. It was the first Western to achieve worldwide popularity that was filmed entirely abroad by a foreign producer in a style that was distinctly and uniquely European. There were many long pauses, many close-ups of the eyes and faces before the gunfights. The unusual sound track by Ennio Morricone (using the pseudonym "Don Savio") was loaded with harsh grating music and noises. The hero was a silent, lonely figure as deadly as a viper and as unkempt in general appearance as ever Charlie King and Slim Whitaker were in the old "B" Westerns where they played the boss heavy's chief henchmen. There was violence, sadism, plenty of corpses, and a story adapted from a Japanese Samurai film, *Yojimbo* (1954).

A Fistful of Dollars grossed big and had a worldwide distribution. Costing approximately $250,000, it has grossed over $11 million. Never before had a continental Western come anywhere close to realizing profits of this sort. In fact, few American Westerns have ever done it either. Was it a fluke? Leone had to find out. He next offered *For a Few Dollars More* (United Artists, 1967), again with the relatively unknown American actor Clint Eastwood as "The Man with No Name." This time there was no attempt to fool audiences into believing the film was American-made. Thus, Leone dropped his pseudonym "Bob Roberts" which had been used in the credits of *A Fistful of Dollars*. The budget was upped to $500,000. World gross receipts have reached $15 million. Leone was riding high in the saddle. He next offered *The Good, the Bad, and the Ugly* (United Artists, 1968), a bloody, long opus with Clint Eastwood ("The Good"), Lee Van Cleef ("The Bad"), and Eli Wallach ("The Ugly") engaged in killing everyone in sight. This time the budget was eight times that for *A Fistful of Dollars*, coming in at around $2 million. But the world gross to date has reached $19 million! United Artists handled the U.S. distribution of these films and spent a lot of money advertising them, but its investment was recovered many times over. The success of these spaghetti Westerns, as they have commonly been called, has been nothing less than phenomenal. In Cinecitta a Western town was built and Italy suddenly had its own Gower Gulch in the shadows of the Vatican and the Colosseum. Cinecitta had been catapulted into the Republic of Europe and hungry actors who had the nerve to mount a horse congregated around the bustling studio.

For a Few Dollars More (United Artists, 1967) — Lee Van Cleef and Clint Eastwood

Treasure of Silver Lake (Columbia, 1965) — Lex Barker and Herbert Lom

The Italian-Spanish Westerns made Eastwood a superstar and advanced the careers of other Hollywood actors who ventured abroad for spaghetti, tortillas, sauerkraut, and rice in the hopes that back home they could feast on bigger and better steaks. Actually, the first Hollywood star to make it big in continental Westerns was Lex Barker, a former Tarzan star; and it is German producers rather than Italian producers who deserve credit for the first commercially successful Westerns made in Europe. When Barker's Hollywood career hit the skids he ventured to Europe for a series of Westerns in Germany. The most popular of these films was *Treasure of Silver Lake* (Columbia, 1965), and the series was based on the Indian novels of Karl May, who never saw the American West but who passionately devoured the novels of Zane Grey. Mainstay of the films was an abundance of well-staged action and the Indian setting filmed in Yugoslavia.

The German Westerns were traditional in story and execution, mainly dealing with stories of legendary Western heroes and the conflict of whites and Indians. They were also naively and awkwardly put together. To American Western aficionados they are pathetic. Italian Westerns, however, quickly took a different turn and became saturated with blatant sex, violence, and anti-heroes. Settings were invariably in the Mexican-dominated sections of the Great Southwest. The same can be said of the Spanish Westerns. Actually, many of the continental Westerns were co-productions of Italy and Spain. The Japanese influence is also found in many of these films as well as in American-made Westerns such as *The Magnificent Seven* (Mirisch, 1960). Japanese Westerns, as such, have not been popular outside of Japan as have the spaghettis.

Many stars familiar to American audiences have appeared in the continental sage-brushers. At the beginning of the Sixties the Italian RAI-TV screened Walt Disney's *Zorro* series starring Guy Williams and George J. Lewis and *Zorro* became the hero of the younger generation. The producers of Cinecitta took advantage of the new success of *Zorro* and the first adventure-drama Westerns filmed in Italy, before *A Fistful of Dollars* revolutionized continental Westerns, were the *Zorro* films. All the continental features on Zorro were Italian or Italian-Spanish co-productions, all low-budget "B" films made in fifteen to thirty days in Cinecitta with some footage shot in Spain. Most were in color and most were never shown in the U.S.

Frank Latimore, an ex-Hollywood actor, made the best foreign *Zorro* films. He had played a dashing swashbuckler, on the order of Fairbanks and Flynn, in several Italian movies and was a popular figure in Europe. Both *Zorro, the Avenger* and *Shades of Zorro* were good films competently directed by J. R. Marchent.

Gordon Scott, another former Tarzan, put aside his loincloth and grapevine to star in *Buffalo Bill, Hero of the Far West,* an Italian-Spanish film, while television's "Wild Bill Hickok," Guy Madison, became "Wyatt Earp" in *Duel at Rio Bravo,* and dignified Englishman Stewart Granger became "Old Surehand," a frontiersman, in *Flaming Frontier.* Lee Van Cleef, invariably a heavy in American films, became the hero in *Sabata* and other spaghettis. Others making the transition to the proliferating Westerns of Europe included Alex Nicol, Cameron Mitchell, Henry Silva, Joseph Cotten, Arthur Kennedy, Jeffrey Hunter, Chuck Connors, Jack Palance, Yul Brynner, and Edd Byrnes.

Sergio Leone tried for a fourth blockbuster with *Once upon a Time in the West* (Paramount, 1967), a long, somewhat tiring Western that was supposed to be an epic Western to equal the best of Hollywood. It was different; it was interesting; and one could even say it was good. But it fell far short of being an epic of any consequence. Stars Henry Fonda, Jason Robards, and Charles Bronson kept it from being a disaster and it showed a good profit in spite of its production cost of several millions of dollars. But receipts also indicated that the charisma of this type of Western was disappearing.

The novelty of the spaghetti-tortilla Westerns was indeed short-lived and their popularity waned in a few years, but their influence was profound on American Westerns. That influence can still be seen in the latest Westerns from Hollywood. And many of the "Hollywood" Westerns made by major American companies are filmed entirely in Europe, principally in Spain.

Since space does not allow for an in-depth exploration of the hundreds of foreign-made Westerns, a select list of such films produced between 1962 and 1977 for release in the United States is presented here in order that the reader will not think the authors completely remiss in their research when a popular foreign film, such as a Sergio Leone vehicle, is looked for and not found in the film lists in the earlier chapters of this book. Such films do not appear there since those chapters are devoted to Westerns made in North America (including Canada and Mexico) for distribution in the United States. The best of the continental Westerns are listed below by title, distribution company, month and year of release in the U.S.A., principal star, and country in which filmed. Films are listed chronologically rather than alphabetically in keeping with the format adopted for this book. They are also assigned numbers with the prefix "FF" (Foreign Film) for purposes of distinguishing them from the American-made Westerns in the general alphabetical listing of all titles at the end of this book.

CONTINENTAL WESTERNS
1962-1977

(A Select List of Westerns Filmed in Europe by Both
Foreign and American Companies)

FF1. THE SAVAGE GUNS
(MGM, October, 1962)
Richard Basehart. Spain

FF2. CAVALRY COMMAND
(Parade, December, 1963)
John Agar. Philippines

FF3. GUNFIGHTERS OF CASA GRANDE
(MGM, May, 1965)
Alex Nicol. Spain

FF4. APACHE GOLD
(Columbia, May, 1965)
Lex Barker. Yugoslavia

FF5. FINGER ON THE TRIGGER
(Allied Artists, May, 1965)
Rory Calhoun. Spain

FF6. GUNMEN OF THE RIO GRANDE
(Allied Artists, June, 1965)
Guy Madison. Spain

FF7. MURIETA
(Warner Bros., September, 1965)
Jeffrey Hunter. Spain

FF8. TREASURE OF SILVER LAKE
(Columbia, November 1965)
Lex Barker. Yugoslavia

FF9. KID RODELO
(Paramount, January, 1966)
Don Murray. Spain

FF10. FRONTIER HELLCAT
(Columbia, March, 1966)
Stewart Granger. Yugoslavia

FF11. LEMONADE JOE
(Allied Artists, March, 1966)
Karel Fiala. Czechoslovakia

FF12. MINNESOTA CLAY
(Harlequin, April, 1966)
Cameron Mitchell. Italy

FF13. THE ROAD TO FORT ALAMO
(World Entertainment Corp., June, 1966)
Ken Clark. Italy

FF14. THE TRAMPLERS
(Embassy, July, 1966)
Joseph Cotten. Italy and Spain

Frontier Hellcat (Columbia, 1966) — Stewart Granger and unidentified players

The Tramplers (Embassy, 1966) — Joseph Cotten (second from left) and Jim Mitchum

FF15. A PLACE CALLED GLORY
(Embassy, August, 1966)
Lex Barker. Spain

FF16. LAST OF THE RENEGADES
(Columbia, September, 1966)
Lex Barker. Yugoslavia

FF17. DESPERADO'S TRAIL
(Columbia, October, 1966)
Lex Barker. Germany

FF18. OLD SHATTERHAND
(Don Kay Associates, September, 1966)
Lex Barker. Spain

FF19. RETURN OF THE SEVEN
(United Artists, October, 1966)
Yul Brynner. Spain

FF20. THE TEXICAN
(Columbia, October, 1966)
Audie Murphy. Spain

FF21. RAMPAGE AT APACHE WELLS
(Columbia, November, 1966)
Stewart Granger. Yugoslavia

FF22. A PISTOL FOR RINGO
(Embassy, November, 1966)
Montgomery Wood. Italy

FF23. SUNSCORCHED
(Feature Film Corp., November, 1966)
Mark Stevens. Unknown

FF24. A FISTFUL OF DOLLARS
(United Artists, January, 1967)
Clint Eastwood. Spain and Italy

FF25. THE TALL WOMEN
(Allied Artists, January, 1967)
Anne Baxter. Spain

FF26. FOR A FEW DOLLARS MORE
(United Artists, May, 1967)
Clint Eastwood. Spain and Italy

FF27. AFRICA, TEXAS STYLE
(Paramount, June, 1967)
Hugh O'Brian. Africa

FF28. THE CHRISTMAS KID
(Producers Releasing Organization, July, 1967)
Jeffrey Hunter. Spain

FF29. THE HELLBENDERS
(Embassy, July, 1967)
Joseph Cotten. Spain

FF30. THE HILLS RUN RED
(United Artists, September, 1967)
Thomas Hunter. Spain and Italy

FF31. JOHNNY YUMA
(Atlantic, September, 1967)
Mark Damon. Spain

FF32. KILL OR BE KILLED
(Rizzoli, September, 1967)
Robert Mark. Italy

FF33. NAVAJO JOE
(United Artists, November, 1967)
Burt Reynolds. Spain and Italy

FF34. ADIOS, GRINGO
(Trans-Lux, November, 1967)
Montgomery Wood. Italy

FF35. UP THE MacGREGORS
(Columbia, November, 1967)
David Bailey. Spain

FF36. FEW DOLLARS FOR GYPSY
(Trans-Lux, December, 1967)
Anthony Steffan. Italy

FF37. THUNDER AT THE BORDER
(Columbia, December, 1967)
Rod Cameron. Yugoslavia

FF38. THE GOOD, THE BAD, AND THE UGLY
(United Artists, January, 1968)
Clint Eastwood. Spain and Italy

FF39. CUSTER OF THE WEST
(Cinerama Releasing Corp., January, 1968)
Robert Shaw. Spain

FF40. FLAMING FRONTIER
(Warner Bros.-7 Arts, February, 1968)
Stewart Granger. Yugoslavia

FF41. A STRANGER IN TOWN
(MGM, April, 1968)
Tony Anthony. Italy and Spain

FF42. 7 GUNS FOR THE MacGREGORS
(Columbia, April, 1968)
Robert Wood. Spain

FF43. A MINUTE TO PRAY, A SECOND TO DIE
(Cinerama Releasing Corp., May, 1968)
Alex Cord. Italy

FF44. VILLA RIDES
(Paramount, June, 1968)
Yul Brynner. Spain

FF45. THE BIG GUNDOWN
(Columbia, August, 1968)
Lee Van Cleef. Italy

FF46. THE STRANGER RETURNS
(MGM, September, 1968)
Tony Anthony. Italy and Spain

FF47. THE UGLY ONES
(United Artists, September, 1968)
Richard Wyler. Italy and Spain

FF48. ANY GUN CAN PLAY
(Raf Industries, September, 1968)
Edd Byrnes. Italy

FF49. A BULLET FOR THE GENERAL
(Avco Embassy, September, 1968)
Gian Maria Volonte. Spain

FF50. SHALAKO
(Cinerama Releasing Organization, November, 1968)
Sean Connery. Spain

FF51. THE MAN FROM NOWHERE
(Gadabout Gaddis Productions, November, 1968)
Giuliano Gemma. Italy

FF52. THE BRUTE AND THE BEAST
(American International, December, 1968)
Franco Nero. Italy

FF53. PAYMENT IN BLOOD
(Columbia, December, 1968)
Edd Byrnes. Italy

FF54. A FEW BULLETS MORE
(Raf Industries, January, 1969)
Peter Lee Lawrence. Italy

FF55. DOLLARS FOR A FAST GUN
(World Enterprises Corp., March, 1969)
Robert Hundar. Unknown

FF56. 100 RIFLES
(20th C. Fox, April, 1969)
Jim Brown. Spain

FF57. DESPERADOS
(Columbia, May, 1969)
Vince Edwards. Spain

FF58. GOD FORGIVES, I DON'T
(American-International, May, 1969)
Terence Hill. Italy

FF59. GUNS OF THE MAGNIFICENT SEVEN
(United Artists, June, 1969)
George Kennedy. Spain

FF60. ONCE UPON A TIME IN THE WEST
(Paramount, July, 1969)
Henry Fonda. Spain

FF61. DEATH RIDES A HORSE
(United Artists, July, 1969)
Lee Van Cleef. Italy and Spain

FF62. ACE HIGH
(Paramount, September, 1969)
Eli Wallach. Spain

FF63. LAND RAIDERS
(Columbia, September, 1969)
Telly Savalas. Spain

FF64. THE RUTHLESS FOUR
(Goldstone, November, 1969)
Van Heflin. Italy

FF65. THIS MAN CAN'T DIE
(Fine Products, February, 1970)
Guy Madison. Italy

FF66. THE 5-MAN ARMY
(MGM, March, 1970)
Peter Graves. Spain and Italy

FF67. A LONG RIDE FROM HELL
(Cinerama, March, 1970)
Steve Reeves. Italy

FF68. THE MERCENARY
(United Artists, March, 1970)
Franco Nero. Spain and Italy

FF69. DAY OF ANGER
(National General, April, 1970)
Lee Van Cleef. Spain and Italy

FF70. A BULLET FOR SANDOVAL
(U.M.C., June, 1970)
Ernest Borgnine. Spain

FF71. NED KELLY
(United Artists, June, 1970)
Mick Jagger. Australia

FF72. SABATA
(United Artists, August, 1970)
Lee Van Cleef. Spain

**FF73. KILL THEM ALL AND
COME BACK ALONE**
(Fanfare, October, 1970)
Chuck Connors. Spain and Italy

FF74. CANNON FOR CORDOBA
(United Artists, October, 1970)
George Peppard. Spain

FF74. MADRON
(Four Star-Excelsior, December, 1970)
Richard Boone. Israel

FF76. A MAN CALLED SLEDGE
(United Artists, March, 1971)
James Garner. Spain and Italy

FF77. VALDEZ IS COMING
(United Artists, March, 1971)
Burt Lancaster. Spain

FF78. THE DESERTER
(Paramount, June, 1971)
Bekim Fehmiu. Spain and Italy

FF79. THE LAST REBEL
(Columbia, August, 1971)
Joe Namath. Italy

FF80. DOC
(United Artists, August, 1971)
Stacy Keach. Spain

FF81. ADIOS, SABATA
(United Artists, September, 1971)
Yul Brynner. Italy and Spain.

**FF82. TODAY WE KILL . . .
TOMORROW WE DIE!**
(Cinerama, September, 1971)
Montgomery Ford. Italy

FF83. THE DIRTY OUTLAWS
(Transvue, September, 1971)
Chip Corman. Spain

FF84. CAPTAIN APACHE
(Scotia, October, 1971)
Lee Van Cleef. Spain

FF85. THEY CALL ME TRINITY
(Avco Embassy, October, 1971)
Terence Hill. Italy.

FF86. CATLOW
(MGM, October, 1971)
Yul Brynner. Spain

FF87. EL TOPO
(ABKCO, November, 1971)
Alexandro Jodorowsky. Mexico

FF88. MAN IN THE WILDERNESS
(Warner Bros., November, 1971)
Richard Harris. Spain

FF89. FIND A PLACE TO DIE
(Gadabout Gaddis Productions, December, 1971)
Jeffrey Hunter. Italy

FF90. BLINDMAN
(20th C. Fox, March, 1972)
Tony Anthony. Italy and Spain

FF91. BOOT HILL
(Film Ventures, March, 1972)
Terence Hill. Italy

FF92. COMPANEROS!
(Cinerama, April, 1972)
Franco Nero. Spain

FF93. JOHNNY HAMLET
(Transvue, May, 1972)
Chip Corman. Spain

FF94. CHATO'S LAND
(United Artists, May, 1972)
Charles Bronson. Spain

FF95. RED SUN
(National General, June, 1972)
Charles Bronson. Spain

FF96. HANNIE CAULDER
(Paramount, July, 1972)
Raquel Welch. Spain

FF97. DUCK, YOU SUCKER
(United Artists, July, 1972)
Rod Steiger. Spain and Italy

FF98. TRINITY IS STILL MY NAME
(Avco Embassy, July, 1972)
Terence Hill. Italy

FF99. FISTFUL OF DYNAMITE
(Same as *Duck, You Sucker*)

FF100. RETURN OF SABATA
(United Artists, September, 1972)
Lee Van Cleef. Italy

FF101. THE PROUD AND THE DAMNED
(Prestige/Columbia, December, 1972)
Chuck Connors. South America

FF102. GO FOR BROKE
(Stellar IV, December, 1972)
John Ireland. Italy

FF103. BAD MAN'S RIVER
(Scotia, December, 1972)
Lee Van Cleef. Spain

FF104. PANCHO VILLA
(Scotia, January, 1973)
Telly Savalas. Spain

FF105. THE LEGEND OF FRENCHIE KING
(K-Tel, May, 1973)
Brigitte Bardot. Spain

FF106. CHARLEY ONE-EYE
(Paramount, May, 1973)
Richard Roundtree. Spain

FF107. HALF BREED
(Hampton, June, 1973)
Lex Barker. Yugoslavia

FF108. DEAF SMITH AND JOHNNY EARS
(MGM, June, 1973)
Anthony Quinn. Spain and Italy

FF109. CUT-THROATS NINE
(United International, August, 1973)
Robert Hundar. Spain.

FF110. THE MAN CALLED NOON
(National General, September, 1973)
Richard Crenna. Spain

FF111. SONNY AND JED
(K-Tel, January, 1974)
Tomas Milian. Italy

FF112. A REASON TO LIVE, A REASON TO DIE
(K-Tel, February, 1974)
James Coburn. Italy

FF113. MAN OF THE EAST
(United Artists, June, 1974)
Terence Hill. Italy (?)

FF114. THOSE DIRTY DOGS
(Cinerama, June, 1974)
Stephen Boyd. Spain (?)

FF115. THE STRANGER'S GUNDOWN
(New Line Cinema, June, 1974)
Anthony Steffan. Italy

FF116. MY NAME IS NOBODY
(Universal, July, 1974)
Henry Fonda. Spain

FF117. DON'T TURN THE OTHER CHEEK
(International Amusement Corp., July, 1974)
Eli Wallach. Spain and Italy

FF118. IT CAN BE DONE . . . AMIGO
(World Wide, November, 1974)
Bud Psencer. Italy

FF119. BEYOND THE LAW
(World Wide, March, 1975)
Lee Van Cleef. Country of filming unknown

FF120. THE STING OF THE WEST
(Film Ventures, June, 1975)
Jack Palance. Italy

FF121. TAKE A HARD RIDE
(20th C. Fox, August, 1975)
Lee Van Cleef. Canary Islands

FF122. WHITE FANG
(American Cinema, September, 1975)
Franco Nero. Believed to be filmed in Italy

FF123. DEEP WEST
(Cambist, November, 1975)
George Hilton. Italy

FF124. ROY COLT AND WINCHESTER JACK
(Libert, December, 1975)
Brett Halsey. Country of filming unknown

FF125. PANHANDLE CALIBRE 38
(Cinegai, December, 1975)
Keenan Wynn. Italy

FF126. RIDE A WILD PONY
(Buena Vista, April, 1976)
Michael Craig. Australia

**FF127. THE STRANGER AND
THE GUNFIGHTER**
(Columbia, April, 1976)
Lee Van Cleef. Spain and Hong Kong

FF128. CHINO
(Intercontinental Releasing Corp., May, 1976)
Charles Bronson. Spain

FF129. ZORRO
(Mondial/Te-Fi/Allied Artists, June, 1976)
Alain Delon. Spain

FF130. MAD DOG
(Cinema Shares, October, 1976)
Dennis Hopper. Australia
(This film also released as *Mad Dog Morgan*)

FF131. THE LEGEND OF FRANK WOODS
(Variety International, May, 1977)
Troy Donahue. Country of filming unknown

FF132. KID VENGEANCE
(Irwin Yablans Company, May, 1977)
Lee Van Cleef. Country of filming unknown

FF133. GOD'S GUN
(Irwin Yablans Company, June, 1977)
Lee Van Cleef. Country of filming unknown

Epilogue

This volume has only faintly scratched the surface in telling the story of Western filmdom, but the filmographies for over 3000 sound Westerns, the brief history, and the photographs should amply stimulate healthful, nostalgic dreaming—hours of it. Psychologists teach that today's reality can best be mastered when one's energies are recharged through short respites from the pressures of that reality. Recalling happier times is one such means of recharging energies, as is evidenced by the current popularity of nostalgia in all forms. For millions of people there have been no happier continuing events to recall than yesterday's Saturdays when, with popcorn and Coke, they sat in rapturous awe engulfed in the bigger-than-life heroics of cinema Westerners ranging from Bronco Billy Anderson and William S. Hart to John Wayne and Randolph Scott and, through fantasizing, juxtaposed their routine lives with those of their screen heroes.

It is perhaps easier merely to shrug one's shoulders and verbalize the cliche, "Beauty is in the eye of the beholder," than it is to try seriously to explain the magnetism of the Western film, for years the only American art form in which the notion of honor retained its full strength. No other film type has captured the imagination of the world as has the American Western. The Western film hero, particularly the "B" star, received an adoration and continuing loyalty of amazing proportions. Why? Because the history of the American Western is the history of a loss of innocence and the traditional mythic Western, epitomized by the "B" programmers, represented a fragment of that lost innocence.

In the pages of this book readers can ride again those musty dream trails overgrown with age and neglect—ride them time and time again, meeting familiar riders from their own age of innocence. They are all here—the heroes, the heroines, the horses, the sidekicks, the good people, and the bad guys. The nostalgic trails are many, and lovin', fightin', shootin', and ridin' can be re-discovered along them as in the days of youth. "Oh, the thrill of it all!" William S. Hart once fervently exclaimed. Hallelujah! Inexorably, the thrill of it all has reverberated through the hearts of millions for three generations.

What is to become of the Western now that there are no longer any heroes to emulate and to spur on to glory with whistles, joyful shouts, and feet stompin'? A good question, but no answer is discernible. The success of recent escapist films such as *Star Wars, The Deep,* and *Jaws* suggests that it may be time for the Western to return to being just what it started out being—escapist entertainment for its own sake and the promulgation of the national Western myth.

Western heroes of the calibre of Buck Jones, Harry Carey, Wally Wales, and Reb Russell were never needed by a new generation as badly as they are needed now. Yet it is certain that there can never be a return to the days of thrills and adventure as found in the "B" programmers and serials of yesterday's Saturdays. But Westerns that espouse the old virtues inherent in the Westerns of those bygone days can be made. They should be made. Cinemaddicts would once again like to see Westerns with heroes riding to the rescue of Sunflower Sues and protecting the pioneers, wagon trains pushing confidently westward, the good guys consistently overcoming the bad guys, and young people toiling and marrying and seeking virtue as its own reward. The heritage of the Western and its traditional nobility is something that must not be allowed to be destroyed by irresponsible filmmakers who would have the nation believe that heroism, decency, individualism, patriotism, and other admirable qualities never existed in the old West. They did.

The Fighting Sheriff (Columbia, 1931)—Buck Jones, Loretta Sayers, and "Silver"

Buck Jones (1941)

Harry Carey (1940)

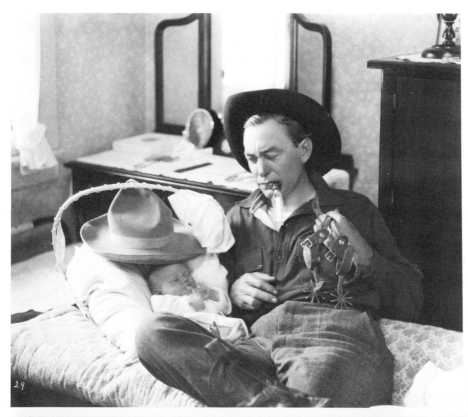

Harry Carey and young friend in un-identified Western

Riders of the Cactus (Big 4, 1931) — Tate Brady and Wally Wales

Wally Wales/Hal Taliaferro (circa 1927)

Alphabetical Listing of Sound Westerns

[**Note:** The first number in parentheses following each title is the year of release; the second number is the entry number in the chronological listing of all films, beginning with the number "1." Thus, any title can quickly be located by reference to the film lists at the ends of Chapters 2-11. Any entry number preceded by "FF" is a foreign film, to be found in the separately numbered list in Chapter 12.]

A

Abilene Town (1946; 1751)
Abilene Trail (1951; 2310)
Ace High (1969; FF62)
Aces and Eights (1936; 623)
Aces Wild (1936; 570)
Across the Badlands (1950; 2257)
Across the Great Divide (1976; 3329)
Across the Plains (1939; 1005)
Across the Rio Grande (1949; 2085)
Across the Sierras (1941; 1229)
Across the Wide Missouri (1951; 2386)
Adios Amigo (1975; 3306)
Adios Gringo (1967; FF34)
Adios, Sabata (1971; FF81)
Advance to the Rear (1964; 3068)
Adventures of Bullwhip Griffin (The) (1967; 3129)
Adventures of Don Coyote (The) (1947; 1883)
Adventures of Frank and Jesse James (1948; 1992)
Adventures of Frontier Fremont (The) (1976; 3307)
Adventures of Red Ryder (1940; 1130)
Adventures of the Masked Phantom (The) (1939; 1037)
Africa, Texas Style (1967; FF27)
Against a Crooked Sky (1975; 3305)
Al Jennings of Oklahoma (1951; 2316)
Alamo (The) (1960; 3005)
Alaska (1944; 1652)
Albuquerque (1948; 1951)
Alias Billy the Kid (1946; 1777)
Alias Jesse James (1959; 2959)
Alias John Law (1935; 511)
Alias the Bad Man (1931; 134)
Allegheny Uprising (1939; 1044)
Along Came Jones (1945; 1700)
Along the Great Divide (1951; 2350)
Along the Navajo Trail (1954; 1744)
Along the Oregon Trail (1947; 1912)
Along the Rio Grande (1941; 1227)
Along the Sundown Trail (1942; 1441)
Alvarez Kelly (1966; 3124)
Ambush at Cimarron Pass (1958; 2900)

Ambush at Tomahawk Gap (1953; 2539)
Ambush Trail (1946; 1766)
Ambush Valley (1936; 672)
American Empire (1942; 1460)
Americano (The) (1955; 2678)
. . . And Now Miguel (1966; 3118)
Angel and the Badman (1947; 1848)
Animals (The) (1971; 3229)
Annie Get Your Gun (1950; 2219)
Annie Oakley (1935; 490)
Any Gun Can Play (1968; FF48)
Apache (1954; 2639)
Apache Ambush (1955; 2720)
Apache Chief (1949; 2139)
Apache Country (1952; 2456)
Apache Drums (1951; 2348)
Apache Gold (1965; FF4)
Apache Kid (The) (1941; 1306)
Apache Kid's Escape (The) (1930; 89)
Apache Rifles (1964; 3077)
Apache Rose (1947; 1858)
Apache Territory (1958; 2936)
Apache Trail (1943; 1534)
Apache Uprising (1966; 3108)
Apache War Smoke (1952; 2491)
Apache Warrior (1957; 2858)
Apache Woman (1955; 2722)
Appaloosa (The) (1966; 3125)
Apple Dumpling Gang (The) (1975; 3297)
Arena (1953; 2551)
Arizona (1940; 1206)
Arizona Bad Man (1935; 512)
Arizona Bound (1941; 1286)
Arizona Bushwhackers (1968; 3149)
Arizona Cowboy (The) (1950; 2196)
Arizona Cyclone (1934; 401)
Arizona Cyclone (1941; 1333)
Arizona Days (1937; 715)
Arizona Frontier (1940; 1158)
Arizona Gangbusters (1940; 1167)
Arizona Gunfighter (1937; 804)

Arizona Kid (The) (1930; 42)
Arizona Kid (The) (1939; 1036)
Arizona Legion (1939; 957)
Arizona Mahoney (1936; 685)
Arizona Manhunt (1951; 2374)
Arizona Nights (1934; 362)
Arizona Raiders (1965; 3103)
Arizona Raiders (The) (1936; 631)
Arizona Ranger (The) (1948; 1982)
Arizona Roundup (1942; 1372)
Arizona Stagecoach (1942; 1429)
Arizona Territory (1950; 2237)
Arizona Terror (1942; 1351)
Arizona Terror (The) (1931; 143)
Arizona Trail (1943; 1541)
Arizona Trails (1935; 513)
Arizona Whirlwind (1944; 1582)
Arizona Wildcat (The) (1939; 962)
Arizonian (The) (1935; 471)
Arkansas Judge (1941; 1223)
Arm of the Law (1932; 211)
Arrow in the Dust (1954; 2626)
Arrowhead (1953; 2565)
At Gunpoint (1955; 2841)
Avenger (The) (1931; 111)
Avenging Rider (The) (1943; 1505)
Avenging Waters (1936; 634)

B

Back in the Saddle (1941; 1238)
Back to God's Country (1953; 2596)
Back to the Woods (1937; 753)
Back Trail (1948; 2000)
Backlash (1956; 2754)
Backtrack (1969; 3175)
Bad Bascomb (1946; 1761)
Bad Company (1972; 3252)
Bad Day at Black Rock (1955; 2674)
Bad Lands (1939; 1025)
Bad Man (The) (1930; 68)
Bad Man (The) (1941; 1241)
Bad Man from Big Bend (1949; 1658)
Bad Man of Brimstone (The) (1937; 822)
Bad Man of Deadwood (1941; 1302)
Bad Man's River (1972; FF103)
Bad Men of Arizona (1936; 631)
Bad Men of Missouri (1941; 1289)
Bad Men of the Border (1945; 1719)
Bad Men of the Hills (1942; 1422)
Bad Men of Thunder Gap (1943; 1482)
Bad Men of Tombstone (1949; 2052)
Badge of Marshal Brennan (The) (1957; 2852)
Badlanders (The) (1958; 2929)
Badlands of Dakota (1941; 1301)
Badlands of Montana (1957; 2845)

Badman from Red Butte (1940; 1126)
Badman's Country (1948; 2933)
Badman's Gold (1951; 2328)
Badman's Territory (1946; 1781)
Baker's Hawk (1976; 3330)
Ballad of Cable Hogue (The) (1970; 3190)
Ballad of a Gunfighter (1964; 3066)
Ballad of Josie (The) (1968; 3148)
Bandido (1956; 2792)
Bandit King of Texas (1949; 2116)
Bandit Queen (1950; 2292)
Bandit Ranger (1941; 1435)
Bandit Trail (The) (1941; 1318)
Bandits and Ballads (1939; 1057)
Bandits of Dark Canyon (1947; 1934)
Bandits of Eldorado (1949; 2132)
Bandits of the Badlands (1945; 1714)
Bandits of the West (1953; 2569)
Bandolero (1968; 3160)
Bar Buckaroos (1940; 1185)
Bar L Ranch (1930; 56)
Bar 20 (1943; 1544)
Bar 20 Justice (1938; 887)
Bar 20 Rides Again (1935; 500)
Bar Z Bad Men (1937; 741)
Barbed Wire (1952; 2471)
Baron of Arizona (1950; 2184)
Barquero (1970; 3194)
Barricade (1950; 2197)
Barrier (The) (1937; 818)
Battle at Apache Pass (The) (1951; 2326)
Battle of Greed (1937; 707)
Battle of Rogue River (1954; 2613)
Battles of Chief Pontiac (The) (1952; 2507)
Battling Buckaroo (1932; 276)
Battling Marshal (1950; 2165)
Battling with Buffalo Bill (1931; 170)
Beast of Hollow Mountain (The) (1956; 2791)
Beau Bandit (1930; 32)
Beauty and the Bandit (1946; 1827)
Behind Southern Lines (1952; 2496)
Belle Le Grande (1951; 2303)
Belle of the Yukon (1944; 1659)
Belle Starr (1941; 1305)
Belle Starr's Daughter (1947; 1927)
Bells of Capistrano (1942; 1432)
Bells of Coronado (1950; 2162)
Bells of Rosarita (1945; 1699)
Bells of San Angelo (1947; 1876)
Bells of San Fernando (The) (1947; 1863)
Below the Border (1942; 1357)
Bend of the River (1952; 2423)
Beneath Western Skies (1944; 1583)
Best of the Badmen (1951; 2352)
Between Fighting Men (1932; 253)
Between Men (1935; 491)
Beyond the Last Frontier (1943; 1540)

Beyond the Law (1930; 74)
Beyond the Law (1934; 375)
Beyond the Pecos (1945; 1686)
Beyond the Purple Hills (1950; 2235)
Beyond the Rio Grande (1930; 40)
Beyond the Rockies (1932; 241)
Beyond the Sacramento (1940; 1191)
Big Bonanza (The) (1944; 1666)
Big Boy Rides Again (1935; 514)
Big Calibre (1935; 515)
Big Country (The) (1958; 2934)
Big Gundown (The) (1968; FF45)
Big Hand for the Little Lady (A) (1966; 3116)
Big Hop (The) (1928; 1)
Big Jake (1971; 3216)
Big Land (The) (1957; 2831)
Big Show (The) (1936; 679)
Big Sky (The) (1952; 2474)
Big Sombrero (The) (1949; 2071)
Big Stampede (The) (1932; 250)
Big Trail (The) (1930; 82)
Big Trees (The) (1952; 2437)
Billy Jack (1971; 3214)
Billy the Kid (1930; 80)
Billy the Kid (1941; 1265)
Billy the Kid in Santa Fe (1941; 1279)
Billy the Kid in Texas (1940; 1175)
Billy the Kid Outlawed (1940; 1147)
Billy the Kid Returns (1938; 908)
Billy the Kid Trapped (1942; 1371)
Billy the Kid vs. Dracula (1966; 3111)
Billy the Kid Wanted (1941; 1315)
Billy the Kid's Fighting Pals (1941; 1252)
Billy the Kid's Gun Justice (1940; 1207)
Billy the Kid's Range War (1941; 1221)
Billy the Kid's Round-Up (1941; 1343)
Billy the Kid's Smoking Guns (1942; 1398)
Bite the Bullet (1975; 3296)
Bitter Creek (1954; 2609)
Black Aces (1937; 800)
Black Arrow (1944; 1642)
Black Bandit (1938; 914)
Black Bart (1948; 1975)
Black Dakotas (The) (1954; 2650)
Black Eagle (1948; 2016)
Black Hills (1947; 1918)
Black Hills Ambush (1952; 2454)
Black Hills Express (1943; 1528)
Black Horse Canyon (1954; 2635)
Black Lash (The) (1952; 2406)
Black Market Rustlers (1943; 1532)
Black Patch (1957; 2871)
Black Rodeo (1972; 3243)
Black Spurs (1965; 3093)
Black Whip (The) (1956; 2818)
Blackjack Ketchum, Desperado (1956; 2755)

Blazing Across the Pecos (1948; 1994)
Blazing Bullets (1951; 2340)
Blazing Frontier (1943; 1536)
Blazing Guns (1935; 516)
Blazing Guns (1943; 1546)
Blazing Justice (1936; 574)
Blazing Saddles (1974; 3274)
Blazing Six Shooters (1940; 1098)
Blazing Sixes (1937; 764)
Blazing Stewardesses (1975; 3294)
Blazing Sun (The) (1950; 2283)
Blazing the Overland Trail (1956; 2785)
Blazing the Western Trail (1945; 1715)
Blazing Trail (The) (1949; 2091)
Blindman (1972; FF90)
Blocked Trail (The) (1943; 1484)
Blood Arrow (1958; 2906)
Blood on the Arrow (1964; 3078)
Blood on the Moon (1948; 2031)
Blue (1968; 3156)
Blue Canadian Rockies (1952; 2508)
Blue Montana Skies (1939; 997)
Blue Steel (1934; 366)
Bob Wills and His Texas Playboys (1944; 1630)
Boiling Point (The) (1932; 262)
Bold Caballero (The) (1936; 582)
Bold Frontiersman (The) (1948; 1969)
Bonanza Town (1951; 2362)
Boot Hill (1972; FF91)
Boot Hill Bandits (1942; 1394)
Boothill Brigade (1937; 789)
Boots and Saddles (1937; 808)
Boots of Destiny (1937; 783)
Border Badmen (1945; 1722)
Border Bandits (1946; 1752)
Border Brigands (1935; 465)
Border Buckaroos (1943; 1515)
Border Caballero (1936; 590)
Border Cafe (1937; 759)
Border City Rustlers (1953; 2589)
Border Devils (1932; 208)
Border Fence (1951; 2375)
Border Feud (1947; 1884)
Border G-Man (1938; 888)
Border Guns (1934; 402)
Border Law (1931; 147)
Border Legion (The) (1930; 53)
Border Legion (The) (1940; 1200)
Border Menace (The) (1934; 403)
Border Outlaws (1950; 2276)
Border Patrol (1943; 1488)
Border Patrolman (The) (1936; 629)
Border Phantom (1937; 763)
Border Rangers (1950; 2268)
Border River (1954; 2604)
Border Romance (1930; 48)
Border Roundup (1942; 1440)

Border Saddlemates (1952; 2442)
Border Treasure (1950; 2259)
Border Vengeance (1935; 517)
Border Vigilantes (1941; 1251)
Border Wolves (1938; 851)
Borderland (1937; 720)
Bordertown Gunfighters (1943; 1545)
Bordertown Trail (1944; 1626)
Born Reckless (1949; 2968)
Born to Battle (1935; 518)
Born to Buck (1968; 3163)
Born to Saddle (1953; 2535)
Born to the West (1937; 826a)
Boss Cowboy (1934; 404)
Boss Nigger (1974; 3284)
Boss of Boomtown (1944; 1604)
Boss of Bullion City (1941; 1216)
Boss of Hangtown Mesa (1942; 1425)
Boss of Lonely Valley (1937; 819)
Boss of Rawhide (1943; 1557)
Boss Rider of Gun Creek (1936; 673)
Both Barrels Blazing (1945; 1690)
Bounty Hunter (The) (1954; 2655)
Bounty Killer (The) (1965; 3102)
Bowery Buckaroos (1947; 1929a)
Boy from Oklahoma (The) (1954; 2610)
Boy's Ranch (1946; 1805a)
Brand of Fear (1949; 2100)
Brand of Hate (1934; 391)
Brand of the Devil (1944; 1623)
Brand of the Outlaws (1936; 642)
Branded (1931; 144)
Branded (1951; 2405)
Branded a Coward (1935; 474)
Branded Men (1931; 166)
Brass Legend (The) (1956; 2819)
Bravados (The) (1958; 2923)
Brave Warrior (1952; 2458)
Breakheart Pass (1976; 3309)
Breed of the Border (1933; 313)
Breed of the West (1930; 87)
Bride Comes to Yellow Sky (The) (1952; 2504)
Brigham Young (1940; 1174)
Brimstone (1949; 2112)
Broken Arrow (1950; 2243)
Broken Lance (1954; 2645)
Broken Land (The) (1962; 3038)
Broken Star (The) (1956; 2759)
Bronco Buster (1952; 2448)
Bronze Buckaroo (The) (1939; 958)
Brothers in the Saddle (1949; 2059)
Borthers of the West (1937; 770)
Brothers O'Toole (The) (1973; 3264)
Brute and the Beast (The) (1968; FF52)
Buchanan Rides Alone (1958; 2930)
Buck and the Preacher (1972; 3241)
Buck Benny Rides Again (1940; 1115)

Buckaroo Broadcast (1938; 869)
Buckaroo from Powder River (1947; 1920)
Buckaroo Sheriff of Texas (1951; 2337)
Buckskin (1968; 3155)
Buckskin Frontier (1943; 1502)
Buckskin Lady (The) (1957; 2856)
Buffalo Bill (1944; 1591)
Buffalo Bill and the Indians (1976; 3318)
Buffalo Bill in Tomahawk Territory (1952; 2418)
Buffalo Bill Rides Again (1947; 1878)
Buffalo Gun (1961; 3030)
Buffalo Stampede (1933; 297)
Bugles in the Afternoon (1952; 2431)
Bulldog Courage (1935; 510)
Bullet Code (1940; 1108)
Bullet for a Badman (1964; 3076)
Bullet for Billy the Kid (1953; 3062)
Bullet for Sandoval (A) (1970; FF70)
Bullet for the General (A) (1968; FF49)
Bullet Is Waiting (A) (1954; 2582a)
Bullets and Ballads (1940; 1080)
Bullets and Saddles (1943; 1551)
Bullets for Rustlers (1940; 1090)
Bullets for Bandits (1942; 1363)
Bullwhip (1958; 2916)
Burning Hills (The) (1956; 2793)
Bury Me Not on the Lone Prairie (1941; 1240)
Bushwackers (The) (1952; 2409)
Butch Cassidy and the Sundance Kid (1969; 3183)
Buzzy and the Phantom Pinto (1941; 1255)
Buzzy Rides the Range (1940; 1209)

C

Cactus Capers (1942; 1392)
Cactus Caravan (1950; 2238)
Cactus Cut-Up (1949; 2076a)
Cactus Kid (The) (1934; 405)
Cactus Makes Perfect (1942; 1368a)
Cahill, United States Marshal (1973; 3266)
Cain's Cut-Throats (1970; 3189)
Cain's Way (1970; 3189)
Calaboose (1943; 1472)
Calamity Jane (1953; 2588)
California (1963; 3054)
California Conquest (1952; 2465)
California Firebrand (1948; 1964)
California Frontier (1938; 940)
California Gold Rush (1946; 1760)
California in 1878 (1930; 94)
California Joe (1943; 1568)
California Mail (The) (1936; 676)
California or Bust (1941; 1330)
California Outpost (1948; 1972)
California Passage (1950; 2289)
California Trail (The) (1933; 302)

Californian (The) (1937; 784)
Call of the Canyon (1942; 1424)
Call of the Desert (1930; 30)
Call of the Forest (1949; 2147)
Call of the Klondike (1950; 2291)
Call of the Prairie (1936; 595)
Call of the Rockies (1931; 133)
Call of the Rockies (1938; 872)
Call of the Rockies (1944; 1616)
Call of the West (1930; 45)
Call of the Wild (1935; 454)
Call of the Yukon (1938; 866)
Call the Mesquiteers (1938; 854)
Callaway Went Thataway (1951; 2402)
Calling Wild Bill Elliott (1943; 1498)
Canadian Mounties vs. Atomic Invaders (1953; 2556)
Canadians (The) (1961; 3017)
Cannon for Cordoba (1970; FF74)
Canyon Ambush (1952; 2490)
Canyon City (1943; 1560)
Canyon Crossroads (1955; 2686)
Canyon Hawks (1930; 65)
Canyon of Missing Men (The) (1930; 49)
Canyon Passage (1946; 1804a)
Canyon Raiders (1951; 2333)
Canyon River (1956; 2788)
Captain Apache (1971; FF85)
Captain John Smith and Pocahontas (1953; 2594)
Captive of Billy the Kid (1952; 2412)
Capture (The) (1950; 2203)
Caravan Trail (The) (1946; 1779)
Cariboo Trail (The) (1950; 2244)
Carolina Cannonball (1955; 2680)
Carolina Moon (1940; 1145)
Carrying the Mail (1934; 406)
Carson City (1952; 2462)
Carson City Cyclone (1943; 1481)
Carson City Kid (The) (1940; 1140)
Carson City Raiders (1948; 1979)
Caryl of the Mountains (1936; 600)
Cassidy of Bar 20 (1938; 852)
Cast a Long Shadow (1959; 2975)
Castaway Cowboy (The) (1974; 3280)
Cat Ballou (1965; 3099)
Catlow (1971; FF86)
Cattle Drive (1951; 2363)
Cattle Empire (1958; 2908)
Cattle King (1963; 3057)
Cattle Queen of Montana (1954; 2664)
Cattle Raiders (1938; 846)
Cattle Stampede (1943; 1529)
Cattle Thief (The) (1936; 621)
Cattle Town (1952; 2509)
Caught (1931; 138)
Cavalcade of the West (1936; 670)
Cavalier of the West (1931; 168)

Cavalry (1936; 661)
Cavalry Command (1963; FF2)
Cavalry Scout (1951; 2341)
Cave of Outlaws (1951; 2388)
Challenge of the Range (1949; 2058)
Charge at Feather River (The) (1953; 2557)
Charley One-Eye (1973; FF106)
Charro! (1969; 3173)
Chato's Land (1972; FF94)
Check Your Guns (1948; 1944)
Cherokee Flash (The) (1945; 1743)
Cherokee Strip (1937; 746)
Cherokee Strip (1940; 1181)
Cherokee Uprising (1950; 2270)
Cheyenne Autumn (1964; 3083)
Cheyenne Cowboy (1949; 2060)
Cheyenne Cyclone (1932; 189)
Cheyenne Kid (The) (1930; 96)
Cheyenne Kid (The) (1933; 322)
Cheyenne Kid (The) (1940; 1083)
Cheyenne Rides Again (1937; 704)
Cheyenne Roundup (1943; 1497)
Cheyenne Social Club (The) (1970; 3195)
Cheyenne Takes Over (1947; 1932)
Cheyenne Tornado (1935; 519)
Cheyenne Wildcat (1944; 1639)
Chief Crazy Horse (1955; 2694)
Chino (1976; FF128)
Chip of the Flying U (1939; 1049)
Chisum (1970; 3198)
Christmas Kid (The) (1967; FF28)
Chuka (1967; 3133)
Cimarron (1931; 106)
Cimarron (1960; 3010)
Cimarron Kid (The) (1952; 2407)
Circle Canyon (1934; 407)
Circle of Death (1935; 462)
Cisco Kid (The) (1931; 167)
Cisco Kid and the Lady (The) (1940; 1067)
Cisco Kid Returns (The) (1945; 1675)
City of Badmen (1953; 2574)
Clancy of the Mounted (1933; 291)
Clearing the Range (1931; 115)
Cliff Edwards and His Musical Buckaroos (1941; 1237)
Cockeyed Cowboys of Calico County (The) (1939; 3193)
Code of Honor (1930; 75)
Code of the Cactus (1939; 970)
Code of the Fearless (1939; 948)
Code of the Lawless (1945; 1726)
Code of the Mounted (1935; 463)
Code of the Outlaw (1942; 1358)
Code of the Prairie (1944; 1640)
Code of the Range (1936; 662)
Code of the Rangers (1938; 862)
Code of the Saddle (1947; 1894)

Code of the Silver Sage (1950; 2193)
Code of the West (1947; 1855)
Cody of the Pony Express (1950; 2199)
Cole Younger, Gunfighter (1958; 2905)
Colorado (1940; 1166)
Colorado Ambush (1951; 2301)
Colorado Kid (The) (1937; 825)
Colorado Pioneers (1945; 1734)
Colorado Ranger (1950; 2215)
Colorado Serenade (1946; 1798)
Colorado Sundown (1952; 2419)
Colorado Sunset (1939; 1021)
Colorado Territory (1949; 2093)
Colorado Trail (The) (1938; 910)
Colt Comrades (1943; 1516)
Colt 45 (1950; 2220)
Column South (1953; 2548)
Comanche (1956; 2753)
Comanche Station (1960; 2989)
Comanche Territory (1950; 2209)
Comancheros (The) (1961; 3033)
Come On, Cowboys (1937; 756)
Come On, Danger (1932; 243)
Come On, Danger! (1942; 1406)
Cone On, Rangers! (1938; 934)
Come On, Tarzan (1932; 240)
Comin' Round the Mountain (1936; 603)
Command (The) (1953; 2525)
Companeros! (1972; FF92)
Concentratin' Kid (1930; 84)
Conquering Horde (The) (1931; 109)
Conquest of Cheyenne (1946; 1805)
Conquest of Cochise (1953; 2575)
Convict Stage (1965; 3094)
Coogan's Bluff (1968; 3164)
Copper Canyon (1950; 2269)
Copper Sky (1957; 2872)
Cornered (1932; 234)
Coroner Creek (1948; 1995)
Corpus Christi Bandits (1945; 1685)
Corral Cuties (1954; 2637a)
Corralling a School Marm (1940; 1132)
Count Three and Pray (1955; 2724)
Country Beyond (The) (1936; 610)
Courage of the North (1935; 520)
Courage of the West (1937; 824)
Courageous Avenger (The) (1935; 508)
Courtin' Trouble (1948; 2033)
Courtin' Wildcats (1929; 21)
Covered Wagon Days (1940; 1109)
Covered Wagon Raid (1950; 2197)
Covered Wagon Trails (1930; 26)
Covered Wagon Trails (1940; 1102)
Cow-Catcher's Daughter (The) (1931; 122a)
Cow Country (1953; 2583)
Cow Town (1950; 2217)
Cowboy (1958; 2901)

Cowboy (The) (1954; 2634)
Cowboy and the Bandit (1935; 446)
Cowboy and the Blonde (The) (1941; 1261)
Cowboy and the Indians (The) (1949; 2120)
Cowboy and the Kid (The) (1936; 619)
Cowboy and the Lady (The) (1938; 931)
Cowboy and the Outlaw (The) (1930; 29)
Cowboy and the Prizefighter (1949; 2153)
Cowboy and the Senorita (1944; 1601)
Cowboy Blues (1946; 1802)
Cowboy Canteen (1944; 1579)
Cowboy Cavalier (1948; 1997)
Cowboy Commandos (1943; 1511)
Cowboy Counsellor (The) (1932; 252)
Cowboy from Brooklyn (The) (1938; 897)
Cowboy from Lonesome River (1944; 1637)
Cowboy from Sundown (The) (1940; 1117)
Cowboy Holiday (1934; 399)
Cowboy in the Clouds (1943; 1567)
Cowboy Millionaire (The) (1935; 435)
Cowboy Serenade (1942; 1359)
Cowboy Star (The) (1936; 680)
Cowboys (The) (1972; 3234)
Cowboys from Texas (1939; 1050)
Cowboy's Holiday (A) (1949; 2117)
Coyote Canyon (1949; 2146)
Coyote Trails (1935; 521)
Crashing Broadway (1933; 319)
Crashing Thru (1939; 1056)
Crashing Thru (1949; 2051)
Crimson Trail (The) (1935; 439)
Cripple Creek (1952; 2466)
Crooked River (1950; 2229)
Crooked Trail (The) (1936; 638)
Crossed Trails (1948; 1968)
Crossfire (1933; 331)
Cry Blood, Apache (1970; 3202)
Culpepper Cattle Company (The) (1972; 3239)
Cupid Rides the Range (1939; 1032)
Curtain Call at Cactus Creek (1950; 2223)
Custer of the West (1968; FF39)
Custer's Last Stand (1936; 696)
Cut-Throats Nine (1973; FF109)
Cyclone Fury (1951; 2368)
Cyclone Kid (1942; 1404)
Cyclone Kid (The) (1931; 161)
Cyclone of the Saddle (1935; 447)
Cyclone on Horseback (1941; 1269)
Cyclone Prairie Rangers (1944; 1647)
Cyclone Ranger (The) (1935; 442)

D

Dakota (1945; 1748)
Dakota Incident (1956; 2781)
Dakota Kid (The) (1951; 2356)

Dakota Lil (1950; 2171)
Dallas (1950; 2296)
Dalton Gang (The) (1949; 2133)
Dalton Girls (The) (1957; 2889)
Dalton That Got Away (1960; 3007)
Daltons Ride Again (The) (1945; 1737)
Daltons' Women (The) (1950; 2181)
Dan Candy's Law (1975; 3298)
Danger Ahead (1940; 1075)
Danger Trails (1935; 522)
Danger Valley (1937; 814)
Dangerous Venture (1947; 1886)
Dangers of the Canadian Mounted (1948; 1971)
Daniel Boone (1936; 665)
Daniel Boone, Trail Blazer (1956; 2802)
Daredevils of the West (1943; 1495)
Daring Caballero (The) (1949; 2094)
Daring Danger (1932; 229)
Dark Command (1940; 1099)
Daughter of the West (1949; 2061)
Davy Crockett and the River Pirates (1956; 2780)
Davy Crockett, Indian Scout (1950; 2161a)
Davy Crockett, King of the Wild Frontier (1955;
  2709)
Dawn at Socorro (1954; 2651)
Dawn on the Great Divide (1942; 1465)
Dawn Rider (The) (1935; 466)
Dawn Trail (The) (1930; 90)
Day of Anger (1970; FF69)
Day of Fury (A) (1956; 2760)
Day of the Bad Man (1958; 2907)
Day of the Evil Gun (1968; 3151)
Day of the Outlaw (1959; 2978)
Days of Buffalo Bill (1946; 1762)
Days of Jesse James (1939; 1062)
Days of Old Cheyenne (1943; 1504)
Dead Don't Dream (The) (1948; 1974)
Dead Man's Gold (1948; 2010)
Dead Man's Gulch (1943; 1476)
Dead Man's Trail (1952; 2469)
Dead or Alive (1944; 1648)
Deadline (1948; 1956)
Deadline (The) (1931; 156)
Deadly Companions (The) (1961; 3025)
Deadly Trackers (The) (1973; 3272)
Deadwood Dick (1940; 1146)
Deadwood Pass (1933; 310)
Deadwood '76 (1965; 3097)
Deaf Smith and Johnny Ears (1973; FF108)
Death Goes North (1939; 971)
Death of a Gunfighter (1969; 3178)
Death Rides a Horse (1969; FF61)
Death Rides the Plains (1943; 1499)
Death Rides the Range (1940; 1078)
Death Valley (1946; 1808)
Death Valley Gunfighter (1949; 2070)
Death Valley Manhunt (1943; 1542)

Death Valley Outlaws (1941; 1309)
Death Valley Rangers (1943; 1562)
Decision at Sundown (1957; 2883)
Deep in the Heart of Texas (1942; 1436)
Deep West (1975; FF123)
Deerslayer (1943; 1559)
Deerslayer (The) (1957; 2870)
Defying the Law (1935; 523)
Demon for Trouble (A) (1934; 377)
Denver and Rio Grande (1952; 2459)
Denver Kid (The) (1948; 2019)
Deputy Marshal (1949; 2136)
Desert Bandit (1941; 1263)
Desert Gold (1936; 601)
Desert Guns (1936; 571)
Desert Horseman (The) (1946; 1800)
Desert Justice (1936; 700)
Desert Man (1934; 408)
Desert Mesa (1935; 424)
Desert of Lost Men (1951; 2392)
Desert Passage (1952; 2457)
Desert Patrol (1938; 883)
Desert Phantom (1936; 597)
Desert Pursuit (1952; 2452)
Desert Trail (The) (1935; 452)
Desert Vengeance (1931; 102)
Desert Vigilante (1949; 2141)
Deserter (The) (1971; FF78)
Desperado (The) (1954; 2638)
Desperadoes (The) (1943; 1508)
Desperadoes of Dodge City (1948; 2013)
Desperadoes of the West (1950; 2293)
Desperadoes' Outpost (1952; 2488)
Desperados (1969; FF57)
Desperados Are in Town (The) (1956; 2808)
Desperado's Trail (1966; FF17)
Desperate Trails (1939; 1033)
Destry (1955; 2675)
Destry Rides Again (1932; 230)
Destry Rides Again (1939; 1064)
Devil Horse (The) (1932; 259)
Devil Riders (1943; 1554)
Devil's Canyon (1935; 525)
Devil's Canyon (1953; 2571)
Devil's Doorway (1950; 2258)
Devil's Mistress (The) (1968; 3152)
Devil's Playground (The) (1946; 1829)
Devil's Saddle Legion (1937; 792)
Devil's Trail (The) (1942; 1399)
Diamond Trail (The) (1932; 275)
Dig That Uranium (1956; 2744a)
Dirty Dingus Magee (1971; 3204)
Dirty Little Billy (1972; 3253)
Dirty Outlaws (The) (1971; FF83)
Disciples of Death (1972; 3248)
Distant Drums (1951; 2403)
Distant Trumpet (A) (1964; 3072)

Doc (1971; FF80)
Dodge City (1939; 987)
Dodge City Trail (1936; 695)
Dollars for a Fast Gun (1969; FF55)
Domino Kid (1957; 2875)
Don Daredevil Rides Again (1951; 2372)
Don't Fence Me In (1945; 1727)
Don't Turn the Other Cheek (1974; FF117)
Doomed at Sundown (1937; 779)
Doomed Caravan (1941; 1217)
Down Dakota Way (1949; 2118)
Down Laredo Way (1953; 2568)
Down Mexico Way (1941; 1321)
Down Rio Grande Way (1942; 1391)
Down Texas Way (1942; 1401)
Down the Wyoming Trail (1939; 1007)
Dragoon Wells Massacre (1957; 2843)
Drango (1957; 2822)
Drift Fence (1936; 584)
Drifter (The) (1944; 1609)
Driftin' Kid (The) (1941; 1323)
Driftin' River (1946; 1820)
Drifing Along (1946; 1756)
Drifting Westward (1939; 959)
Drum Beat (1954; 2663)
Drum Taps (1933; 292)
Drums Across the River (1954; 2636)
Drums in the Deep South (1951; 2381)
Drums of Destiny (1937; 765)
Duchess and the Dirtwater Fox (The) (1976; 3313)
Duck, You Sucker (1972; FF97)
Dude Bandit (The) (1933; 309)
Dude Cowboy (1941; 1342)
Dude Goes West (The) (1948; 1985)
Dude Ranch (1931; 125)
Dude Ranch Harmony (1949; 2123)
Dude Ranger (The) (1934; 383)
Dude Wrangler (The) (1930; 57)
Dudes Are Pretty People (1942; 1388)
Duel at Apache Wells (1947; 2826)
Duel at Diablo (1966; 3114)
Duel at Silver Creek (1952; 2475)
Duel in the Sun (1948; 1963)
Dugan of the Badlands (1931; 130)
Durango Kid (The) (1940; 1160)
Durango Valley Raiders (1938; 905)
Dynamite Canyon (1941; 1294)
Dynamite Pass (1950; 2187)
Dynamite Ranch (1932; 232)

E

Eagle and the Hawk (The) (1950; 2221)
Eagle's Brood (The) (1935; 487)
Echo Ranch (1948; 1965)
El Condor (1971; 3196)

El Diablo Rides (1939; 1052)
El Dorado (1967; 3137)
El Dorado Pass (1948; 2023)
El Paso Kid (The) (1946; 1789)
El Paso Stampede (1953; 2577)
El Topo (1971; FF87)
Empty Holsters (1937; 780)
Empty Saddles (1936; 689)
End of the Trail (1932; 270)
End of the Trail (1936; 669)
Enemy of the Law (1945; 1688)
Escape from Fort Bravo (1953; 2600)
Escape from Red Rock (1958; 2892)
Escort West (1959; 2950)
Everyman's Law (1936; 625)
Eyes of Texas (1948; 1998)

F

Fabulous Texan (The) (1947; 1925)
Face of a Fugitive (1959; 2963)
Face to the Wind (1974; 3281)
Fair Warning (1931; 104)
False Colors (1943; 1555)
False Paradise (1948; 2011)
Fancy Pants (1950; 2265)
Fangs of the Arctic (1953; 2518)
Fangs of the Wild (1954; 2621)
Far Country (The) (1955; 2681)
Far Frontier (The) (1948; 2046)
Far Horizons (The) (1955; 2710)
Fargo (1952; 2484)
Fargo Express (1933; 341)
Fargo Kid (The) (1940; 1202)
Fargo Phantom (The) (1950; 2175)
Fast Bullets (1936; 588)
Fast on the Draw (1950; 2233)
Fastest Guitar Alive (The) (1967; 3139)
Fastest Gun Alive (The) (1956; 2779)
Female Bunch (The) (1971; 3227)
Fence Riders (1950; 2170)
Ferocious Pal (The) (1934; 409)
Feud Maker (The) (1938; 867)
Feud of the Range (1939; 954)
Feud of the Trail (The) (1937; 722)
Feud of the West (1936; 608)
Few Bullets More (A) (1969; FF54)
Few Dollars for Gypsy (1967; FF36)
Fiddlin' Buckaroo (The) (1933; 324)
Fiend Who Walked the West (The) (1958; 2935)
Fight of the Wild Stallions (1947; 1938)
Fighter (The) (1952; 2455)
Fightin' Thru (1930; 94)
Fighting Bill Carson (1945; 1730)
Fighting Bill Fargo (1941; 1340)
Fighting Buckaroo (The) (1943; 1474)
Fighting Caballero (1935; 526)

Fighting Caravans (1931; 107)
Fighting Champ (The) (1932; 271)
Fighting Code (The) (1933; 347)
Fighting Cowboy (The) (1933; 350)
Fighting Deputy (The) (1937; 832)
Fighting Fool (The) (1932; 194)
Fighting for Justice (1932; 258)
Fighting Frontier (1943; 1473)
Fighting Frontiersman (The) (1946; 1841)
Fighting Fury (1935; 390)
Fighting Gringo (The) (1939; 1048)
Fighting Hero (1934; 373)
Fighting Lawman (The) (1953; 2579)
Fighting Legion (The) (1930; 39)
Fighting Mad (1939; 1043)
Fighting Man of the Plains (1949; 2158)
Fighting Marshal (The) (1931; 172)
Fighting Mustang (1948; 1949)
Fighting Parson (The) (1930; 28)
Fighting Parson (The) (1933; 328)
Fighting Pioneers (1935; 458)
Fighting Ranger (The) (1934; 359)
Fighting Ranger (The) (1948; 2005)
Fighting Redhead (The) (1949; 2130)
Fighting Renegade (The) (1939; 1031)
Fighting Shadows (1935; 451)
Fighting Sheriff (The) (1931; 123)
Fighting Stallion (The) (1950; 2191)
Fighting Texan (The) (1937; 772)
Fighting Texans (The) (1933; 326)
Fighting Through (1934; 380)
Fighting to Live (1934; 365)
Fighting Trooper (The) (1934; 388)
Fighting Valley (1943; 1526)
Fighting Vigilantes (The) (1947; 1928)
Fighting with Kit Carson (1933; 327)
Find a Place to Die (1971; FF89)
Finger on the Trigger (1965; FF5)
Fire Creek (1968; 3147)
Firebrand (The) (1962; 3049)
Firebrand Jordan (1930; 25)
Firebrands of Arizona (1944; 1653)
First Texan (The) (1956; 2775)
First Traveling Saleslady (The) (1956; 2790)
Fistful of Dynamite (1972; FF99)
Fistful of Dollars (A) (1967; FF24)
Five Bad Men (1935; 527)
Five Bloody Graves (1970; 3188)
Five Bold Women (1960; 3001)
Five Card Stud (1968; 3162)
Five Guns to Tombstone (1961; 3013)
Five Guns West (1955; 2697)
Five-Man Army (The) (1970; FF66)
Flame of Sacramento (1946; 1791)
Flame of the Barbary Coast (1945; 1692)
Flame of the West (1945; 1701)
Flaming Bullets (1945; 1724)

Flaming Feather (1952; 2415)
Flaming Frontier (1958; 2931)
Flaming Frontier (1968; FF40)
Flaming Frontiers (1938; 881)
Flaming Guns (1932; 273)
Flaming Lead (1939; 1051)
Flaming Star (1960; 3011)
Flap (1970; 3205)
Flashing Guns (1947; 1902)
Flesh and the Spur (1956; 2798)
Flying Lariats (1931; 141)
Fool's Gold (1946; 1757)
For a Few Dollars More (1967; FF26)
For the Love of Mike (1960; 2999)
For the Service (1936; 613)
Forbidden Trail (1932; 263)
Forbidden Trails (1941; 1347)
Forbidden Valley (1938; 847)
Forlorn River (1937; 775)
Fort Bowie (1958; 2897)
Fort Courageous (1965; 3092)
Fort Defiance (1951; 2391)
Fort Dobbs (1958; 2898)
Fort Dodge Stampede (1951; 2370)
Fort Massacre (1958; 2910)
Fort Osage (1952; 2421)
Fort Savage Raiders (1951; 2323)
Fort Ti (1953; 2540)
Fort Utah (1967; 3140)
Fort Vengeance (1953; 2534)
Fort Worth (1951; 2359)
Fort Yuma (1955; 2726)
Forty-Five Calibre Echo (1932; 277)
Forty Guns (1957; 2864)
Forty Guns to Apache Pass (1967; 3132)
Forty-Niners (The) (1932; 257)
Forty-Niners (The) (1954; 2631)
Forty Thieves (1944; 1611)
Four Fast Guns (1960; 2986)
Four for Texas (1964; 3063)
Four Guns to the Border (1954; 2659)
Fourth Horseman (The) (1932; 245)
Freighters of Destiny (1931; 163)
Frenchie (1951; 2297)
Friendly Persuasion (1956; 2812)
Frisco Sal (1945; 1677)
Frisco Tornado (1950; 2266)
From Broadway to Cheyenne (1932; 239)
From Hell to Texas (1958; 2910)
From Noon till Three (1976; 3325)
Frontier Agent (1948; 1981)
Frontier Badman (1943; 1523)
Frontier Crusader (1940; 1127)
Frontier Days (1934; 389)
Frontier Days (1945; 1741)
Frontier Feud (1945; 1738)
Frontier Frolic (1946; 1821)

Frontier Fugitives (1945; 1710)
Frontier Fury (1943; 1518)
Frontier Gal (1945; 1746)
Frontier Gambler (1956; 2795a)
Frontier Gun (1958; 2943)
Frontier Gunlaw (1946; 1758)
Frontier Hellcat (1966; FF10)
Frontier Justice (1936; 659)
Frontier Law (1943; 1556)
Frontier Marshal (1934; 353)
Frontier Marshal (1939; 1020)
Frontier Marshal (1949; 2081)
Frontier Outlaws (1944; 1584)
Frontier Outpost (1950; 2295)
Frontier Phantom (The) (1952; 2416)
Frontier Pony Express (1939; 989)
Frontier Revenge (1948; 2042)
Frontier Scout (1938; 915)
Frontier Town (1938; 853)
Frontier Uprising (1961; 3018)
Frontier Vengeance (1940; 1180)
Frontier Woman (1956; 2778)
Frontiers of '49 (1939; 955)
Frontiersman (The) (1938; 941)
Fugitive (The) (1933; 334a)
Fugitive from Sonora (1943; 1519)
Fugitive of the Plains (1943; 1487)
Fugitive Sheriff (The) (1936; 666)
Fugitive Valley (1941; 1290)
Furies (The) (1950; 2251)
Fury at Gunsight Pass (1956; 2746)
Fury at Showdown (1957; 2837)
Fury in Paradise (1955; 2742a)
Fuzzy Settles Down (1944; 1619)

G

Gallant Defender (1935; 501)
Gallant Fool (The) (1933; 316)
Gallant Legion (The) (1948; 1984)
Galloping Dynamite (1937; 788)
Galloping Kid (The) (1932; 278)
Galloping Romeo (1933; 329)
Galloping Thru (1932; 269)
Galloping Thunder (1946; 1782)
Gambler from Natchez (The) (1954; 2643)
Gambler Wore a Gun (The) (1961; 3022)
Gambling Terror (The) (1937; 718)
Gangs of Sonora (1941; 1278)
Gangster's Den (1945; 1697)
Gangsters of the Frontier (1944; 1636)
Garden of Evil (1954; 2642)
Gas House Kids Go West (1947; 1890a)
Gatling Gun (The) (1972; 3244)
Gaucho Serenade (1940; 1119)
Gauchos of Eldorado (1941; 1325)

Gay Amigo (The) (1949; 2084)
Gay Buckaroo (The) (1932; 193)
Gay Caballero (The) (1932; 198)
Gay Caballero (The) (1940; 1177)
Gay Cavalier (The) (1946; 1773)
Gay Desperado (The) (1936; 660)
Gay Ranchero (The) (1948; 1942)
Gene Autry and the Mounties (1951; 2304)
Gentle Annie (1944; 1663)
Gentleman from Arizona (The) (1939; 1063)
Gentleman from California (The) (1937; 784)
Gentleman from Texas (The) (1946; 1793)
Gentlemen with Guns (1946; 1772)
Geronimo (1940; 1071)
Geronimo (1962; 3041)
Ghost City (1932; 182)
Ghost Guns (1944; 1651)
Ghost of Crossbones Canyon (The) (1952; 2497)
Ghost of Hidden Valley (1946; 1792)
Ghost of Zorro (1949; 2110)
Ghost of Zorro (1959; 2973)
Ghost Patrol (1936; 640)
Ghost Rider (The) (1935; 528)
Ghost Rider (The) (1943; 1489)
Ghost Town (1936; 585)
Ghost Town (1956; 2750)
Ghost Town Gold (1936; 667)
Ghost Town Law (1942; 1383)
Ghost Town Renegades (1947; 1904)
Ghost Town Riders (1938; 942)
Ghost Valley (1932; 235)
Ghost Valley Raiders (1940; 1096)
Giant (1956; 2814)
Girl and the Gambler (The) (1939; 1010)
Girl from Alaska (The) (1942; 1389)
Girl from Gunsight (The) (1949; 2121)
Girl from San Lorenzo (The) (1950; 2180)
Girl of the Golden West (The) (1930; 77)
Girl of the Golden West (The) (1938; 859)
Girl Rush (1944; 1642a)
Girl Trouble (1933; 344)
Git Along Little Dogies (1937; 730)
Glory Guys (The) (1965; 3101)
Glory Trail (The) (1936; 650)
Go for Broke (1972; FF102)
Go West (1940; 1201)
Go West, Young Lady (1941; 1337)
God Forgives, I Don't (1969; FF58)
God's Country (1946; 1776)
God's Country and the Man (1931; 119)
God's Country and the Man (1937; 799)
God's Country and the Woman (1937; 712)
God's Gun (1977; FF133)
Gold (1932; 248)
Gold Fever (1952; 2463)
Gold Ghost (The) (1934; 358a)
Gold Is Where You Find It (1938; 849)

Gold Mine in the Sky (1938; 891)
Gold of the Seven Saints (1961; 3016)
Gold Raiders (1951; 2373)
Gold Strike (1950; 2194)
Golden Stallion (The) (1949; 2144)
Golden Trail (The) (1940; 1143)
Golden West (The) (1932; 268)
Goldtown Ghost Raiders (1943; 2547)
Gone with the West (1976; 3332)
Good Day for a Hanging (1959; 2948)
Good Guys and the Bad Guys (The) (1969; 3184)
Good, the Bad, and the Ugly (The) (1968; FF38)
Goofs and Saddles (1937; 776a)
Gordon of Ghost City (1933; 330)
Grand Canyon Trail (1948; 2028)
Great Adventures of Wild Bill Hickok (The) (1938; 890)
Great American Cowboy (The) (1974; 3278)
Great Bank Robbery (The) (1969; 3180)
Great Day in the Morning (1956; 2765)
Great Divide (The) (1929; 18)
Great Gundown (The) (1977; 3336)
Great Jesse James Raid (The) (1953; 2559)
Great Locomotive Chase (The) (1956; 2773)
Great Man's Lady (The) (1942; 1380)
Great Meadow (The) (1931; 101)
Great Missouri Raid (The) (1951; 2312)
Great Northfield, Minnesota Raid (The) (1972; 3240)
Great Scout and Cathouse Thursday (The) (1976; 3317)
Great Sioux Massacre (The) (1965; 3105)
Great Sioux Uprising (The) (1953; 2560)
Great Stagecoach Robbery (1945; 1674)
Green Grass of Wyoming (1948; 1970)
Guardian of the Wilderness (1976; 3331)
Guilty Trail (1938; 924)
Gun Battle at Monterey (1957; 2879)
Gun Belt (1953; 2562)
Gun Brothers (1956; 2796)
Gun Code (1940; 1153)
Gun Duel in Durango (1957; 2846)
Gun Fever (1958; 2893)
Gun Fight (1961; 3023)
Gun for a Coward (1957; 2833)
Gun Fury (1953; 2585)
Gun Glory (1957; 2861)
Gun Grit (1936; 697)
Gun Hawk (The) (1963; 3059)
Gun Justice (1933; 346)
Gun Law (1933; 304)
Gun Law (1938; 876)
Gun Law Justice (1949; 2066)
Gun Lords of Stirrup Basin (1937; 754)
Gun Packer (1938; 930)
Gun Play (1935; 531)
Gun Ranger (The) (1937; 716)

Gun Runner (1949; 2055)
Gun Smoke (1931; 117)
Gun Smoke (1945; 1676)
Gun Smugglers (1948; 2045)
Gun Street (1961; 3035)
Gun Talk (1947; 1936)
Gun That Won the West (The) (1955; 2721)
Gun the Man Down (1956; 2811)
Gun to Gun (1944; 1574)
Gun Town (1946; 1753)
Gunfight (A) (1971; 3218)
Gunfight at Comanche Creek (1963; 3060)
Gunfight at Dodge City (The) (1959; 2969)
Gunfight at the O.K. Corral (1957; 2851)
Gunfight in Abilene (1967; 3134)
Gunfighter (The) (1950; 2236)
Gunfighters (The) (1947; 1896)
Gunfighters of Abilene (1960; 2985)
Gunfighters of Casa Grande (1965; FF3)
Gunfighters of the Northwest (1954; 2625)
Gunfire (1935; 530)
Gunfire (1950; 2248)
Gunfire at Indian Gap (1957; 2888)
Gunman (The) (1952; 2441)
Gunman from Bodie (The) (1941; 1310)
Gunman's Code (1946; 1813)
Gunman's Walk (1958; 2924)
Gunmen from Laredo (1959; 2956)
Gunmen of Abilene (1950; 2174)
Gunmen of the Rio Grande (1965; FF6)
Gunners and Guns (1935; 372)
Gunning for Justice (1948; 2030)
Gunning for Vengeance (1946; 1771)
Gunplay (1951; 2351)
Gunpoint (1966; 3115)
Guns A'Blazing (1932; 203)
Guns and Guitars (1936; 692)
Guns for Hire (1932; 279)
Guns for San Sebastian (1968; 3153)
Guns in the Dark (1937; 752)
Guns of a Stranger (1973; 3263)
Guns of Fort Petticoat (The) (1957; 2838)
Guns of Hate (1948; 1978)
Guns of the Law (1944; 1590)
Guns of the Magnificent Seven (1969; FF59)
Guns of the Pecos (1937; 706)
Guns of the Timberland (1960; 2990)
Gunsight Ridge (1957; 2863)
Gunslinger (1956; 2770)
Gunslingers (1950; 2200)
Gunsmoke (1947; 1865)
Gunsmoke (1953; 2528)
Gunsmoke in Tucson (1958; 2944)
Gunsmoke Killers (1947; 1865)
Gunsmoke Mesa (1944; 1571)
Gunsmoke on the Guadalupe (1935; 460)
Gunsmoke Ranch (1937; 747)

Gunsmoke Trail (1938; 879)
Gypsy Colt (1954; 2620)

H

Hail to the Rangers (1943; 1539)
Hair-Trigger Casey (1936; 698)
Half Breed (1973; FF107)
Half-Breed (The) (1952; 2449)
Half Way to Hell (1961; 3026)
Hallelujah Trail (The) (1965; 3096)
Halliday Brand (The) (1957; 2825)
Hands Across the Border (1944; 1572)
Hands Across the Rockies (1941; 1270)
Hang 'Em High (1968; 3161)
Hanging Tree (The) (1959; 2955)
Hangman (The) (1959; 2972)
Hangman's Knot (1952; 2505)
Hannah Lee (1953; 2563)
Hannie Caulder (1972; FF96)
Hard Hombre (1931; 148)
Hard Man (The) (1957; 2886)
Harlem Rides the Range (1939; 1013)
Harmony Trail (1944; 1654)
Harvey Girls (The) (1946; 1750)
Haunted Gold (1932; 272)
Haunted Mine (The) (1946; 1767)
Haunted Ranch (1943; 1479)
Haunted Trails (1949; 2114)
Hawaiian Buckaroo (1938; 840)
Hawk of Powder River (The) (1948; 1967)
Hawk of Wild River (The) (1952; 2425)
Hawmps! (1976; 3315)
He Rides Tall (1964; 3067)
Headin' East (1937; 827)
Headin' for the Rio Grande (1936; 690)
Headin' for Trouble (1931; 149)
Headin' North (1930; 85)
Heading West (1946; 1809)
Heart of Arizona (1938; 870)
Heart of the Golden West (1942; 1453)
Heart of the North (1938; 939)
Heart of the Rio Grande (1942; 1374)
Heart of the Rockies (1937; 801)
Heart of the Rockies (1951; 2325)
Heart of the West (1936; 637)
Hearts of the West (1975; 3303)
Heaven Only Knows (1947; 1914)
Heaven with a Gun (1969; 3169)
Heir to Trouble (1935; 509)
Heldorado (1946; 1843)
Hell Bent for Leather (1960; 2987)
Hell Canyon Outlaws (1957; 2877)
Hell Fire Austin (1932; 201)
Hellbenders (The) (1967; FF29)
Hellfire (1949; 2097)

Hellgate (1952; 2482)
Hello Trouble (1932; 227)
Hell's Crossroads (1957; 2836)
Hell's Heroes (1930; 22)
Hell's Outpost (1954; 2668)
Hell's Valley (1931; 112)
Here Comes the Cavalry (1941; 1276)
Heritage of the Desert (1932; 246)
Heritage of the Desert (1939; 979)
Heroes of the Alamo (1937; 794)
Heroes of the Hills (1938; 900)
Heroes of the Range (1936; 644)
Heroes of the Saddle (1940; 1072)
Heroes of the West (1932; 223)
Hiawatha (1952; 2512)
Hidden Danger (1948; 2039)
Hidden Gold (1932; 260)
Hidden Gold (1940; 1128)
Hidden Guns (1956; 2745)
Hidden Valley (1932; 251)
Hidden Valley Days (1948; 1947)
Hidden Valley Outlaws (1944; 1592)
High Lonesome (1950; 2254)
High Noon (1952; 2473)
High Plains Drifter (1973; 3260)
Hills of Oklahoma (1950; 2189)
Hills of Old Wyoming (1937; 738)
Hills of Utah (1951; 2377)
Hills Run Red (The) (1967; FF30)
Hired Gun (The) (1957; 2873)
Hired Hand (The) (1971; 3225)
His Brother's Ghost (1945; 1671)
His Fighting Blood (1935; 488)
Hit the Saddle (1937; 724)
Hittin' the Trail (1937; 732)
Hi-Yo Silver (1940; 1103)
Hollywood Barn Dance (1947; 1892)
Hollywood Bronc Busters (1956; 2821)
Hollywood Cowboy (1937; 757)
Hollywood Round-Up (1937; 815)
Holy Terror (A) (1931; 135)
Hombre (1967; 3130)
Home in Oklahoma (1946; 1826)
Home in San Antone (1949; 2076)
Home in Wyomin' (1942; 1396)
Home on the Prairie (1939; 963)
Home on the Range (1935; 428)
Home on the Range (1946; 1778)
Homesteaders (The) (1953; 2531)
Homesteaders of Paradise Valley (1947; 1873)
Hondo (1953; 2595)
Hondo and the Apaches (1967; 3140a)
Honeychile (1951; 2385)
Honkers (The) (1972; 3236)
Honky Tonk (1941; 1314)
Honor of the Mounted (1932; 224)
Honor of the Range (1934; 363)

Honor of the West (1939; 952)
Hop-a-Long Cassidy (1935; 473)
Hopalong Cassidy Enters (1935; 473)
Hopalong Cassidy Returns (1936; 663)
Hopalong Rides Again (1937; 806)
Hoppy Serves a Writ (1943; 1485)
Hoppy's Holiday (1947; 1903)
Horizons West (1952; 2486)
Horse Soldiers (The) (1959; 2971)
Horsemen of the Sierras (1949; 2148)
Horses' Collars (1935; 529)
Hostile Country (1950; 2192)
Hostile Guns (1967; 3146)
Hot Lead (1951; 2378)
Hour of the Gun (1967; 3142)
How the West Was Won (1963; 3053)
Hud (1963; 3055)
Hudson's Bay (1941; 1213)
Human Targets (1932; 190)
Hurricane Horseman (1931; 154)
Hurricane Smith (1941; 1287)

I

I Killed Geronimo (1950; 2247)
I Killed Wild Bill Hickok (1956; 2771)
I Shot Billy the Kid (1950; 2252)
I Shot Jesse James (1949; 2064)
Idaho (1943; 1483)
Idaho Kid (The) (1936; 641)
Idaho Red (1929; 9)
I'm from the City (1938; 898a)
In Early Arizona (1938; 926)
In Old Amarillo (1951; 2343)
In Old Arizona (1929; 4)
In Old Caliente (1939; 1011)
In Old California (1929; 13)
In Old California (1942; 1408)
In Old Cheyenne (1931; 126)
In Old Cheyenne (1941; 1242)
In Old Colorado (1941; 1239)
In Old Mexico (1938; 911)
In Old Montana (1939; 964)
In Old Monterey (1939; 1026)
In Old New Mexico (1945; 1689)
In Old Oklahoma (1943; 1564)
In Old Sacramento (1946; 1791)
In Old Santa Fe (1934; 393)
Incident at Phantom Hill (1966; 3120)
Indian Agent (1948; 2038)
Indian Fighter (The) (1955; 2739)
Indian Paint (1965; 3091)
Indian Territory (1950; 2264)
Indian Uprising (1952; 2408)
Indians Are Coming (The) (1930; 81)
Invitation to a Gunfighter (1964; 3080)

Irish Gringo (The) (1935; 532)
Iron Mistress (The) (1952; 2506)
Iron Mountain Trail (1953; 2544)
Iron Sheriff (The) (1957; 2839)
Iroquis Trail (The) (1950; 2230)
It Can Be Done . . . Amigo (1974; FF118)
It Happened Out West (1937; 748)
Ivory-Handled Gun (The) (1935; 502)

J

Jack McCall, Desperado (1953; 253b)
Jack Slade (1953; 2586)
Jackass Mail (1942; 1413)
James Brothers of Missouri (The) (1950; 2167)
Jaws of Justice (1933; 342)
Jayhawkers (The) (1959; 2982)
Jeep-Herders (1949; 2125)
Jeremiah Johnson (1972; 3257)
Jesse James (1939; 961)
Jesse James at Bay (1941; 1324)
Jesse James, Jr. (1942; 1381)
Jesse James Rides Again (1947; 1867)
Jesse James vs. the Daltons (1954; 2619)
Jesse James vs. Frankenstein's Daughter (1966; 3112)
Jesse James' Women (1954; 2652)
Jessi's Girls (1975; 3289)
Jiggs and Maggie Out West (1950; 2207)
Joe Dakota (1957; 2865)
Joe Kidd (1972; 3247)
Joe Panther (1976; 3327)
Johnny Concho (1956; 2777)
Johnny Guitar (1954; 2649)
Johnny Hamlet (1972; FF93)
Johnny Reno (1966; 3110)
Johnny Yuma (1967; FF31)
Jory (1972; 3255)
Joshua (1977; 3333)
Journey Through Rosebud (1972; 3237)
Journey to Shiloh (1968; 3159)
Jubal (1956; 2761)
Jubilee Trail (1954; 2632)
Judgement Book (The) (1935; 533)
Junction City (1952; 2468)
Junior Bonner (1972; 3245)
Justice of the Range (1935; 459)
J. W. Coop (1972; 3233)

K

Kansan (The) (1943; 1538)
Kansas Cyclone (1941; 1273)
Kansas Pacific (1953; 2526)
Kansas Raiders (1950; 2284)

Kansas Territory (1952; 2450)
Kansas Terrors (The) (1942; 1038)
Keep Shooting (1942; 1360)
Kentuckian (The) (1955; 2718)
Kentucky Rifle (1956; 2783)
Kettle Creek (1930; 44)
Kid Blue (1973; 3261)
Kid Courageous (1935; 534)
Kid from Amarillo (The) (1951; 2387)
Kid from Arizona (The) (1931; 121)
Kid from Broken Gun (The) (1952; 2478)
Kid from Gower Gulch (The) (1950; 2166)
Kid from Santa Fe (The) (1940; 1122)
Kid from Texas (The) (1950; 2189)
Kid Ranger (The) (1936; 583)
Kid Rides Again (The) (1943; 1471)
Kid Rodelo (1966; FF9)
Kid Vengeance (1977; FF132)
Kid's Last Ride (The) (1941; 1228)
Kill or Be Killed (1967; FF32)
Kill Them All and Come Back Alone (1970; FF73)
King and Four Queens (The) (1956; 2820)
King of Dodge City (1941; 1296)
King of the Arena (1933; 320)
King of the Bandits (1947; 1924)
King of the Bullwhip (1951; 2307)
King of the Cowboys (1943; 1491)
King of the Forest Rangers (1945; 1783)
King of the Grizzlies (1970; 3191)
King of the Mounties (1942; 1445)
King of the Pecos (1936; 596)
King of the Royal Mounted (1936; 649)
King of the Royal Mounted (1940; 1168)
King of the Stallions (1947; 1433)
King of the Texas Rangers (1941; 1316)
King of the Wild Horses (1933; 340)
King of the Wild Horses (1947; 1871)
King of the Wild Stallions (1959; 2970)
Kino, The Padre on Horseback (1977; 3335)
Kiss of Fire (1955; 2725)
Kit Carson (1940; 1163)
Klondike (1932; 238)
Klondike Kate (1943; 1565)
Knife for the Ladies (A) (1973; 3273)
Knight of the Plains (1938; 874)
Knights of the Range (1940; 1084)
Konga, The Wild Stallion (1940; 1104)

L

Lady from Cheyenne (1941; 1247)
Lady from Texas (The) (1951; 2379)
Lady Takes a Chance (A) (1943; 1530)
Land Beyond the Law (1937; 727)
Land of Fighting Men (1938; 857)
Land of Hunted Men (1943; 1486)

Land of Missing Men (The) (1930; 78)
Land of the Lawless (1947; 1880)
Land of the Open Range (1942; 1390)
Land of the Outlaws (1944; 1635)
Land of the Silver Fox (1928; 2)
Land of the Six Guns (1940; 1118)
Land of Wanted Men (1932; 280)
Land Raiders (1969; FF63)
Landrush (1946; 1824)
Laramie (1949; 2087)
Laramie Kid (The) (1935; 535)
Laramie Mountains (1952; 2446)
Laramie Trail (The) (1944; 1593)
Lariats and Sixshooters (1931; 160)
Lasca of the Rio Grande (1931; 165)
Lash (The) (1930; 95)
Last Bandit (The) (1949; 2078)
Last Challenge (The) (1967; 3141)
Last Command (The) (1955; 2719a)
Last Days of Boot Hill (1947; 1926)
Last Frontier (The) (1933; 244)
Last Frontier (The) (1955; 2742)
Last Frontier Uprising (1947; 1854)
Last Gunfighter (The) (1961; 3027)
Last Hard Man (The) (1976; 3316)
Last Horseman (The) (1944; 1610)
Last Hunt (The) (1956; 2747)
Last Musketeer (The) (1952; 2426)
Last of the Badmen (1957; 2830)
Last of the Clintons (The) (1935; 496)
Last of the Comanches (1953; 2521)
Last of the Desperados (1955; 2737)
Last of the Duanes (1930; 66)
Last of the Duanes (1941; 1311)
Last of the Fast Guns (The) (1958; 2925)
Last of the Mohicans (The) (1932; 215)
Last of the Mohicans (The) (1936; 648)
Last of the Pony Riders (1953; 2597)
Last of the Redmen (1947; 1907)
Last of the Renegades (1966; FF16)
Last of the Warrens (1936; 615)
Last of the Wild Horses (1948; 2044)
Last Outlaw (1936; 628)
Last Outpost (1951; 2338)
Last Posse (The) (1953; 2555)
Last Rebel (The) (1968; 3165)
Last Rebel (The) (1971; FF79)
Last Roundup (The) (1934; 364)
Last Round-Up (The) (1947; 1923)
Last Stagecoach West (1957; 2857)
Last Stand (The) (1938; 861)
Last Sunset (The) (1961; 3028)
Last Trail (The) (1933; 333)
Last Train from Gun Hill (1959; 2977)
Last Wagon (The) (1956; 2797)
Law and Jake Wade (The) (1958; 2922)
Law and Lawless (1932; 265)

Law and Lead (1936; 678)
Law and Order (1932; 203)
Law and Order (1940; 1197)
Law and Order (1942; 1426)
Law and Order (1953; 2541)
Law Beyond the Range (1935; 432)
Law Comes to Gunsight (The) (1947; 1887)
Law Comes to Texas (The) (1939; 991)
Law Commands (The) (1937; 749)
Law for Tombstone (1937; 807)
Law Men (1944; 1597)
Law of the Badlands (1945; 1749a)
Law of the Badlands (1951; 2314)
Law of the Barbary Coast (1949; 2102)
Law of the Canyon (1947; 1879)
Law of the 45's (1935; 503)
Law of the Golden West (1949; 2083)
Law of the Lash (1947; 1862)
Law of the Lawless (1964; 3070)
Law of the North (1932; 218)
Law of the Northwest (1943; 1509)
Law of the Pampas (1939; 1041)
Law of the Panhandle (1950; 2261)
Law of the Plains (1938; 875)
Law of the Range (1941; 1271)
Law of the Ranger (1937; 750)
Law of the Rio Grande (1931; 139)
Law of the Saddle (1943; 1533)
Law of the Texan (1938; 925)
Law of the Valley (1944; 1644)
Law of the West (1932; 205)
Law of the West (1949; 2063)
Law of the Wild (The) (1934; 381)
Law of the Wolf (1941; 1256)
Law Rides (The) (1936; 630)
Law Rides Again (The) (1943; 1524)
Law vs. Billy the Kid (The) (1954; 2646)
Law West of Tombstone (The) (1938; 932)
Lawless Borders (1935; 505)
Lawless Breed (1946; 1810)
Lawless Breed (The) (1953; 2520a)
Lawless Code (1949; 2152)
Lawless Cowboys (1951; 2390)
Lawless Eighties (The) (1935; 2918)
Lawless Empire (1945; 1735)
Lawless Frontier (1934; 394)
Lawless Land (1937; 733)
Lawless Nineties (The) (1936; 586)
Lawless Plainsmen (1942; 1376)
Lawless Range (1935; 495)
Lawless Rider (The) (1954; 2640
Lawless Riders (1935; 504)
Lawless Street (A) (1955; 2740)
Lawless Valley (1932; 281)
Lawless Valley (1938; 927)
Lawman (1971; 3226)
Lawman Is Born (A) (1937; 768)

Lay That Rifle Down (1955; 2717)
Leadville Gunslinger (1952; 2434)
Leather Burners (The) (1943; 1510)
Left Handed Gun (The) (1958; 2914)
Left Handed Law (1937; 740)
Legend of Earl Durand (The) (1974; 3282)
Legend of Frank Woods (1977; FF131)
Legend of Frenchie King (The) (1973; FF105)
Legend of Lobo (The) (1962; 3050)
Legend of Nigger Charlie (The) (1959; 3242)
Legend of the Lost (1957; 2890)
Legend of Tom Dooley (1959; 2974)
Legion of the Lawless (1940; 1070)
Lemonade Joe (1966; FF11)
Life and Legend of Buffalo Jones (The) (1976; 3326)
Life and Times of Grizzly Adams (The) (1975; 3287)
Life and Times of Judge Roy Bean (The) (1972; 3256)
Life in the Raw (1933; 321)
Light in the Forest (The) (1958; 2927)
Light of Western Stars (The) (1940; 1105)
Light of the Western Stars (The) (1930; 34)
Lightnin' Bill Carson (1936; 609)
Lightnin' Crandall (1937; 729)
Lightnin' Smith Returns (1931; 142)
Lightning Bill (1934; 410)
Lightning Carson Rides Again (1938; 922)
Lightning Guns (1950; 2288)
Lightning Raiders (1946; 1750a)
Lightning Range (1934; 410a)
Lightning Strikes West (1940; 1139)
Lightning Triggers (1935; 536)
Lightning Warrior (1931; 173)
Lights of Old Santa Fe (1944; 1645)
Lion and the Horse (The) (1952; 2444)
Lion's Den (The) (1936; 635)
Little Big Horn (1951; 2353)
Little Big Man (1971; 3209)
Little Joe the Wrangler (1942; 1451)
Llano Kid (The) (1939; 1055)
Loaded Pistols (1949; 2056)
Local Bad Man (The) (1932; 192)
Lone Avenger (The) (1933; 314)
Lone Bandit (The) (1934; 411)
Lone Cowboy (The) (1934; 355)
Lone Defender (The) (1930; 97)
Lone Gun (The) (1954; 2627)
Lone Hand (The) (1953; 2542)
Lone Hand Texan (The) (1947; 1864)
Lone Prairie (The) (1942; 1446)
Lone Ranger (The) (1938; 860)
Lone Ranger (The) (1956; 2748)
Lone Ranger and the Lost City of Gold (The) (1958; 2921)
Lone Ranger Rides Again (The) (1939; 960)
Lone Rider (The) (1930; 58)
Lone Rider (The) (1934; 412)
Lone Rider Ambushed (The) (1941; 1299)

Lone Rider and the Bandit (The) (1942; 1354)
Lone Rider Crosses the Rio (The) (1941; 1235)
Lone Rider Fights Back (The) (1941; 1329)
Lone Rider in Cheyenne (The) (1942; 1379)
Lone Rider in Frontier Fury (The) (1941; 1295)
Lone Rider in Ghost Town (The) (1941; 1262)
Lone Rider Rides On (The) (1941; 1218)
Lone Star (1952; 2420)
Lone Star Law Men (1941; 1339)
Lone Star Moonlight (1946; 1842)
Lone Star Pioneers (1939; 978)
Lone Star Raiders (1940; 1205)
Lone Star Ranger (1942; 1378)
Lone Star Ranger (The) (1930; 23)
Lone Star Trail (The) (1943; 1525)
Lone Star Vigilantes (The) (1942; 1348)
Lone Texan (1959; 2957)
Lone Texas Ranger (1945; 1691)
Lonely Are the Brave (1962; 3046)
Lonely Man (The) (1957; 2853)
Lonely Trail (The) (1936; 620)
Lonesome Trail (1945; 1742)
Lonesome Trail (The) (1930; 61)
Lonesome Trail (The) (1955; 2715)
Long, Long Trail (The) (1929; 14)
Long Ride from Hell (A) (1970; FF67)
Long Rope (The) (1961; 3014)
Longhorn (The) (1951; 2394)
Loser's End (1934; 413)
Lost Canyon (1943; 1566)
Lost in Alaska (1952; 2480)
Lost Ranch (1937; 781)
Lost Trail (The) (1932; 282)
Lost Trail (The) (1945; 1728)
Love Me Tender (1956; 2810
Lovin' Molly (1974; 3275)
Luck of Roaring Camp (The) (1937; 821)
Lucky Cisco Kid (1940; 1136)
Lucky Larkin (1930; 33)
Lucky Larrigan (1932; 266)
Lucky Terror (1936; 587)
Lucky Texan (The) (1934; 354)
Lumberjack (1944; 1599)
Lure of the Wasteland (1939; 980)
Lust for Gold (1949; 2098)
Lusty Men (The) (1952; 2487)

M

Machismo—40 Graves for 40 Guns (1971; 3220)
Macho Callahan (1970; 3200)
Macintosh and T. J. (1976; 3308)
MacKenna's Gold (1969; 3176)
Mad Dog (1976; FF130)
Madron (1970; FF75)
Magnificent Seven (The) (1960; 3004)

Magnificent Seven Ride (The) (1972; 3249)
Mail Order Bride (1964; 3065)
Major Dundee (1965; 3089)
Man Alone (A) (1955; 2731)
Man and Boy (1971; 3230)
Man Behind the Gun (The) (1953; 2520)
Man Called Gannon (A) (1969; 3174)
Man Called Horse (A) (1970; 3192)
Man Called Noon (The) (1973; FF110)
Man Called Sledge (A) (1971; FF76)
Man from Arizona (The) (1932; 255)
Man from Button Willow (The) (1965; 3090)
Man from Cheyenne (1942; 1355)
Man from Colorado (The) (1948; 2047)
Man from Dakota (The) (1940; 1082)
Man from Death Valley (The) (1931; 146)
Man from Del Rio (1956; 2806)
Man from Galveston (The) (1964; 364)
Man from God's Country (1958; 2899)
Man from Guntown, The (1935; 478)
Man from Hell (The) (1934; 379)
Man from Hell's Edges (1932; 221)
Man from Kitter Ridge (The) (1955; 2711)
Man from Laramie (The) (1955; 2719)
Man from Montana (1941; 1303)
Man from Monterey (The) (1933; 323)
Man from Montreal (1940; 1089)
Man from Music Mountain (1938; 904)
Man from Music Mountain (1943; 1552)
Man from New Mexico (The) (1932; 207)
Man from Nowhere (The) (1968; FF51)
Man from Oklahoma (The) (1945; 1706)
Man from Rainbow Valley (1946; 1795)
Man from Sonora (1951; 2321)
Man from Sundown (The) (1939; 1018)
Man from Texas (1939; 992)
Man from Texas (The) (1947; 1931)
Man from the Alamo (The) (1935; 2566)
Man from the Black Hills (1952; 2439)
Man from the Rio Grande (The) (1943; 1548)
Man from Thunder River (The) (1943; 1513)
Man from Tumbleweeds (The) (1940; 1113)
Man from Utah (The) (1934; 367)
Man in the Saddle (1951; 2396)
Man in the Wilderness (1971; FF88)
Man of Action (1933; 289)
Man of Conquest (1939; 1000)
Man of the East (1974; FF113)
Man of the Forest (1933; 334)
Man of the West (1958; 2940)
Man or Gun (1958; 2917)
Man Trailer (The) (1934; 360)
Man Who Loved Cat Dancing (The) (1973; 3269)
Man Who Shot Liberty Valance (The) (1962; 3039)
Man with the Gun (1955; 2733)
Man with the Steel Whip (1954; 2641)
Man Without a Star (1955; 2695)

Man's Country (1938; 892)
Man's Land (A) (1932; 220)
Many Rivers to Cross (1955; 2683)
Marauders (The) (1947; 1897)
Marauders (The) (1955; 2707)
Mark of the Gun (1969; 3167)
Mark of the Lash (1948; 2024)
Mark of the Renegade (1951; 2364)
Mark of the Spur (1932; 196)
Mark of Zorro (The) (1940; 1186)
Marked for Murder (1945; 1672)
Marked Trails (1944; 1622)
Marksman (The) (1953; 2537)
Marshal of Amarillo (1948; 2001)
Marshal of Cedar Rock (1953; 2522)
Marshal of Cripple Creek (1947; 1910)
Marshal of Gunsmoke (1944; 1576)
Marshal of Heldorado (1950; 2204)
Marshal of Laredo (1945; 1721)
Marshal of Mesa City (1939; 1042)
Marshal of Reno (1944; 1614)
Marshal's Daughter (The) (1953; 2552)
Marshals in Disguise (1954; 2670)
Masked Raiders (1949; 2113)
Masked Rider (The) (1941; 1326)
Mason of the Mounted (1932; 214)
Massacre (1956; 2767)
Massacre Canyon (1954; 2629)
Master Gunfighter (The) (1975; 3300)
Masterson of Kansas (1955; 2676)
Match-Making Marshal (The) (1955; 2702)
Maverick (The) (1952; 2511)
Maverick Queen (The) (1956; 2763)
McCabe and Mrs. Miller (1971; 3222)
McKenna of the Mounted (1932; 236)
McLintock (1963; 3061)
McMasters (The) (1970; 3199)
Medico of Painted Springs (The) (1941; 1275)
Meet Roy Rogers (1941; 1274)
Melody of the Plains (1937; 737)
Melody Ranch (1940; 1193)
Melody Trail (1935; 483)
Men of Texas (1942; 1415)
Men of the North (1930; 70)
Men of the Plains (1936; 655)
Men of the Timberland (1941; 1268)
Men with Steel Faces (1940; 1114)
Men Without Law (1930; 79)
Mercenary (The) (1970; FF68)
Merry Mavericks (1951; 2372a)
Mesquite Buckaroo (1940; 996)
Mexicali Kid (1938; 913)
Mexicali Rose (1940; 983)
Mexican Spitfire Out West (1940; 1194)
Michigan Kid (The) (1947; 1872)
Mine with the Iron Door (The) (1936; 614)
Minnesota Clay (1966; FF12)

Minute to Pray, A Second to Die (A) (1968; FF43)
Miracle of the Hills (The) (1959; 2976)
Miracle Rider (The) (1935; 537)
Misfits (The) (1961; 3015)
Missouri Breaks (The) (1976; 3314)
Missouri Outlaw (A) (1941; 1336)
Missouri Traveler (The) (1958; 2902)
Missourians (The) (1950; 2285)
Mohawk (1956; 2756)
Mojave Firebrand (1944; 1586)
Molly and Lawless John (1973; 3258)
Molly Cures a Cowboy (1940; 1093)
Money, Women and Guns (1959; 2946)
Montana (1950; 2169)
Montana Belle (1952; 2502)
Montana Desperado (1951; 2355)
Montana Incident (1952; 2477)
Montana Kid (The) (1931; 140)
Montana Mike (1947; 1914)
Montana Moon (1930; 36)
Montana Territory (1952; 2460)
Monte Walsh (1970; 3203)
Moon over Montana (1946; 1765)
Moonlight and Cactus (1944; 1632)
Moonlight on the Prairie (1935; 493)
Moonlight on the Range (1937; 833)
Moonlighter (The) (1953; 2578)
More Dead Than Alive (1969; 3168)
Mountain Justice (1930; 44)
Mountain Rhythm (1939; 1015)
Mountain Rhythm (1949; 2107)
Mounted Fury (1931; 174)
Mounted Stranger (The) (1930; 27)
Mrs. Mike (1949; 2156)
Mule Train (1950; 2179)
Murder on the Yukon (1940; 1086)
Murieta (1965; FF7)
Musical Bandit (The) (1941; 1285)
Mustang (1959; 2958)
Mustang Country (1976; 3311)
My Darling Clementine (1946; 1838)
My Friend Flicka (1943; 1492)
My Little Chickadee (1940; 1079)
My Name Is Legend (1975; 3299)
My Name Is Nobody (1974; FF116)
My Outlaw Brother (1951; 2322)
My Pal Ringeye (1947; 1875a)
My Pal, The King (1932; 233)
My Pal Trigger (1946; 1799)
Mysterious Avenger (The) (1936; 573)
Mysterious Desperado (The) (1949; 2119)
Mysterious Rider (The) (1933; 290)
Mysterious Rider (The) (1938; 918)
Mysterious Rider (The) (1942; 1454)
Mystery Man (1944; 1605)
Mystery Mountain (1934; 396)
Mystery of the Hooded Horsemen (The) (1937; 790)

Mystery Ranch (1932; 226)
Mystery Ranch (1934; 361)
Mystery Range (1937; 743)
Mystery Trooper (The) (1931; 178)

N

Naked Dawn (The) (1955; 2734)
Naked Gun (The) (1956; 2808)
Naked Hills (The) (1956; 2772)
Naked in the Sun (1957; 2874)
Naked Spur (The) (1953; 2524)
Navajo Joe (1967; FF33)
Navajo Kid (1945; 1736)
Navajo Run (1964; 3082)
Navajo Trail (The) (1945; 1668)
Navajo Trail Raiders (1949; 2131)
Near the Rainbow's End (1930; 51)
Near the Trail's End (1931; 151)
'Neath Canadian Skies (1946; 1822)
'Neath the Arizona Skies (1934; 400)
'Neath Western Skies (1930; 54)
Nebraskan (The) (1953; 2598)
Ned Kelly (1970; FF71)
Nevada (1935; 499)
Nevada (1944; 1655)
Nevada Badmen (1951; 2345)
Nevada Buckaroo (The) (1931; 150)
Nevada City (1941; 1272)
Nevada Cyclone (1934; 358)
Nevada Smith (1966; 3119)
Nevadan (The) (1950; 2183)
New Frontier (1939; 1024)
New Frontier (The) (1935; 486)
New Mexico (1951; 2344)
Night of the Grizzly (The) (1966; 3113)
Night Passage (1957; 2860)
Night Raiders (1952; 2417)
Night Rider (1962; 3045)
Night Rider (The) (1932; 216)
Night Riders (The) (1939; 990)
Night Riders of Montana (1951; 2315)
Night Stage to Galveston (1952; 2433)
Night Time in Nevada (1948; 2009)
No Man's Range (1935; 538)
No Name on the Bullet (1959; 2952)
Noose for a Gunman (1960; 2994)
North from the Lone Star (1941; 1243)
North of Arizona (1935; 539)
North of Nome (1936; 677)
North of the Rio Grande (1937; 769)
North of the Rockies (1942; 1386)
North of the Yukon (1939; 984)
North to Alaska (1960; 3008)
North to the Klondike (1942; 1356)
North West Mounted Police (1940; 1184)

Northern Frontier (1935; 429)
Northern Patrol (1953; 2558)
Northwest Passage (1940; 1085)
Northwest Rangers (1942; 1457)
Northwest Stampede (1948; 2002)
Northwest Territory (1951; 2398)
Northwest Trail (1945; 1739)
Not Exactly Gentlemen (1931; 113)

O

Oath of Vengeance (1944; 1660)
Oh, Susanna! (1936; 645)
Oh! Susanna (1951; 2320)
Oklahoma! (1955; 2730)
Oklahoma Annie (1952; 2435)
Oklahoma Badlands (1948; 1954)
Oklahoma Blues (1948; 1961)
Oklahoma Cyclone (1930; 62)
Oklahoma Frontier (1939; 1039)
Oklahoma Jim (1931; 153)
Oklahoma Justice (1951; 2369)
Oklahoma Kid (The) (1939; 976)
Oklahoma Outlaws (1943; 1570a)
Oklahoma Raiders (1944; 1585)
Oklahoma Renegades (1940; 1162)
Oklahoma Territory (1960; 2988)
Oklahoma Terror (1939; 1029)
Oklahoma Woman (The) (1956; 2769)
Oklahoman (The) (1957; 2850)
Old Barn Dance (The) (1938; 844)
Old Chisholm Trail (The) (1942; 1461)
Old Corral (The) (1936; 691)
Old Frontier (The) (1950; 2241)
Old Los Angeles (1948; 1972)
Old Louisiana (1937; 723)
Old Oklahoma Plains (1952; 2472)
Old Overland Trail (1953; 2527)
Old Shatterhand (1966; FF18)
Old Texas Trail (The) (1944; 1661)
Old West (The) (1952; 2411)
Old Wyoming Trail (The) (1937; 816)
Old Yeller (1958; 2896)
Ole Rex (1961; 3024)
Omaha Trail (The) (1942; 1428)
O'Malley of the Mounted (1936; 602)
On the Great White Trail (1938; 898)
On the Old Spanish Trail (1947; 1921)
On Top of Old Smoky (1953; 2532)
Once upon a Horse (1958; 2937)
Once upon a Time in the West (1969; FF60)
One-Eyed Jacks (1961; 3020)
One Foot in Hell (1960) 3000)
One Hundred Rifles (1969; FF56)
One Little Indian (1973; 3267)
One Man Justice (1937; 774)

One Man Law (1932; 191)
One Man's Law (1940; 1137)
One More Train to Rob (1971; 3219)
One Way Trail (The) (1931; 157)
Only the Valiant (1951; 2334)
Oregon Passage (1958; 2894)
Oregon Trail (1945; 1703)
Oregon Trail (The) (1936; 572)
Oregon Trail (The) (1939; 1004)
Oregon Trail (The) (1959; 2979)
Oregon Trail Scouts (1947; 1882)
Orphan of the Pecos (1937; 760)
Out California Way (1946; 1840)
Out West with the Peppers (1940; 1138)
Outcast (The) (1954; 2648)
Outcasts of Black Mesa (1950; 2201)
Outcasts of Poker Flat (The) (1937; 739)
Outcasts of Poker Flats (The) (1952; 2451)
Outcasts of the Trail (1949; 2092)
Outlaw (The) (1943; 1480, 1763)
Outlaw Brand (1948; 2027)
Outlaw Country (1949; 2050)
Outlaw Deputy (The) (1935; 467)
Outlaw Express (1938; 885)
Outlaw Gold (1950; 2286)
Outlaw Josey Wales (The) (1976; 3319)
Outlaw Justice (1932; 247)
Outlaw of the Plains (1946); 1818)
Outlaw Queen (1956; 2844)
Outlaw Roundup (1944; 1580)
Outlaw Rule (1935; 437)
Outlaw Stallion (The) (1954; 2644)
Outlaw Tamer (The) (1934; 414)
Outlaw Territory (1953; 2583)
Outlaw Trail (1944; 1595)
Outlaw Treasure (1955; 2706)
Outlaw Women (1952; 2461)
Outlawed Guns (1935; 472)
Outlaw's Daughter (The) (1954; 2660)
Outlaws' Highway (1934; 390)
Outlaws Is Coming! (The) (1965; 3084)
Outlaws of Boulder Pass (1942; 1456)
Outlaws of Pine Ridge (1942; 1449)
Outlaws of Santa Fe (1944; 1594)
Outlaws of Sonora (1938; 865)
Outlaws of Stampede Pass (1943; 1547)
Outlaws of Texas (1950; 2287)
Outlaws' Paradise (1939; 993)
Outlaw's Son (1954; 2671)
Outlaw's Son (1957; 2859)
Outlaws of the Cherokee Trail (1941; 1304)
Outlaws of the Desert (1941; 1328)
Outlaws of the Panhandle (1941; 1234)
Outlaws of the Prairie (1937; 831)
Outlaws of the Range (1936; 605)
Outlaws of the Rio Grande (1941; 1236)
Outlaws of the Rockies (1945; 1716)

Outpost of the Mounties (1939; 1035)
Outrage (The) (1964; 3079)
Outriders (The) 1943; 2205)
Over the Border (1950; 2186)
Over the Santa Fe Trail (1947; 1857)
Overland Bound (1929; 19)
Overland Express (The) (1938; 864)
Overland Mail (1939; 1045)
Overland Mail (1942; 1439)
Overland Mail Robbery (1943; 1558)
Overland Pacific (1954; 2611)
Overland Riders (1946; 1811)
Overland Stage Raiders (1938; 917)
Overland Stagecoach (1942; 1462)
Overland Telegraph (1951; 2399)
Overland to Deadwood (1942; 1437)
Overland Trails (1948; 1945)
Overland with Kit Carson (1939; 1030)
Ox-Bow Incident (The) (1943; 1500)

P

Pack Trail (1953; 2564)
Paint Your Wagon (1969; 3185)
Painted Desert (The) (1931; 100)
Painted Desert (The) (1938; 901)
Painted Stallion (The) (1937; 761)
Painted Trail (The) (1938; 850)
Pal and Gals (1954; 2612)
Pal from Texas (The) (1939; 1040)
Paleface (The) (1948; 2043)
Palomino (The) (1950; 2188)
Pals of the Golden West (1951; 2400)
Pals of the Pecos (1941; 1245)
Pals of the Prairie (1929; 10)
Pals of the Prairie (1934; 415)
Pals of the Range (1935; 448)
Pals of the Saddle (1938; 906)
Pals of the Silver Sage (1940; 1110)
Pals of the West (1934; 416)
Panamint's Bad Man (1938; 893)
Pancho Villa (1973; FF104)
Pancho Villa Returns (1950; 2213)
Panhandle (1948; 1946)
Panhandle Calibre 38 (1975; FF125)
Parade of the West (1930; 24)
Paradise Canyon (1935; 470)
Pardners (1956; 2784)
Pardon My Gun (1930; 76)
Pardon My Gun (1942; 1458)
Park Avenue Logger (1937; 728)
Paroled to Die (1938; 838)
Parson and the Outlaw (The) (1957; 2866)
Parson of Panamint (The) (1941; 1297)
Parting of the Trails (1930; 31)
Partners (1932; 187)

Partners of the Plains (1938; 841)
Partners of the Sunset (1948; 2007)
Partners of the Trail (1931; 136)
Partners of the Trail (1944; 1589)
Passage West (1951; 2357)
Passion (1954; 2657)
Pat Garrett and Billy the Kid (1973; 3262)
Pathfinder (The) (1953; 2514)
Pawnee (1957; 2869)
Payment in Blood (1968; FF53)
Peacemaker (The) (1956; 2813)
Pecos Dandy (The) (1934; 417)
Pecos Kid (The) (1935; 540)
Pecos Pistol (The) (1949; 2135)
Pecos River (1951; 2401)
Perils of the Royal Mounted (1942; 1402)
Perils of the Wilderness (1956; 2744)
Persuader (The) (1957; 2878)
Pest from the West (1939; 1010a)
Phantom Cowboy (The) (1935; 541)
Phantom Cowboy (The) (1941; 1230)
Phantom Empire (The) (1935; 435)
Phantom Gold (1938; 907)
Phantom of Santa Fe (1937; 705)
Phantom of the Desert (1930; 86)
Phantom of the Plains (1945; 1712)
Phantom of the Range (The) (1936; 683)
Phantom of the West (The) (1931; 98)
Phantom Patrol (1936; 656)
Phantom Plainsmen (The) (1942; 1411)
Phantom Rancher (1940; 1097)
Phantom Ranger (1938; 880)
Phantom Rider (The) (1936; 633)
Phantom Rider (The) (1946; 1755)
Phantom Stage (The) (1939; 967)
Phantom Stagecoach (The) (1957; 2840)
Phantom Stallion (1954; 2608)
Phantom Thunderbolt (The) (1933; 299)
Phantom Trails (1955; 2704)
Phantom Valley (1948; 1950)
Phony Express (1943; 1556a)
Pierre of the Plains (1942; 1405)
Pillars of the Sky (1956; 2799)
Pinto Bandit (The) (1944; 1598)
Pinto Canyon (1940; 1112)
Pinto Kid (The) (1941; 1226)
Pinto Rustlers (1936; 617)
Pioneer Days (1940; 1076)
Pioneer Justice (1947; 1895)
Pioneer Marshal (1949; 2149)
Pioneer Trail (1938; 896)
Pioneers (The) (1941; 1259)
Pioneers of the Frontier (1940; 1081)
Pioneers of the West (1940; 1092)
Pirates of Monterey (1947; 1940)
Pirates of the Prairie (1942; 1455)
Pirates on Horseback (1941; 1266)

Pistol for Ringo (A) (1966; FF22)
Pistol Harvest (1951; 2371)
Pistol Packin' Nitwits (1945; 1680a)
Place Called Glory (A) (1966; FF15)
Plainsman (The) (1936; 694)
Plainsman (The) (1966; 3123)
Plainsman and the Lady (The) (1946; 1828)
Plunderers (The) (1948; 2035)
Plunderers (The) (1960; 3009)
Plunderers of Painted Flats (1959; 2951)
Pocatello Kid (The) (1931; 175)
Pocket Money (1972; 3235)
Pony Express (1953; 2543)
Pony Express Days (1940; 1212)
Pony Express Rider (1976; 3328)
Pony Post (1940; 1198)
Pony Soldier (1952; 2503)
Posse (1975; 3291)
Posse from Heaven (1975; 3302)
Posse from Hell (1961; 3021)
Potluck Pards (1934; 352)
Powder River (1953; 2549)
Powder River Gunfire (1948; 1955)
Powder River Rustlers (1949; 2151)
Powderkeg (1971; 3232)
Powdersmoke Range (1935; 484)
Prairie (The) (1947; 1939)
Prairie Badmen (1946; 1801)
Prairie Chickens (1943; 1506)
Prairie Express (1947; 1922)
Prairie Gunsmoke (1942; 1418)
Prairie Justice (1938; 928)
Prairie Law (1940; 1129)
Prairie Moon (1938; 921)
Prairie Pals (1942; 1430)
Prairie Papas (1938; 943)
Prairie Pioneers (1941; 1231)
Prairie Pirates (1950; 2212)
Prairie Raiders (1947; 1888)
Prairie Roundup (1951; 2302)
Prairie Rustlers (1945; 1732)
Prairie Schooners (1940; 1176)
Prairie Spooners (1941; 1224)
Prairie Stranger (1941; 1308)
Prairie Thunder (1937; 802)
Prescott Kid (The) (1934; 392)
Pretty Women (1949; 2159)
Pride of the Plains (1944; 1573)
Pride of the West (1938; 894)
Prince of the Plains (1949; 2075)
Professionals (The) (1966; 3127)
Proud and the Damned (The) (1972; FF101)
Proud Ones (The) (1956; 2766)
Proud Rebel (The) (1958; 2920)
Public Cowboy No. 1 (1937; 795)
Pueblo Terror (1931; 118)
Punchy Cowpunchers (1950; 2161)

Purple Hills (The) (1961; 3034)
Purple Vigilantes (The) (1938; 843)
Pursuit (1975; 3293)

Q

Quantez (1957; 2876)
Quantrill's Raiders (1958; 2909)
Queen of the Yukon (1940; 1161)
Quick Gun (The) (1965; 3069)
Quick on the Trigger (1948; 2037)
Quick Trigger Lee (1931; 171)
Quiet Gun (The) (1957; 2824)
Quincannon, Frontier Scout (1956; 2762)

R

Rachel and the Stranger (1948; 2020)
Racing Blood (1954; 2618)
Racketeer Round-Up (1934; 372)
Racketeers of the Range (1939; 1008)
Rage at Dawn (1955; 2691)
Ragtime Cowboy Joe (1940; 1169)
Raid (The) (1954; 2647)
Raiders (The) (1952; 2494)
Raiders (The) (1964; 3071)
Raiders of Ghost City (1944; 1620)
Raiders of Old California (1957; 2880)
Raiders of Red Gap (1943; 1543)
Raiders of San Joaquin (1943; 1512)
Raiders of Sunset Pass (1943; 1569)
Raiders of the Border (1944; 1577)
Raiders of the Range (1942; 1377)
Raiders of the South (1947; 1850)
Raiders of the West (1942; 1368)
Raiders of Tomahawk Creek (1950; 2274)
Rails into Laramie (1954; 2622)
Rainbow (The) (1929; 5)
Rainbow over Texas (1946; 1786)
Rainbow over the Range (1940; 1151)
Rainbow over the Rockies (1947; 1856)
Rainbow Ranch (1933; 325)
Rainbow Riders (1934; 370)
Rainbow Trail (1932; 184)
Rainbow Valley (1935; 441)
Rainbow's End (1935; 542)
Rainmaker (The) (1957; 2832)
Rampage at Apache Wells (1966; FF21)
Ramrod (1947; 1881)
Ranch House Romeo (1939; 986)
Rancho Deluxe (1975; 3288)
Rancho Grande (1940; 1094)
Rancho Notorious (1952; 2427)
Randy Rides Alone (1934; 371)
Range Beyond the Blue (1947; 1866)

Range Busters (The) (1940; 1159)
Range Defenders (1937; 771)
Range Feud (The) (1931; 169)
Range Justice (1948; 2003)
Range Land (1949; 2157)
Range Law (1931; 155)
Range Law (1944; 1613)
Range Renegades (1948; 1986)
Range Rhythm (1942; 1417)
Range Riders (1934; 418)
Range War (1939; 1034)
Range Warfare (1935; 444)
Ranger and the Lady (The) (1940; 1152)
Ranger Courage (1937; 709)
Ranger of Cherokee Strip (1949; 2140)
Ranger's Code (The) (1933; 332)
Rangers of Fortune (1940; 1173)
Rangers Ride (The) (1948; 1973)
Rangers' Round-Up (The) (1938; 848)
Rangers Step In (The) (1937; 791)
Rangers Take Over (The) (1942; 1466)
Rare Breed (The) (1966; 3109)
Raton Pass (1951; 2330)
Raw Edge (1956; 2794)
Raw Timber (1937; 778)
Rawhide (1938; 863)
Rawhide (1951; 2339)
Rawhide Mail (1934; 368)
Rawhide Rangers (1941; 1284)
Rawhide Romance (1934; 419)
Rawhide Terror (The) (1934; 420)
Rawhide Trail (The) (1950; 2168)
Rawhide Years (The) (1956; 2776)
Ready to Ride (1950; 2267)
Reason to Live, A Reason to Die (A) (1974; FF112)
Rebel City (1953; 2545)
Rebel in Town (1956; 2782)
Rebellion (1936; 668)
Reckless Buckaroo (The) (1935; 543)
Reckless Ranger (1937; 758)
Reckless Rider (The) (1932; 283)
Red Badge of Courage (The) (1951; 2376)
Red Blood of Courage (The) (1935; 464)
Red Desert (1949; 2154)
Red Fork Range (1931; 99)
Red Garters (1954; 2614)
Red Rider (The) (1934; 376)
Red River (1948; 2017)
Red River Range (1938; 945)
Red River Renegades (1946; 1804)
Red River Robin Hood (1943; 1521)
Red River Shore (1953; 2602)
Red River Valley (1936; 591)
Red River Valley (1941; 1341)
Red Rock Outlaw (1950; 2163)
Red Rope (The) (1937; 785)
Red Stallion (The) (1947; 1910a)

Red Stallion in the Rockies (1949; 2082)
Red Sun (1972; FF95)
Red Sundown (1956; 2751)
Red Tomahawk (1967; 3128)
Red, White, and Black (The) (1970; 3207)
Redhead and the Cowboy (The) (1951; 2317)
Redhead from Wyoming (The) (1953; 2515)
Redskins and Redheads (1941; 1248)
Redwood Forest Trail (1950; 2262)
Relentless (1948; 1952)
Renegade (The) (1943; 1531)
Renegade Girl (1946; 1845)
Renegade Ranger (The) (1938; 916)
Renegade Trail (1939; 1019)
Renegades (The) (1946; 1794)
Renegades of Sonora (1948; 2034)
Renegades of the Rio Grande (1945; 1693)
Renegades of the Sage (1949; 2150)
Renegades of the West (1932; 256)
Renfrew of the Royal Mounted (1937; 805)
Reno (1939; 1053)
Reprisal! (1956; 2815)
Requeim for a Gunfighter (1965; 3098)
Restless Breed (The) (1957; 2854)
Return of a Man Called Horse (The) (1976; 3324)
Return of Daniel Boone (The) (1941; 1257)
Return of Frank James (The) (1940; 1155)
Return of Jack Slade (The) (1955; 2728)
Return of Jesse James (1950; 2256)
Return of Sabata (1972; FF100)
Return of the Bad Men (1948; 1999)
Return of the Cisco Kid (The) (1939; 995)
Return of the Durango Kid (1945; 1684)
Return of the Frontiersman (1950; 2231)
Return of the Lash (1947; 1919)
Return of the Rangers (The) (1943; 1549)
Return of the Seven (1966; FF19)
Return of the Texan (1952; 2428)
Return of Wild Bill (The) (1940; 1134)
Return to Warbow (1958; 2895)
Revenge Rider (The) (1935; 443)
Revenger (The) (1972; 3246)
Revolt at Fort Laramie (1957; 2834)
Reward (The) (1965; 3106)
Rhythm of the Rio Grande (1940; 1088)
Rhythm of the Saddle (1938; 929)
Rhythm on the Range (1936; 639)
Rhythm Round-Up (1945; 1696)
Rhythm Wranglers (1937; 829)
Ricochet Romance (1954; 2661)
Riddle Ranch (1936; 699)
Ride a Crooked Trail (1958; 2938)
Ride a Violent Mile (1957; 2887)
Ride a Wild Pony (1976; FF126)
Ride Back (The) (1957; 2847)
Ride Clear of Diablo (1953; 2529)
Ride, Cowboy, Ride (1939; 1036a)
Ride 'Em Cowboy (1936; 652)

Ride 'Em Cowboy (1942; 1365)
Ride 'Em Cowgirl (1939; 956)
Ride Him, Cowboy (1932; 237)
Ride in the Whirlwind (1971; 3223)
Ride Lonesome (1959; 2954)
Ride On, Vaquero (1941; 1249)
Ride Out for Revenge (1957; 2885)
Ride, Ranger, Ride (1936; 657)
Ride, Tenderfoot, Ride (1940; 1164)
Ride the High Country (1962; 3040)
Ride the Man Down (1953; 2516)
Ride to Hangman's Tree (1967; 3138)
Ride, Vaquero! (1953; 2561)
Rider from Tucson (1950; 2228)
Rider of Death Valley (The) (1932; 217)
Rider of the Law (The) (1935; 548)
Rider of the Plains (1931; 120)
Rider on a Dead Horse (1962; 3042)
Riders from Nowhere (1940; 1125)
Riders in the Sky (1949; 2138)
Riders of Black Mountain (1940; 1188)
Riders of Black River (1939; 1028)
Riders of Death Valley (1941; 1277)
Riders of Destiny (1933; 338)
Riders of Pasco Basin (1940; 1100)
Riders of the Badlands (1941; 1345)
Riders of the Black Hills (1938; 884)
Riders of the Cactus (1931; 132)
Riders of the Dawn (1937; 782)
Riders of the Dawn (1945; 1717)
Riders of the Deadline (1943; 1563)
Riders of the Desert (1932; 212)
Riders of the Dusk (1949; 2143)
Riders of the Frontier (1939; 1027)
Riders of the Golden Gulch (1932; 181)
Riders of the Lone Star (1947; 1909)
Riders of the North (1931; 116)
Riders of the Northland (1942; 1412)
Riders of the Northwest Mounted (1943; 1478)
Riders of the Pony Express (1949; 2086)
Riders of the Purple Sage (1931; 162)
Riders of the Purple Sage (1941; 1319)
Riders of the Range (1950; 2176)
Riders of the Rio (1931; 177)
Riders of the Rio Grande (1929; 12)
Riders of the Rio Grande (1943; 1507)
Riders of the Rockies (1937; 776)
Riders of the Sage (1939; 1022)
Riders of the Santa Fe (1944; 1649)
Riders of the Timberline (1941; 1307)
Riders of the West (1942; 1427)
Riders of the Whistling Pines (1949; 2088)
Riders of the Whistling Skull (1937; 708)
Ridin' Down the Canyon (1942; 1468)
Ridin' Down the Trail (1947; 1917)
Ridin' Fool (The) (1931; 127)
Ridin' for Justice (1932; 185)

Ridin' Gents (1934; 378)
Ridin' Law (1930; 47)
Ridin' On (1936; 589)
Ridin' on a Rainbow (1941; 1222)
Ridin' the Cherokee Trail (1941; 1233)
Ridin' the Lone Trail (1937; 813)
Ridin' the Outlaw Trail (1951; 2313)
Ridin' the Trail (1940; 1135)
Ridin' Thru (1935; 498)
Riding Avenger (The) (1936; 626)
Riding Shotgun (1954; 2623)
Riding Speed (1934; 421)
Riding the California Trail (1947; 1847)
Riding the Sunset Trail (1941; 1327)
Riding the Wind (1942; 1369)
Riding Through Nevada (1942; 1442)
Riding Tornado (The) (1932; 213)
Riding West (1944; 1603)
Riding Wild (1935; 468)
Riding with Buffalo Bill (1954; 2662)
Rim of the Canyon (1949; 2108)
Rimfire (1949; 2069)
Rio Bravo (1959; 2960)
Rio Conchos (1964; 3081)
Rio Grande (1938; 938)
Rio Grande (1949; 2160)
Rio Grande (1950; 2279)
Rio Grande Patrol (1950; 2271)
Rio Grande Raiders (1946; 1814)
Rio Grande Ranger (1936; 687)
Rio Grande Romance (1936; 599)
Rio Lobo (1970; 3208)
Rio Rattler (1935; 544)
Rip Roarin' Buckaroo (1936; 664)
River Lady (1948; 1993)
River of No Return (1954; 2615)
River's End (1940; 1154)
River's End (The) (1930; 92)
Road Agent (1941; 1346)
Road Agent (1952; 2438)
Road to Denver (The) (1955; 2712)
Road to Fort Alamo (The) (1966; FF13)
Roamin' Wild (1936; 612)
Roaming Cowboy (The) (1937; 834)
Roar of the Iron Horse (1950; 2222)
Roarin' Guns (1936; 577)
Roaring Frontiers (1941; 1322)
Roaring Guns (1944; 1667a)
Roaring Lead (1936; 686)
Roaring Ranch (1930; 41)
Roaring Rangers (1946; 1764)
Roaring Six Guns (1937; 798)
Roaring Timber (1937; 777)
Roaring West (The) (1935; 475)
Roaring Westward (1949; 2122)
Robbers of the Range (1941; 1250)
Robbers Roost (1933; 287)

Robber's Roost (1955; 2708)
Robin Hood of Eldorado (1936; 592)
Robin Hood of Monterey (1947; 1913)
Robin Hood of Texas (1947; 1901)
Robin Hood of the Pecos (1941; 1219)
Robin Hood of the Range (1943; 1522)
Rock Island Trail (1950; 2216)
Rock River Renegades (1942; 1370)
Rockin' in the Rockies (1945; 1682)
Rockin' Through the Rockies (1940; 1088a)
Rocky Mountain (1950; 2277)
Rocky Mountain Mystery (1935; 438)
Rocky Mountain Rangers (1940; 1124)
Rocky Rhodes (1934; 384)
Rodeo (1952; 2432)
Rodeo Dough (1940; 1187)
Rodeo King and the Senorita (1951; 2361)
Rodeo Rhythm (1942; 1375)
Rogue of the Range (1936; 611)
Rogue of the Rio Grande (1930; 93)
Rogue River (1950; 2280)
Roll Along, Cowboy (1937; 810)
Roll On, Texas Moon (1946; 1815)
Roll, Thunder, Roll (1949; 2115)
Roll, Wagons, Roll (1940; 1156)
Rollin' Home to Texas (1940; 1210)
Rollin' Plains (1938; 895)
Rollin' Westward (1939; 972)
Rolling Caravans (1938; 855)
Rolling Down the Great Divide (1942; 1395)
Romance of the Rio Grande (1929; 15)
Romance of the Rio Grande (1941; 1220)
Romance of the Rockies (1937; 828)
Romance of the West (1935; 569a)
Romance of the West (1946; 1770)
Romance on the Range (1942; 1400)
Romance Rides the Range (1936; 658)
Rooster Cogburn (1975; 3301)
Rootin' Tootin' Rhythm (1937; 751)
Rose Marie (1936; 578)
Rose Marie (1954; 2616)
Rose of Cimarron (1952; 2440)
Rose of the Rancho (1936; 580)
Rose of the Rio Grande (1938; 858)
Rough Night in Jericho (1967; 3143)
Rough Riders of Cheyenne (1945; 1731)
Rough Riders of Durango (1951; 2305)
Rough Riders Round-Up (1939; 977)
Rough Ridin' Justice (1945; 1679)
Rough Riding Ranger (1935; 545)
Rough Riding Rhythm (1937; 793)
Rough Romance (1930; 52)
Rough, Tough West (The) (1952; 2464)
Round Up (The) (1941; 1244)
Round-Up Time in Texas (1937; 742)
Rounders (The) (1965; 3087)
Rovin' Tumbleweeds (1939; 1046)

Roy Dolt and Winchester Jack (1975; FF124)
Royal Mounted Patrol (The) (1941; 1332)
Royal Mounted Rides Again (The) (1945; 1729)
Royal Rider (The) (1929; 6)
Royal Rodeo (The) (1939); 1066a)
Ruggles of Red Gap (1935; 434)
Run for Cover (1955; 2696)
Run of the Arrow (1957; 2867)
Running Target (1956; 2816)
Running Wild (1973; 3270)
Rustlers (1949; 2065)
Rustlers' Hideout (1944; 1631)
Rustlers of Devil's Canyon (1947; 1898)
Rustlers of Red Dog (1935; 427)
Rustlers of the Badlands (1945; 1708)
Rustlers on Horseback (1950; 2272)
Rustlers' Paradise (1935; 455)
Rustler's Roundup (1933; 301)
Rustler's Roundup (1946; 1806)
Rustler's Valley (1937; 787)
Rusty Rides Along (1933; 317)
Ruthless Four (The) (1969; FF64)

S

Sabata (1970; FF72)
Sad Horse (The) (1959; 2964)
Saddle Aces (1935; 546)
Saddle Buster (1932; 204)
Saddle Leather Law (1944; 1665)
Saddle Legion (1951; 2331)
Saddle Mountain Roundup (1941; 1300)
Saddle Pals (1947; 1890)
Saddle Serenade (1945; 1707)
Saddle the Wind (1958; 2904)
Saddle Tramp (1950; 2255)
Saddlemates (1941; 1260)
Saddles and Sagebrush (1943; 1496)
Saga of Death Valley (1939; 1047)
Saga of Hemp Brown (The) (1959; 2983)
Sagebrush Family Trails West (The) (1940; 1073)
Sagebrush Law (1943; 1490)
Sagebrush Politics (1930; 46)
Sagebrush Serenade (1939; 1006)
Sagebrush Trail (1933; 345)
Sagebrush Troubador (The) (1935; 497)
Saginaw Trail (1953; 2581)
Salome, Where She Danced (1945; 1687)
Salt Lake Raiders (1950; 2210)
Sam Whiskey (1969; 3170)
San Antone Ambush (1949; 2126)
San Antonio (1945; 1749)
San Antonio Kid (The) (1944; 1627)
San Fernando Valley (1944; 1633)
San Francisco Story (The) (1952; 2453)
Sandflow (1937; 717)

Santa Fe (1951; 2327)
Santa Fe Bound (1936; 643)
Santa Fe Marshal (1940; 1077)
Santa Fe Passage (1955; 2705)
Santa Fe Rides (1937; 719)
Santa Fe Saddlemates (1945; 1694)
Santa Fe Scouts (1943; 1493)
Santa Fe Stampede (1938; 933)
Santa Fe Trail (1930; 71)
Santa Fe Trail (1940; 1208)
Santa Fe Uprising (1946; 1831)
Santee (1973; 3271)
Saskatchewan (1954; 2617)
Satan's Cradle (1949; 2128)
Saturday Night Square Dance (1949; 2109)
Savage (The) (1952; 2495)
Savage Frontier (1953; 2546)
Savage Guns (The) (1962; FF1)
Savage Horde (The) (1950; 2218)
Savage Red—Outlaw White (1974; 3286)
Savage Sam (1963; 3058)
Scalphunters (The) (1968; 3154)
Scandalous John (1971; 3221)
Scarlet Brand (1932; 209)
Scarlet Horseman (The) (1946; 1754)
Scarlet River (1933; 300)
Scorching Fury (1952; 2513)
Searchers (The) (1956; 2752)
Second Time Around (The) (1961; 3036)
Secret of Convict Lake (The) (1951; 2365)
Secret of Navajo Cave (1976; 3312)
Secret of Outlaw Flats (1953; 2590)
Secret of Treasure Mountain (1956; 2774)
Secret Patrol (1936; 622)
Secret Valley (1937; 710)
Secrets (1933; 349)
Secrets of the Wasteland (1941; 1334)
Seminole Uprising (1955; 2700)
Senor Americano (1929; 17)
Senor Jim (1936; 701)
Senorita from the West (1945; 1723)
Sergeant Rutledge (1960; 2995)
Sergeants 3 (1962; 3037)
Seven Alone (1974; 3285)
Seven Angry Men (1955; 2692)
Seven Bad Men (1955; 2791)
Seven Guns for the MacGregors (1968; FF42)
Seven Guns to Mesa (1958; 2903)
Seven Men from Now (1956; 2786)
Seven Ways from Sundown (1960; 3002)
Seventh Cavalry (1956; 2817)
Shadow of the Hawk (1976; 3323)
Shadow Ranch (1930; 72)
Shadow Valley (1947; 1930)
Shadows of Death (1945; 1683)
Shadows of the West (1949; 2054)
Shadows of Tombstone (1953; 2582)

Shadows on the Range (1946; 1823)
Shadows on the Sage (1942; 1434)
Shakiest Gun in the West (The) (1968; 3157)
Shalako (1968; FF50)
Shane (1953; 2567)
Shark River (1953; 2587)
Sheepman (The) (1958; 2913)
Shenandoah (1965; 3104)
Shepherd of the Hills (The) (1941; 1283)
Sheriff of Cimarron (1945; 1678)
Sheriff of Fractured Jaw (The) (1959; 2947)
Sheriff of Las Vegas (1944; 1667)
Sheriff of Medicine Bow (The) (1948; 2021)
Sheriff of Redwood Valley (1946; 1819)
Sheriff of Sage Valley (1942; 1443)
Sheriff of Sundown (1944; 1646)
Sheriff of Tombstone (1941; 1258)
Sheriff of Wichita (1949; 2053)
Sheriff's Secret (The) (1931; 129)
She Wore a Yellow Ribbon (1949; 2134)
Shine On Harvest Moon (1938; 946)
Shoot Out (1971; 3215)
Shoot Out at Big Sag (1962; 3044)
Shoot-Out at Medicine Bend (1957; 2849)
Shootin' Irons (1943; 1501)
Shooting (The) (1971; 3212)
Shooting High (1940; 1111)
Shootist (The) (1976; 3320)
Short Grass (1950; 2294)
Shot in the Frontier (1954; 2658a)
Shotgun (1955; 2698)
Shotgun Pass (1931; 164)
Showdown (1963; 3056)
Showdown (1973; 3268)
Showdown (The) (1940; 1091)
Showdown (The) (1950; 2249)
Showdown at Abilene (1956; 2800)
Showdown at Boot Hill (1958; 2911)
Shut My Big Mouth (1942; 1367a)
Siege at Red River (The) (1954; 2630)
Sierra (1950; 2225)
Sierra Baron (1958; 2926)
Sierra Passage (1951; 2299)
Sierra Stranger (1957; 2848)
Sierra Sue (1941; 1331)
Sign of the Wolf (The) (1931; 179)
Sign of Zorro (The) (1960; 2996)
Silent Code (The) (1935; 547)
Silent Conflict (1948; 1958)
Silent Men (1933; 298)
Silent Valley (1935; 549)
Silver Bandit (The) (1950; 2178)
Silver Bullet (The) (1935; 457)
Silver Bullet (The) (1942; 1421)
Silver Butte (1949; 2105)
Silver Canyon (1951; 2354)
Silver City (1951; 2395)

Silver City Bonanza (1951; 2318)
Silver City Kid (1944; 1618)
Silver City Raiders (1943; 1553)
Silver Devil (1945; 137)
Silver Horde (The) (1930; 83)
Silver Lode (1954; 2637)
Silver on the Sage (1939; 985)
Silver Queen (1942; 1450)
Silver Raiders (1950; 2250)
Silver Range (1946; 1832)
Silver River (1948; 1983)
Silver Spurs (1936; 579)
Silver Spurs (1943; 1527)
Silver Stallion (1941; 1264)
Silver Star (The) (1955; 2690)
Silver Trail (The) (1937; 721)
Silver Trails (1948; 2008)
Silver Whip (The) (1953; 2523)
Sin Town (1942; 1438)
Sing, Cowboy, Sing (1937; 755)
Sing Me a Song of Texas (1945; 1673)
Singin' in the Corn (1946; 1846)
Singing Buckaroo (The) (1937; 711)
Singing Cowboy (The) (1936; 616)
Singing Cowgirl (The) (1939; 1017)
Singing Dude (The) (1940; 1101)
Singing Guns (1950; 2182)
Singing Hill (The) (1941; 1254)
Singing on the Trail (1946; 1816)
Singing Outlaw (The) (1938; 842)
Singing Sheriff (The) (1944; 1641)
Singing Spurs (1948; 2018)
Singing Vagabond (The) (1935; 506)
Single-Handed Sanders (1932; 197)
Sinister Journey (1948; 1987)
Sioux City Sue (1946; 1834)
Sitting Bull (1954; 2658)
Six Black Horses (1962; 3043)
Six Gun Decision (1953; 2591)
Six Gun Gold (1941; 1292)
Six Gun Gospel (1943; 1535)
Six Gun Justice (1935; 430)
Six Gun Law (1948; 1941)
Six Gun Man (1946; 1759)
Six Gun Mesa (1950; 2208)
Six Gun Music (1949; 2049)
Six Gun Rhythm (1939; 968)
Six Gun Serenade (1947; 1877)
Six Gun Trail (1938; 935)
Six-Shootin' Sheriff (1938; 878)
Skin Game (1971; 3228)
Skipalong Rosenbloom (1951; 2335)
Skull and Crown (1935; 550)
Sky Bandits (1940; 1142)
Sky Full of Moon (1952; 2510)
Slaughter Trail (1951; 2382)
Slim Carter (1957; 2881)

Smith (1969; 3171)
Smoke in the Wind (1975; 3290)
Smoke Lightning (1933; 296)
Smoke Signal (1955; 2687)
Smoke Tree Range (1937; 762)
Smokey Smith (1935; 551)
Smoking Guns (1934; 369)
Smoky (1933; 343)
Smoky (1966; 3122)
Smoky Canyon (1952; 2413)
Smoky Mountain Melody (1948; 2041)
Smoky River Serenade (1947; 1910b)
Smoky Trails (1939; 973)
Snake River Desperadoes (1951; 2346)
Snow Dog (1950; 2240)
Snowfire (1958; 2915)
So You Want to Be a Cowboy (1951; 2333a)
Soldier Blue (1970; 3201)
Sombrero Kid (The) (1942; 1420)
Something Big (1971; 3231)
Somewhere in Sonora (1933; 305)
Son of a Badman (1949; 2077)
Son of Belle Starr (1953; 2553)
Son of Billy the Kid (1949; 2073)
Son of Davy Crockett (The) (1941; 1282)
Son of Geronimo (1952; 2500)
Son of God's Country (1948; 2014)
Son of Oklahoma (1932; 228)
Son of Paleface (1952; 2476)
Son of Roaring Dan (1940; 1148)
Son of the Border (1933; 311)
Son of the Plains (1931; 131)
Son of the Renegade (1953; 2533)
Son of Zorro (1947; 1851)
Song of Arizona (1946; 1768)
Song of Idaho (1948; 1962)
Song of Nevada (1944; 1624)
Song of Old Wyoming (1945; 1733)
Song of Texas (1943; 1514)
Song of the Buckaroo (1939; 950)
Song of the Caballero (1930; 55)
Song of the Drifter (1948; 1943)
Song of the Gringo (1936; 681)
Song of the Prairie (1945; 1718)
Song of the Range (1944; 1657)
Song of the Saddle (1936; 581)
Song of the Sierras (1946; 1836)
Song of the Trail (1936; 598)
Song of the Wasteland (1947; 1889)
Song of the West (1930; 35)
Songs and Saddles (1938; 947)
Sonny and Jed (1974; FF111)
Sonora Stagecoach (1944; 1608)
Sons of Katie Elder (The) (1965; 3100)
Sons of New Mexico (1950; 2164)
Sons of the Pioneers (1942; 1414)
Sons of the Saddle (1930; 60)

Soul of Nigger Charley (The) (1973; 3265)
Soul Soldiers (1970; 3207)
South of Arizona (1938; 899)
South of Caliente (1951; 2383)
South of Death Valley (1949; 2111)
South of Monterey (1946; 1796)
South of Rio (1949; 2103)
South of Santa Fe (1932; 188)
South of Santa Fe (1942; 1367)
South of Santa Fe (1949; 2155)
South Pacific Trail (1952; 2492)
South of the Border (1939; 1058)
South of the Chisholm Trail (1947; 1853)
South of the Rio Grande (1932; 202)
South of the Rio Grande (1945; 1713)
Southward Ho! (1939; 1001)
Southwest Passage (1954; 2628)
Spade Cooley and His Orchestra (1949; 2104)
Spade Cooley, King of Western Swing (1945; 1711)
Spikes Gang (The) (1974; 3276)
Spirit of the West (1932; 200)
Spoilers (The) (1930; 69)
Spoilers (The) (1942; 1387)
Spoilers (The) (1956; 2743)
Spoilers of the Plains (1951; 2309)
Spoilers of the Range (1939; 994)
Spook Town (1944; 1607)
Springfield Rifle (1952; 2493)
Springtime in the Rockies (1937; 820)
Springtime in Texas (1945; 1695)
Springtime in the Sierras (1947; 1900)
Spurs (1930; 64)
Square Dance Jubilee (1949; 2142)
Square Shooter (1935; 426)
Square Shooter (The) (1951; 2335)
Squares (1972; 3238)
Squaw Man (The) (1931; 145)
Stage to Blue River (1951; 2404)
Stage to Chino (1940; 1149)
Stage to Mesa City (1947; 1915)
Stage to Thunder Rock (1964; 3073)
Stage to Tucson (1951; 2298)
Stagecoach (1939; 974)
Stagecoach (1966; 3117)
Stagecoach Buckaroo (1942; 1366)
Stagecoach Days (1938; 886)
Stagecoach Driver (1951; 2360)
Stagecoach Express (1942; 1373)
Stagecoach Kid (1949; 2090)
Stagecoach Outlaws (1945; 1709)
Stagecoach to Dancers' Rock (1962; 3051)
Stagecoach to Denver (1946; 1844)
Stagecoach to Fury (1956; 2805)
Stagecoach to Monterey (1944; 1634)
Stagecoach War (1940; 1144)
Stalking Moon (The) (1969; 3166)
Stallion Canyon (1949; 2095)

Stampede (1936; 682)
Stampede (1949; 2080)
Stand at Apache River (The) (1953; 2576)
Stand Up and Fight (1939; 949a)
Star in the Dust (1956; 2768)
Star of Texas (1953; 2517)
Star Packer (The) (1934; 374)
Starbird and Sweet William (1975; 3295)
Stardust on the Sage (1942; 1403)
Starlight over Texas (1938; 909)
Stars in My Crown (1950; 2214)
Stars over Arizona (1937; 803)
Stars over Texas (1946; 1833)
Station West (1948; 2025)
Stick to Your Guns (1941; 1313)
Sting of the West (The) (1975; FF120)
Stone of Silver Creek (1935; 445)
Storm (The) (1930; 63)
Storm over Wyoming (1950; 2206)
Storm Rider (The) (1957; 2835)
Stormy (1935; 489)
Stormy Trails (1936; 693)
Straight Shooter (1939; 1065)
Strange Gamble (1948; 2022)
Strange Lady in Town (1955; 2699)
Stranger and the Gunfighter (The) (1976; FF127)
Stranger at My Door (1956; 2757)
Stranger from Arizona (The) (1938; 919)
Stranger from Pecos (The) (1943; 1520)
Stranger from Ponca City (The) (1947; 1899)
Stranger from Santa Fe (1945; 1681)
Stranger from Texas (The) (1939; 1061)
Stranger in Town (A) (1968; FF41)
Stranger on Horseback (1955; 2689)
Stranger Returns (The) (1968; FF46)
Stranger Wore a Gun (The) (1953; 2572)
Strangers' Gundown (The) (1974; FF115)
Strawberry Roan (1933; 339)
Strawberry Roan (The) (1948; 2006)
Streets of Ghost Town (1950; 2245)
Streets of Laredo (1949; 2089)
Sudden Bill Dorn (1937; 817)
Sugarfoot (1951; 2319)
Sun Valley Cyclone (1946; 1787)
Sundance Cassidy and Butch the Kid (1975; 3304)
Sundown Kid (1942; 1467)
Sundown in Santa Fe (1948; 2029)
Sundown Jim (1942; 1382)
Sundown on the Prairie (1939; 965)
Sundown Rider (The) (1933; 348)
Sundown Riders (1948; 2015)
Sundown Saunders (1936; 702)
Sundown Trail (1931; 158)
Sundown Trail (The) (1934; 422)
Sundown Valley (1944; 1587)
Sundowners (The) (1950; 2172)
Sunrise Trail (1931; 105)

Sunscorched (1966; FF23)
Sunset Carson Rides Again (1948; 2012)
Sunset in El Dorado (1945; 1720)
Sunset in the West (1950; 2263)
Sunset in Wyoming (1941; 1281)
Sunset of Power (1936; 575)
Sunset on the Desert (1942; 1384)
Sunset Pass (1933; 318)
Sunset Pass (1946; 1803)
Sunset Range (1935; 449)
Sunset Serenade (1942; 1431)
Sunset Trail (The) (1932; 186)
Sunset Trail (1939; 969)
Support Your Local Gunfighter (1971; 3213)
Support Your Local Sheriff (1969; 3172)
Susanna Pass (1949; 2079)
Susannah of the Mounties (1939; 1012)
Sutter's Gold (1936; 606)
Swifty (1935; 507)
Swing, Cowboy, Swing (1944; 1658)
Swing in the Saddle (1944; 1629)
Swing the Western Way (1947; 1893)
Swingin' in the Barn (1940; 1121)

T

Tabasco Kid (The) (1932; 194a)
Taggart (1965; 3085)
Take a Hard Ride (1975; FF121)
Take Me Back to Oklahoma (1940; 1189)
Take Me to Town (1953; 2550)
Talented Tramps (The) (1949; 2124)
Tales of the West #1 (1950; 2242)
Tales of the West #2 (1950; 2253)
Tales of the West #3 (1950; 2273)
Tales of the West #4 (1951; 2306)
Tall in the Saddle (1944; 1656)
Tall Man Riding (1955; 2713)
Tall Men (The) (1955; 2727)
Tall Stranger (The) (1957; 2884)
Tall T (The) (1957; 2841)
Tall Women (The) (1967; FF25)
Taming of the West (1939; 1054)
Target (1954; 2445)
Taza, Son of Cochise (1954; 2606)
Teacher's Pest (1939; 1042a)
Telegraph Trail (The) (1933; 303)
Tell Them Willie Boy Is Here (1970; 3187)
Ten Days to Tulara (1958; 2942)
Ten Wanted Men (1955; 2682)
Ten Who Dared (1960; 3006)
Tenderfoot Goes West (A) (1937; 835)
Tennessee's Partner (1955; 2723)
Tension at Table Rock (1956; 2801)
Tenting Tonight on the Old Camp Ground (1943; 1475)

Terror at Black Falls (1962; 3048)
Terror in a Texas Town (1958; 2939)
Terror of the Plains (1934; 323)
Terror of Tiny Town (1938; 936)
Terror Trail (1933; 293)
Terror Trail (1946; 1835)
Terrors on Horseback (1946; 1785)
Tex Granger (1948; 1966)
Tex Rides with the Boy Scouts (1938; 837)
Tex Takes a Holiday (1932; 267)
Tex Williams and His Western Caravan (1947; 1911)
Texan (The) (1930; 43)
Texan (The) (1932; 284)
Texan Meets Calamity Jane (The) (1950; 2282)
Texans (The) (1938; 902)
Texans Never Cry (1951; 2324)
Texas (1966; 1317)
Texas Across the River (1966; 3126)
Texas Bad Man (1932; 225)
Texas Bad Man (1953; 2603)
Texas Buddies (1932; 254)
Texas City (1952; 2414)
Texas Cyclone (1932; 195)
Texas Desperadoes (1936; 584)
Texas Dynamo (1950; 2226)
Texas Gun-Fighter (1932; 199)
Texas Jack (1935; 552)
Texas Justice (1942; 1407)
Texas Kid (The) (1943; 1561)
Texas Lady (1955; 2736)
Texas Lawmen (1951; 2397)
Texas Man Hunt (1942; 1350)
Texas Marshal (The) (1941; 1280)
Texas Masquerade (1944; 1581)
Texas Panhandle (1945; 1745)
Texas Pioneers (1932; 222)
Texas Rambler (The) (1935; 456)
Texas Ranger (The) (1931; 122)
Texas Rangers (The) (1936; 646)
Texas Rangers (The) (1951; 2349)
Texas Rangers Ride Again (1940; 1203)
Texas Renegades (1940; 1074)
Texas Road Agent (1941; 1346)
Texas Stagecoach (1940; 1123)
Texas Stampede (1939; 966)
Texas Terror (1935; 431)
Texas Terrors (1940; 1195)
Texas to Bataan (1942; 1447)
Texas Tornado (1932; 285)
Texas Trail (1937; 823)
Texas Trouble Shooters (1942; 1409)
Texas Wildcats (1939; 988)
Texican (The) (1966; FF20)
That Texas Jamboree (1946; 1788)
There Was a Crooked Man (1970; 3206)
These Thousand Hills (1959; 2953)
They Call Me Trinity (1971; FF85)

They Came to Cordura (1959; 2984)
They Died with Their Boots On (1942; 1349)
They Rode West (1954; 2666)
Thirteen Fighting Men (1960; 2992)
This Man Can't Die (1970; FF65)
This Savage Land (1965; 3181)
Thomasine and Bushrod (1974; 3277)
Those Dirty Dogs (1974; FF114)
Those Redheads from Seattle (1953; 2584)
Three Desperate Men (1951; 2300)
Three Godfathers (1936; 593)
Three Godfathers (1948; 2036)
Three Guns for Texas (1968; 3158)
Three Hours to Kill (1954; 2656)
Three in the Saddle (1945; 1705)
Three Men from Texas (1940; 1192)
Three Mesquiteers (The) (1936; 653)
Three on the Trail (1936; 607)
Three Outlaws (The) (1956; 2764)
Three-Ten to Yuma (1957; 2868)
Three Texas Steers (1939; 999)
Three Troubledoers (1946; 1782a)
Three Violent People (1957; 2823)
Three Young Texans (1954; 2607)
Thrill Hunter (The) (1933; 308)
Throw a Saddle on a Star (1946; 1769)
Throwback (The) (1935; 482)
Thunder at the Border (1967; FF37)
Thunder in God's Country (1951; 2332)
Thunder in the Desert (1938; 856)
Thunder in the Pines (1948; 2032)
Thunder in the Sun (1959; 2965)
Thunder Mountain (1935; 485)
Thunder Mountain (1947; 1891)
Thunder of Drums (A) (1961; 3032)
Thunder over Arizona (1956; 2787)
Thunder over Texas (1934; 386)
Thunder over the Plains (1953; 2601)
Thunder over the Prairie (1941; 1291)
Thunder Pass (1954; 2654)
Thunder River Feud (1942; 1352)
Thunder Town (1946; 1775)
Thunder Trail (1937; 812)
Thunderbolt (1935; 553)
Thunderhoof (1948; 1996)
Thundering Caravans (1952; 2470)
Thundering Frontier (1940; 1199)
Thundering Gun Slingers (1944; 1588)
Thundering Herd (The) (1933; 297)
Thundering Hoofs (1942; 1419)
Thundering Trail (The) (1951; 2366)
Thundering Trails (1943; 1470)
Thundering West (The) (1939; 951)
Ticket to Tomahawk (1950; 2211)
Tickle Me (1965; 3095)
Tide of Empire (1929; 7)
Timber Country Trouble (1955; 2701)

Timber Stampede (1939; 1016)
Timber Terrors (1935; 554)
Timber Trail (The) (1948; 1988)
Timber War (1935; 494)
Timberjack (1955; 2685)
Time for Killing (A) (1967; 3144)
Tin Star (The) (1957; 2882)
Tioga Kid (The) (1948; 1989)
Titled Tenderfoot (The) (1955; 2703)
To the Last Man (1933; 336)
Today We Kill . . . Tomorrow We Die! (1971; FF82)
Toll of the Desert (1935; 555)
Tomahawk (1951; 2308)
Tomahawk Trail (1957; 2827)
Tomboy and the Champ (1961; 3019)
Tombstone Canyon (1932; 274)
Tombstone Terror (1935; 556)
Tombstone—The Town Too Tough to Die (1942; 1410)
Tonka (1958; 2945)
Tonto Basin Outlaws (1941; 1320)
Tonto Kid (The) (1935; 557)
Too Much Beef (1936; 624)
Top Gun (1955; 2738)
Topeka (1953; 2570)
Topeka Terror (The) (1945; 1670)
Tornado in the Saddle (A) (1942; 1463)
Tornado Range (1948; 1953)
Tough Assignment (1949; 2145)
Toughest Gun in Tombstone (1958; 2912)
Toughest Man in Arizona (1952; 2489)
Town Called Hell (A) (1971; 3224)
Town Tamer (1965; 3107)
Track of the Cat (1954; 2665)
Tracy Rides (1935; 436)
Trail Beyond (The) (1934; 387)
Trail Blazers (The) (1940; 1190)
Trail Drive (The) (1933; 335)
Trail Dust (1936; 688)
Trail Guide (1952; 2422)
Trail of Kit Carson (1945; 1702)
Trail of '98 (1929; 3)
Trail of Robin Hood (1950; 2290)
Trail of Terror (1935; 558)
Trail of Terror (1943; 1537)
Trail of the Arrow (1952; 2498)
Trail of the Hawk (1935; 461)
Trail of the Mounties (1947; 1937)
Trail of the Rustlers (1950; 2173)
Trail of the Silver Spurs (1941; 1214)
Trail of the Vigilantes (1940; 1204)
Trail of the Yukon (1949; 2106)
Trail of Vengeance (1937; 731)
Trail Riders (1942; 1459)
Trail Street (1947; 1861)
Trail to Gunsight (1944; 1628)
Trail to Laredo (1948; 2004)

Trail to Mexico (1946; 1797)
Trail to San Antone (1947; 1852)
Trail to Vengeance (1945; 1740)
Trailin' Trouble (1930; 37)
Trailin' West (1936; 651)
Trailin' West (1949; 2127)
Trailing Danger (1947; 1870)
Trailing Double Trouble (1940; 1179)
Trailing North (1933; 351)
Trailing Trouble (1937; 796)
Trail's End (1935; 560)
Trail's End (1949; 2074)
Trails of Adventure (1935; 559)
Trails of Danger (1930; 73)
Trails of Peril (1930; 73)
Trails of the Golden West (1931; 108)
Trails of the Wild (1935; 476)
Train Robbers (The) (1973; 3259)
Train to Tombstone (1950; 2260)
Traitor (The) (1936; 647)
Tramplers (The) (1966; FF14)
Trap on Cougar Mountain (1972; 3251)
Trapped (1937; 725)
Treachery Rides the Range (1936; 618)
Treachery Rides the Trail (1949; 2067)
Treason (1933; 295)
Treasure of Lost Canyon (1952; 2429)
Treasure of Matecumbe (1976; 3321)
Treasure of Pancho Villa (The) (1955; 2732)
Treasure of Ruby Hills (1955; 2779)
Treasure of Silver Lake (1965; FF8)
Treasure of the Sierra Madre (1948; 1944a)
Trail by Trigger (1944; 1604a)
Trial of Billy Jack (The) (1974; 3283)
Tribute to a Badman (1956; 2758)
Trigger Fingers (1939; 1066)
Trigger Fingers (1946; 1817)
Trigger, Jr. (1950; 2234)
Trigger Law (1944; 1638)
Trigger Pals (1939; 953)
Trigger Smith (1939; 981)
Trigger Tom (1935; 561)
Trigger Trail (1944; 1615)
Trigger Tricks (1930; 50)
Trigger Trio (The) (1937; 811)
Triggerman (1948; 1990)
Trinity Is Still My Name (1972; FF98)
Triple Justice (1940; 1170)
Trooper Hook (1957; 2855)
Trouble at Melody Mesa (1949; 2099)
Trouble Busters (1933; 315)
Trouble in Sundown (1939; 982)
Trouble in Texas (1937; 726)
Trouble on the Trail (1954; 2672)
True Grit (1969; 3177)
True Story of Jesse James (The) (1957; 2829)
Trusted Outlaw (The) (1937; 745)

Tucson Raiders (1944; 1602)
Tulsa Kid (The) (1940; 1157)
Tumbledown Ranch in Arizona (1941; 1253)
Tumbleweed (1953; 2599)
Tumbleweed Tempos (1946; 1839)
Tumbleweed Trail (1942; 1416)
Tumbleweed Trail (1946; 1825)
Tumbleweeds (1939; 1002)
Tumbling Tumbleweeds (1935; 480)
Twenty Mule Team (1940; 1116)
Twilight in the Sierras (1950; 2190)
Twilight on the Prairie (1944; 1617)
Twilight on the Rio Grande (1947; 1874)
Twilight on the Trail (1941; 1312)
Twinkle in God's Eye (The) (1955; 2729)
Twisted Rails (1935; 562)
Two-Fisted Justice (1931; 159)
Two-Fisted Justice (1943; 1469)
Two-Fisted Law (1932; 219)
Two-Fisted Rangers (1940; 1069)
Two-Fisted Sheriff (1937; 767)
Two-Fisted Stranger (1946; 1790)
Two Flags West (1950; 2275)
Two Gun Caballero (1931; 176)
Two-Gun Justice (1938; 873)
Two-Gun Lady (1956; 2804)
Two Gun Law (1937; 734)
Two Gun Man (The) (1931; 124)
Two-Gun Marshal (1953; 2592)
Two Gun Sheriff (1941; 1246)
Two Gun Teacher (The) (1954; 2673)
Two Gun Troubador (1939; 975)
Two Guns and a Badge (1954; 2653)
Two in Revolt (1936; 604)
Two Mules for Sister Sara (1970; 3197)
Two Rode Together (1961; 3029)

U

Ugly Ones (The) (1968; FF47)
Ulzana's Raid (1972; 3254)
Uncivil Warriors (1935; 453a)
Unconquered (1948; 1976)
Unconquered Bandit (1935; 425)
Undefeated (The) (1969; 3186)
Under a Texas Moon (1930; 38)
Under Arizona Skies (1946; 1784)
Under California Stars (1948; 1977)
Under Colorado Skies (1947; 1935)
Under Fiesta Stars (1941; 1298)
Under Mexicali Stars (1950; 2281)
Under Montana Skies (1930; 67)
Under Nevada Skies (1946; 1812)
Under Strange Flags (1937; 736)
Under Texas Skies (1930; 88)
Under Texas Skies (1940; 1171)

Under the Tonto Rim (1933; 306)
Under the Tonto Rim (1947; 1908)
Under Western Skies (1945; 1669)
Under Western Stars (1938; 868)
Undercover Man (1936; 654)
Undercover Man (1942; 1448)
Undercover Men (1935; 563)
Underground Rustlers (1941; 1335)
Unexpected Guest (1947; 1869)
Unforgiven (The) (1960; 2993)
Union Pacific (1939; 998)
Unknown Ranger (The) (1936; 684)
Unknown Valley (1933; 312)
Unsinkable Molly Brown (The) (1964; 3074)
Untamed Breed (The) (1948; 2026)
Untamed Frontier (1952; 2481)
Untamed Heiress (1954; 2624)
Up the MacGregors (1967; FF35)
Utah (1945; 1680)
Utah Blaine (1957; 2828)
Utah Kid (The) (1930; 91)
Utah Kid (The) (1944; 1621)
Utah Trail (1938; 903)
Utah Wagon Train (1951; 2384)

V

Valdez Is Coming (1971; FF77)
Valerie (1957; 2862)
Valiant Hombre (The) (1947; 2040)
Valley of Fear (1951; 1860)
Valley of Fire (1951; 2393)
Valley of Hunted Men (1942; 1452)
Valley of Terror (1937; 713)
Valley of the Lawless (1936; 576)
Valley of the Sun (1942; 1362)
Valley of Vanishing Men (The) (1942; 1464)
Valley of Vengeance (1944; 1600)
Valley of Wanted Men (1935; 564)
Vanishing American (The) (1955; 2735)
Vanishing Frontier (The) (1932; 231)
Vanishing Legion (The) (1931; 128)
Vanishing Men (1932; 210)
Vanishing Outpost (The) (1951; 2389)
Vanishing Riders (The) (1935; 469)
Vanishing Westerner (The) (1950; 2195)
Vanquished (The) (1953; 2554)
Vengeance (1964; 3075)
Vengeance of Rannah (1936; 674)
Vengeance of the West (1942; 1423)
Vengeance Valley (1951; 2311)
Vera Cruz (1954; 2669)
Via Pony Express (1933; 294)
Vigilante (The) (1947; 1885)
Vigilante Hideout (1950; 2246)
Vigilante Terror (1953; 2593)

Vigilantes Are Coming (The) (1936; 671)
Vigilantes of Boomtown (1947; 1859)
Vigilantes of Dodge City (1944; 1650)
Vigilantes Return (The) (1947; 1906)
Vigilantes Ride (The) (1944; 1578)
Villa! (1958; 2941)
Villa Rides (1968; FF44)
Violent Men (The) (1955; 2677)
Virginia City (1940; 1095)
Virginian (The) (1929; 16)
Virginian (The) (1946; 1774)
Viva Cisco Kid (1940; 1107)
Viva Zapata! (1952; 2430)

W

Wackiest Wagon Train in the West (The) (1976; 3322)
Waco (1952; 2424)
Waco (1966; 3121)
Wagon Master (The) (1929; 11)
Wagon Team (1952; 2485)
Wagon Tracks West (1943; 1550)
Wagon Trail (1935; 450)
Wagon Train (1940; 1178)
Wagon Wheels (1934; 382)
Wagon Wheels West (1943; 1570b)
Wagon Wheels Westward (1945; 1747)
Wagonmaster (1950; 2202)
Wagons West (1940; 2467)
Wagons Westward (1940; 1131)
Walk Like a Dragon (1960; 2997)
Walk Tall (1960; 3003)
Walk the Proud Land (1956; 2795)
Walking Hills (The) (1949; 2072)
Wall Street Cowboy (1939; 1023)
Wanderer of the Wasteland (1935; 481)
Wanderer of the Wasteland (1945; 1725)
Wanderers of the West (1941; 1288)
Wanted: Dead or Alive (1951; 2329)
War Arrow (1954; 2604a)
War Drums (1957; 2842)
War of the Wildcats (1943; 1564)
War on the Range (1933; 337)
War Paint (1953; 2573)
War Party (1965; 3088)
War Wagon (The) (1967; 3136)
Warlock (1959; 2961)
Warpath (1951; 2367)
Washington Cowboy (1939; 1046)
Water Rustlers (1939; 949)
Waterhole #3 (1967; 3145)
Way of the West (The) (1934; 324)
Way Out West (1930; 59)
Way Out West (1937; 735)
Way West (The) (1967; 3135)

Webb Pierce and His Wanderin' Boys (1955; 2714)
Welcome to Hard Times (1967; 3131)
Wells Fargo (1937; 830)
Wells Fargo Days (1944; 1606)
Wells Fargo Gunmaster (1951; 2342)
West Is Still Wild/Mulefeathers (The) (1977; 3338)
West of Abilene (1940; 1182)
West of Carson City (1940; 1120)
West of Cheyenne (1931; 110)
West of Cheyenne (1938; 889)
West of Cimarron (1941; 1344)
West of Dodge City (1947; 1868)
West of Eldorado (1949; 2096)
West of Laramie (1949; 2068)
West of Nevada (1936; 636)
West of Pinto Basin (1940; 1196)
West of Rainbow's End (1938; 839)
West of Sonora (1948; 1960)
West of Texas (1943; 1501)
West of the Alamo (1946; 1780)
West of the Brazos (1950; 2227)
West of the Divide (1934; 356)
West of the Law (1934; 324a)
West of the Law (1942; 1444)
West of the Pecos (1934; 397)
West of the Pecos (1945; 1698)
West of the Rio Grande (1944; 1625)
West of the Rockies (1929; 20)
West of the Rockies (1941; 1338)
West of the Santa Fe (1938; 920)
West of Tombstone (1942; 1353)
West of Wyoming (1950; 2177)
West on Parade (1934; 385)
West to Glory (1947; 1875)
Westbound (1959; 2962)
Westbound Mail (1937; 714)
Westbound Stage (1939; 1059)
Western Caravans (1939; 1009)
Western Code (The) (1932; 242)
Western Courage (1935; 492)
Western Cyclone (1943; 1503)
Western Frontier (1935; 477)
Western Gold (1937; 797)
Western Heritage (1948; 1948)
Western Jamboree (1938; 937)
Western Justice (1935; 565)
Western Mail (1942; 1364)
Western Racketeers (1935; 566)
Western Renegades (1949; 2129)
Western Terror (1940; 1209)
Western Trails (1938; 882)
Western Union (1941; 1232)
Western Welcome (A) (1938; 912)
Western Whoopee (1948; 1991)
Westerner (The) (1934; 398)
Westerner (The) (1940; 1172)
Westward Bound (1931; 103)

Westward Ho (1935; 479)
Westward Ho! (1942; 1393)
Westward Ho-Hum (1941; 1306a)
Westward Ho the Wagons! (1957; 2891)
Westward the Women (1952; 2410)
Westward Trail (The) (1948; 1957)
Wheels of Destiny (1934; 357)
When a Man Rides Alone (1933; 288)
When a Man Sees Red (1934; 395)
When a Man's a Man (1935; 433)
When the Daltons Rode (1940; 1150)
When the Legends Die (1972; 3250)
When the Redskins Rode (1951; 2347)
Where the Buffalo Roam (1938; 923)
Where the North Begins (1947; 1933)
Where the West Begins (1938; 845)
Where Trails Divide (1937; 809)
Where Trails End (1942; 1385)
Whirlwind (1951; 2336)
Whirlwind (The) (1933; 307)
Whirlwind Horseman (1938; 871)
Whirlwind Raiders (1948; 1980)
Whirlwind Rider (The) (1935; 567)
Whispering Skull (The) (1944; 1664)
Whispering Smith (1949; 2062)
Whistlin' Dan (1932; 206)
Whistling Bullets (1937; 744)
Whistling Hills (1951; 2380)
White Buffalo (The) (1976; 3334)
White Eagle (1932; 249)
White Eagle (1941; 1225)
White Fang (1975; FF122)
White Feather (1955; 2684)
White Renegade (The) (1931; 152)
White Stallion (1947; 1654)
White Squaw (The) (1956; 2809)
Whoops, I'm an Indian (1936; 649a)
Wichita (1955; 2716)
Wide Open Spaces (1932; 199a)
Wide Open Town (1941; 1293)
Wild and the Innocent (The) (1959; 2966)
Wild and Woolly (1937; 786)
Wild Beauty (1946; 1807)
Wild Bill Hickok Rides (1942; 1361)
Wild Brian Kent (1936; 675)
Wild Bunch (The) (1969; 3179)
Wild Country (1947; 1849)
Wild Country (The) (1971; 3210)
Wild Dakotas (1956; 2749)
Wild Frontier (The) (1947; 1916)
Wild Heritage (1958; 2932)
Wild Horse (1931; 137)
Wild Horse Ambush (1952; 2443)
Wild Horse Canyon (1938; 944)
Wild Horse Mesa (1932; 264)
Wild Horse Mesa (1947; 1929)
Wild Horse Phantom (1944; 1643)

Wild Horse Range (1940; 1133)
Wild Horse Rodeo (1937; 826)
Wild Horse Rustlers (1943; 1477)
Wild Horse Stampede (1943; 1494)
Wild Horse Valley (1940; 1087)
Wild Mustang (1935; 568)
Wild North (The) (1952; 2436)
Wild Rovers (1971; 3217)
Wild Stallion (1952; 2447)
Wild West (1946; 1837)
Wild West Days (1937; 773)
Wild West Whoopee (1931; 114)
Wild Westerners (The) (1962; 3047)
Wildcat of Tucson (1940; 1211)
Wildcat Saunders (1936; 703)
Wildcat Trooper (1936; 632)
Wilderness Mail (1935; 440)
Wildfire (1945; 1704)
Will Penny (1968; 3150)
Winchester (1950; 2239)
Winds of Autumn (The) (1976; 3310)
Winds of the Wasteland (1936; 627)
Wings of the Hawk (1953; 2580)
Wings over Wyoming (1937; 757)
Winners of the West (1940; 1141)
Winning of the West (1953; 2519)
Winterhawk (1975; 3292)
Wishbone Cutter (1977; 3337)
Wistful Widow of Wagon Gap (The) (1947; 1922a)
Without Honors (1932; 183)
Wonderful Country (The) (1959; 2981)
Wolf Call (1939; 1003)
Wolf Dog (1958; 2928)
Wolf Hunters (The) (1949; 2137)
Wolf Riders (1935; 569)
Wolf Song (1929; 8)
Wolves of the Range (1943; 1517)
Woman of the North Country (1952; 2483)
Woman of the Town (The) (1943; 1570)
Woman They Almost Lynched (The) (1953; 2530)
Wrangler's Roost (1941; 1267)
Wyoming (1940; 1165)
Wyoming (1947; 1905)
Wyoming Bandit (The) (1949; 2101)
Wyoming Hurricane (1944; 1596)
Wyoming Mail (1950; 2198)
Wyoming Outlaw (1939; 1014)
Wyoming Renegades (1955; 2693)
Wyoming Roundup (1952; 2501)
Wyoming Whirlwind (1932; 286)
Wyoming Wildcat (1941; 1215)

Y

Yankee Don (1931; 180)
Yaqui Drums (1956; 2803)

Yellow Dust (1936; 594)
Yellow Haired Kid (The) (1952; 2499)
Yellow Mountain (The) (1954; 2667)
Yellow Rose of Texas (1944; 1612)
Yellow Sky (1948; 2048)
Yellow Tomahawk (The) (1954; 2633)
Yellowneck (1955; 2688)
Yellowstone Kelly (1959; 2980)
Yes, We Have No Bonanza (1939; 1001a)
Yodelin' Kid from Pine Ridge (1937; 766)
Young Bill Hickok (1940; 1183)
Young Billy Young (1969; 3182)
Young Blood (1932; 261)
Young Buffalo Bill (1940; 1106)
Young Daniel Boone (1950; 2185)
Young Fury (1965; 3086)
Young Guns (The) (1956; 2789)
Young Guns of Texas (1963; 3052)
Young Jesse James (1960; 2998)

Young Land (The) (1959; 2967)
Yukon Flight (1940; 1068)
Yukon Gold (1952; 2479)
Yukon Manhunt (1951; 2358)
Yukon Patrol (1942; 1397)
Yukon Vengeance (1954; 2605)

Z

Zachariah (1971; 3211)
Zandy's Bride (1974; 3279)
Zorro (1975; FF129)
Zorro Rides Again (1937; 836)
Zorro Rides Again (1959; 2949)
Zorro the Avenger (1960; 3012)
Zorro's Black Whip (1944; 1662)
Zorro's Fighting Legion (1939; 1060)